THE CHINA WHITE PAPER

THE CHINA
WHITE PAPER

August 1949

Originally Issued as

UNITED STATES RELATIONS WITH CHINA
With Special Reference to the Period 1944-1949

Department of State Publication 3573
Far Eastern Series 30

Reissued with the Original Letter of Transmittal to President Truman
from Secretary of State Dean Acheson
and with a New Introduction by
LYMAN P. VAN SLYKE

STANFORD UNIVERSITY PRESS
Stanford, California

The China White Paper was originally issued by the United States Department of State in August 1949 under the title *United States Relations with China, With Special Reference to the Period 1944-1949*. The present edition is identical to the original except for the unnumbered front matter, ending with the Introduction by Lyman P. Van Slyke; the correction of some sixty typographical errors and minor discrepancies of orthography; and the addition of an Index. The Index was prepared for the present edition by Willard A. Heaps.

Stanford University Press
Stanford, California
Introduction and Index © 1967 by the Board of Trustees
of the Leland Stanford Junior University
Printed in the United States of America
L.C. 67-26650

Introduction

by Lyman P. Van Slyke

UNTIL the Japanese attack on Pearl Harbor, American attitudes toward China were shaped by the missionary and the trader, who operated under the system of the unequal treaties forced on China by the Western powers. The United States benefited fully from such treaties—and even contributed to their final form by adding the concept of extra-territoriality—but because Americans had not taken the initiative in setting up and enforcing the treaty system, the American people felt little responsibility for its inequities. In time, Americans came to feel that their behavior in China contrasted favorably with the selfishness of the European powers and Japan, and this feeling was greatly heightened by the idealism and moral fervor of the American missionary effort. The trader and the businessman—advocating free trade and opposing exclusive spheres of influence—represented America's economic stake in China. But this was never more than a very small part of American overseas investment.

In the end, therefore, there grew up a split between our attitudes and our actions. Having no great political or economic stake in China, we were inclined to frame our China policy in moral terms; but for the same reason, we were unwilling to back our policies, however just, against the conflicting policies of nations with higher stakes in the game. There was no conscious duplicity on our part. Our China policy reflected our feelings as a nation; if we were reluctant to back these feelings, it was because our vital interests were not really involved in China.

All this was symbolized by the Open Door policy. Originally an affirmation that every nation should have equality of economic opportunity in China, the Open Door policy was soon redefined as a call for the territorial and administrative integrity of China; but it never led to effective action on our part to ensure China's independence. Nevertheless, thanks to our philanthropic and educational work in China, our willingness to forgo our share of the Boxer indemnity, and our government's repeated expressions of goodwill, we came to think of the United States as China's close friend and benefactor.

Thus, on the eve of Pearl Harbor, although all our sympathies lay with China, we characteristically continued normal relations with Japan. The Japanese attack forced a change in our policies, but it was still impossible to give China much military help. In the first months of the war, there was no matériel to spare; and later it was all but impossible to get supplies to China's isolated armies. Most important, Europe took clear priority over Asia in the Allies' master plan for the war; and in Asia, by 1943 the island-hopping strategy obviously had replaced the strategy of attacking Japan through China. In military terms, China was a sideshow.

To compensate Chiang Kai-shek politically and to keep China actively in the war, Roosevelt pushed China's recognition as one of the Big Four over British objections, and dramatically terminated the unequal treaties in 1943. In these moves, Roosevelt had the enthusiastic support of the American public, which felt that America had done too little for China in the past and which saw the Generalissimo and Madame Chiang as heroic allies against the Japanese aggressor. But once again, United States policy, in its generosity and optimism, did not necessarily reflect the realities of the situation.

While we were committing ourselves to Chinese greatness under Chiang, the Nationalists were becoming increasingly ineffective. Shocking stories of corruption and dictatorial high-handedness came out of Chungking. Friction between the Nationalists and the Communists threatened to erupt into civil war. Chiang also hinted that unless American aid were forthcoming on Chinese terms, China might be forced to make a separate peace, thereby releasing large Japanese forces. The almost unopposed Japanese offensive into the interior of south China in 1944 seemed to confirm all these fears.

By October 1944, when General Joseph W. Stilwell, who favored a tough quid pro quo policy toward Chiang, was recalled at the Generalissimo's insistence, General Patrick J. Hurley had already arrived in China. He expressed clearly the goals of American policy: to keep China in the war, to support Chiang and the National Government, to persuade Chiang to undertake certain reforms, and to promote the unity and democracy to which all Chinese parties proclaimed their dedication. It is clear now that these goals were irreconcilable, for if there was no possibility of withdrawing our support from Chiang, there was no way of getting him to make changes he did not choose to make. America's role as mediator was compromised for the same reason. But this was far from clear at the time, except to those who knew the situation in China most intimately. Americans in 1944-45 were in substantial agreement that China policy, broadly speaking, was being adequately handled. This consensus lasted until well after the war; even Hurley's parting broadside (pp. 581-84) failed to shake it.

Partisanship on the China issue did not really begin until after the Congressional elections of November 1946, which put Republican majorities into both the Senate and the House and marked the low point of the Truman Administration's influence. In January 1947, General George C. Marshall, who had succeeded General Hurley as the President's Special Representative in China, reported the failure of his efforts to arrange a peaceful settlement, and returned home to become Secretary of State. The Republicans—anticipating the Presidency in 1948—used their majorities in Congress to exert an increasingly powerful influence on foreign policy. A group of Congressmen (led by William Knowland and Styles Bridges in the Senate, and by Walter Judd in the House) called for increased aid to the Nationalists in their conflict against the Chinese Communists. Nothing could alter their belief in the greatness of Chiang Kai-shek, or their conviction that the Chinese Communists were Russian puppets.

During 1947 and 1948, the Republicans used the threat of torpedoing the Marshall Plan for the recovery of Europe as a way of getting support for China. Among other things, they argued that if a strategy of massive foreign aid was appropriate to Europe (i.e., Greece), it should also be applied in Asia (i.e., China). So long as this balance of power existed on Capitol Hill, the Administration felt it necessary to make cautious concessions on the China front in order to move ahead with the rest of its foreign program.

Marshall, who was convinced that only all-out military intervention could save Chiang, favored a policy of quiet disengagement from China. Not only were America's resources insufficient for military intervention in his opinion, but the American people would not sanction such a course. And yet disengagement had almost as high a price, thanks not only to the embattled political situation in Washington, but to the accumulated weight of past American relations with China. How could we simply abandon a traditional friend, an ally who had suffered so long, a member of the Big Four by virtue of our own insistence? Marshall wavered, then moved from quiet disengagement back to limited commitment. The principal concessions of the Administration were the resumption of arms shipments to the Chinese Nationalists in early 1947, the dispatch of the Wedemeyer mission later that year, and the China Aid Act of April 1948.

This unstable situation lasted until the unexpected Democratic victory in the 1948 election. With both houses of Congress once more in Democratic hands, the Administration no longer had to buy Republican support for its legislative program at the cost of concessions on China. Instead of reducing partisanship on the China issue, however, the Democratic victory only heightened it. Earlier the Republicans had been overconfident and a little complacent; now, in the bitterness of defeat, they sought to draw blood wherever they could.

As the plight of the Nationalists worsened, Republican attacks on Administration policy became more frequent and more heated. By now, too, a new note had been added—the question of Communist influence on China policy in the State Department. In 1947, the Truman Administration had begun a program of security investigations that it hoped to keep confidential, but a number of sensational cases were receiving publicity all during 1948. Eleven Communist leaders were trading blows with Judge Harold R. Medina in a Smith Act trial in New York City; Judith Coplon of the Justice Department, allegedly a Communist, was under indictment for conspiracy; Klaus Fuchs had confessed to atomic espionage on behalf of the Soviet Union; and the ex-Communist Whittaker Chambers was describing his conspiratorial relations with Alger Hiss, a high official of the State Department. There had been sporadic charges made earlier against certain career China specialists, beginning with Hurley's letter of resignation in 1945, but by 1949 the atmosphere had grown feverish. This was the immediate background for Senator Joseph McCarthy's notorious effort, beginning in early 1950, to discredit the State Department as a whole.

The White Paper was thus published in the midst of acrimonious controversy over United States China policy, the containment of Communism abroad, and the fear of subversion at home.

The idea of a White Paper may have first been suggested by middle-level officers in the State Department's Office of Far Eastern Affairs. Secretary of Defense James V. Forrestal recorded in his diary that at a conference held on November 26, 1948, "Marshall read a paper from some office people in the State Department, who advocated going to the American public now to explain the inadequacies of the Chiang Kai-shek government." Marshall went on to say that he had decided, with the President's approval, to reject this suggestion because he felt it would administer the *coup de grâce* to Chiang.[1] The idea persisted, however, and the following spring, after Dean Acheson's appointment as Secretary of State, Acheson obtained Truman's approval to go ahead with the preparation of a White Paper on China.

When Acheson said later that the White Paper had been published in the belief that "the disasters had already overtaken the Nationalist

---

[1] Walter Millis, ed., *The Forrestal Diaries* (New York: Viking, 1951), p. 534.

government,"[2] he meant that the White Paper could not have hastened a collapse that was already complete. By implication, the decision to publish the White Paper reflected the feeling that since we could no longer effectively influence events in China, we should not be entangled in them. This was the agonizing decision Marshall had shrunk from making a year earlier, when there may still have been grounds for hoping that a Nationalist collapse could be averted. By the spring of 1949, such grounds existed no longer. The Nationalist cause was in ruins: in January, Chiang Kai-shek quit the Presidency and Peiping fell; in April, Communist troops crossed the Yangtze without opposition, and peacefully occupied Shanghai a few days later.

The directive from President Truman and Secretary Acheson to the compilers of the White Paper called for a completely objective record. Yet the Administration plainly hoped this record would show that we had done as much as we could, that our course had been basically correct, and that the impending fall of China to the Communists was in no way attributable to American policy. The White Paper was issued to counter largely Republican criticism. In Truman's words, "The role of this government in its relations with China has been subject to considerable misrepresentation, distortion, and misunderstanding. Some of these attitudes arose because this government was reluctant to reveal certain facts . . ."[3] Truman believed his two goals—objectivity and justification—were compatible. His critics, as it turned out, found the White Paper neither objective nor convincing.

In overall charge of the project was W. Walton Butterworth, who was concurrently Director of the Office of Far Eastern Affairs and Acting Assistant Secretary of State for Far Eastern Affairs. Because of the weight of his duties, Butterworth delegated the actual preparation of the White Paper to his division officers, several of whom he detailed to full-time work on the project. Beginning about March 1949, the White Paper became a round-the-clock effort for those involved. Most of the work of writing and editing was done by five or six officers with recent and extensive experience in China.[4] Only materials in the files of the Department of State were used. To have searched for and sought the release of documents in other agencies—especially the former War Department—would have greatly delayed publication of the White Paper, and Acheson was anxious that it be issued as soon as possible.

[2] U.S. Senate, Committee on Armed Services and Committee on Foreign Relations, *Hearings on the Military Situation in the Far East*, 82d Cong., 1st Sess. (1951), p. 1770.
[3] Department of State, *Bulletin*, Aug. 15, 1949, p. 237.
[4] Many others helped in the preparation of the document, particularly in the Division of Historical Policy Research under G. Bernard Noble, but unless one counts archivists, secretaries, and clerks, the total number was far less than the eighty persons alleged by the journalist Arthur Krock.

This complete reliance on State Department files later led to charges that the White Paper was inadequate in its coverage.

In late June 1949, when the White Paper was nearly finished, Acheson asked Ambassador-at-Large Philip C. Jessup to read the document and suggest changes in it. Jessup, a professor of international law with a distinguished career at Columbia, was at that time the United States representative to the United Nations General Assembly and had been working on negotiations concerning the Berlin blockade. Later, during McCarthy's attacks on Jessup, the erroneous impression was given that the White Paper was largely his creation. Actually, the changes he suggested were few. Jessup did have an active hand, however, in preparing Acheson's Letter of Transmittal, the most controversial document in the volume. The letter subsequently went through many hands and many drafts before Acheson finally reworked it to suit himself.

As one might expect, the White Paper is composed primarily of documents and excerpts from documents, nearly all of which were highly classified before the White Paper was published. This preponderance is greater than appears at first sight, because even the narrative section contains long quotations from documents. Although the period of special reference is from 1944 to 1949, nearly one-fifth of the volume deals with the century from 1844 to 1943. There is very heavy emphasis— about 40 per cent of the total—on 1947 and 1948 (there are only a very few documents dating from early 1949). The volume's coverage is least extensive for 1944 and 1945.[5] Originally scheduled for release at the end of July, the White Paper was held up for about a week by printing difficulties. Because of the rush to publish, no index was prepared. The White Paper was released to the public on August 5, 1949, at a price of three dollars.

In issuing the White Paper, the Administration was proceeding in the belief—or the hope—that the record would speak for itself. Though its principal significance lay in domestic politics, one could expect the White Paper to have a very pronounced impact on both parties in China. Let us consider this impact briefly before turning to its reception in the United States.

The Chinese Communists made the White Paper the center of their first mass anti-American campaign. There had been much Communist-inspired criticism of the United States in the past, but there remained in

---

[5] Extensive and fascinating new documentation covering 1944 is now available in Department of State, *Foreign Relations of the United States, 1944, Vol. VI: China* (Washington, D.C., 1967), 1,206 pp. Similar volumes covering 1941, 1942, and 1943 were published earlier.

China considerable reservoirs of good feeling, particularly among the intellectuals and bourgeoisie in the cities. These reservoirs the Party now set out to drain, as a part of the larger movement to eliminate Western influence from China.

The last five articles in Volume IV of Mao's *Selected Works* denounce the United States in general and the White Paper in particular. Mao's editors describe the goals of the campaign when they say that these pieces "exposed the imperialist nature of United States policy toward China" and "criticized the illusions about U.S. imperialism harbored by some of the bourgeois intellectuals."[6] These articles were the signal for an intense campaign that reached wherever Communist influence was felt. In Nanking, for example, during more than a month following Mao's denunciation, only one issue of the Party paper failed to attack the White Paper, and sometimes additional pages were needed for this purpose. Mass rallies, well-attended by students and American-trained intellectuals, were held in all cities under Communist control.

The campaign sought to discredit the United States for everything it had done in China since the Treaty of Wanghia in 1844, and especially for its recent actions. The Chinese Communists did not find it necessary, or desirable, to translate the White Paper. Instead, they concentrated almost entirely on extracts from Acheson's Letter of Transmittal: the amount of aid given to the Nationalists; the assertion that the United States had done all it could to support Chiang; the claim that the "Communist leaders have foresworn their Chinese heritage" and are subservient to Russia; and above all, the statement that the United States should encourage developments to "throw off the foreign yoke."[7]

In this campaign, John Leighton Stuart, a former president of Yenching University, was particularly singled out, both as our last ambassador on the mainland, and also because he represented so well all that was finest in the American philanthropic and educational tradition in China. In "Farewell, Leighton Stuart!" Mao denounced him as one who "used to pretend to love both the United States and China." The article ends venomously: "Leighton Stuart has departed and the White Paper has arrived. Very good. Very good. Both events are worth celebrating."[8]

In Nationalist circles, the public and official reaction to the White Paper was surprisingly mild. When it became known, late in July, that

[6] Mao Tse-tung, *Selected Works* (Peking: Foreign Languages Press, 1961), IV, 426.
[7] Deliberately or not, one phrase (on p. xvi) was usually mistranslated in such a way that the United States appeared to be calling on Western-trained Chinese to revolt: "ultimately the profound civilization and the democratic individualism [the Communist press here translates 'democratic individualists'] of China will reassert themselves and she will throw off the foreign yoke."
[8] Mao, *Selected Works*, IV, 439.

such a document was about to be published, V. K. Wellington Koo, the Chinese Ambassador, requested postponement. On August 6, he acknowledged that China might have been "guilty of acts of commission and omission in the past" but asserted that "mistakes have not been confined to my country." He stressed the common cause that China was making still with the United States for freedom from Communism.[9] In Canton, Acting President Li Tsung-jen's capital, there was anger and dismay. Officially, however, Foreign Minister George Yeh stated on August 16 that whereas the Nationalists took "serious exception" to the White Paper on many points, "it is not the intention of the Chinese Government to engage in controversy over past issues." He was glad to see, he said, that the two countries agreed completely on at least two points: that the Chinese Communists were "thorough Marxists and tools of Moscow," and that the Soviet Union had violated the Treaty of Friendship and Alliance with China.[10]

Indirectly, the White Paper probably had something to do with the later reforms in the Kuomintang. As Ch'en Ch'eng, then Governor of Taiwan and later Vice-President, said at the time, "The White Paper has awakened us; we must now start on the road to self-help. Hence the publication of the White Paper will not cause us harm."[11] Chiang Kai-shek, then in nominal retirement, made no public statement and advised against an official Nationalist effort to refute the White Paper. Behind the scenes, however, the Nationalists continued to seek United States military aid, and to press their cause through their advocates in this country.

The reaction in the United States was predictably impassioned. No one could assert—or tried to assert—that United States policy in China had been successful. The best the Administration could hope for was acceptance of the White Paper at face value. A few liberal publications, among them the *New Republic* and the *Washington Post*, accepted it on these terms, but their voices went almost unheard in the clamor of criticism. The White Paper was attacked both for the policies it described and as a record of the effort to carry out those policies.

The main charges against the White Paper as a historical document were overall bias, omission and distortion, and premature publication. According to an editorial in the *New York Times*, "This inquest on China is not the work of a serene and detached coroner but of a vitally interested party to the catastrophe." *Time*, speaking for the Luce publications, called it a "lawyer's brief." Patrick Hurley, a vitally interested party himself, denounced it as a "smooth alibi for the pro-

[9] *New York Times*, Aug. 8, 1949, p. 2.
[10] *Ibid.*, Aug. 17, 1949, p. 4.
[11] *Ibid.*, Aug. 8, 1949, p. 2.

Communists in the State Department who have engineered the overthrow of our ally." Many argued that the Administration was trying to put all the blame on Chiang Kai-shek and assume none itself.

The State Department was also accused of deliberately omitting or distorting documents that did not support the Truman-Acheson policy. In the House, Walter Judd alleged sixteen instances of omission, falsification, or distortion. Acheson answered the allegations point by point, and repeated his assertion that the White Paper was a "fair and honest record"; the most important document referred to by Judd, he pointed out, was not held by the State Department and was thus not eligible for inclusion.[12] A few felt that the White Paper was slanted in the other direction. Owen Lattimore, soon to be himself the center of controversy, saw the White Paper as an effort to show "that in pursuit of impeccably anti-Russian aims the United States had engaged in as much intervention as the traffic could possibly bear."[13]

In handling the materials of history, each act of selection is also an act of judgment, and therefore the charge of bias is never completely answerable. But the charge that the White Paper was deliberately slanted is not substantiated by any materials that have since been made public. For the period from 1945 through 1948, the White Paper still stands as our most important single source for the study of United States relations with China.

The White Paper was also criticized for its timing. To some, the Nationalists were "still stubbornly squirming with life," and this document would undermine their efforts to stem the Communist tide. There were also those, including some within the State Department, who agreed with everything about the White Paper except its publication. They felt it was unnecessary and undignified for the United States to rush into public print with matters best handled behind closed doors, and with documents recently composed on the writers' assumption of official privacy.

On the level of policy, critics of the White Paper generally took the line that America's misguided or calculated failure to give Chiang Kai-shek the help he needed to beat the Chinese Communists was leading to Russian control of Asia. This charge broke down into a number of more specific charges: (1) that at Yalta the United States had sold China down the river to bribe Russia to enter a war we had already won; (2) that the Marshall mission's effort to form a coalition government in China had been designed to force the Nationalists into the lethal embrace of the Communists; (3) that in 1947 the Administration had sup-

---

[12] Judd made his charges on August 19. For Acheson's rebuttal, see Department of State, *Bulletin*, Sept. 5, 1949, pp. 350-52, 359.
[13] *The Nation*, Sept. 3, 1949, p. 223.

pressed the Wedemeyer Report, which had recognized the Communist threat to Asia and had called for aid to the Nationalists; (4) that reasonable amounts of military aid, without American military participation except for advisers, would have enabled Chiang to defeat the Chinese Communists; (5) that disloyalty and pro-Communism in the State Department had an evil influence on our China policy.

Although most of these charges remain in some minds controversial to this day, some things seem clearer now than they did twenty years ago. While Yalta, for example, was surely one of Roosevelt's least auspicious exercises in personal diplomacy, the record shows that Russia's participation in the decisive struggle against Japan was still thought absolutely necessary. Furthermore, Chiang had explicitly requested the United States to act as mediator between China and Russia; in order to lure Stalin away from the Chinese Communists, he had offered to make some (not all) of the Yalta concessions that were later so bitterly assailed.

The unification of China by political means (that is, some form of multi-party or coalition government) was the announced aim of both the Nationalists and the Communists even before General Hurley arrived on the scene in 1944. Not only Marshall, but Hurley before him, tried to find some formula that both parties could agree on; indeed, Hurley himself was the principal drafter of a set of proposals for the Chinese Communists to present to the Nationalists.[14] He called its terms "eminently fair," adding that "if there is a breakdown in the parleys it will be the fault of the Government and not the Communists." So far as concessions to the Communist viewpoint are concerned, Hurley's proposal, which the Kuomintang found utterly unacceptable and which Hurley complained to Roosevelt "had not been treated with due consideration," far surpassed any proposal later made by Marshall.

Acheson's Letter of Transmittal stated that the Wedemeyer Report had not been released because it called for Russian participation in a five-power guardianship over Manchuria. But other considerations were probably equally compelling. One was General Wedemeyer's blunt indictment of Nationalist corruption and incompetence, which was about as sweeping in 1947 as the White Paper's two years later. Another was the self-contradictory nature of Wedemeyer's recommendations: he concluded that "until drastic political and economic reforms are undertaken, United States aid cannot accomplish its purpose," yet he called for extensive assistance to China "as early as practicable." A third was Wedemeyer's ill-considered proposal that aid be granted only if China requested advisers with considerable power in "specified economic and military fields." Chiang had never granted such powers in

---

[14] *Foreign Relations, 1944: China*, pp. 666-735, documents under file no. 1049; the two brief quotations in the next sentence are from p. 693 and p. 734.

the past; had he done so now, as Marshall realized, it would have been a long step toward full-scale American involvement in the Chinese civil war.

As for the amount of American aid to China, the whole issue has a quality of unreality. Estimates of our aid to the Nationalist Government ranged from a low of $110 million (Senators Bridges, Knowland, Pat McCarran, and Kenneth Wherry, and the Chinese Embassy in Washington) to a high of $5.9 billion (Mao). The State Department (see pp. 1042-53) showed postwar aid of just over $2 billion, about half of which was classed as military aid. To the Nationalists and their supporters, any amount of aid would have been insufficient if it failed to defeat the Communists. To those who opposed further military aid, the fall of the Kuomintang was the result of its own inadequacies; the waste of past aid showed that future aid would do no good, and nothing in Chiang's record warranted the risk of an open-ended American commitment of unforeseeable size.

Surely the ugliest and probably the most damaging aspect of the furor was the allegation of Communist influence in the State Department. McCarthy's charges finally proved baseless, but in the meantime lives and careers were ruined and lasting harm was done to the conduct of America's foreign policy. The reception of the White Paper instructed many government officials in the value of caution, and persuaded numbers of capable young men to seek careers elsewhere. Some of America's most able and best qualified China specialists were dismissed from the State Department, later to be offered reinstatement and back pay when it was shown that there was no case against them. Others were transferred to less sensitive positions, where often the road to advancement was blocked by their previous association with China. Some were persuaded to accept early retirement. In any case, their long experience and intimate knowledge of China were lost. Among the best known of these men were John Carter Vincent, John Stewart Service, and John Paton Davies. Their reports on China in the 1940's have stood the test of time; by contrast, what few criticisms might be made of their work now seem hardly more than cavils. Many of the reports for which they were later condemned were penetrating insights into Chinese political realities. They saw clearly, and warned their superiors, of the danger of tying the United States irrevocably to a regime that was rapidly discrediting itself and might well be unable to survive. For telling unpleasant truths about the Nationalists, they were later called Communists. Professor John K. Fairbank's tribute to them is no more than just: "These men were true China specialists and we have no one like them today [1967]. In our lifetime we shall never again get this much of a grasp of the Chinese scene."

Almost alone in its judiciousness and insight was Walter Lippmann's reaction to the White Paper.[15] If Acheson was right that nothing the United States had done or left undone had affected the outcome in China (p. xvi), then, Lippmann asked, why did we continue so long and at such cost to support the side we knew was going to lose? At the time, he was one of the very few who saw and described Marshall's dilemma, which reflected in a modern form America's traditional inability to bring its China policy into line with its effective influence in China.

Both critics and supporters of the Truman Administration knew that the White Paper marked the end of an era, and both sides called for a thoroughgoing reappraisal of our Far Eastern policy. Just before the publication of the White Paper, Acheson announced that such a review had been initiated within the State Department, that top-level outside advice was being sought, and that close liaison would be maintained with Congress and other agencies of the executive branch. On October 6-8, 1949, at a closed-door session on Far Eastern policy in Washington some twenty-five China specialists, international businessmen, and public figures (including Marshall, George F. Kennan, and Harold E. Stassen) expressed their opinions on what course American policy should take.[16] Subsequently, the trend of policy, which with certain exceptions represented rather well the sense of these discussions, was to withhold recognition from the Communists while at the same time further dissociating the United States from the Nationalists. The United States also indicated it would regard any Chinese Communist military or political activity beyond the borders of China as a threat to peace.

This policy was plainly expressed in January 1950. In a series of statements, Truman and Acheson indicated that the United States would not provide military aid or advice to "the Chinese forces on Formosa," that we intended to keep "hands off," and that the island, having little strategic significance, lay outside our first line of defense in the Western Pacific. Criticism of the Administration reached a new pitch, fed now by McCarthy's charges, but the policy of disengagement remained in force.

Early in the morning of June 25, 1950, North Korea launched its invasion of South Korea. Truman reacted immediately through the United Nations. Two days later, on June 27, he sent the Seventh Fleet into the Straits of Formosa with orders to prevent any attack on the is-

---

[15] In the columns of the *New York Herald Tribune* on Sept. 6, 8, and 12, 1949.

[16] The transcript of the discussions is contained in U.S. Senate, Committee on the Judiciary, Subcommittee to Investigate the Administration of the Internal Security Act, *Hearings on the Institute of Pacific Relations*, 82d Cong., 1st Sess. (1951), pp. 1551-1682.

land. Our present commitment to the Nationalist Government dates from that order. The Korean War thus brought to a sudden end the policy that the Administration had followed for two years, and committed us once again to involvement in the Chinese civil war.

Because history never repeats itself exactly, no two historical situations are entirely analogous. But a number of parallels between the more recent situation in Vietnam and the earlier situation in China are too striking to be ignored. In both situations, our recognition and support went to a regime with acknowledged shortcomings but to which there seemed to be no adequate alternative. In both there existed the elements of both civil war and international aggression, with a great debate about which was the dominant force. In both there were abundant predictions that limited aid and advice, with direct American military participation, would bring victory in a short period of time. And in both, withdrawal became more difficult as time went on. The obvious difference is that in Vietnam the decision was made to engage. In Vietnam, smaller in size and population than many Chinese provinces, what began as limited and indirect assistance has grown to a half million men and $2 billion per month. In retrospect, it appears that Marshall saw clearly where further intervention would have led in China (p. 382): "The U.S. would have to be prepared virtually to take over the Chinese Government and administer its economic, military and governmental affairs. . . . It would involve this Government in a continuing commitment from which it would be practically impossible to withdraw, and it would very probably involve grave consequences to this nation by making of China an arena of international conflict."

These reflections lead us back to crucial questions, questions that the White Paper raises but cannot fully answer because America itself has not yet given the answers. If in China there was a gap between what we said and what we did, in Vietnam the United States has tried to close this gap not by expressing its goals in less sweeping terms but by pursuing them with vastly greater force. Are the goals of United States Asian policy justified? Is the United States able to achieve such goals? And at what point does the employment of force render meaningless the very goals it seeks? In China as in Vietnam, other issues may have seemed more immediate, but these questions persist. Parts of the answer may lie in a purblind anti-Communism, in the illusion of American omnipotence, and in the force of American self-righteousness. Other answers may lie in the cultural gap across the Pacific and our underestimation of the difficulties involved; and still other answers may suggest themselves to attentive readers of the record that follows. A partial answer is perhaps all we shall have in our time.

THE CHINA WHITE PAPER

United States Relations With

China

With Special Reference
to the Period 1944–1949

BASED ON THE FILES OF THE DEPARTMENT OF STATE

Letter of Transmittal

DEPARTMENT OF STATE
Washington, July 30, 1949

THE PRESIDENT: In accordance with your wish, I have had compiled a record of our relations with China, special emphasis being placed on the last five years. This record is being published and will therefore be available to the Congress and to the people of the United States.

Although the compilation is voluminous, it necessarily covers a relatively small part of the relations between China and the United States. Since the beginning of World War II, these relations have involved many Government departments and agencies. The preparation of the full historical record of that period is by no means yet complete. Because of the great current interest in the problems confronting China, I have not delayed publication until the complete analysis could be made of the archives of the National Military Establishment, the Treasury Department, the Lend-Lease Administration, the White House files and many other official sources. However, I instructed those charged with the compilation of this document to present a record which would reveal the salient facts which determined our policy toward China during this period and which reflect the execution of that policy. This is a frank record of an extremely complicated and most unhappy period in the life of a great country to which the United States has long been attached by ties of closest friendship. No available item has been omitted because it contains statements critical of our policy or might be the basis of future criticism. The inherent strength of our system is the responsiveness of the Government to an informed and critical public opinion. It is precisely this informed and critical public opinion which totalitarian governments, whether Rightist or Communist, cannot endure and do not tolerate.

The interest of the people and the Government of the United States in China goes far back into our history. Despite the distance and broad differences in background which separate China and the United States, our friendship for that country has always been intensified by the religious, philanthropic and cultural ties which have united the two peoples, and has been attested by many acts of good will over a period of many years, including the use of the Boxer indemnity for the education of Chinese students, the abolition of extraterritoriality during the Second World War, and our extensive aid to China during and since the close of the war. The record shows that the United States has consistently maintained and still maintains those fundamental principles of our foreign policy toward China which include the doctrine of the Open Door, respect for the administrative and territorial integrity of China, and opposition to any foreign domination of China. It is deplorable that respect for the truth in the compilation of this record makes it necessary to publish an account of facts which reveal the distressing situation in that country. I have not felt, however, that publication could be withheld for that reason.

The record should be read in the light of conditions prevailing when the events occurred. It must not be forgotten, for example, that throughout World War II we were allied with Russia in the struggle to defeat Germany and Italy, and that a prime object of our policy was to bring Russia into the struggle against Japan in time to be of real value in the prosecution of the war. In this period, military considerations were understandably predominant over all others. Our most urgent purpose in the Far East was to defeat the common enemy and save the lives of our own men and those of our comrades-in-arms, the Chinese included. We should have failed in our manifest duty had we pursued any other course.

In the years since V-J Day, as in the years before Pearl Harbor, military considerations have been secondary to an earnest desire on our part to assist the Chinese people to achieve peace, prosperity and internal stability. The decisions and actions of our Government to promote these aims necessarily were taken on the basis of information available at the time. Throughout this tragic period, it has been fully realized that the material aid, the military and technical assistance, and the good will of the United States, however abundant, could not of themselves put China on her feet. In the last analysis, that can be done only by China herself.

Two factors have played a major role in shaping the destiny of modern China.

The population of China during the eighteenth and nineteenth centuries doubled, thereby creating an unbearable pressure upon the land. The first problem which every Chinese Government has had to face is that of feeding this population. So far none has succeeded. The Kuomintang attempted to solve it by putting many land-reform laws on the statute books. Some of these laws have failed, others have been ignored. In no small measure, the predicament in which the National Government finds itself today is due to its failure to provide China with enough to eat. A large part of the Chinese Communists' propaganda consists of promises that they will solve the land problem.

The second major factor which has shaped the pattern of contemporary China is the impact of the West and of Western ideas. For more than three thousand years the Chinese developed their own high culture and civilization, largely untouched by outside influences. Even when subjected to military conquest the Chinese always managed in the end to subdue and absorb the invader. It was natural therefore that they should come to look upon themselves as the center of the world and the highest expression of civilized mankind. Then in the middle of the nineteenth century the heretofore impervious wall of Chinese isolation was breached by the West. These outsiders brought with them aggressiveness, the unparalleled development of Western technology, and a high order of culture which had not accompanied previous foreign incursions into China. Partly because of these qualities and partly because of the decay of Manchu rule, the Westerners, instead of being absorbed by the Chinese, introduced new ideas which played an important part in stimulating ferment and unrest.

By the beginning of the twentieth century, the combined force of overpopulation and new ideas set in motion that chain of events which can be called the Chinese revolution. It is one of the most imposing revolutions in recorded history and its outcome and consequences are yet to be foreseen. Out of this revolutionary whirlpool emerged the Kuomintang, first under the leadership of Dr. Sun Yat-sen, and later Generalissimo Chiang Kai-shek, to assume the direction of the revolution. The leadership of the Kuomintang was not challenged until 1927 by the Chinese Communist party which had been organized in the early twenties under the ideological impetus of the Russian revolution. It should be remembered that Soviet doctrine and practice had a measurable effect upon the thinking and principles of Dr. Sun Yat-sen, particularly in terms of economics and party organization, and that the Kuomintang and the Chinese Communists cooperated until 1927 when the Third International demanded a predominant position in the Government and the army. It was this demand which precipitated the break between the two groups. To a large extent the history of the period between 1927 and 1937 can be written in terms of the struggle for power between the Kuomintang and the Chinese Communists, with the latter apparently fighting a losing battle. During this period the Kuomintang made considerable progress in its efforts to unify the country and to build up the nation's financial and economic strength. Somewhere during this decade, however, the Kuomintang began to lose the dynamism and revolutionary fervor which had created it, while in the Chinese Communists the fervor became fanaticism.

Perhaps largely because of the progress being made in China, the Japanese chose 1937 as the departure point for the conquest of China proper, and the goal of the Chinese people became the expulsion of a brutal and hated invader. Chinese resistance against Japan during the early years of the war compelled the unqualified admiration of freedom-loving peoples throughout the world. Until 1940 this resistance was largely without foreign support. The tragedy of these years of war was that physical and human devastation to a large extent destroyed the emerging middle class which historically has been the backbone and heart of liberalism and democracy.

In contrast also to the unity of the people of China in the war against Japan were the divided interests of the leaders of the Kuomintang and of the Chinese Communists. It became apparent in the early forties that the leaders of the Government, just as much as the Communist leaders, were still as preoccupied with the internal struggle for power as they were with waging war against Japan. Once the United States became a participant in the war, the Kuomintang was apparently convinced of the ultimate defeat of Japan and saw an opportunity to improve its position for a show-down struggle with the Communists. The Communists, for their part, seemed to see in the chaos of China an opportunity to obtain that which had been denied them before the Japanese war, namely, full power in China. This struggle for power in the latter years of the war contributed largely to the partial paralysis of China's ability to resist.

It was precisely here that two of the fundamental principles of United States policy in regard to China—noninterference in its internal affairs and support of its unity and territorial integrity—came into conflict and that one of them also conflicted with the basic interests of the Allies in the war against Japan. It seemed highly probable in 1943 and 1944 that, unless the Chinese could subordinate their internal interests to the larger interest of the unified war effort against Japan, Chinese resistance would become completely ineffective and the Japanese would be able to deprive the Allies of valuable bases, operating points and manpower in China at a time when the outcome of the war against Japan was still far from clear. In this situation and in the light of the paramount necessity of the most vigorous prosecution of the war, in which Chinese interests were equally at stake with our own, traditional concepts of policy had to be adapted to a new and unprecedented situation.

After Pearl Harbor we expanded the program of military and economic aid which we had inaugurated earlier in 1941 under the Lend-Lease Act. That program, described in chapter I of the attached record, was far from reaching the volume which we would have wished because of the tremendous demands on the United States from all theaters of a world-wide war and because of the difficulties of access to a China all of whose ports were held by the enemy. Nevertheless it was substantial.

Representatives of our Government, military and civilian, who were sent to assist the Chinese in prosecuting the war soon discovered that, as indicated above, the long struggle had seriously weakened the Chinese Government not only militarily and economically, but also politically and in morale. The reports of United States military and diplomatic officers reveal a growing conviction through 1943 and 1944 that the Government and the Kuomintang had apparently lost the crusading spirit that won them the people's loyalty during the early years of the war. In the opinion of many observers they had sunk into corruption, into a scramble for place and power, and into reliance on the United States to win the war for them and to preserve their own domestic supremacy. The Government of China, of course, had always been a one-party rather than a democratic government in the Western sense. The stresses and strains of war were now rapidly weakening such liberal elements as it did possess and strengthening the grip of the reactionaries who were indistinguishable from the war lords of the past. The mass of the Chinese people were coming more and more to lose confidence in the Government.

It was evident to us that only a rejuvenated and progressive Chinese Government which could recapture the enthusiastic loyalty of the people could and would wage an effective war against Japan. American officials repeatedly brought their concern with this situation to the attention of the Generalissimo and he repeatedly assured them that it would be corrected. He made, however, little or no effective effort to correct it and tended to shut himself off from Chinese officials who gave unpalatable advice. In addition to a concern over the effect which this atrophy of the central Chinese administration must have upon the conduct of the war, some American observers, whose reports are also quoted in the attached record, were concerned over the effect which this deterioration of the Kuomintang must have on its eventual struggle, whether political or military, with the Chinese Communists. These observers were already fearful in 1943 and 1944 that the National Government might be so isolating itself from the people that in the postwar competition for power it would prove itself impotent to maintain its authority. Nevertheless, we continued for obvious reasons to direct all our aid to the National Government.

This was of course the period during which joint prosecution of the war against Nazi Germany had produced a degree of cooperation between the United States and Russia. President Roosevelt was determined to do what he could to bring about a continuance in the postwar period of the partnership forged in the fire of battle. The peoples of the world, sickened and weary with the excesses, the horrors, and the degradation of the war, shared this desire. It has remained for the postwar years to demonstrate that one of the major partners in this world alliance seemingly no longer pursues this aim, if indeed it ever did.

When Maj. Gen. Patrick J. Hurley was sent by President Roosevelt to Chungking in 1944 he found what he considered to be a willingness on the part of the National Government and the Chinese Communists to lay aside their differences and cooperate in a common effort. Already they had been making sporadic attempts to achieve this result.

Previously and subsequently, General Hurley had been assured by Marshal Stalin that Russia had no intention of recognizing any government in China except the National Government with Chiang Kai-shek as its leader. It may be noted that during the late war years and for a time afterwards Marshal Stalin reiterated these views to American officials. He and Molotov expressed the view that China should look to the United States as the principal possible source of aid. The sentiments expressed by Marshal Stalin were in large part incorporated in the Sino-Soviet treaty of 1945.

From the wartime cooperation with the Soviet Union and from the costly campaigns against the Japanese came the Yalta Agreement. The American Government and people awaited with intense anxiety the assault on the main islands of Japan which it was feared would cost up to a million American casualties before Japan was conquered. The atomic bomb was not then a reality and it seemed impossible that the war in the Far East could be ended without this assault. It thus became a primary concern of the American Government to see to it that the Soviet Union enter the war against Japan at the earliest possible date in order that the Japanese Army in Manchuria might not be returned to the homeland at the critical moment. It was considered vital not only that the Soviet Union enter the war but that she do so before our invasion of Japan, which already had been set for the autumn of 1945.

At Yalta, Marshal Stalin not only agreed to attack Japan within two or three months after V–E Day but limited his "price" with reference to Manchuria substantially to the position which Russia had occupied there prior to 1904. We for our part, in order to obtain this commitment and thus to bring the war to a close with a consequent saving of American, Chinese and other Allied lives, were prepared to and did pay the requisite price. Two facts must not, however, be lost sight of in this connection. First, the Soviet Union when she finally did enter the war against Japan, could in any case have seized all the territories in question and considerably more regardless of what our attitude might have been. Second, the Soviets on their side in the Sino-Soviet Treaty arising from the Yalta Agreement, agreed to give the National Government of China moral and material support and moreover formalized their assurances of noninterference in China's internal affairs. Although the unexpectedly early collapse of Japanese resistance later made some of the provisions of the Yalta Agreement seem unnecessary, in the light of the predicted course of the war at that time they were considered to be not only justified but clearly advantageous. Although dictated by military necessity, the Agreement and the subsequent Sino–Soviet Treaty in fact imposed limitations on the action which Russia would, in any case, have been in a position to take.

For reasons of military security, and for those only, it was considered too dangerous for the United States to consult with the National Government regarding the Yalta Agreement or to communicate its terms at once to Chungking. We were then in the midst of the Pacific War. It was felt that there was grave risk that secret information transmitted to the Nationalist capital at this time would become available to the Japanese almost immediately. Under no circumstances, therefore, would we have been justified in incurring the security risks involved. It was not until June 15, 1945, that General Hurley was authorized to inform Chiang Kai-shek of the Agreement.

In conformity with the Russian agreement at Yalta to sign a treaty of friendship and alliance with Nationalist China, negotiations between the two nations began in Moscow in July 1945. During their course, the United States felt obliged to remind both parties that the purpose of the treaty was to implement the Yalta Agreement—no more, no less—and that some of the Soviet proposals exceeded its provisions. The treaty, which was signed on August 14, 1945, was greeted with general satisfaction both in Nationalist China and in the United States. It was considered that Russia had accepted definite limitations on its activities in China and was committed to withhold all aid from the Chinese Communists. On September 10, however, our embassy in Moscow cautioned against placing undue confidence in the Soviet observance of either the spirit or letter of the treaty. The subsequent conduct of the Soviet Government in Manchuria has amply justified this warning.

When peace came the United States was confronted with three possible alternatives in China: (1) it could have pulled out lock, stock and barrel; (2) it could have intervened militarily on a major scale to assist the Nationalists to destroy the Communists; (3) it could, while assisting the Nationalists to assert their authority over as much of China as possible, endeavor to avoid a civil war by working for a compromise between the two sides.

The first alternative would, and I believe American public opinion at the time so felt, have represented an abandonment of our international responsibilities and of our traditional policy of friendship for China before we had made a determined effort to be of assistance. The second alternative policy, while it may look attractive theoretically and in retrospect, was wholly impracticable. The Nationalists had been unable to destroy the Communists during the 10 years before the war. Now after the war the Nationalists were, as indicated above, weakened, demoralized, and unpopular. They had quickly dissipated their popular support and prestige in the areas liberated from the Japanese by the conduct of their civil and military officials. The Communists on the other hand were much stronger than they had ever been and were in control of most of North China. Because of the ineffectiveness of the Nationalist forces which was later to be tragically demonstrated, the Communists probably could have been dislodged only by American arms. It is obvious that the American people would not have sanctioned such a colossal commitment of our armies in 1945 or later. We therefore came to the third alternative policy whereunder we faced the facts of the situation and attempted to assist in working out a *modus vivendi* which would avert civil war but nevertheless preserve and even increase the influence of the National Government.

As the record shows, it was the Chinese National Government itself which, prior to General Hurley's mission, had taken steps to arrive at a working agreement with the Communists. As early as September 1943 in addressing the Kuomintang Central Executive Committee, the Generalissimo said, "we should clearly recognize that the Communist problem is a purely political problem and should be solved by political means." He repeated this view on several occasions. Comprehensive negotiations between representatives of the Government and of the Communists, dealing with both military cooperation and civil administration, were opened in Sian in May 1944. These negotiations, in which Ambassador Hurley later assisted at the invitation of both parties between August 1944 and September 1945, continued intermittently during a year and a half without producing conclusive results and culminated in a comprehensive series of agreements on basic points on October 11, 1945, after Ambassador Hurley's departure from China and before General Marshall's arrival. Meanwhile, however, clashes between the armed forces of the two groups were increasing and were jeopardizing the fulfillment of the agreements. The danger of wide-spread civil war, unless the negotiations could promptly be brought to a successful conclusion, was critical. It was under these circumstances that General Marshall left on his mission to China at the end of 1945.

As the account of General Marshall's mission and the subsequent years in chapters V and VI of the underlying record reveals, our policy at that time was inspired by the two objectives of bringing peace to China under conditions which would permit stable government and progress along democratic lines, and of assisting the National Government to establish its authority over as wide areas of China as possible. As the event proved, the first objective was unrealizable because neither side desired it to succeed: the Communists because they refused to accept conditions which would weaken their freedom to proceed with what remained consistently their aim, the communization of all China; the Nationalists because they cherished the illusion, in spite of repeated advice to the contrary from our military representatives, that they could destroy the Communists by force of arms.

The second objective of assisting the National Government, however, we pursued vigorously from 1945 to 1949. The National Government was the recognized government of a friendly power. Our friendship, and our right under international law alike, called for aid to the Government instead of to the Communists who were seeking to subvert and overthrow it. The extent of our aid to Nationalist China is set forth in detail in chapters V, VI, VII and VIII of the record and need not be repeated here. The National Government had in 1945, and maintained until the early fall of 1948, a marked superiority in manpower and armament over their rivals. Indeed during that period, thanks very largely to our aid in transporting, arming and supplying their forces, they extended their control over a large part of North China and Manchuria. By the time General Marshall left China at the beginning of 1947, the Nationalists were apparently at the very peak of their military successes and territorial expansion. The following year and a half revealed, however, that their seeming strength was illusory and that their victories were built on sand.

The crisis had developed around Manchuria, traditional focus of Russian and Japanese imperialism. On numerous occasions, Marshal Stalin had stated categorically that he expected the National Government to take over the occupation of Manchuria. In the truce agreement of January 10, 1946, the Chinese Communists agreed to the movement of Government troops into Manchuria for the purpose of restoring Chinese sovereignty over this area. In conformity with this understanding the United States transported sizable government armies to the ports of entry into Manchuria. Earlier the Soviet Army had expressed a desire to evacuate Manchuria in December 1945, but had remained an additional two or three months at the request of the Chinese Government. When the Russian troops did begin their evacuation, the National Government found itself with extended lines of communications, limited rolling stock and insufficient forces to take over the areas being evacuated in time to prevent the entry of Chinese Communist forces, who were already in occupation of the countryside. As the Communists entered, they obtained the large stocks of matériel from the Japanese Kwantung Army which the Russians had conveniently "abandoned." To meet this situation the National Government embarked on a series of military campaigns which expanded the line of its holdings to the Sungari River. Toward the end of these campaigns it also commenced hostilities within North China and succeeded in constricting the areas held by the Communists.

In the spring of 1946 General Marshall attempted to restore peace. This effort lasted for months and during its course a seemingly endless series of proposals and counterproposals were made which had little effect upon the course of military activities and produced no political settlement. During these negotiations General Marshall displayed limitless patience and tact and a willingness to try and then try again in order to reach agreement. Increasingly he became convinced, however, that twenty years of intermittent civil war between the two factions, during which the leading figures had remained the same, had created such deep personal bitterness and such irreconcilable differences that no agreement was possible. The suspicions and the lack of confidence were beyond remedy. He became convinced that both parties were merely sparring for time, jockeying for military position and catering temporarily to what they believed to be American desires. General Marshall concluded that there was no hope of accomplishing the objectives of his mission.

Even though for all practical purposes General Marshall, by the fall of 1946, had withdrawn from his efforts to assist in a peaceful settlement of the civil war, he remained in China until January 1947. One of the critical points of dispute between the Government and the Communists had been the convocation of the National Assembly to write a new constitution for China and to bring an end to the period of political tutelage and of one-party government. The Communists had refused to participate in the National Assembly unless there were a prior military settlement. The Generalissimo was determined that the Assembly should be held and the program carried out. It was the hope of General Marshall during the late months of 1946 that his presence in China would encourage the liberal elements in non-Communist China to assert themselves more forcefully than they had in the past and to exercise a leavening influence upon the absolutist control wielded by the reactionaries and the militarists. General Marshall remained in China until the Assembly had completed its work. Even though the proposed new framework of government appeared satisfactory, the evidence suggested that there had been little shift in the balance of power.

In his farewell statement, General Marshall announced the termination of his efforts to assist the Chinese in restoring internal peace. He described the deep-seated mutual suspicion between the Kuomintang and the Chinese Communist Party as the greatest obstacle to a settlement. He made it clear that the salvation of China lay in the hands of the Chinese themselves and that, while the newly adopted constitution provided the framework for a democratic China, practical measures of implementation by both sides would be the decisive test. He appealed for the assumption of leadership by liberals in and out of the Government as the road to unity and peace. With these final words he returned to Washington to assume, in January 1947, his new post as Secretary of State.

As the signs of impending disaster multiplied, the President in July 1947, acting on the recommendation of the Secretary of State, instructed Lt. Gen. Albert C. Wedemeyer to survey the Chinese scene and make recommendations. In his report, submitted on September 19, 1947, the General recommended that the United States continue and expand its policy of giving aid to Nationalist China, subject to these stipulations:

1. That China inform the United Nations of her request for aid.

2. That China request the United Nations to bring about a truce in Manchuria and request that Manchuria be placed under a Five-Power guardianship or a trusteeship.

3. That China utilize her own resources, reform her finances, her Government and her armies, and accept American advisers in the military and economic fields.

General Wedemeyer's report, which fully recognized the danger of Communist domination of all China and was sympathetic to the problems of the National Government, nevertheless listed a large number of reforms which he considered essential if that Government were to rehabilitate itself.

It was decided that the publication at that time of a suggestion for the alienation of a part of China from the control of the National Government, and for placing that part under an international administration to include Soviet Russia, would not be helpful. In this record, the full text of that part of General Wedemeyer's report which deals with China appears as an annex to chapter VI.

The reasons for the failures of the Chinese National Government appear in some detail in the attached record. They do not stem from any inadequacy of American aid. Our military observers on the spot have reported that the Nationalist armies did not lose a single battle during the crucial year of 1948 through lack of arms or ammunition. The fact was that the decay which our observers had detected in Chungking early in the war had fatally sapped the powers of resistance of the Kuomintang. Its leaders had proved incapable of meeting the crisis confronting them, its troops had lost the will to fight, and its Government had lost popular support. The Communists, on the other hand, through a ruthless discipline and fanatical zeal, attempted to sell themselves as guardians and liberators of the people. The Nationalist armies did not have to be defeated; they disintegrated. History has proved again and again that a regime without faith in itself and an army without morale cannot survive the test of battle.

The record obviously can not set forth in equal detail the inner history and development of the Chinese Communist Party during these years. The principal reason is that, while we had regular diplomatic relations with the National Government and had the benefit of voluminous reports from our representatives in their territories, our direct contact with the Communists was limited in the main to the mediation efforts of General Hurley and General Marshall.

Fully recognizing that the heads of the Chinese Communist Party were ideologically affiliated with Moscow, our Government nevertheless took the view, in the light of the existing balance of forces in China, that peace could be established only if certain conditions were met. The Kuomintang would have to set its own house in order and both sides would have to make concessions so that the Government of China might become, in fact as well as in name, the Government of all China and so that all parties might function within the constitutional system of the Government. Both internal peace and constitutional development required that the progress should be rapid from one party government with a large opposition party in armed rebellion, to the participation of all parties, including the moderate non-communist elements, in a truly national system of government.

None of these conditions has been realized. The distrust of the leaders of both the Nationalist and Communist Parties for each other proved too deep-seated to permit final agreement, notwithstanding temporary truces and apparently promising negotiations. The Nationalists, furthermore, embarked in 1946 on an over-ambitious military campaign in the face of warnings by General Marshall that it not only would fail but would plunge China into economic chaos and eventually destroy the National Government. General Marshall pointed out that though Nationalist armies could, for a period, capture Communist-held cities, they could not destroy the Communist armies. Thus every Nationalist advance would expose their communications to attack by Communist guerrillas and compel them to retreat or to surrender their armies together with the munitions which the United States has furnished them. No estimate of a military situation has ever been more completely confirmed by the resulting facts.

The historic policy of the United States of friendship and aid toward the people of China was, however, maintained in both peace and war. Since V–J Day, the United States Government has authorized aid to Nationalist China in the form of grants and credits totaling approximately 2 billion dollars, an amount equivalent in value to more than 50 percent of the monetary expenditures of the Chinese Government and of proportionately greater magnitude in relation to the budget of that Government than the United States has provided to any nation of Western Europe since the end of the war. In addition to these grants and credits, the United States Government has sold the Chinese Government large quantities of military and civilian war surplus property with a total procurement cost of over 1 billion dollars, for which the agreed realization to the United States was 232 million dollars. A large proportion of the military supplies furnished the Chinese armies by the United States since V–J Day has, however, fallen into the hands of the Chinese Communists through the military ineptitude of the Nationalist leaders, their defections and surrenders, and the absence among their forces of the will to fight.

It has been urged that relatively small amounts of additional aid—military and economic—to the National Government would have enabled it to destroy communism in China. The most trustworthy military, economic, and political information available to our Government does not bear out this view.

A realistic appraisal of conditions in China, past and present, leads to the conclusion that the only alternative open to the United States was full-scale intervention in behalf of a Government which had lost the confidence of its own troops and its own people. Such intervention would have required the expenditure of even greater sums than have been fruitlessly spent thus far, the command of Nationalist armies by American officers, and the probable participation of American armed forces—land, sea, and air—in the resulting war. Intervention of such a scope and magnitude would have been resented by the mass of the Chinese people, would have diametrically reversed our historic policy, and would have been condemned by the American people.

It must be admitted frankly that the American policy of assisting the Chinese people in resisting domination by any foreign power or powers is now confronted with the gravest difficulties. The heart of China is in Communist hands. The Communist leaders have foresworn their Chinese heritage and have publicly announced their subservience to a foreign power, Russia, which during the last 50 years, under czars and Communists alike, has been most assiduous in its efforts to extend its control in the Far East. In the recent past, attempts at foreign domination have appeared quite clearly to the Chinese people as external aggression and as such have been bitterly and in the long run successfully resisted. Our aid and encouragement have helped them to resist. In this case, however, the foreign domination has been masked behind the façade of a vast crusading movement which apparently has seemed to many Chinese to be wholly indigenous and national. Under these circumstances, our aid has been unavailing.

The unfortunate but inescapable fact is that the ominous result of the civil war in China was beyond the control of the government of the United States. Nothing that this country did or could have done within the reasonable limits of its capabilities could have changed that result; nothing that was left undone by this country has contributed to it. It was the product of internal Chinese forces, forces which this country tried to influence but could not. A decision was arrived at within China, if only a decision by default.

And now it is abundantly clear that we must face the situation as it exists in fact. We will not help the Chinese or ourselves by basing our policy on wishful thinking. We continue to believe that, however tragic may be the immediate future of China and however ruthlessly a major portion of this great people may be exploited by a party in the interest of a foreign imperialism, ultimately the profound civilization and the democratic individualism of China will reassert themselves and she will throw off the foreign yoke. I consider that we should encourage all developments in China which now and in the future work toward this end.

In the immediate future, however, the implementation of our historic policy of friendship for China must be profoundly affected by current developments. It will necessarily be influenced by the degree to which the Chinese people come to recognize that the Communist regime serves not their interests but those of Soviet Russia and the manner in which, having become aware of the facts, they react to this foreign domination.   One point, however, is clear. Should the Communist regime lend itself to the aims of Soviet Russian imperialism and attempt to engage in aggression against China's neighbors, we and the other members of the United Nations would be confronted by a situation violative of the principles of the United Nations Charter and threatening international peace and security.

Meanwhile our policy will continue to be based upon our own respect for the Charter, our friendship for China, and our traditional support for the Open Door and for China's independence and administrative and territorial integrity.

Respectfully yours,

DEAN ACHESON

Contents

CHAPTER IV

The Yalta Agreement and the Sino-Soviet Treaty of 1945

CHAPTER V

The Mission of General George C. Marshall, 1945–1947

CHAPTER VII

The Military Picture, 1945–1949

LIST OF ANNEXES

Page

CHAPTER VII

The Military Picture, 1945–1949

Chronology of Principal Events Affecting Sino-American Relations

1844
July 3   Treaty of Wanghia, first Sino-U.S. treaty (Cushing Treaty)

1858
June 18   Treaty of Tientsin (Reed Treaty)

1868
July 28   Treaty of Washington (Burlingame Treaty)

1899
Sept.–Mar.   Secretary Hay's Open Door notes
   1900

1900
July 3   U.S. policy on preservation of Chinese territorial and administrative entity announced

1903
Oct. 8   Sino-U.S. Commercial Treaty signed at Shanghai

1905
Sept. 5   Treaty of Portsmouth, ending Russo-Japanese War

1908
Nov. 30   Root-Takahira Agreement

1909
Nov.–Dec.   Knox "neutralization" of Manchurian railways proposal

1911
Oct. 10   Start of Chinese Revolution

1912
Feb. 12   Abdication of Manchu dynasty and establishment of Chinese Republic

1915
Mar. 13   Secretary Bryan's statement of opposition to Japanese Twenty-One Demands on China
May 11   Secretary Bryan's statement of nonrecognition of Sino-Japanese agreements impairing American treaty rights in China

1917
Aug. 14   Chinese declaration of war against Germany
Nov. 2   Lansing-Ishii Agreement

1921
May — Foundation meeting of Chinese Communist Party held at Shanghai

1922
Feb. 6 — Nine-Power Treaty signed at Washington Conference

1927
Jan. 27 — Secretary Kellogg's statement expressing sympathy with Chinese nationalism and U.S. policy of noninterference in Chinese internal affairs

Apr.–July — Development of Kuomintang-Communist breach

1928
June 8 — Peking taken by Nationalist forces led by Yen Hsi-shan

July 6 — Unification of China under Kuomintang announced by Chiang Kai-shek

July 25 — U.S. recognition of the National Government of the Republic of China

1931
Sept. 18 — Beginning of Japanese conquest of Manchuria

1932
Jan. 7 — Secretary Stimson's announcement of policy of nonrecognition of territorial changes brought about by force

Feb. 23 — Secretary Stimson's letter to Senator Borah outlining U.S. policy in the Sino-Japanese dispute

1934
Apr. 29 — U.S., in note to Japan, reasserted its treaty rights in China

July 7 — U.S. protest to Japan regarding the creation of a petroleum monopoly in Manchuria

1936
May 5 — Draft Chinese Constitution promulgated

Dec. 12 — Generalissimo Chiang Kai-shek "arrested" by Chang Hsueh-liang at Sian, Shensi

Dec. 25 — Generalissimo Chiang released from Sian "captivity"

1937
July 7 — Start of Japan's undeclared war on China

Sept. 22 — Manifesto of Central Committee of Communist Party regarding formation of "united front" with Kuomintang

Sept. 23 — Statement by Generalissimo Chiang Kai-shek welcoming manifesto

Oct. 5 — President Roosevelt's "quarantine" speech in Chicago

Nov. 3–24 — Brussels Conference convened in virtue of article VII of Nine-Power Treaty of 1922

1938
Oct. 6 — U.S. protest regarding Japanese nonobservance of the Open Door in China

1939
July 26 — U.S. gave notice of termination of Japan-U.S. Commercial Treaty of Feb. 21, 1911

1940

Mar. 30   U.S. denounced setting up of Wang Ching-wei regime in Nanking

1941

May 6   China declared eligible by President Roosevelt for lend-lease assistance

July 26   United States froze Japanese assets in United States

Dec. 7   Japanese attack upon Pearl Harbor

Dec. 8   U.S. declaration of war against Japan

1942

Jan. 29–30   Soong-Stimson exchange of notes regarding appointment of General Stilwell as Chief of Staff of Generalissimo Chiang's Joint Staff, and United States Army Representative in China

Feb. 2   Letter orders issued by General Marshall ordering General Stilwell to Chungking to serve under Supreme Command of Generalissimo Chiang

Feb. 7   U.S. loan to China of $500,000,000 authorized

Mar. 6   General Stilwell reported to Generalissimo Chiang

1943

Jan. 11   Sino-U.S. treaty providing for relinquishment of American extraterritoriality signed at Washington

Oct. 30   Declaration of Four Nations on General Security signed by U.K., U.S., U.S.S.R. and China at Moscow

Nov. 22–26   Cairo Conference of Roosevelt, Churchill and Chiang Kai-shek

Nov. 28–   Tehran Conference of Roosevelt, Churchill and Stalin
Dec. 1

Dec. 1   Cairo Declaration issued by U.S., U.K. and China

Dec. 17   Repeal by U.S. Congress of discriminatory legislation regarding Chinese immigration and naturalization

1944

June   Vice President Henry A. Wallace's mission to China

Aug. 18   General Patrick J. Hurley appointed Personal Representative of President Roosevelt to China

Aug. 31   General Hurley's conversation with Molotov in Moscow

Oct. 24   Recall of General Stilwell from China announced

1945

Jan. 8   General Hurley presented credentials as American Ambassador to China to Generalissimo Chiang Kai-shek

Feb. 4–11   Yalta Conference of Roosevelt, Churchill and Stalin

Feb. 11   Yalta Agreement signed by Roosevelt, Churchill and Stalin

Apr. 15   Ambassador Hurley conferred with Stalin and Molotov at Moscow regarding settlement of Kuomintang-Communist question

May 8   V–E Day

July 17–   Berlin Conference of U.S., U.K. and U.S.S.R.
Aug. 1

July 26   Potsdam Declaration calling upon Japan to surrender unconditionally issued by U.S., U.K., and China

Aug. 9   Soviet Union entered war against Japan

Aug. 14   Surrender of Japan

1945

Aug. 14	Sino-Soviet Treaty of Friendship and Alliance and related agreements signed at Moscow
Oct. 11	Summary of National Government-Communist conversations issued
Nov. 27	Resignation of Ambassador Hurley announced
Nov. 27	Appointment of Gen. George C. Marshall as President Truman's Special Representative to China announced
Dec. 15	Statement of United States policy on China issued by President Truman
Dec. 16–27	Moscow Conference of Foreign Ministers of U.S., U.K., and U.S.S.R.

1946

Jan. 7	First meeting of the Committee of Three
Jan. 10	Committee of Three agreement regarding cessation of hostilities
Jan. 10–31	Meeting of the Political Consultative Conference
Jan. 13	Effective date of the cessation-of-hostilities agreement
Jan. 14	Executive Headquarters at Peiping began official functions
Jan. 31	Resolutions adopted by Political Consultative Conference
Feb. 25	Agreement reached on basic plan for military reorganization and integration of Communist forces into the National Army
Mar. 1–17	Meeting of the Kuomintang Central Executive Committee
Mar. 11	General Marshall left China for U.S. to report to the President
Apr. 18	General Marshall returned to China
Apr. 18	Occupation of Changchun by Chinese Communist forces
May 5	Transfer of National Government from Chungking to Nanking
May 19	Occupation of Ssupingchieh by National Government troops
May 23	Occupation of Changchun by National Government troops
June 7	Beginning of truce period in Manchuria
June 27	Joint China-U.S. Agricultural Mission commenced operations
June 30	Expiration of the truce; negotiations at an apparent stalemate
July 11	Senate confirmation of J. Leighton Stuart as American Ambassador to China
July 29	Communist ambush of U.S. Marine convoy near Peiping
Aug. 10	Joint statement on situation in China issued by General Marshall and Ambassador Stuart
Aug. 30	Conclusion of Sino-American surplus-property sale agreement
Oct. 11	Occupation of Kalgan by National Government troops
Nov. 2	Sino-U. S. Treaty of Friendship, Commerce and Navigation signed at Nanking
Nov. 15– Dec. 25	Meeting of the National Assembly to adopt a Constitution
Dec. 18	Statement by President Truman of American policy toward China

1947

Jan. 6	General Marshall's recall announced
Jan. 7	General Marshall's nomination as Secretary of State announced
Jan. 29	U. S. announced termination of its connection with the Committee of Three and Executive Headquarters

1947

Feb. 11	Chinese Government notified Communist delegation in Nanking that its presence was no longer desired
Feb. 28	Uprising in Taiwan
Mar. 1	Reorganization of the Legislative Yuan and the Control Yuan announced
Mar. 19	Occupation of Yenan by National Government troops
Apr. 17	Reorganization of the Executive Yuan and the State Council announced
June 30	Extraordinary meeting of the Standing Committee of the Kuomintang Central Executive Committee
July 9	President Truman instructed General Wedemeyer to proceed to China on a fact-finding mission
Aug. 24	General Wedemeyer's statement on his departure from China
Sept. 9	Fourth Plenary Session of the Kuomintang Central Executive Committee opened
Sept. 19	General Wedemeyer submitted his report to the President
Oct. 28	The Democratic League outlawed

1948

Mar. 12	Occupation of Ssupingchieh by Chinese Communist forces
Mar. 29	Meeting of the National Assembly
Apr. 3	China Aid Act of 1948 approved by President Truman
July 3	Agreement signed covering terms of American economic aid to China
Aug. 5	Exchange of notes providing for establishment of Sino-American Joint Commission on Rural Reconstruction in China
Aug. 19	Economic reform decrees issued by National Government
Sept. 23–24	Occupation of Tsinan by Chinese Communist forces
Oct. 15	Occupation of Chinchow by Chinese Communist forces
Oct. 20	Occupation of Changchun by Chinese Communist forces
Nov. 1	Occupation of Mukden by Chinese Communist forces
Dec. 1	Occupation of Hsuchow by Chinese Communist forces
Dec. 31	Formation of Sun Fo's cabinet

1949

Jan. 1	New Year's messages by Generalissimo Chiang Kai-shek and Prime Minister Sun Fo
Jan. 8	Chinese request for Big Four mediation
Jan. 12	U.S. declination to act as an intermediary
Jan. 15	Occupation of Tientsin by Chinese Communist forces
Jan. 21	Chiang Kai-shek announced his decision to retire; Li Tsung-jen became Acting President
Jan. 31	Occupation of Peiping by Chinese Communist forces
Feb. 5	Most of the Chinese Government's offices moved to Canton
Mar. 12	Ho Ying-chin became Prime Minister in Canton
Mar. 24	Occupation of Taiyuan by Chinese Communist forces
Apr. 14	Extension of China Aid Act of 1948
Apr. 20	Crossing of Yangtze River by Communist forces
May 16–17	Occupation of Hankow by Chinese Communist forces
May 25	Occupation of Shanghai by Chinese Communist forces
June 2	Occupation of Tsingtao by Chinese Communist forces
June 3	Yen Hsi-shan became Prime Minister in Canton

UNION OF SOVIET

M O

⊛Tihwa

S I N K I A N G

T S I N G H A I

T I B E T

S I K A N G

N E P A L

I N D I A

BHUTAN

Ledo ○

PAKISTAN

Y ü

Lashio ○

B U R M A

BAY
OF
BENGAL

S I A M

CHINA

·—··—·	International boundary
———··—··	Provincial boundary
★ Nanking	National Capital
⊛ Tsinan	Provincial Capital or
	Special Municipality
○ Poshan	Other City

0   100   200   300   400   500
Statute miles

0   100 200 300 400 500
Kilometers

70   80   90   100

50

40

30

80

20

100

REPUBLICS

110   120   130

HEILUNGKIANG

HSINGAN

HOKIANG

Tsitsihar

NUNKIANG   Harbin
                   Mutanchiang
                   SUNGKIANG

LIAOPEH   KIRIN
                   Kirin
           Changchun
Fenghua
Ssupingkai

JEHOL   ANTUNG   Tunghua

Chihfeng   Mukden
            LIAONING

Chengte   Chinchow
Kalgan   Yingkow
Hwaian   Kupeikou   Hulutao
Tatung   Lukouchiao   Chinhuangtao
          Peiping Tientsin
                   Tangku   Dairen
                                 Port Arthur
                   Chefoo   Weihaiwei

HOPEH

Taiyüan   Tsinan
                   Weihsien   YELLOW
Yenan   Poshan
           Tungo Taian   Tsingtao   SEA

                   SHANTUNG

Sian   Kaifeng Hsuchow   KIANGSU
Loyang Chengchow

HONAN   Huaian

HUPEH   Pengpu
                   Pukow
                   Nanking   Shanghai   EAST CHINA

Hankow   Wuhu   SEA
Wuchang
                   Fenghua
           CHEKIANG

HUNAN   KIANGSI

           FUKIEN
                         Taipei
KWEICHOW   Keelung
                         TAIWAN
                         (FORMOSA)
                   Amoy

KWANGSI   KWANGTUNG   PHILIPPINE
           Canton   SEA

           Hong Kong (Br.)
           Macau
           (Port.)

           SOUTH CHINA
                   SEA

110   120

The international boundaries shown on this map do not necessarily
correspond in all cases to the boundaries recognized by the
U. S. Government.

SEA
OF
JAPAN

KOREA

CHUAN
gtu
ngking
gtze

Yellow River

River

PHILIPPINE
ISLANDS

CHAPTER I

A Century of American Policy, 1844–1943

I. INTRODUCTION

For more than half a century the policy of the United States toward China has been based on the twin principles of (1) equality of commercial opportunity, and (2) the maintenance of the territorial and administrative integrity and political independence of China. Although the United States has at times recognized the special relations between China and neighboring countries, it has also recognized and asserted that the domination of China by any one Power or any group of Powers is contrary to the interests both of China and of the United States. The United States has advocated a policy of noninterference in the internal affairs of China. The United States has taken the position that the Chinese people should be given time to develop those political institutions which would best meet their needs in the modern world. The United States has also sought to prevent third Powers from utilizing disturbances within China as an opportunity for individual or collective aggrandizement. The United States has long been interested in the creation of conditions which would permit the development of a stable Chinese political organism, and in its relations with China has supported the principle of peaceful settlement of disputes in accordance with the generally recognized precepts of international law.

II. DEVELOPMENT OF BASIC AMERICAN POLICY

EQUALITY OF COMMERCIAL OPPORTUNITY

During the nineteenth century United States policy toward China was expressed by treaties and ordinary diplomatic procedures designed to secure equality of trading rights in China. The fundamental principle underlying American relations with China—equality of commercial opportunity—was incorporated in the first treaty between the two Powers, the Treaty of Wanghia signed on July 3, 1844, in the

1

form of a most-favored-nation clause.[1] This provision guaranteed that whatever treaty rights other Powers gained with respect to trade, residence, religious activity, tariffs or other commercial regulations would automatically accrue to the United States. The most-favored-nation clause was retained in the subsequent commercial treaties negotiated with China in the nineteenth century, namely the Treaty of Tientsin of 1858[2] and the Burlingame Treaty of 1868.[3] The principle of equality of commercial opportunity worked well until the late 1890's, when new imperialistic pressures seemed to threaten a division of China into spheres of interest among the other Great Powers.

ENUNCIATION OF THE OPEN DOOR POLICY

Under the circumstances the United States resorted to a new approach, using another formula to secure its objectives. The Open Door notes of Secretary of State John Hay to the Powers during the period from September to November 1899 gave concrete expression to the principle of equality of opportunity.[4] Hay asked the Powers involved in the struggle over China to give guarantees that in their respective "spheres of influence or interest" they would not interfere with the equality of rights of nationals of other countries in matters of tariffs, railroad charges, and harbor dues. The replies to these notes were somewhat equivocal or conditional, the Russian reply being the most evasive of all. Nevertheless the diplomatic language of the replies made it possible for Hay to announce to the world that the policy of the Open Door had been accepted, and that it was the governing policy in China.

The anti-foreign disturbances in China in 1900, usually referred to as the Boxer Rebellion, afforded the United States (which had participated with the other Powers in a joint expeditionary force sent to rescue the beleaguered legations in Peking) an opportunity to make a statement of policy which went a step beyond the Open Door notes of the preceding year. In a circular note to the participating Powers, dated July 3, 1900, Hay declared that the "policy of the Government of the United States is to seek a solution" of the difficulties in China which would "preserve Chinese territorial and administrative entity" and "safeguard for the world the principle of equal and impartial trade with all parts of the Chinese Empire."[5] Thus the principle of the maintenance of Chinese territorial and administrative entity be-

---

[1] See annex 1.
[2] See annex 2.
[3] See annex 3.
[4] See annex 4.
[5] See annex 5.

came the policy of the United States. This policy was helpful in achieving a solution of the difficulties between China and the Powers arising from the destruction of property and loss of foreign lives in the course of the Boxer Rebellion. The terms of settlement of the incident were contained in the Protocol of Peking, signed September 7, 1901, which, among other things, required China to pay, over a period of years, an indemnity amounting to 333 million dollars. Of this the United States claimed only 25 million dollars, which proved to be more than adequate to indemnify American nationals. Under arrangements provided through Congressional action in 1908 and 1924 the United States remitted all Boxer indemnity payments not allocated to claimants. Altogether the United States returned approximately 18 million dollars to the Chinese Government, which placed the money in a trust fund for the education of Chinese youths in China and in the United States. On January 11, 1943, the United States yielded all further claims to indemnity payments.

EARLY EFFORTS TO MAINTAIN THE OPEN DOOR

Since the turn of the century the United States has sought to maintain, by diplomacy, the twin principles of equal commercial opportunity and Chinese territorial and administrative integrity on numerous occasions. At the same time the United States extended the Open Door doctrine by interpreting it to prohibit exclusive mining or railway privileges and commercial monopolies. These extensions were initially aimed largely at Russia, which was pushing down through Manchuria and threatening Chinese control over that vast territory. After the Russo-Japanese War, 1904–1905, the principles were turned more sharply against Japan, which had taken Russia's place in the southern half of Manchuria as a menace to Chinese territorial and administrative integrity.

When Russia endeavored through pressure upon China to obtain a privileged position in Manchuria, the United States circularized the Powers on February 1, 1902, protesting that such action was contrary to the Open Door policy. The American memorandum stated:

"An agreement by which China cedes to any corporation or company the exclusive right and privilege of opening mines, establishing railroads, or in any other way industrially developing Manchuria, can but be viewed with the gravest concern by the Government of the United States. It constitutes a monopoly, which is a distinct breach of the stipulations of treaties concluded between China and foreign powers, and thereby seriously affects the rights of American citizens; it restricts their rightful trade and exposes it to being discriminated against, interfered with, or otherwise jeopardized, and strongly tends toward permanently impairing the sovereign rights of China in this part of the Empire, and seriously interferes with her ability to meet her international obligations. Furthermore, such concession on the part of China will undoubtedly be followed by demands from other powers for similar and equal exclusive advantages in other parts of the Chinese Empire, and the inevitable result must be the complete wreck of the policy of absolute equality of treatment of all nations in regard to trade, navigation, and commerce within the confines of the Empire.

"On the other hand, the attainment by one power of such exclusive privileges for a commercial organization of its nationality conflicts with the assurances repeatedly conveyed to this Government by the Imperial Russian Ministry of Foreign Affairs of the Imperial Government's intention to follow the policy of the Open Door in China, as advocated by the Government of the United States and accepted by all the treaty powers having commercial interests in that Empire."

When, in the following year, the United States learned that Russia was pressing China for a bilateral convention which would have prohibited treaty ports and foreign consuls in Manchuria and would have excluded all foreigners except Russians from Chinese public service in North China, the United States protested to Russia on April 25, 1903, that such action was contrary to the Open Door policy and injurious to the legitimate interests of the United States in China. The Sino-American Treaty of Commerce, signed October 8, 1903, reaffirmed the concept of the Open Door and was accompanied by the opening of Mukden and Antung in Manchuria to foreign trade, thus thwarting Russian attempts to close it.[6]

The Russo-Japanese War of 1904–1905, which was fought mainly on Chinese soil, afforded the United States an opportunity to restate the basic principles of its China policy. Upon the outbreak of the war, Hay on February 10, 1904, appealed to both belligerents to limit as much as possible their military operations and to respect the neutrality and "administrative entity" of China.[7] Subsequently he circularized the Powers in the interests of the integrity of China and the Open Door in the Orient on January 13, 1905:

"It has come to our knowledge that apprehension exists on the part of some of the powers that in the eventual negotiations for peace between Russia and Japan claim may be made for the concession of Chinese territory to neutral powers. The President would be loathe to share this apprehension, believing that the introduction of extraneous interests would seriously embarrass and postpone the settle-

---

[6] See annex 6.
[7] See annex 7.

ment of the issues involved in the present contest in the Far East, thus making more remote the attainment of that peace which is so earnestly to be desired. For its part, the United States has repeatedly made its position well known, and has been gratified at the cordial welcome accorded to its efforts to strengthen and perpetuate the broad policy of maintaining the integrity of China and the 'open door' in the Orient, whereby equality of commercial opportunity and access shall be enjoyed by all nations. Holding these views the United States disclaims any thought of reserved territorial rights or control in the Chinese Empire, and it is deemed fitting to make this purpose frankly known and to remove all apprehension on this score so far as concerns the policy of this nation, which maintains so considerable a share of the Pacific commerce of China and which holds such important possessions in the western Pacific, almost at the gateway of China." [8]
President Theodore Roosevelt offered his good offices to bring about peace negotiations between Russia and Japan. The resultant Treaty of Portsmouth, September 5, 1905, pledged the two signatories to restore Manchuria to China and to observe measures "which apply equally to all nations" in the commerce and industry of Manchuria.

THE ROOT-TAKAHIRA AGREEMENT, 1908

A few years later, in an exchange of notes between the Secretary of State and the Japanese Ambassador in Washington, Japan subscribed to the twin principles of United States policy toward China. By the Root-Takahira Agreement, November 30, 1908, the United States and Japan mutually agreed (1) to maintain the *status quo* in the Pacific and to respect each other's territorial possessions in that region; (2) to uphold the Open Door in China; and (3) to support by pacific means the "independence and integrity of China." [9]

THE KNOX "NEUTRALIZATION" PROPOSALS, 1909

In an effort to strengthen the Open Door principle and at the same time to discourage the further penetration of Manchurian trade and commerce by Russia and Japan, the United States suggested in 1909 that the Manchurian railroads be taken out of international politics. President Taft and Secretary of State Knox saw that the territorial integrity and political independence of China in Manchuria were being menaced by the railway concessions granted to Japan and Russia, and were convinced that this was contrary to the spirit and letter of the Open Door. Knox circularized the Powers in November–December 1909 as follows:

---

[8] See annex 8.
[9] See annex 9.

"Perhaps the most effective way to preserve the undisturbed enjoyment by China of all political rights in Manchuria and to promote
the development of those Provinces under a practical application of
the policy of the Open Door and equal commercial opportunity would
be to bring the Manchurian highways, the railroads, under an economic,
scientific, and impartial administration by some plan vesting in China
the ownership of the railroads through funds furnished for that purpose by the interested powers willing to participate."

Knox also proposed that the nationals of the participating Powers
should supervise the railroad system during the term of the loan, and
that the Governments concerned should enjoy for such period "the
usual preferences for their nationals and materials" upon an equitable
basis among themselves.[10]   Great Britain, Germany, and China
indicated a willingness to accede in principle to the Knox proposal,
which was almost brutally rebuffed by Russia and Japan.   The result
of the Knox neutralization scheme was to draw Russia and Japan more
closely together in defense of their interests in Manchuria and Inner
Mongolia.   Although using the language of the Open Door and the
territorial integrity of China, they entered into treaty engagements
on July 4, 1910, and June 25, 1912, which in effect seemed designed
ultimately to close the door to others and to threaten the integrity
of China.

III. WORLD WAR I AND POST-WAR SETTLE-MENTS

HOSTILITIES IN CHINA

World War I had repercussions in China even prior to the Chinese
declaration of war (August 14, 1917) against Germany.   At the outbreak of the war China, on August 3, 1914, asked the United States to
assist in preventing the spread of hostilities to Chinese soil, where
the belligerents had foreign settlements and leased areas.   The United
States accepted this request and informed the British Government on
August 11, 1914, of the American "desire to preserve the *status quo*
in China."   When Japan entered the war against Germany, Secretary
of State Bryan on August 19, 1914, informed the Japanese Government that the United States "notes with satisfaction that Japan, in
demanding the surrender by Germany of the entire leased territory of
Kiaochow does so with the purpose of restoring that territory to
China, and that Japan is seeking no territorial aggrandizement in
China."   Bryan reminded Japan of its pledge to support "the inde-

---

[10] See annex 10.

pendence and integrity of China and the principle of equal opportunities for the commerce and industry of all nations in China" as contained in the Root-Takahira Agreement of November 30, 1908.

THE TWENTY-ONE DEMANDS, 1915

Early in 1915 Japan secretly presented to China the Twenty-One Demands, which, if accepted in full, would have made China a virtual protectorate of Japan. Not only did the Japanese Government demand further economic and political rights in Manchuria, Shantung, and Inner Mongolia, but it also sought exclusive mining and industrial rights in the Yangtze valley and actually demanded supervisory control over Chinese social and political institutions, including not only schools and churches but even the Government itself. When the United States learned of the Demands it took the opportunity to reaffirm its traditional policy toward China. In a note of March 13, 1915, to the Japanese Ambassador in Washington Bryan reviewed American policy since the Open Door notes of 1899, called attention to the various international undertakings concerning China, and argued that Japan's Demands were inconsistent with its past pronouncements regarding the sovereignty of China. The Secretary stated that the United States relied upon the "repeated assurances" of Japan in regard to "the independence, integrity and commerce of China" and on Japan's taking "no steps" which would be "contrary to the spirit of those assurances." The Secretary pointed out that the activity of Americans in China "has never been political, but on the contrary has been primarily commercial with no afterthought as to their effect upon the governmental policy of China." Bryan also stated:

"While on principle and under the treaties of 1844, 1858, 1868 and 1903 with China the United States has grounds upon which to base objections to the Japanese 'demands' relative to Shantung, South Manchuria, and East Mongolia, nevertheless the United States frankly recognizes that territorial contiguity creates special relations between Japan and these districts."

The Secretary asserted, however, that the United States "could not regard with indifference the assumption of political, military or economic domination over China by a foreign Power", and expressed the hope that Japan would find it consonant with its interests "to refrain from pressing upon China an acceptance of proposals which would, if accepted, exclude Americans from equal participation in the economic and industrial development of China and would limit the political independence of that country." The Secretary concluded his note with the statement that the policy of the United States "is directed to the maintenance of the independence, integrity and commercial freedom of China and the preservation of legitimate American rights and interests in that Republic." [11]

Despite these expressed American views and Chinese resistance, Japan persisted and forced China, under the pressure of an ultimatum, to agree to revised Demands which represented a retreat from the extreme position taken when the original Demands were put forth. Thereupon Bryan notified both Tokyo and Peking in identic notes on May 11, 1915, that the United States "cannot recognize any agreement or undertaking which has been entered into or which may be entered into between the Governments of Japan and China, impairing the treaty rights of the United States and its citizens in China, the political or territorial integrity of the Republic of China, or the international policy relative to China commonly known as the Open Door policy".[12]

THE LANSING-ISHII AGREEMENT, NOVEMBER 2, 1917

As a result of its entrance into World War I, the United States found itself associated with Japan. Once more the two Powers sought to record a joint policy toward China, which had declared war against Germany on August 14, 1917, by an exchange of notes between the American Secretary of State and the Japanese Special Ambassador. By the Lansing-Ishii Agreement of November 2, 1917, the United States and Japan reaffirmed their respect for the principles of the Open Door and the independence and territorial integrity of China. The Agreement read in part:

"The Governments of the United States and Japan recognize that territorial propinquity creates special relations between countries, and consequently the Government of the United States recognizes that Japan has special interests in China, particularly in the part to which her possessions are contiguous.

"The territorial sovereignty of China, nevertheless, remains unimpaired, and the Government of the United States has every confidence in the repeated assurances of the Imperial Japanese Government that while geographical position gives Japan such special interests they have no desire to discriminate against the trade of other nations or to disregard the commercial rights heretofore granted by China in treaties with other powers." [13]

---

[11] See annex 11.
[12] See annex 12.
[13] See annex 13.

By a secret protocol, withheld from the published exchange of notes, but which the United States considered an inseparable part of the Agreement, the two Powers agreed that they would "not take advantage of the present conditions to seek special rights or privileges in China which would abridge the rights of the subjects or citizens of other friendly states." The Lansing-Ishii Agreement was formally annulled by an exchange of notes, dated April 14, 1923, following the coming into force of the Nine-Power Treaty.

SETTLEMENT OF THE SHANTUNG QUESTION

At the Washington Conference of 1921–1922 the United States, in concert with the United Kingdom, exercised its good offices in bringing about a settlement of the Shantung controversy between China and Japan. Early in World War I Japan seized the German leased territory of Kiaochow Bay and subsequently extended its control over the entire Shantung peninsula. Japan promised ultimately to restore Shantung Province to the sovereignty of China. During the war, however, Japan managed, through various treaties, to obtain recognition of its dominant position in Shantung by China and the Allies. At the Paris Peace Conference in 1919 China demanded the return of the German leasehold and German economic privileges in the province. Japan, on the other hand, insisted upon a treaty clause which would recognize Japanese succession to all German rights and privileges, including the railway, in Shantung. The American Delegation at Paris supported China, protested against the transfer, and offered an alternative plan to cede the former German holdings to the Allied and Associated Powers, which were to make the proper disposition of them later. President Wilson was not able to hold out against the Japanese demands, and a clause was included in the Treaty of Versailles by which Germany renounced in favor of Japan its rights in Shantung. China thereupon refused to sign the treaty. The controversy was not resolved during the intervening years. At the Washington Conference the Chinese and Japanese delegates met with British and American observers to consider the problem. As a result of these direct negotiations Japan and China signed a treaty on February 4, 1922, which provided for the restoration of Shantung in full sovereignty to China, and for the purchase by China of the Tsingtao-Tsinan Railway with funds obtained from Japanese bankers in the form of a fifteen-year loan secured by a lien on the railroad. The reassertion of Chinese sovereignty over Shantung, achieved with United States assistance, was a considerable victory for China, although the terms of the Japanese railway loan did not greatly disturb Japan's economic supremacy in that province.

THE NINE-POWER TREATY, FEBRUARY 6, 1922

After the close of World War I the United States succeeded in having the twin principles of its policy toward China written into a treaty. The Powers participating in the Washington Conference signed the Nine-Power Treaty on February 6, 1922. The signatories, other than China, agreed to respect the sovereignty, the independence, and the territorial and administrative integrity of China, and to uphold the principle of the Open Door. The Powers, other than China, also agreed "to refrain from taking advantage of conditions in China in order to seek special rights or privileges which would abridge the rights of subjects or citizens of friendly states, and from countenancing action inimical to the security of such states." [14]

Mention should be made of the related naval arrangements concluded at the Washington Conference. The Five-Power Naval Treaty, signed on February 5, 1922, provided for the reduction and limitation of naval forces, including those of the United States in the Pacific which, together with the provision for the non-fortification of United States possessions in the Far East, gave evidence that the policy and purpose of the United States in the Far East was only defensive.

By the Nine-Power Treaty traditional American policy was given a broad, nine-power base. This treaty provided a sort of charter governing the relations between China and the Powers for almost two decades. The treaty was one of the principal points at issue with Japan after the seizure of Manchuria in 1931–1933, and was the subject of the Brussels Conference called in 1937 pursuant to a League of Nations resolution after the outbreak of the undeclared war between Japan and China. The Brussels Conference, supported by the United States, adopted a resolution on November 24, 1937, which, after reviewing Far Eastern developments since the Washington Conference, reaffirmed the principles of the Nine-Power Treaty "as being among the basic principles which are essential to world peace and orderly progressive development of national and international life." The Brussels Conference recommended suspension of hostilities between Japan and China and expressed the hope, which was not realized, that the conference might be reconvened at a later date.

IV. NON-INTERFERENCE IN CHINESE INTERNAL AFFAIRS—THE WASHINGTON CONFERENCE AND AFTER

The Nine-Power Treaty of February 6, 1922, also contained a provision by which the signatory Powers, other than China, agreed "to

---

[14] See annex 14.

provide the fullest and most unembarrassed opportunity to China to develop and maintain for herself an effective and stable government". This was in accordance with the long-held view of the United States that China should be given time to progress along the road of national development. The United States sympathized with the efforts of Chinese people to achieve those political institutions which would best meet their needs in the modern world and had followed a policy of strict neutrality on internal Chinese developments. When the Manchu dynasty had been challenged by the Republican revolution in October 1911, the United States had maintained its neutrality in the incipient civil war and had helped neither the recognized government at Peking nor the Republican revolutionists in the Yangtze Valley. Following the abdication of the Manchus, the Chinese Republic was established on February 12, 1912. *De jure* recognition by the United States of the Republican Government followed on May 2, 1913.

STATEMENT BY SECRETARY KELLOGG, JANUARY 27, 1927

Subsequently in the 1920's when the Chinese Nationalists, under the leadership of the Kuomintang, were driving northward through the Yangtze Valley in an effort to unite all China, Secretary of State Frank B. Kellogg restated American sympathy with Chinese nationalism and the American policy of non-interference in the internal affairs of China. The statement by the Secretary of State, made public on January 27, 1927, said in part:

"The United States has always desired the unity, the independence and prosperity of the Chinese nation. It has desired that tariff control and extraterritoriality provided by our treaties with China should as early as possible be released. . . .

"The Government of the United States has watched with sympathetic interest the nationalistic awakening of China and welcomes every advance made by the Chinese people toward reorganizing their system of Government.

"During the difficult years since the establishment of the new regime in 1912, the Government of the United States has endeavored in every way to maintain an attitude of the most careful and strict neutrality as among the several factions that have disputed with one another for control in China. . . . This Government wishes to deal with China in a most liberal spirit. It holds no concessions in China and has never manifested any imperialistic attitude toward that country. It desires, however, that its citizens be given equal opportunity with the citizens of the other Powers to reside in China and to pursue their legitimate occupations without special privileges, monopolies or spheres of special interest or influence." [15]

Following the Nanking "incident" of March 24, 1927, when foreigners were subjected to indignities at the hands of Chinese Nationalist forces and were rescued by Western gunboats, the United States strove to settle the matter in such a way as to compensate the Powers for the injuries resulting from the civil strife, but without punitive measures against the Chinese nation. Chinese xenophobia had previous manifestations, the Boxer Rebellion in 1900 being the best-known example. Sporadic outbreaks of anti-foreignism occurred in various parts of China during the Chinese Nationalist movement of the 1920's. Despite these manifestations of Chinese xenophobia the United States dealt sympathetically with the new regime, made its peace with the new central government, and ultimately extended recognition to it.

RECOGNITION OF THE NATIONAL GOVERNMENT, 1928

After China had achieved a degree of unity under the Kuomintang leadership of General Chiang Kai-shek, the United States recognized the National Government of the Republic of China on July 25, 1928, by concluding with that Government a treaty restoring tariff autonomy to China—the first nation to do so.[16] In connection with the negotiation of this treaty Mr. Kellogg stated:

"The good will of the United States toward China is proverbial and the American Government and people welcome every advance made by the Chinese in the direction of unity, peace and progress. We do not believe in interference in their internal affairs. We ask of them only that which we look for from every nation with which we maintain friendly intercourse, specifically, proper and adequate protection of American citizens, their property and their lawful rights, and, in general, treatment in no way discriminatory as compared with the treatment accorded to the interests or nationals of any other country."

V. THE SINO-SOVIET DISPUTE IN 1929

As the tide of Chinese nationalism swept northward in 1928 and 1929 it came into conflict with the rights and privileges of the Soviet Union in Manchuria. In mid-1929 a dispute developed between China and the Soviet Union over the Chinese Eastern Railway in Manchuria. The United States immediately took the lead in attempting to achieve

---

[15] See annex 15.
[16] See annex 16.

a peaceful solution. The efforts of Secretary of State Stimson failed to arrest intermittent armed clashes along the Manchurian border. In mid-November Russian troops invaded Manchuria in force.

Eventually, following direct negotiations, the U.S.S.R. and China on December 22, 1929, signed a Protocol under which the controversy was settled on the basis of restoring the *status quo ante*, and the Soviet Union retained the special privileges in the Chinese Eastern Railway zone originally acquired by the Czarist Government in the 1890's but subsequently redefined in the Sino-Soviet Treaties of 1924.

VI. JAPANESE EXPANSION INTO CHINA FROM 1931

THE NON-RECOGNITION DOCTRINE OF SECRETARY STIMSON

When Japan embarked upon a policy of forcible expansion in Manchuria in September 1931, the United States in cooperation with the League of Nations, of which it was not a member, sought a peaceful solution of the controversy.

As it became evident that Japan was determined to persist in its course of conquest, Mr. Stimson addressed notes to both Japan and China on January 7, 1932, in which he announced the policy of non-recognition of territorial changes brought about by force. In identic notes the Secretary informed the two Powers that the United States "cannot admit the legality of any situation *de facto* nor does it intend to recognize any treaty or agreement entered into between those Governments, or agents thereof, which may impair the treaty rights of the United States or its citizens in China, including those which relate to the sovereignty, the independence, or the territorial and administrative integrity of the Republic of China, or to the international policy relative to China, commonly known as the open door policy; and that it does not intend to recognize any situation, treaty or agreement which may be brought about by means contrary to the covenants and obligations of the Pact of Paris of August 27, 1928, to which Treaty both China and Japan, as well as the United States, are parties." [17]

After hostilities had been extended to Shanghai and Manchurian independence had been proclaimed, Mr. Stimson sought world-wide support for this position in a letter to Senator Borah, Chairman of the Senate Committee on Foreign Relations, dated February 23, 1932, which was made public the next day. At the same time the Secretary reaffirmed the policy of his predecessor as regards American sympathy

---

[17] See annex 17.

with Chinese nationalism and non-interference in Chinese internal affairs. After tracing the development of traditional United States policy toward China since the turn of the century, Mr. Stimson commented on the principles underlying the Nine-Power Treaty as follows:

"This Treaty thus represents a carefully developed and matured international policy intended, on the one hand, to assure to all of the contracting parties their rights and interests in and with regard to China, and on the other hand, to assure to the people of China the fullest opportunity to develop without molestation their sovereignty and independence according to the modern and enlightened standards believed to maintain among the peoples of this earth. At the time this Treaty was signed, it was known that China was engaged in an attempt to develop the free institutions of a self-governing republic after her recent revolution from an autocratic form of government; that she would require many years of both economic and political effort to that end; and that her progress would necessarily be slow. The Treaty was thus a covenant of self-denial among the signatory powers in deliberate renunciation of any policy of aggression which might tend to interfere with that development. It was believed—and the whole history of the development of the 'Open Door' policy reveals that faith—that only by such a process, under the protection of such an agreement, could the fullest interests not only of China but of all nations which have intercourse with her best be served."

In stressing the obligations assumed by the signatories of the Nine-Power Treaty, Mr. Stimson pointed out that it was but one of several "interrelated and interdependent" treaties negotiated at the Washington Conference. He stated that the "willingness of the American Government to surrender its then commanding lead in battleship construction and to leave its positions at Guam and in the Philippines without further fortifications, was predicated upon, among other things, the self-denying covenants contained in the Nine-Power Treaty which assured the nations of the world not only of equal opportunity for their Eastern trade but also against the military aggrandizement of any other power at the expense of China." Calling attention to the enlightened principles embodied in the Kellogg-Briand Pact and the Nine-Power Treaty, Secretary Stimson continued: "We believe that this situation would have been avoided had these covenants been faithfully observed, and no evidence has come to us to indicate that a due compliance with them would have interfered with the adequate protection of the legitimate rights in China of the signatories of those treaties and their nationals." He suggested that the rest of the world join the United States in applying the non-recognition principle to "any situation, treaty or agreement entered into" by Japan and China "in violation of the covenants of these treaties, which affect the rights of our Government or its citizens in China." If other Governments were to do so "a caveat will be placed upon such action which, we believe, will effectively bar the legality hereafter of any title or right sought to be obtained by pressure or treaty violation."

The Secretary concluded his letter with the statement:

"In the past our Government, as one of the leading powers on the Pacific Ocean, has rested its policy upon an abiding faith in the future of the people of China and upon the ultimate success in dealing with them of the principles of fair play, patience, and mutual goodwill. We appreciate the immensity of the task which lies before her statesmen in the development of her country and its government. The delays in her progress, the instability of her attempts to secure a responsible government, were foreseen by Messrs. Hay and Hughes and their contemporaries and were the very obstacles which the policy of the Open Door was designed to meet. We concur with those statesmen, representing all the nations, in the Washington Conference who decided that China was entitled to the time necessary to accomplish her development. We are prepared to make that our policy for the future." [18]

The non-recognition principle enunciated by Secretary Stimson, which was also accepted by the League of Nations, remained the basis of United States policy and was reaffirmed on numerous occasions during the years between the time of its enunciation and American involvement in World War II following the Japanese attack on Pearl Harbor.

DEFENSE OF AMERICAN TREATY RIGHTS IN CHINA

The United States continued in the following years to assert its treaty rights in China in the face of the extension of Japanese activities. When a Japanese Foreign Office spokesman (Mr. Eiji Amau) issued a statement on April 17, 1934, proclaiming (1) Japanese "special responsibilities in East Asia" and (2) Japanese political guardianship of China, and warning the Powers against financial, political, or commercial undertakings prejudicial to Japanese interests in China, the United States quickly replied. In a carefully worded note delivered in Tokyo on April 29, 1934, the United States reaffirmed its treaty

[18] See annex 18.

rights. Secretary Hull restated American policy toward China as follows:

"The relations of the United States with China are governed, as are our relations with Japan and our relations with other countries, by the generally accepted principles of international law and the provisions of treaties to which the United States is a party. In international law, in simple justice, and by virtue of treaties, the United States has with regard to China certain rights and certain obligations. In addition, it is associated with China or with Japan or with both, together with certain other countries, in multilateral treaties relating to rights and obligations in the Far East, and in one great multilateral treaty to which practically all the countries of the world are parties.

"Entered into by agreement, for the purpose of regulating relations between and among nations, treaties can lawfully be modified or be terminated—but only by processes prescribed or recognized or agreed upon by the parties to them.

"In the international associations and relationships of the United States, the American Government seeks to be duly considerate of the rights, the obligations and the legitimate interests of other countries, and it expects on the part of other governments due consideration of the rights, the obligations and the legitimate interests of the United States.

"In the opinion of the American people and the American Government, no nation can, without the assent of the other nations concerned, rightfully endeavour to make conclusive its will in situations where there are involved the rights, the obligations and the legitimate interests of other sovereign states."

During this time the puppet regime in Manchuria planned to establish an official monopoly, the Manchurian Petroleum Company, for the distribution of oil products in Manchuria. The United States protested to Tokyo on July 7, 1934, and asked the Japanese Government to "use its influence to discourage the adoption by the Manchurian authorities of measures which tend to violate the principle of the Open Door and the provisions of various treaties which the authorities in Manchuria have agreed to respect." A number of notes on the subject were exchanged in the following months in which the Japanese Government refused to accept responsibility for the actions of the Manchurian officials, while the United States continued to maintain the principle of the Open Door. Finally, the United States summarized its position in this controversy in a note to the Japanese Government, dated April 15, 1935, as follows:

"The American Government greatly regrets that the Japanese Government has not seen its way clear to use the influence which it possesses through its close and peculiar relations with the present regime in Manchuria to uphold in practice the principle of the Open Door and the fulfillment of the treaty obligations which both the Japanese Government and the authorities in Manchuria have on numerous occasions declared that they would maintain.

". . . the American Government is constrained to express its considered view that upon the Japanese Government must rest the ultimate responsibility for injury to American interests resulting from the creation and operation of the petroleum monopoly in Manchuria."

STATEMENT BY SECRETARY HULL, DECEMBER 5, 1935

Japan persisted in penetrating deeper into China. The attempt by Japan, late in 1935, to convert the five northern provinces of Hopei, Chahar, Suiyuan, Shansi, and Shantung into an autonomous area caused no change in the American attitude. In a statement to the press on December 5, 1935, Mr. Hull reiterated the position of the United States:

"Unusual developments in any part of China are rightfully and necessarily of concern not alone to the Government and people of China but to all of the many powers which have interests in China. For, in relations with China and in China, the treaty rights and the treaty obligations of the 'treaty powers' are in general identical. The United States is one of those powers.

"In the area under reference the interests of the United States are similar to those of other powers. In that area there are located, and our rights and obligations appertain to, a considerable number of American nationals, some American property, and substantial American commercial and cultural activities. The American Government is therefore closely observing what is happening there.

"Political disturbances and pressures give rise to uncertainty and misgiving and tend to produce economic and social dislocations. They make difficult the enjoyment of treaty rights and the fulfillment of treaty obligations.

"The views of the American Government with regard to such matters not alone in relation to China but in relation to the whole world are well known. As I have stated on many occasions, it seems to this Government most important in this period of world-wide political unrest and economic instability that governments and peoples keep faith in principles and pledges. In international relations there must be agreements and respect for agreements in order that there may be the confidence and stability and sense of security which are essential to orderly life and progress. This country has abiding faith in the fundamental principles of its traditional policy. This Government adheres to the provisions of the treaties to which it is a party and continues to bespeak respect by all nations for the provisions of treaties solemnly entered into for the purpose of facilitating and regulating, to reciprocal and common advantage, the contacts between and among the countries signatory." [19]

VII. THE JAPANESE UNDECLARED WAR OF 1937

At the start of the undeclared war of Japan in China, following a clash between Japanese and Chinese troops on July 7, 1937, at the Marco Polo Bridge outside Peiping, Mr. Hull urged a policy of self-restraint upon the Japanese Government. On July 16, 1937, the Secretary issued a statement on fundamental principles of international policy containing the precepts advocated by the United States in international relations which were applicable to the Sino-Japanese controversy. The statement by Mr. Hull enumerated such principles as maintenance of peace; abstinence from the use of force in relations between states; abstinence from interference in the internal affairs of other nations; adjustment of problems in international relations by processes of peaceful negotiation and agreement; faithful observance of international agreements; modification of provisions of treaties by orderly processes carried out in a spirit of mutual helpfulness and accommodation; respect by all nations for the rights of others and performance by all nations of established obligations; promotion of economic security and stability throughout the world; and effective equality of commercial opportunity and application of the principle of equality of treatment. These principles were reaffirmed in a later statement issued by the Department of State on August 23, 1937, in which it was made clear that the United States regarded these principles as being applicable to the Pacific area.

During the interval between the first and second statements mentioned above, the United States sought ways and means of bringing about an amicable settlement between China and Japan. Besides urging both disputants to seek a peaceful solution the United States on August 10, 1937, informally offered its good offices to Japan in an effort to settle the controversy. This offer contemplated providing neutral ground where Japanese and Chinese representatives might meet to negotiate, and giving assistance in adjusting the difficulties

---

[19] See annex 19.

which might develop during the negotiations. As Japan did not respond to the offer, the United States Government felt that no useful purpose would be served in making a similar approach to the Chinese Government.

THE "QUARANTINE" SPEECH OF PRESIDENT ROOSEVELT
OCTOBER 5, 1937

As Japanese military operations in China increased in intensity it became evident that Japan was bent upon solving the controversy by force. In an address delivered at Chicago on October 5, 1937, President Roosevelt, without mentioning any Power by name, condemned the Japanese resort to undeclared war against China. The President cited the spreading "epidemic of world lawlessness" and drew the parallel that in case of an epidemic of physical disease the community joins in a "quarantine" of the patients in order to protect the health of the community against the spread of the disease. The President stated that war was a "contagion whether it be declared or undeclared", and that it "can engulf states and peoples remote from the original scene of hostilities." The following day the Department of State underscored American sympathy with China by issuing a statement which said in part:

"In the light of the unfolding developments in the Far East, the Government of the United States has been forced to the conclusion that the action of Japan in China is inconsistent with the principles which should govern the relationships between nations and is contrary to the provisions of the Nine-Power Treaty of February 6, 1922, regarding principles and policies to be followed in matters concerning China, and to those of the Kellogg-Briand Pact of August 27, 1928." [20]

DEFENSE OF THE PRINCIPLE OF THE OPEN DOOR

During the undeclared war the United States on numerous occasions protested against the violation of its treaty rights in China by Japan. The United States included within the term "treaty rights" protection of American missionaries and their property, as well as protection of Americans engaged in commercial activity. In the course of their campaigns, Japan's military forces frequently violated American missionary property either by outright seizure for occupation purposes or by bombing and shelling of the property. It appeared that Japanese violation of American missionary property was part of a deliberate attempt to eradicate American cultural influence in China, inasmuch as

[20] See annex 20.

American missionaries, through their religious, educational, and medical work, had played a very large part in spreading Western concepts of thought ever since the opening of China to intercourse with the West, and in developing a close cultural tie between the United States and China. Although the mission stations, frequently located in the interior, were for the most part conspicuously marked with the American flag, the Japanese usually disregarded such marking. The United States protested these violations of American property in China, but received as little satisfaction from the Japanese Government on this aspect as it had in answer to its protests on violations of commercial interests.

In a note to Japan, dated October 6, 1938, the United States called attention to the "categorical assurances" given by the Japanese Government that the Open Door would be maintained in China. The note reviewed numerous instances in which actions by Japanese agencies in China had contravened these assurances and interfered with American treaty rights in China. The note closed with a request that Japan implement its "assurances already given with regard to the maintenance of the Open Door and to non-interference with American rights" by taking the following effective measures:

"1. The discontinuance of discriminatory exchange control and of other measures imposed in areas in China under Japanese control which operate either directly or indirectly to discriminate against American trade and enterprise;

"2. The discontinuance of any monopoly or of any preference which would deprive American nationals of the right of undertaking any legitimate trade or industry in China or of any arrangement which might purport to establish in favor of Japanese interests any general superiority of rights with regard to commercial or economic development in any region of China; and

"3. The discontinuance of interference by Japanese authorities in China with American property and other rights including such forms of interference as censorship of American mail and telegrams and restrictions upon residence and travel by Americans and upon American trade and shipping." [21]

In its reply of November 18, 1938, Japan denied the American contention that Japanese actions in China violated American treaty rights or discriminated against American interests in China. The note from the Japanese Foreign Minister to the American Ambassador in Japan indicated that Japan did not interpret the principle of the Open Door

---

[21] See annex 21.

in the same way as did the United States. The reply of the Japanese Foreign Minister of November 18, 1938, concluded as follows:

"At present Japan, devoting its entire energy to the establishment of a new order based on genuine international justice throughout East Asia, is making rapid strides toward the attainment of this objective. The successful accomplishment of this purpose is not only indispensable to the existence of Japan, but also constitutes the very foundation of the enduring peace and stability of East Asia.

"It is the firm conviction of the Japanese Government that now, at a time of the continuing development of new conditions in East Asia, an attempt to apply to present and future conditions without any changes concepts and principles which were applicable to conditions prevailing before the present incident does not in any way contribute to the solution of immediate issues and further does not in the least promote the firm establishment of enduring peace in East Asia.

"The Imperial Government, however, does not have any intention of objecting to the participation in the great work of the reconstruction of East Asia by your Excellency's country or by other Powers, in all fields of trade and industry, when such participation is undertaken with an understanding of the purport of the above stated remarks; and further, I believe that the regimes now being formed in China are also prepared to welcome such participation." [22]

The American note of December 30, 1938, delivered by the Ambassador in Tokyo to the Japanese Foreign Minister, challenged Japan's interpretation of the Open Door principle and reaffirmed the views contained in the previous communication of October 6, 1938. The United States again called upon Japan to observe its treaty obligations. The United States denied that its treaty rights in China could be abrogated by the unilateral action of Japan, and stressed the fact that it was always ready and willing to discuss treaty revision by orderly processes of negotiation and agreement among the parties thereto. The note of December 30, 1938, stated:

"The admonition that enjoyment by the nationals of the United States of non-discriminatory treatment in China—a general and well established right—is henceforth to be contingent upon an admission by the Government of the United States of the validity of the conception of Japanese authorities of a 'new situation' and a 'new order' in East Asia, is, in the opinion of this Government, highly paradoxical. . . .

[22] See annex 22.

"Whatever may be the changes which have taken place in the situation in the Far East and whatever may be the situation now, these matters are of no less interest and concern to the American Government than have been the situations which have prevailed there in the past, and such changes as may henceforth take place there, changes which may enter into the producing of a 'new situation' and a 'new order', are and will be of like concern to this Government. This Government is well aware that the situation has changed. This Government is also well aware that many of the changes have been brought about by the action of Japan. This Government does not admit, however, that there is need or warrant for any one Power to take upon itself to prescribe what shall be the terms and conditions of a 'new order' in areas not under its sovereignty and to constitute itself the repository of authority and the agent of destiny in regard thereto. . . .

"The United States has in its international relations rights and obligations which derive from international law and rights and obligations which rest upon treaty provisions. Of those which rest on treaty provisions, its rights and obligations in and with regard to China rest in part upon provisions in treaties between the United States and China and in part on provisions in treaties between the United States and several other powers including both China and Japan. These treaties were concluded in good faith for the purpose of safeguarding and promoting the interests not of one only but of all of their signatories. The people and the Government of the United States cannot assent to the abrogation of any of this country's rights or obligations by the arbitrary action of agents or authorities of any other country.

"The Government of the United States has, however, always been prepared and is now prepared to give due and ample consideration to any proposals based on justice and reason which envisage the resolving of problems in a manner duly considerate of the rights and obligations of all parties directly concerned by processes of free negotiation and new commitment by and among all of the parties so concerned. There has been and there continues to be opportunity for the Japanese Government to put forward such proposals. This Government has been and it continues to be willing to discuss such proposals, if and when put forward, with representatives of the other powers, including Japan and China, whose rights and interests are involved, at whatever time and in whatever place may be commonly agreed upon.

"Meanwhile, this Government reserves all rights of the United States as they exist and does not give assent to any impairment of any of those rights." [23]

This and subsequent protests regarding violation of American treaty rights in China were equally unproductive of positive results. From the beginning of Japan's undeclared war the sympathies of the American people were with China. Despite this fact, and despite Japanese violations of American treaty rights in China, the United States continued to sell war supplies to Japan for about two and a half years after the commencement of Sino-Japanese hostilities in accordance with the traditional theory of freedom of trade, and the then existing concepts of neutrality and freedom of the seas. Furthermore, during these years the United States tried to steer a course which would not involve it in hostilities in the Far East.

DEFENSE OF CHINESE INTEGRITY

United States interest in the maintenance of Chinese administrative integrity under existing arrangements continued unabated throughout the undeclared war. Beginning in the fall of 1937, the United States repeatedly made representations to Japan regarding the failure of the latter to maintain the integrity of the Chinese Maritime Customs Administration [24] and the Chinese Salt Administration, the revenues from both of which had been pledged to service foreign loans, including American loans. The representations did not deter Japan from its course, which included setting up various "autonomous" regimes in those parts of China occupied by the Japanese Army.

Late in 1939 the United States learned that Japan was considering setting up a Chinese central regime at Nanking under Wang Ching-wei. The United States took the position that such a regime would be a purely artificial creation, lacking any broad Chinese popular support; that it would be designed primarily to serve the special purposes of Japan; and that it would result in depriving the people and the Government of the United States, as well as those of other third countries, of long established rights of equal opportunity and fair treatment in China which were legally theirs. When the new regime was set up in March 1940 the United States announced that it would continue to recognize the National Government of the Republic of China whose capital was then at Chungking. In a forceful

[23] See annex 23.
[24] The United States in 1928 had been the first country to restore tariff autonomy to China.

public statement on March 30, 1940, Mr. Hull denounced the use of force in setting up the new Chinese regime under Japanese auspices as follows:

"In the light of what has happened in various parts of China since 1931, the setting up of a new regime at Nanking has the appearance of a further step in a program of one country by armed force to impose its will upon a neighboring country and to block off a large area of the world from normal political and economic relationships with the rest of the world. The developments there appear to be following the pattern of other regimes and systems which have been set up in China under the aegis of an outside power and which in their functioning especially favor the interests of that outside power and deny to nationals of the United States and other third countries enjoyment of long-established rights of equal and fair treatment which are legally and justly theirs.

"The Government of the United States has noted statements of high officials of that outside power that their country intends to respect the political independence and the freedom of the other country and that with the development of affairs in East Asia this intention will be demonstrated. To this Government the circumstances, both military and diplomatic, which have attended the setting up of the new regime at Nanking do not seem consistent with such an intention.

"The attitude of the United States toward use of armed force as an instrument of national policy is well known. Its attitude and position with regard to various aspects of the situation in the Far East have been made clear on numerous occasions. That attitude and position remain unchanged.

"This Government again makes full reservation of this country's rights under international law and existing treaties and agreements." [25]

UNITED STATES SUPPORT OF CHINESE RESISTANCE

By way of moral and material support to China in its resistance to Japan's undeclared war, the United States gave notice to Japan on July 26, 1939, of its desire to terminate the Treaty of Commerce and Navigation between the United States and Japan signed on February 21, 1911. As a result of this action, after January 26, 1940, the United States was in a position to resort to successive economic measures against Japan. After the termination of the commercial treaty the United States increasingly restricted the shipment of oil, scrap iron, machinery, machine tools, and other war matériel to Japan. (A moral embargo on the shipment of aircraft, aircraft parts and ac-

---

[25] See annex 24.

cessories, and aerial bombs to Japan had been in effect since mid-1938.) On July 26, 1941, President Roosevelt issued an Executive Order freezing Japanese assets in the United States, thereby virtually cutting off all trade with Japan.

The United States also supported China with positive measures in its resistance against Japanese conquest. American aviators on active duty were permitted to enter the Reserves and to join the Chinese armed forces, a military mission was sent to China, and China was declared eligible for lend-lease assistance on May 6, 1941. In addition, there were various economic measures which are discussed later in this chapter.

AMERICAN-JAPANESE INFORMAL CONVERSATIONS IN 1941

Beginning in the spring of 1941 the United States and Japan entered into informal, exploratory conversations for a comprehensive and peaceful settlement of the various political and economic problems of the Far East. During these conversations, which lasted until December 7, 1941, an effort was made to draft an agreement containing the principles on which peace could be maintained in the Pacific area. The United States remained firm in its conviction that an agreement should contain the following principles which were to be supported by both Powers:

1. The principle of the inviolability of territorial integrity and sovereignty of each and all nations.

2. The principle of non-interference in the internal affairs of other countries.

3. The principle of equality, including equality of commercial opportunity and treatment.

4. The principle of reliance upon international cooperation and conciliation for the prevention and pacific settlement of controversies and for improvement of international conditions by peaceful methods and processes.[26]

The United States proposed that all Japanese forces in China be withdrawn, and that the National Government of the Republic of China be supported—militarily, politically, and economically—as against any other regime in China. The United States was willing to reestablish normal trade relations with Japan and to improve economic relations between the two countries. Japan, on the other hand, sought to obtain recognition from the United States of Japanese hegemony in the Far East. Among other things, Japan wanted the United States to discontinue furnishing aid to the Nationalist

---

[26] See annex 25.

regime in Chungking which was resisting Japanese onslaughts. The United States refusal to stop its support of China and the unwilling-ness of the United States to compromise on the principle of Chinese sovereignty were among the immediate motivations of the Japanese attack upon Pearl Harbor on December 7, 1941. This Japanese aggression abruptly terminated the bilateral informal conversations.

VIII. WORLD WAR II

Following the attack on Pearl Harbor the United States and China fought side by side against Japan. The United States had already been giving assistance to China, in accordance with the American policy of extending aid to nations resisting aggression, but now that assistance was accelerated and increased in scope. It included lend-lease, and military and financial assistance.

THE LEND-LEASE PROGRAM, 1941–1943

On March 15, 1941, four days after the passage of the Lend-Lease Act, President Roosevelt made an address in which he said: "China likewise expresses the magnificent will of millions of plain people to resist the dismemberment of their Nation. China, through the Generalissimo, Chiang Kai-shek, asks our help. America has said that China shall have our help." After a lend-lease program to meet the emergency needs of China had been developed following consultations between Chinese and American officials, the President, on May 6, 1941, in accordance with the provisions of the Act, declared the defense of China to be vital to the defense of the United States. A Master Lend-Lease Agreement with China was not signed, however, until June 2, 1942.[27]

Lend-lease aid to China was begun in 1941, and was aimed particularly at improving transport over the Burma Road, the only artery through which goods could flow into unoccupied China. The first lend-lease shipments consisted primarily of trucks, spare parts, motor fuel, and lubricants for use on the Burma Road and material for the development of the highway. At the request of Generalissimo Chiang Kai-shek a mission of American traffic experts was sent to China in June 1941, to survey the Burma Road and make recommendations for increasing traffic over it. On the basis of these recommendations the Chinese Government undertook a number of measures to improve the administration of the road. Additional spare parts and repair equipment were furnished to China under lend-lease, and a number of

---

[27] See annex 26.

American motor-traffic technicians were recruited in the United States and sent to China at lend-lease expense. The United States also furnished road-building equipment and asphalt under lend-lease to assist China in hard-surfacing the Burma Road. As a result of these efforts and of the arrival of large numbers of American trucks, the tonnage carried over the Burma Road by November 1941, was almost four times greater than it had been during the early months of 1941. The quantity of material carried was increased from 4,000 tons a month at the beginning of 1941 to 15,000 tons in November 1941.

While the capacity of the Burma Road was being expanded, lend-lease was helping in the attempt to open a second route into China. During 1941 lend-lease funds amounting to 15 million dollars were allocated to China for use in constructing a railroad from Burma into China which had been started by the Chinese Government in 1938, and which would have made possible a great increase in the volume of supplies transported to China through the Burmese port of Rangoon. The completion of this project was prevented, however, by successful Japanese military operations in Burma.

The fall of Burma and the seizure of the southern portion of the Burma Road by the Japanese early in 1942 left air transport as the only effective means of getting supplies into China. Great progress was made, particularly during 1943, in the development of an air-transport route into China. In the month of December 1943, for example, twice as much cargo (13,450 short tons) was flown into China as in all 1942 (5,258 short tons). In January 1944, the tonnage of goods flown into China was seven times that of January 1943—14,472 short tons as compared to 1,923 short tons—and the monthly tonnage continued to increase. It should be pointed out, however, that a very large proportion of the supplies flown into China during this period was destined for the United States miiltary forces then operating in China. Some of this traffic was carried by planes operated by the China National Aviation Corporation, part of whose fleet of cargo planes was furnished to China through lend-lease channels. The bulk of the supplies which were flown from India to China was, however, transported by the Tenth United States Air Force between April and December 1942, and subsequently by the United States Air Transport Command, which, beginning in December 1942, operated a ferry service 500 miles long between Assam, India and the Yunnan plateau, over the towering "Hump" of the Himalayas—the most difficult supply operation of the entire war.

At the same time efforts were made under the lend-lease program to develop new land supply routes to China. By the end of 1943 American engineers were constructing the Ledo Road from Assam in

India across upper Burma to China. (This road, renamed the Stilwell Road, was finally opened early in 1945.) India became the great supply base for operations whose objectives were the expulsion of Japan from Burma and the reopening of land transportation through that area for supplies for China. Stockpiles in India of material for China, awaiting shipment as soon as new transportation routes were opened, were steadily growing by the end of 1943.

The total value of lend-lease supplies transferred to China through December 31, 1943, amounted to 201 million dollars, of which 175.6 million dollars represented goods and 25.4 million dollars represented services rendered. In addition, goods valued at 191.7 million dollars were consigned to the American commanding general in the China-Burma-India Theater for transfer to China.[27a]

MILITARY AID, 1941–1943

The United States began to give military aid to China even before the United States became a belligerent in World War II. The lend-lease supplies that were provided China between the time of the cutting of the Burma Road and the end' of 1943 had the effect of greatly increasing this form of assistance. Early in 1941 the United States and China developed a project under lend-lease for equipping and training large numbers of Chinese forces. The United States Government subsequently organized a military mission composed of specialists in all phases of modern warfare to advise Chinese authorities on the use of the materials provided in connection with this project. This mission, which arrived in China in November 1941, was supported by lend-lease funds.

Unfortunately, little of the equipment intended for China's ground forces under this program ever reached its intended destination. The United States was more successful, however, in furnishing China with assistance in the air. Early in 1941 this Government approved a plan which permitted American fighter planes piloted by volunteer American airmen and serviced by American ground crews to fight against Japan in the service of China. The American Volunteer Group (the "Flying Tigers"), under the command of Major General Claire L. Chennault, was formally constituted as a unit of China's armed forces by an order issued by Generalissimo Chiang Kai-shek on August 1, 1941. During the time that it was in existence the American Volunteer Group provided an effective air defense for southwest China and rendered invaluable assistance to hard-pressed Chinese and other forces in Burma. The American Volunteer Group

---

[27a] For further information concerning lend-lease and the Lend-Lease Pipeline Agreements, see chapters V and VII.

was disbanded in July 1942, when its personnel was incorporated into the United States Tenth Air Force, which had been organized in the China-Burma-India Theater early in 1942. In recognition of its increasingly important role the United States air unit in China was formally activated as the Fourteenth United States Air Force on March 10, 1943. This force kept control of the air over unoccupied China, engaged in expanding operations against the Japanese, and ably performed the vital mission of protecting the terminal bases of the air transport route into China. The activities of this force helped to maintain China's military position and morale throughout the war.

In addition to furnishing China with fighter planes and pilots, the United States took steps to put into effect a program for building a strong and well-equipped Chinese Air Force. In May 1941 an American Air Mission headed by General Clagett was sent to China to survey the situation. Among other things, the report of the Air Mission recommended that a program to train Chinese pilots and mechanics be developed, inasmuch as China did not have enough men trained to fly or maintain the planes that were needed to defend China from Japanese air attacks.

Because of the difficulties that would be encountered in trying to establish aviation training centers in China, a program was developed, using lend-lease funds, to implement this recommendation by training Chinese flyers in the United States. In October 1941 the first group of fifty students arrived in the United States to take the standard United States Air Force training course for pilots at Thunderbird Field in Arizona. Other groups of Chinese pilots came to the United States for training during the war. The United States Army also trained Chinese aviation personnel in India.

The program for training Chinese aviation personnel had an important bearing on operations against Japan. In November 1943 the formation of a Chinese-American Composite Wing of the Chinese Air Force was announced. This wing, composed of Chinese and American airmen and ground units and equipped with fighter and bombing planes, formed the nucleus for a strong Chinese Air Force, and as the Chinese personnel gained experience the American personnel was gradually withdrawn.

Soon after its entry into the war, the United States, at the formal request of the Chinese Government, sent Lieutenant General Joseph W. Stilwell to China.[27b] In addition to being Commanding General of United States Forces in the China-Burma-India Theater, and of

---

[27b] For the Stimson-Soong exchange of letters with respect to General Stilwell's assignment, see annex 27 (a) and (b).

such Chinese troops as Generalissimo Chiang Kai-shek might assign to him, General Stilwell was also to be Chief of Staff of the Generalissimo's proposed Joint Staff—an Allied staff made up of officers representing the United States, the United Kingdom, China, and the Netherlands. Although no Allied personnel were ever assigned to this Joint Staff because of the later change of attitude of the Chinese Government, nonetheless General Stilwell drew his formal authority in the Chinese military hierarchy from his continuing position as its Chief. General Stilwell thus served concurrently with General Ho Ying-chin, who was Chief of Staff of the Chinese Army, as one of two Chiefs of Staff to the Generalissimo. Under General Stillwell an extensive program for equipping and training Chinese ground forces was undertaken in India, and attempts were made to overcome the reluctance of the Chinese Government to cooperate in such a program in China.

At these training centers in India large numbers of Chinese ground forces were equipped, through lend-lease, with the latest types of American weapons. Some of the personnel thus trained by American Army officers demonstrated their combat efficiency in operations in northern Burma beginning in 1943. This program provided not only complete tactical units but also cadres for the training of Chinese divisions beyond the mountains in China proper.

Beginning in April 1943, United States Army officers, each of whom was a specialist in some phase of modern warfare, also operated training centers for Chinese officers in China. A field-artillery center, for example, graduated more than 5,000 officers and an infantry center, more than 3,000 officers by the end of the year. American officers also went into the field with units of the Chinese Army to serve as instructors, advisers, and observers; and American ordnance officers, with the assistance of Chinese mechanics, engaged in the work of restoring worn Chinese equipment. Mention should also be made of the American field-hospital units which were sent to China and to northern Burma to aid the Chinese forces, and of United States Army engineers and other specialists sent to China to help improve communications and air-base facilities. The United States Army also cooperated with Chinese forces in the protection of the advancing Stilwell Road against Japanese attacks.

United States military assistance up to the end of 1943 made possible much more effective United States-Chinese combined operations, ground and air, on the Asian continent in the later stages of World War II.[27c]

[27c] For subsequent military aid, see chapter VII.

FINANCIAL AID 1937-1943 [27d]

United States financial aid to China, like lend-lease and other military assistance, antedated the Japanese attack on Pearl Harbor. The Secretary of the Treasury, using the United States Stabilization Fund, entered into stabilization agreements in 1937 and 1941 to further the monetary and financial cooperation of the two Governments and the stabilization of the United States dollar–Chinese yuan rate of exchange. In an agreement of July 14, 1937, with the Central Bank of China, the Secretary of the Treasury agreed to purchase Chinese yuan up to an amount equivalent to 50 million dollars, with the proviso that all such yuan purchased were to be fully collateralized by gold. By February 1938, yuan equivalent to 48 million United States dollars had been purchased. Repurchase of this amount was completed by October 1942.

On April 1, 1941, the Secretary of the Treasury entered into a second agreement with the Government of China and the Central Bank of China to purchase Chinese yuan up to an amount equivalent to 50 million United States dollars. This agreement did not provide for collateralization of such purchases. It was further agreed at this time that a Stabilization Board be established, to which the Chinese Government banks were to contribute 20 million dollars. Purchase of yuan under this agreement amounted to 10 million dollars, and was repaid in April 1943.

At approximately the same time China concluded a similar agreement with the United Kingdom by which the latter extended to China a stabilization loan (£5,000,000) to be administered by the same Stabilization Board. Although the Sino-American and the Sino-British stabilization agreements were technically distinct, it had been agreed that all stabilization operations were to be carried on by a single Board composed of five members: three Chinese, one British, and one American.

On July 26, 1941, only a few months after the establishment of the Stabilization Board, the President of the United States issued a freezing order under whose terms the assets of China and Japan in the United States were placed under the supervision of the Treasury Department. The freezing of Chinese funds was undertaken at the specific request of Generalissimo Chiang Kai-shek. The administration of the controls with respect to Chinese assets was conducted with a view to facilitating the operations of the Stabilization Board and otherwise strengthening the foreign trade and exchange position of the Chinese Government.

[27d] See annex 28 (parts a–ii).

Besides aiding China in its efforts at currency stabilization, the United States extended credits to China through the Export-Import Bank. In general these were commodity credits which were used to purchase a considerable variety of American industrial and agricultural products and services. Credits aggregating 18.9 million dollars were authorized in 1936 and 1937. Four Export-Import Bank credits were granted between December 13, 1938, and November 30, 1940, amounting to 120 million dollars. In accordance with the agreements governing these four credits payment was made in large part by the sale to the United States of such Chinese products as tung oil, tin, tungsten, wolframite, and antimony. The credit had been repaid almost entirely by June 30, 1949.

Shortly after the United States became a belligerent in World War II President Roosevelt, in accordance with a request by the Generalissimo, asked the Congress to extend further financial aid to China. In a letter to the Congress dated January 31, 1942, the President declared: "Responsible officials both of this Government and of the Government of China have brought to my attention the existence of urgent need for the immediate extension to China of economic and financial assistance, going beyond in amount and different in form from such aid as Congress has already authorized. I believe that such additional assistance would serve to strengthen China's position as regards both her internal economy and her capacity in general to function with great military effectiveness in our common effort." The President enclosed a draft of a joint resolution which he urged Congress to pass authorizing the Secretary of the Treasury, with the approval of the President, "to loan or extend credit or give other financial aid to China in an amount not to exceed in the aggregate $500,000,000." The joint resolution was promptly passed by Congress and was signed by the President on February 7, 1942 (Public Law 442).[28] Less than a week later the money to implement this resolution was appropriated. The United States and China signed an agreement on March 21, 1942, establishing this amount as a credit in the name of the Chinese Government.[28a]

At the time of the extension of this credit the Japanese offensive in the Pacific and in southeast Asia was in full swing and land communications with China were being severed. It was important to the United States that China should be strengthened and encouraged to continue the war against Japan. Since opportunities for giving

---

[28] For President Roosevelt's message to Generalissimo Chiang immediately upon the enactment of Public Law 442, see annex 29 (a).

[28a] For a fuller treatment of this agreement, see annexes 28 and 29 (b).

effective material aid to China, such as was being rendered to Allies in more accessible areas through lend-lease, were not great, the 500 million dollar credit was characterized by the Secretary of the Treasury as the "finanial counterpart of lend-leasing war materials."

The funds provided under the agreement of March 21, 1942, were used by the Chinese Government mainly to purchase gold for sale in China as an anti-inflationary measure and to provide backing for the issuance of Chinese Government savings and victory bonds denominated in United States dollars. A total of 220 million dollars was withdrawn in gold, much of which was shipped to China, principally during 1945, to be sold internally in an effort to control inflation by reducing currency in circulation and keeping down the price of gold.

A total of 200 million dollars was reserved for the redemption of Chinese Government securities issued in United States dollars—100 million dollars for payment of Chinese United States dollar savings certificates, and another 100 million dollars earmarked for the payment of Chinese United States dollar victory bonds. This earmarking was abandoned in 1946 and the funds became available for imports and other foreign payments as measures were promulgated governing payment of foreign currency bonds held in China which provided that such bonds would be redeemed in Chinese currency. It was also provided, however, that registered bond-holders outside China would be paid in foreign currency.

Of the 80 million dollar balance of this loan the sum of 55 million dollars was spent for the purchase of bank notes in the United States, and 25 million dollars for textiles imported into China.

The Chinese Government made use of this credit entirely on its own initiative and discretion. Efforts had been made to incorporate in the agreement a clause calling for consultation regarding use of the credit but the United States Government acceded to strenuous objections by the Chinese on this point. Although Chinese officials did offer informal assurances regarding consultation, they seldom availed themselves of the opportunity for United States advice in this regard and disregarded that which was obtained.

A more detailed treatment of the origin and uses of this credit, and of other war-time financial relations between the United States and China, together with pertinent documents, is attached as an annex.[28b]

Final determination of the terms upon which this financial aid was given was deferred, under the agreement of March 21, 1942, until after the war.

[28b] See annex 28.

RELINQUISHMENT OF AMERICAN EXTRATERRITORIALITY IN CHINA

Following the outbreak of war between the United States and Japan, the United States Government took a number of important steps which demonstrated the desire and intention of the United States to treat China as an equal among the Major Powers and to contribute to the strengthening of the Chinese nation.

On October 9, 1942, the United States took the initiative and suggested to China that a treaty be negotiated providing for the relinquishment of American extraterritorial rights in China and for the settlement of related questions. Provisions for such action had been included in the Sino-American Commercial Treaty of October 8, 1903, Article XV of which had provided:

"The Government of China having expressed a strong desire to reform its judicial system and to bring it into accord with that of Western nations, the United States agrees to give every assistance to such reform and will also be prepared to relinquish extra-territorial rights when satisfied that the state of the Chinese laws, the arrangements for their administration, and other considerations warrant it in so doing."

From that time on, it was the established policy of the United States to move toward relinquishment of American extraterritorial rights in China, but during the first quarter of the twentieth century conditions did not warrant such action.

The question of a general relinquishment of extraterritorial jurisdiction in China by the Treaty Powers was brought up at the Washington Conference in 1921–1922. The Conference adopted a resolution providing for the establishment of a Commission "to inquire into the present practice of extraterritorial jurisdiction in China, and into the laws and the judicial system and the methods of judicial administration of China" with a view to making recommendations to the respective Governments regarding the relinquishment of extraterritoriality.

The Commission on Extraterritoriality met in China in 1926. The Commission reported its findings of fact as a result of its investigations into the practice of extraterritorial jurisdiction and into Chinese laws and the Chinese judicial system and recommended improvements in the Chinese legal, judicial, and prison systems. The Commissioners expressed the opinion that "when these recommendations shall have been reasonably complied with, the several Powers would be warranted in relinquishing their respective rights of extraterritoriality." Subsequently, the Chinese Government adopted a program with regard to the Chinese judicial system and Chinese prisons directed toward meeting the recommendations of the Commission.

The United States and China entered into active negotiations in 1930 looking toward the relinquishment of American extraterritorial rights in China. These discussions were far advanced when in 1931 they were suspended as a consequence of the Japanese military occupation of Manchuria, which was followed by Japanese disruptive activities in China south of the Great Wall in 1932 and 1935. The United States was giving renewed favorable consideration to the question of proceeding toward a relinquishment of extraterritorial jurisdiction in 1937 when Japan commenced its undeclared war by invading North China and subsequently Central and South China.

From the Japanese invasion of China in July 1937 until the outbreak of war between the United States and Japan in December 1941, the extraterritorial system operated to the advantage of the United States, China, and the other countries opposed to Japanese aggressive activities, by providing protection for recognized treaty rights which the Japanese effort at monopoly violated. Although conditions did not favor taking active steps toward relinquishment of extraterritorial rights in China, the United States policy remained firm that such steps should be taken as soon as practicable.

This policy was reaffirmed on several occasions by officials of the United States Government. In a statement to the press on July 19, 1940, the Acting Secretary of State, Sumner Welles, said:

"It has been this Government's traditional and declared policy and desire to move rapidly by process of orderly negotiation and agreement with the Chinese Government, whenever conditions warrant, toward the relinquishment of extraterritorial rights and of all other so-called 'special rights' possessed by this country as by other countries in China by virtue of international agreements. That policy remains unchanged." [29]

In reply to a letter from the appointed Chinese Minister for Foreign Affairs, Dr. Quo Tai-chi, Secretary Hull wrote, on May 31, 1941:

"As you are also aware, the Government and people of the United States have long had a profound interest in the welfare and progress of China. It goes without saying that the Government of the United States, in continuation of steps already taken toward meeting China's aspirations for readjustment of anomalies in its international relations, expects when conditions of peace again prevail to move rapidly by processes of orderly negotiation and agreement with the Chinese Government, toward relinquishment of the last of certain rights of

[29] See annex 30.

a special character which this country, together with other countries, has long possessed in China by virtue of agreements providing for extraterritorial jurisdiction and related practices." [30]

The question of the relinquishment of extraterritorial jurisdiction in China was included in the informal conversations between the United States and Japan during 1941. The outline of a proposed basis for agreement between the two countries which the Secretary of State handed to the Japanese Ambassador on November 26, 1941, contained the following provision:

"5. Both Governments will give up all extraterritorial rights in China, including rights and interests in and with regard to international settlements and concessions, and rights under the Boxer Protocol of 1901.

"Both Governments will endeavor to obtain the agreement of the British and other governments to give up extraterritorial rights in China, including rights in international settlements and in concessions and under the Boxer Protocol of 1901."

Immediately after the outbreak of war between the United States and Japan in December 1941, all energies were directed toward the prosecution of the war. While the United Nations were suffering serious military reverses in the Far East it was felt that any action toward relinquishment of extraterritorial jurisdiction in China would have been interpreted widely as a gesture of weakness. Even before the tide of battle in the Pacific turned in favor of the United Nations, however, the United States in the spring of 1942 started to give active consideration to the question of relinquishing extraterritoriality in China before the termination of hostilities.

After the Japanese thrusts into the Central and Southwest Pacific had been halted and United Nations forces were on the offensive in the Pacific and Chinese theaters, the United States took the initiative and suggested to the Chinese Government on October 9, 1942, that a treaty be concluded to provide for the relinquishment by the United States of extraterritorial and related rights in China. On October 24, 1942, the Secretary of State handed the Chinese Ambassador in Washington a draft text of the proposed treaty. Following negotiations between the two Governments, the treaty was signed on January 11, 1943, and became effective with the exchange of ratifications on May 20, 1943.[31] This treaty, together with a similar Sino-British treaty which was negotiated at the same time, was warmly approved by Chinese leaders.

---

[30] See annex 31.
[31] See annex 32.

REPEAL OF CHINESE EXCLUSION ACTS, 1943

As a further indication of American policy, the President, on December 17, 1943, signed an Act, which had been passed by large majorities of both Houses of Congress, removing long-standing legislative discriminations against Chinese. The Act repealed the Chinese exclusion laws, established an annual Chinese immigration quota, and made legally admitted Chinese eligible to naturalization as American citizens. The enactment of this legislation had been specifically recommended by President Roosevelt in order to "correct an historic mistake" and give "additional proof that we regard China not only as a partner in waging war but that we shall regard her as a partner in days of peace."

AMERICAN ACKNOWLEDGMENT OF CHINA AS A GREAT POWER

American recognition of the status of China as one of the Great Powers was demonstrated on two other occasions in the fall of 1943. The United States insisted that China be included as a signatory, together with the United Kingdom, the U.S.S.R., and the United States, of the Declaration of Four Nations on General Security, signed in Moscow on October 30, 1943, which recognized the right and responsibility of China to participate jointly with the other great powers in the prosecution of the war, the organization of the peace, and the establishment of machinery for post-war international cooperation.[32] The Cairo Declaration, issued on December 1, 1943, by President Roosevelt, Prime Minister Churchill, and Generalissimo Chiang Kai-shek, following their meeting at Cairo, Egypt, in the latter part of November 1943, declared their "purpose" that "Manchuria, Formosa, and the Pescadores shall be restored to the Republic of China."[33] On his return from the Cairo Conference President Roosevelt could say, in his Christmas Eve message to the Nation: "Today we and the Republic of China are closer together than ever before in deep friendship and in unity of purpose."

---

[32] Subsequently China participated as a Great Power in the Dumbarton Oaks conversations in the summer and fall of 1944, and was one of the sponsoring Powers of the United Nations Conference on International Organization, which met at San Francisco in 1945, and which formulated the Charter of the United Nations. The Charter granted China a permanent seat on the Security Council.

[33] See annex 33.

CHAPTER II

A Review of Kuomintang-Chinese Communist Relations, 1921–1944

I. INTRODUCTION

Various internal factors arising from or influencing the course of the Chinese revolution have played a major role in the growth and development of American policy toward China. The rise of Asiatic nationalism, the impact of the West, the loss by the decadent Ch'ing Dynasty of what the Chinese call the "Mandate of Heaven," and the consequent struggle for succession to power have all been factors which inevitably modified and conditioned the efforts of the United States to conduct its relations with China in accordance with its traditional policies outlined in chapter I.

It is impossible here to analyze all these factors; but it is necessary at this point, if one is to understand the course and purposes of American actions in China since 1944, to pause and review at least in outline the long and tortuous relationship between the Kuomintang and the Chinese Community Party. This struggle for the acquisition and retention of power has played a major role in the internal Chinese scene for a quarter of a century, even at the expense of the prosecution of the war against Japan; it has been utilized by Major Powers in the pursuit of their own objectives and rivalries and in turn has affected them; and it has been a significant influence on the course of relations between China and the various Powers. In the crowded events of the last few years and the bitter readjustments of the postwar period it is easy to forget the origins and development of the Kuomintang-Communist struggle for supremacy; but they must be recalled if one is to understand and place in proper perspective the course of American policy since V–J Day. This struggle has had a great effect on American actions and attitudes.

II. BASIC FACTORS

THE KUOMINTANG PROGRAM

The ideological basis of the Kuomintang was formulated by Dr. Sun Yat-sen during his years of conspiracy against the Manchu regime and was elaborated in various of his writings after the 1911 revolution. Dr. Sun tried to make use of Western thought while constructing a solution specifically for China which would retain what he thought valuable in the Chinese tradition. His program has continued to form the theoretical basis of Kuomintang political thought.

Dr. Sun conceived of the Chinese revolution as taking place in three distinct stages: (1) military unification, (2) "political tutelage" and (3) constitutionalism.[1] The first stage was to be a period of military dictatorship. As soon as order should be restored, the second stage was to begin, during which the people were to be trained by the Kuomintang in the exercise of their political rights. Finally, the third stage of constitutional government was to be reached and the revolutionary process completed.

The long-term program that Dr. Sun Yat-sen hoped to put into effect in China was detailed in many of his writings, of which the *San Min Chu-I*, the "Three Principles of the People," is the best known. Briefly, his "Three Principles," are: (1) *min ts'u*, or "people's nationalism," under which China would regain her national integrity and cultural unity; (2) *min ch'uan*, or "people's democracy," under which the people would exercise the "four political powers" (suffrage, recall, initiative and referendum), by which they control the government, which in its turn exercises the "five governing powers" (legislative, judicial, executive, "examination" and censorial) ; and (3) *min sheng*, or "people's livelihood," a form of socialism involving equalization of land ownership, regulation of capital and avoidance of the class struggle.

Although Dr. Sun was impressed by the Bolshevik success in 1917 and although he accepted the tactical aid and advice of the Third International, he never subscribed to Communist ideas such as the class struggle; indeed, he stressed repeatedly that the class struggle could and should be avoided in China. Dr. Sun invited and accepted the aid and collaboration of the U.S.S.R., the Third International and the Chinese Communist Party only with the expressed understanding that "the Communist order or even the Soviet System cannot actually be introduced into China"[2] and that "in joining the Kuomintang,

---

[1] Sun Yat-sen, "Outline [Fundamentals] of National Reconstruction" (*Chien Kuo Ta Kang*), given in Leonard Shih Lien-hsu, *Sun Yat-sen: His Political and Social Ideas* (Los Angeles, 1933), and in Arthur N. Holcombe, *The Chinese Revolution* (Cambridge, 1930).

[2] Joint statement by Sun Yat-sen and Adolph Joffe, representative of Soviet Russia, in Shanghai, January 1923. See Chinese Ministry of Information, *China Handbook, 1937–1945* (official publication of the Ministry of Information of the Kuomintang) (New York, The Macmillan Company, 1947), p. 66.

Communists of the Third International are to obey Kuomintang discipline." [3]

THE COMMUNIST PROGRAM

The Chinese Communist program for the Chinese revolution is based on the Leninist theories of imperialism and revolution in semi-colonial countries. Although the theories have undergone changes at the hands of men like Mao Tse-tung, Chairman of the Central Committee of the Chinese Communist Party, basically they correspond to the orthodox concepts of Lenin and Stalin. Innovations introduced by Chinese Communist theoreticians have concerned details of the revolutionary time-table and not basic revolutionary principles. The long-term objectives of Chinese Communism are the orthodox Marxian goals of socialism and, ultimately, the classless, communist society.

In all countries the "bourgeois-democratic revolution" is considered by the Leninist theory to be "progressive" within certain limits, and even to be a prerequisite of eventual socialist revolution. The first objective of revolution in a colonial or semi-colonial country, however, is what the Communists call the liberation of the country from imperialism and feudalism. During this period even the development of capitalism is "progressive" but as the "bourgeois-democratic revolution" progresses, inherent class antagonisms will come to the fore and the bourgeoisie will come to ally itself with imperialism and feudalism against the working class. At this point, according to Lenin, collaboration between the bourgeoisie and the working class must cease. In a frequently quoted passage Lenin said:

"The Communist International should form *temporary understandings*, even *alliances*, with the bourgeois democracy of the colonies and the backward countries, but not merge with it, unconditionally preserving the independence of the proletarian movement, even in its most embryonic form . . . We, as Communists, must and will *support bourgeois emancipation* movements in the colonial countries only in those cases when these movements are really revolutionary, when their representatives will not hinder us in educating and organizing the peasantry and the large masses of the exploited in the revolutionary spirit." [4]

The Chinese Communist advocacy of democracy during the early stages of the Chinese revolution must be considered in terms of the

---

[3] Statement by Li Ta-chao, one of the top-ranking Chinese Communists, *ibid.*, p. 66.

[4] E. Burns, *Handbook of Marxism* (New York, 1935), p. 896. The concluding sentence is used by Liu Shao-ch'i in his pronouncement "On Nationalism and Internationalism," broadcast by the Chinese Communist North Shensi radio, Nov. 9 and 10, 1948. Italics as given in Burns, *op. cit.*

theory of "New Democracy" as propounded by Mao Tse-tung according to the Leninist formula. The Communist party, he wrote, has a role to perform even during the "bourgeois-democratic" stage of the Chinese revolution:

"The first stage of this revolution in colonial and semicolonial countries—though according to its social nature, it is fundamentally still a bourgeois-democratic one, of which the objective requirements still basically call for the clearance of the way to capitalistic development— yet, despite this, this revolution is no longer the old, wholesale bourgeois-led revolution for the building of capitalist society and a state of the bourgeois-dictatorship type, but a new type of revolution, wholly or partly led by the proletariat, the first stage of which aims at the setting up of a new democratic society, a new state of the combined dictatorship of all classes. The fundamental character of this revolution will never vary until the arrival of the stage of Socialist revolution, though during its progress, it may pass through several minor stages in accordance with the possible changes in the attitude of enemies and allies." [5]

The tactics to be followed by the Chinese Communist Party during the early stages of the revolution are implicit in the Communist analysis of the nature of the "bourgeois-democratic revolution." The Communist Party will in theory ally itself with such parties, groups, or classes as it considers "progressive," in order to hasten the revolution against feudalism and imperialism. But the great fear of the Communist Party is that it may lose the initiative and the leadership in the revolution to nationalists, reformers, or social-democrats. Communist tactics in China have steered a precarious course between the danger of "right opportunism," through which the initiative is lost, and that of "left extremism," which, according to Communist thinking, prematurely attempts to turn the "bourgeois-democratic revolution" into a socialist revolution and thus causes the Communists to lose their influence in the "bourgeois" revolution before the socialist revolution can be successfully prosecuted.

FOUNDATION OF THE COMMUNIST PARTY, 1921

The first Communist groups in China were formed in Peking in 1919 and 1920 by Ch'en Tu-hsiu and various students, among whom was Mao Tse-tung. In 1920 at Baku, the Comintern convened a "Congress of Oriental Nations," at which China was represented. In May 1921

---

[5] Mao Tse-tung, "China's New Democracy," 1940, is included in the appendix to *The Strategy and Tactics of World Communism*, Supplement III (H. Doc. 154, part 3, 81st Cong., 1st sess.).

the foundation meeting of the Chinese Communist Party was convened in Shanghai by Ch'en Tu-hsiu and Li Ta-chao. During the following months the Chinese Communist Party was organized in various provinces and cities in China. Other Chinese Communist Groups were formed among Chinese students in France, Germany, Russia and Japan. In 1923 the Third Congress of the Communist Party met in Canton and, in accordance with a previous decision of the Comintern, decided to enter the Kuomintang and create a "united front" against the northern militarists.

REORGANIZATION OF THE KUOMINTANG, 1924

Meanwhile Dr. Sun Yat-sen, whose appeals for foreign aid had gone unanswered except by Russia and whose attempts to unify China through alliances with southern war-lords had ended in his being forced to flee from Canton to Shanghai, was carrying on discussions with Adolph Joffe, a representative of Russia. In January 1923 Dr. Sun and Joffe issued a joint statement setting forth the principles under which Russia and the Communist International were to aid the Chinese revolution during the ensuing years:

"Dr. Sun Yat-sen holds that the Communist order or even the Soviet system cannot actually be introduced into China because there do not exist here the conditions for the successful establishment of either communism or sovietism. This view is entirely shared by Mr. Joffe, who is further of the opinion that China's paramount and most pressing problem is to achieve national unification and attain full national independence, and regarding this task, he has assured Dr. Sun Yat-sen that China has the warmest sympathy of the Russian people and can count on the support of Russia." [6]

In partial fulfillment of this pledge of aid to Dr. Sun Yat-sen, Michael Borodin was sent to Canton in September 1923. Borodin quickly became the principal Kuomintang adviser. Under his direction the Kuomintang was reorganized at the First National Party Congress in January 1924 along the lines of the Russian Communist Party with centralized control extending from headquarters into the smallest subdivisions. The Kuomintang was now able to function with disciplined efficiency for the first time in its history. At the same Congress it was resolved that Communists who were willing to take an oath of obedience to the Kuomintang authorities and who accepted the principles of the Kuomintang should be admitted to the Party as individuals. Li Ta-chao declared in this connection:

---

[6] *China Handbook, 1937–1945*, p. 66.

"In joining the Kuomintang, communists of the Third International are to obey Kuomintang discipline and to participate in the national revolution. They have not the slightest intention of turning the Kuomintang into a communist party. Those Communists who join the Kuomintang do so as individuals and not on a party basis."[7]

The objectives of the Kuomintang-Communist collaboration were declared to be the elimination of feudalism (i. e. at that time, the regime of the northern militarists) and the unification of the country so that China would be able to stand up against foreign Powers on a basis of equality.

III. KUOMINTANG-COMMUNIST COLLABORATION, 1924–1927

In collaboration with the Communists and the Comintern advisers, the Kuomintang was able to accomplish a shift from the tactics of conspiracy it had previously employed to those of revolution. The Kuomintang assumed the leadership over the new forces that had been unleashed by the spread of nationalism in China. Through the use of propaganda among the peasant and working masses, the Kuomintang was able to turn its military campaigns into popular uprisings. Its army was put under the leadership of officers trained according to Soviet methods at the newly established Whampoa Academy, and achieved a degree of efficiency never before equaled in modern China.

Following the death of Dr. Sun Yat-sen in 1925, General Chiang Kai-shek, director of the Whampoa Academy, became the leading figure in the Kuomintang. In 1926 he commanded the "Northern Expedition," a campaign to unify China by destroying the power of the warlords in the north. The revolutionary forces, preceded by propaganda corps, made rapid progress, and toward the end of the year the Kuomintang capital was established at Hankow. A split in the party between the left wing at Hankow and the right wing under the leadership of General Chiang, however, was becoming increasingly evident. The latter was anxious to obtain the support of the middle classes, particularly the commercial and banking community of Shanghai, while the Communists were attempting to turn the Nationalist revolution into social revolutionary channels. In April 1927 the Generalissimo set up a government at Nanking rivaling that of the left faction of the Kuomintang which had gained dominance in Hankow. Following the capture of Shanghai in March 1927 he carried out a purge of the Communists in Shanghai, and somewhat later conducted a similar

---

[7] *Ibid.*, p. 66.

one in Canton. These purges involved several hundred thousand deaths. It should also be remembered that leading figures on both sides were still in comparable positions twenty years later, which inevitably added great personal bitterness to the other factors which complicated the later negotiations.

Meanwhile the position of Borodin and the Communists in Hankow was becoming more difficult. Conflicting and ill-advised orders from Moscow, which was at the time in the throes of the Stalin-Trotsky controversy, did not help the position of the Communists. The crisis was precipitated when the Kremlin forced the Chinese Communists to demand majority control of the Kuomintang and separate workers and peasant armies. Borodin knew better than to present such a demand, but Roy, the Indian watchdog of the Third International, went over his head. By July, the Communist cause had collapsed and Borodin was forced to retire from China, while purges of the Communist element in Hankow were being carried out.

IV. CIVIL WAR, 1927–1936

Although the Communists had been expelled from both wings of the Party, unity within the Kuomintang was not restored until February 1928 when the Party was reorganized under the control of General Chiang Kai-shek. In June 1928 Kuomintang forces took Peking, completing the official unification of China and destroying the power of the northern warlords. After 1927, the principal obstacle to stability in China was the existence of Chinese Communist districts and troops in open rebellion against the National Government of China.

Once they had been purged from the cities and had lost their proletarian base, the Communist leadership concentrated on a small area in south Kiangsi which remained the remnant of a much larger South China peasant base. Since the economy of this area was wholly agrarian, Communist tactics shifted to exploitation of peasant difficulties. This was the forerunner of later Communist expansion and successes. It also represented the triumph of the Mao Tse-tung faction which opposed the urban policy of Li Li-san and favored an agrarian emphasis. Li Li-san, who had gone to Moscow, was not to return to prominence until the Russian army brought him to Manchuria in 1945.

In five major "bandit suppression campaigns," starting in December 1930 and lasting until 1935, the Generalissimo attempted to exterminate the Communist forces in China. These campaigns were launched as follows: (1) December 1930, under Lu Ti-p'ing; (2) May 1931, under Ho Ying-ch'in; (3) June 1931, under Chiang Kai-shek;

(4) April 1933, under Ch'en Ch'eng; (5) October 1933, under Chiang Kai-shek.

The fourth and particularly the fifth campaigns were planned with the assistance of the German military advisers Von Seeckt and after him Von Falkenhausen. Hundreds of thousands of troops were mobilized by the Nationalists. The campaigns did not succeed in exterminating the Communists, but the Generalissimo was able to dislodge them from their bases in southern China, forcing them to flee to a base in the northwest in the "long march" of 1934–1935. An incidental effect of the anti-Communist campaigns was the consolidation of Nationalist political control over many of the provinces that had previously maintained a degree of regional autonomy.

V. THE KUOMINTANG-COMMUNIST ENTENTE, 1937–1944

BACKGROUND OF THE ENTENTE

While the National Government was engaged in the problem of suppressing Communism, Japan embarked upon a series of encroachments on Chinese territory, beginning with occupation of Manchuria in 1931 and leading up to the Marco Polo Bridge incident on July 7, 1937.

The Japanese actions aroused large sectors of Chinese opinion. The effect of this aggression was similar in many ways to the effect of the earlier Twenty-one Demands and the insistence by Japan at the Paris Peace Conference that it be ceded the German rights in the Shantung peninsula. Again there was an upsurge of nationalism, particularly after 1935, when the loss of the northern provinces was threatened. The revival of patriotism included most of politically conscious China—elements ranging from warlords to students. Resistance against Japanese aggression became a popular slogan exploited not only by leftist intellectuals, such as those united in the National Salvation League, but also by dissident militarists.

The Chinese Communists had declared "war" on Japan as early as 1932 while their main force was still concentrated in Kiangsi, hundreds of miles from the nearest Japanese troops.[8] Although demands for a "united front" became a factor in the Communist propaganda, the Chinese Communist Party at first offered no concessions to other groups to make possible a true "united front" but insisted on retaining

---

[8] See the "Circular Telegram of the Provisional Central Government of the Soviet Republic of China Declaring War Against Japan," given in V. A. Yakhontoff, *The Chinese Soviets* (New York, 1934), pp. 236–38.

full control over any anti-Japanese coalition. In 1935 the Seventh World Congress of the Comintern officially proclaimed the new policy of the "united front" and offered the cooperation of Communist parties to other groups willing to fight fascism. At that time, the Chinese Communist Party was criticized because it had "not yet succeeded in carrying out these tactics [of the united front] really consistently and without mistakes," and because the concept of the "united front" had not been broad enough. The Chinese Communist Party was specifically censured for failing to unite with the dissident anti-Japanese militarists who had rebelled against the Nanking government in Fukien Province in 1933.[10] Following the Congress, the first serious offers of a "united front" were made to the Kuomintang. In January 1936 the Chinese Communist Party publicly offered the "hand of friendship" to Generalissimo Chiang Kai-shek if he would take up arms against Japan. On August 26, 1936, the Chinese Communist Party proclaimed to the Kuomintang, "we are prepared to form a strong revolutionary united front with you as was the case during . . . the great Chinese Revolution of 1925–1927 . . . [that] is the only proper way to save our country today."

Coming at a time of growing patriotic resentment against Japanese aggression, the stepped-up demands for a "united front" by the Chinese Communist Party were an effective propaganda weapon for use against the troops to which the National Government had assigned the task of "bandit suppression" in northwest China. By the end of 1936 the army of Chang Hsueh-liang, the former warlord of Manchuria, was in no mood to fight against the Communist forces. In December 1936 the Generalissimo and his staff visited Sian in Shensi Province to map out a sixth "Bandit Suppression" campaign. Rather than carry out Nationalist orders to resume operations against the Communists, Chang Hsueh-liang decided to "arrest" the Generalissimo. In this move he was acting in league with the commander of the "Hsipei" (Northwestern) troops, Yang Hu-ch'eng, and the subordinate commanders of both the Hsipei army and his own "Tungpei" (Manchurian) army.

On the day of the *coup* the commanders of the "Tungpei" and "Hsipei" armies issued a circular telegram stating the demands of "national salvation," consisting of eight points: reorganization of the Nanking government and admission of parties to share the joint responsibility of national salvation; end of the civil war and armed resistance against Japan; a release of the leaders of the patriotic move-

---

[10] Wang Ming, *The Revolutionary Movement in the Colonial Countries, Report to the VII World Congress of the Communist International, August 7, 1935* (New York, 1935).

ment in Shanghai; pardon of all political prisoners; a guarantee of liberty of assembly; safeguard for the people's rights of patriotic organization and political liberty; putting into effect the will of Dr. Sun Yat-sen; and convening a National Salvation Conference.[11]

These points corresponded generally to a program of "national salvation" advocated by the Communist Party in a telegram issued earlier in December. They also resembled a manifesto issued by the "All-China Federation of National Salvation" on May 31, 1936.

The details of the Sian incident have been obscured by the personal considerations involved in the available accounts. According to one version, Chang Hsueh-liang and some of his associates considered the Generalissimo their leader and merely wished to awaken him to the danger of Japanese aggression, although other more radical officers of the "Tungpei" army favored executing him. The Chinese Communist Party, whose representatives were called to Sian immediately after his capture, at first favored the execution of the Generalissimo, but, apparently on orders from Moscow, shifted to a policy of saving his life. The Chinese Communist concept, inspired from Moscow, became one of promoting a "united front" with the Generalissimo and the National Government against the Japanese; this concept seems to have played a considerable role in saving the life of the Generalissimo. At any rate, on December 25, 1936, the Generalissimo returned to Nanking, accompanied by his captor Chang Hsueh-liang, who expressed sentiments of repentance. It seems certain that no agreement between the Generalissimo and the Communist or Tungpei leaders was signed. It seems equally certain, however, that an understanding of some kind was reached by the groups involved. After the Sian incident the establishment of an entente between the Chinese Communists and the Kuomintang moved rapidly ahead.[12]

The wartime entente between the Kuomintang and the Chinese Communist Party was never formalized by a written alliance, but rested upon a series of parallel documents issued by the two parties, by which the Kuomintang announced the change in Chinese Government policy from one of military suppression of communism to that of seeking a political settlement, and by which the Chinese Communist Party proclaimed the abandonment of forceful insurrection and sovietization in favor of cooperation with the Government against Japanese aggression. These documents are (1) the telegram from the

---

[11] See annex 34.

[12] A first-hand account of the Sian incident is given in Mme. Mei-ling (Soong) Chiang, *China at the Crossroads; an Account of the Fortnight in Sian, when the Fate of China Hung in the Balance* (London, Faber and Faber, 1937). This work was also published with varying titles in New York and Shanghai.

Central Committee of the Chinese Communist Party to the Third Plenary Session of the Kuomintang Central Executive Committee on February 10, 1937; (2) the resolution of February 21, 1937 of the Third Plenary Session of the Kuomintang Central Executive Committee; (3) the manifesto of September 22, 1937 by the Central Committee of the Communist Party; and (4) the statement on the following day by Generalissimo Chiang Kai-shek commenting on the Communist manifesto.

THIRD PLENARY SESSION OF THE KUOMINTANG CENTRAL EXECUTIVE COMMITTEE, 1937

Shortly after the return of the Generalissimo from Sian, the Third Plenary Session of the Fifth Central Executive Committee of the Kuomintang was held in Nanking. On February 10, 1937, five days before the session opened, the Central Committee of the Chinese Communist Party addressed a telegram to the session which recommended a program including the suspension of civil war and the concentration of the national strength against external aggression, a guarantee of civil rights, the calling of a "national salvation" conference, the preparation for armed resistance and improvement in living conditions of the people. If these points were approved, the Communist Party declared itself prepared to make certain alterations in the policies that had characterized its activities:

1. to stop the program of armed uprisings throughout the country for the overthrow of the National Government in Nanking;

2. to change the Chinese Soviet Government into the Government of the Special Region of the Republic of China and the Red Army into the National Revolutionary Army under the direct leadership of the Military Affairs Commission in Nanking;

3. to enforce the democratic system of universal suffrage within the special regions under the regime of the Government of the Special Regions;

4. to put an end to the policy of expropriating the land of the landlords and to execute the common program of the anti-Japanese united front.[13]

The question of reconciliation with the Communists was dealt with at length by the Third Plenary Session in a resolution passed on February 21, 1937. The resolution reviewed the original leniency of Sun Yat-sen in admitting Communists to the Kuomintang in 1924

---

[13] Text in *New China* (Yenan, Mar. 15, 1937). See annex 35.

and their "subsequent treasonable and rebellious activities" up to the time of the session, when the "Communist bandits, reduced to straits in the Northwest, have begun to announce alleged willingness to surrender." The resolution stated that the Kuomintang would give the Communists a chance to "reform" on four conditions:

1. Abolition of the separate army and its incorporation into the united command of the nation's armed forces.

2. Dissolution of the so-called "Chinese Soviet Republic" and similar organizations and unification of the government power in the hands of the National Government.

3. Absolute cessation of Communist propaganda and acceptance of the Three People's Principles.

4. Stoppage of the class struggle.[14]

These points corresponded closely to the changes in policy the Communist Party had declared itself willing to make. After having laid down the conditions on which the Communists would be permitted to "start life anew", the session in its closing manifesto blamed the Communists for terroristic activities since 1927, "thus undermining the nation's strength which otherwise would have been employed in resisting the invader." The cardinal policy of the Kuomintang was declared to be the eradication of the Communist scourge. However, the achievement of unity through peaceful means was to be the guiding principle, although the Chinese people were warned against the fallacious theories of the class struggle.[15]

These documents established the basic conditions for the entente. During the ensuing months negotiations betwen the parties continued. Chou En-lái held discussions with the Generalissimo and other Kuomintang officials at Kuling, summer capital of China. Other meetings were held within Chinese Communist territory.

Many of the conditions of the entente were implemented during the course of the negotiations. The civil war ceased. The Communist policies of land confiscation were suspended, and Communist propaganda was preparing the people for the united front. The Kuomintang was making active preparations for increased democratization, including the calling of a People's National Congress for November 1937 to inaugurate a new constitution.[16] Many, though by no means all, of the political prisoners held by the Kuomintang were released.

---

[14] *The China Year Book, 1938*, pp. 532, 470; *China Handbook, 1937–1945*, p. 66.

[15] *China Handbook, 1937–1945*, p. 66.

[16] Because of the war and repeated postponements this Congress did not meet until November 1946.

MANIFESTO OF THE CHINESE COMMUNIST PARTY, SEPTEMBER 22, 1937

Apparently public announcement of the entente was originally scheduled for the middle of July 1937, when a Chinese Communist manifesto was handed to the Kuomintang, declaring that Chinese unity had been restored for the purpose of resisting Japan. Publication of the manifesto was delayed until September 22, 1937, because of the outbreak of hostilities with Japan after the Marco Polo Bridge incident of July 7, 1937.

The manifesto of the Central Committee of the Communist Party, published on September 22, 1937, stated that the Communist Party had "on the basis of peace and national unity and joint resistance against foreign aggression, reached an understanding with the Kuomintang" and proposed the following objectives:

"(1) Struggle for the independence, liberty and emancipation of the Chinese nation by promptly and swiftly preparing and launching the national revolutionary campaign of resistance. . . .

"(2) Enforce democracy based on the people's rights and convoke the National People's Congress in order to enact the Constitution and decide upon the plans of national salvation.

"(3) Improve the well-being and enrich the livelihood of the Chinese people. . . ."

The manifesto expressed the belief that the whole country would support these objectives, although the program would meet with numerous difficulties, particularly from Japanese imperialism, and declared:

"(1) The *San Min Chu-I* enunciated by Dr. Sun Yat-sen is the paramount need of China today. This Party is ready to strive for its enforcement.

"(2) This Party abandons its policy of overthrowing the Kuomintang of China by force and the movement of sovietization, and discontinues its policy of forcible confiscation of land from landowners.

"(3) This Party abolishes the present Soviet Government and will enforce democracy based on the people's rights in order to unify the national political machinery.

"(4) This Party abolishes the Red Army, reorganizes it into the National Revolutionary Army, places it under the direct control of the National Government, and awaits orders for mobilization to share the responsibility of resisting foreign invasion at the front." [17]

---

[17] Full text given in annex 36.

STATEMENT BY GENERALISSIMO CHIANG KAI-SHEK, SEPTEMBER 23, 1937

On September 23, 1937, the day following the publication of the Communist manifesto, the Generalissimo issued a formal statement welcoming the change in Communist policies:

"The Manifesto recently issued by the Chinese Communist Party is an outstanding instance of the triumph of national sentiment over every other consideration. The various decisions embodied in the Manifesto, such as the abandonment of a policy of violence, the cessation of Communist propaganda, the abolition of the Chinese Soviet Government and the disbandment of the Red Army are all essential conditions for mobilizing our national strength in order that we meet the menace from without and guarantee our own national existence.

"These decisions agree with the spirit of the Manifesto and resolutions adopted by the Third Plenary Session of the Kuomintang. The Communist Party's Manifesto declares that the Chinese Communists are willing to strive to carry out the Three Principles. This is ample proof that China today has only one objective in its war efforts." [18]

IMPLEMENTATION OF THE AGREEMENTS, 1937-1938

During 1937 and 1938 a number of concrete steps were taken to implement the entente and to further the united resistance against the Japanese invasion. By order of the National Government the Chinese Communist Army was reorganized as the Eighth Route Army, and later into the 18th Group Army, with the Communist generals Chu Teh and P'eng Te-huai as commander and vice-commander, and Lin Piao, Ho Lung, and Liu Po-ch'eng as division commanders. The Eighth Route Army was designated to garrison the area of the Shensi-Kansu-Ninghsia (Shen-Kan-Ning) border region, the former Communist area. Shortly afterwards the Communists, whose area of control was expanding as a result of their guerrilla warfare efforts, established the Shansi-Chahar-Hopei (Chin-Cha-Chi) border region government under the National Government. The Chin-Cha-Chi regional government received the sanction of the National Government in January, 1938; it was the only Communist-dominated local government to receive such formal sanction. During the first three years of the entente the Communist armies received a monetary subsidy from the National Government, as well as a small allotment of ammunition.

In addition the National Government carried out a number of measures regarding civil rights and greater democratization, although

---

[18] Full text in annex 37.

due to wartime conditions it did not call the National Assembly into session to act on a new Chinese constitution. The Communist Party was permitted to publish its own newspaper, the *Hsin Hua Jih-Pao* (*New China Daily*) in Hankow.[18a] Chou En-lai was one of the seventeen members of the presidium of the Extraordinary National Congress of the Kuomintang in March 1938 and was appointed Vice-Minister of the Political Training Board of the National Military Council, a position he held until 1940.

Among the more important steps towards increased democracy and freedom of discussion taken by the Kuomintang during this period was the creation by the Extraordinary National Congress of the Kuomintang in March 1938 of the People's Political Council (PPC), with powers to discuss and question all important Government measures and to make proposals to the Government. Although the People's Political Council was purely advisory, the prestige of its members and the caliber of its discussions made it a significant body.

The most important policies of this period are embodied in the "Program of Armed Resistance and National Reconstruction," which was adopted by the Kuomintang Party Congress on April 1, 1938, and subsequently by the People's Political Council. The "Program" was accepted by both the Kuomintang and the Chinese Communist Party as the basic outline of principles to be followed by the wartime entente, subsidiary only to the *San Min Chu-I* (Three People's Principles).[19] The Program pledged China to play a just role in world affairs, urged intensified military activity, called for governmental reforms, increased economic growth and the organization of the people.

The period during which the National Government was located at Hankow marked the high point of Kuomintang-Communist cooperation. In spite of continued defeats of the Chinese armies by Japan, the solidarity of the Chinese people created a spirit of optimism. The Generalissimo emerged as the symbol of national unity and of eventual victory.

DETERIORATION OF KUOMINTANG-COMMUNIST RELATIONS, 1938-1941

In the latter half of 1938 relations between the Kuomintang and the Chinese Communist Party began to deteriorate. At the end of August the Hankow-Wuchang Defense Headquarters outlawed three Communist-sponsored mass organizations because it feared the Communists would use them to gain influence in Nationalist territory.

[18a] This Communist paper continued to be published in Nationalist territory throughout the war.

[19] Text is given in *China Handbook, 1937-1945*, pp. 61-62.

After the fall of Hankow in October 1938 Communist-Kuomintang relations worsened steadily. More Communist organizations were suppressed. The Communists were attacked for failing to yield control over their area in Shensi Province to the National Government, and for not allowing the National Government to exercise direct command over the Communist armies in the field and to direct their training.

In the following years relations between the two parties remained strained, and charges and countercharges of failure to abide by the promises of 1937 became increasingly violent, often leading to local clashes between Chinese National and Communist forces. The one policy common to both parties was resistance against the Japanese invasion, and even this was often neglected amid the jockeying for advantage between the two parties. However the resumption of open hostilities on a large scale was avoided. During 1939 the National Government, at that time located in Chungking, began to enforce a rigid military blockade of the Communist areas to prevent Communist infiltration into Nationalist China. The expansion of Communist military forces into areas outside the regional defense zones assigned them by the National Government led to incidents and continuous skirmishes between the Communists and Nationalists. The arguments and fighting over the demarcation between Communist and Nationalist military zones culminated in the "New Fourth Army Incident" of January 1941, the most serious wartime clash between Nationalist and Communist armies and the real beginning of civil strife. The fighting reached such proportions that it received world-wide attention. The Government version of the incident was that it had issued orders for the Communist New Fourth Army to move north of the Yangtze and engage the Japanese in the Yellow River area, but the orders had been ignored because the Communists wished to expand their holdings in the south. For reasons of discipline it was therefore necessary to disarm them. It was the Communist contention that the Government purpose was to restrict Communist areas and at the same time place the New Fourth Army in a hopeless military position.

KUOMINTANG-COMMUNIST NEGOTIATIONS, 1941–1944

In spite of the frequent military friction between the Communist and Nationalist forces, the Government policy remained that of seeking a political settlement with the Communists. On March 6, 1941, in a reference to the "New Fourth Army Incident" in a speech to the People's Political Council, the chief arena in which attempts were made to settle the issue between the Communists and Kuomintang, the Generalissimo said:

".. . the Government is solely concerned with leading the nation against the Japanese invaders and extirpating the traitors, and is utterly without any notion of again taking up arms to 'suppress the Communists.' . . . Provided unity can be preserved and resistance carried on to the end, the Government will be ready to follow your direction [i. e., the directions of the PPC] in the settlement of all outstanding questions." [20]

No settlement was reached between the Kuomintang and the Chinese Communist Party, however, and the relations between the two armies continued strained, with periodic fighting, while at the meetings of the People's Political Council a group of minor parties continued attempts at mediation. These minor parties had formed the "United National Construction League" [21] at the end of 1939, with the principal object of preserving Kuomintang-Communist cooperation. Minor parties played an important, if unsuccessful, role in the negotiations between the Communists and the Kuomintang prior to the offer of American good offices in 1944 by Major General Patrick J. Hurley, the Personal Representative of President Roosevelt.

Attempts to settle the Kuomintang-Communist differences were not limited to discussions and statements before the PPC. On a number of occasions direct negotiations between Communist and Nationalist officials took place. The first of these occasions was the talks between General Ho Ying-ch'in, Minister of War in the National Government, and Chin Pang-hsien (Po Ku), a member of the Chinese Communist Party's Central Committee, early in 1940.

In September 1943 the Generalissimo gave explicit instructions to the Eleventh Plenary Session of the Fifth Central Executive Committee of the Kuomintang that the Chinese Communist problem should be handled by peaceful means:

"After hearing the Secretariat's report on the question of the Chinese Communist Party and the views expressed by various members of the Central Executive Committee, I am of the opinion that first of all we should clearly recognize that the Communist problem is a purely political problem and should be solved by political means. Such ought to be the guiding principle for the Plenary Session in its effort to settle this matter." [22]

Following the Eleventh Plenary Session, Communist General Lin Piao conducted negotiations in Chungking during November 1943 on the reorganization of the Communist forces.

---

[20] This speech is given in full in annex 38.

[21] This League went through several reorganizations and finally became known as the Democratic League.

[22] The full text is given in annex 39.

More comprehensive discussions between representatives of the Chinese Government and the Chinese Communist Party began in Sian on May 4, 1944. The Government was represented at these talks by General Chang Chih-chung of the National Military Council and Dr. Wang Shih-chieh, then Minister of Information. The Communists were represented by Lin Tzu-han, an important member of the Central Committee of the Chinese Communist Party. Chang, Wang and Lin returned to Chungking on May 14, 1944, and continued the negotiations through an exchange of memoranda until September, when the negotiations were discussed in detailed reports to the PPC by Chang Chih-chung and Lin Tzu-han.

During these discussions the following major points were brought up:

1. The disposition, size, command, and training of the Communist armies.

2. The relationship between Communist-organized regional governments and the National Government.

3. Problems connected with civil rights and especially the legalization of the Communist Party and its activities in Nationalist areas.

Incidental to these points a number of problems arose which were connected with the implementation of various pledges made by the Communist Party and the Kuomintang throughout the period of Kuomintang-Communist entente. During these discussions the question of constitutional government arose, and suggestions for "coalition government" were brought forth for the first time.

Although no settlement was reached on the basis of these discussions, it is clear that from May to September 1944 the Chinese Government and the Chinese Communist Party were seeking a peaceful settlement of their disputes through political negotiations.[23]

THE WALLACE MISSION, 1944

During the spring of 1944, President Roosevelt appointed Vice President Henry A. Wallace to make a trip to China to see what he could do toward consolidating the Chinese war effort against Japan. Mr. Wallace took this opportunity to visit Soviet Central Asia for a brief inspection of agricultural developments, and arrived in Chungking the latter part of June. In the course of this visit Mr. Wallace had several long conversations with the Generalissimo on matters of mutual interest. The notes made on these conversations indicate that

---

[23] See annexes 40, 41, and 42.

a wide range of topics was discussed of which the majority have no bearing on the events and issues described in this present paper.[24]

In a conversation on June 21 with the Generalissimo, Mr. Wallace stated that the President had indicated to him that if the Kuomintang and the Communists could not get together they might "call in a friend". The President had indicated that he might be that friend. John Carter Vincent, in a conversation the next morning, said that Stalin had agreed with Ambassador Harriman in Moscow that support of the Generalissimo was desirable during the prosecution of the war and expressed keen interest in a settlement between the Kuomintang and the Communists, basing his interest on the practical matter of more effective fighting against Japan rather than upon any ideological considerations, and adding that he felt the United States should assume a position of leadership in the Far East.

During a conversation on the afternoon of June 22, the General-issimo launched into a lengthy complaint against the Communists, whose actions, he said, had had an unfavorable effect on Chinese morale. He added that the Chinese people regarded them more as internationalists than as Chinese, despite the nominal dissolution of the Third International. He then added that the Communists desired the breakdown of Chinese resistance against Japan because this would strengthen their own position. They did not fear such a development because they were now convinced that Japan would be defeated without Chinese resistance. The Generalissimo deplored propaganda to the effect that they were nothing more than agrarian democrats and remarked that they were more communistic than the Russians. He said that a settlement with the Communists would be simple if they would agree to support the Government and accept a peaceful and political role in the administration of the country. He urged that the United States maintain an attitude of "aloofness" toward the Communists which would encourage them to show a greater willingness to reach a settlement with Kuomintang. The Foreign Minister, who was present at the conversation, interposed at this stage to say that whereas the Government required the Communists to submit to its authority, it was not its intention to interfere in local administration or remove officials or army officers who showed themselves to be cooperative. In conclusion, the Generalissimo said that he understood the policy of President Roosevelt and requested that the

---

[24] See annexes 43 and 44, for summary notes of these conversations made by John Carter Vincent, then Chief of the Division of Chinese Affairs of the Department of State, who accompanied the Vice President to China. The Department is not aware of any written record which Mr. Wallace himself may have made.

President be informed that he, the Generalissimo, desired a political solution of the Communist problem.

It was in a conversation on the following morning, June 23, that the Generalissimo suddenly reversed his previous refusal to permit Americans in Communist territory and agreed that an American military observer mission could proceed.[25] Later in the conversation the question of Russia again rose. Mr. Wallace stressed the point that no situation should be permitted in China which might lead to conflict with Russia. The Generalissimo agreed and added that anything not detrimental to Chinese sovereignty would be done to avoid such a conflict. Mr. Wallace again said that the United States could not be expected to be a party to any negotiations. The Generalissimo expressed his concurrence and said that China would seek an early opportunity for discussions with Russia. In another conversation later in the day, the Generalissimo asked that the following message be conveyed to the President: "If the United States can bring about better relations between the U. S. S. R. and China, and can bring about a meeting between Chinese and Soviet representatives, President Chiang would very much welcome such friendly assistance." [26]

During the ride to the airport on June 24, the Generalissimo twice expressed his appreciation that Mr. Wallace, as a representative of President Roosevelt, should lend his efforts for the improvement of Sino-Soviet relations. The Generalissimo also said he would welcome the assistance of the President in the settlement of the Communist problem, even though it was an internal one. He also expressed his conviction that the Communists were not men of good faith, but that if the President were willing to take the risk of helping he would be happy to have such assistance and would not consider it as meddling in internal affairs.

CONCLUSION

In September 1944 the negotiations went into a new phase with the arrival of General Hurley as the Personal Representative of the President of the United States with the mission of promoting harmonious relations between Generalissimo Chiang and General Stilwell, and of performing certain other duties in connection with military supplies. It was only a few months later after the termination of the original

---

[25] Unsuccessful attempts had been made previously by the United States Army to secure Chinese permission for an observer group to go to Communist territory. On June 22 Mr. Wallace mentioned the subject and received an evasive answer from the Generalissimo.

[26] These views should be considered in connection with chapter IV.

mission that the Kuomintang-Communist struggle, with the entrance of the United States on the scene, due to the need for prosecuting the war against Japan, took on an international aspect, which it had not possessed since the expulsion of the Russian Mission in 1927. The intervening seventeen years of bitter civil war and subsequent reluctant cooperation, under external threat, had created deep-seated hatreds, suspicions, differences of approach and objective, and a reluctance to forget the past which, more severely than was perhaps realized at the time, limited what could usefully be contributed by outside assistance.

CHAPTER III

The Ambassadorship of Major General Patrick J. Hurley, 1944–1945

I. IMMEDIATE BACKGROUND OF THE HURLEY MISSION

INTRODUCTION

Major General Patrick J. Hurley was appointed Personal Representative of the President to China on August 18, 1944. He arrived in Chungking on September 6, 1944. Mr. Clarence E. Gauss resigned as Ambassador to China on November 1, 1944, and General Hurley was nominated for the position on November 30, 1944. He presented his credentials on January 8, 1945.

To understand the reasons for the mission of General Hurley to China it is necessary to take into account the conditions which existed internally in China in 1943 and 1944. As indicated above, the Chinese record of opposition to Japanese aggression had been a distinguished and enviable one which commanded the admiration and sympathy of all peoples throughout the world who were opposing aggression. By 1943, however, the devitalizing effects of six years of war were beginning to make themselves felt. This trend in 1944 became pronounced to an alarming degree.

The long years of war were taking a heavy economic toll. Many of the most productive areas of China had been occupied by Japan. Inflation began to set in and the new Chinese middle class which had been the backbone of Kuomintang liberalism found itself being progressively beggarized. In this situation the extreme right wing and reactionary elements in the Kuomintang came to exercise increasing power and authority. The regular and periodic political reports of the Embassy in Chungking indicated a steady deterioration in the economic situation and a growing paralysis within the governmental administrative hierarchy. It was symptomatic that the Embassy reported that the Twelfth Plenary Session of the Fifth Kuomintang

Central Executive Committee had met in May 1944 but apparently accomplished little and had resulted in a serious setback for liberal elements in the Party. The Embassy also reported that liberal elements in the Party were discouraged by the trend but hoped that developments would support their contention that Kuomintang leadership was bankrupt.

The protracted background of developments outlined in chapter II contributed to the particular state of relations between the Chinese Communists and the National Government which existed when General Hurley embarked on his mission. As has already been pointed out, following the Sian incident in late 1936 the Chinese National Government and the Chinese Communist Party had indicated their intention to present a united front against the Japanese invaders and to settle their differences by political means. Negotiations between the Communists and the National Government had been proceeding over a period of seven years prior to General Hurley's mission to China. In his instructions to the Eleventh Plenary Session of the Fifth Central Executive Committee of the Kuomintang held in September 1943, the Generalissimo had stated that he was of the opinion that "first of all we should clearly recognize that the Chinese Communist problem is a purely political problem and should be solved by political means",[1] that is, through negotiations rather than through force. Accordingly, in the spring of 1944, active negotiations had been conducted at Sian by the National Government represented by Dr. Wang Shih-chieh and the Chinese Communist Party represented by Lin Tsu-han.

Despite the announced intention of the Chinese Government and the Chinese Communist Party to seek a political, that is a negotiated, solution of their differences, and notwithstanding the fact that negotiations were being actively conducted to that end, the Chinese military effort against Japan was increasingly handicapped by internal disunity.

In a conversation on July 3 with an officer of the Embassy, Dr. Sun Fo, President of the Legislative Yuan, said he had discussed the situation frankly with the Generalissimo. He had told him that the Chinese armies must be rehabilitated if they were to be effective. He also pointed out that one of the principal obstacles to effective prosecution of the war was the immobilization of some 300,000 of the Government's best troops to watch the Chinese Communists. This factor, he said, also immobilized large Chinese Communist forces which had fought well against Japan and could do so again. Dr. Sun said he had told the Generalissimo that the Chinese Communists did

[1] *China Handbook, 1937–1945*, p. 67.

not want to communize or dominate China, that it would in any case be impossible for them to do so and that what they wanted was a settlement which would enable them to cooperate with the Nationalist Government against Japan. Dr. Sun added to the Embassy officer that the Generalissimo was used to making decisions himself and not taking advice. Dr. Sun felt, however, that his remarks had had some effect and that the Generalissimo was actually seeking in his own mind for means of reorienting some of his ideas. Dr. Sun felt that American opinion could be of assistance in this process if it did not appear to be bringing pressure on the Generalissimo.

However discouraged other elements may have been by the internal deterioration and stalemate in the Chinese war effort against Japan, no such note appeared in the words or actions of the General-issimo. In his Double Tenth speech of October 10, 1944, he reiterated his determination to fight to the end and to preserve his leadership in the struggle for the consolidation of China. He also showed himself sensitive to foreign criticisms of internal developments and in a rather ominous note implied that foreign powers would be well advised not to interfere in the internal affairs of China, particularly in the relations of the National Government with the Chinese Communists.

The foregoing considerations were repeatedly reflected in the reports made in 1944 by the American Ambassador, Mr. Gauss. As he often emphasized, these factors were having a disastrous effect upon the Chinese effort in the war against Japan. His comments and obser-vations were substantiated by periodic reports he received from Ameri-can consular officials in such widely diversified areas as Fukien, Kweilin, Kunming, Chengtu, Sian and Lanchow.

Other American observers in China were becoming increasingly apprehensive over the fact that neither the Chinese Government nor the Chinese Communists were directing their main efforts against Japan. Congressman Mansfield in January of 1945 in his report to Congress following his return from his mission to China summarized this opinion: "On the basis of information which I have been able to gather, it appears to me that both the Communists and the Kuomintang are more interested in preserving their respective Parties at this time and have been for the past two years than they are in carrying on the war against Japan. Each Party is more interested in it own status because both feel that America will guarantee victory."

CHINESE UNITY AND THE WAR EFFORT

Ambassador Gauss had emphasized this point of view in a conver-sation with the Generalissimo on August 30, 1944.[2] He reported that

---

[2] See annex 45.

the Generalissimo had sent for him and had discussed the Chinese Communist problem for an hour and a half, saying that Washington did not understand the problem and it was the duty of the Ambassador to see that it did. In addition to making charges of bad faith and treachery against the Chinese Communists, General Chiang stated that the attitude of the American Government in urging China to resolve its differences with the Chinese Communists served only to strengthen the latter in their recalcitrance. He said that the Communist demands were equivalent to asking the Government to surrender unconditionally to a party known to be under the influence of a foreign power. He added that the United States should tell the Communists to settle their differences with and submit to the National Government. Ambassador Gauss stated that, being assured that he might speak frankly and openly, he was able to emphasize that the American Government was not interested in the cause of the Chinese Communists but that it was interested in seeing a solution of a Chinese internal problem which found Chinese armed forces facing each other rather than facing and fighting the Japanese and that this was of outstanding importance in that critical period of the war. He expressed his complete sympathy with the difficult task facing the Generalissimo in the solution of the Chinese Communist problem and added:

"We have not suggested that the Chinese Government should capitulate to Communist demands. Our interest is solely in the unification of China and the dissipation of the present critical situation. Our hope is that a peaceful solution can be found to this problem by the Chinese themselves."

The Ambassador reported that he made the personal observation that while the Generalissimo said that the Chinese Communists were not to be trusted, the Embassy had long heard the Chinese Communists complain equally that the Kuomintang Government could not be trusted. It seemed to him that an effort should be made to dissipate this mutual mistrust and that it was his personal opinion that a solution might be found in some measure which would bring the most competent representatives of the several groups and parties to participate in and share the responsibilities of the Government. He was of course aware of the Kuomintang contention that there could at that time be one-party government only. He indicated, however, that he would like to see the difficulty overcome. Even if it could not be overcome on a broad basis to give representation in the Government to minor parties, perhaps a limited solution might be found under which able representatives of the parties or special groups might be provided for, with these persons being invited to share in some form of responsible war council which planned and carried out plans to meet the serious war crisis taking place in China. In conclusion the Ambassador said that in such sharing of responsibility perhaps there could be developed a disposition toward cooperation for unification of China. The Generalissimo commented that this suggestion might at least be worth studying.

In response to the Ambassador's report of this conversation, Secretary of State Hull informed Mr. Gauss that the President and he had given careful consideration to the report and agreed that a "positive, frank, and free approach to Chiang on the subject of governmental and related military conditions in China should be made at this time." The Secretary indicated that the Generalissimo's suggestion that the Chinese Communists should be told to settle their differences with the Government was similar to his previous suggestion to Vice President Wallace and that the general argument of the Generalissimo as set forth to the Ambassador showed a discouraging lack of progress in the thinking of the Generalissimo in view of his own professed desire to reach a settlement with the Chinese Communists and in view of dissident developments in other areas not under Chinese Communist influence. The Secretary then suggested that the Ambassador might tell the Generalissimo that if the latter would arrange a meeting the Ambassador would be prepared to speak to the Communist representative in Chungking along the same general lines as the Ambassador and the Vice President had spoken to him; that the Ambassador would point out to the Communist representative that unity in China in prosecuting the war and in preparing for the peace was urgently necessary; that a spirit of tolerance and good will—of give and take—was essential in achieving such unity; that Chinese of every shade of political thinking should cooperate now to defeat the Japanese; and that differences could be settled if the major objective of victory was kept firmly in mind. The Ambassador was requested to inform Chiang (1) that the President and the Secretary felt that Mr. Gauss' suggestion for a coalition council was deserving of careful consideration; (2) that they were concerned, not only regarding non-settlement with the Chinese Communists, but also with regard to reports of discontent and dissidence in other parts of the country among non-Communist Chinese; (3) that they were not interested in the Communists or other dissident elements as such, but were anxious that the Chinese people develop and utilize, under the leadership of a strong representative and tolerant government, the physical and spiritual resources at their command in carrying on the war and establishing a durable democratic peace.[3]

___

[3] See annex 46.

PESSIMISM OF AMBASSADOR GAUSS

Although Ambassador Gauss transmitted this message to Chiang Kai-shek, he doubted that the Generalissimo would take the necessary steps or was even capable of doing so. He was also pessimistic over the prospects for negotiation with the Communists in view of the deep suspicion on both sides and inability to recognize realities. He even questioned the Chinese desire to cooperate actively in the war against Japan. The reports from the Embassy during October and early November present a depressing picture of a deteriorating situation, characterized by internal squabbles and apathy.

The discouraging conclusions of Ambassador Gauss were further reinforced from a source other than the Embassy or the Consulates. Several Foreign Service officers, all specialists in the Far East, at the request of the United States Army, were attached to the staff of the Commanding General of the China-Burma-India (later China) Theater for liaison duties. These officers had a unique opportunity, through travel and contacts with American and Chinese Military authorities, to observe conditions and report their reactions. These reports were made available to American officials concerned. The memoranda of these officers were prepared on a wide range of subjects and during a period of over two years, from early 1943 to early 1945, when the end of the war with Japan was not yet recognized as imminent. They show the development of the following themes:

1. Russian intentions with respect to the Far East, including China, are aggressive.

2. The Chinese Communists have a background of subservience to the U. S. S. R., but new influences—principally nationalism—have come into play which are modifying their outlook.

3. The Chinese Communists have become the most dynamic force in China and are challenging the Kuomintang for control of the country.

4. The Kuomintang and National Government are disintegrating.

5. The rivalry between these two forces threatens to culminate in a civil war which (a) would hamper the conduct of the war against Japan, (b) would press the Communists back into the arms of the U. S. S. R. and (c) might well lead eventually to American Soviet involvement and conflict.

6. The Communists would inevitably win such a war because the foreign Powers, including the United States, which would support the Government, could not feasibly supply enough aid to compensate for the organic weaknesses of the Government.

7. In this unhappy dilemma, the United States should attempt to prevent the disaster of a civil war through adjustment of the new align-

ment of power in China by peaceful processes. The desirable means to this end is to encourage the reform and revitalization of the Kuomintang so that it may survive as a significant force in a coalition government. If this fails, we must limit our involvement with the Kuomintang and must commence some cooperation with the Communists, the force destined to control China, in an effort to influence them further into an independent position friendly to the United States. We are working against time because, if the U. S. S. R. enters the war against Japan and invades China before either of these alternatives succeeds, the Communists will be captured by the U. S. S. R. and become Soviet satellites.

8. A policy of this description would also—and this is a decisive consideration in the war against Japan—measurably aid our war effort.[4]

THE MILITARY FACTOR

As serious as were the other factors which contributed to the general deterioration during 1944 the most crucial point certainly, and the one which loomed largest in official American thinking, was the disintegration of the military situation which threatened the collapse of the entire Chinese war effort. It was this military factor which most immediately concerned American officials. Signs of military disintegration appeared in the spring, assumed major proportions during the summer, and eventuated in disaster during the fall. On April 17 the Japanese launched an attack southward across the Yellow River which marked the beginning of their campaign to open the Peiping-Hankow Railroad. On May 18 Loyang in the Yellow River area was captured and the remnants of Tang En-po's troops were set upon by the local populace. With the capture of Kaifeng the entire Honan front collapsed.

On May 27 the Japanese opened the drive southward into Hunan Province across the Yangtze and along the Hankow-Canton Railroad. On June 6, Huan-Chiang was occupied and the important center of Changsha was flanked to the west. On June 18 Changsha was captured and ten days later Hengyang was surrounded, though it did not fall until August 8. This placed the Japanese forces in a position to mount an offensive against the strategic air base Kweilin. In mid-August the Japanese mounted a new offensive in the coastal province of Chekiang. This drive resulted in the capture of Lishui on August 28. In mid-September Japanese forces crossed from Hunan into Kwangsi Province.

During the ensuing weeks Japanese forces from the north and southeast converged on Kweilin, which fell on November 12. With this

---

[4] See annex 47.

development the entire East China front had collapsed and there was little reason to believe that the Japanese if they so elected would not have the capability of attacking Chungking and the vitally important American base at Kunming. The situation was further complicated by reverses on the Salween front in Burma. Increasingly it had become apparent that the Chinese war effort had largely ceased to be an effective factor in China and that to a disturbing extent the Chinese will to fight had vanished. The main Nationalist effort was being concentrated on containment of Communists in the north and in internal political squabbles in Chungking. It was only in Burma, where the Chinese troops were under the direct command of General Stilwell, that Chinese ground forces were making a distinct military contribution.

PRESIDENT ROOSEVELT'S MESSAGES TO GENERALISSIMO CHIANG KAI-SHEK, JULY-AUGUST 1944

It was particularly this rapidly disintegrating military situation in East China which gave the most serious concern to President Roosevelt. As he saw it the first step in the solution would be the appointment of an American general to the command of all Chinese armies. On July 7, 1944, the President sent the following message to the Generalissimo:

"The critical situation which now exists in my opinion calls for the delegation to one individual of the powers to coordinate all the Allied military resources in China, including the Communist forces. . . . I am promoting Stilwell to the rank of full General and I recommend for your most urgent consideration that you recall him from Burma and place him directly under you in the command of all Chinese and American forces, and that you charge him with the full responsibility and authority for the coordination and direction of the operations required to stem the tide of the enemy's forces. I feel that the case of China is so desperate that if radical and promptly applied remedies are not immediately effected, our common cause will suffer a disastrous setback."

The Generalissimo agreed to this proposal in principle but suggested that as a preliminary step a high ranking American official well acquainted with political as well as military matters and having the complete confidence of the President be sent to Chungking to discuss the problem. On July 15 the President replied as follows:

"I am very glad to learn that in principle you are in agreement with the proposal to place General Stilwell in absolute command under you of the Chinese troops without any hindrance. . . I am searching for a personal representative with far sightedness and political ability to collaborate with you. . . In the meantime I again urge you to take all steps to pave the way for General Stilwell's assumption of command at the earliest possible moment."

The President followed up this message with another one of August 10:

"I have this proposal to make: That General Patrick J. Hurley . . . be designated by me as my personal representative with you. . . He should be of great service in adjusting relations between you and General Stilwell. . . ."

The President also proposed that Mr. Donald Nelson accompany General Hurley to deal with lend-lease and other economic matters. The Generalissimo accepted the proposal.

On August 23 the President again urged on the Generalissimo the appointment of General Stilwell to the command of all Chinese Armies in the following message:

"I am glad that you find General Hurley and Mr. Nelson acceptable for the important mission they will perform for us. Now that my personal representatives to you have been decided upon, I think we should proceed immediately to take the positive steps demanded by the military situation. I urge that you take the necessary measures to place General Stilwell in command of the Chinese forces, under your direction, at the earliest possible date. . . . I feel certain, however, that between General Hurley and General Stilwell there will be an adequate comprehension of the political problems you face. I am urging action in the matter of Stilwell's appointment so strongly because I feel that, with further delay, it may be too late to avert a military catastrophe tragic both to China and to our allied plans for the early overthrow of Japan. . . . I do not think the forces to come under General Stilwell's command should be limited except by their availability to defend China and fight the Japanese. When the enemy is pressing us toward possible disaster, it appears unsound to reject the aid of anyone who will kill Japanese. . . . I feel sure that General Hurley will be highly useful in promoting relations which will facilitate General Stilwell's exercise of command and his understanding of the related political problems. . . ."

Despite his earlier agreement in principle, the Generalissimo had still failed to place General Stilwell in command and the relations between the two men became increasingly bad. By early September, the military picture had become so ominous that the President felt compelled to send still another message to the Generalissimo:

"After reading the last reports on the situation in China my Chiefs of Staff and I are convinced that you are faced in the near future with the disaster I have feared. . . . I have urged time and again in recent months that you take drastic action to resist the disaster which has been moving closer to China and to you. Now, when you have not yet placed General Stilwell in command of all forces in China, we are faced with a loss of a critical area in East China with possible catastrophic consequences."

REPORTS BY GENERAL STILWELL

On September 22, General Stilwell reported to the Chief of Staff in Washington his estimate of the Generalissimo's actions:

"Chiang Kai-shek is following his usual policy. At first he readily agreed to the command arrangement and also by inference agreed to use the communist army under my command, then he began the delaying action, which still continues. He protests that there are many difficulties which have to be smoothed out and this takes time. Actually, he believes that our advance in the Pacific will be swift enough and effective enough to spare his further effort, and he would like to avoid the bitter pill of recognizing the communists and putting a foreigner in command of the army. . . ."

On September 26, General Stilwell again reported to the Chief of Staff as follows:

"Chiang Kai-shek has no intention of making further efforts to prosecute the war. Anyone who crowds him toward such action will be blocked or eliminated . . . Chiang Kai-shek believes he can go on milking the United States for money and munitions by using the old gag about quitting if he is not supported. He believes the war in the Pacific is nearly over, and that by delaying tactics, he can throw the entire burden on us. He has no intention of instituting any real democratic regime or of forming a united front with the communists. He himself is the main obstacle to the unification of China and her cooperation in a real effort against Japan . . . I am now convinced that, for the reasons stated, the United States will not get any real cooperation from China while Chiang Kai-shek is in power. I believe he will only continue his policy and delay, while grabbing for loans and postwar aid, for the purpose of maintaining his present position, based on one-party government, a reactionary policy, or the suppression of democratic ideas with the active aid of his gestapo."

Shortly before his departure from China, General Stilwell gave yet another estimate of the crisis involving himself to the Chief of Staff:

"It is not a choice between throwing me out or losing Chiang Kai-shek and possibly China. It is a case of losing China's potential effort if Chiang Kai-shek is allowed to make removals now. I believe that the solution to the problem lies in insisting on the acceptance of our proposals yet at the same time giving the Generalissimo a boost in prestige which will permit him to give his agreement without loss of face or offense to the Chinese Nationalist spirit."

By this time it had become apparent to General Hurley that the relations between the Generalissimo and General Stilwell had reached a point where no kind of a third party intervention could possibly remedy the damage already done except by the removal of General Stilwell, and furthermore, that no progress could be made in other outstanding questions until a new American Supreme Commander had been appointed. President Roosevelt accepted this point of view and Major General Albert C. Wedemeyer was designated to replace General Stilwell. There was seemingly no real effort made subsequently to have General Wedemeyer named to command all Chinese armies. It should be remembered in this connection that by the end of the year it was apparent that the Japanese did not intend to push beyond Kweilin for the capture of Chungking, and furthermore that the serious military situation which had developed in Burma early in the summer had been considerably alleviated.

In his final report to the War Department, General Stilwell made the following comments in appraisal of the controversy in which he had been a principal figure:

"However, as the level of command rose, national policies and politics entered the picture with resulting deterioration in sincerity and in cooperation. With the one exception of the Chinese Army in India where General Stilwell had been given direct command of the forces, the Americans enjoyed no command functions in the Chinese Army. Elsewhere the Theater Commander lacked the right of 'order'. Consequently, having no overall control, he could neither form the strategy nor direct the tactics. Holding in general to a purely advisory role, the Americans were often regarded with a jaundiced look of suspicion. In some instances our honest efforts, and our impartial action demonstrated an altruistic motive which won the respect and trust of certain field commanders. This favorable reaction to our conduct did not always hold true in the Chungking Government. In high places we were generally regarded as interlopers of cunning demeanor distributing largesse, most of which failed to materialize.

" 'Aid to China', once undertaken, should have been vigorously prosecuted. Fortified with a full knowledge of China's governmental venality, her economic chaos, her military weakness, a written agreement to a plan committing her to a vigorous prosecution of the war under American supervision and material assistance should have been signed before we tendered any aid.

"It became increasingly obvious that a more frank and vigorous foreign policy would have helped to gain China's whole-hearted cooperation, and her acknowledgment that our cooperation depended upon determined action on her part. The genial, parental admonishments of our government had failed to persuade the head of China's Central Government to recognize his political opponents—not even as a concession to the United States who regarded such recognition as important to the war effort. Certain factors entered into the picture, illuminating the fallacy of political placation, vain promise, and shabby support of a vacillating policy which drained public funds into a futile transfusion.

"Japanese aggression imposed a temporary unity on the various elements in struggling to determine whether China would progress along democratic or authoritarian lines. Of these elements Chiang Kai-shek was the strongest, and public opinion compelled him to assume the symbol of national unified will.

"Faced with the Japanese offensive designed to disintegrate China and bring about its collapse, Chiang chose to abandon national unity and to steer a course seeking to dominate rather than to unify and lead. He sought to dominate because he had no appreciation of what genuine democracy means.

"The Kuomintang party, of which he is the leader, was once the expression of genuine nationalistic feeling, but is now an uncertain equilibrium of decadent, competing factions, with neither dynamic principles nor a popular base. Chiang controls by manipulating these functions with an adroit political sense. His seat is insecure. His reluctance to expand military strength, his preoccupation with the security of domestic supremacy, his suspicion of everyone around him, and his increasing emotional instability betrayed a realization of this. He became a hostage of the forces he manipulated.

"Nowhere does Clausewitz's dictum that war is only the continuation of politics by other methods apply with more force that it did in CBI. In handling such an uncertain situation as existed in that theater of war, the Americans would have done well to avoid committing themselves unalterably to Chiang, and adopted a more realistic attitude toward China itself. We could gain little by supporting the attitude of the Chiang regime. We could have gained much by exerting pressure on Chiang to cooperate and achieve national unity, and if he proved unable to do this, then in supporting those elements in China which gave promise of such development." [4a]

[4a] The present treatment of the controversy surrounding General Stilwell does not purport to be a full and complete account of that crisis. Only that material has been used which would serve as background for the Mission of General Hurley. It is the understanding of the Department of State that the National Military Establishment is preparing a full history of World War II and that this period will be more fully treated therein.

It was primarily to prevent that which did finally happen that General Hurley was dispatched to China by President Roosevelt. Once that crisis had been resolved with the appointment of General Wedemeyer, General Hurley undertook to lend his good offices in other problems.

GENERAL HURLEY'S INSTRUCTIONS

According to General Hurley's report to the Department of State his instructions from the White House dated August 18 were (1) to serve as personal representative of the President to Generalissimo Chiang Kai-shek; (2) to promote harmonious relations between Chiang and General Joseph Stilwell and to facilitate the latter's exercise of command over the Chinese armies placed under his direction; (3) to perform certain additional duties respecting military supplies; and (4) to maintain intimate contact with Ambassador Gauss. A few months later, after his appointment as Ambassador, General Hurley outlined his understanding of his mission and of United States policy in China in the following terms: "(1) To prevent the collapse of the National Government, (2) to sustain Chiang Kai-shek as President of the Republic and Generalissimo of the Armies, (3) to harmonize relations between the Generalissimo and the American Commander, (4) to promote production of war supplies in China and prevent economic collapse, and (5) to unify all the military forces in China for the purpose of defeating Japan."

GENERAL HURLEY'S TALK WITH MR. MOLOTOV

In company with Mr. Donald Nelson, chairman of the War Production Board, and a Special Representative of President Roosevelt, General Hurley had flown to Chungking by way of Moscow, where they had discussed the Chinese situation with Foreign Minister Molotov. According to Mr. Nelson's report of this conversation, he explained that his main business in China concerned economic matters and that General Hurley's concerned military matters; that Chinese cooperation in the war was of "vital importance"; and that to achieve this the United States Government must support Generalissimo Chiang and effect complete unity in China. In response to Mr. Nelson's request for Soviet opinion on this subject, Mr. Molotov replied that it was difficult to judge the Chinese situation from Washington or Moscow but that he would be willing to express some off-the-record thoughts. Mr. Molotov's remarks were summarized in the report as follows:

"Molotov then talked at length on the Generalissimo's imprisonment at Sian in 1936 and said that relations between China and the

Soviet Union were tense at that time. However, he said that the Soviet Government had turned its back on the Chinese revolutionary groups led by Chang Hsueh-liang and Wang Ching-wei which included many Communists and which looked to the Soviet Union for sympathy and aid and had issued a statement to the effect that Japanese provocation had been the cause of the uprising in Sian and other events in China. Due to the political and moral support of the Soviet government, Chiang had been allowed to return to the seat of his government and the revolutionary leader (Chang Hsueh-liang) had been arrested. The Soviets had hoped as a result of their action that Soviet-Chinese relations would change for the better. However, the Chinese had shown little interest in strengthening relations which had on the contrary deteriorated in recent years.

"Although he said that the Soviet government had unjustifiably been held responsible for various happenings in China during recent years, Molotov stressed that it would bear no responsibility for internal affairs or developments in China. Molotov then spoke of the very impoverished conditions of the people in parts of China, some of whom called themselves Communists but were related to Communism in no way at all. It was merely a way of expressing dissatisfaction with their economic condition and they would forget this political inclination when their economic condition improved. The Soviet government should not be associated with these 'communist elements' nor could it in any way be blamed for this situation. The solution of the entire situation was to make the Chinese government work in the common interest and cope with the tasks before it and to make life more normal in China. Molotov said in conclusion that the Soviets would be glad if the United States aided the Chinese in unifying their country, in improving their military and economic condition and in choosing for this task their best people. . . . Molotov's satisfaction at being consulted was clearly indicated. He gave little new information but he confirmed statements made previously that his government would be glad to see the United States taking the lead economically, politically, and militarily in Chinese affairs. Molotov made it clear also that until Chiang Kai-shek tried by changes in his policies to improve Sino-Soviet relations, the Soviet government did not intend to take any interest in Chinese governmental affairs."

The importance of this conversation is apparent from the frequent references in General Hurley's subsequent reports to Molotov's expression of Soviet policy toward China.

II. THE EFFORT AT MEDIATION

INITIAL STEPS

Upon arriving at Chungking in September, General Hurley came to the conclusion that the success of his mission "to unify all the military forces in China for the purpose of defeating Japan" was dependent on the negotiations already under way for the unification of Chinese military forces. Accordingly, shortly after his arrival he undertook active measures of mediation between the Chinese National Government and the Chinese Communist Party.

In December 1944 General Hurley commented as follows regarding his early efforts at reconciliation:

"At the time I came here Chiang Kai-shek believed that the Communist Party in China was an instrument of the Soviet Government in Russia. He is now convinced that the Russian Government does not recognize the Chinese Communist Party as Communist at all and that (1) Russia is not supporting the Communist Party in China, (2) Russia does not want dissensions or civil war in China, and (3) Russia desires more harmonious relations with China.

"These facts have gone far toward convincing Chiang Kai-shek that the Communist Party in China is not an agent of the Soviet Government. He now feels that he can reach a settlement with the Communist Party as a Chinese political party without foreign entanglements. When I first arrived, it was thought that civil war after the close of the present war or perhaps before that time was inevitable. Chiang Kai-shek is now convinced that by agreement with the Communist Party of China he can (1) unite the military forces of China against Japan, and (2) avoid civil strife in China."

With respect to specific steps taken by him, General Hurley reported in December 1944 that with the consent, advice and direction of the Generalissimo and members of his Cabinet and on the invitation of leaders of the Communist Party, he had begun discussions with the Communist Party and Communist military leaders for the purpose of effecting an agreement to regroup, coordinate and unite the military forces of China for the defeat of Japan. He continued: "The defeat of Japan is, of course, the primary objective, but we should all understand that if an agreement is not reached between the two great military establishments of China, civil war will in all probability ensue."

THE FIVE-POINT DRAFT AGREEMENT, NOVEMBER 10, 1944

Following discussions with Chinese Government and Chinese Communist representatives in Chungking, General Hurley on November 7, 1944, flew to Yenan for a two-day conference with Mao Tse-tung, the Chairman of the Central Executive Committee of the Chinese Communist Party. The Communist leaders were impressed by the fact that General Hurley had taken the initiative in making this flight and cordial relations were established at once. As a result of these discussions there was evolved at Yenan a five-point draft, entitled "Agreement Between the National Government of China, the Kuomintang of China and the Communist Party of China," which was signed by Mao Tse-tung as Chairman of the Central Executive Committee of the Chinese Communist Party on November 10, 1944, and by General Hurley as a witness. This important agreement read as follows:

"(1) The Government of China, the Kuomintang of China and the Communist Party of China will work together for the unification of all military forces in China for the immediate defeat of Japan and the reconstruction of China.

"(2) The present National Government is to be reorganized into a coalition National Government embracing representatives of all anti-Japanese parties and non-partisan political bodies. A new democratic policy providing for reform in military, political, economic and cultural affairs shall be promulgated and made effective. At the same time the National Military Council is to be reorganized into the United National Military Council consisting of representatives of all anti-Japanese armies.

"(3) The coalition National Government will support the principles of Sun Yat-sen for the establishment in China of a government of the people, for the people and by the people. The coalition National Government will pursue policies designed to promote progress and democracy and to establish justice, freedom of conscience, freedom of press, freedom of speech, freedom of assembly and association, the right to petition the government for the redress of grievances, the right of writ of habeas corpus and the right of residence. The coalition National Government will also pursue policies intended to make effective the two rights defined as freedom from fear and freedom from want.

"(4) All anti-Japanese forces will observe and carry out the orders of the coalition National Government and its United National Military Council and will be recognized by the Government and the Military Council. The supplies acquired from foreign powers will be equitably distributed.

"(5) The coalition National Government of China recognizes the legality of the Kuomintang of China, the Chinese Communist Party and all anti-Japanese parties."

THE THREE-POINT PLAN

General Hurley felt that this Five-Point Draft Agreement, which he promptly submitted to the National Government, offered a practical plan for settlement with the Communists. National Government leaders, however, said that the Communist plan was not acceptable. The National Government submitted as counter-proposal a Three-Point Agreement reading as follows:

"(1) The National Government, desirous of securing effective unification and concentration of all military forces in China for the purpose of accomplishing the speedy defeat of Japan, and looking forward to the post-war reconstruction of China, agrees to incorporate, after reorganization, the Chinese Communist forces in the National Army who will then receive equal treatment as the other units in respect of pay, allowance, munitions and other supplies, and to give recognition to the Chinese Communist Party as a legal party.

"(2) The Communist Party undertakes to give their full support to the National Government in the prosecution of the war of resistance, and in the post-war reconstruction, and give over control of all their troops to the National Government through the National Military Council. The National Government will designate some high ranking officers from among the Communist forces to membership in the National Military Council.

"(3) The aim of the National Government to which the Communist Party subscribes is to carry out the Three People's Principles of Dr. Sun Yat-sen for the establishment in China of a government of the people, for the people and by the people and it will pursue policies designed to promote the progress and development of democratic processes in government.

"In accordance with the provisions of the *Program of Armed Resistance and National Reconstruction*, freedom of speech, freedom of the press, freedom of assembly and association and other civil liberties are hereby guaranteed, subject only to the specific needs of security in the effective prosecution of the war against Japan."

REPLY OF THE CHINESE COMMUNISTS

This proposal was handed to General Chou En-lai, the Communist representative in Chungking, on November 22 and was taken by him to Yenan early in December. Following his arrival in Yenan, General Chou wrote General Hurley a letter, which the latter reported as follows:

"The refusal of the Generalissimo and the National Government of our minimum five point proposal, clearly showing disagreement with our suggestions for a coalition government and united military council and the submission of the three point counter-proposal, preclude the possibility of my returning to Chungking for further negotiations. We find it impossible to see any fundamental common basis in these new proposals. We feel that publication of our five-point proposal is now called for in order to inform the public and to bring out the changing attitude of the Government.

"Despite the fact that President Chiang has so limited the question of military cooperation between us that no easy solution can be achieved, we completely desire to continue to discuss with you and General Wedemeyer [5] the concrete problems of our future military cooperation and to continue the closest contact with the United States Army Observers Section in Yenan. Chairman Mao Tse-tung has especially asked me to express his deep thanks and appreciation for your sympathy and energetic efforts on behalf of unity in China."

General Hurley reported that he was conferring daily with the Generalissimo and members of his cabinet "endeavoring to liberalize the counter-proposal. We are having some success. The Generalissimo states that he is anxious that the military forces of the Communist Party in China and those of the National Government be united to drive the invaders from China. The Communist leaders declare this is also their objective. I have persuaded Chiang that in order to unite the military forces in China and prevent civil conflict it will be necessary for him and the Kuomintang and the National Government to make liberal political concessions to the Communist Party and to give them adequate representation in the National Government."

General Hurley, who reported that all his communications with Yenan without exception were sent with the full knowledge and consent of the high officials of the National Government, wrote Chou En-lai that it was his understanding that the five-point offer of settlement proposed by the Chinese Communists was to form the basis of discussion and was not a "take it or leave it" proposition; that the Communist Party was willing to consider suggestions for amendments by the National Government and that the three-point offer in response to the Communist proposal was not the final word of the National

---

[5] General Wedemeyer had replaced General Stilwell in November as commander of United States forces in the China Theater.

Government. He regarded both instruments as steps in the negotiations and it was his understanding that publication of the five-point
Communist proposal would be withheld while negotiations were pending. He did not believe that negotiations had been terminated unless
General Chou so wished them, and he knew that the National Government was disposed to make every effort to unify China. He felt
it would be a great tragedy if the door were closed at this critical hour
to further discussions.

General Chou replied to General Hurley on December 16, 1944,
stating that the unexpected and flat rejection by the Kuomintang of
the Communist five-point proposal caused a deadlock in the negotiations and rendered his return to Chungking useless. He indicated
that this could not be construed as Communist discontent with the
United States and that he agreed with the advice of General Hurley
against the publication of the five points, but insisted that they should
be made public when the appropriate time came. The one fundamental difficulty with respect to these negotiations, he felt, was the
unwillingness of the Kuomintang to forsake one-party rule and accept
the proposal for a "democratic coalition government."

General Hurley replied to General Chou En-lai in a telegram on
December 21, 1944, stating his belief that chances for success along
the general lines of the Communist proposals would be "brighter
than ever before if he would come again to Chungking." On December 24, Mao Tse-tung telegraphed General Hurley stating that General
Chou was occupied with "important conference preparations" which
made his departure from Yenan difficult. Mao stated that the National
Government had not shown sufficient sincerity to warrant continuing
negotiations on the basis of the five-point proposal and he suggested
a conference in Yenan. On December 28, General Chou wrote General
Hurley that the Communists would not be willing to continue abstract
discussions on the question of accepting their proposal for a "democratic coalition government." He proposed instead the following
four additional points which he requested the Ambassador to communicate to the Chinese Government authorities "to see whether they
are determined to realize democracy and unity": (1) The release of
all political prisoners; (2) the withdrawal of Kuomintang forces surrounding the border region and those attacking the new Fourth Army
and the South China Anti-Communist column; (3) the abolition of
all oppressive regulations restricting the people's freedom; and (4)
cessation of all secret service activity.

Ambassador Hurley replied in a letter dated January 7, 1945, addressed to Mao Tse-tung and Chou En-lai, stating that the additional
four points outlined in the latter's letter of December 28 constituted

a departure from "our original agreed procedure which was to arrive at an agreement on general principles before discussing specific details." The Ambassador also stated that he was convinced that the National Government was sincerely desirous of making such concessions as would make a settlement possible, but that such matters could not be discussed by telegram or letter. He suggested, after obtaining the approval of the National Government, that he make a brief visit to Yenan, accompanied by Dr. T. V. Soong, Dr. Wang Shih-chieh, and General Chang Chih-chung, to discuss matters in person and that Mao Tse-tung and Chou En-lai might return with the foregoing group to Chungking if agreement in principle were reached as a result of the discussions in Yenan.

THE CONFERENCE AT CHUNGKING

In a reply to this proposal, on January 11, Mao Tse-tung stated that the proposal for a conference between both parties at Yenan was greatly appreciated but that he felt that nothing could be achieved thereby. He proposed that a preparatory conference be called in Chungking for the purpose of convening a National Affairs Conference; that the preparatory conference include Kuomintang, Communist and Democratic League delegates; that the proceedings of the conference be made public; and that "the delegates have equal standing and freedom to travel." He added that if the National Government found these proposals acceptable General Chou would proceed to Chungking for discussions. On January 20, the Ambassador wrote Mao Tse-tung with the knowledge and approval of the Generalissimo outlining certain changes that were contemplated in the National Government. General Hurley added "it may well be that this measure together with the other measures that have been offered by the National Government may not be sufficient to satisfy the Chinese Communists, but I think it would be a great pity if such far-reaching government proposals were rejected out of hand without due consideration. As a friend of China I suggest you send General Chou En-lai or any other representative you may select to Chungking for a brief visit to talk matters over with the Government. It need not take long; if he is busy two or three days would be sufficient." On January 23, the Ambassador was informed by Mao Tse-tung in reply that General Chou was being sent to Chungking to negotiate with the Government.

THE NATIONAL GOVERNMENT'S PROPOSAL

Following the arrival of General Chou in Chungking on January 24 a series of conferences were held in which Dr. T. V. Soong, Acting President of the Executive Yuan and Minister for Foreign Affairs,

Dr. Wang Shih-chieh, Minister of Information, and General Chang Chih-chung, Director of Political Training of the National Ministries Council, represented the National Government. General Chou represented the Chinese Communist Party and General Hurley attended on the invitation of both parties. Dr. Wang Shih-chieh stated that the National Government was prepared to take the following measures, in addition to its previous three-point proposal:

"1. The Government will set up, in the Executive Yuan, an organ whose nature resembles a war cabinet, with a membership of from seven to nine men, to act as the policy making body of the Executive Yuan. The Chinese Communist Party and other parties will be given representation on this organ.

"2. The Generalissimo of the National Military Council will appoint two Chinese Army officers (of whom one will be an officer of the Chinese Communist troops) and one American Army officer to make recommendations regarding the reorganization, equipment and supplies of Chinese Communist troops, for approval by the Generalissimo of the National Military Council.

"3. The Generalissimo of the National Military Council will appoint one American Army officer as the immediate commander of Chinese Communist troops for the duration of the war against Japan. The said immediate commander of Chinese Communist troops shall be responsible to the Generalissimo of the National Military Council. He shall insure the observance and enforcement of all government orders, military or nonmilitary, in the area under his control."

THE COMMUNIST PARTY'S REACTION

Ambassador Hurley stated that he had no authority from his Government to agree that an American Army officer would participate as indicated in the National Government's proposal. General Chou objected that Dr. Wang was not yet fully aware of the fundamental aims of the Communists. Despite the Generalissimo's New Year's speech, in which he had spoken of the necessity for adopting a constitution at an early date and returning the control of the Government to the people, it appeared to General Chou that Dr. Wang's proposal represented merely concessions made by the Kuomintang while that party still retained control of the Government. General Chou repeated the position which he and Mao Tse-tung had expressed to General Hurley when they had negotiated the original Five-Point Agreement, namely, that the Communist Party would not submit the command of its troops to the Kuomintang Party although it was prepared to turn over command of its troops to the National Government when the one-party rule of the Kuomintang had been abolished and the Government had been reconstituted as a coalition administration representing all parties. He would favor at such time establishing a military commission to reorganize the Chinese armed forces, but he would not agree that such a commission should be permitted to reorganize only Communist troops. The entire Chinese military establishment should be reorganized and he would be glad to see an American serve on such a commission.

CONFERENCE WITH THE GENERALISSIMO

This Communist Party position was made known to Generalissimo Chiang at a conference attended by Ambassador Hurley, Dr. T. V. Soong, and Dr. Wang Shih-chieh. The Ambassador reported that Chiang pointed out that he was calling a meeting for May 4, in keeping with the will of Dr. Sun Yat-sen, for the purpose of taking steps to draft a constitution, to pass the control of the National Government to the people, and to abolish the one-party rule of the Kuomintang. The Generalissimo made the definite statement that in his opinion all the political parties in China including his own constituted less than 2 percent of the Chinese people. He believed that it would not be for the best interest of China to turn the control of the Government over to any political group or to a coalition of political groups. He felt it to be his duty to have a democratic constitution for China adopted by a convention in which all the people of China, and not alone the organized political minorities, would participate. He expressed his belief that the Chinese Communist Party was not in fact a democratic party and that it professed to be democratic only for the purpose of trying to achieve control of the administration of the National Government. The Ambassador suggested to the Generalissimo that he was losing valuable time and again said that he could afford to make political concessions and shorten the period of transition in order to obtain control of the Communist forces. Ambassador Hurley stated that the Generalissimo's most important objective at the moment should be unification of the Communist military forces with those of the National Government. This would be the first step toward China's major objectives, namely: (1) unification of all military forces to defeat Japan; (2) unification of China to prevent outside forces from keeping China divided against itself; (3) prevention of civil war in China and (4) a united, free, democratic China under a democratic constitution adopted by a convention of the Chinese people.

After extended discussions Dr. Wang Shih-chieh and General Chou En-lai were appointed to form a committee to draw up a proposal which "would make action possible." On February 3 Dr. Wang Shih-chieh presented the following draft to the Ambassador:

"In order to intensify our war effort against the enemy and strengthen our national unity, it is agreed that the National Government should invite the representatives of the Kuomintang and other parties, and some non-partisan leaders, to a consultative meeting. This meeting is to be named the Political Consultation Conference, and its membership is not to exceed ———— persons.

"The function of this conference is to consider: (a) steps to be taken in winding up the period of political tutelage and establishing constitutional government, (b) the common political program to be followed in the future and the unification of armed forces, and (c) the form in which members of parties outside the Kuomintang will take part in the National Government.

"If the said Political Consultation Conference succeeds in reaching a unanimous conclusion, it will be submitted to the National Government for consideration and execution. During the Political Consultation Conference, all parties should refrain from recriminations of any kind."

General Chou En-lai informed the Ambassador that he was sending a copy of the draft by telegram to Yenan and he added that for the first time he felt that a basis for cooperation was being reached. General Hurley reported that he discussed the draft with Generalissimo Chiang Kai-shek on February 4. In reporting this discussion the Ambassador stated that the Generalissimo said he had consented to the proposal but he felt that the Communists had obtained what they had been endeavoring to obtain all along. Ambassador Hurley told him "very frankly" that the only instrument heretofore with which he could have worked with the Communists was the five-point agreement; that if he had revised that agreement at the time it was offered, the Communists would probably have accepted reasonable revision; and that it was still the only document in which there was a signed agreement by the Communists to submit control of their armed forces to the National Government.

SUMMARY OF KUOMINTANG VIEWS

In the middle of February 1945 the Ambassador summarized the views of the representatives of the Chinese Government during these discussions. According to his report, the Government representatives stated that the real purpose of the Chinese Communist Party was not the abolition of the one-party rule by the Kuomintang but rather, as indicated by all the maneuvers made by the Chinese Communists, to overthrow control by the Kuomintang Party and obtain a one-party rule of China by the Chinese Communist Party. The Kuomintang desired to have a democratic constitution adopted and to return the government to the people. It would not surrender its authority in these troublous times to a coterie of parties in a so-called coalition government. It would appoint a bi-partisan war cabinet with policy-making powers but would retain control of the Government until control was returned to the people under a democratic constitution. The Generalissimo stated that he wanted the Communists to accept the latest offer of the Government, which was made in good faith and with every possible guarantee that their armed forces would not be destroyed or discriminated against. He said that the Chinese Communists aimed to effect a *coup* by which they would take control of the National Government and convert it into a one-party Communist Government similar to that of Russia. He felt that the Chinese Communist Party's hopes for success were based on the fact that they believed that if Russia entered the war in Asia it would support the Chinese Communists against the National Government. Chiang pointed out that notwithstanding all this, the Government had decided to undertake this bold measure for returning rule to the people in the midst of war; that now the Government invited the Communists and other Party representatives, with complete freedom of travel, to meet on an equal status for the purpose of intensifying efforts against the enemy and strengthening national unity and to provide a program for completing the period of tutelage and establishing a democratic constitutional government.

ADJOURNMENT OF THE CONFERENCE

In concluding his report on these negotiations, General Hurley stated: "I am convinced that our Government was right in its decision to support the National Government of China and the leadership of Chiang Kai-shek. I have not agreed to any principles or supported any method that in my opinion would weaken the National Government or the leadership of Chiang Kai-shek. I have, however, on many occasions, advised the Generalissimo and Soong that China must furnish her own leadership, make her own decisions and be responsible for her own domestic and international policies."

General Chou En-lai left Chungking for Yenan on February 16. Prior to his departure he informed the Ambassador that he believed that his Party would agree to the Political Consultation Conference provided for in the proposal of the Chinese Government. He expressed the opinion, however, that one-party rule should be immediately ended and that a coalition administration should be instituted to guide China in forming a democratic government based upon a democratic constitution adopted by a people's convention. General Hurley departed from Chungking on February 19, 1945, for consultation in Washington.

THE GENERALISSIMO'S STATEMENT OF MARCH 1, 1945

Generalissimo Chiang, in a public address on March 1, 1945 before the Commission for the Inauguration of Constitutional Government, reaffirmed his conviction that the solution of the Communist question must be through political means and outlined the steps which the Government had taken looking toward such solution. He stated:

"I have long held the conviction that the solution of the Communist question must be through political means. The Government has labored to make the settlement a political one. As the public is not well informed on our recent efforts to reach a settlement with the Communists, time has come for me to clarify the atmosphere.

"As you know, negotiations with the Communists have been a perennial problem for many years. It has been our unvarying experience that no sooner is a demand met than fresh ones are raised. The latest demand of the Communists is that the Government should forthwith liquidate the Kuomintang rule, and surrender all power to a coalition of various parties. The position of the Government is that it is ready to admit other parties, including the Communists as well as non-partisan leaders, to participate in the Government, without, however, relinquishment by the Kuomintang of its power of ultimate decision and final responsibility until the convocation of the People's Congress. We have even offered to include the Communists and other parties in an organ to be established along the lines of what is known abroad as a 'war cabinet'. To go beyond this and to yield to the Communist demand would not only place the Government in open contravention of the Political Program of Dr. Sun Yat-sen, but also create insurmountable practical difficulties for the country.

"The Government has not hesitated to meet the issues raised by the Communists squarely. During his recent visit the Communist representative, Chou En-lai, was told that the Government would be prepared to set up in the Executive Yuan a policy-making body to be known as the Wartime Political Council, to which other parties, including the Communists, would have representation. In addition, he was told that the Government would be ready to appoint a Commission of three officers to make plans for the incorporation of the Communist forces in the National Army, composed of one Government officer, one Communist and one American, provided that the United States Government would agree to allow an American officer to serve. If the

United States Government could not agree, some other means of guaranteeing the safety of the Communist forces, and non-discrimination in their treatment, could doubtless be evolved.

"No one mindful of the future of our four hundred and fifty million people and conscious of standing at the bar of history would wish to plunge the country into a civil war. The Government has shown its readiness and is always ready to confer with the Communists to bring about a real and lasting settlement with them.

"I have explained the Government's position on the Communist problem at length, because today that is the main problem to unity and constitutional government.

"I now turn to the concrete measures which the Government proposes to take to realize constitutional government which I wish to announce briefly:

"1. The People's Congress to inaugurate constitutional government will be convened on November 12 this year (the 80th birthday of Dr. Sun Yat-sen) subject to the approval by the Kuomintang National Congress which is due to meet in May.

"2. Upon the inauguration of constitutional government, all political parties will have legal status and enjoy equality. (The Government has offered to give legal recognition to the Communist Party as soon as the latter agrees to incorporate its army and local administration in the National Government. The offer still stands.)

"3. The next session of the People's Political Council with a larger membership as well as more extensive powers will soon be sitting. The Government will consider with the council the measures in regard to the convening of the People's Congress and all related matters." [6]

THE COMMUNIST PARTY'S REPLY, MARCH 9, 1945

On March 12, 1945, the American Embassy at Chungking was requested to transmit the following letter,[7] dated March 9 from General Chou to General Hurley, who was then in Washington:

"Your kind message of 20 February has been received.

"Under instructions from the Central Committee of my party and from Chairman Mao Tse-tung I have sent a letter on the 9th of March to Dr. Wang Shih-chieh, representative of the National Government, containing the following two points of which I especially would like to inform you about:

---

[6] For complete text, see *China Handbook, 1937–1945*, p. 73.

[7] This message and a preceding one of Feb. 18 from General Chou to General Hurley concern the question of Chinese Communist participation on the Chinese delegation to the San Francisco Conference. For texts of Feb. 18 message and reply by General Hurley, see annexes 48 (a) and 48 (b).

"1. The Central Committee of my party was originally planning to draft our proposals in answer to Dr. Wang Shih-chieh's proposal of calling a political consultation conference, in order to facilitate the discussions, and so it was all the more unexpected that President Chiang Kai-shek on March 1, should have made a public statement opposing the abolition of one-party rule, the convening of an inter-party conference and also the establishment of a coalition government, announcing instead the one-party Kuomintang government is preparing to call on November 12 of this year that one-party controlled, deceitful, China splitting, so-called National Congress, based on conditions to which the people have no freedom, in which political parties and groups have no legal status, and in which large areas of the country have been lost making it impossible for the majority of the people to take part.

"This clearly demonstrates that the Kuomintang government is obstinately insisting on having their own way alone, thus on the one hand showing that they have not the least sincerity of wanting to carry out democratic reforms, and on the other it leaves no basis on which negotiations between the Communist Party and the other democratic parties and the Kuomintang government can be continued in these circumstances.   The Central Committee of my party considers that there is no longer the need to draft proposals in answer to Wang Shih-chieh.

"2. The Central Committee of my party and Chairman Mao Tsetung are decidedly of the opinion that if Chinese delegates are to represent the common will of the whole Chinese people at the San Francisco Conference in April, then they must consist of representatives of the Chinese Kuomintang, the Chinese Communist Party and the Chinese Democratic League; and definitely there should not be only Kuomintang government delegates attending the meeting. America and England both have announced that their delegations will consist of representatives from all important political parties while your Honorable President has made known that the American delegation will consist of an equal number from both the Democratic and Republican parties; but since the Chinese situation is so lacking in unity, then, if the Kuomintang should try to monopolize the entire delegation, this would be not only unjust or unreasonable, but it would show that their standpoint is for wanting to split China.   My party has already officially put forth the above demands to the Kuomintang government and suggested that Chou En-lai, Tung Pi-wu and Chin Pang-hsien, three members of our Central Committee, join the Chinese delegation.   If this is not accepted by the Kuomintang government, then my party will determinedly oppose the Kuomin-

tang splitting measure and reserve the right of expression on all opinions and the actions of the monopolized delegation of the Kuomintang
government at the conference of the United Nations at San Francisco.

"Please inform your Honorable President of the above two proposals
as soon as possible and also express my deep appreciation for his interest on behalf of Chinese unity. I extend to you my deepest personal
regards."

In view of this sharp reaction by the Chinese Communist Party, active negotiations between the Communists and the National Government leaders looking toward the unification of China were broken off
at this time and were not resumed until the following summer. In
commenting on these negotiations, Ambassador Hurley stated:

"I pause to observe that in this dreary controversial chapter, two
fundamental facts are emerging: (1) the Communists are not in fact
Communists, they are striving for democratic principles; and (2)
the one party, one man personal Government of the Kuomintang is
not in fact fascist, it is striving for democratic principles. Both the
Communists and the Kuomintang have a long way to go, but if we
know the way, if we are clear minded, tolerant and patient, we can be
helpful. But it is most difficult to be patient at a time when the unified
military forces of China are so desperately needed in our war effort."

III. THE PROBLEM OF MILITARY ASSISTANCE

AMBASSADOR HURLEY'S RECOMMENDATION AGAINST
AMERICAN AID TO THE CHINESE COMMUNISTS

Meanwhile, another problem had arisen shortly before the Ambassador's departure for Washington. This was the problem of supplying American arms and equipment to groups in China other than the
National Government. The Ambassador recommended that "all such
requests, no matter how reasonable they may seem to be, be universally
refused until or unless they receive the sanction of the National Government and of the American Government." It was his "steadfast
position that all armed warlords, armed partisans and the armed forces
of the Chinese Communists must without exception submit to the control of the National Government before China can in fact have a
unified military force or unified government." The Ambassador followed this policy in connection with a request from General Chu Teh
in January 1945 that the United States Army lend the Communist
forces 20 million dollars in United States currency for use in procuring the defection of officers and men of the Chinese puppet government together with their arms and for use in encouraging sabotage

and demolition work by puppet troops behind the Japanese lines. General Chu informed General Wedemeyer that his forces would assume full responsibility for repayment of the loan following victory over Japan and in support of his request submitted a document claiming that during 1944 Communist forces won over 34,167 Chinese puppet troops with 20,850 rifles, sidearms, mortars, field pieces, etc. The document estimated that with American financial help puppet defections during 1945 could be increased to 90,000 men. In commenting on this proposal the Ambassador stated:

"While financial assistance of the type requested by General Chu might in the end prove to be more economical than importing a similar quantity of arms and ammunition from the United States for use against Japan, I am of the firm opinion that such help would be identical to supplying arms to the Communist armed Party and would, therefore, be a dangerous precedent. The established policy of the United States to prevent the collapse of the National Government and to sustain Chiang Kai-shek as president of the Government and Generalissimo of the Armies would be defeated by acceptance of the Communist Party's plan or by granting the lend-lease and monetary assistance requested by General Chu Teh."

THE AMERICAN CHARGÉ'S RECOMMENDATIONS

Shortly after the arrival of General Hurley in Washington for consultation the question of supplying arms and military equipment to the Chinese Communist forces was raised by the American Chargé d'Affaires at Chungking, George Atcheson, in the communication to the Department of State paraphrased below. The Chargé had reported on February 26 that since the conclusion of negotiations with the Communists there had been a growing impression among observers there that for various reasons the Generalissimo had greatly stiffened his attitude toward the Communists and toward the continuing faint hopes held by some liberals that a settlement might still eventually be possible.

It appears that the situation in China is developing in some ways which are neither conducive to the future unity and peace of China nor to the effective prosecution of the war.

A necessary initial step in handling the problem was the recent American endeavor to assist compromise between the factions in China through diplomatic and persuasive means. Not only was unity correctly regarded as the essence of China's most effective conduct of the war, but also of the speedy, peaceful emergence of a China which would be united, democratic, and strong.

However, the rapid development of United States Army plans for rebuilding the armies of Chiang Kai-shek, the increase of additional aid such as that of the War Production Board, the cessation of Japanese offensives, the opening of the road into China, the expectation that the Central Government will participate at San Francisco in making important decisions, the conviction that we are determined upon definite support and strengthening of the Central Government alone and as the sole possible channel for assistance to other groups, the foregoing circumstances have combined to increase Chiang Kai-shek's feeling of strength greatly. They have resulted in lack of willingness to make any compromise and unrealistic optimism on the part of Chiang Kai-shek.

Among other things, this attitude is reflected in hopes of an early settlement with the Soviet Union without settlement of the Communist problem, when nothing was ultimately offered except an advisory inter-party committee without place or power in the Government, and in recent appointments of a military-political character, placing strong anti-Communists in strategic war areas, and naming reactionaries to high administrative posts, such as General Ho Kuo Kuang, previously Commander-in-Chief of Gendarmerie, as Chairman of Formosa; and Admiral Chan Chak, Tai Li subordinate, as mayor of Canton.

On their part, the Communists have arrived at the conclusion that we are definitely committed to the support of Chiang Kai-shek alone, and that Chiang's hand will not be forced by us so that we may be able to assist or cooperate with the Communists. Consequently, in what is regarded by them as self-protection, they are adopting the course of action which was forecast in statements made by Communist leaders last summer in the event they were still excluded from consideration, of increasing their forces actively and expanding their areas to the south aggressively, reaching southeast China, regardless of nominal control by the Kuomintang. We previously reported to the Department extensive movements and conflicts with forces of the Central Government already occurring.

It is the intention of the Communists, in seizing time by the forelock, to take advantage of East China's isolation by the capture of the Canton-Hankow Railway by Japan to render themselves as nearly invincible as they can before the new armies of Chiang Kai-shek, which are being formed in Yunnan at the present time, are prepared; and to present to us the dilemma of refusing or accepting their assistance if our forces land at any point on the coast of China. There is now talk by Communists close to the leaders of the need of seeking Soviet aid. Active consideration is being given to the creation of a unified council of their various independent guerrilla governments by the party itself, which is broadcasting demands for Communist and other non-Kuomintang representations at San Francisco.

Despite the fact that our actions in our refusal to aid or deal with any group other than the Central Government have been diplomatically correct, and our intentions have been good, the conclusion appears clear that if this situation continues, and if our analysis of it is correct, the probable outbreak of disastrous civil conflict will be accelerated and chaos in China will be inevitable.

It is apparent that even for the present this situation, wherein we are precluded from cooperating with the strategically situated, large and aggressive armies and organized population of the Communist areas, and also with the forces like the Li Chi-shen–Tsai Ting-k'ai group in the southeast, is, from a military standpoint, hampering and unsatisfactory. From a long-range viewpoint, as set forth above, the situation is also dangerous to American interests.

If the situation is not checked, it is likely to develop with increasing acceleration, as the tempo of the war in China and the entire Far East is raised, and the inevitable resolution of the internal conflict in China becomes more imperative. It will be dangerous to permit matters to drift; the time is short.

In the event the high military authorities of the United States agree that some cooperation is desirable or necessary with the Communists and with other groups who have proved that they are willing and in a position to fight Japan, it is our belief that the paramount and immediate consideration of military necessity should be made the basis for a further step in the policy of the United States. A favorable opportunity for discussion of this matter should be afforded by the presence of General Wedemeyer and General Hurley in Washington.

The initial step which we propose for consideration, predicated upon the assumption of the existence of the military necessity, is that the President inform Chiang Kai-shek in definite terms that we are required by military necessity to cooperate with and supply the Communists and other suitable groups who can aid in this war against the Japanese, and that to accomplish this end, we are taking direct steps. Under existing conditions, this would not include forces which are not in actual position to attack the enemy, such as the Szechwan warlords. Chiang Kai-shek can be assured by us that we do not contemplate reduction of our assistance to the Central Government. Because of transport difficulties, any assistance we give to the Communists or to other groups must be on a small scale at first. It will be less than the natural increase in the flow of supplies into

China, in all probability. We may include a statement that we will furnish the Central Government with information as to the type and extent of such assistance. In addition, we can inform Chiang Kai-shek that it will be possible for us to use our cooperation and supplies as a lever to restrict them to their present areas and to limit aggressive and independent action on their part. Also we can indicate the advantages of having the Communists assisted by the United States instead of seeking direct or indirect help or intervention from the Soviet Union.

Chiang Kai-shek might also be told, if it is regarded as advisable, at the time of making this statement to him, that while our endeavor to persuade the various groups of the desirability of unification has failed and it is not possible for us to delay measures for the most effective prosecution of the war any longer, we regard it as obviously desirable that our military aid to all groups be based upon coordination of military command and upon unity, that we are prepared, where it is feasible, and when requested, to lend our good offices to this end, and although we believe the proposals should come from Chiang Kai-shek, we would be disposed to support the following:

First, formation of something along the line of a war cabinet or supreme war council in which Communists and other groups would be effectively represented, and which would have some part in responsibility for executing and formulating joint plans for war; second, nominal incorporation of Communist and other forces selected into the armies of the Central Government, under the operational command of United States officers designated by Chiang Kai-shek upon General Wedemeyer's advice, upon agreement by all parties that these forces would operate only within their existing areas or areas which have been specifically extended. However, it should be clearly stated that our decision to cooperate with any forces able to assist the war effort will neither be delayed by nor contingent upon the completion of such internal Chinese arrangements.

It is our belief that such a *modus operandi* would serve as an initial move toward complete solution of the problem of final entire unity, and would bridge the existing deadlock in China. The principal and over-riding issues have become clear, as one result of the recent negotiations. At the present time, Chiang Kai-shek will not take any forward step which will mean loss of face, personal power, or prestige. Without guarantees in which they believe, the Communists will not take any forward step involving dispersion and eventual elimination of their forces, upon which depend their strength at this time and their political existence in the future. The force required to break this deadlock will be exerted on both parties by the step we propose to take. The *modus operandi* set forth in these two proposals should initiate concrete military cooperation, with political cooperation as an inevitable result, and consequently furnish a foundation for increasing development toward unity in the future.

The political consultation committee plan, which could function, if adopted, side by side with the Government and the war council, would not be excluded by these proposals. It should be anticipated that the committee would be greatly strengthened, in fact.

Of course, the statements to the Generalissimo should be made in private, but the possibility would be clearly understood, in case of his refusal to accept it, of the logical, much more drastic step of a public expression of policy such as that which was made by Churchill with reference to Yugoslavia.

The fact of our aid to the Communists and other forces would shortly become known throughout China, however, even if not made public. It is our belief that profound and desirable political effects in China would result from this. A tremendous internal pressure for unity exists in China, based upon compromise with the Communists and an opportunity for self-expression on the part of the now repressed liberal groups. Even inside the Kuomintang, these liberal groups such as the Sun Fo group, and the minor parties, were ignored in recent negotiations by the Kuomintang, although not by the Communists, with whom they present what amounts to a united front, and they are discouraged and disillusioned by what they regard as an American commitment to the Kuomintang's existing reactionary leadership. We would prove we are not so committed by the steps which we proposed, we would markedly improve the prestige and morale of these liberal groups, and the strongest possible influence would be exerted by us by means of these internal forces to impel Chiang Kai-shek to make the concessions required for unity and to put his own house in order.

Such a policy would unquestionably be greatly welcomed by the vast majority of the people of China, even though not by the very small reactionary minority by which the Kuomintang is controlled, and American prestige would be increased by it.

The statement has been made to a responsible American by Sun Fo himself that if Chiang Kai-shek were told, not asked, regarding United States aid to Communists and guerrillas, this would do more to make Chiang Kai-shek come to terms with them than any other course of action. It is believed by the majority of the people of China that settlement of China's internal problems is more a matter of reform of the Kuomintang itself than a matter of mutual concessions. The Chinese also state, with justification, that American non-intervention in China cannot avoid being intervention in favor of the conservative leadership which exists at the present time.

In addition, by a policy such as this, which we feel realistically accepts the facts in China, we could expect to obtain the cooperation of all the forces of China in the war; to hold the Communists to our side instead of throwing them into the arms of the Soviet Union, which is inevitable otherwise in the event the U.S.S.R. enters the war against Japan; to convince the Kuomintang that its apparent plans for eventual civil war are undesirable; and to bring about some unification, even if not immediately complete, that would furnish a basis for peaceful development toward complete democracy in the future.

General Hurley strongly opposed the course of action recommended above and it remained the policy of the United States to supply military matériel and financial support only to the recognized Chinese National Government.[8]

IV. CHINA AND THE SOVIET UNION

AGENDA FOR DR. SOONG'S MOSCOW CONVERSATIONS

Shortly before his visit to Washington Ambassador Hurley had raised the question of negotiations between the Chinese National Government and the Soviet Government. On February 4 the Ambassador reported to the Department of State that the Chinese Government contemplated sending Dr. T. V. Soong to Moscow for a conference as a personal representative of the Generalissimo. He transmitted a tentative agenda for the conference which the Chinese Government had prepared and added that the Chinese Government had asked for changes or suggestions in the agenda. His telegram concluded as follows:

"In connection with this situation bear in mind that early last September Ambassador Harriman, Mr. Nelson and myself conferred with Mr. Molotov on the Soviet attitude toward the Communists in China, believing that understanding of this was essential to settlement of the Chinese Communist and National Government controversy. Mr. Molotov stated roughly as follows:

---

[8] For a detailed account of United States aid to China prior to, during and subsequent to this period, see chapter I, pp. 26-28, the sections on military aid and financial aid in Chapters V and VIII, and annexes 171 and 185.

"(1) The so-called Chinese Communists are not in fact Communists at all.

"(2) The Soviet Government is not supporting the Chinese Communists.

"(3) The Soviets do not desire dissensions or civil war in China.

"(4) The Soviets complain of Chinese treatment of Soviet citizens in China but frankly desire closer and more harmonious relations in China. . . . The Chinese are anxious to ascertain if the Soviet attitude continues as outlined last September by Molotov. On this I am unable to give any definite assurances for the simple reason that I do not know."

In response to this report the Acting Secretary of State, Joseph C. Grew, informed the Ambassador on February 6 as follows:

"On the subject of your telegram, we feel, and believe you will concur in our opinion, that while we are at all times anxious to be helpful to the Chinese Government we should not permit the Chinese Government to gain the impression that we are prepared to assume responsibility as 'advisor' to it in its relations with the USSR. Former Vice President Wallace, with the subsequent approval of the President, indicated clearly last summer to Chiang Kai-shek in response to a suggestion by Chiang that the United States could not be expected to act as 'mediator' between China and Russia. Furthermore, the President in a message to the Generalissimo [9] transmitted through the Embassy in July 1944 stated that a conference between Chinese and Russian representatives would be greatly facilitated if, prior thereto, the Chinese Government had reached a working arrangement with the Chinese Communists for effective prosecution of the war against Japan. In a message to the Embassy at Chungking in September 1944, the President and the Secretary expressed views, for communicating by Ambassador Gauss to Chiang Kai-shek with regard to importance of reaching such a 'working arrangement'.

"With particular reference to the proposed agenda, we feel that the Chinese must reach their own decision with regard to what questions they should (or should not) discuss with the Russians and that we ought not take it upon ourselves to place a caveat upon or to sponsor discussion of any particular question. . . . With reference to your final and ultimate paragraphs, we have no concrete information which runs counter to the four points mentioned by you. We appreciate receiving your report on this matter and hope that you will keep us

[9] This message and related ones concern the conversations between Vice President Wallace and the Generalissimo. They will be found in annex 43 to chapter II.

informed of developments. You will, of course, know best how to handle discussions on the subject with the Chinese in a manner which will be helpful to them and unprejudicial to our position."

By telegram dated February 18 General Hurley answered:

"I had prepared a reply to your message which I did not send. In your message you appear to have reduced my role in these negotiations to the position of merely making a suggestion without implementing the suggestion. That is the method followed by Ambassador Gauss when he transmitted the President's and the Secretary of State's message on September 9 last. That message, as you now know, obtained no results whatever because it lacked vigorous implementation. I decided, however, not to send the telegram as I hoped to see you and discuss the situation more fully. It is my earnest desire to be amenable to every suggestion from the State Department even when I believe our position is weakened and accomplishment postponed by lack of vigorous implementation of suggestions. Perhaps this respite in negotiations and my visit with the State Department will clarify in my mind the distance I will be able to go in promotion of the war effort by inducing or compelling the unification of Chinese armed forces and the coordination of effort to assist us in the defeat of Japan."

AMBASSADOR HURLEY'S INTERVIEW WITH MARSHAL STALIN, APRIL 15, 1945

After consultation in Washington, the Ambassador departed on April 3, 1945, for Chungking. He travelled by way of London and Moscow in order to discuss American policy in China with British and Soviet leaders. He reported to the Department of State that on the night of April 15, 1945, he had concluded a conference with Marshal Stalin and Foreign Minister Molotov in which the Ambassador, Mr. Harriman, had also participated. With respect to this conference General Hurley reported to the Department that he had recited for Marshal Stalin in the presence of Mr. Molotov his analysis of Mr. Molotov's earlier statement respecting the Soviet attitude toward the Chinese Communist Party and the National Government. His report, dated April 17, continued:

"My analysis was briefly as follows: 'Molotov said at the former conference that the Chinese Communists are not in fact Communists at all. Their objective is to obtain what they look upon as necessary and just reformations in China. The Soviet Union is not supporting the Chinese Communist Party. The Soviet Union does not desire internal dissension or civil war in China. The Government of the Soviet Union wants closer and more harmonious relations in China. The

Soviet Union is intensely interested in what is happening in Sinkiang and other places and will insist that the Chinese Government prevent discriminations against Soviet Nationals.' Molotov agreed to this analysis. I then outlined for Stalin and Molotov existing relations between the Chinese Government and the Chinese Communist Party. I stated with frankness that I had been instrumental in instituting conferences and negotiations between the Chinese Communist Party and the Chinese Government. I then presented in brief form an outline of the negotiations, of the progress which had been made and of the present status. I informed Stalin that both the Chinese Government and the Chinese Communist Party claimed to follow the principles of Sun Yat-sen for the establishment of a government of the people, by the people and for the people in China. I continued that the National Government and the Chinese Communist Party are both strongly anti-Japanese and that the purpose of both is to drive the Japanese from China.- Beyond question there are issues between the Chinese Communist Party and the Chinese Government, but both are pursuing the same principal objective, namely, the defeat of Japan and the creating of a free, democratic and united government in China. Because of past conflicts there are many differences on details existing between the two parties. I made clear American insistence that China supply its own leadership, arrive at its own decisions, and be responsible for its own policies. With this in mind, the United States had endorsed China's aspirations to establish a free, united government and supported all efforts for the unification of the armed forces of China. I informed him that President Roosevelt had authorized me to discuss this subject with Prime Minister Churchill and that the complete concurrence of Prime Minister Churchill and Foreign Secretary Eden had been obtained in the policy of endorsement of Chinese aspirations to establish for herself a united, free, and democratic government and for the unification of all armed forces in China in order to bring about the defeat of Japan. To promote the foregoing program it had been decided to support the National Government of China under the leadership of Chiang Kai-shek. Stalin stated frankly that the Soviet Government would support the policy. He added that he would be glad to cooperate with the United States and Britain in achieving unification of the military forces in China. He spoke favorably of Chiang Kai-shek and said that while there had been corruption among certain officials of the National Government of China, he knew that Chiang Kai-shek was 'selfless', 'a patriot' and that the Soviet in times past had befriended him. I then related to Stalin and Molotov the request made by the Chinese Communists for representation at the San Francisco Conference. I told them that before leaving China I had advised the Chinese Communists that the conference at San Francisco was to be a conference of governments and not of political parties and that I had advised the Communists to request representation at San Francisco through the National Government of the Republic of China. I told him that this decision had been upheld by President Roosevelt and that the President had advised Chiang Kai-shek of the advisability of the National Government's permitting the Chinese Communist Party to be represented on the Chinese National Government's delegation to the conference at San Francisco. I told the Marshal that it was a very hopeful sign when Chiang Kai-shek offered a place on the delegation to San Francisco to a Chinese Communist and that the appointment had been accepted. I told Stalin that I thought it was very hopeful that a leading member of the Chinese Communist Party would be a delegate of the Chinese National Government at San Francisco. Stalin agreed that this development was very significant and he approved. I told him that President Roosevelt and Prime Minister Churchill had indicated their approval of the policy outlined. The Marshal was pleased and expressed his concurrence and said in view of the over-all situation, he wished us to know that we would have his complete support in immediate action for the unification of the armed forces of China with full recognition of the National Government under the leadership of Chiang Kai-shek. In short, Stalin agreed unqualifiedly to America's policy in China as outlined to him during the conversation."

COMMENTS ON AMBASSADOR HURLEY'S REPORT

Although Mr. Harriman was present during the conversation reported in the foregoing communication, he departed for Washington on consultation before the communication was sent. The Chargé d'Affaires in Moscow, George Kennan, sent a telegram dated April 23 to Mr. Harriman personally in Washington commenting in part as follows:

"In view of your familiarity with the matter and the opportunity that you now have for stating your own views to the Department I am of course making no comment on my own to the Department regarding the report of Ambassador Hurley nor did I make any to him since your views were not known to me, but I do want to let you know that it caused me some concern to see this report go forward. I refer specifically to the statements which were attributed to Stalin to the effect (1) that he expressed unqualified agreement with our policy in China as Ambassador Hurley outlined it to him, (2) that this policy would be supported by the Soviet Government and (3) that we would have his complete support, in particular, for immediate action directed toward the unification of the armed forces of China with full recognition of the Chinese National Government under the leadership of Generalissimo Chiang Kai-shek. . . .

"There was, of course, nothing in Ambassador Hurley's account of what he told Stalin to which Stalin could not honestly subscribe, it being understood that to the Russians words mean different things than they do to us. Stalin is of course prepared to affirm the principle of unifying the armed forces of China. He knows that unification is feasible in a practical sense only on conditions which are acceptable to the Chinese Communist Party. . . .

"Actually I am persuaded that in the future Soviet policy respecting China will continue what it has been in the recent past: a fluid resilient policy directed at the achievement of maximum power with minimum responsibility on portions of the Asiatic continent lying beyond the Soviet border. This will involve the exertion of pressure in various areas in direct proportion to their strategic importance and their proximity to the Soviet frontier. I am sure that within the framework of this policy Moscow will aim specifically at: (1) Reacquiring in substance, if not in form, all the diplomatic and territorial assets previously possessed on the mainland of Asia by Russia under the Czars. (2) Domination of the provinces of China in central Asia contiguous to the Soviet frontier. Such action is dictated by the strategic necessity of protecting in depth the industrial core of the U.S.S.R. (3) Acquiring sufficient control in all areas of north China now dominated by the Japanese to prevent other foreign powers from repeating the Japanese incursion. This means, to the Russian mind, the maximum possible exclusion of penetration in that area by outside powers including America and Britain. . . .

"It would be tragic if our natural anxiety for the support of the Soviet Union at this juncture, coupled with Stalin's use of words which mean all things to all people and his cautious affability, were to lead us into an undue reliance on Soviet aid or even Soviet acquiescence in the achievement of our long term objectives in China."

On April 19, 1945, Ambassador Harriman discussed General Hurley's report with Mr. E. F. Stanton of the Office of Far Eastern Affairs of the Department of State.

The memorandum of conversation indicated that Mr. Harriman felt that General Hurley's report, while factually accurate, gave a "too optimistic impression of Marshal Stalin's reactions." Mr. Harriman was certain that Marshal Stalin would not cooperate indefinitely with Chiang Kai-shek and that if and when Russia entered the conflict in the Far East he would make full use of and would support the Chinese Communists even to the extent of setting up a puppet government in Manchuria and possibly in North China if Kuomintang-Communist differences had not been resolved by that time. He indicated that he had impressed on General Hurley the fact that statements made by Stalin endorsing our efforts in China did not necessarily mean that the Russians would not pursue whatever course of action seemed to them best to serve their interests. Mr. Harriman feared that Ambassador Hurley might give Chiang Kai-shek an "over-optimistic account of his conversations with Stalin" and he thought it might be advisable to suggest to General Hurley that he should be careful "not to arouse unfounded expectations." On April 23 Secretary Stettinius instructed Ambassador Hurley as follows:

"I attach great importance to Marshal Stalin's endorsement at the present time of our program for furthering the political and military unity of China under Generalissimo Chiang Kai-shek. However, at the same time I feel, as I have no doubt you do also, the necessity of facing the probability that Marshal Stalin's offer is given in direct relation to circumstances that are existing now and that may not long continue. The U.S.S.R. is at present preoccupied in Europe and the basis for her position in Asia following the war is not yet affected by the Communist-Kuomintang issue to an appreciable degree. In view of these circumstances I can well appreciate the logic of Marshal Stalin's readiness to defer to our leadership and to support American efforts directed toward military and political unification which could scarcely fail to be acceptable to the U.S.S.R. If and when the Soviet Union begins to participate actively in the Far Eastern theater, Chinese internal unity has not been established and the relative advantages of cooperation with one side or the other become a matter of great practical concern to the future position of the Soviet Union in Asia, it would be equally logical, I believe, to expect the U.S.S.R. to reexamine Soviet policy and to revise its policy in accordance with its best interests. Consequently I believe that it is of the utmost importance that when informing Generalissimo Chiang Kai-shek of the statements made by Marshal Stalin you take special pains to convey to him the general thought expressed in the preceding paragraph in order that the urgency of the situation may be fully realized by him. Please impress upon Generalissimo Chiang Kai-shek the necessity for early military and political unification in order not only to bring about the successful conclusion of the Japanese war but also to establish a basis upon which relations between China and the Soviet Union may eventually become one of mutual respect and permanent friendship."

AMBASSADOR HURLEY'S REVIEW OF SOVIET–CHINESE COMMUNIST RELATIONS

General Hurley following his return to Chungking, in a report discussing negotiations between the Chinese Government and the Chinese Communist Party stated early in July 1945:

"We are convinced that the influence of the Soviet will control the action of the Chinese Communist Party. The Chinese Communists do not believe that Stalin has agreed or will agree to support the National Government of China under the leadership of Chiang Kaishek. The Chinese Communists still fully expect the Soviet to support the Chinese Communists against the National Government. Nothing short of the Soviet's public commitment will change the Chinese Communists' opinion on this subject. . . . Before the Yalta Conference,[9a] I suggested to President Roosevelt a plan to force the National Government to make more liberal political concessions in order to make possible a settlement with the Communists. The President did not approve the suggestion.

"I believe the Soviet's attitude toward the Chinese Communists is as I related it to the President in September last year and have reported many times since. This is also borne out by Stalin's statement to Hopkins and Harriman. Notwithstanding all this the Chinese Communists still believe that they have the support of the Soviet. Nothing will change their opinion on this subject until a treaty has been signed between the Soviet and China in which the Soviet agrees to support the National Government. When the Chinese Communists are convinced that the Soviet is not supporting them, they will settle with the National Government if the National Government is realistic enough to make generous political settlements. The negotiations between the National Government and the Communist Party at this time are merely marking time pending the result of the conference at Moscow.[10]

"The leadership of the Communist Party is intelligent. When the handwriting is on the wall, they will be able to read. No amount of argument will change their position. Their attitude will be changed only by inexorable logic of events. The strength of the armed forces of Chinese Communists has been exaggerated. The area of territory controlled by the Communists has been exaggerated. The number of

---

[9a] See chapter IV.

[10] This refers to the negotiations between T. V. Soong and Molotov in Moscow which began early in July, and were continued intermittently throughout July and August culminating in the signing of the Sino-Soviet Treaty of Friendship and Alliance and related agreements in Moscow on Aug. 14, 1945. These negotiations are discussed in chapter IV.

Chinese people who adhere to the Chinese Communist Party has been exaggerated. State Department officials, Army officials, newspaper and radio publicity have in a large measure accepted the Communist leaders' statements in regard to the military and political strength of the Communist Party in China. Nevertheless, with the support of the Soviet the Chinese Communists could bring about civil war in China. Without the support of the Soviet the Chinese Communist Party will eventually participate as a political party in the National Government."

V. FURTHER GOVERNMENT-COMMUNIST NEGOTIATIONS

SIXTH KUOMINTANG CONGRESS, MAY 1945

The Sixth Plenary Session of the Kuomintang Congress was inaugurated in Chungking in May 1945. In commenting on the opening address of the session by Generalissimo Chiang, the Ambassador noted that the Generalissimo made no direct reference to the Communist program although he obviously did nothing to close any door against Communism. The Generalissimo had recently held two conferences with the Ambassador on the subject of unification of all anti-Japanese armed forces in China and had stated that while the situation was not moving as rapidly as desired, progress with the Communists was being made.

On May 17, 1945, the Kuomintang Congress passed a resolution concerning the Chinese Communist problem. This resolution stated that the Kuomintang had consistently striven for China's freedom and equality through national unity and the prosecution of the war, while the Chinese Communist Party, despite its pledges of 1937, "had persisted in armed insubordination." The resolution pointed out that with the convening of the National Assembly in sight it would be possible to establish a constitutional government "in the not distant future." It was hoped that the Communists would not fail to appreciate the difficulties confronting the nation and that an amicable solution would be reached.

In another resolution adopted on May 16, 1945, the Kuomintang Congress stated that China harbored no territorial ambitions; that all China wanted was the preservation of its territorial and administrative integrity and fair and equal treatment for all its nationals overseas; that it was hoped that the five great powers would continue to cooperate after the war; that friendly cooperation between the Soviet Union and China was especially necessary; that China would do everything possible to ensure the success of the San Francisco Conference; and that national unity and a constitutional government were the cherished objectives of Kuomintang endeavor.

In a report to the Department, early in June, 1945, Ambassador Hurley stated:

"In the view of the Chinese government the principal achievements of the recently concluded Sixth Kuomintang Congress are as follows:

"1. All Kuomintang Party headquarters in the army will be abol-.ished within three months. Similar action will be taken in the schools.

"2. Within six months local representation councils will be established in all provinces and districts in free China on the basis of popular elections.

"3. A law to give legal status to political parties will be promulgated and the government hopes that the Communist Party will qualify thereunder. In this connection, the government has re-iterated its intention to seek settlement of the Communist problem through negotiations.

"4. Measures have been decided upon with a view to improving the position of peasant farmers; reduction of renting; questions of land tenure and land taxation.

"5. A decision to hold a national assembly was confirmed and it is scheduled to convene on November 12, 1945.

"The question of membership in the National Assembly will be referred to the People's Political Council on which it is anticipated that all parties will be represented." [11]

---

[11] General Hurley subsequently reported that the First Plenary Session of the Fourth People's Political Council convened in Chungking on July 7, 1945, with 218 of 290 members present. The eight Communist members were not present; a few of the twelve Democratic League Members attended. He further reported that on July 19 the Council adopted the following resolutions (as published in the Central News Agency): "(1) The date for the convocation of the National Assembly is to be left to the discretion of the government. (2) The membership of the Assembly with due regard to the legal and practical aspects of the issue and in accord with the opinions of the P. P. C. members should provide the fullest possible representation of all classes of the people in the country. (3) When a constitution is adopted, a constitutional government shall be inaugurated. (4) Prior to the convocation of the Assembly, the government should continue to improve all available political means for obtaining national unity and solidarity, to insure freedom of opinion, of publication, of assembly, and of organized political societies and should enforce the Habeas Corpus Act, recognize the legal status of various political parties and cause the setting up of people's representative organs in all provinces of free China in order to lay a solid foundation for local self-government."

THE COMMITTEE OF SEVEN

Late in June, the Ambassador reported that pursuant to measures adopted by the Sixth Kuomintang Congress the Government had appointed a committee of seven persons including members of the Kuomintang and of the Democratic League and political independents to negotiate with the Communists. The Ambassador said that the Government thereupon sent a message to Mao Tse-tung, Chairman of the Chinese Communist Party, and Chou En-lai, Vice Chairman, offering to have this committee negotiate with representatives of the Communist Party for a unification of the armed forces of China for the purpose of defeating Japan. The Government had agreed to the recognition of the Communists as a political party in China but declined to recognize it as an armed belligerent or insurrection group. The Communists did not immediately answer and put forth considerable propaganda including a "somewhat defiant" broadcast from Yenan on June 20 saying among other things that the Chinese Communist Party would not participate in either the People's Political Council meeting to be held in Chungking beginning July 7 or the November Assembly. The Ambassador said that the Government had just received a reply from Mao Tse-tung and Chou En-lai, indicating that they would resume negotiations with the Government. Ambassador Hurley added:

"Although the Communist Party of China had unquestionably been endeavoring recently to bring about clashes between the Communist troops and those of the Government (and has succeeded in causing some clashes, the importance of which had been exaggerated in some quarters), the logic of events seems to now be convincing the Communists that their best interests as a political party may be served by coming to an agreement with the National Government rather than attempting to destroy it. The decision to resume negotiations does not mean that the conflict has been solved. The end is not as yet in sight but the situation seems definitely improved."

The members of the committee referred to above called on the Ambassador on June 27, 1945, and informed him that the committee had been formed to discuss the problem of unifying China, stating that the three political independents had been appointed by the People's Political Council and that the others had volunteered their services. They added that they had called upon the Ambassador to seek his assistance and advice. The Ambassador replied that while he wished to be helpful, the Chinese "should not ask a foreigner to make their decisions for them." His report of this meeting added:

"I suggested that the committee should go over all the proposals and counter-proposals made by the Kuomintang and the Communists during the past six months or so, and from them endeavor to evolve a formula which might be acceptable to both sides. I believed that, as American Ambassador, it would not be proper for me to express an opinion on the merits of the Five-Point Communist Proposal or the Three-Point Kuomintang Proposal. . . . I said that, when the committee had concluded its deliberations in Chungking, I would be glad to provide a plane to take them to Yenan for discussions with the Communists. I stated that if, when discussions were under way at Yenan, both the Communists and others wished me to join in the conversations, I would be happy to do so. I urged that all Chinese taking part in the deliberations and discussions should not do so as members of the Kuomintang, Democratic League, Communist Party, or any other party or group, but as patriotic Chinese who were endeavoring earnestly to bring about a free, united, and democratic China."

On June 28, 1945, General Wang Jo-fei, the ranking Chinese Communist in Chungking at the time, called on the Ambassador. The Counselor of the Embassy, who was also present during the discussion, made a summary of their conversation. The Ambassador recalled to General Wang that he had been instrumental in obtaining the inclusion of a Communist delegate in the Chinese Government delegation to the San Francisco Conference. He recalled also that he had made a trip to Yenan to confer with Mao Tse-tung and had brought Chou En-lai and others to Chungking twice for the purpose of negotiating with the Government for a settlement. The Ambassador said that he had done more in an effort to bring about a just settlement between the Communists and the Government than any other one man. He said he had been presented in the Communist press in China and elsewhere as being opposed to the Chinese Communists. The Ambassador said that he realized that much of the abuse was coming from people who were opposed to the National Government of China and did not desire the unification of National and Communist armies in China. He said that notwithstanding all these unjust and untrue accusations he was the best friend the Chinese Communists had in Chungking.

The Ambassador recalled that he had assisted them in drafting the Communist Five-Point Proposal. He had presented that proposal to the Generalissimo. The Ambassador said that he believed the press and other attacks on him constituted an attempt to keep the Communists and the Kuomintang apart by persons who wished, for their own selfish reasons, to prevent the creation of a free, united, democratic and strong China. General Wang stated frankly that real communism in China under present conditions was impossible.

The General stated, however, with perfect candor that the Party now supported democratic principles but only as a stepping stone to a future communistic state.

The Ambassador said that he had provided a plane to take the Committee of Seven and General Wang to Yenan on July 1; that the committee had requested his assistance in the discussion, but that he would not do so unless requested by the Communists. The Ambassador inquired whether the Communists would be willing to join a steering committee to advise throughout the transition period (remainder of the "period of tutelage" which would presumably end with the adoption of a constitution by the National Assembly opening on November 12) and suggested ways and means to improve the Government. General Wang replied that this would depend on whether the committee had real power; if it were only to be a committee without real authority, then it would not be acceptable.

The Ambassador recalled that he had brought the Communist Five-Point Proposal to Chungking where some Government officials had told him that he had "been sold a bill of goods" by the Communists. However, he felt that he was making progress in convincing the Generalissimo that the proposals were generally reasonable.

General Chou En-lai had asked that the four conditions he had proposed on December 28, 1944, be met by the National Government as conditions precedent to any agreement by the Communists on the Five Points which they themselves had submitted through the Ambassador. The Ambassador remarked that the Government had already withdrawn some sixty thousand troops from the north; there was considerable freedom of speech and press (the Communist newspaper was allowed to be published in Chungking); the secret police were necessary in war time to deal with important security matters as witness the FBI and England's Scotland Yard. The Ambassador said that if the Five-Point Proposal were agreed to, the Communists would then be a part of the Government and would themselves take a hand in the settlement of the questions included in the Four-Point Proposal which Chou En-lai had sent to General Hurley on December 28, 1944.

General Wang believed that the Five-Point Proposal with some alterations would still be acceptable to the Communists as a basis for negotiations, indicating, however, that they would like to see the four points accepted before agreeing on the five points. The Ambassador told General Wang that he believed the Five-Point Proposal of the Communists and the Three-Point Proposal of the Government contained in themselves sufficient basis for an agreement between the parties.

General Wang requested that, while the Committee of Seven was engaged in conversations with the Communists at Yenan, the Ambassador endeavor to persuade the Generalissimo to accept the Four-Point Proposal as a condition precedent to further negotiations. The Ambassador replied that for the reasons already stated, he could not do so. Action on the four points should come after and not before an agreement with the armed Communist Party. The Ambassador stated frankly that nearly everyone familiar with the situation was of the opinion that if the Generalissimo conceded the four points prior to an agreement, the Communists would not enter into any agreement at all.

The above-mentioned committee went to Yenan by air on July 1, 1945, and returned on July 5 bearing a document containing new Communist proposals. According to Dr. Wang Shih-chieh, then Minister of Information of the Chinese Government, these proposals covered principally two main points: (1) that the National Chinese Government call off the National Assembly scheduled for November 12, 1945, and (2) that the Chinese Government summon a political conference composed on a basis of equality of three members of the Kuomintang, three members of the Chinese Communist Party and three members of the Democratic League, with an additional three members to be chosen from independent political parties or organizations. General Hurley's own opinion was that this was the Communists' way of playing for time awaiting the results of the Soong Conference at Moscow.

AMBASSADOR HURLEY'S DEPARTURE

Negotiations between the Communist representatives and the National Government continued throughout August. Mao Tse-tung accompanied by General Hurley who had gone to Yenan for this purpose, arrived in Chungking on August 28, 1945, and remained for about a month. The unexpected acceptance by Mao of the invitation to visit Chungking may well have been precipitated in part by the announcement of the Sino-Soviet Treaty of August 14, 1945, which pledged Russian support of the National Government as the only government of China. The Ambassador departed from Chungking for consultation in the United States on September 22, 1945, and arrived in Washington four days later. Shortly before his departure he submitted the following report regarding the negotiations then being conducted in Chungking between the National Government and Communist representatives:

"(1) The negotiators have agreed that they will collaborate for the establishment of a democratic government in China for the reconstruction of China and the prevention of civil war.

"(2) Both have agreed to support the leadership of Chiang Kai-shek as President of the Republic.

"(3) They have further agreed that both parties will support the doctrines of Sun Yat-sen and will cooperate for the establishment in China of a strong, democratic government.

"(4) The Communists have agreed that they will recognize the Kuomintang as the dominant party in control of the government and will cooperate with that party during the period of transition from the present form of government to a democratic regime.

"(5) Numerous other questions, including the release of political prisoners, freedom of person, speech, press, belief, assembly and association were agreed upon.

"There are two important points on which the conferees are not yet in agreement, although both parties have made concessions toward making agreement possible. One point is that the Communists claim the right to appoint, select, or elect any Communist governors or mayors in certain provinces. The Government contends that until a constitution has been adopted and a democratic government inaugurated the prerogative of appointing governors and officials is vested in the President of the Republic. . . . The Government considers that this should not be changed until the transitory period from the present government to a constitutional government has been achieved. Both parties agree to work together during the transitional period. The next point on which the parties have approached an agreement but have not finally agreed is the number of Communist troops that are to be included in the National peace-time army of China. The Communists first contended that they should have 48 Communist divisions. It was pointed out by the Government that the present plan calls for a peace-time army consisting of 80 to 100 divisions, and that the Communists, who the Nationalists claim are in minority, are claiming the right to approximately one-half of the peace-time army. . . . This, the Nationalists refuse to agree to, but they have offered the Communists 20 divisions, or what will constitute approximately one-fifth of the planned peace-time army. Chairman Mao Tse-tung said that they did not reject the offer but that the Communists wanted to give it further consideration.

"The overall achievement in this conference has been to keep the Communists and the Nationalists talking peace-time cooperation during the period for which civil war has been predicted by nearly all the elements who are supporting a policy to keep China divided against herself. The conferences will continue. Mao Tse-tung is remaining in Chungking. The Generalissimo had given Mao his word and pledged his character for the safe conduct of Mao and his·party. He has agreed to give Mao and his party transportation to Yenan at any time they wish to discontinue the conferences.

"I told the Communists and Government negotiators last night that in my opinion they were attempting to settle too many details. . . . I said that if they could agree on basic overall principles, details could be worked out in accordance with such principles.

"The spirit between the negotiators is good. The rapprochement between the two leading parties of China seems to be progressing, and the discussion and rumors of civil war recede as the conference continues."

The Embassy at Chungking reported that the Ambassador had delayed his departure from September 18 to September 22, to remain in China an additional four days upon the earnest request of both the Chinese Communist representatives and the Chinese Government negotiators "to render assistance in reaching agreement." The Embassy added "for the Department's information, both parties have expressed deep appreciation of the cooperation and assistance of the Ambassador. They have agreed upon a paragraph to be included in their proposed final resolution thanking the Ambassador for his great services to China in bringing about the conference and in his general helpfulness as mediator during the negotiations." In a letter to President Truman dated September 17, 1945, President Chiang stated that "General Hurley's wise statesmanship and human qualities have won the respect and affection of the Chinese people who see in him a fitting symbol of American foreign policy of fair-play and justice. I have talked with General Hurley at length and with perfect frankness regarding the policy of my government on various questions, and have asked him to acquaint you, Mr. President, with the various aspects which have a bearing on the implementation of continued close collaboration between China and the United States in the maintenance of peace and order in the Far East."

CONTINUING NEGOTIATIONS AT CHUNGKING

Negotiations continued in Chungking between the Chinese Communists and the National Government following the departure of the Ambassador. Early in October, Dr. K. C. Wu, the Minister of Information of the Chinese Government, requested the Embassy at Chungking to convey the following message to General Hurley:

"The Chinese Communists have agreed to accept the proposal by the National Government that they be allotted 20 divisions in the National Army. A military commission will decide how soon the forces of the Chinese Communists can be organized into 20 divisions.

The Chinese Communists will be represented on this commission by the Chief of Staff, General Yeh Chien-ying and certain other officers designated by him. The National Government will be represented by General Lin Wei-wen, Vice Minister of War, and General Liu Pei, Vice Minister of Military Operations.

"Furthermore, agreement has been reached that prior to the establishment of a constitutional government the National Government will organize a political council of 37 members. This council will represent independents and all parties. The council will consider and make recommendations regarding (1) a draft constitution for submission to a people's congress, (2) whether a people's congress should be convened on November 12 as planned or postponed to a later date, and (3) a policy for peaceful reconstruction.

"The Chinese Communists proposed that the council adopt a 'system of absolute veto'. The representatives of the National Government have not yet agreed to this proviso which would mean that all proposals would have to receive unanimous approval before they became effective,

"Discussions of the political council shall be open to the public and not secret. Decisions adopted by it shall be final and conclusive. Resolutions which are adopted by it shall be carried out in accordance with due process of law by the National Government."

Mao Tse-tung returned to Yenan by plane on October 11, 1945. Just prior to his departure, General Chou En-lai discussed the progress of negotiations with a member of the staff of the American Embassy. From this conversation it appeared that a joint Government-Communist statement, which would probably be made public on the day of Mao's departure for Yenan, was being prepared. The points of agreement were set forth in an official statement issued on October 11. Chou said that the only principal point remaining on which some sort of agreement had not been reached was the question of the government of liberated areas which were then under control of the Chinese Communists; in particular he mentioned the provinces of Hopei, Shantung, and Chahar. According to Chou the Chinese Communist Party desired that the governors of the liberated areas be appointed by a council which would be elected from districts and villages. He added that the Government was agreeable to elections in the districts and villages but insisted that the Central Government appoint directly provincial governors. In the opinion of the Embassy the two sides were far from agreement on the basic question of political control in the liberated areas now dominated by the Chinese Communists. On October 11 the Government released the text of the agreement with the

Communists.[12] The important feature of this agreement was that it called for the convening of the Political Consultation Conference for the implementation of the agreed general principles. General Marshall was later to assist in this effort.

In mid-October 1945 the Embassy at Chungking reported that it had been informed that Wang Jo-Fei had returned from Yenan, that Governor Chang Chun of Szechwan would arrive in Chungking in a few days and that upon his arrival he, together with Dr. Wang Shih-chieh, then Minister of Foreign Affairs, and Shao Li-tze, Secretary General of the People's Political Council, would represent the Chinese Government in renewed conversations with the Communists, Chou En-lai and Wang Jo-Fei. The conversations would cover matters relating to the following subjects: (1) the Political Consultative Council; (2) liberated areas; and (3) the National Assembly. It was expected that the conversations would last for about ten days. Upon conclusion of the conversations Chou En-lai would carry back the proposals to Yenan for decision by the Chinese Communist authorities. The Chinese Communist authorities would then appoint delegates who would come to Chungking to attend the Political Consultative Conference, which it was anticipated would be held early in November. It had been decided that General Yeh Chien-ying, Chief of Staff of the 18th Army Group, would come to Chungking with the Communist delegates, probably as a delegate himself and also to serve as a Communist member of the subcommittee of three to discuss military questions. The Embassy at Chungking felt that the Communist representative was "definitely much more optimistic" than he had previously been with respect to the likelihood of an eventual agreement between the Central Government and the Communists, and had expressed great satisfaction over the announcement in the press that Ambassador Hurley would shortly return to China.

Although a published statement issued by Dr. K. C. Wu, the Chinese Minister of Information, on October 27 indicated that the Government-Communist conversations were "progressing in a cordial atmosphere," Wang Ping-nan, a Communist representative at Chungking, informed the Embassy that recent negotiations had made no progress. He expressed the opinion that the Government apparently intended to play for time while securing military control over areas liberated by the Communists, and he voiced the Communist resentment of what he termed "American intervention" in landing troops at many points in North China to hold them pending the arrival of Government troops, large elements of which had been flown north by the United States Air Force.[13] According to the Embassy, he at first

---

[12] See annex 49.
[13] For an account of military operations in 1945 see chapter VII.

parried a query in regard to the Manchurian situation but afterwards said there were in that area a few Eighth Route Army personnel. In the main, he said, there had been a rising up of the common people. He expressed the view that the U.S.S.R. would not interfere in internal conflicts in China, preferring to let the Chinese work out their own problems unless the United States should give active aid to the Kuomintang, in which event the U. S. S. R. might find some action necessary.

CLASHES BETWEEN COMMUNIST AND NATIONAL TROOPS

On November 4, the Embassy at Chungking reported that in the opinion of the Military Attaché the threat of widespread civil war in China seemed to be growing. The Embassy pointed out that the gravity of the situation was demonstrated by the postponement of the convocation in Chungking of the newly organized Political Consultative Conference in deference to discussions between the National Government and the Communists regarding a military truce. The principal weapon of the Communists in their efforts to prevent the Central Government from occupying areas dominated by them was the effectiveness of Communist troops against the railroads in those areas. The Embassy had learned that the Communists had offered to refrain from attacking lines of communication only if the Government promised to stop the movement of Government troops into North China. Since the Government had flatly refused so to do, the Embassy felt that the situation seemed "almost hopeless."

POSTPONEMENT OF THE POLITICAL CONSULTATIVE
CONFERENCE

On November 10, 1945, Dr. K. C. Wu informed the Embassy in Chungking that on October 30 the Government had made the following six proposals in writing to the Communists:

"(1) Both sides to give orders to their troops to remain wherever they are and not to attack the other side; (2) the Communists to withdraw their troops from places along railways which they have been raiding and the Government will undertake not to send troops to those places—these sections to be guarded entirely by railway police; (3) a communications supervisory committee to be organized by the People's Political Council with members of the People's Political Council as well as other disinterested representatives from the various concerned localities to carry out inspections along the railway lines and report their findings about the situation; (4) in case the Government finds it necessary to move troops along the Peiping-Suiyuan Railroad, the Tatung-Puchow, the Tsingtao-Tsinan, the northern section of the

Pinghan Railroad, the eastern section of the Lunghai Railroad and the northern section of the Tientsin-Pukow, the Government will consult the Communists first in order to reach agreement; (5) both sides should endeavor earnestly within one month to reach a fundamental arrangement about reorganization of Communist troops and the allotment of places where they will be stationed; (6) the proposed People's Consultative Council should be convened at once." In connection with the last point, Dr. Wu said that everyone but the Communists had already named delegates to the Political Consultative Conference, which would consist of 8 Government, 7 Communist, 13 Third Party, and 9 non-partisan members.

Dr. Wu stated that the Communists had not replied until November 8 and that their reply took the form of counter-proposals which were highly unsatisfactory to the National Government.

The Political Consultative Conference scheduled to meet on November 20 failed to convene with resulting increased pessimism in Chungking regarding further negotiations. On November 25, General Chou En-lai departed from Chungking for Yenan and on the following day Wang Ping-nan followed him. On November 27, a provisional list of delegates to the Political Consultative Conference was finally released to the press.

On December 1, Wang Ping-nan returned to Chungking; on December 3, he called at the Embassy at Chungking and said that the Chinese Communist leaders had definitely decided to participate in the Political Consultative Conference and that five of the seven Communist delegates had been selected. He said that the remaining two would be selected and the group would fly to Chungking for a meeting to be held possibly about December 10. He would not venture an opinion as to the outcome of the Conference but admitted the great importance of the meeting to the future of China. In this connection, he said that future developments in China depended even to a greater extent, however, on American policy toward China and that therefore the Communists were eagerly awaiting the arrival of General Marshall and an expected clarification of the American position."[14] The Embassy at Chungking reported that during this conversion "Wang made a particular point of stating that Soviet policy is one thing but that Chinese Communist policy is their own and independent of the Soviet policy. In an apparent effort to counter recent charges in the Chinese Government press, he emphasized that the Chinese Communists are particularly desirous of maintaining cordial relations with the United

---

[14] On Nov. 27, 1945, President Truman announced the appointment of General Marshall as his Special Representative in China. For an account of General Marshall's mission, see chapter V.

States, recognizing that China must have American assistance in the postwar period." The Communist representatives to the Political Consultative Conference failed, however, to arrive in Chungking until December 17 with resulting delay in the convocation of the Conference.

VI. THE RESIGNATION OF AMBASSADOR HURLEY

Meanwhile, Ambassador Hurley had submitted his resignation in a letter to the President, dated November 26, and his resignation had been accepted by the President in a letter of the following day.[15] The post remained vacant until the appointment of Ambassador Stuart on July 11, 1946.

---

[15] For text of General Hurley's letter, see annex 50. On December 7, 1945, Secretary of State Byrnes answered in a public hearing before the Senate Foreign Relations Committee the charges against certain officers of the Department of State which General Hurley had raised in his letter of resignation and which he had amplified before the same committee on December 5 and 6.

CHAPTER IV

The Yalta Agreement and the Sino-Soviet Treaty of 1945

I. THE YALTA AGREEMENT, FEBRUARY 11, 1945

TEXT OF THE AGREEMENT

On behalf of the United States, Great Britain and the U.S.S.R. on February 11, 1945, Roosevelt, Churchill and Stalin signed at Yalta an agreement containing the political conditions upon which the Soviet Union would enter the war against Japan.[1] This agreement reads as follows:

"The leaders of the three Great Powers—the Soviet Union, the United States of America and Great Britain—have agreed that in two or three months after Germany has surrendered and the war in Europe has terminated the Soviet Union shall enter into the war against Japan on the side of the Allies on condition that:

"1. The status quo in Outer-Mongolia (The Mongolian People's Republic) shall be preserved;[2]

"2. The former rights of Russia violated by the treacherous attack of Japan in 1904 shall be restored, viz:

"(a) the southern part of Sakhalin as well as all the islands adjacent to it shall be returned to the Soviet Union,

---

[1] As background to the Yalta Agreement, see chapter I concerning the Cairo Declaration and chapter II on the conversations of Vice President Henry A. Wallace with Generalissimo Chiang Kai-shek in Chungking during June 1944, in which the latter requested the assistance of the United States in bringing about an improvement in Sino-Soviet relations. A summary of these conversations, prepared by a member of the Vice Presidential party, is published as annex 43. At the first formal meeting of the Tehran Conference Marshal Stalin declared that the Soviet Union would enter the war against Japan "once Germany was finally defeated." The question of making Dairen a "free port under international guaranty" and Soviet use of the Manchurian railways were discussed informally during the Tehran Conference.

[2] The Soviet Union as a result of the insertion of "(The Mongolian People's Republic)" later claimed this provision meant independence. The Chinese position was based on the Sino-Soviet Treaty of 1924 which had recognized Chinese sovereignty in Outer Mongolia. For the outcome of the discussion on this point see p. 117.

"(b) the commercial port of Dairen shall be internationalized, the preeminent interests of the Soviet Union in this port being safeguarded [3] and the lease of Port Arthur as a naval base of the U.S.S.R. restored,[4]

"(c) the Chinese-Eastern Railroad and the South-Manchurian Railroad which provides an outlet to Dairen shall be jointly operated by the establishment of a joint Soviet-Chinese Company it being understood that the preeminent interests of the Soviet Union shall be safeguarded [5] and that China shall retain full sovereignty in Manchuria;

"3. The Kurile islands shall be handed over to the Soviet Union.

"It is understood, that the agreement concerning Outer-Mongolia and the ports and railroads referred to above will require concurrence of Generalissimo Chiang Kai-shek. The President will take measures in order to obtain this concurrence on advice from Marshal Stalin.

"The Heads of the three Great Powers have agreed that these claims of the Soviet Union shall be unquestionably fulfilled after Japan has been defeated.

"For its part the Soviet Union expresses its readiness to conclude with the National Government of China a pact of friendship and alliance between the U.S.S.R. and China in order to render assistance to China with its armed forces for the purpose of liberating China from the Japanese yoke."

DISCUSSIONS AT YALTA

From the available evidence, it is clear that the primary motivation of the Yalta Agreement was military. This aspect is indicated by the fact that Mr. Stettinius, then Secretary of State, was informed by President Roosevelt that since this was predominantly a military matter he (the President) and Mr. Harriman would handle the negotia-

---

[3] A controversy was later to arise over this wording, the origin and authorship of which are still obscure. Mr. Harriman, the American Ambassador at Moscow, who was a participant in the discussions, subsequently stated that "there is no reason from the discussions leading up to the Yalta agreements to presume that the safeguarding of the 'preeminent interests of the Soviet Union' should go beyond Soviet interests in the free *transit* of exports and imports to and from [*sic*] the Soviet Union. . . ." (Italics in the original.)

[4] Mr. Harriman has commented on this provision as follows: "I believe President Roosevelt looked upon the lease of Port Arthur for a naval base as an arrangement similar to privileges which the United States has negotiated with other countries for the mutual security of two friendly nations."

[5] As regards this provision Mr. Harriman has also stated his conviction that President Roosevelt had in mind only transit traffic and not any general Russian interest in Manchuria.

tions. Mr. Harriman has subsequently stated that Admiral King was aware of the projected arrangements and considered them the most important outcome of the Yalta Conference.

In a conversation between President Roosevelt and Marshal Stalin on Far Eastern matters during the Yalta Conference, the latter brought up the subject of the political conditions upon which the Soviet Union would enter the war against Japan. In the course of the conversation Marshal Stalin indicated that the political conditions would have to be met because Soviet entry into the Pacific war "would have to be justified to Russian 'public opinion.' "

In general terms the Russian conditions were conceded. It should be remembered that at this time the atomic bomb was anything but an assured reality; the potentialities of the Japanese Kwantung Army in Manchuria seemed large; and the price in American lives in the military campaign up the island ladder to the Japanese home islands was assuming ghastly proportions. Obviously military necessity dictated that Russia enter the war against Japan prior to the mounting of Operation Olympic (the assault upon Kyushu), roughly scheduled for November 1, 1945, in order to contain Japanese forces in Manchuria and prevent their transfer to the Japanese home islands.

There was historical precedent for the specific provisions of the Yalta Agreement, and the subsequent Sino-Soviet Treaty and related agreements of 1945 provided adequate legal guarantees. It was, however, unfortunate that China was not previously consulted. President Roosevelt and Marshal Stalin, however, based this reticence on the already well-known and growing danger of "leaks" to the Japanese from Chinese sources due to the debilitating and suppurative effects of the war. Here again military exigency was the governing consideration. At no point did President Roosevelt consider that he was compromising vital Chinese interests.

SOVIET VIEWS ON THE AGREEMENT

At the end of May 1945 Harry Hopkins, at the request of President Truman, visited Moscow. Among other topics he discussed the Far Eastern situation. During the discussions Marshal Stalin stated that the reconstruction of China would depend largely on the United States since Russia would be preoccupied with its own reconstruction; that he proposed no alteration over the sovereignty of Manchuria or any other part of China, either Sinkiang or elsewhere; that the Soviet system was not in existence in Mongolia; that Generalissimo Chiang Kai-shek was the only Chinese leader qualified to undertake the unification of China; that the Chinese Communist leaders were not as good or as well qualified to undertake the task; and that he would welcome

Chinese civilian participation in the administrative taking over of Manchuria.

President Truman in Washington on June 14 repeated the foregoing to Dr. T. V. Soong, then Premier and Foreign Minister of China, who expressed his gratification. Dr. Soong pointed out that, even though the Yalta Agreement referred to the re-establishment of Russian rights lost in the Russo-Japanese War of 1904, by the Sino-Soviet Treaty and related agreements of May 31, 1924 and the Agreement of September 20, 1924, with Chang Tso-lin, then war lord of Manchuria, Russia had renounced special concessions including extraterritoriality. He said that these points would have to be clarified.

On June 15, 1945, Ambassador Hurley informed Generalissimo Chiang Kai-shek of the provisions of the Yalta Agreement pursuant to instructions from the President of June 9, 1945. At the same time the Ambassador communicated to the Generalissimo Marshal Stalin's categorical assurances regarding Chinese sovereignty in Manchuria and his oral concurrence to the principle of the Open Door in China, both of which Stalin had given to the President via Harry Hopkins, who had been on special mission to Moscow in May-June 1945. From the Generalissimo's reaction it was apparent that the Russians had already made the Yalta Agreement known to him.

II. THE SINO-SOVIET TREATY OF FRIENDSHIP AND ALLIANCE, AUGUST 14, 1945

NEGOTIATION OF THE TREATY

Sino-Soviet negotiations between Dr. T. V. Soong and Marshal Stalin and Foreign Minister Molotov began in Moscow during the first week in July 1945. Following their interruption by the Berlin Conference, negotiations were resumed in August with Dr. Wang Shi-chieh, the new Chinese Foreign Minister, replacing Dr. Soong as chief Chinese plenipotentiary. Dr. Soong, however, assisted Dr. Wang in the August negotiations. At the outset the United States informed the participants that it expected to be consulted prior to the signature of any Sino-Soviet agreement, in view of its role at Yalta. The American position was that the Yalta Agreement should be complied with—no more, no less.

Difficulties over the interpretation of the provisions of the Yalta Agreement arose from the very beginning, with the Soviet Union interpreting the agreement to suit its own purposes. As the Soviet interpretation of the Yalta Agreement became increasingly apparent, the United States finally felt compelled to inform both parties that certain Soviet proposals exceeded the Yalta provisions. At the beginning of the negotiations the Soviet Union asked (1) for a controlling Soviet interest in the Chinese Eastern and South Manchurian Railways; (2) that the boundaries of the Dairen and Port Arthur leases be those of the Kwantung Peninsula lease prior to the Russo-Japanese War of 1904; and (3) the recognition of the independence of Outer Mongolia. The Chinese believed, and the United States agreed, that these proposals exceeded the provisions of the Yalta Agreement. Secretary of State Byrnes, with the approval of the President, then advised the Chinese Government against making any concessions beyond the terms of the Yalta Agreement. On August 10, 1945, Mr. Harriman, acting on instructions, informed Dr. Soong as a matter of record that the United States Government considered that the proposals which he had already made fulfilled the Yalta Agreement and that any further concessions would be with the understanding that they were made by the Chinese Government because of the value it attached to obtaining Soviet support in other directions. Mr. Harriman reported that Dr. Soong "thoroughly understood and accepted the correctness of this position."

A Treaty of Friendship and Alliance between the Republic of China and the U.S.S.R. was signed on August 14, 1945. At the same time notes were exchanged and agreements signed on various individual and related matters.[6] The Treaty pledged mutual respect for their respective sovereignties and mutual noninterference in their respective internal affairs. In the exchange of notes the Soviet Union promised to give moral support and military aid entirely to the "National Government as the central government of China" and recognized Chinese sovereignty in Manchuria; and China agreed to recognize the independence of Outer Mongolia if a plebiscite after the defeat of Japan confirmed that that was the desire of the Outer Mongolian people.[7] The agreement on Dairen committed China to declare Dairen a free port "open to the commerce and shipping of all nations" and provided for Chinese administration of the port; but it exceeded Yalta by granting the Soviet Union a lease of half of the port facilities, free of charge. This agreement has not been put into effect, since Nationalist military and civil officials have been prevented from functioning in the Kwan-

---

[6] For full texts see annexes 51–59.

[7] One of the main preoccupations of Dr. Soong during the negotiations was to secure Soviet recognition of Chinese sovereignty in Outer Mongolia, even though this had in fact ceased to exist many years before. The Soviet Union had been the controlling *de facto* force there since the middle 1920's despite the Sino-Soviet Treaty of 1924. (See footnote 2 to this chapter.) Dr. Soong was apparently willing to agree to other significant and important concessions in return for Outer Mongolia and it was with some difficulty that he was persuaded by Mr. Harriman to accept substance in place of form.

tung Peninsula area because of the attitude of the Russians and the Chinese Communists. The agreement on Port Arthur provided for the joint use of the area as a naval base by the two Powers and extended the boundary of that area farther than the United States expected, though not to the pre-1904 boundary which the U.S.S.R. would have preferred. The railway agreement provided for joint ownership and operation of the Chinese Eastern and South Manchurian Railways. The Treaty and the agreements regarding Dairen, Port Arthur, and the railroads were to run for thirty years.[8]

ASSURANCES ON THE OPEN DOOR

On July 28 in Berlin Mr. Harriman, in a memorandum to Secretary Byrnes, had pointed out that since the United States Government had taken the initiative in inducing China to discuss matters of mutual interest with the Soviet Union, it was incumbent upon the United States to obtain recognition of the principle of the Open Door policy in Manchuria and to make certain that the resulting Sino-Soviet arrangements did not have the effect of giving the Soviet Union special advantages over American and other foreign commerce with Manchuria, or of shutting out foreign trade from that part of China. He therefore recommended that the Soviet Union be requested to give written assurances of support for the Open Door policy. This suggestion was approved by the Department of State on August 5, 1945. On August 14, however, Mr. Harriman reported that, according to Mr. Molotov, Generalissimo Stalin did not believe there was then any need for a public statement on the Open Door, "especially as he had given his assurances that the Open-Door Policy would be maintained."

The Department on August 22 instructed the Ambassador in Moscow as follows:

"1. The President desires that you arrange to see Stalin or, if this proves impracticable, Molotov, as soon as possible and present to him our views as given below regarding the issuance of a statement affirming respect for the Open-Door policy in connection with the Soong-Stalin agreements.

"2. The oral assurances given by Stalin, as you have indicated to Molotov, are satisfactory to the President. However, you should explain clearly and forcefully the situation in this country where public opinion and public reaction to events of concern to the United States

---

[8] About Aug. 10, 1945, Dr. Soong told Mr. Harriman that agreement had been reached on all outstanding points. Mr. Harriman reported that Dr. Soong was "very grateful for our support and is convinced that unless we had taken an active part in the negotiations he would have had to concede to all Stalin's demands."

have great weight and where the public expects and is entitled to be given as full a knowledge as practicable on foreign affairs which may affect the interests of this country.   It follows, therefore, that the oral assurances by Stalin do not meet the situation.   You may also emphasize the deep interest which the American public has in Far Eastern events and particularly in developments pertaining to China, including Manchuria.   In reply to Molotov's assertion that the agreements would make it clear that no restriction would be imposed on foreign commerce, you may state that in so far as the agreements might fail to give assurances regarding full equality of opportunity and freedom from any form of discrimination they would fall short of what we would consider satisfactory.   In reply to his point that no such statement had been foreseen at Yalta, you may say that we do not consider it reasonable that, simply because at Yalta the desirability of such assurances was not mentioned, we are therefore not entitled to request these assurances.

"3. With regard to the manner in which Stalin's assurances might be given public form, we suggest and would prefer that the Soviet and Chinese governments issue a statement, at the time of the publication of the agreements, affirming adherence to the policy of the Open-Door, equality of opportunity and non-discrimination in matters relating to the management and operation of the railways and the free port of Dairen.   We do not insist upon the particular language of the suggested statement as communicated by you to Stalin, but we do feel that any statement issued should give in clear and unequivocal terms the assurances we have requested and which Stalin had agreed to give.

"4. We understand that the Chinese are prepared to issue such a statement and you are authorized to urge on Stalin the desirability of a similar statement by the Soviet Government."

Mr. Harriman on August 27 delivered this message to Stalin, who agreed that the Soviet Union would make a public statement expressing support of the Open Door policy in China, including Manchuria, equal opportunity for trade and commerce, and freedom from discrimination for all free countries.   Mr. Harriman assured Generalissimo Stalin that the Chinese Government would make a similar statement after Stalin expressed a preference for separate statements in lieu of a joint Sino-Soviet one.   In the same conversation Stalin said that he expected the National Government to send Chinese troops to Manchuria in the near future to take over from the Russians.   He added that the Russian Army had as yet found no Chinese Communist guerrilla units in Manchuria and that he believed the National Government and the Chinese Communists would reach agreement, since it was in the interests of both sides to do so.

In a conversation on August 31 the Minister-Counselor of the American Embassy discussed the proposed statement with the Chief of the American Section of the Soviet Foreign Office. The latter seemed to be under the impression that the United States had in mind a statement concerning China in general. The Minister emphasized, however, that the United States was concerned with Manchuria since the statement was intended to relate to the Sino-Soviet arrangements regarding the Russian position in that area.

On September 6 General Hurley informed the Department that the suggestions for a statement had been made at a time when the attitude of the Soviet Union toward the National Government of China had not been publicly and officially stated. The Ambassador believed that publication of the Sino-Soviet Treaty and related agreements had altered the situation: "The publication of these documents has demonstrated conclusively that the Soviet Government supports the National Government of China and also that the two governments are in agreement regarding Manchuria."

In mid-September Mr. Harriman reported a conversation a few days earlier between the Chinese Ambassador in Moscow and Andrei Vyshinsky, Soviet Deputy Foreign Minister, in which the latter had asked for a draft of the proposed statement by the Chinese Government. The Chinese Ambassador added that Dr. Soong was most anxious to have the statement issued but that when he (the Chinese Ambassador) had informed Chungking of the request from Vyshinsky he had been informed that the question had been referred to Dr. Wang Shih-chieh, the Chinese Foreign Minister, who was then in London attending the First Session of the Council of Foreign Ministers. In the end, however, the Chinese Government seemingly took the position that the Sino-Soviet Treaty constituted a sufficient guarantee, since it did not again raise the question. The Soviet Union, which from the beginning had been reluctant, also seems to have allowed the question to lapse.

CHINESE REACTION TO THE TREATY

On August 16, 1945, Generalissimo Chiang Kai-shek informed Ambassador Hurley that agreement had been reached with the Soviet Union and that he was "generally satisfied with the treaty." In reporting this conversation to the Department Ambassador Hurley added that his reports "showed the Generalissimo has always doubted the Soviet's position in regard to relations with the Chinese Communists. Yesterday he thanked me for the basis that I had helped him to lay for rapprochement with the Soviets. He admitted that the Sino-Soviet treaty indicates (1) an intention on the part of the

Soviets to assist in bringing about unification of the armed forces in China; (2) an intention to support Chinese efforts to create a strong, unified and democratic government; and (3) an intention to support the National Government of China." In conclusion, General Hurley said that "Chiang Kai-shek will now have an opportunity to show realistic and genuine leadership. He will have an opportunity to show his qualifications for leadership of the Chinese people in peace as well as in war. I am with the Generalissimo frequently. I insist continuously that the Chinese people must be responsible for their own policies, select their own leadership, and make their own decisions."

In a conversation of August 21 with Ambassador Hurley the Chinese Foreign Minister, Dr. Wang Shih-chieh, who had just returned to Chungking, "expressed himself as being satisfied with the results and said that proceedings would commence at once for the approval of the treaty and the notes exchanged between the Soviet and Chinese Governments."

On August 29, Madame Chiang Kai-shek, who was then in the United States, called on the President. She complimented him on the results of the Sino-Soviet conversations and expressed appreciation to the United States Government for the assistance which it had given to the Chinese plenipotentiaries in working out these agreements. The President said that that had been one of his principal objectives in going to Berlin and that he felt strongly that China should be supported in working out the arrangements which had been initiated by President Roosevelt.

Despite criticism of the Sino-Soviet arrangements of August 14, 1945, and as indicative of the value which the Chinese Government attached to them, Dr. Wang Shih-chieh as late as September 14, 1947, in a conversation with General Marshall, then Secretary of State, concerning the question of the veto power as applied to the Japanese peace treaty, expressed his opposition to the elimination of the veto power because of his fears that the Soviet Union "would interpret this, for its own convenience, as virtually cancelling the Sino-Soviet Treaty." The Foreign Minister was concerned at the reaction this would have on the situation in China.

Editorial comment in both Nationalist and Chinese Communist territory expressed approval of the Sino-Soviet Treaty and related agreements at the time they were made public.

UNITED STATES REACTION TO THE TREATY

At the time that the Sino-Soviet Treaty and related agreements were made public the United States supported the arrangements. In a statement issued on August 27, 1945, Secretary Byrnes said that he believed that the treaty and accompanying agreements constituted an "important step forward in the relations between China and the Soviet Union." He added that the United States welcomed this development "as a practical example of the continuing unity and mutual helpfulness which should characterize the acts of members of the United Nations in peace as well as in war."

Nevertheless early in September the American Embassy in Moscow registered a note of caution regarding the significance of the Sino-Soviet arrangements and their relation to the historic course of Russian imperialism. In a telegram of September 10, 1945, to the Department the American Embassy in Moscow summarized its views with respect to Russian intentions in the Far East as follows:

"1. The pact was not necessary for the achievement of any immediate objectives now being obtained by the Red Army. Regardless of the existence of the pact these objectives, including the military occupation of Manchuria and the Liaotung Peninsula, could and would have been achieved.

"2. The effect of the agreements concerning Manchuria should cause no illusion. Russian willingness to withdraw its forces and to admit Chinese to civil affairs control reflects mature statesmanship on the part of Stalin and his Moscow advisers. The initial Russian position as an occupying power, together with greater proximity and the far greater discipline of Russian power, should make it easy for the Russians to remain masters of the situation even after Russian troops have withdrawn. It was tacitly understood by both parties to the Moscow negotiations that Chinese officials in Manchuria would for the most part have to be amenable to Russian influence. Chinese Communist forces, according to recent broadcasts, have been ordered to enter Manchuria and in cooperation with the Russian army, to accept the Japanese surrender. Logically, the Russian authorities and their sympathizers will encourage the use of these Communist forces in the administration of Manchuria after the evacuation of the Russian Army. It should also be realized that local Russian authorities, in matters concerning the internal affairs of neighboring countries, do not always exercise the same restraint as does the Kremlin.

"3. Nothing in the internal regime of Outer Mongolia will be changed with its independence. The only effect will be its elimination as a possible source of future Chinese irredentism and an increase in its usefulness as an instrument for future Russian expansion.

"4. Russian assurances of support to the National Government and of non-interference in internal Chinese affairs reaffirms what has existed for some time. It is probable that any Kremlin control over the Chinese Communists has been through the Party apparatus and not through government channels.   It seems likely that this situation will obtain in the future—namely, control through the Party.   The bargaining position of the Chinese Communists on the basis of implied military support is undoubtedly weakened by the Russian assurances. On the other hand, these assurances (a) remove any excuse for a Sino-American crusade against the Chinese Communists as a spearhead of Russian penetration of China, (b) to a considerable extent dispel general suspicion of Russian intentions in China and thus disarm average critics of the Russian role there, and (c) place Russian policy in China on a high and disinterested moral plane.   In the meantime, the Russian Communist Party can continue to support the Chinese Communist program of "democratization," and to exert political pressure on the National Government to compromise.

"5. There should be no misunderstanding of Russian intentions toward Japan and Korea simply because of superficial Russian moderation on Manchuria.   In the Russian zone of Korea Communist-trained Korean elements are already being given responsibility for civil affairs. It is a natural tendency or even a deliberately conceived policy for the Russians to seek maximum internal influence in near-by areas through use of persons trained to accept their discipline and to share their ideology."

SOVIET ATTITUDE TOWARD MANCHURIAN INDUSTRIES

About the same time the United States became disturbed over developments in Manchuria.   Upon the defeat of Japan, the Soviet Union accepted the surrender of Japanese forces in Manchuria, as well as in southern Sakhalin and the Kurile Islands.   While its troops were in Manchuria, the Soviet Government removed considerable Japanese-owned industries and equipment from Manchuria, on the ground that such property was "war booty" because it had been used to support the Japanese war effort.   The United States protested these removals to the Soviet Union on a number of occasions, objecting not only to the inclusion of these industries in the concept of war booty, but also to the unilateral action of the Soviet Government in removing Japanese industries from Manchuria.   The United States took the position that the disposition of Japanese property in Manchuria should be decided by an Inter-Allied Reparations Commission for Japan on the same basis as for Japanese external assets located in other countries.[8a]

When the Soviet Union proposed to China early in 1946 that control of Japanese industrial enterprises in Manchuria be shared by agreement between the two states, the United States informed both China

---

[8a] See annex 60.

and the Soviet Union that the establishment of such exclusive bilateral control would be contrary to the principle of the Open Door and would constitute clear discrimination against Americans who might wish to participate in the development of Manchurian industry.

DISCUSSIONS AT THE MOSCOW CONFERENCE, 1945

At the Moscow Conference of the Foreign Ministers of the United Kingdom, the United States and the Soviet Union, in December 1945, the United States proposed that the question of transfer of control of Manchuria to the Chinese National Government be included on the agenda of the Conference. Mr. Molotov, the Soviet Foreign Minister, would not agree to the inclusion of this question. He explained that it was not necessary inasmuch as the Soviet Union had a special agreement with China concerning Manchuria and that there were no differences between the two countries on the subject. He said that the evacuation of Russian troops from South Manchuria was completed and that the evacuation from North Manchuria would have been completed if the Chinese Government had not requested that it be delayed for a month. Mr. Molotov insisted, however, on discussing the presence of United States troops in North China. Secretary Byrnes agreed to do so in connection with the disarming of Japanese forces in North China.

During the several meetings at which this question was discussed, Mr. Byrnes made the point that American forces in China were merely assisting in the demobilization of Japanese troops and their deportation from the area. He indicated that this task had been assumed from a feeling of responsibility for the maintenance of peace in North China which was one of the motives prompting the dispatch of General Marshall on special mission. Mr. Molotov stated that the evacuation of Russian troops from Manchuria would be completed by February 1, 1946, and that the Chinese simply wanted to get others to do their work. He added that it was intolerable that there were still Japanese forces which had not yet been disarmed. He called attention to a Soviet memorandum of December 21 which objected to "other foreign troops" assisting in the disarming of Japanese forces in China and demanded that the United States agree with the Soviet Union on a date not later than the middle of January 1946 for simultaneous evacuation of their respective forces from China. In this memorandum the Soviet Government declared that it adhered to a policy of non-interference in the internal affairs of China and indicated that "other states" should do likewise. Mr. Byrnes reiterated that the United States was merely carrying out its responsibilities and denied that the United States was interfering in Chinese internal affairs. He emphasized that the United States desired a unified and united China, and asked for Soviet cooperation to that end. In a subsequent conversation with Secretary Byrnes, Generalissimo Stalin also objected to the use of American troops in the demobilization of Japanese forces in China.

The communiqué issued at the close of the Moscow Conference contained the following statement regarding China:

"The three Foreign Secretaries exchanged views with regard to the situation in China. They were in agreement as to the need for a unified and democratic China under the National Government, for broad participation by democratic elements in all branches of the National Government, and for a cessation of civil strife. They reaffirmed their adherence to the policy of noninterference in the internal affairs of China.

"Mr. Molotov and Mr. Byrnes had several conversations concerning Soviet and American armed forces in China.

"Mr. Molotov stated that the Soviet forces had disarmed and deported Japanese troops in Manchuria but that withdrawal of Soviet forces had been postponed until February 1st at the request of the Chinese Government.

"Mr. Byrnes pointed out that American forces were in north China at the request of the Chinese Government, and referred also to the primary responsibility of the United States in the implementation of the Terms of Surrender with respect to the disarming and deportation of Japanese troops. He stated that American forces would be withdrawn just as soon as this responsibility was discharged or the Chinese Government was in a position to discharge the responsibility without the assistance of American forces.

"The two Foreign Secretaries were in complete accord as to the desirability of withdrawal of Soviet and American forces from China at the earliest practicable moment consistent with the discharge of their obligations and responsibilities."

AMERICAN PROTESTS ON DAIREN

Because Dairen was not opened to commercial vessels in the months following the surrender of Japan, the United States on two occasions during 1947 protested to the Soviet Government on the grounds that American commercial activity was hindered by the·port's not being opened to traffic. The Soviet Union replied by referring to the provision of the agreement regarding Dairen of August 14, 1945, which stated that, in case of war with Japan, Dairen was to come under the control of the military regime authorized for the Port Arthur naval base area. The Soviet Union added that in as much as the war with

Japan had not been terminated, there being no peace treaty, Dairen came under the administration of the Port Arthur naval base. The Soviet Government also stated that it "sees no basis for a change of the regime" under which Dairen remained closed to commercial intercourse with other countries. Thus the United States protests were of no avail.

CONCLUSION

At the time that the Sino-Soviet Treaty and related agreements were concluded they were generally considered in the most favorable light. It was thought that the arrangements would provide a firm basis for peaceful and harmonious relations between the two countries. The Yalta Agreement had, of course, been dictated by military necessity and the vital importance of ensuring the entry of the Soviet Union into the Far Eastern war before the Allied invasion of Japan which had been set for the autumn of 1945. Although the unexpectedly early collapse of Japanese resistance later made some of the provisions of the Yalta Agreement seem unnecessary, the Agreement and the subsequent Sino-Soviet Treaty in fact imposed legal limitations on the action which Russia would, in any case, have been in a position to take. At Yalta, Marshal Stalin not only agreed to declare war on Japan within two or three months after V–E Day but limited his "price" with reference to Manchuria substantially to the position which Russia had occupied there prior to 1904. In the Sino-Soviet Treaty, furthermore, the Soviets agreed to give the National Government of China moral and material support and moreover formalized their assurances of noninterference in Chinese internal affairs. In view of world developments since the conclusion of hostilities against Japan, especially in recent years, there is no evidence to suggest that the absence of such arrangements would have restrained the Soviet Union from pursuing Russia's long-range traditional objectives. Even though the Soviet Union has not seen fit to honor its signed agreements in practice, their existence has had, as the National Government itself has admitted, moral and legal advantage for that Government.

CHAPTER V

The Mission of General George C. Marshall
1945–1947 [1]

I. THE ECONOMIC, MILITARY AND POLITICAL SETTING

INTRODUCTION

After the successful termination of the war against Japan, and at the time General Hurley left Chungking, there were several elements in the situation which plausibly argued that prospects for peace and reconstruction in China were reasonably good. The negotiations between the National Government and the Chinese Communists had reached a stage of agreement on general principles and General Hurley himself felt that agreement on details and implementation was by no means impossible. Both participants in the negotiations still professed their desire and intention to seek a political settlement and there could be little doubt that the overwhelming popular demand was for peace.

Perhaps the most important factor immediately after V–J Day was the economic situation, which, despite the brutal and devastating effects of eight years of war, was surprisingly good and contained many elements of hope.

GENERAL ECONOMIC SITUATION IMMEDIATELY AFTER V–J DAY

In China proper, although there had been serious wartime disruption in certain sectors of the economy, the productive potential of agriculture, mining, and industry in most of the area taken from the Japanese was not substantially different from that of 1937. The expulsion of the Japanese from Manchuria and Formosa promised to increase several-fold the national industrial plant and to contribute to the achievement of national self-sufficiency in food. Such economic problems as could be foreseen in the late summer of 1945 related less

---

[1] The bulk of the material for this chapter has been drawn from the files of General Marshall's Mission.

to the reconstruction of productive equipment than to the organization of production and distribution through facilities already available.

Except in those parts of Central and South China which had been subjected to active military operations in 1944–1945, production of foodstuffs was at or near prewar levels, but agricultural production had shifted significantly away from cash crops, such as cotton, to food crops for local consumption. Heavy losses were inflicted on inland and coastal shipping during the war years, and the railroad from Peiping to Canton and others in South China had suffered serious damage, but the efficiency of the greater portion of railroad facilities was only moderately impaired. The number of motor vehicles in operation had actually increased somewhat during the war. Coal production had increased by about 25 percent under Japanese management. On the other hand, electric power supply in China proper decreased significantly because of the loss of over one-quarter of prewar generating capacity.

Wartime changes in industrial capacity were not important, except in the iron and cotton textile industries. Despite destruction of facilities at Hankow by retreating Chinese forces, total pig iron capacity was increased by about 50 percent over prewar levels during the occupation. Cotton spinning capacity, however, fell sharply. A full year after Japanese surrender little more than half of the prewar total of nearly 5 million spindles was in operation. An additional 1.4 million spindles were reparable but were not expected to be brought into production for another year. The principal economic effects of eight years of war and invasion appear to have been not so much the destruction of wealth or the diversion of production into new channels as the suspension of the process of industrialization and the disruption of the new national monetary system.

In regaining Manchuria, China would inherit the extensive industrial complex built by the Japanese and a rich agricultural area capable of producing a substantial export surplus. With about one-fourth of the total area and one-ninth the population, Manchuria had come to possess an industry over four times as large as that of China proper, and an electric generating capacity nearly three times as large. The density of Manchuria's rail net was over four times as great as that of China proper.

China's economic gains in resuming administration over Formosa after a lapse of 50 years were smaller than, but similar in nature to those in prospect on V–J Day in Manchuria. Formosa also had traditionally a large export surplus of agricultural products. Japanese industrial achievements were less impressive in Formosa than in Manchuria, but a wartime boom had given Formosa a substantial productive capacity in aluminum, petroleum products, and electric power, in addition to its older capacity in sugar refining and other food exporting industries. Both agriculture and industry in Formosa, however, had suffered severely during the war. Irrigation works and crops themselves had suffered heavy typhoon damage in 1944 and 1945, and food production had declined for lack of adequate fertilizer. Industry, the electric power distribution system, and harbor facilities were crippled by Allied bombing in the last months of the war.

CHINA'S FINANCIAL POSITION

China's foreign exchange holdings at the conclusion of the war with Japan were by far the largest in the history of that country. The principal fiscal asset of the Chinese Government at the end of the war against Japan was its unprecedentedly large reserves of gold and U. S. dollar exchange, which were estimated to total over 900 million United States dollars on December 31, 1945. The accumulation of these reserves had been made possible by virtue of the nondisbursement of a substantial portion of the 500 million dollar American credit authorized in 1942, and by United States Government payments during the war of approximately 400 million dollars to the Chinese Government against advances of Chinese currency and Chinese Government expenditures on behalf of the 'United States Army. In addition to these reserves of the Chinese Government, private Chinese held very substantial foreign exchange assets, most of which could be used to finance imports into China. Although complete data regarding private Chinese holdings of gold, silver and other foreign exchange assets is not available, it has been estimated conservatively that such holdings on V–J Day amounted to at least several hundred million United States dollars.

Optimism based upon China's very favorable foreign exchange position was tempered by realization of the magnitude of the reconstruction task in some parts of the economy, as well as the necessity of immediate large-scale imports of food and industrial raw material. Pending the re-establishment of normal internal trade, industrial production could be maintained and consumer welfare protected only by the purchase abroad of relatively large quantities of such essential commodities as cotton and grain. Reconstruction was most urgently needed in the field of transportation. Substantial assistance in obtaining the abnormal volume of imports needed in connection with postwar reconstruction and rehabilitation was anticipated from UNRRA. The ultimate soundness of the international financial position of the Chinese Government depended, however, on the speed with which export industries and remittances from Chinese overseas regained their prewar levels.

The Chinese Government also faced financial problems of a largely domestic nature. Inflationary methods of finance had been resorted to during the war as the only means of maintaining resistance against the Japanese in the face of the loss of the richest part of the national territory, the disruption of normal trade, and the disorganization of public administration. Bringing the wartime inflation to a halt was essential to post-war economic recovery, but such action depended upon an expansion of revenues and a reduction in military expenditures. After the war, the Government regained control of the greatest revenue producing areas of China proper, and, of course, looked forward to the Manchurian and Formosan economies as rich sources of revenue. The extensive industrial properties taken over from the Japanese promised to provide the Government with a new and non-inflationary source of funds. No accurate appraisal of the value of these properties is available but, in addition to the major Government properties acquired in Manchuria and Formosa, the Chinese Government fell heir to Japanese cotton mills in China proper with a total of almost two million spindles, representing nearly half of the nation's cotton spinning industry, as well as various other Japanese-owned industrial facilities.

In prospect, the Government's financial position on V–J Day was reasonably bright. The inter-related problems that it faced both domestically and internationally were sizable, but at the same time it possessed assets which appeared capable of making a large contribution to their solution.

UNFAVORABLE ELEMENTS

Despite the favorable elements in the negotiations and in the economic situation there was reason during the fall of 1945 for grave concern that the prospects of peace and stability in China were in serious jeopardy. The Chinese Communists had refused to recognize orders issued by the National Government concerning acceptance of surrender of Japanese and Chinese puppet troops and were proceeding, insofar as their capacity permitted, to accept such surrender, to seize enemy matériel, and to occupy enemy territory. The result was a series of increasingly frequent and widespread clashes between the armed forces of the Government and of the Chinese Communist Party. These clashes spread to other areas as well, to such an extent that competent observers had grave doubts as to the possibility of a peaceful settlement.

GENERAL WEDEMEYER'S REPORTS

On November 14, 1945, Lieutenant General Albert C. Wedemeyer, Commanding General, China Theater, reported to Washington that the National Government was completely unprepared for occupation of Manchuria in the face of Communist opposition. He also reported his recommendation to the Generalissimo that the Chinese should adopt the immediate objective of consolidating the areas south of the great wall and north of the Yangtze and of securing the overland line of communications in that area prior to entry into Manchuria.

Again on November 20, 1945, he reported as follows:

"I have recommended to the Generalissimo that he should concentrate his efforts upon establishing control in north China and upon the prompt execution of political and official reforms designed to remove the practice of corruption by officials and to eliminate prohibitive taxes."

General Wedemeyer also recommended the utilization of foreign executives and technicians, at least during the transition period. He then added:

"Chinese Communist guerrillas and saboteurs can and probably will, if present activities are a reliable indication, restrict and harass the movements of National Government forces to such an extent that the result will be a costly and extended campaign. . . . Logistical support for National Governmental forces and measures for their security in the heart of Manchuria have not been fully appreciated by the Generalissimo or his Chinese staff. These facts plus the lack of appropriate forces and transport have caused me to advise the Generalissimo that he should concentrate his efforts on the recovery of north China and the consolidation of his military and political position there prior to any attempt to occupy Manchuria. I received the impression that he agreed with this concept."

Among General Wedemeyer's conclusions at that time were the following:

"1. The Generalissimo will be able to stabilize the situation in south China provided he accepts the assistance of foreign administrators and technicians and engages in political, economic and social reforms through honest, competent civilian officials.

"2. He will be unable to stabilize the situation in north China for months or perhaps even years unless a satisfactory settlement with the Chinese Communists is achieved and followed up realistically by the kind of action suggested in paragraph 1.

"3. He will be unable to occupy Manchuria for many years unless satisfactory agreements are reached with Russia and the Chinese Communists.

"4. Russia is in effect creating favorable conditions for the realization of Chinese Communist and possibly their own plans in north China and Manchuria. These activities are violations of the recent Sino-Russian Treaty and related agreements.

"5. It appears remote that a satisfactory understanding will be reached between Chinese Communists and the National Government."

The final recommendation of General Wedemeyer was the establishment by the United States, Great Britain and Russia of a trusteeship over Manchuria until such time as the National Government had become sufficiently strong and stabilized to assume responsibility of full control over the area. One of the principal reasons which led General Wedemeyer to the above conclusions was his conviction that National Government abuses and malpractices had already created serious discontent among the local population in areas taken over from the Japanese, and even this soon after the end of the war against Japan had seriously alienated a considerable amount of sympathy for the National Government.

It is against this checkered background that the mission of General Marshall should be considered.

GENERAL MARSHALL'S APPOINTMENT AND INSTRUCTIONS

When President Truman announced on November 27, 1945, his acceptance of Ambassador Hurley's resignation, he announced also the appointment of General of the Army George C. Marshall as his Special Representative in China, with the personal rank of Ambassador. In the instructions which he addressed to General Marshall on December 15,[1a] the President asked the General to bring to bear the influence of the United States to the end that the "unification of China by peaceful, democratic methods" might be achieved as soon as possible and concurrently to endeavor to effect a cessation of hostilities, particularly in North China. To assist in the accomplishment of this mission General Marshall was authorized to speak to Generalissimo Chiang Kai-shek and other Chinese leaders "with the utmost frankness" and to state that "a China disunited and torn by civil strife" was not a proper place for American economic assistance in the form of credits or technical assistance nor for American military aid.

[1a] See annexes 61, 62.

THE PRESIDENT'S POLICY STATEMENT OF DECEMBER 15, 1945

A portion of General Marshall's instructions, in the form of a Presidential statement on United States policy toward China, was released on December 15 for publication the following day.[1b] Stating that a "strong, united, and democratic China" was of the utmost importance to world peace, the President declared that it was "in the most vital interest of the United States and all the United Nations that the people of China overlook no opportunity to adjust their internal differences promptly by methods of peaceful negotiation." He called for a cessation of hostilities in China, but pledged that there would be no American military intervention to influence the Chinese civil fighting, explaining the presence of American troops in North China in terms of the necessity for disarming and evacuating surrendered Japanese troops still on Chinese soil.

President Truman further urged the convening in China of a national conference of the major Chinese political elements to develop a solution to the problems of China which would not only end internal strife but would also bring about unification of the country on terms which would give all major political elements fair and effective representation in the Chinese Government. This obviously meant modification of the Kuomintang's system of "political tutelage" and the broadening of the base of government. The President pointed out that the detailed steps necessary to the achievement of political unity in China must be worked out by the Chinese themselves and disowned any intention of intervening in these matters. He declared, however, that China and all parties and groups in China had a clear responsibility to the other United Nations to eliminate armed civil conflict, which was a threat to world stability and peace.

The President concluded by promising American assistance, as China moved toward peace and unity, in the rehabilitation of the country, in the improvement of the industrial and agrarian economy, and in the establishment of a military organization "capable of discharging China's national and international responsibilities for the maintenance of peace and order."

THE BEGINNING OF THE MARSHALL MISSION

In the light of these instructions General Marshall undertook the execution of his mission immediately upon his arrival in Chungking. The complex problems in China fell largely under three heads—political, military and economic—but they frequently became so entangled that discussion of them cannot be separated. This was particularly true of the political and military problems, for the two

---

[1b] For full text see annex 62.

principal Chinese parties to the negotiations in which General Marshall took part, the National Government and the Chinese Communist Party, frequently made military action or inaction a *sine qua non* for a political concession, or vice versa.

The President's Special Representative acted both as an intermediary between Generalissimo Chiang Kai-shek and the representatives of the Chinese Communist Party and as an adviser to or member of certain bodies, or committees, which were established in the effort to reach agreement on China's problems. He also exercised initiative in giving each side impartially and confidentially the benefit of his analysis of the situation as it developed, and in drafting various statements and agreements which he thought might move the negotiations forward.

Throughout his mission General Marshall kept the President and the Secretary of State fully informed of the progress of the negotiations, of his actions in connection with these negotiations and of his estimate of the situation in China. His actions and decisions had the unqualified support and approval of the President and the Secretary of State.

The negotiations themselves were most difficult and most complex. As it turned out General Marshall was often unable to bring the two sides to complete agreement on a set of terms before the situation changed, frequently as a result of what he considered bad faith on one side or the other, and a new set of proposals based on the new situation became the basis of discussion. This chapter largely forms a narrative, therefore, of the constantly shifting situations, proposals, counterproposals, and discussions, starting with the political and military situation which General Marshall found in China upon his arrival. Economic matters concerning Sino-American relations during the period of the Marshall mission, however, have been separated from the rest of this narrative insofar as possible and grouped together toward the end of the chapter.

RECAPITULATION OF CHINESE POLITICAL BACKGROUND FOR THE MISSION

Dr. Sun Yat-sen's program for China had envisaged a period of "political tutelage" under the Kuomintang as the necessary preparation for the establishment of constitutional government in China. The Kuomintang had thus been committed to end its one-party control of government and to convene a National Assembly for the purpose of adopting a constitution and forming a new government, and a draft constitution had actually been promulgated by the National Government on May 5, 1936. A National Assembly had been scheduled to be convened in November 1937 to adopt the constitution, but the outbreak of hostilities with Japan had resulted in a postponement of this Assembly. Preparations for the convening of the Assembly had continued, however, during the war with Japan and at a meeting of the Kuomintang Central Executive Committee in September 1943, Generalissimo Chiang Kai-shek had indicated that with the establishment of representative institutions the Kuomintang would lose all special privileges and other parties would be equal to it in rights and freedoms. The Generalissimo had also stated on September 13, 1943:

". . . I am of the opinion that first of all we should clearly recognize that the Chinese Communist problem is a purely political problem and should be solved by political means."

The Central Executive Committee had accordingly passed a resolution providing that within one year after the conclusion of the war the National Government was to convene a National Assembly to adopt and promulgate a constitution. Shortly thereafter, the Generalissimo appointed a committee of 53, including 2 Communist representatives, to lay the groundwork for constitutional government. In May 1944 a Communist representative held preliminary conversations at Sian with two high-ranking National Government representatives and later proceeded to Chungking where further discussions were held for a settlement of the differences between the Government and the Chinese Communists.

In subsequent discussions between the National Government and the Chinese Communist Party at Chungking shortly after V–J Day agreement was reached regarding steps to be taken toward the establishment of a constitutional government. The exact formula was set forth in the Text of the Summary of National Government-Communist Conversations issued at Chungking on October 11, 1945, and referred to above.[2]

This text provided that questions which were not settled during these conversations should be referred to a "Political Consultative Conference."

It will be noted that President Truman's statement of December 15, 1945, was entirely consonant with the publicly stated pledges of the Chinese Government and the Generalissimo regarding a peaceful settlement of the Communist problem and with the agreement reached between that Government and the Chinese Communist Party in October 1945 providing for the convening of the "Political Consultative Conference" to discuss measures looking toward the establishment of

---

[2] See chapter III.

a constitutional Government. A provisional list of the delegates to this Conference had been published at Chungking on November 27. On December 31, 1945, the National Government announced that the Generalissimo had decided that the Political Consultative Conference would convene at Chungking on January 10, 1946.

II. THE AGREEMENTS OF JANUARY AND FEBRUARY 1946

THE CEASE-FIRE AGREEMENT OF JANUARY 10, 1946

Prior to the convening of the Conference, the National Government presented to the Chinese Communist Party a proposal for the cessation of hostilities, in which it suggested the formation of a committee composed of a representative of the National Government and a representative of the Chinese Communist Party, with General Marshall as Chairman, to discuss the question of the cessation of hostilities and related matters. The Chinese Communist Party having agreed to the formation of this committee, General Chang Chun was appointed as the National Government representative and General Chou En-lai as the Chinese Communist Party representative. This Committee, called the Committee of Three, held its first formal meeting on January 7, 1946.

During the early conversations of General Marshall with National Government leaders and Chinese Communist Party representatives in Chungking the basic distrust between the two groups was apparent. The National Government was convinced that the U.S.S.R. had obstructed the efforts of the National Government to assume control over Manchuria in spite of the provisions of the Sino-Soviet Treaty of August 1945 and that the Chinese Communists were tools of the U.S.S.R. The Chinese Communist Party was suspicious of the Kuomintang and believed that its aim was the destruction of the Chinese Communist Party. The Government leaders were unwilling to permit Communist participation in the Government until the Communists had given up their armed forces, while the Communists believed that to do so without guarantees of their legal political status would end in their destruction.

In the light of the statement of American policy toward China, which pointed out that the United States, the United Kingdom, and the U.S.S.R. were committed by various agreements with the Chinese Government to the return of all China, including Manchuria, to Chinese control, General Marshall envisaged a solution which would be in accord with these agreements and which would result in bringing this area under the control of a unified China.

With that end in view, he had informed General Chou En-lai on January 4 that the United States Government was committed to the movement of National Government troops to Manchuria. General Chou expressed his agreement to the inclusion of an exception in the cessation of hostilities agreement to permit the movement of National Government troops into Manchuria and added that the movement of such troops conformed to American policy and to the Sino-Soviet Treaty of August 1945.

The Committee of Three reached an agreement on January 10 for the cessation of hostilities. In accordance with this agreement, both the Generalissimo and Mr. Mao Tse-tung, Chairman of the Chinese Communist Party, issued orders to their respective armed forces to cease hostilities and halt all movements of troops, with certain exceptions which were included in stipulations regarding the cease-fire order and were made public in a press release.[3] These stipulations provided for the movement of National Government troops into and within Manchuria for the purpose of restoring Chinese sovereignty and for the movement of National Government troops south of the Yangtze River in connection with the Government military reorganization plan. The cease-fire order was to be effective at midnight on January 13, thus allowing time for the transmission of the order to commanders in the field. The order further provided for the cessation of destruction of and interference with all lines of communication and for the removal of obstructions placed against or interfering with such lines.

The agreement also provided for the establishment of an Executive Headquarters at Peiping to carry out the agreement for the cessation of hostilities.[4] This headquarters, which began its official functions on January 14, was to consist of three commissioners, one representing the National Government, one representing the Chinese Communist Party, and one representing the United States. The National Government and the Chinese Communist Party were to have equal representation in the operations section of the Executive Headquarters and in the teams to be sent to the field to carry out on the spot the provisions of the cease-fire order and the directives of the headquarters. The necessary instructions and orders agreed upon unanimously by

---

[3] See annex 63.

[4] See annex 71 for full text of the document establishing the Executive Headquarters and for a memorandum on operations of the Executive Headquarters. American military and naval personnel in China were also charged with certain functions concerning repatriation of Japanese, a task which was fulfilled with the highest degree of effectiveness so that by the end of 1946 a total of almost 3,000,000 Japanese military personnel and civilians had been repatriated to Japan. A memorandum on this operation is also included in annex 71.

the three commissioners were to be issued in the name of the President of the Republic of China. It was made clear that American participation in the headquarters was solely for the purpose of assisting the Chinese members in the implementation of the cease-fire order.

THE POLITICAL CONSULTATIVE CONFERENCE

The agreement for the cessation of hostilities enabled the Political Consultative Conference (hereafter called the PCC) to convene in an atmosphere of peace. The PCC, which was in session at Chungking from January 10 to 31, 1946, was composed of representatives of the Kuomintang, the Chinese Communist Party, the Democratic League, and the Youth Party and of non-party delegates. It met as a consultative body without any legal authority to enforce its decisions. Morally, all groups represented were obligated to accept the decisions, but legally the PCC resolutions were subject to approval by the central committees or governing bodies of the various parties represented.

At the opening session of the PCC, Generalissimo Chiang Kai-shek announced the decision of the Government to grant immediately certain fundamental democratic rights. They included freedom of speech, assembly, and association; equal legal status for all political parties; the holding of popular elections; and the release of political prisoners. On January 31, the PCC held its final session and released to the press the text of the resolutions agreed upon.[5] These resolutions were divided into five main headings as follows: (1) Government Organization; (2) Program for Peaceful National Reconstruction; (3) Military Problems; (4) Agreement on the National Assembly; and (5) the 1936 Draft Constitution.

In his address to the closing session of the PCC, the Generalissimo made the following statements regarding the PCC resolutions:[6]

"I wish to declare first on behalf of the Government that they will be fully respected and carried out as soon as the prescribed procedures have been completed. I pledge at the same time that I will uphold this program faithfully and will also see to it that all the military and civil subordinates follow it strictly. From now on, I will, whether in the Government or out of it, faithfully and resolutely observe, as a citizen should, all the decisions of this Conference."

In contrast to the Generalissimo's statements, however, there were indications of strong opposition to the PCC resolutions among powerful reactionary groups in the Kuomintang. Minority party reaction to the decisions of the PCC was shown in the issuance of categorical

---

[5] See annexes 64, 65, 66, 67, 68.
[6] As reported by the Kuomintang Ministry of Information.

statements by the Chinese Communist Party, the Democratic League, and the Youth Party of their intention to carry out the PCC resolutions.

General Marshall did not act as a mediator or participate in the discussions of the Political Consultative Conference. In accordance with the Generalissimo's request, he did, however, have prepared a brief draft of an act for possible promulgation by the National Government which included a bill of rights, a provision for drawing up a constitution to be submitted to the National Assembly in May and a provision for the establishment of an interim coalition government reposing in the Generalissimo power of control as the President of all China prior to the formation of the constitutional government. This draft was presented to the Generalissimo on a confidential basis on January 23.

THE PCC RESOLUTIONS

The PCC resolutions provided for convening a National Assembly on May 5, 1946, for the purpose of adopting a constitution and for the formation of a Constitution Draft Committee to draw up a detailed plan for revision of the 1936 Draft Constitution based on the principles agreed upon by the PCC, as well as recommendations of various associations connected with the promotion of constitutionalism in China. This plan was to be submitted to the National Assembly for adoption. The PCC resolutions also provided that, pending the convening of the National Assembly, the Kuomintang would revise the organic law of the National Government to make the State Council the supreme organ of the Government in charge of national affairs. This Council was to be composed of 40 members, who would be chosen by the Generalissimo from Kuomintang and non-Kuomintang members. Half of the Councillors would be members of the Kuomintang and half members of other parties and non-party personnel. The specific allotment of seats of non-Kuomintang Councillors was to be the subject of separate discussion after the adjournment of the PCC. The PCC resolutions regarding the State Council empowered the President to veto any decision of the Council, and such a veto could be overridden only by a three-fifths vote of the Council. General resolutions would require a majority vote of the Councillors present, but any resolutions involving changes in the administrative policy would be required to have a two-thirds vote of the members present for approval. However, a majority vote of the members present would be sufficient to decide whether a resolution involved a change in administrative policy. The PCC resolutions regarding the membership of the State Council and the question of the veto power subsequently played an important part in the negotiations between the Chinese Government and the Chinese Communist Party. The question of the veto power arose in discussions regarding membership in the State Council. The Chinese Communist Party began to advance claims for control of at least 14 seats in the Council among its own members and friendly nominees. With this number the Chinese Communist Party would have sufficient voting strength to exercise a veto to prevent changes in the PCC resolutions.

Under the Program for Peaceful National Reconstruction of the PCC resolutions, the equality and legality of all political parties were recognized and all parties were pledged to recognize the national leadership of President Chiang Kai-shek. The program provided *inter alia* for the maintenance of the *status quo* in liberated areas where the government was under dispute until a settlement should be made by the National Government after its reorganization, a point of considerable importance in later negotiations.

Under the PCC resolutions on military problems, provision was made for reorganization and reduction of the armies and the creation of a national army belonging to the State in which no political parties would be allowed to carry on political activities. It was also provided that the "Three-Man Military Commission" should agree upon practical methods for the reorganization of the Chinese Communist armies at an early date. It was further provided that, when the reorganization of both the National Government and Communist armies should be completed, all armies should again be reorganized into 50 or 60 divisions.

THE MILITARY REORGANIZATION AGREEMENT OF FEBRUARY 25, 1946

On January 10 the National Government suggested the formation of a military committee to draw up measures for the reorganization and redisposition of the Chinese armies. Such a committee had already been agreed to by the National Government and the Chinese Communist Party during the negotiations ending in October 1945. The Chinese Communist Party representatives agreed to this proposal and both the Chinese Government and the Chinese Communist Party expressed their approval of General Marshall's participation in this committee as an adviser. This committee, known as the Military Subcommittee, was composed of General Chang Chih-chung as the National Government representative, General Chou En-lai as the Chinese Communist Party representative and General Marshall as adviser.

The Military Subcommittee held its first meeting on February 14, 1946, and on February 25 reached an agreement entitled "Basis for Military Reorganization and for the Integration of the Communist Forces into the National Army." In the press release announcing the agreement,[7] it was explained that the purpose of the agreement was to facilitate the economic rehabilitation of China and at the same time to furnish a basis for the development of an effective military force capable of safeguarding the security of the nation, including provisions to safeguard the rights of the people from military interference. It was also pointed out that the Executive Headquarters at Peiping would be charged with responsibility for supervising the execution of orders necessary to the implementation of the agreement and that the measures to be decided upon by the Military Subcommittee for the execution of the terms of the agreement would be carried out over a period of 18 months.

The terms of the agreement envisaged the reduction of the National Government armies to 90 divisions at the end of 12 months and the reduction of the Chinese Communist forces to 18 divisions during that same period. A further reduction at the end of the following 6 months provided for 50 National Government divisions and 10 Communist divisions, the total of 60 divisions of not more than 14,000 men each to be formed into 20 armies. The process of integration was provided for initially during the seventh month. The National Government and the Chinese Communist Party were required under the agreement to make provisions for the supply, movement and employment of their respective demobilized personnel, the National Government to assume this responsibility for all demobilized personnel as soon as practicable. For purposes of integration and deployment, China was divided into five general areas as follows: Northeast China, Northwest China, North China, Central China and South China (including Formosa) and a specific number of armies was provided for each area at the end of the 12-month period and again at the end of the full 18-month period. Provision was made for the following distribution of the armed forces at the end of 18 months: Northeast China (Manchuria)—14 National Government divisions' and 1 Communist division; Northwest China—9 National Government divisions; North China—11 National Government divisions and 7 Communist divisions; Central China—10 National Government divisions and 2 Communist divisions; and South China (including Formosa)—6 National Government divisions.

In discussions leading to this agreement, General Marshall endeavored to emphasize as strongly as possible the necessity of creating in China a national, nonpolitical military force along the lines of western military tradition, to be used as a democratic army and not as an authoritarian weapon. The agreement reached was based upon the general principle of separating the army from politics and, although

---

[7] See annex 69.

this idea was not expressly stated in the agreement, the various articles adhered to this general plan. This principle was of the greatest importance in China, where political power in the final analysis was dependent upon the possession of military force and where the military constantly interfered with civil administration or were themselves legally in control of civil administration by appointment to office. In a brief speech at the time of the signing of this agreement General Marshall made the following statement: "This agreement, I think, represents the great hope of China. I can only trust that its pages will not be soiled by a small group of irreconcilables who for a selfish purpose would defeat the Chinese people in their overwhelming desire for peace and prosperity."

The agreement required the National Government to prepare and submit to the Military Subcommittee, within 3 weeks of the promulgation of the agreement, a list of the 90 divisions to be retained and the order of demobilization of units during the first 2 months. Such a list was submitted on March 26. The agreement similarly provided for the preparation and submission to the Committee by the Chinese Communist Party, within 3 weeks of the promulgation of the agreement, of a complete list of all its military units, together with a list of the 18 divisions to be retained and the order of demobilization of units during the first 2 months—a provision with which the Communists never complied. It was further provided that within 6 weeks after the promulgation of this agreement both the National Government and the Chinese Communist Party should furnish to the Committee lists of the units to be demobilized.

Agreement was reached by the Military Subcommittee on February 27, 1946, on a directive [8] to the Executive Headquarters implementing the basic plan for military reorganization and integration of the Communist armies into the National Army. The directive, signed on March 16, 1946, established the Executive Headquarters as the agency for the execution of the basic plan and provided for the formation of a group in the headquarters, composed of National Government, Chinese Communist Party, and United States personnel, to plan and supervise the execution of the plan. The directive also provided for the complete disbandment within 3 months of Chinese puppet units who had served the Japanese and for the establishment of a 12-week basic training program for the National Government and Communist Party divisions to be retained. The directive recommended the establishment of a Demobilized Manpower Commission, which should coordinate its efforts with those of the Government, the Communist

---

[8] See annex 70.

Party, civilian agencies, relief organizations, and the Executive Headquarters.[8a]

The conclusion of the agreement for military reorganization marked the third major step in bringing peace to China and in establishing a basis for unification of the country.   The cessation of hostilities agreement was designed to bring to a halt actual fighting in order that negotiations for a political and military settlement could be carried on in an atmosphere of peace.   The PCC resolutions represented an agreement on the questions of governmental reorganization and the establishment of a constitutional government.   The Basis for Military Reorganization similarly provided an agreement on the question of integration of the Communist Party armed forces into the National Army and the reorganization of all armies in China on a democratic base.

It should be noted that the political and military agreements recognized the preponderant strength of the Kuomintang position in the National Government.   In the interim State Council, which was to function until the establishment of constitutional government through action of the National Assembly, the Kuomintang was allocated 20 of the 40 seats.   The President was empowered to veto any decision of the Council and his veto could be overriden only by a three-fifths vote of the members of the Council.   Under the military reorganization plan, the preponderant strength of the National Government was recognized by provision for a National Government superiority of 5 to 1 in relation to the Communist forces, by which at the end of the 18-month reorganization and integration period the National Army would have 50 Government and 10 Communist divisions.

CHINESE PUBLIC REACTION

The immediate reaction of the Chinese public to the cessation of hostilities and the announcement of the PCC resolutions was one of enthusiastic approval, tempered by the realization that the implementation of the resolutions would be the acid test by which the sincerity of the two rival parties could be gauged.   The indication of strong resentment against the PCC on the part of powerful groups within the Kuomintang and the opposition by a powerful group of National Government Army generals to any reorganization of the armies which would threaten their position were seen as obstacles, on the Kuomintang side, to successful implementation of the resolutions.   Disquieting incidents, such as an attack by alleged Kuomintang plain-clothes men on a mass meeting held at Chungking to celebrate the success of the PCC, police interference with minority party delegates to the PCC, and an attack on the Communist Party news-

[8a] See Annex 71.

paper premises at Chungking, all served to strengthen the fears of opposition to the PCC by irreconcilable elements in the Kuomintang.

KUOMINTANG ACTION ON THE PCC RESOLUTIONS

The next step in connection with the PCC resolutions of January 31 was that of obtaining legal action by the National Government to approve these resolutions. The Central Executive Committee (hereafter called the CEC) of the Kuomintang met at Chungking from March 1 to 17 for the purpose of passing upon the PCC resolutions. Simultaneously with the CEC sessions, there were also held at Chungking meetings of the PCC Steering Committee and the PCC Constitutional Reviewing Committee, in which discussions were held of points which the CEC reportedly wished to have revised. Although the CEC announced at the end of its sessions that it had approved the PCC resolutions *in toto*,[9] there were indications that approval had been hedged by reservations and that irreconcilable elements within the Kuomintang were endeavoring to sabotage the PCC program. Their efforts were reportedly directed toward revisions of the principles approved by the PCC as the basis for revising the Draft Constitution and toward obtaining close adherence to the May 1936 Draft Constitution, on which the Kuomintang had originally insisted in the PCC sessions.

Discussions regarding the PCC resolutions continued in the PCC Steering Committee after the adjournment of the Kuomintang CEC on March 17. During this period the Communist Party and Democratic League representatives maintained the general position that the PCC resolutions had been agreed upon by duly authorized representatives of all parties and indicated that they would oppose any major changes in the resolutions. The Communist Party and Democratic League, therefore, refused to nominate members to the State Council for participation in a reorganized government until the Kuomintang should publish a statement of any revisions of the PCC resolutions agreed upon and of a definite commitment by the Kuomintang to implement the PCC program as revised. In the meantime, the Communist Party postponed its Central Committee meeting, originally scheduled for March 31 for the purpose of passing upon the PCC resolutions. Under these circumstances the PCC Constitutional Reviewing Committee suspended its work upon preparation of a revised constitution to submit to the National Assembly, still scheduled to meet on May 5, but later postponed and not convened until November.

---

[9] See annex 72.

GENERAL MARSHALL'S RECALL FOR CONSULTATION

Following the signing of the military reorganization agreement General Marshall had recommended to President Truman that he be recalled to Washington for a brief visit. He felt that he should report to the President on the situation in China and he was particularly anxious to take up the question of the transfer of surplus property and shipping and the problem of loans to China. He also wished to make a personal presentation of the situation in China regarding UNRRA and famine conditions. He was of the opinion that he should make a brief visit to obtain financial and economic facilities to aid China and return to China in time to assist in adjusting differences which were certain to arise over the major problems connected with the agreements reached. It was his opinion that steps had to be taken to assist China and its people in the increasingly serious economic situation and to facilitate the efforts being made toward peace and unity in China and toward the establishment of a unified defense force. General Marshall felt that Chinese political and military unity could only be consolidated and made lasting through the rehabilitation of the country and the permanent general improvement of economic conditions. President Truman approved the recommendation and formally recalled him to Washington for these purposes. He accordingly departed for Washington on March 11, 1946.

III. THE MANCHURIAN CRISIS

FIELD TEAMS FOR MANCHURIA

The cease-fire agreement of January 10, 1946, made no mention of any exemption of any part of China from its provisions, except in regard to the movement of troops, and there was no implication or indication in the meetings of the Committee of Three that Manchuria was not included within the scope of the cessation of hostilities order. General Marshall felt very strongly that the authority of the Executive Headquarters in Manchuria should be asserted in order to avoid possible future clashes and difficulties between the two opposing Chinese forces if the Russian troops should withdraw from Manchuria. The matter was complicated by the continued delay in the withdrawal of Russian troops, resulting in suspicion on the part of the National Government of Russian intentions and aims in Manchuria and in the consequent inability of the National Government to assume control in that area.

With these circumstances in mind and as a result of reports of fighting at Yingkow, a port in south Manchuria, General Marshall proposed on January 24, 1946, that an Executive Headquarters field team be sent immediately to Yingkow and that in the event of future incidents of this kind similar action be taken.[10]   The National Government was unwilling to agree to this proposal, although the Chinese Communist Party gave its approval.   On February 20 General Marshall again, but without success, proposed that field teams be sent to Manchuria, pointing out the need of such teams both in stopping possible conflicts and in establishing a basis for the demobilization of the armies under the plan for military reorganization and integration.   While the Chinese Communist Party acquiesced in this proposal, the National Government remained adamant in spite of a deterioration of the situation in Manchuria.   At this stage the National Government seemed determined to incur no restraints on its freedom of action in Manchuria and appeared bent on a policy of complete military occupation of the area and elimination of the Chinese Communist forces if they were encountered, even though it did not have the military capability of achieving these objectives.

It was not until March 11, the day of General Marshall's departure for Washington, that the Generalissimo finally agreed to the entry of Executive Headquarters field teams into Manchuria, but with numerous conditions stipulated, so that agreement on a directive for the entry of the teams into Manchuria was not reached until March 27.[11] This directive was not, however, sufficiently broad to enable the teams to bring about a cessation of the fighting, which meanwhile was developing into a dangerous situation for the National Government forces.

In addition to this difficulty, there was a justified complaint by the Chinese Communists that the National Government commander at Canton had violated the terms of the cessation of hostilities order by refusing to recognize the authority of the Executive Headquarters in his area of command, and that the Supreme Headquarters of the National Government armies at Nanking had failed to carry out the specific stipulation of the cease-fire order to report all movements of the National Government troops to the Executive Headquarters at Peiping.   There had been, of course, a number of minor infractions of the cease-fire order by subordinate commanders on both sides. There was also a difficult problem in the north Hupeh–south Honan area where about 60,000 Communist troops, encircled by Government troops, were having difficulty in obtaining food supplies.

The extended delay in the sending of teams to Manchuria, caused first by the National Government's refusal to give its approval for such

---

[10] See annex 73.
[11] See annex 74.

action and later by the inability of the two Chinese representatives to agree on a suitable directive for the teams, had already resulted in a serious situation. The Chinese Communist Party in Manchuria was steadily extending the area of its control. The Russian withdrawal from Manchuria, originally scheduled to be completed by December 3, 1945, had been postponed until February 1, 1946, in accordance with an agreement between the Chinese and Soviet Governments. In early March, however, the Chinese Government formally requested the withdrawal of the Russian forces from Manchuria. Subsequent to this request, the Soviet Government agreed to the progressive and complete withdrawal of its armies beginning on April 6 and ending on April 29. When the Russian troops did withdraw toward the north, the National Government found itself with extended lines of communication and limited railroad rolling stock. Although it had approximately 137,000 troops in Manchuria and the adjoining areas of Jehol Province by mid-March, these were insufficient to move into all the areas evacuated by the Russian armies in time to prevent their occupation by the Chinese Communists. The Chinese Communist forces were moving both into areas from which Russian troops were withdrawing and into the hinterland between the lines of communication where there had been no occupation forces. The movement of National Government troops into and within Manchuria for the purpose of restoring Chinese sovereignty had been provided for in the cease-fire agreement. The entry of the Chinese Government forces had, however, been seriously impeded by the Russian refusal to permit their use of Dairen as the port of entry and their continued advance subsequent to their entry had been blocked by the delay in the Russian withdrawal. This delay also had the effect of giving the Chinese Communists time to build up their forces in Manchuria, which had apparently been reinforced by the movement of hastily organized or reinforced units from Chahar and Jehol Provinces. While these movements had begun in August and September 1945, there was evidence of the unauthorized continuation of the movement after January 13, 1946. Chinese Communist political infiltration was also facilitated by the delayed Russian withdrawal. In addition, the Chinese Communists were enabled to take over and put into use among their troops stores of weapons and military supplies possessed by the Japanese at the time of their surrender and made available directly or indirectly by the Russians.

Further delay and increased distrust between the National Government and the Chinese Communists had resulted from the actions of the National Government commander in Manchuria in seeking to establish military control in the rural areas removed from the main lines of communication, there being no Executive Headquarters field teams to moderate or regulate the procedure where National Government and Chinese Communist forces were in contact. These tactics had brought him in violent conflict with Chinese Communist forces in the hinterland, who were thus in a position to level the accusation that his chief aim was to eliminate their forces rather than to restore Chinese sovereignty in Manchuria.

This situation made a solution of the political impasse immeasurably more difficult, as it created considerable misgivings among the Chinese with regard to the relationship of the Chinese Communists to the Soviet Union and strengthened the position of irreconcilable elements within the Kuomintang, which would have been opposed to the political solution offered by the PCC resolutions under any circumstances. The situation in Manchuria, however, presented them with a plausible excuse for resisting any limitation of Kuomintang governmental authority under such circumstances. Chinese Communist resentment and suspicions, in turn, were aroused by the obvious intention of the National Government to assume complete military and political control in Manchuria through new administrative appointees for Manchurian posts from among the most anti-Communist elements in the Kuomintang.

In spite of the deterioration in the general situation, agreement was reached in the PCC Steering Committee on April 1 in regard to the National Assembly. Following this agreement, however, subsequent meetings of the PCC Steering Committee ended in a virtual stalemate and, with the worsening of the situation in Manchuria, it became apparent that no real settlement of governmental and constitutional questions in China could be reached so long as the Manchurian problem remained unsolved. This meant an indefinite postponement of the National Assembly, originally scheduled for May 5. Matters were further complicated by the continued refusal of the Chinese Communist Party to submit a complete list of its military units in accordance with the Military Reorganization Agreement of February 25.

In spite of agreement authorizing the entry of Executive Headquarters field teams into Manchuria, the National Government offered obstructions to the functioning of the teams, first by the refusal of the Commanding General in Manchuria to permit the teams to enter Manchuria and later by the refusal of the National Government members of the teams to take any action on the basis that they had no authority. It was not until April 8 that the field teams proceeded to areas of conflict in Manchuria, where the situation was complicated by developments connected with the Russian withdrawal. Subsequent to their withdrawal from Mukden, for example, the Russian military authorities refused to approve the National Government's use of the rail line north toward Changchun for the transportation of Chinese troops, alleging that it was prohibited by the terms of the Sino-Soviet Treaty of August 1945.   It was also reported that the Russian authorities had rejected a request by the Chinese Government for the retention of small Russian garrisons in the points then being evacuated by Russian troops until the National Government's troops should arrive to take over sovereignty at such places.

Another phase of the Manchurian situation, one which was the subject of frequent propaganda attacks by the Chinese Communist Party, was the transportation of National Government troops by American facilities.   On March 31 the Chinese Communists protested the further transportation of Chinese Government armies into Manchuria by American vessels on the ground that the military reorganization plan of February 25 restricted the number of Government troops in Manchuria to 5 armies.   It was pointed out to General Chou En-lai that the limitation of Government troops in Manchuria, set forth in the military reorganization plan, was not to be effective until the end of 12 months and that the movement of National Government armies into Manchuria had been authorized by the cessation of hostilities order of January 10.

CHINESE COMMUNIST OCCUPATION OF CHANGCHUN

On April 15, 1946, the day after the withdrawal of Russian troops from Changchun, the Chinese Communist forces attacked the city, and occupied it on April 18.   This action was a flagrant violation of the cessation of hostilities order and an act which was to have serious consequences.   It made the victorious Chinese Communist generals in Manchuria overconfident and less amenable to compromise, but even more disastrous was the effect upon the National Government. It greatly strengthened the hand of the ultra-reactionary groups in the Government, which were then in a position to say that the Communists had demonstrated that they never intended to carry out their agreements.

At the time of General Marshall's return to China on April 18, the impasse was complete, except that the Chinese Communists were willing to submit the future military dispositions and local political reorganization to negotiations if the fighting were terminated.   The National Government declined such compromises, on the grounds that the cessation of hostilities order clearly gave National Government troops the right to proceed anywhere in Manchuria necessary to establish sovereignty, and stated that negotiations regarding political questions would be considered only after sovereignty had been established along the railway mentioned in the Sino-Soviet Treaty of August

1945. The Government was militarily powerless, however, to enforce such demands. General Marshall submitted a proposal to the Generalissimo in keeping with what he believed to be the Generalissimo's view that the Government could not and would not advance farther north, but discovered that the Generalissimo had in mind the use of force to occupy Changchun and overpower the Chinese Communist troops in that region.

At the beginning of May the Generalissimo finally came to the point of proposing the same conditions for a settlement of the Manchurian problems that the Chinese Communists had actually proposed about six weeks earlier, before the Communists had captured Changchun. It was also demanded that Chinese Communist forces evacuate Changchun and permit Government troops to occupy it, indicating that following the occupation of Changchun negotiations would begin regarding military dispositions and political reorganization.

The successful Chinese Communist commanders in the Changchun region, however, had been strengthened by their acquisition of Japanese military equipment and stores, including medium artillery and tanks, while the National Government's military position grew weaker as its forces advanced, owing to the great distances over which its troops had to move in proceeding northward. The Chinese Communists therefore did not accept the Government's terms and General Chou En-lai urged General Marshall to withdraw shipping support from the National Government armies in order to force the hand of the Generalissimo. The Generalissimo's advisers were urging a policy of force which they were not capable of carrying out, even with American logistical support and the presence of United States Marines in the North China ports of Tsingtao and Tientsin and up the railway line toward the port of Chinhuangtao, from which the coal essential for the industries of the lower Yangtze Valley area was shipped south.

GENERAL MARSHALL'S APPRAISAL OF THE SITUATION

In conversations with National Government leaders General Marshall endeavored to emphasize the seriousness of the situation. He pointed out that many of the existing difficulties could have been avoided earlier by the National Government but that the situation was now reversed; that there was a complete lack of faith and a feeling of distrust on both sides and that each side saw behind all proposals from the other an evil motive; that the National Government had blocked the sending of field teams into Manchuria which might have been able to control the situation; that while the Communists said that the cessation of hostilities order of January 10 applied to all of

China, the National Government resisted its application to Manchuria; that when the National Government troops moved into Manchuria they attempted to destroy the Chinese Communist forces in the hinterland; and that the Generalissimo's military advisers had shown very poor judgment. He continued that in many instances the National Government authorities had offered opportunities to the Communist Party to make accusations against their good faith: (1) the situation north of Hankow, where Communist troops were surrounded by large Government concentrations; (2) the movement of Government troops toward Chihfeng, Jehol Province, under orders issued by the National Government military headquarters at Chungking in violation of the cease-fire order; (3) the refusal of the Commanding General at Canton to recognize the existence of Communist troops in that area as well as the orders of the Executive Headquarters and the National Government at Chungking regarding Executive Headquarters' investigation of the situation in this area; (4) the failure of the National Government Army Headquarters to submit daily reports of its troop movements south of the Yangtze River, as was clearly required by the cessation of hostilities order; (5) the search of homes of Chinese Communist Party personnel and closure of Chinese Communist newspaper offices at Peiping; (6) the "buzzing" of the airfield at Yenan by National Government planes; and (7) the detention of Chinese Communist field team personnel at the airfield at Mukden. General Marshall characterized these acts as stupid actions of no benefit to the National Government, which not only served as ammunition to the Chinese Communists, but, what was far more serious, stimulated their suspicion of Government intentions. He said that the Kuomintang had had an opportunity to have peace in Manchuria but had not utilized the opportunity, and concluded that the Chinese Communists were now taking advantage of the existing situation and were becoming stronger daily, thus placing the National Government in a very dangerous military position with over-extended lines and a constantly increasing dispersion of forces.

The reaction of the Chinese Communists was revealed by their desire to change the ratio of military strength in Manchuria. General Chou En-lai informed General Marshall that the Communist Party wished to revise the ratio of 1 Communist division to 14 Government divisions in Manchuria provided for in the military reorganization agreement at the end of 18 months, and was adamantly opposed to the movement of additional Government troops in Manchuria. General Marshall explained that, when the United States had completed the movement of the seven National Government armies into Manchuria which it was committed to transport to that area, a total of 228,000

Government troops would have been moved by American facilities. However, the total National Government strength at the end of 12 months authorized for Manchuria in the military reorganization agreement would be approximately 240,000 men.

In further discussions with General Chou En-lai, General Marshall stated that in his opinion the fundamental difference between the positions of the two sides lay in the question of sovereignty in Manchuria; that sovereignty implied control and control could not be held by the National Government unless it occupied Changchun; and that the Generalissimo had made a significant concession to the Chinese Communists by his willingness to hold open for negotiation problems relating to the remainder of Manchuria provided the Communist forces evacuated Changchun. He further stated that he had done his best in an effort to negotiate this critical problem but that the matter had virtually passed out of his hands. He added that he did not see that he could accomplish anything more through mediation, since at that time his position in endeavoring to persuade the Government to take various actions had been heavily compromised by the Communist attack on Changchun.

GENERAL MARSHALL'S TEMPORARY WITHDRAWAL FROM MEDIATION

At this point General Marshall withdrew from formal mediation between the two parties for a settlement of the Manchurian problem. He did, however, continue to hold separate conferences with representatives of the two sides and to act as a channel of communication between them. The diminishing effectiveness of the Executive Headquarters field teams was a matter of particular concern at this time. Executive Headquarters reports during this period revealed the complete opposition of the Communist members, at the operations level in the Headquarters and in the field teams, toward any common sense action which should be taken by the teams. United States Army officers had originally been impressed by the high degree of cooperation by the Communists, but the Communist tactics of blocking action had lowered American confidence in their sincerity. In view of these difficulties the Committee of Three discussed the matter and on May 14 reached agreement on a document designed to ensure more prompt investigation of reported violations of the cessation of hostilities order.[12]

During his discussions with National Government leaders, General Marshall continued to point out that the time element was of great importance. The situation in North China was becoming more serious

---

[12] See annex 75.

with two major irritants affecting the situation there—the unsettled question of the destruction of railway fortifications and the failure of the National Government to report its routine troop movements to the Executive Headquarters. The situation in North China was, of course, dominated by the outcome in Manchuria, and continued failure to find a solution in Manchuria would probably make the Executive Headquarters completely ineffective. A solution was made more difficult by the repeated insistence of the Generalissimo in discussions with General Marshall that he would not sign or agree to any settlement that did not provide for evacuation of Changchun by the Communists and its occupation by the Government and that he would accept nothing less than complete National Government sovereignty in Manchuria. Under these circumstances General Marshall considered it unwise for him to re-enter the negotiations in the capacity of mediator, since there was no basis for agreement by the Chinese Communist Party and he did not wish to be placed in a position where he would have no power to avert an otherwise certain stalemate.

SUGGESTED COMPROMISE SOLUTION

At the request of the Generalissimo for his views General Marshall suggested that a compromise solution of the Manchurian issues be reached which would provide for Communist withdrawal from Changchun and the establishment of an advance echelon of the Executive Headquarters at that city as a basis for terminating the fighting preliminary to entering into negotiations. This solution would also envisage the occupation of Changchun by the Government troops within a maximum time of six months, preferably much sooner. General Marshall's conclusions as communicated to the Generalissimo, were as follows:

The Government's military position was weak in Manchuria and the Communists had the strategical advantage there. The psychological effect of a compromise on the part of the Government to achieve peace would not injure its prestige but would indicate that the Generalissimo was making every effort to promote peace. The proposal to utilize the Executive Headquarters in Changchun would bolster the conviction that the Generalissimo was striving for peace. Finally some compromise must be reached as quickly as possible or China would be faced with a chaotic situation, militarily, financially and economically.

General Marshall suggested the same general solution on May 13 to General Chou En-lai, who said that he would transmit the proposal to Yenan. General Marshall emphasized that, unless he could be reasonably certain of the position of the Communist Party on military and political issues, it would be impossible for him to resume the role of mediator and that he could not again place himself in the position of being a party to an agreement which included provision for negotiations regarding vital or fundamental differences unless he had reasonable assurance of a favorable outcome. The Chinese Communist reply to this proposal indicated apprehension that the Government might raise the question of other cities, such as Harbin, once it occupied Changchun. The Communists also stated that they desired to have five divisions in Manchuria instead of the one division authorized in the military reorganization agreement.

Daily discussions between the Generalissimo and General Marshall were held at this time regarding the detailed terms for a military settlement, the redistribution of troops as a condition precedent to the issuance of a cease-fire order, and tentative arrangements whereby the Communists would voluntarily evacuate Changchun and an advance section of the Executive Headquarters would assume control of the city, pending a further settlement of problems relating to Changchun and the areas north of that city. On May 22 the Generalissimo informed General Marshall that he had not heard from his military commanders in Manchuria for three days and that he feared that following their capture of Ssupingchieh on May 19 (after fighting lasting over a month) they were advancing toward Changchun. The Generalissimo expressed agreement with General Marshall's view that occupation of Changchun at a time when the basis of an agreement with the Communists was practically completed would be inadvisable and said that he was leaving for Mukden on May 24 in order to keep control of the situation. General Marshall pointed out the danger of a delay and expressed the hope that the Generalissimo would return as soon as possible in order that the negotiations could be carried to completion. Generalissimo Chiang Kai-shek departed for Mukden on May 23, his departure on this 11-day trip being the first of a chain of events which were almost completely disastrous in their effect on the situation. The fact that the Generalissimo requested and received the use of General Marshall's official airplane for the trip served to heighten the public impression of General Marshall's close connection with the trip and to add to the embarrassment that later developed.

On May 23 General Marshall conveyed to General Chou En-lai three points set forth by the Generalissimo prior to his departure as conditions precedent to any general agreement: (1) The Chinese Communist Party must make every effort to facilitate the restoration of communications; (2) in any agreement regarding Manchurian issues, provision must be made for carrrying out the military demobilization and reorganization plan within specified dates; and (3) the Generalissimo would not commit himself to further agreements without an understanding that when field teams or high staff groups reached an impasse, the final decision would be left to the American member. General Marshall also asked General Chou En-lai whether the Communist Party would agree to the proposal for the evacuation of Changchun by the Communist troops, the entry into Changchun of the advance section of the Executive Headquarters, and the cessation of further advances of Government troops.

General Chou En-lai stated that the Communist Party would agree to the three proposals suggested by General Marshall but that the Generalissimo's three conditions were new. He added that he would endeavor to solve the communications problem with the National Government representative and that he had no objection to the second condition. With respect to authority for decision by American members, he said that this would have to be discussed with his associates.

NATIONAL GOVERNMENT CAPTURE OF CHANGCHUN

On May 23 the National Government's forces entered Changchun, following a Communist withdrawal from that city and little or no opposition from the Communist forces after the Government capture of Ssupingchieh on May 19. The absence of the Generalissimo from Nanking and the difficulty of communication with him by General Marshall made for an extremely unsatisfactory situation at a most critical moment. The Generalissimo's presence in Mukden at the time of the capture of Changchun conveyed the impression of a journey timed to coincide with a previously planned military triumph, and public pronouncements by the Generalissimo in Mukden tended to heighten this impression. In spite of General Marshall's appeals by radio for the issuance of an order for the cessation of offensive operations, the Generalissimo took no action toward that end, although his earlier insistence had been on the evacuation of Changchun and its occupation by Government forces as a precedent to further negotiation and the issuance of a cease-fire order. To make matters more serious, the Government troops, after their occupation of Changchun, continued to advance north along the rail line toward Harbin and toward Kirin to the east, and the result was to increase Communist suspicion and distrust of Government promises and to place General Marshall's impartial position as a possible mediator in a questionable light insofar as the Communists were concerned. The positions were now reversed. Where formerly difficulties arose from the Communist attack on Changchun in open violation of the cease-fire order and the consequent stronger stand taken by the Chinese Communist generals in Manchuria, the new situation played directly into the hands of the National Government military commanders in Manchuria, who now felt certain that they could settle the problem by force and were therefore disinclined to compromise with the Communists.

GENERALISSIMO CHIANG'S PROPOSALS OF MAY 24, 1946

On May 24 the Generalissimo forwarded to General Marshall from Mukden his formal conditions for the restoration of peace. He demanded the execution of the cessation of hostilities agreement of January 10, which specifically related to freedom of action for the Nanking Government in taking over sovereignty in Manchuria, and of the agreement for military reorganization of February 25. The Generalissimo placed first importance on a Communist demonstration of good faith by permitting National Government agencies to restore communications in North China and stipulated again that in the Executive Headquarters and its field teams American members should cast the deciding vote. He also asked General Marshall whether he would guarantee Communist good faith in carrying out agreements. No mention was made by the Generalissimo of his intention or willingness to issue an order halting troop movements or to agree to the establishment of an advance section of the Executive Headquarters at Changchun, both of which had been proposed by General Marshall at the time of the Generalissimo's departure for Mukden with the suggestion that the Generalissimo might reach a decision while in Mukden and inform General Marshall.

General Marshall, therefore, dispatched a message to the Generalissimo at Mukden requesting explanatory details regarding his general statements, proposing the immediate movement of a section of the Executive Headquarters to Changchun and urging him to issue an order immediately directing the cessation of attacks, pursuits, or advances while the details of a truce were being arranged. General Marshall urged him to avoid the painful results of previous mistakes in forging ahead in Manchuria without granting permission for the presence of field teams to prevent unnecessary skirmishing and the more recent unfortunate results of the attitude of the belligerent Chinese Communist commanders at Changchun. General Marshall also asked for an explanation of the meaning of the Generalissimo's use of the word "guarantee" in reference to General Marshall's role.

On May 28 the Generalissimo again communicated with General Marshall, repeating the terms previously set forth but agreeing to a qualification General Marshall had suggested regarding the power of decision of Americans in the Executive Headquarters and its field teams. The Generalissimo also stated that, with respect to the method of recovering sovereignty in Manchuria, the National Government could not abandon the taking over of administration in any area, but might agree to send forward, after military advances had ceased, only administrative officials and such military and police forces as would be absolutely necessary for the maintenance of local order and communications. He explained that, by use of the word "guarantee," he meant that General Marshall would set time limits for putting into effect all agreements which General Marshall had signed and would assume the responsibility of supervision over the strict observance of such agreements on the part of the Chinese Communists.

Not having received this second message from the Generalissimo, on May 29 General Marshall sent a further message to the Generalissimo at Mukden, informing him that the continued advances of the National Government troops in Manchuria in the absence of any action to terminate the fighting, other than the terms indicated by him in his first message from Mukden, was making General Marshall's services as a possible mediator extremely difficult and might soon make them virtually impossible. No reply having been received to this message,[13] General Marshall dispatched an additional message to the Generalissimo on May 31 at Peiping, where the latter had just arrived, repeating the substance of his previous message and stating that a point was being reached where the integrity of his position was open to serious question. General Marshall again requested the Generalissimo, therefore, to issue immediately an order terminating advances, attacks or pursuits by the National Government troops and to authorize the immediate departure of an advance section of the Executive Headquarters to Changchun.

In a message of June 1 from Peiping the Generalissimo informed General Marshall that in all decisions he had kept in mind the difficulty of General Marshall's position and was doing everything in his power to facilitate and assure the success of his work. He said that he was prepared to agree to the proposal to send an advance section of the Executive Headquarters to Changchun in the event of his not being able immediately to issue orders to National Government troops to terminate their advance.

During this period General Marshall continued to have conferences with General Chou En-lai, National Government leaders, and representatives of the minority parties. These representatives had offered certain proposals for settlement of the Manchurian problem, but they were not approved by either the National Government or the Chinese Communist Party.

---

[13] It later developed that General Marshall's message of May 29 had missed the Generalissimo in Mukden and was long delayed in delivery.

ARRANGEMENTS FOR A TRUCE

On June 3 the Generalissimo returned to Nanking. A discussion of the situation with General Marshall indicated that a misunderstanding on the part of the Generalissimo caused by mistranslation of General Marshall's message had prevented the immediate establishment of an advance section of the Executive Headquarters in Changchun. General Marshall, therefore, immediately directed its establishment. The Generalissimo agreed to issue an order to his armies in Manchuria to cease advances, attacks or pursuits—in other words. aggressive action—for a period of ten days to afford the Communists an opportunity to prove their sincerity by completing negotiations with the National Government during that period on the following points: (1) detailed arrangements to govern a complete termination of hostilities in Manchuria; (2) definite detailed arrangements, with time limits, for the complete resumption of communications in North China; and (3) a basis for carrying out without further delay the agreement for military reorganization of February 25.

The Generalissimo first stipulated one week in which to complete these negotiations but finally agreed to a period of 10 days. He informed General Marshall that this would be his final effort at doing business with the Communists, that the present indeterminate situation with communications blocked, coal barely obtainable in sufficient quantities, and cities starving, could not be endured economically or otherwise, and that all-out war would be preferable.

When the Generalissimo's terms were presented to General Chou En-lai by General Marshall, General Chou immediately asked for an extension of the 10 days to one month but finally reduced his request to 15 days on the ground that there were many complicated plans to be agreed to and General Chou would have to fly to Yenan at least once for conferences with Chinese Communist leaders.

On June 6 the Generalissimo and the Chinese Communist Party issued separate announcements of orders halting advances, attacks, or pursuits by their troops in Manchuria for a 15-day period beginning at noon on June 7.[13a] They also announced that during this period agreements were to be reached regarding arrangements for the complete termination of hostilities in Manchuria, complete resumption of communications in China, and execution without delay of the agreement for military reorganization of February 25.

Constant negotiations followed the promulgation of these orders. General Chou En-lai consulted the Communist leaders in Yenan and returned to Nanking for discussions. An agreement for the resump-

---

[13a] See annex 76.

tion of communications was reached after detailed discussions.[14] Little trouble was anticipated in reaching agreement on the detailed arrangements for formal termination of hostilities in Manchuria. The great difficulties to be resolved related to demobilization, reorganization, and particularly redistribution of troops, especially in Manchuria and Shantung Province. General Marshall's problems during this period also related to sporadic but violent fighting in various localities, mostly in North China, which could not be halted on short notice, since many of the actions had evidently been planned and ordered a week or more in advance.

The rather virulent Communist propaganda attacks against the United States and the alleged support by General Marshall of the National Government in the fighting at this time were due to a continuation of an effort (1) to arouse American opposition to any military representation in China and (2) to offset in the United States the effect of the Generalissimo's proposal to give American officers the deciding vote in case of disagreements. The fact that just as an agreement seemed to be on the verge of being reached the Generalissimo remained absent in Mukden and Peiping for a considerable period while his armies exploited their successful action south of Changchun aroused great suspicion against his good faith and particularly against the impartiality of General Marshall's attitude, since General Marshall had advanced proposals to the Chinese Communists for Communist evacuation of Changchun and the cessation of further advances by National Government troops which the Communists had accepted.

NEGOTIATIONS DURING THE TRUCE PERIOD

Negotiations during the truce period proceeded very slowly, due to the reluctance of either side to commit itself in advance of the other regarding reorganization and particularly redistribution of troops. Fighting in Shantung Province, arising from a Communist offensive at the beginning of the truce period and lasting for about a week, proved to be a very disturbing factor, causing increased bitterness and unwillingness to make concessions.

Several members of the PCC asked General Marshall to suggest the convening of the PCC Steering Committee at this time to work simultaneously on political problems while the Committee of Three handled the military problems. General Marshall informed them that this did not come within the scope of his authority. The Generalissimo had often said that he would not negotiate on political problems

---

[14] See annex 77.

until he had occupied Manchuria. He had, however, later said that after Government occupation of Changchun he would be prepared to negotiate both political and military questions. General Chou En-lai indicated that it would be preferable to omit discussion of political matters and to preserve the *status quo* in the various areas. He pointed out to General Marshall that, although the latter had been reluctant to accept the Generalissimo's proposal that the Committee of Three be empowered to solve administrative problems, he felt that this matter should be given further consideration. He added that, since General Marshall did not wish to be involved in political decisions, the problem could be solved by action to be taken by the reorganized Government.

On June 17 the Generalissimo indicated to General Marshall, for transmission to General Chou En-lai, the nature of his demands. The National Government proposals required the evacuation of Chinese Communist forces from Jehol and Chahar Provinces before September 1, 1946; the occupation by Government forces of Chefoo and Weihaiwai in Shantung Province; the reinforcement of Tsingtao with one National Government army to permit the withdrawal of the United States Marines stationed at that city; the evacuation by the Chinese Communists before July 1, 1946, of all localities in Shantung Province forcibly occupied by Communist troops after noon of June 7, 1946; the immediate occupation of these localities by Government garrisons; and the reinforcement of the Tientsin region by one Government army, commencing September 1, 1946, to permit the withdrawal of the United States Marine forces in that area. With respect to Manchuria, the National Government proposals provided for Government occupation of various points then held by Communist forces, such as Harbin, Antung, Tunghwa, Mutankiang, and Paicheng.

General Chou En-lai, after preliminary study of these proposals, informed General Marshall that they were entirely too demanding to admit of acceptance by the Chinese Communist Party. He stated that, except for the restoration of the *status quo* in Shantung Province prior to June 7, none of the points could be considered, and pointed out that the date of June 7 should be applied to Manchuria only, in accordance with the orders issued by both sides halting advances, attacks or pursuits by their troops in Manchuria, beginning on that date, while the restoration of original positions in China proper should be based on January 13, in accordance with the cessation of hostilities order of January 10. General Marshall also discussed the situation with the Generalissimo and told him that there seemed to be no likelihood that the Chinese Communists would accept his terms without considerable modification. General Marshall had suggested to General Chou En-lai that he fly to Yenan to consult with the leaders of his party, but after General Chou held a conference with Nationalist Government officials he stated that nothing had occurred in this conference to justify a trip to Yenan.

The principal stumbling block presented by the National Government proposals did not appear to be in regard to readjustments in Manchuria. Communist resentment was more aroused by the National Government stipulations regarding North China, which required Communist evacuation of provinces and cities then under their occupation and subsequent entry of Government troops into these areas.

The negotiations had again reached an impasse, and there remained only a few days before the truce period would expire. The situation was extremely critical and had not been helped throughout by the belief, freely expressed by some of the National Government military officers and politicians, that only a policy of force would satisfy the situation and that the Chinese Communists could be quickly crushed. General Marshall considered the latter view a gross underestimate of the possibilities, as a long and terrible conflict would be unavoidable, and conveyed his views to the Generalissimo on this subject.

At the suggestion of General Marshall, the Generalissimo agreed to extend the truce period until noon of June 30 for the purpose of permitting further time to negotiate matters referred to in his original 15-day truce order. At the same time the Generalissimo presented two additional terms: (1) The Communists were to withdraw from the Tsinan-Tsingtao Railway before August 1, 1946, and (2) the procedure of unanimous vote in the Committee of Three and the Executive Headquarters was to be revised before June 30, 1946.

Negotiations during the extended truce period proceeded in formal meetings of the Committee of Three with some prospect of success. These meetings marked the formal re-entry of General Marshall into the negotiations as mediator. The Chinese Communists made concessions in granting the deciding vote to Americans on teams and in Executive Headquarters regarding matters pertaining to cessation of hostilities procedures, interpretation of agreements, and their execution. This did not apply, however, to the Committee of Three, since General Marshall thought that the United States Government should not bear the heavy responsibility through his actions in regard to matters of great importance beyond the interpretation of agreements.

It was difficult to predict the rate of progress and eventual outcome because of the effect of heavy sporadic fighting, the carelessly expressed desire of some important Government leaders to settle issues by force, unfortunate propaganda, and mutual suspicion and distrust.

On June 24, the Committee of Three reached agreement on a document entitled "Stipulations for the Resolution of Certain Disagreements among the Field and Communication Teams, and Executive Headquarters in Changchun and Peiping." [15]   Under this agreement certain authority was granted to American officers on teams and at the Executive Headquarters which was expected to facilitate greatly control of the situation in areas of hostilities in the future.   The most difficult problem was that of redisposition and reduction of troops in Manchuria and North and Central China.   The Manchurian phase then seemed to be the least difficult to compose.

CESSATION OF HOSTILITIES IN MANCHURIA

By June 26 an agreement had been reached in the Committee of Three for the cessation of hostilities in Manchuria, entitled "Directive for the Termination of Hostilities in Manchuria." [16]   This Directive provided for the application to Manchuria of the cessation of hostilities agreement of January 10, except as modified in the Directive or later by the Committee of Three; for the separation from contact of troops in close or hostile contact; for the readjustment of troops on the basis of the situation believed to have existed at noon of June 7, 1946; for the cessation of all tactical movements; for the punishment of commanders who failed to carry out the terms of the Directive; and for the submission by both sides to the Advance Section of the Executive Headquarters, within 15 days of the effective date of the Directive, of lists of all units, strengths and locations in Manchuria.

Agreement on this document marked the settlement of the second of the three major issues to be decided during the 15-day truce period, which had now been extended to June 30.   It was understood, however, that agreements on individual issues would not be operative unless agreement on all major issues was reached in accordance with a stipulation to that effect by the Generalissimo.

REVISION OF THE MILITARY REORGANIZATION AGREEMENT AND RELATED POLITICAL PROBLEMS

When the discussions revealed the impossibility of reaching agreement for revision of the basic military reorganization agreement of February 25 prior to the expiration of the extended truce period, negotiations were centered on a preliminary agreement covering only the principal issues, with the understanding that formal revision would be negotiated after the completion of the preliminary document.

[15] See annex 78.
[16] See annex 79.

The question of troop dispositions was complicated by the fact that little demobilization had taken place in North China. The National Government had confined its demobilization to South and West China and further demobilization would be largely confined to North China and Manchuria. This National Government demobilization had been carried out by reducing divisions which lacked full strength to brigades, the officer personnel of divisions headquarters and headquarters troops having been demobilized. The real point was that under the present Government proposals very heavy troop demobilization on both sides would be involved between July 1, 1946, and January 1, 1947.

On June 21, General Chou En-lai had stated that the Chinese Communist Party proposed that: (1) the Committee of Three should immediately stop the fighting in Manchuria and China proper and a new order for the termination of hostilities should be issued with the additional stipulation that American members of field teams should have the power to execute this order and to decide upon investigations to be made by the teams; (2) after the cessation of fighting, the Committee of Three should work out a plan for the restoration of communications and the Chinese Communists pledged that the repair of railways would have first priority; (3) after the cessation of hostilities, the Committee should work out arrangements for the reorganization and demobilization of armies in all China, including Manchuria, and the staffs of both parties under the leadership of the American staff should work out a plan for the Committee of Three's approval; and (4) a second session of the Committee of Three should be convened to discuss the reorganization of the Government, the protection of the people's rights and a solution of the people's livelihood, and local governments should be reorganized and elections held. General Chou expressed the belief that the Generalissimo was most concerned over the problems of army reorganization, integration, and training and pointed out that the Generalissimo presented demands in connection with these problems which caused concern to the Chinese Communist Party because if the Chinese Communist Party accepted these demands there would still be no assurances on the many other problems which had not been discussed. General Chou considered this the crucial point at issue. He suggested, therefore, that during the period of army reorganization the Communist troops be reorganized in Communist areas and Government troops in Government territory and that training be carried out by American officers, who, he said, were trusted by both sides, the two forces to be brought together and integrated after this interim period.

General Marshall pointed out to General Chou that the Generalissimo had stated very clearly, in his announcement of the truce period on June 6, that a basis should be established for carrying out without further delay the agreement of February 25 for the demobilization, reorganization and integration of Chinese armies and that the Generalissimo had this in mind when he presented his proposals. General Marshall emphasized that there must be a definite understanding of Chinese Communist demands regarding the redistribution of troops in North China and that this should have been decided upon in March and April, when the Chinese Communists were to have submitted a list of their troops for demobilization. He continued that the National Government had submitted such lists but the Communist Party had not done so. In the absence of these lists, the staffs had been unable to draw up a plan for troop redistribution in North China.

After learning of the decision of the Generalissimo to extend the truce period, General Chou En-lai agreed to include the questions of redistribution of troops in North and Central China in the agenda for discussion since this problem was the greatest gap between the two parties. In conversations on this subject, General Marshall pointed out that when General Chou referred to the attitude of Government military commanders in Manchuria, he should remember General Marshall's statements about the Chinese Communist generals in Manchuria at the time of their occupation of Changchun, and that he should also remember that he himself had frequently used the expression "conditions have changed" in justifying some proposal, just as this expression was now being used by the National Government in presenting its new stipulations.

On June 26 General Marshall informed General Chou that the Government, pursuant to the Communist Party demand, was willing to agree to a revision of troop strengths in Manchuria to allow the Communists to have 3 divisions as against the Government's 15 divisions but would not agree to 5 Communist divisions.

General Chou said that the Chinese Communist Party's difficulty was that, while it was entering into agreements on military matters, it did not know what the Government attitude would be later in regard to political questions. He then explained the views of the Chinese Communist Party as follows:

Army units would have no connection with civil administration, and after the reorganization of the Central Government and local governments the Communist armies would be assembled in areas under Communist control and Government armies in areas under its control. The army would be separated from civil administration through the establishment of local self-government and elections. The Government view that political administration should be adjusted according to the identity of the troops in control of a particular area was a violation of the principle of subordination of the army to civil administration. Under the Government proposals, Government troops would in many cases move into Communist areas and change the civil administrations. The movement of Government armies into Communist-held areas for the purpose of demobilization would mean occupation of Communist territory through negotiation as a substitute for occupation by force. This procedure was incompatible with the PCC resolutions on this subject and with the general agreements. The Communists were willing to withdraw from some areas in order to erase Government fear of a Communist threat, but such areas should be left ungarrisoned. Both Jehol and Shantung Provinces were largely under Communist control and it was more logical to expect the Government to evacuate these provinces than to demand that the Communists do so.

On June 27 the Generalissimo told General Marshall that political adjustments were at this time difficult, if not impossible, unless military readjustments were effected as a means of avoiding clashes, and presented specific proposals for such readjustments: The Chinese Communist Party should, within ten days, evacuate north Kiangsu Province, the Tsinan-Tsingtao Railway, Chengte and Kupeikou, Antung Province, and Harbin, these places to be occupied by Government troops within one month; the Communists should withdraw in one month from other places to be evacuated, but the entry of Government troops might be delayed for two or three months; and as a compromise measure, Communist officials in Hsin Heilungchiang, Hsingan, and Nenchiang Provinces in Manchuria, and Chahar Province, might be accepted by the Government as a temporary arrangement which would receive consideration at the time of political reorganization.

In commenting upon the Generalissimo's terms, General Chou En-lai expressed the following views: Garrison troops must not interfere with the local administration in areas where they were stationed. While the Chinese Communist Party was willing to consider a readjustment regarding Harbin and the detailed problems involved in stationing Government and Communist troops in specified areas, it was not in a position to accept the Government claim to the Tsinan-Tsingtao Railway, Chengte, Kupeikou, and the other places. However, if the Government felt that the Communist forces along the rail line in north Kiangsu and Shantung constituted a menace to the Government, the Communists were willing to reduce their forces in such areas or withdraw them altogether, but the Government troops should not enter Communist areas.   The Communists were willing to garrison north Kiangsu with a small force by reducing the number of troops provided for in the military reorganization agreement of February 25. They would withdraw their forces from the Tsinan-Tsingtao Railway if the Government would agree to garrison only Tsinan, Weihsien, and Tsingtao. All Communist troops would be withdrawn from the Tsaochuang coal mines, leaving no garrison troops and freeing the railway line for operation in connection with the coal mines, the latter to be controlled by a committee established for that purpose.   These withdrawals should, however, in no way prejudice the local administrations established by the Communists in those areas.

Subsequent conversations on the subject of troop dispositions indicated that the Government was adamant regarding its demand for the withdrawal of Communist forces from Chengte and for the stationing at Yenki of the Communist forces in eastern Manchuria and was insistent on having sizable Government garrison troops in Harbin. The Communist Party was equally adamant that areas to be evacuated by the Communists during the period of army reorganization should not be occupied by Government forces.

GENERAL MARSHALL'S DRAFT AGREEMENT ON THE ARMY REORGANIZATION PLAN

After these discussions General Marshall drew up a draft proposal entitled "Preliminary Agreement to Govern the Amendment and Execution of the Army Reorganization Plan of February 25, 1946" [17] as a basis of discussion by the two Chinese sides with the hope that agreement might be reached on this final document prior to the expiration of the extended truce period on noon of June 30.   As stated in the document, it established conditions for the purpose of committing the National Government and the Chinese Communist Party to certain understandings in order to facilitate the preparation and acceptance of the formal documents required and to permit the immediate issuance of instructions for the final termination of hostilities.

The chief points of this document were:

1. Provision for the specific disposition of Government and Communist troops, by definite localities, in Manchuria and China proper.

2. No change in 5-to-1 ratio of troop strengths.

3. The previously established period of 12 months for the assignment of troops to specified localities to be altered to 6 months.

4. The Executive Headquarters to determine immediately localities occupied by Government and Communist forces in China proper since

---

[17] See annex 80.

January 13, 1946, and troops involved to evacuate such areas within 20 days, unless specifically directed otherwise.

5. The Executive Headquarters to determine immediate localities occupied by Government and Communist forces in Manchuria after noon of June 7, 1946, and troops involved to evacuate such areas within 10 days unless specifically directed otherwise.

6. The Communist Party to agree to a Government garrison in Harbin of 5,000 men.

7. The Communist Party to concentrate its troops in specified localities, Government troops not to move into areas vacated in China proper and existing local governments and Peace Preservation Corps for maintenance of local security to be continued.

An annex to this document specified areas in which Communist troops were not to be garrisoned or concentrated, leaving for discussion the time period within which these troops were to be withdrawn.

In commenting on this draft proposal, the Generalissimo expressed unwillingness to confine paragraph 5 to Manchuria only. Regarding paragraph 6, which dealt with the status of Harbin, he agreed to appoint a civilian mayor and to name a person acceptable to the Communist Party. In regard to paragraph 7 he first expressed complete disapproval and his final attitude was not clearly indicated. He agreed to Communist local governments, but could not accept such an arrangement in Kiangsu Province because of the numerous refugees, who, he said, would be mistreated by the existing local governments. He accepted the idea of Peace Preservation Corps on the basis of strengths similar to those of local security troops in a *hsien*. The Generalissimo would not accept partial occupation by the Government of north Kiangsu but insisted that the Communist evacuation should be carried out as far north as Huaian within 6 weeks and, within 3 to 6 months, north of the Lunghai Railway. He also stipulated that the Communist evacuation of the Tsinan-Tsingtao Railway should include the coal mines along that line, particularly Poshan (on a spur running south from Changtien). He was unbending in regard to the Communist evacuation of Chengte and said that the Communists should evacuate areas in Jehol Province south of the latitude of Chengte within 1 month and the city itself within 3 months. He stipulated that Antung Province should be evacuated within 1 month and concluded that a paragraph should be added to the document requiring the completion of amendments to the military reorganization of February 25 within 10 days. In regard to the Manchuria Annex,[18] which had been presented to General Chou En-lai on June 17 with National Government approval as an annex to the amendment of the

---

[18] See annex 81.

agreement of February 25, the Generalissimo stated that the entire demobilization and integration program in Manchuria should be completed before November 1, 1946, the original document having provided for its completion by January 1, 1947.

On June 29 General Chou En-lai commented as follows to General Marshall on this document and the reservations of the Generalissimo to the document: The Chinese Communist Party could not agree to the Generalissimo's desire to make an exception of north Kiangsu, although it would be willing to station only minimum forces in that area. Nor was the Communist Party in a position to accept the time limits desired by the Generalissimo because it was not sufficiently informed of actual conditions to know how much time would be required to effect the concentration of Communist troops in the areas indicated. He suggested, therefore, a period of 1 to 3 months—in some cases it would require the minimum and in others more.

As Shantung Province was almost entirely under Communist occupation, the Communists should have some cities on the Tientsin-Pukow line if they withdrew entirely from the Tsinan-Tsingtao Railway. Although the Communists had no intention of stationing troops at the coal mines along the Tsinan-Tsingtao Railway, the stipulation that they should give up all these coal mines was not acceptable in principle. Further concessions regarding Chengte were impossible. The Communists had made many concessions to the Government without presenting any demands, except the proposal for an increase of a few divisions in Manchuria, and he was asking Yenan for authorization to withdraw that proposal. Since he had previously thought that the National Government's demand regarding Antung referred to the city rather than the Province, he would have to refer this question to his colleagues in Manchuria before giving a reply.

After further discussion, General Chou said that he was prepared to consider any formula except that for civil administration involving the withdrawal of the Communist forces from north Kiangsu and Government occupation of that region. He continued that the main text of the document was almost entirely acceptable to the Communist Party except for one or two minor points.

Thus the only important issue on which agreement had not been reached at this time was the question of the status of the local governments in the areas from which the Chinese Communist forces would be withdrawn. The settlement of this issue would virtually have assured an agreement on the preliminary document for the amendment of the military reorganization plan, which, in turn, would have led to the signing of all the documents discussed during the June truce periods, the Generalissimo having stipulated that all the documents on which agreement should be reached be signed simultaneously.

On the following day the Generalissimo indicated that he was willing to compromise somewhat in the matter of Chengte but insisted that the evacuation of Kiangsu by the Communists to the north of the Lunghai Railway be completed within one month. General Marshall pointed out that it would be impossible logistically to evacuate to the north of the Lunghai line in one month and that the most serious factor was the Communist insistence on the continuation of the local administrations and a Peace Preservation Corps. He then suggested that a compromise solution be found on the basis of the continuation of the local governments, including the establishment of some specially selected group to arrange an agreement regarding a modification of these governments and the matter of the Peace Preservation Corps.

General Marshall pointed out to the Generalissimo that statements issued by his military leaders indicated that the Government was washing its hands of any democratic procedure and was pursuing a dictatorial policy of military force. He further informed the Generalissimo that comparison of the army dictatorship in Japan, which led to the destruction of that nation, with the present procedure of the Chinese military leaders would be inevitable. General Marshall informed the Generalissimo that in his opinion an extension of the existing form of partial truce would probably result in violent military ruptures due to the tense and explosive situation, the bitterness of the commanders in the field, and the strong desire of Government military leaders to settle matters by force, for which the National Government plans were complete and fairly well known to the Communist Party.

The Generalissimo finally announced that he had already issued instructions continuing in effect his orders against aggressive action by his troops. On June 30, the Kuomintang Minister of Information publicly announced that, while the truce period had expired at noon on June 30 and although no satisfactory agreement had been reached between the two parties, the Government had requested General Marshall to continue mediation with a view to reaching a peaceful settlement and that the Government would not initiate any attacks against Communist forces but would order its troops to remain on the defensive and await the settlement of pending issues.

On July 1 an announcement was made that the Generalissimo had issued orders continuing the prohibition against aggressive action by his armies.[19] General Chou En-lai subsequently furnished Gen-

---

[19] See annex 82.

eral Marshall a copy of a similar order issued on July 1 by the Chinese Communist Party leaders.[20]

DISINTEGRATION OF THE TRUCE ARRANGEMENT

The situation was further complicated by the renewed public expression by several National Government leaders of a desire to settle the issue by force and by mass meetings in Shanghai carefully organized to stir up anti-American feeling, related in particular to the then current Congressional consideration of lend-lease matters.

The Chinese Communists professed to regard measures for aid to China and official statements in Washington as proving their contention that American economic and military support to the Chinese Government would continue to be given irrespective of whether the National Government offered the Communists a fair and reasonable basis for settlement of military and political differences. The Communists maintained that new legislation intended to aid China which was then under consideration in the United States Congress [21] was reinforcing the National Government's tendency to deal with the Communists by force and was thus contributing to all-out civil war. At the same time some reactionary Kuomintang elements in inner Government circles were utilizing American measures as a basis for pressing the Generalissimo to push forward with a campaign of extermination against the Communists. Yet these and other Kuomintang extremists appeared to be joining in anti-American agitation on the grounds that American economic pressure was causing American imports to displace Chinese products, bankrupt Chinese industrialists and prevent Chinese recovery. These Kuomintang groups were also antagonistic to the restraint exercised by General Marshall and his assistants on the National Government with regard to an anti-Communist military campaign and were even using the Communist line against American intervention in pursuance of their aim to free the National Government from any American impediment to drastic anti-Communist action. The agitation and propaganda resulting from the activity of the different factions was being manifested in mass demonstrations, press campaigns and mob actions. One such incident involved a Shanghai peace delegation, consisting of educators, businessmen, students, and labor representatives and including therein representatives of women's organizations, which

---

[20] See annex 83.

[21] Under his wartime powers, the President had directed the establishment of a small military advisory group in China. The proposed legislation would have provided legislative authority for such a group and the military assistance under the new legislation would have been carried out in accordance with the military reorganization agreement of Feb. 25, 1946. See chapter VII.

proceeded to Nanking on June 24 for the publicly stated purpose of petitioning the Government to avoid civil war. This peace delegation was met at the railway station and restrained from leaving by an organized group of Kuomintang secret police, who confined the delegates in a room and in the course of a disturbance lasting several hours mauled and beat the delegates so severely that they were hospitalized. Government gendarmes who were present at the beginning of the incident failed to intervene and soon disappeared and the delegates were not rescued until several hours later.

During July there began a gradual worsening of the military situation with the spread of hostilities to various points in China proper.[22] The Commissioners of the Executive Headquarters had endeavored to keep the situation under control by dispatching a message on July 5 to all field teams and to the advance section at Changchun, in which it was stated that the National Government and the Chinese Communist Party had announced that the truce was to be continued throughout China pending the outcome of further negotiations. The Commissioners directed all commanders to refrain from aggressive action, including advances, attacks, and pursuits. The effect of this order was short-lived, however, and other events occurred which gave indication of further deterioration in the situation, both militarily and politically.

On July 7 the Chinese Communist Party issued a manifesto containing a bitter attack on American policy toward China and a protest against what the Communists termed American military and financial aid to the National Government, which encouraged the civil-war policy of the Kuomintang. General Marshall had previously refrained from comment on such propaganda attacks, but the coincidence of events led him to inform General Chou En-lai of the serious blow to the negotiations such propaganda attacks represented, paralleling as they did similar propaganda releases from Moscow, and of the impossibility of his serving any useful purpose in mediation and in the termination of hostilities while such attacks continued.

Matters were not helped at this stage by the departure of the Generalissimo from Nanking for Kuling on July 14, which meant that negotiations would be greatly handicapped during his absence. There were increasing signs of the gravity of the situation from a military standpoint, as hostilities spread in various areas. Each side accused the other of responsibility for offensive action and movements of troops. Accompanying the deterioration in the military situation

---

[22] Meetings were held in early July of a special group of National Government and Chinese Communist representatives to discuss the problem of local government but no agreement could be reached.

were evidences of efforts on the part of certain Kuomintang officials to suppress open criticism of the Government. Two well-known Chinese members of the Democratic League, one of them a prominent university professor, were assassinated by unknown persons (later revealed to be members of the Kunming Garrison Headquarters' secret police) and there were indications that Kuomintang secret police were intimidating leading Democratic League members and Chinese liberals in other parts of the country.

Communist activities during this period, in line with the Yenan propaganda attack on the United States policy toward China, began to be centered on the United States Marines in China and in mid-July the first serious incident involving the Communists and United States Marines occurred—the kidnapping of 7 Marines in east Hopei and their detention by the Communists for several days before being released. This was followed at the end of the month by a deliberate Communist ambush of a United States Marine-escorted motor convoy bound from Tientsin to Peiping, during which 3 Americans were killed and 12 wounded.[22a]

[22a] Following the Communist ambush on July 29 of the United States Marine convoy near Peiping, a fact-finding team of selected personnel from the Executive Headquarters was formed at the personal request of the Generalissimo and of General Chou En-lai to determine the responsibility and to submit a report on the incident. General Marshall delayed the formation of this team until the United States Marine Corps investigation of the incident had been completed and the Communists had made a personal request for such a team because of the anticipated charge by the Communists that the National Government representative on the investigating team would automatically side with the American member. General Marshall explained this reason to General Chou En-lai.

The investigation by the fact-finding team from Executive Headquarters encountered great, although anticipated, difficulties. The Communists employed delaying tactics and vicious propaganda. General Marshall finally told General Chou En-lai that he would not tolerate further delays and misrepresentations. He characterized Communist tactics regarding the investigation of this incident in emphatic terms and informed General Chou that if there were further delays he would withdraw the American representative from the investigating team and make a public statement of the facts. General Marshall was reluctant to take such action, however, since it would play directly into the hands of the small group in the Kuomintang which was blocking his efforts to terminate the fighting, would virtually end the usefulness of the Executive Headquarters, and might result in a general military conflagration. When General Chou stated that the reports received from Communist representatives were completely at variance with those from the Americans, General Marshall emphasized to him that it was quite impossible for the United States Army, Navy or Marine Corps personnel to involve themselves in deliberate misrepresentation in such an investigation. He further said that the American investigators had made no attempt, and did not intend, to conceal facts or bend them to their advantage and that he wished to emphasize the importance of straightforward action without delay. The testimony of the

IV. THE APPOINTMENT OF J. LEIGHTON STUART AS AMBASSADOR TO CHINA

The deterioration of the situation in China and what appeared to be the decisive influence of the reactionary political and military group around the Generalissimo convinced General Marshall of the desirability of obtaining the assistance in the mediation effort of an American of unquestioned character and integrity and with long experience in China. With this view in mind, General Marshall recommended the appointment of Dr. J. Leighton Stuart, President of Yenching University at Peiping, as American Ambassador to China. President Truman acted upon this recommendation and on July 11, 1946, the United States Senate confirmed the nomination of Dr. Stuart as Ambassador to China.

On July 26, shortly after Dr. Stuart's arrival at Nanking, General Chou En-lai proposed that an order for the unconditional cessation of hostilities be issued immediately and that at the same time the various arrangements worked out during the negotiations in June be put into effect. He further proposed that National Government and Communist Party representatives then meet with Dr. Stuart for preliminary discussion of the reorganization of the Government and local government problems and that any agreement reached be submitted to the PCC Steering Committee for approval since the reorganization of the Government required the approval of all parties.

In frank discussions at this time with a high-ranking National Government official, General Marshall endeavored to impress upon him the gravity of the situation. He informed him that the principal loss, in his opinion, was the lowering of the Generalissimo's prestige and that this was particularly tragic since the Generalissimo represented perhaps the greatest asset China had at this time. He continued that the Generalissimo's advisers were giving him such narrow and prejudiced advice that the situation seemed hopeless and that comments had been made to him privately by the Generalissimo's own associates which they could not make openly. He described the weakness of the financial and economic structure of the country, which argued strongly against civil war, and said that, if the Generalissimo continued in his present attitude toward negotiations, civil war was

---

two Chinese sides regarding the incident was conflicting and General Marshall finally instructed the United States personnel of the investigating team to withdraw and submit their own report. This report was to the effect that a Communist force had ambushed the motor convoy of Executive Headquarters and UNRRA supplies escorted by a United States Marine unit, that it had killed three Marines and wounded 12 others and that no National Government troops were present or involved in the incident.

inevitable. General Marshall pointed out that while the Generalissimo believed that the military situation would develop favorably during this lull in negotiations, developments might not occur in accordance with his belief. He said that the Generalissimo's military commanders were leading him into an uncontrollable situation and that when such a situation materialized these same commanders would be appealing for aid which would not be forthcoming. General Marshall emphasized that the United States would not underwrite a Chinese civil war.

In later conversations with this same official, General Marshall emphasized that the tactics being followed by the Government were such that in its efforts to prevent communism the Government was creating conditions favorable for a Communist regime. He cited as an example the existing financial and economic situation which would be made more serious by continuation of military operations and added that civil war, accompanied by economic chaos, would provide fruitful breeding grounds for communism.

Meanwhile, economic developments were providing grave portents of the rapid deterioration that was to come. The resumption of military operations was progressively isolating agricultural and mining areas from urban centers of consumption and export, and required a steady expansion of the currency in circulation to meet the Government's swollen budgetary requirements. These factors combined to stimulate a rapid, although not yet explosive, inflation, the consequences of which were universal commodity speculation and hoarding, a low level of exports and emigrant remittances and, in turn, the steady depletion of the Government's foreign exchange reserves.

V. ORGANIZATION OF THE STATE COUNCIL

PROPOSAL FOR A FIVE-MAN COMMITTEE

On August 1 Dr. Stuart in a long conference with the Generalissimo at Kuling proposed the organization of a special committee, including National Government and Communist Party representatives, with Dr. Stuart as Chairman, for the purpose of reaching an agreement for the immediate organization of the State Council.[23] In view of the apparent impossibility of obtaining the Generalissimo's agreement to the issuance of an order for the termination of hostilities, General Marshall and Dr. Stuart considered it advisable to approach the problem from another angle. It was their belief that if some progress were made by this committee the Generalissimo would be

---

[23] For the PCC resolution on the State Council, see annex 64.

willing to agree to a cessation of hostilities, which were at this time increasing in extent throughout North China and were threatening to spread into Manchuria.   The Generalissimo utilized the Communist attack on the United States Marine convoy as a reason for delaying decision but agreed to consider the matter.   General Marshall and Dr. Stuart were of the opinion that there was urgent necessity for creating the State Council, which, in effect, would give a form of genuine legislative action for control or guidance of the Government.

On August 5 the Generalissimo gave his agreement to the formation of a small informal five-man committee to be composed of Government and Communist Party representatives, under Dr. Stuart as Chairman, for the purpose of reaching an agreement for organization of the State Council.   On the following day he stipulated five preliminary conditions which the Communists would have to accept and carry out within a month to six weeks: (1) The Communist forces in north Kiangsu should withdraw north of the Lunghai Railway; (2) Communist forces should withdraw from the Tsinan-Tsingtao Railway; (3) Communist forces should withdraw from Chengte and areas in Jehol Province south of that city; (4) Communist forces should withdraw into 2½ provinces in Manchuria (Hsin Heilungchiang, Nenchiang, and Hsingan); and (5) Communist forces should withdraw from places in Shansi and Shantung Provinces occupied after June 7.   These terms were more exacting than those at the end of June when the stalemate had been reached.

The Chinese Communist Party replied that the National Government made no mention of local government and that the Communist Party's refusal to accept Government demands for taking over local administration in areas to be evacuated by Communist troops, which had led to the impasse at the end of June, was based on the grounds that such a procedure was contrary to the PCC resolutions.[24]   The Communist Party was willing to agree to the holding of political and military discussions simultaneously but would not accept the five Government conditions as a condition which must be agreed to prior to discussion of political matters.

THE MARSHALL-STUART STATEMENT OF AUGUST 10, 1946

At this point in the negotiations, on August 10, 1946, General Marshall and Ambassador Stuart issued a joint public statement in an

---

[24] Annex 1 of the PCC resolution entitled "Program for Peaceful National Reconstruction": "In those recovered areas where the local government is under dispute the *status quo* shall be maintained until a settlement is made according to Articles 6, 7 and 8 of Chapter III on Political Problems in this Program by the National Government after its reorganization."

effort to bring both sides and the Chinese public to a realization of the issues and to arouse public pressure for the termination of hostilities. Pointing out that the fighting threatened to pass out of control and that the economic situation was most serious, they stated that both the Government and the Communist leaders wished to put an end to the fighting but that there was still lack of agreement on certain issues. The redisposition of troops was one of the issues mentioned, but General Marshall and the Ambassador informed the Chinese public that a more fundamental issue concerned the character of local governments following such a redisposition.[25]

In very frank conversations with the Generalissimo at this time General Marshall outlined his estimate of the situation as follows: Events during the weeks following his final talk with the Generalissimo prior to the latter's departure for Kuling in July corresponded almost exactly with his predictions at that time. The Generalissimo had said that he could control the situation in Manchuria and that fighting in North China would be local and that, if General Marshall were patient, the Communists would appeal for a settlement and would be willing to make compromises necessary for such a settlement. Fighting in North China would, however, under present circumstances soon be completely out of control. Once it spread to Jehol Province, Manchuria would be affected, and the result would be a civil war beyond his or Communist control. This would be a catastrophe in that it would afford an ideal opportunity for the Communists to expand and for the U.S.S.R. to support the Chinese Communists, either openly or secretly. The Government had much to lose and little to gain from hostilities at this time, which might end in the collapse of the Government and of the country's economy. The Generalissimo must remember that the long lines of communication and the terrain favored the employment of Communist guerrilla tactics. General Marshall's objective, beyond that of a unified and rejuvenated China, was not what some of the Generalissimo's advisers seemed to think—that is, to put the Communist Party in control. He opposed the policy of the Generalissimo and his immediate advisers because he thought that the procedure of the National Government would probably lead to Communist control in China; the chaotic conditions then developing would not only weaken the Kuomintang but would also afford the Communists an excellent opportunity to undermine the Government. Information reaching General Marshall from a wide variety of sources indicated a serious lowering of Kuomintang prestige, and criticism of Kuomintang governmental procedure was increasing daily. The most

---

[25] See annex 84.

serious consequence of the situation was its profound injury to the prestige of the Generalissimo, which was perhaps China's greatest asset.

GENERALISSIMO CHIANG KAI-SHEK'S POSITION

After frequent conferences the Generalissimo indicated his willingness to make an effort to reach agreement with the Chinese Communists for the organization of the State Council through the Five-Man Committee, but he was not willing to agree to a termination of the fighting until his five conditions had been met. The Generalissimo informed General Marshall that even this concession was a great one and involved a military risk on the part of the Government. General Marshall did not agree with this view and considered that the greater risk was involved in the continuation of the fighting.

On August 13 the Generalissimo issued a public statement which was indicative of his attitude.[26] The entire blame for the breakdown in the negotiations and the economic distress in the country was laid at the door of the Chinese Communists. He described the Government's policy as follows: (1) the ending of the period of political tutelage and establishment of constitutional government; (2) adherence to the PCC resolutions; (3) broadening of the basis of the Government by the inclusion of members of all parties and non-party persons to carry out the PCC Program of Peaceful National Reconstruction; (4) adherence to the cessation of hostilities agreement of January 10, with the proviso that the Communists withdraw from areas "where they threaten peace and obstruct communications"; (5) the use of political means to settle political differences, but only if the Communists gave assurance and evidence that they would carry out the various agreements reached; and (6) the protection and security of the people and their properties and the removal of any threat to peace.

MAJOR FACTORS OF DISAGREEMENT

On August 22 General Chou En-lai expressed his willingness to participate in the meetings of the Five-Man Committee to discuss the organization of the State Council. There were two issues connected with this question: (1) the allocation of seats on the Council among the political parties and the non-party group and (2) the veto power in the Council in connection with the carrying out by the reorganized Government of the Program for Peaceful National Reconstruction agreed upon by the PCC and constituting one of the PCC resolutions.

---

[26] See annex 85.

The military situation was growing more serious day by day and there was at this time an immediate threat of an outbreak of fighting in Jehol Province, northeast of Peiping. The Chinese Communist Party had issued a general mobilization order, which the Communists contended was a defensive measure against what they considered to be the purpose of the National Government to settle issues by military force. The fact of the matter was that each side took the stand with General Marshall that the other was provoking the fighting and could not be trusted to go through with an agreement. The effort of General Marshall and Ambassador Stuart with respect to the State Council was another move, on a higher level, to break the stalemate and make it possible to terminate hostilities.

In late August the Generalissimo gave his formal agreement to the creation of the Five-Man Committee to pave the way for the formation of the State Council and also agreed that the conclusions of this group would be presented to the PCC Steering Committee for approval in accordance with the PCC resolutions. Shortly thereafter he appointed the National Government's two members of the Committee. At the same time he indicated that he had not in any way moderated his insistence on the five conditions to be met by the Communists in order to bring about a cessation of hostilities. In view of these five conditions General Chou En-lai expressed doubt regarding the proposal for creating the State Council, contending that it would only serve to give false encouragement to the public since the Generalissimo had no intention of facilitating the cessation of hostilities by moderating his previous terms.

Under these circumstances, General Marshall and Ambassador Stuart were concentrating on the measures to create the State Council as at least one definite step toward governmental reorganization that might exert an influence sufficient to furnish a basis for the termination of the fighting. The Generalissimo informed General Marshall that all that was necessary was for the Chinese Communists to stop fighting and abide by the terms of the cease-fire order of January 10, although under questioning he admitted that he was not moderating his five conditions.

In the meantime the National Government continued its offensive in north Kiangsu, cleared the Communists from the Tsinan-Tsingtao Railway and captured Chengte, capital of Jehol Province, on August 29. These were all points covered by the five Government conditions. The Communist forces launched an attack along the Lunghai Railway between Hsuchow and Chengchou and began their siege of Tatung in early August.

VI. THE TRUMAN-CHIANG MESSAGES OF AUGUST 1946

PRESIDENT TRUMAN'S MESSAGE OF AUGUST 10

In the meantime, on August 10, 1946, President Truman had forwarded to the Generalissimo a personal message, in which the President had expressed his concern at the deteriorating situation in China and at the actions of selfish interests of extremist elements, equally in the Kuomintang and the Chinese Communist Party. The President described the growing conviction that an attempt was being made to settle major social issues by resort to force rather than by democratic procedures. He pointed out that it was still the firm desire of the American Government and people to assist China to achieve lasting peace and a stable economy under a truly democratic government, but that unless convincing proof were shortly forthcoming that genuine progress was being made toward a peaceful settlement of internal Chinese problems, it would be necessary for the President to redefine and explain the position of the United States to the American people.[27]

GENERALISSIMO CHIANG'S REPLY OF AUGUST 28

To this the Generalissimo replied on August 28.[28] The reply placed the blame for the fighting on the Communists and charged that the aim of Communist policy was to use armed force to seize political power, overthrow the Government, and install a totalitarian regime. He stated that while mistakes had been made by some National Government subordinates they had been minor in scale compared with the flagrant violations of the Communists and that the National Government had dealt sternly with its offenders. The Generalissimo proclaimed his policy of broadening the basis of the National Government by the inclusion of all parties and non-party personnel and said that success must depend upon the sincerity of the Communists in responding to the National Government's appeals.

PRESIDENT TRUMAN'S MESSAGE OF AUGUST 31

In view of the generally unsatisfactory nature of Generalissimo Chiang Kai-shek's reply of August 28 to President Truman's personal message and the continued deadlock in the negotiations, the President forwarded a further message to the Generalissimo in which he emphasized that the prompt end of the threat of civil war in China

---

[27] See annex 86.
[28] See annex 87.

through the establishment of political unity would make it feasible for the United States to proceed with its plans further to aid China in the rehabilitation of its industrial and agricultural economy.[29]

VII. THE DRIFT TOWARD ALL-OUT STRIFE

COMMUNIST RESENTMENT OF AMERICAN AID TO CHINA

The signing of an agreement between the Chinese and United States Governments on August 30, 1946, for the sale of United States Government surplus property in various islands of the Pacific was the occasion for the issuance of a statement by the Chinese Communist Party at Shanghai attacking the United States for extending large-scale military aid to the National Government. General Marshall had explained to General Chou En-lai the background of the negotiations leading to the signing of this agreement prior to its actual completion and had explained that the surplus property in question did not contain combat matériel but consisted of machinery, motor vehicles, communications equipment, rations, medical supplies and various other items which would be of considerable value in the rehabilitation of the Chinese economy. The transaction could not be held in abeyance until the two Chinese groups settled internal differences which had existed over a long period of years. The alternative was to deprive China and its people of the opportunity to acquire materials beneficial to its reconstruction.

In view of continued Chinese Communist propaganda attacks on the surplus property agreement of August 30, 1946, General Marshall gave a very detailed explanation of this transaction to the Communist Party representative. He pointed out that this transaction had been under discussion since the beginning of 1946 and had almost been settled at the time of General Marshall's departure for the United States in March. During his visit to the United States he had ironed out most of the difficulties involved and the failure to reach an agreement on this transaction in February had resulted from Chinese Government efforts to improve the terms. The alternative to completing an agreement with China for the sale of this surplus property was the immediate disposal of the property to other governments in the Far East or dumping it in the ocean, courses of action which would have deprived China of material of considerable importance in the economic rehabilitation of the country. General Marshall continued that Chinese Communist propaganda had imputed to this transaction every evil purpose possible and that great harm had thus

---

[29] See annex 88.

been done. He concluded that while he accepted this propaganda as inevitable, he was greatly disturbed when a proposal such as that for the informal Five-Man Committee was being destroyed as a result of such propaganda. The Chinese Communist Party representatives, however, continued to be critical of the surplus property agreement on the grounds that items such as trucks, communications equipment and army rations and uniforms would be used for civil war purposes and other items would be sold on the market and the proceeds thereof expended for military purposes.

With respect to United States military aid programs [30] General Marshall was being placed in the untenable position of mediating on the one hand between the two Chinese groups while on the other the United States Government was continuing to supply arms and ammunition to one of the two groups, namely, the National Government. Action was therefore taken in August to suspend certain portions of these programs which might have a bearing on the continued prosecution of hostilities in China. Licenses were not granted for the export to China of combat type items of military equipment and in late September shipments of combat items from the Pacific area to China were temporarily suspended. (On October 22, 1946, the suspension was lifted to permit the delivery of civilian type items for the Chinese Air Force.) This ban was imposed at a time when the National Government was gradually increasing the tempo of its military campaign and when its reserves of matériel were ample. The ban apparently had little effect, since it was not until November, when the National Government had reached the peak of its military holdings, that the National Government issued an order for the cessation of hostilities. By that time the Government's forces had occupied most of the areas covered by its demands to the Chinese Communists in June and during later negotiations and had reached what turned out to be the highest point of its military position after V–J Day.

PROBLEMS RELATING TO THE FIVE-MAN COMMITTEE

By September 3 both Chinese groups had named their representatives to the informal Five-Man Committee. Agreement on the composition of the Committee did not, however, mean that Committee meetings were assured. The Chinese Communist Party continued to insist on the receipt of assurances from the Government that the latter would issue orders for the cessation of hostilities when agreement should be reached in the Committee.

---

[30] See chapter VII.

In referring to the informal Five-Man Committee General Marshall pointed out to the Chinese Communist Party representative that, when this proposal was presented to the Generalissimo, the latter had said that it would not be an effective procedure since the Communists would immediately introduce other matters which would so complicate the discussions that no progress would be made. General Marshall had informed the Generalissimo that Dr. Stuart would act as chairman of the Committee only during discussion of State Council issues and that if other issues were brought up Dr. Stuart would withdraw from the discussions. General Marshall further explained to the Communist Party representative that he had exerted every effort and every argument to end the impasse and obtain a cessation of hostilities and that he had ignored the attacks on him personally, both those made publicly by the Communists and those made by individuals within the Government who were opposed to almost everything he had been trying to accomplish.

The Chinese Communist Party attitude toward the proposal for the informal Five-Man Committee was that it would agree to participate in the discussions of the Committee upon the receipt of a guarantee that cease-fire arrangements would be made and that the Government would drop its five conditions after the Committee reached a formula for Government reorganization. The Communist representative also stated that the Communist Party would not name its members to the State Council while fighting continued because the Government apparently wished to have the State Council decide upon cease-fire arrangements. He pointed out that if the matter were left to the State Council, the Kuomintang, together with the Youth Party, would have a majority of the votes and any cease-fire arrangements would thus be on Kuomintang terms. The Communists desired that the Committee of Three handle such arrangements. In brief, the Communist Party position was that it would participate in the discussions in the Five-Man Committee provided that, when a basis of agreement should be reached, a cease-fire order would be issued. It desired that an unconditional cease-fire order be issued or that the Committee of Three meet immediately to discuss this question.

Following several days of conferences at Kuling between the Generalissimo and General Marshall, the former indicated that certain terms were acceptable to him. He agreed that the settlement of the military terms for the cessation of hostilities would be made by the Committee of Three and not by the State Council provided the Communist Party agreed to have the Committee of Three take action on the various issues discussed by that Committee in June. These were the questions of restoration of communications, the terms for the termination of hostilities and the redistribution of troops in Manchuria and the military reorganization of the armed forces which would stipulate the places where Communist troops were to be stationed. The Generalissimo had yielded on one important point by agreeing that the question of local government could be referred to the State Council after its establishment. He also expressed his willingness to have the Constitutional Reviewing Committee resume its work when the Five-Man Committee had reached agreement and its conclusions had been approved by the PCC Steering Committee but said that, prior to the issuance of a cease-fire order, the Communist Party must name its representatives to the National Assembly. General Marshall had gained the impression from statements by the Generalissimo that he considered that practically all the points covered by his five conditions would be automatically taken care of by his insistence on continued Government military occupation of places recently occupied by its troops. It was also the impression of General Marshall that reorganization of the Executive Yuan would take place after the convening of the National Assembly.

When these terms were transmitted to General Chou En-lai, he expressed the view that, except for the proposal for the Five-Man Committee to discuss the reorganization of the State Council, the entire procedure in connection with political considerations outlined by the Generalissimo was contrary to the PCC resolutions. The Communist Party asked, therefore, that the Committee of Three be convened immediately to find some basis for the issuance of a cease-fire order.

General Marshall considered that the Communist Party proposal meant a return to the impasse at the end of June which Dr. Stuart and he had been endeavoring to break through by the proposal for the reorganization of the State Council. He pointed out that unless the Committee of Three meeting were paralleled or preceded by efforts to reorganize the State Council, the situation had merely returned to the previous deadlock. It was General Marshall's position that the stand taken by the Chinese Communist Party was harmful to it, as the Government probably wanted all the time possible for military operations and time was thus to its advantage.

During this period the Communist representatives continued to insist on two points: (1) assurances from the Government that the Communists would be able to control sufficient votes in the State Council to veto any revision of the PCC resolutions, and (2) the early issuance of a cease-fire order.

The Generalissimo indicated at this time that he would not agree to a meeting of the Committee of Three until the Five-Man Committee should meet and give indication of reaching an agreement for the organization of the State Council and all that it was necessary for the Communists to do in connection with the National Assembly was to submit a list of their delegates. The Generalissimo also indicated that he would not agree to informal discussions of the State Council issues by Government members of the Five-Man Committee prior to the formal meetings of the Committee, but that he would agree specifically that the two questions of the allocation of seats in the Council and the veto power would be the subjects for that Committee to discuss and settle.

On September 16 General Chou En-lai departed from Nanking for Shanghai. Prior to his departure he forwarded to General Marshall three memoranda. The first memorandum outlined United States aid to the Chinese Government, described it as contributory to civil war, protested the sale of United States Government surplus property to the Chinese Government, and demanded that the United States Government freeze all supplies and shipping covered by the surplus property agreement pending a settlement in China and the restoration of peace and unity and establishment of a coalition government. The second memorandum requested the convening of the Committee of Three to discuss the issuance of an order for the cessation of hostilities.[31] The third memorandum announced the departure of General Chou for Shanghai and said that he would return as soon as a meeting of the Committee of Three should be convened.[32]

The Generalissimo, when informed of the situation, said that he would not agree to Government participation in the Committee of Three until the Five-Man Committee had been convened and had given some indication of reaching an agreement. He did agree, however, to a compromise proposal presented by General Marshall regarding the allocation of seats in the State Council, which would have given the Communists within one vote of a veto power to block revision of the PCC resolutions, on the assumption that there was certain to be at least one liberal-minded, independent councillor who would vote independently.

NEITHER SIDE YIELDS MEASURABLY

During this period of negotiations, there had been little change in the position of the Chinese Communists. They continued to insist that a solution for the cessation of hostilities issue was a prerequisite to their participation in the Five-Man Committee discussions looking toward the organization of the State Council, although they did finally

---

[31] See annex 89.
[32] See annex 90.

agree to enter into Committee discussions provided the Committee of Three should meet simultaneously to discuss the cessation of hostilities; they demanded that the Generalissimo's five conditions be dropped after a basis for the State Council should have been reached in the Five-Man Committee; they stated their refusal to name their members of the State Council, in the event of agreement on a formula for the Council, until hostilities should cease; and they indicated their desire that the PCC Steering Committee should discuss the reorganization of the Executive Yuan. The greatest concern of the Communists during this period was for the cessation of hostilities and for assurances that the PCC resolutions would not be modified; to this latter end they insisted on some formula in the veto power arrangement which would ensure that the PCC resolutions would not be changed, as they apparently felt that their safety lay in the retention of the decisions of the PCC.

The Government position during this period was less fixed: The Government first placed the blame on the Communists for the initiation of the fighting and thus insisted that there was no need to issue a cease-fire order; the Government stated at the beginning of September that it would not abandon the Generalissimo's five conditions; and Government spokesmen indicated that all issues regarding a truce and the settlements in various areas were to be discussed in the State Council. Subsequently, however, after an earlier refusal to consider the convening of the Committee of Three, the Generalissimo agreed to permit that Committee to settle the cessation of hostilities issue provided the Communists would carry out certain tentative agreements reached during June and, in effect, abandoned the five conditions through agreement to permit the Kiangsu local government problem to be settled by the State Council. Government military advances had in any case more or less made the carrying out of most of these five conditions a *fait accompli*. The Generalissimo also agreed to the summoning of the Constitutional Reviewing Committee as soon as the Five-Man Committee should have reached an agreement and this agreement should have been confirmed by the PCC Steering Committee, thus providing some assurance to the Communists of conformity with PCC procedures. He had, however, posed an additional condition by stipulating that he would not agree to the cessation of hostilities until the Communists should have named their delegates to the National Assembly, a procedure which the Communists characterized as not in conformity with the PCC resolutions; and he had indicated that the Executive Yuan would not be reorganized until the National Assembly should have convened, although the PCC resolutions envisaged the reorganization of the Executive Yuan prior to that time. The Generalissimo also indicated that he contemplated continued Government military occupation of the places occupied in its military campaign. Toward the end of this period of negotiations, the Generalissimo agreed to the convening of the Committee of Three when the Five-Man Committee should have given evidence of having reached agreement on the State Council, but he would not agree to informal meetings of the Five-Man Committee prior to its formal meetings.

The positions of the two parties thus continued irreconcilable. General Marshall and Dr. Stuart had endeavored to break the deadlock through the proposal for the Five-Man Committee as a step leading toward the cessation of hostilities. They had exerted strong pressure on the Generalissimo in an effort to obtain his concurrence to this proposal only to meet with Communist refusal to participate in the meetings of the Committee. Propaganda campaigns, as usual, played a part in wrecking their efforts, as they led to confusion and misunderstandings. The most bitter of these campaigns was that directed by the Communist Party against the American Government and the surplus-property transaction. Communist distrust and Communist practices of distortion and disregard of the truth imputed to this transaction an evil purpose intended to further civil war in China, which was utterly contrary to the facts. The Generalissimo had frankly told General Marshall that the conclusion of an agreement for the termination of hostilities was his final trump card in forcing the Communist Party to name its delegates to the National Assembly. Since the Communist Party considered this as a sixth condition to be added to the previously announced five conditions, they were pressing for the more immediate issue, as they saw it, of terminating the fighting.

On September 19, in response to an oral request from the Communist Party representative at Nanking, General Marshall communicated to General Chou En-lai at Shanghai the National Government reaction to General Chou's request for a meeting of the Committee of Three.[33] In a further memorandum from Shanghai, General Chou again repeated his request for a meeting of the Committee of Three and indicated that unless the meeting were convened he would be compelled to make public all the important documents in the negotiations since the June truce period.[34] General Marshall made it very clear to the Communist Party representative at Nanking at this time that in view of the vicious Communist propaganda attacks directed against his personal integrity and honesty of purpose, which were

---

[33] See annex 91.
[34] See annex 92.

being paralleled by repeated private requests from the Communists that he continue his mediation efforts, he wished to emphasize that such a procedure would no longer be tolerated—if the Communists doubted his impartiality as a mediator, they needed only to notify him accordingly and he would immediately withdraw from the negotiations.

In discussions of the situation with high-ranking National Government representatives at this time, General Marshall impressed upon them the delicacy of the situation and the possibility that, if the situation continued to deteriorate, the Communists would be driven to seek and be dependent upon outside support, such as Russian aid, which would make the task of peaceful settlement much more difficult.

Since the Generalissimo was expected to return to Nanking from Kuling, where he had been since mid-July, General Marshall and Dr. Stuart addressed a joint letter to General Chou En-lai at Shanghai asking that he also return to Nanking in order that further efforts could be made to achieve a peaceful arrangement.[35] General Chou maintained in his reply his previous stand that he would prefer to await the convening of the Committee of Three.[36]

Upon the return of the Generalissimo to Nanking and pursuant to his request for advice regarding the issuance of a public statement, General Marshall suggested on September 27 that the Government propose the convening of the Five-Man Committee and the Committee of Three with the understanding that the agreements tentatively reached in June be carried out, that the Committee of Three decide the problem of the military reorganization and integration agreement, that the PCC Steering Committee confirm whatever conclusions were reached by the Five-Man Committee, that all local government issues be settled by the State Council and that concurrently with the cessation of hostilities the Communist Party publish the list of its delegates to the National Assembly. General Marshall set forth these procedures in a draft statement for approval by the Generalissimo and possible use.[37] General Marshall suggested that these arrangements be accompanied by Government action to secure the immediate cessation of hostilities.

It was the view of General Marshall that, if the Communists expressed agreement to the general terms and procedures outlined, an order for the cessation of hostilities should be immediately issued and the Five-Man Committee and the Committee of Three should meet at once. The Generalissimo subsequently informed General Marshall that after study of this suggestion he had come to the

[35] See annex 93.
[36] See annex 94.
[37] See annex 95.

conclusion that the several agreements indicated should be completed prior to the cessation of hostilities—in brief, the Committee of Three would have to reach complete agreement on the redisposition of troops for demobilization and integration of the armies and the Five-Man Committee would also have to reach an agreement prior to the issuance of a cease-fire order. It was the opinion of General Marshall that such a procedure would completely vitiate the entire purpose of his suggestion. The Generalissimo later informed General Marshall that he had decided not to release any public statement at that time.

NATIONAL GOVERNMENT MILITARY ACTIVITIES

During this period the National Government began an advance against Kalgan, an important Communist-held city northwest of Peiping. The Chinese Communists, who had been beseiging Tatung (north Shansi) since early August, announced the formal lifting of the siege of that city in order to meet the Government charge that Kalgan was being attacked because the Communists were threatening Tatung. On September 30 the Kuomintang Central News Agency announced that Government forces had begun operations for the purpose of capturing Kalgan. On the same day the Communist Party announced publicly its refusal to name its delegates to the National Assembly unless certain PCC procedures were observed.

It was against this background that General Chou En-lai addressed a memorandum to General Marshall on September 30 pointing to the Government attack on Kalgan, one of the political and military centers of the Communist Party, and stating that if the National Government did not cease military operations against Kalgan the Communist Party would be compelled to presume that the Government was giving public indication of a "total national split" and its abandonment of a peaceful settlement.[38] The Communist Party representatives stated orally that the cessation of the Government drive against Kalgan was a prerequisite to Communist participation in simultaneous meetings of the Committee of Three and the Five-Man Committee.

FURTHER DETERIORATION IN THE NEGOTIATIONS

On October 1, 1946, in a conference with Chinese Communist Party representatives at Nanking, General Marshall made it clear to them that he was in agreement with neither the Communist Party's course of action nor that of the National Government. He said that the situation had almost reached the point where he would not continue in the position of a mediator and that he could no longer continue to be a middleman in a prolonged series of accusations and counter-

---

[38] See annex 96.

accusations, of proposals and counterproposals. General Marshall stated that he had to give first consideration to the position of the Government that he represented. He pointed out that while he was struggling with the Chinese Government in an effort to have terms proposed which would have a fair chance of acceptance by the Chinese Communist Party, the latter had come forward with an announcement of refusal to name its delegates to the National Assembly. While he was struggling with the Chinese Communists in an effort to reach a basis for agreement, the Government had publicly announced its attack on Kalgan. This type of procedure had continued week after week and month after month. He said that he wished to emphasize that the procedure followed by the Communists was inevitably productive of long delay during which military operations were continuing. He concluded, however, that he was willing to discuss General Chou's memorandum of September 30 with the Government and would do his best to prevail upon the Government to take action which would increase the possibility of peaceful settlement.

General Marshall decided at this time that he would not carry oral messages to the Chinese Communists but would transmit only written communications from the Government.

He felt that the United States Government could not continue to be a third party to the existing procedure under which the Government had been proceeding with its "local operations" for 3 months. He thought it apparent that the National Government's campaign against Kalgan could be justified only on the basis of a policy of force. He felt that he could not put himself in the position of mediating during a continued series of military campaigns and that he must have positive assurances from the National Government that there was a reasonable basis for compromise which offered possibility of success.

GENERAL MARSHALL CONSIDERS WITHDRAWING

In view of the existing situation, General Marshall addressed a memorandum to the Generalissimo on October 1, in which, after stating that he was not in agreement with the present course of the Government or of the Communist Party, he concluded:

"I wish merely to state that unless a basis for agreement is found to terminate the fighting without further delays of proposals and counterproposals, I will recommend to the President that I be recalled and that the United States Government terminate its efforts of mediation."

Earlier in the memorandum General Marshall stated that he had carefully considered all the factors involved in the current status of negotiations and military operations and had also taken into consideration the most recent developments, such as the Communist Party's announcement of its refusal to submit a list of Communist delegates to the National Assembly unless certain PCC procedures were met, the Kuomintang Central News Agency announcement of the Government operations against Kalgan, certain informal proposals presented by Dr. T. V. Soong, and the memorandum of September 30 from General Chou En-lai.[39]

On the following day the Generalissimo gave Ambassador Stuart an oral account of the reply which he expected to make to General Marshall's memorandum. He indicated that he was aware of General Marshall's embarrassment in the existing situation and that he always kept his problems in mind. He felt, however, that it was absolutely essential to the national welfare that the Government gain control of Kalgan and that the occupation of this city by the Government would do much to prevent further military action by the Chinese Communists. The Generalissimo's statement served to convince General Marshall almost completely that the time had come for his recall from China since the Generalissimo was certainly following a definite policy of force under cover of the protracted negotiations. The Generalissimo had now completely reversed the position he had taken in June when he had agreed that the Communists would be permitted to retain possession of Kalgan, which they had occupied shortly after V–J Day.

On October 2 the Generalissimo forwarded to General Marshall a reply to the latter's memorandum.[40] Referring to General Marshall's memorandum the Generalissimo said that

"the Government hereby, with all frankness, expresses its maximum concessions in regard to the solution of the present problem".

These "maximum concessions" were as follows: (1) While the Government had originally agreed that the Communist Party be allocated 8 seats and the Democratic League 4 seats on the State Council, it would now offer 1 seat to a member of the independent group who would be recommended by the Chinese Communist Party and agreed upon by the Government. This would make a total of 13 seats held by Councillors satisfactory to the Communist Party, which should without delay submit the lists of its members on the State Council and of its delegates to the National Assembly. (2) The location of the Communist troops under the military reorganization plan should be determined immediately and the Communist forces should enter such locations according to agreed dates, the foregoing to be decided upon

---

[39] See annex 97.
[40] See annex 98.

by the Committee of Three and carried out under the supervision of the Executive Headquarters. The memorandum concluded that if the Communists agreed to these two proposals "a cease-fire order should be issued by both sides, when agreement has been reached thereon."

The reply of the Generalissimo involved lengthy procedures during which the attack on Kalgan would be carried to its conclusion and it omitted any reference to the disposition of Government troops, which was a requirement of the military reorganization agreement of February 25. General Marshall did not think that the United States Government could afford to be a party to a course of questionable integrity and he felt that this fact should be made unmistakably clear to the Chinese Government.

In a long conference on October 4, the Generalissimo informed General Marshall that his departure from China was unthinkable and that he could not possibly cease his efforts at mediation, since the crisis in China was the most important in the world and his efforts were of great historic significance. General Marshall explained that his own actions and position and those of the United States Government as represented by him were in question under the existing situation. He stated that he was convinced that a campaign of force was in progress and that negotiations could be described as a cover for this campaign—under such circumstances he could no longer participate in the negotiations. He continued that in June the Government had agreed that Kalgan would be left in Communist hands at a time when the Government was in a much weaker military position than at this time—Chengte had now been captured, most of Hopei and Jehol Provinces had been occupied, Government troops had advanced well beyond Peiping in the direction of Kalgan and Government forces were on the verge of occupying Chihfeng and Tolun, both important strategic points. The present procedure, said General Marshall, clearly meant a campaign of force and not a settlement by negotiation. General Marshall pointed out that at the end of June he had opposed the whole procedure in prospect for July and August, when the Generalissimo had declined to accept the agreements openly reached and had stated there would be only local fighting in China proper and no fighting in Manchuria. He continued that he had not only disagreed with that conception but had thought that it inevitably meant the development of a full-fledged civil war beyond Government or Communist control for a long time to come. This conference ended without any indication on the part of the Generalissimo that he would halt the drive against Kalgan. General Marshall informed the Generalissimo in conclusion that he regretted to inform him that nothing had transpired in the discussion to cause him to alter his point of view—in fact, he was the more convinced that the United States Government was being placed in a position where the integrity of its actions could be successfully questioned and that he must, therefore, recommend to President Truman his recall.

On the following day General Marshall forwarded a message to Washington recommending his recall, the pertinent portions of which are as follows:

"I feel that despite the present vicious Communist propaganda of misrepresentation and bitter attacks and despite the stupid failure of the Communists to agree to the Five-Man Committee under Dr. Stuart, actuated in our opinion through fear of the very delays which have resulted from this refusal, the United States Government cannot afford before the world to have me continue as mediator and should confidentially notify the Generalissimo accordingly. I believe that this is the only way to halt the military campaign and to dispel the evident belief of the Government generals that they can drag along the United States while carrying out their campaign of force. It is suggested for your approval that the following message be sent by the President to the Generalissimo:

" 'General Marshall recommends that his mission be terminated and that he be recalled. He has explained to you that he feels that a continuation of mediation under present circumstances of extensive and aggresive military operations would place the United States Government in a position where the integrity of its actions as represented by him would be open to serious question. I deplore that his efforts to bring peace to China have been unsuccessful, but there must be no question regarding the integrity of his position and actions which represent the intention and high purpose of the United States Government. I, therefore, with great regret have concluded that he should be immediately recalled.' "

When word reached the Generalissimo through Ambassador Stuart of General Marshall's action, the Generalissimo expressed his willingness to stop military advances against Kalgan for a period of five days, possibly even longer if the American mediators insisted, on condition that the Communist Party would immediately participate in meetings of both the Five-Man Committee and the Committee of Three and that Kalgan would be the first issue negotiated. The Generalissimo also requested that General Marshall and Dr. Stuart discuss the matter with him on the following morning. Upon the receipt of this message from the Generalissimo, General Marshall requested the Department of State not to transmit to the President his recommendation that he be recalled, pending the receipt of further instructions.

THE KALGAN TRUCE PROPOSAL

In discussion with the Generalissimo of the Kalgan truce proposal, General Marshall made clear that a short truce would not allow time for successful negotiations, particularly with the threat of the resumption of aggressive military action, and a long truce would be too difficult to control in view of the complications to be faced by the military commanders in the field and their own aggressive attitudes. General Marshall suggested that the proposal which he had presented to the Generalissimo on September 27 be considered—this involved an immediate cessation of hostilities once the Communist Party agreed to the procedure specified. The Generalissimo said that he was unwilling to agree to this proposed procedure, and insisted that the cessation of hostilities must depend upon the successful completion of the meetings of the Committee of Three and the Five-Man Committee. The Generalissimo said he would, however, order a truce of five days on the basis of Communist agreement to meetings of the Committee of Three and the Five-Man Committee as outlined in his memorandum of October 2. After some discussion, the Generalissimo agreed to extend the truce period to 10 days and indicated that if, as the end of the truce approached, it appeared that the Chinese Communists were in a mood to negotiate, he would lengthen the period. He requested that the truce be announced as a proposal from General Marshall and Ambassador Stuart rather than from the National Government. General Marshall and Dr. Stuart agreed to this request even though it was not their proposal—it merely represented the best terms they could obtain.

General Marshall prepared a memorandum [41] outlining the conditions of the truce as agreed to by the Generalissimo and sent it to Dr. Stuart, who communicated it orally to a Chinese Communist Party representative, and on the following day sent a copy to this Communist representative and an additional copy to General Chou En-lai at Shanghai. The conditions of the truce were as follows: (1) The purpose of the truce was "to carry out the two proposals of the Generalissimo" in his communication to General Marshall of October 2; (2) during the truce period Executive Headquarters field teams would check on its observance; and (3) public announcement of the truce would be made by Dr. Stuart and General Marshall without any announcement from the two parties.

At the same time General Marshall requested the Department of State to inform President Truman of the foregoing events and of General Marshall's decision to withdraw the recommendation for his recall.

---

[41] See annex 99.

The Chinese Communist Party rejected this truce proposal on the grounds that there should be no time limit to the truce period and that discussions in the Committee of Three and the Five-Man Committee should not be limited to the two proposals in the Generalissimo's memorandum of October 2 since discussion of these topics during a truce would be considered as negotiation under military coercion.[42]

THE MARSHALL-STUART STATEMENT OF OCTOBER 8, 1946

The Chinese Communist Party's rejection of the truce proposal placed General Marshall in a position entirely opposite from the one he had previously held in opposing continued aggressive military action.   It was now the Government which had offered at least a temporary cessation of hostilities and the Communists who declined. General Marshall and Ambassador Stuart then issued a joint public statement on October 8 in regard to the situation.[43]   The statement began with a description of General Chou En-lai's memorandum of September 30 on Government military operations against Kalgan and the Communist attitude thereto.   It was a recital of the negotiations from the time of the receipt of General Chou's memorandum asking for a cessation of the attack on Kalgan to the time of the Communist Party rejection of the 10-day truce proposal.

THE COMMUNIST POSITION

In discussions with General Marshall and Dr. Stuart, Communist Party representatives stated the Communist views: The Communist Party wanted a definite cessation of the attack on Kalgan and the only way for the Government to show its sincerity was to withdraw its troops to their original positions.   The Communists had hoped that General Marshall and Dr. Stuart would be able to make the Government realize that it was assuming the role of a victor over the vanquished and that they would also be able to make the Government change its policy of war, but the Communists had now lost hope.   They appreciated very much the efforts of General Marshall and Dr. Stuart, but China, they said, was now in the midst of civil war. The Communists hoped that General Marshall and Dr. Stuart would, on the one hand, have the United States Government cease its aid to the Chinese Government and, on the other hand, "have a fair mediating process which would be acceptable to both sides."   General Marshall replied that he did not accept this statement regarding the United States Government and that he did not like the inference of the second portion of this statement.   He concluded that he very much feared that his efforts in the negotiations had terminated.

---

[42] See annex 100.
[43] See annex 101.

In view of the unsatisfactory nature of this conversation and with the desire to do everything possible at this critical period, General Marshall proceeded to Shanghai to see General Chou En-lai. In their conversation it developed that some misunderstanding had arisen from the wording of the terms of the truce proposal which had led to uncertainty whether the Communist Party was to give consideration to the two proposals of the Generalissimo or to "carry out" such proposals. General Chou indicated that the two proposals of the Generalissimo were from the Communist viewpoint unacceptable conditions. One of them, he said, meant that the Communist Party could not exercise the veto power to prevent revision of the PCC resolutions and the other proposal meant that, while the Communist troop locations would be fixed, the Government armies would be free to move. General Chou concluded that it was the view of the Communist Party that only a lasting truce would demonstrate that the Government did not desire a "total split." He then presented to General Marshall a three-point military and eight-point political proposal which, he said, represented the Communist stand on military and political issues. The military proposal required that all troops resume the positions held in China proper as of January 13 and in Manchuria as of June 7, that the location of all troops until the time of army reorganization should be fixed and that Government troops moved after January 13 should be returned to their original locations. The political proposal consisted of detailed points for discussion by the Five-Man Committee and the PCC Steering Committee, which all were related to the PCC resolutions.

General Marshall emphasized to General Chou that the Generalissimo had not planned the truce for the purpose of gaining time for the movement of troops and munitions, and concluded that after hearing the views of General Chou it would seem that his mediation efforts were futile and there was no practical basis for further action on his part. General Marshall reminded him that some time ago he had indicated that if the Communist Party did not trust his impartiality as mediator it had merely to say so and he would withdraw. General Chou said that he would make a written reply to the Generalissimo, and that, although he had not welcomed the joint statement issued by Ambassador Stuart and General Marshall, he wished to make clear that he did not cast any reflection on General Marshall's actions throughout the entire period of mediation.

On October 9 General Chou En-lai replied to the Generalissimo's memorandum of October 2 and the Kalgan truce proposal in a memorandum addressed to General Marshall.[44] This memorandum con-

---

[44] See annex 102.

cluded that the Government should cease its attack on Kalgan and that if the Government should permanently call off such an attack, the Communist Party was willing to participate in meetings of the Committee of Three and the Five-Man Committee or the PCC Steering Committee to have simultaneous discussions of (1) the cessation of hostilities and (2) the implementation of the PCC resolutions. The memorandum also included the military and political proposals made by General Chou to General Marshall at Shanghai.

GENERALISSIMO CHIANG'S STATEMENT OF OCTOBER 10, 1946

On October 10, 1946, the anniversary of the founding of the Chinese Republic, the Generalissimo made a speech,[45] in which, referring to the negotiations, he made statements along the following general lines:

The Government asked the Communist Party to abandon its plot to achieve regional domination and distintegration of the country by military force and to participate along with all other parties in the National Government and the National Assembly. It was the hope of the Government that the various political parties and groups would submit their lists of candidates to the State Council and of delegates to the National Assembly. The Government desired a total and permanent cessation of hostilities, but during the past 3 months the Communists had rejected all the proposals of the Generalissimo and had also turned down the truce proposal presented by General Marshall and Dr. Stuart; the Government was not, however, going to abandon its policy of a peaceful settlement. It would continue to hope and seek for a settlement by mediation and consultation.

THE FALL OF KALGAN AND THE SUMMONING OF THE NATIONAL ASSEMBLY

During this period a group of representatives of the Democratic League and the China Youth Party proceeded to Shanghai for the purpose of inducing General Chou En-lai to return to Nanking. Just as it appeared that their efforts would succeed, a series of events occurred which aroused bitter feeling on the part of the Chinese Communists and one of which created strong opposition from all minority parties. On October 10, Government forces captured Kalgan with little or no opposition from Communist troops and on the same day occupied Chihfeng, the last Communist stronghold in Jehol Province. Government troops at this time were also reported to be on the verge of occupying additional Communist-held towns in north Kiangsu. On the same day the Government announced the resumption of na-

---

[45] See annex 103.

tionwide conscription, which had been suspended following the Japanese surrender in August 1945.   Even after these events, General Chou En-lai was said by Dr. Sun Fo, President of the Legislative Yuan, to be ready to return to Nanking, but the issuance by the Government on October 11 of a mandate announcing that the National Assembly would be convened on November 12, as scheduled, caused General Chou to cancel his plans.   This announcement also resulted in strong criticism from the other minority parties, as they considered it evidence of unilateral and dictatorial action on the part of the Government.   They asserted that agreement had been reached on April 24 in discussion between representatives of all parties and the Generalissimo for postponement of the National Assembly, then scheduled for May 5, and that it was understood that the date for convening the Assembly would be decided by discussion among all parties.   The National Government explained that its action was in accordance with Kuomintang regulations, which required formal notification and confirmation of the date of the National Assembly one month prior to its convocation.   The result of this series of events was to cause the cancellation of the plans for the return of General Chou and the minority party representatives to Nanking.

DRAFT STATEMENT PREPARED FOR THE GENERALISSIMO

The Generalissimo on October 13 indicated to General Marshall and Ambassador Stuart that he wished them to consider the possibility of his making a statement, such as that previously suggested by General Marshall on September 27, but modified in accordance with recent changes in the situation.   General Marshall, referring to changes in the situation, pointed out that the important factor was the immediate cessation of hostilities and that, even if the Communists were forced to submit to various agreements by the pressure of Government military action, there could be no healthy results from political negotiations and reorganization of the Government as the bitterness engendered thereby would be too deep and the spirit of revenge and distrust too great.   The Generalissimo replied that he could not agree to an unconditional cessation of hostilities without some evidence for the people and the Government leaders that some advantage had been gained for the reorganization of the Government.   He mentioned the submission by the Communists of their list of delegates to the National Assembly as an example.

General Marshall reminded the Generalissimo that in early July the latter had said that it was first necessary to deal harshly with the Communists and later, after 2 or 3 months, to adopt a generous attitude. It seemed to General Marshall that after more than 3 months with the

Government in possession of all the important strategic points, that the time had come for the generous attitude of which he had spoken. The Generalissimo agreed to this but repeated his previous statement regarding the necessity of obtaining certain advantages prior to the cessation of hostilities.

Pursuant to the Generalissimo's suggestion, General Marshall and Dr. Stuart drew up and forwarded to the Generalissimo a draft of a statement for release by him, including therein the demand by the Generalissimo for submission of the names of the Communist delegates to the National Assembly. This draft statement, based upon the previous draft presented to the Generalissimo by General Marshall on September 27, contained the following points: [46]

The Five-Man Committee and the Committee of Three to hold simultaneous meetings immediately with the following understandings:

The various agreements tentatively reached by the Committee of Three during the June negotiations to be put into effect and the tentative agreement reached at the same time for the redisposition of troops in Manchuria to be confirmed.

Government troops north of the Yangtze River to continue in occupation of places now under their control until the Committee of Three reached agreement for the redistribution, reorganization and demobilization of the armed forces.

The PCC Steering Committee to confirm without delay any understanding reached by the Five-Man Committee.

Questions of local government to be settled by the newly organized State Council.

The Constitutional Reviewing Committee to be reconvened immediately and the agreed draft to be submitted to the National Assembly as the basis for its action.

Concurrent with the cessation of hostilities, which was to be effected immediately following the Communist Party's agreement to the foregoing procedure, the Communist Party to announce its intention of participating in the National Assembly by publishing the list of its delegates thereto.

EIGHT-POINT PROPOSAL BY THE GENERALISSIMO, OCTOBER 16, 1946

On October 16 the Generalissimo made a public statement [47] in which he announced the Government's views and presented an eight-point proposal, upon acceptance of which by the Chinese Communist Party the National Government was prepared to arrange for the immediate cessation of hostilities. The Generalissimo referred to his public state-

---

[46] See annex 104 for full text.
[47] See annex 105.

ment on October 10, in which he had said "the Government has always adhered to the political solution of our domestic political problem and would not give up this policy of peaceful settlement under whatever circumstances," and continued that, despite the recent Communist rejection of Government proposals, the Government would not abandon its policy of "peaceful settlement" and would still seek a settlement by mediation and consultation. The Generalissimo's eight-point proposal was very similar to the proposals set forth in the draft statement prepared by General Marshall and Dr. Stuart, the chief difference being (1) the deletion of the point regarding the separation of opposing troops in close contact upon which tentative agreement had been reached in June and (2) the exclusion of Manchuria from the proposal providing for the settlement of the question of local government by the State Council. One point required that the tentative agreement reached for the redisposition of troops in Manchuria be carried out in accordance with a fixed schedule without delay while the draft statement had provided only that this tentative agreement was to be confirmed. The proposals by the Generalissimo were also forwarded to General Marshall for transmission to the Chinese Communist representatives on October 17.

Despite the similarity of the Generalissimo's eight-point proposal to the draft statement submitted to him on September 27 by General Marshall, the lapse of time and the military events intervening, such as the occupation of Kalgan and the opening of a Government attack on Antung and Chefoo at the time of the announcement of this eight-point proposal, largely nullified most of the possibilities for good results.

THE COMMUNIST REPLY

The initial Communist reaction to the Generalissimo's eight-point proposal was unfavorable, as indicated by General Chou En-lai at Shanghai to a group of minority party leaders and by a Communist radio broadcast from Yenan. The Third Party Group (minority party leaders) were endeavoring to persuade General Chou to return to Nanking from Shanghai and three high-ranking National Government officials had also gone to Shanghai to confer with General Chou. General Marshall was of the opinion that the American mediators should stand aside at this time and encourage Chinese efforts to reach a settlement, with the Third Party Group in the position of the middleman. On October 20 General Chou En-lai and the members of the Third Party Group decided to return to Nanking on the following day. Apparently no new understanding had been reached, but the spirit of the conferences in Shanghai appeared to have offered the possibility of continued negotiations.

In early October the Generalissimo had informed General Marshall of his plans to proceed to Formosa for a brief visit on October 20. When, however, it was learned that General Chou En-lai and the Third Party Group had decided to return to Nanking, the General-issimo remained in Nanking until their arrival and had a brief talk with them before departing for Formosa on the same day. Prior to his departure, he informed General Marshall that he would be absent for only a few days and that he would return at any moment if his presence in Nanking were desirable in connection with the negotiations.

During this period fighting continued in various parts of North China, although the situation remained relatively quiet in Manchuria except for small-scale actions and Communist disruption of lines of communication. Communist actions along the Peiping-Hankow Railway line, intermingled with general fighting in the southern Hopei area crossed by this line, were reportedly devoted largely to the destruction of the rail lines. Government forces were apparently centering their attention on coal mining areas and they occupied two important coal mining centers during this period. Other high lights of this period were the Communist-organized mass demonstrations in Harbin and Tsitsihar in northern Manchuria directed toward the withdrawal of American troops from China and criticism of Ameri-can interference in internal Chinese affairs. Further indications of a deterioration in the situation were seen in the gradual evacuation of Communist Party personnel from Nanking, Shanghai and Chung-king to Yenan in United States Army planes furnished at the request of the Communist delegation in Nanking.

There still remained, however, some basis for hope in the situation in that General Chou En-lai had finally returned to Nanking from Shanghai and in that the Third Party Group, whose chief weapon in the discussions both with the Government and the Communists was the question of participation or nonparticipation in the National Assem-bly, was actively engaged in the mediation effort. This enabled the American mediators to remain in the background.

On October 24, General Chou En-lai informed Ambassador Stuart that the Chinese Communists could not accept the Government eight-point proposal.

THE SPREADING OF HOSTILITIES

In the meantime military activity showed no signs of abating. Gov-ernment forces occupied the last of the main stations on the Tsinan-Tsingtao Railway and Government forces were moving north along the Peiping-Hankow Railway in southern Hopei. Most serious was the opening of a Government drive on Antung in Manchuria, from which the Generalissimo was now insisting that the Communists withdraw within 15 days after the issuance of a cease-fire order. Communist propaganda attacks on the United States continued, demanding the immediate withdrawal of all American troops and of American support from the National Government. Further indications of the deterioration in the situation were seen in the reduction of Communist personnel at the Executive Headquarters at Peiping to the point that the Communist branch was practically inoperative. The Communists had also withdrawn their members from all field teams in Government-occupied areas in China proper except at four points.

ATTEMPT AT MEDIATION BY THE THIRD PARTY GROUP

In a discussion of the situation with General Marshall on October 26, General Chou En-lai said that if the Government military advances continued there would be no necessity for continued negotiations and the Committee of Three should take action in this matter. Further questioning revealed that General Chou did not consider a meeting of the Committee of Three the issue, although he did not object in any way to such a meeting. This conversation revealed the extent to which his attitude was governed by the deep suspicion of any terms presented by the National Government, even when it was pointed out to him that certain of the National Government's eight points represented terms desired by the Communists on which the National Government had not previously agreed. General Marshall pointed out to him that the distrust was so great on both sides that there was all the more need to find some method on which both could agree for the termination of the hostilities.

He continued that the situation presented an almost impossible prospect for agreement unless divested of every detail not vital to either party and that it was hoped that the Third Party Group might be able to find some basis for compromise, a course infinitely better than a mediation procedure by Americans since it would then be a settlement by the Chinese themselves.

General Chou indicated that if the Third Party Group could produce a compromise proposal with a sound basis he would discuss it with them, but that, in view of the military situation and Government attacks in various areas, there would be no basis for any negotiations if this situation continued. In that event, he said, his presence in Nanking would be useless.

General Marshall pointed out that he and Dr. Stuart had tried every possible means of stopping the hostilities without success—their proposal for the Five-Man Committee, to which the Government finally agreed but to which General Chou would not agree; the

Kalgan truce proposal, which General Chou had characterized as capitulation; and now another somewhat similar situation in which it was hoped that hostilities could be ended through the efforts of the Third Party Group.

The continued absence of the Generalissimo from Nanking, together with the open resumption of the Government military campaign in Manchuria, was detrimental to the whole situation. The Third Party Group was becoming discouraged since its three-point proposal [48] for a settlement of the differences had been rejected by the Generalissimo, who had told them that they should have adopted his eight-point proposal of October 16. General Chou En-lai had unofficially accepted practically all of this proposal, but the news of the Government capture of Antung caused him to say that he must await instructions from Yenan. The Third Party Group then recommended that there be an informal discussion by National Government, Communist, and Third Party Group representatives. The Generalissimo agreed but insisted that his eight-point proposal constitute the agenda. General Chou En-lai agreed and the meeting was scheduled for November 4.

On October 28 in a discussion of the situation with the Generalissimo, General Marshall described the deep seated distrust the Communist Party had of the motives of the Generalissimo and the Kuomintang leaders, to which had been added their distrust of the American mediators. He pointed out that the Communists had no intention of surrendering and that, while they had lost cities, they had not lost armies, nor was it likely that they would lose their armies since they had no intention of making a stand or fighting to a finish at any place. He continued that the Generalissimo might be able to take Harbin but that the Government would then be in for endless trouble.

The Generalissimo replied that the time had come to halt the fighting but he did not wish this to be conveyed to the Third Party Group. General Marshall then explained that this group appeared to be the only hope in the situation and urged the Generalissimo to show them every consideration and build up their prestige by making concessions and encouraging them to speak frankly to him. He further pointed out that they had become so discouraged by the failure of their efforts that they had expressed the desire to withdraw from the negotiations and return to Shanghai.

On October 30 the Generalissimo informed Ambassador Stuart that he was willing to make two additional concessions:

---

[48] See annex 106.

(1) The cease-fire order would apply to Manchuria as well as to China proper. Military redispositions would follow the June settlement and local administration would be dealt with uniformly in all of China.

(2) Cities and *hsien* along the Changchun Railway trunk line, except for those already under occupation by the Government, would not be taken over before the reorganization of the Government.

The arguments of the Communist Party at this time were not consistent. They had insisted that the Government military leaders were determined to settle the issues by force, yet the Communists were apparently risking the continuation and expansion of the fighting in the hope that the Government would make concessions in order to obtain the list of Communist delegates to the National Assembly. Furthermore, the issues of the State Council and local government were not now at this stage as difficult to solve as they had been in June and it seemed that the principal outstanding issue was the reorganization of the Executive Yuan. The Communists and the Democratic League seemed to attach great importance to this issue as a condition precedent to the convening of the National Assembly. In view of the discouragement of the Third Party Group, the problem was to make this Group aware of the fact that the military settlement was greatly affected by political issues and that the members of the Group should stand together and remain strong under the pressure of the Government and the Communist Party to divide them. The Government continued to be unwilling to agree to the cessation of hostilities until the Communists submitted a list of their delegates to the National Assembly and the Communists were willing to submit such a list only to a reorganized Government, which to them meant the reorganization of the Executive Yuan. The Generalissimo had indicated that he would not reorganize the Executive Yuan until after the meeting of the National Assembly.

Several developments at this time had a bearing on the negotiations. General Chou En-lai had agreed to return to Nanking from Shanghai only if the Third Party Group would stand with the Communist Party in refusing to nominate delegates to the National Assembly until the Government had been reorganized in strict accordance with the PCC resolutions. This was proving very embarrassing to the Third Party Group. The Group were urging General Marshall and Dr. Stuart to take the lead again in the negotiations, but the American mediators declined to do so because it was very important that, if possible, a Chinese neutral group act in mediation, at least on political questions.

Although the National Government had agreed to participate in an informal discussion of the various issues with the Communists and the Third Party Group, the Government representatives did not attend the meeting on November 4 and the Third Party Group merely asked General Chou to state the Communist demands. This he did very completely, covering every issue.

On November 5 the Generalissimo informed General Marshall and Ambassador Stuart that the absence of the Government members from the meeting previously agreed to had resulted from a number of indications that the Communists wished to eliminate American mediation. General Marshall expressed regret that the failure of the National Government to participate in the meeting was due to this reason and stated that the Communist Party either accepted the American mediators or did not—they either trusted the American mediators or did not trust them and Government action could not force a decision in this particular manner. The Generalissimo then said that the time had come to stop the fighting and that he was prepared for an unconditional termination of hostilities. He expressed a desire to have General Marshall and Ambassador Stuart advise him with respect to the announcement of the cessation of hostilities, together with a reference to the convening of the National Assembly, which he hoped the minority parties would attend.

GENERALISSIMO CHIANG'S STATEMENT OF NOVEMBER 8, 1946

General Marshall and Dr. Stuart, therefore, prepared a draft statement which represented the views of the Generalissimo regarding the termination of hostilities and met the issues which were certain to be raised by the minority parties regarding conditions under which the National Assembly would meet and adopt a constitution. (At the request of the Generalissimo, General Marshall had frequently, during the negotiations, prepared for his consideration and possible use drafts of statements or of proposals which might be introduced into the discussions. In so doing, General Marshall had acted as a staff officer might on behalf of the Generalissimo in drawing up documents containing the latter's views.) Meanwhile, they received a draft of a statement prepared by the Generalissimo which they believed would further complicate the situation since it was highly provocative, lengthy, argumentative and difficult to understand. Furthermore it would not terminate the fighting in a way that promised more than a threat of future use of force.

On November 7 General Marshall and Dr. Stuart met with the Generalissimo at the latter's request and presented to him a Chinese translation of their draft.[49] They expressed the opinion that his draft statement would merely aggravate the situation in China. The Gen-

---

[49] See annex 107.

eralissimo then explained that in preparing the draft he had had to take into consideration a number of important points:

(1) While there had previously been a divided opinion in the Government regarding the proper course to be followed, there was at this time a complete unanimity of opinion that a policy of force was the only course to follow.

(2) He must give careful consideration in the organization of the National Assembly to the delegates who had been legally elected in 1936 and were now assembled in Nanking and not emphasize the dominant importance of the PCC resolutions in contrast to the 1936 draft constitution.

(3) He must also give careful consideration to the morale of the Army, considering the losses that had been recently sustained, if they were to be greeted by the announcement of an unconditional cessation of hostilities which amounted to the virtual unconditional surrender of the National Government's position and contentions.

The Generalissimo continued that he could not support the statement in the draft prepared by General Marshall and Dr. Stuart regarding an unconditional termination of hostilities before his military and political leaders and further explained that he stood practically alone in the belief that matters could be settled by peaceful negotiations and the fighting stopped. The Generalissimo then asked General Marshall and Dr. Stuart to reconsider their draft in the light of his statements and advise him accordingly. General Marshall replied that he would need an opportunity to consider with Dr. Stuart the points of view expressed by the Generalissimo as he was seriously concerned whether he should participate, as a representative of the United States Government, in the preparation of a paper in accordance with the points of view he had indicated, which were contrary to the views of General Marshall and those, he thought, of the United States Government.

In submitting a redraft of the statement to the Generalissimo on November 8, General Marshall stated that it should be clearly understood that the redraft did not have his approval as a representative of the United States Government. He continued that he had merely endeavored to help the Generalissimo as staff officers might assist him in drafting his views in the least provocative manner but that the redraft did not have his approval since he was in almost complete disagreement with the attitude of the Government military leaders.

The statement issued by the Generalissimo on November 8 was modified, but the method proposed for stopping the fighting was inconclusive and still held, in effect, a threat of renewed battle to force a political decision.[49a]   The statement expressed hope that the State Council would be reorganized while the final redraft prepared by General Marshall and Dr. Stuart had indicated that it should be reorganized in order to carry out its functions for the reorganization of the Government in accordance with the PCC resolutions.   This would include the reorganization of the Executive Yuan, but the Generalissimo's statement merely said that such a reorganization would not take place prior to the meeting of the National Assembly and made no mention of the PCC resolutions.   As a result of a meeting between General Chou En-lai and the Third Party Group, the former, under date of November 8, forwarded to General Marshall a letter [50] which, in effect, constituted a reply to the eight-point proposal of the Generalissimo.   The letter was noncommittal and referred only casually to the eight points, but it did hold open the door for continued negotiations and peace.   General Marshall transmitted a copy of this letter to the National Government on the same day.

CEASE-FIRE ORDER BY THE NATIONAL GOVERNMENT

During the period preceding the announcement by the Generalissimo of his issuance of a cease-fire order to Government troops, there had been no improvement in the military picture.   Fighting continued in North China and the Government forces occupied Tunghua in Manchuria, which had been one of the cities from which the Government had demanded the withdrawal of Communist forces at the time of the Generalissimo's absence in Formosa.   Another factor of considerable importance in the situation was the decreased effectiveness of the Executive Headquarters as a result of the vicious Communist propaganda attacks on the Americans and the anti-American demonstrations and campaigns staged in Communist-held areas.

The issuance by the Generalissimo of a cease-fire order set the stage, however, for the convening of the National Assembly against a background of peace.   The Government approach to the National Assembly was not, however, sufficiently in accordance with the PCC resolutions and meant that, if all the delegates appeared, the Kuomintang would have an overwhelming majority, and a simple majority vote could determine the character of the constitution without much consideration of the fundamental guarantees agreed to in the PCC.   The Government had been unwilling to agree to any temporary adjournment after the formal convocation, as proposed by General Marshall and Dr. Stuart, and had passed up an excellent

[49a] See annex 108.
[50] See annex 109.

opportunity of capitalizing in a conciliatory manner on the proposal to stop the fighting.

CONVENING OF THE NATIONAL ASSEMBLY, NOVEMBER 15, 1946

On November 10 the National Government requested a meeting of the Committee of Three. In view of the failure to reach any agreement regarding the National Assembly, General Chou En-lai was reluctant to attend the meeting but finally agreed to an informal meeting which was held on November 11.

General Chou En-lai stated that it appeared futile to proceed with arrangements for the termination of hostilities when unilateral action of the Government in convening the National Assembly contrary to the PCC resolutions meant a definite "split" in China. After the Government representative presented its proposal in detail, General Chou finally agreed to transmit the proposal to Yenan for prompt reply and indicated that he would study the matter and proceed on the basis that whatever the political impasse at this time, he would join in working for an agreement for the formal termination of hostilities.

Meanwhile an informal meeting of the PCC Steering Committee was held, the first since April 24, at which the Communist Party requested a postponement of the National Assembly until the end of November. This request was transmitted to the Generalissimo by a prominent nonparty member of the Third Party Group.

The PCC Steering Committee also practically reached agreement on the composition of the State Council and the Committee appeared to have agreed that the reorganization of the Executive Yuan should be planned for prior to the National Assembly but not announced until after the adjournment of the Assembly. At this point the Government stopped the meetings of the Committee, but an informal meeting was held on November 12 which may have had some connection with the decision by the Generalissimo on November 11 to delay the convening of the National Assembly for three days. He informed Dr. Stuart that at the urgent request of the non-party delegates he had agreed to this postponement and that they had promised that, if such a delay were granted, the Third Party Group would submit their lists of delegates and possibly the Communist Party would also do so. The Communist Party informed the Government, however, on November 12 that it would not participate in nor did it approve of the National Assembly since it had been convened and also postponed unilaterally by the Kuomintang.

The National Assembly was formally convened on November 15 with a decidedly limited representation from non-Kuomintang groups.

The names of additional delegates from non-party and Youth Party personnel were submitted on the night of November 15, but the Communist Party and the Democratic League were not represented. The postponement for 3 days had resulted in the promise of attendance by some of the Third Party Group, but it had had the effect of disrupting the unity of action of that Group and had seriously, if not fatally, weakened their influence for good as a balance between the two major parties.

The address of the Generalissimo at the opening of the Assembly was mild in tone and was devoted chiefly to the achievements and objectives of the National Government.[51] General Chou En-lai, however, on November 16 issued a statement to the press regarding the National Assembly, in which he was strongly critical of the Kuomintang, charged that its action in convening the Assembly was contrary to the PCC resolutions, and gave notice that the Communist Party did not recognize the Assembly. He also stated that the door of negotiations had been "slammed" by the Kuomintang authorities.[52]

THE END OF AMERICAN MEDIATION

General Chou En-lái called on General Marshall on November 16 and asked for transportation for himself and other Communist representatives to Yenan during the following week. He indicated that he was leaving some members of the Communist delegation at Nanking and that he expected to study the situation with the Communist leaders at Yenan. He expressed the wish that the Executive Headquarters be continued for the time being even though there was little it could do. He expressed fear that the National Government would undertake offensive operations against Yenan and said that if this occurred it would mean the end of all hope for a negotiated peace. He also asked that transportation be provided for Communist personnel in the Executive Headquarters in Peiping and Changchun and in Nanking and Shanghai to evacuate them to points of safety. General Marshall stated that American planes would be provided for the purposes requested by General Chou and added that, while he had had no information of National Government plans for an attack on Yenan, he would deplore such action and oppose it strongly. He also said that if such an attack occurred he would consider that it terminated his mission.

In conclusion, General Marshall asked General Chou En-lai to take up with the Communist leaders the question of his continued mediation. He said that it was useless for him to endeavor to mediate if he

[51] See annex 110.
[52] See annex 111.

were not trusted as being sincere in an effort to be impartial and that under such circumstances it would be useless for him to remain in China. General Marshall stated that he wished General Chou to determine formally from the Communist leaders at Yenan whether specifically they wished him to continue in his mediation role and asked that the matter be viewed as a plain business proposition without regard to Chinese considerations of "face" since he was not interested in "face." He explained that his sole interest was the question of whether he could render some service to China by way of mediation. General Chou stated that he sympathized with the request by General Marshall and that he would place the question before the appropriate Communist authorities at Yenan.

General Chou En-lai departed for Yenan on November 19 in a United States Army plane. His departure brought to an end the long period of negotiations and discussions begun in January 1946. The door had not been closed to further negotiation by either side, but it seemed likely that a fresh start would have to be made before there would be any possibility of bringing about an understanding between the two parties. The attitude of the Communist Party and the Democratic League indicated their belief that the PCC resolutions had been totally destroyed and that it would be necessary to convene another conference of all parties similar to that held in January.

It seemed apparent to General Marshall that the Government military leaders were in the saddle and were thoroughly convinced that the Communists would not carry out any agreement reached. The strong political clique in the Kuomintang was firmly convinced that the Communists would merely disrupt any government in which they participated. With these two forces working together and the Communist repulse of every overture General Marshall and Dr. Stuart had persuaded the Government to make, the existing tragic situation had developed. It seemed to General Marshall that the Government had been using the negotiations largely for its own purposes. Following the breakdown of the negotiations in June, the Government had been waging war on a constantly increasing scale, heavily absorbing Government funds. These military expenditures, which were consuming about 70 percent of the total Government budget, served to increase inflation at the same time the Chinese Government was asking the United States for large loans.

The expanded currency continued to go into commodity speculation and hoarding on an increasing scale, and wholesale prices had risen about seven times during the year. In an abortive effort to combat inflation by absorbing currency from circulation, the Government engaged in heavy sales of gold taken from its reserves. In addition, despite the very considerable imports that were made available through UNRRA and other foreign aid measures, the Government's foreign exchange reserves were drawn on to procure imports for which the depressed level of exports and inward remittances had failed to provide the necessary means of payment. At the end of 1946, official Chinese reserves of gold and United States dollars had been depleted by approximately 450 million dollars, or about 50 percent.

On the other side, the Communist Party had, in General Marshall's opinion, defeated itself through its own suspicions, refusing to agree to possible procedures which might well have resulted in a settlement of the issues. This had been particularly true of its rejection of the proposal for the Five-Man Committee under Ambassador Stuart, which might have led to organization of the State Council and the carrying out of the other PCC agreements, and of its almost contemptuous rejection of the Kalgan truce proposal. It had misconstrued each overture arranged by General Marshall and Dr. Stuart and had apparently been convinced by its own campaign of public misrepresentation of American intentions and actions. It also chose to ignore in discussion and in criticisms of Government actions its own military and other actions that were violations of agreements.

At this time a high-ranking Government official was urging upon General Marshall the need for American financial assistance to meet the serious economic situation. General Marshall was very emphatic in stating to him that it was useless to expect the United States to pour money into the vacuum being created by the Government military leaders in their determination to settle matters by force and that it was also useless to expect the United States to pour money into a Government dominated by a completely reactionary clique bent on exclusive control of governmental power.

Another ranking Government official approached General Marshall at this time in regard to action taken by the Export-Import Bank to reject General Marshall's recommendation, approved by the Department of State, for the extension of loans for the Canton-Hankow Railway and for the Yellow River bridge in north Honan. General Marshall explained that the Bank had given as the reason for this action that there was not sufficient prospect of amortization to justify the loans. When the Government official said that he did not understand why the loans had been rejected since they had nothing to do with the Government military campaign, General Marshall pointed out that it was the open corruption of the Government as well as its military policy which entered into consideration.

GENERAL MARSHALL'S VIEWS ON THE SITUATION IN CHINA

On December 1 General Marshall held a long conference with the Generalissimo, which revealed the wide divergence of their views on what course should be followed to reach a peaceful settlement in China. General Marshall pointed out that in his opinion the complete distrust of the National Government in the good intentions of the Communist Party during the past spring had been replaced by an overwhelming distrust on the part of the Communists of the good intent of any proposal advanced by the Government toward a peaceful settlement of the differences. In the recent negotiations, General Marshall and Ambassador Stuart had found it impossible to convince the Communists of the good intentions of the Government or even of the integrity of action of the American mediators. It was General Marshall's view that even the most tolerant approaches of the National Government, notably that represented by the Generalissimo's eight-point proposal of October 16, had been neutralized by military action—in this particular case an attack on Antung and Chefoo at the time of the announcement of this proposal. In regard to the economic situation General Marshall pointed out that military expenditures were reported to be consuming about 70 percent of the National Government's budget, thus creating a vacuum in Government assets in order to support extensive military efforts at the same time that he was being pressed to recommend various loans by the United States Government. He informed the Generalissimo that in the event of a financial collapse the Kuomintang would be imperiled and a fertile field would be created for the spread of communism. General Marshall observed that the National Government's military commanders in the field were wholly unaccustomed to any consideration of financial restrictions. He said that the Communists were aware of the approaching crisis and that this entered into their calculations in forming plans. Directly opposed to this economic problem was the view of the National Government military leaders that the issues could be settled by force. General Marshall said that he not only disagreed with this view from a military standpoint but also felt that before sufficient time could elapse to prove the accuracy of such a view there would be a complete economic collapse. He pointed out that the inability of the National Government to keep open the railway between Tientsin and Chinhuangtao since the withdrawal of the United States Marines in September was one example; another was the fact that sections of Hopei Province, presumably reoccupied by the National Government forces, were still dotted throughout with Communist headquarters. General Marshall summed up the situation with the statement that the Communists were too large a military and civil force to be ignored and that, even if one disregarded the brutality of the inevitable procedure necessary to destroy them, they probably could not be eliminated by military campaigning. He believed, therefore, that it was imperative that efforts be made to bring them into the Government and that the greatest care should be taken to avoid having military action disrupt the procedure of negotiations.

The Generalissimo said that he was firmly convinced that the Communists never intended to cooperate with the National Government and that, acting under Russian influence, their purpose was to disrupt the National Government. He felt that it was necessary to destroy the Communist military forces and believed that if this were done there would be no difficulty in handling the Communist question. He went on to say that the situation was different from that existing during early campaigns against the Communist forces in that roads were available this time to permit freedom of military movement; he felt confident, therefore, that the Communist forces could be exterminated in from 8 to 10 months. The Generalissimo, referring to the economic situation, said that, while it was more serious in the cities, the Chinese economy was based largely on the agrarian population and there was no danger for a long time of an economic collapse.[53]

At this point General Marshall briefly, but firmly, restated his view that this large Communist group could not be ignored and that the National Government was not capable of destroying it before the country would be faced with a complete economic collapse. General Marshall did not discuss what was to him of vital concern: the possibility of a collapse of the Kuomintang and the evident growing disapproval of the character of the local government, or misgovernment, that the Kuomintang was giving the country.

Under date of December 4 the Communist representative at Nanking forwarded to General Marshall a message from General Chou En-lai at Yenan setting forth, for transmission to the Generalissimo, the Communists' terms for reopening negotiations:[54] (1) the dissolution of the National Assembly and (2) the restoration of troop positions held as of January 13 in accordance with the cessation of hostilities agreement. General Marshall forwarded a copy of this message without comment to the National Government. General Chou En-lai's message made no reply to General Marshall's request for an indication by the Communist Party of its attitude toward his mediation efforts and posed conditions which the National Government obviously could not be expected to accept. It appeared that the Communist Party had, in effect, rejected American mediation.

---

[53] See below, pp. 220–229.
[54] See annex 112.

The Generalissimo had in early December indicated the Chinese Government's desire to obtain General Marshall's services as an adviser. General Marshall had declined the offer since he believed it unreasonable to expect that his services as adviser to the National Government could materially promote a beneficial reaction within the Government when as a mediator with full backing from the United States Government he had been unable to influence the Chinese Government. General Marshall was struggling with two problems—the power of the reactionaries in the Government and the difficulty of dealing with the Communist Party with its immense distrust of the Kuomintang. The best defense against communism in his opinion was for the existing Government in China to carry out reforms which would gain for it the support of the people. He was concerned over the destructive influence of the reactionaries in the Government and felt that the Generalissimo's own feelings were so deep and his associations of such long standing that it was most difficult to separate him from the reactionary group. He considered that the solution called for the building up of the liberals under the Generalissimo while at the same time removing the influence of the reactionaries. In considering the Generalissimo's desire for American advice, General Marshall felt that American advice could be helpful in many matters but that corruption within the Government could not be eliminated through advice but rather through the existence of an effective opposition party.

He therefore endeavored, in conversations with National Government leaders, to emphasize the importance and necessity of the adoption by the National Assembly of a constitution in keeping with the PCC resolutions, which would be at least an initial step in the direction of representative government in China. It was the opinion of General Marshall that if this kind of constitution were adopted and the State Council reorganized with seats left vacant for the Communists and the Democratic League, and if the reorganization of the Executive Yuan were then begun, it might be possible to discuss with the Communists ways of their coming into the National Assembly.

In furtherance of the idea of endeavoring to build up a liberal group in China to a position of influence, General Marshall took every opportunity in conversations with minority and non-party Chinese to emphasize the necessity of the unification of the minority parties and the organization of a liberal group which could serve as a balance between the two major parties. He pointed out that the liberal Chinese should band together in a single liberal patriotic organization devoted to the welfare of the people and not to the selfish interests of minority party group leaders. They would then be able to exert influence in the political situation, an influence which would increase as the group gained prestige. Such a group could stand between the Kuomintang and the Communist Party and neither of them could normally take a decisive step without the support of the liberal party. The minority parties, however, had allowed themselves to be divided and were consequently unable to influence the situation or prevent the use of military force by the Government or the promotion of economic collapse by the Communists. In the midst of this deplorable situation stood the Chinese people alone bearing the full weight of the tragedy.

In conversations with the Generalissimo at this juncture General Marshall noted definite inconsistencies. The Generalissimo said that he would do everything he could to bring the Communists into the Government by peaceful negotiation, but when discussing the question of reopening the two main railways in North China he said that it was useless to attempt to negotiate with the Communists on this question, which would have to be solved by force. He also said that if the railways were taken by force, the Communists would then be compelled to come to terms. He had taken a similar attitude in June, when he had said that "given time, the ripe apple will fall into our laps," and again in August, when he had said that "if hostilities are stopped, there would be no way to force the Communists to attend the National Assembly."

THE WORK OF THE NATIONAL ASSEMBLY

Following the departure of General Chou En-lai for Yenan and the termination of the negotiations, attention was centered chiefly on the National Assembly and the question of the type of constitution it might adopt. There were early indications that the Kuomintang reactionaries were opposed to the adoption of a constitution along the lines of the PCC resolutions and that they were endeavoring to obtain approval of the May 5, 1936 constitution in substantially unchanged form. These circumstances required that the Generalissimo take a strong stand if the constitution to be adopted were to be in general accord with the PCC resolutions.

The Generalissimo did exercise a determined personal leadership, assisted by almost all other groups and individuals in the Assembly, in opposing the extreme right-wing clique. The Assembly adjourned on December 25 with the Generalissimo in full and confident control of the situation, having demonstrated his ability to override the Kuomintang reactionaries and having restored his prestige through his action in securing the adoption of a constitution of a democratic character in reasonable accord with the PCC resolutions.

While the new constitution was on its face a democratic document, General Marshall was concerned with the degree and manner of its enforcement. The passage of the constitution was only the beginning and the only guarantee of an honest reorganization of the Government and a genuine enforcement of the constitution lay in the development of a truly liberal group in China. General Marshall feared that if the minority and non-party liberal groups continued to operate individually, the reorganization of the Government might be a synthetic one. He continued, therefore, to emphasize the importance of the organization of the Chinese liberals into an effective force, which would have as its objective the support of whatever appeared to be a good government.

THE COMMUNIST PARTY'S REACTION

The Chinese Communist Party was apparently adamant in refusing to recognize the National Assembly and the new constitution and on demanding the acceptance of its two conditions as prerequisites to further negotiation. Communist propaganda attacks on the United States grew stronger during this period and Communist spokesmen indicated the probable Communist strategy—the use of constant harassing tactics on Kuomintang weak points to prevent the reopening of lines of communication and the refusal of further negotiation until the Government had become weakened by economic deterioration. The Communists still had made no reply to General Marshall's inquiry regarding his mediation role.

Although there appeared to be slight prospect for the renewal of negotiations, General Marshall and Ambassador Stuart, pursuant to the Generalissimo's request, suggested that definite proposals be presented to the Communist Party without any attendant publicity. They indicated that, with the adoption of a sound constitution, if the Government proceeded with the establishment of the State Council and began a genuine reorganization of the Executive Yuan, the Generalissimo might send a few representatives of importance and liberal standing to Yenan to discuss with the Communists the question of reopening negotiations for the cessation of hostilities and Communist participation in the reorganization of the Government. However, before the good faith of the Government had been at least partially established by the adoption of a constitution in accord with the PCC resolutions, news of the Government purpose had become known. The Communist reaction was unfavorable and there were indications that they would resent reorganization of the State Council and the Executive Yuan prior to consultation with them, apparently feeling that this would close the door on any possibility of responsible participation on their part.

On December 27 General Marshall, in reply to the Generalissimo's request for his comments on the situation, made the following remarks: It was unlikely that the Communists would commit themselves to an agreement at this time due to their overwhelming suspicion that it was the Government's intention to destroy them by military force. The Government's military commanders had erred considerably in their optimistic estimate of what they could achieve toward suppression of the Communists. They had stated in June that Kiangsu Province would be cleared of Communist forces within two months and the Province had not yet been cleared. At the same time they had said that the Communists could be brought to terms from a military standpoint within three months. That had not occurred after six months. The Government refusal to terminate hostilities in order to force the Communists to participate in the National Assembly had failed of its purpose. If the Communists would not renew negotiations, the Government should go ahead with the reorganization, leaving the door open for Communist and Democratic League participation. The Generalissimo, by his leadership in the National Assembly in opposing the reactionaries and securing the adoption of a reasonably sound constitution, had gained a great moral victory which had rehabilitated, if not added to his prestige. It was most important, therefore, that he demonstrate at this time that the new constitution was not a mere collection of words and that he was determined to institute a democratic form of government. He must by his own indirect leadership father a coalition of the minority groups into a liberal party, since, unless such sizable minority groups existed, his efforts in the National Assembly to secure a sound constitution would be regarded as mere camouflage for an intention to proceed with one-party government. The various minority groups could not of themselves manage an amalgamation and such action would require his active assistance. He should also call on the minority party leaders to nominate men for various posts rather than follow previous practices of neutralizing the opposition leaders by bribing them with attractive appointments. If he did not take such action, there could be no genuine two-party government and his integrity and position would be open to serious attack. The organization of the minority parties into a large liberal group would assist him greatly and he could place himself in the position of the father of his country rather than continue merely as the leader of the Kuomintang one-party government.

VIII. THE END OF THE MARSHALL MISSION

GENERAL MARSHALL'S REFUSAL TO CONTINUE AS MEDIATOR

General Marshall remained in China during this period in the hope that he might be able to use his influence toward the adoption of a genuinely democratic constitution. In the past he had often felt that the National Government had desired American mediation as a shield for its military campaigns and at this time the Communists had no desire for further American mediation but feared being placed in an unfavorable position if they were to reject formally such mediation. He was not willing to allow himself thus to be used by either party, nor did he intend to serve as an umpire on the battlefield. He felt that his continued usefulness as a negotiator had practically been wrecked by the recent Communist rejection of all Government overtures, actions which played directly into the hands of the reactionaries in the Government, from whom his chief opposition had always come.

General Marshall was of the opinion that, if the Communists declined to reopen negotiations and repulsed the Government's overtures, the Executive Headquarters should be dismantled. He also believed that he should be recalled to give a first-hand report to the President on the situation. It was his hope that by issuing a very frank statement at the time of his recall he might be able to weaken the power of the reactionaries and strengthen the position and influence of the better elements, and he believed that the time had come when it was going to be necessary for the Chinese themselves to do the things he had endeavored to persuade them to do. He hoped, therefore, that by a frank statement of Chinese Communist misrepresentations and vicious propaganda against the United States he might be able to give some guidance to misinformed people both in China and in the United States.

GENERAL MARSHALL'S RECALL AND FINAL STATEMENT

On January 6, 1947, the President announced that he had directed General Marshall to return to Washington to report in person on the situation in China. General Marshall left China en route to the United States on January 8, and shortly after his departure the Department of State made public the personal full and frank statement referred to above. The greatest obstacle to peace in China, the General stated, was the almost overwhelming suspicion with which the Kuomintang and the Chinese Communists regarded each other. Other important factors which he blamed for the breakdown of negotiations included the opposition of the dominant group of Kuomintang reactionaries, the efforts of the extreme Communists to produce an economic situation which would facilitate the overthrow or collapse of the Government, and the dominating influence of the military in China. "The salvation of the situation," he reported, "would be the assumption of leadership by the liberals in the Government and in the minority parties and successful action on their part under the leadership of the Generalissimo would lead to unity through good government." [55]

In conclusion, General Marshall said that he had spoken very frankly because in no other way could he hope to bring to the American people even a partial understanding of the complex problem and that he was expressing his views publicly, as was his duty, to present his estimate of the situation and its possibilities to the American people.

Prior to his departure from China, General Marshall had conversations with several high-ranking Government officials. He stressed the necessity of removing the dominant military clique and the reactionaries from the Government structure. He explained that the frank statement he expected to make would arouse bitterness, particularly among the radicals, the reactionaries and the irreconcilables. He said that he had exerted every effort to create an opportunity for the better elements in China to rise to the top, and he hoped that his statement would assist in making possible the organization of a patriotic liberal group under the indirect sponsorship of the Generalissimo. He continued that he considered such action imperative from the standpoint of the Generalissimo since he needed a respectable opposition party in order to prove to the world his sincerity in establishing a democratic form of government in China. General Marshall pointed out that such an opposition party would be a strong force for good, which the Generalissimo could use to wipe out graft, corruption and incompetence in the Government and in the Kuomintang and which would provide an effective check on the existing dictatorial control of the military leaders.

PRESIDENT TRUMAN'S STATEMENT OF DECEMBER 18, 1946

Shortly before General Marshall's recall to Washington, President Truman on December 18, 1946, after full consultation with his Special Representative in China, issued a further statement on China. He reaffirmed American policy as laid down in his statement of December 15, 1945, and reviewed events in China in relation to that policy during the intervening year. He restated the American belief that a "united and democratic China" was of the utmost importance to world peace and that a broadening of the base of the Chinese Government

---
[55] See annex 113 for full text.

to make it representative of the Chinese people would further China's progress toward that goal.   He expressed deep regret that China had not yet been able to achieve unity by peaceful methods but hoped that the Chinese Government would yet find a solution.   He characterized as still sound the plans for political unification and military reorganization agreed upon early in 1946 but never fully implemented.   Stating that the United States would give careful and sympathetic consideration to ways and means which were presented for constructive aid to China, the President laid down a continued policy of avoiding involvement in Chinese civil strife and of persevering in a policy of "helping the Chinese people to bring about peace and economic recovery in their country." [56]

The Kuomintang press generally interpreted this statement as an endorsement of the National Government's policy and position while the Communist Party radio attacked it as "mainly an apology for the United States Government's reactionary policy toward China since March of this year."

AMERICAN WITHDRAWAL FROM THE COMMITTEE OF THREE AND EXECUTIVE HEADQUARTERS

On January 7, 1947, President Truman announced the nomination of General Marshall as Secretary of State.   Shortly after General Marshall's assumption of office the decision was reached to terminate the connection of the United States with the Committee of Three and to withdraw American personnel from Executive Headquarters.[57]   This action made it possible to withdraw all United States Marines from North China, except for a guard contingent at Tsingtao, the location of the United States Naval Training Group engaged in training Chinese naval personnel.   In issuing an announcement regarding the termination of the Executive Headquarters, the National Government expressed its appreciation of the American efforts to achieve peace and unity in China.

CONCLUSION

The termination of the American mediation effort did not change the traditional attitude of the United States toward China.   That effort had failed to bring peace and unity to China.   There was a point beyond which American mediation could not go.   Peace and stability in China must, in the final analysis, be achieved by the efforts of the Chinese themselves.   The United States had endeavored to assist in attaining those goals and in the process had been sub-

---

[56] See annex 114.
[57] See annex 115.

jected to bitter attack by many groups, both in China and abroad—attacks which had, deliberately or otherwise, misrepresented the intentions and purposes of the United States Government. The issue at this point was squarely up to the Chinese themselves. It was General Marshall's opinion that only through the existence of a liberal opposition group in China could there be a guarantee of good government and of progress toward stability. The future efforts of the Chinese themselves would determine whether it was possible to give peace and stability to the people of China. It was General Marshall's belief that the United States should continue to view sympathetically the problem facing the Chinese and should take any action, without intervening in China's internal affairs, that would assist China in realizing those aims which represented the hopes and aspirations of the Chinese people as well as those of the United States.

IX. ECONOMIC DEVELOPMENTS DURING THE MARSHALL MISSION

EFFECTS OF INTERNAL CONFLICT

The economic situation in 1946, while not decisive, did influence developments; more importantly, it carried serious implications for the future and in no small measure indicated National Government capabilities. The discouraging lack of progress toward a political and military settlement in 1946 was matched by a steady deterioration of the National Government's economic position. In contrast to the relatively bright situation prevailing on V–J Day, China, 16 months later, was gripped by a mounting inflation, its reserves of foreign exchange had been partially depleted, and no real beginning had been made on the task of internal rehabilitation and economic development. Rather, the outbreak of widespread fighting between Nationalist and Communist forces had resulted in general damage to mining and transportation facilities and in the progressive isolation of mineral and agricultural production from centers of consumption and export. The nature of the struggle in China made it possible for the Chinese Communists to better their relative position by tactics aimed at destruction and economic stagnation, while the National Government was faced with the task of attempting to maintain a military front and economy extending over vast areas and linked by exposed and lengthy lines of communication. These considerations had been in the mind of General Marshall when he warned the National Government against the consequences of a full-scale civil war.

One of the important blows to the National Government's economic prospects, however, was not traceable to Chinese actions or, initially, to the outbreak of civil strife. After the Japanese surrender, Russian occupation forces systematically stripped equipment and parts from key plants in the Manchurian industrial complex. As a result, China did not acquire a functioning industrial system in Manchuria, but rather, a damaged heavy industry, poorly integrated and partially inoperable. When Manchuria became the first major area of civil fighting, transport disruption became a chronic problem. The few railroad lines operating in Nationalist-held areas of Manchuria were severely handicapped by shortages of rolling stock and by damaging Communist raids. Cities were separated from the areas from which they normally obtained their food supplies and fuel. Manchuria increasingly became a major economic liability to the National Government.

In China proper, the paramount post-war economic problem was the continuing inflation. During the war with Japan the Government had financed a large part of its expenditures by the issuance of paper currency. The result had been a steady inflation of prices which in turn had as one of its consequences the destruction of the savings and the economic position of middle class Chinese. The inflationary process, far from being arrested in 1946, was accelerated. Wholesale prices in Shanghai increased more than seven times during the year. The official exchange rate between the Chinese National currency dollar and the United States dollar was raised in August from 2,020 to 1 to 3,350 to 1. By December the open market dollar rate had risen to 6,500 to 1.

Financial policies followed by the National Government were an important factor in the inflation. Of total Government expenditures in the postwar period, less than 25 percent were financed through taxation and other recurring sources of revenue. Another 10 percent were met by the partial liquidation of official gold and United States dollar reserves and former enemy properties. The deficit of approximately 65 percent of the total budget was covered by currency expansion. The course of the inflation was fostered furthermore by a gradually declining public confidence in both the Government and its monetary unit. The resulting general reluctance to hold Chinese currency impeded the production and movement of goods and induced speculation and hoarding of commodities on a grand scale, all of which served to intensify greatly the scarcity of commodities brought about directly by military operations.

It would have been unreasonable to expect the National Government to make the transition from war to peace, involving as it did the reoccupation of areas long under enemy control, without a measure of inflation. With the outbreak of civil strife and the resulting high level of military outlays, continuing inflation could scarcely have been avoided. The budgetary and fiscal operations of the National Government, however, were of such a nature as to accentuate inflationary developments. Government expenditures were largely uncontrolled. Funds were dissipated by inefficient military commanders and in the maintenance of excessively large and wholly unproductive garrison forces. Much of the tax revenue nominally accruing to the Government failed to reach the Government's treasury because of malpractices prevalent throughout the administrative hierarchy.

DEVELOPMENTS IN CHINA'S FOREIGN EXCHANGE AND TRADE POLICIES

Associated with the domestic inflation was a steady depletion of the Government's foreign exchange reserves. Domestic inflation had the effect of inhibiting exports and of enhancing the demand for imports which could serve as a hedge against rising prices. In the months immediately following the Japanese surrender, the Government permitted the abnormal demand for imported commodities to operate without restriction. In March 1946, action was taken to prohibit the importation of certain luxury items and to place a larger list of non-essential imports under licensing. In November, control of imports was tightened by an expansion of the prohibited list, by the imposition of quotas upon important import items and by the extension of licensing to all other permitted imports.

At the same time, however, the maintenance of unrealistic foreign exchange rates had the effect of subsidizing imports and penalizing exports. Moreover, the proliferation of local taxes and other artificial barriers to domestic trade tended to reduce drastically the flow of goods into China's great coastal cities. Thus, the dependence of Chinese urban areas on foreign imports was greatly increased while foreign exchange receipts were simultaneously diminished. Other factors contributing to the unfavorable balance-of-payments position and a flight of capital abroad included the widespread smuggling of exports, the undervaluation of declared exports and the transmittal of inward remittances through illegal channels.

The cumulative result of the various influences bearing upon China's import-export position and of the National Government's policy of open-market sales of gold as a counterinflationary device was a decline in official reserves of United States dollar exchange and gold from the V-J Day level of 900 million dollars to an estimated figure of approximately 450 million dollars at the end of 1946. This use of official assets unfortunately did not involve an over-all expansion through purchases abroad of productive plant and equipment in China or an adequate inflow of repair and replacement parts for existing plant.

EFFECTS OF RESTRICTIONS ON TRADE AND SHIPPING

Chinese regulations governing foreign trade and foreign exchange transactions hampered China's foreign trade because of the character of the regulations and their administration as well as because of the direct restrictions they imposed. These regulations were highly complex, they varied considerably in their application as between different Chinese ports and they were often made effective immediately upon their announcement with consequent hardship to importers. It was recognized that the Chinese were confronted with a situation which required the husbanding of foreign exchange resources. There was, however, a general belief among foreign traders that the Chinese administrative mechanism charged with enforcing trade and exchange regulations was unnecessarily cumbersome and arbitrary. Charges were frequently leveled against the Chinese Government for alleged corruption and favoritism, open or indirect, to privileged Chinese firms. Some of the complaints of private foreign firms may have been occasioned by curtailment of trade due to the stringent foreign exchange situation which affected all business in greater or less degree, or by the natural tendency, following the relinquishment by foreign Powers of extraterritoriality, for Chinese firms to be given a larger share of China's foreign trade. While due allowance must be made for these qualifying circumstances, many of the charges of favoritism and inefficiency appeared to be well grounded.

In the field of shipping, the Chinese Government took the highly nationalistic position that, contrary to general international practice, no foreign flag vessels could carry cargoes from abroad to Chinese ports not designated as ocean ports. This position excluded foreign flag vessels from the Yangtze River beyond Shanghai and required transshipment in the Shanghai area of all cargoes being carried between ports up the Yangtze, such as the major commercial center of Hankow, and foreign countries. In consequence, the transportation of such cargoes in Chinese waters was much more costly than it should have been, and the process of transshipment in the Shanghai area frequently made that port a bottleneck for commodities urgently needed in the interior of China.

ECONOMIC TREATY RELATIONS

Despite the increasingly severe controls imposed by the Chinese Government on foreign trade, and the malpractices associated with enforcement of such controls, China contributed during this period to creating a framework in which effective international economic relations might eventually be conducted. China's negotiation of a commercial treaty and an aviation agreement with the United States, and its adherence to the General Agreement on Tariffs and Trade, were important steps in this regard. A modern comprehensive treaty of friendship, commerce and navigation was negotiated in 1946 to replace the old treaty of 1903 and other treaties which had been based on the previously existing extraterritorial arrangements between the United States and China. Ratifications were exchanged and the treaty became effective on November 30, 1948. The treaty was based on the principles of mutuality and nondiscrimination; in general it provided that each Government shall assure to nationals of the other, with some exceptions and subject to its general laws, the same treatment and rights enjoyed by its own nationals and provided also that the nationals of either in the territories of the other shall be entitled to any rights or privileges which may be granted to the nationals of a third country. The trade and commerce of the two countries with each other were also guaranteed similar rights to most-favored-nation treatment. Thus the treaty was in reciprocal terms and provided for no rights or privileges for nationals of the United States in China which it did not equally confer on Chinese nationals in the United States.

Also in 1946 preliminary steps were taken for the negotiation of a reciprocal trade agreement with China. This agreement was eventually consummated in 1947 when the United States negotiated with China and 21 other countries a multilateral reciprocal trade agreement (the General Agreement on Tariffs and Trade) which reaffirmed the principle of most-favored-nation treatment, incorporated various general provisions governing trade relationships and provided for tariff concessions resulting in mutual reductions or bindings of duties on certain tariff classifications of the respective countries. This agreement became effective with respect to China on May 22, 1948.

A bilateral air transport agreement between the United States and China was signed in Nanking on December 20, 1946. This agreement is based on standard clauses drawn up at the Chicago International Civil Aviation Conference of 1944 and incorporates the so-called Bermuda principles contained in the bilateral air transport agreement between the United States and the United Kingdom. It is to be noted that conclusion of the latter agreement in February 1946 marked the establishment of a pattern of air transport agreements which, with slight deviations, the United States has negotiated ever since. The pattern of these air agreements involves in general the following factors: routes, privileges (accorded to an air carrier of one nation in the air space of a second), rates, frequency of operation, and capacity of aircraft. With the exception of prescribed routes over which aircraft of each contracting party operate, the remainder of the agreement is relatively standard and grants full reciprocity to each signatory country. The bilateral air transport agreements negotiated by the United States are purely commercial aviation agreements for the reciprocal exchange of commercial air rights. The United States–China air agreement makes no provision for base rights for either Government in the territory of the other. Under this agreement the airlines of each country are accorded the right to operate services to the other over three different routes. Since the conclusion of the agreement the United States has utilized two of the routes granted to it in services to Shanghai, while China has exercised its route privileges for the operation of a mid-Pacific route to San Francisco.

FOREIGN AID IN 1946

During 1945 and 1946 a series of measures were taken by foreign governments which provided China with very substantial external economic aid.[58] The commodities and services made available by these various measures contributed to meeting China's abnormal need following the Japanese surrender for food, clothing, medical supplies and raw materials and provided the capital equipment necessary to begin the rehabilitation and reconstruction of Chinese agriculture and of certain key industrial and transportation facilities.

The China program of the United Nations Relief and Rehabilitation Administration represented the largest single measure of foreign aid to China during this period and was the largest program that UNRRA carried out for any one country. UNRRA began its shipments to China in November 1945 and by the end of that year had shipped approximately 300,000 tons of supplies. The UNRRA program for China continued throughout 1946 and 1947, and a few deliveries took place thereafter. The value of goods delivered to China under the UNRRA program, including shipping and insurance costs, is estimated at 658.4 million dollars. The United States contribution to the world-wide UNRRA fund was approximately 72 percent. It may therefore be said that the United States contribution to the UNRRA China program amounted to 72 percent of 658.4 million dollars, or 474 million dollars. UNRRA's China program consisted chiefly of food and clothing and of a wide variety of capital goods and materials important to the rehabilitation of China's agriculture and industries. In addition, UNRRA provided large numbers of technical and super-

---

[58] See annex 181.

visory personnel who assisted the Chinese in the distribution of consumption commodities and the installation of capital goods.

During the latter part of 1945, the Chinese Government approached the Export-Import Bank with applications for the extension of credits to cover a variety of rehabilitation needs. No action was taken on these requests, however, and in January 1946 the National Advisory Council, acting in accordance with General Marshall's recommendations, decided that a major program of financial assistance to China must await satisfactory political and economic developments in that country. General Marshall was therefore able to use the possibility of American economic aid as a bargaining point in trying to achieve his political objectives. By early 1946, the progress of the negotiations between the National Government and the Chinese Communists made it appear that a peaceful settlement might be reached which would provide a basis for gradual stabilization and rehabilitation of the Chinese economy. Consequently, the Export-Import Bank gave favorable consideration, upon the recommendation of General Marshall and the Department of State, to a number of Chinese applications and during the first quarter of 1946 authorized a total of 66.8 million dollars in credits to the Chinese Government. These credits were primarily for cargo vessels, railway repair materials, electric-power generating equipment and raw cotton, and they were all on a long-term basis except for the cotton credit, which was to be repaid in 24 months. A credit of 16 million dollars previously authorized for the Yungli Chemical Industries was not finalized by guaranty of the Chinese Government until 1947. This brought the total of Export-Import Bank credits actually made available to China after V–J Day to 82.8 million dollars.

In recognition of the magnitude of Chinese requirements for reconstruction and the possibilities for economic development under orderly conditions, the United States Government gave consideration during the same period to setting aside substantial funds to assist China in this task. In April 1946, following the recommendation of General Marshall and approval by the National Advisory Council, the Export-Import Bank authorized the earmarking until June 30, 1947, of 500 million dollars of the Bank's funds for the possible extension of individual credits to the Chinese Government and private Chinese interests. It was contemplated that such credits would be confined to particular projects and would be subject to the usual criteria governing the Bank's lending operations. No implementing agreements were consummated, however, between the Bank and the representatives of the Chinese Government.

During the latter months of 1946, General Marshall and the Department of State recommended favorable consideration of certain Chinese projects by the Export-Import Bank. The Bank refused at this time to take favorable action on Chinese credit proposals chiefly because of the outbreak in mid-1946 of widespread fighting between the Chinese Communists and National Government forces and the clear implications that this development carried for Chinese economic prospects. In this situation, the Bank was unable to find reasonable assurances of repayment regarding which it had a statutory obligation.

In February 1946 the Canadian Government extended a long-term credit of 60 million dollars to the Chinese Government. Of the total credit, 25 million dollars was to be used to purchase (a) supplies and equipment originally requested by China from Canada as mutual aid but undelivered as of V–J Day, (b) other commodities in production in Canada on September 1, 1945, which were surplus to Canadian requirements, and (c) certain used industrial equipment, together with (d) the cost of reconverting and processing such equipment. The remaining 35 million dollars of the credit was to be used for equipment, supplies and services required by the Chinese Government for reconstruction and other post-war purposes.

The United States extended a credit to the Chinese Government, somewhat similar to the Canadian credit referred to above, in an agreement of June 14, 1946, commonly referred to as the Lend-Lease "Pipeline" Credit Agreement. This agreement provided for the delivery on a long-term credit basis, pursuant to section 3 (c) of the Lend-Lease Act, of civilian-type equipment and supplies contracted for but undelivered on V–J Day under the wartime lend-lease program for China. It was subsequently determined that a total of 51.7 million dollars in equipment and supplies could be furnished under contracts covered by this agreement.

The sale to China of United States civilian-type war surplus property with an estimated procurement value of 900 million dollars was authorized or recognized under an agreement of August 30, 1946, between the two Governments. [59] The property was located in India and China and on 17 Pacific islands and consisted in large measure of small ships and marine equipment, fixed installations, vehicles of all types, construction equipment and air-force supplies and equipment. The remainder of the property comprised a wide variety of communications equipment, tools, shop equipment, industrial machinery, electrical equipment, medical equipment and supplies and chemicals. The agreed realization to the United States for this property was 175 million

---

[59] For the Chinese Communist reaction to this agreement see p. 180.

dollars. Of this amount 55 million dollars was to be repaid in Chinese currency on a long-term credit basis, 20 million dollars of which the United States Government was in turn to use for cultural and educational activities in China. The balance of this credit, 35 million dollars, was to be made available in Chinese currency for acquisition by the United States Government of real property in China for diplomatic and consular use and for other American governmental expenses in China. To this credit was added an agreed offset of 150 million dollars against the United States wartime indebtedness to China arising out of expenditures by the Chinese Government for the United States Army. While these considerations totaled 205 million dollars, the United States as a part of the agreement established a fund of 30 million dollars to be used by China for shipping and technical services arising out of the property transfer. This 30-million-dollar fund reduced the total United States realization to the net figure of 175 million dollars

In October 1945 the Government of China had presented to the United States a proposal for technical collaboration in agriculture and forestry. In the course of the ensuing discussions it was agreed to establish a joint China–United States Agricultural Mission to make an intensive study of the problems of agricultural improvement in China, with special attention to be given those agricultural commodities which play an important role in Sino-American trade. The President of China stressed the importance of the mission's assignment and technical collaboration in general in a letter to the President of the United States which read in part as follows:

"We have been for centuries primarily an agricultural nation. The farmer is traditionally regarded with affection and respect. During recent times, unfortunately, our agricultural technique has fallen behind due to delay in the adoption and application of new scientific methods. I am keenly conscious of the fact that unless and until Chinese agriculture is modernized, Chinese industry cannot develop; as long as industry remains undeveloped, the general economy of the country cannot greatly improve. For this reason, I heartily agree with you that any plan for cooperation in economic development between our two countries should include agriculture."

The United States Government dispatched 10 agricultural experts to China for the mission, the Government of China appointed 13 and work was commenced on June 27, 1946. Conferences were held with Government officials, businessmen and agricultural specialists at Shanghai and Nanking, and field trips were made through 14 provinces and the island of Taiwan. One group concentrated on the broad aspects of the mission's assignment—education, research, and rural economic and social problems—while other smaller sections studied the production and marketing of specific commodities including tung oil, silk, tea, carpet wool and fish.

The mission submitted its report jointly to the two Governments late in 1946, and its recommendations were received by the United States Government as the conclusions of independent technical experts.

The report outlined in some detail a comprehensive and long-range program that the Chinese Government might undertake for the improvement of China's agriculture. The mission's recommendations included the following points: (1) greater emphasis on fertilizer production, development of irrigation, improvement of plants and animals, development of forestry, and production of fruits, vegetables and livestock to improve diets; (2) adjustment of the exchange rate, reduction in costs of transportation and credit, and improvement of standardization and quality to encourage the production and export of important agricultural commodities; (3) provision of adequate farm credit, improvement of tenancy conditions, advancement of land surveys, registration, and appraisal, and enforcement of the Land Law of 1946 with respect to taxation of land; (4) furthering of programs relating to general education, public health, transportation, river conservancy, and flood control; (5) emphasis on agricultural instruction, research and extension work within an integrated system; (6) creation of a single Government bank to serve agricultural needs; (7) consideration of measures to guard against a rapid increase in the growth of population.

In his statement of December 18, 1946, President Truman had renewed the offer of American assistance in implementing the recommendations of the mission in so far as feasible.

Despite the continuing efforts of the American Government to elicit Chinese action few constructive measures were taken by the Chinese Government in the field of agricultural improvement. Several of the recommendations of the Joint Mission, however, were later embodied in the program of the Joint Commission for Rural Reconstruction in China, established under the terms of the China Aid Act of 1948.[60]

[60] See chapter VIII.

CHAPTER VI

The Ambassadorship of John Leighton Stuart, 1947–1949

I. THE POLITICAL AND MILITARY SITUATION

FURTHER EFFORTS AT NEGOTIATION

The American mediation effort described in chapters III and V had ended, but the Chinese Government did not at once cease its attempts to find some method for the resumption of political negotiations. On January 15, 1947, the Generalissimo informed Ambassador Stuart that he had been meeting for several days with prominent Government leaders in an attempt to determine some means of reopening negotiations. These consultations resulted in four agreements within the Chinese Government which were given to the Ambassador. The points listed were as follows:

(1) The National Government desired to send a delegation to Yenan or would invite the Communist Party to send one to Nanking to continue discussions, or it would agree to a round-table conference at any mutually acceptable place.

(2) The Government and the Communists should at once issue a cease-fire order and confer on its implementation.

(3) The Government desired to resume discussions of practicable plans for the reorganization of the army and the restoration of communications based on the principles of the Committee of Three.

(4) The Government expressed a desire to reach an immediate agreement with the Communists on the political control of disputed areas.

The Generalissimo asked the Ambassador to get in touch with the principal Communist delegate still in Nanking, Mr. Wang Ping-nan, to ascertain if the Communists would invite a Government peace delegation to Yenan. Dr. Stuart was specifically requested not to disclose the foregoing four points, but if asked he could say that tentatively General Chang Chih-chung, Governor of Sinkiang, would represent the Government. Dr. Stuart could also state, if asked, that the Government attached no conditions to peace discussions. It

230

was the avowed hope of the Generalissimo that discussions without conditions might be more fruitful than previous ones and that the original spirit of the Political Consultative Conference agreements could be recaptured.

On January 16 the Ambassador saw Wang Ping-nan, who asked the anticipated questions and received the replies which the Generalissimo had authorized. The Ambassador took particular pains to make it clear that he was acting only as a transmitting medium and not as a direct participant. The Chinese Communist reply was prompt and categorical to the effect that if the Government would agree to the two previously stipulated conditions (that is, the abrogation of the constitution and the restoration of the military positions held January 13, 1946, the effective date of the cease-fire agreement) the negotiations could be resumed in Nanking; if not, nothing could be gained by sending a delegation to Yenan. The Communist representative insisted, however, that this reply was not intended to break off negotiations but rather to clear the ground for subsequent resumption. The Ambassador on January 23 informed the Department of State that it was his belief that the Chinese Communists meant what they said on this point as they were militarily confident and believed that the Government would be forced within the ensuing few months to reopen discussions on Communist terms.

On January 20 the Ministry of Information, on behalf of the National Government, published a long statement outlining the course of negotiations with the Chinese Communists. It stated, *inter alia:*

"As far back as the beginning of the war of resistance, in order to pool together the nation's efforts, the Government called the People's Political Council consisting of representatives of all political parties and independents.

"From start to finish, the Government has regarded the Communist problem as a political problem. The Kuomintang at its Tenth Central Executive Committee Plenary Session in 1942 and Eleventh Plenary Session the following year persistently advocated an early solution through political means.

"After May 1944 the Government has been negotiating with the Communist Party without let-up in the hope that a peaceful settlement could be reached."

The Ministry of Information concluded its statement with the announcement that the Chinese Government would make another appeal to the Chinese Communists for additional conversations and listed the four-point proposal, which had previously been communicated to the Communist representatives. The Communists replied publicly on

January 29, charging that the four points of the Government were nothing but a fraud which rejected the real prerequisites for peace negotiations. The Communists refused to accept the Nationalist offer until their previous two conditions, namely abrogation of the constitution and a return to the military *status quo* of January 13, 1946, had been accepted. On the following day the Nationalist Ministry of Information repeated its previous offer but added that the two conditions demanded by the Communists would have the effect of destroying the Chinese Republic. The Government therefore felt that ít had no alternative but to proceed with its own program for political democratization. It appealed to all groups and factions to join in the work of the reconstruction and rehabilitation of China. The Generalissimo, on February 16, 1947, followed up this plea with one of his own, pledging his Government to a 10-point program of economic rehabilitation and asking for the cooperation of all citizens of China.[1] On February 11, the Government notified the Communist delegation in Nanking that its presence in Government areas was no longer desired.

REVERSAL OF COMMUNIST POLICY

Indications of the attitude of the Chinese Communist Party were given in statements which appeared early in 1947. The first was a statement by Chou En-lai [2] which, together with the other documents, represented a major change in the public official Communist line and a distinct reversal of policy as previously set down in 1945 by Mao Tse-tung, as Chairman of the Central Committee, in his report to the Seventh Party Congress entitled *The New Democracy*. The second document was a statement by Lu Ting-yi, head of the Department of Information of the Chinese Communist Party and a member of the Central Committee, in which he aligned the Chinese Communists with Russia on foreign policy and denounced the United States as the heir of German and Japanese Fascists.[3] On February 1, the Central Committee issued a strong denunciation of the National Government, accused the Government of selling out China to foreign interests and announced that the Chinese Communists would refuse to recognize any agreements and understandings reached by the National Government subsequent to January 10, 1946.[4]

---

[1] For full text of these statements see annex 116 (a)–(d).

[2] See annex 117.

[3] See annex 118.

[4] Full text in annex 119. The length to which this change has gone is indicated in a speech by Mao Tse-tung given on June 30, 1949, which is included as annex 120.

THE SOVIET PROPOSAL OF MARCH 10, 1947

On March 10, at a meeting of the Council of Foreign Ministers at Moscow, the Soviet Foreign Minister, Mr. Molotov, proposed that problems relating to the settlement of the civil war in China be included in the agenda of the meeting of the Council. The United States Government did not concur in the Soviet proposal. This view was reinforced by the instantaneous reaction of the Chinese Government. The Chinese Foreign Minister, Dr. Wang Shih-chieh, on March 11 informed General Marshall that China would strenuously object to having its internal affairs placed on the agenda of the Moscow Conference. At the same time the Foreign Minister issued a similar statement to the press. The Chinese Communists took their cue from Moscow and issued a statement favoring inclusion of China on the Moscow Conference agenda, but insisted that the Chinese Communists themselves should be represented at any such discussions. In view of the opposition to the Soviet proposal, it was dropped.

Dr. Wang also informed the American Ambassador that on March 8 the Soviet Ambassador had called with two requests: (1) that China take over the administration of Dairen and Port Arthur and (2) that joint operation be undertaken of the railway line from Dairen through Mukden to Changchun. Subsequently a Chinese Government Mission under strict Russian surveillance did visit Dairen to survey the situation. The negotiations reached an impasse over the questions of armed police and the admission of Chinese troops into the area and were not renewed.

REORGANIZATION OF THE LEGISLATIVE YUAN AND THE CONTROL YUAN, MARCH 1, 1947

In the meantime, the functioning of the National Government had been paralyzed to a considerable extent by the slowness with which its projected reorganization was proceeding. The new Constitution of China had been adopted by the National Assembly on December 25, 1946, with the provision that it would go into effect one year from the date of its adoption. During the interim period a transition government would be organized to prepare the country for constitutional government, to eliminate one-party rule by termination of the period of political tutelage, and to prepare other groups for participation in the national political life. The organization of this new government proved to be far more difficult than had been anticipated.

The difficulties principally arose from the inability of the Kuomintang and the third parties to agree in their negotiations upon the division of the principal positions in the Five Yuan and the State Council. It should be noted, parenthetically, that throughout these negotiations a certain number of positions were reserved for the Communist Party if it should choose to participate. There was at no time, however, any indication that the Communists had any intention of participating and, in fact, all their public announcements were emphatic in stating that it would be impossible for them to participate under what they called "an illegal constitution."

At a fairly early stage in the negotiations it also became apparent that the Democratic League, the third largest party, had so far associated itself with the stand taken by the Communists that it too would not participate. This reduced the negotiations, apart from the internal manipulations within the Kuomintang itself, which became the most important phase, to a division of positions between the Kuomintang on the one hand and the Youth Party and the Social Democrats on the other. These two minor parties commanded so small a following that the efforts to get them in the Government could be considered important only in a symbolic sense of nominally ending one-party rule.

At midnight, March 1, the Government announced the appointment of 50 new members to the Legislative Yuan, of whom 17 were Kuomintang, 13 Youth Party, 12 Social Democrats, and 8 non-partisan. At the same time 25 new members were named to the Control Yuan, of whom 9 were Kuomintang, 6 Youth Party, 7 Social Democrats, and 3 non-partisan. Forty-four new members were added to the People's Political Council, of whom 11 were Kuomintang, 11 Youth Party, 11 Social Democrats, and 11 non-partisan. These new members added to the old membership gave the third parties a minority representation, but nonetheless one much larger proportionately than their actual political following.

The next day Dr. T. V. Soong, following a frank conversation with the Generalissimo, resigned as Prime Minister. Ambassador Stuart interpreted this development and its background to the Department of State in the following terms on March 3:

"T. V. Soong had a long talk with Generalissimo on the afternoon of the evening that he handed in his resignation. At any rate the latter interview was not unamicable and the Generalissimo, although urging him to maintain his position as chairman of the Supreme Economic Council, readily accepted his resignation as President of the Executive Yuan and then without much ado as the chairman of the Supreme Economic Council as well. My surmise from available information is that Generalissimo propounded to T. V. Soong in the first conversation his military plans for intensification of the civil war which *inter alia* will require, in view of recent price increases, a rise in pay and supply allotments for the Army in the near future.

Hemmed in on the one side by relentless demands of civil war and on the other by increasingly painful limitations which his growing unpopularity was imposing on his freedom of action, he decided to save his reputation—if not his face—by chucking in his hand before it was called and he was well smeared.

"My belief is that the Generalissimo has determined to embark on an all-out military campaign to free as much of China proper from Communist control as possible to the end that after about three months, the Communists would be chastened (where they are now blatantly bumptious) and concentrated in a much smaller area. My guess is that feeling as he does about Communists, the Generalissimo, although nervous about the Moscow Conference, does not envisage any improvement promising permanency in Soviet-American relations and therefore is not without hope that the United States will in due course come in some fashion and to some degree to the Government's assistance. There is no doubt that he is now increasingly concerned about the rate of financial deterioration and the ability of Communists to prolong the struggle and create havoc. However, he has made a point of telling Chinese who call upon him that China must stand on its own feet and face the future without American assistance. I have a sense that the CC Clique [5] work on him in this wise and, concomitantly, to the effect that he will be getting the worst of both worlds if he weakens himself domestically and fails to achieve compensatory aid from the United States. That his mood is exigent and bitter is evident as indicated in today's speech. As I see it, these next few days are important for the reorganization plans—important in that this fight-it-all-alone mood should not find reflection in the appointments and powers of the State Council and the Executive Yuan."

AMBASSADOR STUART'S SUMMARY OF DEVELOPMENTS

On March 12, Ambassador Stuart summarized the developments of late February and early March, together with his interpretation as given below, this being of particular importance in view of the impending Third Plenary Session of the Central Executive Committee of the Kuomintang which would have an important bearing on future developments:

"Events have moved so rapidly in China during the past 10 days and have included so many complicating factors that it might be useful at this time to present a brief over-all summary drawing together

---

[5] The CC Clique is the extreme right-wing faction of the Kuomintang and is completely dominated by two brothers, Chen Li-fu and Chen Kuo-fu, who have long been closely associated with the Generalissimo. The latter has relied on them to discipline the rank and file of the Party.

and correlating previous telegrams. The two main aspects are, of course, the military and the political-economic, with the former giving a kind of desperate urgency to the need for political adjustment because the continuance of civil war is an increasing drain on the national economy, making a mockery of attempts to move in the direction of normal economic development.

"The current military campaigns have surpassed in scope anything seen in many months. The Government obviously wanted, and badly needed, a major military victory in Shantung. This it has failed to obtain. Communists took the initiative in Manchuria, managing to force their way to the very gates of Changchun. They have now been turned back by Nationalist reinforcements and in this sense have suffered a defeat if, as has been suggested, their objective was a territorial victory to strengthen the hand that they hope the Soviets will play for them at the Moscow meeting. If, on the other hand, the principal objective was further to sap Nationalist strength, then they have achieved a victory. The Military Attaché's intelligent guess on casualties is 10,000 for the Government and 20,000 for the Communists in Manchuria, and 40,000 for the Government and 20,000 for the Communists in other areas, mainly Shantung.

"The establishment of general headquarters at Hsuchow seems to be a desirable and long-needed development from the Government standpoint in that it puts it in a better position to direct and control operations. The Military Attaché also states he sees signs on both sides of a decreasing desire to fight and more particularly by Government forces. Even high-ranking officers have said to him that whereas there seemed to be some point in endless fighting when the enemy was Japan, there is not much stomach for fighting when it is against Chinese. This lack of morale appears to be reflected among the troops who do not understand what the civil war is all about and who, in some instances, have been susceptible to Communist appeals to lay down their arms. The Generalissimo's insistence on increased pay to improve troop morale played a part in Soong's resignation.

"Against this grim background have been the political changes of the last 10 days, which, so far, are inconclusive. The reorganization of the State Council and the Executive Yuan is still in the negotiation stage. The stumbling block is whether and on what terms the Social Democrats will participate . . . .

"In the excitement of other events, the announcement by the Government of additional government, third party and non-partisan members to the Legislative and Control Yuan, the PPC, and the Standing Committee for the Enforcement of the Constitution caused only a minor ripple. The Government stand that this development constitutes a significant step in the direction of relinquishing one-party control has received little attention and is not likely to do so pending reorganization of the State Council and the Executive Yuan.

"The heightened tempo of repressive police activities all over the country, and particularly in areas where the Communists have been most active has been widely reported and variously interpreted, depending on the political views of the commentator. This development has been strongly condemned in independent and left-wing circles. At the same time the attitude has been general that however reprehensible these activities may be, the Government can hardly be expected to loosen its controls as long as it is engaged in a life and death struggle. Concomitantly, there is general belief that with the return of all Communist delegations to their own territory the possibility of peace negotiations and political settlement has been indefinitely postponed, making all the more improbable any prospect of halting economic deterioration."

THE CAPTURE OF YENAN

The Generalissimo in his statement of February 16, indicating the intention of the Government to consolidate its current positions, had said: "On its part the Government will confine its military efforts to the protection and restoration of communication systems so necessary for the economic life of the nation and we shall spare no efforts to continue to seek for a political solution of the Communist problem." At that time Dr. T. V. Soong had categorically stated to the American Ambassador that both he and the Generalissimo were of the same mind, that Yenan should not be attacked. Subsequently the Military Attaché was similarly advised by the G–2 section of the Ministry of National Defense. It was therefore not without significance that the Government chose the middle of March to launch an attack on Yenan and capture the already largely evacuated Communist capital. The military claims of the Government subsequently proved to be exaggerated, but the psychological effect in non-Communist China at a critical point was important. From a strictly long-range military standpoint, the capture of Yenan served principally to over-extend Government lines and drain the national economy. The Ambassador commented as follows on this subject:

"Although the Government claims it routed over 100,000 Communist troops, this appears to be a gross exaggeration since American observers during the return of Communist mediation personnel reported the virtual evacuation of Yenan. It has long been apparent that the Communists have prepared well for this eventuality and that they never had any real intention of defending Yenan should such action appear to be costly. Rather it is more in keeping with their long developed tactics to evacuate any given point in the face of enemy pressure, draw him into a pocket, and thereafter gradually sap his strength with guerrilla tactics. Furthermore, Government lines are seriously extended into territory which can be counted upon to be hostile in all respects."

Indicative of Government confidence in a settlement by force was the public claim by the Chief of Staff at this time that the Communists would be defeated in six months. Coincidentally, the Generalissimo told Dr. Stuart that by the end of August or the beginning of September the Communist forces would either be annihilated or driven into the far hinterland.

STUDENT DEMONSTRATIONS

It was symptomatic of the growing popular discontent that May and June should witness the most serious outburst of student demonstration and violence since the end of the war against Japan. In every major academic center of China students, for the most part with much sympathy from University faculties, went on strike, demanding an end of the civil war, effective action by the Government to improve national economic conditions and relief for their own increasingly desperate economic plight. Numerous deaths resulted from these demonstrations and it was only because of skillful handling of the situation in such key areas as Peiping and Shanghai by certain key individuals and the opportune ending of the school year, which permitted the Government to close the universities for the summer, that more serious disturbances were avoided. The Government was no doubt concerned over the implications of these disorders as indicative of mounting popular discontent. The situation was further complicated by a series of relatively minor but potentially dangerous rice riots coming at a time when the new crop had not yet been harvested and the stocks of the previous year were rapidly being exhausted.[6]

The Ambassador reported as follows on May 29:

"Over-all political scene which continues to be dominated largely by the economic and military situation, is deteriorating at an accelerated rate. Within recent weeks existing bad rice situation, brought about in the main by military requirements and hoarding, has added to the spreading unrest. On May 18 the Government issued an edict prohibiting student demonstrations which was immediately disobeyed in major urban centers and has resulted in further loss of prestige by

[6] See annexes 121 and 122 for Embassy reports of May 20 and June 4, 1947.

the Government. At the present time the students are actively agitating for a nation-wide general strike to commence June 2, but the student movement has thus far been characterized by considerable indecision and has not fallen under the control of any single group or party. There are strong indications, however, that the student movement will assume larger proportions and eventually come under the leadership of anti-Government groups, particularly of the Democratic League if not the Communists. . . .

"As general unrest and disillusionment increases, Communist prestige is enhanced, largely through recent military successes in north China and Manchuria. Although completely reliable information is not yet available, it is reasonably clear that in Manchuria the Central Government has suffered reverses along the Chinese Changchun Railway and at least a partial Government withdrawal in the Northeast may become necessary. Recent Communist military activities in Manchuria have been well coordinated with large-scale raids on north China and Jehol rail lines assisted in a large degree by the military blunderings of General Tu Li-ming. An important aspect of the north China situation is the evident Communist capability of disrupting communications between the Kailan mines and the sea which will have continual effect upon the coal supply situation, especially for Shanghai.

"Although anti-civil war sentiment is increasing, largely among student, academic and business groups, it has thus far not reached a point where it will be decisive in influencing the Government as evidenced by the character of the two statements issued by the Generalissimo this week. The fact that he felt called upon to issue any statement speaks for itself. One indication that there is growing sentiment among liberal Kuomintang members of the Government for peace negotiations was a resolution presented to the Legislative Yuan recently by some twenty of its members, calling for the resumption of peace talks and reportedly having the tacit approval of Dr. Sun Fo. On May 27, the PPC adopted a resolution to invite the Communists to resume peace talks which can be interpreted as largely a Kuomintang maneuver stemming from recent military reverses and growing anti-civil war sentiment, and designated to pin sole responsibility for continuation of the civil war on the Communists. In the face of Communist military successes, it seems unlikely that the Communists would be prepared to join in peace talks except on terms much more favorable than the Government is apparently now willing to accept.

"Nor is there any basis for believing that the Communists do not regard time and tide as working for them or that they would be willing at this time to accept equitable and feasible proposals.

"For the immediate future the gravest danger to the Government would result in this atmosphere if disaffection commences among National troops with the Government unable to supply adequate rations. There has been fairly steady deterioration of morale in the Government forces, especially in the Northeast, but for the time being it is believed that the Government can hold the loyalty of the best trained and equipped troops. It may be anticipated that Government efforts will be bent towards supplying these troops adequately and in expectation that civilian unrest can be held in check or quelled by a show of force."

CONTINUED DETERIORATION OF THE GOVERNMENT'S POSITION

The Ambassador further reported on June 7 as follows:

"It is obvious that the Government faces in Manchuria the probability of a military debacle of large proportions. It has already withdrawn from substantial areas previously under Government control. Judging from the ineptitude and incompetence thus far demonstrated by General Tu Li-ming, it is probable that the Government's defeat may assume even larger proportions. It seems to lie within the Communists' power either to continue to bleed the Government's strength in Manchuria or to force further Government withdrawal."

It was also symptomatic of popular uneasiness and confusion that the People's Political Council, which had played such a significant role during the war against Japan as a sounding-board of public opinion, should on May 26, in its last session before it passed out of existence, pass by a large majority a resolution inviting Communist representatives to come to Nanking for discussions on ways and means of bringing about the termination of the civil war. The Embassy pointed out that this resolution represented the growing discontent of Chinese intellectuals with the Government and the mounting demand for some kind of a peace settlement.[7] The People's Political Council at the same session, however, passed a resolution demanding continuation of the punitive action against the Chinese Communists.

The invitation of the People's Political Council was promptly and summarily rejected by the Communists as another evidence of Government insincerity. The Ambassador on June 18 reflected popular speculation on further developments in the following report:

"President Chiang believes that he had conclusive evidence of a Communist plot to create widespread disorders on June 2 and is no less convinced that the measures taken thwarted this. He unquestionably over-estimated the Communist influence in the recent student

[7] See annex 123.

demonstrations and probably realizes this now himself. There were divergencies in what occurred in the principal cities. The tragic death of three students in Wuhan University and the serious wounding of three others, together with a number of minor casualties were on the initiative of the Hankow garrison commander, who has been summarily dismissed.

"The PPC peace resolutions have been presented through the Standing Committee of that body to the State Council, which approved them in principle but has asked that they be made more concrete for final action at the next meeting of the State Council. . . .

"In contrast with almost all the other high officials President Chiang is maintaining his calm self-control and a somewhat sobered confidence. There is a general feeling of frustration among the others due primarily to the objective facts with which they are all familiar but intensified by the nervous fear of the Communists. . . .

"It requires a certain temerity to attempt any forecasts, but it would seem that one of three possible consequences will follow without much delay from the present critical conditions:

"1. President Chiang will assert himself as the leader of an attempt to settle the Communist issue either by securing their assent to renew negotiations or by demonstrating that they are in effect an armed rebellion and as such opposed to the national welfare. I have been hoping that he would be able to do this in a dramatic, revolutionary way that would catch the imagination of his people. This is probably expecting too much, but he has gone so far in discarding his earlier preconceptions and adopting progressive ideas that I believe he can be influenced to further advance. This will perhaps be slower and much less satisfactory than a more spectacular procedure but it has real possibilities and is perhaps by all odds the most hopeful solution.

"2. With the threatening catastrophe drawing closer it is quite possible that a nucleus of enlightened, non-partisan leaders may emerge who will attract the more liberal elements from within the Kuomintang, be supported by the politically conscious public and come to terms with the Communists. President Chiang would presumably disappear from the scene, Premier Chang Chun, T. V. Soong, or some other outstanding figure might assume leadership, and an *ad interim* coalition government be established. Among the disadvantages would be the inexperience of the new group and the inability, especially conspicuous among Chinese, of a loosely-formed body to cooperate effectively.

"3. There will be complete disintegration of the present Central Government with the Communists in control of their own territory, which they would use every effort to extend. Sectional governments would be established under the strongest man or group in the area with all the evils of such chaotic and unstable conditions."

Evidence of growing deterioration in the general situation and of increasing popular dissatisfaction with the Government and its conduct of the civil war was being received not only from the better-known urban centers such as Shanghai, Nanking and Peiping, but was also disturbingly obvious throughout all sections of the country. Perhaps the most disturbing report received by the Embassy came the last week in June from the American Consul General in Mukden. He reported the gradual worsening of the Government's military position, personal squabbling between military commanders, growing Communist initiative which kept Government forces disorganized and off-balance, the tightening of the economic situation and the slackening popular morale, which made the local populace increasingly receptive to almost any change which might offer some prospect of stabilization. It was a picture of Government corruption, inefficiency and aimlessness in the face of a major disaster.[8]

The downward course of the economic and financial situation in China during 1947 is described in more detail in chapter VIII, where the question of further extension of aid by the United States is also discussed. It was impossible for the United States Government to consider that question apart from the problem of reforms in the Chinese Government, since without such reforms no financial aid could provide a remedy.

II. AMERICAN EFFORTS TO ENCOURAGE REFORMS BY THE CHINESE GOVERNMENT

During the war against Japan the United States endeavored to encourage the Chinese Government to effect various reforms which would serve to strengthen the Government and thus contribute to the fight against a common enemy as well as lay the foundation for stability and progress in the post-war period. At the request of the Chinese Government, the United States Government sent American advisers and technical experts to China to assist the Chinese Government in various fields, such as soil conservation, public health, cooperatives, animal husbandry, industrial production and medicine.

AMBASSADOR STUART'S REPORTS

During the period of General Marshall's mission to China, both he and Ambassador Stuart repeatedly emphasized to the Chinese Government leaders the desirability and also the necessity of formulating

---

[8] See annex 124.

and carrying out measures of reform which would improve governmental administration and efficiency, win for it popular support and confidence and contribute to the effective use of American aid.

Following General Marshall's departure from China and in continuation of his efforts, Ambassador Stuart took every opportunity, in conversations with Government leaders, to stress the need for action by the Government which would result in the emergence of liberal elements to positions of leadership, the lessening of the influence of the reactionary group and the carrying out of basic measures of reform. It was felt that only through such action could the Government successfully meet the challenge of the Chinese Communists and be able to prevent dissipation of its own resources and to make effective use of American aid.

In the light of these considerations, great importance was attached to the outcome of the efforts and plans being made for reorganization of the Government. The Third Plenary Session of the Central Executive Committee of the Kuomintang met during March and its meetings gave some indication of the struggle for power between conservative and liberal factions of the Party. The two principal points of interest were (1) the efforts of certain factions within the Kuomintang to obstruct reorganization of the Government and (2) the struggle for power and position between the reactionary CC Clique and the loosely knit Political Science Group. On the first point, the Generalissimo, supported by the liberal elements, was successful in blocking the drive to stop reorganization. In the struggle between factions, the Generalissimo emerged in a stronger position than before, but at the same time the CC Clique continued in control at all levels of the Party machinery.

This intra-Party struggle for personal power occurred against the background of the deterioration of the Government's prestige and position and apparently without regard for its effect on the Government and unity of purpose. The Ambassador commented on March 12:

"Evidence of CC Clique expansion into the financial field will not increase banking and business confidence in the Government—it is also additional evidence of the Generalissimo's tactics of not allowing any one group to gain exclusive control over the finance of the country."

The Ambassador pointed out on April 5 some of the difficulties connected with the efforts for governmental reorganization and the Generalissimo's part therein:

"The tragic paradox of his position, of which he may be unaware, is that he is being compelled by circumstances to utilize the qualifications which the CC Clique can offer. At the same time this Clique exploits its preferred position to render more firm its hold on the Party and the country; and with time the Generalissimo, therefore, may well become less and less able to dispense with them or to circumscribe their activities which can only serve to aggravate those social conditions basically giving rise and strength to the Communist movement." [11]

The Ambassador also commented:

"The Foreign Minister remarked the other day on the irony of a situation where the Generalissimo, having been made self-conscious about his ability to dictate a political settlement and consequently reluctant to use bludgeoning tactics, finds himself in endless political dickering which only delays that reorganization which his liberal advisors have been urging on him."

The Ambassador also reported that the CC Clique was attempting to build itself up in the popular mind as the truly liberal and revolutionary element of the Party; that the CC Clique was putting its main effort into preparation for the elections which would precede the coming into effect of the constitution on December 25, 1947; and that preparations were proceeding for the termination of political tutelage.

The Central Executive Committee of the Kuomintang issued a manifesto on March 24 prior to the conclusion of its session. This manifesto did little to clarify the situation beyond general statements on broadening the basis of the Government, removing obstacles to national unification, stabilizing the national economy, striving for world peace and building up the potential strength of the country for national reconstruction." [12]

REORGANIZATION OF THE EXECUTIVE YUAN AND STATE COUNCIL, APRIL 17, 1947

On April 17 the reorganization of the Executive Yuan and the State Council was announced, with General Chang Chun as President of the Executive Yuan or Prime Minister. At the same time, Dr. Sun Fo, son of the founder of the Chinese Republic, was elected Vice President. Nominations by the Generalissimo for the other four Yuan showed no change. A series of official statements accompanied this completion of the reorganization. President Chiang, in a statement on April 18, hailed the reorganization as another step in the ending of political tutelage and again offered the Communists

---

[11] See annex 125.
[12] See annex 126.

an opportunity to participate in the Government if they would abandon their policy of seizing power by force. At the same time the political program of the National Government was announced, which largely followed the earlier outline of the manifesto of the Central Executive Committee of the Kuomintang, with the addition of guarantees for civil liberties. On April 23 the Minister of Information in his weekly press conference made a similar announcement on behalf of his Government that the Kuomintang had ended the period of political tutelage. The same evening the new Prime Minister, General Chang Chun, pledged himself and his Government to the fulfillment of the obligations which the Government had undertaken publicly during the preceding days."

In commenting on the reorganization of the Government, the Ambassador stated that it was too early to assess with any accuracy the eventual effect of the State Council reorganization and that any such assessment must be approached with caution in the light of a series of past Chinese Government reorganizations which had been largely for external effect and had brought little effective change to the Chinese domestic scene, even though the majority of Kuomintang members were forward-looking modern Chinese. The Ambassador further stated:

"In summary, the composition of the State Council is as regards the Kuomintang and independents as good as could be expected in the circumstances. Whether or not the State Council, which will constitute itself on April 23, if its members can reach Nanking by that date, will assert itself in such a manner as to bring about substantial social and economic reform in China remains, of course, a question depending upon many factors, not the least one being the attitude of the Generalissimo toward it and his ability to control the Kuomintang as the still dominant political party in China."

The Ambassador noted with some concern the establishment at this time of a separate Kuomintang political committee, the secretary general of which was Chen Li-fu, the leader of the CC Clique, and pointed out that it was a safe assumption that this committee would have an important role in controlling the Kuomintang political machine and establishing party policies. He concluded:

"In final analysis the major imponderable is whether or not the Generalissimo will be capable of seeking and being guided by the advice of liberal-progressive public servants rather than acceding to the reactionary henchmen personally loyal to him." [14]

---

[13] See annex 127 (a)–(d) for full text of statements.

[14] See annex 128.

While the governmental reorganization was a step in the right direction and gave some hope for improvement, the behind-the-scenes political maneuvering for power without regard for the position of the Government itself continued to hamper efforts toward improvement in administration. This disunity and the political machinations, despite the serious situation with which the Government was confronted, were reflected in the circumstances surrounding the student demonstrations which occurred on a nation-wide scale in May. The Ambassador's comment on these demonstrations evidenced their character:

"Leadership and motivation of the demonstrations have shown definite signs of changing. Most competent observers believe the original impetus was given by the CC Clique which was desirous of inciting a series of disorders which would in time publicly discredit a Political Science Group-dominated Government by proving it incapable of maintaining order, and in the long run provide the justification for a strong-arm, right-wing government coming into power either through a coup d'etat or through sweeping the elections to be held this fall."

These activities, of course, played into the hands of anti-Government elements and as stated by the Ambassador: "It must be assumed that the Communists are present and, if not already active, are prepared to exploit the situation should it become necessary or desirable."

On May 29 the Embassy reported on developments to the Department as follows:

"The reorganized Executive Yuan under Chang Chun is more strongly based than the previous T. V. Soong regime, but the political maneuvers of the CC Clique and the pace of economic and military developments have tied its hands to date. Furthermore, in the face of existing problems, non-Kuomintang participants in the reorganized Government have thus far shown no capacity for initiative. However, outlook for next few months is not, in the Embassy's opinion, for any spectacular collapse but in the direction of increasing deterioration in Government authority and control. In the meantime, general Government sentiment will continue to look to American aid as a means of staving off further economic and military deterioration."

Further indication of the need for positive measures by the Chinese Government to restore popular confidence was contained in the Ambassador's comments on the situation on June 18:

"The growing discontent with or even hostility toward the Government has been stimulated among intellectuals by the extremely harsh measures against students and among the unthinking masses by the mounting costs of livelihood. In its simplest terms the complaints center around freedom and food."

The Ambassador further commented:

"President Chiang has been thinking very earnestly both over the situation as he is compelled to recognize its realities and over advice given him which, so far as I can gather, has all been very much to the same effect. In general, this is that the demand for peace is widespread and insistent, and the Government should be able either to persuade the Communists to stop fighting and resume peace discussions or to place the responsibility for continuing the civil war upon them, and furthermore that the Government should win back popular confidence by official statements calculated to keep the people much better informed than they have been hitherto of the problems and intentions of the Government. In my personal conversations with President Chiang I have been as frank as seemed permissible and have been cheered especially during the latest interview by what seemed to be on his part something more than a general assent in principle."

The Ambassador also observed:

"Actually much of the apparent strength of Chinese Communism is due chiefly to the inefficiency and corruption of the Kuomintang and—with an alarming acceleration—to popular loss of faith in the Government. One can be reasonably certain that with sufficient evidence of competent statesmanship and determined moral reforms the Government could recover its hold alike on the intellectuals and the masses."

THE POLITICAL SITUATION IN MANCHURIA

The same struggle for power and the intra-party rivalry which was hampering the National Government was vitally affecting the Government's position in Manchuria. During the latter half of June the Consul General at Mukden reported as follows:

"Rivalry (if not enmity) between General Hsiung Shih-hui, the Generalissimo's representative, and General Tu Li-ming, Commanding the Northeast Combat Command, is openly discussed and the absence of closely integrated military and economic planning is attributed to it."

The Consul General also described the attitude of Chinese Government representatives in Manchuria and the effect upon the Government as follows:

"Nationalist southern military forces and civil administrators conduct themselves in Manchuria as conquerors, not as fellow countrymen, and have imposed a 'carpet-bag' regime of unbridled exploitation on the areas under their control."

He continued that the result was to make the local populace in the countryside so antagonistic toward outsiders as to affect the morale of non-Manchurian troops and at the same time arouse vindictiveness in southern military officers and civil administrators. Commenting on the food problem at Mukden the Consul General said:

"Puerile efforts have been made toward price control and to combat hoarding, but in general, the results of these efforts have been largely to enforce requisitioning of grain at bayonet point for controlled prices and enable the resale of requisitioned grain at black market prices for the benefit of the pockets of rapacious military and civil officials."

It was thus inevitable that, as reported by the Consul General:

"Evidence is growing daily that the people of Manchuria are not only prepared for but are keenly desirous of a change in government. But what change? Most are undecided even though voluble in discontent of the present way of living and the trend of events. It is safe to state that the overwhelming majority in the nation are dissatisfied with, dislike and would welcome freedom from the present Nationalist regime."

When on June 19 the Generalissimo summoned the Ambassador and, after describing to him his estimate of the seriousness of the situation in Manchuria, asked for the Ambassador's opinion, Dr. Stuart made the following reply:

"I replied that it might be that the time had come for him to take emergency measures such as organizing a small but carefully selected group to work with himself, men respected by all and able to take responsibility as well as to form a team; to reduce expenditures by at least discontinuing all measures not needed for the emergency period; to make an announcement to the people that if the Communist Party finally refused the latest peace proposals the people of the country should hold them responsible; if they wished to preserve the democratic way of life as to be effected soon under constitutional government they should all work together to save the nation from the threatened danger; to this end all should work for the common purpose and contribute what they could of service or wealth; the Government should, respecting civil liberties, carry out the most immediate reforms with the courage and ruthless impartiality required by the crisis and in all such ways win back popular support or ask to be relieved of the task; that I had always believed that such a revolutionary program would attract the thinking people, especially students and other supposed leftists; that he should allocate responsibility (for instance, military affairs) with a minimum of red tape, and himself tour the country making speeches and arousing the populace to rally to the new movement; that with the people behind him he need not fear the Communist military strength nor their other activities and should continue to keep the door wide open for a resumption of peace negotiations; that hopelessness and defeatism were paralyzing those who wanted to do something for the nation but under some such determined, progressive leadership they could be inspired to new hope and effort; and finally that I felt sure such a program would win abundant sympathy in America and elsewhere over the world. At the end, he said that he had been thinking along very much the same lines."

CHINESE MOVES TOWARD REFORM

In the face of a situation calling for the most resolute and clearsighted action, the powerful Standing Committee of the Central Executive Committee of the Kuomintang on June 30 held an extraordinary and previously unannounced session to discuss general Party policy. After five hours of discussion, the Committee adopted three resolutions: (1) to continue and expand the "punitive action against the Communists"; (2) to draw up and put into effect plans for integrating the San Min Chu I Youth Corps into the Kuomintang; and (3) to set in motion preparations for the fall elections. Such inadequate measures at this critical time would have been farcical had they not been so tragic in their implications of a lack of driving force and determination to see the civil war through to a successful conclusion.

There was, however, apparently an awareness of the need for drastic action on the part of the National Government, as indicated by the resolution on general national mobilization passed by the State Council on July 4, which stated, *inter alia:*

"It is proposed that the State Council order a national general mobilization and encourage the people to help in its execution. Plans concerning the acceleration of economic reconstruction, the reform of local governments, the mobilization of manpower and resources, the improvement of food and conscription administrations, the maintenance of social order, the mitigation of the people's sufferings, the protection of their basic rights, the practice of thrift, the increases of agricultural and industrial production, and the amelioration of the treatment of officers and men shall be carefully drafted by the competent authorities and enforced in accordance with law. The competent authorities shall also be instructed to guard against abuses in the execution of those plans." [15]

This awareness was also reflected in statements made at this time by the Generalissimo and General Chang Chun, the Prime Minister. In an address to the nation on July 6 the Generalissimo said:

"Simultaneously, we must exert all-out efforts in effecting national reforms and improvements. While we are suppressing the Communist brigands with military means, the nation must also at the same time effect internal reforms."

The President admitted

"that the Government in itself is not perfect while in the body of the Chinese society also are found many weak points, made all the weaker by the Communist rebellion. But, however difficult it may be for the nation to accomplish its goal, reforms and improvements must be effected."

The official Central News Agency gave the following account of General Chang Chun's statements on this same subject in a press interview on July 5: "During the period of national general mobilization, the Government will see that all orders are faithfully and promptly carried out," he said. "Government officials should win the confidence and cooperation of the people and coordination among various Government departments should be further strengthened. Corruption and delinquency among Government officials and armed forces should be wiped out," General Chang emphasized. [15a]

The Generalissimo again reflected this increasing awareness of current needs in his radio broadcast on July 7, the tenth anniversary of the beginning of Sino-Japanese hostilities:

"Unless drastic reforms are introduced, China may not be able to exist in the family of nations. Therefore, political, educational, economic and social reforms, which should be made, shall not be delayed until the conclusion of the suppression campaign, but will be initiated right away. . . . It was for the purpose of concentrating our efforts to effect an over-all reform and remove all obstacles in the way of national reconstruction that national general mobilization was ordered." [16]

[15] See annex 129.
[15a] See annex 130.
[16] See annex 131.

THE COMMUNISTS PROCLAIMED TO BE IN OPEN REBELLION, JULY 4, 1947

The resolution on general national mobilization adopted by the State Council on July 4 also proclaimed the Chinese Communists to be in open rebellion against the National Government and demanded that the resources of the country be devoted to their suppression. This part of the resolution was reinforced by statements issued shortly thereafter by the Generalissimo and the Prime Minister, General Chang Chun, in which it was emphasized that the Government was determined to carry out and make effective the national mobilization and suppress the Chinese Communist rebellion. It is interesting to note that the Generalissimo said, "We have never attempted to castigate Communism as a theory or idea. . . . The Government was willing to give full consideration to their opinions, but no peace talk— no mediation—has succeeded in dissuading the Communists from staging a rebellion."

Thus ended a long chapter in Kuomintang-Communist relations, begun in 1937, during which there had been alternate periods of negotiations and military clashes. The Chinese Government had now abandoned its previous publicly expressed policy of seeking to solve the Communist problem by political means and was proclaiming the Chinese Communists to be rebels against the Government's authority who were to be suppressed by military force.

On July 19, the Central News Agency published the text of "The Outline for the Implementation of Mobilization to Suppress Rebellion and Complete Constitutional Government," which was adopted by the State Council on July 18, to become effective immediately. Its 18 articles were general in scope but provided an adequate framework if the Government should succeed in implementing them effectively.[17]

SECRETARY MARSHALL'S MESSAGE OF JULY 6, 1947

On July 6, Ambassador Stuart had delivered to the Generalissimo a message from Secretary of State Marshall, as follows:

"We have been following closely the situation in China and are perturbed over the economic deterioration resulting from the spread of hostilities. We are keenly aware of China's needs and the Generalissimo is thoroughly familiar with the general tenor of my ideas. I cannot presume in my position to offer advice as to how he should deal with the specific situation in Manchuria. In all frankness I must point out that he was forewarned of most of the present serious difficulties and advised regarding preventive measures.

---

[17] See annex 132.

"In the final analysis the fundamental and lasting solution of China's problems must come from the Chinese themselves.   The United States cannot initiate and carry out the solution of those problems and can only assist as conditions develop which give some beneficial results. Please assure the Generalissimo of my continued deep personal concern over events in China and of my earnest desire to find ways of being helpful."

In transmitting this message to the Generalissimo, Ambassador Stuart stressed his confidence that the United States wished to assist and strengthen China as a free nation, but pointed out that it was a most difficult task to decide upon an effective kind of aid and methods by which it might be rendered.   The Ambassador further said that military aid alone would not lead toward the type of development in China which the United States held essential for China's own good. The Generalissimo informed Dr. Stuart that he thoroughly understood the meaning of the message, that he had heard these points from General Marshall when he was in China and that he was grateful for this renewed expression.

In reply to the Generalissimo's inquiry as to the Ambassador's interpretation of the message, Dr. Stuart said that he had many times outlined to the Generalissimo the type of adjustments which were considered prerequisites to a more positive policy and assistance on the part of the United States.   He said that the type of change which he had in mind centered around basic reform through constitutional institutions within the body of the Government, including the delegation of more authority, the establishment and visible maintenance and protection of civil liberties, and the actual development of a more intimate working relationship between the Government and the people. Dr. Stuart stated that the State Council's general national mobilization resolution had in some of its parts certain of the ideas for reform which his Government thought were so necessary, but that there was no assurance that this new order would mean more than many which had previously been issued.   The Ambassador again emphasized the need for drastic over-all reform.   The Generalissimo replied that he understood what was meant and that he would undertake to do something along these lines as soon as possible.

AMBASSADOR STUART'S OBSERVATIONS ON NORTH CHINA AND MANCHURIA

Following a brief trip to Peiping, the Ambassador on July 15, at the request of the Generalissimo, described to him conditions in North

China and Manchuria as he found them. His report of these observations to the Generalissimo is as follows:

"Independent Chinese and American reports from Manchuria agree that conditions are extremely serious not merely from a military point of view but because of the hostility of the people alike toward Communists and the Central Government. Military officers of the Central Government of all ranks are exploiting the populace, enriching themselves, and consequently there are stirrings of separatist feelings. I said that it was my strong opinion that reliance on trusted local leaders with a large measure of autonomy would strengthen the Government position and neutralize Communist success in using these same methods.

"I said I found the north China people somewhat relieved because temporary Government gains in Manchuria removed immediate threat, but discontent was almost as intense as in the northeast. This discontent seemed generally true throughout the country and was becoming rapidly intensified.

"The Generalissimo remarked that economic conditions accounted largely for this, to which I replied that fiscal and economic deterioration was more a symptom and that it was the general feeling of hopelessness and impending disaster that led to increasing military graft, especially in Manchuria. In short, war weariness and increasing forebodings were paralyzing military efforts. I smilingly charged the Generalissimo with having used in his latest statement my own language about a new revolution but without my emphasis on reform and constitutional liberties, restricting his own statement in effect to one of fighting Communists. The Generalissimo agreed somewhat more heartily than usual with my statements and admitted that others could see developments sometimes more clearly than he and asked that I draft specific suggestions. In this latter connection I am taking no action for the time being."

On August 11, Ambassador Stuart again repeated his plea to the Generalissimo that radical reforms be undertaken.[18] On August 19, in a report on the situation,[19] Dr. Stuart spoke of the growing number, both within the Government and outside it, who admitted the logic of the pleas that the Chinese should adopt self-help measures and put their own house in order, but who felt utterly impotent in view of the conservatism, feudalistic ideas, selfishness, narrow prejudices and similar limitations prevalent among those who had the power to effect reforms. He also said that while the signs of willingness

[18] See annex 139.
[19] See annex 140.

and ability to institute progressive reforms were still sadly lacking there were some such signs.

Following a brief visit to Peiping, the Ambassador reported to the Department on September 8 his impressions of conditions in North China as follows:

"The prevailing attitude of students, is `. . . quite revealing, especially when they are thought of as a rough register of the trend in public opinion. In both Tsing Hua and Yenching Universities the anti-Communist element is reported as certainly 90% and more probably 95%, and the anti-Kuomintang-Government proportion as fully 90%. In the University of Peiping, Government sympathizers claim that the percentage opposed to the present administration is much lower. My guess would be that these figures are a fair index of student thinking generally over the country. The obvious conclusion would seem to be that the people—even the more radical and immature—are instinctively against Communism and could easily be won to support a truly reformed National Government. Among the students Chiang Kai-shek, as the symbol of Kuomintang rule, has lost greatly in esteem. To most of them he is frankly finished.

"Another impression is the extent to which Soviet inspired literature is being read by students and the unthinking way with which they accept and quote assertions, about the United States for instance, which are palpably untrue. If we are to undertake a program of active assistance to China I earnestly hope that it will be accompanied by provision for carefully planned publicity.

"Conditions in Communist controlled territory are described to me as follows. The more intelligent country people live not so much in actual discontent or hardship as in fear of what might happen to them at any time. The others accept relative economic insecurity and the regulations imposed on them rather passively. The children are growing up with more or less enthusiasm for the existing regime and are taught to believe all that is evil of the National Government and America. The situation is still somewhat plastic but will become fixed with time. There is general agreement that better local administration with complete assurance that there would be no danger of the certain reprisals if the Communists came back would result in a welcome for the National Government. Economic distress is widely prevalent but there is food for everyone.

"There is great satisfaction in North China over the appointment of General Chen Cheng to supreme authority in Manchuria and the dismissal of Hsiung Shih-hui. The purging of army officers and other reforms, as reported in the local press, have made a fine impression.

"Marshal Li Tsung-jen is gaining in public confidence. There seems no reason to credit rumors of his disaffection toward the National Government. Governor Sung Lien-chung complains—as usual—of having insufficient troops under his command to cope with the Communists in Hopei. The Mayor is working diligently to arouse interest in the coming elections and has drafted college professors and others to visit the different precincts of the city and give lectures on the subject. But he is discouraged by the small numbers registering for casting ballots. It is not clear how much of this apathy is due to fear and how much to indifference or ignorance."

III. THE WEDEMEYER MISSION

INTRODUCTION

While the situation continued to deteriorate and popular discontent with and criticism of the Government increased, the Chinese Government seemed incapable of taking, or unwilling to take, effective steps to meet the serious problems confronting it. There seemed to be rather a feeling of apathy, defeatism and spiritual bankruptcy which led inevitably to a complete psychological dependence upon external aid as the sole means of solving China's problems with little regard to the realities of a situation in which Chinese efforts and measures of self-help were the essential and basic need.

GENERAL WEDEMEYER'S INSTRUCTIONS

In view of these circumstances, the President on July 9, 1947, pursuant to the recommendation of the Secretary of State, instructed Lieutenant General Albert C. Wedemeyer to proceed immediately to China and Korea on a fact-finding mission. This decision was announced on July 11.

The President instructed General Wedemeyer to

"proceed to China without delay for the purpose of making an appraisal of the political, economic, psychological and military situations—current and projected. In the course of your survey you will maintain liaison with American diplomatic and military officials in the area. In your discussions with Chinese officials and leaders in positions of responsibility you will make it clear that you are on a fact-finding mission and that the United States Government can consider assistance in a program of rehabilitation only if the Chinese Government presents satisfactory evidence of effective measures looking towards Chinese recovery and provided further that any aid which may be made available shall be subject to the supervision of representatives of the United States Government.

"In making your appraisal it is desired that you proceed with detachment from any feeling of prior obligation to support or to further official Chinese programs which do not conform to sound American policy with regard to China. In presenting the findings of your mission you should endeavor to state as concisely as possible your estimate of the character, extent, and probable consequences of assistance which you may recommend, and the probable consequences in the event that assistance is not given."

CHINESE REACTION TO THE APPOINTMENT

The reaction in China was mixed. Dr. Wang Shih-chieh, Minister for Foreign Affairs, expressed the views of his Government as follows:

"The Chinese Government as well as President Chiang Kai-shek welcome the appointment of General Albert C. Wedemeyer as special envoy representing the President of the United States on a fact-finding mission to China and Korea. He is a staunch old friend of China. When he served in the China theatre during the latter part of the war, his contributions to Sino-American collaboration and his achievement in strengthening the China theatre were widely appreciated.

"It is my belief that his coming visit will vastly facilitate a more complete understanding of the Chinese situation by the American people, further strengthen Sino-American friendship and cooperation and be conducive to general stabilization of the situation in the Far East."

The Chinese Government believed that General Wedemeyer's mission would result in immediate and substantial economic and military aid. For the same reason, liberal and opposition groups were skeptical of the mission, fearing that aid would only prolong the civil war. Chinese Communist reaction was bitterly hostile.

GENERAL WEDEMEYER'S STATEMENTS OF AUGUST 22 AND 24, 1947

During the month that General Wedemeyer and his mission remained in China they visited the principal centers of the country and talked with a very large number of people, both in and out of the Government, and representing all shades of opinion and interests, as well as with American and other non-Chinese businessmen and officials. On August 22, in accordance with the Generalissimo's suggestion, General Wedemeyer delivered an address to a joint meeting of the State Council and all the Ministers of the National Government, at which the Generalissimo and Madame Chiang and the American Ambassador were also present. In this address he was strongly critical of the military effort of the Government and of the corruption and inefficiency prevalent in its ranks. He said in substance that the National Government could not defeat the Chinese Communists by force but could win the loyal, enthusiastic and realistic support of the Chinese people only by improving the political and economic situation immediately. He stressed that the effectiveness and timeliness of these improvements would determine whether the National Government would stand or fall.[20] Although the General prefaced and concluded his remarks with expressions of genuine friendship for China, Ambassador Stuart reported that those present at the gathering, predominantly of the old scholar class, generally regarded the remarks as offensive. President Chiang was also apparently offended and, in bidding the General farewell, chided him for allegedly refusing to see certain groups of substantial persons in the cities visited. General Wedemeyer, however, protested his desire to see as many different types as his schedule permitted. President Chiang also renewed his request that the Genral provide him with a list of names of Chinese with large financial holdings abroad, but General Wedemeyer felt that since the names had been given him in strictest confidence, he would have to refuse.

General Wedemeyer reinforced his views by a statement issued at Nanking on August 24 at the time of his departure from China:

"In China today I find apathy and lethargy in many quarters. Instead of seeking solutions of problems presented, considerable time and effort are spent in blaming outside influences and seeking outside assistance.

"It is discouraging to note the abject defeatism of many Chinese, who are normally competent and patriotic and who instead should be full of hope and determination.

"Weakened and disrupted by long years of war and revolution, China still possesses most of the physical resources needed for her own rehabilitation. Recovery awaits inspirational leadership and moral and spiritual resurgence which can only come from within China. . . .

" . . . the existing Central Government can win and retain the undivided, enthusiastic support of the bulk of the Chinese people by removing incompetent and/or corrupt people who now occupy many positions of responsibility in the Government, not only national but more so in provincial and municipal structures.

"There are honorable officials who show high efficiency and devotion to duty, who strive to live within ridiculous salaries and such

---

[20] See annex 133.

private means as they possess, just as there are conscientious business-men who live up to a high code of commercial ethics. But no one will misunderstand my emphasis upon the large number whose conduct is notoriously marked by greed, incompetence or both.

"To regain and maintain the confidence of the people, the Central Government will have to effect immediately drastic, far-reaching political and economic reforms. Promises will no longer suffice. Performance is absolutely necessary. It should be accepted that military force in itself will not eliminate communism." [21]

CHINESE REACTION TO GENERAL WEDEMEYER'S STATEMENTS

The reaction in China to General Wedemeyer's statement of August 24 was in general unfavorable except among the liberal opposition groups. Typical of the reaction was an interview given by the Prime Minister to the United Press in which he charged that General Wedemeyer had failed to understand the situation in China and had not impartially sought his information. [22] The announcement of General Wedemeyer's Mission had led to expectations of immediate aid and the effect of his speech to the State Council meeting and his parting statement had served to dispel hopes of substantial assistance and had in turn caused resentment. The Chinese Communists, apparently fearful of American aid, were also bitter and in a broadcast of August 28 attacked General Wedemeyer in strong terms. [23]

Ambassador Stuart reported that on August 25, his own personal secretary, Philip Fugh, had been quizzed by the Generalissimo regarding the background of the Wedemeyer Mission, as to why it was regarded as necessary, and whether it meant that the United States wished to force his (Chiang's) retirement or removal. This inquiry may have been prompted by General Wedemeyer's reference to the need for "inspirational leadership" in China. Ambassador Stuart concluded that the General's talk had been a "rude shock to the Chinese Government," but he felt that "most politically conscious non-partisan and liberal Chinese undoubtedly largely endorse all that the Mission has said." [24]

General Wedemeyer was seriously concerned at the reaction to his final press statement and to his talk before the State Council. A letter which he wrote to the Ambassador on August 30 indicated his surprise at the reaction:

[21] See annex 134.
[22] See annex 136.
[23] See annex 137.
[24] For full text of the Ambassador's report, see annex 141.

"The members of my mission and I have carefully perused the Chinese and American reaction to our final press statement. You know and the Generalissimo should know that the objective was to assist him in instituting reforms and reorganizing his government to facilitate economic and political stability. You can reassure him that all the members of my mission are friendly to China.

"As far as the reaction to my talk before the State Council and the Ministers is concerned, the Generalissimo asked me to make this talk and urged complete frankness. The Generalissimo's Secretary strongly reiterated that the Generalissimo wanted a frank appraisal of my observations. You personally confirmed my hope when we were returning from the talk that my frank appraisal was sorely needed and was well received. You added that my statements were made courteously and with due regard for the sensibilities of those venerable officials who were present.

"The members of my Mission again join in thanking you and the members of your staff for the assistance and courtesies they received."

General Wedemeyer on September 8 repeated his concern over the reaction in a letter to the Secretary of State as follows:

"Reference is made to Ambassador Stuart's resume of my talk to assembled Chinese officials, including the Generalissimo, members of State Councils, and Ministers. The Generalissimo strongly and repeatedly urged this talk and Ambassador Stuart concurred. At the conclusion the Ambassador stated that if my Mission served no other useful purpose, the value of the talk fully justified the presence of the Mission in China. I was particularly careful in presenting the data in a courteous manner in order not to offend the finer sensibilities of the venerable gentlemen and high officials present. I emphasized that I made the talk upon the repeated request of the Generalissimo to whom I had previously related observations. I refrained meticulously from any hint or suggestion concerning my conclusions or projected recommendations. This visibly piqued and disappointed Chinese officialdom. I prefaced the talk with the statement that I was appearing before the assembled officials as a friend and not as a Presidential envoy. My action requires no defense or apology. However, the above information appears pertinent in the light of Ambassador Stuart's messages concerning the subject and also in view of both favorable and unfavorable Chinese reactions."

Prior to his departure the Chinese Government had handed General Wedemeyer a memorandum setting forth an account of Kuomintang accomplishments in the thirties, a justification of the Government position and a reaffirmation of the Government's determination to see the civil war through to a successful conclusion. In this memorandum the Government claimed that it had already undertaken most of the internal reforms recommended by the United States.[25]

RECOMMENDATIONS OF THE WEDEMEYER REPORT

Following a brief visit to Korea, General Wedemeyer returned to Washington and on September 19 presented his confidential report to President Truman.[26]

The controversy in the United States surrounding this Report arose largely from the fact that the United States Government did not make it public. The President had originally requested this appraisal of the situation in China for his own guidance and that of the Secretary of State and not for public use. General Wedemeyer's analysis of the situation in China was in general similar to that submitted to the Department of State in numerous reports by the American Embassy and American consular officers in China and by General Marshall himself. Among the recommendations of the Report, however, was one requiring immediate action by the United Nations to place Manchuria under a Guardianship of Five Powers including the Soviet Union, or a United Nations Trusteeship. It was the conviction of the President and the Secretary of State that any such recommendation, if made public at that time, would be highly offensive to Chinese susceptibilities as an infringement of Chinese sovereignty, and representing the Chinese Government as incapable of governing Chinese territory. It was also believed that it would no doubt be rejected by the Chinese Government as it would in a sense represent at least a partial alienation of Chinese territory to a group of powers including the Soviet Union. In any event, they believed that to place upon the United Nations responsibility for action to implement such a recommendation might well seriously endanger the future of that organization, which at that time was already confronted with other grave and pressing problems. The Generalissimo was confidentially advised by the Secretary of State of the impediments this recommendation had placed in the way of the publication of the Report, and vouchsafed no comment.

The Wedemeyer Report recommended in general that the United States provide military and economic aid to China under a program of assistance over a period of at least five years requiring Congressional authorization. It also provided for financial assistance to China for reconstruction projects and eventually for currency stabilization, while at the same time recognizing: "The present fiscal situa-

---

[25] See annex 138.

[26] See annex 135 for full text of those portions of the Wedemeyer Report dealing with China.

tion is inopportune for the introduction of a new currency or the adoption of even an intermediate step towards stabilization."

The Report indicated that improvement of the economic situation through American aid should open the way for further constructive support in the future from existing agencies, such as the Export-Import Bank, the International Bank and Monetary Fund and private Chinese and foreign capital. In its military phases the Report recommended that military advice and supervision be extended in scope to include field forces, training centers and particularly logistical agencies, but it recognized the desirability of avoiding direct United States involvement in the civil war by indicating: "Although advice indicated above does provide advice indirectly to tactical forces, it should be carried on outside operational areas to prevent the criticism that American personnel are actively engaged in fratricidal warfare."

In addition to the stipulations regarding action by the United Nations, reference to which has been made previously, the Report recommended other stipulations as precedent to United States aid:

"That China make effective use of her own resources in a program for economic reconstruction and initiate sound fiscal policies leading to reduction of budgetary deficits.

"That China give continuing evidence that the urgently required political and military reforms are being implemented.

"That China accept American advisors as responsible representatives of the U. S. Government in specified military and economic fields to assist China in utilizing U. S. aid in the manner for which it is intended."

IV. INTERNAL DEVELOPMENTS IN CHINA

FOURTH PLENARY SESSION OF THE KUOMINTANG CENTRAL EXECU-
TIVE COMMITTEE

The Fourth Plenary Session of the Central Executive Committee of the Kuomintang opened at Nanking on September 9, 1947, with the announced purpose of consolidating the San Min Chu I Youth Corps with the Kuomintang. There was, however, much speculation that the Session would have a more important task. According to reliable information the Generalissimo in his opening address, which was largely a repetition of remarks he had made to the Standing Committee the preceding June, said that for twenty years he had been attempting to implement the principles of Sun Yat-sen and that he had to admit failure but was determined to continue. But he scathingly denounced the Party for failing to solve China's problems and absolved himself from all responsibility. From this point he proceeded to charge that the members of the Kuomintang had also failed, that the Communists had proved themselves abler and more devoted and that without reform and rejuvenation the Kuomintang was doomed to extinction. The Generalissimo asserted that China would never again be dependent on the United States for assistance. He said that China's policy toward Japan was in line with that of the Soviet Union, with which country China would have to strengthen its relations, while preserving its traditional tie of friendship with the United States. It is noteworthy that an elaborate if general program of reform was proposed during the Session and that it was expected to be adopted. At one of the final meetings, however, the Generalissimo demanded that the reform program be dropped and that in its place the Kuomintang proceed to carry out unfulfilled promises made during the previous two years. The final manifesto of the Fourth Plenary Session, published on September 13,[27] did not indicate any specific accomplishments of the meeting.

On September 20 the Embassy reported its appraisal of the meeting to the Department of State: [28] The reported reform was believed to be related to the Wedemeyer Mission and to the desire to comply with American requirements for assistance. The consolidation of the Youth Corps was sought, however, in order to draw the younger elements into the Party, and to eliminate the growing friction between the Kuomintang and the Youth Corps. The consolidation achieved by the meeting was reportedly not very successful, and the Central Executive Committee accomplished very little. The Session involved a sparring for position, which might lead to a purge. The CC Clique emerged in a stronger position than previously, owing to its control of the Youth Corps and its ability to exploit internal and international conditions. The disappointing outcome of the Wedemeyer Mission played an important role in the Session, for it belied the expectations of the Government, which had expected substantial aid or at least specific promises from that Mission.

In a further report on September 20 [29] regarding the general situation the Embassy pointed out that the most disheartening feature of the Chinese situation, in economic as well as in other fields, was the overt reliance upon American aid to extricate China from its pressing problems and a corresponding lack of self-reliance and self-help in meeting these problems. The political, military, and economic position of the Central Government was said to be continuously

[27] See annex 142.
[28] For full text of this report, see annex 143.
[29] For full text, see annex 144.

deteriorating, and the failure of the expected assistance from the Wedemeyer Mission to materialize, combined with renewed Communist military activity, was intensifying a tendency to panic. Supporting the Generalissimo's reference to the Soviet Union, thinly veiled suggestions were emanating from high officials of the Chinese Government to the effect that China might have to seek assistance from that country, and that the Soviet Ambassador to China might be asked to mediate in the civil war. Such talk was regarded as primarily for effect on the United States, and secondarily as a reflection of a feeling of desperation among Chinese leaders. There was also an increasing Chinese fear that the United States was tending to shift the center of gravity of its Far Eastern policy from China to Japan. The large-scale raid of Liu Po-cheng into Anhwei and southern Honan was a matter of great concern, and the military situation in Shantung had deteriorated. The military situation in Manchuria was said to be quiescent, but a sixth Communist offensive was thought to be imminent. The expected Communist offensive would probably be coordinated with one in North China. Communist radio broadcasts had stated that the offensive to "liberate" China north of the Yangtze had been launched, but it was not thought that this objective would be attained "within the foreseeable future." It was disheartening to see the Chinese reliance on the *deus ex machina* of American aid, as illustrated by the presumption that the deficit in China's balance of payments would be met by the United States in one form or another.

On September 27 the American Consul General in Shanghai reported that the CC Clique there was increasing its power and dominating the Kuomintang's preparations to ensure that the successful candidates in the coming election were "elite party supporters plus such few political beggars as it may seem expedient to accept as window dressing." In this connection the Consul General forwarded reports that T. V. Soong had made a bargain with the CC Clique which involved his appointment as Governor of Kwangtung and that H. H. Kung was presumably involved in the bargain. Shanghai reports also indicated that the Government's anti-Americanism at this time had been inspired by the right wing of the Kuomintang, which found it an effective method of weakening the Political Science group.

AMBASSADOR STUART'S REPORT OF SEPTEMBER 29, 1947

Two days later, Dr. Stuart reported to the Department as follows:

"There is not much evidence yet of success in dealing with graft, which is becoming more prevalent in the worsening economic situation.

But President Chiang is at least trying to tackle the problem. The Control Yuan has been given considerably more authority with instructions to exercise it in this matter. One hears constantly of those who have been brought to trial. An instance, which is a somewhat acid test for any Chinese official, is the son of an old and honored friend of President Chiang, now at the head of the Postal Administration but charged with flagrant speculation, whom President Chiang ordered to be punished according to law regardless of all other considerations.

"The powers of the local police are being enlarged as part of the plan for eliminating or at least restricting the activities of military police and secret service men. . . .

"There are not a few hard-working, public-spirited progressives in the Government who share our dissatisfaction with it and who earnestly desire for their country all that we have expressed as our hope for China. But their difficulties are very real. Just to mention one of many, the members of the two minority parties brought in to broaden the basis of the Government are showing themselves to be even more rapacious for office and its perquisites than many of the Kuomintang, with no improvement in administrative efficiency. These progressives and their many sympathizers outside would be immensely heartened by some indication of our intention to assist them and would, in my opinion, be the nucleus through which we can go a long way toward realizing our aims for China and for a stable peace in this part of the world. But they do not see much hope without such aid from us and any authoritative indication of our policy would be very reassuring."

On October 11, members of the Military Affairs Committee of the American House of Representatives who were visiting in China called on the Generalissimo. In answer to their questions he stated his belief that the Chinese Communists were thorough-going Communists, working in collusion with and taking orders from Moscow, and that they constantly received supplies from Russia. He repeated his request for greater American aid and then said that "the predicament in Manchuria was an American responsibility." In conclusion he said that if the Government were finally defeated it would not be because of Russia or the Chinese Communists, but because the United States had failed to give promised assistance at a time of desperate need.

In a report to the Department on October 29, Ambassador Stuart found no reason to change his previous estimates.[30]

---

[30] See annex 145.

OUTLAWING OF THE DEMOCRATIC LEAGUE, OCTOBER 28, 1947

Additional developments concerned the minor parties. Partly as a result of Government pressure, and partly as an indication of dissension within its own ranks, Carson Chang's Social Democratic Party was bitterly split during August and September and ended up as two separate groups with consequent diminution of such influence as it had possessed. Henceforth little was to be heard of it except for that faction which joined with the Government and became largely a rubber-stamp of the Kuomintang.

During September and October there were increasingly frequent reports that the Government was planning action against the Democratic League on charges that it was subservient to the Communists. Finally, on October 28, an official decree outlawed the League and made it subject to the provisions of the General National Mobilization Order of July 4.[31]

The prominent leaders of the party were not arrested and, as a result of negotiations between the League and the Government, the League on November 6 announced its formal dissolution.[32] The Government decree was never revoked and it was apparent that the Generalissimo was determined to eliminate the League from public activities.[33]

POSSIBILITY OF RESUMPTION OF PEACE NEGOTIATIONS

During the winter of 1947–1948 rumors of peace negotiations with the Chinese Communists again became current. This time the possibility of Russian mediation was injected. On December 20, 1947, General Chang Chih-chung, who had played a leading role in the negotiations while General Marshall was in China, told the American Ambassador that he had recently discussed the situation with the Generalissimo. He had argued with the Generalissimo that the only solution lay in the resumption of the PCC resolutions, but the latter remonstrated that he could not take the initiative—though he would not object if General Chang made cautious inquiries. General Chang also told Ambassador Stuart that prior to his conversation with the Generalissimo he had approached the Soviet Embassy in Nanking for help in persuading the Chinese Communists to resume peace talks. He had warned the Russians that China could never be won over to Russia against the United States, and had insisted that in aiding China the United States had no ulterior motives against the Russians. He said the Russians seemed impressed, and in reply to their inquiry

[31] See annex 146.
[32] See annex 147.
[33] See annex 148.

as to what they might do, he said that they might advise the Chinese Communists to stop fighting.

On the other hand a statement was issued on December 25 by Chairman Mao Tse-tung of the Central Committee of the Chinese Communist Party.[34] The statement was one of triumph and confidence, as well as a series of vitriolic attacks on the United States as the great enemy of the world and the agent responsible for continuing the civil war in China.

Subsequently the private secretary to the Generalissimo confirmed to the Embassy that the Russians had offered to mediate in the Chinese situation. The secretary stated emphatically, however, that the Generalissimo had not given his approval to the activities of General Chang Chih-chung and that the Chinese Government neither desired nor believed possible any accommodation with the Chinese Communists at that time. However, it was increasingly apparent during January 1948 that there were elements in the Chinese Government which favored a political settlement. The Embassy on January 23 reported to the Department its belief that something might come of this trend in favor of negotiations because of the increasingly unfavorable position of the Government, and the apparent determination of the Chinese Communists to carry the fighting to Central and South China. It was clear that responsible Chinese Government officials were also concerned by this latter possibility.

On February 6 the Ambassador found that the Chinese Foreign Minister was seriously perturbed over the military situation in Manchuria. The Foreign Minister stated that he believed the renewed attacks by the Chinese Communist forces on Mukden arose from the Chinese refusal of the Russian offer of mediation. He told the Ambassador that the Soviet Chargé d'Affaires, acting on instructions, had requested protection for Russian citizens in Manchuria. When the Chargé remonstrated that the Soviet Union had never given China cause for misgiving, the Foreign Minister reminded him of the behavior of Russian troops after entering Manchuria in August 1945.

On March 8 the Embassy at Nanking commented as follows on these and related developments:

"There is increasing evidence that despite the announced intention of present Government leadership to continue the civil war, strong opposition to this policy by civil and military officials, as well as by the general public, particularly the intellectuals, may soon become sufficiently strong to compel present leadership to abandon this policy in favor of negotiated peace or face the threat of being

---

[34] See annex 149.

discarded. It is difficult at the moment to define precisely the scope of this opposition or its strength, but the fact of its existence or of its growth can hardly any longer be denied. The disintegration and decay which has characterized all phases of the Government's activities during the past several years continues and in recent weeks has been accentuated. It is increasingly apparent that the Government is over-extended militarily, with resulting inability to prevent continued economic deterioration and has reached a point where its overall political control is imperiled.

"The Government now exerts only a tenuous control over approximately one per cent of Manchuria and not more than ten or fifteen per cent of that part of China proper north of the Yellow River. Between the Yellow River and the Yangtze there are strong Communist elements and there has been infiltration even south of the Yangtze. Government forces are hard pressed and on the defensive in practically every theater. There is increased demoralization, a fatalistic feeling that collapse of the government is inevitable, and a decided trend toward regionalism; each regional leader is looking about for means to defend himself against the Communists when he can no longer call on Nanking.

"With this alarming situation there is need for inspired leadership which is not forthcoming. Those in control of the government seem almost frantic in their search for solution, yet incapable of taking the necessary initiative. Increasingly, it is the Generalissimo who must make the decisions and he continues the slave of his past and unable to take the drastic measures required. He may be expected, we believe, doggedly to continue the fight with the idea that if worse comes to worst, he can withdraw to Canton where T. V. Soong is engaged in building a stronghold, and let regionalism again prevail. There is, however, likelihood that opposition within the Government may not permit this course of action. This opposition is well aware of the perils of Soviet mediation, but appears inclined to prefer such mediation to a continuation of the current struggle, the only end to which they increasingly fear will be a Communist-dominated China.

"Such a negotiated settlement would likely require the disappearance from the political scene of the present dominant leadership, including the Generalissimo. Yet, we cannot rule it out. While present criminally inept and wasteful strategy can postpone temporarily the loss of major strategic points, it cannot do so indefinitely. By far the greater part of the Government's military and economic resources have been committed to Manchuria and North China. Despite the scale of this commitment it has not forced, and shows no sign of forcing, a decision on the Government's behalf. Failing

American economic aid on an impossibly large scale, failing active American military aid, and failing competent Chinese leadership and planning, there may be revolt within the ranks of the Kuomintang and acceptance of the Soviet offer to mediate in the forlorn hope that such a compromise would give a breathing spell for regrouping, consolidation, and the emergence of some dynamic quality that would again create the will to victory now lacking. The dangers of coalition with Communists are well known to those in opposition. Most likely accommodation would, therefore, be on a purely territorial basis which would, in effect, be but a temporary, though perhaps prolonged, truce. In any case, we feel it is entirely possible that non-Communist elements released by such event from the dead traditional hand of present leadership, might rally to American assistance with a complementary possibility of the development of political, economic and spiritual resources, which might eventuate in stable non-Communist government in Central and South China."

ELECTIONS TO THE NATIONAL ASSEMBLY

In the meantime, the principal internal preoccupation apart from the civil war had been, as it would continue to be for the next six months, the elections for the National Assembly—the Assembly itself was to establish the first constitutional government—and the struggle within the Kuomintang for power. This interest was manifested in a series of political crises. Despite predictions and speculation to the contrary, the Government held the elections late in 1947 according to schedule. In the absence of the Communists and the Democratic League, these elections were between the various factions in the Kuomintang and the two minor parties, the Social Democrats and the Youth Party, which had agreed to participate. For a number of reasons the results were slow in coming in, though there was little doubt as to the eventual outcome. In the end it was apparent that majority influence in the new National Assembly and the Legislative Yuan would lie with the CC Clique, the extreme right-wing faction of the Kuomintang. It was precisely here that the Government found itself confronted with an ironic situation. It was publicly committed to a certain proportional representation by the minor parties, but when the results were tabulated it was seen that practically none of the minor party candidates had been successful, and that they had lost to either the CC Clique or independent Kuomintang candidates. The Government was faced with the difficult and embarrassing necessity of persuading successful candidates to withdraw after they had won, in order to comply with the commitment on broadening the Government. This was only made possible by an *ex post facto* declaration that only those Kuomintang candidates would be considered successful who had prior approval of the Party. This decision was later to create difficulty for the Generalissimo at the spring meeting of the National Assembly, which decided to rebel against his authority. Even the over-all victory of the CC Clique would later prove, in part, illusory on a national scale. It also became apparent that the real strength of the CC Clique lay in its control over local administrations.

DISTURBANCES IN SHANGHAI

Early in February there was an outbreak of disturbances in Shanghai, attended by some loss of life and destruction of property. The discontent this time did not center in any one particular group but appeared to be fairly general throughout the city and to be a general reflection of discontent with the manner in which the Government was prosecuting the war and handling civil administration. Neither the Embassy nor the Consulate General in Shanghai believed, however, that these disturbances forecast any imminent over-all breakdown of law and order, especially in view of the determined and imaginative action by the mayor. They felt, rather, that the disturbances were more the signs of things to come.[35]

V. REDEFINITION OF AMERICAN POLICY

CONSIDERATIONS UNDERLYING THE FORMULATION OF A PROGRAM OF AID TO CHINA

For several months prior to October 1947, the Department of State, together with the National Advisory Council, had been making studies of China's balance-of-payments position with a view to its bearing on a program of further aid to China. In the latter part of October the Department of State began the formulation of such a program.

In this connection several basic factors had to be taken into consideration: It was recognized that in the main the solution of China's problems must largely be a task for the Chinese themselves. A United States program of aid to China should not be such as would place the United States in the position of direct responsibility for the conduct of the fighting in China or for the Chinese economy. The United States Government could not virtually take over the Chinese Government and administer its economic and military affairs. Any such undertakings would have involved the United States in a continuing commitment from which it would have been practically impossible to withdraw regardless of circumstances or of Chinese Government actions.

---

[35] See annex 150 (a) and (b).

Account also had to be taken of the heavy burden of foreign aid which the United States was assuming elsewhere and of the limitations on the extent to which American resources could be drawn upon for foreign aid under the peacetime organization of its economy.

Secretary Marshall reflected these considerations when, during the hearings on the China aid program in February 1948, he stated that an attempt to underwrite the Chinese economy and the Chinese Government's military effort represented a burden on the United States economy and a military responsibility which he could not recommend as a course of action for this Government. Nevertheless, it was believed that the United States should do what was feasible under existing circumstances and that the proposed program of aid for China would, as the President stated to the Congress on February 18, 1948, "assist in retarding rapid economic deterioration and thus give the Chinese Government a further opportunity to initiate the measures necessary to the establishment of more stable economic conditions. But it is, and has been, clear that only the Chinese Government itself can undertake the vital measures necessary to provide the framework within which efforts toward peace and true economic recovery may be effective."

The new proposal did not call for a long-term recovery program extending over 5 years, as recommended by General Wedemeyer. As Secretary Marshall stated before the House Committee on Foreign Affairs on February 20, 1948, "it is very necessary to have in mind that a proposal at the present time cannot be predicated upon a definite termination for the necessity of such assistance as in the case of the European Recovery Program." It was evident that no long-range recovery program could be developed until the Chinese Government had demonstrated its capacity to take, with substantial United States assistance, initial steps toward laying the basis for further constructive efforts. The Department of State's program thus called for aid over a 15-month period during which the Chinese Government would have a further opportunity to take initial steps to this end.

With respect to the question of military aid, as recommended by General Wedemeyer, the Department of State's proposed aid program, calling for 570 million dollars in economic assistance, was sufficiently large to free the major portion of the Chinese Government's own foreign exchange assets for the purchase of such military supplies as it might wish to obtain from foreign sources. It was not considered desirable that the United States embark upon a military aid program calling for the use of United States military advisers in combat areas or upon measures of military aid which would have led to United States military intervention in China or to direct United States involvement in China's civil strife. For these reasons, it was considered that the Chinese Government's requirements for military matériel from foreign sources should be met through purchases from its own resources, largely freed for such use through the proposed program of economic aid, and that the existing United States military advisory groups in China would enable the United States to extend advice and assistance within the framework of the considerations outlined above.

It was against the background of these considerations that the Department of State's proposed China aid bill was presented to the Congress in February 1948. The Congress passed legislation authorizing aid for China on April 2, 1948, the title of which was the China Aid Act of 1948. The Department's proposals for a program of aid to China and Congressional action on these proposals are described in greater detail in chapter VIII.

SECRETARY MARSHALL'S PRESS CONFERENCE OF MARCH 10, 1948

Meanwhile the question of American policy toward China was again suddenly and inadvertently raised. In an interview with an American correspondent early in March, the remarks made by the American Ambassador were misinterpreted to mean that he favored a coalition government. Despite his clarification on the following day, some confusion persisted. At Secretary Marshall's regular press conference on March 10, a correspondent, referring to Congressman Fulton's statement before the House Foreign Affairs Committee that there had never been a disavowal of American policy favoring a coalition government in China to include the Communists and that this apparently was still American policy, asked the Secretary if this were so. Secretary Marshall replied that the principals, Chiang Kai-shek and the head of the Communist Party, Mao Tse-tung, had reached a partial agreement in September 1945. Then, he said, in November 1945 they had reached a formal agreement for a meeting of the Political Consulative Conference, and on December 17 there had been another agreement between Mao Tse-tung and Chiang Kai-shek, the basis of it being that it was to bring all Chinese parties together in a discussion to endeavor to settle the problem by political means. On December 15 President Truman had announced his statement of the policy of the United States Government. Secretary Marshall pointed out that the terms had been expressed in very broad language, that is, that the Chinese should widen the basis of their government and give representation on a broad basis. Asked if this were still our policy, Secretary Marshall replied in the affirmative, pointing out that it was not intended to force the Chinese to do this on the basis of any issues which had previously arisen.

For the background of the correspondents, Secretary Marshall pointed out certain essential differences between the situation in China and the situation in European countries. In China a single party, the Kuomintang, and the Government had been practically identical for some time. The problem of "coalition" in the European sense, where various established parties exist, did not really arise in the Chinese situation. What did arise was the question which the Chinese themselves had been discussing for some time of granting parties other than the Kuomintang, including the Communist Party, some representation in at least the legislative branches of the Government. Neither the Communist nor any other party except the Kuomintang had had any representation in the legislative branch. The Secretary explained that, when he was in China, the Chinese Nationalist Government was following a policy of settling its disputes with the Communists as a political matter on the basis of negotiation instead of using force for their suppression. He had participated as a mediator in these discussions.

Since these remarks also were misinterpreted, the Department of State issued the following release on March 11:

"In view of misunderstandings that have arisen concerning the Secretary's statements about China at his March 10 press conference, it is pointed out that the Secretary referred to President Truman's statement of December 15, 1945. That statement expressed the belief of the United States 'that peace, unity and democratic reform in China will be furthered if the basis of this Government (China's) is broadened to include other political elements in the country'. The Secretary said that this statement still stands. When asked specifically whether broadening the base of the Chinese Government meant we favored the inclusion of the Chinese Communist Party, he replied that the Communists were now in open rebellion against the Government and that this matter (the determination of whether the Communists should be included in the Chinese Government) was for the Chinese Government to decide, not for the United States Government to dictate."

PRESIDENT TRUMAN'S PRESS CONFERENCE OF MARCH 11, 1948

On the same day, questions were put to the President at his press conference concerning the inclusion of Chinese Communists in the Chinese Government. The President was specifically asked whether he still supported the statement he had made on December 15, 1945. The President replied that this statement still stood. In answer to further questions, he explained that it was not the policy of the United States to urge the National Government of China to take Communists into the Government, but that the policy of the United States, which had further been carried out by General Marshall on his mission to China, was to assist the Chiang Kai-shek Government to meet the situation with which it was confronted. He expressed his hope that the Chinese liberals would be taken into the Government, but stated that "we did not want any Communists in the Government of China or anywhere else if we could help it."

VI. CHANGES IN THE CHINESE GOVERNMENT

ELECTION OF PRESIDENT CHIANG AND VICE PRESIDENT LI TSUNG-JEN

Events were now moving toward the first constitutional Assembly, which was to meet on March 29 for the election of the President and the Vice President. It was anticipated that this meeting would be a crucial one for the Government, and the Embassy in its reports of March 17 and March 31 saw nothing to warrant any optimism.[36] Practically the entire time and attention of prominent members of the Government during these days were taken up with the struggle for allocation of seats in the Assembly and, subsequently, in the jockeying for position over the election for President and Vice President. The struggles reached such extremes that at one point certain disappointed aspirants to the National Assembly staged a hunger strike at a Nanking hotel. Actions such as this at this desperate point in the history of the Government only served to increase dissatisfaction with and criticism of the Government and, in particular, the Generalissimo. In answer to this criticism the Generalissimo made it clear that he would not accept the office of President. He offered to serve his country in any other capacity but it was known that he was considering the presidency of the Executive Yuan and would allow the office of President to become similar to that of the President of France. Early in April, he instructed the Party to vote for Dr. Hu Shih, the distinguished Chinese scholar and former Ambassador to the United States, as President, and Dr. Sun Fo, son of the founder of the Republic, as Vice President. The immediate reaction was an almost unanimous demand in the Assembly that the Generalissimo reverse his position and accept the office. Bowing to the popular will which acclaimed him as the only possible choice, he accepted. This resulted in a great

---

[36] See annex 151 (a) and (b).

increase in his prestige, though not sufficient to enable him to impose his will in the vice-presidential election.

The three leading contenders for the Vice Presidency were Dr. Sun Fo, who was the choice of the Generalissimo; General Ch'eng Chien, one of the oldest and highest ranking generals of the army and Governor of Hunan; and General Li Tsung-jen, a member of the Kwangsi Clique and for many years one of the most prominent members of the Kuomintang. General Li had staged a highly successful campaign and had succeeded in rallying around himself most of the liberal and other elements in the Assembly strongly desirous of reform and changes in the Government. Resolution of this conflict required many days of political juggling and several ballots, but in the end General Li won, despite all the pressure which the Generalissimo brought to bear on recalcitrant members of the Assembly. Immediately following this election there was widespread hope that a genuine and inspired reform movement would now arise to bring about those changes which all agreed were necessary if the National Government were to avoid disaster. In time, however, it became apparent that nothing of the sort would happen.

General Li himself took no action, despite all rumors, and claimed that he could do nothing because the Generalissimo still controlled the Party machine, Government finances, and the army. It was typical of the manner in which the Generalissimo set about disciplining the Party rebellion that at the Presidential inauguration the newly-elected Vice President was left entirely in the background, and when the Presidential party drove off after the inaugural ceremonies he was ignored. These developments did not augur well for the future of unity in prosecuting the war against the Communists, and the hopes aroused by the election of General Li on what was, in effect, a popular movement for change and reform, were soon shattered.[37]

THE SEARCH FOR A NEW EXECUTIVE YUAN

The struggle for power within the Kuomintang was carried over into the search for a new Prime Minister and Executive Yuan. The names most prominently mentioned for the premiership were those of General Ho Ying-chin; the incumbent, General Chang Chun; Dr. T. V. Soong; and the Foreign Minister, Dr. Wang Shih-chieh. The Generalissimo appears to have favored General Ho but refused to meet his conditions. In the end the compromise selection was Dr. Wong Wen-hao, an eminent geologist, chairman of the National Resources Commission, and a man of unquestioned personal integrity, but totally without political following. It was apparent that the new Govern-

---

[37] See annex 152 (a)–(n).

ment was composed of loyal followers of the Generalissimo and that he would continue to have the final word on all decisions. Public reaction to the new Government was generally unfavorable and the preliminary reports of the Government and the Legislative Yuan gave little hope for confidence.[38]

The Ambassador reported to the Department on June 24 as follows:

"The crucial problem is still the personality of President Chiang. He is fully cognizant of the current deterioration. He listens patiently to warnings as to the inevitability of disaster unless new policies are adopted and to suggestions regarding these. He seems sincerely determined to act in accordance with the theory of his new office and under constitutional procedure. But there is actually very little change in his methods.

"I had been hoping that with the appointment of General Ho Ying-ch'in as Minister of National Defense the military operations would be delegated to him with real authority and that General Barr could work closely with him.[39] I had urged this course upon the President and had received his assurance of agreement provided only he were kept constantly informed. I had also discussed the matter more than once with General Ho who heartily concurred in the advisability of this plan and promised that he would do his best. Yet the President has just issued an order that all operations are to be carried out under instructions from him through the Chief-of-Staff—the incompetent Ku Chu-t'ung!

"General Pai Ch'ung-hsi had been relieved of his post as Minister of National Defense, presumably for helping in the election of Li Tsung-jen. He was then offered the important task of commanding the troops in the five provinces between the Yellow and Yangtze Rivers and after long hesitation accepted, only to learn that he would not be allowed to organize local militia in this area—a feature which he has always strongly advocated—and that certain regions, such as that surrounding the Wu Han cities, would be out of his jurisdiction. He thereupon withdrew his acceptance and left in disgust for Shanghai. The President showed no regret and remarked that this was of no importance. He seems suspicious that the Kwangsi Clique have designs against him and is thus alienating, or at least losing the effective cooperation of, men who by every test have been loyal both to him and to the national cause.

"These instances of recent happenings will seem grimly familiar to you. I have more than ever a sense of frustration in endeavoring to

---

[38] See annex 153 (a)–(e).

[39] General Barr's mission is discussed below, chapter VII.

influence the President's thinking. I have an easy access to him and am invited to say anything to him without reserve. No Chinese dares to say to him what many even among his closer associates are now thinking and they are looking to me with a pathetic expectancy. And yet I feel impotent to accomplish anything that helps to reverse the downward trend.

"There is a very wide-spread anti-American sentiment crystallizing in protests against our efforts to strengthen Japan. This is being revealed by the vehement attacks upon my message to the students.[40] It is rather puzzling to account for this phenomenon. To explain it as due entirely to Communist or Soviet instigation is an oversimplification. This has of course helped to create it by skillful propaganda and to organize it by agents planted both among faculties and students. But there must be a receptive mood to have produced so general a response and among so many who are normally pro-American. This is perhaps caused in large part by a fear of Japan which began in the closing years of the last century and has become instinctive as well as deeper than we can readily imagine. It is aggravated by distorted reports of our activities in Japan, including those from Chinese official sources, by misconceptions and false inferences, by the publication of the Draper [report on the industrial potential and reconstruction of Japan] and similar reports, by the cynical assumption that we would not hesitate to sacrifice China in preparing for our private war with Russia, and of course by deliberate, unremitting and malicious propaganda. Another very real factor is the all but universal dissatisfaction with the present Government and the irrational but easily understandable association of America with its existence or its failings. The students, more highly sensitized than other elements of the population, are utterly dispirited and with no proper outlet for their patriotic urgings. An agitation against America for restoring their old enemy to a position of becoming again a potential menace has a curious appeal under these depressing circumstances. Apart entirely from these forebodings and their utilization by Communist and other anti-Government factions are the selfish and shortsighted commercial or industrial groups which seek to avoid Japanese competition. The extremely profitable and perhaps none too efficient Shanghai textile industry, for instance, wishes to maintain for itself the Chinese and Southeastern Asia markets. Thus strangely enough the extreme left and crassly capitalistic interests unite in disapproving our intentions in Japan. We cannot be too careful in carrying out those intentions to give no slightest cause for reasonable misapprehension."

---

[40] See below, p. 277.

STUDENT RIOTS

The students, to whose attitude Ambassador Stuart referred, made known their discontent in a series of riots and demonstrations which extended throughout the length and breadth of the country and even into Manchuria, wherever student groups were found. As usual, the disturbances began in May as examination time approached, and there were many who again thought that they would die down when the examination period had passed. But this time there was more substance to the agitation, and it continued with greater or lesser intensity deep into the summer. The students had learned the lesson of previous years of Government repression of their activities and this time, instead of attacking the Government to reveal their dissatisfaction with their situation, they chose to attack the Government indirectly by protesting American policy in Japan. In this campaign they were abetted by other groups who honestly or for ulterior reasons disapproved of that policy. By early June the anti-American demonstrations had become so violent and irrational that Dr. Stuart felt compelled to appeal to his long relationship with Chinese academic groups. He therefore on his own initiative issued a statement,[41] which had a sobering effect on many of those to whom it was addressed, but the agitators who had seized control of the movement for other purposes managed to keep the disturbances going for many weeks. With the passage of weeks, interest shifted to other and more pressing subjects. On August 17 the Executive Yuan issued an order forbidding disturbances which were calculated to give aid and comfort to the enemy,[41a] and the movement quickly collapsed.

During July the Embassy and the Consulates, in a series of reports to the Department, had outlined in some detail the situation and their concern with it.[42] On July 30 the Ambassador summarized his views as follows:

"We can be quite certain that no amount of military advice or material from us will bring unity and peace to China unless indeed there are reforms sufficiently drastic to win back popular confidence and esteem. That these could even be attempted by those now in power or that the improvements could be rapid and radical enough to reverse the prevailing attitude is scarcely to be hoped for. But without this assurance the intention to give increased military aid ought to be carefully considered in all its implications. Even under the most hopeful conditions such aid would probably require some two years

---

[41] See annex 154.
[41a] See annex 155.
[42] See annex 156 (a)–(d).

or more from next January to accomplish its objective in view of the basic necessity of training new divisions and of recovering lost territory and morale."

ECONOMIC REFORM DECREES OF AUGUST 19, 1948

In a desperate move to stem the tide of economic deterioration, the Government on August 19 promulgated a series of drastic reform measures, which are treated in greater detail elsewhere in this paper.[43] These measures produced a temporary boost in morale in many parts of the country and public opinion in China initially felt that if they were forcefully implemented there was a chance of salvaging the situation. The test case was Shanghai, where the Generalissimo appointed his son, General Chiang Ching-kuo, as economic czar. At the outset young Chiang gave every indication that he would carry out his orders ruthlessly and he announced that special privilege would receive no consideration. Before many weeks had elapsed, however, it became apparent that he was attacking vested interests stronger than himself. The basic fallacy of the August decrees was that they failed to provide the necessary and sufficient measures for a genuine currency reform or to take account of the conditions which had created the crisis. Instead, they attempted to freeze the situation by the imposition of police measures which paralyzed the economic life of Shanghai and other urban centers and in the end further worsened the situation of small and medium businessmen without appreciably affecting the major operators.[43a] Repression could hold the line for a few weeks, but as trade came to a standstill, as the note circulation increased and as the refusal of producers to send stocks of foodstuffs into Shanghai created an emergency food shortage, the artificial controls gave way to pent-up economic pressures and the tempo of economic deterioration reached an unprecedented rate. The military disasters which were about to strike served to accentuate the deterioration. On November 1 Chiang Ching-kuo resigned.[44]

It was symptomatic of the situation that on November 4 the official Kuomintang organ, the *Chung Yang Jih Pao*, should publish an editorial highly critical of the Government suggesting that it might well learn something from the Chinese Communists.[45]

As the situation became worse for the National Government, the Communists in their turn not only reflected growing confidence but also a heightened stridency in their attacks on the United States. Fol-

---

[43] See p. 396.

[43a] See annex 157 (a)-(c).

[44] For his statement at the time of his resignation, see annex 158.

[45] See annex 159.

lowing a period of seeming conciliation, they returned to their former line that the United States was the great enemy. In so doing their statements came more and more to resemble the Kremlin propaganda line.[46]

VII. ALTERNATIVES OF AMERICAN POLICY

SECRETARY MARSHALL'S POLICY DIRECTIVES OF AUGUST 12 AND 13, 1948

During these depressing and disastrous months the Government increased its efforts to secure additional American aid, not only through direct approach but also through publicity. Both the Embassy and the Department of State felt an increasing need to review American policy and to determine what, if any, changes should be made.

On August 10 the Embassy, after reviewing the military, economic, and psychological factors of the situation, recommended (1) that "American efforts be designed to prevent the formation of a coalition government" including Communists in the light of the history of such coalitions in other areas of the world and that continued or increased support of the National Government was the best means to this end, although it was possibly already too late; (2) that, if the march of events resulted in some kind of an accommodation with the Chinese Communists, American "influence should be used to arrange a cessation of hostilities on a basis of a very loose federation with territorial division which would leave as large an area of China as possible with a government or governments free of Communist participation"; and (3) that, in the event of a return to regionalism in China, American economic aid be given to strengthen regional governments so as to "permit basic anticommunist Chinese characteristics to reassert themselves and correspondingly weaken sympathy for the Communists." [47]

The Secretary of State on August 12, 1948, outlined the following points for the Embassy's general guidance:

"1. The United States Government must not directly or indirectly give any implication of support, encouragement or acceptability of coalition government in China with Communist participation.

"2. The United States Government has no intention of again offering its good offices as mediator in China.

---

[46] See annex 160. For a recent statement in this vein by Mao Tse-tung, see annex 120.

[47] For full text of the Embassy's report, see annex 161.

"Overt United States opposition to Chinese Government compromise with the Chinese Communists (or even secretly expressed opposition, which would likely become known) would at this juncture provide ammunition in China for propaganda alleging that the United States was encouraging and prolonging the civil war. It could also mislead the Chinese Government to expect unlimited aid which could not eventuate under the existing world situation and in any circumstances would require congressional action. Any informal expression of United States Government attitude toward these questions should, at this stage of developments in China, be confined to the two points outlined above. You should, of course, overlook no suitable opportunity to emphasize the pattern of engulfment which has resulted from coalition governments in eastern Europe."

On August 13 Secretary Marshall observed:

"While the Department will keep actively in mind the questions raised, it is not likely that the situation will make it possible for us at this juncture to formulate any rigid plans for our future policy in China. Developments in China are obviously entering into a period of extreme flux and confusion in which it will be impossible with surety to perceive clearly far in advance the pattern of things to come and in which this Government plainly must preserve a maximum freedom of action."

POLICY REVIEW OF OCTOBER 1948

Toward the end of October the Embassy again pointed out the continuing deterioration and inquired whether there had been any changes in Washington. To this the Secretary replied:

"There is general agreement with your assumption that the United States purposes in the Far East would as in the past be best served by the existence of political stability in China under a friendly Government, and American policy and its implementation have been consistently directed toward that goal. However, underlying our recent relations with China have been the fundamental considerations that the United States must not become directly involved in the Chinese civil war and that the United States must not assume responsibility for underwriting the Chinese Government militarily and economically. Direct armed intervention in the internal affairs of China runs counter to traditional American policy toward China and would be contrary to the clearly expressed intent of Congress, which indicated that American aid to China under the $125,000,000 grants [47a] did not in-

---

[47a] See chapter VIII.

volve the use of United States combat troops nor United States personnel in command of Chinese troops.   Public statements in Congress by leaders of the Senate Foreign Relations Committee, which initiated Section 404 (b) of the China Aid Act, indicated that aid to China under the $125,000,000 grants must be completely clear of the implication of the United States underwriting the military campaign of the Chinese Government, since any such implication would be impossible over so vast an area.

"Our China Aid Program was designed to give the Chinese Government a breathing spell to initiate those vital steps necessary to provide the framework within which the base for economic recovery might be laid and essential for its survival.   It was clear that in the main solution of China's problems was largely one for the Chinese themselves and the aid was intended to give the Chinese Government further opportunity to take measures of self-help.

"The general basic considerations governing our approach to the China problem were set forth in my statement before the Senate Foreign Relations and House Foreign Affairs Committees executive sessions, a copy of which was forwarded to you.   The United States Government must be exceedingly careful that it does not become committed to a policy involving the absorption of its resources to an unpredictable extent as would be the case if the obligations are assumed of a direct responsibility for the conduct of the civil war in China or for the Chinese economy, or both.   To achieve the objective of reducing the Chinese Communists to a completely negligible factor in China in the immediate future, it would be necessary for the United States virtually to take over the Chinese Government and administer its economic, military and governmental affairs.   Strong Chinese sensibilities regarding infringement of China's sovereignty, the intense feeling of nationalism among all Chinese, and the unavailability of qualified American personnel in large numbers required argue strongly against attempting such a solution.   It would be impossible to estimate the final cost of a course of action of this magnitude.   It certainly would be a continuing operation for a long time to come.   It would involve the United States Government in a continuing commitment from which it would practically be impossible to withdraw, and it would very probably involve grave consequences to this nation by making of China an arena of international conflict.   Present developments make it unlikely that any amount of United States military or economic aid could make the present Chinese Government capable of reestablishing and then maintaining its control throughout all China. There is little evidence that the fundamental weaknesses of the Chinese Government can be basically corrected by foreign aid.   These considerations were set forth in my statement in February and they are certainly no less true under present circumstances.

"Despite American aid since V–J Day, including the China Aid Program, deterioration has continued to a point, as you say in your report of October 22, where the present regime has lost the confidence of the people, reflected in the refusal of soldiers to fight and the refusal of the people to cooperate in economic reforms. This description is generally consistent with that given in previous Embassy reports and Shanghai's report of October 21, which quotes [a high Government official], a strong supporter of the Generalissimo, as saying that 99 percent of the people are against the Government, and Taipei's report of October 22 which quotes [a high official] as saying that unless the Government gets out of office soon the people themselves are about ready to throw them out.

"In your report of May 26 you state that the present Government lacks the capability to halt the spread of Communism and will continue to lack the capability unless, as seems unlikely, it can find the inspired leadership needed to rally people and restore to the National armies the will to fight. You also say that the Generalissimo cannot be expected to provide that leadership as he seems incapable of change and gives every evidence of intention to persist in personal rule which has resulted in the present sad state of affairs.

"Furthermore, in your report of June 14 you described the Generalissimo's assurance of agreement with your recommendation regarding the conduct of military operations by General Ho Ying-chin with General Barr's close collaboration and his subsequent instructions to the contrary that all operations were to be carried out under the Generalissimo's instructions through his 'incompetent' Chief of Staff.

"Your report of June 22 states that it would appear that the Generalissimo's predisposition to appoint his old and personally trusted comrades, regardless of their proven corruption or lack of ability, to posts of responsibility still outweighs his desire for good government.

"Your report of August 10 states there is no longer faith that the present Government can bring a return to an even bearable standard of living without some radical reorganization; that without the Generalissimo disintegration seems inevitable, yet long experience with him suggests that he is no longer capable of changing and reforming or discarding inefficient associates in favor of competent ones; that one would expect the Government to clutch at any means of improving the situation but it ignores competent military advice and fails to take advantage of military opportunities offered, due in a large part to the fact that the Government and the military leadership continue to deteriorate as the Generalissimo selects men on the basis of personal reliability rather than military competence; and that there is awareness of the desperate military situation yet no evidence of the will or capability to cope with it.

"In your report of August 20 you state that General Barr's advice to the Generalissimo on specific problems arising from the conduct of current military operations has in general been ignored and that the grave difficulties encountered by General Barr in the accomplishment of his mission originate entirely in the failure of the Chinese high command to perform its functions.

"In your report of August 10 you state we must recognize that the present Government or any anti-Communist Chinese combination can scarcely be expected to completely eliminate the Communist menace by military or any other means.

"Your report of October 16 states that there are not many Chinese who continue with conviction to support the Generalissimo except his immediate followers and certain ranking military officers, and that the Government, but especially the Generalissimo, is more unpopular than ever and is increasingly denounced. You also say that it is difficult to see at this late date how any efforts on our part, short of armed intervention on a very large scale, can avert further military disaster, with the likelihood that coalition in some form will result.

"In your report of October 22 you say 'our military advisers' feel that the Nationalist military establishment has very likely already suffered too great losses in manpower, matériel and morale to make any such effort successful, that there is just no will to fight left in the Nationalist forces and that you can find no effective way to change the situation. You further state that a moral resurgence of Chinese will to resist Communist aggression is required and that the requisite leadership just is not available.

"The foregoing picture of the China situation and its possible developments is generally borne out by some fifteen other Embassy reports between May and October. This appraisal is also borne out by other information reaching the Department, such as Tientsin's report of October 14.

"Recent Nationalist military reverses support the foregoing picture. Tsingtao's report of October 1 states that the majority of Government troops at Tsinan did not want to fight, while those that did fight found their position made impossible by the disaffected, and that the Government forces at Tsinan had ample ammunition and food, and assurance of further supplies in the event of a protracted siege. Mukden's report of October 19 gives a similar picture of the fall of Chinchow, stating that the early collapse of Chinchow's defenses was caused by the defection of two divisions of the Government's 93rd

Army. The fall of Changchun was similarly aided by the defection of Government units. In each case the fall of the cities was reportedly accompanied by the loss of considerable quantities of military matériel through the defection and surrender of sizable numbers of Government troops.

"Possibly pressing the Generalissimo for removal of incompetents does not appear promising in the light of his recent appointment, as you reported on October 19, of General Tu Li-ming to command in the Northeast in the face of repeated American advice against placing him in a responsible command. The reference to increased JUSMAG [Joint United States Military Advisory Group in China] personnel, functions and authority after prior agreement by the Generalissimo on the acceptance and implementation of JUSMAG advice as the price of stepped-up aid flies in the face of all previous experience of American advisers in China. You will recall the decisions regarding United States military advisers reached in my meeting with Secretary Royall, Undersecretary Draper, General Bradley, General Wedemeyer and others on June 11, when it was agreed that United States military advisers should not be placed with Chinese units in operational areas.

"With reference to shipments of arms and ammunition as quickly as possible, the United States National Military Establishment is making every effort to speed delivery of military matériel being purchased from the $125,000,000 grants. The Department of the Army states informally that the loading of nearly all the ammunition covered by the Chinese request for 37.8 million dollars of arms and ammunition is expected to be completed on the West Coast about mid-November and the shipment should reach China by early December. Every effort is being made to expedite the shipment of other matériel under this program. The National Military Establishment is also endeavoring to arrange shipment of all arms and ammunition which SCAP can advance and delivery of this matériel is expected to be made during November. Authorization for the disbursement of the $103,000,000 requested by the Chinese Government from the $125,000,000 grants has been transmitted by the Department to the Treasury Department and the latter has paid to the Chinese Government, or to the United States Departments of the Army, Navy and Air Force, as directed by the Chinese, $97,000,000 of this total, the balance of $6,000,000 to be paid October 25. You will realize no means exist to extend military aid to China other than United States assistance to the Chinese Government under the $125,000,000 grants.

"In summary, adoption of a course of increased aid would violate all basic considerations underlying American policy toward China, would involve the United States directly in China's civil war, would commit this Government to underwriting the Chinese Government militarily and economically at a cost which it would be impossible to estimate at a time when the United States has heavy commitments throughout the world in connection with foreign aid programs and would not, in the light of appraisals of the situation submitted by the Embassy and consular offices in China over a period of several months, achieve its avowed objectives."

In another inquiry on October 23, the Ambassador suggested a number of possible alternatives and requested instructions:

"(A) Will we continue to recognize and support the Nationalist Government should they be forced to move elsewhere in China because of continuing military reverses?

"(B) Would we advise the retirement of the Generalissimo in favor of Li Tsung-jen or some other national political leader with better prospects of forming a republican non-Communist government and of more effectively prosecuting the war against the Communist rebels?

"(C) Would we approve the retirement of the Generalissimo in favor of some Chinese leader who could bring an end to the civil war on the best possible terms for the Nationalist forces and the non-Communist political parties?

"(D) In the latter course would we recognize and support a coalition government resulting from termination of hostilities and involving cooperation with the Communists for a united China? or,

"(E) Would we give *de facto* recognition to such governments, the while withholding any Eca or other support?

"I appreciate the difficulties which these seemingly hypothetical questions pose for you and your advisers. However in the acute crisis which I foresee for the Generalissimo and his government I feel that I must have the benefit of your most recent thinking on the above specific points or in more general terms if you prefer in order adequately to represent the views of the United States in this critical phase of our relations with China."

To this, the Secretary replied as follows:

"With respect to the hypothetical questions raised by you on October 23, the United States Government cannot place itself in a position of advising the retirement of the Generalissimo or the appointment of any other Chinese as head of the Chinese Government. To offer such advice is to accept responsibility for developments arising from the acceptance thereof and inferentially to commit the United States Government to support the succeeding regime regardless of United States interests. The difficulty of our position in the event the Generalissimo and his Government raise such questions is appreciated but it is not in the national interest to vouchsafe cut and dried answers to these oversimplified questions. . . . What can be said in answer to your questions is that the United States Government will certainly continue to support the National Government as long as it remains an important factor on the Chinese scene. What course we would adopt should it move from Nanking, collapse, disappear or merge in a coalition with the Communists would have to be decided at the time in the light of United States interests and the then existing situation.

"As stated in my instruction of August 13, it is not likely that the situation will make it possible for us at this juncture to formulate any rigid plans for our future policy in China. Developments in China are obviously entering into a period of extreme flux and confusion in which it will be impossible with surety to perceive clearly far in advance the pattern of things to come and in which this Government plainly must preserve maximum freedom of action."

In the development of his thinking on the problem facing the United States, the Ambassador on October 28 observed to the Department that:

"What we really object to in Communism is not its admittedly socialized reforms but its intolerance, its insidious reliance on fifth column and similar secretive methods, its ruthless suppression of all thought or action that does not conform, its denial of individual human rights, its unscrupulous reliance on lying propaganda and any other immoral means to attain its ends, its fanatical dogmatism including its belief in the necessity for violent revolution. All these evils plus the fact that policy is directed from Moscow, apply to Chinese Communism as truly as elsewhere. Our problem is how to retard or expose or neutralize their influence in China.

"Evil in Communism is moral or political rather than military. Predominance of the latter aspect in China is largely a historical accident. Even if we had been able to assist the Chiang Government by military means to clear an area of militant communism—which is all we could have hoped to do at best—we would still have been obliged to assist in educational and other processes by which the non-Communist section would be able to demonstrate superiority of genuine democracy. Otherwise, military gains would have proved self-defeating."

CHINESE REQUESTS FOR FURTHER MILITARY ASSISTANCE

During November, at the Paris session of the General Assembly of the United Nations, Dr. T. F. Tsiang, then head of the Chinese Delegation, approached Secretary of State Marshall on behalf of the Chinese Foreign Minister to inquire regarding the possibility of the appointment of American Army officers to actual command of Chinese Army units under the guise of advisers and the appointment of an officer of high rank to head a special mission. In the reply given to this request attention was called to the inherent difficulties involved in an attempt on the part of a newly appointed foreign official to advise the Chinese Government regarding its courses of action even if such an official were completely conversant with all the numerous difficulties of the situation and the even greater difficulties for a foreign official not familiar with China. Dr. Tsiang also inquired as to the possibility of expediting the deliveries of military matériel, and was assured that all possible was being and would be done. In reply to his inquiry regarding the desirability of an appeal to the United Nations, he was informed that this was a matter for decision by the Chinese themselves.[48]

The Generalissimo then addressed a letter to President Truman,[49] in which he asked for increased aid on the grounds that China was in danger of being lost to the cause of democracy. He said that the most fundamental factor in the general deterioration of the military situation was the nonobservance by the Soviet Union of the Sino-Soviet Treaty of Friendship and Alliance, which, "as Your Excellency will doubtless recall, the Chinese Government signed as a result of well-intentioned advice from the United States." He also asked for a high-ranking military officer as adviser, and a firm statement of American policy in support of the cause for which his Government was fighting.

The reply of the President was delivered on November 13.[50] It stated that all possible was being done to expedite the shipment of supplies and repeated what Secretary Marshall had told Dr. Tsiang regarding an adviser. The President called attention, however, to the fact that Major General Barr, Director of the Joint United States Military Advisory Group in China, was conversant with the current situation and that his advice had always been available to the Generalissimo. The President adverted to his statement of March 11, 1948, which, he said, made the position of the United States abundantly clear. He concluded that it was with the hope of supporting the cause of peace and democracy throughout the world that the United States had extended assistance to the Chinese Government and that the United States Government would continue to exert every effort to expedite the implementation of the program of aid for China.

---

[48] See annex 162 (a) and (b).

[49] See annex 163.

[50] See annex 164.

The estimate of the military situation furnished the Department by the Embassy at Nanking on November 6 made it impossible to expect that the appointment of a high-ranking United States military officer could cause any change in the situation:

"We gathered together senior military personnel JUSMAG and Service Attachés, who, after discussing military situation, were unanimous that short of actual employment of United States troops no amount of military assistance could save the present situation in view of its advanced stage of deterioration. Agreeing that employment of United States troops was impossible, it was the conclusion of the group that there was no military step China or the United States could take in sufficient time to retrieve the military situation."

From then until the end of the year high officials of the Chinese Government approached the Ambassador in varying degrees of pessimism, asking his advice and assistance. To all such approaches he expressed assurances of continuing American sympathy but made it clear that the American Government could not assume responsibility for decisions which properly lay with the Chinese Government.[51]

It was against this background that a new cabinet was formed in December 1948 with Dr. Sun Fo as the new President of the Executive Yuan or Prime Minister.[52]

VIII. CHINESE DEVELOPMENTS IN 1949

PRESIDENT CHIANG'S NEW YEAR'S MESSAGE

At the beginning of the year there were rumors that the Generalissimo would withdraw from the presidency and turn over control to the Vice President, General Li Tsung-jen. Rumors of his withdrawal were strengthened by his New Year's message to the nation [53] in which he indicated that the National Government would be willing to enter into peace negotiations with the Chinese Communists and that, if peace could be secured, he would not be concerned about his own position.

The Ambassador on January 3 commented as follows on this New Year's message:

"My first reaction was favorable. It was dignified and conciliatory. There was less abuse of the Communists than usual. In assuming

---

[51] See annexes 165 (a)–(h).

[52] See annex 166 for a series of chronicle round-up reports written by the Embassy in Nanking during 1948. These informal reports give a summary account of the over-all situation during the year.

[53] See annex 167.

blame for the national distress the Generalissimo was in the best tradition and in indicating his readiness either to continue or retire he was in accord with new democratic concepts.

"But on further thought the fatal flaws reveal themselves. It was too much a literary composition in the grand manner. It has the gracious tone of a powerful ruler dealing with troublesome rebels. In this it ignored unpleasant realities: the virtual collapse of military capacity, the failure of the latest monetary measures, the almost universal desire for peace and the impossibility of it as long as he stays in office.

"The other flaw was more serious. In a sense he has made concessions but in doing so has not gone far enough. His stubborn pride, his anger over the Communist war criminal list which he heads, the influence of . . . irreconcilables led him to retract his forthright decision made earlier in the week to resign and leave the Vice President free to adopt any policy that might seem to him to be for national welfare. Yet the pressure was too strong and his original intention too definite for him to avoid any reference to his own willingness to retire. This will destroy what ever is left of will to fight among his troops. There was at once division of opinion among military officers. The position taken seems to be the result of compromise among the various groups in the Kuomintang. Each of the Generalissimo's five conditions may be taken to represent emphasis of one of these factions. In attempting to reconcile them all he may further intensify internal disagreements. Communist reaction can be easily surmised. Their attitude will doubtless be uncompromising. Flushed with success and with victory in sight they want to complete the task of eradicating once and for all the evil influence of the Kuomintang, precisely as Chen Li-fu and his supporters have consistently argued regarding the Communists. Whether by this the Communists mean only the present leadership and structural organization of the Kuomintang can only be learned from their future behavior. But it will seem that the Kuomintang at any rate must succumb to the dynamic purpose of the Communists and because of its own shortcomings. Once the Communists have eliminated this source of opposition they might propose some inclusive form of coalition and attempt a political settlement with political resistance groups in the outlying provinces.

"In any event a movement was started on New Year's day which would seem to be the beginning of the end of military conflict on a national scale."

PRIME MINISTER SUN FO'S NEW YEAR'S MESSAGE

On New Year's Day also Dr. Sun Fo, the Prime Minister, broadcast a message to the Chinese people repeating the Generalissimo's statement regarding the desire of the Chinese Government for peace. Of some interest was his reference to the period of peace negotiations in 1946:

"You will recall that, shortly after V–J Day, a political consultative conference was called, which was attended by representatives of all political parties and leading independents. The Government decided to call this conference because it was generally realized that the country and the people needed recuperation and peace so that rehabilitation work could be started. After three weeks of concerted efforts, and thanks to the good offices of General George Marshall as President Truman's Special Envoy to China, a program for the settlement of all disputes was worked out.

"Had these measures been carried out at that time, all of us would have seen more prosperity and happiness in our midst. Unfortunately, all the parties concerned could not completely abandon their own selfish ends, and the people in general did not exert sufficient influence in promoting this peace movement."

CHINESE REQUEST FOR FOREIGN MEDIATION

On January 8, 1949, the Chinese Foreign Minister requested the American, British, French and Soviet Governments to act as intermediaries in the initiation of negotiations with the Chinese Communist Party with a view to obtaining a restoration of peace.[54]

On January 12 the United States replied to the Chinese request in the following *aide-mémoire:*

"The United States Government has received and has given careful consideration to the aide-memoire delivered by the Chinese Minister for Foreign Affairs to the United States Ambassador at Nanking on January 8, 1949.

"It is noted in the aide-memoire that the Chinese Government is most anxious that the internal situation in China should not in any way become an impediment to the progress of world peace. It is also noted that the Chinese Government took steps immediately following the Japanese surrender to initiate and carry on peace negotiations with the Chinese Communist Party.

"It will be recalled that these negotiations in September and October 1945 resulted in agreement for the convening of a Political Consultative Conference, to be composed of representatives of all political

---

[54] For text of *aide-mémoire* of Jan. 8, 1949, see annex 168.

parties as well as non-party Chinese leaders, for the purpose of forming a constitutional government in which all Chinese parties and groups would be represented. It will also be recalled that subsequent to these negotiations clashes between the armed forces of the Chinese Government and of the Chinese Communist Party became increasingly widespread. It was at this juncture in December 1945 that the United States Government, motivated by the same anxiety as that expressed in the Chinese Government's aide-memoire under acknowledgment with respect to the danger to world peace from the internal situation in China and desirous of doing everything within its power to assist in bringing peace to China, offered its good offices in the hope that a peaceful settlement of their differences could be achieved by the Chinese themselves along the lines of the agreement reached in September and October. In furtherance of that Chinese agreement and with the consent of the Chinese Government and the Chinese Communist Party, General Marshall shortly after his arrival in China on December 21, exerted his good offices in assisting the Chinese Government and the Chinese Communist Party to reach an agreement for a cessation of hostilities with the hope that discussions by the Chinese of their differences could be conducted in an atmosphere of peace.

"Following the convening of the Political Consultative Conference and its approval of resolutions providing for the settlement of political differences and the establishment of a constitutional government to include all parties and groups in China, General Marshall again exerted his good offices in connection with the agreement reached for the reorganization of all Chinese armed forces and their amalgamation into a national army responsible to a civilian government.

"The negotiations between the Chinese Government and the Chinese Communist Party subsequently broke down and the various agreements were not implemented. The United States Government, therefore, after having made every effort to assist the Chinese in bringing peace to China through implementation of the fundamental political agreements arising out of the Chinese Government's negotiations with the Chinese Communist Party immediately after the Japanese surrender, considered that it had no alternative to withdrawal from its position as an intermediary.

"In the light of the foregoing, it is not believed that any useful purpose would be served by the United States Government's attempting, in accordance with the Chinese Government's suggestion, to act as an intermediary in the present situation."

The Ambassador was instructed that if he were asked any questions he should limit his reply to the confines set by the President's message to Congress of February 18, 1948, and the statement by the Secretary of State to the House Foreign Affairs Committee on February 20.[55] He was also to assure the Foreign Minister of the sympathetic interest and genuine friendship of the American people for the people of China. On the same day, the Chinese Ambassador in Washington called on the Acting Secretary of State to ascertain if, in the event the Chinese request were refused, the United States would consider issuing a statement indicating that the Chinese Government sincerely desired a peaceful settlement. He was informed that such action would be inappropriate. France, Great Britain and the Soviet Union also refused the Chinese request for mediation.

THE RETIREMENT OF THE GENERALISSIMO

By the end of 1948 the Chinese Communist forces were in strength in the Pengpu area north of Nanking and the best of the Nationalist forces had been withdrawn through Nanking south of the Yangtze River. The grave military position of the National Government was reflected in the estimate submitted in December by General Barr, Director of the JUSMAG in China, that only a policy of unlimited United States aid, including the immediate employment of the United States armed forces, which he said he did not recommend, would enable the National Government to maintain a foothold in South China against a determined Chinese Communist advance. By the latter part of January the Chinese Communist forces had moved to the north bank of the Yangtze in the Nanking-Shanghai area and were in position to attempt a crossing of the river.

On January 21 the Generalissimo issued a statement announcing his decision to retire and left Nanking for Fenghua, his birthplace. He declared:

"With the hope that the hostilities may be brought to an end and the people's sufferings relieved, I have decided to retire. As from January 21st, Vice-President Li Tsung-jen will exercise the duties and powers of the President in accordance with Article 49 of the constitution which provides that 'in the event the President is for any reason unable to perform his functions, his duties and powers shall be exercised by the Vice President.'"

The Generalissimo's action was, in effect, recognition of the overwhelming desire of the Chinese people for peace. As he stated: "Since I issued my New Year message urging the restoration of peace, the entire nation with one accord has echoed its unreserved support."

On January 24, 1949, the Chinese Ambassador at Washington offi-

---

[55] See pp. 379–380.

cially notified the Department of State of the Generalissimo's decision
and of the assumption of office by Vice President Li Tsung-jen.

THE POSITION AND POLICIES OF ACTING PRESIDENT LI

On January 23 a representative of the Acting President called on
Ambassador Stuart to request a public statement of support from the
United States. This representative said that General Li had been in
touch with the Soviet Embassy and had worked out a tentative three-
point draft agreement between China and the Soviet Union which the
Soviet Ambassador had taken with him to Moscow a few days earlier.
The three points were: (1) strict Chinese neutrality in any future
international conflict; (2) the elimination of American influence to as
great an extent as possible in China; (3) the establishment of a basis
of real cooperation between China and Russia. General Li had agreed
to these three points in principle and felt that his hand would be
strengthened in negotiating on them if he had a statement of American support. The Department at once replied that it considered it
"incredible that Li Tsung-jen should seek a United States statement
indicating support for the purpose of strengthening his position while
at the same time arranging a tentative agreement with Russia calling
for elimination of American influence from China." The Ambassador
was instructed to make these views known to General Li.

In the meantime, the Acting President had directed General Chang
Chun, General Chang Chih-chung and Mr. Chen Li-fu to seek a direct
approach to the Chinese Communist Party. The Acting President
also summoned an unofficial peace mission to fly to Peiping to arrange
for the subsequent reception of an official peace mission. With his encouragement an unofficial Shanghai peace delegation proceeded to
Peiping to discuss peace arrangements with the Chinese Communists.
The Chinese Communist Party continued to hold to its publicly announced eight-point peace terms as the basis of a settlement:

1. Strict punishment of war criminals.
2. Abolition of the constitution.
3. Abolition of the Kuomintang legal system.
4. Reorganization of Nationalist troops according to democratic
   principles.
5. Confiscation of "bureaucratic" capital.
6. Reformation of the land system.
7. Abolition of "treasonous treaties."
8. Convocation of a Political Consultative Conference with nonparticipation of "reactionary elements," establishment of democratic coalition government, taking over all authority of the
   "Kuomintang reactionary government" and all its strata.

These terms were equivalent to unconditional surrender, but the Government's condition was so serious that it felt compelled to make an effort toward negotiation with a view to obtaining modification.

On February 5, pursuant to a decision of the Executive Yuan, the Chinese Government moved most of its offices to Canton, although the Acting President remained in Nanking and requested the return to that city of the heads of certain ministries. The American Embassy established an office at Canton headed by the Minister-Counselor to maintain contact with those Chinese Government agencies which had moved to that city.

After Acting President Li had assumed office, several high-ranking Chinese Government officials, erstwhile strong supporters of the Generalissimo, approached the Ambassador to ask for assistance in dissuading the Generalissimo from interfering in governmental and military affairs. They considered that the Generalissimo was hampering the Acting President's peace negotiations and various reform measures, as well as the formulation of measures for the defense of the Yangtze River in the event of the breakdown of efforts to reach a peaceful settlement with the Chinese Communists. The Ambassador reported these overtures to the Department with the statement that he was, of course, taking no action with respect to these pleas.

On February 9 the Minister-Counselor at Canton reported as follows:

"Chen Tai-chu has again approached me with respect to encouragement of potential resistance elements when peace talks have failed. He said it would be most helpful if I could meet informally with various groups in Canton who were laboring under the impression that we are disinterested in continued resistance and perfectly prepared to recognize a Communist regime and talk to those groups along the line of my conversations with him. If U. S. Government could not make public statements at this stage, my remarks, which would inevitably reach the press and be attributed to me, would be helpful. I told him I would have to think the matter over.

"If the arguments I used in previous conversation with Chen and as used in my conversation with Chen Li-fu shortly before leaving Nanking and reported to the Department conform with thinking in Washington, such informal meetings as those suggested might prove beneficial to our interests. There are undoubtedly many liberal Chinese who desperately do not want to come under a Communist regime, but who see no alternative unless assistance is to be forthcoming from the U. S. I have insisted that although I could, of course, not commit the Congress, I found it difficult to believe further assistance would be forthcoming until there was some tangible resistance movement giving signs of effectiveness and to which help from the U. S. might bring success. Chen Tai-chu believes the discussions he has suggested might encourage potential resistance elements sufficiently that active measures would be undertaken to find a leader or leaders capable of reviving the will to resistance in free China.

"I should appreciate urgently the Department's instructions."

The Department replied as follows:

"Approach described in your message is similar in nature to other feelers during recent weeks and appear to be part and parcel of political jockeying for advantage by various groups. In the light of General Barr's estimate, with which you are familiar, that in the absence of unlimited U. S. aid, including the immediate use of U. S. armed forces, the Chinese Government cannot maintain a foothold in south China against a determined Communist advance, it seems unrealistic to believe that either a public U. S. Government statement or even statements attributed to you could serve any useful purpose. If resistance to the Communist advance is to be effective, it must obviously be based upon genuine Chinese effort and not upon the issuance of statements from outside China. In any event, you will recall the President's reply to the Generalissimo's message which dealt with this question.

"In view of the continued implementation of the China Aid Act, it is difficult to understand the impression conveyed to you that the U. S. is disinterested in continued resistance and is perfectly prepared to recognize a Communist regime."

As the struggle continued between the Acting President and his followers on the one hand and the Generalissimo and his supporters, together with the Canton faction headed by the Prime Minister, on the other hand, the Ambassador reported on February 20, 1949, as follows:

"The Department may care to take measures publicly or otherwise for refuting the mistaken impressions created by press accounts of forthcoming large scale American military aid. These reports, which were prominently published in vernacular and English language press in China, have the effect of inciting the Generalissimo and his irreconcilables to re-take the leadership now in a renewed resistance movement. He is already being influenced, I hear, by arguments of his indispensability from a small group of die-hard supporters whose motives are not entirely disinterested.

"Meanwhile the Generalissimo is interfering in military affairs, thus hampering rather than helping the Yangtze defense. Li Tsung-jen may eventually be sufficiently thwarted by these factors to feel forced to retire south, prematurely abandoning peace efforts. The only hope for public support for renewed resistance against the Communists lies in convincing the Chinese people that the Chinese Communist Party does not desire peace on any tolerable basis. Li is presently endeavoring to put this to thoroughgoing test. The U. S. can, I feel, help most at this stage by avoidance of public debate and objective appraisal of the coming developments. The tone of the Secretary's recent statements on China have been very useful in this regard."

The Department took no action on the Ambassador's suggestion that a statement be issued.

The Ambassador's report of February 23 served to high-light the difficulties with which the Acting President was confronted:

"In the struggle for power between Li Tsung-jen and the 'Canton' faction headed by Sun Fo, Li is in a fundamentally weak position because he does not control the larger portion of the Army, lacks financial resources and does not command the allegiance of that considerable portion of the Kuomintang bureaucracy controlled by the Generalissimo and the CC politicians. This fundamental weakness has been frankly acknowledged, and probably somewhat exaggerated, by Pai's Headquarters to the American Consulate General at Hankow appealing for U. S. aid.

"However, he has made some preparations recently in mobilizing popular support for his peace program. The most important single evidence of this is the decision of the Legislative Yuan to meet in Nanking rather than in Canton. This is, of course, in direct defiance of the Premier's publicly expressed wishes. At the Yuan Session, Sun Fo is certain to be violently denounced, both for his sponsorship of the Government move south and for speculations he is alleged to have committed. A significant indication of the feeling of many legislators was the press report that the legislators resident at Shanghai had passed a resolution accusing Sun Fo of 'deserting' the Acting President and calling for the return of the Executive Yuan to Nanking.

"Further tangible demonstrations that Li is making progress are the meeting of the Control Yuan here and their resolution to support him, the announcement that the Executive Yuan joint office will soon open at Nanking, and the arrival of the Ho Ying-chin in the capital. Li also has the backing of important newspapers in Shanghai and Nanking, which praise his twin program of peace and reform while condemning the Kuomintang for ineptitude and corruption and censuring the Sun Fo cabinet for 'running away'. Insofar as can be determined, support for Li is growing among banking and business circles in Shanghai and Nanking and among that large but inarticulate section of the population who disregard the larger issues and are principally interested in keeping the destruction of war from their homes.

"Li's present position is similar in some ways to that he occupied while campaigning for Vice-President. At that time he became the symbol of revolt against arbitrary dictation by the Generalissimo and the party and succeeded in uniting behind him all the dissident (and often mutually incompatible) factions for the purpose of his election. He has again become a symbol, this time a symbol of the yearning for peace that pervades this war-weary country. So long as his peace efforts make perceptible progress, or even succeed in delaying (or seeming to delay) the Communist assault on the Yangtze, he should be able to maintain and utilize for his support this mobilized public opinion.

"Li is aware of the basic weakness of his position, but is astutely capitalizing on the support of those who see him as the chief hope for peace, in order either to heal the breach between himself and the Canton group, or at least win over to his side as many as possible of the powerful leaders in the Kuomintang. He is also endeavoring to bolster his position in concrete ways by making overtures for U. S. aid and planning economic and political reform. The extent to which he succeeds in these efforts will determine his strength either as negotiator with the Communists or subsequently as the leader of resistance should the Communists renew the attack."

On February 21 the Ambassador reported that the Acting President had expressed to him a desire to have an American adviser for the Ministry of Finance and also an American expert on public administration to help reduce and reorganize the whole structure of the Government. In view of the state of disorganization of the Chinese Government and the lack of unity between the rival groups, the Department of State instructed the Ambassador to inform the Acting President that the appropriate channel for the employment of American advisers would be through the Chinese Embassy at Washington, particularly since the presence in the United States of Pei Tsu-yi, formerly Governor of the Central Bank, as Chief of the Chinese Technical Mission, would offer the Embassy an excellent opportunity to locate personnel with the necessary qualifications and experience. The Ambassador was also instructed to state that the Department would be pleased to afford appropriate assistance and facilities as requested by the Chinese authorities.

On February 28 Acting President Li Tsung-jen forwarded the following message to President Truman:

"Since assuming office as Acting President, I have had in mind a message to you expressing the hope that the historic friendship between our two countries may be maintained, and assuring you of my appreciation for all that has been done for China under your administration."

The President replied as follows:

"I wish to express my sincere appreciation of your kind message of February 28 and to assure you of my very real desire to see a continuation of the traditional and close ties of friendship which have existed between the peoples and Governments of our two countries."

The unofficial Shanghai peace delegation returned from Peiping and issued a statement sufficiently optimistic to give encouragement to the peace-hungry public and to strengthen the hands of those advocating an all-out effort to obtain peace. The Acting President succeeded in having the Legislative Yuan hold its session in Nanking at the end of February and, following his trip to Canton, the Prime Minister and the Vice President of the Executive Yuan, who was also the Foreign Minister, returned to Nanking. All this signified a temporary political victory for the Acting President and a concerted effort to present a united front on the part of the Government to the nation and the Chinese Communists. On March 3 it was announced that the National Government had named a ten-man peace preparation committee headed by Dr. Sun Fo.

On March 6 the Ambassador reported a conversation with the Chinese Foreign Minister as follows:

"He said that Lapham [55a] had not been responsive to the Chinese request for a silver loan. I pointed out that ECA had no authority in such matters and added that it was improbable that the Congress would feel itself in a position to make a loan to China in the light of current circumstances.

"Wu T'ieh-chen then asked what were our anxieties re China and the Chinese Government. I replied that these were two: (1) disunity within the Government and (2) the lack of public support for the Government. In response to his question if I referred to differences between Nanking and the Canton group, I replied that this interpretation was inevitable but that there was also considerable confusion with respect to relations between the retired President and the Acting President, that the American public did not understand what the actual relationship between these two was. After exhausting the usual 'official' explanations, the Foreign Minister frankly admitted that it is difficult for a man who had held power so long suddenly

---

[55a] Roger Lapham, Chief of the ECA China Mission.

to become inactive. He continued that there had been some very serious discussions recently and that the Government leaders were determined to start a new system centering authority in the Cabinet which would from now on be responsible with the President being relegated to his 'constitutional' status. The Generalissimo would thus become an 'elder statesman' consulted on occasion but restrained from giving orders. To make the move less pointed it is proposed that several other of the older Kuomintang leaders would be similarly treated. I expressed hope that there would be some success in putting these measures into effect."

The second week in March was marked by a cabinet crisis which resulted in the resignation of Dr. Sun Fo as Prime Minister. The Legislative Yuan's resolution calling for meetings of the Cabinet at Nanking during the period of peace efforts reduced Canton, although it was still nominally the seat of the National Government, to a position of only administrative importance on the national scene. These developments strengthened the political position of the Acting President and his efforts to unify the Government forces around himself. But the power of the Generalissimo continued to be felt as was indicated by the Acting President's sending of an emissary to Fenghua to see the Generalissimo, by the failure of certain Kuomintang leaders to accept the Acting President's invitation to come to Nanking and by the arrest, under orders from one of the Generalissimo's loyal military commanders, of a Chinese newspaper editor at Nanking for publication of an editorial criticizing the Generalissimo's interference in governmental affairs.

IX. RENEWED CONSIDERATION OF ADDITIONAL AMERICAN AID

RECOMMENDATION FROM TIENTSIN

On March 12, 1949, the Consul General at Tientsin forwarded to the Department the text of a memorandum from the American Chamber of Commerce at that city strongly opposing further aid to the Chinese Government. On March 15 the Consul General commented as follows on this memorandum:

"Americans in Tientsin who had the unhappy experience two months ago of witnessing the capture of Tientsin by Communist armies equipped almost entirely with American arms and other military equipment handed over practically without fighting by Nationalist armies in Manchuria, have expressed astonishment at radio reports from the U. S. during the last two or three days to the effect that a bill may be presented to the Congress to extend further military and economic aid to the Nationalist Government in the sum of a billion and a half dollars.

"Americans in Tientsin feel the only result of further U. S. aid to a Government which has proved so ineffective that most of our previous aid has passed to the Communists will be to further strengthen the Communists. They feel that the apparent retirement of the Generalissimo has had little effect on the character of the Nationalist Government, particularly in view of the reported selection as new Premier of General Ho Ying-chin, considered the archetype of the Chinese who have brought the National Government to its present sorry state. They feel that our global policy of opposition to Communism should not oblige us to support a hopelessly inefficient and corrupt government which has lost the support of its people. They believe that at this juncture it would be useless to extend further aid to a government which is so far gone. They feel that the present situation must be solved by the Chinese and that for the time being we should adopt a hands-off policy."

COMMENTS BY THE EMBASSY OFFICE AT CANTON

The Embassy Office at Canton on March 22 commented as follows on the question of further aid to China which was then being considered by the Department of State.

"As I analyze the situation at the moment, we may expect the Communists to continue the deployment of troops on the north bank of the Yangtze and when they are ready to attempt the crossing we may anticipate an announcement of their willingness to negotiate peace on the terms they will stipulate and which may be expected to be a reiteration of Mao Tse-tung's eight points. Their announced willingness to negotiate will likely be in the form of an ultimatum threatening to cross the Yangtze if the terms are not accepted within the time limit. It is unlikely that the terms will be acceptable to the Kuomintang leaders although they will appear reasonable to the war-weary Chinese masses.

"Even though rumors of Communist morale difficulties may have foundation, it may be anticipated that the Communist troops will fight. On the contrary, however, there appears little likelihood that the Nationalist troops can be reinspired with the will to resist. Chang Chun may, as he claims, be able to rally forces in the southwest to defend themselves, but it will unlikely be defense of a character long to delay the Communists, once they have determined on an advance. There is even some thought that with the breakdown of peace negotiations, the process of regional fragmentation will be accelerated, with each area seeking to fend for itself, thus making more easy the Communist task.   The dissident Kwangtung Legislative Yuan members remaining at Canton demanding defense of the constitution' are an indication of this trend.

"As I see it, when the Communists have deployed their troops and issued their ultimatum and had it rejected, they may be expected to cross the Yangtze, meeting little resistance and occupying urban centers of the Yangtze Valley.   They will then have the capability of continuing their advance in the southwest or the south, overcoming without too much difficulty any regional resistance they may encounter. Whether they will proceed to the task immediately or delay for months or years rests solely for their determination.

"In a previous telegram I suggested the possibility that Li Tsungjen might supply effective leadership.   I am now less inclined to that view.   He has increased tremendously in stature; has greatly increased his following, yet the centripetal forces in free China remain too strong for him to overcome.   The deep-seated Chinese characteristic of family solidarity is too strong and we are witnessing a frantic search by each individual to save himself and his family first, then maybe his province, with little if any thought to the principles involved, or the nation.   Also, if, as alleged, the cruiser *Chungking* has been put out of action by the Chinese Air Force, we may still see the Generalissimo re-emerge in his Foochow-Amoy-Taiwan triangle.

"I have been chided of late by many Chinese officials, from the Vice Premier and the Foreign Minister down, for what they term our 'wait and see' policy in respect to China. . . . I have put forward the arguments outlined in the Department's letter to Senator Connally [56] and have stressed the need for the Chinese to demonstrate the possibility of effective resistance to Communist expansion before expecting the U. S. to make further investments in National China.   In each case I have been given the impression of utter inability of China to cope unaided with the situation.   In other words, the sole means of turning the tide in China would, as the Department suggests, require the use of 'large U. S. forces in actual combat, contrary to our traditional policy and our national interests'."

DIFFICULTIES CONFRONTING ACTING PRESIDENT LI

Following the resignation of Dr. Sun Fo, General Ho Ying-chin was named Prime Minister, or President of the Executive Yuan. This appointment gave the Acting President a Prime Minister of his own choosing and served to strengthen Government unity.   A new

[56] For text of letter from Secretary Acheson to Senator Tom Connally on March 15, see annex 186.

Cabinet was quickly formed and steps were taken to appoint National Government peace delegates and to propose the early opening of peace discussions with the Chinese Communists.

The increasingly serious position of the Chinese Government was reflected in military developments which included the fall of Tientsin on January 15, the final occupation of Peiping on February 3, and the subsequent National Government reverses in the Hsuchow area, thus placing the Chinese Communists forces on the north bank of the Yangtze where they represented a direct threat to Nanking and Shanghai.   On March 24 the Acting President presented a draft peace formula and the names of the Government's official peace delegates to the Executive Yuan for approval.   On March 26 the Chinese Communist Party announced the names of its delegates for the peace negotiations, and Peiping was named as the locale of the negotiations.   The National Government peace delegates arrived at Peiping on April 2, and after some informal discussion were presented by the Chinese Communist Party with an ultimatum setting a deadline of April 12 for the acceptance of the Chinese Communist conditions and stating that whether in war or in peace the Communist forces would cross the Yangtze River.   This ultimatum was subsequently withdrawn as an exchange of messages occurred between the Acting President and Mao Tse-tung.

On April 6 the Ambassador reported as follows:

"I referred to the analogous problem of munitions from the U. S. with reference to a Chinese Government request for a grant of United States silver. The Acting President and the Premier had suggested that ships bringing the last consignments be diverted to Hong Kong or Canton for the equipment of Pai Chung-hsi and Chang Fa-kuei. I pointed out that there were technical difficulties in such procedures, and that in any event it seemed unnecessary, since there were ample stores of munitions in warehouses at Keelung. The problem in both cases was, of course, that the Generalissimo controlled the greater share of the national treasury reportedly stored in Taiwan and that through his appointed Governor of Taiwan he also controlled the warehouses full of munitions there. I added that from the record of the past three years, there was slight hope of effective resistance to the Communists under this leadership. I continued that if the Acting President and the Premier had responsibilities for government, they should also have the authority to utilize all the available government resources. I was aware of the difficulties and the embarrassment for them and of the danger to the peace negotiations by forcing the issue with the Generalissimo now. Nonetheless, this was a problem that sooner or later would have to be faced. It was, I added, a Chinese problem which they should not look to us to solve for them. The emissary understood that my remarks were only for the ears of the President and the Premier and I believe he also understood their import." [55b]

The following report from the Consul General at Shanghai, on April 4, serves to point up some of the difficulties confronting the Acting President:

"Despite the steady increase of Li's prestige and popularity, his actual power should not be overestimated. There is little indication that he has been able to infuse any new fighting spirit into the Nationalist armies, or indeed that he has been able to introduce any substantial reforms which might eventually lead to that result. In the military field his principal contribution has probably been to decrease the anxiety of the Communist rank and file to fight and thereby relatively to increase the strength of the Nationalists. However, until we have positive indications whether or not there is any real fight left in the Nationalists, it cannot be said that any great improvement in the military position has taken place.

"A second weakness which Li has had to face is his limited power to enforce his orders and to hold in check centrifugal forces among Nationalist leaders. The Generalissimo, though outwardly cooperating, is maintaining in effect independent political and military authority. The Kuomintang leaders in Canton are playing their own game, as are other provincial leaders. Though Li has accomplished miracles in asserting his authority in ever widening sectors, he still does not have unified authority over Nationalist China. It is important both to appreciate this and to realize how far he has come since he was given his present responsibility with practically none of the Nationalist assets—political, military and economic—to carry them out."

On April 15, the Ambassador reported as follows:

"The Acting President has sent another appeal to me for assistance. He asked if it would not be possible for the U.S. Government to make some kind of statement deterring the Communists from crossing the Yangtze. What he has in mind apparently is a statement by the President or the Secretary to the effect that a Communist crossing of the Yangtze would be considered a threat to the security of the U. S. and that should such a military operation be undertaken the U. S. would have to give consideration to the appropriate measures to be taken. A statement in a press conference in reply to a pertinent question might prove the most suitable method or some interested

---

[55b] With reference to a Chinese request for silver aid see chapter VIII which contains a more complete account of United States economic and financial aid during this period.

Senator such as Connally might give his views on the implications of the Communists coming south of the river.

"I have every sympathy with the Acting President in his efforts to contain the Communists north of the Yangtze. His appeal is further evidence of the desperate position of the Nationalist Government vis-a-vis the Communists and of the small confidence he places in the peace negotiations at Peiping. Any statement of sympathy from the U. S. at this time would encourage him enormously. I am not, however, able to support Li's request unless the U.S. Government is prepared to back up such a statement by some kind of effective assistance. Since the Acting President's request requires a reply, I would be grateful for the Department's instructions."

X. THE WITHDRAWAL OF THE GOVERNMENT FROM NANKING

THE COMMUNIST DEMANDS OF APRIL 15, 1949

On April 15 the National Government at Nanking was informed of the Chinese Communist Party's terms, according to which the Government would be given until April 20 to accept or reject the draft agreement presented by the Chinese Communists. The Ambassador was informed by Chinese Government officials that the draft had been prepared by the Chinese Communist Party and had been given to the Nationalist peace delegation at Peiping in the early stages of the negotiations. After days of discussions the Nationalist delegates succeeded in achieving slight drafting changes but nothing of substance and they emphasized to the Government at Nanking that this draft, which was based in general upon the Chinese Communists' eight-point proposals originally made public in January, and was tantamount to unconditional surrender, would have to be accepted without change. The Communist Party indicated that if its terms were not accepted at the time of the expiration of the deadline, it would break off negotiations. The Acting President explained the foregoing circumstances to the Ambassador and some of his foreign colleagues on April 17. On the following day the Ambassador reported as follows:

"General Pai Chung-hsi called on me this morning to report that the Acting President, in view of the latest Communist demands, will propose to the Generalissimo that, peace being impossible, he should either resume full responsibilities of the presidency or leave China, turning over all authority and national resources to Li Tsung-jen. By such steps the Acting President will seek to force the Generalissimo to end by a clear-cut decision the present state of confusion which the latter, himself, has created."

On April 20 the Ambassador further reported as follows:

"The Minister of Education called with an additional message from the Finance Minister who is thoroughly discouraged over the chaotic financial conditions in Nationalist territory and trying to resign. Han Li-wu did not renew Liu's request for immediate financial assistance but did ask what the U. S. attitude would be should the Nationalist forces put up a spirited defense of the Yangtze, prevent the Communists from crossing, and thereby recapture popular support generally for continued resistance to the Communists southward advance. He asked if under these circumstances there would be a possibility of American financial assistance to stabilize the local currency, or a substantial silver loan for payment of the troops defending Nationalist territory. I replied along the lines previously reported, pointing out that a considerable treasure of gold, silver and foreign currency did exist and that it was an internal Chinese problem for the present Government to obtain control of all of it."

THE CROSSING OF THE YANGTZE

Prior to the expiration of the deadline of April 20, the National Government requested an extension of time to April 25 to enable it to consider the Chinese Communist Party's draft peace agreement and on April 20 sent a message to the Chinese Communists rejecting the draft peace agreement but requesting a cease-fire order so that further negotiations might be held. In the meantime the Chinese Communists informed the Nationalist peace delegates at Peiping that if the Government's reply to their proposal were negative, or if no reply were received by April 20, the Communists would consider the negotiations ended and would begin the crossing of the Yangtze. At midnight, on April 20, the Chinese Communist forces crossed the Yangtze River at several strategic points, a crossing which was described by the Embassy at Nanking, on April 23, in the following terms:

"The ridiculously easy Communist crossing of the Yangtze was made possible by defections at key points, disagreements in the High Command, and the failure of the Air Force to give effective support."

While these events were occurring, the Minister-Counselor at Canton reported as follows, on April 21:

"Chen Li-fu says that the decision last night at Canton of the Central Executive Committee and that of the Government at Nanking to reject the Communist terms were both unanimous. He is sanguine that the bickering between the various elements of the Kuomintang has terminated and that the Party will rally as a unit for renewed resistance. He envisages the complete removal of the Government to Canton, leaving the Commander-in-Chief of the Armed Forces with Headquarters at Nanking. He is confident that the Air Force and the Navy will cooperate with the Ground Forces and that the Yangtze crossing on any important scale can be delayed for months, if not prevented. So far as he is aware, the Generalissimo continues his willingness to send complete support to Li Tsung-jen with no present intention of resuming authority himself.

"With the closing of the ranks of the Kuomintang, Chen is sanguine of effective resistance to the Communist advance, yet desperately wants assurances of further U. S. aid. After reviewing the unhappy results of our past efforts to help China, and our failure largely because China refused to help itself, I cautioned him not to count upon further U.S. aid unless and until the Government had first demonstrated its ability with a broadened basis to rally support in territory it still controls for further and effective resistance on a scale giving promise of the ability eventually to retake the offensive. I mentioned our axiom 'God helps him who helps himself', of which there is a Chinese equivalent, and said that the American people could not be expected to invest any more money in the Kuomintang regime until it gave promise of offering an effective alternative to Communism. Chen tried unsuccessfully to pin me down as to what would be considered effective resistance. Obviously, his back was to the wall and he, like others in his position, is determined upon desperate measures to avoid the almost inevitable Communist domination of all China. Now that those who thought peace possible have been disillusioned, he is sanguine that the Kuomintang, with united ranks, will be able to rally sufficient support to prolong the struggle until the U.S. can be persuaded once again to intervene. Should that time come, he hopes that we will lay our cards frankly on the table and demand a definite *quid pro quo* for anything we give. That is the only way, he said, we could assure the accomplishment of the ends we desire."

On April 21 the Department sent the following message to the Ambassador at Nanking in reply to his report of April 15 conveying an appeal from the Acting President for a statement by the United States Government to deter the Chinese Communists from crossing the Yangtze River:

"The Acting President's request appears to be overlapped by the meeting between him and you and your foreign colleagues on April 17, and to be overtaken by events . . .

"As you are aware, the only Congressional authority presently existing for aiding the Chinese Government is the legislation extending the availability of the residual China Aid Act funds. The Department's views on this subject were set forth in the Secretary of State's letter to Senator Connally, of March 15, re the McCarran proposal. For your information, the text of the letter to Senator Connally was not released by the Department which wished to avoid possible adverse effect on the Chinese Government and Li's position in the negotiations with the Communists."

On April 23 the Acting President, the Prime Minister and the remaining officials of the Ministry of National Defense left Nanking for Shanghai, en route to Canton. The Chinese Communist forces were by this time across the Yangtze River in strength and Nationalist Armies deployed for the defense of the river had been ordered to withdraw to the south. Chinese Communist forces occupied Nanking on April 24 and were in a position to move toward Shanghai. In succession, the Communist forces occupied Hankow on May 16–17, Shanghai on May 25, and Tsingtao on June 2.

The general effect of these developments on the National Government's position was described by the Embassy in a report of May 1:

"Despite the desperate plight of the Government and agreement among all leaders of the necessity of continuing resistance to the Communists, the basic conflict of authority between Li and the Generalissimo has not been resolved. The Generalissimo came out with a public statement expressing confidence in final victory, though the war may continue for three years, and pledging support to Li. However, there is no indication he really intends to relinquish power and Li and Pai are increasingly bitter. This struggle probably will continue to hamstring Government resistance."

XI. FORMOSA

The case of Formosa is a pertinent one in the record of American efforts to encourage reform within the Chinese Government. By the terms of the Cairo Declaration of December 1, 1943, the United States and China declared their intention that Formosa should be restored to China. In September 1945 the administration of the island was taken over from the Japanese by Chinese forces assisted by small

American teams pursuant to the Japanese Instrument of Surrender and General Order No. 1 issued by the Japanese Government at the direction of the Supreme Commander for the Allied Powers, dated September 2, 1945.

China found Formosa in favorable circumstances since Japan had made constructive use of the great natural resources of the island and the living standards of the population were higher than anywhere on the Chinese mainland. It possessed a good industrial complex and was more than self-sufficient in foodstuffs. The native population for 50 years had been under the rule of a foreign invader and therefore welcomed the Chinese forces as liberators. During the Japanese occupation the principal hope of the people had been reunion with the mainland. Instead of utilizing this highly favorable situation to its own advantage the National Government appointed to the governorship General Chen Yi, a long-time associate of the Generalissimo, who some years before had given up the governorship of Fukien under curious circumstances. The new Governor arrived with an imposing retinue who proceeded with great efficiency to exploit Formosa. In addition the local population was ruthlessly excluded from any important role in public life and was made to feel that it was again under the rule of a conqueror.

The economic deterioration of the island and the administration of the mainland officials became so bad that on February 28, 1947, popular resentment erupted into a major rebellion. In the ensuing days the Government put down the revolt in a series of military actions which cost thousands of lives. Order was restored but the hatred of the mainland Chinese was increased.

After the rebellion the American Ambassador in Nanking attempted to persuade the Generalissimo that National Government tactics in the long run could never succeed and that the Government by its policy was destroying a source of wealth it desperately needed at that time. The Generalissimo, who professed to be unaware of conditions as they were reported to him by the Ambassador, and who relied on the findings of a Chinese investigating mission whose findings were in large part published and exonerated Chen Yi, was led to request that a memorandum be prepared for him setting forth in detail conditions as American officials saw them. This was done.[57]

The facts set forth were such that General Chen Yi had finally to be relieved of his post as Governor, and in May 1947 a civilian, Wei Taoming, former Ambassador to the United States, was named as his successor. During the ensuing year and a half, Governor Wei made an

---

[57] For text of memorandum to the Generalissimo, see annex 169.

honest and earnest effort to remedy the situation. The military was kept out of sight, some Formosans were taken into the Government, encouragement was given to the local economy and the Governor himself attempted to isolate the island from the inflationary and destructive forces on the mainland, though many of the key officials were not responsive to his authority. Although it cannot be said that economic conditions improved, it can be said that the situation did not become measurably worse.

During his Mission to China, General Wedemeyer on August 17, 1947, reported to the Secretary of State as follows:

"Our experience in Formosa is most enlightening. The administration of the former Governor Chen Yi has alienated the people from the Central Government. Many were forced to feel that conditions under autocratic rule were preferable. The Central Government lost a fine opportunity to indicate to the Chinese people and to the world at large its capability to provide honest and efficient administration. They cannot attribute their failure to the activities of the Communists or of dissident elements. The people anticipated sincerely and enthusiastically deliverance from the Japanese yoke. However, Chen Yi and his henchmen ruthlessly, corruptly and avariciously imposed their regime upon a happy and amenable population. The Army conducted themselves as conquerors. Secret police operated freely to intimidate and to facilitate exploitation by Central Government officials. . . .

"The island is extremely productive in coal, rice, sugar, cement, fruits and tea. Both hydro and thermal power are abundant. The Japanese had efficiently electrified even remote areas and also established excellent railroad lines and highways. Eighty percent of the people can read and write, the exact antithesis of conditions prevailing in the mainland of China. There were indications that Formosans would be receptive toward United States guardianship and United Nations trusteeship. They fear that the Central Government contemplates bleeding their island to support the tottering and corrupt Nanking machine and I think their fears well founded."

In January 1949, as the Communists were preparing to cross the Yangtze, Governor Wei was summarily removed and replaced by General Chen Cheng, who proceeded to restore military rule. In recent months the population of Formosa has been increased by an estimated 400,000 civilians and over 300,000 military refugees from the mainland. With them they brought the mainland inflation and increased the population to a point which the island may not be able to support. In March 1949 American officials who had surveyed the economic deterioration reported that "mounting economic dislocation will intensify economic friction leading to increased political tension unless remedial action is taken."

In summary, the views of American officials have been that the island is badly and inefficiently run at a time when the best possible efforts are needed unless developments on the mainland are simply to be transferred to Formosa.

CHAPTER VII

The Military Picture, 1945–1949

Although military aspects of the civil strife in China have been mentioned throughout the preceding five chapters, it will be convenient to summarize here the military picture since 1945 as background for a description of the military assistance of all types rendered by the United States to the Chinese Government since V–J Day. This assistance has included the supply of arms and other matériel, credits for military purchases, transportation of Chinese troops and military advice, but it has scrupulously excluded the use of American personnel in combat operations between the Nationalist Government forces and the Communists or their presence in combat areas.

I. MILITARY OPERATIONS

OPERATIONS IN 1945

With the formal surrender of the Japanese in September 1945, the Chinese Nationalists and the Chinese Communists began a contest for the control of Japanese-held areas of China. Forces of the National Government which had borne the brunt of Japanese thrusts were concentrated in Central and South China in those areas to which the Japanese advance had penetrated. The Communists, on the other hand, organized as guerrilla units, were widely dispersed throughout Central, North and coastal China, operating in the countryside through which ran the Japanese lines of communication. In the race for the control of those areas which the Japanese had occupied the Communists thus held a certain geographic advantage. The Government at that time, however, possessed an estimated five to one superiority in combat troops and in rifles, a practical monopoly of heavy equipment and transport, and an unopposed air arm.

In order to assist the Government in reoccupying Japanese-held areas and opening lines of communication, the United States immediately after V–J Day transported three Nationalist armies by air to key sectors of East and North China, including Shanghai, Nanking and Peiping, and likewise during the ensuing months provided water

311

transport for an additional large number of troops until, according to Department of the Army figures, between 400,000 and 500,000 Chinese soldiers had been moved to new positions. The plans for these operations and the planes and vessels to carry out the moves were provided through Headquarters, United States Forces China Theater. In order to assist the Government further in maintaining control of certain key areas of North China and in repatriating the Japanese, and at the request of the National Government, over 50,000 United States Marines were landed in North China and occupied Peiping, Tientsin, and the coal mines to the north, together with the essential railroads in the area. With such American assistance, forces of the Generalissimo, who had been designated by SCAP as the sole agent to receive the surrender of Japanese forces in China proper, were able to effect the surrender of the great majority of the 1,200,000 Japanese troops stationed there, together with their equipment and stocks of military matériel.[1]

Prior to V–J Day the American Government had embarked on programs to equip an air force commensurate with the Chinese Government's needs and a 39-division army. Following V–J Day, transfers were continued to provide for an 8⅓ group air force, and under an authorization to assist in equipping reoccupation forces, transfers of military matériel for ground troops were continued until, by the end of December 1945, according to Department of the Army records, sufficient equipment had been transferred to complete by tonnage the requirements of the 39-division program. Other lend-lease transfers included quantities of vehicles and quartermaster items which were of major significance in giving the Nationalist armies mobility and in equipping them for operations in North China and Manchuria.

The Communists for their part, despite the attempts of the National Government to enforce the order that all Japanese in China should surrender only to the Generalissimo, were able to force the surrender of numbers of Japanese in Central and North China. However, their greatest assistance was to come later from Manchuria, which the Russians had occupied and where, while engaged in the stripping of Manchurian industries, they were effecting the surrender of the Japanese. Upon the withdrawal of the Russian forces from that area in 1946, the arriving Government forces, hitherto prevented from occupying Manchuria, found themselves facing Chinese Communist forces already organized in the area and equipped with former Japanese weapons.

---

[1] This was in accordance with General Order No. 1 issued by General MacArthur, Supreme Commander for the Allied Powers (SCAP).

As a result of military operations in the closing months of 1945 the Government was able to clear the Lunghai Railway (Lienyunkang and Paochi) and most of China south of it. To the north the Government held Peiping, Tientsin and the line of communications to the Manchurian border, Taiyuan, Tatung, and the western portion of the Pingsui Railway (Peiping and Paotow). It had not, however, gained control of any of the major north-south railway lines, a serious handicap since forces in North China depended for their logistical support on bases in Central China.

The Government was faced with the alternatives of postponing the attempt to reoccupy Manchuria or of overextending its military forces in attempting to reoccupy it. This was in no case an easy decision to make. United States military advisers pointed out the dangers of occupying Manchuria in view of the logistical difficulty of supporting operations there while attempting to pacify China proper. The Chinese Government in deciding to put its best armies and main effort into reoccupying Manchuria at the end of a 1,000-mile-long supply line committed itself to a scale of operations it could not support, and opened the way to the eventual piecemeal destruction by the Communists of its widely scattered military units.

OPERATIONS IN 1946

During the period of General Marshall's mission in China, the Government considerably improved its military holdings. Government armies in mid-1946 comprised approximately 3,000,000 men, opposed by something over 1,000,000 Communists of whom an estimated 400,000 were not regular troops. In the first part of that year the Nationalists succeeded in clearing important lines of communication including the Lunghai in Central China, parts of the Pinghan (Peiping and Hankow) and connecting north-south communications, and railway lines into Manchuria as far as Changchun. The Communists, routed at Ssupinghchieh in Manchuria, saved their forces from annihilation only by a rapid retreat across the Sungari River. The Communists for their part during the first half of 1946 extended their holdings west into Kansu and Ninghsia, and somewhat increased their control of areas in Shansi and along the Ping-sui Railway. In general, however, major areas of combat were limited to Manchuria where, as previously indicated, Communist gains were made as a result of the withdrawal of the Russians from Manchuria, handled in such a way as to facilitate Communist acquisition of this territory and the Japanese equipment therein. During the latter part of 1946 the Nationalists made impressive gains, clearing most of Shensi, Kansu, north Shansi, south Chahar, part of northern

Hopeh and Jehol and nearly all of Kiangsu. The Government seized Kalgan, Tatung, Chengte, and gained control of the Ping-sui Railroad.

In Shantung the Nationalists achieved a major advance, clearing much of the Tsin-pu Railway (Tientsin and Pukow). Communist gains during this period were limited to minor advances into Honan and Hupeh, and infiltration around Government positions in Manchuria. By the close of 1946 the superiority of the Government's forces was in most areas as yet unchallenged.

The gains of the Government from V–J Day to the end of 1946 appeared impressive when viewed solely from the standpoint of areas occupied and lines of communication cleared. The Government desire to occupy Manchuria with its concentration of heavy industries is understandable. It was essential, however, for it to control the lines of communication to and in the areas it was clearing, for unlike the Communists operating as guerrillas and living off the country, Government forces were supplied from bases in Central China. In occupying Manchuria and in garrisoning such extensive lines of communication and the major cities along them, the Government overextended itself both militarily and politically, with neither the troops to garrison such holdings nor the personnel to administer them. The occupation of these areas without the ability to draw support from their resources meant a loss rather than a gain. In this sense the Nationalists found themselves in a position not dissimilar from that of the Japanese during their war with China, when, though holding the lines of communication, they found themselves unable to bring the conflict to a successful conclusion. The Communists, on the other hand, making no effort to hold specific positions, retreated before Government forces and succeeded in keeping their own units intact and mobile for eventual concentration and use at points of their own choosing against Government units tied to the defense of fixed positions.

Department of the Army figures indicate that at the end of 1946 the Government had 2,600,000 men under arms. Communist strength at this time was over 1,100,000 men, the acquisition of Japanese stocks in Manchuria having made possible the development of more effective forces. The Government still, however, enjoyed a marked superiority in rifles variously estimated at from three or four to one. That the Government, possessing this superiority in men and equipment, should so soon be forced on the defensive was less attributable to the admitted skill of the Communists in planning their campaigns to conform to their resources than to the military ineptness of the Government in initially overestimating its capabilities, and subsequently refusing to adjust to the realities of the situation.

OPERATIONS IN 1947

In 1947 the strategic initiative passed from the Government to the Communists and the latter carried the conflict from Manchuria and North China into areas which had supposedly been cleared by the Government. Activity which marked the turning point in the strife included the mounting by the Communists of a series of minor offensives in Manchuria and the successful blunting of a major Government drive into Shantung. The first Communist offensive in Manchuria was mounted early in 1947 and lasted for only a few weeks, but it and three successive drives wore down the Government units defending key positions. The fifth Communist offensive mounted in May covered most of Manchuria, netting the Communists over 20,000 captured rifles in its opening operations, lowering Government troop morale in proportion to the increase in Communist morale, and leaving the Government units in Kirin, Changchun, and Ssupingchieh surrounded. The reasons for the Communist victories must be sought in an appraisal of National failings rather than in positive Communist accomplishments. Observers in the summer of 1947 noted that the Communists had met no Nationalist resistance, with the result that the Communists completely possessed the initiative. Several factors contributed to the lack of any will to resist on the part of Government troops. American military and diplomatic observers in China reported that there was a rift in the Chinese Nationalist high command in Manchuria which produced indecisive leadership; that troops who for a year had been performing garrison duties had lost their offensive spirit; that during this period of military occupation friction had developed between Government military personnel drawn mainly from Central and South China, who considered themselves conquerors and conducted a carpet-bag regime of exploitation, and the local populace who had so recently greeted them as liberators from both the Japanese and the Russians.

The Consul General at Mukden on May 30, 1947, forwarded the following appraisal of the situation to the Department of State:

"In past two months morale Nationalist forces has deteriorated at rapidly accelerating pace. Present serious state of their demoralization has been confirmed to us by many sources (including various other Chinese contacts, UNRRA officials, Americans just arrived from Kirin, and indirectly NECC [2] quarters) and has become matter of wide public knowledge and talk. It is reflected in jumpy nerves of military garrison, efforts to evade conscription, and reliable information from all sectors of Nationalist territory (including points distant from cur-

---

[2] North East Combat Command.

rent fighting) indicating that Nationalists in a panicky state are fever-
ishly building trench systems everywhere with only 'Maginot' defense
strategy in mind. There is good evidence that apathy, resentment, and
defeatism are spreading fast in Nationalist ranks causing surrenders
and desertions. Main factors contributing to this are Communists ever
mounting numerical superiority (resulting from greater use native recruits, aid from underground and Korean units), National soldiers
discouragement over prospects getting reinforcements, better solidarity and fighting spirit of Communists, losses and exhaustion of
Nationalists, their growing indignation over disparity between officers
enrichment and soldiers' low pay, life, and their lack of interest in
fighting far from home among 'alien' unfriendly populace (whereas
Communists being largely natives are in position of fighting for native
soil).

"This does not mean Manchurian collapse is necessarily imminent.
It does mean, however, that Nationalist morale has reached a point
where there is the possibility of a sudden debacle laying all Manchuria
open to the Communists whenever they choose to take it. In such an
event the Communists might close in immediately for the kill or prefer
to wait, while preparing the ground psychologically and ruining the
government's morale which is not yet fully reflected in the military
picture."

The Communists in seizing the initiative brought superior forces
to bear at points of greatest Government overextension, destroyed
isolated bodies of troops, cut communications and seized arms. At
this period the Government appears to have had two alternatives:
to reinforce its units sufficiently to enable them to assume the offensive,
closing with, and if possible destroying, the enemy, or to withdraw
before constant attrition made disaster inevitable. Any compromise
course offered the double penalty of both the loss of Manchuria and
the armies defending it. Reinforcements which could ill be spared
from other areas were sent to Manchuria, but these were not adequate
to compensate for losses sustained in the spring offensive. The Government's further attempts to replace losses with recruitment from
Manchuria failed dismally, a marked indication of its failure to win
the support of the local populace. Though the Communists were not
yet strong enough to dislodge the Government from its main strongholds, the Government's units, isolated and with their lines of communication threatened, took on the aspect of beleaguered garrisons
waiting for reinforcements which would never come.

The failure of the Government to use properly the American trained
and equipped armies which it had sent to Manchuria, far superior to

any Communist units, indicated that in this particular area faulty generalship counted more heavily than fire power, and troop morale more than superiority of equipment.

In other areas of China, Government forces in general kept the initiative well into 1947. Large areas of Shantung were occupied and by October the Government had seized Chefoo. In the west Government forces attacked and seized Yenan, the Communist capital, using an estimated 75,000 troops in this operation. Widely heralded as a great victory, this was in reality an expensive and empty one, for the Communists, contrary to Government procedure, were unwilling to violate sound military policy by committing major forces in combat for a city which had symbolic but not military significance. The Communists evacuated Yenan without a struggle, leaving the Government to support its troops in the mire of the deserted Shensi area.

By mid-summer the Communists had started a southward movement across the Lunghai and toward the Yangtze. This process, at first an infiltration rather than a general movement, forced the Government to abandon some of its gains in Shantung in order to reinforce its positions along the Lunghai. In commencing this movement south while the Government had large forces concentrated in Manchuria and Shantung, the Communists were operating on what appears to have been an effective appraisal of Nationalist intentions and capabilities, a realization that the Government was committed to positional warfare, was overextended, that for reasons of prestige it would not withdraw or consolidate, and that mobility and the initiative lay with their own forces. By late 1947 the Communists had concentrated such a considerable force in Central China that only a major Government offensive could have dislodged it. Committed to the holding of widespread areas the Government had no reserves for such operations, though Government forces now comprised 2,700,000 men facing 1,150,000 Communists according to the best available estimates of American military personnel.

By the close of 1947 Communist units lay in strength along the railroads from North China to Manchuria, constantly threatening interdiction of traffic on these lines; they had occupied portions of the Tsinan-Tsingtao Railroad in Shantung, had extended their holdings along the Ping-han, and were preparing operations which in the following months would interdict traffic on the Lunghai. The Communists held the rail lines in Manchuria north of Mukden and as the year closed were conducting operations which cut permanently the railroad south of that city. For Government forces, which had not succeeded in developing local resources, the supply and replacement problems were critical. Government forces thus effectively compartmented by the interdiction of their lines of communication were to be dealt with separately in the coming year.

OPERATIONS IN 1948 AND 1949

A Communist offensive mounted late in December of 1947 severed all railway connections into Mukden and isolated all the major Nationalist garrisons in Manchuria. The Government withdrew the bulk of its forces from Kirin and Changchun in order to reinforce its Mukden garrison. To supply the 150,000 to 200,000 troops within the immediate Mukden area, the Government resorted to costly airlift operations. Though the forces garrisoning Mukden included the New First and the New Sixth Armies, the two best units available, the Government feared to commit these troops to offensive operations lest the forces operating in the open country defect to the enemy, or lest attrition or defeat endanger the entire Government position in Manchuria. The Communists refrained from costly attacks on entrenched Government forces.

Elsewhere in China the Communists pushed their advantages. In Shensi they reoccupied Yenan in mid-April. In the course of this and subsequent operations they destroyed or captured the Government units which had originally captured Yenan, together with considerable reinforcements, meeting little resistance in this operation, during which many Government troops defected to the Communists. Government fear of further defections became a restraining influence in the planning of operations and tended to constrict Government forces even more deeply in their defensive positions.

Communist forces in Central China remained comparatively quiet but in the spring moved against and seized several points along the Lunghai including Loyang and Kaifeng, at which they met only token resistance and from which they acquired considerable stores. In Shantung the Communists took the offensive, the first major test in this territory coming with the seizure of Weihsien. The senior officer of the United States Military Advisory Group in China, Major General David Barr, in a report on his duty in China, made certain observations on this engagement, the substance of which follows:

In this battle the Nationalists' commander, in order to preserve his forces intact, withdrew them from the main areas of conflict into the east city. In a subsequent attempt to evacuate his forces, he was caught and his troops were destroyed. While the battle for the city was being joined orders were issued for Government columns to move from Tsinan and Tsingtao to relieve the city. The column from Tsinan, three divisions strong, met inferior Communist forces and made no serious attempt to fight through to Weihsien. The column from Tsingtao returned to that city without having engaged the enemy. The Government's defeat at Weihsien revealed that disloyalty, poor morale and lack of will to fight marked the Government units involved.

An Eca mission studying conditions in China expressed the following views in a report dated July 23, 1948:

"The Mission was really startled by the facts about the military situation in China and to find such an enormous gap between what they had supposed to be the case and the actual truth. We were surprised at the wide gulf between the combined opinion of our own competent military in China supported by the Ambassador and the present military and related policy of the Chinese Government in Nanking. This was despite repeated and continued efforts on the part of the Ambassador with the support of the American military advisers to persuade the Government to a change in its military strategy and tactics."

The Nationalists, however, clung to their defensive strategy, making possible a major Communist victory in Shantung at Tsinan, where 85,000 to 100,000 Government troops took refuge behind the strong natural and constructed fortifications of the city. The best available estimates indicate that the Communists brought to bear against Tsinan's defenders a margin of superiority not normally adequate to justify hope of victory in conflict for such a strong position. After a brief period of fighting, marked by the defection of units of the Nationalist 84th Division, the Communists took the city on September 23–24, 1948. With this victory they acquired an estimated 50,000 rifles and considerable stocks of ammunition.

The Consul General at Tsingtao submitted the following evaluation of the causes for the Government's defeat:

"Prime cause for swift loss of city is psychological rather than material or military. Nationalist garrison had been isolated for two months with no possibility ground support. Previous Nationalist defeats in which Nationalist troops failed fight known to Tsinan garrison and people. Communist victory at Tsinan felt inevitable in view record of failure of Nationalists and consistent victories of Communists who at Tsinan used many of best troops. Nationalist soldiers and population Shantung in general no longer consider Nationalist Government merits continued support in civil war, loss of lives and economic chaos. These factors expressed themselves in outright defection to Communists, immediate surrenders, and failure to stand and fight. Those soldiers willing to fight were unable to trust other units to support them.   No mutuality of feelings between regular forces and local Peace Preservation Corps troops.   Nationalist regulars were largely from Central and South China and had little interest in defending strange city and people.   Communists undoubtedly had organized support within city.   No real attempt made defend perimeter at distance outside of city wall.   Antiquated custom of falling back to city walls was speedily observed by Nationalist defenders.   Other military causes were poor intelligence, failure to take initiative against Communists when concentrating for campaign and thus keeping them off balance.   Belated inadequate improper air support.

"In a summary, majority troops at Tsinan did not want to fight while those that did fight found their position made impossible by the disaffected.   Defection of Wu Hua-wen was merely the manifestation of a general phenomenon.   His treason was not of itself the cause of defeat.

"Nationalists at Tsinan had ample ammunition and food and assurance of further supplies in event protracted siege."

The Communists encouraged by this victory rapidly moved against Chinchow, supply base for Government forces in Manchuria.   At this city the Government had over 70,000 troops including units of the recently brought up Eighth Army under General Fan Han-chieh, reputedly one of the ablest Chinese generals.   Against these troops the Communists, availing themselves of their superior mobility, concentrated a numerically stronger force.   The Government at Mukden, 120 miles distant, had 150,000–200,000 men, including its best armies. It had complete control of sea lanes and had available the port of Hulutao to which reinforcements could and were eventually sent for this key battle.   It was obvious that the supply of units in Manchuria, totaling some 300,000 men, would become vastly more difficult if Chinchow fell and that its loss meant the eventual loss of Manchuria.

The commander of the Nationalist forces at Mukden, General Wei Li-huang, was ordered to commence a movement to relieve Chinchow by September 25.   Wei delayed his departure from Mukden until October 9 and then moved out slowly and without his complete forces. Strong reinforcements were landed at Hulutao but only a portion of them moved toward Chinchow; on meeting opposition these were committed piecemeal and never reached their objective.   According to Department of the Army reports, Government units of the 93rd Army defending the city defected to the Communists and on October 15, 1948, the Communists occupied it.   In this victory the Communists acquired not only the rifles and equipment of the defending forces but also great quantities of stores which had been stockpiled for the use of Government forces in Manchuria.

The Generalissimo at this time flew to Peiping and assumed direction of field operations. This placed the actual commander miles from the scene of fighting with no adequate information on the condition of his forces or on the forces of the enemy. Commands were sent direct to the commanding general of the units involved, eliminating the normal coordinating staff levels. Though military observers considered that the general plan of action evolved was sound, the lack of any coordinating procedure produced complete confusion on all operating levels. In a belated attempt to save the forces in Manchuria, orders were issued for them to evacuate that area.

Events of the immediately following days have not yet been clearly reconstructed. While Government units were operating in the field, the Communists struck at the headquarters controlling their movements and captured or killed its ranking officers. With no coordinated direction, the previously American trained and equipped units which had won such an illustrious record against the Japanese, disintegrated. A few stragglers found their way back to Mukden, which was surrendered to the Communists without a fight. A few thousands succeeded in reaching Yingkow and were evacuated by ship, but the overwhelming majority of the Government forces in the Mukden area surrendered without a fight to the Communists.

The Government in occupying Manchuria took steps contrary to the advice of competent United States military observers who were aware that the Government could not reoccupy Manchuria and pacify the rest of China as well. As indicated previously Government forces in Manchuria were supplied from bases in China proper. A contributing factor to the supply difficulties was the Russian occupation of Dairen which denied to the Government the use of Manchuria's most efficient port and connecting railway line (though other ports were available at Hulutao and Yingkow). After initial offenses had been blunted, the Government fell back on the defensive. Officers and troops of the Government never obtained the support of the people on whom they were billeted. The loss of Manchuria was a tragedy for the Government for it meant the loss of China's most highly developed industrial area, the prize which had originally drawn the Government there. Of even greater significance was the loss of the forces and resources without which successful resistance in North China became impossible. The loss of Manchuria was the most striking illustration of the Government's overestimation of its capabilities.

The Chinese Air Force, which had played no essential part in assisting the Government forces during these battles, appeared after the Communists had occupied Mukden and engaged in bombing from such altitudes that competent military observers considered the operation a complete waste.

The tempo of the civil war after the fall of Mukden increased rapidly. The Communists immediately moved against Hsuchow, where the Government had maintained twenty-odd divisions spread out along the Lunghai Railway. In an attempt to save the forces in this area an evacuation was ordered, but the action taken was neither decisive nor on time, and before the evacuation had been completed the Government forces were surrounded by the Communists. In early November General Barr reported to the Department of the Army:

"Deterioration of military situation in the Hsuchow area previously reported has worsened due to known defection to the Communists of two Nationalist Divisions with the suspected defection of an additional three. As this defection becomes known to other Government units it can be anticipated that it will spread rapidly not only in the Hsuchow area but elsewhere."

Both the former Hsuchow garrison and a force which had moved up to reinforce it were isolated and destroyed after a minimum of conflict.

Tientsin fell on January 15, 1949, after a brief siege; Peiping surrendered without a fight at the end of January.

In a review of military developments from January 1, 1948, through January of 1949 the Intelligence Division of the Department of the Army stated:

"The Nationalists entered 1948 with an estimated strength of 2,723,000 troops. Recruitment and replacement of combat losses kept this figure constant through mid-September. By 1 February 1949, however, heavy losses had reduced Nationalist strength to 1,500,000, of which approximately 500,000 are service troops. This represents a reduction of 45 percent of the Nationalist Government's total troop strength, in a 4½-month period.

"Communist strength, estimated at 1,150,000 a year ago, has mounted to 1,622,000, virtually all combat effectives. This increase of approximately 40 percent represents the creation of new units, particularly in Manchuria and East Central China. Whereas the Nationalists began 1948 with almost a three-to-one numerical superiority, the Communist forces now outnumber the total Nationalist strength and have achieved better than a one-and-a-half-to-one superiority in combat effectives. The expansion was accompanied by continued reorganization of the military forces along more uniform and orthodox lines.

"The events of the last year, and more specifically those of the last four and one-half months, have resulted in such overwhelming losses to the National Government that, acting alone, its military position has declined beyond possible recoupment. On the other hand, these same events have so enhanced the position and capabilities of the Communists that they are now capable of achieving a complete military victory over the Nationalist forces. Other considerations, particularly those of a political character, may affect the speed with which this capability is exercised."

The Military Attaché at Nanking estimated that during this 4½-month period Government forces lost over 140,000 American rifles. Losses of other than American rifles are estimated to have been several times this figure—practically all of which fell undamaged to the Communists. Military estimates indicated that during this same period the Communists effectively integrated into their own forces approximately 200,000 former Government troops who could be used as combatants, with possibly 400,000 more captured Nationalist troops being integrated into Communist service units.

On April 20, 1949, the Communists crossed the Yangtze without effective opposition by either the Chinese Army or the Chinese Air Force and, having occupied Nanking, moved rapidly toward Shanghai, which fell on May 25. Communist units which had crossed the Yangtze to the west of Shanghai pushed forward rapidly meeting no resistance from Government forces, which withdrew from their advance. By the second week in May the Communists had pushed some twenty armies 120 miles south of the Yangtze and were continuing to advance without opposition. Since then Hankow has fallen, and Sian, gateway to the northwest, has been captured.

Department of the Army estimates indicate that Government forces remaining in China prior to the fall of Nanking and Shanghai consisted of 315,000 in those areas; 175,000 at Sian, described by Chinese Government officials as unreliable; 120,000 under General Pai Chung-hsi in the Hankow area; an estimated 120,000 in the northwest without equipment or the industrial facilities to provide it; and possibly 120,000 to 150,000 others scattered elsewhere throughout China in isolated garrisons.

II. AMERICAN OPERATIONAL ADVICE TO THE CHINESE

DIRECTIVES TO GENERAL BARR ON ADVISORY ACTIVITIES

In 1946 there had been established in China a United States Advisory Group to assist in the implementation of certain phases of

American policy. It was kept in existence until late 1948. During the latter part of its existence it was under the command of Major General David Barr. The functions and operations of the Advisory Group are described in subsequent sections of this chapter. Though unwilling to assume responsibility for Chinese Government strategic plans and operations, the United States Government determined in the fall of 1947 to authorize the senior officer of the Army Advisory Group to make his advice available to the Generalissimo on an informal and confidential basis. Instructions from Secretary of State Marshall to the Ambassador in this sense were forwarded on November 28, 1947, reading as follows:

"You may rest assured premise is fully accepted here that military expenditures on present war scale are incompatible with balancing of Chinese Government budget which in turn is prerequisite to controlling of inflation. You may recall it was in anticipation of ultimate consequences for China of such a situation that as long as two years ago this Government attempted to prevent civil war in China. Furthermore it is a moot question whether military expenditures could in fact be cut during a period of civil war if present forces were reduced but remaining numbers given adequate care and equipment; it seems evident that only well led and well trained and cared for divisions imbued with improved spirit would be capable of assuming and holding initiative against Chinese forces.

"I am willing that General Barr should make his advice available to Generalissimo on informal and confidential basis and that Army Advisory Group should supply advice with respect to reorganization of Chinese Army Services of Supply should that be desired. I am however not willing that we should accept responsibility for Chinese strategic plans and operations. I think you will agree that implications of our accepting that responsibility would be very far-reaching and grave and that such responsibility is in logic inseparable from authority to make it effective. Whatever the Generalissimo may feel moved to say with respect to his willingness to delegate necessary powers to Americans, I know from my own experience that advice is always listened to very politely but not infrequently ignored when deemed unpalatable."

Prior to his departure from the United States, General Barr, later to be appointed director of JUSMAG, received additional oral instructions from the Secretary of State authorizing him to give this advice on a personal and confidential basis. Following a conference with the Generalissimo, arrangements were made whereby the Chinese Ministry of National Defense provided General Barr information on

Chinese operations, and channels were established through which General Barr could make known to the Chinese his recommendations.

GENERAL BARR'S REPORT

The section following relates some of the recommendations made by General Barr and the manner in which the Chinese received and acted upon this advice. The section consists of quotations from a report submitted by General Barr early in 1949, with the occasional explanatory material added by the Department of State enclosed in brackets.

Report of Operational Advice Given to the Generalissimo, the Minister of National Defense and the Chief of the Supreme Staff by Major General David Barr

An early estimate of the situation, prior to the first formal meeting of the select combined group, convinced me of the futility of continuing to hold isolated Manchurian cities which were totally dependent upon air for both civilian and military supply. The combined air-lift capacity of Chinese civilian and military transports fell far short of the enormous tonnage requirements. The cost of air-lift replacement, maintenance and fuel—in a country bereft of gold credits— could only result in economic disaster, while making only ineffectual contributions to the supply effort.

Early in March, therefore, when the Communists had withdrawn their main forces from the vicinity of Changchun and Mukden, after their winter offensive, I strongly urged the Generalissimo to take advantage of this opportunity to make a progressive withdrawal from Manchuria. He was aghast at this proposal, stating that no circumstances would induce him to consider such a plan. Hopeful of a compromise, I suggested the withdrawal into Mukden of the Changchun, Kirin and Ssupingchieh garrisons. To this the Generalissimo replied that political considerations precluded the abandonment of Changchun, the ancient capital of Manchuria, but that he would consider a plan for withdrawing the Kirin garrison into Changchun. The Kirin garrison was accordingly withdrawn at a later date.

In my next conference with the Generalissimo, and after his reiterated determination not to consider a withdrawal from Manchuria, I proposed that an early offensive be launched to open rail communications between Chinchow and Mukden. The Generalissimo enthusiastically concurred, and instructed his staff to prepare a plan in consultation with my assistants.

At a meeting at the Ministry of National Defense War Room on 8 March 1948 General Lo indicated that a general plan for the opening of a corridor to Mukden had been prepared and approved by the Generalissimo. . . . On 5 May 1948, a coordinated attack from Mukden and Chinchow would be mounted to open a corridor along the railroad between those two points.

The lack of a broad strategic plan for operations was so obviously missing that I inquired if such a plan existed. I was told that the Chinese Armed Forces were then operating under a "Six Months' Plan" and that a "Two Year Plan" had been prepared but was not yet approved by the Generalissimo.

During the period between the date of the above meeting and 17 March 1948, the following events occurred:

The Nationalist 69th Army evacuated Kirin on 12 March and withdrew into Changchun.

Ssupingchieh was captured by the Communists on the night of 12 March.

Air lift of 23,000 Nationalist troops from the Kaifeng-Loyang area to Sian was initiated. For this air lift, all available military transport aircraft was employed, the operation extending over several weeks to the detriment of other operations I considered more important. General Hu Tsung-nan, an old friend of the Generalissimo, had prevailed upon him to reinforce his Sian garrison to an extent which was later to prove disastrous to the Nationalists in East Central China. The loss to the Communists of the Kaifeng-Chenghsien-Loyang area was a direct result of this shift of troops to the west. It has been my contention throughout that the strategic importance of Sian was highly overrated. To this day, a large number of Nationalist troops remain at Sian which could have been far more profitably employed elsewhere.

The greater part of two Nationalist divisions were destroyed in the mountains northeast of Sian because of poor reconnaissance and no march security.

A meeting was held at the Ministry of National Defense War Room on 17 March 1948. In discussing the coming offensive to open a corridor to Mukden, the Chinese stated that it would take six months to repair the railroad between Chinchow and Hsinmin.

On being questioned as to the amount of destruction the Nationalists were able to achieve prior to the evacuation of Kirin, the Chinese were vague. I pointed out that a large amount of the arms and ammunition in the hands of the Communists was captured Nationalist equipment and that the practice of permitting such material to fall into the hands of the Communists was prolonging the war. Although I stressed this point many times after that, it was of little avail. The Chinese seemed inherently unable to destroy anything of value.

At a meeting with the Generalissimo on 24 March, I discussed with him the following subjects, among others:

(1) The food situation in Mukden and our ability to assist by immediate delivery of 12 United States C–46's out of a total of 20 available in Japan for turnover to the Chinese.

(2) That United States ammunition from the Pacific, destined for Mukden, had not yet been moved to that city although it had arrived in Shanghai.

(3) The necessity of a definite and detailed plan for the opening of a line of communication to Mukden. In this connection, the Generalissimo again assured me that he intended to hold Mukden at all cost.

(4) The Generalissimo stressed the need for .45 caliber ammunition for use in the large number of submachine guns being used in the Nationalist Army.

In connection with paragraphs (1) and (4) above, I was able to forward a memorandum to the Generalissimo on 29 March informing him that 1 million rounds of .45 caliber ammunition were being made available to him and that the transfer of 16 to 20 United States C–46's had been approved.

A meeting was held at the Ministry of National Defense War Room on 16 April. . . . Following the above meeting, I called on General Yu Ta-wei, Minister of Communications, and learned that his office had received no instructions regarding the reconstruction of the Chinchow-Hsinmin railroad. He stated, however, that he had been informed of the plan and was going ahead with his preparations.

On the 29th of April, at a conference with the Supreme G–3, he again assured my staff that the Mukden attack would be launched on 5 May. He stated that the Generalissimo had ordered the attack to jump off not later than the 5th day of May. . . .

On the 30th of April, my staff interviewed an officer of the Combined Service Forces installation in Mukden. He had only been in office 4 days but had been sent to Nanking by Wei Li-huang to plead with the Ministry for food and gasoline and additional air transport to carry it in. He stated that the Army had food for about 3 weeks and that he needed 3 million gallons of gasoline. He stated that he had had a meeting with the Supreme Staff and that he could get no cooperation from the Chinese Air Force but had arranged with the civilian air lines to fly in an additional month's supply of food. (Comment: Each day brought new facts to confirm my belief that General Wei Li-huang had no intention of mounting the proposed attack on 5 May.)

On 1 May 1948 my staff, in conference with the Supreme G–3, was informed of a victory northwest of Sian in which parts of the 2d, 4th and 6th Communist columns in that area were destroyed by the 82d Nationalist Division and other troops of General Ma. A dispatch from General Li, Deputy Supreme G–3, then in Mukden, stated that Wei Li-huang wanted reinforcements from North China before staging his attack. General Lo Tseh-Kai, Supreme G–3, did not believe then that the attack would be mounted. He stated that Wei Li-huang was coming to Nanking to confer with the Generalissimo. (COMMENT: I determined then that if the attack did not take place as planned, I would recommend to the Generalissimo that Mukden be evacuated quickly before the Communists could stage their spring offensive, since Mukden and Changchun could not be indefinitely supplied by air.)

Having been notified that General Chiang, Deputy Chief of Staff of the Mukden Headquarters was in Nanking, I arranged a conference with him at the Ministry on 4 May 1948. General Chiang led off with a lengthy description of recent Communist movements from the north towards the Mukden area, of their excellent state of supply and training and of the assistance they were receiving from Russia. It was obvious that he was leading up to the news that the proposed Nationalist attack to open the corridor to Chinchow would not be mounted.

He stated that the morale of the Mukden forces was high and ...i they wanted to fight and defeat the Communists. When asked "why not then fight now before it is too late?", General Chiang answered that reinforcements from North China were necessary. He stated that a strong defense of the Mukden-Chinchow areas should be made at that time and a coordinated attack to open a corridor be made later. He advised to sit tight until the Communist intentions became clear and then take action. This was undoubtedly the policy Wei Li-huang would pursue in spite of all orders to the ontrary from the Generalissimo and the Supreme Staff. The opportunity to take the initiative away from the Communists had been lost. It was extremely doubtful if a later attempt to open a corridor would be successful.

I attended the conference mentioned above, on the afternoon of the 5th of May at the Generalissimo's home. Present were the Generalissimo and Madame Chiang Kai-shek, the three Mukden Generals mentioned above and several members of the Supreme General Staff. After a lengthy discourse by the Mukden Generals as to the reasons the long awaited Manchurian operations could not then be staged, the Generalissimo asked for my opinions. I told him that I had heard nothing but reasons why the attack could not be mounted. That at a later date I was convinced the same excuses would be given plus those that would develop during the interim. I recommended that the attack be mounted then and that if this could not be accomplished then Manchuria should be evacuated while an opportunity still offered itself. I pointed out that Communist strength in Manchuria was increasing and that if success was uncertain at this time, it was definitely impossible later. I further pointed out that Changchun and Mukden could not be indefinitely supplied by air. The Generalissimo stated that because General Fu Tso-yi could not spare two armies from North China at that time to reinforce the Chinchow garrison, a reinforcement being considered necessary to the success of the operation, he had decided to postpone the attack to 1 August 1948. He further stated that the troops then available in Manchuria would be the only ones that could be counted upon and enjoined the Mukden commanders to use the time available for the intensive training of these troops. (I would like to point out at this time that the Generalissimo had directed General Wei Li-huang as early as the preceding winter to prepare plans and ready himself for an attack early in May to open a corridor from Mukden to Chinchow. That the Supreme G–3 and members of his division had made six separate trips to Mukden in an effort to press preparations for this attack. That both myself and my staff had continuously urged the Chinese towards this effort since early February. That General Wei Li-huang was able to get away with such complete disobedience of orders without punishment or even censure, as far as I know, points out one reason why the Nationalists are losing the present war.)

On 6 May 1948, the Supreme G–3 had a conference with the three visiting Mukden Generals. General Chao had told him that the Communists had learned of the proposed Nationalist attempt to open the corridor and were moving troops to intercept the attack. He insisted that more time was needed to train and organize more troops. His main theme was to *defend* Mukden and Chinchow thus containing large masses of Manchurian Communists which in turn meant the salvation of North China. The G–3 disagreed and pointed out that another such opportunity to wrest the initiative from the Communists and defeat them would not occur again.

At a meeting on 29th May I asked whether there was any intention or thought being given to a withdrawal from Manchuria and was given a negative answer. I stated that if Chinchow fell as a result of inaction at Mukden, then Mukden was surely lost and that this should be made clear to Wei Li-huang. The Chief of Staff informed me that an agreement was reached at the Generalissimo's headquarters that if Wei Li-huang failed to assist the Chinchow garrison, he would be severely punished.

During the month of May 1948, certain political and military developments occurred which are of interest. The National Assembly adjourned on 1 May after electing Chiang Kai-shek and Li Tsung-jen President and Vice President respectively. On 10 May the Executive Yuan resigned en bloc which brought most government efforts to a standstill and made decisions difficult to obtain. A new Cabinet was not appointed until after Inaugural Day, 20 May. General Ku Chu-tung, Commander of the Ground Forces, was named Supreme Chief of Staff during the week ending 14 May and General Yu Han-mou was named as Commander of the Ground Forces. The selection of these officers to fill these highly important military posts was a disappointment to me. Their military background left much to be desired. They were staunch supporters of the Generalissimo and it was obvious that their appointment was for political expediency rather than ability. I had met them both before and had been impressed by their lack of personality.

[In view of the Chinese determination not to abandon Manchuria and following an inspection of certain areas there by American officers, General Barr on June 2, 1948, submitted new proposals for offensive action in Manchuria.]

During the period from the 20th to the 30th of June, my staff in personal conferences with the Supreme G–2 and G–3, were made acquainted with the following facts:

Because of the serious situation forming in East Central China, the Generalissimo flew to Chienhsien, west of Kaifeng to personally direct operations. On the 24th of June he held an important military commanders' meeting at Sian. In connection with this and other such meetings, the Minister of National Defense, General Ho Ying-chin, complained to me, with some bitterness, that the Generalissimo often issued operational orders direct without informing him or the Supreme General Staff. This is a well known failing of the Generalissimo's. It was reported to my staff that the Chinese Air Force in a weak effort to support the defenders of Kaifeng, strafed Communist columns from elevations well above 2,000 feet. This failing was mentioned to the Chinese on innumerable occasions without apparent result. Not only did they strafe from ineffective heights, but they also bombed from ridiculous elevations. It was also reported that Kaifeng was bombed during the Communist occupation, which was later proven untrue or at least the results were very ineffective.

Decision was made by the Generalissimo to defend isolated Tsinan to the last. (Such decisions have been costly to the Nationalists in troops and supplies.) I pointed out again to the Generalissimo and to the Supreme Staff the futility of attempting to hold cities from within restricted perimeters by purely defensive measures against overpowering enemy forces. Tsinan at this time was isolated from Hsuchow by Communist forces at Yenchow and Taian. Although in considerable strength in this area the main Communist force was still on the Honan plains, southeast of Kaifeng. An opportunity existed to do one of two things. By offensive action north from Hsuchow and south from Tsinan, the Nationalist forces were capable of destroying the Communists and reopening the corridor between Hsuchow and Tsinan. The Nationalists were also capable at this time of evacuating Tsinan and withdrawing into Hsuchow. Having no confidence in the will to fight of the Tsinan garrison after their ineffective attempt to recapture Weihsien, and having heard reports of the questionable loyalty of some of the senior commanders, I recommended that the city be evacuated, and the troops be withdrawn to Hsuchow. Again, as in the case of Changchun, I was told that because of political reasons, Tsinan, the capital of Shantung Province, must be defended.

On July 2, 1948, at the invitation of the American Military Attaché, Brig. Gen. Robert H. Soule, I flew over Kaifeng and the area to the southeast thereof where heavy fighting was reported to be in progress. Reports of destruction in Kaifeng by the Chinese Air Force bombing and fire were proven untrue. With the exception of a few bomb craters outside the city walls, no effects of the bombing could be seen. We circled at low altitude all over the reported battle area southeast of the city, but with the exception of a few burning houses in scattered villages, a few mortar shell bursts, some marching troops and two fighter planes flying higher than we were, there was little evidence of the reported clash of half a million men.

At a meeting in the Ministry of National Defense War Room on 14 September 1948, the following observations were made by the Chinese:

The G–3 stated that although completely surrounded and isolated, food was still coming to Tsinan from the countryside. He believed that an additional division could be air lifted into Tsinan to assist in the defense. I recommended strongly against this believing that the city was lost and that it only meant the loss to the Nationalists of an additional division. One had already been air lifted in from Tsingtao. I recommended, that rather than fly in additional troops, the present Tsinan garrison be air lifted to Hsuchow.

On 24 September 1948 I learned that Tsinan had been captured by the Communists. The unexpectedly early fall of the city was the result of a defection to the Communists of an entire Nationalist division which had been entrusted with the defense of the western approaches to the city. This division, former puppet troops, had been suspected and should have previously been relieved.

At a meeting with the Generalissimo on the 29th of September, the following matters, among others, were discussed:

The Generalissimo expressed deep disappointment over the outcome of the battle of Tsinan and stated that its fall was unexpected. He said that it was necessary for a study to be made on Chinese strategy, tactics, training and organization of field units in order that the mistakes committed at Tsinan would not be repeated. He said that the old strategy of holding strong points or key cities at all cost would have to go.

The Generalissimo said that my reasoning was very sound and expressed the hope that I would attend the weekly military operational conference held each Wednesday in the Ministry of Defense War Room. He asked that I give his operational officers the benefit of my experience and advice. I stated that I would be glad to comply with his request.

[In view of Communist activity around Chinchow the Generalissimo had ordered General Wei in Mukden to take aggressive offensive action to relieve the pressure further south. General Barr made the following comment on a meeting held October 1 in the Ministry of National Defense War Room:]

I pointed out that the situation in Chinchow was extremely critical, that five days had passed since General Wei Li-huang had received orders to attack to the west and that there had been no indication of such an attack getting under way. I recommended that the Mukden troops break out to the west of their position at once, ready or not.

At a luncheon meeting on 7 October 1948 the following matters were discussed and recommendations made:

General Ho Ying-chin announced that it had been determined to organize, train and equip an additional 28 strategic reserve divisions (three regiments in each) over and above the nine presently being organized and trained. I pointed out that little progress had been made in the original plan to form nine divisions and asked how he expected to handle 28 more. He replied that there were that many in the south and west that had been depleted in combat, were partially equipped, and could be brought up to strength and equipped with United States aid supplies supplemented by Chinese production. He stated that his representatives would confer shortly with Brigadier General Laurence Keiser, my Ground Division Senior Adviser, on the plan. This was another example of Chinese grandiose planning without thought or regard to the possibility of its implementation.

General Ho stated that the Generalissimo was in Peiping. (The Generalissimo did not return to Nanking until after the fall of Mukden and Chinchow. He directed this operation from Peiping without the assistance of his Supreme Staff whom he failed to keep informed as to what was taking place. In spite of this unorthodox procedure, the plans made and orders given were sound and had they been obeyed, the results would probably have been favorable.)

At a meeting in the Ministry of National Defense War Room on 13 October 1948, the following matters were discussed:

General Wei Li-huang had used only 11 divisions in his breakout to the west instead of 15 as ordered. He had been directed to employ his 52d Army to reinforce his operations. The attack had commenced on 9 October, 13 days after receipt of orders to attack immediately. Progress had been very slow to date.

In discussing the situation at Changchun, I learned that the garrison commander, General Cheng Tung-kuo, had received instructions from Wei Li-huang to coordinate his breakout with Wei Li-huang's attack, immediately before, during or immediately after. To date there had been no indications of any effort on his part to comply with these confused instructions and the situation at Changchun was obscure.

At a meeting in the Ministry of National Defense War Room on the 20th of October 1948, the following matters were discussed:

A briefing by the Supreme G–2 and G–3 disclosed the loss to the Communists on 20 October of Changchun after the defection of the majority of the garrison and the suicide of the garrison commander, General Cheng Tung-kuo. This report of suicide was later found to be untrue. It was reported also that Chinchow had fallen with four of the victorious Communist columns already moving south towards Hulutao. The efforts of the Nationalists to attack north from the Chinsi-Hulutao area had been completely unsuccessful while the movement southwest from Mukden of General Wei Li-huang's armies was disappointingly slow.

I asked whether or not plans had been prepared for the evacuation of the Chinsi-Hulutao area and upon being answered in the negative, I recommended that plans be made then to include shipping necessary for the evacuation of heavy equipment and supplies, and suggested that the troops fight south down the corridor.

I asked if it was known what General Wei Li-huang intended to do, since Chinchow had fallen, and suggested that he should evacuate Mukden entirely and fight southwest with the idea of entering North China. I pointed out that if he returned into Mukden, the Nationalist Government could not supply him much longer by air and that his position would deteriorate into a second Changchun. General Ho Ying-chin agreed and stated that he had put this question up to the Generalissimo who was still in Peiping, but had received no reply.

In a visit to G–3 on the morning of 28 October 1948, my staff learned of the defeat of General Wei Li-huang's forces west of Mukden on 27 October. I recommended that the 11 Nationalist divisions then in the Chinsi-Hulutao area, be evacuated by sea at once or make a determined effort to fight their way south into north China before the main Communist strength could return to prevent it. I further recommended that the troops in Yinkow, and all that could reach Yinkow from Mukden, also be evacuated by sea at once. I could not refrain from pointing out that if Wei Li-huang had moved southwest promptly after receiving his orders on the 25th of September, instead of delaying until the 9th of October, and then had moved with speed in the attack, he would have saved Chinchow and could have brought all his strength into North China. General Ho admitted that I was correct, but stated that his hands were tied and that the Generalissimo had directed the entire operations alone from Peiping without reference to him or to the Supreme Staff. In this, of course, the Generalissimo was wrong, but the orders he issued to General Wei Li-huang for the conduct of operations in Manchuria were sound. Had they been carried out with determination and speed there was every chance of success. Chinchow, though sorely pressed, held out against the Communists long enough to enable the Mukden and the Hulutao-Chinsi forces to converge to their rescue had they moved promptly and fought with sufficient determination to get there in time. The Nationalist troops, in Manchuria, were the finest soldiers the Government had. The large majority of the units were United States equipped and many soldiers and junior officers still remained who had received United States training during the war with Japan. I am convinced that had these troops had proper leadership from the top the Communists would have suffered a major defeat. The Generalissimo placed General Tu Yu-ming, an officer of little worth, in charge of field operations, properly relegating to General Wei Li-huang over-all supervision from Mukden where he could do little harm. But Tu Yu-ming also fought the battle from Mukden, placing the burden of active command in the field to General Liao Yao-hsiang, Commanding General of the 9th Army Group. Liao was a good general but was killed early in the action. Without top leadership and in the confusion that followed the Communists were able to segment the Nationalist forces and destroy them piecemeal. General Wei Li-huang and General Tu Yu-ming deserted the troops and were safely in Hulutao at the end. The efforts of the troops in the

Chinsi-Hulutao area to relieve Chinchow were also futile. Instead of mounting an all-out attack with full force initially, which could have swept aside the Communists who were weakened by withdrawals sent against Wei Li-huang, the attack was developed slowly with troops being thrown in piecemeal. The attack soon bogged down with the troops showing little will to fight. The loss of Manchuria and some 300,000 of its best troops was a stunning blow to the Government. To me, the loss of the troops was the most serious result. It spelled the beginning of the end. There could be no hope for North China with an additional 360,000 Communist troops now free to move against its north flank.

[Following the loss of forces in Manchuria the center of activity shifted to Hsuchow.]

At a meeting in the Ministry of National Defense War Room on the 25th of November 1948, the following matters were discussed:

The Supreme G–2 and G–3 briefed the assembly on the current military situation. The strength of the Hsuchow garrison was given as 270,000. Regarding supplies, it was stated that ammunition was sufficient but a food shortage existed. I strongly recommended that Hsuchow be evacuated at once and that its troops move south against the rear of the Communists forces below Shusien. The G–2 reported that the Mukden-Chinchow railroad had been restored. It had taken the Communists just 25 days to restore this line, a project the Nationalists had insisted would take 6 months when discussions were under way concerning the proposed Nationalist 5 May attack which never materialized.

At a meeting in the Ministry of National Defense War Room on 1 December 1948, the following subjects were discussed:

The usual G–2—G–3 briefing disclosed that four of the nine Nationalist armies at Hsuchow were not being employed in the attack to the south. I recommended that the attack be an all-out one and that all troops be employed with a view toward evacuating the city entirely. I again stressed the necessity for speed. General Ho Ying-chin stated that the orders issued had been to that effect.

[Despite belated efforts of the forces in the Hsuchow area to withdraw to more easily defensible positions these forces were surrounded and destroyed by the Communists as were units moving to their relief. As it became apparent that the remaining military forces of the Government were powerless to stop the Communist armies and that their defeat was inevitable, steps were taken to decrease the size of JUSMAG, for American military personnel associated with it did not have the diplomatic immunity accorded attachés. With the certainty that Nanking would fall in the immediate future and with the disorganized condition of the Chinese armies, its period of usefulness had passed and orders were issued for its removal from China. On December 18 in a telegram to the Department of the Army General Barr stated in part: "Marked by the stigma of defeat and the loss of face resulting from the forced evacuation of China, north of the Yangtze, it is extremely doubtful if the National Government could muster the necessary popular support to mobilize sufficient manpower in this area (South China) with which to rebuild its forces even if time permitted. Only a policy of unlimited United States aid including the immediate employment of United States armed forces to block the southern advance of the Communists, which I emphatically do not recommend, would enable the Nationalist Government to maintain a foothold in southern China against a determined Communist advance. . . . The complete defeat of the Nationalist Army . . . is inevitable."]

[General Barr summarized his views of the causes for the Government's defeat as follows:]

Many pages could be written covering the reasons for the failure of Nationalist strategy. I believe that the Government committed its first politico-military blunder when it concentrated its efforts after V–J Day on the purely military reoccupation of the former Japanese areas, giving little consideration to long established regional sentiments or to creation of efficient local administrations which could attract wide popular support in the liberated areas. Moreover, the Nationalist Army was burdened with an unsound strategy which was conceived by a politically influenced and militarily inept high command. Instead of being content with consolidating North China, the Army was given the concurrent mission of seizing control of Manchuria, a task beyond its logistic capabilities. The Government, attempting to do too much with too little, found its armies scattered along thousands of miles of railroads, the possession of which was vital in view of the fact that these armies were supplied from bases in central China. In order to hold the railroads, it was also necessary to hold the large cities through which they passed. As time went on, the troops degenerated from field armies, capable of offensive combat, to garrison and lines of communication troops with an inevitable loss of offensive spirit. Communist military strength, popular support, and tactical skill were seriously under-estimated from the start. It became increasingly difficult to maintain effective control over the large sections of predominantly Communist countryside through which the lines of communication passed. Lack of Nationalist forces qualified to take the field against the Communists enabled the latter to become increasingly strong. The Nationalists, with their limited resources, steadily lost ground against an opponent who not only shaped his strategy around available human and material resources, but also capitalized skillfully on the Government's strategic and tactical blunders and economic vulnerability.

Initially, the Communists were content to fight a type of guerrilla warfare, limiting their activities to raids on lines of communication and supply installations. The success of their operations, which were purely offensive, instilled in them the offensive attitude so necessary to success in war. On the other hand, the Nationalist strategy of defense of the areas they held, developed in them the 'wall psychology' which has been so disastrous to their armies. As the Communists grew stronger and more confident, they were able, by concentrations of superior strength, to surround, attack, and destroy Nationalist units in the field and Nationalist held cities. It is typical of the Nationalists, in the defense of an area or a city, to dig in or retire within the city walls, and there to fight to the end, hoping for relief which never comes because it cannot be spared from elsewhere. The Chinese have resisted advice that, in the defense of an area or a city, from attack by modern methods of warfare, it is necessary to take up positions away from the walls where fire and maneuver is possible. Further, they have been unable to be convinced of the necessity for withdrawing from cities and prepared areas when faced with overpowering opposition and certain isolation and defeat, while the opportunity still existed for them to do so. In some cases their reasons for failure to withdraw and save their forces were political, but in most cases, they were convinced that by defensive action alone, they could, through attrition, if nothing else, defeat the enemy. Because of this mistaken concept and because of their inability to realize that discretion is usually the better part of valor, large numbers of Nationalist troops were lost to the Government.

It must be understood that all through the structure and machinery of the Nationalist Government there are interlocking ties of interest peculiar to the Chinese—family, financial, political. No man, no matter how efficient, can hope for a position of authority on account of being the man best qualified for the job; he simply must have other backing. In too many cases, this backing was the support and loyalty of the Generalissimo for his old army comrades which kept them in positions of high responsibility regardless of their qualifications. A direct result of this practice is the unsound strategy and faulty tactics so obviously displayed in the fight against the Communists.

Cooperation among and coordination of effort between the Armed Forces leaves much to be desired. The Ground Forces, being the old and dominant arm, is the source from which the large majority of top military positions are filled. These officers, mostly old and loyal contemporaries of the Generalissimo, have little or no knowledge of the newer arms: the Air Force and the Navy. The Chinese Air Force, consisting of 8⅓ groups, is far in excess of what a country bereft of gold credits can support. Although it has among its personnel over five thousand United States trained pilots, it accomplished little, other than air-lifting troops and operating its transports for personal gains. There was an ever present reluctance to take a chance on losing equipment or personnel, which was clearly reflected in their constant refusal to operate at other than high altitudes. There was an ingrained resentment in the Chinese Air Force against killing Chinese Communists who had no air support. All of these factors are important and unfortunate because the Chinese Air Force, unopposed, could have rendered invaluable support in ground operations had its capabilities been properly employed. From a military viewpoint, the case of the Navy is not so important since its employment, right or wrong, could have had little effect on the final outcome; all operations were land based. From an economic viewpoint, the Navy could have been of inestimable value in suppressing smugglers in Hong Kong-Canton waters had it been willing to suppress and not participate. It was completely relieved of this mission in March 1948, and reputedly millions of dollars in customs revenue continue to be lost to the Government.

It might be expected that the Communists, being Chinese themselves, would also suffer from these faulty Nationalist traits and characteristics, and to a certain extent they do, but they have wisely subordinated them and made their ideology of Communism almost a fetish. By means of total mobilization in the areas they control, propaganda, and the use of political commissars within their armed forces, they maintain loyalty to the established order. Their leaders are men of proven ability who invariably out-general the Nationalist commanders. The morale and fighting spirit of the troops is very high because they are winning.[3]

III. AMERICAN ADVISORY GROUPS IN CHINA

LEGISLATION AND AGREEMENTS

As of V–J Day American forces in China numbered approximately 60,000 men. Though redeployment to the United States was commenced soon thereafter, Headquarters, United States Forces China Theater, and its component units continued to provide assistance to the Chinese Government, planning and implementing the redeploy-

---

[3] This concludes the quoted portion of General Barr's report.

ment of the Chinese Nationalist Army, supervising the turnover to the Chinese of military supplies, and conducting and assisting in the repatriation of Japanese forces. Simultaneously the Marines in North China were repatriating Japanese and maintaining control for the Government of the lines of communication in that vital area, a service of great military significance in view of the fact that all available Chinese and American facilities were being strained to enable the Chinese to occupy other key areas and in view of the logistical difficulties which would have faced the Chinese if they had occupied this area at an early date and depended for supplies on Central China, to which no railroad connections had been opened.

Concurrent with this assistance plans were prepared for the formation of military advisory groups which had been requested by the National Government. Annex 170 sets forth a memorandum of conversation between President Truman and Dr. T. V. Soong on September 14, 1945, in which the question of American military assistance to China was discussed. It was the original intention of the United States in 1945 that military assistance would be designed to assist in the reorganization and consolidation of the various Chinese armies under the terms of general principles which had already been agreed to by the National Government and the Chinese Communists. This whole concept was implicit in the mission of General Marshall. It was the hope at that time that civil strife could be avoided and, therefore, no American military assistance could, as President Truman stated, be diverted to fratricidal warfare or to support undemocratic administration.

With this in view the Nanking Headquarters Command was activated on February 20, 1946. On February 25, 1946, the President issued a directive to the Secretaries of State, War, and the Navy as follows:

"The Secretaries of War and the Navy are authorized and directed to establish jointly a U. S. Military Advisory Group to China. The strength of the Advisory Group shall not exceed one thousand officers and men except as authorized by me in the light of possible future political and military developments.

"The Secretary of State will conduct the necessary negotiations with the Chinese Government.

"The object of this Advisory Group will be to assist and advise the Chinese Government in the development of modern armed forces for the fulfillment of those obligations which may devolve upon China under her international agreements, including the United Nations Organization, for the establishment of adequate control over liberated areas in China, including Manchuria, and Formosa, and for the maintenance of internal peace and security."

Pursuant to the receipt of this directive the military services moved to formalize the status of the advisory groups as such and to assign them appropriate missions. There were initially two groups—an Army Advisory Group which included army, air and supply advisers, and a Naval Advisory Group. Legislation was likewise requested in order to provide authorization for their operation after the expiration of the President's wartime powers under which they were initially being established. A bill to provide military advice and assistance to the Republic of China was introduced in the Senate on June 13, 1946, as S. 2337 of the 79th Congress, 2d session. A similar bill was introduced into the House on June 14, 1946, as H.R. 6795. The Committee on Foreign Affairs of the House reported favorably on H.R. 6795, but no other action was taken in the 79th Congress on these bills, both bills dying with the termination of the 2d session of the 79th Congress. A Military and Naval Missions Bill (H.R. 2313 and S. 759, 80th Congress) providing for the detail of such missions to foreign countries was introduced in the succeeding Congress, passing the House but not the Senate, where it was referred to the Senate Armed Services Committee. The Navy obtained legislative authorization for the establishment of a Naval Advisory Group through Public Law 512 of the 79th Congress, which authorized the transfer of 271 ships and craft to China and the detailing of 300 navy personnel to assist the Chinese in naval matters. Pending the procurement of legislative authorization for the other components of the advisory group and pending decision on the advisability of establishing joint or separate groups, it was determined not to negotiate a formal agreement with the Chinese Government. Informal discussions, however, resulted in a draft agreement which governed Sino-American relations in this regard during the existence of the groups. On September 17, 1948, advisory personnel in China were charged with the establishment of a joint advisory group, known as JUSMAG–China, consisting of Army, Navy, and Air units, together with a Combined Services Group and a Joint Advisory Staff. JUSMAG was formally activated on November 1, 1948; because of the deteriorating military situation its removal from China was ordered prior to the end of the year.

THE JOINT ADVISORY STAFF

In order to coordinate the activities of the separate components of JUSMAG in their dealings with various agencies of the Chinese Government, the Joint Advisory Staff was established. This group was charged with the responsibility of reviewing advisory papers being transmitted to the Chinese Minister of Defense, and of providing advice to appropriate officers of the Ministry of Defense and of the Supreme Staff. In view of the conflicting lines of authority which had existed under the duplicating divisions of the old National War Council, the Chinese Minister of National Defense faced a difficult problem in establishing clearly defined operating procedures. Among the projects embarked on by the Joint Advisory Staff were the forwarding of advice on the operations and functions of the Supreme Staff, and on the various personnel, intelligence, training and supply activites which it supervised in its overall direction of all the armed forces of China.

THE NAVAL ADVISORY DIVISION

The Navy Advisory Group, and its successor, the Naval Advisory Division of JUSMAG, were primarily concerned with assisting the Chinese Government in naval matters, training Chinese crews to man the ships transferred under Public Law 512 (131 such ships were eventually transferred) and rendering the Chinese technical advice on the operation and maintenance of these vessels. The activities of the group were designed to place the Chinese Government in a better position to protect and improve the safety of navigation in its waters and to make it possible for the Chinese to assume naval responsibility in that area, particularly with regard to the repatriation of Japanese and the movement of Chinese armies. To accomplish these objectives a Naval Advisory Staff was established at Nanking and a joint advisory organization was initiated through which advice was forwarded to the Chinese Ministry of National Defense. The senior member of this group advised the ranking officers of the Chinese Government on purely naval matters and similar staff advisory relationships existed on all levels of the organization. A training group was established at Tsingtao to form and train Chinese crews which were to operate the ships transferred to the Chinese Navy. This unit provided not only afloat training of crews but also conducted shore-based schools. It assisted the operating units of the Chinese Navy in maintenance, repair, and spare parts procurement and in every way had an immediate and direct influence on the indoctrination and training of the Chinese Navy. Other units of this group were established at Shanghai to assist in the activities being carried on at the Kiangwan Dockyard, and at Canton to assist in anti-piracy and anti-smuggling operations. A final report prepared by Naval Advisory Division personnel listed among the accomplishments of the Naval Advisory Mission the following, to name only the most significant:

The initial rehabilitation of the Chinese naval force and the introduction of modern naval thought into the various levels of the Navy with a resultant reorganization of Chinese Naval Headquarters; introduction of an elemental operating system, an operating corps, and an officer training program for this corps; establishment of a modern naval medical service; assistance in the organization of systematic personnel procedures; establishment of a modern naval training center, and the ultimate training in this center of over 300 Chinese officers and 3,000 Chinese enlisted men.

Since the Chinese Navy was not opposed by a Chinese Communist Navy it was never combat tested, though the assistance provided by the Naval Advisory Group enabled the Chinese Navy to reach operating standards it would not otherwise have achieved. The Chinese Navy did not satisfactorily perform what could have been a major service, the complete interdiction of junk traffic by which Communist forces in Shantung received supplies and reinforcements, nor did it perform satisfactory service in those operations in the Gulf of Chili when by bombardment it could have rendered notable assistance to ground forces engaging the Communists in the Hulutao area.

During the closing months of 1948 and the early months of 1949 there was evidence that the morale of Chinese naval personnel was so low and the will to fight so lacking that Chinese Naval Headquarters had hesitated to permit naval vessels freedom of operations lest they desert to the Communists.

THE AIR ADVISORY DIVISION

The Air Division of the Army Advisory Group, forerunner of the Air Advisory Division of Jusmag, was established to assist in the modernization of the Chinese Air Force and to provide the Chinese technical advice on the maintenance and operation of such an air force. During the war United States and Chinese air force personnel had been integrated into a Chinese-American Composite Wing of the 14th Air Force, and in combat operations conducted by this unit the Chinese performed creditably. Chinese personnel to man this unit and the post war Chinese Air Force were for the most part American-trained under a program through which, according to the Department of the Air Force, prior to and succeeding V–J Day over 5,000 Chinese received intensive instruction under a United States supervised training program.

During the war transfers of airplanes and other air matériel were initiated in order to provide the Chinese Government with an air force commensurate with its needs. After V–J Day transfers of planes and equipment were continued under a program designed to provide the Chinese with an 8⅓ group air force, until a total of 936 planes had been made available, the bulk of these after V–J Day. Because of the close wartime cooperation between American and Chinese air force personnel the establishment of an air force unit in the Advisory Group represented a continuation of certain wartime assistance. After the inactivation of the Chinese-American Composite Wing, United States Army Air Corps cadres were placed with 13 Chinese Air Force units and these advisory units were already in operation, when on February 26, 1946 establishment of a Military Advisory Group was authorized by the President.

Though the ultimate objective of the Air Division was to assist in the development of a modern air force, much of its early activities consisted of giving the Chinese Air Force advice on receiving, storing, and maintaining the vast amounts of United States surplus air equipment made available to it. Simultaneously, steps were taken to lay the groundwork for an air force organization fitted to Chinese needs and capabilities. Work in this regard continued throughout the existence of the Air Division and as experience dictated, changes in organization were recommended.

In August 1946, Air Division teams advising Chinese fighter groups actively engaged in combating the Communists were withdrawn on the order of General Marshall to prevent further involvement in the Chinese civil conflict. Advice and guidance continued, however, on problems such as planning an adequate training system for the Chinese Air Force, establishing an adequate personnel management system, instituting coordinated supply procedures, developing suitable tables of organization and equipment for the Chinese Air Force, and developing proper operational procedures.

Air Division teams were established at certain Chinese Air Force bases such as Peiping, Chengtu and Hankow, and personnel were assigned to provide appropriate advice to units such as the Chinese Flying School at Hangchow and the Air Technical Service Command at Shanghai.

Despite the advisory assistance provided, the Chinese Air Force never attained satisfactory operating standards. Bombing operations were usually conducted from such an altitude that accurate bombing of military targets was impossible; strafing of enemy troops was carried on at altitudes of from 1,500 to 2,000 feet; supply drops to beleaguered garrisons and units were made from such altitudes that considerable quantities of the supplies dropped fell into the hands of the beseiging Communists.

In the final report prepared by the Air Advisory Division the following comments were made:

"Without a doubt China's ravaged economy cannot support an establishment based on 8⅓ tactical groups even if the present exorbitant personnel overhead were pared in half. Without some economic recovery it cannot afford an air force of any size. Their air plans appear to take no cognizance of national economy nor do they indicate a sense of values with respect to the internal economy of the air force. A big organization for face-building purposes is uppermost in their thinking. Aid through low cost support or outright grants encourages this prodigality.

"The CAF has questionable value as a military ally mainly because of their inability to conduct their administrative and logistical functions satisfactorily. It will take years of basic and specialized education to correct this deficiency. Direct supervision by U. S. personnel down to the departmental level in squadrons would be necessary to produce acceptable results. Their fighting qualities in the civil war have been of an extremely low order. However, during the Japanese War when they had a cause in which they believed, they performed creditably while following American flight leaders.

"An advisory program is inextricably tied to an aid program. Advisors invariably find that aid assists them to accomplish their mission. Advisory groups are used by the recipient nations, purposely or not, as a powerful means of fostering increases or in obtaining favorable action on aid requests. If the recipient requests advice merely to get aid, the advisory relationship is not sound and should not be undertaken. It is believed that China presently falls in this category.

"It is not believed that an objective of 'a China that is militarily strong' can be attained in the foreseeable future even if it is desirable. Therefore an advisory program based on this objective as a consideration is not considered feasible."

THE COMBINED SERVICE FORCES ADVISORY DIVISION

The Combined Services Division of the Army Advisory Group, later reorganized under JUSMAG as the Combined Service Forces Advisory Division, was established to advise and assist the Combined Service Forces of the Republic of China in the development of effective supply techniques and procedures.

During the closing year of the war against the Japanese, through the efforts of Headquarters, United States Forces China Theater, United States and Chinese forces in China cooperated closely in the development of an efficient supply system under the direction of a combined Chinese-American staff. Chinese commanders had traditionally been hesitant to commit their forces and equipment to battle since men and rifles lost in combat were usually not replaced, and the commander would find himself without a unit commensurate with his rank. Because of this particular fact, the development of supply and replacement procedures was necessary in order to instill in commanders a willingness to risk their units in combat. In developing such a supply system during the war, American personnel participated with Chinese in all phases of supply work. The establishment after V–J Day of a Combined Services Division represented, therefore, a continuation of wartime assistance. This group, among other contributions, rendered the following assistance:

Provision of advice on the development of an organizational pattern for a Chinese supply system;

Provision of advice and assistance on the organization and conduct of training courses for all service schools;

Provision of advice and assistance in the inventory, requisitioning, withdrawal, and disposition of United States surplus equipment sold to China and being handled by the Board of Supply of the Executive Yuan;

Provision of advice and guidance for such vital activities as the medical, finance, ordnance, signal, transportation, and engineering services.

THE GROUND FORCES ADVISORY DIVISION

The most important of the various components of JUSMAG and its predecessor organizations was the Ground Forces Advisory Division, successor to the Army Advisory Group which was established to provide an organization to advise and assist the Chinese Ground Forces. In this connection a brief review of the activities along these lines being conducted under the direction of Headquarters, United States Forces China Theater, as of V–J Day is pertinent. In order to develop a Chinese Army capable of effective operations against the Japanese, General Stilwell had embarked on a program initially conceived on a more limited scale by the Magruder Mission, to train and equip 39 ground-force divisions. Under his direction five such divisions were trained and equipped in Burma, subsequently performing creditably in combat, and an organization was established in China to carry on similar activities there, though little had been accomplished in the latter area because of the limited military supplies being flown over the hump. Under General Wedemeyer the 39-division program was carried forward. The additional number of personnel and the added tonnage of supplies arriving in China made possible its rapid implementation. Another and by far the most significant factor in its successful development was the close cooperation which existed under the direction of Headquarters, United States Forces China Theater, between Chinese and American personnel on all levels. This mutual cooperation was of significance since the prime problem facing

United States forces in China under the command of General Wedemeyer was the combination of Chinese manpower and resources with American equipment and training to develop military forces capable of meeting the Japanese in combat.

In order to assist in the development of integrated plans between the Chinese and American units then operating in China, joint Chinese-American staff meetings were held at Chungking and at other appropriate centers, though command of the forces of each country remained solely with the officers of that country. Schools were established to prepare Chinese military personnel for all phases of work with ground forces operations. United States officers were assigned to ground units to give operational advice on all levels and under all conditions, including active combat. This program to train and equip Chinese divisions progressed so satisfactorily that by mid-August 1945 Chinese forces were concentrated in South China for a major offensive operation—which was overtaken by V–J Day prior to its initiation. Thus, as of V–J Day, there existed effective United States–Chinese cooperation on all phases of ground force activity.

Following V–J Day United States forces in China continued certain assistance to the Chinese Government, particularly in the redeployment of Chinese armies, the repatriation of the Japanese, and in effecting arrangements for the transfer of surplus military material. The Ground Forces Section, Nanking Headquarters Command, was the agency originally established to continue providing advice and assistance after the inactivation of major United States headquarters. This section, organized in April of 1946, was succeeded by the Army Advisory Group. Initially the advice and assistance which it could render were limited to the organization and functioning of Chinese Ground Forces Headquarters, and to the establishment and operation of schools. The Division was not authorized to make recommendations concerning the organization or equipment of ground force units, nor to carry on advisory activities directly involved in the training of the Chinese units. These functions were the responsibility of the Peiping Executive Headquarters in connection with its efforts to reduce the size of the Nationalist and Communist armies under the terms of the Tripartite Agreement. Following the inactivation of the Peiping Executive Headquarters, the restriction on advice concerning the organization and equipment of Government units was lifted. The prohibition against advisory activities directly concerned with the training of Chinese Government units and the operation of training centers was relaxed later to permit Army Advisory participation in various Chinese Ground Forces training centers. The prohibition against participation in training activities north of the

Yangtze River (except for the Cavalry School at Tienshui and the Army School at Hsuchow) was never relaxed. Consideration will be given later to the policy determination underlying the decisions not to relax certain of the provisions governing advisory group activities.

In a report prepared by the Ground Forces Advisory Division of JUSMAG immediately prior to its inactivation, the following analysis of projects accomplished and unfulfilled was presented:

"The tangible results of the advice and assistance given to the Chinese Ground Forces during this period are in general terms:

"a. The development of the Ground Forces Headquarters into an organization capable of operating in a barely satisfactory manner.

"b. The establishment of the Ground Forces School system and the operation of the Infantry and Artillery Schools and the Ground Staff College in a fairly efficient manner.

"c. The establishment of the system of Training Centers.

"d. Training of the 204th and 205th Divisions at Taiwan.

"e. A decided improvement in the operation of the Army Military Academy at Chengtu, and its branch Officer Training Classes at Taiwan and Hankow, and in the operation of the Cadre Schools at Taiwan, Nanking, and Canton.

"The principal accomplishment of the Ground Forces Advisory Division during this period was the indoctrination of thousands of Chinese officers with United States principles of organization, with United States staff methods and procedures, and with United States methods of instruction. The results of this indoctrination together with the benefits which may result from the close association of many Chinese officers with United States Army officers cannot be evaluated at this time. Those results would have become increasingly apparent during the next two or three years.

"The Ground Forces Advisory Division did not accomplish those things which it was hoped would be accomplished by the end of 1948. The progress of the Chinese Ground Forces as a whole has not been satisfactory. The following have adversely affected the desired progress of the Chinese Ground Forces to a degree far greater than was expected in the summer of 1946.

"a. The requirements for the prosecution of the civil war.

"b. The continued deterioration of Chinese currency in terms of its purchasing power.

"c. The lack of funds and the consequent lack of equipment, supplies, housing, etc.

"d. The lack of positive 'command pressure.'

"e. The passive and, at times, active resistance to change when that change would reduce the power or prestige of the individual affected.

"f. The fact that each decision was not based primarily on military considerations alone, but was influenced to a considerable degree by 'political' and 'personality' considerations and the desires (at times, almost the demands) of subordinate commanders.

"g. Incompetence of individuals occupying key positions and, until early 1948, the physical absence from Ground Forces Headquarters of the Chief, Chinese Ground Forces.

"h. The failure of commanders of all echelons to delegate authority and responsibility to their staffs and subordinate commanders."

The activities of the Group most directly concerned with assisting the Chinese Government in its civil strife were those connected with advisory group participation in Chinese training centers. In July 1947 the Chinese Ministry of National Defense issued a directive establishing a ground force training center in Taiwan and in December 1947 it ordered additional centers established. In October 1947 the Department of State informed the War Department that it agreed to the participation of the Army Advisory Group in the training activities of the Taiwan divisional training center.

The memorandum to the War Department setting forth the position of the Department of State read as follows:

"The Department of State is prepared to agree to participation by the AAG in the training center at Takao provided that (1) AAG will not participate in any other similar training center without prior concurrence of the Department; (2) the assistance in the form of materials supplied by the U.S. will be limited to training aids; (3) every effort will be made to minimize publicity to the effect that this action constitutes direct U. S. participation in the civil war; (4) arrangements be made that U. S. officers concerned shall be briefed by the Embassy on the political situation in Formosa to the end that they will so conduct themselves as to avoid AAG and the training center from being drawn into the controversy which has developed between the island inhabitants and the authorities of the Central Government."

The 205th Chinese Division was selected as the first unit to be trained in this center, but it was not until the middle of November that arrangements for this had been completed by the Chinese. The first group of American advisers arrived in Taiwan for permanent duty in December 1947. In March 1948 authorization was granted for advisory group participation in the training activities of the Nanking Training Center, and in July further authorization was granted for participation in the training work of Chinese Army Centers at Canton, Hankow, and Chengtu. Limited participation in the Hsuchow Center was likewise authorized.

The final report of the Ground Forces Advisory Division contained an evaluation of the work of these training centers, the substance of which is given in the following paragraphs:

Of these Chinese training centers, only the one at Taiwan produced satisfactory results. In this center two divisions, the 204th and 205th, were highly trained according to Chinese standards, and two additional ones, the 201st and 206th, received training which was average by Chinese standards. At Canton the 154th division likewise received training judged average by Chinese standards, but unsatisfactory by American standards. These were the only significant results produced, although the center at Nanking made a valuable contribution in the training of cadres for certain of the other training centers. Operations were handicapped by a lack of funds and technical equipment, the failure to relieve units south of the Yangtze to participate in training activities, and the failure of the Chinese to attempt to implement effectively this program despite the Generalissimo's directive that a modern training and replacement system would be operated. The Nanking center, primarily designed to train individual replacements for divisions which could not be relieved from front line duty to receive training, was likewise handicapped by the indifference of the Chinese to this need and their unwillingness to implement the Generalissimo's directive initiating such a training program. Though over 17,000 replacements were passed through the center, none received any significant degree of training owing to the unwillingness of the Chinese to leave them in the center for any appreciable period. The failure of the military to carry out the Generalissimo's directive in this instance was typical of many similar situations where orders issued by senior Chinese officers after consultation with advisory group personnel were successfully evaded by subordinate officers.

Though the center at Hankow could have accomplished its mission of training individual replacements, it suffered from the same difficulty as the one at Nanking. The Canton training center, primarily designed to train cadres, was ordered established in December 1947. In the next two to three months Chinese staff members were assigned, but prior to the end of May little else was accomplished, when officers from the advisory group were permitted to inspect the area, which proved completely unsuited for the projected activities. The center was moved to Canton in June and on July 1 American advisers departed to assume duties there. A preliminary cadre training course initiated in early August of 1948 was highly successful due to the fact that 19 American trained instructors were available. However, this school did not start regular operations until the first of November because the three divisions concerned did not furnish their cadres until that time, nor were the cadres ever made available simultaneously for full and effective training.

The unsatisfactory results which attended the efforts of United States advisory personnel to develop in the Chinese Army effective training and replacement procedures may be attributed in part to the Chinese attitude toward replacements and their training. Recruitment was at all times disorganized. Separate commanders were frequently authorized to go into an area to procure "recruits," generally conscripts or men impressed into duty. Provincial governors who had their own replacement problems gave little heed to Government levies. Conscripts enroute to army centers would frequently be impressed by local commanders. Those who did arrive at army centers were frequently assigned immediately to units without further training. Attempts to modernize this system met with widespread opposition, and it was at one time reported that field commanders had demanded that no drastic change be made in the Chinese system. At various times in many of the Ground Forces Advisory Division projects it became apparent that the lack of positive command pressure made successful operations difficult, if not impossible. In view of the resistance to change to more efficient procedures which would have reduced the prestige of individuals affected, this lack of command pressure doomed many projects to incompletion. Operations were influenced therefore to a large degree not by military necessity but by political and personal factors, and the desires of the individuals concerned rather than the basic military needs of the country.

This inability to prod the Government into effective action where personal interests were involved was accentuated by the incompetence of the individuals occupying high positions in the military chain of command. Advisory activities were further complicated and hindered by the fact that the Chief of the Ground Forces, General Ku Chutung, was not present at Ground Forces Headquarters but remained in command of a field unit. No decision could be made by his senior officers without prior reference of the question to him.

Similar unsatisfactory results met the advisory group's efforts in May 1948 to encourage the Chinese in the establishment south of the Yangzte of a 38-division strategic reserve to be composed of divisions not involved in combat, which were to be trained to high standards for use against future eventualities. Lack of adequate planning by appropriate Chinese headquarters for personnel and transportation, and failure to develop the training centers previously described hindered any effective action on this plan. When military conditions became critical in October 1948 the Government, recognizing the need for such a strategic reserve force, requested further assistance from the advisory group, but attempts to initiate action on this program were overtaken by the rapidly developing military situation. In the final advisory group report it was noted that because of the Chinese characteristics of not agreeing to decentralized authority, unwillingness to place responsibility on command levels, and a tendency to compartmentalize all work, a large number of advisers would be required to carry such a project forward. The conclusion set forth in this report was that effective advisory results in such a situation depended on advisory assistance and indirect control at least down to the regimental level.

COMPARISON OF AID TO CHINA WITH AID TO GREECE

As it became evident to all observers that the Communists were winning the war, despite American aid and assistance to the National Government in the form of the advisory mission and transfers of equipment and grants, the role of the advisory groups was reviewed. A frequently recurring suggestion was that it be increased in size, that considerable additional quantities of military equipment be made available for transfer to the Chinese through it, and that the directive governing its operations be relaxed, to permit more direct United States involvement in the training and operations of Chinese army. The most frequently raised suggestion was that China be put in the same category as Greece with respect to the receipt of military aid and advisory assistance.

In this connection a brief comparison of the commitments involved if this had been embarked upon is pertinent. Greece, a country of about 51,000 square miles, has a population of 7.4 million, approximately that of greater Shanghai and its environs. China is comprised of approximately 450 million people. In Greece, armed forces of between 150,000 to 200,000 men have been opposing guerrilla units containing approximately 20,000 effectives, holding no cities or centers of population and being restricted for the most part to mountain border areas. It is recognized, however, that the Greek guerrillas received supplies from the Communist countries to the north of Greece. The Chinese Nationalists by late 1947 had a superiority over the Communists of only about 2½ to 1, with 2½ to 3 million Government troops facing 1 to 1½ million Communists, who at that time controlled approximately one fourth of China's lands and people. To have supported the Government's military operations in China to the same comparative degree as those in Greece were supported would have required an advisory group of many thousands, unpredictably large amounts of equipment, and the involvement of United States advisers in the direction of modern large-scale war, and rather than representing a calculated risk it would have represented an incalculable risk. To have embarked on such a project this Government would have justly felt that there should have been more assurances of possible success than had been provided by the previous record of the Chinese Government in its military operations. There was no reason to think that the furnishing of additional military assistance would substantially alter the pattern of military developments in China unless a great number of Americans were involved, possibly in actual combat, and unless this Government were prepared to underwrite permanently the success of the Chinese Government's military operations. Nor was there any evidence that the means were in sight to enable the Chinese Government, even with extensive United States economic assistance, to delay more than temporarily the rapid deterioration of economic and political conditions. Further involvement of this nature would, however, have been most acceptable to the Chinese Government.

In this connection it should be noted that during consideration by the Congress of an aid program for China in 1948, the House in the enabling bill placed China in the same category as Greece with regard to the receipt of military aid. The Senate Foreign Relations Committee, however, rewrote the proposed bill, specifically wording the portion dealing with additional aid through grants in order to avoid having China placed in the same category as Greece with respect to military aid.

During debate in the Senate on March 29, 1948, regarding the China aid program, Arthur H. Vandenberg, Chairman of the Committee on Foreign Relations of the Senate, made the following statements:

"The Committee on Foreign Relations wishes to make it unmistakably clear, in this, as in all other relief bills, that there is no implication that American aid involves any continuity of obligation beyond specific, current commitments which Congress may see fit to make. . . . We do not—we cannot—underwrite the future. . . . It is a duty to underscore this reservation in the case of China because we find here many imponderables as a result of the military, economic and social pressures which have understandably undermined her stabilities, and prevented or postponed the internal reforms which even her surest friends readily concede to be not only desirable but essential for the Chinese people and for the Nationalist Government. . . . We cannot deal with the Chinese economy on an over-all basis, as we have done in the European recovery program. China is too big. The problem is too complicated. . . . As in the case of Greece and Turkey, your Committee recognizes that military aid is necessary in order to make economic aid effective. It proposes to make military supplies available, at China's option. For this or any other purpose, at China's option, a grant of $100,000,000 is included in the bill.   . . .   Your Committee believes, as a matter of elementary prudence, that this process must be completely clear of any implication that we are underwriting the military campaign of the Nationalist Government.   No matter what our heart's desire might be, any such implication would be impossible over so vast an area.   Therefore, for the sake of clarity, we prefer to leave the initiative, in respect to these particular funds, in the hands of the Nationalist Government.   . . .   Under another law, the United States will continue to furnish military advisers to the Government of China at her request.   . . .   Their capacity is advisory only.   Nothing in the pending bill alters these limitations in any aspect.   . . .   We have undertaken to write this new provision into the law in a fashion which **at least commits us to make military cooperation on our own responsibility."**

During the same debate Senator Connally said:

"There is an item of $100,000,000 which is not earmarked.   . . . It is in the nature of an outright grant to China for her use, under her own responsibility for whatever great and critical need may arise. There is not a word in the bill regarding military supplies or military aid.   It is, of course, entirely probable that the $100,000,000 grant may, if the exigency should arise, be utilized by the Central Government of China for the purchase of munitions, equipment and arms. . . .   This measure is the best plan or device we could bring about in the Committee to extend aid to China, without making hard and fast commitments which we did not feel it was wise to make."

The Greek-Turkish proviso was deleted by the Congress prior to the passage of the enabling bill.   Following passage of the enabling legislation the House of Representatives inserted into the appropriation bill passed by it on June 4, 1948, the proviso that aid being extended to China be placed in the same particular category as that being extended to Greece and Turkey.   On June 15, 1948, the Senate approved certain amendments to the foreign-aid appropriation bill, 1949, one of which removed the Greek-Turkish proviso contained in the House bill.   On June 19, 1948 the foreign-aid appropriation bill was sent to conference.   The conference report shows that the total amount of aid to China was reduced from $463 million to $400 million, the Greek-Turkish proviso was removed, and the $125 million grants were thus to be made available to China in accordance with section 404 (b) of the China Aid Act of 1948.   The Foreign Aid Appropriation Act, 1949, was then passed by the Congress on the same day.[4]

---

[4] For an explanation of these various figures, see chapter VIII.

IV. MILITARY MATÉRIEL AND SERVICES PROVIDED THE CHINESE GOVERNMENT SINCE V-J DAY[ª]

SUMMARY

Any assessment of military aid provided to the Chinese Government by the United States since V-J Day must take into account the fact that no dollar value can be put on three of the most vital forms of aid—that rendered by Headquarters, United States Forces China Theater, in planning the redeployment of the Chinese Army and the repatriation of the Japanese, aid rendered by the Marines in North China in occupying key areas and maintaining control for the Government of essential lines of communication, and aid provided by the advisory groups.

Apart from these forms of aid, the American Government since V-J Day has authorized military aid for the Chinese Government in the form of grants and credits totaling approximately 1 billion dollars. During this same period an additional 1 billion dollars of economic aid has been authorized. It was, of course, inevitable that economic assistance had indirect military value.

There is set forth in annex 172 a detailed account with accompanying tables of the various categories of this American aid. Among the most important of these were 781 million dollars of post-V-J Day lend-lease aid, including sufficient matériel to complete the remaining 50 percent of the wartime program designed to equip 39 Chinese divisions, 101 million dollars of surplus military equipment including over 300 aircraft and very large quantities of ammunition, and 125 million dollars under the China Aid Act of 1948, expended largely for military equipment during 1948 and 1949.

It is evident from a review of these transfers of military equipment that American aid to the Chinese Government since V-J Day in the form of matériel and services has been extensive. It has likewise been continuing except for that period starting during General Marshall's mediation efforts when there was a ban on the export of munitions from this country and its Pacific bases.

SECRETARY MARSHALL'S TESTIMONY ON THE 1946 EMBARGO

The prohibition on the export of munitions from the United States to China was placed at a time when the truce between the armies of the Chinese Government and the Chinese Communists was breaking down and hostilities were increasing on a wide scale. In this connection

---

[ª] See annex 171 for a study of American military matériel and services provided to the Chinese Government since V-J Day.

Secretary Marshall's testimony before the House Committee on Foreign Affairs on February 20, 1948, is of interest.   Certain portions of the testimony follow:

"Mr. Vorys.   As I understand it, we had an embargo for 10 months on shipment of arms to China and then the ammunition that we did authorize to be shipped, which they purchased, has not gotten to the troops yet.   Now, why is that?

"Secretary Marshall. Do you mean the original embargo and then the later developments?

"The embargo was in August, 1946, and the release was in May of 1947.

"Mr. Vorys. That is about 10 months.

"Secretary Marshall. Yes.

"Mr. Vorys. As I understand it, the so-called generalissimo ammunition which was authorized to be shipped has not gotten to the troops yet.   I am informed that part of it had not left the United States. Now, why is that?   They cannot fight without ammunition.

"Secretary Marshall. That is quite evident.

"This particular matter is a shipping proposition.   Mr. Butterworth can give you some of the details but I can state some of the things offhand.[5]

"In the first place, the embargo was placed in August, I think, of 1946, by me, because at that time the situation was threatening to break down entirely.   The fighting in north China had been held pretty largely in abeyance since the agreements reached on January 10, 1946, except in Manchuria, where a new focus of fighting had developed.

"In the endeavor to mediate this, and prevent its spreading all over North China, we were put in the position of acting in a mediatory position on the one hand and shipping in military supplies on the other. At that time the Chinese Government had sufficient munitions for their armies and there was no embarrassment to them.

---

[5] Details were given in the following letter of Feb. 24, 1948, from Secretary Marshall to Representative Charles A. Eaton:

"You will recall that in the course of the public hearings on February 20, 1948, before the Foreign Affairs Committee of the House of Representatives on the China aid bill Mr. Vorys queried whether the Chinese Government had received the so-called generalissimo (7.92) ammunition sold to the Chinese Government by the Foreign Liquidation Commissioner under a contract dated June 25, 1947.

"It has been ascertained from the Department of the Army that the Chinese Government shipped this ammunition from Seattle to China on July 14 and August 11, 1947.   The first shipment represented slightly more than one-third of the ammunition and the second shipment covered the balance.

"Would you please be so good as to apprise Mr. Vorys of this information and to incorporate it in the record of the hearings."

"There were incidents, such as the explosion of the dump in Shanghai, and more particularly the very heavy reported losses of munitions to the Communist forces by defeats suffered in the field by the Government forces. When the release date was given which was effected bv taking off any refusal to grant export licenses—

"Mr. VORYS (interposing). I may have used the word 'embargo' improperly.

"Secretary MARSHALL. It was in effect an embargo, on military supplies. There were amendments to that in relation to spare parts for airplanes, and items of that sort.

"Of course, there was a great deal that was coming in through the surplus property transactions, to the degree that we could reach a settlement with the Chinese authorities who were negotiating the surplus property agreements.

"Then we come to the period in May, when that export license embargo was removed. Since that time I think there was only one important commercial contract made by the Chinese Government."

The prohibition on the export of munitions from the United States or its Pacific bases to China became effective in the United States on July 29, 1946, and in the Pacific in mid-August 1946. On October 22, 1946, the ban was modified to permit the Chinese to purchase civilian end-use items under the 8⅓ Group Program for the Chinese Air Force and on October 31, 1946, the Far Eastern field office of the OFLC [6] was authorized to notify the Chinese Government that it was ready to negotiate the sale of such civilian end-use items. The Chinese informed the OFLC that they were interested in procuring these items only if eventual provision of items for this program was likewise assured, though civilian end-use items would have been valuable in the maintenance and operation of transport planes and airport installations. The Chinese concluded no contracts covering these items until over a year later on November 6, 1947.

In April and May 1947, prior to the lifting of the ban on the export of arms and ammunition, the United States Marines turned over (abandoned) to the Chinese Government forces in North China the considerable quantities of small arms and artillery ammunition mentioned in annex 171. These and similar transfers continued during the summer months until by early September approximately 6,500 tons of ammunition had been transferred at no charge to the Chinese.

On May 26, 1947, the Secretary of State directed that the prohibition on the issuance of export licenses covering the shipment of arms and ammunition be removed.

---

[6] Office of the Foreign Liquidation Commissioner.

There is set forth in annex 173 a description of the principal contracts for surplus military equipment and commercial contracts which the Chinese Government concluded during the year following the lifting of the embargo. As will be noted these contracts covered very considerable quantities of arms, ammunition and combat planes.

AMERICAN EQUIPMENT CAPTURED BY THE CHINESE COMMUNISTS

Much of the equipment furnished by the United States to China prior to and after V–J Day has fallen into the hands of the Communists—the greatest losses starting in mid-September 1948, though substantial losses had occurred before that time. In a report of early November 1948, the Embassy stated that in the battles of Tsinan, the Liaoaning Corridor, Changchun and Mukden, the Nationalists lost 33 divisions, over 320,000 men, including 8 divisions 85 percent United States equipped. Losses of equipment included approximately 100,000 American rifles and 130,000 rifles of other origin, together with large quantities of military matériel. It was indicated that there was virtually no destruction of equipment accomplished by the Nationalists prior to their defeats during the period under consideration.

In early December 1948 the Military Attaché at Nanking reported that "seventeen originally United States equipped divisions have been totally lost—Chinese Communist forces claims are that 70 per cent of United States equipped forces lost by November 2. After the fall of Manchuria CSF [Combined Service Forces of Chinese Nationalist Army] high ranking officer told an American officer 80 per cent of United States equipment had been lost by capture and attrition. It is believed the figure of 80 per cent loss of all United States equipment is a sound basis on which to determine amounts lost—of this amount at least 75 per cent exclusive of ammunition has been captured by the Communists." It is now estimated that in the 4½ months from the fall of Tsinan in September to the fall of Peiping at the end of January, the Government lost approximately a million men and 400,000 rifles. Losses since the end of January include those in the Nanking-Shanghai area in April and May. Losses of air force matériel, while not so serious, have occurred, and it is at present known that the Communists have acquired by defection a number of planes of American origin.

The most significant loss of naval equipment was that of the cruiser *Chungking*, transferred to the National Government by the British, though there have likewise been defections of minor naval units.

There is some question as to whether the Russians supplied the Communists with Russian equipment. It is certain, however, that large stocks of Japanese equipment were abandoned in Manchuria in such a way as to enable the Communists to gain possession of them. Charges have been made in the press that the Russians utilized Japanese equipment from Manchuria to manufacture Japanese-type equipment for the Communists. As indicated previously, of the Japanese stocks in China on V–J Day the Government seized by far the larger portion. Also bearing on the question of equipment is the relative capacity of arsenals operated by the Nationalists and the Communists. Until the Government's military collapse in the fall of 1948, the major arsenals in China and Manchuria were held by the Government—15 major arsenals and 5 subarsenals producing quantities of small arms and small arms ammunition adequate to sustain normal operations of the Chinese Army. The Government also had access to arms markets in foreign countries other than the United States and in the years following V–J Day purchased considerable quantities of military matériel through such sources.

ADEQUACY OF THE GOVERNMENT'S MILITARY SUPPLIES

Prior to the defeats suffered late in 1948, the Government enjoyed a marked superiority in equipment over the Communists in all types of equipment. This fact confirms the statements of military observers, including General Barr, that the defeats suffered by the Chinese Nationalist armies were not attributable to a lack of equipment.[7]

General Barr on November 16 reported to the Department of the Army as follows:

"I am convinced that the military situation has deteriorated to the point where only the active participation of United States troops could effect a remedy. It has been obvious to me for some time that nothing short of a United States organization with the authority and facilities available to you on V–J day including a United States fed and operated supply pipeline could remedy the situation. Military matériel and economic aid in my opinion is less important to the salvation of China than other factors. No battle has been lost since my arrival due to lack of ammunition or equipment. Their military debacles in my opinion can all be attributed to the world's worst leadership and many other morale destroying factors that lead to a complete loss of will to fight. The complete ineptness of high military leaders and the widespread corruption and dishonesty throughout the Armed Forces, could, in some measure, have been controlled and directed had the above authority and facilities been available. Chinese leaders completely lack the moral courage to issue and enforce an unpopular decision. . . .

"I do not believe that the United States should advise or assist in any way such a [coalition] government, with its Communist domi-

---

[7] See annex 174.

nated Armed Forces, and recommend, that in this event, JUSMAG be withdrawn in accordance with plans outlined . . . [on] 13 November. . . .

"The Generalissimo has lost much of his political and popular support. It is unknown to what extent the nation would support his attempt to continue the present government in a new move. It is believed that such a move will only delay the end of the war and that the Communist forces will eventually overwhelm the government wherever it locates itself. This will occur before the Government, even with United States assistance, can train, equip, and put into the field sufficient forces to stem the tide. For this reason unless all-out United States military assistance, including employment of United States Forces, which I certainly do not recommend, is given the government in its new location, I recommend that JUSMAG be withdrawn in accordance with present plans."

In the final report of JUSMAG the portion dealing with the 125 million dollar grants contains this statement: "In general troops in combat have had adequate supplies of weapons and ammunition, and their reverses are attributable to other causes than lack of equipment."

CHAPTER VIII

The Program of American Economic Aid 1947–1949

The economic and financial assistance given to China by the United States during World War II, beginning with the lend-lease assistance of 1941 has been outlined in chapter I. The problem of additional assistance has been noted in other intervening chapters, especially in chapter VI. The aid in money and supplies given in support of the military efforts of the Chinese Government has been described in chapter VII. This chapter continues the account of economic and financial assistance rendered during 1947, 1948, and the first months of 1949. Before this assistance is described, however, it will be helpful to present a brief survey of the economic situation in China in 1947.

I. THE ECONOMIC SITUATION IN 1947

INTERNAL ECONOMIC FACTORS

Fundamental in the situation which caused the United States Government to press for comprehensive reforms was the increasingly serious economic situation during the first half of 1947. Mention has previously been made of the accelerating pace of inflation which was occasioned primarily by the financing of large Government budgetary deficits with new currency notes. The domestic price level in China had risen steadily throughout the war with Japan. This process had continued without any real check through 1946. Indeed, the rate of price increases had far outstripped the rate at which new currency was being issued, a signal that public confidence in the monetary unit had fallen significantly.

This continuing depreciation in the value of the Chinese currency was of course a matter of concern to the responsible officials of the National Government. Through 1946 and into 1947, the Government sought to maintain control of the inflationary process by open market sales of gold from official reserves. This provided opportunities, of which advantage reputedly was taken frequently, for collusion

360

between informed Government officials and speculators. While the Government's absorption of currency by means of gold sales undoubtedly allayed somewhat the rate of price increase, the policy had no effect upon the basic inflationary forces, while it dissipated the Government's foreign exchange assets without a compensating inflow of commodities. Although there was no sharp, panicky decline in the value of the currency through 1946 as in later years, prices rose steadily during 1946 at an average rate of about 12 percent per month. The absence of explosive price rises was due, in large part, to the great influx of imported consumer goods (including UNRRA stocks) in the immediate post-war period.

In January 1947 the Shanghai price level rose at a rate well above the 1946 average and in early February there occurred a violent upheaval in the Shanghai money market, marked most spectacularly by a rise in the price of the United States dollar in terms of C. N. C. (Chinese National Currency), from approximately 7,700 to 18,000. This "crisis" apparently was brought on by a wave of speculative activity in Shanghai rather than by the introduction of any important new factor. It came, however, as a severe shock to the National Government and was a factor contributing to the resignation in March of the Prime Minister, Dr. T. V. Soong. The Government's action, which came promptly, was drastic and initially effective. It outlawed speculative activity in gold and foreign exchange, abandoned the gold sales policy, and fixed a new official exchange rate of C. N. 12,000 to the United States dollar. The police measures against exchange and gold speculators were successful only temporarily, as was true in a later experiment of the same nature, but the immediate crisis was in fact surmounted.

CHINESE REQUESTS FOR AMERICAN AID

It was during this period of inflationary upsurge that the National Government renewed its requests for American aid. On February 4, Prime Minister Soong called on the Ambassador to express his concern and alarm over the deteriorating economic situation. On February 6, he gave to the Ambassador an *aide-mémoire* dealing directly with the need for American financial aid:

"I am not trying to be an alarmist. Last summer when people were freely predicting that economic collapse would come in a matter of weeks, I told General Marshall and yourself that it would be a question of many months before the eventuality had to be faced.

"Even as General Marshall was leaving, I expressed the hope that although the economic situation in China is particularly difficult to predict and while 1947 will be a year of terrific difficulties, it might be possible to hold through because there were then visible signs of improvement particularly in exports and in prospects of increased agricultural production. The rapid turn for the worse during the last few weeks as evidenced by the figures I have given you have radically altered the picture.

"We had all hoped that we would not have to approach the United States Government for financial assistance until the State Council and the Executive Yuan have been reorganized. The economic situation, however, has forced our hands.

"In fact, the economic situation has led the minor parties to sit on the fence, as they would naturally not like to be identified with a government that might collapse. Moreover, this situation has undoubtedly stimulated the Communists to greater efforts to weaken the government and refuse to be in a conciliatory mood.

"I am convinced that only one thing will steady the economic situation and improve the political outlook and that is some concrete form of American assistance and support. Perhaps the simplest, most helpful form of assistance would be an immediate credit of $150 million for cotton or cotton and wheat for a term of ten years as it would immediately favorably affect our balance of payments, secure the withdrawal of fapi [1] as the products are sold, assure the people of concrete American assistance. Politically it will encourage the wavering elements in the minor parties to join the government, and it would encourage the progressive members of the Government to press forward for a speedy reorganization. A smaller sum than the figure mentioned will not have the effect necessary in this emergency.

"On the other hand the nature of this credit goes as far as possible from any charge of direct aid for military use.

"In addition if someone like Blandford, in whom the Chinese Government had confidence and had given access to all economic information could visit the United States immediately before General Marshall leaves for Moscow, he would be able to explore what further American financial and advisory assistance might be given and under what circumstances this aid might come.

"I consider this particularly important as it would mean continuing aid with a definite program of action for both China and the United States."

At this point the immediately critical aspect of the Chinese economic problem was related closely to the state of domestic public opinion and public confidence within China. As has been noted, the underlying factors in the situation were almost without exception heavily unfavorable: a grossly unbalanced budget, a large deficit on current

---

[1] Fapi is a Chinese term for national currency.

balance of payments account, widespread disruption of inland transportation, and a low volume of internal industrial production and trade. On the other hand, China still had official reserves of gold and United States dollars in excess of 400 million dollars. Foreign exchange assets of private Chinese citizens probably were at least as large. Cessation of domestic gold sales by the Chinese Government meant that it would be possible to finance essential imports out of official reserves for a considerable period without depleting these reserves below the point of minimum working balances. The mobilization of privately held foreign exchange assets obviously presented difficult problems, but it could be hoped that some additional resources could be obtained through this means. The National Government still held important industrial assets taken over from the Japanese, notably a large portion of the cotton textile industry. If placed on the market for sale on terms inducive to private buyers, these assets might have provided an important counterinflationary source of revenue while beginnings were being made upon a reform of the hopelessly inadequate budgetary and tax-collecting mechanisms.

Moreover, substantial programs of external assistance to China were either at the peak of their implementation or represented significant potential contributions to the Chinese economy. The UNRRA program for China had got under way slowly. This had been due, in large measure, to the limited absorptive capacity of China, particularly the inadequacy of distribution facilities at Shanghai, and in part to the shipping strike on the west coast of the United States during the fall of 1946. As a result of its delayed implementation, it was clear that the large UNRRA China program would be carried on throughout 1947, considerably beyond the cessation of UNRRA in other areas of the world. Scheduled deliveries of UNRRA goods to China during 1947 amounted to a total value at Chinese ports of close to 300 million dollars.

The Lend-Lease "pipe line" credit from the United States of 51.7 million dollars, and the Canadian credit of 60 million dollars, had been only partially drawn upon by January 1947. Surplus property under the 1946 bulk sale agreement was just beginning to arrive in China. Of authorized Export-Import Bank credits for China, 54.6 million dollars had not been drawn. In April 1947 the United States Maritime Commission authorized the sale to China of surplus warbuilt merchant vessels on terms involving credits of 16.5 million dollars. All these programs made available a continuing flow of usable and salable resources into the Chinese economy.

Despite the substantial volume of external resources, both Chinese and foreign, available to China during this period, it was recognized by the Department of State that additional assistance to China might serve in some degree to strengthen public confidence in the National Goverment and to aid that Government in obtaining the support of minor political parties.

CONSIDERATION OF EXPORT-IMPORT BANK CREDITS

One possibility was the extension of credits by the Export-Import Bank, which still had under earmark for China the sum of 500 million dollars recommended by General Marshall in 1946. Earlier discussions of credits to China with officials of the Bank had met with a negative response, the Bank view being based mainly upon the fact that developments in China cast the gravest doubts upon the National Government's capacity to service additional loans. On March 4, 1947, Secretary Marshall directed that discussions between the Department and the Bank be resumed, specifically with reference to loans for reconstruction of the Canton-Hankow Railway, the development of a new harbor at Tangku, and for rehabilitation of certain coal mines. The Bank expressed its continuing skepticism regarding China's ability to repay additional loans and its doubts as to the appropriateness of the policy of using Export-Import Bank funds for reconstruction purposes. Nevertheless, it was stated that the Bank was ready to consider specific applications for credits.

At this time, however, the National Government was preparing the details of a request not for individual project credits but for a large-scale comprehensive program of financial assistance. This was made known to the American Embassy in Nanking on April 12, and on May 8 Ambassador Koo in a conversation with Secretary Marshall asked on instructions from his Government that a loan of 1 billion dollars be advanced to China. On May 13 Ambassador Koo sent to the Secretary of State an informal memorandum summarizing his earlier statement and adding that details of the plan for the proposed loan would be submitted "when it becomes clear that the request for the loan is acceptable in principle to the United States Government."

Acceptance "in principle" of the Chinese loan proposal was felt to be impracticable in the absence of information as to the details of the proposal. The Chinese Embassy was so informed on May 22. At the same time, the Department of State made it clear that a more detailed explanation of the Chinese proposal would receive careful examination.

Subsequently, on May 27, the Chinese Embassy submitted a further memorandum requesting that the 500 million dollars earmarked by the Export-Import Bank for China be advanced to finance the purchase of equipment and materials for a list of reconstruction projects, and that an additional 500 million dollars be sought from the Congress, to be available over a three-year period, for the purchase of commodities such as cotton, wheat, and petroleum, which, upon their sale in China, would provide the Chinese currency needed to meet internal costs of the reconstruction program.

China's need for foreign financial aid was sharply distinguished by the Department of State from that of certain European countries for which the extension of assistance was being actively considered by the United States Government. The virtually complete exhaustion of the foreign exchange resources of these European countries made it imperative that aid be given on an emergency basis if they were to be able to continue the import of vital necessities. China's foreign exchange reserves in mid-1947 were, by contrast, still substantial in relation to the minimum import deficit of that country. Thus, it was apparent that a request to Congress for the appropriation of funds for a large-scale program of aid to China could not be justified at that time as an emergency measure to enable continued importation of essential commodities. This was among the considerations reflected in Secretary Marshall's statement to Congress on May 20 that no further requests for foreign-aid funds were contemplated during the current session. The Chinese Embassy was informed of this statement with reference to its request for 500 million dollars to be authorized by Congress.

The question of renewal of the earmark of 500 million dollars by the Export-Import Bank was already under consideration, quite apart from the Chinese Embassy's request for extension of credits by the Bank in that amount. It was concluded by the Export-Import Bank that there was no realistic prospect that China could receive or effectively use 500 million dollars for reconstruction projects within the coming fiscal year, and that the earmark as such should not be continued beyond its expiration on June 30. The Department of State concurred in this decision, at the same time making clear its position that the lapse of the earmark should not preclude consideration of specific requests for credits to China. In connection with the lapse of the earmark, the Export-Import Bank on June 27 issued the following statement:

". . . the Bank is prepared to consider the extension of credits for specific projects in China notwithstanding the expiration on June 30 of the earmarking of $500,000,000 of the Bank's fund in April 1946 for possible further credit to Chinese Government agencies and private enterprises.

"The Bank has heretofore taken action to bring to an end its program of large emergency reconstruction credits and is reverting to its primary objective of financing and facilitating specific American exports and imports, including the financing of American equipment and technical services for productive enterprises abroad which will contribute generally to foreign trade expansion.

"In its consideration of any application, the Bank will observe the basic principles which guide its lending activities in all areas of the world.   In pursuance of the policy laid down by Congress, the Bank will make only loans which serve to promote the export and import trade of the United States, which do not compete with private capital but rather supplement and encourage it, which are for specific purposes, and which, in the judgment of the Board of Directors, offer reasonable assurance of repayment.   As a general rule, the Bank extends credit only to finance purchases of materials and equipment produced or manufactured in the United States and technical services of American firms and individuals, as distinguished from outlays for materials and labor in the borrowing country."

Prior to this announcement, the Department of State on June 17 informed the Chinese Embassy of the decision to permit expiration of the earmark.   It was noted, however, that the Department was prepared to support early and favorable consideration of loans to China for individual reconstruction projects.

Pursuant to the conversation with representatives of the Department of State on June 17, the Chinese Ambassador on June 27 submitted to the Export-Import Bank a list of credit applications totalling 268.3 million dollars for reconstruction projects.   These were not accompanied by an indication of priority nor were they in general supported by sufficient financial and economic analyses to provide an adequate basis for conclusive consideration by the Bank.   On July 31 the Ambassador requested an Export-Import Bank credit of 200 million dollars for purchases of raw cotton during 1947 and 1948.   This application was refused by the Bank on the ground that China's available cotton supplies were adequate for mill requirements until mid-1948.   The Bank, however, indicated its readiness to consider an application for a cotton credit in the spring of 1948.

At the time of the Bank's consideration of the proposed cotton credit, the Department of State representative on the Board of Directors, while concurring in the above action, recalled that when the earmark of 500 million dollars was permitted to lapse, a press release had been issued expressing the Bank's willingness to consider individual credits to China.   He went on to make the following general statement which he requested be incorporated in the records of the Bank:

"From the standpoint of U.S. foreign policy the Department of State urges early and favorable consideration of individual Export-

Import Bank credits to China in accordance with the statutes which guide the Bank's lending activities. The Department is concerned because of the urgency of the situation in China and regards it as highly desirable from the standpoint of U.S. foreign policy that there be some prompt manifestation of economic assistance to that country. The Department hopes that the Board of Directors of the Export-Import Bank will at an early date conclude their consideration of the individual loan applications which have been submitted by the Chinese Government or by private enterprise, with a view to decision as to the extent to which such projects can qualify for Export-Import Bank financing."

During the late winter and early spring, the Congress had been considering the proposed United States Foreign Relief Program, which was intended to meet the requirements of individual countries for emergency assistance in the post-UNRRA period. Although the case of China was not identical with that of certain European countries—in the sense that unless emergency aid were made available to certain European countries, essential imports could not have been obtained—the Department of State nevertheless believed that China's inclusion in the program was justified on the ground that it would be desirable to assist China to conserve its dwindling reserves of foreign exchange for purchases other than commodities needed for current consumption. Of the 322 million dollars appropriated by the Congress, therefore, a sum of 27.7 million dollars was earmarked for a China program and an agreement to govern the extension of this aid was concluded with the Chinese Government on October 27, 1947. This amount, plus an additional sum of 18 million dollars set aside for China in a supplemental appropriation in December, was expended for purchases of rice, wheat, wheat flour and medical supplies for distribution in China's coastal cities where, at the instigation of the Department of State, rationing systems were instituted.

PROPOSALS FOR A SILVER LOAN

Concurrent with its consideration of Chinese requests for Export-Import Bank and Congressional loans, the United States Government was confronted with a tentative Chinese proposal for large-scale assistance as an extreme measure to bring about currency stabilization in China. The rapidly deepening Government budgetary deficit had sent the note issue and prices to astronomical figures. In its search for a remedy, the Chinese Government made cautious inquiries of the United States Embassy in Nanking regarding the possibility of a large United States loan of silver which it was proposed should be minted and introduced into circulation as a partial substitute for and stabilizing influence on the paper currency. During the second week of June 1947, the Governor of the Central Bank approached officers of the Embassy with proposals along this line. He emphasized that they were purely tentative and informal, that no detailed plans had been worked out, and that he would prefer to await Washington's informal response before drawing up more specific plans. At the same time he submitted an undated and unsigned "memorandum on the Chinese currency" for transmittal to Washington. The Embassy, in forwarding the memorandum, described it as "a hasty and rough job which somewhat cursorily disposes of some of the technical comments" that the Embassy had made, but suggested that, in view of the deterioration in the Chinese currency situation, careful consideration be given to any reasoned proposal advanced by the Governor concerning use of silver.

Four days later the Secretary of State made a request of Secretary of the Treasury Snyder for the opinion of Treasury experts as to whether or not a silver loan to China would be practical and would establish among the Chinese people their former confidence in the silver dollar to offset their existing lack of confidence in paper currency. He emphasized that he did not believe that a silver loan to China would be favorably considered by Congress at its current session; that he did not have in mind proposing such a loan to Congress; but that he wanted to clarify for himself the various possibilities without regard to these considerations.

Pursuant to Secretary Marshall's inquiry, officers of the Treasury and State Departments jointly considered the Chinese silver proposal. They reached a conclusion that was sent to the Embassy for transmittal to the Chinese Government in the following message of July 9, 1947:

"It is thought that a loan for currency stabilization is not possible at this stage. Such a loan would, in any case, require Congressional action. It is recognized here that reintroduction of silver coins may ultimately provide a means of achieving stabilization, but it is considered that (1), no monetary measure could have an appreciable effect in the face of continued massive deficit spending, and (2), as the proposal sketched in the Central Bank Governor's memorandum indicates, if adopted, the flight from fapi might be more seriously accentuated."

This view was subsequently confirmed and elaborated by the Treasury Department, which, in response to Secretary Marshall's inquiry, stated:

"The Treasury Department is of the opinion that there is little merit to the proposal to introduce silver currency in China under existing conditions. Opportunities for graft and favoritism are involved in this proposal such as were afforded under the gold sales program of 1942. The depreciation in the value of the paper currency would occasion a drain upon the government stocks of silver coins, a large part of which may go directly into hoarding. It is our view that the completion of the program of substituting silver coins for paper currency might involve an impossibly large volume of silver coins under such circumstances. It is also possible that the introduction of silver coins on a partial scale such as is proposed by the Chinese Government might actually bring about a situation where the paper currency would depreciate in value faster than it would without the silver coins, and accelerate the deterioration in Chinese fiscal conditions. Any association on the part of this Government in the provision of an initial stock of silver coins might involve it in a moral responsibility to provide much larger amounts of silver which would be required for the development of a new currency.

"In the presently thin world silver market, any program for the remonetization of silver in China would inevitably drive up the price of silver, and entail an outlay on the order, possibly, of half a billion dollars. Even if the presently circulating paper currency were completely replaced by silver coins there is no present indication that the Chinese government's budget would be balanced and that the government would not again resort to the issuance of paper currency to finance its deficit.

"China's basic economic difficulties are a cause rather than a result of the increasing instability of her currency. I do not need to elaborate on this theme—the heavy government deficits which are being met by continuous expansion of the paper currency, and the lack of internal peace are at the root of China's troubles. In our opinion, the appropriate time for a revision of the Chinese monetary system will come when a broad program of internal reform is developed. A remonetization of silver at that time would have advantages and disadvantages which would need to be reviewed in the light of existing circumstances, and other possible financial and monetary measures which might be taken."

THE MOUNTING ECONOMIC CRISIS IN CHINA

Meanwhile, the economic situation in China had continued to worsen. After the initial brake to inflation provided by the emergency measures in February, prices had resumed their upward trend. By August the Shanghai wholesale price index had reached a point 300 percent above the February level, and the open market price for the United States dollar had risen to 45,000 C.N. In September and October this upward movement continued without check. No serious effort had been made to institute even the minimum improvements in budgetary and fiscal practices needed to alter the conditions giving rise to inflation.

Similarly, the drain on China's foreign exchange reserves had continued. By October official gold and United States dollar reserves were estimated to have fallen to a level of about 300 million dollars, with no prospect that their eventual depletion could be avoided. Private exchange holdings had not been tapped. A step toward a more realistic approach to the import-export problem had been taken when the principle of a fixed dollar exchange rate was abandoned in August in favor of a policy of flexible official rates. After giving an initial impetus to exports, however, exchange policy gradually reverted to the previous practice of more or less rigid official exchange rates.

Progress had been made in certain sectors of the Chinese economy. Food production had increased, the textile industry was producing at higher levels than in 1946, and the Chinese shipping industry had been fully restored. These developments, unfortunately, were more than counterbalanced by the spread of civil strife, the continuing and widespread disruption of inland transportation, and the progressive reduction in the volume of domestic trade.

At this stage, as at every point in the gradual deterioration of the Chinese economy, the downhill movement could have been halted only by vigorous action on the part of the Chinese Government. Civil strife by this time had become an irrevocable commitment. To wage it effectively, there was needed a drastic overhaul of the Government's economic mechanism. Critically needed were controls over the expenditure of funds by the military, a drive to tap noninflationary sources of revenue, moves to end the waste of assets flowing in from earlier foreign aid programs, and, above all, the development of a national economic program geared to the requirements of large-scale military operations.

Action in these directions obviously was uniquely a responsibility of the Chinese Government. At the same time, it was recognized by the Department of State that, even if all practicable steps were undertaken by the National Government, there would be an interim period before significant results could be expected. This deteriorating economic situation was a vital significant part of the over-all picture which led Secretary Marshall to recommend in July to President Truman that a comprehensive survey be made by General Wedemeyer.[2]

---

[2] See pp. 255 ff.

II. PREPARATION IN THE UNITED STATES OF THE CHINA AID PROGRAM

INTRODUCTION

For some months in mid-1947 the Department of State had been working with the National Advisory Council on International Monetary and Financial Problems in making studies of China's balance of payments position for possible use in connection with an aid program for China. By September 1947 it had become apparent that the foreign exchange assets of the Chinese Government would by early 1948 have been reduced to a point at which they would be insufficient to finance a flow of imports essential to continuation of a minimum level of economic activity and civil order in the coastal cities. This observation was based on the belief that the foreign exchange resources which would then be available to the Chinese Government (approximately 234 million dollars in gold and United States dollars on January 1, 1948, as reported by the Chinese Government) represented the minimum amount required for purchase of military imports and for maintenance of working balances. It was estimated conservatively that private Chinese gold, silver and other foreign exchange assets had increased to at least 500 million dollars, but mobilization of such assets in support of China's foreign exchange position appeared unlikely.

SECRETARY MARSHALL'S RECOMMENDATIONS TO CONGRESS

In consideration of China's need for funds to substitute for the Chinese Government's rapidly diminishing foreign exchange assets, the Department of State in October 1947 undertook the formulation of an economic assistance program for China to be presented to the Congress during the early part of its 1948 session. This undertaking was not based upon the premise that additional foreign aid would or could solve China's economic problems. Rather, it reflected the view that it was necessary to assist the Chinese Government so that that Government might be provided with an additional opportunity to initiate measures directed toward a fundamental improvement of its position. On November 10, in a statement before a joint session of the Senate Committee on Foreign Relations and the House Committee on Foreign Affairs, Secretary of State Marshall announced the intention of the Department to present to Congress a program of aid for China:

"The situation in China continues to cause us deep concern. The civil war has spread and increased in intensity. The Chinese Communists by force of arms seek control of wide areas of China.

"The United States and all other world powers recognize the National Government as the sole legal government of China. Only the Government and people of China can solve their fundamental problems and regain for China its rightful role as a major stabilizing influence in the Far East. Nevertheless we can be of help and, in the light of our long and uninterrupted record of friendship and international cooperation with China, we should extend to the Government and its people certain economic aid and assistance."

On the following day, during hearings before the Senate Committee on Foreign Relations, Secretary Marshall, in reply to a question regarding the funds that would be involved in a program of aid for China, stated that it would be very difficult to give any firm estimate at that time but that he would tentatively say that the amount would be in the neighborhood of 25 million dollars a month or a total of some 300 million dollars. During hearings before the House Committee on Foreign Affairs on the next day, Secretary Marshall said of the situation in China:

"It is very decidedly one where we have found the greatest difficulty in trying to calculate a course where money could be appropriated with, as I put it, a 70 percent probability of effective use in the situation.

"Now, that is what we have been trying to develop. We could not—and I add this to what I said earlier this morning—find through the ordinary agencies, the Export-Import Bank, any basis for getting ahead with certain enterprises in China which we thought would be helpful; so it is going to be necessary to turn to Congress for action on its part. What we have in mind, very briefly, is in relation to their import program from overseas outside of China, to see what can be done toward a stay of execution in the deterioration of their monetary situation so as to give them a chance, with reasonable action on their part, and very energetic action on their part, to take some measures toward restoring the financial situation."

PREMIER CHANG CHUN'S REQUEST OF NOVEMBER 17, 1947

On November 17 General Chang Chun, the Chinese Premier, addressed the following letter to the Secretary of State:

"At this moment when you are shouldering the heavy responsibility of formulating the initial plans for aiding Europe and China, I feel compelled to send you this message for your personal consideration.

"For over six months I have been in charge of the Executive Yuan. While I am in no wise in despair of the eventual outcome of the fight which the Generalissimo and my colleagues are putting up, I must frankly admit that both the military and economic situations are today far more critical than at the time when I assumed office. Though the Government forces have retaken the Shantung Peninsula, thereby depriving the Communists of one of their strongholds and bases of supply, the dislodged and scattering Communist units are now operating in more and wider areas than before. This not only calls for greater military efforts but also for fresh and urgent economic measures. Furthermore, the Government position in Manchuria, if allowed to remain too long on the defensive may become out of control, politically as well as militarily. This explains why there is such an outcry on the part of the Chinese public to see China given both emergency assistance and a long-range aid program. I am sure that in whatever form or language this desire may be expressed, you will regard it with understanding and sympathy. In sending these words to you, I am fully conscious of my own responsibility in helping China merit the effort which you have so generously exerted in the past and which you are continuing to exert now."

To this message the Secretary replied as follows:

"Thank you for your letter of November 17, in which you give me your views on the present situation in China. As Dr. Wang Shih-chieh doubtless told you, we are taking steps to complete the 8⅓ Group Program insofar as the equipment is still available and are making arrangements for China to be able to purchase ammunition from supplies in the Pacific Islands as well as from manufacturers in the United States.[2a]

"A program to provide economic and financial assistance to China is being prepared for presentation to the Congress.

"I am confident that despite the special difficulties which you face and the enormity of China's needs, you will appreciate that we are endeavoring to be of all possible help within the limits imposed by existing conditions in China, the United States and elsewhere.

"I send you my warm personal greetings with assurance that I will do within my power all that I can to be of assistance."

THE CHINESE REQUEST OF NOVEMBER 21 AND 24, 1947

On November 24 the Chinese Embassy at Washington handed the Department of State a memorandum quoting an informal aide-mémoire, requesting American aid, which had been presented to the American Ambassador at Nanking three days before:

"1. The Chinese Government welcomes Secretary Marshall's statement that the American Government should extend economic and

---

[2a] The military aspects are discussed in chapter VII.

financial aid to China and that a definite proposal is under consideration for early action. Such aid is indeed essential if China is to avoid financial and economic breakdown and achieve stability.

"2. Secretary Marshall indicated tentatively that American aid might be of the order of U. S. $300,000,000 of which U. S. $60,000,000 might be available prior to June 30, 1948, and that he hoped that definite proposals would be ready when Congress meets next January. The prospect of such aid is gratifying, but the most recent data show that the financial situation has become so critical that emergency aid is immediately needed and cannot wait until April of next year. These data were informally supplied to the American Government through its Nanking Embassy on November 18. The Chinese Government therefore earnestly hopes that, pending the working out of a comprehensive program as mentioned below, the American Government may find it possible to provide by action of Congress interim emergency aid to cover the deficit in China's international balance of payments at the rate of at least U. S. $25,000,000 monthly beginning with January next.

"3. The Chinese Government fully recognizes that, in order to deal with the present and prospective situation in China, a comprehensive and carefully prepared program is needed in which external aid and internal measures of self-help are closely integrated. The immediate need is for emergency aid and action to check the inflation and prevent a breakdown. But it is also clear that the time has come for China to embark upon a program of fundamental internal reform. The program should cover currency and banking, public revenues and expenditures, the armed forces, foreign trade, land policy and rural conditions, rehabilitation of essential industries and communications and administrative methods. As a result of China's sufferings and losses during eight years of war and the subsequent Communist rebellion, China cannot carry out such a program unaided. The Chinese Government, therefore, in keeping with the long history of Chinese-American cooperation, hopes it may count upon American material and technical assistance in carrying out this program.

"4. For the purpose of discussing interim emergency aid and devising plans for further action on the lines indicated above, the Chinese Government would be prepared to send to Washington a small technical mission or to receive in Nanking a similar mission from the American Government.

"The Chinese Government would appreciate an early reply from the American Government concerning the views indicated above."

The Department of State replied to the Chinese request as follows:

"The Department of State has given sympathetic consideration to the memorandum from the Chinese Embassy dated November 24, 1947, and desires to support steps by which U.S. Government assistance can be integrated with internal measures of self-help in China in order to contribute toward an effective program for economic recovery.

"In accordance with statements made at the conference on November 13 between the Secretary of State and the Chinese Ambassador, the Department of State is actively proceeding with formulation of definite proposals for submission to the Congress in January. It is contemplated that there should be consultation between our two Governments at an early date with respect to various aspects of these proposals. If, at that time, the Chinese Government desires, the United States would welcome a small technical mission in Washington."

AMBASSADOR STUART'S COMMENTS

During the course of work on the China aid program, Ambassador Stuart on November 24, 1947, sent the following pertinent general comment to the Department:

"I have the honor to comment further on some of the spiritual or human factors in the civil war as they are revealing themselves more clearly in the midst of rapidly deteriorating military and fiscal trends. The Communist organizers have a fanatical faith in their cause and are able to inspire their workers and to a large extent their troops and the local population with belief in its rightness, practical benefits and ultimate triumph. As against this the Government employees are becoming ever more dispirited, defeatist, and consequently listless or unscrupulously self-seeking. This of course still further alienates the liberal elements who ought to be the Government's chief reliance. Even the higher officials are beginning to lose hope. The effect on military morale is disastrous. In this drift toward catastrophe they clutch at American aid as at least postponing the inevitable. This is all that such monetary aid can do unless there is also among the Kuomintang leaders a new sense of dominating purpose, of sacred mission, of national salvation, expressing itself in challenging slogans, arousing them to fresh enthusiasms, leading them to forget their personal fears, ambitions and jealousies in the larger, more absorbingly worthwhile cause. It seems to me that this idea can be urged upon them under two emphases.

"(1) *Freedom.* There can be absolutely no freedom of thought or action under Communist rule. The contentment that comes from a measure of economic security is conditioned on mute acceptance of party dictation. The zeal is generated by what is in large measure false and malicious indoctrination. If the Kuomintang could appreciate the propagandist value of exposing this and go to the opposite extreme in guaranteeing freedom of speech, publication and assembly, at whatever seeming risk of subversive activities, it would win the loyalty of the intellectuals as nothing else could. The really harmful agitation of Communist agents in newspaper offices, schools or even in Government bureaus, could be safely left to the constructive elements in each unit concerned. An aggressive ideological warfare over this issue by the Kuomintang might be made tremendously effective. But the Government would have to take an adventurous leap and cease to rely upon its secret service and other suppressive agencies.

"(2) *The People's Livelihood.* The third of the famous *Three Principles* is being constantly honored in speeches and published articles. The Communists have gone a long way toward its realization but the Government shows up lamentably in comparison. True, it has had incessant foreign and domestic conflicts, but making all allowance for its difficulties the record to date has been extremely discreditable. If, however, all who do not want China to be communized could be enlisted in a movement to support the Government in effecting better local administration, there might well be a resurgent revolutionary movement that would attack at once graft and the inefficiency among Government officials and the wantonly destructive policy of the Communists. Both could alike be described as the present form of treasonable or unpatriotic activity, to be resisted and eliminated as they would a foreign foe by all who love their country.

"American aid could be based on the desire to help the populace in Government territory to have the twin benefits of the freedom essential to democracy and the economic welfare which is the only protection against Communist penetration. If conditioned upon hearty Government determination to achieve these two objectives for its people, it would first of all supply the new hope without which the leaders could scarcely recover from their depression of spirit and would give us the strongest leverage in furnishing the desperately needed aid as at each stage there is evidence of progress or in stopping it whenever the forces of reaction or of corruption assert themselves. . . ."

"SOME FUNDAMENTAL CONSIDERATIONS ON AMERICAN AID TO CHINA"

On December 22, 1947 the Chinese Government handed Ambassador Stuart the following memorandum entitled "Some Fundamental Considerations on American Aid to China":

"1. The American plan for aid to China should be a long-range four-year project, the purpose of which would be to assist China to achieve political and economic stability, including currency reform.

To attain this object, the funds for relief and rehabilitation to be obtained from the United States would require U.S. $500,000,000 for the first year, the same amount for the second year, U.S. $300,000,000 for the third year, and U.S. $200,000,000 for the fourth year, totaling one and one-half billion U.S. dollars.

"2. With regard to the relief fund obtained under the plan, the Chinese Government should appropriate a fund in Chinese currency, equivalent to the value of relief commodities supplied by the United States. This fund should be put to such uses as to benefit production and to curb inflation. There should be consultation and agreement between China and the United States in mapping out schemes for spending of this fund; and the American Government should receive full information concerning its actual disbursement.

"3. China will, on her accord, employ experienced American personnel to assist her in the planning for financial, monetary, and other administrative reforms. She will likewise employ American technical experts to participate in the execution of certain construction undertakings. The Chinese Government itself will express the aforesaid intention to the American Government at an appropriate moment, with the request that the latter will assist in the selection of such personnel. The employment of these personnel will not, however, be made an international legal obligation of the Chinese Government in order to avert infringement on China's sovereignty and administrative integrity.

"4. The American aid to China plan shall contain no political condition other than what may be stipulated in the aid plan for Europe. On the other hand, terms which will be stipulated in the aid plan for Europe may apply, wherever practicable, to China.

"5. As regards the supply of military equipment and ammunition, China should be allowed to purchase in the form of loans the surplus and other military material from the American Government. The total of such loans is tentatively estimated at U.S. $100,000,000 for the year 1948. Prior to the submission of lists for such purchases, the Chinese Government will consult the American Military Advisory Group in China."

WASHINGTON DISCUSSIONS WITH CHINESE REPRESENTATIVES

During the last quarter of 1947, concurrent with the preparation of a China aid program, a number of conferences were held between officers of the Department of State and two representatives of the Chinese Government who had come to Washington to offer technical assistance in the drafting of the program: Dr. Arthur Young, an American who for twenty-odd years had been an adviser to the Chinese Ministry of Finance, and Dr. Kan Lee, a special representative of the Ministry of Foreign Affairs. In discussing with them its plans for United States assistance to China, the Department stressed the great importance it attached to the execution by the Chinese Government of "rough and ready" measures of financial, economic and administrative reform. It was recommended to Young and Lee that they urge upon the Chinese Government the immediate preparation of such measures with a view to their prompt application, both prior to and concurrent with the anticipated extension of American aid, in order that the effectiveness of the aid might be maximized.

In January 1948 the Chinese Government, pursuant to the invitation of the Department of State, despatched a small technical mission to Washington. This mission, headed by Pei Tsu-yi, former Governor of the Central Bank of China, met frequently with representatives of the Department of State and other agencies concerned with formulation of the China aid program. The mission submitted for review with United States Government representatives a presentation of Chinese economic difficulties and remedial measures that might be instituted by the Chinese Government.

PREMIER CHANG CHUN'S STATEMENT OF JANUARY 28, 1948

On January 28, 1948, the Chinese Premier, General Chang Chun, issued a widely publicized statement expressing the Chinese Government's determination to undertake sweeping reforms in administrative, financial, economic and military fields. The statement read as follows:

"As a result of her suffering and losses during more than 8 years of war and the subsequent Communist rebellion, China is now facing unprecedented economic difficulties. In order to overcome these difficulties, the Chinese Government, in the light of the long history of Chinese-American friendship, has requested economic and technical assistance from the United States. It was with gratification that the Chinese Government noted the inclusion of China in the interim-aid bill and the announced intention of the United States Government to take early action during the present session of the Congress to provide substantial aid for China. The Chinese Government fully recognizes that in order to secure the maximum benefit from external aid an adequate and practicable program of domestic measures of self-help is needed. This program should at the beginning lay stress on financial and economic measures of immediate importance which will be followed or accompanied by certain other reforms in the fields of general administration and military reorganization.

The main financial and economic reform measures which the Chinese Government intends to undertake are:

"(1) Control and readjustment of Government expenditures both in Chinese national currency and foreign currencies so as to realize all practicable economies.

"(2) Improvement of the national, provincial and local tax systems and the administration thereof with the dual object of increasing the yield and placing the tax burden upon economic groups that are best able to pay.

"(3) With a view to insuring greater efficiency in the performance of their duties, the treatment of civil servants as well as officers and men will be gradually raised. Simultaneously, a program will be enforced for the gradual reduction of Government personnel.

"(4) Strengthening and extension of control over the supply of essential commodities of daily necessity with a view to checking speculation and the abnormal rise of prices.

"(5) In order to insure the maximum effectiveness of external aid, every effort will be made toward laying the basis for a more stable monetary system.

"(6) Banking and credit systems to be reformed through the centralization of control in the Central Bank of China and the maintenance of a counter-inflationary policy.

"(7) Promotion of exports through removal of obstacles to export movements.

"(8) Improvement of import control; but as soon as conditions permit, the emergency control measures shall be modified.

"(9) Improvement of agricultural production and rural conditions and land reforms through the adoption of such recommendations of the China–United States Agricultural Mission as are suitable for early introduction.

"(10) Rehabilitation of communications and essential industries as far as conditions permit in order to increase production and reduce dependence upon abnormal imports."

PRESENTATION OF THE CHINA AID PROGRAM TO CONGRESS

Following a period of detailed planning by the Department of State in consultation with other departments concerned, and final review by the National Advisory Council, a program of economic aid for China was submitted to the Congress by the President on February 18, 1948. The presentation of the program was accompanied by a special message from the President, and the Secretary of State testified on February 20 before the House Committee on Foreign Affairs in support of the program.[3] At the same time, the Ambassador issued a pub-

---

[3] See annex 175 (a) and (b).

lic statement in China designed to explain the purpose of the proposed program of American assistance.[3a] The program as presented called for an appropriation of 570 million dollars to be available for expenditure until June 30, 1949, a period of approximately 15 months considering the time that would be required for Congressional action. It was envisaged that 510 million dollars of the total would be used to finance minimum imports of essential civilian types of commodities chiefly foodstuffs and industrial materials, while 60 million dollars would be programed for a few selected industrial and transportation reconstruction projects to be initiated prior to June 30, 1949.

Subsequent to the public presentation of the China aid program to Congress, the Secretary of State read the following statement to the Committees on Foreign Affairs and Foreign Relations in executive session:

I am assuming your familiarity with the general outline of the Chinese program which I presented at the opening hearing on this subject. There is a great deal that directly bears on the problem which is not in the public interest of this country, and particularly of the Chinese Government, to state for the open record. A public statement of many of the factors which have led to the failures of the Chinese Government in both the military and economic field, however accurate, would be destructive of morale to that Government and its army. Moreover, it would actually be helpful, even stimulating, to the morale of the Communist Party, and especially the Communist army. Therefore, it has been very difficult to make a frank public statement of the case.

Considering the military aspects of the problem it was clear from V–J Day in 1945 that the Chinese Government was confronted by a military situation which made it, in the opinion of virtually every American authority, impossible to conquer the Communist armies by force. Geographically, the odds were too heavy against the Government—thousands of miles of communications bordered by mountains affording easy retreats for guerrilla forces, numerous vulnerable river crossings and tunnels easily subject to destruction; the strategical and tactical characteristics of guerrilla warfare permitting a concentration of guerrilla forces at a desired point where the Government was weakest; and the governmental military necessity of covering all points, therefore all weakly and thus vulnerable to surprise attack.

There was constant insistence on the part of the Generalissimo and his high military and political group that the only way the issue could be settled was by force. I had endeavored to persuade them time after time that it was not within their capability to settle the matter by force. The odds were too heavy against them. Furthermore, there was conspicuous ineptitude and widespread corruption among the higher leaders. The consequent low morale of the Chinese Government armies has been a factor of great importance to the military situation.

We have had many proposals for this Government to support the Chinese military program. That is easy to say, but extraordinarily difficult and dangerous to do. It involves obligations and responsibilities on the part of this Government which I am convinced the American people would never knowingly accept. We cannot escape the fact that the deliberate entry of this country into the armed

---

[3a] See annex 176.

effort in China involves possible consequences in which the financial cost, though tremendous, would be insignificant when compared to the other liabilities inevitably involved.

So far, I have been discussing the Government military forces. On the other side, the Communist forces have brought about terrible destruction and virtually wrecked the economy of China. This was their announced purpose—to force an economic collapse. The development of the situation was predicted by me to the Chinese Government frankly and forcibly many times in the summer and fall of 1946. The Government failures have been even worse than I anticipated.

We have furnished important aid to China since V–J Day. Military aid included the transportation by U.S. facilities of Chinese Government troops from points in west China to the major cities of central and north China and from coastal points to the port of entry into Manchuria for the reoccupation of Japanese-held areas. At the end of the war the U.S. had largely equipped and partially trained 39 Chinese divisions. Additional equipment was transferred to the Chinese to complete these divisions and to replace worn-out equipment. Military lend-lease aid to the Chinese Government amounted to more than $700 million. The Chinese Government obtained the arms and equipment of the surrendering Japanese armies in China proper (below the Great Wall) and Formosa, a total of approximately 1,235,000 men. The Chinese Communists obtained large quantities of Japanese arms in Manchuria, through direct or indirect Soviet connivance; the number of surrendering Japanese troops in Manchuria is estimated at 700,000.

The National Government has had its own arsenals, which, while small by U.S. standards, did represent an effective addition to its military potential. Japanese-armed Chinese puppet troops with their equipment were taken over by the Chinese Government in large numbers—estimated as 780,000.

Under Public Law 512 the U.S. has transferred to the Chinese Navy as a gift 97 naval craft and has trained Chinese naval personnel to man these vessels. The U. S. Military Advisory Group at Nanking has furnished advice and assistance on a staff level to the Chinese Government in organizational and training matters and is now participating in training of Chinese troops on a division level in Formosa.

The U. S. Marine Corps landed about 55,000 men in north China after V–J Day. In addition to disarming the Japanese, the Marines guarded railways and coal mines in north China until September 1946 to ensure an adequate supply of coal for the vital industrial areas in north and central China. At the time of their withdrawal in the spring and summer of 1947, the Marines "abandoned" certain military matériel, including munitions, to the Chinese Government forces. The U. S. Army and Marine Corps were largely responsible for the removal of approximately 3,000,000 Japanese soldiers and civilians from China.

We have been supplying munitions under surplus property arrangements and the Chinese have made some purchases of munitions commercially. In recent months the Chinese have concluded contracts with OFLC for most of the U. S. military surplus suitable to Chinese needs, including ammunition, transport planes and other military matériel. Arrangements are now being completed to sell to the Chinese under surplus arrangements the remaining available ammunition in Hawaii and in the Zone of the Pacific.

There have been long delays in completing the necessary contracts largely because the Chinese officials concerned persisted in time-consuming maneuvers to secure an even greater bargain than our people felt authorized to agree to.

On the civilian side, commercial vessels have been transferred to the Chinese Government and large amounts of civilian goods valuable to the Chinese economy were sold to the Chinese Government under surplus arrangements at prices representing only a small fraction of their procurement cost. The Export-Import Bank has extended credits to the Chinese for reconstruction purposes and the import of cotton. The U.S. contributed a major share of the UNRRA program for China. Authorized U.S. aid from V–J Day until the present date, exclusive of surplus property sales, totals $1,432,000,000, at least half of which was military assistance.

The Chinese Government has received aid from other foreign sources. The non-U.S. share of the UNRRA program and certain foreign credits together total approximately $250 million. The Chinese Government obtained the large Japanese industrial and other holdings in China having a roughly estimated value in 1945 dollars of $3,600,000,000. (This figure allows for a 50 percent reduction of the value of Japanese holdings in Manchuria due to Soviet removals, civil war and related damage and general under-maintenance in the post-war period.)

All of the foregoing means, at least to me, that a great deal must be done by the Chinese authorities themselves—and that nobody else can do it for them— if that Government is to maintain itself against the Communist forces and agrarian policies. It also means that our Government must be exceedingly careful that it does not become committed to a policy involving the absorption of its resources to an unpredictable extent once the obligations are assumed of a direct responsibility for the conduct of civil war in China or for the Chinese economy, or both.

There is another point that I wish to mention in consideration of this matter. There is a tendency to feel that wherever the Communist influence is brought to bear, we should immediately meet it, head on as it were. I think this would be a most unwise procedure for the reason that we would be, in effect, handing over the initiative to the Communists. They could, therefore, spread our influence out so thin that it could be of no particular effectiveness at any one point.

We must be prepared to face the possibility that the present Chinese Government may not be successful in maintaining itself against the Communist forces or other opposition that may arise in China. Yet, from the foregoing, it can only be concluded that the present Government evidently cannot reduce the Chinese Communists to a completely negligible factor in China. To achieve that objective in the immediate future it would be necessary for the United States to underwrite the Chinese Government's military effort, on a wide and probably constantly increasing scale, as well as the Chinese economy. The U.S. would have to be prepared virtually to take over the Chinese Government and administer its economic, military and governmental affairs.

Strong Chinese sensibilities regarding infringement of China's sovereignty, the intense feeling of nationalism among all Chinese and the unavailability of qualified American personnel in the large numbers required argue strongly against attempting any such solution. It would be impossible to estimate the final cost of a course of action of this magnitude. It certainly would be a continuing operation for a long time to come. It would involve this Government in a continuing commitment from which it would practically be impossible to withdraw, and it would very probably involve grave consequences to this nation by making of China an arena of international conflict. An attempt to underwrite the Chinese economy and the Chinese Government's military effort represents a burden on the U.S. economy and a military responsibility which I cannot recomend as a course of action for this Government.

On the other hand we in the Executive Branch of the Government have an intense desire to help China. As a matter of fact, I have struggled and puzzled over the situation continuously since my return. Our trouble has been to find a course which we could reasonably justify before Congress on other than emotional grounds. It has been a long struggle to concoct an economic program and clear it through the various Government agencies—the National Advisory Council, and, of course, the Budget Bureau, where they properly have to be very factual.

We are already committed by past actions and by popular sentiment among our people to continue to do what we can to alleviate suffering in China and to give the Chinese Government and people the possibility of working out China's problems in their own way. It would be against U.S. interests to demonstrate a complete lack of confidence in the Chinese Government and to add to its difficulties by abruptly rejecting its request for assistance. The psychological effect on morale in China would be seriously harmful.

We hope that the program we are presenting to Congress will assist in arresting the accelerating trend of economic deterioration to provide the Chinese Government with a further opportunity to lay the groundwork for stabilizing the situation. In these circumstances, I consider that this program of economic assistance, proposed with full recognition of all the unfavorable factors in the situation, is warranted by American interests.

The problem of U.S. aid to China must be considered in the light not only of the foregoing but also in its relation to other important factors.

China does not itself possess the raw material and industrial resources which would enable it to become a first-class military power within the foreseeable future. The country is at present in the midst of a social and political revolution. Until this revolution is completed—and it will take a long time—there is no prospect that sufficient stability and order can be established to permit China's early development into a strong state. Furthermore, on the side of American interests, we cannot afford, economically or militarily, to take over the continued failures of the present Chinese Government to the dissipation of our strength in more vital regions where we now have a reasonable opportunity of successfully meeting or thwarting the Communist threat, that is, in the vital industrial area of Western Europe with its traditions of free institutions.

Present developments make it unlikely, as previously indicated, that any amount of U.S. military or economic aid could make the present Chinese Government capable of reestablishing and then maintaining its control throughout all of China.

The issues in China are thoroughly confused. The Chinese Communists have succeeded to a considerable extent in identifying their movement with the popular demand for change in present conditions. On the other hand, there have been no indications that the present Chinese Government, with its traditions and methods, could satisfy this popular demand or create conditions which would satisfy the mass of Chinese people and prevent further violence and civil disobedience.

I know from my own personal experience that large numbers of young Chinese, college graduates, have gone over to the Communist Party, not because they favored the ideology of the Party but because of their complete disgust with the corruption among the officials of the Chinese Government. In the opinion of these young men, the Communist Party was trying to do something for the common people, and no one accuses the Communist leaders or officials of personal graft. For this reason the Communist military forces are not all of the same way of thinking. I have recently been told by our representatives in Manchuria and other places that it is quite apparent that considerable groups are within the ranks of the Communist army because they are opposed to the iniquities of the political party in power, the Kuomintang, and its failure to do anything constructive for the common people and not because of any belief in Communist ideology.

At present, the Chinese Government is not only weak but is lacking in self-discipline and inspiration. There is little evidence that these conditions can be basically corrected by foreign aid. In these circumstances, any large-scale U.S. effort to assist the Chinese Government to oppose the Communists would most probably degenerate into a direct U.S. undertaking and responsibility, involving the commitment of sizeable forces and resources over an indefinite period. Such a dissipation of U.S. resources would inevitably play into the hands of the Russians, or would provoke a reaction which could possibly, even probably, lead to another Spanish type of revolution or general hostilities.

In these circumstances, the costs of an all-out effort to see Communist forces resisted and destroyed in China would, as indicated above, be impossible to estimate; but the magnitude of the task and the probable costs thereof would clearly be out of all proportion to the results to be obtained.

It was not intended that American aid should be equated with China's total foreign exchange deficit. In the first place, no reliable estimate of China's total foreign exchange expenditures over the next 15 months was available. Such an estimate would have had to include expenditures for military purposes as well as for civilian imports, but the Chinese Government had spent very little since the war for imports of military equipment and supplies and had not formulated a program of military procurement. It was believed that necessary military expenditures could be financed in the discretion of the Chinese Government out of its own foreign exchange reserves and due allowance was made for this contingency. Furthermore, China's receipts of foreign exchange from exports and remittances were so erratic that it was extremely difficult to project the capacity of the Chinese Government to pay for its essential civilian imports out of current earnings.

There were, however, certain available criteria which were applied in formulating the program. The capacities of China's cotton mills were known and their needs for raw cotton could be estimated, as could the petroleum requirements of selected industries and transportation facilities. Thus, a floor and a ceiling as well were available for two major categories of China's import requirements. Experience gained in previous aid programs had demonstrated that China's capacity for effective internal distribution of other commodities, such as food and fertilizer, was extremely limited due to high costs generated by inflation and to the cumbersome and inefficient administrative structure of many Chinese organizations. It was decided, therefore, to program aid imports of commodities other than petroleum and cotton on the basis of past imports as modified by Chinese Government estimates of minimum import requirements.

It was recognized that the comprehensive reconstruction of Chinese industry and transportation would require foreign capital of great magnitude. It was evident, however, that a large scale reconstruction program could not be carried out successfully amidst the existing disorganization and hyperinflation. A high proportion of the cost of each reconstruction project would have to be met in Chinese currency to cover domestic expenditures for labor and materials. Thus, the inflationary consequences of an ambitious reconstruction program might well have been so extreme as to have crippled the program itself and substantially increased the rate of economic deterioration in the economy as a whole. It was decided therefore to concentrate on a few of the most serious obstacles to permanent improvement of the Chinese economic situation. These obstacles were the shortage of electric power, coal and fertilizer, and the serious disrepair existing in China's railroad facilities.

Other considerations, such as the availability of specific commodities and competing demands upon American resources, were of course brought to bear on the exact amount of aid requested. The total amount programed, however, was estimated as approximating the maximum of commodities that China could absorb effectively within a limited time period and, on the basis of conservative estimates of prospective exports and remittances, this amount was believed to be beyond China's means to finance out of current earnings. Such improvement as China could have effected in exports and remittances would have increased the amount of foreign exchange available to the Chinese Government for additional imports or for accumulation of reserves.

The Secretary of State had stated in his initial testimony on the aid program before the House Foreign Affairs Committee that "provision of a currency stabilization fund would, in the opinion of our monetary experts, require large sums which would be largely dissipated under the present conditions of war financing and civil disruption." Nevertheless, in the course of Committee hearings, interest was evidenced in the possibility of lending stability to the Chinese currency through a United States loan or grant of silver for monetary circulation within China. Pursuant to a request from the House Foreign Affairs Committee, the Department of State in late March submitted to Chairman Eaton of that Committee a statement analyzing the silver proposal with reference to China. The statement had been prepared in collaboration with the Treasury Department and the Federal Reserve Board and was entitled "Possible Use of Silver for Monetary Stabilization in China in Connection with China Aid Program."[4] A copy of the statement also was submitted to the Senate Committee on Foreign Relations. The analysis led to negative conclusions which were stated briefly in the opening summary paragraph of the statement as follows: "The China Aid Program does not provide for the use of silver to bring about monetary stability in China. It does not do so for three main reasons: *one*, because conditions in China do not now furnish a basis for any lasting currency stabilization; *two*, because even if basic conditions now favored stabilization of the currency and price level it would not be practical to restore the silver standard in China; and *three*, because the introduction of silver as an emergency measure at this time would involve such technical difficulties as to make it a costly and uncertain venture."

It was clear that the proposed aid program could not, of itself, bring about a decided change for the better in the rapidly deteriorating Chinese economic picture. Other factors remaining equal, it was believed that the proposed aid would serve to prevent an acceleration of the inflation that was certainly in prospect in the absence of aid. The expendable commodities would help to prevent starvation in the coastal cities, maintain employment in the cotton mills, and keep other industry and transportation from breaking down, while the capital goods would make possible some permanent improvement in important sectors of the economy. Moreover, receipts from the sale of these goods within China by the Chinese Government would to some extent merely serve to maintain the level of income that the Government had been receiving. There would still remain a very large budgetary deficit that the Chinese Government had been meeting by the issuance of currency. Nor would the extension of American material aid affect the other major problems of China's civil and military administration that represented the basic deterrents to effective organization of the economy and prosecution of the Government's military program.[4a]

Thus, it was apparent at the time this aid program was presented to the Congress that no amount of outside material assistance or advice could substitute for the far-reaching steps that would have to be taken by the Chinese Government itself if it were to survive. This was widely recognized by many Chinese individuals and officials of the Chinese Government including the then Premier Chang Chun, who had, as stated above, issued on January 28, 1948, a statement of intention to undertake measures of domestic reform. This state-

[4] See annex 177.
[4a] See annex 178 (a) and (b).

ment by the Chinese Government lent some encouragement to the Administration and the Congress in support of the hope that a program of United States aid might be augmented sufficiently by the Chinese themselves so that a basis could be laid for economic improvement and political stability.

These circumstances dictated that an initial United States aid program for China should be limited approximately to the period of a year rather than authorized for five years as had been recommended by General Wedemeyer, or for four years as was requested by the Chinese Government. The proposed China aid program differed sharply in this respect from the European Recovery Program which was considered simultaneously by the Congress. In the case of both Western Europe and China, the effectiveness of United States aid depended primarily upon the performance of the Government through which aid would be extended. But in the European situation, economic and political conditions, and the administrative structure of the governments concerned, made it possible to develop a long-range economic reconstruction plan, whereas in China such planning was clearly impossible, and the capacity of the Chinese Government to carry out sweeping measures necessary to permanent economic improvement was a highly uncertain factor. Authorization of a long-range aid program would have represented a commitment by the United States Government from which it would have been extremely difficult, if not impossible, to withdraw, regardless of future developments. The China aid program was regarded by the Department of State as a measure which might become either the first stage of larger and more constructive endeavors or the conclusion of large-scale United States aid to the Chinese Government. These alternative possibilities, and the fact that their determination would depend heavily on actions of the Chinese Government, were pointed out by the Secretary in testimony before Congress and subsequently by the United States Embassy to officials of the Chinese Government.

III. THE CHINA AID ACT OF 1948

The President's request for authorization and appropriation of 570 million dollars for economic aid to China was considered during March by the Senate Committee on Foreign Relations and the House Committee on Foreign Affairs. The House of Representatives was the first to pass legislation for aid to China, incorporated in an omnibus bill dealing with foreign aid on a world-wide basis. The House bill authorized two separate appropriations for China totaling 570 million dollars for a 15-month period. One authorization provided 420 million dollars for economic aid and the other amended the legislation under which Greece received aid to authorize 150 million dollars for military assistance to China to be supervised by an American military mission on the same basis as that which underlay provision of United States military aid in Greece. This would have required assumption of responsibility by the United States Government for programing, procurement and delivery of military supplies for the Chinese Government and for detailed supervision of their use in China, including operational advice to Chinese combat forces in the field.

The Senate dealt with aid to China in an individual bill which authorized the appropriation of 463 million dollars to be available for obligation for the period of one year. Of this total, 363 million dollars was to be provided as economic aid while the balance, 100 million dollars, was to be set aside for grants on such terms as the President might decide. The legislative history of this bill made it clear that this special fund was to be disbursed at the discretion of the Chinese Government, although it was assumed that the Chinese Government probably would elect to use it largely for procurement of military supplies. The Senate bill, however, made no reference to military aid in providing for this special grant and the report of the Senate Foreign Relations Committee stated:

"In view of the Chinese requirement for military supplies, it may be assumed that the Chinese Government, on its own option and responsibility, would seek this grant for such supplies. With intelligent planning, and careful conservation and efficient utilization the Chinese Government could achieve much with this sum. . . . [It] will be extended in the form of grants to be used by the Chinese Government without any of the conditions and controls which will prevail with respect to the expenditure of the remaining $363,000,000. Presumably, therefore, this amount can be used for the procurement of military supplies and equipment if the National Government so desires. The committee agreed, however, that the broad language of section 3 (b) of the present bill should not be interpreted to include the use of any of the armed forces of the United States for combat duties in China."

Thus, the Senate and House bills differed sharply in the degree to which they would place responsibility on the United States Government for supervision of Chinese Government military planning and operations. This difference was reconciled by the House and Senate conferees in favor of the Senate bill. The conference bill, which was passed by the Congress on April 2, 1948, followed substantially the form of the Senate bill but changed the amounts authorized for one year to 338 million dollars for economic aid and 125 million dollars for special grants to be used in the discretion of the Chinese Government. The conference bill became the China Aid Act of 1948 [5] and was incorporated as Title IV of Public Law 472 entitled the Foreign Assistance Act of 1948.[6]

Congress subsequently appropriated the full 125 million dollars authorized for special grants to the Chinese Government. However, despite testimony by the Department of State that the full amount of the President's original request for 570 million dollars was needed for economic aid, the Congress appropriated only 275 million dollars for this purpose. The 570 million dollar program for 15 months presented by the President, if scaled down proportionately to a 12-month period, would have come to approximately 463 million dollars. Thus, the appropriation represented an actual reduction of 188 million dollars below the amount requested for economic aid.

The preamble to the China Aid Act of 1948 declared it to be the policy of the people of the United States to encourage the Republic of China and its people to exert sustained common efforts to achieve internal peace and economic stability, to maintain the genuine independence and administrative integrity of China and to sustain and strengthen principles of individual liberty and free institutions in China through a program of assistance based on self-help and co-operation. It further declared it to be the policy of the United States that assistance provided under the act should at all times be dependent upon Chinese cooperation in furthering the programs. Finally, the preamble emphasized that any assistance furnished under the act

". . . shall not be construed as an express or implied assumption by the United States of any responsibility for policies, acts, or undertakings of the Republic of China or for conditions which may prevail in China at any time."

Section 405 of the act provided that

". . . an agreement shall be entered into between China and the United States containing those undertakings by China which the Secretary of State, after consultation with the Administrator of Economic Cooperation, may deem necessary to carry out the purposes of this title and to improve commercial relations with China".

In addition to the supply of expendable commodities and provision

---

[5] See annex 179. It received the President's approval on Apr. 3, 1948.

[6] Title I (the Economic Cooperation Act of 1948) of this omnibus act authorized the European Recovery Program, and titles II and III dealt with the International Children's Emergency Fund and the Greek-Turkey aid programs respectively.

of capital goods for reconstruction projects envisaged in the program presented by the President, the Congress in section 407 of the act provided for a program of assistance for reconstruction in rural areas of China. This section authorized the Secretary of State to conclude an agreement with China establishing a Joint Commission on Rural Reconstruction in China to be composed of two Americans and three Chinese. It was apparent that such a program would have to be largely educational in character and, therefore, that the funds required for its operation would, for the most part, be Chinese currency. Consequently, this section provided that the rural reconstruction program might be financed by "an amount equal to not more than 10 per centum of the funds made available" for economic aid to China, and that "such amount may be in U.S. dollars, proceeds in Chinese currency from the sale of commodities made available to China" as economic aid, or both.

IV. IMPLEMENTATION OF THE CHINA ECONOMIC AID PROGRAM

INITIATION OF THE PROGRAM

By virtue of an advance by the Reconstruction Finance Corporation, the Economic Cooperation Administration was able to launch the authorized program of commodity assistance to China before Congress acted on its appropriation. The China Aid Act of 1948 provided for an RFC advance of 50 million dollars, and the President decided that this amount should be divided between economic aid and the program of special grants to the Chinese Government in the same proportion that the total authorized appropriations for these two purposes bore to each other. Thus, 36.5 million dollars of the 50 million dollars was allocated by the Bureau of the Budget to ECA, and 13.5 million dollars was allocated to the Treasury for disbursement upon request by the Chinese Government. ECA extended assistance initially in accordance with the terms of notes exchanged on April 30, 1948, between the Secretary of State and the Chinese Ambassador in Washington. These notes provided that, pending the negotiation of a bilateral economic aid agreement, the extension of American aid would be governed by the agreement of October 27, 1947, negotiated in connection with the United States Foreign Relief Program, subject to such modifications as might be agreed by the two governments.

Negotiations regarding the terms of a bilateral economic aid agreement between China and the United States were begun in May of 1948 between the American Embassy in Nanking and the Chinese Ministry of Foreign Affairs. The Act specified that aid should be provided to China ". . . under the applicable provisions of the Economic Cooperation Act of 1948 (Title I) which are consistent with the purposes" of the China Aid Act (Title IV). Thus, it was necessary that the Department of State negotiate, after consultation with ECA, an agreement with China which adhered as closely as possible to the terms specified by Title I for aid to countries participating in the Organization for European Economic Cooperation. At the same time, due allowance had to be made for certain aspects of the Chinese situation that were basically different from conditions obtaining in Western Europe. Variation was called for particularly in regard to those sections of Title I which prescribed various undertakings in the field of economic self-help to be required of European governments. It would have been futile, for example, to require that the Chinese Government, in the midst of civil strife, rampant inflation and administrative disorganization, attempt to achieve objectives in the field of industrial reconstruction and financial stabilization as rigorous as those indicated by Title I for commitment by Western European countries.

Negotiations were satisfactorily concluded in the first days of July and the Agreement was signed on July 3, 1948, by Ambassador Stuart and the Chinese Minister of Foreign Affairs, Wang Shih-chieh.[7] In general, the Agreement followed the pattern of the bilateral agreements which were negotiated simultaneously with Western European countries. The language of certain articles was made almost identical for those undertakings specified by Title I which applied in principle to the Chinese as well as to the European situation. Where circumstances differed substantially, however, some standard articles were modified considerably in the China Agreement, or unique provisions were added.

UNDERTAKINGS BY THE CHINESE GOVERNMENT

The undertakings by the Chinese Government in the Agreement which were most significant in terms of their relevance to the basic problems confronting that Government, or in terms of their unique character, can be summarized as follows:

1. In order to achieve the maximum improvement of economic conditions through the employment of American assistance, the Chinese Government agreed to (a) take the measures necessary to ensure efficient and practical use of economic resources available to it, including effective use of United States aid goods and appropriate use of private Chinese assets in the United States, (b) promote the development of industry and agriculture on a sound economic basis, (c) take the

---

[7] See annex 181.

financial, monetary, budgetary and administrative measures necessary to create more stable currency conditions, and (*d*) cooperate with other countries to increase the international exchange of goods and services and to reduce public and private barriers to foreign trade.

2. The Chinese Government agreed to make all practicable efforts to improve commercial relations with other countries, with particular reference to the conditions affecting foreign trade by private enterprises in China. This undertaking was unique to the China Agreement and was required specifically by section 405 of the China Aid Act. The article containing this undertaking was made fairly general in character, partly out of deference to the sensitivities of the Chinese Government, and also because the Chinese Government on May 22, 1948, had put into effect the provisions of the General Agreement on Tariffs and Trade, which detailed principles of foreign commercial relations.

3. The Chinese Government agreed that all United States aid goods should be processed and distributed according to terms and conditions and prices agreed upon between the Chinese and United States Governments. The Chinese Government also undertook to achieve fair and equitable distribution of United States aid goods and similar commodities, in so far as possible through rationing and price control systems in the urban centers of China. This also was an undertaking unique to the China Agreement, but it was believed that provisions for joint supervision over the distribution of United States aid goods within China by the two Governments was essential to minimize dissipation of such goods in the disorganized situation that existed.

The commitments in the Agreement by the Chinese Government to take action in the field of economic self-help represented major undertakings towards large objectives. They were, however, general in character and expressed in relative rather than absolute terms. The American Government was fully appreciative of the enormous difficulties which confronted the Chinese Government. It did not expect perfection or near perfection in the performance of that Government. Nevertheless, it was evident that unless the Chinese Government and people themselves were to take effective initial steps as a necessary basis for the progressive solution of their economic and administrative difficulties, American aid, whether economic or military, would accomplish little of permanent value. The China Aid Act was designed particularly to afford the Chinese Government an opportunity to execute desperately needed measures of self-help. It was therefore incumbent on the American Government to make use of its program of aid, to the maximum extent possible and appropriate, to represent to the Chinese Government the essentiality of its undertaking those measures of self-help indispensable to its survival.

It was recognized that the self-help undertakings expressed by the Chinese Government in the bilateral aid agreement were so general that they provided little guidance for concrete action and offered considerable latitude for Chinese failure to act. General undertakings to initiate basic reforms had been undertaken unilaterally by the Chinese Government in the past with little to show for them. What was really called for in the circumstances was the formulation of specific measures and the early and progressive translation of such measures into a coherent program of concrete action. As indicated above, the Chinese Premier, Chang Chun, had voluntarily issued a general statement in January 1948 of intention to carry through sweeping reform measures. The prompt and practical implementation of the Premier's statement had been urged by the United States Government as soon as the statement was issued, but after 3 months there was no evidence that the statement had occasioned the initiation of first steps directed toward basic reforms. The American Government believed that it should take the occasion of the negotiation of the aid agreement vigorously to persuade the Chinese Government to formulate specific measures for concrete action, and that it should urge the Chinese Government continuously throughout the period of the aid program to carry out such measures.

Consideration was given by the Department of State to the inclusion of more specific Chinese commitments in the bilateral aid agreement, or to obtain separate written commitments from the Chinese Government. It was decided, however, that insistence on a formalization of detailed commitments in this manner would prove unworkable even if attained. This decision reflected recognition of the fact that, while it was appropriate to call for formal general commitments on self-help by the Chinese Government in connection with extension of a large United States aid program, the specific implementation of such commitments was, in a purely formal as well as in a very real sense, the exclusive responsibility of the Chinese Government. A requirement of written pledges on matters of detailed administration by the Chinese Government as a prerequisite to United States aid would place on the United States Government the responsibility for supervising the implementation of the pledges and the obligation to suspend or to withdraw aid if the specific commitments were not met. This would have been an undertaking by the American Government which probably would have led to the employment of American supervisory personnel in China in large numbers, and which unquestionably would have been regarded in China and elsewhere as an extreme infringement of Chinese sovereignty. It would have involved the American Government, in effect, in an attempt to force the Chinese Government to do in its own self-interest those things which only that Government itself was in a position to initiate and which, in the last analysis, only the Chinese Government itself could administratively perform.

In view of the above considerations, the Department of State decided that efforts should be intensified on an informal basis to persuade the Chinese Government of the necessity of early concrete measures in implementation of the general undertakings proposed for inclusion in the aid agreement. Consequently, the Embassy in Nanking was instructed to hold a special series of informal discussions with Chinese Government leaders corollary to negotiations on the aid agreement, such discussions to be related in substance to the agreement but to be held apart from the formal negotiations. The Department indicated that, in such discussions, the Chinese should be pressed for oral assurances regarding specific measures intended.

SPECIFIC ECONOMIC MEASURES RECOMMENDED TO CHINA

On May 15, 1948, the Department of State transmitted to the Embassy at Nanking for use in corollary discussions with Chinese Government leaders a list of the principal specific measures regarding which it was believed the Chinese Government should initiate concrete steps. The list was not meant to be comprehensive, nor did it attempt to detail the administrative steps that would be involved. It was felt that the Embassy was in a better position to judge the more detailed actions that would be required. In any event, the Embassy was advised to encourage the Chinese to set forth their own proposals for general and concrete action, reserving the Embassy's comments for emphasis or addition if significant points were neglected by the Chinese. The following measures were those contained in the instruction from the Department of State to the Embassy: [8]

1. *Government Expenditures*

(*a*) Establishment of budgetary control and standardization of accounting, based on short-term projections, in the hands of a central fiscal authority with power to make allocations for all expenditures and with sufficient political strength to resist demands for unnecessary expenditures.

(*b*) Elimination of nonproductive expenditures not essential to efficient civil administration and prosecution of the war, such as padded army rolls, troops garrisoned in sheltered areas, Kuomintang Party activities, and so forth.

---

[8] See annex 182.

2. *Government Receipts*

(*a*) Administrative improvements in taxation.

(*b*) Expansion of measures to protect tax revenue from currency depreciation, such as the use of multiplication factors, ad valorem taxes and taxation at source.

(*c*) Expeditious sale of Government assets which could be operated more appropriately and efficiently by private enterprise.

3. *Civil and Military Administration*

(*a*) Adoption or continuation of a realistic cost of living index as a standard for ensuring more adequate pay for civil employees and soldiers.

(*b*) Drastic and impartial weeding out of civil and military officials guilty of gross inefficiency or corruption.

(*c*) Conscientious reduction of civil and military rolls to eliminate unnecessary employees.

(*d*) Coordination and elimination of duplication in civil and military agencies.

4. *Distribution of Staple Commodities*

Improved administration of, or extension of, distribution controls or incentives to maintain and expand the flow of consumer goods into rural areas as necessary to increase production and movement of agricultural goods for urban consumption and export.

5. *Banking and Credit*

Adjustment of the banking system in order:

(*a*) to give the Central Bank complete control of banking and credit policy for the purpose of checking speculation and ensuring more adequate credit for essential productive economic activity;

(*b*) to establish a clearer demarcation between the functions of Government and private banks and to prevent favoritism to Government banks;

(*c*) to eliminate uneconomic banking operations, such as the Central Cooperative Bank.

6. *Agricultural Improvement*

Implementation of recommendations of the Joint U.S.-China Agricultural Mission, with special reference to enforcement of reductions in rents and interest rates.

7. *Foreign Trade and its Controls*

(*a*) Administrative improvements in import and exchange controls including coordination throughout China of control procedures.

(*b*) More realistic exchange rate policies.

(*c*) Provision of adequate credit for production and marketing of export goods.

(*d*) Improvement in quality and standardization of export goods.

8. *Encouragement to Private Enterprise*

(*a*) Clarification, by action as well as by statement, of fields open to private enterprise without governmental intrusion.

(*b*) Elimination of special privilege in foreign trade and domestic enterprise.

In addition to the measures of self-help listed above, the Department instructed the Embassy to request that the Chinese Government permit foreign flag vessels carrying American aid cargo destined for inland water ports to discharge their cargo at such ports. It was believed that this permission was necessary for the effective implementation of American aid to interior points of China. After lengthy consideration, the Chinese Government indicated its willingness to grant such permission on a case by case basis, but the effect of the decision was not great for, by the time it was made, foreign shipping firms had become reluctant to risk transportation up the Yangtze.

In discussing the shipping problem with Chinese officials, the Embassy pointed out, *inter alia*, that general Chinese permission for foreign commercial vessels to carry international cargo on China's major inland waterways would clearly be to China's economic interest; that, while all sovereign powers enjoyed full control over national inland waterways, a large majority of nations had for reasons of economic self-interest granted foreign commercial vessels right of access to some or all of their inland ports.

In commenting on the Department's instructions, the Embassy indicated that while measures of self-help had frequently been the subject of pointed discussions with Chinese leaders in the past, it agreed that an intensive effort should now be made to urge the overwhelming importance of immediate reforms.[9] On May 22, 1948, Ambassador Stuart, during a conversation with President Chiang Kai-shek, handed him a memorandum dealing with the problems of domestic reform in China.[10] The memorandum was represented, not as an official document, but as the Ambassador's views as to what basic steps should be taken. It covered many of the points made in the Department's instruction of May 15, but the contents of the memorandum were arranged to correspond to the ten points of reform made in Premier

---

[9] See annex 180.
[10] See annex 182.

Chang Chun's statement of January 28, 1948. The Ambassador's memorandum subsequently was used by members of the Embassy as the basis for informal discussions with numerous other high Chinese Government officials, to whom the points were elaborated in greater detail with emphasis on the urgent need for early actions of specific and concrete character.

Informal contacts similar to the "corollary discussions" were maintained with various Chinese Government officials by members of the United States Embassy and by officers of the ECA mission in China throughout the period of the economic aid program. It was considered that American advisory assistance to the Chinese Government could be arranged more appropriately in this manner than by the designation of American officials as advisers to various Government agencies. The experience of foreign advisers to the Chinese Government, of whom there had been many in the past, provided little ground for believing that the results of such designation would be fruitful, nor did it seem wise that the American Government should be burdened in this manner, even by implication, with responsibility for actions, or failure to act, by the Chinese Government. It appeared axiomatic that, if Chinese leaders were disposed to accept advice, they would do so whether the advice was given in an official capacity or on an informal basis. Moreover, the Chinese Government was understandably sensitive to the type and degree of American guidance that might be associated with American aid. It was recalled that the Chinese Government stated in its memorandum of December 22, 1947, that while it intended to employ, on its own accord, American personnel to assist in planning for financial, monetary and other administrative reforms, "the employment of these personnel will not, however, be made an international legal obligation of the Chinese Government in order to avert infringement on China's sovereignty and administrative integrity."

On August 5, 1948, notes were exchanged between the United States and Chinese Governments [11] providing for the establishment of a Joint Commission on Rural Reconstruction in China and defining the scope and terms of the program which the Commission might undertake. Authority was given the Commission to formulate and carry out a broad program, with emphasis on the educational aspects of improving agricultural techniques in rural areas. The three Chinese members of the Commission were appointed immediately after the exchange of notes and the two American members on September 16, 1948. The Commission formally assembled in Nanking on October

[11] See annex 183.

1 and, in accordance with a provision in the agreement, elected one of the Chinese members as its chairman.

PROGRESS OF THE ECONOMIC AID PROGRAM

The following brief summary of the accomplishments of the. economic aid program is taken from a detailed account of the program published by the Economic Cooperation Administration in February 1949 entitled *Economic Aid under the China Aid Act of 1948:* [12]

"Food has been provided through a controlled ration system to nearly 13,000,000 inhabitants of seven major Chinese cities. Cotton financed under the program has kept the mills operating in China's largest industry, providing cloth for direct consumption, for barter to encourage the bringing of indigenous food into the cities, and for export to earn foreign exchange that can be used to pay for more imports. Petroleum has kept in operation basic industries, and also provided goods for which the farmers in the countryside are prepared to exchange their produce. Fertilizer imports have been planned for use in the production of spring crops in 1949. A Joint Commission on Rural Reconstruction has been established, and has formulated principles and a program for attacking some of the root causes of poverty and unrest among China's vast rural population. An industrial program of replacement machinery and reconstruction projects has been initiated with the participation of private American engineering firms; although actual procurement and construction had to be suspended for the most part due to uncertainties connected with the civil war, much useful engineering survey work has been done. A 'counterpart' fund in local currency, established by agreement with the Chinese Government and managed jointly by Chinese and Americans, has been used to maintain many hospitals, welfare programs, and dike-building projects.

"In spite of the growing chaos around them, these activities, by and large, have been managed with care and have been carried out successfully within their own limited terms of reference. In the case of the commodity program particularly, the supplies provided have been an important and at times crucial factor in keeping unrest to a minimum in the main cities of the coastal areas controlled by the Nationalist Government. In this narrow but significant sense, therefore, the efforts of ECA in China have been constructive and useful. Supplies financed by the United States have been and are being effectively distributed to the people intended to receive them."

Of the total 275 million dollar appropriation for economic aid to

[12] See annex 184.

China, Eca originally had earmarked 203.8 million dollars for commodities, 67.5 million dollars for industrial and transportation reconstruction and replacement projects, 2.5 million dollars for dollar expenditures of the Joint Commission on Rural Reconstruction, and 1.2 million dollars for Eca administration. By April 3, 1949, the expiry date of the China Aid Act of 1948, 215.0 million dollars had been authorized for procurement of commodities, and about 139.2 million dollars of these supplies had arrived in China.

During the period of these expenditures, the economy of Nationalist China continued to deteriorate at an accelerating pace. The budgetary deficit was unquestionably much more serious in 1948 than in preceding years. The loss of territory to Communist forces, the further dislocation of transportation and productive facilities and a sharp increase in smuggling combined to reduce receipts from taxes, Government-operated enterprises and customs duties. Increased military expenditures were incurred as the civil war spread and mounted in intensity.

Prices in August 1948, as measured by the Shanghai wholesale price index, were more than 3 million times those of the prewar half year, January to June 1937. In the first 7 months of 1948 prices increased more than 45 times and the black market rate for United States dollar notes increased over 50 times. Moreover the rate of price increase for the period progressively exceeded the rate of expansion of the note issue, as confidence in the currency diminished, and accordingly the value of the total currency outstanding contracted in terms of purchasing power. This contraction of the purchasing power of an expanding note issue has been observed in the later stages of currency inflation in other countries.

Private capital was almost wholly directed into nonproductive channels of financial speculation and hoarding of commodities, and banks demonstrated an increasing reluctance to extend long-term credit for industrial investment. The loss of economic resources through contraction of the area controlled by the National Government was illustrated most significantly by the abandonment in December 1948 of the Kailan mines located near Tientsin. These mines had been supplying more than half of the coal consumed in all of Nationalist-controlled China.

In the mid-summer of 1948 there was a sharp increase in the velocity of currency circulation which sent prices to astronomical figures. The Chinese Government was unwilling to print new currency notes of sufficiently large denominations to keep pace with prices, and it had become impossible to print adequate quantities of currency of lower denominations, which had to be used in such bulk that bushel baskets were required for currency transactions. The currency had become almost worthless as a medium of exchange.

On August 19, 1948, the Chinese Government announced the introduction of a new gold yuan currency to replace the old Chinese National currency at a ratio of G.Y.1 to C.N. 3 million. The rate of exchange for one United States dollar was set at G.Y. 4. The Government emphasized that introduction of the gold yuan would be accompanied by drastic financial reforms to curtail expenditures and increase revenue. It was represented that these reforms would reduce the budgetary deficit and the need for new note issue with the result that the internal purchasing power and the foreign exchange value of the new currency could be maintained.

Domestic prices and foreign exchange rates were pegged and drastic penalties prescribed for black market operations. The public was required to sell its gold, silver, and foreign currency notes in China to the Government at the pegged rates, and Chinese nationals were instructed to register with the Government all holdings of foreign exchange abroad. To bolster public confidence in the measures, the Government announced that, although the new currency was inconvertible, it was to be backed by gold, silver and other official foreign exchange holdings amounting to 200 million dollars and by the securities of certain Government-owned enterprises valued at 300 million dollars. Moreover, it was stated that the new note issue would be limited to G.Y. 2 billion.

The combination of stringent police measures and initial public confidence served for a few weeks to keep the Chinese economy functioning at the frozen price and foreign exchange levels of the August 19 reforms. The Government reported collection of more than 150 million dollars in foreign exchange for which it paid out new gold yuan.

It became evident shortly, however, that the Chinese Government was taking no effective action to curtail expenditures or to increase revenue, for new currency continued to be issued in the previous volume to cover the budgetary deficit. In addition, large quantities of gold yuan had been exchanged for foreign currencies and gold, much of which had heretofore been hoarded, and this added greatly to the total volume of currency competing for goods. Between August 19 and October 1 the note issue had increased almost five times.[13]

The continuing inflationary pressures revealed themselves first in West and North China where police enforcement was relatively ineffective. At Shanghai, however, Chiang Ching-kuo, the Gen-

---

[13] See annex 157 (a)-(c).

eralissimo's son, pursued a ruthless enforcement campaign. The price differential between the coastal cities and the hinterland and the maintenance of increasingly artificial foreign exchange rates, seriously impeded the movement of food and raw materials for urban consumption and export. Insistence on maintenance of the August 19 price levels, which was almost fanatical at Shanghai, resulted in the depletion of food and other commodity stocks in the cities to dangerously low levels, and brought about an almost complete stagnation of economic activity. Finally, the regulations became so ineffective and disruptive of economic activity that they were revoked officially in the face of a downward slide of the gold yuan which continued thereafter at a rapid rate. By late April and early May, 1949, the gold yuan, which had been introduced at a ratio of G.Y. 4 to U.S. $1, had depreciated in the open market to quotations ranging between G.Y. 5 million and 10 million to U.S. $1.

The ECA helped to alleviate the food crisis brought about by the extremes to which the Chinese Government's emergency reform measures of August 19 were carried. Steps were taken to speed up ECA deliveries of cereals and this proved to be of crucial importance in allaying unrest in the major cities. However, even after the reform measures were revoked, Chinese Government procurement of food for its share of the city rationing programs continued to lag seriously, and ECA thereafter provided a major portion of the ration requirements.

During the fall of 1948, the growing seriousness of the military situation in North China and Manchuria made it necessary for ECA to suspend preparatory work on industrial reconstruction and replacement projects located in those areas. In view of the rapid disintegration of the National Government military position which occurred shortly thereafter, the ECA Administrator announced on December 21, 1948, that work on the entire industrial program was, to a large extent, being suspended. At the time of suspension, all the projects were still in the preliminary engineering stage, no funds having been actually committed for procurement.

The impending fall of Peiping and Tientsin to Chinese Communist control confronted ECA with the problem of how its operations in North China should be handled in that event. ECA referred the matter to the Department of State, which took the position that ECA aid should be discontinued to areas of China that came under Chinese Communist control. On December 30, 1948, the President orally communicated to the Acting Secretary of State his confirmation of the

Department's position, which was recorded in the Department as follows:

"1. That this Government would continue to support through the implementation of the China Aid Act the present Chinese Government or a legal successor Government. However, should a government come into power which comes to terms with the Chinese Communists, all aid should cease irrespective of whether the Communists are in numerical ascendency or not.

"2. When the Chinese Communists either directly or indirectly through a coalition government take control over any area, all ECA supplies ashore or in the process of being unloaded can be distributed under conditions similar to those now prevailing. However, ECA supplies which have not yet reached such ports should be diverted elsewhere.

"3. That the military supplies under the China Aid Act should be delivered in so far as possible in accordance with the advice of our military authorities in China."

The intention of the second sentence of numbered paragraph (1) quoted above was that aid should cease to those areas that came under the control of a government in which the Chinese Communists participated. On January 14, 1949, the President's decision was reviewed by the Cabinet, with the ECA Administrator present, at which time it was reaffirmed.

Tientsin fell to Chinese Communist assault on January 15, 1949, and a peaceful takeover of Peiping by the Chinese Communists occurred during the last days of January. Although ECA stocks in both cities were small at the time, the ECA representatives were prepared in accordance with the President's decision, to complete their distribution of existing stocks through channels previously agreed upon and under appropriate supervision. In both cities, however, the Chinese Communists seized ECA stocks of wheat and flour, which they distributed to selected groups of civilian workers rather than to the population generally. ECA stocks of cotton yarn and cloth at Tientsin were sealed by the Chinese Communists and ECA officers were unable to make any disposition of these stocks before their departure from the area on March 21, 1949.

Meanwhile, Generalissimo Chiang Kai-shek had retired from the scene in Nanking on January 21 and the reconstituted cabinet under the leadership of Acting President Li Tsung-jen was endeavoring to find a basis upon which peace negotiations could be carried on with the Chinese Communists. (These developments are treated in detail in chapter VI.)

The Chinese Government's official foreign exchange reserves at this time consisted in large part of gold and silver bullion in China. The Central Bank reported at the end of the first quarter of 1949 total gold and silver holdings of approximately 160 million dollars, although other reliable sources indicated that such holdings were as much as 250 million dollars. The bulk of the bullion had been removed to Taiwan and Amoy before the Generalissimo retired. The Acting President later sent an emissary to see the Generalissimo to arrange for the return of the gold and silver and on April 15 the Control Yuan at Nanking passed a bill requesting their return to the Government. Although the Generalissimo subsequently made available to the Government at Nanking 17 million silver coins from stores at Amoy, efforts to obtain the use of the reserves at Amoy and Taiwan for emergency expenditures by Nanking were generally unavailing.

The Government at Nanking, in its search for means to retain some semblance of order in the increasingly chaotic administrative and financial conditions obtaining in the lower Yangtze valley, approached the United States Government frequently during the late winter and spring of 1949 seeking to obtain silver with which to meet its military and administrative expenditures. The proposals varied in detail from time to time, but essentially they all amounted to the advance of silver by the United States Government to underwrite the Chinese Government's budgetary deficit. The Departments of State and Treasury gave no encouragement to these Chinese proposals.

On March 23, the Embassy commented on a Chinese proposal for silver aid as follows:

"Although we agree that the financial situation is growing increasingly perilous, we can find no support on economic grounds for a currency stabilization loan. The intensifying currency crisis essentially arises from the internal budget deficit and not from the shortage of foreign exchange. The ECA commodity import program has substantially answered the latter phase of the problem.

"Any 'stabilization loan' at this time would be merely budget deficit assistance. The deficit is an internal Chinese problem and the Government has consistently proved unable or unwilling to act either to increase Government revenues or reduce expenses. The fact of the deficit alone is not the cause but the symptom of the fundamental imbalance between the tremendous demand arising from the weight of the Government's military structure, administrative incompetence and corruption, upon increasingly limited goods and services. No fiscal program involving quantitative money manipulations of the type monotonously recurring in the past as 'financial reform' can significantly affect this imbalance. We know of no Chinese Government fiscal program proposed or in prospect which offers any possibility of effective results in meeting the monetary difficulties."

On April 6, the Ambassador reported as follows: "Both the Acting President and the Premier have again and separately raised the question of U. S. financial and economic assistance. The Prime Minister is still hoping to secure a silver loan from the U. S. and suggested a lien on the island of Taiwan, or on its products, as security. The Acting President, through his emissary . . . emphasized the imminent danger of collapse of the Government because of the fiscal situation; he asked if this did not warrant American aid sufficient to keep the Nationalist Government going at least through the peace talks. In response to the latter's comment, I felt compelled to speak frankly. I pointed out the difficulties from the American standpoint in securing financial assistance. I called attention to the well-known fact that the Chinese Government had reportedly something less than 300 million dollars in gold and silver bullion and foreign exchange; that most of this reserve existed, or was made possible, because of previous American aid; that it would seem natural to draw upon this fund for the present emergency. Our officials in Washington were, of course, fully aware of this reserve fund. I continued that if peace could be secured, it would not be too difficult for the new Government to build up a fresh reserve in an atmosphere of peace and a period of productive activity, that if the fighting were renewed, these reserves would either fall under control of the Communists or be consumed within a brief period of time in efforts toward further resistance."

CONTINUATION OF ECONOMIC AID BEYOND APRIL 3, 1949

On March 31 the Chinese Ambassador submitted to the Department of State proposals for the interim extension of the ECA Program beyond April 3 to June 30, 1949, and for a new economic aid program of 420 million dollars during the fiscal year 1950. These proposals were received while consideration was being given by Congress to recommendations from ECA and the Department of State regarding limited extension of the economic aid program for China. Careful consideration had been given during the early months of 1949 by ECA and the Department of State to the question of what recommendations should be made to Congress for continuation or cessation of American aid to China before the authority contained in the China Aid Act of 1948 expired on April 3, 1949. These studies were continued in early 1949. The following facts and observations were fundamental to a decision on this question.

Foreign aid authorized for the Chinese Government since V–J Day had amounted to approximately 2,254 million dollars, of which the United States had provided 90 percent or slightly more than 2 billion dollars in the form of grants and credits. Aid authorized by the United States had been divided almost equally between military and economic purposes. Total American grants and credits since V–J Day had been equivalent in value to more than 50 percent of the monetary expenditures of the Chinese Government and was of proportionately greater magnitude in relation to the budget of that Government than the United States had provided to any nation of Western Europe since the end of the war. In addition to its aid in the form of grants and credits, the United States had sold the Chinese Government large quantities of military and civilian type surplus property for a nominal return. Surplus property with a total estimated procurement cost of over 1 billion dollars had been sold China for an agreed realization to the United States of 232 million dollars. Moreover, the United States had assisted the Chinese Government through the provision of military advisory personnel, and had "abandoned" and transferred substantial quantities of military material in China, for which there is no estimated dollar value. Finally, between V–J Day and the end of 1947, the Chinese Government had drawn down the largest gold and United States dollar reserves it had ever held by approximately 700 million dollars to finance commodity imports and the sale of gold within China.

The following summary table lists the various measures of foreign economic and military aid authorized for China since V–J Day. A more detailed description of the U. S. Government measures listed below is contained in annex 185.

I. *U. S. Government Grants and Credits*

Grants: (Millions of U. S. dollars)

Lend-lease	$513. 7
Military aid under Sino-American Cooperative Organization Agreement	17. 7
U. S. contribution to Unrra China program .	474. 0
U. S. share of Unrra contribution to Botra .	3. 6
Ammunition abandoned and transferred by U. S. Marines in North China (over 6,500 tons) (no estimate of value available).	
Transfer of U.S. Navy vessels (P. L. 512) (valued at procurement cost)	141. 3
U. S. foreign relief program	46. 4
Eca program	275. 0
$125 million grant under China Aid Act of 1948	125. 0
TOTAL GRANTS	$1,596. 7

I. *U. S. Government Grants and Credits*—Continued

Credits: (*Millions of U. S. dollars*)

Lend-lease	$181. 0
Lend-lease "pipe line" credit	51. 7
Export-Import Bank credits	82. 8
Surplus property sales for credit:	
Sale of excess stocks of U. S. Army in West China	20. 0
OFLC dockyard facilities sales	4. 1
Civilian surplus property transfers (under August 30, 1946, bulk sale agreement)	55. 0
Maritime Commission Ship Sales	16. 4

TOTAL CREDITS	$411. 0	
TOTAL GRANTS AND CREDITS		$2, 007. 7

II. *Other Foreign Grants and Credits*

Balance of UNRRA China program	$184. 4	
Balance of UNRRA contribution to BOTRA	1. 4	
Canadian credit	60. 0	
TOTAL OTHER FOREIGN AID		$245. 8
TOTAL FOREIGN GRANTS AND CREDITS SINCE V–J DAY . . .		$2, 253. 5

III. *U. S. Government Surplus Property Sales*

(in millions of U. S. dollars)

	Procurement cost	Agreed realization to U. S.
Sale of excess stocks of U. S. Army in West China .	(Not available)	$20
OFLC dockyard facilities sales.	" "	4. 1
Civilian surplus property transfers (under August 30, 1946, agreement)	$900	175.
Maritime Commission ship sales	77. 3	26. 2
Military surplus property transfers	100. 8	6. 7
TOTAL SURPLUS PROPERTY SALES	$1, 078. 1	[1] $232. 0

[1] Includes $95.5 million to be paid on credit terms as indicated in Table I above under *credits.*

Despite provision of this foreign aid, the position of the Chinese Government had deteriorated steadily, both militarily and economically. The Chinese Government had failed to demonstrate its capacity to cope with the immense and complicated forces at work in China. In the fields of economic policy and civil and military administration, the Chinese Government had undertaken no effective initial steps directed toward correcting the basic maladjustments of the Chinese economy and the malpractices of its administration. Governmental expenditures and the issuance of the fiat paper money had proceeded at an uncontrolled and increasing rate. There had been no evidence of successful measures to augment revenue, nor had there been any evidence of elimination of maladministration in the civilian and military bureaucracy. The measures of attempted financial reform by the Government were poorly conceived, and in effect, had increased rather than retarded the rate of economic deterioration.

By March 1949, the military position of the Chinese Government had collapsed to the point where the Chinese Communists controlled the major centers of population and the railroads from Manchuria south to the Yangtze Valley and were in a position to take control of Nanking, Hankow and Shanghai by military or political means within a relatively short period of time, and on their own terms. The military collapse of the Chinese Government had for the most part been the consequence of inept leadership and lack of will to fight on the part of its armies, rather than of inadequate military supplies. The loss and abandonment of military matériel by Chinese Government forces had constituted a large source of military supply for the Chinese Communists. It was apparent that, unless there were an unexpected and unprecedented improvement in the administrative and military operations of the National Government and in the will to fight of its armies, the Chinese Communists would not have difficulty in expanding their control throughout the south and west of China if, as soon as they consolidated their position in the north, they chose to move southward. It was the considered judgment of responsible American Government observers in China that only the extension of unlimited American economic and military aid, involving extensive control of Chinese Government operations by American military and administrative personnel, and including the immediate employment of United States armed forces to block the southern advance of the Communists, would enable the National Government to maintain a foothold in South China against a determined advance by the Chinese Communists. It was believed that under the existing circumstances, however, involvement of the United States in the Chinese civil war by such action would be clearly contrary to American interests.

The above considerations led the Department of State to view unfavorably a bill (S. 1063) that had been introduced in the Senate calling for 1.5 billion dollars of military and economic aid for China. Upon a request by the Senate Foreign Relations Committee for comment on the bill, Secretary of State Acheson stated the Department's views in a letter of March 15, 1949, to Senator Tom Connally, Chairman of the Committee.[14]

Although the relative military capabilities of the Chinese Government and the Chinese Communists were evident, the political situation was highly uncertain. Acting President Li Tsung-jen had entered into peace negotiations with the Chinese Communists, thus reflecting a widespread desire among the Chinese people for peace at all costs. The intentions of the Chinese Communists were far from clear. Although there was little that the United States could do to influence the course of events in China, it would have been inconsistent with the traditional relations between the United States and China for the United States, in the face of extreme adversity for the Chinese people, abruptly to cease on April 3, 1949, economic aid to the Chinese Government which it continued to recognize. It was believed that the United States should certainly continue its economic relief until the next harvest in areas of China that remained free of Communist domination.

The Department of State therefore supported an ECA proposal that Congress be requested to amend the China Aid Act of 1948 to permit obligation of existing appropriations until December 31, 1949. It was estimated that by April 3 there would remain approximately 54 million dollars unobligated, and that this sum would enable continuation of the commodity assistance program at the existing level to Central and South China and Taiwan substantially until the midsummer harvest became available; that if, in the meantime, Nanking and Shanghai should come under Chinese Communist control, remaining funds might prove to be sufficient to continue commodity assistance for a longer period in South China and Taiwan. It was also believed that, in so far as funds were available, the rural reconstruction program should be continued in coastal and interior areas of China so long as circumstances made it possible to do so.

On April 14, 1949, the Congress passed legislation which, in effect, carried out the recommendations of ECA and the Department of State. Rather than amending the China Aid Act of 1948, Congress wrote new legislation which made available to the President such portion of the appropriation for economic aid as remained unobligated on April 3, 1949, or might subsequently be released from obligation. In view of the extreme fluidity and uncertainty of the situation in China, the new legislation authorized the President to use these funds in such manner and on such terms and conditions as he might determine for aid to those areas of China that remained free of

---

[14] See annex 186.

Chinese Communist control.   Moreover, the funds were made available for obligation through February 15, 1950, in order that the expiration of authority would occur while the next Congress was in session.

THE APPRAISAL OF ACTING PRESIDENT LI

Perhaps the aptest and most tragic summary of American intentions toward China and of the reasons for the present predicament of China was given by the Acting President, General Li Tsung-jen, himself.   The first three paragraphs of a letter he wrote to President Truman on May 5, 1949, concern the events of the period with which this paper is concerned and read as follows:

"Throughout our war of resistance against Japanese aggression, the United States of America continuously extended to us her moral and material assistance, which enabled our country to carry on an arduous struggle of eight long years until final victory was achieved. The sincere friendship thus demonstrated by the United States has contributed not only to strengthen further the traditional ties between our two countries but to win the deep gratitude and unbounded goodwill of the people of China.

"This policy of friendly assistance was continued when some years ago General George C. Marshall, under instructions from your good self, took up the difficult task of mediation in our conflict with the Chinese Communists, to which he devoted painstaking effort. All this work was unfortunately rendered fruitless by the lack of sincerity on the part of both the then Government and the Chinese Communists.

"In spite of this, your country continued to extend its aid to our Government.   It is regrettable that, owing to the failure of our then Government to make judicious use of this aid and to bring about appropriate political, economic and military reforms, your assistance has not produced the desired effect.   To this failure is attributable the present predicament in which our country finds itself."

Annexes

Annexes to Chapter I: A Century of American Policy, 1844–1943

1

Treaty of Wanghia (Cushing Treaty), July 3, 1844[1]

[Extract]

ARTICLE II

Citizens of the United States resorting to China for the purposes of commerce will pay the duties of import and export prescribed in the Tariff, which is fixed by and made a part of this Treaty. They shall, in no case, be subject to other or higher duties than are or shall be required of the people of any other nation whatever. Fees and charges of every sort are wholly abolished, and officers of the revenue, who may be guilty of exaction, shall be punished according to the laws of China. If the Chinese Government desire to modify, in any respect, the said tariff, such modifications shall be made only in consultation with Consuls or other functionaries thereto duly authorized in behalf of the United States, and with consent thereof. And if additional advantages or privileges, of whatever description be conceded hereafter by China to any other nation, the United States, and the citizens thereof, shall be entitled thereupon, to a complete, equal, and impartial participation in the same.

2

Treaty of Tientsin (Reed Treaty), June 18, 1858[2]

[Extract]

ARTICLE XXX

The contracting parties hereby agree that should at any time the Ta Tsing Empire grant to any nation, or the merchants or citizens of any nation, any right, privilege or favor, connected either with navigation, commerce, political or other intercourse, which is not conferred by this treaty, such right, privilege and favor shall at once freely inure to the benefit of the United States, its public officers, merchants and citizens.

---

[1] Hunter Miller, ed., *Treaties and Other International Acts of the United States of America*, vol. 4, pp. 559, 560.
[2] *Ibid.*, vol. 7, pp. 793, 804.

3

Treaty of Washington (Burlingame Treaty), July 28, 1868 [3]

[Extract]

ARTICLE VI

Citizens of the United States visiting or residing in China shall enjoy the same privileges, immunities or exemptions in respect to travel or residence as may there be enjoyed by the citizens or subjects of the most favored nation ; and, reciprocally, Chinese subjects visiting or residing in the United States shall enjoy the same privileges, immunities and exemptions in respect to travel or residence as may there be enjoyed by the citizens or subjects of the most favored nation. But nothing herein contained shall be held to confer naturalization upon citizens of the United States in China, nor upon the subjects of China in the United States.

4

The Open Door Notes

Secretary Hay to the Ambassador in Great Britain (Choate) [4]

WASHINGTON, *September 6, 1899*

SIR: The Government of Her Britannic Majesty has declared that its policy and its very traditions precluded it from using any privileges which might be granted it in China as a weapon for excluding commercial rivals, and that freedom of trade for Great Britain in that Empire meant freedom of trade for all the world alike. While conceding by formal agreements, first with Germany and then with Russia, the possession of "spheres of influence or interest" in China in which they are to enjoy special rights and privileges, more especially in respect of railroads and mining enterprises, Her Britannic Majesty's Government has therefore sought to maintain at the same time what is called the "open-door" policy, to insure to the commerce of the world in China equality of treatment within said "spheres" for commerce and navigation. This latter policy is alike urgently demanded by the British mercantile communities and by those of the United States, as it is justly held by them to be the only one which will improve existing conditions, enable them to maintain their positions in the markets of China, and extend their operations in the future. While the Government of the United States will in no way commit itself to a recognition of exclusive rights of any power within or control over any portion of the Chinese Empire under such agreements as have within the last year been made, it can not conceal its apprehension that under existing conditions there is a possibility, even a probability, of complications arising between the treaty powers which may imperil the rights insured to the United States under our treaties with China.

This Government is animated by a sincere desire that the interests of our citizens may not be prejudiced through exclusive treatment by any of the con-

---

[3] William M. Malloy, ed., *Treaties, Conventions, International Acts, Protocols and Agreements Between the United States of America and Other Powers,* vol. I, pp. 234, 236.

[4] *Foreign Relations of the United States,* 1899, p. 131. Similar instructions were sent to American Diplomatic Representatives at Paris, Berlin, St. Petersburg, Rome, and Tokyo.

trolling powers within their so-called "spheres of interest" in China, and hopes also to retain there an open market for the commerce of the world, remove dangerous sources of international irritation, and hasten thereby united or concerted action of the powers at Pekin in favor of the administrative reforms so urgently needed for strengthening the Imperial Government and maintaining the integrity of China in which the whole western world is alike concerned. It believes that such a result may be greatly assisted by a declaration by the various powers claiming "spheres of interest" in China of their intentions as regards treatment of foreign trade therein. The present moment seems a particularly opportune one for informing Her Britannic Majesty's Government of the desire of the United States to see it make a formal declaration and to lend its support in obtaining similar declarations from the various powers claiming "spheres of influence" in China, to the effect that each in its respective spheres of interest or influence

First. Will in no wise interfere with any treaty port or any vested interest within any so-called "sphere of interest" or leased territory it may have in China.

Second. That the Chinese treaty tariff of the time being shall apply to all merchandise landed or shipped to all such ports as are within said "sphere of interest" (unless they be "free ports"), no matter to what nationality it may belong, and that duties so leviable shall be collected by the Chinese Government.

Third. That it will levy no higher harbor duties on vessels of another nationality frequenting any port in such "sphere" than shall be levied on vessels of its own nationality, and no higher railroad charges over lines built, controlled, or operated within its "sphere" on merchandise belonging to citizens or subjects of other nationalities transported through such "sphere" than shall be levied on similar merchandise belonging to its own nationals transported over equal distances.

The recent ukase of His Majesty the Emperor of Russia, declaring the port of Ta-lien-wan open to the merchant ships of all nations during the whole of the lease under which it is to be held by Russia, removing as it does all uncertainty as to the liberal and conciliatory policy of that power, together with the assurances given this Government by Russia, justifies the expectation that His Majesty will cooperate in such an understanding as is here proposed, and our ambassador at the court of St. Petersburg has been instructed accordingly to submit the propositions above detailed to His Imperial Majesty, and ask their early consideration. Copy of my instruction to Mr. Tower is herewith inclosed for your confidential information.

The action of Germany in declaring the port of Kiaochao a "free port," and the aid the Imperial Government has given China in the establishment there of a Chinese custom-house, coupled with the oral assurance conveyed the United States by Germany that our interests within its "sphere" would in no wise be affected by its occupation of this portion of the province of Shang-tung, tend to show that little opposition may be anticipated from that power to the desired declaration.

The interests of Japan, the next most interested power in the trade of China, will be so clearly served by the proposed arrangement, and the declaration of its statesmen within the last year are so entirely in line with the views here expressed, that its hearty cooperation is confidently counted on.

You will, at as early date as practicable, submit the considerations to Her Britannic Majesty's principal secretary of state for foreign affairs and request their immediate consideration.

I inclose herewith a copy of the instruction sent to our ambassador at Berlin bearing on the above subject.[5]

I have the honor to be [etc.]   JOHN HAY.

Secretary Hay to American Diplomatic Representatives at London, Paris, Berlin, St. Petersburg, Rome, and Tokyo [6]

WASHINGTON, *March 20, 1900*

SIR: The ——— Government having accepted the declaration suggested by the United States concerning foreign trade in China, the terms of which I transmitted to you in my instruction No. ——— of ———, and like action having been taken by all the various powers having leased territory or so-called "spheres of interest" in the Chinese Empire, as shown by the notes which I herewith transmit to you,[7] you will please inform the Government to which you are accredited that the condition originally attached to its acceptance—that all other powers concerned should likewise accept the proposals of the United States—having been complied with, this Government will therefore consider the assent given to it by ——— as final and definitive.

You will also transmit to the minister for foreign affairs copies of the present inclosures,[7] and by the same occasion convey to him the expression of the sincere gratification which the President feels at the successful termination of these negotiations, in which he sees proof of the friendly spirit which animates the various powers interested in the untrammeled development of commerce and industry in the Chinese Empire, and a source of vast benefit to the whole commercial world.

I am [etc.]   JOHN HAY.

5

Secretary Hay to American Diplomatic Representatives at Berlin, Paris, London, Rome, St. Petersburg, Vienna, Brussels, Madrid, Tokyo, The Hague, and Lisbon [8]

WASHINGTON, *July 3, 1900*

In this critical posture of affairs in China it is deemed appropriate to define the attitude of the United States as far as present circumstances permit this to be done. We adhere to the policy initiated by us in 1857 of peace with the Chinese nation, of furtherance of lawful commerce, and of protection of lives and property of our citizens by all means guaranteed under extraterritorial treaty rights and by the law of nations. If wrong be done to our citizens we propose to hold the responsible authors to the uttermost accountability. We regard the condition at Pekin as one of virtual anarchy, whereby power and responsibility are practically devolved upon the local provincial authorities. So long as they are not in overt collusion with rebellion and use their power to protect foreign life and property, we regard them as representing the Chinese people, with whom we seek to remain in peace and friendship. The purpose of the President is, as it has been heretofore, to act concurrently with the other

---

[5] Not printed.
[6] Foreign Relations, 1899, p. 142.
[7] Not printed.
[8] Foreign Relations 1900, p. 299.

powers; first, in opening up communication with Pekin and rescuing the American officials, missionaries, and other Americans who are in danger; secondly, in affording all possible protection everywhere in China to American life and property; thirdly, in guarding and protecting all legitimate American interests; and fourthly, in aiding to prevent a spread of the disorders to the other provinces of the Empire and a recurrence of such disasters. It is of course too early to forecast the means of attaining this last result; but the policy of the Government of the United States is to seek a solution which may bring about permanent safety and peace to China, preserve Chinese territorial and administrative entity, protect all rights guaranteed to friendly powers by treaty and international law, and safeguard for the world the principle of equal and impartial trade with all parts of the Chinese Empire.

You will communicate the purport of this instruction to the minister for foreign affairs.

JOHN HAY.

6

Treaty Between the United States and China for the Extension of the Commercial Relations Between Them, Signed at Shanghai, October 8, 1903 [9]

The United States of America and His Majesty the Emperor of China, being animated by an earnest desire to extend further the commercial relations between them and otherwise to promote the interests of the peoples of the two countries, in view of the provisions of the first paragraph of Article XI of the final Protocol signed at Peking on the seventh day of September, A. D. 1901, whereby the Chinese Government agreed to negotiate the amendments deemed necessary by the foreign Governments to the treaties of commerce and navigation and other subjects concerning commercial relations, with the object of facilitating them, have for that purpose named as their Plenipotentiaries:—

The United States of America—

   Edwin H. Conger, Envoy Extraordinary and Minister Plenipotentiary of the United States of America to China—

   John Goodnow, Consul-General of the United States of America at Shanghai—

   John F. Seaman, a Citizen of the United States of America resident at Shanghai—

And His Majesty the Emperor of China—

   Lü Hai-huan, President of the Board of Public Works—

   Sheng Hsüan-huai, Junior Guardian of the Heir Apparent. Formerly Senior Vice-President of the Board of Public Works—

who, having met and duly exchanged their full powers which were found to be in proper form, have agreed upon the following amendments to existing treaties of commerce and navigation formerly concluded between the two countries, and upon the subjects hereinafter expressed connected with commercial relations, with the object of facilitating them.

---

[9] *Ibid.*, 1903, p. 91.

Article I

In accordance with international usage, and as the diplomatic representative of China has the right to reside in the capital of the United States, and to enjoy there the same prerogatives, privileges and immunities as are enjoyed by the similar representative of the most favored nation, the diplomatic representative of the United States shall have the right to reside at the capital of His Majesty the Emperor of China. He shall be given audience of His Majesty the Emperor whenever necessary to present his letters of credence or any communication from the President of the United States. At all such times he shall be received in a place and in a manner befitting his high position, and on all such occasions the ceremonial observed toward him shall be that observed toward the representatives of nations on a footing of equality, with no loss of prestige on the part of either.

The diplomatic representatives of the United States shall enjoy all the prerogatives, privileges and immunities accorded by international usage to such representatives, and shall in all respects be entitled to the treatment extended to similar representatives of the most favored nation.

The English text of all notes or dispatches from United States officials to Chinese officials, and the Chinese text of all from Chinese officials to United States officials shall be authoritative.

Article II

As China may appoint consular officers to reside in the United States and to enjoy there the same attributes, privileges and immunities as are enjoyed by consular officers of other nations, the United States may appoint, as its interests may require, consular officers to reside at the places in the Empire of China that are now or that may hereafter be opened to foreign residence and trade. They shall hold direct official intercourse and correspondence with the local officers of the Chinese Government within their consular districts, either personally or in writing as the case may require, on terms of equality and reciprocal respect. These officers shall be treated with due respect by all Chinese authorities, and they shall enjoy all the attributes, privileges and immunities, and exercise all the jurisdiction over their nationals which are or may hereafter be extended to similar officers of the nation the most favored in these respects. If the officers of either government are disrespectfully treated or aggrieved in any way by the authorities of the other, they shall have the right to make representation of the same to the superior officers of their own government who shall see that full inquiry and strict justice be had in the premises. And the said consular officers of either nation shall carefully avoid all acts of offense to the officers and people of the other nation.

On the arrival of a consul duly accredited at any place in China opened to foreign trade it shall be the duty of the Minister of the United States to inform the Board of Foreign Affairs, which shall, in accordance with international usage, forthwith cause the proper recognition of the said consul and grant him authority to act.

Article III

Citizens of the United States may frequent, reside and carry on trade, industries and manufactures, or pursue any lawful avocation, in all the ports or localities of China which are now open or may hereafter be opened to foreign residence and trade; and, within the suitable localities at those places which have been or may be set apart for the use and occupation of foreigners, they may rent or purchase houses, places of business and other buildings, and rent or lease in perpetuity land and build thereon. They shall generally enjoy as to their persons and property all such rights, privileges and immunities as are or may hereafter be granted to the subjects or citizens of the nation the most favored in these respects.

ARTICLE IV

The Chinese Government, recognizing that the existing system of levying dues on goods in transit, and especially the system of taxation known as *likin*, impedes the free circulation of commodities to the general injury of trade, hereby undertakes to abandon the levy of *likin* and all other transit dues throughout the Empire and to abolish the offices, stations and barriers maintained for their collection and not to establish other offices for levying dues on goods in transit. It is clearly understood that, after the offices, stations and barriers for taxing goods in transit have been abolished, no attempt shall be made to re-establish them in any form or under any pretext whatsoever.

The Government of the United States, in return, consents to allow a surtax, in excess of the tariff rates for the time being in force, to be imposed on foreign goods imported by citizens of the United States and on Chinese produce destined for export abroad or coastwise. It is clearly understood that in no case shall the surtax on foreign imports exceed one and one-half times the import duty leviable in terms of the final Protocol signed by China and the Powers on the seventh day of September, A. D. 1901; that the payment of the import duty and surtax shall secure for foreign imports, whether in the hands of Chinese or foreigners, in original packages or otherwise, complete immunity from all other taxation, examination or delay; that the total amount of taxation, inclusive of the tariff export duty, leviable on native produce for export abroad shall, under no circumstances, exceed seven and one-half per centum *ad valorem*.

Nothing in this article is intended to interfere with the inherent right of China to levy such other taxes as are not in conflict with its provisions.

Keeping these fundamental principles in view, the High Contracting Parties have agreed upon the following method of procedure.

The Chinese Government undertakes that all offices, stations and barriers of whatsoever kind for collecting *likin*, duties, or such like dues on goods in transit, shall be permanently abolished on all roads, railways and waterways in the nineteen Provinces of China and the three Eastern Provinces. This provision does not apply to the native Customs offices at present in existence on the seaboard, at open ports where there are offices of the Imperial Maritime Customs, and on the land frontiers of China embracing the nineteen Provinces and the three Eastern Provinces.

Wherever there are offices of the Imperial Maritime Customs, or wherever such may be hereafter placed, native Customs offices may also be established, as well as at any point either on the seaboard or land frontiers.

The Government of the United States agrees that foreign goods on importation, in addition to the effective five per centum import duty as provided for in the Protocol of 1901, shall pay a special surtax of one and one-half times the amount of the said duty to compensate for the abolition of *likin*, of other transit dues besides *likin*, and of all other taxation on foreign goods, and in consideration of the other reforms provided for in this article.

The Chinese Government may recast the foreign export tariff with specific duties, as far as practicable, on a scale not exceeding five per centum *ad valorem;* but existing export duties shall not be raised until at least six months' notice has been given. In cases where existing export duties are above five per centum, they shall be reduced to not more than that rate. An additional special surtax of one-half the export duty payable for the time being, in lieu of internal taxation of all kinds, may be levied at the place of original shipment or at the time of export on goods exported either to foreign countries or coastwise.

Foreign goods which bear a similarity to native goods shall be furnished by the Customs officers, if required by the owner, with a protective certificate for each package, on the payment of import duty and surtax, to prevent the risk of any dispute in the interior.

Native goods brought by junks to open ports, if intended for local consumption, irrespective of the nationality of the owner of the goods, shall be reported at the native Customs offices only, to be dealt with according to the fiscal regulations of the Chinese Government.

Machine-made cotton yarn and cloth manufactured in China, whether by foreigners at the open ports or by Chinese anywhere in China, shall as regards taxation be on a footing of perfect equality. Such goods upon payment of the taxes thereon shall be granted a rebate of the import duty and of two-thirds of the import surtax paid on the cotton used in their manufacture, if it has been imported from abroad, and of all duties paid thereon if it be Chinese grown cotton. They shall also be free of export duty, coast-trade duty and export surtax. The same principle and procedure shall be applied to all other products of foreign type turned out by machinery in China.

A member or members of the Imperial Maritime Customs foreign staff shall be selected by the Governors-General and Governors of each of the various provinces of the Empire for their respective provinces, and appointed in consultation with the Inspector General of Imperial Maritime Customs, for duty in connection with native Customs affairs to have a general supervision of their working.

Cases where illegal action is complained of by citizens of the United States shall be promptly investigated by an officer of the Chinese Government of sufficiently high rank, in conjunction with an officer of the United States Government, and an officer of the Imperial Maritime Customs, each of sufficient standing; and, in the event of it being found by the investigating officers that the complaint is well founded and loss has been incurred, due compensation shall be paid through the Imperial Maritime Customs. The high provincial officials shall be held responsible that the officer guilty of the illegal action shall be severely punished and removed from his post. If the complaint is shown to be frivolous or malicious, the complainant shall be held responsible for the expenses of the investigation.

When the ratifications of this Treaty shall have been exchanged by the High Contracting Parties hereto, and the provisions of this Article shall have been accepted by the Powers having treaties with China, then a date shall be agreed upon when the provisions of this Article shall take effect and an Imperial Edict shall be published in due form on yellow paper and circulated throughout the Empire of China setting forth the abolition of all *likin* taxation, duties on goods in transit, offices, stations and barriers for collecting the same, and of all descriptions of internal taxation on foreign goods, and the imposition of the surtax on the import of foreign goods and on the export of native goods, and the other fiscal changes and reforms provided for in this Article, all of which shall take effect from the said date. The Edict shall state that the provincial high officials are responsible that any official disregarding the letter or the spirit of its injunction shall be severely punished and removed from his post.

ARTICLE V

The tariff duties to be paid by citizens of the United States on goods imported into China shall be as set forth in the schedule annexed hereto and made part of this Treaty, subject only to such amendments and changes as are authorized by Article IV of the present convention or as may hereafter be agreed upon by the High Contracting Parties hereto. It is expressly agreed, however, that citizens of the United States shall at no time pay other or higher duties than those paid by the citizens or subjects of the most favored nation.

Conversely, Chinese subjects shall not pay higher duties on their imports into the United States than those paid by the citizens or subjects of the most favored nation.

ARTICLE VI

The Government of China agrees to the establishment by citizens of the United States of warehouses approved by the proper Chinese authorities as bonded warehouses at the several open Ports of China, for storage, re-packing, or preparation for shipment of lawful goods, subject to such necessary regulations for the protection of the revenue of China, including a reasonable scale of fees according to commodities, distance from the custom house and hours of working, as shall be made from time to time by the proper officers of the Government of China.

ARTICLE VII

The Chinese Government, recognizing that it is advantageous for the country to develop its mineral resources, and that it is desirable to attract foreign as well as Chinese capital to embark in mining enterprises, agrees, within one year from the signing of this Treaty, to initiate and conclude the revision of the existing mining regulations. To this end China will, with all expedition and earnestness, go into the whole question of mining rules; and, selecting from the rules of the United States and other countries regulations which seem applicable to the condition of China, will recast its present mining rules in such a way as, while promoting the interests of Chinese subjects and not injuring in any way the sovereign rights of China, will offer no impediment to the attraction of foreign capital nor place foreign capitalists at a greater disadvantage than they would be under generally accepted foreign regulations; and will permit citizens of the United States to carry on in Chinese territory mining operations and other necessary business relating thereto provided they comply with the new regulations and conditions which will be imposed by China on its subjects and foreigners alike, relating to the opening of mines, the renting of mineral land, and the payment of royalty, and provided they apply for permits, the provisions of which in regard to necessary business relating to such operations shall be observed. The residence of citizens of the United States in connection with such mining operations shall be subject to such regulations as shall be agreed upon by and between the United States and China.

Any mining concession granted after the publication of such new rules shall be subject to their provisions.

ARTICLE VIII

Drawback certificates for the return of duties shall be issued by the Imperial Maritime Customs to citizens of the United States within three weeks of the presentation to the Customs of the papers entitling the applicant to receive such drawback certificates, and they shall be receivable at their face value in payment of dutes of all kinds (tonnage dues excepted) at the port of issue; or shall, in the case of drawbacks on foreign goods re-exported within three years from the date of importation, be redeemable by the Imperial Maritime Customs in full in ready money at the port of issue, at the option of the holders thereof. But if, in connection with any application for a drawback certificate, the Customs authorities discover an attempt to defraud the revenue, the applicant shall be dealt with and punished in accordance with the stipulations provided in the Treaty of Tientsin, Article XXI, in the case of detected frauds on the revenue. In case the goods have been removed from Chinese territory, then the consul shall inflict on the guilty party a suitable fine to be paid to the Chinese Government.

ARTICLE IX

Whereas the United States undertakes to protect the citizens of any country in the exclusive use within the United States of any lawful trade-marks, provided that such country agrees by treaty or convention to give like protection to citizens of the United States:—

Therefore the Government of China, in order to secure such protection in the United States for its subjects, now agrees to fully protect any citizen, firm or corporation of the United States in the exclusive use in the Empire of China of any lawful trade-mark to the exclusive use of which in the United States they are entitled, or which they have adopted and used, or intend to adopt and use as soon as registered, for exclusive use within the Empire of China. To this end the Chinese Government agrees to issue by its proper authorities proclamations, having the force of law, forbidding all subjects of China from infringing on, imitating, colorably imitating, or knowingly passing off an imitation of trade-marks belonging to citizens of the United States, which shall have been registered by the proper authorities of the United States at such offices as the Chinese Government will establish for such purpose, on payment of a reasonable fee, after due investigation by the Chinese authorities, and in compliance with reasonable regulations.

ARTICLE X

The United States Government allows subjects of China to patent their inventions in the United States and protects them in the use and ownership of such patents. The Government of China now agrees that it will establish a Patent Office. After this office has been established and special laws with regard to inventions have been adopted it will thereupon, after the payment of the prescribed fees, issue certificates of protection, valid for a fixed term of years, to citizens of the United States on all their patents issued by the United States, in respect of articles the sale of which is lawful in China, which do not infringe on previous inventions of Chinese subjects, in the same manner as patents are to be issued to subjects of China.

ARTICLE XI

Whereas the Government of the United States undertakes to give the benefits of its copyright laws to the citizens of any foreign State which gives to the citizens of the United States the benefits of copyright on an equal basis with its own citizens:—

Therefore the Government of China, in order to secure such benefits in the United States for its subjects, now agrees to give full protection, in the same way and manner and subject to the same conditions upon which it agrees to protect trade-marks, to all citizens of the United States who are authors, designers or proprietors of any book, map, print or engraving especially prepared for the use and education of the Chinese people, or translation into Chinese of any book, in the exclusive right to print and sell such book, map, print, engraving or translation in the Empire of China during ten years from the date of registration. With the exception of the books, maps, etc., specified above, which may not be reprinted in the same form, no work shall be entitled to copyright privileges under this article. It is understood that Chinese subjects shall be at liberty to make, print and sell original translations into Chinese of any works written or of maps compiled by a citizen of the United States. This article shall not be held to protect against due process of law any citizen of the United States or Chinese subject who may be author, proprietor, or seller of any publication calculated to injure the well-being of China.

Article XII

The Chinese Government having in 1898 opened the navigable inland waters of the Empire to commerce by all steam vessels, native or foreign, that may be specially registered for the purpose, for the conveyance of passengers and lawful merchandise, citizens, firms, and corporations of the United States may engage in such commerce on equal terms with those granted to subjects of any foreign power.

In case either party hereto considers it advantageous at any time that the rules and regulations then in existence for such commerce be altered or amended, the Chinese Government agrees to consider amicably and to adopt such modifications thereof as are found necessary for trade and for the benefit of China.

The Chinese Government agrees that, upon the exchange of the ratifications of this treaty, Mukden and Antung, both in the province of Sheng-king, will be opened by China itself as places of international residence and trade. The selection of suitable localities to be set apart for international use and occupation and the regulations for these places set apart for foreign residence and trade shall be agreed upon by the Governments of the United States and China after consultation together.

Article XIII

China agrees to take the necessary steps to provide for a uniform national coinage which shall be legal tender in payment of all duties, taxes, and other obligations throughout the Empire by the citizens of the United States as well as Chinese subjects. It is understood, however, that all customs duties shall continue to be calculated and paid on the basis of the Haikwan Tael.

Article XIV

The principles of the Christian religion, as professed by the Protestant and Roman Catholic Churches, are recognized as teaching men to do good and to do to others as they would have others do to them. Those who quietly profess and teach these doctrines shall not be harassed or persecuted on account of their faith. Any person, whether citizen of the United States or Chinese convert, who, according to these tenets, peaceably teaches and practices the principles of Christianity shall in no case be interfered with or molested therefor. No restrictions shall be placed on Chinese joining Christian churches. Converts and non-converts, being Chinese subjects, shall alike conform to the laws of China; and shall pay due respect to those in authority, living together in peace and amity; and the fact of being converts shall not protect them from the consequences of any offense they may have committed before or may commit after their admission into the church, or exempt them from paying legal taxes levied on Chinese subjects generally, except taxes levied and contributions for the support of religious customs and practices contrary to their faith. Missionaries shall not interfere with the exercise by the native authorities of their jurisdiction over Chinese subjects; nor shall the native authorities make any distinction between converts and non-converts, but shall administer the laws without partiality, so that both classes can live together in peace.

Missionary societies of the United States shall be permitted to rent and to lease in perpetuity, as the property of such societies, buildings or lands in all parts of the Empire for missionary purposes and, after the title deeds have been found in order and duly stamped by the local authorities, to erect such suitable buildings as may be required for carrying on their good work.

Article XV

The Government of China having expressed a strong desire to reform its judicial system and to bring it into accord with that of Western nations, the United States agrees to give every assistance to such reform and will also be prepared to relinquish extra-territorial rights when satisfied that the state of the Chinese laws, the arrangements for their administration, and other considerations warrant it in so doing.

Article XVI

The Government of the United States consents to the prohibition by the Government of China of the importation into China of morphia and of instruments for its injection, excepting morphia and instruments for its injection imported for medical purposes, on payment of tariff duty, and under regulations to be framed by China which shall effectually restrict the use of such import to the said purposes. This prohibition shall be uniformly applied to such importation from all countries. The Chinese Government undertakes to adopt at once measures to prevent the manufacture in China of morphia and of instruments for its injection.

Article XVII

It is agreed between the high contracting parties hereto that all the provisions of the several treaties between the United States and China which were in force on the first day of January, A. D. 1900, are continued in full force and effect except in so far as they are modified by the present treaty or other treaties to which the United States is a party.

The present treaty shall remain in force for a period of ten years, beginning with the date of the exchange of ratifications and until a revision is effected as hereinafter provided.

It is further agreed that either of the high contracting parties may demand that the tariff and the articles of this convention be revised at the end of ten years from the date of the exchange of the ratifications thereof. If no revision is demanded before the end of the first term of ten years, then these articles in their present form shall remain in full force for a further term of ten years reckoned from the end of the first term, and so on for successive periods of ten years.

The English and Chinese texts of the present Treaty and its three annexes have been carefully compared; but, in the event of there being any difference of meaning between them, the sense as expressed in the English text shall be held to be the correct one.

This Treaty and its three annexes shall be ratified by the two High Contracting Parties in conformity with their respective constitutions, and the ratifications shall be exchanged in Washington not later than twelve months from the present date.

In testimony whereof, we, the undersigned, by virtue of our respective powers, have signed this Treaty in duplicate in the English and Chinese languages, and have affixed our respective seals.

Done at Shanghai, this eighth day of October in the year of our Lord one thousand nine hundred and three, and in the twenty ninth year of Kuang Hsü eighth month and eighteenth day.

EDWIN H. CONGER [SEAL.]

JOHN GOODNOW [SEAL.]

JOHN F. SEAMAN [SEAL.]

Signatures and seal of Chinese Plenipotentiaries.

    [LÜ HAI-HUAN]

    [SHENG HSÜAN-HUAI]

ANNEX I

As citizens of the United States are already forbidden by treaty to deal in or handle opium, no mention has been made in this Treaty of opium taxation.

As the trade in salt is a government monopoly in China, no mention has been made in this Treaty of salt taxation.

It is, however, understood, after full discussion and consideration, that the collection of inland dues on opium and salt and the means for the protection of the revenue therefrom and for preventing illicit traffic therein are left to be administered by the Chinese Government in such manner as shall in no wise interfere with the provisions of Article IV of this treaty regarding the unobstructed transit of other goods.

EDWIN H. CONGER [SEAL.]

JOHN GOODNOW [SEAL.]

JOHN F. SEAMAN [SEAL.]

Signatures and seal of Chinese Plenipotentiaries.

    [LÜ HAI-HUAN]

    [SHENG HSÜAN-HUAI]

ANNEX II

Article IV of the Treaty of Commerce between the United States and China of this date provides for the retention of the native Customs offices at the open ports. For the purpose of safeguarding the revenue of China at such places, it is understood that the Chinese Government shall be entitled to establish and maintain such branch native Customs offices at each open port, within a reasonable distance of the main native Customs offices at the port, as shall be deemed by the authorities of the Imperial Maritime Customs at that port necessary to collect the revenue from the trade into and out of such port. Such branches, as well as the main native Customs offices at each open port, shall be administered by the Imperial Maritime Customs as provided by the Protocol of 1901.

EDWIN H. CONGER   [SEAL.]
JOHN GOODNOW   [SEAL.]
JOHN F. SEAMAN   [SEAL.]

Signatures and seal of Chinese Plenipotentiaries.
     [LÜ HAI-HUAN]
     [SHENG HSÜAN-HUAI]

ANNEX III

The schedule of tariff duties on imported goods annexed to this Treaty under Article V is hereby mutually declared to be the schedule agreed upon between the representatives of China and the United States and signed by John Goodnow for the United States and Their Excellencies Lü Hai-huan and Sheng Hsüan-huai for China at Shanghai on the sixth day of September, A. D. 1902, according to the Protocol of the seventh day of September, A. D. 1901.

EDWIN H. CONGER   [SEAL.]
JOHN GOODNOW   [SEAL.]
JOHN F. SEAMAN   [SEAL.]

Signatures and seal of Chinese Plenipotentiaries.
     [LÜ HAI-HUAN]
     [SHENG HSÜAN-HUAI]

7

Secretary Hay to American Diplomatic Representatives at Peking, St. Petersburg, and Tokyo [10]

WASHINGTON, *February 10, 1904*

You will express to the minister of foreign affairs the earnest desire of the Government of the United States that in the course of the military operations which have begun between Russia and Japan the neutrality of China and in all practicable ways her administrative entity shall be respected by both parties, and that the area of hostility shall be localized and limited as much as possible, so that undue excitement and disturbance of the Chinese people may be prevented and the least possible loss to the commerce and peaceful intercourse of the world may be occasioned.

JOHN HAY.

8

Secretary Hay to American Diplomatic Representatives at Vienna, Brussels, Paris, Berlin, London, Rome, and Lisbon [11]

WASHINGTON, *January 13, 1905*

It has come to our knowledge that apprehension exists on the part of some of the powers that in the eventual negotiations for peace between Russia and Japan claim may be made for the concession of Chinese territory to neutral

[10] *Ibid.*, 1904, p. 2.
[11] *Ibid.*, 1905, p. 1.

powers. The President would be loath to share this apprehension, believing that the introduction of extraneous interests would seriously embarrass and postpone the settlement of the issues involved in the present contest in the Far East, thus making more remote the attainment of that peace which is so earnestly to be desired. For its part, the United States has repeatedly made its position well known, and has been gratified at the cordial welcome accorded to its efforts to strengthen and perpetuate the broad policy of maintaining the integrity of China and the "open door" in the Orient whereby equality of commercial opportunity and access shall be enjoyed by all nations. Holding these views the United States disclaims any thought of reserved territorial rights or control in the Chinese Empire, and it is deemed fitting to make this purpose frankly known and to remove all apprehension on this score so far as concerns the policy of this nation, which maintains so considerable a share of the Pacific commerce of China and which holds such important possessions in the western Pacific, almost at the gateway of China.

You will bring this matter to the notice of the government to which you are accredited, and you will invite the expression of its views thereon.

JOHN HAY.

9

Root-Takahira Agreement, November 30, 1908

The Japanese Ambassador (Takahira) to Secretary Root [12]

Washington, November 30, 1908.

SIR: The exchange of views between us, which has taken place at the several interviews which I have recently had the honor of holding with you, has shown that Japan and the United States holding important outlying insular possessions in the region of the Pacific Ocean, the Governments of the two countries are animated by a common aim, policy, and intention in that region.

Believing that a frank avowal of that aim, policy, and intention would not only tend to strengthen the relations of friendship and good neighborhood, which have immemorially existed between Japan and the United States, but would materially contribute to the preservation of the general peace, the Imperial Government have authorized me to present to you an outline of their understanding of that common aim, policy, and intention:

1. It is the wish of the two Governments to encourage the free and peaceful development of their commerce on the Pacific Ocean.

2. The policy of both Governments, uninfluenced by any aggressive tendencies, is directed to the maintenance of the existing status quo in the region above mentioned and to the defense of the principle of equal opportunity for commerce and industry in China.

3. They are accordingly firmly resolved reciprocally to respect the territorial possessions belonging to each other in said region.

4. They are also determined to preserve the common interest of all powers in China by supporting by all pacific means at their disposal the independence and integrity of China and the principle of equal opportunity for commerce and industry of all nations in that Empire.

5. Should any event occur threatening the status quo as above described or the principle of equal opportunity as above defined, it remains for the two

[12] *Ibid.,* 1908, p. 510.

Governments to communicate with each other in order to arrive at an understanding as to what measures they may consider it useful to take.

If the foregoing outline accords with the view of the Government of the United States, I shall be gratified to receive your confirmation.

I take [etc.]   K. TAKAHIRA.

Secretary Root to the Japanese Ambassador (Takahira)[13]

Washington, November 30, 1908.

EXCELLENCY: I have the honor to acknowledge the receipt of your note of to-day setting forth the result of the exchange of views between us in our recent interviews defining the understanding of the two Governments in regard to their policy in the region of the Pacific Ocean.

It is a pleasure to inform you that this expression of mutual understanding is welcome to the Government of the United States as appropriate to the happy relations of the two countries and as the occasion for a concise mutual affirmation of that accordant policy respecting the Far East which the two Governments have so frequently declared in the past.

I am happy to be able to confirm to your excellency, on behalf of the United States, the declaration of the two Governments embodied in the following words:

1. It is the wish of the two Governments to encourage the free and peaceful development of their commerce on the Pacific Ocean.

2. The policy of both Governments, uninfluenced by any aggressive tendencies, is directed to the maintenance of the existing status quo in the region above mentioned, and to the defense of the principle of equal opportunity for commerce and industry in China.

3. They are accordingly firmly resolved reciprocally to respect the territorial possessions belonging to each other in said region.

4. They are also determined to preserve the common interests of all powers in China by supporting by all pacific means at their disposal the independence and integrity of China and the principle of equal opportunity for commerce and industry of all nations in that Empire.

5. Should any event occur threatening the status quo as above described or the principle of equal opportunity as above defined, it remains for the two Governments to communicate with each other in order to arrive at an understanding as to what measures they may consider it useful to take.

Accept [etc.]   ELIHU ROOT.

10

Memorandum by Secretary Knox on the Neutralization of the Manchurian Railways [14]

Now that there has been signed and ratified by an unpublished imperial decree an agreement by which American and British interests are to cooperate in the financing and construction of the Chin Chou Tsitsihar Aigun Railroad, the

---

[13] *Ibid.* 1908, p. 511.

[14] *Ibid.,* 1910, p. 234.   The Ambassador at London was instructed, on Nov. 6, 1909, to deliver the memorandum to the British Government.   On Dec. 14, 1909, the American Diplomatic Representatives at Paris, Berlin, St. Petersburg, Tokyo, and Peking were instructed to present this proposal to the respective governments to which they were accredited.

Government of the United States is prepared cordially to cooperate with the British Government in diplomatically supporting and facilitating this, so important alike to the progress and the commercial development of China.

The Government of the United States would be disposed to favor ultimate participation to a proper extent on the part of other interested powers whose inclusion might be agreeable to China and which are known to support the principle of equality of commercial opportunity and the maintenance of the integrity of the Chinese Empire.

However, before the further elaboration of the actual arrangement the Government of the United States asks the British Government to give their consideration to the following alternative and more comprehensive projects:

1. Perhaps the most effective way to preserve the undisturbed enjoyment by China of all political rights in Manchuria and to promote the development of those Provinces under a practical application of the policy of the open door and equal commercial opportunity would be to bring the Manchurian highways and the railroad under an economic and scientific and impartial administration by some plan vesting in China the ownership of the railroads through funds furnished for that purpose by the interested powers willing to participate. Such loan should be for a period ample to make it reasonably certain that it could be met within the time fixed, and should be upon such terms as would make it attractive to bankers and investors. The plan should provide that nationals of the participating powers should supervise the railroad system during the term of the loan, and the Governments concerned should enjoy for such period the usual preferences for their nationals and materials upon an equitable basis *inter se.*

The execution of such a plan would naturally require the cooperation of China and of Japan and Russia, the reversionary and the concessionaries, respectively, of the existing Manchurian railroads, as well as that of Great Britain and the United States, whose special interests rest upon the existing contract relative to the Chin Chou Aigun Railroad.

The advantages of such a plan to Japan and to Russia are obvious. Both those powers, desiring in good faith to protect the policy of the open door and equal opportunity in Manchuria, and wishing to assure to China unimpaired sovereignty, might well be expected to welcome an opportunity to shift the separate duties, responsibilities, and expenses they have undertaken in the protection of their respective commercial and other interests for impartial assumption by the combined powers, including themselves, in proportion to their interests. The Government of the United States has some reason to hope that such a plan might meet favorable consideration on the part of Russia, and has reason to believe that American financial participation would be forthcoming.

2. Should this suggestion not be found feasible in its entirety, then the desired end would be approximated if not attained by Great Britain and the United States diplomatically supporting the Chin Chou Aigun arrangement and inviting interested powers friendly to the complete commercial neutrality of Manchuria to participate in the financing and construction of that line and of such additional lines as future commercial development may demand, and at the same time to supply funds for the purchase by China of such of the existing lines as might be offered for inclusion in this system.

The Government of the United States hopes that the principle involved in the foregoing suggestions may commend itself to His Britannic Majesty's Government. That principle finds support in the additional reasons that the consummation of some such plan would avoid the irritations likely to be engendered by the uncontrolled direct negotiations of bankers with the Chinese Government, and also that it would create such community of substantial interest in China as would facilitate a cooperation calculated to simplify the problems, fiscal and monetary—reforms now receiving such earnest attention by the Imperial Chinese Government.

11

Secretary Bryan to the Japanese Ambassador (Viscount Chinda)[15]

WASHINGTON, *March 13, 1915*

EXCELLENCY: On February 8 last your excellency left with me at the Department a memorandum setting forth the demands which the Imperial Japanese Government felt obliged to make upon China, and on the 22d day of the same month your excellency delivered to me an additional memorandum presenting certain "requests" affecting the relations between the two countries which the Imperial Government has urged China to consider.

The American Government is glad to learn from these two communications of the Imperial Government that the "requests" were not presented to China as "demands" but that they were but "wishes" for which "friendly consideration" was asked on the part of China. The American Government understands from this distinction between the "demands" and the "requests" that the latter are not to be pressed if the Chinese Government should decline to consider them.

Inasmuch as these requests appear to have a bearing upon the traditional attitude of both the United States and Japan towards China, I desire to present to your excellency the following considerations of the Government of the United States relative to the effect which, it is thought, these demands and requests may have upon the relations of the United States with the Chinese Republic.

Reciprocating the frank and friendly character of the statements of the Imperial Japanese Government, the Government of the United States of America believes that an expression of its views with respect to these matters will be received by the Imperial Government in the same friendly spirit in which it is offered.

It will be recalled that in the year 1899 the Government of the United States requested the Governments of France, Germany, Great Britain, Italy, Russia and Japan to give their formal consent to three proposals:

First. They will in no way interfere with any treaty port or any vested interest within any so-called "sphere of interest" or leased territory they may have in China.

Second. The Chinese treaty tariff of the time being shall apply to all merchandise landed or shipped to all such ports as are within said "sphere of interest" (unless they be "free ports"), no matter to what nationality it may belong, and that duties so leviable shall be collected by the Chinese Government.

Third. They will levy no higher harbor dues on vessels of another nationality frequenting any port in such "sphere" than shall be levied on vessels of their own nationality, and no higher railroad charges over lines built, controlled, or operated within such "sphere" on merchandise belonging to citizens or subjects of other nationalities transported through such "sphere" than shall be levied on similar merchandise belonging to their own nationals transported over equal distances.

---

[15] *Ibid.,* 1915, p. 105.

On December 26, 1899, the Minister for Foreign Affairs addressed a note to the American Minister at Tokyo assuring the Minister—

> that the Imperial Government will have no hesitation to give their assent to so just and fair a proposal of the United States, provided that all the other Powers concerned shall accept the same.

A similar acceptance was given on behalf of the other Powers approached.

On July 3, 1900, having been consulted by other Powers as to the course to be pursued in China as a result of the Boxer disturbances, this Government expressed its views in a circular communication to Austria-Hungary, France, Germany, Great Britain, Italy, Japan and Russia, stating that—

> the policy of the Government of the United States is to seek a solution which may bring about permanent safety and peace to China, preserve Chinese territorial and administrative entity, protect all rights guaranteed to friendly Powers by treaty and international law, and safeguard for the world the principle of equal and impartial trade with all parts of the Chinese Empire.

In reply the Minister for Foreign Affairs of the Imperial Government expressed through the American Minister at Tokyo views in accord with those of the United States Government.

In the following month Great Britain and Germany signed an agreement defining their mutual policy in China:

> I. It is a matter of joint and permanent international interest that the ports on the rivers and littoral of China should remain free and open to trade and to every other legitimate form of economic activity for the nationals of all countries without distinction, and the two Governments agree on their part to uphold the same for all Chinese territory so far as they can exercise influence.
>
> II. Her Britannic Majesty's Government and the Imperial German Government will not on their part make use of the present complication to obtain for themselves any territorial advantages in Chinese dominions and will direct their policy towards maintaining undiminished the territorial conditions of the Chinese Empire.

This agreement being communicated by those Powers to Japan was acknowledged by the Imperial Government in a note containing the following language:

> The Imperial Government having been assured by the contracting Powers that in adhering to the agreement in question they would be placed in relation to it in the same position as if they had been a signatory thereto, do not hesitate to declare formally their adherence to the said agreement and their acceptance of the principles embodied therein.

In 1901, when the Manchurian Convention was being negotiated by the Russian and Chinese Governments, involving the grant of certain exclusive privileges relating to the opening of mines and the building of railroads in Manchuria, the Japanese Minister called on the Secretary of State of the United States and said that the Japanese Government considered that the convention was a most undesirable thing because it was a violation of the understanding among all the Powers that the integrity of the Chinese Empire should be preserved, and that the Japanese Government was anxious that some means should be taken by the different Powers to induce China to delay the final signature of the convention beyond the period assigned by Russia as an ultimatum for signing.

On the same subject a circular note was sent by the United States to Belgium, China, France, Germany, Great Britain, Italy, Japan, the Netherlands, Russia and Spain, as follows:

An agreement by which China cedes to any corporation or company the exclusive right and privilege of opening mines, establishing railroads, or in any other way industrially developing Manchuria, can but be viewed with the gravest concern by the Government of the United States. It constitutes a monopoly, which is a distinct breach of the stipulations of treaties concluded between China and foreign Powers, and thereby seriously affects the rights of American citizens; it restricts their rightful trade and exposes it to being discriminated against, interfered with or otherwise jeopardized, and strongly tends towards permanently impairing the sovereign rights of China in this part of the Empire, and seriously interferes with her ability to meet her international obligations. Furthermore, such concession on the part of China will undoubtedly be followed by demands from other Powers for similar and equally exclusive advantages in other parts of the Chinese Empire, and the inevitable result must be the complete wreck of the policy of absolute equality of treatment of all nations in regard to trade, navigation, and commerce within the confines of the Empire.

On the other hand, the attainment by one Power of such exclusive privileges for a commercial organization of its nationality conflicts with the assurances repeatedly conveyed to this Government by the Imperial Russian Ministry of Foreign Affairs of the Imperial Government's intention to follow the policy of the open door in China, as advocated by the Government of the United States and accepted by all the Treaty Powers having commercial interests in that Empire.

It is for these reasons that the Government of the United States, animated now, as in the past, with the sincerest desire of insuring to the whole world the benefits of full and fair intercourse between China and the nations on a footing of equal rights and advantages to all, submits the above to the earnest consideration of the Imperial Governments of China and Russia, confident that they will give due weight to its importance and adopt such measures as will relieve the just and natural anxiety of the United States.

The foregoing constitute the beginnings of the policy of the United States and other Powers interested in the welfare of China for the maintenance of the territorial integrity and administrative entity of China, and equal opportunities in commerce and industries in her behalf. To this policy the Powers have generally given their formal acceptance and support.

It is only necessary to refer to the British-Japanese Treaty of 1902, the Japanese Declarations at the opening of the Russo-Japanese war, the British-Japanese Treaty of 1905, the Russo-Japanese Treaty of Portsmouth, of 1905, the Franco-Japanese Entente of 1907, and the Russo-Japanese Treaty of 1907, in which Japan confirmed her special interest in maintaining the political independence and territorial integrity of the Empire of China, and in securing equal opportunities to all nations in the commercial and industrial development of China.

Finally, the United States and Japan declared their policy in the Far East by an exchange of notes on November 30, 1908, between the Honorable Elihu Root, then Secretary of State, and Baron Kogoro Takahira, the Ambassador of Japan. These notes contain the following language:

4. They are also determined to preserve the common interest of all Powers in China by supporting by all pacific means at their disposal the independence and integrity of China and the principle of equal opportunity for commerce and industry of all nations in that Empire.

5. Should any event occur threatening the status quo as above described or the principle of equal opportunity as above defined, it remains for the two Governments to communicate with each other in order to arrive at an understanding as to what measures they may consider useful to take.

I assume that it is because they wish to act in the spirit of this agreement to communicate with each other in reference to any event which may threaten these principles that your excellency's Government has informed this Government of the above-mentioned proposals which have been made to China. It is with the same purpose also, and on the further ground that the United States feels itself under a moral obligation to the Powers whose pledges are deposited with it not to pass over in silence any threatened violation of these pledges, that I address this communication to you with a view to carrying out the agreement of 1908 in accordance with that mutual regard and friendship which inspired it.

The United States, confident that the principle of mutuality will be preserved by Japan, believes that it may rely upon the often repeated assurances of your excellency's Government relative to the independence, integrity and commerce of China, and that no steps will be taken contrary to the spirit of those assurances.

For two generations American missionaries and teachers have made sacrifices in behalf of religious and educational work in China. American capital has been invested and industries have been established in certain regions. The activity of Americans has never been political, but on the contrary has been primarily commercial with no afterthought as to their effect upon the governmental policy of China. As an outgrowth of these two interests Americans have become concerned in the legitimate participation in the economic development of China along broader lines. Many projects which in other countries are left to private enterprise are in China conducted necessarily under government direction. United States citizens and capital are thus engaged in certain public improvements, such as the Huai River conservancy, the Hukuang Railway project, etc. A fourth matter of great moment to the United States is its broad and extensive treaty rights with China. These in general relate to commercial privileges and to the protection of Americans in China. In view of these treaty rights and its increasing economic interests in China, this Government has noted with grave concern certain of the suggestions which Japan has, in the present critical stage of the growth and development of the new Republic, considered it advisable to lay before the Chinese Government. While on principle and under the treaties of 1844, 1858, 1868 and 1903 with China the United States has ground upon which to base objections to the Japanese "demands" relative to Shantung, South Manchuria, and East Mongolia, nevertheless the United States frankly recognizes that territorial contiguity creates special relations between Japan and these districts. This Government, therefore, is disposed to raise no question, at this time, as to Articles I and II of the Japanese proposals. Further, as to Article IV, and Article V, paragraphs 2, 5 and 7, this Government perceives no special menace to the existing rights and interests of the United States or of its citizens in China. On the other hand Article V, paragraph 4, restricting the purchase of arms and ammunition to purchases from Japan, and paragraph 6 contemplating a monopoly of the development of the province of Fukien, the United States Government considers, would, if they should become operative, be violations of the principle of equal opportunity for the commerce and industries of other nations. American citizens may claim a right to share in the commercial development not only in Fukien but in other provinces as well. The United States is not unmindful that many serious disadvantages would result to its commercial and industrial enterprises if special preference is given to one nation in the matter of concessions. An example is shown in the operation of the South Manchuria Railway whereby discriminations have been made for some time against freight brought into Manchuria in other than Japanese vessels. This case indicates the embarrassing results of concessions of a broad preference or option. The United States, as well as every other nation, has the right to have its citizens free to make contracts with the Central and Provincial Governments without having the exercise of their rights interrupted or regarded as unfriendly by a third power ; for each American enterprise in China is treated on its own merits as to its usefulness and prospective benefit, and without any regard to the possible effect it might have on China's future political status in the Orient.

The rights and privileges, which are set forth in these two paragraphs and which Japan seeks to obtain from China, are in conflict with rights of Americans secured by treaties between the United States and China.

Article XV of the Treaty of 1844 reads as follows :

> The former limitation of the trade of foreign nations to certain persons appointed at Canton by the ·Government and commonly called Hong-merchants, having been abolished, citizens of the United States, engaged in the purchase or sale of goods of import or export, are admitted to trade with any and all subjects of China without distinction ; they shall not be subject to any new limitations, nor impeded in their business by monopolies or other injurious restrictions.

Article XXX of the Treaty of 1858 reads as follows :

> The contracting parties hereby agree that should at any time the Ta Tsing Empire grant to any nation or the merchants or citizens of any nation, any right, privilege or favor, connected either with navigation, commerce, political or other intercourse which is not conferred by this treaty, such right, privilege and favor shall at once freely enure to the benefit of the United States, its public officers, merchants and citizens.

Article VIII of the Treaty of 1868 reads as follows :

> The United States, always disclaiming and discouraging all practices of unnecessary dictation and intervention by one nation in the affairs or domestic administration of another, do hereby freely disclaim and disavow any intention or right to intervene in the domestic administration of China in regard to the construction of railroads, telegraphs or other material internal improvements. On the other hand, his Majesty, the Emperor of China, reserves to himself the right to decide the time and manner and circumstances of introducing such improvements within his dominions. With this mutual understanding it is agreed by the contracting parties that if at any time hereafter his Imperial Majesty shall determine to construct or cause to be constructed works of the character mentioned within the empire, and shall make application to the United States or any other western Power for facilities to carry out that policy, the United States will, in that case, designate and authorize suitable engineers to be employed by the Chinese Government, and will recommend to other nations an equal compliance with such application, the Chinese Government in that case

protecting such engineers in their persons and property, and paying them a reasonable compensation for their service.

Articles III and VII of the Treaty of 1903 read as follows:

Article III. Citizens of the United States may frequent, reside and carry on trade, industries and manufactures, or pursue any lawful avocation, in all the ports or localities of China which are now open or may hereafter be opened to foreign residence and trade; and within the suitable localities at those places which have been or may be set apart for the use and occupation of foreigners, they may rent or purchase houses, places of business and other buildings, and rent or lease in perpetuity land and build thereon. They shall generally enjoy as to their persons and property all such rights, privileges and immunities as are or may hereafter be granted to the subjects or citizens of the nation the most favored in these respects.

Article VII. The Chinese Government, recognizing that it is advantageous for the country to develop its mineral resources, and that it is desirable to attract foreign as well as Chinese capital to embark in mining enterprises, agrees, within one year from the signing of this treaty, to initiate and conclude the revision of the existing mining regulations. To this end China will, with all expedition and earnestness, go into the whole question of mining rules; and, selecting from the rules of the United States and other countries regulations which seem applicable to the condition of China, will recast its present mining rules in such a way as, while promoting the interests of Chinese subjects and not injuring in any way the sovereign rights of China, will offer no impediment to the attraction of foreign capital nor place foreign capitalists at a greater disadvantage than they would be under generally accepted foreign regulations; and will permit citizens of the United States to carry on in Chinese territory mining operations and other necessary business relating thereto provided they comply with the new regulations and conditions which will be imposed by China on its subjects and foreigners alike, relating to the opening of mines, the renting of mineral land, and the payment of royalty, and provided they apply for permits, the provisions of which in regard to necessary business relating to such operations shall be observed. The residence of citizens of the United States in connection with such mining operations shall be subject to such regulations as shall be agreed upon by and between the United States and China.

Any mining concessions granted after the publication of such new rules shall be subject to their provisions.

It is manifest that these articles including "most favored nation" treatment entitle Americans to claim from China the same rights as those which Japan now seeks to have granted exclusively to her subjects.

It remains to call attention to Article III forbidding the alienation or lease of any port, harbor or island on the coast of China, and to Article V, paragraph 1, requiring China to employ competent Japanese subjects as advisers for conducting administrative, financial and military affairs, and paragraph 3 suggesting the joint policing of China, "where it is deemed necessary."

With reference to the first of these three proposals, Baron Kato has explained to the American Ambassador at Tokyo that Japan has no desire for a naval station on the coast of China, either at Tsingtau, or south of that point, as it would be valueless to her, but that it would however object to another nation having such a station. With reference to the employment of advisers the United States believes it may be assumed that the Chinese Government will not discriminate unfairly in their selection, although it should be pointed out that this Government understands that Japan has six out of twenty-five advisers to the Republic representing eight nations.   In respect to the proposed joint policing of certain places where there has been some friction between Japanese and Chinese, this Government feels apprehensive that this plan, instead of tending to lessen such friction might create greater difficulties than those which it is desired to remove.

But what is more important is the fact that these proposals, if accepted by China, while not infringing the territorial integrity of the Republic, are clearly derogatory to the political independence and administrative entity of that country.   The same is in a measure true of Paragraph 4 of Article V relative to the purchase of arms.   It is difficult for the United States, therefore, to reconcile these requests with the maintenance of the unimpaired sovereignty of China, which Japan, together with the United States and the Great Powers of Europe, has reaffirmed from time to time during the past decade and a half in formal declarations, treaties and exchanges of diplomatic notes.   The United States, therefore, could not regard with indifference the assumption of political, military or economic domination over China by a foreign Power, and hopes that your excellency's Government will find it consonant with their interests to refrain from pressing upon China an acceptance of proposals which would, if accepted, exclude Americans from equal participation in the economic and industrial development of China and would limit the political independence of that country.

The United States is convinced that an attempt to coerce China to submit to these proposals would result in engendering resentment on the part of the Chinese and opposition by other interested Powers, thereby creating a situation which this Government confidently believes the Imperial Government do not desire.

The United States Government embraces this opportunity to make known that it has viewed the aspirations of Japan in the Far East with that friendship and esteem which have characterized the relations of the two nations in the past. This Government cannot too earnestly impress upon your excellency's Government that the United States is not jealous of the prominence of Japan in the East or of the intimate cooperation of China and Japan for their mutual benefit. Nor has the United States any intention of obstructing or embarrassing Japan, or of influencing China in opposition to Japan.   On the contrary the policy of the United States, as set forth in this note,.is directed to the maintenance of the independence, integrity and commercial freedom of China and the preservation of legitimate American rights and interests in that Republic.

Accept [etc.]   W. J. BRYAN.

12

Secretary Bryan to the Ambassador in Japan (Guthrie)[16]

WASHINGTON, May 11, 1915—5 p. m.

Please call upon the Minister for Foreign Affairs and present to him a note textually as follows:

"In view of the circumstances of the negotiations which have taken place and which are now pending between the Government of Japan and the Government of China, and of the agreements which have been reached as a result thereof, the Government of the United States has the honor to notify the Imperial Japanese Government that it cannot recognize any agreement or undertaking which

[16] *Ibid.,* 1915, p. 146.

has been entered into or which may be entered into between the Governments of Japan and China, impairing the treaty rights of the United States and its citizens in China, the political or territorial integrity of the Republic of China, or the international policy relative to China commonly known as the open door policy.

"An identical note has been transmitted to the Government of the Chinese Republic."   BRYAN.

13

Lansing-Ishii Agreement, November 2, 1917

Secretary Lansing to Viscount Ishii, Japanese Ambassador on Special Mission [17]

WASHINGTON, *November 2, 1917.*

EXCELLENCY: I have the honor to communicate herein my understanding of the agreement reached by us in our recent conversations touching the questions of mutual interest to our Governments relating to the Republic of China.

In order to silence mischievous reports that have from time to time been circulated, it is believed by us that a public announcement once more of the desires and intentions shared by our two Governments with regard to China is advisible.

The Governments of the United States and Japan recognize that territorial propinquity creates special relations between countries, and, consequently, the Government of the United States recognizes that Japan has special interests in China, particularly in the part to which her possessions are contiguous.

The territorial sovereignty of China, nevertheless, remains unimpaired and the Government of the United States has every confidence in the repeated assurances of the Imperial Japanese Government that while geographical position gives Japan such special interests they have no desire to discriminate against the trade of other nations or to disregard the commercial rights heretofore granted by China in treaties with other powers.

The Governments of the United States and Japan deny that they have any purpose to infringe in any way the independence or territorial integrity of China and they declare, furthermore, that they always adhere to the principle of the so-called "open door" or equal opportunity for commerce and industry in China.

Moreover, they mutually declare that they are opposed to the acquisition by any Government of any special rights or privileges that would affect the independence or territorial integrity of China or that would deny to the subjects or citizens of any country the full enjoyment of equal opportunity in the commerce and industry of China.

I shall be glad to have your excellency confirm this understanding of the agreement reached by us.

Accept [etc.]   ROBERT LANSING.

Viscount Ishii, Japanese Ambassador on Special Mission, to Secretary Lansing [18]

WASHINGTON, *November 2, 1917.*

SIR: I have the honor to acknowledge the receipt of your note of to-day, communicating to me your understanding of the agreement reached by us in our

---

[17] *Ibid.*, 1917, p. 264.
[18] *Ibid.*

recent conversations touching the questions of mutual interest to our Governments relating to the Republic of China.

I am happy to be able to confirm to you, under authorization of my Government, the understanding in question set forth in the following terms:

In order to silence mischievous reports that have from time to time been circulated, it is believed by us that a public announcement once more of the desires and intentions shared by our two Governments with regard to China is advisable.

The Governments of Japan and the United States recognize that territorial propinquity creates special relations between countries, and, consequently, the Government of the United States recognizes that Japan has special interests in China, particularly in the part to which her possessions are contiguous.

The territorial sovereignty of China, nevertheless, remains unimpaired and the Government of the United States has every confidence in the repeated assurances of the Imperial Japanese Government that while geographical position gives Japan such special interests they have no desire to discriminate against the trade of other nations or to disregard the commercial rights heretofore granted by China in treaties with other Powers.

The Governments of Japan and the United States deny that they have any purpose to infringe in any way the independence or territorial integrity of China and they declare, furthermore, that they always adhere to the principle of the so-called "open door" or equal opportunity for commerce and industry in China.

Moreover, they mutually declare that they are opposed to the acquisition by any government of any special rights or privileges that would affect the independence or territorial integrity of China or that would deny to the subjects or citizens of any country the full enjoyment of equal opportunity in the commerce and industry of China.

I take [etc.] K. Ishii

14

Nine-Power Treaty Signed at Washington, February 6, 1922 [19]

The United States of America, Belgium, the British Empire, China, France, Italy, Japan, the Netherlands and Portugal:

Desiring to adopt a policy designed to stabilize conditions in the Far East, to safeguard the rights and interests of China, and to promote intercourse between China and the other Powers upon the basis of equality of opportunity;

Have resolved to conclude a treaty for that purpose and to that end have appointed as their respective Plenipotentiaries;

The President of the United States of America:
Charles Evans Hughes,
Henry Cabot Lodge,
Oscar W. Underwood,
Elihu Root,
citizens of the United States;

His Majesty the King of the Belgians:
Baron de Cartier de Marchienne, Commander of the Order of Leopold and of the Order of the Crown, His Ambassador Extraordinary and Plenipotentiary at Washington;

---

[19] *Ibid.*, 1922, vol. I, p. 276.

His Majesty the King of the United Kingdom of Great Britain and Ireland and of the British Dominions beyond the Seas, Emperor of India:

The Right Honourable Arthur James Balfour, O. M., M. P., Lord President of His Privy Council;

The Right Honourable Baron Lee of Fareham, G. B. E., K. C. B., First Lord of His Admiralty;

The Right Honourable Sir Auckland Campbell Geddes, K. C. B., His Ambassador Extraordinary and Plenipotentiary to the United States of America;

and

for the Dominion of Canada:

The Right Honourable Sir Robert Laird Borden, G. C. M. G., K. C.;

for the Commonwealth of Australia:

Senator the Right Honourable George Foster Pearce, Minister for Home and Territories;

for the Dominion of New Zealand:

The Honourable Sir John William Salmond, K. C., Judge of the Supreme Court of New Zealand;

for the Union of South Africa:

The Right Honourable Arthur James Balfour, O. M., M. P.;

for India:

The Right Honourable Valingman Sankaranarayana Srinivasa Sastri, Member of the Indian Council of State;

The President of the Republic of China:

Mr. Sao-Ke Alfred Sze, Envoy Extraordinary and Minister Plenipotentiary at Washington;

Mr. V. K. Wellington Koo, Envoy Extraordinary and Minister Plenipotentiary at London;

Mr. Chung-Hui Wang, former Minister of Justice.

The President of the French Republic:

Mr. Albert Sarraut, Deputy, Minister of the Colonies;

Mr. Jules J. Jusserand, Ambassador Extraordinary and Plenipotentiary to the United States of America, Grand Cross of the National Order of the Legion of Honour;

His Majesty the King of Italy:

The Honourable Carlo Schanzer, Senator of the Kingdom;

The Honourable Vittorio Rolandi Ricci, Senator of the Kingdom, His Ambassador Extraordinary and Plenipotentiary at Washington;

The Honourable Luigi Albertini, Senator of the Kingdom;

His Majesty the Emperor of Japan:

Baron Tomosaburo Kato, Minister for the Navy, Junii, a member of the First Class of the Imperial Order of the Grand Cordon of the Rising Sun with the Paulownia Flower;

Baron Kijuro Shidehara, His Ambassador Extraordinary and Plenipotentiary at Washington, Joshii, a member of the First Class of the Imperial Order of the Rising Sun;

Mr. Masanao Hanihara, Vice Minister for Foreign Affairs, Jushii, a member of the Second Class of the Imperial Order of the Rising Sun;

Her Majesty the Queen of The Netherlands:

Jonkheer Frans Beelaerts van Blokland, Her Envoy Extraordinary and Minister Plenipotentiary;

Jonkheer Willem Hendrik de Beaufort, Minister Plenipotentiary, Chargé d'Affaires at Washington;

The President of the Portuguese Republic:

Mr. José Francisco de Horta Machado da Franca, Viscount d'Alte, Envoy Extraordinary and Minister Plenipotentiary at Washington;

Mr. Ernesto Julio de Carvalho e Vasconcellos, Captain of the Portuguese Navy, Technical Director of the Colonial Office.

Who, having communicated to each other their full powers, found to be in good and due form, have agreed as follows:

ARTICLE I

The Contracting Powers, other than China, agree:

(1) To respect the sovereignty, the independence, and the territorial and administrative integrity of China;

(2) To provide the fullest and most unembarrassed opportunity to China to develop and maintain for herself an effective and stable government;

(3) To use their influence for the purpose of effectually establishing and maintaining the principle of equal opportunity for the commerce and industry of all nations throughout the territory of China;

(4) To refrain from taking advantage of conditions in China in order to seek special rights or privileges which would abridge the rights of subjects or citizens of friendly States, and from countenancing action inimical to the security of such States.

ARTICLE II

The Contracting Powers agree not to enter into any treaty, agreement, arrangement, or understanding, either with one another, or, individually or collectively, with any Power or Powers, which would infringe or impair the principles stated in Article I.

ARTICLE III

With a view to applying more effectually the principles of the Open Door or equality of opportunity in China for the trade and industry of all nations, the Contracting Powers, other than China, agree that they will not seek, nor support their respective nationals in seeking—

(a) any arrangement which might purport to establish in favour of their interests any general superiority of rights with respect to commercial or economic development in any designated region of China;

(b) any such monopoly or preference as would deprive the nationals of any other Power of the right of undertaking any legitimate trade or industry in China, or of participating with the Chinese Government, or with any local authority, in any category of public enterprise, or which by reason of its scope, duration or geographical extent is calculated to frustrate the practical application of the principle of equal opportunity.

It is understood that the foregoing stipulations of this Article are not to be so construed as to prohibit the acquisition of such properties or rights as may be necessary to the conduct of a particular commercial, industrial, or financial undertaking or to the encouragement of invention and research.

China undertakes to be guided by the principles stated in the foregoing stipulations of this Article in dealing with applications for economic rights and privileges from Governments and nationals of all foreign countries, whether parties to the present Treaty or not.

ARTICLE IV

The Contracting Powers agree not to support any agreements by their respective nationals with each other designed to create Spheres of Influence or to provide for the enjoyment of mutually exclusive opportunities in designated parts of Chinese territory.

ARTICLE V

China agrees that, throughout the whole of the railways in China, she will not exercise or permit unfair discrimination of any kind. In particular there shall be no discrimination whatever, direct or indirect, in respect of charges or of facilities on the ground of the nationality of passengers or the countries from which or to which they are proceeding, or the origin or ownership of goods or the country from which or to which they are consigned, or the nationality or ownership of the ship or other means of conveying such passengers or goods before or after their transport on the Chinese Railways.

The Contracting Powers, other than China, assume a corresponding obligation in respect of any of the aforesaid railways over which they or their nationals are in a position to exercise any control in virtue of any concession, special agreement or otherwise.

ARTICLE VI

The Contracting Powers, other than China, agree fully to respect China's rights as a neutral in time of war to which China is not a party; and China declares that when she is a neutral she will observe the obligations of neutrality.

ARTICLE VII

The Contracting Powers agree that, whenever a situation arises which in the opinion of any one of them involves the application of the stipulations of the present Treaty, and renders desirable discussion of such application, there shall be full and frank communication between the Contracting Powers concerned.

ARTICLE VIII

Powers not signatory to the present Treaty, which have Governments recognized by the Signatory Powers and which have treaty relations with China, shall be invited to adhere to the present Treaty. To this end the Government of the United States will make the necessary communications to nonsignatory Powers and will inform the Contracting Powers of the replies received. Adherence by any Power shall become effective on receipt of notice thereof by the Government of the United States.

ARTICLE IX

The present Treaty shall be ratified by the Contracting Powers in accordance with their respective constitutional methods and shall take effect on the date of the deposit of all the ratifications, which shall take place at Washington as soon as possible. The Government of the United States will transmit to the other Contracting Powers a certified copy of the *procès-verbal* of the deposit of ratifications.

The present Treaty, of which the French and English texts are both authentic, shall remain deposited in the archives of the Government of the United States, and duly certified copies thereof shall be transmitted by that Government to the other Contracting Powers.

In FAITH WHEREOF the above-named Plenipotentiaries have signed the present Treaty.

DONE at the City of Washington the Sixth day of February One Thousand Nine Hundred and Twenty-Two.

	CHARLES EVANS HUGHES	[SEAL]
	HENRY CABOT LODGE	[SEAL]
	OSCAR W UNDERWOOD	[SEAL]
	ELIHU ROOT	[SEAL]
	BARON DE CARTIER DE MARCHIENNE	[SEAL]
	ARTHUR JAMES BALFOUR	[SEAL]
	LEE OF FAREHAM	[SEAL]
	A. C. GEDDES	[SEAL]
	R. L. BORDEN	[SEAL]
	G. F. PEARCE	[SEAL]
	JOHN W SALMOND	[SEAL]
	ARTHUR JAMES BALFOUR	[SEAL]
	V S SRINIVASA SASTRI	[SEAL]
[SEAL]	SAO-KE ALFRED SZE	
[SEAL]	V. K. WELLINGTON KOO	
[SEAL]	CHUNG-HUI WANG	
[SEAL]	A SARRAUT	
[SEAL]	JUSSERAND	
[SEAL]	CARLO SCHANZER	
[SEAL]	V. ROLANDI RICCI	
[SEAL]	LUIGI ALBERTINI	
	T. KATO	[SEAL]
	K. SHIDEHARA	[SEAL]
	M. HANIHARA	[SEAL]
	BEELAERTS VAN BLOKLAND	[SEAL]
	W. DE BEAUFORT	[SEAL]
	ALTE	[SEAL]
	ERNESTO DE VASCONCELLOS	[SEAL]

15

Statement by Secretary Kellogg, January 27, 1927 [20]

At this time, when there is so much discussion of the Chinese situation, I deem it my duty to state clearly the position of the Department of State on the questions of tariff autonomy and the relinquishment of extraterritorial rights.

The United States has always desired the unity, the independence and prosperity of the Chinese nation. It has desired that tariff control and extraterritoriality provided by our treaties with China should as early as possible be released. It was with that in view that the United States made the declaration in relation to the relinquishment of extraterritoriality in the Treaty of 1903 and also entered into the Treaty of Washington of February 6, 1922, providing for a Tariff Conference to be held within three months after the coming into force of the Treaty.

---

[20] *Ibid.*, 1927, vol. II, p. 350.

The United States is now and has been, ever since the negotiation of the Washington Treaty, prepared to enter into negotiations with any Government of China or delegates who can represent or speak for China not only for the putting into force of the surtaxes of the Washington Treaty but entirely releasing tariff control and restoring complete tariff autonomy to China.

The United States would expect, however, that it be granted most favored nation treatment and that there should be no discrimination against the United States and its citizens in customs duties, or taxes, in favor of the citizens of other nations or discrimination by grants of special privileges and that the open door with equal opportunity for trade in China shall be maintained; and further that China should afford every protection to American citizens, to their property and rights.

The United States is prepared to put into force the recommendations of the Extraterritoriality Commission which can be put into force without a treaty at once and to negotiate the release of extraterritorial rights as soon as China is prepared to provide protection by law and through her courts to American citizens, their rights and property.

The willingness of the United States to deal with China in the most liberal spirit will be borne out by a brief history of the events since making the Washington Treaty. That Treaty was ratified by the last one of the Signatory Powers on July 7, 1925, and the exchange of ratifications took place in Washington on August 6, 1925. Before the treaties finally went into effect and on June 24, 1925, the Chinese Government addressed identic notes to the Signatory Powers asking for the revision of existing treaties. On the first of July 1925, I sent instructions to our Minister in Peking, which instructions I also communicated to all the other Governments, urging that this should be made the occasion of evidencing to the Chinese our willingness to consider the question of treaty revision. I urged that the Powers expedite preparations for the holding of the Special Conference regarding the Chinese customs tariff and stated that the United States believed that this special tariff conference should be requested, after accomplishing the work required by the Treaty to make concrete recommendations upon which a program for granting complete tariff autonomy might be worked out. The Delegates of the United States were given full powers to negotiate a new treaty recognizing China's tariff autonomy. At the same time, I urged the appointment of the Commission to investigate extraterritoriality, with the understanding that the Commission should be authorized to include in its report recommendations for the gradual relinquishment of extraterritorial rights. Prior to this, the Chinese Government urged the United States to use its influence with the interested Powers to hasten the calling of the Conference on Tariff Matters and the appointment of the Extraterritorial Commission and for each Government to grant to its representatives the broad power to consider the whole subject of the revision of the treaties and to make recommendations upon the subject of the abolition of extraterritorial rights. This was in harmony with the views of the United States. Accordingly, on September 4, 1925, the United States and each of the other Powers having tariff treaties with China evidenced their intention to appoint their delegates to the Tariff Conference. By a note which has been published, the Powers informed China of their willingness to consider and discuss any reasonable proposal that might be made by the Chinese Government on the revision of the treaties on the subject of the tariff and also announced their intention of appointing their representatives to the Extraterritorial Commission for the purpose of considering the whole subject of extraterritorial rights and authorizing them to make recommendations for the purpose of enabling the governments concerned to consider what, if any, steps might be taken with a view to the relinquishment of extraterritorial rights. Delegates were promptly appointed and the Chinese Tariff Conference met on October 26, 1925.

Shortly after the opening of the Conference and on November 3, 1925, the American Delegation proposed that the Conference at once authorize the levying of a surtax of two and one-half per cent on necessaries, and, as soon as the requisite schedules could be prepared, authorize the levying of a surtax of up to five per cent on luxuries, as provided for by the Washington Treaty. Our Delegates furthermore announced that the Government of the United States was prepared to proceed at once with the negotiation of such an agreement or agreements as might be necessary for making effective other provisions of the Washington Treaty of February 6, 1922. They affirmed the principle of respect for China's tariff autonomy and announced that they were prepared forthwith to negotiate a new treaty which would give effect to that principle and which should make provision for the abolition of likin, for the removal of tariff restrictions contained in existing treaties and for the putting into effect of the Chinese National Tariff Law. On November 19, 1925, the Committee on Provisional Measures of the Conference, Chinese delegates participating, unanimously adopted the following resolution:

"The Delegates of the Powers assembled at this Conference resolve to adopt the following proposed article relating to tariff autonomy with a view to incorporating it, together with other matters, to be hereafter agreed upon, in a treaty which is to be signed at this Conference.

"The Contracting Powers other than China hereby recognize China's right to enjoy tariff autonomy; agree to remove the tariff restrictions which are contained in existing treaties between themselves respectively and China; and consent to the going into effect of the Chinese National Tariff Law on January 1st, 1929.

"The Government of the Republic of China declares that likin shall be abolished simultaneously with the enforcement of the Chinese National Tariff Law; and further declares that the abolition of likin shall be effectively carried out by the First Day of the First Month of the Eighteenth Year of the Republic of China (January 1st, 1929)."

Continuously from the beginning of the Conference, our delegates and technical advisers collaborated with the delegates and technical advisers of the other Powers, including China, in an effort to carry out this plan,—viz. to put into effect the surtaxes provided for in the Washington Treaty, and to provide for additional tariff adequate for all of China's needs until tariff autonomy should go into effect. Until about the middle of April 1926, there was every prospect for the successful termination of the Conference to the satisfaction of the Chinese and the other Powers. About that time the Government which represented China at the Conference was forced out of power. The delegates of the United States and the other Powers, however, remained in China in the hope of continuing the negotiations and on July 3, 1926, made a declaration as follows:

"The Delegates of the foreign Powers to the Chinese Customs Tariff Conference met at the Netherlands Legation this morning. They expressed the unanimous and earnest desire to proceed with the work of the Conference at the earliest possible moment when the Delegates of the Chinese Government are in a position to resume discussion with the foreign Delegates of the problems before the Conference."

The Government of the United States was ready then and is ready now to continue the negotiations on the entire subject of the tariff and extraterritoriality or to take up negotiations on behalf of the United States alone. The only question is with whom it shall negotiate. As I have said heretofore, if China can agree upon the appointment of delegates representing the authorities or the people of the country, we are prepared to negotiate such a treaty. However, existing treaties which were ratified by the Senate of the United States cannot be abrogated by the President but must be superseded by new treaties negotiated with somebody representing China and subsequently ratified by the Senate of the United States.

The Government of the United States has watched with sympathetic interest the nationalistic awakening of China and welcomes every advance made by the Chinese people toward reorganizing their system of Government.

During the difficult years since the establishment of the new regime in 1912, the Government of the United States has endeavored in every way to maintain an attitude of the most careful and strict neutrality as among the several factions that have disputed with one another for control in China. The Government of the United States expects, however, that the people of China and their leaders will recognize the right of American citizens in China to protection for life and property during the period of conflict for which they are not responsible. In the event that the Chinese Authorities are unable to afford such protection, it is of course the fundamental duty of the United States to protect the lives and property of its citizens. It is with the possible necessity for this in view that American naval forces are now in Chinese waters. This Government wishes to deal with China in a most liberal spirit. It holds no concessions in China and has never manifested any imperialistic attitude toward that country. It desires, however, that its citizens be given equal opportunity with the citizens of the other Powers to reside in China and to pursue their legitimate occupations without special privileges, monopolies or spheres of special interest or influence.

16

Treaty Between the United States and China Regulating Tariff Relations, Signed at Peiping, July 25, 1928 [21]

The United States of America and the Republic of China, both being animated by an earnest desire to maintain the good relations which happily subsist between the two countries, and wishing to extend and consolidate the commercial intercourse between them, have, for the purpose of negotiating a treaty designed to facilitate these objects, named as their Plenipotentiaries:—

The President of the United States of America:

J. V. A. MacMurray, Envoy Extraordinary and Minister Plenipotentiary of the United States of America to China;

and the Government Council of the Nationalist Government of the Republic of China:

T. V. Soong, Minister of Finance of the Nationalist Government of the Republic of China;

who, having met and duly exchanged their full powers, which have been found to be in proper form, have agreed upon the following treaty between the two countries:

---

[21] *Ibid.*, 1928, vol. II, p. 475.

ARTICLE I

All provisions which appear in treaties hitherto concluded and in force between the United States of America and China relating to rates of duty on imports and exports of merchandise, drawbacks, transit dues and tonnage dues in China shall be annulled and become inoperative, and the principle of complete national tariff autonomy shall apply subject, however, to the condition that each of the High Contracting Parties shall enjoy in the territories of the other with respect to the above specified and any related matters treatment in no way discriminatory as compared with the treatment accorded to any other country.

The nationals of neither of the High Contracting Parties shall be compelled under any pretext whatever to pay within the territories of the other Party any duties, internal charges or taxes upon their importations and exportations other or higher than those paid by nationals of the country or by nationals of any other country.

The above provisions shall become effective on January 1, 1929, provided that the exchange of ratifications hereinafter provided shall have taken place by that date; otherwise, at a date four months subsequent to such exchange of ratifications.

ARTICLE II

The English and Chinese texts of this Treaty have been carefully compared and verified; but, in the event of there being a difference of meaning between the two, the sense as expressed in the English text shall be held to prevail.

This treaty shall be ratified by the High Contracting Parties in accordance with their respective constitutional methods, and the ratifications shall be exchanged in Washington as soon as possible.

In testimony whereof, we, the undersigned, by virtue of our respective powers have signed this Treaty in duplicate in the English and Chinese languages and have affixed our respective seals.

Done at Peiping, the 25th day of July, 1928, corresponding to the 25th day of the 7th month of the 17th year of the Republic of China.

[SEAL]   J. V. A. MacMURRAY

[SEAL]   TSE VEN SOONG

17

Secretary Stimson to the Ambassador in Japan (Forbes)[22]

WASHINGTON, *January 7, 1932—noon.*

7. Please deliver to the Foreign Office on behalf of your Government as soon as possible the following note:

"With the recent military operations about Chinchow, the last remaining administrative authority of the Government of the Chinese Republic in South Manchuria, as it existed prior to September 18th, 1931, has been destroyed. The American Government continues confident that the work of the neutral commission recently authorized by the Council of the League of Nations will facilitate an ultimate solution of the difficulties now existing between China and Japan. But in view of the present situation and of its own rights and obligations therein, the American Government deems it to be its duty to notify both the Imperial

---

[22] *Foreign Relations of the United States, Japan,* 1931–1941, vol. I, p. 76.

Japanese Government and the Government of the Chinese Republic that it cannot admit the legality of any situation *de facto* nor does it intend to recognize any treaty or agreement entered into between those Governments, or agents thereof, which may impair the treaty rights of the United States or its citizens in China, including those which relate to the sovereignty, the independence, or the territorial and administrative integrity of the Republic of China, or to the international policy relative to China, commonly known as the open door policy; and that it does not intend to recognize any situation, treaty or agreement which may be brought about by means contrary to the covenants and obligations of the Pact of Paris of August 27, 1928, to which Treaty both China and Japan, as well as the United States, are parties."

State that an identical note is being sent to the Chinese government.

STIMSON

18

Secretary Stimson to Senator Borah, Chairman of the Committee on Foreign Relations of the Senate, February 23, 1932 [23]

You have asked my opinion whether, as has been sometimes recently suggested, present conditions in China have in any way indicated that the so-called Nine Power Treaty has become inapplicable or ineffective or rightly in need of modification, and if so, what I considered should be the policy of this Government.

This Treaty, as you of course know, forms the legal basis upon which now rests the "Open Door" policy towards China. That policy, enunciated by John Hay in 1899, brought to an end the struggle among various powers for so-called spheres of interest in China which was threatening the dismemberment of that empire. To accomplish this Mr. Hay invoked two principles (1) equality of commercial opportunity among all nations in dealing with China, and (2) as necessary to that equality the preservation of China's territorial and administrative integrity. These principles were not new in the foreign policy of America. They had been the principles upon which it rested in its dealings with other nations for many years. In the case of China they were invoked to save a situation which not only threatened the future development and sovereignty of that great Asiatic people, but also threatened to create dangerous and constantly increasing rivalries between the other nations of the world. War had already taken place between Japan and China. At the close of that war three other nations intervened to prevent Japan from obtaining some of the results of that war claimed by her. Other nations sought and had obtained spheres of interest. Partly as a result of these actions a serious uprising had broken out in China which endangered the legations of all of the powers at Peking. While the attack on those legations was in progress, Mr. Hay made an announcement in respect to this policy as the principle upon which the powers should act in the settlement of the rebellion. He said

"The policy of the Government of the United States is to seek a solution which may bring about permanent safety and peace to China, preserve Chinese territorial and administrative entity, protect all rights guaranteed to friendly powers by treaty and international law, and safeguard for the world the principle of equal and impartial trade with all parts of the Chinese Empire."

He was successful in obtaining the assent of the other powers to the policy thus announced.

---

[23] *Ibid.*, p. 83.

In taking these steps Mr. Hay acted with the cordial support of the British Government. In responding to Mr. Hay's announcement, above set forth, Lord Salisbury, the British Prime Minister expressed himself "most emphatically as concurring in the policy of the United States."

For twenty years thereafter the Open Door policy rested upon the informal commitments thus made by the various powers. But in the winter of 1921 to 1922, at a conference participated in by all of the principal powers which had interests in the Pacific, the policy was crystallized into the so-called Nine Power Treaty, which gave definition and precision to the principles upon which the policy rested. In the first article of that Treaty, the contracting powers, other than China, agreed

1. To respect the sovereignty, the independence and the territorial and administrative integrity of China.

2. To provide the fullest and most unembarrassed opportunity to China to develop and maintain for herself an effective and stable government.

3. To use their influence for the purpose of effectually establishing and maintaining the principle of equal opportunity for the commerce and industry of all nations throughout the territory of China.

4. To refrain from taking advantage of conditions in China in order to seek special rights or privileges which would abridge the rights of subjects or citizens of friendly states, and from countenancing action inimical to the security of such states.

This Treaty thus represents a carefully developed and matured international policy intended, on the one hand, to assure to all of the contracting parties their rights and interests in and with regard to China, and on the other hand, to assure to the people of China the fullest opportunity to develop without molestation their sovereignty and independence according to the modern and enlightened standards believed to maintain among the peoples of this earth. At the time this Treaty was signed, it was known that China was engaged in an attempt to develop the free institutions of a self-governing republic after her recent revolution from an autocratic form of government; that she would require many years of both economic and political effort to that end; and that her progress would necessarily be slow. The Treaty was thus a covenant of self-denial among the signatory powers in deliberate renunciation of any policy of aggression which might tend to interfere with that development. It was believed—and the whole history of the development of the "Open Door" policy reveals that faith—that only by such a process, under the protection of such an agreement, could the fullest interests not only of China but of all nations which have intercourse with her best be served.

In its report to the President announcing this Treaty, the American Delegation, headed by the then Secretary of State, Mr. Charles E. Hughes, said

"It is believed that through this Treaty the 'Open Door' in China has at last been made a fact."

During the course of the discussions which resulted in the Treaty, the Chairman of the British delegation, Lord Balfour, had stated that

"The British Empire delegation understood that there was no representative of any power around the table who thought that the old practice of 'spheres of interest' was either advocated by any government or would be tolerable to this conference. So far as the British Government was concerned, they had, in the most formal manner, publicly announced that they regarded this practice as utterly inappropriate to the existing situation."

At the same time the representative of Japan, Baron Shidehara, announced the postion of his government as follows:

"No one denies to China her sacred right to govern herself. No one stands in the way of China to work out her own great national destiny."

The Treaty was originally executed by the United States, Belgium, the British Empire, China, France, Italy, Japan, the Netherlands and Portugal. Subsequently it was also executed by Norway, Bolivia, Sweden, Denmark and Mexico. Germany has signed it but her Parliament has not yet ratified it.

It must be remembered also that this Treaty was one of several treaties and agreements entered into at the Washington Conference by the various powers concerned, all of which were interrelated and interdependent. No one of these treaties can be disregarded without disturbing the general understanding and equilibrium which were intended to be accomplished and effected by the group of agreements arrived at in their entirety. The Washington Conference was essentially a disarmament conference, aimed to promote the possibility of peace in the world not only through the cessation of competition in naval armament but also by the solution of various other disturbing problems which threatened the peace of the world, particularly in the Far East. These problems were all interrelated. The willingness of the American government to surrender its then commanding lead in battleship construction and to leave its positions at Guam and in the Philippines without further fortification, was predicated upon, among other things, the self-denying covenants contained in the Nine Power Treaty, which assured the nations of the world not only of equal opportunity for their Eastern trade but also against the military aggrandizement of any other power at the expense of China. One cannot discuss the possibility of modifying or abrogating those provisions of the Nine Power Treaty without considering at the same time the other promises upon which they were really dependent.

Six years later the policy of self-denial against aggression by a stronger against a weaker power, upon which the Nine Power Treaty had been based, received a powerful reinforcement by the execution by substantially all the nations of the world of the Pact of Paris, the so-called Kellogg-Briand Pact. These two treaties represent independent but harmonious steps taken for the purpose of aligning the conscience and public opinion of the world in favor of a system of orderly development by the law of nations including the settlement of all controversies by methods of justice and peace instead of by arbitrary force. The program for the protection of China from outside aggression is an essential part of any such development. The signatories and adherents of the Nine Power Treaty rightly felt that the orderly and peaceful development of the 400,000,000 of people inhabiting China was necessary to the peaceful welfare of the entire world and that no program for the welfare of the world as a whole could afford to neglect the welfare and protection of China.

The recent events which have taken place in China, especially the hostilities which having been begun in Manchuria have latterly been extended to Shanghai, far from indicating the advisability of any modification of the treaties we have been discussing, have tended to bring home the vital importance of the faithful observance of the covenants therein to all of the nations interested in the Far East. It is not necessary in that connection to inquire into the causes of the controversy or attempt to apportion the blame between the two nations which are unhappily involved; for regardless of cause or responsibility, it is clear beyond peradventure that a situation has developed which cannot, under any circumstances, be reconciled with the obligations of the covenants of these two treaties, and that if the treaties had been faithfully observed such a situation could not have arisen. The signatories of the Nine Power Treaty and of the Kellogg-Briand Pact who are not parties to that conflict are not likely to see any reason for modifying the terms of those treaties. To them the real value of the faithful performance of the treaties has been brought sharply home by the perils and losses to which their nationals have been subjected in Shanghai.

That is the view of this Government. We see no reason for abandoning the enlightened principles which are embodied in these treaties. We believe that this situation would have been avoided had these covenants been faithfully observed, and no evidence has come to us to indicate that a due compliance with them would have interfered with the adequate protection of the legitimate rights in China of the signatories of those treaties and their nationals.

On January 7th last, upon the instruction of the President, this Government formally notified Japan and China that it would not recognize any situation, treaty or agreement entered into by those governments in violation of the covenants of these treaties, which affected the rights of our Government or its citizens in China. If a similar decision should be reached and a similar position taken by the other governments of the world, a caveat will be placed upon such action which, we believe, will effectively bar the legality hereafter of any title or right sought to be obtained by pressure or treaty violation, and which, as has been shown by history in the past, will eventually lead to the restoration to China of rights and titles of which she may have been deprived.

In the past our Government, as one of the leading powers on the Pacific Ocean, has rested its policy upon an abiding faith in the future of the people of China and upon the ultimate success in dealing with them of the principles of fair play, patience, and mutual goodwill. We appreciate the immensity of the task which lies before her statesmen in the development of her country and its government. The delays in her progress, the instability of her attempts to secure a responsible government, were foreseen by Messrs. Hay and Hughes and their contemporaries and were the very obstacles which the policy of the Open Door was designed to meet. We concur with those statesmen, representing all the nations in the Washington Conference who decided that China was entitled to the time necessary to accomplish her development. We are prepared to make that our policy for the future.

Very truly yours,   HENRY L. STIMSON

19

Statement by Secretary Hull, December 5, 1935 [24]

In reply to inquiries by press correspondents in regard to the "autonomy movement" in North China, Chinese and Japanese activities in relation thereto, and the American Government's attitude, the Secretary of State said:

There is going on in and with regard to North China a political struggle which is unusual in character and which may have far-reaching effects. The persons mentioned in reports of it are many; the action is rapid and covers a large area; opinions with regard to it vary; what may come of it no one could safely undertake to say; but, whatever the origin, whoever the agents, be what they may the methods, the fact stands out that an effort is being made—and is being resisted—

---

[24] *Ibid.,* p. 240.

to bring about a substantial change in the political status and condition of several of China's northern provinces.

Unusual developments in any part of China are rightfully and necessarily of concern not alone to the Government and people of China but to all of the many powers which have interests in China. For, in relations with China and in China, the treaty rights and the treaty obligations of the "treaty powers" are in general identical. The United States is one of those powers.

In the area under reference the interests of the United States are similar to those of other powers. In that area there are located, and our rights and obligations appertain to, a considerable number of American nationals, some American property, and substantial American commercial and cultural activities. The American Government is therefore closely observing what is happening there.

Political disturbances and pressures give rise to uncertainty and misgiving and tend to produce economic and social dislocations. They make difficult the enjoyment of treaty rights and the fulfillment of treaty obligations.

The views of the American Government with regard to such matters not alone in relation to China but in relation to the whole world are well known. As I have stated on many occasions, it seems to this Government most important in this period of world-wide political unrest and economic instability that governments and peoples keep faith in principles and pledges. In international relations there must be agreements and respect for agreements in order that there may be the confidence and stability and sense of security which are essential to orderly life and progress. This country has abiding faith in the fundamental principles of its traditional policy. This Government adheres to the provisions of the treaties to which it is a party and continues to bespeak respect by all nations for the provisions of treaties solemnly entered into for the purpose of facilitating and regulating, to reciprocal and common advantage, the contacts between and among the countries signatory.

20

Press Release Issued by the Department of State on October 6, 1937 [25]

The Department of State has been informed by the American Minister to Switzerland of the text of the report adopted by the Advisory Committee of the League of Nations setting forth the Advisory Committee's examination of the facts of the present situation in China and the treaty obligations of Japan. The Minister has further informed the Department that this report was adopted and approved by the Assembly of the League of Nations today, October 6.

Since the beginning of the present controversy in the Far East, the Government of the United States has urged upon both the Chinese and the Japanese Governments that they refrain from hostilities and has offered to be of assistance in an effort to find some means, acceptable to both parties to the conflict, of composing by pacific methods the situation in the Far East.

The Secretary of State, in statements made public on July 16 and August 23, made clear the position of the Government of the United States in regard to international problems and international relationships throughout the world and as applied specifically to the hostilities which are at present unfortunately going on between China and Japan. Among the principles which in the opinion of the Government of the United States should govern international relationships,

[25] *Ibid.*, p. 396.

if peace is to be maintained, are abstinence by all nations from the use of force in the pursuit of policy and from interference in the internal affairs of other nations; adjustment of problems in international relations by process of peaceful negotiation and agreement; respect by all nations for the rights of others and observance by all nations of established obligations; and the upholding of the principle of the sanctity of treaties.

On October 5 at Chicago the President elaborated these principles, emphasizing their importance, and in a discussion of the world situation pointed out that there can be no stability or peace either within nations or between nations except under laws and moral standards adhered to by all; that international anarchy destroys every foundation for peace; that it jeopardizes either the immediate or the future security of every nation, large or small; and that it is therefore of vital interest and concern to the people of the United States that respect for treaties and international morality be restored.

In the light of the unfolding developments in the Far East, the Government of the United States has been forced to the conclusion that the action of Japan in China is inconsistent with the principles which should govern the relationships between nations and is contrary to the provisions of the Nine Power Treaty of February 6, 1922, regarding principles and policies to be followed in matters concerning China, and to those of the Kellogg-Briand Pact of August 27, 1928. Thus the conclusions of this Government with respect to the foregoing are in general accord with those of the Assembly of the League of Nations.

21

The Ambassador in Japan (Grew) to Prince Konoye, Japanese Prime Minister and Minister for Foreign Affairs [26]

No. 1076   TOKYO, *October 6, 1938.*

EXCELLENCY: On the occasion of the interview which Your Excellency accorded me on October 3, when I had the honor to convey orally the views and desires of my Government with regard to conditions in China being brought about by agencies or representatives of the Japanese Government, which are violative of or prejudicial to American rights and interests in China, I undertook to set forth and to extend those views and desires in a note to be presented shortly thereafter. In fulfilment of that undertaking and under instruction from my Government, I now have the honor to address Your Excellency as follows:

The Government of the United States has had frequent occasion to make representations to Your Excellency's Government in regard to action taken and policies carried out in China under Japanese to which the Government of the United States takes exception as being, in its opinion, in contravention of the principle and the condition of equality of opportunity or the "open door" in China. In response to these representations, and in other connections, both public and private, the Japanese Government has given categorical assurances that equality of opportunity or the open door in China will be maintained. The Government of the United States is constrained to observe, however, that notwithstanding the assurances of the Japanese Government in this regard violation by Japanese agencies of American rights and interests has persisted.

As having by way of illustration a bearing on the situation to which the Government of the United States desires to invite the attention of the Japanese

---

[26] *Ibid.,* p. 785.

Government, it is recalled that at the time of the Japanese occupation of Manchuria the Japanese Government gave assurances that the open door in Manchuria would be maintained. However, the principal economic activities in that area have been taken over by special companies which are controlled by Japanese nationals and which are established under special charters according them a preferred or exclusive position. A large part of American enterprise which formerly operated in Manchuria has been forced to withdraw from that territory as a result of the preferences in force there. Arrangements between Japan and the regime now functioning in Manchuria allow the free movement of goods and funds between Manchuria and Japan while restricting rigidly the movement of goods and funds between Manchuria and countries other than Japan.

This channeling of the movement of goods is effected primarily by means of exchange control exercised under the authority of regulations issued under an enabling law which provide expressly that for the purposes of the law Japan shall not be considered a foreign country nor the Japanese yen a foreign currency. In the opinion of my Government equality of opportunity or open door has virtually ceased to exist in Manchuria notwithstanding the assurances of the Japanese Government that it would be maintained in that area.

The Government of the United States is now apprehensive lest there develop in other areas of China which have been occupied by Japanese military forces since the beginning of the present hostilities a situation similar in its adverse effect upon the competitive position of American business to that which now exists in Manchuria.

On April 12, 1938 I had occasion to invite the attention of Your Excellency's predecessor to reports which had reached the Government of the United States indicating that discrimination in favor of Japanese trade with North China was likewise to be by means of exchange control and to ask for assurances that the Japanese Government would not support or countenance financial measures discriminating against American interests. Although the Minister for Foreign Affairs stated then that the Japanese Government would continue to support the principle of equal opportunity or open door in China no specific reply has yet been made by the Japanese Government on the subject of these representations.

The Government of the United States now learns that the Japanese authorities at Tsingtao have in effect established an exchange control, that they are exercising a discretionary authority to prohibit exports unless export bills are sold to the Yokohama Specie Bank, and that the Bank refuses to purchase export bills except at an arbitrary rate far lower than the open market rate prevailing at Tientsin and Shanghai. A somewhat similar situation apparently prevails at Chefoo. Furthermore, reports continue to reach the American Government that a comprehensive system of exchange control will soon be established throughout North China. Control of foreign exchange transactions gives control of trade and commercial enterprise, and the exacting, either directly or indirectly, by the Japanese authorities of control of exchange in North China would place those authorities in position to thwart equality of opportunity or free competition between Japan and the United States in that area. In such a situation, imports from and exports to the United States, as well as the choice of dealers in North China, would be entirely subjected to the dispensation of the Japanese authorities. Notwithstanding the short time that exchange control has been enforced in Tsingtao, two cases of discrimination have already been brought to the attention of the Government of the United States. In one instance an American dealer in a staple commodity has been unable to export to the United

States because Japanese authorities there have insisted that his export bills be sold to a Japanese bank at a price so far below the current rate of exchange of the Chinese currency in the open market that such transaction would involve a loss rather than a profit; but a Japanese competitor recently completed a large shipment invoiced at a price in United States dollars which was equivalent to the local market price calculated at the current open market rate. In the other instance, an American firm was prevented from purchasing tobacco in Shantung unless it should purchase so-called Federal Reserve notes or yen currency with foreign money and at an arbitrary and low rate of exchange, conditions not imposed upon the company's Japanese or Chinese competitors.

The Government of the United States has already pointed out to the Japanese Government that alterations of the Chinese customs tariff by the regimes functioning in those portions of China occupied by Japanese armed forces and for which the Japanese Government has formally assured its support are arbitrary and illegal assumptions of authority for which the Japanese Government has an inescapable responsibility. It is hardly necessary to add that there can be no equality of opportunity or open door in China so long as the ultimate authority to regulate, tax, or prohibit trade is exercised, whether directly or indirectly, by the authorities of one "foreign" power in furtherance of the interests of that power. It would appear to be self-evident that a fundamental prerequisite of a condition of equality of opportunity or open door in China is the absence in the economic life of that country of preferences or monopolistic rights operating directly or indirectly in favor of any foreign country or its nationals. On July 4 I spoke to General Ugaki of the desire of the American Government that there be avoided such restrictions and obstacles to American trade and other enterprises as might result from the setting up of special companies and monopolies in China. The Minister was so good as to state that the open door in China would be maintained and that the Government of the United States might rest assured that the Japanese Government would fully respect the principle of equal opportunity.

Notwithstanding these assurances, the Provisional regime in Peiping announced on July 30th the inauguration as of the following day of the China Telephone and Telegraph Company, the reported purpose of this organization being to control and to have exclusive operation of telephone and telegraph communications in North China. There was organized in Shanghai on July 31st the Central China Telecommunications Company, and the Special Service Section of the Japanese army has informed foreign cable and telegraph companies that the new company proposes to control all the telecommunications in Central China. According to a semi-official Japanese press report, there was organized at Shanghai on July 28 the Shanghai Inland Navigation Steamship Company to be controlled by Japanese the reported object of which is to control water transportation in the Shanghai delta area. According to information which has reached my Government, a Japanese company has been organized to take over and operate the wharves at Tsingtao which have hitherto been publicly owned and operated. Should such a development occur, all shipping of whatever nationality would become dependent upon a Japanese agency for allotments of space and stevedoring facilities. The wool trade in North China is now reported to be a Japanese monopoly and a tobacco monopoly in that area is reported to be in process of formation. Moreover, according to numerous reports which have been reaching my Government, the Japanese Government is proceeding with the organization of two special promotion companies which it has chartered and which it will control with the object of investing in, unifying, and regulating the administration of certain large sectors of economic enterprise in China.

The developments of which I have made mention are illustrative of the apparent trend of Japanese policy in China and indicate clearly that the Japanese authorities are seeking to establish in areas which have come under Japanese military occupation general preferences for, and superiority of, Japanese interests, an inevitable effect of which will be to frustrate the practical application of the principle of the open door and deprive American nationals of equal opportunity.

I desire also to call Your Excellency's attention to the fact that unwarranted restrictions placed by the Japanese military authorities upon American nationals in China—notwithstanding the existence of American treaty rights in China and the repeated assurances of the Japanese Government that steps had been taken which would insure that American nationals, interests and property would not be subject to unlawful interference by Japanese authorities—further subject American interests to continuing serious inconvenience and hardships. Reference is made especially to the restrictions placed by the Japanese military upon American nationals who desire to reenter and reoccupy properties from which they have been driven by the hostilities and of which the Japanese military have been or still are in occupation. Mention may also be made of the Japanese censorship of and interference with American mail and telegrams at Shanghai and of restrictions upon freedom of trade, residence and travel by Americans, including the use of railways, shipping, and other facilities. While Japanese merchant vessels are carrying Japanese merchandise between Shanghai and Nanking, those vessels decline to carry merchandise of other countries, and American and other non-Japanese shipping is excluded from the lower Yangtze on the grounds of military necessity. Applications by American nationals for passes which would allow them to return to certain areas in the lower Yangtze valley have been denied by the Japanese authorities on the ground that peace and order have not been sufficiently restored, although many Japanese merchants and their families are known to be in those areas.

American nationals and their interests have suffered serious losses in the Far East arising from causes directly attributable to the present conflict between Japan and China, and even under the most favorable conditions an early rehabilitation of American trade with China cannot be expected. The American Government, therefore, finds it all the more difficult to reconcile itself to a situation in which American nationals must contend with continuing unwarranted interference with their rights at the hands of the Japanese authorities in China and with Japanese actions and policies which operate to deprive American trade and enterprise of equality of opportunity in China. It is also pertinent to mention that in Japan, too, American trade and other interests are undergoing severe hardships as a result of the industrial, trade, exchange and other controls which the Japanese Government has imposed incident to its military operations in China.

While American interests in the Far East have been thus treated at the hands of the Japanese authorities, the Government of the United States has not sought either in its own territory or in the territory of third countries to establish or influence the establishment of embargoes, import prohibitions, exchange controls, preferential restrictions, monopolies or special companies—designed to eliminate or having the effect of eliminating Japanese trade and enterprise. In its treatment of Japanese nationals and their trade and enterprise, the American Government has been guided not only by the letter and spirit of the Japanese-American Commercial Treaty of 1911 but by those fundamental principles of international law and order which have formed the basis of its policy in regard to all peoples and their interests; and Japanese commerce and enterprise have continued to enjoy in the United States equality of opportunity.

Your Excellency cannot fail to recognize the existence of a great and growing disparity between the treatment accorded American nationals and their trade and enterprise by Japanese authorities in China and Japan and the treatment accorded Japanese nationals and their trade and enterprise by the Government of the United States in areas within its jurisdiction.

In the light of the situation herein reviewed the Government of the United States asks that the Japanese Government implement its assurances already given with regard to the maintenance of the open door and to non-interference with American rights by taking prompt and effective measures to cause,

(1) The discontinuance of discriminatory exchange control and of other measures imposed in areas in China under Japanese control which operate either directly or indirectly to discriminate against American trade and enterprise;

(2) The discontinuance of any monopoly or of any preference which would deprive American nationals of the right of undertaking any legitimate trade or industry in China or of any arrangement which might purport to establish in favor of Japanese interests any general superiority of rights with regard to commercial or economic development in any region of China; and

(3) The discontinuance of interference by Japanese authorities in China with American property and other rights including such forms of interference as censorship of American mail and telegrams and restrictions upon residence and travel by Americans and upon American trade and shipping.

The Government of the United States believes that in the interest of relations between the United States and Japan an early reply would be helpful.

I avail myself [etc.]   JOSEPH C. GREW

22

The Japanese Foreign Minister (Arita) to the Ambassador in Japan (Grew) [27]

[Translation]

No. 102, American I   [TOKYO,] *November 18, 1938.*

EXCELLENCY: I have the honor to inform Your Excellency that I have carefully perused the contents of Your Excellency's note no. 1076, dated October 6th, addressed to the then Minister for Foreign Affairs Prince Konoye, concerning the rights and interests of the United States in China.

In this note, Your Excellency sets forth, on the basis of information in the possession of the Government of the United States, various instances in which Japanese authorities are subjecting American citizens in China to discriminatory treatment and are violating the rights and interests of the United States.

The views held by the Japanese Government with regard to these instances may be stated as follows:

1. According to the information in the possession of the Imperial Government, the circumstances which led to the adoption of such measures as those at present enforced in Tsingtao concerning export exchange, and the present situation being as set forth below, it is believed that those measures cannot be construed as constituting any discrimination against American citizens.

[27] *Ibid.,* p. 797.

A short time ago the Federal Reserve Bank of China was established in North China. This bank's notes, with foreign exchange value fixed at one shilling and two pence to one yuan, already have been issued to an amount of more than one hundred million yuan, and are being widely circulated. These bank notes being the legal currency required by the Provisional Government, the maintenance of their value and their smooth circulation is regarded as an indispensable basis for the conduct and development of economic activities in North China. Since the Japanese Government has, therefore, taken a cooperative attitude, all Japanese subjects are using those notes, and accordingly, even in their export trade are exchanging them at the rate of one shilling and two pence. On the other hand, the former legal currency still circulating in these areas has depreciated in exchange value to about eight pence per yuan. Consequently those who are engaged in export trade and are using this currency, are enjoying improper and excessive profits, as compared with those who are using Federal Reserve notes and carrying on legitimate transactions at the legally established rate of exchange. Japanese subjects and others who are using Federal Reserve notes have been suffering unreasonable and excessive losses as compared with those persons who use exclusively the former legal currency although residing and carrying on their businesses in the areas under the jurisdiction of the Provisional Government of North China. Furthermore, the existence of the above mentioned disparity between the foreign exchange value of the Federal Reserve notes and that of the former legal currency, which currency the Federal Reserve Bank has been and is exchanging at a rate almost on a par with its own notes, is bound to exert an unfavourable effect upon the exchange value of the Federal Reserve notes, and eventually also upon the exchange value of the Japanese yen. The Japanese Government therefore can not remain indifferent to such a situation.

In order to place the users of the former legal currency who have been obtaining improper and excessive profits on an equal footing with those using the Federal Reserve notes and at the same time to assist in the maintenance of the exchange value of the Federal Reserve Bank notes, represents an objective of those export exchange measures adopted at Tsingtao. Inasmuch as the application of the measures makes no differentiation according to nationality they are not at all discriminatory. As a matter of fact, it is through these measures that those users of the Federal Reserve notes who had in a sense been discriminated against have been placed on an equal footing with the others, and thus, for the first time on equal footing, are enabled to compete on an entirely equitable basis.

2. Some time ago the new regimes in North and Central China revised the Customs tariff rates seeking to secure a rational modification of the former tariff rates enforced by the Nationalist Government, because those rates were unduly high and not suitable for the promotion of the economic recovery and general welfare of the Chinese people. In any case, the schedule adopted is the one that was readily approved by the Powers in 1931, and was not calculated to inure to the benefit of any particular country. Accordingly no complaint has been heard from foreign residents of any nationality in China. The Japanese Government is, of course, in favor of the purpose of this revision, and believes that it will serve to promote effectively the trade of all countries with China.

3. As for the organization of certain promotion companies in China, the restoration and development of China's economic, financial and industrial activities following the present incident is a matter of the most urgent necessity for the welfare of the Chinese people. Moreover, the Japanese Government,

for the sake of the realization of a new order in East Asia, is exceedingly anxious for the prompt inauguration and progress of undertakings looking toward such restoration and development, and is devoting every constructive effort to realize this objective. The fact that the North China Development Company and the Central China Promotion Company were established represents nothing other than an offer to China of the necessary assistance for this restoration, and at the same time, an attempt to contribute to the development of the natural resources of China. It does not in any way impair the rights and interests of nationals of Your Excellency's country or in any way discriminate against their enterprises. The Japanese Government therefore, of course, has no intention of opposing, but rather welcomes heartily, the participation of third Powers which intend to cooperate on the basis of the new conditions.

The telecommunication companies in North and Central China, the inland navigation steamship company at Shanghai and the wharfage company at Tsingtao have also been established to meet the imperative need of an early restoration of communications, transportation, and harbor facilities which were destroyed as a result of the incident. It is proper that the telecommunications enterprise, not only because of its nature as a public utility but also in view of its relation to the maintenance of peace and order and to national defense, should be undertaken by special companies. However, all other enterprises being ordinary Chinese or Japanese juridical persons, do not have the objectives of discrimination against Your Excellency's country or third powers or of the gaining of monopolistic profits. As regards the wool trade, while the control of purchasing agencies was enforced in the Mongolian region, it now has been discontinued. There is at present no plan of any sort for the establishment of a tobacco monopoly.

4. Concerning the return of American citizens to the occupied areas, in North China there is no restriction on their returning, except in special cases where the personal safety of those who return would be endangered. Your Excellency is aware that in the Yangtze Valley large numbers of Americans have already returned. The fact that permission to return has not yet been made general is, as has been repeatedly communicated to Your Excellency, owing to considerations of the danger involved on account of order not yet being restored, or because of the impossibility of admitting nationals of third Powers on account of strategic necessities such as the preservation of military secrets. Further, the various restrictions enforced in the occupied areas concerning the residence, travel, enterprise and trade of American citizens, constitute the minimum regulations possible consistent with military necessities and the local conditions of peace and order. It is the intention of the Japanese Government to restore normal conditions as soon as circumstances permit.

5. The Japanese Government is surprised at the allegation that there exists a fundamental difference between the treatment accorded to Japanese in America and the treatment accorded to Americans in Japan. While it is true that in this period of emergency, Americans residing in this country are subject to various economic restrictions, these restrictions are, needless to say, imposed not upon Americans alone but also equally upon all foreigners as well as upon Japanese subjects. A statement of the views of the Japanese Government concerning the opinion as set forth in Your Excellency's note, regarding the treatment of Japanese subjects in American territory, is reserved for another occasion.

While the Japanese Government with the intention of fully respecting American rights and interests in China, as has been frequently stated above, has been making every effort in that direction, in view of the fact that military operations on a scale unprecedented in our history are now being carried out in East Asia, I am of the opinion that the Government of Your Excellency's country also should recognize the fact that occasionally obstacles arise hindering the effecting of the intention of respecting the rights and interests of Your Excellency's country.

At present Japan, devoting its entire energy to the establishment of a new order based on genuine international justice throughout East Asia, is making rapid strides toward the attainment of this objective. The successful accomplishment of this purpose is not only indispensable to the existence of Japan, but also constitutes the very foundation of the enduring peace and stability of East Asia.

It is the firm conviction of the Japanese Government that now, at a time of the continuing development of new conditions in East Asia, an attempt to apply to present and future conditions without any changes concepts and principles which were applicable to conditions prevailing before the present incident does not in any way contribute to the solution of immediate issues and further does not in the least promote the firm establishment of enduring peace in East Asia.

The Imperial Government, however, does not have any intention of objecting to the participation in the great work of the reconstruction of East Asia by Your Excellency's country or by other Powers, in all fields of trade and industry, when such participation is undertaken with an understanding of the purport of the above stated remarks; and further, I believe that the regimes now being formed in China are also prepared to welcome such participation.

I avail myself [etc.] HACHIRO ARITA

23

The Ambassador in Japan (Grew) to the Japanese Foreign Minister (Arita) [28]

No. 1153 TOKYO, December 30, 1938.

EXCELLENCY: Acting under the instructions of my Government I have the honor to address to Your Excellency the following note:

The Government of the United States has received and has given full consideration to the reply of the Japanese Government of November 18 to this Government's note of October 6 on the subject of American rights and interests in China.

In the light of facts and experience the Government of the United States is impelled to reaffirm its previously expressed opinion that imposition of restrictions upon the movements and activities of American nationals who are engaged in philanthropic, educational and commercial endeavors in China has placed and will, if continued, increasingly place Japanese interests in a preferred position and is, therefore, unquestionably discriminatory in its effect against legitimate American interests. Further, with reference to such matters as exchange control, compulsory currency circulation, tariff revision, and monopolistic promotion in certain areas of China the plans and practices of the Japanese authorities imply an assumption on the part of those authorities that the Japanese Government or the regimes established and maintained in China by Japanese armed forces are entitled to act in China in a capacity such as flows from rights of sovereignty and further in so acting to disregard and even to declare non-

---

[28] *Ibid.*, p. 820.

existent or abrogated the established rights and interests of other countries including the United States.

The Government of the United States expresses its conviction that the restrictions and measures under reference not only are unjust and unwarranted but are counter to the provisions of several binding international agreements, voluntarily entered into, to which both Japan and the United States, and in some cases other countries, are parties.

In the concluding portion of its note under reference, the Japanese Government states that it is firmly convinced that "in the face of the new situation, fast developing in Asia, any attempt to apply to the conditions of today and tomorrow inapplicable ideas and principles of the past neither would contribute toward the establishment of a real peace in East Asia nor solve the immediate issues" and that "as long as these points are understood Japan has not the slightest inclination to oppose the participation of the United States and other Powers in the great work of reconstructing East Asia along all lines of industry and trade."

The Government of the United States in its note of October 6 requested, in view of the oft reiterated assurances proffered by the Government of Japan of its intention to observe the principles of equality of opportunity in its relations with China and in view of Japan's treaty obligations so to do, that the Government of Japan abide by these obligations and carry out these assurances in practice. The Japanese Government in its reply appears to affirm that it is its intention to make its observance of that principle conditional upon an understanding by the American Government and by other governments of a "new situation" and a "new order" in the Far East as envisaged and fostered by Japanese authorities.

Treaties which bear upon the situation in the Far East have within them provisions relating to a number of subjects. In the making of those treaties, there was a process among the parties to them of give and take. Toward making possible the carrying out of some of their provisions, others among their provisions were formulated and agreed upon: toward gaining for itself the advantage of security in regard to certain matters, each of the parties committed itself to pledges of self-denial in regard to certain other matters. The various provisions agreed upon may be said to have constituted collectively an arrangement for safeguarding, for the benefit of all, the correlated principles on the one hand of national integrity and on the other hand of equality of economic opportunity. Experience has shown that impairment of the former of these principles is followed almost invariably by disregard of the latter. Whenever any government begins to exercise political authority in areas beyond the limits of its lawful jurisdiction there develops inevitably a situation in which the nationals of that government demand and are accorded, at the hands of their government, preferred treatment, whereupon equality of opportunity ceases to exist and discriminatory practices, productive of friction, prevail.

The admonition that enjoyment by the nationals of the United States of non-discriminatory treatment in China—a general and well-established right— is henceforth to be contingent upon an admission by the Government of the United States of the validity of the conception of Japanese authorities of a "new situation" and a "new order" in East Asia, is, in the opinion of this Government, highly paradoxical.

This country's adherence to and its advocacy of the principle of equality of opportunity do not flow solely from a desire to obtain the commercial benefits which naturally result from the provisions of that principle. They flow from a firm conviction that observance of that principle leads to economic and political stability, which are conducive both to the internal well-being of nations and to mutually beneficial and peaceful relationships between and among nations; from a firm conviction that failure to observe that principle breeds international friction and ill-will, with consequences injurious to all countries, including in particular those countries which fail to observe it; and from an equally firm conviction that observance of that principle promotes the opening of trade channels thereby making available the markets, the raw materials and the manufactured products of the community of nations on a mutually and reciprocally beneficial basis.

The principle of equality of economic opportunity is, moreover, one to which over a long period and on many occasions the Japanese Government has given definite approval. It is one to the observance of which the Japanese Government has committed itself in various international agreements and understandings. It is one upon observance of which by other nations the Japanese Government has of its own accord and upon its own initiative frequently insisted. It is one to which the Japanese Government has repeatedly during recent months declared itself committed.

The people and the Government of the United States could not assent to the establishment at the instance of and for the special purposes of any third country of a regime which would arbitrarily deprive them of the long established rights of equal opportunity and fair treatment which are legally and justly theirs along with those of other nationals.

Fundamental principles such as the principle of equality of opportunity which have long been regarded as inherently wise and just which have been widely adopted and adhered to, and which are general in their application are not subject to nullification by a unilateral affirmation.

With regard to the implication in the Japanese Government's note that the "conditions of today and tomorrow" in the Far East call for a revision of the ideas and principles of the past, this Government desires to recall to the Japanese Government its position on the subject of revision of agreements.

This Government had occasion in the course of a communication delivered to the Japanese Government on April 29, 1934, to express its opinion that "treaties can lawfully be modified or be terminated—but only by processes prescribed or recognized or agreed upon by the parties to them".

In the same communication this Government also said, "In the opinion of the American people and the American Government, no nation can, without the assent of the other nations concerned, rightfully endeavor to make conclusive its will in situations where there are involved the rights, the obligations and the legitimate interests of other sovereign states". In an official and public statement on July 16, 1937, the Secretary of State of the United States declared that this Government advocates "adjustment of problems in international relations by processes of peaceful negotiation and agreement".

At various times during recent decades various powers, among which have been Japan and the United States, have had occasion to communicate and to confer with regard to situations and problems in the Far East. In the conducting of correspondence and of conferences relating to these matters, the parties involved have invariably taken into consideration past and present facts and they have not failed to perceive the possibility and the desirability of changes in the situation. In the making of treaties they have drawn up and have agreed upon provisions intended to facilitate advantageous developments and at the same time to obviate and avert the arising of friction between and among the various powers which, having interests in the region or regions under reference, were and would be concerned.

In the light of these facts, and with reference especially to the purpose and the character of the treaty provisions from time to time solemnly agreed upon for the very definite purposes indicated, the Government of the United States deprecates the fact that one of the parties to these agreements has chosen to embark—as indicated both by action of its agents and by official statements of its authorities—upon a course directed toward the arbitrary creation by that power by methods of its own selection, regardless of treaty pledges and the established rights of other powers concerned, of a "new order" in the Far East. Whatever may be the changes which have taken place in the situation in the Far East and whatever may be the situation now, these matters are of no less interest and concern to the American Government than have been the situations which have prevailed there in the past, and such changes as may henceforth take place there, changes which may enter into the producing of a "new situation" and a "new order", are and will be of like concern to this Government. This Government is well aware that the situation has changed. This Government is also well aware that many of the changes have been brought about by the action of Japan. This Government does not admit, however, that there is need or warrant for any one Power to take upon itself to prescribe what shall be the terms and conditions of a "new order" in areas not under its sovereignty and to constitute itself the repository of authority and the agent of destiny in regard thereto.

It is known to all the world that various of the parties to treaties concluded for the purpose of regulating contacts in the Far East and avoiding friction therein and therefrom—which treaties contained, for those purposes, various restrictive provisions—have from time to time and by processes of negotiation and agreement contributed in the light of changed situations toward the removal of restrictions and toward the bringing about of further developments which would warrant in the light of further changes in the situation, further removals of restrictions. By such methods and processes, early restrictions upon the tariff autonomy of all countries in the Far East were removed. By such methods and processes the rights of extraterritorial jurisdiction once enjoyed by Occidental countries in relations with countries in the Far East have been given up in relations with all of those countries except China; and in the years immediately preceding and including the year 1931, countries which still possessed those rights in China including the United States were actively engaged in negotiations—far advanced—looking toward surrender of those rights. All discerning and impartial observers have realized that the United States and others of the "treaty powers" have not during recent decades clung tenaciously to their so-called "special" rights and privileges in countries of the Far East but on the contrary have steadily encouraged the development in those countries of institutions and practices in the presence of which such rights and privileges may safely and readily be given up; and all observers have seen those rights and privileges gradually being surrendered voluntarily through agreement by the Powers which have possessed them. On one point only has the Government of the United States, along with several other governments, insisted: namely, that new situations must have developed to a point warranting the removal of "special" safeguarding restrictions and that the removals be effected by orderly processes.

The Government of the United States has at all times regarded agreements as susceptible of alteration, but it has always insisted that alterations can rightfully be made only by orderly processes of negotiation and agreement among the parties thereto.

The Japanese Government has upon numerous occasions expressed itself as holding similar views.

The United States has in its international relations rights and obligations which derive from international law and rights and obligations which rest upon treaty provisions. Of those which rest on treaty provisions, its rights and obligations in and with regard to China rest in part upon provisions in treaties between the United States and China and in part on provisions in treaties between the United States and several other powers including both China and Japan. These treaties were concluded in good faith for the purpose of safeguarding and promoting the interests not of one only but of all of their signatories. The people and the Government of the United States cannot assent to the abrogation of any of this country's rights or obligations by the arbitrary action of agents or authorities of any other country.

The Government of the United States has, however, always been prepared and is now prepared to give due and ample consideration to any proposals based on justice and reason which envisage the resolving of problems in a manner duly considerate of the rights and obligations of all parties directly concerned by processes of free negotiation and new commitment by and among all of the parties so concerned. There has been and there continues to be opportunity for the Japanese Government to put forward such proposals. This Government has been and it continues to be willing to discuss such proposals, if and when put forward, with representatives of the other powers, including Japan and China, whose rights and interests are involved, at whatever time and in whatever place may be commonly agreed upon.

Meanwhile, this Government reserves all rights of the United States as they exist and does not give assent to any impairment of any of those rights.

I avail myself [etc.]   JOSEPH C. GREW

24

Statement by Secretary Hull, March 30, 1940 [29]

In response to inquiries with regard to the attitude and position of the Government of the United States in the light of the setting up at Nanking of a new regime, the Secretary of State made a statement as follows:

"In the light of what has happened in various parts of China since 1931, the setting up of a new regime at Nanking has the appearance of a further step in a program of one country by armed force to impose its will upon a neighboring country and to block off a large area of the world from normal political and economic relationships with the rest of the world. The developments there appear to be following the pattern of other regimes and systems which have been set up in China under the aegis of an outside power and which in their functioning especially favor the interests of that outside power and deny to nationals of the United States and other third countries enjoyment of long-established rights of equal and fair treatment which are legally and justly theirs.

"The Government of the United States has noted statements of high officials of that outside power that their country intends to respect the political independence and the freedom of the other country and that with the development of affairs in East Asia this intention will be demonstrated. To this Government

[29] *Ibid.*, vol. II, p. 59.

the circumstances, both military and diplomatic, which have attended the setting up of the new regime at Nanking do not seem consistent with such an intention.

"The attitude of the United States toward use of armed force as an instrument of national policy is well known. Its attitude and position with regard to various aspects of the situation in the Far East have been made clear on numerous occasions. That attitude and position remain unchanged.

"This Government again makes full reservation of this country's rights under international law and existing treaties and agreements.

"Twelve years ago the Government of the United States recognized, as did other governments, the National Government of the Republic of China. The Government of the United States has ample reason for believing that that Government, with capital now at Chungking, has had and still has the allegiance and support of the great majority of the Chinese people. The Government of the United States of course continues to recognize that Government as the Government of China."

25

Document Handed by Secretary Hull to the Japanese Ambassador (Nomura) on November 26, 1941 [30]

Strictly Confidential,
Tentative and Without
Commitment

WASHINGTON, *November 26, 1941*

OUTLINE OF PROPOSED BASIS FOR AGREEMENT BETWEEN THE UNITED STATES AND JAPAN

SECTION I

Draft Mutual Declaration of Policy

The Government of the United States and the Government of Japan both being solicitous for the peace of the Pacific affirm that their national policies are directed toward lasting and extensive peace throughout the Pacific area, that they have no territorial designs in that area, that they have no intention of threatening other countries or of using military force aggressively against any neighboring nation, and that, accordingly, in their national policies they will actively support and give practical application to the following fundamental principles upon which their relations with each other and with all other governments are based:

(1) The principle of inviolability of territorial integrity and sovereignty of each and all nations.

(2) The principle of non-interference in the internal affairs of other countries.

(3) The principle of equality, including equality of commercial opportunity and treatment.

(4) The principle of reliance upon international cooperation and conciliation for the prevention and pacific settlement of controversies and for improvement of international conditions by peaceful methods and processes.

The Government of Japan and the Government of the United States have agreed that toward eliminating chronic political instability, preventing recurrent economic collapse, and providing a basis for peace, they will actively support and practically apply the following principles in their economic relations with each other and with other nations and peoples:

---
[30] *Ibid.*, p. 768.

(1) The principle of non-discrimination in international commercial relations.

(2) The principle of international economic cooperation and abolition of extreme nationalism as expressed in excessive trade restrictions.

(3) The principle of non-discriminatory access by all nations to raw material supplies.

(4) The principle of full protection of the interests of consuming countries and populations as regards the operation of international commodity agreements.

(5) The principle of establishment of such institutions and arrangements of international finance as may lend aid to the essential enterprises and the continuous development of all countries and may permit payments through processes of trade consonant with the welfare of all countries.

SECTION II

Steps To Be Taken by the Government of the United States and by the Government of Japan

The Government of the United States and the Government of Japan propose to take steps as follows:

1. The Government of the United States and the Government of Japan will endeavor to conclude a multilateral non-aggression pact among the British Empire, China, Japan, the Netherlands, the Soviet Union, Thailand and the United States.

2. Both Governments will endeavor to conclude among the American, British, Chinese, Japanese, the Netherland and Thai Governments an agreement whereunder each of the Governments would pledge itself to respect the territorial integrity of French Indochina and, in the event that there should develop a threat to the territorial integrity of Indochina, to enter into immediate consultation with a view of taking such measures as may be deemed necessary and advisable to meet the threat in question. Such agreement would provide also that each of the Governments party to the agreement would not seek or accept preferential treatment in its trade or economic relations with Indochina and would use its influence to obtain for each of the signatories equality of treatment in trade and commerce with French Indochina.

3. The Government of Japan will withdraw all military, naval, air and police forces from China and from Indochina.

4. The Government of the United States and the Government of Japan will not support—militarily, politically, economically—any government or regime in China other than the National Government of the Republic of China with capital temporarily at Chungking.

5. Both Governments will give up all extraterritorial rights in China, including rights and interests in and with regard to international settlements and concessions, and rights under the Boxer Protocol of 1901.

Both Governments will endeavor to obtain the agreement of the British and other governments to give up extraterritorial rights in China, including rights in international settlements and in concessions and under the Boxer Protocol of 1901.

6. The Government of the United States and the Government of Japan will enter into negotiations for the conclusion between the United States and Japan of a trade agreement, based upon reciprocal most-favored-nation treatment and reduction of trade barriers by both countries, including an undertaking by the United States to bind raw silk on the free list.

7. The Government of the United States and the Government of Japan will, respectively, remove the freezing restrictions on Japanese funds in the United States and on American funds in Japan.

8. Both Governments will agree upon a plan for the stabilization of the dollar-yen rate, with the allocation of funds adequate for this purpose, half to be supplied by Japan and half by the United States.

9. Both Governments will agree that no agreement which either has concluded with any third power or powers shall be interpreted by it in such a way as to conflict with the fundamental purpose of this agreement, the establishment and preservation of peace throughout the Pacific area.

10. Both Governments will use their influence to cause other governments to adhere to and to give practical application to the basic political and economic principles set forth in this agreement.

26

Master Lend-Lease Agreement Between the United States and China, Signed at Washington June 2, 1942 [31]

Whereas the Governments of the United States of America and the Republic of China declare that they are engaged in a cooperative undertaking, together with every other nation or people of like mind, to the end of laying the bases of a just and enduring world peace securing order under law to themselves and all nations;

And whereas the Governments of the United States of America and the Republic of China, as signatories of the Declaration by United Nations of January 1, 1942, have subscribed to a common program of purposes and principles embodied in the Joint Declaration made on August 14, 1941 by the President of the United States of America and the Prime Minister of the United Kingdom of Great Britain and Northern Ireland, known as the Atlantic Charter;

And whereas the President of the United States of America has determined, pursuant to the Act of Congress of March 11, 1941, that the defense of the Republic of China against aggression is vital to the defense of the United States of America;

And whereas the United States of America has extended and is continuing to extend to the Republic of China aid in resisting aggression;

And whereas it is expedient that the final determination of the terms and conditions upon which the Government of the Republic of China receives such aid and of the benefits to be received by the United States of America in return therefor should be deferred until the extent of the defense aid is known and until the progress of events makes clearer the final terms and conditions and benefits which will be in the mutual interests of the United States of America and the Republic of China and will promote the establishment and maintenance of world peace;

And whereas the Governments of the United States of America and the Republic of China are mutually desirous of concluding now a preliminary agreement in regard to the provisions of defense aid and in regard to certain considerations which shall be taken into account in determining such terms and conditions and the making of such an agreement has been in all respects duly authorized, and all acts, conditions and formalities which it may have been necessary to perform, fulfil or execute prior to the making of such an agreement in conformity with the

---

[31] 56 Stat. 1494.

laws either of the United States of America or of the Republic of China have been performed, fulfilled or executed as required;

The undersigned, being duly authorized by their respective Governments for that purpose, have agreed as follows:

ARTICLE I

The Government of the United States of America will continue to supply the Government of the Republic of China with such defense articles, defense services, and defense information as the President of the United States of America shall authorize to be transferred or provided.

ARTICLE II

The Government of the Republic of China will continue to contribute to the defense of the United States of America and the strengthening thereof and will provide such articles, services, facilities or information as it may be in a position to supply.

ARTICLE III

The Government of the Republic of China will not without the consent of the President of the United States of America transfer title to, or possession of, any defense article or defense information transferred to it under the Act of March 11, 1941 of the Congress of the United States of America or permit the use thereof by anyone not an officer, employee, or agent of the Government of the Republic of China.

ARTICLE IV

If, as a result of the transfer to the Government of the Republic of China of any defense article or defense information, it becomes necessary for that Government to take any action or make any payment in order fully to protect any of the rights of a citizen of the United States of America who has patent rights in and to any such defense article or information, the Government of the Republic of China will take such action or make such payment when requested to do so by the President of the United States of America.

ARTICLE V

The Government of the Republic of China will return to the United States of America at the end of the present emergency, as determined by the President of the United States of America, such defense articles transferred under this Agreement as shall not have been destroyed, lost or consumed and as shall be determined by the President to be useful in the defense of the United States of America or of the Western Hemisphere or to be otherwise of use to the United States of America.

ARTICLE VI

In the final determination of the benefits to be provided to the United States of America by the Government of the Republic of China full cognizance shall be taken of all property, services, information, facilities, or other benefits or considerations provided by the Government of the Republic of China subsequent to March 11, 1941, and accepted or acknowledged by the President on behalf of the United States of America.

In the final determination of the benefits to be provided to the United States of America by the Government of the Republic of China in return for aid furnished under the Act of Congress of March 11, 1941, the terms and conditions thereof shall be such as not to burden commerce between the two countries, but to promote mutually advantageous economic relations between them and the betterment of world-wide economic relations. To that end, they shall include provision for agreed action by the United States of America and the Republic of China, open to participation by all other countries of like mind, directed to the expansion, by appropriate international and domestic measures, of production, employment, and the exchange and consumption of goods, which are the material foundations of the liberty and welfare of all peoples; to the elimination of all forms of discriminatory treatment in international commerce; to the reduction of tariffs and other trade barriers; and, in general, to the attainment of economic objectives identical with those set forth in the Joint Declaration made on August 14, 1941, by the President of the United States of America and the Prime Minister of the United Kingdom.

At an early convenient date, conversations shall be begun between the two Governments with a view to determining, in the light of governing economic conditions, the best means of attaining the above-stated objectives by their own agreed action and of seeking the agreed action of other like-minded Governments.

ARTICLE VIII

This Agreement shall take effect as from this day's date. It shall continue in force until a date to be agreed upon by the two Governments.

Signed and sealed at Washington in duplicate this second day of June, 1942.

FOR THE GOVERNMENT OF THE UNITED STATES OF AMERICA

CORDELL HULL   [SEAL]
Secretary of State
of the United States of America

FOR THE GOVERNMENT OF THE REPUBLIC OF CHINA

TSE VUNG SOONG   [SEAL]
Minister for Foreign Affairs
of China

27 (a)

Secretary Stimson to the Chinese Minister for Foreign Affairs
(Soong)

WASHINGTON, *January 29, 1942*

MY DEAR MR. SOONG: In furtherance of the plan for sending to the Generalissimo a high ranking United States Army officer to act as his Chief of Staff and as Commanding Officer of United States Army forces in that region, it is necessary to have certain points quite clearly understood, so that essential arrangements with the British Chiefs of Staff may be completed. In accordance with our previous conversations and correspondence on this subject, it is my understanding that the functions of the United States Army Representative are to be generally as follows:

To supervise and control all United States defense-aid affairs for China.

Under the Generalissimo to command all United States forces in China and such Chinese forces as may be assigned to him.

To represent the United States Government on any International War Council in China and act as the Chief of Staff for the Generalissimo.

To improve, maintain and control the Burma Road in China.

If the above represents the understanding and agreement of the Generalissimo on the functions of the United States Army Representative, the British will agree to cooperate in Burma and India so as to promote the effectiveness of the United States Army Representative's efforts.

A particular point involving personnel on which clarification is sought is as follows:

The message from the Generalissimo dated January 21st stated that the United States representative should bring with him an Air officer of high rank. We were prepared to make such an assignment but have since learned, informally, that the Generalissimo might like to retain Colonel Chennault as the highest ranking American Air officer in China. If this should be the case, the arrangement will be quite agreeable to the War Department and Chennault's promotion to the grade of Brigadier General will be accomplished at the proper time.

I request that you give me an early reply since we are making every effort to place the general plan into prompt execution.

Sincerely yours,

HENRY L. STIMSON

27 (b)

The Chinese Minister for Foreign Affairs (Soong) to Secretary of War Stimson

WASHINGTON, *January 30, 1942*

MY DEAR MR. STIMSON: I have to acknowledge with thanks the receipt of your letter of January 29th and wish to confirm our understanding that the functions of the United States Army Representative are to be generally as follows:

To supervise and control all United States defense-aid affairs for China.

Under the Generalissimo to command all United States forces in China and such Chinese forces as may be assigned to him.

To represent the United States Government on any International War Council in China and act as the Chief of Staff for the Generalissimo.

To improve, maintain and control the Burma Road in China.

With reference to the appointment of an Air officer of high rank, the Generalissimo would indeed like if possible to retain Colonel Chennault as the highest ranking American Air officer in China, because of his signal services to both our countries, and much appreciates your kind consideration in the matter.

I am glad to learn of your intention to promote Colonel Chennault to the grade of Brigadier General in due course.

Yours sincerely,

T. V. SOONG

28

Five Hundred Million Dollar Financial Aid of 1942 and Other Wartime Financial Relationships

INTRODUCTION

The documents and other materials appearing in this annex provide background (a) on the negotiations and discussions leading up to the passage of the Joint Resolution of February 7, 1942, authorizing financial aid to China (Public Law 442, 77th Cong., 56 Stat. 82) and the signing of the financial aid agreement of March 21, 1942, pursuant thereto by the Governments of the United States and the Republic of China, (b) on the uses of the financial aid provided by the United States and (c) on negotiations concerning the financing of expenditures in Chinese currency by or on behalf of the United States Army in China during the war.

Transfers to Chinese accounts from the financial aid authorized in 1942 were as follows:

Date of Transfer	Purpose	Amount (millions)
1. April 15, 1942	Establishment of fund for redemption of U. S. dollar security issues.	$200
2. February 1, 1943	Purchase of gold	20
3. March 2, 1943	Purchase of bank notes and supplies	20
4. October 13, 1944	Purchase of gold	20
5. May 22, 1945	Purchase of gold	60
6. June 12, 1945	Purchase of gold	60
7. July 18, 1945	Purchase of textiles	10
8. July 27, 1945	Purchase of gold	60
9. August 3, 1945	Purchase of bank notes	35
10. February 7, 1946	Purchase of textiles	1. 5
11. March 13, 1946	Purchase of raw cotton	13. 5
	TOTAL	500. 0

On March 24, 1941, the Chinese Government announced in Chungking its plan to issue U.S. $100 million of 4 percent ten year National Government Allied Victory Bonds and U.S. $100 million of one, two and three year savings certificates with interest at 3 percent, 3½ percent and 4 percent, respectively. Following the announcement the Chinese Government requested the immediate transfer of 200 million dollars for the establishment of a fund for the redemption of these issues. As noted above, the transfer was made on April 15, 1942.

These issues were denominated in United States dollars, were sold for Chinese currency and were repayable at maturity in United States dollars or in Chinese currency at the option of the holder. It is believed that the most of the savings certificates were redeemed in United States dollars. Provision for U.S. dollar redemption of the ten year Allied Victory bonds, however, was revoked in 1946. except for registered bond holders outside China. It is not known how many bonds of this issue have been redeemed in United States dollars.

Of the 220 million dollars in gold purchased by China from the 500 million dollar credit of 1942, 158.6 million dollars had been shipped to China by V–J Day. Shipments in 1943 amounted to 10.5 million dollars and in 1944 to 15.2

million dollars, and the remainder was shipped in the first eight months of 1945. From late 1943 to June 30, 1945, the Chinese Government sold gold to the public for Chinese currency in an effort to combat inflation. Approximately 100 million dollars in gold (valued at $35 per ounce) was sold up to June 30, 1945, when gold sales were temporarily suspended. Some gold was sold on an advance basis. On June 30, 1945, the Chinese Government imposed a tax, payable in gold or Chinese currency on such sales as had not then been completed. Data are lacking as to how much gold was retained by this device.

Gold sales were resumed in September 1945 and terminated in February 1947 and were resumed intermittently in 1948 and 1949. Data are unavailable as to the amount of gold sold since September 1945.

Payments to the Chinese Government for Chinese currency supplied to or expended on behalf of the United States Army during the war were as follows:

	(Millions of dollars)
1. Through February 1944 at the official rate of 20 yuan equals US $1	155
2. Lump sum settlement for advances in 1944 through September	210
3. Lump sum settlement for fourth quarter, 1944	45

Settlement for advances of Chinese currency in 1945 and up to August 30, 1946, was provided in the Surplus Property Sales Agreement of the latter date between the United States and China.

The documents which follow are arranged substantially in chronological order.

28 (a)

The Ambassador in China (Gauss) to Secretary Hull

CHUNGKING, *December 30, 1941*

Today I called on General Chiang at his request. After briefly reviewing recent measures for political and military collaboration with the United States and Great Britain, he passed on to the economic situation in substantially the following terms:

While there is no lack of confidence on the part of intelligent Chinese that the anti-Axis Powers will be victorious in the end, there is such lack of confidence among the uninformed masses, the sceptics, and the associates of the Chinese traitors. Morale has been affected by the early Japanese successes and by the way the Japanese have exploited them for purposes of propaganda. Specific mention was made of the radio appeal for Asiatic solidarity against westerners which was recently made to Chiang by the Prime Minister of Thailand. China can contribute fighting man power to the common cause but the United States and Great Britain must give China financial help in order to prevent further deterioration in economic fundamentals, loss of confidence in the Chinese currency, etc. Such help would do much toward strengthening morale and to silence the critical and doubtful elements. The credit he wants is about one billion United States dollars, of which he has through the British Ambassador asked the British Government to provide about one-half or one hundred million pounds, expecting America to provide the rest or about five hundred million dollars.

Chiang asked that in transmitting his request to my Government I should emphasize the importance such aid at this time would have to Chinese morale in overcoming Japanese propaganda and because of the needed support it would give to the economic structure of China. He pointed out that the present currency issue exceeds thirteen billion paper dollars and that the 1942 budget shows a deficit of at least nine billion Chinese dollars, and said that the proposed loan would be used partially to support a domestic bond issue intended to curb inflation.

I replied that of course I would faithfully and immediately report his request and his discussion to my Government which I was confident would be disposed to consider with sympathy any reasonable proposals to aid China in resisting Japan. However, I suggested that to assist consideration of his request and in approaching Congress for legislation necessary to authorize participation by the United States in a credit or loan to China, a carefully prepared outline of the needs of the situation on the basis of the studies and recommendations of the financial advisers and experts of the Chinese Government should be submitted together with an outline of the measures contemplated to be undertaken to meet the situation including the measures which China will take to help herself. I explained that what I was suggesting was not an outline of the terms of any proposed loan but an outline of the needs of the situation and of the definite measures which should be taken to meet these needs.

Chiang said that experts and advisers were working out plans for the use of the proposed credit or loan but that he desired me in the meanwhile to make the proposal to my Government. The proposals for application of the loan could be put forward when the loan is assured.

I learned from the British Ambassador that he was approached for a loan of one hundred million pounds from Great Britain and has referred the matter to his Government. He equally lacked any specific proposals as to how the loan, if granted, would be applied to the difficulties of the economic situation of China; Chiang had said that he considered it an urgent necessity that he should be enabled to demonstrate to the Chinese people and armies that the British Government had sufficient faith in victory to give quick and effective aid to China.

28 (b)

A. Manuel Fox, U.S. Member on the Chinese Stabilization Board, to Secretary of the Treasury Morgenthau

CHUNGKING, *January 3, 1942*

(A) In Yunnanfu and Chungking I find a great deal of talk of a loan to China by Great Britain and the United States. I am informed that the subject has already been raised with each of the Governments by the Generalissimo. In Chinese Government circles the talk is of a loan by Britain of one hundred million pounds and a loan of the United States amounting to five hundred million United States dollars.

(B) For some time prior to the outbreak of the war I have felt that a new loan to China was needed due to the extreme gravity of the internal economic situation here. My feeling has been reinforced since December 8 in view of (1) the effect on Chinese political opinion of the initial Japanese successes; and (2) the perceptible strengthening of defeatist elements in Chinese Government circles; and (3) the probable effect of temporary Japanese successes in southeast Asia in the near future. In this situation in order to keep China going as an Anti-Axis power a substantial loan (the bigger the better) would be invaluable. An argument in favor of making the loan as big as possible is the very fact that the larger portion of such a loan could not be used.

(C) The internal economic effects of such a loan would be beneficial, after the first psychological effects have worn off, although because of the physical difficulties in the importing of goods they might not be commensurate with its size. The fact that the political advantages would be very great is of more importance. A loan might make all the difference between a Chinese defeatist victory (lukewarm as they are) and the neutralization of the defeatists. The actual outlay would be much smaller than the nominal amount of the loan, as already indicated. It would be desirable to use the loan as an occasion for insisting on strengthening and improving the Central Bank and the Chinese banking system, but the political effects of the loan could be reinforced by not requiring any specific guarantees.

(D) The following uses could be made of the loan: (1) To retard the infla-tionary spiral by guaranteeing an attractive issue of Government bonds to absorb fapi and make it unnecessary for the future that the Government of China issue more currency to cover its budgetary deficit; (2) To insure the maintenance of an inflow of imports by promoting trade with India (as long as the Burma Road remains open) and with Russia. I am not in a position to evaluate from a political standpoint the aspects of financing trade with Russia but certainly there would be an accrual of economic advantages; (3) the financing of loans, if possible, for the promotion of the internal small scale production which is greatly needed and for agricultural production. Retardation of rise in prices would be aided by the effects of both (2) and (3) in increasing the supply of goods; and perhaps (4) the provision of foreign exchange backing for the note issue which would temporarily affect beneficially internal confidence in the cur-rency. If it were possible to link the Stabilization Board in some way with the loan it might be desirable to do so because, if for no other reason, it might be easier for the Board than for the Chinese Government itself to secure confidence.

(E) The Board has received a scheme submitted by the Ministry of Finance which proposes that its remaining U.S. dollar and sterling assets be used as a guarantee fund for an issue of Chinese Government bonds on the lines of I (D). I see three objections to this: 1. The amount involved would not be sufficient to contribute substantially to the absorption of fapi; 2. taking into consideration the terms of agreements instituting the fund, there is some doubt as to the legality of the suggested procedure; 3. The Board would be deprived of its function of providing foreign exchange for imports. (This function must be performed so long as imports are possible.)

28 (c)

The Ambassador in China (Gauss) to Secretary Hull

CHUNGKING, *January 8, 1942*

I have the honor to refer to my message on the subject of finance-economic con-ditions in China and to my earlier messages in regard to the Chinese Government's request for an American credit of half a billion dollars and a British credit for one hundred million pounds, and to enclose for the Department's information (1) a memorandum of my conversation with General Chiang on December 30 when he asked me to place his request for a loan before the American Govern-ment,[32] (2) paraphrase of a telegram sent by the British Ambassador to his govern-

---

[32] See annex 28 (a).

ment on the reference subject,[33] (3) copy of a memorandum of Mr. Vincent's conversation with Mr. Hall-Patch, financial attache of the British Embassy,[33] and (4) copy of a confidential memorandum prepared by Mr. Chang Chia-ngau, Minister of Communications, for General Chiang and Dr. Kung in regard to the financial situation in China.[33]

I had suggested previously that the Congress might be asked to authorize a credit to China up to a specified amount for utilization under agreements or arrangements to be made by the executive branch of the Government after the presentation and consideration of definite proposals to be put forward by the Chinese Government.

I am convinced that credits of the magnitude requested by General Chiang (a total of about one billion U. S. dollars) are out of all proportion to the needs of the situation viewed from the political-psychological or the finance-economic standpoint—or both. While, in the absence of any definite proposals supported by factual data, only a rough estimate can be made, I feel that credits (American and British) of at most no more than a half billion dollars would generously satisfy all the requirements of the situation, psychological and financial, and that credits in excess of such an amount would be misleading and invite attempts at misuse. They would be misleading in that they might lead to popular expectation of practical results commensurate with the size of the credits, which would not be the case, because in present circumstances there is no practicable way in which such large credits could be effectively and legitimately utilized. They would invite attempts at misuse on the part of self-seeking banking and government elements who would find it difficult to resist the temptation to draw on such excessive credits for their own gain.

Aside from the broad idea of supporting government credit and retarding currency inflation, I am not informed with regard to any program for using the credits requested. Conversations with Dr. Fox and with Sir Otto Niemeyer lead me to believe that the Chinese Government has not formulated plans for coping with the serious internal situation and is therefore hardly in a position to indicate with any exactness the use it expects to make of desired foreign credits. Mr. Chang Chia-ngau sets forth in very general terms the need and usefulness of an internal bond issue supported by foreign credits and the Vice Ministers of Finance speak of "reconstruction" even more vaguely, and unconvincingly in so far as immediate needs are concerned. These, I fear, are examples illustrative of the government approach to the problem. The attitude and ideas of the Minister of Finance and the Minister of Economics are no more encouraging.

In the absence of technical studies on the subject, it is difficult for the Embassy to arrive at even a relatively precise idea of the reasonably constructive uses to which the credit might be put. However, it may serve some purpose to indicate in purely suggestive terms the Embassy's thoughts in the matter based on general observation.

A domestic bond issue, supported by foreign credits, would seem to be theoretically sound and advisable. No approximately definite figures as to the amount of such bonds that might be marketed are obtainable. The figure of two billion Chinese dollars is the one most often mentioned and under favorable conditions the amount might increase to four billions. Distribution primarily among the investing public would seem to be essential to accomplish the ends desired; that is, the withdrawal of currency from circulation and the release of goods now being hoarded. Obviously no public benefit would result from the

---

[33] Not printed.

government banks' exchanging currency in their vaults and newly issued currency for bonds backed by foreign currency at a fixed rate.

Encouragement of agricultural and small industrial production is wanting and badly needed. If it is feasible to do so, a portion of the credit might be used to support loans or grants to agricultural interests for the reclamation and improvement of farm land and to home and community industrial enterprises. The Chinese Government, notwithstanding the obvious advantages of such action, has been slow and reluctant to give assistance but it might be induced to do so if credits were set aside available only to support loans or grants of the kind. Only a very rough guess can be made as to the amount that might be earmarked for this purpose. Although there is slight likelihood that it would all be used, one hundred million dollars might be designated for the purpose of supporting grants or loans up to a billion Chinese dollars for small scale production and a like amount for agricultural improvement.

Dr. Fox, suggests,[34] inter alia (to the Secretary of the Treasury), use of a portion of the credit to promote imports from Russia into China. (He makes a similar suggestion with regard to imports from India). I am not in a position to evaluate the practical features of such a plan but I know that any opportunity to encourage the inflow of goods into China at this time should not be overlooked. One hundred million dollars of the credit might be set aside for this purpose in the hope that some portion could be used to accomplish the desired results.

The Central Executive Committee of the Kuomintang, at its meeting in December last, passed a resolution calling for "The execution of a land policy and the institution of government machinery to deal exclusively with land registration and the equalization of land ownership. . .". Various Kuomintang organs and committees have in the past passed similar resolutions, the effect of which has been inconsequential. To encourage implementation of the resolution quoted above, a practical step would seem to be the earmarking of a portion of the credit (one hundred million dollars is suggested as a generous estimate) for the support of the necessary financing of the agrarian reform contemplated.

The Generalissimo stresses the psychologically beneficial effect of a large political loan or credit at this time but he offers no program for its use, stating that a program will be forthcoming after the credit is given. I concur in his statement as to the need and the effect of a credit (while differing with regard to the amount) but I am convinced of the advisability, from the Chinese point of view as well as our own, of earmarking portions of the credit for certain purposes. Designation of portions of the credit for support of measures suggested above may be ill-received in banking and some governmental quarters but I believe that, viewing the situation as a whole from the standpoint of general public welfare and from the standpoint of strengthening the country's economic structure for continued resistance to Japan, it will produce more constructive results than the granting of a large lump credit or loan without designation as to use. It is well not to overlook the beneficial psychological effect upon the Chinese people of support for measures mentioned above (in particular measures for increased production and agrarian reform) ; and the practical effects of even partial application and implementation of such measures would fully justify our support. Probably no more than half the amounts suggested would be effectively used for the purposes mentioned and no doubt there would be administrative difficulties and inefficiencies, but even so, urgent requirements would at least be partially met—production of commodities would be increased (thereby remov-

---

[34] See annex 28 (b).

ing some of the curse from currency inflation) and a start towards long overdue agrarian reform would be made. And those elements in China which have been urging such measures and the infinitely greater number that would benefit therefrom would be encouraged and strengthened in their resolve to support active prosecution of the war against Japan, having received a practical demonstration that they are fighting *for* something. The alternative is purchase of the support of the retrogressive, self-seeking, and, I fear, fickle elements in and intimately associated with the government through the granting of a "free" credit, for I am convinced that a substantial credit should be granted.

I cannot too strongly emphasize my feeling that we should clearly and forcefully make known to the Chinese Government, in connection with financial aid that we may extend to China, our opposition to the use of any portion of such aid, directly or indirectly for the financing of expensive and harmful monopolies. This is a matter which calls for no clarification on my part in as much as I am sure that the Department is fully aware of the dangers of the situation.

28 (d)

The Chinese Minister of Finance (Kung) to Secretary of the Treasury Morgenthau

CHUNGKING, *January 9, 1942*

China has been fighting a war of resistance with heavy strain on her resources and with untold sacrifices for four and one-half years. At the present time, China's economic and financial situation is in a precarious condition. The livelihood of the people is difficult, because of increasing prices; and the brave soldiers at the front are ill-clothed and ill-fed. It is necessary to retain control of currency and prices without production being curtailed. It would be impossible to carry on the war if the already very critical economic and financial front should collapse.

Since the survival and existence of democratic countries are interdependent, present world war developments render it imperative for these countries to pool their economic and military resources. Consequently, I appeal to you for a political war loan of five hundred million dollars. Great Britain has also been approached by us for a loan of one hundred million pounds for the purpose of covering the total sum required. We are awaiting a reply from Great Britain. If you will lead, I am confident they will follow your example. This loan is requested for the purpose of replenishing reserve so as to restore confidence in currency, to offset diminished imports by increased production, to restrain prices, and to meet additional urgent war requirements. There are sound justifications for the loan on economic grounds, and also from the standpoint of joint military front. Frankly, however, my reason for approaching you is political above all; and the import of a loan of this nature is even more important than the Lend-Lease Bill's import. The essence of such a move is timeliness, so as to demonstrate that China's confidence in the allied powers is matched by equal confidence in China of the allied powers, in the most crucial months of emergency immediately before us. In addition to electrifying public opinion, early announcement of the loan would have an immediate effect throughout Asia, including our common enemy, Japan. My appreciation of your continuing keen interest in China provides me with confidence in sending you this message.

28 (e)

Secretary Hull to Secretary of the Treasury Morgenthau

WASHINGTON, *January 10, 1942*

MY DEAR MR. SECRETARY: Reference is made to Generalissimo Chiang Kai-shek's request of December 30, 1941 that the United States Government provide China with $500,000,000 of financial help in order to support Chinese morale and prevent the effects of further depreciation of the Chinese currency and deterioration of the fundamental economic situation in China.

The Generalissimo's proposal has been given very careful consideration. I feel that, as an act of wartime policy and to prevent the impairment of China's military effort which would result from loss of confidence in Chinese currency and depreciation of its purchasing power, it is highly advisable that the United States extend financial assistance to the Government of China in amounts up to $300,000,000 at the present time. I believe that a determination of this Government's policy to this effect need not await ascertainment of the attitude to be taken by Great Britain on the similar Chinese proposal with reference to sterling credits.

I feel that the greatest possible expedition in reaching a position where an announcement can be made is highly important. I feel also that it would seem to be highly desirable that the British Government be kept currently informed of our views and decisions in regard to this matter in order that the British Government may be afforded opportunity, should it so desire, to take simultaneous and comparable action.

Sincerely yours,

CORDELL HULL

28 (f)

Generalissimo Chiang Kai-shek to Secretary of the Treasury Morgenthau

CHUNGKING, *14th January, 1942*

DEAR MR. SECRETARY: I have requested Mr. Fox to inform you in person of China's present financial and economic realities and needs. Throughout these critical years your support of China's cause has been most enthusiastic and sympathetic. You are now naturally more than ever concerned with our problems and difficulties, especially at the moment when our interests and destiny are absolutely identical.

If China's finance and economics fail to be improved and strengthened, our power of resistance against Japanese aggression will be so adversely affected that the entire war front of the allied Powers will inevitably suffer. My Government and people earnestly hope that your Government will give us the speediest and most effective assistance, and that, in compliance with my request and in accordance with the plan prepared by our Minister of Finance, you will exert your utmost to procure the desired loan for China. In view of actual war-time requirements this loan is not large.

I feel certain that in his verbal report Mr. Fox will enter fully into the military, financial and economic situations in China, and will explain in detail what bearing they have in the attainment of our common victory.

With best wishes,

Yours sincerely,

CHIANG KAI-SHEK

28 (g)

The Chinese Minister for Foreign Affairs (Soong) to Secretary of the Treasury Morgenthau

[WASHINGTON,] *January 21, 1942*

MY DEAR MR. SECRETARY: During your absence from Washington I received the enclosed message for you from the Generalissimo.

Since Mr. Fox is due to arrive in Washington shortly, it occurs to me that you may like to have an opportunity of seeing him and hearing from him of the situation in China before you renew discussions with me. However I am at your disposal at any time, should you wish to see me earlier.

Sincerely yours,

T. V. SOONG

[Enclosure]

The Generalissimo deeply appreciates Secretary Morgenthau's efforts which have materialized in a proposal that the U. S. Government would undertake to pay for the maintenance of part of the Chinese army in U. S. Dollar notes. After careful consideration, however, he doubts whether this scheme is practicable. Payment of Chinese soldiers in U. S. currency would tend to create a cleavage between the army and the general economic structure in China which may actually hasten the collapse of the Chinese currency. Before Mr. Fox left Chungking the Generalissimo had a long discussion with him in which he pointed out a number of reasons why he considered the scheme difficult of application and which he asked Mr. Fox to convey to Secretary Morgenthau.

The Generalissimo urgently requests that careful consideration be given to his original proposal that the United States grant to China a political loan of 500 million U. S. dollars, which would be the only means to prevent an impending economic collapse. This loan should be regarded in the light of an advance to an ally fighting against a common enemy, thus requiring no security or other prearranged terms as to its use and as regards means of repayment.

28 (h)

Minutes [35] *of a Meeting in the Office of the Secretary of State, January 30, 1942*

[Extract]

Present : Secretary Hull
          Secretary Morgenthau
          Dr. Viner
          Mr. White
Later Joined By: Mr. Berle
          Mr. Hornbeck
          Mr. Hamilton
          Mr. Feis

Secretary Hull asked for opinions as to which of the several methods suggested by the Treasury would be the best medium for giving help. He said he himself was not interested in the method. He said that should be the Treasury's business.

---

[35] Prepared at the Treasury Department.

He was solely interested in seeing that China did get aid in the present critical situation.

Mr. Hornbeck stated that he thought the ideal method of helping would be a Congressional statute providing for an extension of financial aid to China. He said that might, however, cause undue delay. He was not certain that legislation was the most practical method of approaching the problem. He stated that he did not think the matter was so urgent or acute that a matter of days were critical, but that if it were to take several weeks for Congress to pass such legislation, it would be too late. If legislation could be passed in a few days he favored legislation.

Mr. Hornbeck went on to say that he thought that the sum should be $500 million instead of the $300 million which Secretary Hull had indicated in his letter to Secretary Morgenthau. Mr. Hornbeck thought that a reduction in the portion which the United States was prepared to give to $300 million would be too great a reduction from the sum which Chiang-Kai-Shek was asking. He felt Chiang-Kai-Shek should be given what he asked for, namely $500 million from the United States. Secretary Morgenthau agreed with Hornbeck, as did the others, and it was therefore decided that the sum which they would recommend would be $500 million.

28 (i)

Secretary of the Treasury Morgenthau to Generalissimo Chiang Kai-shek

WASHINGTON, *February 16, 1942.*

DEAR GENERALISSIMO CHIANG: I read with great interest your letter of January 14, 1942, transmitted to me in person by Mr. Fox. The unanimity and promptness with which my Government responded to the appeal for financial assistance is evidence that your confidence in the support of the United States is well founded. It also demonstrated that the American people have faith in the Chinese people and know that you and your Government will continue to play a vital part in the common effort against our foes.

I wish you to know that here in the United States Generalissimo Chiang Kai-shek is looked upon as the personification of the heroism and courage of the Chinese people who, under the most difficult circumstances and at tremendous odds, have successfully defended their country against invasion. No one doubts in the United States that your leadership has secured for China the unity of purpose and will, without which China would have fallen victim to the Japanese aggressor. Moreover, the people of the United States clearly understand that China's unceasing resistance will not only bring freedom and independence to itself, but will play a major part in achieving victory and peace for free men everywhere.

Sincerely yours,

H. MORGENTHAU, Jr.

28 (j)

Initial Draft of United States-China Financial Aid Agreement [36]

WHEREAS, the Governments of the United States of America and of the Republic of China are engaged, together with other nations and peoples of like mind, in a

---

[36] Handed to the Chinese Minister for Foreign Affairs, T. V. Soong, by the Treasury Department, Feb. 21, 1942.

cooperative undertaking against common enemies, to the end of laying the bases of a just and enduring world peace securing order under law to themselves and all nations, and

WHEREAS, the United States and China are signatories to the Declaration of United Nations of January 1, 1942, which declares that "each government pledges itself to employ its full resources, military or economic, against those members of the Tripartite Pact and its adherents with which such government is at war"; and

WHEREAS, the Congress of the United States, in unanimously passing Public Law No. 442, approved February 7, 1942, has declared that financial and economic aid to China will increase China's ability to oppose the forces of aggression and that the defense of China is of the greatest possible importance, and has authorized the Secretary of the Treasury of the United States, with the approval of the President, to give financial aid to China, and

WHEREAS, such financial aid will enable China to strengthen greatly its war efforts against the common enemies by helping China to

(1) strengthen its currency, monetary, banking and economic system;

(2) finance and promote increased production, acquisition and distribution of necessary goods;

(3) retard the rise of prices, promote stability of economic relationships, and otherwise check inflation;

(4) prevent hoarding of foods and other materials;

(5) improve means of transportation and communication;

(6) effect further social and economic measures which will safeguard the unity of the Chinese people; and

(7) meet military needs and take other appropriate measures in its war effort.

In order to achieve these purposes, the undersigned, being duly authorized by their respective Governments for that purpose, have agreed as follows:

ARTICLE I.

The Secretary of the Treasury of the United States agrees to establish forthwith on the books of the United States Treasury a credit in the name of the Government of the Republic of China in the amount of 500,000,000 U.S. dollars. The Secretary of the Treasury .shall make transfers from his credit, in such amounts and at such times as the Government of the Republic of China shall request, to an account or accounts in the Federal Reserve Bank of New York in the name of the Government of the Republic of China or any agencies designated by it. Such transfers may be requested by and such accounts at the Federal Reserve Bank of New York may be drawn upon by the Government of the Republic of China either directly or through such persons or agencies as it shall authorize.

ARTICLE II.

China desires to keep the Secretary of the Treasury of the United States informed as to the use of the funds herein provided and to consult with him from time to time as to such uses. The Secretary of the Treasury of the United States desires to make available to the Government of the Republic of China technical and other appropriate advice as to ways and means of effectively employing these funds to achieve the purposes herein described. Technical problems that may from time to time arise in effectuating the financial aid herein provided will be subjects of discussion between the Secretary of the Treasury of the United States and the Government of the Republic of China.

ARTICLE III.

The final determination of the terms upon which this financial aid is given, including the benefits to be rendered the United States in return, is deferred until the progress of events makes clearer the final terms and benefits which will be in the mutual interest of the United States and China and will promote the establishment of lasting world peace and security. In determining the final terms and benefits no interest charges shall be made for the financial aid herein provided and full cognizance shall be given to the desirability of maintaining a healthy and stable economic and financial situation in China in the post-war period as well as during the war and to the desirability of promoting mutually advantageous economic and financial relations between the United States and China and the betterment of world-wide economic and financial relations.

ARTICLE IV.

This Agreement shall take effect as from this day's date.

Signed and sealed at Washington, District of Columbia, in duplicate this _____ day of _____, 1942.

On behalf of the United States of America

Secretary of the Treasury

On behalf of the Republic of China

----

28 (k)

The Ambassador in China (Gauss) to Secretary Hull

CHUNGKING, *March 1, 1942.*

Strictly confidential information has reached the Embassy that a draft Sino-American loan agreement has been received from Washington by the Ministry of Finance and has been discussed. It is said that the Ministry resents on the ground that a measure of control is contemplated the provision for consultation by the Government of China with the Treasury Department concerning expenditures under the loan. The Ministry has been disappointed to find that the loan is not granted, as the Press has stated, as an absolute gift in recognition of China's contribution to the War effort in general.

I am not prepared to express an opinion on the question of policy whether or not we should provide for some means of repayment. I have been privately told by a prominent and intelligent Chinese banker that the obtainment of the loan was too easy for the loan to be appreciated or for provision for its effective use to be insured. There is a perceptible assumption on the part of Chungking officials and bankers that it is a compensation which was due to China for its past and present resistance to Japan and for what the Chinese regard as our past and present shortcomings.

It is my conviction that for the purpose of having some measure of control over the matter in which so large a loan is expended we should firmly insist on retaining the provision for consultation. It is my opinion as I have indicated in previous telegrams that the best interests of China and our own best interests as well would be served by controls and allocation of parts of the loan for specific purposes.

28 (I)

The Chinese Minister for Foreign Affairs (Soong) to Under Secretary of the Treasury Bell

[WASHINGTON,] *March 3, 1942*

DEAR MR. BELL: I am in receipt of a reply on the draft of the Loan Agreement from the Generalissimo dated February 25th, which I delayed presenting to you owing to a visit to Canada.

The Generalissimo is very appreciative of the generous spirit that characterized the draft Agreement and desires me to convey his grateful appreciation to the Secretary.

As to details he suggested the following points:

1. Reactions in Chungking as to Article II appear to be that the U. S. Government will in some way pass judgment on the uses to which the Loan may be put, and thereby limits in some degree the freedom of making disbursement.

As China in any case would like to keep the Secretary informed, and as the Secretary has in the past without any agreement always exerted himself on every occasion to help China, he suggests that Article II is unnecessary, since it makes of such voluntary acts mandatory. He therefore hopes that Article II may be dropped.

2 (a) As the whole energy of the people is concentrated on winning the war, he hopes that the final determination of the terms upon which the financial aid is given should be left until after the war. He suggests that the phrase "after the war" should appear in Article III, coming after the phrase "deferred until the progress of events" in the opening sentence.

2 (b) Although greatly appreciative of the United States waiving interest, he believes that the lofty plane of cooperation between the United States and China would be aided by dropping all reference to interest through deleting the clause "no interest charges shall be made for the financial aid herein provided".

2 (c) For the purpose of clarification that the final determination of the terms upon which the financial aid is given should be a bilateral and not a unilateral measure, he would suggest that in the final sentence of Article III the words the "United States and China shall take full cognizance of" should come after the words "In determining the final terms and benefits".

In order to make the suggestions clearer I am enclosing the draft Agreement with such alterations as are suggested in the telegram.

The Generalissimo again bids me to say that such textual changes as he suggested are only to heighten the impression of the Chinese people at this unprecedentedly generous act of the American Government and people.

Would you be good enough to pass on the suggestions to your colleagues for their kind consideration.

Yours sincerely,

T. V. SOONG

28 (m)

Acting Secretary Welles to Secretary of the Treasury Morgenthau

WASHINGTON, *March 11, 1942.*

MY DEAR MR. SECRETARY: I refer to your letter of March 10 on the subject of the draft of the proposed agreement regarding the extension of financial aid to China.

All parties concerned are in agreement that the purposes of the extension of this financial aid are predominantly political, diplomatic, and military.

The draft which you submitted to Dr. T. V. Soong for consideration contains in its four articles provisions which make readily available to the Chinese Government without restrictive commitments the $500,000,000 which the Congress appropriated for the making of a loan, the extending of a credit or the giving of other financial aid to China. It does not in fact impair or restrict the Chinese Government's freedom of action in the making of disbursements.

In his letter to Mr. Bell of March 3 Dr. Soong suggests, on behalf of Generalissimo Chiang Kai-shek, the making of a number of changes. In my opinion, we can readily accept most of these suggestions and proceed accordingly. With regard, however, to the suggestion that Article II be omitted in its entirety, it seems to me that there is ample warrant for a discussion of the matter and that we should endeavor to cause Dr. Soong and the Generalissimo to realize that provisions such as appear in the draft of that article are desirable from point of view not only of this Government but of the Chinese Government.

With regard to procedure, I would suggest that there first be made a redraft of the proposed Article II and that there then be communicated to Dr. Soong a statement by you that we are in complete concurrence with his comments and the changes which he has suggested except as regards that article, and that, in the light of his comments on that article, there is submitted to him for his consideration a possible alternative form.

Toward facilitating procedure along that line, I submit here attached for your consideration a draft of a possible substitute for Article II.

Another possible line of procedure which might be considered would be that of putting the substance of this suggested alternative draft of Article II into letters which might be exchanged between you and Dr. Soong.

In as much as the only delay which has occurred in connection with the attention which has been given this matter has been delay on the part of the Chinese, I would further suggest that, in whatever communication you make to Dr. Soong, you indicate to him that all officers of this Government who are concerned with the negotiating of this agreement are eager to bring the matter to a mutually satisfactory conclusion with the utmost possible expedition.

Sincerely yours,

SUMNER WELLES

[Enclosure—Draft]

ARTICLE II

As a manifestation of the cooperative spirit which underlies the common war effort of China and the United States, appropriate officials of the two Governments will confer from time to time regarding technical problems which may arise in connection with the financial aid herein provided and will exchange information and suggestions regarding ways and means of most effectively applying these funds toward achieving the purposes which are envisaged by the two nations.

28 (n)

The Chinese Minister for Foreign Affairs (Soong) to Under Secretary of the Treasury Bell

[WASHINGTON,] *March 19, 1942*

DEAR MR. BELL: Confirming our conversation, I have to inform you that I have received a reply from the Generalissimo with reference to your proposal to re-insert Article II of the proposed loan agreement in a modified form.

The Generalissimo states that after carefully consulting his colleagues he feels that even in the modified form Article II is generally construed as limiting the freedom of action in the use of the proceeds, and would therefore adversely affect the public response to bonds, savings deposits and other measures that are to be based on the loan.

In addition, among his soldiers, who have been tremendously heartened by the generous and unconditional assistance as revealed in the exchange of messages between the President and himself, the inclusion of Article II would create the impression that the terms are not as clear-cut as they envisaged.

The Generalissimo therefore feels that the civilian and military reactions are such as to justify his request that Article II be dropped completely, and I shall be grateful if you will transmit his message to your colleagues for their consideration.

With kind regards,
    Yours sincerely,

T. V. SOONG

28 (o)

The Chinese Minister for Foreign Affairs (Soong) to Secretary of the Treasury Morgenthau

[WASHINGTON,] *March 21, 1942*

MY DEAR MR. SECRETARY: In connection with the Agreement concluded today between the Governments of the United States of America and the Republic of China regarding financial aid to China, as a manifestation of the cooperative spirit which underlies the common war effort of our two countries, I wish to inform you that it is the intention of my Government, through the Minister of Finance, to keep you fully informed from time to time as to the use of the funds provided in the said Agreement.

Sincerely yours,

T. V. SOONG

28 (p)

[For the Joint Statement by Secretary of the Treasury Morgenthau and the Chinese Minister for Foreign Affairs (Soong), March 21, 1942, see post, annex 29 (b).]

28 (q)

The Chinese Minister of Finance (Kung) to Secretary of the Treasury Morgenthau

[CHUNGKING,] *April 20, 1942*

With reference to keeping the Treasury informed on all developments relating to the loan I have done so and intend to do so in the future. For example, I told Adler on the 18th of March about the plan to put out savings certificates and bonds and he must have cabled this to the Treasury. I welcome any counsel the Treasury is willing to offer and if the Secretary cares to make any suggestions every consideration will be given to them. It was essential to request the shift of funds to the Central Bank in order to convince the people that use was being made of the loan without delay to prevent inflation.

28 (r)

Secretary of the Treasury Morgenthau to the United States Treasury Representative, American Embassy at Chungking

WASHINGTON, *December 29, 1942*

One. With reference to your cable in which you report that Dr. Kung is willing to accept any decision the Treasury may desire to make in connection with the amount of gold which should be purchased from the Treasury by China, whether it be twenty, thirty, forty, or fifty million dollars, due to the considerations set forth in the following, the Treasury believes that the more appropriate sum would be the amount already agreed upon, U.S. twenty million dollars.

A. Treasury does not perceive in what manner the Chinese government would benefit by purchasing additional gold on which the required charges would have to be paid by the government of China.

B. It would seem to be indicated by the information received from Mr. Hsi and from you with respect to the attitude of Dr. Kung on purchasing additional gold that Dr. Kung does not feel any urgent requirement for additional gold exists.

C. Additional gold purchase by the government of China would entail raising funds to purchase the additional gold by the United States Treasury. It would be necessary for the Government of the United States to pay interest on the funds raised at a time when the Government is already engaged in the task of borrowing tremendous amounts in order to meet its current fiscal requirements.

D. The Treasury would have difficulty in justifying to the public an increase in the indebtedness of the United States Government so as to render it possible for the Chinese government to buy gold for earmarking here, unless China would benefit in some way by the purchase of additional gold.

Two. Kindly advise Dr. Kung of the foregoing.

28 (s)

Message Received from the Chinese Minister of Finance (Kung), July 8, 1943

During the six years of our war of resistance China's military expenditure has been increasing continuously. According to the national budget of the current year, the estimated expenditure was originally placed at 36,200,000,000 yuan, while the estimated income was given as 23,200,000,000 yuan, representing about 65% of the total expenditure. The remaining 35% is entirely met by increased note issue.

Owing to military requirements and the requests made by the American Military Mission, the Chinese Government has undertaken to build, or improve, the airfields in various parts of the country and to increase their equipment, as well as to improve the Yunnan-Burma highway and other necessary highways and railways. Each enterprise often necessitated the expenditure of 4,000,000,000 to 5,000,000,000 yuan, making a total of additional requirements amounting to over 30,000,000 yuan.

Furthermore, owing to the difficulties of transportation and the small volume of supplies received under the American Lend-Lease Act, the Chinese Government has been obliged to provide ways and means of increasing the production of military supplies in order to meet the demands of the war. All such expenses are beyond what is provided by the budget, and the Chinese Government is compelled to further increase its note issue in order to meet the situation. For these reasons there has been constant tendency toward inflation. In order to remedy the situation and to stabilize the price of commodities, it is necessary to adopt measures having the effect of checking inflation. Through increased taxation and other means, the Government has withdrawn a certain portion of the notes in circulation, but there is still by far the larger portion in the hands of the people which is being used toward the purchase and accumulation of commodities, resulting in the further rising of prices and in making livelihood increasingly difficult.

The chief purpose for the proposed purchase and sale of gold is to withdraw large quantities of notes now in circulation. The fact that each ounce of gold is worth now about 8,000 yuan shows the psychology of Chinese people toward gold. To obtain the desired result, it is only necessary for the time being to have bullion which can be handled easily. However, the question of coinage is being given careful study and can be best taken up at the time of reorganization of Chinese currency.

According to Madam Chiang, the proposal which we are making—that is, the purchase of 200,000,000 dollars' worth of gold with the United States loan—has received the approval of President Roosevelt and Secretary Morgenthau in principle. It is earnestly hoped that it can be realized at an early date. We always appreciate and welcome suggestions and advices from Secretary Morgenthau and Dr. White, but in this particular case we are influenced by actual conditions in China, and we feel that it has to be done in the way we suggested in order to reap the desired benefits. It is earnestly hoped that we shall not lose this good opportunity of checking inflation.

28 (t)

Memorandum to President Roosevelt from Secretary of the Treasury Morgenthau

[WASHINGTON,] *July 15, 1943*

On July 14, 1943, we sent a message to Dr. H. H. Kung, the Chinese Minister of Finance, informing him that the Treasury is prepared in principle to agree to the Chinese request to purchase $200 million of gold out of the $500 million financial aid as a means of helping to check inflation in China. Dr. Kung was also informed that a formal request was, of course, necessary before any definitive decision and action could be taken.

The Chinese Government has already drawn on the Treasury to the extent of $240 million out of the $500 million financial aid:—$200 million has been set aside as backing for Chinese Government savings certificates and bond issues; $20 million was used to purchase gold, and $20 million is being used for the printing of banknotes and the purchase of relative materials. The purchase of gold with an additional $200 million will mean that in total the Chinese will have used $440 million out of the $500 million financial aid.

In the message to Dr. Kung, as well as in discussions with the representatives of the Chinese Government in Washington, it has been made clear that the Treasury is acquiescing to the Chinese proposal because the Government of China deems that the sale of gold to the public will aid its war effort by helping to fight inflation and hoarding and that, therefore, the decision to purchase the gold is primarily the responsibility of the Chinese Government. Furthermore, the Chinese have been urged to give careful consideration to the best ways of using the gold, particularly because of the great costs, difficulties and dangers inherent in the use of gold as a means of checking inflation under conditions existing in China at present. We especially stressed the fact that the Chinese Government will by this step be sacrificing large amounts of foreign exchange, which could be used in the post-war period to pay for imports needed for reconstruction and rehabilitation.

The use of gold coins as against bullion for the purpose was carefully considered. It was felt both by us and by the Chinese Government that this technique for selling the gold to the public would not be feasible in the present instance, primarily because it would be necessary to give the gold coins a fixed monetary value, while it is contemplated that the price of gold in terms of yuan will change frequently and substantially as time goes on.

The suggestion was therefore made to the Chinese representatives in Washington that the gold might be sold to the public in China in small bars of one or two ounces in order to reach the widest possible section of the Chinese public and such bars might have some engraving which might suggest the United States origin of the financial aid, if the Government of China so wished.

28 (u)

Secretary of the Treasury Morgenthau to the Chinese Minister of Finance (Kung)

WASHINGTON, *July 27, 1943*

The Treasury agrees to the request of the Government of China transmitted to me by Ambassador Wei Tao-ming that $200 million be made available from the credit on the books of the Treasury in the name of the Government of the Republic of China for the purchase of gold.

In order to avoid unnecessary raising of funds by the United States Treasury, it is suggested that transfers from the credit of the Chinese Government for the purchase of gold be made at such time and in such amounts as are allowed by existing facilities for the transportation to China of the equivalent amount of gold. Since it is intended that this gold will be sent to China for sale to the public, this procedure should not interfere with the program outlined in your message of July 23, 1943.

On receipt of requests from the Government of China that a specific amount should be transferred from the credit of the Government of China on the books of the Treasury and be used for the purchase of gold, the necessary action will be taken to consummate these requests. The details of the arrangements will be discussed with Dr. P. W. Kuo and Mr. Hsi Te-mou.

Sincerely yours,

H. MORGENTHAU, Jr.

28 (v)

Memorandum to President Roosevelt from Secretary of the Treasury Morgenthau

[WASHINGTON,] *December 18, 1943*

You have spoken of the request of Generalissimo Chiang-Kai-Shek for an additional $1 billion of financial aid to China to be used to help control inflation and for postwar reconstruction.

I

The facts regarding inflation in China and the possibility of its control through the use of dollar resources are as follows:

Inflation in China, as you well know, arises from the grave inadequacy of production for war needs and essential civilian consumption. Supplies have been drastically reduced by enemy occupation and the cutting off of imports except the small amounts that come by air or are smuggled from occupied territory.

The Chinese Government cannot collect sufficient taxes or borrow from the people in adequate amounts. As a consequence, the Government has been issuing 3.5 billion yuan a month, twice the rate of a year ago.

The official exchange rate for yuan is now 5 cents; before China entered the war it was 30 cents. The open market rate for yuan in U. S. paper currency is one cent and in terms of gold one-third of a cent.

You have suggested the possibility of our selling dollar currency for yuan to be resold to China after the war at no profit to us. No doubt something could be done to alleviate inflation through the sale of gold or dollar currency in China. I have received the following message from Dr. Kung dated December 14:

"You will be pleased to hear that the recent gold shipment is one of the outstanding factors contributing to the strengthening of fapi, because people believe that the arrival of gold has increased the much needed reserve of our currency, thereby influencing the stability of prices. The action of the United States Government re-affirms to the Chinese people that, despite difficulties arising from the blockade and the cumulative effects of over six years of war against the invasion, China has a powerful friend desirous of strengthening China's economy as conditions permit."

However, while something could be done to retard the rise in prices, the only real hope of controlling inflation is by getting more goods into China. This, you know better than I, depends on future military operations.

II

China has tried two similar monetary remedies for alleviating inflation without marked success.

1. The Chinese Government issued and sold dollar securities for yuan, setting aside $200 million of the aid granted by this country for the redemption of the securities. (These securities were sold at exorbitant profit to the buyers. For instance, a person holding $100 in United States currency could have quadrupled his money in less than two years by selling the currency for yuan on the open market and buying the dollar securities issued by the Chinese Government.) I believe that the program made no significant contribution to the control of inflation.

2. The Chinese Government has recently been selling gold at a price in yuan equivalent to $550 an ounce, about fifteen times the official rate. We have shipped to China more than $10 million of gold and they have sold about $2 million of gold for yuan. This program has not been tried sufficiently to warrant any definite conclusion as to its possible effect.

China now has $460 million of unpledged funds in the United States and is getting about $20 million a month as a result of our expenditures. China could use these funds in selling gold or dollar assets for yuan, although in my opinion such schemes in the past have had little effect except to give additional profits to insiders, speculators and hoarders and dissipate foreign exchange resources that could be better used by China for reconstruction.

Under the circumstances, a loan to China for these purposes could not be justified by the results that have been obtained. It is my opinion that a loan is unnecessary at this time and would be undesirable from the point of view of China and the United States. Large expenditures on ineffective measures for controlling inflation in China would be an unwise use of her borrowing capacity which should be reserved for productive uses in other ways. On reconstruction, it is too soon for us to know the best use or the best form of the aid we might give to China.

RECOMMENDATIONS

For the past five years I have had a deep admiration for the valiant fight that the Chinese people, under the leadership of Chiang-Kai-Shek, have waged against Japanese aggression. Therefore, I am in complete sympathy with your position that no stone be left unturned to retard the rise in prices. Using the tools we have at hand, I recommend the following:

1. All United States expenditures in China, currently $400 million yuan a month and rising rapidly, be met through the purchase of yuan with gold or dollar currency at whatever price we can get them for in the open market. This is equal to more than 10 percent of the present rate of issue.

2. Accelerate the shipment of gold purchased by China to twice the amount we have previously planned to send. It should be possible to raise gold shipments from $6 million a month to about $12 million. At the present price for gold in the open market this would be equal to the present 3.5 billion of yuan currency that is being issued.

The impact of this two-fold program should contribute to retarding inflation, always bearing in mind that the basic reason for inflation in China is the shortage of goods.

28 (w)

The Ambassador in China (Gauss) to Secretary Hull

CHUNGKING, *December 23, 1943*

I called last evening in company with Atcheson upon President and Madame Chiang at their request. The only other person present was Wang Chung Hui who had been with them at Cairo. In reply to Chiang's question, which he asked significantly, whether I had received any telegrams recently I said none of importance. The Generalissimo then asked my opinion of the situation in China, especially economic developments, and he observed that he would welcome any advice that I might offer and hear any plan I might suggest.

In referring to the seriousness of economic conditions, he reiterated his suggestion that I put forward any plan for amelioration. He then went on to say that in his country the coming year would be most crucial and that the faith of the Chinese people in China's national currency had so far prevented an economic collapse. Chiang said that it was essential that there be an early reopening of the Burma Road for so long as this road remains unopened the desperate economic situation of China renders it essential to support the value of the currency of China and maintain the rate of exchange.

In reply to Chiang's question as to whether I have studied the problem of the financial difficulties of China, I said that we try to keep up with the financial situation in the light of whatever information is available and that from the American point of view one aspect which has lately been causing me much concern is the effect which the rate of exchange is having on the expenditures by the American Government for the American military forces with which China is being assisted; those expenditures are now attaining high figures and when converted at the artificial rate of exchange are costing the American Government twenty million dollars and over a month in American currency, which, while benefitting China by accumulating a currency reserve in the United States, make for expenditures by the United States eight to ten times as great as we would have to spend in the United States or elsewhere for services and facilities of a comparable character such as advance airbase facilities which our forces urgently require. I expressed my concern that as this became known in our country it might cause serious criticism that the American Government and Army are being exploited and that such criticism would operate to the injury of China as well as of our war effort in China.

The Generalissimo firmly affirmed that the exchange rate for Chinese currency cannot be altered. I replied that I entirely understood his position on that point. I suggested however that there might be adopted without involving a change in the exchange rate other proposals toward a solution of the problem, such as reverse Lend-Lease, or the proposal that the Secretary of the Treasury had made to Dr. Kung regarding the sale of gold. Madame Chiang observed that as there was no market for gold, the efforts of the Chinese Government to sell gold had proved a failure. The Generalissimo affirmed that he had given study to the question of reverse Lend-Lease, that the whole financial situation had been causing Kung and himself much anxiety, that it is not possible to change the exchange rate and that support must be given to the value of Chinese currency. He asked that I see Dr. Kung again and just before leaving the room in the way that is his custom requested with a manifestation of some exasperation and emphasis that I make it known to our Treasury and military authorities that both the economic and military collapse of China would result from a failure to support the currency of China.

Madame Chiang indicated during the course of the conversation that the President had been made acquainted at Cairo with the Generalissimo's views on the seriousness of the situation. After Chiang had left she expressed herself emphatically in regard to China's economic difficulties and remarked with some bitterness that about 200 Chinese dollars were being paid by China for the maintenance of every American soldier in China. She indicated that as our forces are augmented the cost would become intolerable and added that it is becoming more and more impossible to find sufficient pigs, chickens, and cattle to feed the American troops (needed to supplement the amounts of supplies which we ourselves bring in). She said that it was imperative that sufficient backing be accorded Chinese currency.

Two. It is my belief that last evening's stage was set for soliciting the support of the Department of State for request of an additional American loan and that such a request was not put forward because of the diversion made to the subject of our expenditures for military purposes. On December 20 I was informed by Stilwell that a billion dollar loan had been requested by Chiang and that an answer was expected by Chiang that day. That he told me and no more. I assume that the request was made through military channels and in connection with military talks.

It is unfortunate that the Embassy is not kept fully advised of developments occurring in relations between the United States and China.

In my recent telegram there was carefully set forth the Embassy's view in regard to a further loan to China at this time. It is my firm opinion that we should take a firm stand at this time on this question. In regard to military plans for a Burma campaign calculated to restore overland transportation to China, believed by experts here to be the only possible measure for bettering the abnormal economic situation, I have no information. I am ready to believe that although the foreign exchange rate is not of concern to the masses of the people, hoarders and speculators would avail themselves of any substantial change in that rate to accelerate rising prices still further.

Nothing substantial has actually been done by the Chinese Government to find and deal with these speculators and hoarders. Nevertheless, I am of the opinion that China possesses substantial reserves of U. S. currency at this time and there might be taken, without reference to exchange rate as such, probably within the framework of the sale of gold and reverse Lend-Lease, reasonable measures to cope with the situation affecting our military expenditures in China.

Although I do not pretend to pass judgment in matters of a military character, I should stress what we have repeatedly reported previously, namely, that economic and military conditions in China are deteriorating so fast that, in order to prevent collapse of China in due course, military measures to restore the Burma Road and reopen land transportation to China are imperative at an early date. The economic situation in China will not be helped by a loan from the United States at this juncture. It can only be helped by successful military operations on an extensive scale.

28 (x)

Secretary of the Treasury Morgenthau to Secretary Hull

WASHINGTON, *December 31, 1943*

MY DEAR MR. SECRETARY: This is to acknowledge receipt of your letter of December 29th enclosing a report of December 23, 1943 from Ambassador Gauss. I appreciate your sending me this telegram and have found it of considerable interest.

I see that Ambassador Gauss is in agreement with the views expressed in our Memorandum to the President, a copy of which I sent to you in letter dated December 20, 1943.

It would seem that no further steps can be taken regarding the Chinese request for a loan until we have received a reply to our Memorandum which, as you probably know, the President said he was going to forward to President Chiang Kai-shek.

Sincerely yours,

H. MORGENTHAU, Jr.

28 (y)

Generalissimo Chiang Kai-shek to President Roosevelt [37]

I have received your recent telegram forwarded through Ambassador Gauss and am happy that you have recovered from your indisposition. I appreciate the fact that you have been endeavoring to find a solution to the economic problems of China even during your illness.

To my mind the proposals made by the Treasury Department are not those of one allied nation to another but rather are in the nature of a commercial transaction. If put into practice these proposals would not increase China's economic strength in the prosecution of the war. On the contrary the impairment of the Chinese people's confidence in *fapi* would only add to her economic difficulties. I would not make this urgent appeal to you were it not for the fact that we are entering a most critical stage. I have reached the following conclusions after giving mature consideration to the future perilous economic situation in this war theater:

(1) An out and out loan of one billion dollars from the United States would enable us partly to meet the deficit of the coming war budget and also through reciprocal aid to meet a part of American military expenses in China, such as the repair and construction of airfields and necessary installations, the feeding of American troops and the transportation of war materials, et cetera.

(2) If it is the opinion of the Treasury Department that it is not able to accept the above proposal I suggest that such expenditures as are incurred by United States forces in China should be borne by the American Government. The Central Bank of China will facilitate exchange at the official rate of US$1 equals 20 yuan. The rate is unalterable in as much as we cannot afford to shake the confidence of the people in *fapi*, which is a stabilizing factor amidst a world of uncertainty brought about by the vicissitudes of war. It is only thus that we can directly maintain the credit of *fapi* and indirectly save China from economic collapse. Such collapse would seriously affect the whole military posi-

---

[37] Transmitted by the Ambassador in China from Chungking, Jan. 16, 1944.

tion of the Allies because of China's inability to continue resistance for any considerable length of time.

The second of these proposals is outright help which the Chinese people and army would appreciate and when it is considered that the United States has been feeding even British and Russian civilians this would be entirely in accordance with the Allied strategy of pooling resources. As an example, I might point out here that following the battle of Changteh 300,000 houses in that area were left in ruins and less than 10 buildings still remain. In this respect the people of China have suffered incalculable losses since the commencement of our war of resistance seven years ago. Our sacrifice in men and materials both civil and military is convincing proof of our willingness to give all that we are and everything that we have to the Allied cause. One of the crack units of China, 57th Division, has been entirely sacrificed.

I felt keenly when I saw you in Cairo that with your vision and wisdom you completely comprehended the critical situation which now faces this country and that you were eager to extend to our people every means of practical help in order to enable them to march forward shoulder to shoulder with the American people to common victory. I was so encouraged that I hastened to reassure the Chinese people of the solidarity and strength of our united efforts. I still feel sure that as leader of the Allied nations you will do all in your power to help China to continue her resistance and to do her full part in the global war. You realize, I am sure, that I will do all in my power to rally the support of the Chinese nation to bring about speedy victory and that I have even gone to the length of delaying the reopening of the Burma route so that essential amphibious equipment might be diverted to the European theater, thereby disappointing all classes of my countrymen who still bear in their memories the scar of the defeat suffered in the last Burma campaign as a result of which China lost large quantities of men and equipment through no fault of her own.

In the event that the Treasury Department feels unable to agree to either of the above two proposals then China will be compelled to pursue the only course open to her, namely, to continue resistance against our common enemy Japan with all her available strength and for as long as possible, thus in a way discharging her responsibilities as a member of the United Nations. In that eventuality she would have to permit her wartime economy and finances to follow the natural course of events. In such a case the Chinese Government would have no means at its disposal to meet the requirements of United States forces in China and consequently the American Army in China would have to depend upon itself to execute any and all of its projects, for to our great regret we would be placed inevitably in a position in which we could not make any further material or financial contribution, including the construction of works for military use.

28 (z)

The Ambassador in China (Gauss) to Secretary Hull

CHUNGKING, *January 16, 1944*

The Generalissimo requested that the Ambassador inform the Departments of State, Treasury and War that China would not be asking for anything were it not for the critical military and economic situation because China has pride in helping herself and in being self-sufficient; that the Generalissimo assured the Ambassador that any financial or material assistance rendered China by the

United States would not be hoarded for post-war purposes; that China would not take advantage of any situation to profit thereby and that China is neither a petty thief nor a robber baron. The Generalissimo said China had not asked for assistance last year or the year before. But the situation now is very much worse than a year ago and the cost of assisting American forces in China has become such a great strain that China is unable to keep up such assistance and that if the Treasury Department cannot help China financially, the American Army in China will have to depend on itself after March 1. The Generalissimo said that the United States forces have six weeks to make preparations and that after March 1 China could not be of material or financial assistance in connection with any project the American forces might have in mind. The Ambassador inquired whether this meant China would be unable to cooperate militarily with the United States forces in China. The Generalissimo replied that what he meant was that after March 1 American forces must look after themselves. Mr. Atcheson said he assumed this meant that the American forces must finance themselves and also make necessary arrangements for the purchase of supplies, construction materials and labor. The Generalissimo replied in the affirmative and said that China would of course continue to fight as long as she could and that as indicated in the latter part of his message to the Press she will carry on until the inevitable military and economic collapse and then will do the best possible under existing circumstances. Generalissimo Chiang said that within the past two weeks he had approved requests of United States Army headquarters that China undertake airfield projects which would cost the enormous sum of 13 billion dollars and that China simply could not finance such projects. (Madame Chiang said as an interesting sidelight that every American soldier in China cost the Chinese Government three hundred Chinese dollars per day; that there are several thousand American soldiers and that a great increase in the number of these is contemplated. She said furthermore that at the current cost of military rice 300 Chinese dollars would feed a Chinese soldier for a month; that after March 1 the United States Army would also have to feed its own soldiers and that the United States will have to depend upon itself. Madame Chiang said that date of March first was an implementation of the Generalissimo's statement set forth in the last paragraph of his message to the President.)

The Ambassador stated that it was his impression that it is the view of American economists that no amount of American money to the credit of China in the United States could remedy China's economic and financial situation any more than would be the case if our entire output of machine guns were hypothecated to China but remained in the United States. The Generalissimo replied that American economists know American economy and world economy in general but do not understand Chinese economy or Chinese psychology, the latter having a great deal to do with the situation in China. The Generalissimo said that the exchange rate is absolutely unalterable; that a maintenance of *fapi* is necessary to maintain public confidence; that a loan even though the actual cash remained in the United States would be regarded by the Chinese people as a reserve for *fapi*.

In reply to Mr. Atcheson's inquiry the Generalissimo said that the question of the Commission proposed by Mr. Morgenthau was covered in that section of his message referring to the Treasury's proposals. Mr. Atcheson pointed out that this was a suggestion made by the President. The Generalissimo replied that the Commission would be acting under directions of the Treasury and along the lines of the proposals made by the Treasury.

The Ambassador reported further that after his return to the Embassy Madame Chiang telephoned him to say that if the Commission planned to discuss the proposals made by the Treasury there was no use in its coming but if it was sent out to discuss the two proposals made by the Generalissimo it would be welcome. Among various arguments advanced by Madame Chiang was one to the effect that the expenditures of the United States forces in China amounting to approximately U. S. $20,000,000 per month could not be dumped on the black market in a day and that dumping of even U. S. $1,000,000 would swiftly and extensively lower the black market rate.

The Ambassador added that his comments would follow.

The Ambassador reported that while the Generalissimo rejected the suggestion of sending a commission to China to confer on the proposals made by the Treasury, he has not closed the door entirely to such a commission provided it comes to discuss the Generalissimo's proposals, namely, a loan or assumption by our Army of all expenses incurred by it in the China theater without financial or material assistance from the Chinese Government.

The Ambassador stated that if he knew of any possible means which the United States could utilize to provide aid to China at this time either to transform her contribution to the general war effort into something affirmative or to support the present economic situation which continues rapidly to deteriorate he would heartily advocate it. The Ambassador said he would at all times prefer to see us operate in China without Chinese aid; that we could completely justify our heavy expenditures in China on the basis of spiraling prices which China must also meet in her own operations; but to be compelled to increase these heavy expenditures another five times because of the unrealistic attitude on the exchange rates creates a situation which might readily lead to a charge of exploitation and react unfavorably for China if it became known in the United States.

The Ambassador said that since he had not been informed in regard to commitments or military and other plans he could not suggest how far if at all pressure might be brought to bear upon China, but expressed the opinion that, however unpleasant these developments may be, and however unfortunate it may be that disagreements with China over money matters should have arisen, we should maintain a firm position declining to be coerced by petulant gestures or threats.

The Ambassador concluded his message by stating that the conversation held the preceding evening was calm and friendly on both sides and that the Generalissimo and Madame Chiang were most cordial throughout.

28 (aa)

Message From General Stilwell to General Somervell, March 27, 1944

[Extract]

We are now hoping that the Chinese may take a more realistic attitude on money matters. The Generalissimo is pressing Kung to effect agreement although mention of the phrase "exchange rate" sends the Generalissimo into a tailspin. We would like to have permission to explore the possibilities of the following plan, the only one which has a chance of success at the present time.

That the Chinese continue to advance CN to U. S. Army according to our needs and their ability. At the beginning of each three-month period, the U. S. to decide on a sum of U. S. dollars which will be advanced to the Chinese during the period.

For the next three-month period this sum to be figured between 100 and 200, probably between 125 and 165, U. S. requirements in CN to be kept secret, while the Chinese may publicize our "contribution" if they think wise for stabilization purposes. The rate of exchange will not come into the transaction, and the decision on final benefit derived by the Chinese and U. S. respectively will be left to postwar negotiation.

We think that the "tri-monthly ratio" between the two contributions will become the de facto rate of final settlement, since postwar stabilization of rate must certainly be at a much lower figure. To raise a portion of their contribution to U. S. in the least inflationary manner the Chinese to be urged to sell gold and U. S. dollars on joint account. This procedure is preferable to our sale on our own account since the sales will probably produce only 20 percent of our requirement. We fully realize the disadvantage of postwar negotiation on final rate, but think that the dangers are more imaginary than real.

28 (bb)

Secretary of War Stimson to President Roosevelt

WASHINGTON, *May 26, 1944*

DEAR MR. PRESIDENT: I submit herewith a chronological résumé of the negotiations with the Chinese Government with respect to the rates of exchange covering our expenditures in China. Since the résumé necessarily is somewhat long, I am also summarizing herewith its context.

When our troops first arrived in China they found an agreed exchange rate of $20 (Chinese) for $1 (U.S.), which even then had no realistic relationship to the purchasing value of the Chinese yuan. However, our requirements for food and housing were small and the expenditures were assumed by the Chinese Government which also undertook the requisite airport construction. In the fall of 1943 when General Somervell visited Chungking, this situation had changed and important construction was delayed, as the Chinese Government had not provided sufficient funds. General Stilwell was making direct expenditures to obtain necessary speed in completing urgently needed facilities.

General Somervell proposed to Dr. Kung the establishment of a more favorable exchange rate. He suggested a rate of 100 to 1 in comparison with the then black market rate of 120 to 1. He proposed that we continue to procure $20 (Chinese) for each $1 (U.S.) with the Chinese either to donate or to make available under reverse lend-lease $80 (Chinese) for each $1 (U.S.).

At the Cairo Conference the United States agreed to finance further construction expenditures. However the exchange rate was not discussed. The Generalissimo on his return cabled you requesting either a loan of $1,000,000,000 (U.S.), or the payment of Chinese expenditures at a 20 to 1 rate. As this would have made our expenditures in China astronomical, you disapproved the proposal and urged the Generalissimo to accept proposals offered by our representatives.

The Chinese had been threatening to discontinue construction. With the receipt of your message, they agreed to provide $2,500,000,000 (Chinese) and we in turn agreed to deposit $25,000,000 to Chinese account in this country. This was in effect a 100 to 1 rate, but the Chinese would not continue the arrangement on a monthly basis. We also forwarded $20,000,000 (U.S.) at Chinese request for purchase by the Chinese in the black market to lower the rate. There was little confidence in this proposal and the money has not as yet been turned over to the Chinese. Nevertheless, the Chinese continued to advance funds for the construction program subject to our shipment of $5,000,000,000 (Chinese) per month into China. This is continuing and work to date has not been held up.

The Chinese have advanced us $7,000,000,000 (Chinese) and have received in partial payment the one deposit of $25,000,000. Manifestly, they are worried as to the rate for repayment. For the first time we occupy the favorable position. We have advised the Chinese consistently of our willingness to bear these expenditures at a reasonable exchange rate. The 60 to 1 rate recently proposed by Dr. Kung with $20 (Chinese) to be purchased for each $1 (U.S.) and $40 (Chinese) to be provided under reverse lend-lease is not realistic in view of the present black market rate. We are not adverse to a reverse lend-lease arrangement of this type, though we do object to an unrealistic rate; and although it would result in the Chinese obtaining a greater credit for future settlement, it would appear most unlikely that funds received under reverse lend-lease at any rate approaching realism would at any time even closely approach the dollar value of direct lend-lease aid.

Perhaps our war program in China has contributed somewhat to inflation. However, the number of our troops and the magnitude of our construction are not sufficient to have a major effect. The Chinese report expenditures at approximately $10,000,000,000 (Chinese) for support of our troops and for construction prior to the Cairo Conference. They have advanced $7,000,000,000 (Chinese) for construction authorized at Cairo. In turn the United States has lend-leased goods valued at $413,000,000 (U.S.). The Treasury Department granted a credit to the Chinese Government of $500,000,000 (U.S.), against which it drew $243,000,000. The FEA has purchased goods for $48,000,000 (U.S.) at a 20 to 1 rate. Our forces in China have expended through February 1944 a total of $155,000,000 (U.S.) at the rate of 20 to 1. The financial contribution of the United States has been most substantial and greatly in excess of the Chinese expenditures even at the 20 to 1 rate. A settlement of the $7,000,000,000 (Chinese) construction advance alone at the 20 to 1 rate would involve a premium payment of over $300,000,000 (U.S.) compared with a rate of 150 to 1, and the latter is below current black market.

The black market is continuing to rise. The rate at the present time should not be less than 150 to 1 and even this rate should be revised periodically unless the Chinese Government controls inflation.

The War Department believes that our representatives should continue to stand firm for a realistic rate. In view of the effect of any rate on military planning, commitments should not be made in Chungking without clearance in Washington by the Treasury Department and your approval.

Respectfully yours,

HENRY L. STIMSON

[Enclosure]

RÉSUMÉ OF CHINESE EXCHANGE SITUATION, 19 MAY 1944

1. The exchange situation in China first was brought to the attention of the War Department by General Stilwell early in 1943, at which time he reported that the official rate of exchange of 20 to 1 was not realistic, inasmuch as the open market rate at that time was around 40 to 1 and increasing rapidly. He called attention to the fact that with the large expenditures contemplated by the Army, definite steps should be taken to have a new official rate established.

2. The official rate of exchange of 20 to 1 was established in August 1941 and has been supported by the U. S. Government as a measure of making effective the stabilization agreement entered into with China at the same time. This stabilization agreement expired in January 1944.

3. When the matter of the rate was first reported by General Stilwell the Treasury Department was requested to give some consideration to having the Chinese effect a change in the rate and during the latter part of 1943, that department endeavored to obtain some relief in the matter. . These efforts included a change in the official rate, the granting of a special rate to the United States or the sale of gold at an advantageous price to use the proceeds to decrease the excessive costs of the War Department's expenditures in China because of the unrealistic rate.

4. With a knowledge of the State and Treasury Department and undoubtedly with the full knowledge of the Chinese Government, the War Department has been paying its personnel in China U. S. currency and permitting that personnel to go into the open or black market and purchase Chinese currency at any available rate. Later, the State and Treasury Department requested the War Department to ship United States currency to China for use in paying personnel and operating expenses. The War Department has been reluctant to having its soldiers dealing in black market operations, but for morale purposes, it could not do other than authorize such a procedure in view of its failure to find other means of giving its men in China sufficient local currency to offset the unrealistic exchange rate. In addition to the morale factor, there has been the ever increasing expenditures by the War Department for supplies and construction.

5. Failing to secure relief through a change in the official rate, the War Department, early in 1943 felt the need for a reciprocal Lend-Lease agreement with China and the Chinese Government indicated that they may be willing to enter into such an agreement. Accordingly, an agreement was drafted for submission to the Chinese. In view of the exchange situation and the fact that the Treasury Department expressed the view that efforts up to that time to secure a better official rate of exchange had proved fruitless, it was decided to include in the reciprocal Lend-Lease agreement, in addition to the provisions to direct aid in kind, a section to the effect that the Chinese Government would provide funds in Chinese currency to be used by the U. S. in direct purchase of supplies, materials, facilities and services in lieu of reciprocal aid in kind and to meet the essential governmental and military needs for Chinese currency. The understanding was that this currency received under the agreement could be used in reducing the excessive cost to the U. S. of expenditures for personnel and other purposes on account of the unrealistic Chinese exchange rate. This reciprocal Lend-Lease agreement was presented to Dr. Soong, Foreign Minister of the Chinese government by the State Department in Washington in May 1943 with a memorandum explaining the purpose of the financial provisions thereof. The agreement was submitted to General Stilwell in China and was concurred in by him in view of the apparent impossibility of securing a proper exchange rate.

6. In October 1943 General Somervell visited Chungking. He was advised by General Stilwell that delays occurring in construction necessitated direct contractual expenditures by United States forces. The artificial exchange rate of 20 to 1 as compared with a black market rate of 120 to 1 was resulting in exorbitant costs. General Stilwell believed that a better arrangement was essential to our planned operations. General Somervell, with the knowledge and consent of the Ambassador, proposed to Dr. Kung, subject to ratification

by the U. S. authorities in Washington, that the Chinese Government make available to our forces the requisite Chinese currency to support these forces and the military construction under one of two alternatives:

a. The United States would deposit to Chinese account in the United States $1 U. S. for each $100 CN furnished, this deposit to be credited against an official exchange rate of 20 to 1, with the remaining $80 CN to be a contribution of the Chinese Government to our joint war effort (this arrangement would protect publicly the 20 to 1 official rate) ; or,

b. The Chinese Government would provide the requisite funds with the United States depositing to Chinese account $1 U.S. for $20 CN of each $100 CN made available, the remaining $80 CN to be provided under a reverse lend-lease agreement.

Dr. Kung appeared to view these proposals as feasible and promised to place them before the Generalissimo for approval.

7. Shortly after General Somervell's return to the United States in November, and before the proposals could be carried further, the Cairo Conference was held. The Generalissimo attended this conference. It is understood that he was advised that the United States was prepared to bear the cost of its military effort in China. It is not understood that the question of exchange rates was considered. Subsequent to the conference, as indicated in the report of Ambassador Gauss, January 16, 1944, the Generalissimo in a message to the President urged that a loan of $1,000,000,000 U.S. be made to China, or that, otherwise, the United States assume full responsibility for its expenditures in China at a 20 to 1 rate.

8. The Treasury Department was then negotiating with the Chinese Government with a view to transporting gold to China for purchase of Chinese currency in the open market to control inflation and to secure a better exchange rate. These negotiations did not appear to be progressing rapidly. The Secretary of Treasury recognizing the urgency of the airport construction program authorized the War Department to proceed with its own negotiations.

Representatives of the State Department concurred in this arrangement. Our military representatives were authorized to advise the Chinese that the United States was prepared to accept full responsibility for its military expenditures subject to the establishment of a reasonable exchange rate which would have some relationship to the actual purchasing power of the Chinese dollar. On 15 January our Commanding General in China and State Department representatives were advised to press for an early completion of a reverse lend-lease agreement concurrently with an agreement to be presented by military representatives with respect to the funds to be made available by the Chinese Government to cover our military expenditures. The military representatives were advised to keep in constant touch with the State Department and Treasury Department representatives so that any action taken in Chungking would be jointly understood. Mr. Edward C. Acheson was sent to China to assist the Commanding General in presenting the proposed fiscal arrangement.

9. In reply to the Generalissimo's request, referred to above, the President urged the acceptance of the proposal submitted by our military and diplomatic representatives. It is to be noted that the authorities in this country were in agreement that there was little merit in the proposed loan to China.

10. Our military and diplomatic representatives proceeded with the negotiations. In the latter part of January estimates became available with respect to the substantial construction costs involved in the new airport projects. Meanwhile the black market exchange rate had continued to advance and payments in

American dollars at a 20 to 1 rate would have become astronomical in comparison to the value received in work. The War Department would have found it necessary to have requested additional funds for the purpose from Congress and was apprehensive that the exorbitant costs would have serious repercussions. Again on 24 January our military representatives were advised to maintain a firm stand, but to inform the Chinese Government that the United States was prepared to place to Chinese account the U.S. dollar equivalent of any Chinese funds made available under general arrangements which they would suggest to the Chinese Government.

11. Dr. Kung was designated by the Generalissimo to receive the United States' proposals. Our representatives proposed as an interim measure that the United States would purchase $1,000,000,000 CN at the rate of 40 to 1 through the deposit of $25,000,000 U.S. to Chinese account in this country. The Chinese Government would add $1,500,000,000 CN to this account. This proposal would have established an interim exchange rate of 100 to 1. The Chinese Government did advance the first funds and the $25,000,000 U.S. in payment thereof was deposited to Chinese account. However the Chinese Government did not accept the proposal as a continuing measure. On 3 February Dr. Kung made a counter-proposal to continue the official exchange rate of 20 to 1 with the Central Government contribution $10 CN more for each $1 U.S. under reverse lend-lease. Our representatives turned down this proposal. They advised us on 12 February that they could see no benefit in further proposals. However, Dr. Kung was asked to advance $1,000,000,000 CN per month during the remainder of the negotiations with the repayment rate to be decided during negotiations.

12. Report of expenditures at this time indicated that our own expenditures in China had increased from $400,000 in January 1943 to $23,000,000 in December. Estimates for airport and other construction indicated a requirement of approximately $2,500,000,000 CN monthly. Payment for these funds at a 20 to 1 rate as compared with the proposed 100 to 1 rate would have resulted in an annual premium to the Chinese Government in excess of $1,000,000,000. However, the proposed rate of 100 to 1 was still below the real purchasing value which was more adequately expressed by the black market rate which had reached 150 to 1. On February 20 General Stilwell was advised that he must continue to take a firm stand while still expressing the willingness of the United States to bear full costs at a reasonable exchange rate. On February 25 we were advised by our military representatives that Dr. Kung had asked for $20,000,000 U. S. to be flown to China as an advance to the Chinese account with the rate to be determined later. These funds Dr. Kung proposed to use for the purchase of Chinese currency in the black market in an effort to drive down the black market rate. At the suggestion of our representatives, and with the approval of the Treasury Department, this money was flown to India in the understanding that $5,000,000 U. S. was to be made available to the Chinese Government to test the effect of the proposed purchases prior to utilizing the full amount. These funds have not as yet been turned over to the Chinese Government as our representatives on the ground felt that the transfer might prove detrimental in view of the existing status of negotiations.

13. On March 2 our representatives advised us that the Chinese Government had agreed to furnish not to exceed $5,000,000,000 CN per month to our forces provided the requisite money in Chinese currency was shipped from the United States, with March and April requirements to be shipped by air. Arrangements were made to meet this request.

14. During the period of negotiations the construction work has been proceeding satisfactorily. As our proposal with respect to the deposit of $25,000,000 U. S. per month to the Chinese account in the United States in exchange for $2,500,-000,000 CN had not been accepted by the Chinese Government, only the initial deposit was made. Since we are obtaining all of the funds needed without an exchange commitment, our representatives in China believed it undesirable to submit further proposals to the Chinese. They awaited counter-proposals from the Chinese Government. On May 7 our representatives advised us that the Chinese were pressing hard for a financial agreement at a 60 to 1 rate, $40 CN of each $60 CN furnished to be credited as reverse lend-lease. As the black market was continuing to rise, our representatives were unwilling to accept this offer and insisted on a three months' agreement for a rate of 150 to 1. Our representatives in the field reported that the Chinese Government would make a direct appeal to the United States.

15. It is important to note that the Chinese Government has receded considerably from its stand taken in 1943, and from its even more adamant stand taken in December 1943 and January 1944, as a result of the firm position taken by the United States. While the work undertaken by the American forces and payment therefor may aggravate the distress of the Chinese economy, it is very doubtful if its influence on the inflation difficulties is a major contributing factor. In local areas where work is being carried on, our expenditures will have more serious effect on inflationary difficulties than elsewhere, but even there our expenditures are not the primary cause of their economic disturbance. In any event, it is difficult to understand the effect of the rate of exchange on this economy as the United States funds made available to China would accumulate as a credit to be drawn against after the war. It would be difficult to justify an artificial exchange rate which would make the cost of American participation in the war in China out of all proportion to the actual value of the work received, particularly taking into consideration the relatively low cost of labor in China as compared with the United States.

16. The extent of United States aid to China must also be taken into consideration in determining the exchange rate which is to be accepted. Lend-Lease aid to China has aggregated more than $400,000,000 U.S., although some of the Lend-Lease material is still stock piled in India as transportation has not been available for its movement to China. At a realistic rate, this Lend-Lease expenditure alone is equivalent to $60,000,000,000 CN.

In addition thereto, the Treasury Department granted a credit to the Chinese Government of $500,000,000 U.S. in March 1942 against which $243,000,000 has been drawn at the end of 1943.

The Foreign Economic Administration will have purchased in China from 1941 through June 1944 approximately $48,000,000 U.S. which at the official rate would purchase $960,000,000 CN worth of merchandise (strategic materials). At a realistic rate of 100 to 1 as a conservative average for the period, these purchases would have cost only $9,600,000 U.S. This means that over the period the Chinese Government had been benefited as a result of the unrealistic exchange rate by a premium of $38,400,000 U.S.

Likewise, our forces in China have expended for the period 1 January 1943 to include February 1944 a total of $155,550,000 U.S. which at the official rate of exchange total $3,111,000,000 CN. Expenditures during the month of March and April 1944 have been on the basis of the new agreement, whereby the Chinese advanced to us the currency required for our needs and we in turn deposited U. S. currency to the credit of the Chinese Government in such amount as the

Commanding General, U. S. Forces reports as properly due. The total amount reported by the Commanding General, U. S. Forces under this agreement to have been received up to April 23 is $7,680,000,000 CN. (How much of this should be credited as a Chinese contribution to the war effort, and how much the United States Government is expected to reimburse the Chinese cannot be determined in Washington at this time in view of the fact that negotiations in this respect are being carried on by General Stilwell in China.) This is a total expenditure in Chinese currency to date of $10,791,000,000 CN. This would cost the U. S. at the official rate of 20 to 1 $539,550,000 U.S. whereas at a realistic rate of 150 to 1 it would cost only $72,000,000. This means that the U. S. pays a premium on these expenditures of $467,550,000 due to the unrealistic rate.

Dr. Kung in a letter to the Secretary of War has reported Chinese expenditures during part of February and all of March and April as aggregating $7,016,000,000 CN. The Chinese state, however, in addition to this amount the Chinese Government has paid out since September 1942 for construction of airfields, barracks, air force supplies and improvement of roads at the request of the United States authorities a total of $10,878,260,457 CN.

While the cost of the services furnished the United States forces in China cannot be verified, his estimate of construction cost in 1944 of $7,000,000,000 CN is in agreement with our own figures. The United States has deposited against this advance of $7,000,000,000 CN the sum of $25,000,000 U.S. to Chinese credit in the United States.

17. In view of the large sums involved and the continuing expenditures, it is apparent that the agreed exchange rate may have a decided influence on military operations and on military planning. While it is desirable for a firm agreement to be effected at the earliest possible date, the importance of such agreement to contemplated military operations warrants its careful consideration in Washington before it is accepted formally. It is suggested, therefore, that any arrangements which may be proposed in Chungking be tentative until their effect on military operations can be studied by our Government in Washington so that all factors may be taken into consideration. It is apparent that the American position has constantly improved during the progress of the negotiations as a result of the firm stand taken by all of our representatives working in close agreement. Meanwhile, military construction has proceeded without delay.

28 (cc)

Minutes of a Meeting on Chinese Gold Purchases [38]

Present: Mr. White
Mr. Bernstein
Mr. Hsi Te-mou
Mr. T. L. Soong
Mr. Y. C. Koo
Mr. Adler

Mr. Hsi gave Mr. White a copy of the following telegram from K. K. Kwok:

"As Federal Reserve Bank of New York advised having shipped balance by plane thus exhausting our $20 million and as sales still extremely heavy and recent arrivals far from being adequate to meet outstanding contracts, please request

[38] Held in the office of Mr. H. D. White, Director of the Division of Monetary Research, Treasury Department, on Oct. 2, 1944.

U. S. Treasury immediately transfer US$20 million or if possible more out of $200 million and ship by plane. Please contact Adler and give him my best regards."

Mr. White raised the general question of the merits of selling US$200 million of gold in the existing situation. He pointed out that China's gold would be an enormous asset to her after the war if still conserved as it could provide a base for economic reconstruction as well as for reorganization of the currency. If it were sold now it might have some little psychological effect but could not substantially retard rising prices or the basic economic situation which was due to the acute scarcity of goods. Moreover, much of the gold would disappear into hoards and might emerge from those hoards either very slowly or not at all. Mr. White asked who was buying the gold and Mr. Koo replied that it was distributed from Chungking to Sian, Lanchow, Chengtu, etc. where it was bought by farmers and amahs.

Mr. Y. C. Koo indicated that sale of gold had had some beneficial effect and that the cessation of the sale of gold would send prices skyrocketing. The question was then raised of the discrepancy between the price at which gold was sold by the Central Bank and the black market price. Mr. White pointed out that with the existence of such a spread sometimes amounting to CN$5–6,000 somebody was making a profit and it was not the government. The Secretary had shown some interest in this question. Mr. Soong expressed surprise that the spread had been so high, Mr. Adler adding that it had been as much as 60% of the official price in the early part of September and then had dropped to CN$1,500 with the arrival of gold. There was some discussion of the relationship between spot and forward prices, Messrs. Koo and Soong claiming that the main reason for the discrepancy between the price at which the Central Bank sold and the black market price was the non-availability of supplies in Chungking. If there were sufficient supplies of gold, the discrepancy could be obliterated. Mr. Hsi pointed out that even with current arrivals, forward sales exceeded Central Bank's supplies of gold. It was also pointed out that the existence of high rates of interest might explain part of the discrepancy between spot and forward but after some comment by Mr. White and Mr. Bernstein, Messrs. Soong and Koo emphasized that the market's lack of confidence in the Central Bank's ability to procure adequate supplies was apparently the main reason.

Mr. White pointed out that it was cheaper for the Central Government to print fapi than to absorb fapi in exchange for gold at a time when the dent that was being made by the sale of gold was not significantly large. Mr. Koo stated that in the month of July two billion fapi had been absorbed by the sale of gold, Mr. Adler adding that the note issue in July was 9 billion fapi. Mr. Y. C. Koo mentioned that U.S. Army expenditures had been the major factor in the deterioration of the economic situation and alluded to the good relations that had existed between the Treasury and the Ministry of Finance during the past ten years. Mr. White said there was no question of that; in fact were it not for these good relations the Treasury would not be interested in how China utilized her gold. He was anxious to see that she got the maximum advantage from such utilization.

He asked how much gold China had left. Mr. Hsi replied that she had US $10 million left from a previous account and that Dr. Kung was anxious to get more gold through use of the half billion dollar loan. In fact, Dr. Kung was asking for $50 million of gold for sale of gold bullion and $100 million of gold for minting token coins. Mr. Koo and Mr. Soong stressed the fact that the cessation of the sale of gold would have very serious effects at this time. Mr. White asked whether people who bought forward could receive cash for their delivery certificates and the answer was in the affirmative. Mr. White pointed out this fact should reduce the spread between spot and forward. Mr. Adler asked why the price of gold had been lowered in July. Mr. Koo and Mr. Hsi said they would cable to Chungking for an explanation, Mr. Hsi confessing that it appeared to have been a mistake.

Mr. Hsi expressed the desire to take up the question of the minting of coins. Mr. White indicated that it should be taken up with Mr. Adler and the people from the Mint.

Mr. White concluded the meeting by saying that he would take up the matter with the Secretary and get in touch with the Chinese again.

28 (dd)

Memorandum by Secretary of the Treasury Morgenthau[39]

1. This memorandum does not deal with the questions of textiles and trucks which were included in the program which was presented to this Government. The urgency of China's need for these items and their bearing upon inflation are recognized. They are omitted because our supply authorities are in the process of making an over-all determination of requirements and supplies and are not yet in a position to make a decision respecting China's requests.

2. We are agreed that any program to stabilize the currency and to check inflation should comprise a broad series of measures in the following categories:

  (a) Monetary and banking rehabilitation.
  (b) Foreign exchange stabilization.
  (c) Fiscal and administrative reforms.
  (d) Increase of supplies and improvement in their distribution.

3. We are anxious to give full support to an effective anti-inflationary program for China. It is therefore recommended that a Currency Stabilization Fund of $500 million be constituted for this purpose from the remaining $240 million of the United States loan to China and from China's existing dollar balances. Such an allocation of this remainder of the United States loan would be in strict accordance with the spirit and the letter of the 1942 financial agreement. The Fund would be set aside with firm mutual commitment on the part of China and the United States as to its purposes and availability.

It is envisaged that the uses to which this Currency Stabilization Fund would be put would be part of a broad concerted program for combatting inflation and for currency stabilization and these uses would be subject to joint agreement. The time at which the Fund's operations would start would be discussed at a later date.

The Treasury stands ready to advise and consult with the Chinese Government on the content and timing of such anti-inflationary and stabilization program. We are strongly of the opinion that the initiation of a Currency Stabilization Fund would strengthen the financial position of the Chinese Government and would inspire confidence both at home and abroad in its future economic and financial stability. The existence of such a Fund would give the Chinese people a real sense of security with respect to their ability to cope with their grave problems of reconstruction.

---

[39] Handed to Dr. T. V. Soong on May 8, 1945.

It should be noted that this proposal relates to only one portion of the foreign exchange assets presently available to China and that it would leave a relatively large amount of dollar exchange for helpful intermediate measures and for meeting China's current foreign exchange requirements.

4. We believe that the Chinese Government should terminate the program of forward sales of gold. As you know, the U. S. Treasury was not consulted when this program was initiated. In view of the difficulties of shipping gold, the limited effects of sales upon price rises in China, the public criticism of such sales and the desirability of using foreign exchange resources to achieve maximum effects, this program is ill-advised.

5. The Treasury will endeavor, as in the past, to make available limited quantities of gold for shipment to China during the next few months, having due regard to the need for restricting gold shipments where these endanger lives or use scarce transport facilities. However, in consideration of points 2 and 3 above, it is believed that further shipments should be financed out of foreign exchange assets other than those proposed to be earmarked for currency stabilization.

6. China should investigate and cancel sales to speculators and illicit purchasers and insure that only bona fide purchasers will receive such gold as is available. If gold arrivals are still not sufficient to meet past commitments, it is suggested that China may offer to place dollar credits (at about $35 per ounce) for the time being from her existing assets to the accounts of purchasers of gold to whom she cannot temporarily make delivery.

7. It is most unfortunate that the impression has arisen in the United States that the $200 million of U. S. dollar certificates and bonds and the gold sold in China have gone into relatively few hands with resultant large individual profits and have failed to be of real assistance to the Chinese economy.

28 (ee)

Minutes of a Meeting on Gold Fund for China [40]

Present: Secretary Morgenthau
Mr. D. W. Bell ⎫
Mr. Coe   ⎪
Mr. Adler   ⎬ Treasury
Mr. Friedman ⎭
Mr. Clayton ⎫
Mr. Collado ⎬ State
Mr. T. V. Soong ⎫
Mr. Tsu-yee Pei ⎬ China
Mr. W. Y. Lin   ⎭

Before Dr. Soong, Mr. Pei and Mr. Lin joined the meeting, there was a brief discussion of what the Chinese would be told. In this discussion Mr. Coe made the point that he still favored the establishment of the $500 million fund and pointed out that our memorandum was not inconsistent with our commitment to the Chinese. The Secretary indicated that he was prepared to give them the remainder of the $200 million of gold.

When Dr. Soong, Mr. Pei and Mr. Lin joined the meeting, the Secretary asked Dr. Soong for the answer to his questions on how much gold China would need

---
[40] Held in the office of the Secretary of the Treasury, Mr. Morgenthau, on May 9, 1945.

for the next three months. Dr. Soong replied that in addition to the outstanding commitments the Chinese planned to sell about 1 million ounces during the next three months. The Secretary asked the "experts" to agree on the figures after the meeting.

Dr. Soong then read a memorandum proposing a reconstruction fund which, in effect, indicated that the Chinese wanted much larger loans from the United States.

The Secretary replied that we would give their proposal our careful consideration. He then went on to say that the establishment of a $500 million Fund would assist him in furthering China's interest before Congress. At this time, he said he was asking Dr. Soong to reconsider their decision to see whether they could not see their way clear to the establishment of such a Fund.

Dr. Soong replied that he could not do it; that he could only consider it if the Fund was established out of new loans. He, moreover, could not be responsible for the mistakes made in his absence and these mistakes were now being overcome. He, Dr. Soong, had not objected to the publicity on the mishandling of the Funds. He had not opposed sale of U.S. dollar savings certificates and bonds, but it had been stupid to stick to the original 20 to 1 rate.

The Secretary pointed out that he would like to be helpful and that, in effect, it was merely a matter of re-arrangement of Chinese bookkeeping in order to set up this Fund. If Dr. Soong decided not to accept the proposal on the $500 million Fund, the Secretary would obviously be disappointed. However, the commitment to make available the remainder of the $200 million of gold was not tied up with the fund proposal and the Treasury would study ways of accelerating gold shipments.

28 (ff)

The Chinese Minister for Foreign Affairs (Soong) to Secretary of the Treasury Morgenthau

[WASHINGTON] *May 9, 1945*

MY DEAR MR. SECRETARY: May I express my appreciation of the frank talk we had at luncheon, and the helpful attitude you showed at the conference this afternoon.

I have cabled to the Generalissimo your suggestion of setting up a $500 million Reconstruction Fund, and will let you know as soon as I have his reply. I added that you recognized that the above suggestion and the question of gold delivery are two separate matters; that there is no question of the validity of your prior commitment; that you are ready to meet it; and that gold will be made available.

In view of the urgency of the situation, I shall appreciate it if you will kindly designate some member of your Department to discuss the details with my assistants, Mr. Tsu-yee Pei and Dr. W. Y. Lin, so that the necessary shipments could be made at once.

As Mr. Clayton said this afternoon, I have to return to San Francisco to meet my engagements there, accordingly I shall be grateful for your prompt reply.

Faithfully yours,

T. V. SOONG

28 (gg)

Acting Secretary of State Grew to Secretary of the Treasury Morgenthau

WASHINGTON, *May 16, 1945*

MY DEAR MR. SECRETARY: The Department has given careful attention to the request of the Chinese Foreign Minister, Dr. T. V. Soong, for the delivery during the remainder of 1945 of about $190,000,000 of gold from the unused balance of the $500,000,000 credit approved by the Congress in January 1942.

It is the Department's view, which it understands is shared by the Treasury, that the sale of gold by China has not proved and is not likely to prove a very effective anti-inflationary device. Moreover, it believes that the establishment of a $500,000,000 fund for combating inflation and stabilizing the Chinese currency which you proposed last week to Dr. Soong would, if adopted by the Chinese Government, be of considerable short and long run benefit to China.

The Chinese Government believes, however, that the immediate political and psychological as well as real economic effects of a continued and accelerated gold sale policy will have a vital importance in the critical situation confronting it, and strongly requests the delivery of the gold in question in accordance with the terms of the understanding between the two governments of July 1943. Since there appears to be no doubt that the Chinese Government attaches a greater importance to the immediate delivery of the gold than to the longer run benefits which might result from the establishment of the fund which you have proposed and since the continued stability of China and her increasing military efforts in the war against the common enemy are of great concern to the United States, the Department recommends that the Treasury, if transportation is available, deliver the gold to China in accordance with the time schedules put forward by Dr. Soong.

Sincerely yours,

JOSEPH C. GREW

28 (hh)

Secretary of the Treasury Morgenthau to the Chinese Minister for Foreign Affairs (Soong)

WASHINGTON, *May 16, 1945*

DEAR MR. SOONG: This is to confirm what I told you today. In accordance with your memorandum of May 11, the Treasury is prepared to authorize the shipment of the balance of the $20 million of gold which is on earmark with the Federal Reserve Bank of New York for the Central Bank of China and to transfer the balance of $180 million to the account of the Central Bank of China with the Federal Reserve Bank of New York, in three equal monthly installments of $60 million from May to July 1945. The Treasury accepts the schedule of gold shipments contained in your memorandum of May 11, 1945 and is making arrangements with the Army to carry out the shipments of the gold according to that schedule. The preliminary arrangements to ship the requested amount for the month of May have already been made. These steps are being taken in accordance with our Financial Aid Agreement of March 1942 and my letter to Dr. Kung of July 27, 1943.

At this time it seems to me necessary and desirable to point out that the purpose of the $500 million of financial aid to China, and particularly my agreement in July 1943 to ship gold to China, was to assist in an anti-inflationary program which would strengthen confidence in the Chinese Government and its finances and thereby help maintain the Chinese economy. As you know, it is my opinion that the sale of gold by China has not proved effective in combating inflation, and I am doubtful that it will prove effective. Also as I have told you, the manner in which the gold sales have been conducted and the consequent public criticism of them in China are not conducive to achieving the purposes for which our financial aid was granted.

Therefore, I would respectfully ask the Chinese Government to consider carefully the matters proposed to you in my memorandum of May 8, 1945. In particular I would reiterate my suggestion that China constitute a $500 million fund for combating inflation and stabilizing the currency from its foreign exchange assets. I think that this step would be of considerable short and long-run benefit to China and would inspire confidence in the Chinese Government's handling of its difficult economic situation.

The Treasury has noted with great interest the intention of the Chinese Government, as stated in your memorandum to the Secretary of State, to effectuate reforms relating to financial and economic matters. We think that the carrying out of these reforms will do more to insure confidence among the people and give a measure of stability to the present economic and financial situation than the gold program.

I know that you and your Government will take these friendly suggestions in the spirit in which they are offered. As I told you, we intend to carry out faithfully our financial agreement of 1942. However, the Chinese Government's response to our proposal to institute a $500 million fund and her conduct of the gold sales program will be important considerations in our financial relations with China.

This Government has as prime objectives the defeat of Japan and the liberation of China. As an old friend of China, I believe that our faith and confidence in China will be justified.

Very truly yours,

H. MORGENTHAU, Jr.

28 (ii)

Information Requested in Connection with the Uses of the 1942 $500 Million China Aid Credit [41]

I. U. S. dollar allocations of the $500 million aid by purpose and amount.
    A. Redemption of U. S. dollar securities issued in China in 1942.
        1. Types of securities issued, maturity, rate of interest, exchange rate at which sold and at which redeemed, whether or not negotiable, and the pertinent regulations, if any, concerning their use as collateral from 1942 to date.
        2. Breakdown with respect to each type of security issued of:
            a. The U.S. dollar value of sales to date.
            b. The U.S. dollar face value of the securities redeemed to date.

---

[41] Enclosure in a letter from J. Burke Knapp, Director, Office of Financial and Development Policy, Department of State, to Dr. Shao-Hwa Tan, Minister, Chinese Embassy at Washington, June 9, 1948. To date, the information requested has not been received.

  c. The actual amount of U.S. dollars paid out for the redemption of securities by months and the total to date.

  e [d]. The actual amount of U.S. dollars paid out in interest on the securities by months and the total to date.

  f [e]. The amount of U.S. dollars the Chinese Government expects to pay out in interest and principal in the future on outstanding securities.

  g [f]. The U.S. dollar value of purchases of securities by foreigners from the Central Bank of China and from other banks authorized to market the securities.

 3. Breakdown with respect to each type of security of:

  a. The U.S. dollar value of sales to government and semi-government institutions by months and the total to date.

  b. The actual amount of U.S. dollars paid out to government and semi-government institutions for the redemption of securities owned by these institutions.

B. Sales of gold purchased by the Chinese Government out of the $500 million financial aid.

 1. Breakdown of the amount of gold sold in the form of spot gold, forward gold, and gold certificates by months and the total to date, with prices at which sold.

 2. The amount of gold delivered to purchasers by months and the total to date, with details of the proceeds of the tax in gold and Chinese currency and of the impact on deliveries of gold to purchasers of the 40 percent tax on undelivered gold imposed in July 1945.

 3. Breakdown of the amount of gold sold in the form of spot gold, forward gold, and gold certificates to government and semigovernment institutions and the amount delivered by months and the total to date.

 4. Regulations, if any, concerning the status of gold as collateral from 1943 to date.

C. Breakdown of all other dollar expenditures by the Chinese Government out of the $500 million financial aid by purpose, by amount and by months and total to date.

II. Chinese currency proceeds of the sales of U. S. dollar securities, gold, and other assets procured from the 1942 financial aid.

A. Amount of Chinese currency receipts.

 1. Breakdown of amount of Chinese currency receipts by source (U.S. securities, gold, etc.), by months and by fiscal years and the total to date.

 2. Percentage of total government revenue constituted by Chinese currency receipts of sales of U.S. securities, gold, etc. by months and fiscal years to date.

B. Uses of Chinese currency receipts.

 1. Amounts of government expenditures financed by these Chinese currency receipts by months and the total to date.

 2. Percentage of total government expenditures constituted by B. 1 by months and fiscal years to date.

C. Amounts of Chinese currency, if any, paid out for interest on and for the redemption of U. S. dollar securities.

29(a)

President Roosevelt to Generalissimo Chiang Kai-shek, February 7, 1942 [42]

It is a source of great gratification to me and to the Government and people of the United States that the proposal which I made to the Congress that there be authorized for the purpose of rendering financial aid to China in the sum of $500,000,000 was passed unanimously by both the Senate and the House of Representatives and has now become law.

The unusual speed and unanimity with which this measure was acted upon by the Congress and the enthusiastic support which it received throughout the United States testify to the wholehearted respect and admiration which the Government and people of this country have for China. They testify also to our earnest desire and determination to be concretely helpful to our partners in the great battle for freedom. The gallant resistance of the Chinese armies against the ruthless invaders of your country has called forth the highest praise from the American and all other freedom loving peoples. The tenacity of the Chinese people, both armed and unarmed, in the face of tremendous odds in carrying on for almost five years a resolute defense against an enemy far superior in equipment is an inspiration to the fighting men and all the peoples of the other United Nations. The great sacrifices of the Chinese people in destroying the fruits of their toil so that they could not be used by the predatory armies of Japan exemplify in high degree the spirit of sacrifice which is necessary on the part of all to gain the victory toward which we are confidently striving. It is my hope and belief that use which will be made of the funds now authorized by the Congress of the United States will contribute substantially toward facilitating the efforts of the Chinese Government and people to meet the economic and financial burdens which have been thrust upon them by an armed invasion and toward solution of problems of production and procurement which are essential for the success of their armed resistance to what are now our common enemies.

I send you my personal greetings and best wishes. I extend to you across land and sea the hand of comradeship for the common good, the common goal, the common victory that shall be ours.

29 (b)

Joint Statement by Secretary of the Treasury Morgenthau and Dr. T. V. Soong, Chinese Minister for Foreign Affairs, March 21, 1942

The United States and China have today entered into an Agreement giving effect to the Act of Congress unanimously passed by the Senate and House of Representatives authorizing $500,000,000 of financial aid to China. The Agreement, approved by the President and by Generalissimo Chiang Kai-shek, was signed by Secretary Morgenthau on behalf of the United States and by Dr. Soong on behalf of China.

This financial aid will contribute substantially towards facilitating the great efforts of the Chinese people and their government to meet the financial and

[42] *Department of State Bulletin,* Feb. 7, 1942, p. 142.

economic burdens which have been imposed upon them by almost five years of continuous attack by Japan.

This Agreement is a concrete manifestation of the desire and determination of the United States, without stint, to aid China in our common battle for freedom.

The final determination of the terms upon which this $500,000,000 financial aid is given to China, including the benefits to be rendered the United States in return, is deferred until the progress of events after the war makes clearer the final terms and benefits which will be in the mutual interest of the United States and China and will promote the establishment of lasting world peace and security.

The text of the Agreement is as follows:

"WHEREAS, The Governments of the United States of America and of the Republic of China are engaged, together with other nations and peoples of like mind, in a cooperative undertaking against common enemies, to the end of laying the bases of a just and enduring world peace securing order under law to themselves and all nations, and

"WHEREAS, The United States and China are signatories to the Declaration of United Nations of January 1, 1942, which declares that 'Each government pledges itself to employ its full resources, military or economic, against those members of the Tripartite Pact and its adherents with which such government is at war'; and

"WHEREAS, the Congress of the United States, in unanimously passing Public Law No. 442, approved February 7, 1942, has declared that financial and economic aid to China will increase China's ability to oppose the forces of aggression and that the defense of China is of the greatest possible importance, and has authorized the Secretary of the Treasury of the United States, with the approval of the President, to give financial aid to China, and

"WHEREAS, such financial aid will enable China to strengthen greatly its war efforts against the common enemies by helping China to

"(1) strengthen its currency, monetary, banking and economic system:

"(2) finance and promote increased production, acquisition and distribution of necessary goods;

"(3) retard the rise of prices, promote stability of economic relationships, and otherwise check inflation;

"(4) prevent hoarding of foods and other materials;

"(5) improve means of transportation and communication;

"(6) effect further social and economic measures which promote the welfare of the Chinese people; and

"(7) meet military needs other than those supplied under the Lend-Lease Act and take other appropriate measures in its war effort.

"In order to achieve these purposes, the undersigned, being duly authorized by their respective Governments for that purpose, have agreed as follows:

ARTICLE I.

"The Secretary of the Treasury of the United States agrees to establish forthwith on the books of the United States Treasury a credit in the name of the Government of the Republic of China in the amount of 500,000,000 U. S. dollars. The Secretary of the Treasury shall make transfers from this credit, in such amounts and at such times as the Government of the Republic of China shall request, through the Minister of Finance, to an account or accounts in the Federal Reserve Bank of New York in the name of the Government of the Republic of China or any agencies designated by the Minister of Finance. Such transfers may be requested by and such accounts at the Federal Reserve Bank of New York may be drawn upon by the Government of the Republic of China either directly or through such persons or agencies as the Minister of Finance shall authorize.

ARTICLE II.

"The fiinal determination of the terms upon which this financial aid is given, including the benefits to be rendered the United States in return, is deferred by the two contracting parties until the progress of events after the war makes clearer the final terms and benefits which will be in the mutual interest of the United States and China and will promote the establishment of lasting world peace and security. In determining the final terms and benefits full cognizance shall be given to the desirability of maintaining a healthy and stable economic and financial situation in China in the post-war period as well as during the war and to the desirability of promoting mutually advantageous economic and financial relations between the United States and China and the betterment of world-wide economic and financial relations.

ARTICLE III.

"This Agreement shall take effect as from this day's date.

"Signed and sealed at Washington, District of Columbia, in duplicate this 21st day of March, 1942.

"On behalf of the United States of America
HENRY MORGENTHAU, Jr.
Secretary of the Treasury

"On behalf of the Republic of China
T. V. SOONG
Minister for Foreign Affairs."

30

Statement by Acting Secretary Welles, July 19, 1940 [43]

In response to inquiries from press correspondents with regard to the British Prime Minister's comments upon the question of extraterritoriality in China included in his statement of July 18, the Acting Secretary of State, Mr. Sumner Welles, commented as follows:

"The most recent statement of this Government on this subject is contained in a note presented on December 31, 1938, to the Japanese Government, which mentions *inter alia* the progress made toward the relinquishment of certain rights of a special character which the United States together with other countries has long possessed in China. In 1931 discussions of the subject between China and each of several other countries, including the United States, were suspended because of the occurrence of the Mukden incident and subsequent disrupting developments in 1932 and 1935 in the relations between China and Japan. In 1937 this Government was giving renewed favorable consideration to the question when there broke out the current Sino-Japanese hostilities, as a result of which the usual processes of government in large areas of China were widely disrupted.

"It has been this Government's traditional and declared policy and desire to move rapidly by process of orderly negotiation and agreement with the Chinese Government, whenever conditions warrant, toward the relinquishment of extra-

---

[43] *Foreign Relations of the United States, Japan,* 1931–1941, vol. I, p. 927.

territorial rights and of all other so-called 'special rights' possessed by this country as by other countries in China by virtue of international agreements. That policy remains unchanged."

31

Secretary Hull to the Appointed Chinese Minister for Foreign Affairs (Quo Tai-chi) [44]

WASHINGTON, *May 31, 1941.*

MY DEAR MR. MINISTER: I acknowledge the receipt of and thank you for your letter of May 26, 1941 in regard to your visit to Washington and to our conversations during your short sojourn here.

We greatly enjoyed your visit.

It is very gratifying to receive in your letter reaffirmation of the endorsement by the Chinese Government and people of the general and fundamental principles which this Government is convinced constitute the only practical foundation for an international order wherein independent nations may cooperate freely with each other to their mutual benefit.

As you know, the program in which the Government and people of the United States put their trust is based upon and revolves about the principle of equality of treatment among nations. This principle comprehends equality in international relations in a juridical sense, nondiscrimination and equality of opportunity in commercial relations, and reciprocal interchange in the field of cultural developments. Implicit in this principle is respect by each nation for the rights of other nations, performance by each nation of established obligations, alteration of agreements between nations by processes not of force but of orderly and free negotiation, and fair dealing in international economic relations essential to peaceful development of national life and the mutually profitable growth of international trade. One of the purposes of this program is to effect the removal of economic and other maladjustments which tend to lead to political conflicts.

As you are also aware, the Government and people of the United States have long had a profound interest in the welfare and progress of China. It goes without saying that the Government of the United States, in continuation of steps already taken toward meeting China's aspirations for readjustment of anomalies in its international relations, expects when conditions of peace again prevail to move rapidly, by processes of orderly negotiation and agreement with the Chinese Government, toward relinquishment of the last of certain rights of a special character which this country, together with other countries, has long possessed in China by virtue of agreements providing for extraterritorial jurisdiction and related practices.

This Government welcomes and encourages every advance made by lawful and orderly processes by any country toward conditions of peace, security, stability, justice and general welfare. The assurances given in Your Excellency's letter under acknowledgment of China's support of the principle of equality of treatment and nondiscrimination in economic relations should have wholesome effect both during the present period of world conflict and when hostilities shall have ceased.

The Government of the United States is dedicated to support of the principles in which the people of this country believe. Without reservation, we are con-

---

[44] *Ibid.*, p. 929.

fident that the cause to which we are committed along with China and other countries—the cause of national security, of fair dealing among nations and of peace with justice—will prevail.

With kindest regards [etc.]

Sincerely yours,   CORDELL HULL

32

Treaty Between the United States and China for the Relinquishment of Extraterritorial Rights in China and the Regulation of Related Matters, Signed at Washington, January 11, 1943, With Accompanying Exchange of Notes [45]

The United States of America and the Republic of China, desirous of emphasizing the friendly relations which have long prevailed between their two peoples and of manifesting their common desire as equal and sovereign States that the high principles in the regulation of human affairs to which they are committed shall be made broadly effective, have resolved to conclude a treaty for the purpose of adjusting certain matters in the relations of the two countries, and have appointed as their Plenipotentiaries:

The President of the United States of America,

Mr. Cordell Hull, Secretary of State of the United States of America, and

The President of the National Government of the Republic of China,

Dr. Wei Tao-ming, Ambassador Extraordinary and Plenipotentiary of the Republic of China to the United States of America;

Who, having communicated to each other their full powers found to be in due form, have agreed upon the following articles:

ARTICLE I

All those provisions of treaties or agreements in force between the United States of America and the Republic of China which authorize the Government of the United States of America or its representatives to exercise jurisdiction over nationals of the United States of America in the territory of the Republic of China are hereby abrogated. Nationals of the United States of America in such territory shall be subject to the jurisdiction of the Government of the Republic of China in accordance with the principles of international law and practice.

ARTICLE II

The Government of the United States of America considers that the Final Protocol concluded at Peking on September 7, 1901, between the Chinese Government and other governments, including the Government of the United States of America, should be terminated and agrees that the rights accorded to the Government of the United States of America under that Protocol and under agreements supplementary thereto shall cease.

The Government of the United States of America will cooperate with the Government of the Republic of China for the reaching of any necessary agreements with other governments concerned for the transfer to the Government of the Republic of China of the administration and control of the Diplomatic Quarter at Peiping, including the official assets and the official obligations of the Diplomatic Quarter, it being mutually understood that the Government of the Repub-

_____

[45] 57 Stat. 767.

lic of China in taking over administration and control of the Diplomatic Quarter will make provision for the assumption and discharge of the official obligations and liabilities of the Diplomatic Quarter and for the recognition and protection of all legitimate rights therein.

The Government of the Republic of China hereby accords to the Government of the United States of America a continued right to use for official purposes the land which has been allocated to the Government of the United States of America in the Diplomatic Quarter in Peiping, on parts of which are located buildings belonging to the Government of the United States of America.

ARTICLE III

The Government of the United States of America considers that the International Settlements at Shanghai and Amoy should revert to the administration and control of the Government of the Republic of China and agrees that the rights accorded to the Government of the United States of America in relation to those Settlements shall cease.

The Government of the United States of America will cooperate with the Government of the Republic of China for the reaching of any necessary agreements with other governments concerned for the transfer to the Government of the Republic of China of the administration and control of the International Settlements at Shanghai and Amoy, including the official assets and the official obligations of those Settlements, it being mutually understood that the Government of the Republic of China in taking over administration and control of those Settlements will make provision for the assumption and discharge of the official obligations and liabilities of those Settlements and for the recognition and protection of all legitimate rights therein.

ARTICLE IV

In order to obviate any questions as to existing rights in respect of or as to existing titles to real property in territory of the Republic of China possessed by nationals (including corporations or associations), or by the Government, of the United States of America, particularly questions which might arise from the abrogation of the provisions of treaties or agreements as stipulated in Article I, it is agreed that such existing rights or titles shall be indefeasible and shall not be questioned upon any ground except upon proof, established through due process of law, of fraud or of fraudulent or other dishonest practices in the acquisition of such rights or titles, it being understood that no right or title shall be rendered invalid by virtue of any subsequent change in the official procedure through which it was acquired. It is also agreed that these rights or titles shall be subject to the laws and regulations of the Republic of China concerning taxation, national defense, and the right of eminent domain, and that no such rights or titles may be alienated to the government or nationals (including corporations or associations) of any third country without the express consent of the Government of the Republic of China.

It is also agreed that if it should be the desire of the Government of the Republic of China to replace, by new deeds of ownership, existing leases in perpetuity or other documentary evidence relating to real property held by nationals, or by the Government, of the United States of America, the replacement shall be made by the Chinese authorities without charges of any sort and the new deeds of ownership shall fully protect the holders of such leases or other documentary evidence and their legal heirs and assigns without diminution of their prior rights and interests, including the right of alienation.

It is further agreed that nationals or the Government of the United States of America shall not be required or asked by the Chinese authorities to make any payments of fees in connection with land transfers for or with relation to any period prior to the effective date of this treaty.

ARTICLE V

The Government of the United States of America having long accorded rights to nationals of the Republic of China within the territory of the United States of America to travel, reside and carry on trade throughout the whole extent of that territory, the Government of the Republic of China agrees to accord similar rights to nationals of the United States of America within the territory of the Republic of China. Each of the two Governments will endeavor to have accorded in territory under its jurisdiction to nationals of the other country, in regard to all legal proceedings, and to matters relating to the administration of justice, and to the levying of taxes or requirements in connection therewith, treatment not less favorable than that accorded to its own nationals.

ARTICLE VI

The Government of the United States of America and the Government of the Republic of China mutually agree that the consular officers of each country, duly provided with exequaturs, shall be permitted to reside in such ports, places and cities as may be agreed upon. The consular officers of each country shall have the right to interview, to communicate with, and to advise nationals of their country within their consular districts; they shall be informed immediately whenever nationals of their country are under detention or arrest or in prison or are awaiting trial in their consular districts and they shall, upon notification to the appropriate authorities, be permitted to visit any such nationals; and, in general, the consular officers of each country shall be accorded the rights, privileges, and immunities enjoyed by consular officers under modern international usage.

It is likewise agreed that the nationals of each country, in the territory of the other country, shall have the right at all times to communicate with the consular officers of their country. Communications to their consular officers from nationals of each country who are under detention or arrest or in prison or are awaiting trial in the territory of the other country shall be forwarded to such consular officers by the local authorities.

ARTICLE VII

The Government of the United States of America and the Government of the Republic of China mutually agree that they will enter into negotiations for the conclusion of a comprehensive modern treaty of friendship, commerce, navigation and consular rights, upon the request of either Government or in any case within six months after the cessation of the hostilities in the war against the common enemies in which they are now engaged. The treaty to be thus negotiated will be based upon the principles of international law and practice as reflected in modern international procedures and in the modern treaties which the Government of the United States of America and the Government of the Republic of China respectively have in recent years concluded with other governments.

Pending the conclusion of a comprehensive treaty of the character referred to in the preceding paragraph, if any questions affecting the rights in territory of the Republic of China of nationals (including corporations or associations), or of the Government, of the United States of America should arise in future and if these questions are not covered by the present treaty, or by the provisions of existing treaties, conventions, or agreements between the Government of the United States of America and the Government of the Republic of China not abrogated by or inconsistent with this treaty, such questions shall be discussed by ᴙepresentatives of the two Governments and shall be decided in accordance with generally accepted principles of international law and with modern international practice.

ARTICLE VIII

The present treaty shall come into force on the day of the exchange of ratifications.

The present treaty shall be ratified, and the ratifications shall be exchanged at Washington as soon as possible.

Signed and sealed in the English and Chinese languages, both equally authentic, in duplicate, at Washington, this eleventh day of January, one thousand nine hundred forty-three, corresponding to the eleventh day of the first month of the thirty-second year of the Republic of China.

CORDELL HULL
WEI TAO-MING

Secretary Hull to the Chinese Ambassador (Wei Tao-ming)

WASHINGTON, *January 11, 1943.*

EXCELLENCY:

In connection with the treaty signed today between the Government of the United States of America and the Government of the Republic of China in which the Government of the United States of America relinquishes its extraterritorial and related special rights in China, I have the honor to acknowledge the receipt of your note of today's date reading as follows:

"Excellency: Under instruction of my Government, I have the honor to state that in connection with the treaty signed today by the Government of the Republic of China and the Government of the United States of America, in which the Government of the United States of America relinquishes its extraterritorial and related special rights in China, it is the understanding of the Government of the Republic of China that the rights of the Government of the United States of America and of its nationals in regard to the systems of treaty ports and of special courts in the International Settlements at Shanghai and Amoy and in regard to the employment of foreign pilots in the ports of the territory of China are also relinquished. In the light of the abolition of treaty ports as such, it is understood that all coastal ports in the territory of the Republic of China which are normally open to American overseas merchant shipping will remain open to such shipping after the coming into effect of the present treaty and the accompanying exchange of notes.

It is mutually agreed that the merchant vessels of each country shall be permitted freely to come to the ports, places, and waters of the other country which are or may be open to overseas merchant shipping, and that the treatment accorded to such vessels in such ports, places, and waters shall be no less favorable than that accorded to national vessels and shall be as favorable as that accorded to the vessels of any third country.

It is mutually understood that the Government of the United States of America relinquishes the special rights which vessels of the United States of America have been accorded with regard to the coasting trade and inland navigation in the waters of the Republic of China and that the Government of the Republic of China is prepared to take over any American properties that may have been engaged for those purposes and to pay adequate compensation therefor. Should either country accord the rights of inland navigation or coasting trade to vessels of any third country such rights would similarly be accorded to the vessels of the other country. The coasting trade and inland navigation of each country are excepted from the requirement of national treatment and are to be regulated according to the laws of each country in relation thereto. It is agreed, however, that vessels of either country shall enjoy within the territory of the other country with respect to the coasting trade and inland navigation treatment as favorable as that accorded to the vessels of any third country.

It is mutually understood that the Government of the United States of America relinquishes the special rights which naval vessels of the United States of America have been accorded in the waters of the Republic of China and that the Government of the Republic of China and the Government of the United States of America shall extend to each other the mutual courtesy of visits by their warships in accordance with international usage and comity.

It is mutually understood that questions which are not covered by the present treaty and exchange of notes and which may affect the sovereignty of the Republic of China shall be discussed by representatives of the two Governments and shall be decided in accordance with generally accepted principles of international law and with modern international practice.

With reference to Article IV of the treaty, the Government of the Republic of China hereby declares that the restriction on the right of alienation of existing rights or titles to real property referred to in that article will be applied by the Chinese authorities in an equitable manner and that if and when the Chinese Government declines to give assent to a proposed transfer the Chinese Government will, in a spirit of justice and with a view to precluding loss on the part of American nationals whose interests are affected, undertake, if the American party in interest so desires, to take over the right or title in question and to pay adequate compensation therefor.

It is mutually understood that the orders, decrees, judgments, decisions and other acts of the United States Court for China and of the Consular Courts of the United States of America in China shall be considered as *res judicata* and shall, when necessary, be enforced by the Chinese authorities. It is further understood that any cases pending before the United States Court for China and the Consular Courts of the United States of America in China at the time of the coming into effect of this treaty shall, if the plaintiff or petitioner so desires, be remitted to the appropriate courts of the Government of the Republic of China which shall proceed as expeditiously as possible with their disposition and in so doing shall in so far as practicable apply the laws of the United States of America.

It is understood that these agreements and understandings if confirmed by Your Excellency's Government shall be considered as forming an integral part of the treaty signed today and shall be considered as effective upon the date of the entrance into force of that treaty.

I shall be much obliged if Your Excellency will confirm the foregoing.

I avail myself of this opportunity to renew to Your Excellency the assurances of my highest consideration."

I have the honor to confirm that the agreements and understandings which have been reached in connection with the treaty signed today by the Government of the United States of America and the Government of the Republic of China are as set forth in the above note from Your Excellency.

I avail myself [etc.]   CORDELL HULL

33

Statement on Conference of President Roosevelt, Generalissimo Chiang Kai-shek, and Prime Minister Churchill, Cairo, December 1, 1943 [46]

The several military missions have agreed upon future military operations against Japan. The Three Great Allies expressed their resolve to bring unrelenting pressure against their brutal enemies by sea, land, and air. This pressure is already rising.

The Three Great Allies are fighting this war to restrain and punish the aggression of Japan. They covet no gain for themselves and have no thought of territorial expansion. It is their purpose that Japan shall be stripped of all the islands in the Pacific which she has seized or occupied since the beginning of the first World War in 1914, and that all the territories Japan has stolen from the Chinese, such as Manchuria, Formosa, and the Pescadores, shall be restored to the Republic of China. Japan will also be expelled from all other territories which she has taken by violence and greed. The aforesaid three great powers, mindful of the enslavement of the people of Korea, are determined that in due course Korea shall become free and independent.

With these objects in view the three Allies, in harmony with those of the United Nations at war with Japan, will continue to persevere in the serious and prolonged operations necessary to procure the unconditional surrender of Japan.

---

[46] *Department of State Bulletin,* Dec. 4, 1943, p. 393.

Annexes to Chapter II: A Review of Kuomintang–Chinese Communist Relations, 1921–1944

34

"*Telegram to the Nation*" (*Manifesto on the Seizure of Chiang Kai-shek*) *December 12, 1936* [1]

Ever since the loss of the North-Eastern Provinces five years ago, our national sovereignty has been steadily weakened, and our territory has dwindled day by day. We suffered national humiliation at the time of the Shanghai Truce, and again with the Tangku Truce and the Ho-Umetsu Agreement. There is not a single citizen who does not feel sick at heart because of this.

Recently there have been startling changes in the international situation. Certain Powers are intriguing with one another, and using our nation and our people as a sacrifice. When hostilities began in East Suiyuan, popular resentment reached its height, and our soldiers everywhere were very indignant.

At this juncture, our Central Leader ought to encourage both military and civilians to organize the whole people in a united war of national defence. But while those soldiers at the front endure death and bloodshed in the defence of our national territories, the diplomatic authorities are still seeking compromises.

Ever since the unjust imprisonment of the patriotic leaders in Shanghai, the whole world has been startled; the whole of our people has been filled with anger and distress. To love one's country is an offence! This is a terrifying prospect.

Generalissimo Chiang Kai-shek, surrounded by a group of unworthy advisers, has forfeited the support of the masses of our people. He is deeply guilty for the harm his policies have done the country. We, Chang Hsueh-liang and the others undersigned, advised him with tears to take another way; but we were repeatedly rejected and rebuked.

Not long ago, the students in Sian were demonstrating in their National Salvation movement, and General Chiang set the police to killing these patriotic children. How could anyone with a human conscience bear to do this? We his colleagues of many years' standing, could not bear to sit still and witness it.

Therefore we have tendered our last advice to Marshal Chiang, while guaranteeing his safety, in order to stimulate his awakening.

The Military and Civilians in the North-West unanimously make the following demands:

1. Reorganize the Nanking Government, and admit all parties to share the joint responsibility of saving the nation.

2. Stop all kinds of civil wars.

---

[1] James Bertram, *First Act in China; the Story of the Sian Mutiny* (New York, The Viking Press, 1938), pp. 126–127.

3. Immediately release the patriotic leaders arrested in Shanghai.

4. Release all political prisoners throughout the country.

5. Emancipate the patriotic movement of the people.

6. Safeguard the political freedom of the people to organize and call meetings.

7. Actually carry out the Will of Dr. Sun Yat-sen.

8. Immediately call a National Salvation Conference.

The eight items above are the points of National Salvation unanimously maintained by us and by all the Military and Civilians throughout the North-West.

We, therefore, hope that you gentlemen will stoop to meet public sentiment and sincerely adopt these demands, so as to open one line of life for the future, and remedy past mistakes that have been the ruin of the country. The great cause is before us: it does not permit glancing backward. We hope to carry out the policies here maintained only for the liberation and benefit of the country. As to our merit or guilt, we leave this to the judgment of our fellow-countrymen.

In sending this telegram, we urgently await your order.

SIANFU, *December 12, 1936.*

35

The Central Committee of the Chinese Communist Party to the Third Plenary Session of the Fifth Central Executive Committee of the Kuomintang, February 10, 1937

[On February 10, 1937 (five days before the Session's opening) the Central Committee of the Chinese Communist Party addressed a telegram to the Third Plenary Session of the Fifth Central Executive Committee of the Kuomintang in which it agreed to make the following alteration in the policies which have characterized the activities of the Communist Party in China:]

"(1) to stop our program of conducting armed uprisings throughout the country for the overthrow of the National Government in Nanking; (2) to change the Soviet Government into the Government of the Special Region of the Republic of China and the Red Army into the National Revolutionary Army under the direct leadership of the Central Government and the Military Affairs Commission in Nanking; (3) to enforce the thorough democratic system of universal suffrage within the special regions under the regime of the Government of the Special Region; and (4) to put an end to the policy of expropriating the land of landlords and to execute persistently the common program of the anti-Japanese united front."

[The telegram then recommended the following five-point program:]

"(1) suspension of civil wars of all sorts and concentration of all the national strength for unanimous resistance to external aggression; (2) freedom of speech, assembly, organization, etc. and release of all political prisoners; (3) convocation of a congress of various parties, factions, military groups and organizations in order to concentrate capable leaders of the country as a whole for the joint salvation of the country; (4) immediate accomplishment of the preparatory work for a war of resistance against Japan; and (5) amelioration of the living conditions of the people at large."

36

Manifesto on Unity by the Central Committee of the Chinese Communist Party, September 22, 1937 [2]

Beloved Compatriots—The Central Executive Committee of the Communist Party of China respectfully and sincerely issues the following Manifesto to all fathers, brothers and sisters throughout the country or:

At the present juncture when the country is facing extreme danger and the fate of the nation is in the balance, in order to save the country from extinction, we have, on the basis of peace and national unity and joint resistance against foreign aggression, reached an understanding with the Kuomintang of China, and are determined to participate in the concerted effort for overcoming the national emergency. This has a profound significance on the future of the great Chinese nation. For we all know that, when the national existence is endangered, only through internal unity can the aggression of imperialistic Japan be overcome. The foundation of national solidarity is now already laid, and the campaign of national emancipation launched. The Central Executive Committee of the Communist Party of China congratulates itself on the brilliant future of the nation. However, in order to transform this future into the realization of a New China, independent, free and happy, all descendants of Huangti (the first Chinese Emperor) must patiently and unceasingly participate in the concerted struggle.

The Central Executive Committee of the Communist Party of China avails itself of this opportunity to propose the following general objectives for the common struggle of the entire people or:

(1) Struggle for the independence, liberty and emancipation of the Chinese nation by promptly and swiftly preparing and launching the national revolutionary campaign of resistance with a view to recovering the lost territories and restoring the integrity of territorial sovereign rights.

(2) Enforce democracy based on the people's rights and convoke the National People's Congress in order to enact the Constitution and decide upon the plans of national salvation.

(3) Improve the well-being and enrich the livelihood of the Chinese people by relieving famines and other calamities, stabilizing the people's livelihood, consolidating national defense and economy, removing the sufferings of the people and bettering their living conditions.

These are the urgent requirements of China, for which the struggle is aimed. We believe that they will receive the whole-hearted support of the entire people. The Communist Party of China is ready to co-operate fully with their compatriots for the attainment of these objectives.

The Communist Party of China fully realizes that this programme is likely to meet with numerous difficulties. The first obstacle will come from Japanese Imperialism. In order to deprive the enemy of all pretext for aggression and dispel doubts on the part of friends, the Central Executive Committee of the Communist Party of China solemnly declares the following in connection with national emancipation:

[2] Lawrence K. Rosinger, *China's Wartime Politics, 1937–1944* (Princeton, Princeton University Press, 1944), pp. 96–97.

(1) The San Min Chu-I (Three People's Principles) enunciated by Dr. Sun Yat-sen is the paramount need of China to-day. This Party is ready to strive for its enforcement.

(2) This Party abandons its policy of overthrowing the Kuomintang of China by force and the movement of sovietization and discontinues its policy of forcible confiscation of land from landowners.

(3) This Party abolishes the present Soviet Government and will enforce democracy based on the people's rights in order to unify the national political machinery.

(4) This Party abolishes the Red Army, reorganizes it into the National Revolutionary Army, places it under the direct control of the Military Affairs Commission of the National Government, and awaits orders for mobilization to share the responsibility of resisting foreign invasion at the front.

Beloved compatriots, the sincerity, honesty and faithfulness of the attitude of this Party have already been manifested before the entire people in both words and action, and have received the approval of the people. In order to secure closer unity with the Kuomintang of China, consolidate national peace and unity, and carry out this sacred revolutionary war, we have decided immediately to translate into action those parts of our words which have not yet been enforced, such as the abolition and reorganization of the Red Army in the Soviet Area, in order to facilitate unified command for resisting the enemy.

The enemy have penetrated into our country; the moment is critical. Compatriots, let our 400 million people rise and unite. Our nation, with its long history, cannot be conquered. Rise and struggle for the consolidation of national unity and overthrow of Japanese oppression. Victory will be ours. Long live the victory for resisting Japan. Long live the independence, liberty and welfare of new China.

37

Statement by Generalissimo Chiang Kai-shek on Kuomintang-Communist Unity, September 23, 1937 [3]

The aim of the Nationalist Revolution is to seek freedom and equality for China. Dr. Sun Yat-sen said that the San Min Chu I are fundamental principles of national salvation. He earnestly hoped that all our people would strive with one heart to save the state from its perils. Unfortunately, during the past ten years not all of our countrymen have had a sincere and unwavering faith in the Three Principles of the People, nor have they fully realized the magnitude of the crisis confronting our country. The course of the Revolution in its efforts at national reconstruction has been blocked by many obstacles. The result has been waste in our national resources, widespread suffering among the people, increasing humiliations from outside, and growing dangers to the state.

During the past few years the National Government has been calling ceaselessly upon the nation to achieve genuine internal solidarity, and to face unitedly the national crisis. Those who have in the past doubted the Three Principles of the People have now realized the paramount importance of our national interests, and have buried their differences for the sake of internal unity. The

---

[3] Chiang Kai-shek, *Resistance and Reconstruction; Messages During China's Six Years of War, 1937–1943* (New York and London, Harper & Brothers, 1943), pp. 20–21. In this volume the date is erroneously given as Sept. 24, 1937. (*The Chinese Year Book, 1938–1939*, p. 340.)

Chinese people today fully realize that they must survive together or perish together, and that the interests of the nation must take precedence over the interests of individuals or groups.

The Manifesto recently issued by the Chinese Communist Party is an outstanding instance of the triumph of national sentiment over every other consideration. The various decisions embodied in the Manifesto, such as the abandonment of a policy of violence, the cessation of Communist propaganda, the abolition of the Chinese Soviet Government, and the disbandment of the Red Army are all essential conditions for mobilizing our national strength in order that we may meet the menace from without and guarantee our own national existence.

These decisions agree with the spirit of the Manifesto and resolutions adopted by the Third Plenary Session of the Kuomintang. The Communist Party's Manifesto declares that the Chinese Communists are willing to strive to carry out the Three Principles. This is ample proof that China today has only one objective in its war efforts.

In our revolution we are struggling not for personal ambitions or opinions, but for the realization of the Three Principles of the People. Especially during this period of national crisis, when the fate of China lies in the balance, we ought not to argue over the past, but should try as a nation to make a new start. We should earnestly strive to unite, so that as a united nation we may safeguard the continued existence of the Republic.

If a citizen believes in the Three Principles and works actively for the salvation of the state, the Government should not concern itself with his past, but should give him opportunity to prove his loyalty in service to the Republic. Likewise, the Government will gladly accept the services of any political organization provided it is sincerely working for the nation's salvation, and is willing under the banner of our national revolution to join with us in our struggle against aggression.

The Chinese Communist Party, by surrendering its prejudices, has clearly recognized the vital importance of our national independence and welfare. I sincerely hope that all members of the Communist Party will faithfully and unitedly put into practice the various decisions reached, and under the unified military command that is directing our resistance, will offer their services to the state, fighting shoulder to shoulder with the rest of the nation for the successful completion of the Nationalist Revolution.

In conclusion, I may say that the foundation of the Chinese state rests firmly on the Three Principles first expounded by Dr. Sun Yat-sen. This foundation is one that cannot be shaken or changed. Now that the entire nation is awakened and solidly united, it will boldly follow the unswerving policy of the Government, and will mobilize the entire resources to resist the tyrannical Japanese and save the state from its imminent peril.

Enlightened people the world over now realize that China is fighting not merely for her own survival, but also for world peace and for international faith and justice.

38.

Message of Generalissimo Chiang Kai-shek to the People's Political Council, March 6, 1941 [4]

I intend, as a representative of the Government, to explain today its attitude toward the conditions laid down by the Communist members of the Council. Before I make any report I wish to state that the Government did not originally intend to declare publicly its stand on its relations with the Chinese Communist Party. Now that the latter has, however, formally telegraphed these demands to the Council, which is an organ of national opinion, it has acted in a manner quite unlike that usually characterizing its words and deeds. It is, therefore, incumbent upon the Government and the Council to make a formal declaration of their attitude in the interests of the nation, the War of Resistance and the future of national reconstruction. A nation, and more especially when it is engaged in mortal combat with an aggressor, depends for its very life upon the maintenance of discipline, order and the necessity of the Government's writ being obeyed. Given a sound framework of discipline and legality it will be able to overcome whatever perils and difficulties come in its way. If, on the other hand, its military command is not unified and its authority questioned, it will meet with defeat no matter how strong its armed forces may be. We are now pitting the whole strength of the nation against the Japanese militarists in a life-and-death struggle. The fate of our nation is hanging in the balance. It is a time when we must give the most scrupulous attention to the upholding of order and authority in the State. In all matters—whether political, social or party problems—not involving conflict with, or obstruction to national order and authority, there is room for frank and open adjustment of differences in search of rational solutions. This has always been the policy and attitude of the Government in relation to the Chinese Communist Party; the achievement of unity by means of mutual concessions in the face of external aggression and the attainment of success in resistance and reconstruction.

I understand that the Secretariat of the Council has received two sets of demands from the Chinese Communist Party entitled: firstly, "rehabilitation measures;" and secondly, "measures for a provisional settlement"—each set containing twelve points. I can assert that though these demands were received by members of the Council before it assembled, no government institution or individual member of the Government, nor I myself, received them. Now that we have seen them we are, first of all, astonished at the wording of the titles and next, at the formal resemblance of the contents to the demands made by the Japanese prior to the Lukouchiao Incident. One is particularly and painfully reminded of the so-called "Three Principles" announced by the Japanese at that unhappy time. The Chinese Communists are as much citizens of the Chinese Republic as we all are, and yet their presentation of such demands at such a time as this would seem clearly to indicate their intention of taking up a hostile attitude to the National Government and the People's Political Council. We think, therefore, the least said the better, and do not regard it as necessary to rebut each point in detail. It is sufficient to classify the sense of the demands into three main categories of "military," "political," and "party" affairs. The first eight points of the first set of demands regarding "rehabilitation measures" and the first, sixth, seventh, eighth, ninth and tenth points of the second set

---

[4] Chiang Kai-shek, *op. cit.*, pp. 235–241.

regarding "measures for a provisional settlement" belong to the category of military affairs. The ninth and twelfth points of the first set and the third, fourth and fifth points of the second set belong to the category of political affairs, while the tenth and eleventh points of the first set and the eleventh and twelfth points of the second set belong to the category of party affairs. A brief explanation of the bearing of the sense of the demands under each of these three heads upon resistance and reconstruction is indispensable.

Firstly, the demand is, in effect, that the Government should not suppress disobedient and rebellious troops, that government authorities should be punished for so doing and that the losses of the mutineers in such rebellions should be compensated.

Secondly, the implication is that the Government should establish special areas outside the sphere of its authority, recognize the existence of anomalous political organizations and restrict its power to check illegal activities on the part of organizations or individuals. Recognition of a so-called "democratic authority in the enemy's rear" is also demanded. The logical outcome of all this would be disaster—such a disaster as must invariably follow any attempt by a party to take advantage of enemy invasion in order to seize supreme power.

Thirdly, the sense of the demands is that the Communist Party should enjoy a special status and special rights and that the Government should not deal with the Communist members of the Council on the same footing as it deals with all other members belonging to other parties or to none. The Government not being ready to comply, the Communists have refused to attend the present meeting of the People's Political Council. In essence this is really what the demands amount to. I think that when the Communist Party produced them it did not perhaps realize they were of so drastic a nature. But were the Government to accept them without protest, China would scarcely be any longer worthy of being called a nation or the People's Political Council an organ of the national will.

Now I shall further expound the attitude of the Government towards these three categories of demands.

In the category of military affairs the consistent policy of the Government has been to nationalize our armies. That is, under the supreme command of the National Government there is but one system of national armies, and there can be no second system of armies under the control of individual parties or private persons. I can categorically assure the Council that the national revolutionary army is the army of the State and in no way the army of any particular party whatever. It is, therefore, absolutely out of the question to regard a section of it as belonging to the Communist Party. There can be but one source of command. Should a second presume to assert itself, it would be indistinguishable from the "military council" of Wang Ching-wei's puppet regime and accordingly detested and abjured by the whole country. It is inconceivable that the Communists, if devoted to the cause of resistance, should take up such a position.

Next, the political principle of the Government is to democratize the national political system. All citizens, individually or in organized bodies, while they conform to discipline, should shoulder their responsibilities, fulfill their duties and enjoy their rights, possess all due freedom of action, but sovereignty is indivisible. If a second source of political authority were to be allowed to exist outside the Government—such, for example, as might be called by the name of a "democratic authority behind the enemy lines," mentioned in these demands—it would not differ from the traitorous administrations in Nanking and Manchuria. Not only would the Government find it intolerable, but the whole country would see in it an irreconcilable enemy.

Although as a result of the nation's historical development there is now but one party exercising administrative power, while others of varying size and permanency are "in opposition," yet all parties exist in a spirit of equality with one another, this being nowhere more markedly visible than in this democratic institution, the People's Political Council. Here all are equal rather as citizens than as parties. There could be no room for a special status of one party or demands for special rights, such as would vitiate the sprouting of our democratic institutions. I hope that all of you councillors will fully comprehend the nature of this considered and unvarying stand of the Government regarding its relationship with political parties.

Now I would like to elaborate somewhat upon the military aspect of the matter. From the time in 1938 when the 18th Army Corps, in defiance of the orders of the High Command, arbitrarily withdrew to the right bank of the Yellow River and forcibly carried out an illegal occupation of the Sui-Teh district, the Government has been loath to consider this move as instigated solely by the Communist Party, or to hold that party guilty of sabotaging resistance; nor did it think that any such motive was necessarily behind the 18th Army Corps' insubordination. Nevertheless, the effect extended even to the rear where it created general uneasiness on account of the potential dangers it threatened. The result was highly damaging to the whole prosecution of the war, putting a weapon into the hands of the enemy and imperilling the nation in the gravest manner. During the past two years or more the Government has been simultaneously unifying the fighting efforts of the whole army at the front and stabilizing the internal condition of the nation in the southwest and northwest of the rear. It is an exceedingly distressing fact that while all other countries in the world present a united front to external aggression, with us the Government finds added to the task of waging war on an invader that of settling internal troubles. Surely such a state of affairs is not to be paralleled in the history of any other revolutionary country. However, the precautions taken by the Government have been such as to avert any disaster either at the front or in the rear and the country may reckon this as great good fortune. Despite this danger, we find our capacity to withstand the enemy strong enough to ensure our final victory and also a sound and formidable foundation laid for stability in the rear. Had it been otherwise and had timely measures not been taken, by now the provinces of the south and northwest, if not long overrun by the enemy, would have been ruined by the escapades of rebels and antisocial elements; and the people in the rear would be living in such insecurity as those suffer in provinces behind the enemy lines, in Hopei, Chahar, Shantung and Kiangsu where the National Government and its armed forces cannot protect them from the double oppression of the Japanese and the puppets.

However, the fact remains that the forces of resistance are considerably weakened by the enforced retention in the rear of large numbers of troops who might be fighting at the front. This also imposes a grievously depressing weight upon the spirits of the whole army and people. The problem is one that is really not difficult to solve. All that is required is a complete change in the attitude and actions of the Communist Party, in no longer regarding the 18th Army Corps as its peculiar possession or as an instrument for the obstruction of other sections of the national forces to the detriment of resistance. Let the Communists carry out the declaration they themselves made in 1937 wherein they said: (1) Dr. Sun's Three Principles of the People serve the needs of present-day China and the Chinese Communist Party is prepared to strive for their complete fulfillment; (2) they would abandon all violent action and policy aimed at the overthrow of the Kuomintang, the movement for the propagation of communism in China, and the policy of violent confiscation of landowners' holdings; (3) they would abolish the then Chinese Soviet government in the Northwest and work towards a united democratic government for the whole country; (4) they would abolish the name and status of the Red Army and permit its incorporation into the national revolutionary army under the command of the National Military Council of the National Government. If they would now but faithfully carry out their original intention to comply with these conditions and move all the troops connected with their party according to the plans laid down by the National Military Council into the areas appointed for them to defend, the whole country could be united to meet the invader, there would be an end of internal obstacles and anxieties, and it would be possible to deal the exhausted enemy a tremendous blow which I am convinced would bring about within a short time a most sensational victory. At least we could restore the lines held in the autumn of 1938; of this the military authorities are in no doubt. Then lost territory would be recovered and our fellow-countrymen delivered from their sufferings. This would be an immense contribution of the 18th Army Corps to the national cause and the whole country would admire the patriotism of the Communists. Our Government has no other demand to make of the Communist Party and the troops connected with it save this one fervent wish that they will carry out the obligations into which they themselves freely entered and support the Program of Resistance and Reconstruction to which the People's Political Council gave its unanimous endorsement. It merely hopes that the Communists will cast off all party prejudice and put the interests of the nation first by obeying orders, maintaining discipline and working in harmony with all their comrades-in-arms.

There are also two other groups of these demands which have an intimate relation with military affairs: what the Communists call the "prevention of provocation," the "withdrawal of the anti-Communist forces in Central China" and the "immediate cessation of all attacks on us." These three points call for some remark. This sort of senseless, mendacious, misleading and malicious propaganda vilifies our Government and deliberately injures the sacred mission of resistance, but, more than that, it offers insult to the pure spirit of the whole country's united battle against aggression. I need scarcely assert that our Government is solely concerned with leading the nation against the Japanese invaders and extirpating the traitors, and is utterly without any notion of again taking up arms to "suppress the Communists." It desires never again to hear of that ill-omened term which now has a place only in Chinese history. Let them obey orders, give up their attacks on their comrades-in-arms and cease all their provocative acts; the Government will then treat them with all possible consideration. The Government is, moreover, desirous of showing generosity and of letting bygones be bygones. In defense of our national interest it cannot, however, fail to punish and check insubordination, for it would otherwise fail in its duty to the nation. For loyal soldiers it has such a loving solicitude that the charge of provocation and attack is absurd. I can make myself responsible for the statement in your presence that at no future time could there conceivably be another campaign for the suppression of the Communists. I hope that you will address an appeal to Mao Tse-tung, Tung Pi-wu and the other Communist members of this Council to effect a change in the attitude of their party so that we can discuss here all together the questions they have raised and arrive at some reasonable solution of them. You represent the will of the nation and your bounden duty is to strive for the success of resistance and reconstruction and national unity. If the Communist Party will only accept your advice, and say and do nothing in future contrary to the Program of Resistance and Reconstruction and their own manifesto of 1937, the Government will undoubtedly respect whatever resolutions you may adopt for the settlement of the incident and see that they are carried fully into effect without delay.

In conclusion, provided unity can be preserved and resistance carried on to the end, the Government will be ready to follow your directions in the settlement of all outstanding questions. I call upon the Communist members of the Council to realize the national danger at this time of mortal combat with the invader and, acting in the spirit of the saying "brothers quarrel at home but go out together to repel assault from without," to accept the judgment of this Council and make their contribution to national solidarity. This is the fervent prayer of the whole people, and it would moreover deal the enemy a mighty blow. Out of solicitude for the Communist Party and in the desire to see it play its full part in the history of this life-and-death struggle of our country, we beg it to continue in its mission of reconstruction and resistance against aggression.

39

Statement by Generalissimo Chiang Kai-shek to the Fifth Central Executive Committee of the Kuomintang, September 13, 1943 [5]

After hearing the secretariat's report on the question of the Chinese Communist Party and the views expressed by various members of the Central Executive Committee I am of the opinion that first of all we should clearly recognize that the Chinese Communist problem is a purely political problem and should be solved by political means. Such ought to be the guiding principle for the Plenary Session in its effort to settle this matter. If you share my views you should maintain the policy of leniency and forbearance which we have consistently pursued in dealing with our domestic affairs with the expectation that the Chinese Communist Party will be moved by our sincerity and magnanimity no matter in what way they may slander us nor in what manner they may try to create trouble.

In spite of provocations we should abide by the manifesto of the Tenth Plenary Session: "In the case of those who sincerely believe in the Three People's Principles, obey laws and orders, do not hinder prosecution of the war, do not attempt to upset social order and do not seize our national territory in defiance of Government decrees, the Central Government would overlook their past record either in thought or in deed and should respect their opportunities, be they individuals, or political groups, to serve the country." We should, now as ever, continue to be tolerant in strict conformity with the manifesto and earnestly expect the Communist Party eventually to realize and correct their errors. We should make it clear that the Central Government does not have any particular demand to make on the Chinese Communist Party but hopes that it will abandon its policy of forcibly occupying our national territory and give up its past tactics of assaulting National Government troops in various sectors, thus obstructing the prosecution of the war.

We also hope that the Chinese Communist Party will redeem its pledge made in its declaration of 1937 and fulfill the four promises solemnly announced in that

---

[5] *China Handbook, 1937–1945*, pp. 67–68. The Fifth Central Executive Committee was then holding its eleventh plenary session.

document: "(1) To struggle for the realization of the Three People's Principles; (2) To abandon the policy of overthrowing the Kuomintang regime by force, give up the Communist movement and discard the policy of confiscating land by force; (3) To dissolve the present government organization and by carrying into practice the principles of democracy thus held to bring about the political unity of the whole nation; (4) To disband the Red Army by incorporating it into the National Army under the direct command of the Military Council of the National Government. The troops thus reorganized will await orders to move to the front to undertake the tasks of fighting the enemy."

If the Chinese Communist Party can prove its good faith by making good its promises the Central Government, taking note of its sincerity and loyalty in carrying on our war of resistance, will once more treat it with sympathy and consideration so that we may accomplish hand in hand the great task of resistance and reconstruction.

40

Report by the Representative of the National Government [6] to the People's Political Council, September 15, 1944 [7]

Members of the People's Political Council requested a report on the conversations concerning the Chinese communist problem. As a representative of the Government, I shall make a simple and concise statement:

On January 17, 1944, Kuo Chung-yung, Liaison Officer of the National Military Council stationed with the 18th Group Army, telegraphed the Board of Military Operations, reporting: "On the 16th of this month, Mao Tse-tung in a talk with me expressed the opinion that the Communist Party would send either Chou En-lai, or Lin Tsu-han, or Commander-in-chief Chu Teh, or all of them, to Chungking to see the Generalissimo for instructions. He asked me to report and seek approval." On February 2, the Board of Military Operations sent a telegram in reply to Liaison Officer Kuo, saying: "Messrs. Chu, Chou, and Lin are welcome. Please telegraph again before their departure." Later, a telegram came from Liaison Officer Kuo stating that, according to Chu Teh, Chou En-lai, and Lin Tsu-han, Lin was scheduled to leave on April 28. The National Government, upon receipt of the information, on May 1 delegated Dr. Wang Shih-chieh and myself to Sian to conduct preliminary conversations with Mr. Lin. We arrived in Sian on May 2 simultaneously with Mr. Lin. Between May 4 and 11, five conversations were held in Sian. The opinions expressed by Mr. Lin during the conversations were all recorded and the minutes were sent to Mr. Lin who, after reading them and making corrections and revisions, handed the minutes back to us in person and signed them. At that time, Mr. Lin inquired whether we could also sign the minutes. In our opinion, these minutes contain the opinions expressed by Mr. Lin or part of our opinions agreed to by Mr. Lin and should be signed by Mr. Lin only. As to the opinions of the National Government, we should formally present them after we returned to Chungking and had consulted with higher authorities. The following is the original text of the minutes signed by Mr. Lin:

---

[6] Gen. Chiang Chih-chung, Minister of Political Training of the National Military Council.
[7] *China Handbook, 1937–1945*, pp. 81–90.

"POINTS RAISED DURING THE CONVERSATIONS BETWEEN MAY 4 AND MAY 8

"A.   *On Military Matters*

"1. The 18th Group Army and troops formerly belonging to the 'New Fourth Army' should obey the orders of the National Military Council.

"2. The Communist troops should be reorganized into at least four armies consisting of 12 divisions, as proposed by General Lin Piao last year.

"3. After reorganization, the troops will take up the defense of their original positions, but they should follow the direction of the commanders of the war zones in which they are stationed. When the war is victoriously concluded, they should abide by orders of transfer issued by the National Government to designated defense areas.

"4. After the reorganization of the troops, their commander, in accordance with the regulations governing personnel promulgated by the National Government, may recommend personnel for appointment.

"5. After its reorganization, the said Army should abide by the rules and regulations governing military supplies, as applied to other armies under the National Government.

"B.   *On the Shensi-Kansu-Ningsia Border Area Question*

"1. Its name shall be changed to the Northern Shensi Administrative Area.

"2. This Administrative Area shall be under the direct jurisdiction of the Executive Yuan and shall not be under the Shensi Provincial Government.

"3. The said Administrative Area should embrace the original area (map attached) and its boundaries should be fixed jointly by representatives of the National Government and the Chinese Communist Party.

"4. This Administrative Area should faithfully carry out the Three People's Principles, the *Program of Armed Resistance and National Reconstruction* and the laws and orders of the National Government. Other laws and regulations which are deemed necessary, due to local circumstances, should be submitted to the National Government for approval before promulgation.

"5. The annual budget of the Administrative Area should be submitted to the National Government for approval.

"6. The Administrative Area and the 18th Group Army, after being authorized to receive Government appropriations, should not issue local bank-notes. All the previously issued bank-notes should be properly disposed of by the Ministry of Finance.

"7. The Kuomintang may conduct Party activities and publish newspapers in the Administrative Area and set up a radio station in Yenan. At the same time, the Kuomintang should recognize the legal status of the Communist Party in China and permit the latter to set up a radio station in Chungking to facilitate exchange of opinions between the two Parties and the Government.

"8. The existing organization of the Shensi-Kansu-Ningsia Border Area is not to be changed for the time being.

"C.   *On the Party Problem*

"As provided by the *Program of Armed Resistance and National Reconstruction* the Chinese Communist Party should be granted legal status. There should be no more unlawful arrests and no more suppression of books and newspapers, while freedom of speech and democracy should be promoted. Those persons who were arrested on account of the New Fourth Army Incident as well as all imprisoned members of the Chinese Communist Party including Liao Cheng-chih and Chang Wen-ping should be immediately released. Order should be given to protect the families of members of the 18th Group Army and the New Fourth Army.

"D. *On Other Matters*

"1. The Communist Party should express its desire to continue faithfully to keep the four-point pledge and support the war of resistance and the program of national reconstruction under the leadership of Generalissimo Chiang Kai-shek, while the Kuomintang in turn should express its willingness to seek a just and rational readjustment of the relations between the two Parties by political means.

"2. The military blockade on the Shensi-Kansu-Ningsia Border Area should be lifted. As at present, trade and transportation should be given priority.

"3. Military, political and economic problems in guerilla areas behind enemy lines should be solved to the advantage of the war under the direction of the National Government and the National Military Council.—(*Signed*) Lin Tsu-han, May 11, 1944."

"*Appendix: Four Points Proposed by Divisional Commander Lin Piao*

"1. With regard to the Party issue, we wish to obtain a legitimate status under the *Program of Armed Resistance and National Reconstruction* and to enforce the Three People's Principles. The National Government on the other hand may conduct Party activities and run Party papers in the Chinese Communist areas.

"2. With regard to the problem of troops, we desire that our troops should be reorganized into four armies with 12 divisions and be accorded the same treatment as the National Government troops.

"3. The North Shensi Border Area, in its original form, should be turned into an administrative area, while other areas should be reorganized and the laws and decrees of the National Government should be enforced there.

"4. With regard to the area of operations, we accept in principle the National Government's decision that our troops be dispatched to the north of the Yellow River. However, at present we can only make necessary preparations. We guarantee that the decision will be put into effect as soon as the war is terminated. Should war conditions permit (as in the case of a general counter-offensive) arrangements may be made for the transfer of our troops to other areas."

II

Since Lin Tsu-han had expressed concrete opinions, we returned to Chungking on May 17, together with Mr. Lin. At that time, the Central authorities were making preparations for the 12th Plenary Session of the Central Executive Committee of the Kuomintang and the National Administrative Conference. Despite busy preparations, we submitted a report to the National Government on the results of the Sian conversations and the opinions expressed by Lin Tsu-han so as to enable the Government to consider measures for the solution of this problem. On June 5, we met Lin Tsu-han and handed to him the memorandum of the National Government concerning the solution of the Chinese Communist problem through political methods. The original text of the memorandum is as follows:

"Memorandum of the National Government concerning the Solution of the Chinese Communist Problem through Political Means, June 5, 1944."

With the opinions expressed by Representative Lin Tsu-han at Sian as a basis, the following memorandum was drawn up:

"A. *Military Problems*

"1. The 18th Group Army and its units stationed in various localities should be reorganized into four armies consisting of ten divisions with their designations to be decided by order of the National Government.

"2. The said Army must obey the orders of the National Military Council.

"3. The strength of the said Army should be fixed in accordance with the organization of the national armies (orders to be issued by the Ministry of War). The said Army should not form extra echelons, detachments or other units. All such extra units already in existence must be disbanded within a specific date set by the National Government.

"4. In matters pertaining to personnel the said Army may make recommendations to the National Government regarding appointments in accordance with regulations governing personnel.

"5. The said Army should be given military expenses in the same way as other national armies by the National Government, and the independence of the commissariat should be upheld in accordance with the Military Management Act.

"6. The said Army must carry on its training work in accordance with the training program and orders issued by the National Government, which has the right to send men to inspect its training work.

"7. All units of the said Army must be concentrated for service within a certain specified period.   Until then the units in the various war zones must be placed under the direction of the war area commanders concerned.

"B. *The Shensi-Kansu-Ningsia Border Area Problem*

"1. The Shensi-Kansu-Ningsia Border Area shall be renamed the North Shensi Administrative Area, and its administrative organ called the North Shensi Administrative Office.

"2. The said Administrative Area should be within the confines of the territory it embraces at present.   But its exact territory should be fixed by representatives of the National Government and the Communist Party jointly.

"3. The said Administrative Office should be under the direct control of the Executive Yuan.

"4. The said Administrative Area should carry out the laws and orders of the National Government.   Other laws and orders which are deemed necessary because of local peculiar circumstances should be submitted to the National Government for approval before promulgation.

"5. Appointment or removal of the Chairman of the said Administrative Area should be made by the National Government, whereas its commissioners and magistrates may be appointed by the National Government upon the recommendation of the chairman.

"6. The organization of the said Administrative Area should be submitted to the National Government for approval.

"7. The budget of the said Administrative Area should be submitted annually to the National Government for approval.

"8. In the said Administrative Area and the places where the units of the 18th Group Army are stationed, no local bank-notes should be issued.   The notes already issued should be disposed of by arrangement with the Ministry of Finance.

"9. All administrative organizations set up by the Chinese Communists themselves in other places should be taken over and dealt with by the provincial governments concerned.

"C. *The Party Problems*

"1. Party affairs for the duration of the war should be conducted in accordance with the *Program of Armed Resistance and National Reconstruction*, while after the conclusion of the war, according to the National Government's decision, a People's Congress should be convened to adopt a constitution and enforce constitutional government. The Chinese Communist Party should obey the laws of the National Government and enjoy the same treatment as other political parties.

"2. The Chinese Communist Party must reaffirm its sincerity to carry out its four pledges."

After handing the National Government's Memorandum to Lin Tsu-han, we stated that, in case the Chinese Communist Party agrees to put the above-mentioned measures into affect, (1) the National Government will consider the withdrawal of the garrison troops in the defense areas and the restoration of the trade communications between these areas and their neighboring districts; and (2) members of the Chinese Communist Party arrested on charges of violating the law will be leniently treated and released on bail by the National Government. Mr. Lin then took a letter from his pocket enclosing a document entitled "Suggestions for the Solution of Some Current Urgent Problems Made by the Central Committee of the Chinese Communist Party to the Central Executive Committee of the Kuomintang." He handed the document to us for reading. Following is the original text:

"Suggestions made by the Central Committee of the Chinese Communist Party to the Central Executive Committee of the Kuomintang concerning the solution of some of the current urgent problems.

"The Kuomintang and the Communist Party have cooperated in the war of resistance already for seven years. That the Chinese Communist Party. has been sincere in its effort to promote the welfare of the nation, fought valiantly in the war of resistance, enforced the *San Min Chu I*, fulfilled the four-point pledge and consistently supported the National Government and Mr. Chiang Kai-shek in armed resistance and national reconstruction, must be apparent to all. But at present, when the war situation is becoming very critical and the Japanese invaders are continuing their attacks, the internal political condition and the Kuomintang-Communist relationship have not followed the right track to keep pace with the war requirements.

"With a view to overcoming the present difficulties, repulsing the Japanese invaders and seriously preparing for a counter-offensive, the Chinese Communist Party considers that the only way to achieve these objectives is to adopt democracy and strengthen national unity. For this purpose, the Chinese Communist Party hopes that the Government will solve the following extremely urgent problems. These problems, some of which concern national political affairs and others the outstanding issues between the two Parties, are candidly listed as follows:

"A. *Problems Pertaining to National Political Affairs*

"1. The Government is requested to adopt democracy and safeguard the freedoms of speech, the press, assembly, association and person.

"2. The Government is requested to lift the ban on political parties, recognize the legal status of the Chinese Communist Party and the various anti-Japanese parties and groups, and set free political offenders.

"3. The Government is requested to permit the people to enforce local self-government in name as well as in fact.

"B. *Problems Pertaining to the Outstanding Issues Between the Two Parties*

"1. In consideration of the needs of resistance against Japan, the record of achievements in the war of resistance and the present strength of the troops, the Government is requested to organize the Chinese Communist troops into 16 armies consisting of 47 divisions with 10,000 troops per division. As a compromise, the Government is requested to approve of the organization of at least five armies of 16 divisions.

"2. The Government is requested to recognize the Shensi-Kansu-Ningsia Border Government and the popularly-elected anti-Japanese governments in bases in North China as legally-constituted local governments and to recognize all measures taken to meet war exigencies.

"3. During the period of the war of resistance, the *status quo* be maintained in areas garrisoned by the Communist troops and readjustments be considered after the conclusion of the war.

"4. The Government is requested to give full material aid to the 18th Group Army and the New Fourth Army. Since 1940, the Government has given them not one bullet, not one pill of medicine, not one cent of money or one grain of rice. It is requested that this situation be immediately remedied.

"5. With regard to the weapons, munitions, and medicines furnished China by the Allied countries, the Government is requested to apportion and distribute them equitably among the various armies of China and the 18th Group Army and the New Fourth Army should be given the share due them.

"6. The Government is requested to order its military and political organs to lift the military and economic blockades of the Shensi-Kansu-Ningsia Border Area and the various anti-Japanese bases.

"7. The Government is requested to order its military organs to cease armed attacks on the New Fourth Army in Central China and the guerillas in Kwangtung.

"8. The Government is requested to order the Party and military organs to set free persons arrested in various places, such as Yeh Ting and officers and men of the New Fourth Army in the South Anhwei Incident, Liao Cheng-chih and Chang Wen-ping in Kwangtung, Hsu Chieh, Hsu Min-chiu, Mao Tse-nin, Yang Tse-hua and Pan Chueh in Sinkiang, Lo Shih-wen, Yao Hsien, Li Chun, and Chang Shao-ming in Szechwan, Ho Ping and others in Hupeh, Liu Yin in Chekiang, Hsuan Hsia-fu, Shih Tso-hsiang, Li Yu-hai, Chen Yuan-ying and Chao Hsiang in Sian. These men are all patriots and they should be set free in order to further the interests of war against Japan.

"9. The Government is requested to permit the Chinese Communist Party to conduct party activities and publish party papers in various places in the entire country while the Chinese Communist Party will also permit the Kuomintang to conduct party activities and publish party papers in the Shensi-Kansu-Ningsia Border Area and the various anti-Japanese democratic border areas behind the enemy lines.

"The foregoing concerns only the principal points. The Chinese Communist Party sincerely hopes that the National Government will give them a reasonable and most speedy settlement. As the war against Hitler in the West might be victoriously concluded this year, the counter-offensive against Japan in the East can surely be unfolded next year. Furthermore, the Japanese invaders are now launching large-scale attacks to threaten our anti-Japanese front. If our two parties can not only continue to cooperate but also readjust our internal political affairs and improve the party relationship, not only will the present general situation be greatly improved but we will have bright prospects of victory when our country, in coordination with our Allies, launches a large-scale counter-offensive next year. It is hoped that our Government will give the foregoing its serious and favorable consideration.—Lin Tsu-han, Representative of the Chinese Communist Party."

Then and there we said to Lin Tsu-han : "We did not receive the 20 proposals brought up by you on May 22, and they were withdrawn by you, because there was a wide difference between these proposals and the opinions expressed by you at Sian. Your present 12 proposals, though fewer in number, are similar in content. We ought not to accept this document from you, but as we do not want to disregard your wish we can only agree to keep it. However, we cannot forward it to higher authorities." Mr. Lin said, "Then you may keep it in your place for reference."

III

On June 6, we received a letter from Lin Tsu-han. In this letter two points were raised. First, he thought that the difference between the Government memorandum and the proposals of the Chinese Communist Party of June 4 was too great. Besides reporting the memorandum to the Central Committee of the Chinese Communist Party, he requested us to forward the 12-point proposal of the Chinese Communists to the National Government for a rational solution of the problem. Second, he regarded as contrary to fact the phrase, "based on the opinions expressed by Representative Lin Tsu-han at Sian," appearing in the beginning of the Government memorandum. He regarded the minutes of the Sian conversations as "preliminary opinions, finally reached after joint discussions." He agreed that "each Party should refer to its own central authorities for instructions before making a final decision." So he still hoped the National Government would consider the latest proposals made by the Chinese Communist Party. On June 8, we sent Mr. Lin a letter answering the two points he had brought up. First, we had made it clear that we would not submit Mr. Lin's letter dated June 5 to higher authorities because the difference between the original opinions and the proposals made by Mr. Lin later was too great. Mr. Lin finally said : "You may keep the letter in your place for reference." Therefore, we only consented at that time to keep Mr. Lin's letter and again made it clear that the letter could not be submitted to higher authorities. Second, the opinions recorded in the minutes of the Sian conversations, and corrected and revised by Mr. Lin, who intimated that he would make clean copies and sign again, were duly submitted to the National Government. Therefore the Government memorandum was based on Mr. Lin's opinions and it accepted as many of his opinions as possible. We hoped that he could completely accept the memorandum.

IV

We received another letter from Mr. Lin on June 11. He said that he thought the two points in our reply of June 8 were "quite difficult to comprehend." First, he said that, since we had recognized him as the representative of the Chinese Communist Party, we should not refuse to report to the National Government the opinions formally expressed by the Chinese Communist Party, and yet he was unilaterally asked to accept personally the memorandum of the National Government. How could he make a decision all by himself? Second, he admitted that the 12 points suggested by the Chinese Communist Party and handed to us by him on June 5 are "slightly different" from the opinions obtained during our conversations at Sian, but seeing that the Government memorandum was also different from the Sian conversations, he felt that such divergences of views common to both sides in the conversations were nothing surprising. Now that he had reported the Government memorandum to the Central Committee of the Chinese Communist Party by wire, we should not refuse to forward the opinions formally brought up by the Chinese Communist Party to the National Government for instructions.

In fact, the two points which Mr. Lin said were incomprehensible are very plain. It is because Mr. Lin is the representative of the Chinese Communist Party, that the opinion expressed by him can be counted upon. As to the 12 points raised by the Chinese Communist Party, their contents greatly differ from Mr. Lin's opinions. Moreover, there was no indication of the Chinese Communist Party's intention to carry out the fundamental idea of obeying military command and political orders. What it brought up were one-sided demands. Therefore, it is quite understandable that we declared then that we could not forward the proposal. Nevertheless, hoping to seek an early solution to the problem and especially unwilling to create any misunderstanding, we forwarded the 12 points as handed to us by Mr. Lin to the National Government. Afterwards we received instructions from the National Government stating, "the National Government on June 5 sent its memorandum to Representative Lin for transmission to the Chinese Communist Party. Those of the opinions of the Chinese Communist Party which can be accepted by the National Government have already been embodied in the memorandum to the fullest extent. It is hoped that the Chinese Communist authorities will accept the memorandum."

We informed Mr. Lin by letter on June 15 of the instructions of the National Government. We also explained that the fundamental spirit of the present conversations should follow the principle of the unity of military command and political orders as the prerequisite of improving the current situation and strengthening national unity. But the 12 points raised by the Chinese Communist Party made no mention of how to carry out military and political orders of the National Government, how to improve administrative measures, and how to readjust and reorganize armed units. As to the number of armed units to be reorganized, we said at Sian that the possible number was three armies with eight divisions. Now the Government in the memorandum has decided to increase it to four armies with ten divisions—an increase of two divisions as compared with the figure we mentioned. This shows the readiness of the National Government to compromise as much as possible.

V

After we answered Mr. Lin's letter on June 15, for more than ten days the Chinese Communist Party gave no answer to the Government memorandum. On July 3, Mr. Lin asked us to meet him and verbally raised two points. First, in political affairs he hoped that the National Government would take a broader view of "democracy." Second, concerning the question of troops he hoped that the Communist army could be increased to five armies with 16 divisions. Simultaneously he told us that he had received a wire from Yenan welcoming us to that city for further discussions.

At that time we immediately made an explanation: Regarding the question of democracy, the Government had been adopting various measures to hasten the realization of democratic government. For instance, it had abolished the compulsory system of censoring books and magazines before publication, strictly ordered all the provinces in the rear to complete the establishment of local representative bodies, and was about to promulgate the Regulations for Safe-Guarding the Freedom of the Human Person, and a number of other democratic measures were under consideration, which we need not enumerate. As to the increase of army units, the National Government was now enforcing a policy of emphasizing the quality of soldiers and has been reducing the number of armed units as much as possible. It has gone to the utmost limit to accept the demands of the Chinese Communist Party. Its sympathetic readiness to compromise can be understood if one compares the number of national troops at the beginning of the war with their present total. Finally we believed that if the conversations proceed like this, there appeared to be deliberate intention to protract them. It seemed necessary to give a comprehensive and definite answer to the Government memorandum and then use it as a basis of concrete discussion. It was not advisable to continue empty talks and bargaining lest further complications should arise. We also indicated that if the conversations could come to a conclusion in Chungking, we would consider a visit to Yenan.

VI

Mr. Lin visited us again on July 13. He again requested the National Government to give some instructions in connection with the 12 proposals of the Chinese Communists. He made, however, no mention of how they were going to answer the memorandum given to them by the National Government. As the problems raised by Mr. Lin had been explained in the past and did not need further explanation, we only told him that we understood the purpose of his visit. The meeting was closed after we arranged a date for further conversations.

VII

On July 23, Mr. Lin sent us a letter. He again inquired whether we had asked for instructions for a reply to the 12 proposals brought up by the Chinese Communists. In addition he invited us to go to Yenan.

We met Mr. Lin again on July 25. We gave a comparatively more detailed verbal explanation concerning the problems listed in his 12 proposals. We told him that the memorandum of the National Government represented the National Government's concrete views, and that it was the Chinese Communist Party which had not given an answer after much delay. We also stated that such an attitude on the part of the Chinese Communist Party seemed to indicate its deliberate intention in putting off the matter and its unwillingness to find a solution for the problem.

VIII

During this period, we continued to study the question and considered that, following the previous verbal answer, we should give a written reply so as to put our explanations in more concrete form. We met Mr. Lin again on August 5, telling him that we were going to turn into a written reply our opinions given verbally during the previous meeting. We added, "When you have given a definite answer to the Government memorandum, we shall consider further conversations and the question whether we shall go to Yenan or not."

After this talk, on August 10 we sent Mr. Lin a letter based on our previously expressed opinions. Its gist is as follows:

"Three months have elapsed since we had the honor of consulting with you at Sian. For more than two months we have been waiting for the Chinese Communist Party to give a definite reply to the memorandum of the National Government handed to you on June 5 and this prolonged silence was quite beyond our expectation. Regarding the contents of the memorandum, the National

Government not only accepted almost in total the requests of Divisional Commander Lin Piao but also most of your opinions expressed recently at Sian. Since the Chinese Communist Party supports the unification and solidarity of the nation, please urge it to accept the memorandum.

"In connection with the 12 points raised by the Chinese Communist Party, Articles 1 to 3 of the memorandum pointed out that the Government would carry out during the war the *Program of Armed Resistance and National Reconstruction* as accepted by the Chinese Communist Party and other parties and realize within one year after conclusion of the war constitutional government which will give an equal status to all political parties. This statement is clear and concrete. If vague and empty phrases were employed in addition to this statement, they would only cause further discord in the future. The present fixed policy of the National Government is to enlarge gradually the scope of the people's freedom and to promote local self-government step by step in accord with the progress of the war, the approach of victory, and the stability of society. At the same time the National Government hopes that, after its acceptance of the Government memorandum, the Chinese Communist Party will from time to time express its opinion for the effective enforcement of the *Program of Armed Resistance and National Reconstruction* and actively participate in the work of the People's Political Council and the Commission for the Inauguration of Constitutional Government. It is hoped that the views of both parties will thus be reconciled and true unification and solidarity of the nation brought about. Here lies the true significance of the solution of the problem through political means.

"In the 12-point proposal, there are four articles regarding the organization and stationing of the troops and their food and war supplies. The 18th Group Army originally consisted of three divisions. The National Government now promises to allow it to increase to four armies with ten divisions. In permitting this the National Government has taken a very liberal attitude, for the Government is now adopting the policy of 'quality first' and has ordered the reduction in size of other units. Regarding the stationing of troops, the National Government asserts the principle of concentration for service on the one hand and on the other provides for a system of adjustment, training and command prior to their concentration. The Government has indeed taken into consideration all phases of the problem. ꞌRegarding their pay, the National Government promises that the troops will be given the same treatment as the national army. As to the supply of arms, the National Government will from time to time make fair distributions among the armies according to their needs and the duties they perform.

"Another article in the 12-point proposal demands that the National Government recognize the 'Shensi-Kansu-Ningsia Border Area' and the 'Anti-Japanese Governments Elected by the People in Bases in North China.' The National Government in its memorandum has already set forth very liberal measures. Other administrative organs in any other areas should be handed over to the various provincial governments concerned in accordance with the memorandum so as to avoid any discord.

"As for other demands they are either at variance with facts or unreasonable, and we shall not repeat them here since we have given you verbal explanations."

IX

Afterwards we received Mr. Lin Tsu-han's letter of August 30 in which he answered our letter of August 10 under instructions of the Chinese Communist Party. It may be summed up as follows:

"1. The letter of August 10 seems to be written in a reproachful tone blaming the Chinese Communist Party for the unreasonable delay. This is entirely contrary to facts and is a misinterpretation. For, the National Government's memorandum is too far apart in principle from the Chinese Communist Party's 12 written points and eight verbal points. It is pointed out that (a) in the memorandum nothing is mentioned about the establishment of a constitutional Government, recognition of the legal status of various political parties and the setting free of political offenders; (b) The memorandum mentions only the number of reorganized troops, the abolition of units other than the reorganized troops and the concentration of the armies for war service; (c) Only strict observance of laws and orders of the National Government for war purposes is required of the Border Government, making no mention of the realization of the Three People's Principles and giving no recognition to the various existing measures and laws; (d) The democratic governments organized by the people in various anti-Japanese bases are to be abolished. All these are cited as facts showing the vast divergence of the opposing views.

"2. Regarded as the obstacle to the fundamental solution of this problem is the wide gap existing between the viewpoints of the National Government, and the Chinese Communist Party and the 'great masses of the people.' For the Government has been persistently reluctant to realize immediately the Three People's Principles and the democratic system of government.

"3. It is hoped that the National Government will give primary attention to national interests in the solution of the country's political problems and questions regarding the relationship of the Kuomintang and the Chinese Communist Party. It should start from a standpoint that is beneficial to national solidarity in armed resistance and the promotion of democracy." The letter again emphasizes the "political problems," "military problems," and problems concerning "Border area" and "North China, Central China and South China anti-Japanese bases." It reaffirms its attitude toward the various issues mentioned under the first item and simultaneously expands considerably their scopes.

"4. The letter asserts that the Chinese Communist Party is persistent in faithfully carrying out its four pledges, faithfully practising the Three People's Principles, and adhering to the policy of democratic consolidation and political settlement, and does not wish to break off the conversations."

We were greatly surprised to read Mr. Lin's letter of August 30. I believe you gentlemen can all form a very appropriate judgment as to how much truth is in the points listed in that letter and it is not necessary for me to elaborate it. Since we received orders to discuss concrete problems, during the period from our visit to Sian to the present moment, the more we have discussed the problems, the greater the difference of opinions has become. The reason why the divergence of opinions has become greater and greater can be seen from the above-mentioned documents. We cannot help regretting the situation, but do not lose hope. In order to make the Chinese Communist Party really understand our ideas, we sent another reply, the gist of which is as follows:

"The purpose of our conversations with you by order of the National Government is to seek national unification. In other words, to request the Chinese Communist Party to fulfil faithfully its four pledges, and to support faithfully the political unity of the nation. If the Chinese Communist Party had, as you said, faithfully carried out its four pledges, why have there been so many cases of attacks on national troops in different localities by the Chinese Communists? And why is it necessary for the National Government at present to instruct us to discuss with you such questions as the obeying of military command and political orders?

"The National Government, in instructing us to confer with you about unification, aims at laying a solid foundation for the realization of constitutionalism and the Three People's Principles in their entirety. The National Government in its memorandum has made definite statements on the questions of democracy and political parties. In addition, detailed explanations are given in our letter of August 10. How can you say nothing was mentioned? Your letter says that the Chinese Communist Party has thoroughly applied the Three People's Principles in the border area and anti-Japanese bases behind the enemy lines. It also says that the people and anti-Japanese organizations in all the Chinese Communist areas enjoy all forms of freedom and rights. But many facts compel us to deny your statements. Take for instance democracy and freedom. The separation of the five powers as taught by the Father of our Republic is the right way to democracy and is the safeguard for the people's freedom. But is there any factual proof of the independence of judicial power and control power in areas under the Chinese Communist Party? Is there any guarantee of freedom of the press and person for the people in the Communist area, and even for members of the Chinese Communist Party? In our last letter we said that we hoped that no vague and abstract demands in connection with the problems of democracy and freedom would be brought up. Instead, we requested the Chinese Communist Party to discuss thoroughly at any time the means of solving the different problems with the National Government, the People's Political Council and the Commission for the Inauguration of Constitutional Government. Such steps are considered not only appropriate but also necessary.

"We pointed out that answers have already been given one by one to the questions in your letter. It is absolutely true that the National Government's memorandum has accepted most of the opinions put forward by Divisional Commander Lin Piao last year and those raised by you at Sian recently. Yet you still emphatically stated that the divergence of views is too great. But the real reason for the divergence is the steady increase in the number of requests of the Chinese Communist Party. What you asked for at Sian was more than what Divisional Commander Lin asked for last year. The 12 points raised by the Chinese Communist Party outnumber the requests you made at Sian. The present letter adds the eight so-called verbal requests to the 12 points. Since requests increase with time, the divergence of views naturally widens. Take for instance the question of the North Shensi Border Area and other anti-Japanese bases. Divisional Commander Lin requested that the North Shensi Border Area be turned into an administrative area within its original area, and all the other areas be reorganized and obey the laws and orders of the National Government. The document you signed at Sian did not contain other anti-Japanese bases. The 12-point proposal of the Chinese Communist Party asks for the recognition of the Shensi-Kansu-Ningsia Border Area and Anti-Japanese Governments Elected by the People in North China Bases. Your letter now seeks the recognition of Shensi-Kansu-Ningsia Border Area and the Anti-Japanese Governments Elected by the People in Anti-Japanese Bases behind the enemy lines in North, Central, and South China. Under such conditions of steady changes and gradual expansion of requests, which side should be responsible if the conversations cannot be brought to a successful conclusion?

"We have explained that the National Government and the Kuomintang do not place the interest of one single party above the interests of the country and people. It is earnestly hoped that the Chinese Communist Party can share in the observance of this principle.

"Finally we say that we shall be glad to go to Yenan if it would serve any useful purpose. We wish to know whether the Chinese Communist Party can send responsible representatives to Chungking to solve the present problem and who will be appointed to accompany us back to Chungking should we go to Yenan.

"The four pledges made by the Chinese Communist Party in September, 1937:

"(1) The Chinese Communist Party is prepared to fight for the thorough realization of Dr. Sun Yat-sen's Three People's Principles which answer the present-day needs of China.

"(2) The policy of insurrection which aims at the overthrow of the Kuomintang political power shall be abolished. The policy of land-confiscation by force and the policy of Communist propaganda shall be discontinued.

"(3) With the dissolution of the Chinese Soviet Government, a system of political democracy shall be put into practice so that the country may be politically unified.

"(4) The name and designations of the Red Army shall be abolished and the troops shall be reorganized as part of the National Revolutionary Army subject to the control of the National Military Council, and shall be waiting for instructions to take up frontline duties in the war of resistance against Japan."

X

The foregoing is a report on the conversations and the important contents of the related documents. Today the entire nation ardently hopes to arrive at a rational solution of the Chinese Communist problem at an early date in order to achieve national solidarity and unity, the winning of victory, the success of national reconstruction. Entrusted with the mission to carry on the conversations, we naturally have the greatest enthusiasm and hope. What the National Government is seeking is unity of military command and political orders. In this way we can attain real unity and bring about the concerted efforts of the entire army and people of the nation to defeat the enemy. Only thus can our program of resistance and reconstruction be benefited.

In view of this all-important prerequisite, the National Government is always ready to take actual facts into consideration, to arrive at the best possible solution, and to accept the opinions of the Chinese Communist Party as much as possible. This can be clearly seen from the Government memorandum.

As to the problem of democracy and freedom, the National Government has always been realistic and has always tried to do something instead of indulging in empty talks. Under the principles embodied in the *Program of Armed Resistance and National Reconstruction,* it has undertaken to give freedom to the press, to safeguard the people's liberty and to widen the powers of the people's representative organs. It will continue to exert its efforts along this line so that constitutionalism can be successfully adopted after the war. By that time, the question of political parties will be automatically solved. Although the Chinese Communist Party has not yet made any indication of willingness to accept the Government memorandum or to obey the military command and political orders of the Government, we hope the Chinese Communist Party will abide by the principles of solidarity and armed resistance, and realize the true unity of the nation by actual deeds. The National Government will never alter its policy of seeking a political solution. In fact, it is sincerely awaiting an announcement by the Chinese Communist Party that it will revise its standpoint and solve this problem at an early date so as to satisfy the expectations of the entire nation.

Realizing your interest and concern in this problem, I have come here to report on the conversations and to explain the attitude and wishes of the National Government. Your attention to the matter will be appreciated.

41

Report by the Representative of the Central Committee of the Chinese Communist Party [8] to the People's Political Council, September 15, 1944 [9]

Gentlemen, I have been asked by the Presidium to make a report regarding the conversations which were held during the past four months between Dr. Wang Shih-chieh and General Chang Chih-chung on behalf of the National Government and myself on behalf of the Central Committee of the Chinese Communist Party. I feel greatly honored.

To rectify the relationship between the Kuomintang and the Chinese Communist Party, a just and reasonable readjustment should be made. This is a thing of great political importance. Not only are the members of the People's Political Council concerned over this problem, but it is also receiving the attention of all of our fellow countrymen. What I am going to report at this meeting today concerns what we discussed in the last four months. Connected with my talks with Dr. Wang and General Chang, there were seven documents which are rather important. Copies of these documents have been printed for your information.

Throughout the conversations on this occasion, the Yenan government displayed an attitude of sincerity. We hoped that the National Government would solve all the problems, we also hoped that we would be able to report oftener to the Generalissimo. Although no final decision regarding these problems has been reached, the conversations are being continued with Dr. Wang and General Chang in the most friendly atmosphere. This is because we are all anxious to solve the three main problems.

The first problem relates to military command. Both Dr. Wang and General Chang believe that this problem should be settled by all means. The Chinese Communist Party likewise wished to see a solution. But up to now a solution has not yet been found. Although details cannot be disclosed at the present moment, in general I may say that divergent opinions still exist. But we should frankly tell you gentlemen of the P. P. C. that difference of opinion is the main reason for failing to reach a solution.

There are two points in the documents which, from our viewpoint, are highly important. The first is how to solve these problems fundamentally. That is to say, in the face of the grave national crisis, we should unite under the leadership of Generalissimo Chiang and should exert all our efforts in the prosecution of the war of resistance. Unified, our strength can be increased. I believe that our country has the strength. We have 450,000,000 people and that is strength.

As to how we can bring about unification, the answer is by the ushering in of a democratic form of government even during the war. To have a democratic government certainly can avert national calamity. We have suggested the car-

---

[8] Lin Tsu-han.
[9] *China Handbook, 1937–1945,* pp. 90–94.

rying out of the Three People's Principles, the *Program of Armed Resistance and National Reconstruction*; and the Ten-Point Program of the Chinese Communist Party. If these could be carried out, then the people throughout the country would be unified and the fighting strength would be enhanced.

At the beginning of the war, the Generalissimo declared that "the entire land, irrespective of locality, and the entire people, irrespective of age, must be united and defend the country. Only in this way can we expect to increase our national strength." It is necessary for us to realize that our enemy Japan, well-developed industrially, is strong. It is not that China does not have the strength. Our strength can be secured only by adopting the democratic form of government. Our war is fought for justice and against aggression. We must have a democratic government because our war is an all-out people's war.

The second point involves some military demands which the Chinese Communist Party has put before the Government. Before the outbreak of the war we brought up certain things which we hoped that the Kuomintang would do and certain other things which we hoped that the Chinese Communist Party would do. To mention the more important ones, we hoped that, politically, the National Government would give the people of the entire nation freedom of speech, of the press, and of person; permit the lawful existence of political parties and organizations; and carry out local self-government. Now that the war has entered upon its eighth year, many developments and changes in the military and political situation have taken place. On September 22, 1937, shortly after the war broke out the Chinese Communist Party issued a declaration. Then the Generalissimo issued a statement on September 23. Both declaration and statement aimed at solving all the problems.

Take the army question, for instance. In northern Shensi there were 80,000 men. The National Government gave permission to reorganize them into three divisions with 45,000 men. Soldiers are needed for the prosecution of the war. When the province of Hopei was occupied by the enemy and Taiyuan was lost, the National Government ordered the 18th Group Army to move deep into the area behind the enemy line to destroy the puppet regime and harass the enemy. The 18th Group Army has done all these things, and has done them well.

During that period the 18th Group Army penetrated into Shansi, Hopei and Chahar. It seriously undermined the puppet regimes in various enemy occupied areas and brought these places under the national flag. In the course of more than seven years of war, the Communist military force has developed along the right tracks and consists now of an army of 475,000 men and a people's militia force of 2,200,000 men. Therefore, we hope that the National Government will give us five armies with 16 divisions. This is the demand we have brought up in military affairs.

Second, regarding political administration. The Chinese Communist Party has established in areas behind the enemy line a number of political administrations. There are 15 such units in Hopei, Shantung and Suiyuan, and they serve as bases for the war of resistance. In these places the system of popular election has been adopted. The number of people practicing this kind of civil right is 88,000,000. In some of these places the people have already held two elections, while in other places one election has taken place. We hope that our National Government will administer these political set-ups and direct the exercise of civil rights. This is our demand regarding the people's rights.

Third, we want a lawful existence. In the past the Communist Party hoped that the National Government would give different facilities to different things it undertook. Since other political parties and organizations can lawfully exist, the Chinese Communist Party asks for an open, lawful existence. This point is rather important. The other problems mentioned in our correspondence need not be mentioned here *seriatim*.

Our conversations have centered around two things—one concerns the basic problem of democratic government; the other the solution of some pending questions regarding the Chinese Communist Party. The points which we believe to be important have been brought up in the conversations. The National Government has a memorandum and General Chang Chih-chung told me that we should follow that memorandum.

We feel that there are still differences between our proposal and the Government memorandum, and no solution has yet been made. I shall mention only the more important points here, as all the minor points can be seen from our correspondence.

There are differences in our respective opinions. Where do the differences lie? For instance, I have just said that our aim is to fight the enemy. To fight the enemy we must have troops. At present there are on the guerilla battle fronts behind the enemy lines in North, Central and South China a total of 470,000 regular forces under the leadership of the Chinese Communist Party. In addition there are 2,000,000 men in the people's militia corps. According to these figures, as many as 47 divisions can be organized. At a memorial meeting on March 12, 1944, the death anniversary of Dr. Sun Yat-sen, Chou En-lai said that, in view of the National Government's total planning, we had decided only to ask for the designation of 18 divisions grouped into six armies, although the size of our forces warranted the organization of 47 divisions. In repeated talks afterwards, we were told that there were still difficulties. The Chinese Communist Party then reduced the number to five armies with 16 divisions. But the National Government memorandum calls for only four armies with ten divisions. As most of our armed forces are in war areas behind the enemy line, it would be difficult to direct them if they were divided into too few units. Hence we have asked for an increase in their numerical strength. According to the Government memorandum, these troops after reorganization will be concentrated for war duties, while those which have not been placed under reorganization will be disbanded without delay. We are fighting all the time and it is impossible to cease fighting. It would be very difficult to concentrate the troops.

As to lawful existence of political parties and organizations and other questions in connection with democracy, we believe that there is the necessity of discussing them. For example we have been trying to give freedom of speech and publication, but up to the present session of the People's Political Council this hope has not yet been realized. Another example is found in the case of freedom of person. Although the Regulations for Safe-Guarding the Freedom of the Human Person was promulgated in July, it has not been enforced. For instance, those involved in the New Fourth Army Incident were arrested without a trial. Yeh Ting is not a Communist and at that time he came out at the request of the Chinese Communist authorities. Then there are Liao Cheng-chih, Chang Wen-ping and others who were detained in Kwangtung. We hope that these men as well as many other political offenders will be released simultaneously. Now that the Regulations have been promulgated, we hope that the Central Government will prove its existence by action.

The foregoing is comparatively a basic analysis. Our hope is different from the National Government's memorandum and we hope that the memorandum can be brought nearer to our viewpoint. What I have just mentioned are the more important points. Of course there are things of secondary importance. For instance, when we were at Sian, General Chang and Dr. Wang said that the conversations would be used as preliminary suggestions which, when put in written form, would serve for the reference of the two Parties. But the Central Government's memorandum says that it was the opinion expressed by Representative Lin. This is a misunderstanding on the part of General Chang and Dr. Wang. We discussed this matter only for three hours before a decision was made. Since both General Chang and Dr. Wang have often mentioned this case, I welcome the opportunity to make an explanation here, pointing out the slight discrepancy.

I shall now come to the story of the conversations. Last year a resolution was adopted by the Kuomintang at its 11th Plenary Session to solve the Communist problem by political means. This news was received in Yenan with enthusiasm, and given wholehearted support. Since the New Fourth Army Incident of 1940, the relationship between the two Parties has been a deadlock. Although I am a member of the People's Political Council, I was unable to come out because of the blockade. After the 11th Plenary Session we came out with permission from the National Government. But, owing to the spring sowing movement in the border area, my departure from Yenan was delayed until April 29. Upon my arrival in Sian, I unexpectedly met General Chang and Dr. Wang. As there was then no airplane scheduled to fly to Chungking, we began our conversations in Sian on May 4. We had altogether five talks which served as a preliminary exchange of opinions before reporting to the National Government.

At that time General Chang and Dr. Wang asked me for my opinions. I replied that the National Committee of the Chinese Communist Party likewise discussed the questions related to the conversations. Chou En-lai's speech made in Yenan at the memorial meeting on the anniversary of Dr. Sun Yat-sen's death on March 12, 1944, could serve as the basis of the conversations. This speech dealt with two things—one in connection with democracy and constitutional government; the other about the solution of many impending issues between the Kuomintang and the Chinese Communist Party.

General Chang and Dr. Wang said that these matters would have to be discussed after our arrival in Chungking and that at present emphasis should be laid on military affairs. The military question consists of (1) reduction of the scope of the organization system and (2) reduction of the numerical strength of the forces. I said that we had 470,000 troops and I asked to what size they were to be reorganized with the permission of the National Government. General Chang discussed the matter with me and I said that we should have six armies with 18 divisions. Too many, said General Chang. That question alone we discussed for three days.

Two years ago Divisional Commander Lin Piao proposed that our forces should be reorganized into four armies with 12 divisions. General Chang, who had brought with him the minutes of the talk with Lin Piao, mentioned the old proposal. I told him that I could report that suggestion to the Central Committee of the Chinese Communist Party for consideration. Many other questions discussed concerned political affairs. They are all mentioned in the documents.

Minutes of the last conversation were kept, and the other day Lei Cheng showed me the minutes with the title, "Results of the Conversations with Lin Tsu-han," and asked me to sign. I told him that the minutes contained opinions of both parties concerned, and that I would sign after making revisions and would ask both General Chang and Dr. Wang to sign also. They said that it was not necessary to sign because it was not a set of terms and that all they had to do was to forward the minutes to the National Government for instructions. So much for the preliminary conversations.

We flew to Chungking on May 17. After receiving our telegram, the Central Committee of the Chinese Communist Party promptly drafted 20 articles on May 20 on the basis of my telegram. The first article dealt with democracy, expressing the hope that the Government would immediately grant the freedom of speech, publication, and person. The second article asked for the recognition of the lawful existence of the Chinese Communist Party and the release of political offenders. The third article dealt with local self-government. The other articles concerned some minor questions.

On May 22 I showed these articles to General Chang and Dr. Wang. After reading the articles, they felt that some of the minor questions were provocative in nature and returned the paper to me. I asked them their opinion, whereupon they replied that the articles had better be changed to 12 articles with the remaining eight articles concerning minor questions to be presented verbally. Although these eight articles on minor questions may not seem of great consequence, they are major issues to Yenan circles.

After receiving my message, the Yenan authorities on June 3 sent me another 12 articles which I delivered to General Chang and Dr. Wang on June 4. Later, I also forwarded to Yenan the 18-point memorandum of the National Government. General Chang and Dr. Wang said that they could not accept my letter. As representative of the Chinese Communist Party I thought that my letter should be sent to Generalissimo Chang. On June 11 I wrote to General Chang and Dr. Wang and received a reply from them saying that my letter had been forwarded to the National Government.

After a long period of time, Minister H. C. Liang declared at a press conference that the Kuomintang-Communist conversations had come to a standstill and the Chinese Communist Party should realize the situation. Several correspondents came to question me and I said that we would do anything that is beneficial to the war of resistance. On July 16 Minister Liang again issued a statement in English. His statement, containing four items, said that some points in the present conversations had been solved while others could not be settled, but there would be no civil war. Several correspondents again came to see me. On August 13, Chou En-lai issued a statement to the effect that the Chinese Communist Party wishes to have the problem solved. In addition he expressed the hope that General Chang and Dr. Wang could go to Yenan to carry on the conversations. I forwarded this message to General Chang and Dr. Wang and, in their opinion, the matter could be given consideration. On August 14 they gave me a reply and on August 30 another reply, making a total of seven documents. Gentlemen, you will understand clearly what has happened during our conversations by referring to the documents.

I have come to Chungking because my comrades in the Chinese Communist Party are anxious to secure a solution of the problem and I am very sincere in purpose. I have been here four months and am still in close touch with General Chang and Dr. Wang, who have exchanged views with me on the matter. But the issue is still pending, even to the present moment. The Chinese Communist Party hopes that the National Government will find a solution. The nation needs unification, especially unification among political parties and organizations. But the fact is quite clear to you, gentlemen : there is still a divergence of opinion between the two Parties after four months of conversations.

42

Statement by the Chinese Minister of Information (Liang)[10]

May I add a few remarks here concerning Lin Tsu-han's report on the Kuomintang-Communist conversations in the People's Political Council?

In the first place, Mr. Lin said in his report, published in the local newspapers on September 16 and in the *Sin Hua Jih Pao* on September 17, "Minister H. C. Liang once stated in a press conference that conversations between the Kuomintang and Communists have come to a standstill." This is a misrepresentation, as I never said a thing like that. What I did say is "the conversations are still continuing," and "though the conversations are not progressing at a pace as anticipated, it would be incorrect to say that they are running altogether smoothly."

Secondly, Mr. Lin reported, "Minister Liang told the pressmen of Chungking at a press conference held on July 26 that a part of the Kuomintang-Communist problem has been solved but another part is insoluble." Words again differed from my original version which says "Under the present circumstances, a part of the Kuomintang-Communist problem has been solved but it is too much to expect a total solution yet." You may recall that I made these remarks in a statement on the possible trend of the Kuomintang-Communist conversations, and made them on your repeated request.

43

Summary Notes of Conversations Between Vice President Henry A. Wallace and President Chiang Kai-shek, June 21–24, 1944[11]

CONVERSATION AT PRESIDENT CHIANG'S RESIDENCE, JUNE 21—5 p. m.

Present: President Chiang
Vice President Wallace
Dr. T. V. Soong (translating)

President Chiang asked Mr. Wallace whether he had any message from President Roosevelt. Mr. Wallace replied that he had nothing in writing but that he had notes on a conversation with President Roosevelt just prior to his departure from Washington. Mr. Wallace said that President Roosevelt had mentioned the inflationary situation in China but that he (Wallace) did not wish to discuss the subject in Chungking due to the absence in America of the Minister of Finance, Dr. Kung. Mr. Wallace said that President Roosevelt had talked about the Communists in China. President Roosevelt had assumed that, in as much as the Communists and the members of the Kuomintang were all Chinese, they were basically friends and that "nothing should be final between friends". President Roosevelt had cited the Bryan Treaty and had quoted Al Smith and Charles Francis Adams to support his point. President Roosevelt had indicated that if the parties could not get together they might "call in a friend" and had indicated that he might be that friend.

---

[10] Issued at a press conference of Sept. 20, 1944 (*China Handbook, 1937-1945*, p. 94).

[11] By John Carter Vincent, Chief of the Division of Chinese Affairs, who accompanied the Vice President to China. The files of the Department do not contain any indication of the existence of a report in written form made by Mr. Wallace to President Roosevelt or of the nature of any oral report made.

. . . Mr. Wallace expressed the opinion that there should not be left pending any question which might result in conflict between China and the U.S.S.R. President Chiang suggested that President Roosevelt act as an arbiter or "middleman" between China and the U.S.S.R. (NOTE: President Chiang's suggestion was apparently prompted by Mr. Wallace's earlier statement that President Roosevelt was willing to act as an arbiter between the Communists and the Kuomintang. Mr. Wallace made no comment at the time. However, after discussing the matter with Mr. Vincent that evening, Mr. Wallace made it clear to President Chiang the next morning before breakfast that President Roosevelt had not suggested acting as arbiter between China and the U.S.S.R. and that, whereas he felt that the United States would be quite willing to use its good offices to get the U.S.S.R. and China together, it could not undertake the role of "middleman" in negotiations between the U.S.S.R. and China or become a party or guarantor of any agreement reached between China and the U.S.S.R.)

Mr. Wallace said that he felt that the people of the United States were deeply interested in seeing an increase in Chinese agricultural efficiency which will permit a sound industrialization. The United States desires a strong, democratic China which would make for a healthy political situation in the country. The United States had always had this idea and it felt most strongly in that regard now. Mr. Wallace believed that no matter how dark the present situation was in China, if China exerted herself to the utmost, it could with help from the United States and a kindly attitude on the part of Great Britain, realize its destiny. There would be no time to lose in effecting improvements once the war was over.

President Chiang expressed a desire for friendly understanding with the U.S.S.R. Mr. Wallace mentioned a conversation which he had had in Tashkent with Ambassador Harriman. Ambassador Harriman had told Mr. Wallace of a recent discussion he had had with Mr. Stalin during which China was discussed. President Chiang asked to see a copy of the memorandum which Mr. Wallace had mentioned. Mr. Wallace said he did not have a copy. He recalled that Mr. Stalin had stressed the need for a united China eager to carry on the war against Japan. Mr. Wallace suggested that Dr. Soong discuss the matter with Mr. Vincent, who probably had a better idea of the contents of the memorandum since he had had a number of conversations with Ambassador Harriman. (NOTE: That evening Dr. Soong asked Mr. Vincent about the matter, requesting to see any notes that Mr. Vincent might have made. Mr. Vincent said that he had only his memory to rely upon and informed Dr. Soong of those portions of the memorandum which he thought it appropriate and judicious to give him. Specifically he told Dr. Soong that Mr. Stalin had agreed to President Roosevelt's point that support of President Chiang was advisable during the prosecution of the war; that Mr. Stalin had expressed a keen interest in there being reached a settlement between the Kuomintang and the Chinese Communists, basing his interest on the practical matter of more effective fighting against Japan rather than upon any ideological considerations; that Mr. Stalin had criticized the suspicious attitude of the Chinese regarding the Sakhalin Agreement with Japan; and that Mr. Stalin felt the United States should assume a position of leadership in the Far East.)

Toward the end of the conversation Mr. Wallace described to President Chiang the developments in agriculture which he had observed in Siberia. The discussion ended sometime after 6 p. m.

DISCUSSION WITH PRESIDENT CHIANG, JUNE 22—4 : 30 p.m.

Present : President Chiang
        Madame Chiang
        Vice President Wallace
        Dr. T. V. Soong
        Dr. Wang Shih-chieh
        Messrs. Vincent, Lattimore, and Hazard

Mr. Wallace mentioned the poor showing the Chinese troops had made. He referred specifically to a story he had heard about the Chinese peasants attacking the soldiers in the Honan campaign because they were running away from the Japanese. President Chiang then undertook to explain the situation. He said that Chinese reverses were due to a loss of morale on the part of the soldiers ; that this loss of morale was to a large extent due to the economic situation. Mr. Vincent asked President Chiang whether he understood correctly that it was the morale of the troops rather than lack of equipment which had caused the reverses. President Chiang replied, "both". (NOTE: The next day, at the request of Madame Chiang, President Chiang explained his reference to the effect of the economic situation on the morale of the troops. He said that the soldiers at the front were worried about their families who were suffering at home because of the inflation. He also said that the condition of the troops themselves was adversely affected by inflationary high prices and scarcity of goods. In this latter connection he stated however that the situation was better now than it had been some months ago.)

President Chiang then described what he considered to be basic in the present unfortunate military situation in China. He said that the Chinese people have fought for seven years under conditions of great hardship, and that they had expected help from abroad ; that they had expected an all-out Burma campaign early this year and this would have resulted in bringing relief to the Chinese Army ; and that the failure to initiate an all-out Burma campaign had had a decidedly adverse effect on Chinese morale. The Chinese people felt that they had been deserted. President Chiang then referred to his conversations with President Roosevelt at Cairo. He said that President Roosevelt had promised an all-out campaign in Burma early in 1944 but that at Tehran President Roosevelt had reversed his decision, indicating that the necessary amphibious landing craft would not be available for such a campaign. President Chiang said that this reversal of decision had had a very unfortunate reaction in China. He referred to his conversation with President Roosevelt, at which time he had told President Roosevelt that, unless very early action were taken to open up Burma he could not count upon a continuance of effective Chinese resistance to the Japanese. Recent developments had proven him correct in his estimate. Mr. Wallace said that he recalled having a conversation with President Roosevelt, either personally or in a Cabinet meeting, regarding this matter but that he did not recall the details. He asked Mr. Vincent regarding the matter but Mr. Vincent said he did not have any detailed information concerning the Cairo conversations. (NOTE: The day of Mr. Wallace's departure— June 24th—President Chiang asked Mr. Wallace to inform President Roosevelt that he, President Chiang, understood the necessity under which President Roosevelt was working when he reversed his decision regarding the Burma campaign ; that he was therefore not criticizing President Roosevelt for his decision ; but that he wished to remind President Roosevelt that the prediction which he, President Chiang, had made at the time was sound.)

President Chiang then discussed his relations with the American Army in China. He said that American army officers clearly indicated their lack of confidence in China but that he, President Chiang, "continued to have full confidence in his army". He asked Mr. Wallace to report this to President Roosevelt and to tell him that, in spite of the attitude of the American Army, he would be guided by the advice of President Roosevelt. President Chiang, somewhat apologetically, (but with obvious intent to get across a point) mentioned what he described as a minor incident involving General Stilwell. He said that in the early stages of the Honan campaign he had asked General Stilwell for diversion to his air force of 1,000 tons of gasolene, but that General Stilwell had very abruptly refused the request, saying that the Chinese Army could get the gasolene from its own "over the hump" supplies. President Chiang indicated that it was difficult for him to operate in the face of such an uncooperative attitude. In response to Mr. Wallace's query, President Chiang said that he lacked confidence in General Stilwell's judgment. He went on to say that critical comment in the American press of the Chinese Army and the attitude of the American Army in China had adverse effects on Chinese morale but that he retained the confidence of his army and confidence in his army. Mr. Wallace commented upon the remarkable degree of faith which China had in the Generalissimo. At this point (5 p. m.) President Chiang, Mr. Wallace, Dr. Soong, Dr. Wang Shih-chieh, and Mr. Vincent went into the drawing room to continue the discussion, which lasted until 7:30 p. m.

Mr. Vincent made a brief recapitulation of that portion of the preceding conversation which had dealt with the military situation in China and the question of the present unfavorable position of the Chinese Army and asked President Chiang whether he had any suggestions with regard to measures which might effect an improvement. President Chiang said that he had nothing to suggest at that time. He, President Chiang, went back again to the Cairo Conference decision regarding the Burma campaign, stating that if it could have been carried out the effect on morale in China would have been very great even though the material assistance which might have been afforded China would not have been large, and that the current defeats would have been avoided.

Mr. Wallace asked President Chiang about the "New Life" movement. President Chiang gave a brief description of the movement, stating that its purpose was to train the people in having more disciplined lives and to raise their standards of thinking and conduct.

President Chiang next referred to criticism of China appearing in the American press and said that this criticism should be stopped. He said that the Chinese people were losing hope of receiving aid from abroad.

President Chiang next launched forth into a lengthy complaint against the Chinese Communists. He said that China suffered greatly because of the Communists. He said that the people of the United States did not understand the situation. Although the Communists were not entirely responsible for the situation in China, their subversive actions and propaganda had had a very unfavorable effect on Chinese morale. He referred to the first year of the war when he had received the cooperation of the Communists "within the law", but said that the Communists now were not subject to discipline and refused to obey his orders. He said that the attitude of the Chinese toward the Communists was an important factor in the situation; that the Chinese people did not regard the Communists as Chinese, but regarded them as "internationalists", subject to the orders of the Third International. Mr. Wallace mentioned the fact that the Third International had been dissolved but President Chiang indicated that the situation had not been altered by that fact.

Mr. Wallace mentioned remarks that were made to him by Mr. Martel Hall, Manager of the Peking branch of the National City Bank of New York, who had traveled from Peking through Communist territory to Chungking in 1943. Mr. Hall had spoken in terms of high praise of the Communists, had said that they continued to have confidence in the Generalissimo, but that they felt the Generalissimo was not correctly informed with regard to the situation in Communist areas. President Chiang said that Mr. Hall, like many other Americans, (he mentioned specifically Colonel Carlson) was under the influence of Communist propaganda. President Chiang said that he did not like to use harsh language regarding the Communists; that he would welcome them back into the Government fold; but that the fact was that the low morale of the people and the army was due to Communist propaganda. He said that the Communists desired a breakdown of Chinese resistance against the Japanese because this would strengthen their own position. Mr. Wallace expressed amazement at this statement. President Chiang admitted that the Communists desire the defeat of Japan but that they were now convinced that this defeat could be accomplished without Chinese resistance. They therefore hoped for the collapse of the Kuomintang prior to the end of the war because such a collapse would enable them to seize power, whereas, if the Kuomintang continued in power until peace the Communists would have no opportunity to supplant it. President Chiang referred to the clever Communist propaganda to the effect that they were not tied to the U. S. S. R., that they were in fact nothing more than agrarian democrats. As a matter of fact, the Communists follow the orders of the Third International. The Chinese Government cannot openly criticize the Communists for their connection with the Third International because it is afraid of offending the U. S. S. R. Mr. Wallace referred to the patriotic attitude of the Communists in the United States and said that he could not understand the attitude of the Chinese Communists, as described by President Chiang. President Chiang said that this difference in the attitude of the American and the Chinese Communists might be explained by the fact that there was no possibility of the American Communists seizing power, whereas the Chinese Communists definitely desired to do so in China. He then said that the United States was far removed from the U. S. S. R. but that the U. S. S. R. would not feel safe if the Communists were not in power in China. He then laughingly remarked that the Chinese Communists were more communistic than the Russian Communists.

Mr. Vincent inquired as to the progress of conversations between the Communist representative in Chungking, Lin Tzu-han, and the Kuomintang representatives of which Dr. Wang Shih-chieh was chief. President Chiang said he desired to make the Communists live up to their propaganda in regard to their desire for cooperation and offensive action against the Japanese. He said that there had been Communist proposals for a settlement and Kuomintang counterproposals. The Kuomintang proposal was very simple: support the President, support the Government, and support the war effort. The Chinese Government requires obedience from the Communists and incorporation of the Communist Army within the Chinese Army as its first essential to a settlement. Secondly, the Chinese Government requires that territory now under Communist control become an integral part of China administratively. If the Communists would accede to these two demands they would receive equal treatment with other Chinese in China, they would be guaranteed political amnesty, and given the right to continue as a political party with freedom of assembly and discussion. President Chiang also said that if the Communists would accede to these requirements, the group of American officers would be allowed to proceed to North China as requested. They would not have direct contact with the Communists but would go under the auspices of the Chinese Government to train "converted" Communist troops. Mr. Wallace asked President Chiang whether he was optimistic with regard to a settlement.. President Chiang said it was possible if the Communists showed sincerity. If a settlement were reached President Chiang said he could carry out his program for democracy earlier than now expected. He said that he would try his best to reach a settlement.

President Chiang again reverted to the subject of Communist propaganda. He asked Mr. Wallace to inform President Roosevelt that Communist propaganda has his highest respect. President Roosevelt should bear in mind that the Communists could not openly use the U.S.S.R. for support but that they could and did use the U.S.A. (opinion) to force the Kuomintang to accede to their demands. Such tactics make a settlement difficult. The best assistance that the United States could give in this matter would be to display "aloofness" to the Communists. They would then show a greater willingness to reach a settlement with the Kuomintang.

At this juncture, Dr. Wang Shih-chieh said he wished to offer some explanation on the Chinese Government's proposal to the Communists. He said that whereas the Chinese Government required that the Communists submit to its authority it was not the intention to interfere in local administration and that it was not the intention to remove local officials or even army officers who showed themselves cooperative.

Mr. Wallace said that the Generalissimo's description of the situation filled him with "hope and fear". He said that China's relations with the U.S.S.R. were threatened by the attitude demonstrated in conversations which he had had with Mr. Wei and Admiral Shen (Minister of Agriculture) and by President Chiang's remarks. Mr. Wallace did not mention what it was in the situation that filled him with "hope".

Mr. Wallace stated that American Army officers felt that Chinese interpretation of the significance of the transfer of Japanese troops from Manchuria to China was incorrect. Mr. Wallace also pointed out that if, as President Chiang stated, the Chinese Communists were linked with the U.S.S.R., then there was even greater need for settlement. He also expressed his appreciation of the frankness with which President Chiang had spoken.

President Chiang again advised that we adopt an attitude of "coolness" toward the Communists. He said that the United States Army was anxious that all military power in China be utilized against the Japanese but the United States Army did not realize the threat which the Communists constituted to the Chinese Government and overestimated the utility of the Communists against the Japanese. He went on to say that he understood President Roosevelt's policy and asked that President Roosevelt be informed that he, President Chiang, desired a political solution of the problem.

Mr. Wallace asked whether it was not possible to reach an understanding on a "lower level" with a view to maximum use of forces in the north. Mr. Vincent asked what President Chiang thought would be the adverse effects of sending the United States Army intelligence group to Communist areas *now* without awaiting a settlement. President Chiang said that "haste does not make for speed". He said, "please do not press; please understand that the Communists are not good for the war effort against Japan". With this evasive reply the conversation was concluded.

DISCUSSION WITH PRESIDENT CHIANG, JUNE 23—9 A. M.

Present: President Chiang
Vice President Wallace
Dr. Hollington Tong (translating)
Dr. Wang Shih-chieh
Mr. Lattimore (assisting in translating)
Mr. Vincent

Mr. Wallace reported conversations with General Marshall and with Secretary Stimson before leaving America in regard to China's situation in an endeavor to persuade President Chiang that we are not interested in "Chinese Communists" but are interested in the prosecution of the war. (He and Mr. Vincent had decided upon this line of approach the night before in order to avoid further lengthy discussion of the Communists *per se*.) He spoke of the military situation in East Asia in general terms and of the need for taking all steps that might further hasten the end of the war and reduce the loss of American lives. He felt that the United States Army intelligence group in North China would be able to gather intelligence which would save the lives of American aviators. Mr. Vincent again stressed the point that whereas he appreciated that President Chiang was faced with a very real problem in handling negotiations for a settlement with the Communists, the American Army was also faced with a very real problem with regard to obtaining intelligence from North China. He mentioned specifically the need for intelligence by the B–29 group at Chengtu. He pointed out that the American Army had no interest whatsoever in Communists but that it had for very urgent reasons an interest in carrying on the war against Japan from China. He urged that President Chiang's problem of reaching a settlement with the Communists and the United States Army problem of obtaining intelligence be treated as separate—as indeed they were.

President Chiang, completely reversing his position of the evening before, said "that can be done". He said that the group could go as soon as it was organized without reference to a settlement with the Communists. He said, however, that they must go under the auspices of the National Military Council rather than under the auspices of the United States Army, and added that Chinese officers must go with them. He then stressed the point that the Communists did not take his orders and gave concrete illustrations. He said with some feeling that the United States Army must realize how essential it is to have a unified command. Much pressure has been brought to bear by the United States Government to have the Chinese Government reach a settlement with the Communists but the United States Government has exerted no pressure upon the Communists. He said that the American Government should issue a statement that the Communists should come to terms with the Chinese Government. He said that the United States Army attitude supported the Communists and requested Mr. Wallace upon his return to America to make it clear that the Communists should come to terms with the Chinese Government. In response to a remark by Mr. Wallace, President Chiang said there were no present questions which would cause conflict with the U.S.S.R. Mr. Vincent again pointed out that solution of President Chiang's important problems of relations with the Communists and the U.S.S.R. need not precede the despatch of military observers to North China. President Chiang said that the military observers would be permitted to go.

President Chiang said, "I am confident that what President Roosevelt stands for is good for China and for the furtherance of the war." "But," he said, "one of the things for which we are fighting this war is the maintenance of order. Please tell President Roosevelt that I will follow his advice but I must insist on the maintenance of law and order and upon the observance of discipline."

Mr. Wallace again stressed the point that there should be no situation in China which might lead to conflict with the U.S.S.R. President Chiang said that the Chinese Government had gone far out of its way to come to an agreement with the Communists in order to avoid conflict with the U.S.S.R. and added that anything not detrimental to the sovereignty of the Chinese Government would be done to avoid conflict with the U.S.S.R. At this point Mr. Wallace again said that the United States could not be expected to be a party to negotiations between China and the U.S.S.R. He also said that President Chiang's formula for settlement with the Communists might prove transitory unless China reached an understanding with the U.S.S.R. He referred again to Ambassador Harriman's discussion with Mr. Stalin as indicating the necessity for an agreement with the U.S.S.R. President Chiang stated that he fully shared Mr. Wallace's views and that the Chinese Government would seek an early opportunity to have discussions with the Government of the U.S.S.R. Although Mr. Wallace had indicated that the United States might not be able to assist in the negotiations he continued to hope that there could be found ways whereby the United States could be of assistance.

Mr. Wallace stated that another reason why a settlement with the Communists might prove temporary was the economic situation in China and expressed a hope that measures could be taken as soon as possible to improve the economic lot of the Chinese people. President Chiang endorsed this view. Mr. Wallace said that in so far as the Communists have power and influence it is due to economic conditions. He said that the Communist revolution in Russia in 1916 was brought about primarily by economic distress. He admitted that it was very difficult to do anything now after seven years of war, but he pointed out how easy it would be to attribute to the Communists social unrest in China when actually this unrest would be due to economic distress.

President Chiang indicated that the making of concessions to the Communists did not matter as long as discipline could be maintained. Mr. Wallace said that unity should express itself in welfare of the people if communism was to be avoided. Mr. Vincent suggested that the best defense against communism in China was agrarian reform. Mr. Wallace said that when the war was over it would take much energy and foresight for the Chinese Government to avoid the fate of the Kerensky government in Russia. President Chiang said that the Chinese Government was proceeding with these considerations in mind.

The conversation ended at 11 a. m. and was resumed at 5 p. m. In the meantime, Mr. Wallace had visited the Embassy in Chungking, had received a message from President Roosevelt advising him to press President Chiang to permit the despatch of the Army observer group, and had arranged that General Ferris join the conversation in the afternoon. Participants were: President Chiang, Mr. Wallace, Dr. Soong (translating), Dr. Wang Shih-chieh, Mr. Lattimore (assisting in translating), Mr. Vincent, General Ferris and Mr. John Service (aide to General Ferris).

Mr. Wallace read to President Chiang President Roosevelt's message. Mr. Vincent made a brief recapitulation of the morning's conversation and asked President Chiang whether his understanding was correct that the observer group might proceed to North China as soon as it was organized. President Chiang replied in the affirmative. Mr. Vincent then asked for an explanation of the conditions under which the group might proceed. There ensued some discussion as to whether the word "auspices" was a correct translation of President Chiang's Chinese term describing the relationship of the National Military Council to the United States Army group. It was decided that whereas "auspices" was not an exact translation, it was about as good as any that could be found and that whatever the translation, President Chiang did not intend that the group would have to operate under orders from the National Military Council.

General Ferris then asked for clarification on a number of points: whether the United States Army group would be allowed direct communication facilities with the American command. President Chiang said they would be. General Ferris said that all information gathered would be made available to the Chinese military authorities. General Ferris asked a number of questions. President Chiang said that he should confer with General Ho Ying-chin in regard to details. General Ferris asked for President Chiang's full support and received the President's assurances in that respect. President Chiang referred to the use of the word "mission" in describing the group and said that he did not believe that it should be so called. At Madame Chiang's suggestion (she had joined the group some minutes before) it was decided to call the group the "United States Army Investigation Section".

President Chiang said that he wanted the American Army authorities to bear in mind that in as much as the Communists did not accept orders from him he could not guarantee the protection of the group while in Communist territory but that he would give all possible aid. General Ferris asked when the group might go. President Chiang said it could go as soon as it was organized. General Ferris said that it would probably comprise 15–20 men. He asked President Chiang whether there would be Chinese officers accompanying the group, and whether the group would be allowed freedom of movement. He pointed out that the members of the group would not of course remain together but would "fan out" on individual assignments. President Chiang said that General Ferris should see General Ho with regard to the composition of the group. General Ferris expressed the hope that General Ho would place no impediments in the way of the group's carrying out its mission. President Chiang said, "See General Ho tomorrow at 4 p. m. He will have my instructions." (NOTE: At this point General Ferris and Mr. Service withdrew.)

Mr. Wallace presented to President Chiang a scroll sent by President Roosevelt to the people of Chungking. President Chiang said, "Representing the people of Chungking, I accept this scroll as a priceless symbol which they will hold forever in gratitude and reverence."

President Chiang then said he had a few questions to raise with Mr. Wallace. He requested Mr. Wallace to mention to President Roosevelt the question of Allied Military Government of Occupied Territories (AMGOT) in the Far East, and suggest to President Roosevelt that there be an agreement between British, American and Chinese authorities on this question. President Chiang said that at Cairo he had raised with President Roosevelt the question of a Chinese-American economic commission to handle projects of post-war reconstruction in China. He hoped that Dr. Kung would have an opportunity to discuss this matter while he was in Washington and requested Mr. Wallace to lend whatever assistance he could. Mr. Wallace expressed approval of the idea and said he would do what he could.

Mr. Wallace referred to a comment he had made to President Chiang soon after his arrival in Chungking regarding the absence of any Russian territorial ambitions in the Far East. Without modifying that statement he wished to add an explanation which had occurred to him since the first conversation. He said that the U.S.S.R. wanted a warm water port in the Far East and that President Roosevelt had suggested that Dairen might be made a free port. Mr. Wallace said that in making this remark he was not acting under instructions from President Roosevelt or speaking officially. President Chiang said that he had discussed the matter with President Roosevelt at Cairo and had indicated his agreement provided the U.S.S.R. cooperated with China in the Far East and provided there was no impairment of Chinese sovereignty.

President Chiang referred to the present economic distress (lack of consumer products) in China and said that Dr. Kung was going to ask for an increase of "over the hump" tonnage to provide for the importation of 2,000 tons of civilian supplies each month. He said that it was very important that this request be granted from the military as well as the economic point of view. In response to Mr. Wallace's question President Chiang said that these civilian supplies would be comprised of cloth, medicines and spare parts. Mr. Wallace mentioned the possibility of using C–54s now that Myitkyina was in Allied hands but he pointed out that it might prove very difficult to persuade the American Army to permit civilian supplies to take up air cargo space. President Chiang asked Mr. Wallace to take a personal interest in the matter.

President Chiang asked Mr. Wallace to inform President Roosevelt as follows: "If the United States can bring about better relations between the U.S.S.R. and China and can bring about a meeting between Chinese and Soviet representatives, President Chiang would very much welcome such friendly assistance." If the United States would "sponsor" such a meeting President Chiang would go more than halfway in reaching an understanding with the U.S.S.R. A conference with regard to Pacific affairs was desirable and the United States would be the logical place for such a conference. Madame Chiang interpolated to suggest that it be called the "North Pacific Conference". Mr. Vincent inquired whether they were not speaking of two related but separate matters, that is, discussions between Chinese and Soviet representatives in regard to their problems, and a conference of nations bordering on the North Pacific to discuss more general problems. He said that it would seem desirable to have the Sino-Soviet discussions prior to any North Pacific conference. Dr. Soong said that a North Pacific conference might be used as a cloak for discussions between Chinese and Soviet representatives. Mr. Wallace said that Dr. Soong would be of value in Washington in laying the foundation for such a conference. President Chiang said that he could not be spared from Chungking and added, laughingly, that with Dr. Kung gone and Madame Chiang planning to go abroad, Dr. Soong was his only mouthpiece in speaking to Americans.

The conversation ended at this point—7 p. m.

———

June 24th—During the hour's ride from President Chiang's residence to the airport (10 to 11 a. m.) President Chiang made the following comments (Madame Chiang interpreting) which he requested Mr. Wallace to consider as a message from himself to President Roosevelt:

1. The attitude of President Roosevelt at the Cairo Conference, his warmth, etc., has immense historic value to the people and army of China.

2. President Chiang is gratified over the abrogation of the unequal treaties and efforts on behalf of the Exclusion Act.

3. Mr. Wallace's visit to China, as the representative of President Roosevelt, to bring about accord with Russia shows great friendship for China.

4. Mr. Wallace's visit at this dark hour will help the morale of the troops and give hope that America will continue to aid China.

5. Assure the President that President Chiang understands the necessity under which the President acted when he changed plans at Tehran. Nevertheless, President Chiang foresaw what the change meant. When President Chiang sent a strong, frank memorandum to President Roosevelt it was because he foresaw what is now happening. If the Generalissimo sees that China's collapse will come he will tell the President, but China has not yet arrived at the state of collapse which he predicted to the President. Things are not today as bad as he feared.

6. President Chiang greatly respects the President's character, his views, etc.

7. President Chiang was deeply touched when Mr. Wallace told him about how badly the President felt about the Tehran change relating to the Generalissimo personally. Therefore, he again appreciates most deeply that Mr. Wallace should come out on behalf of Russo-Chinese friendship.

8. The Chinese Communist question is an internal political problem but he would nevertheless welcome the President's assistance. He feels that the Chinese Communists are not men of good faith. Their signature is no good. He would not like to see the President blamed for Communist failure to carry out commitments. Just the same he is happy to have the President's help if the President, after mature consideration, decides he would like to give his help. The Generalissimo would not consider the President's participation as meddling in China's internal affairs, but the Generalissimo is a true friend who knows the Chinese Communists through and through and thinks that no matter what the Communists say they will do, it will not be carried out, in which case the President's prestige would suffer a great loss. The Generalissimo wants the President to know that the conflict between the Communists and the Central Government is not like that between capitalism and labor in the United States—the situations are not analogous.

9. The Generalissimo is eager to have closer cooperation and understanding with the President—but how? Too many channels through State Department. Churchill has personal representative in Carton de Wiart who handles both political and military matters. Could President Roosevelt pick someone like this? He could perform an invaluable service. Today military cooperation is very difficult because of personnel. He feels that Chennault is most cooperative. Stilwell has improved, but has no understanding of political matters—he is entirely military in outlook.

10. The Generalissimo has the utmost confidence in Dr. Kung. In helping Dr. Kung the President will be helping the Generalissimo.

11. The Generalissimo is shaping everything toward the democratic path. He wrote *China's Destiny* to get the Communists to fall into line. The Generalissimo wants the Communists to be a political party. He plans such advances in agrarian program that the Communists will have no opportunity to stir up social unrest.

12. He hopes after the war to get the interest rate for farmers down to 10 per cent and hopes to promote land ownership by breaking up large land holdings.

44

President Roosevelt to President Chiang Kai-shek

[WASHINGTON?] *July 14, 1944*

Vice President Wallace has handed me your telegram of July 8 in reply to his letter to you of June 27 [12] I have also received with much interest the Vice President's full report of his conversations with you. Mr. Wallace has told me of the twelve points which you requested that he bring to my attention, and I am grateful for the friendliness and frankness with which your views have been expressed.

With regard to the negotiations now in progress with the Chinese Communists, I have noted with particular satisfaction your assurance that only political means will be employed in seeking a solution. Also I welcome the indication given me by Mr. Wallace of your desire for improved relations between the U.S.S.R. and China, and your suggestion that I use my good offices to arrange for a conference between Chinese and Russian representatives is being given serious thought. It occurs to me that any such conference would be greatly facilitated if a working arrangement had been reached beforehand between the Chinese Government and the Chinese Communists for effective prosecution of the war against the Japanese in North China. The Vice President has also informed me, in this connection, of your encouraging remark that it would be possible to carry out your democratic program earlier than expected if a settlement with the Communists could be secured.

It is with regret that I have received reports of Madame Chiang's ill health and I trust that she will have a speedy recovery.

With warm regards and best wishes,

Sincerely yours,

FRANKLIN D. ROOSEVELT

---

[12] The letter from Vice President Wallace of June 27 and the reply from Generalissimo Chiang Kai-shek of July 8 have not been found.

Annexes to Chapter III: The Ambassadorship of Major General Patrick J. Hurley, 1944–1946

45

The Ambassador in China (Gauss) to Secretary Hull

893.00/8–3144   CHUNGKING, *August 31, 1944*

Yesterday evening President Chiang Kai-shek sent for me. For an hour and a half he talked about the Communist problem, stating that it is not understood in Washington, and it is my duty to be sure the problem is understood. Set forth below are the principal points of the argument which Chiang constantly emphasized and repeated, in addition to the usual charges of bad faith and treachery against the Communists:

In the matter of world problems, China is disposed to follow our lead; and it is not unfriendly for us to suggest that China should improve relations with the Soviet Union. China should receive the entire support and sympathy of the United States Government on the domestic problem of Chinese Communists. Very serious consequences for China may result from our attitude. In urging that China resolve differences with the Communists, our Government's attitude is serving only to intensify the recalcitrance of the Communists. The request that China meet Communist demands is equivalent to asking China's unconditional surrender to a party known to be under a foreign power's influence (the Soviet Union). The Communists are growing arrogant and refuse to continue negotiations since our observer group arrived in Yenan. The United States should tell the Communists to reconcile their differences with and submit to the national government of China.

This could be done by our observer group as well as by the Embassy in any contact we have with representatives of the Communists at this point. In addition, the strength of Communist armies could be determined by observer group. The need of Communist forces to defeat Japan should not be stressed by us. The Chinese Communists are under the influence of a foreign power; neither that power nor the Communists dares condemn it, since to do so would condemn the Communists before the people of China in general. The Communists' expansionist ambitions are what brought about assignment of troops to prevent expansion of this nature; prove all Communists cannot be trusted. Furthermore, Chiang Kai-shek commented that the problem of Communist cooperation would not be solved by introduction of a foreign commander of Chinese armies. Chiang stated that there are persons in Washington who seem to believe that it is merely a matter of issuing military orders to have them obeyed and said that the Communists have not obeyed, although he has ordered them to attack the Japanese.

Since I had been assured that I might speak openly and frankly, it was possible for me to stress that the United States Government is not interested in the Chinese Communists' cause; however, we are interested in seeing a prompt solution of a Chinese internal problem which finds the armed forces of China facing one another instead of facing and making war upon Japan, and, in the present critical period of the war, this is of outstanding importance. My statement to Chiang was that our observation, and reports to Washington, showed a definite breakdown in negotiations between the Kuomintang and the Communists prior to the organization of our army observer group to go to Yenan, that the observer group is in Yenan only for purposes of military intelligence, that the group has no political mission, and what has been described as arrogant refusal to continue negotiations cannot have resulted from their presence.

Answering a question as to whether I believed the people of China favor the Communists, I replied that I did not. However, I remarked that at the present time, the Communist Party is reported not to be practicing or preaching communism, but to be following and supporting the Kuomintang principles of improvement of conditions of the masses and democracy. My statement was that, if I might speak frankly, many believe the Kuomintang Party in power has not in recent years kept their principles first and foremost in mind, and the Embassy has not failed to hear of some of the disaffection, both in military and in other circles, which resulted. The Generalissimo stated that only the Communists obstruct and defy his government, and if reports or suggestions of dissatisfaction exist at other points, it is merely the machination of Communists utilizing stooges removed from themselves to convey propaganda of this nature.

My entire sympathy with the difficult task confronting Chiang Kai-shek in solving the Communist problems was expressed; and I stated we have not suggested that the Chinese Government should yield to the demands of the Communists. The interest of the United States Government is only in dissipation of the existing critical situation and in the unification of China, and it is our hope that a peaceful solution for this situation can be found among themselves by the Chinese.

Having received permission to speak frankly, I continued with the personal observation that although Chiang Kai-shek states that the Communists cannot be trusted, for a long time we have heard equal complaints from the Communists that it is not possible to trust the Kuomintang government. In my opinion, effort should be exerted to clear up this mutual distrust, and it was my own view that a solution might be reached in some measure which would result in sharing of and participation in the responsibilities of the government by competent representatives of other parties and groups. Of course, I was familiar with the contention of the Kuomintang that there can now be only one party government; and I should like to see the difficulty surmounted, but even if it were not possible to overcome it on a broad basis, giving representation in the government to minor parties, it might be that a limited solution could be reached which might provide for able representation of special groups or parties, and these individuals should be invited to come and participate in some form of responsible war council planning and carrying out the plans to meet the serious war crisis by which China is faced at the present time. Perhaps it might be possible to develop, through such a sharing of responsibility, a situation which would overcome existing criticism and mistrust, and a disposition to work together for China's unification, whereupon Chiang Kai-shek commented that the suggestion might be worth studying, at least.

The conversation was an entirely friendly one; most of the talking was done by Chiang Kai-shek, and the conversation ended with Chiang reiterating his arguments as set forth in the opening portion of this message.

GAUSS

46

Secretary Hull to the Ambassador in China (Gauss)

893.00/8–3144

WASHINGTON, *September 9, 1944*

1. Careful consideration has been accorded to your messages by the President and by me, and we are in agreement with you that at the present time, a frank, friendly, and positive approach should be made to Chiang Kai Shek on the matters of governmental and related military conditions in China.

2. The Generalissimo's suggestion that Chinese Communists should be instructed to settle their differences with the government has been noted by us. Chiang Kai Shek made a like suggestion to the Vice President, and Chiang's argumentation in general, as set forth in your previous message, is strikingly like that used with Vice President Wallace; would indicate a discouraging lack of progress in the Generalissimo's thinking, in consideration of dissident developments reported in other areas not under the influence of the Communists, and in the light of Chiang's own professed desire to come to a settlement with the Communists.

3. Unless you regard the step as inadvisable, it is suggested that you inform Chiang if he will arrange for a meeting, you are prepared to talk with the Communist representative in Chungking along the same general lines as you and Vice President Wallace have talked with Chiang; that you will indicate to the Communist representative the urgent need for unity in China in carrying on the war and in making ready for the peace; that to achieve such unity a spirit of good will and tolerance, of give and take, is essential; that at the present time, Chinese of every shade of political thought should cooperate for the defeat of Japan, and that if the principal objective of victory is kept firmly in mind, differences can be settled. The foregoing may be told to Chiang as from the President and from me. You may add that we concur in your comments to Chiang Kai Shek as reported. In addition, please tell Chiang that the observer group in north China is on a military mission and we do not consider it advisable to use it for the purpose which he suggested.

4. Further, we note with approval that you utilized the opportunity afforded by conversation with Chiang to mention your idea of a coalition council as described by you. Please tell Chiang that the President and I feel your suggestion is timely as well as practical, and worthy of careful consideration; that we are concerned not alone with reference to non-settlement with the Chinese Communists but also with regard to reports of dissidence and dissatisfaction among non-Communist Chinese in other areas of the country; that we are not concerned with Chinese Communists or other dissident elements as such, but are anxious, on behalf of the United Nations and on our own behalf, and also on behalf of China, that, under the leadership of a strong but tolerant and representative government, the people of China develop and use the spiritual and physical resources at their command to carry on the war and to establish a lasting democratic peace, and to achieve this, factional differences can, and should be,

settled and merged by intelligent cooperation and conciliation. It is our belief that a most effective means to achieve this end would be a council or some body which represents all influential elements in China, with full powers, under the leadership of Chiang Kai Shek. However, we recognize that Chiang may have in mind some means of achieving the same result which would be equally or more effective.

Further, you may make use as you wish of such portions of the cogent arguments expressed in your telegrams, as coming from us, and also the views which were well expressed by Atcheson on August ninth in his conversation with Sun Fo.

Kindly inform General Hurley, General Stilwell, and Mr. Nelson with regard to the matter. You are authorized to invite one or more of them to go with you to call upon Chiang if you feel that it would serve a useful purpose.

HULL

47

Memoranda by Foreign Service Officers in China, 1943–1945

[Extracts] [1]

1. Soviet intentions with respect to the Far East, including China, are aggressive.

September 17, 1943 (Davies)

"It is perhaps not too early to suggest that Soviet policy will probably be directed initially at establishing frontiers which will insure Russian security and at rehabilitation of the U. S. S. R. There is no reason to cherish optimism regarding a voluntary Soviet contribution to our fight against Japan, whether in the shape of air bases or the early opening of a second front in Northeast Asia. The Russians may be expected to move against the Japanese when it suits their pleasure, which may not be until the final phases of the war—and then only in order to be able to participate in dictating terms to the Japanese and to establish new strategic frontiers."

January 15, 1944 (Davies)

"We need to dispatch immediately, while it is still welcome, a military and political observers' mission to Communist China to collect enemy information, assist in and prepare for certain limited operations from that area, obtain accurate estimates of the strength of Communist armies, report on Russian operations in North China and Manchuria should Russia attack Japan, and assess the possibility of North China and Manchuria developing into a separate Chinese state—perhaps even as a Russian satellite."

April 7, 1944 (Service)

"We must be concerned with Russian plans and policies in Asia because they are bound to affect our own plans in the same area. But our relations with Russia in Asia are at present only a subordinate part of our political and military relations with Russia in Europe in the over-all United Nations war effort and post-war settlement. We should make every effort to learn what the Russian aims in Asia are. A good way of gaining material relevant to this will be a

---

[1] These extracts from reports by John P. Davies, Jr., Raymond P. Ludden and John Stewart Service are grouped in order of the several themes as summarized on pp. 64–65.

careful first-hand study of the strength, attitudes and popular support of the Chinese Communists. . . .

"Chiang unwittingly may be contributing to Russian dominance in Eastern Asia by internal and external policies which, if pursued in their present form, will render China too weak to serve as a possible counter-weight to Russia. By so doing, Chiang may be digging his own grave; not only North China and Manchuria, but also national groups such as Korea and Formosa may be driven into the arms of the Soviets."

2. The Chinese Communists have a background of subservience to the U. S. S. R., but new influences—principally nationalism—have come into play which are modifying their outlook.

June 24, 1943 (Davies)

"Chinese Communist policy appears to have followed the Comintern line. In its initial expression the policy adhered to the program of world revolution. With the Comintern's abandonment of this program, the Chinese Communists embraced in 1935, in compliance with Moscow directives, the policy of the united front.

"The new line, so far as it applied to Asia, was in all probability prompted by the Kremlin's realistic appraisal of the Soviet Union's position in the Far East. Russia was threatened by Japan. The Japanese Army had with its Manchurian adventure apparently decided upon a policy of continental expansion. Confronted by a strong Russian Army in eastern Siberia, the Japanese seemed to be intent upon outflanking the Russians through China. China could not be expected to offer strong resistance to Japanese expansion so long as it was torn by internal dissension. It was therefore evident that China should become unified and actively resist Japanese pressure westward.

"As the Chinese Communists moved away from world revolution to nationalism they also moved in the direction of more moderate internal political and economic policy. Whether these other moves were in compliance with Comintern dictates is less material than that they were historically and evolutionarily sound.

"The trend toward nationalism is believed to be strongest among the troops and guerrillas who have been fighting the national enemy. Although we have no accurate information on the subject, it is suspected that the political leaders of the Party retain their pro-Russian orientation and that they are, notwithstanding the dissolution of the Comintern, likely to be susceptible to Moscow direction. This probable schism within the Party may prove at some later date to be of major importance."

August 3, 1944 (Service)

"The Chinese Communist Party claims that it is Marxist. By this the Communists mean that their ideology, their philosophical approach, and their dialectical method are based on Marxist materialism. Marxism thus becomes to them chiefly an attitude and approach to problems. It is a long-term view of political and economic development to which all short-term considerations of temporary advantage or premature power are ruthlessly subordinated.

"The Communists actively support the war because this gives them an opportunity to mobilize, organize and indoctrinate the people, and to create and train an efficient army.

"They operate by preference in the areas behind the Japanese lines because there they are relatively free from Kuomintang interference.

"Such policies as the abandonment of land confiscation are useful temporary expedients to help them carry on the war and to win unified popular support in the areas of their operations. It also has strong propaganda appeal in other areas.

"Their espousal of democracy appeals to the great majority of the people of China and is a good club for beating the Kuomintang. They realize that popular support must be their principal weapon against the superior arms of the Kuomintang in any contest of strength.

"Their democratic claims, their engagement in guerrilla warfare behind the enemy lines, and their proclamation of liberal economic policies based on private property are also useful in appealing to foreign sympathy and in winning the foreign support which they realize will be necessary, at least for a time, in the economic rehabilitation and development of China following the war."

3. The Chinese Communists have become the most dynamic force in China and are challenging the Kuomintang for control of the country.

October 9, 1944 (Service)

"Reports of two American officers, several correspondents, and twenty-odd foreign travelers regarding conditions in the areas of North China under Communist control are in striking agreement. This unanimity, based on actual observation, is significant. It forces us to accept certain facts, and to draw from those facts an important conclusion.

"*The Japanese are being actively opposed*—in spite of the constant warfare and cruel retaliation this imposes on the population. This opposition is gaining in strength. The Japanese can temporarily crush it in a limited area by the concentration of overwhelming force. But it is impossible for them to do this simultaneously over the huge territory the Communists now influence.

"*This opposition is possible and successful because it is total guerrilla warfare aggressively waged by a totally mobilized population.* In this total mobilization the regular forces of the Communists, though leaders and organizers, have become subordinate to the vastly more numerous forces of the people themselves. They exist because the people permit, support and wholeheartedly fight with them. There is complete solidarity of Army and people.

"*This total mobilization is based upon and has been made possible by what amounts to an economic, political and social revolution.* This revolution has been moderate and democratic. It has improved the economic condition of the peasants by rent and interest reduction, tax reform and good government. It has given them democratic self-government, political consciousness and a sense of their rights. It has freed them from feudalistic bonds and given them self-respect, self-reliance and a strong feeling of cooperative group interest. *The common people, for the first time, have been given something to fight for.*

"The Japanese are being fought now not merely because they are foreign invaders but because they deny this revolution. *The people will continue to fight any government which limits or deprives them of these newly won gains.*"

November 7, 1944 (Davies)

"The Chinese Communists are so strong between the Great Wall and the Yangtze that they can now look forward to the postwar control of at least North China. They may also continue to hold not only those parts of the Yangtze valley which they now dominate but also new areas in Central and South China. The Communists have fallen heir to these new areas by a process, which has been operating for seven years, whereby Chiang Kai-shek loses his cities and principal lines of communication to the Japanese and the countryside to the Communists.

"The Communists have survived ten years of civil war and seven years of Japanese offensives. They have survived not only more sustained enemy pressure than the Chinese Central Government forces have been subjected to, but also a severe blockade imposed by Chiang.

"They have survived and they have grown. Communist growth since 1937 has been almost geometric in progression. From control of some 100,000 square kilometers with a population of one million and a half they have expanded to about 850,000 square kilometers with a population of approximately 90 million. And they will continue to grow.

"The reason for this phenomenal vitality and strength is simple and fundamental. It is mass support, mass participation. The Communist governments and armies are the first governments and armies in modern Chinese history to have positive and widespread popular support. They have this support because the governments and armies are genuinely of the people."

January 4, 1945 (Davies)

"The Current situation in China must afford the Kremlin a certain sardonic satisfaction.

"The Russians see the anti-Soviet Government of Chiang Kai-shek decaying—militarily, politically and economically. They observe the Chinese Communists consolidating in North China, expanding southward in the wake of Chiang's military debacles and now preparing for the formal establishment of a separatist administration.

"It is equally evident to the Russians that the Chinese Communists will not in the meantime be idle. The Communists have amply demonstrated a capacity for independent, dynamic growth. However Marshal Stalin may describe the Chinese Communists to his American visitors, he can scarcely be unaware of the fact that the Communists are a considerably more stalwart and self-sufficient force than any European underground or partisan movement."

4. The Kuomintang and National Government are disintegrating.

June 20, 1944 (Service)

"B. *The position of the Kuomintang and the Generalissimo is weaker than it has been for the past ten years.*

"China faces economic collapse. This is causing disintegration of the army and the government's administrative apparatus. It is one of the chief causes of growing political unrest. The Generalissimo is losing the support of a China which, by unity in the face of violent aggression, found a new and unexpected strength during the first two years of the war with Japan. Internal weaknesses are becoming accentuated and there is taking place a reversal of the process of unification.

"1. Morale is low and discouragement widespread. There is a general feeling of hopelessness.

"2. The authority of the Central Government is weakening in the areas away from the larger cities. Government mandates and measures of control cannot be enforced and remain ineffective. It is becoming difficult for the Government to collect enough food for its huge army and bureaucracy.

"3. The governmental and military structure is being permeated and demoralized from top to bottom by corruption, unprecedented in scale and openness.

"4. The intellectual and salaried classes, who have suffered the most heavily from inflation, are in danger of liquidation. The academic groups suffer not only the attrition and demoralization of economic stress; the weight of years of political control and repression is robbing them of the intellectual vigor and leadership they once had.

"5. Peasant resentment of the abuses of conscription, tax collection and other arbitrary impositions has been widespread and is growing. The danger is ever-increasing that past sporadic outbreaks of banditry and agrarian unrest may increase in scale and find political motivation.

"6. The provincial groups are making common cause with one another and with other dissident groups, and are actively consolidating their positions. Their continuing strength in the face of the growing weakness of the Central Government is forcing new measures of political appeasement in their favor.

"7. Unrest within the Kuomintang armies is increasing, as shown in one important instance by the 'Young Generals conspiracy' late in 1943. On a higher plane, the war zone commanders are building up their own spheres of influence and are thus creating a 'new warlordism.'

"8. The break between the Kuomintang and the Communists not only shows no signs of being closed, but grows more critical with the passage of time: the inevitability of civil war is now generally accepted.

"9. The Kuomintang is losing the respect and support of the people by its selfish policies and its refusal to heed progressive criticism. It seems unable to revivify itself with fresh blood, and its unchanging leadership shows a growing ossification and loss of a sense of reality. To combat the dissensions and cliquism within the Party, which grows more rather than less acute, the leadership is turning toward the reactionary and unpopular Chen brothers clique.

"10. The Generalissimo shows a similar loss of realistic flexibility and a hardening of narrowly conservative views. His growing megalomania and his unfortunate attempts to be 'sage' as well as leader—shown, for instance, by 'China's Destiny' and his book on economics—have forfeited the respect of many intellectuals, who enjoy in China a position of unique influence. Criticism of his dictatorship is becoming outspoken.

"In the face of the grave crisis with which it is confronted, the Kuomintang is ceasing to be the unifying and progressive force in Chinese society, the role in which it made its greatest contribution to modern China.

"C. *The Kuomintang is not only proving itself incapable of averting a debacle by its own initiative: on the contrary, its policies are precipitating the crisis.*

"Some war-weariness in China must be expected. But the policies of the Kuomintang under the impact of hyperinflation and in the presence of obvious signs of internal and external weakness must be described as bankrupt. This truth is emphasized by the failure of the Kuomintang to come to grips with the situation during the recently concluded plenary session of the Central Executive Committee.

"1. *On the internal political front the desire of the Kuomintang leaders to perpetuate their own power overrides all other considerations.* The result is the enthronement of reaction.

"The Kuomintang continues to ignore the great political drive within the country for democratic reform. The writings of the Generalissimo and the Party press show that they have no real understanding of that term. Constitutionalism remains an empty promise for which the only "preparation" is a half-hearted attempt to establish an unpopular and undemocratic system of local self-government based on collective responsibility and given odium by Japanese utilization in Manchuria and other areas under their control.

"Questions basic to the future of democracy such as the form of the Constitution and the composition and election of the National Congress remain the dictation of the Kuomintang. There is no progress toward the fundamental conditions of freedom of expression and recognition of non-Kuomintang groups. Even the educational and political advantages of giving power and democratic character to the existing but impotent Peoples Political Council are ignored.

"The Kuomintang shows no intention of relaxing the authoritarian controls on which its present power depends. Far from discarding or reducing the paraphernalia of a police state—the multiple and omnipresent secret police organizations, the Gendarmerie, and so forth—it continues to strengthen them as its last resort for internal security.

"2. *On the economic front the Kuomintang is unwilling to take any effective steps to check inflation which would injure the landlord-capitalist class.*

"It is directly responsible for the increase of official corruption which is one of the main obstacles to any rational attempt to ameliorate the financial situation. It does nothing to stop large-scale profiteering, hoarding and speculation—all of which are carried on by people either powerful in the Party or with intimate political connections.

"It fails to carry out effective mobilization of resources. Such measures of war-time control as it has promulgated have remained a dead letter or have intensified the problems they were supposedly designed to remedy—as for instance ill-advised and poorly executed attempts at price regulation.

"It passively allows both industrial and the more important handicraft production to run down, as they of course must when it is more profitable for speculators to hold raw materials than to have them go through the normal productive process.

"It fails to carry out rationing except in a very limited way, or to regulate the manufacture and trade of luxury goods, many of which come from areas under Japanese control. It shows little concern that these imports are largely paid for with strategic commodities of value to the enemy.

"It fails to make an effective attempt to reduce the budgetary deficit and increase revenue by tapping such resources as excess profits and incomes of landlords and merchants. It allows its tax-collecting apparatus to bog down in corruption and inefficiency—to the point that possibly not more than one-third of revenues collected reach the government. It continues to spend huge government funds on an idle and useless Party bureaucracy.

"At best, it passively watches inflation gather momentum without even attempting palliative measures available to it, such as the aggressive sale of gold and foreign currency.

"It refuses to attack the fundamental economic problems of China such as the growing concentration of land holdings, extortionate rents and ruinous interest rates, and the impact of inflation.

D. *These apparently suicidal policies of the Kuomintang have their roots in the composition and nature of the Party.*

"In view of the above it becomes pertinent to ask *why* the Kuomintang has lost its power of leadership; *why* it neither wishes actively to wage war against Japan itself nor to cooperate whole-heartedly with the American Army in China; and *why* it has ceased to be capable of unifying the country.

"The answer to all these questions is to be found in the present composition and nature of the Party. Politically, a classical and definitive American description becomes ever more true; the Kuomintang is a congerie of conservative political cliques interested primarily in the preservation of their own power against all outsiders and in jockeying for position among themselves. Economically, the Kuomintang rests on the narrow base of the rural-gentry-landlords and militarists, the higher ranks of the government bureaucracy, and merchant bankers having intimate connections with the government bureaucrats. This base has actually contracted during the war. The Kuomintang no longer commands, as it once did, the unequivocal support of China's industrialists, who as a group have been much weakened economically, and hence politically, by the Japanese seizure of the coastal cities.

"The relations of this description of the Kuomintang to the questions propounded above is clear.

"The Kuomintang has lost its leadership because it has lost touch with and is no longer representative of a nation which, through the practical experience of the war, is becoming both more politically conscious and more aware of the Party's selfish shortcomings.

"It cannot fight an effective war because this is impossible without greater reliance upon and support by the people. There must be a release of the national energy such as occurred during the early period of the war. Under present conditions, this can be brought about only by reform of the Party and greater political democracy. What form this democracy takes is not as important as the genuine adoption of a democratic philosophy and attitude; the threat of foreign invasion is no longer enough to stimulate the Chinese people and only real reform can regain their enthusiasm. But the growth of democracy, though basic to China's continuing war effort, would, to the mind of the Kuomintang's present leaders, imperil the foundations of the Party's power because it would mean that the conservative cliques would have to give up their closely guarded monopoly. Rather than do this, they prefer to see the war remain in its present state of passive inertia. Thus are they sacrificing China's national interests to their own selfish ends.

"For similar reasons, the Kuomintang is unwilling to give whole-hearted cooperation to the American Army's effort in China. Full cooperation necessarily requires the broad Chinese military effort which the Kuomintang is unable to carry out or make possible. In addition, the Kuomintang fears the large scale, widespread and direct contact by Americans with the Chinese war effort will expose its own inactivity and, by example and personal contacts, be a liberalizing influence."

5. The rivalry between these two forces threatens to culminate in a civil war which (a) would hamper the conduct of the war against Japan, (b) would press the Communists back into the arms of the U.S.S.R. and (c) might well lead eventually to American-Soviet involvement and conflict.

January 23, 1943 (Service)

"It is now no longer wondered whether civil war can be avoided, but rather whether it can be delayed at least until after a victory over Japan.

"The dangers and implications of this disunity are obvious and far-reaching. Militarily, the present situation is a great hindrance to any effective war effort by China. Its deterioration into civil war would be disastrous. The situation therefore has direct relationship to our own efforts to defeat Japan.

". . . there can be no denial that civil war in China, or even the continuation after the defeat of Japan of the present deadlock, will greatly impede the return of peaceful conditions. This blocking of the orderly large scale rehabilitation of China will in itself seriously and adversely affect American interests. Even if a conflict is averted, the continuance, or, as is probable in such an event, the worsening of the already serious economic strains within the country may result in economic collapse. If there is civil war the likelihood of such an economic collapse is of course greater.

"There is also the possibility that economic difficulties may make the war-weary, over-conscripted and over-taxed farmers fertile ground for Communist propaganda and thus bring about a revolution going beyond the moderate democracy which the Chinese Communists now claim to be seeking. Such a Communist government would probably not be democratic in the American sense. And it is probable, even if the United States did not incur the enmity of the Communists for alleged material or diplomatic support of the Kuomintang, that this Communist government would be more inclined toward friendship and cooperation with Russia than with Great Britain and America."

June 24, 1943 (Davies)

"Basis for Conflict"

"The Kuomintang and Chiang Kai-shek recognize that the Communists, with the popular support which they enjoy and their reputation for administrative reform and honesty, represent a challenge to the Central Government and its spoils system. The Generalissimo cannot admit the seemingly innocent demands of the Communists that their party be legalized and democratic processes be put into practice. To do so would probably mean the abdication of the Kuomintang and the provincial satraps.

"The Communists, on the other hand, dare not accept the Central Government's invitation that they disband their armies and be absorbed in the national body politic. To do so would be to invite extinction.

"This impasse will probably be resolved, American and other foreign observers in Chungking agree, by an attempt by the Central Government to liquidate the Communists. This action may be expected to precipitate a civil war from which one of the two contending factions will emerge dominant. . . ."

"Chiang Kai-shek and his Kuomintang lieutenants fully realize the risks of an attack on the Communists. This may explain the reported statements of high officials in Chungking that they must prepare not only for the coming civil war but also for the coming war with Russia. Chiang and his Central Government recognize that they cannot defeat the Communists and the Soviet Union without foreign aid. Such aid would naturally be sought from the United States and possibly Great Britain.

". . . we may anticipate that Chiang Kai-shek will exert every effort and resort to every stratagem to involve us in active support of the Central Government. We will probably be told that if fresh American aid is not forthcoming all of China and eventually all of Asia will be swept by communism. It will be difficult for us to resist such appeals, especially in view of our moral commitments to continued assistance to China during the post-war period.

"It is therefore not inconceivable that, should Chiang attempt to liquidate the Communists, we would find ourselves entangled not only in a civil war in China but also drawn into conflict with the Soviet Union."

June 20, 1944 (Service)

"Obsessed by the growing and potential threat of the Communists, who it fears may attract the popular support its own nature makes impossible, the Kuomintang, despite the pretext—to meet foreign and Chinese criticism—of conducting negotiations with the Communists, continues to adhere to policies and plans which can only result in civil war. In so doing it shows itself blind to the facts: that its internal political and military situation is so weak that success without outside assistance is most problematic; that such a civil war would hasten the process of disintegration and the spread of chaos; that it would prevent the prosecution of any effective war against Japan; and that the only parties to benefit would be Japan immediately and Russia eventually."

December 9, 1944 (Davies)

" . . . The Generalissimo realizes that if he accedes to the Communist terms for a coalition government, they will sooner or later dispossess him and his Kuomintang of power. He will therefore not, unless driven to an extremity, form a genuine coalition government. He will seek to retain his present government, passively wait out the war and conserve his strength, knowing that the Communist issue must eventually be joined.

"The Communists, on their part, have no interest in reaching an agreement with the Generalissimo short of a genuine coalition government. They recognize that Chiang's position is crumbling, that they may before long receive substantial Russian support and that if they have patience they will succeed to authority in at least North China. . . ."

6. The Communists would, inevitably, win such a war because the foreign powers, including the United States, which would support the Government, could not feasibly supply enough aid to compensate for the organic weaknesses of the Government.

January 23, 1943 (Service)

". . . Assuming that open hostilities are for the time being averted, the eventual defeat and withdrawal of the Japanese will leave the Kuomintang still confronted with the Communists solidly entrenched in most of North China (East Kansu, North Shensi, Shansi, South Chahar, Hopei, Shantung, North Kiangsu and North Anhwei). In addition the Communists will be in position to move into the vacuum created by the Japanese withdrawal from Suiyuan, Jehol and Manchuria, in all of which areas there is already some Communist activity. In the rest of China they will have the sympathy of elements among the liberals, intellectuals, and students.

". . . There is undoubtedly a strong revulsion in the mind of the average, non-party Chinese to the idea of renewed civil war and the Kuomintang may indeed have difficulty with the loyalty and effectiveness of its conscript troops."

October 9, 1944 (Service)

"Just as the Japanese Army cannot crush these militant people now, so also will Kuomintang force fail in the future. With their new arms and organization, knowledge of their own strength, and determination to keep what they have been fighting for, these people—now some 90 million and certain to be many more before the Kuomintang can reach them—will resist oppression. They are not Communists. They do not want separation or independence. But at present they regard the Kuomintang—from their own experience—as oppressors; and the Communists as their leaders and benefactors.

"With this great popular base, the Communists likewise cannot be eliminated. Kuomintang attempts to do so by force must mean a complete denial of democracy. This will strengthen the ties of the Communists with the people: a Communist victory will be inevitable. . . .

"From the basic fact that the Communists have built up popular support of a magnitude and depth which makes their elimination impossible, *we must draw the conclusion that the Communists will have a certain and important share in China's future* . . . I suggest the future conclusion that unless the Kuomintang goes as far as the Communists in political and economic reform, and otherwise proves itself able to contest this leadership of the people (none of which it yet shows signs of being willing or able to do), the Communists will be the dominant force in China within a comparatively few years."

November 7, 1944 (Davies)

"Only if he is able to enlist foreign intervention on a scale equal to the Japanese invasion of China will Chiang probably be able to crush the Communists. But foreign intervention on such a scale would seem to be unlikely. Relying upon his dispirited shambling legions, his decadent corrupt bureaucracy, his sterile political moralisms and such nervous foreign support as he can muster, the Generalissimo may nevertheless plunge China into civil war. He cannot succeed, however, where the Japanese in more than seven years of determined striving have failed. The Communists are already too strong for him.

"If the Generalissimo neither precipitates a civil war nor reaches an understanding with the Communists, he is still confronted with defeat. Chiang's feudal China can not long coexist alongside a modern dynamic popular government in North China.

"The Communists are in China to stay. And China's destiny is not Chiang's but theirs."

7. In this unhappy dilemma, the United States should attempt to prevent the disaster of a civil war through adjustment of the new alignment of power in China by peaceful processes. The desirable means to this end is to encourage the reform and revitalization of the Kuomintang so that it may survive as a significant force in a coalition government. If this fails, we must limit our involvement with the Kuomintang and must commence some cooperation with the Communists, the force destined to control China, in an effort to influence them further into an independent position friendly to the United States. We are working against time because, if the U.S.S.R. enters the war against Japan and invades China before either of these alternatives succeeds, the Communists will be captured by the U.S.S.R. and become Soviet satellites.

June 20, 1944 (Service)

"We must seek to contribute toward the reversal of the present movement toward collapse and to the rousing of China from its military inactivity. This can be brought about only by an accelerated movement toward democratic political reform within China. Our part must be that of a catalytic agent in this process of China's democratization. It can be carried out by the careful exertion of our influence, which has so far not been consciously and systematically used.

"This democratic reform does not necessarily mean the overthrow of the Generalissimo or the Kuomintang. On the contrary—if they have the vision to see it—their position will be improved and the stability of the Central Government increased. The democratic forces already existing in China will be strengthened, the reactionary authoritarian trends in the Kuomintang will be modified, and a multi-party United Front Government will probably emerge. It is almost certain that the Generalissimo and the Kuomintang would continue to play a dominant part in such a government.

"It goes without saying that this democratization of China must be brought about by, and depend on, forces within the country. It cannot be enforced by us— or by any foreign nation—

". . . If we come to the rescue of the Kuomintang on its own terms we would be buttressing—but only temporarily—a decadent regime which by its existing composition and program is incapable of solving China's problems. Both China and ourselves would be gaining only a brief respite from the ultimate day of reckoning."

October 10, 1944 (Service)

"In the present circumstances, the Kuomintang is dependent on American support for survival. *But we are in no way dependent on the Kuomintang.*

". . . by continued and exclusive support of the Kuomintang, we tend to prevent the reforms and democratic reorganization of the government which are essential for the revitalization of China's war effort. Encouraged by our support the Kuomintang will continue in its present course, progressively losing the confidence of the people and becoming more and more impotent. Ignored by us, and excluded from the Government and joint prosecution of the war, the Communists and other groups will be forced to guard their own interests by more direct opposition."

November 15, 1944 (Davies)

"We should not now abandon Chiang Kai-shek. To do so at this juncture would be to lose more than we could gain. We must for the time being continue recognition of Chiang's Government.

"But we must be realistic. We must not indefinitely underwrite a politically bankrupt regime. And, if the Russians are going to enter the Pacific War, we must make a determined effort to capture politically the Chinese Communists rather than allow them to go by default wholly to the Russians. Furthermore, we must fully understand that by reason of our recognition of the Chiang Kai-shek Government as now constituted we are committed to a steadily decaying regime and severely restricted in working out military and political cooperation with the Chinese Communists.

"A coalition Chinese Government in which the Communists find a satisfactory place is the solution of this impasse most desirable to us. It provides our greatest assurance of a strong united, democratic, independent and friendly China—our basic strategic aim in Asia and the Pacific. If Chiang and the Communists reach a mutually satisfactory agreement, there will have been achieved from our point of view the most desirable possible solution. If Chiang and the Communists are irreconcilable, then we shall have to decide which faction we are going to support.

"In seeking to determine which faction we should support we must keep in mind these basic considerations: Power in China is on the verge of shifting from Chiang to the Communists.

"If the Russians enter North China and Manchuria, we obviously cannot hope to win the Communists entirely over to us, but we can through control of supplies and post-war aid expect to exert considerable influence in the direction of Chinese nationalism and independence from Soviet control."

8. A policy of this description would also—and this is a decisive consideration in the war against Japan—measurably aid our war effort.

December 12, 1944 (Davies)

"The negotiations looking to an agreement between the Generalissimo and the Chinese Communists have failed. It is not impossible, however, that one or the other side may in the near future revive the negotiations with a new proposal.

"So long as the deadlock exists, or new negotiations drag on, it is reasonable to assume that the Generalissimo will continue to refuse us permission to exploit militarily the Chinese Communist position extending into the geographical center of Japan's inner zone. With the war against Japan proving so costly to us, we can ill afford to continue denying ourselves positive assistance and strategically valuable positions.

"It is time that we unequivocally told Chiang Kai-shek that we will work with and, within our discretion, supply whatever Chinese forces we believe can contribute most to the war against Japan. We should tell him that we will not work with or supply any Chinese unit, whether Central Government, Provincial or Communist, which shows any inclination toward precipitating civil conflict. We should tell him that we propose to keep him, as head of the recognized government, informed of what supplies we give the various Chinese forces.

"It is time that we make it clear to Chiang-Kai-shek that we expect the Chinese to settle their own political differences; that we refuse to become further involved in and party to Chinese domestic political disputes. We greatly hope and desire that China will emerge from this war unified, democratic, independent and strong. We feel that this goal is to be achieved most expeditiously and with the least possible expenditure of Chinese and American blood and treasure if the United States bends its efforts in China primarily toward working with and assisting whatever elements can contribute most to the speedy defeat of Japan."

February 14, 1945 (Ludden and Service)

"American policy in the Far East can have but one immediate objective: the defeat of Japan in the shortest possible time with the least expenditure of American lives. To the attainment of this objective all other considerations should be subordinate.

"The attainment of this objective demands the effective mobilization of China in the war against Japan. Operating as we are in a land theater at the end of a supply line many thousands of miles in length, the human and economic resources of China increase in importance as we draw closer to Japan's inner zone of defense. Denied the effective use of these resources the attainment of our primary objective will be unnecessarily delayed.

"There is ample evidence to show that to the present Kuomintang Government the war against Japan is secondary in importance to its own preservation in power. China's military failure is due in large part to internal political disunity and the Kuomintang's desire to conserve such military force as it has for utilization in the maintenance of its political power. The intention of the Generalissimo to eliminate all political opposition, by force of arms if necessary, has not been abandoned. In the present situation in China, where power or self-preservation depend upon the possession of military force, neither the Kuomintang nor opposition groups are willing to expend their military resources against the Japanese through fear that it will then *vis-à-vis* other groups.

"The aim of American policy as indicated clearly by official statements in the United States is the establishment of political unity in China as the indispensable preliminary to China's effective military mobilization. The execution of our policy has not contributed to the achievement of this publicly stated aim. On the contrary, it has retarded its effect because our statements and actions in China have convinced the Kuomintang Government that we will continue to support it and it alone. The Kuomintang Government believes that it will receive an increasing flow of American military and related supplies which, if past experience is any guide, it will commit against the enemy only with great reluctance, if at all.

"We cannot hope for any improvement in this situation unless we understand the objectives of the Kuomintang Government and throw our considerable influence upon it in the direction of internal unity. We should be convinced by this time that the effort to solve the Kuomintang-Communist differences by diplomatic means has failed; . . . .

"At present there exists in China a situation closely paralleling that which existed in Yugoslavia prior to Prime Minister Churchill's declaration of support for Marshal Tito. That statement was as follows:

" 'The sanest and safest course for us to follow is to judge all parties and factions dispassionately by the test of their readiness to fight the Germans and thus lighten the burden of Allied troops. This is not a time for ideological preferences for one side or the other.'

"A similar public statement issued by the Commander in Chief with regard to China would not mean the withdrawal of recognition or the cessation of military aid to the Central Government; that would be both unnecessary and unwise. It would serve notice, however, of our preparation to make use of all available means to achieve our primary objective. It would supply for all Chinese a firm rallying point which has thus far been lacking. The internal effect in China would be so profound that the Generalissimo would be forced to make concessions of power and permit united-front coalition. The present opposition groups, no longer under the prime necessity of safeguarding themselves, would be won wholeheartedly to our side and we would have in China, for the first time, a united ally."

48 (a)

The Vice Chairman of the Central Committee of the Chinese Communist Party (Chou) to the Ambassador in China (Hurley)

February 18, 1945

DEAR GENERAL HURLEY: I am ever grateful for the kindness extended to me while I was in Chungking. After my return to Yenan I have made a detailed report to the Central Committee of my Party and to Chairman Mao Tze-tung. Since at present the Democratic Coalition Government has not yet come into existence in China and the existing National Government is completely a one-Party dictatorship of the Kuomintang which can represent neither the 10 million people of the Chinese liberated areas nor the common will of the broad masses of people in areas under Kuomintang control; consequently in the United Nations Conference which is to be convened on April 25 in San Francisco, China cannot be represented by a delegation sent by the Kuomintang Government only. While I was in Chungking you told me that the delegation to the San Francisco Conference should consist of the representatives of the Kuomintang, the Communist Party and the Democratic League. The Central Committee of our Party and Chairman Mao Tze-tung are in complete agreement with you. We consider furthermore that the representatives of the Kuomintang should be limited to ⅓ of the delegation. The other ⅔ of the delegation should be sent by the Communist Party and the Democratic League. Only then can the common will of the Chinese people be fairly represented; otherwise that delegation could never be in a position to settle any problem in the conference on behalf of China. Will you be so kind as to transmit this message to the President of the United States. With my best regards and respects,

CHOU EN-LAI.

48 (b)

The Ambassador in China (Hurley) to the Vice Chairman of the Central Committee of the Chinese Communist Party (Chou)

February 20, 1945

Thanks for your kind telegram. I was happy to hear from you. I did discuss with you the coming conference at San Francisco but I made it clear to you that only the National Government of China has been invited to participate in that conference. I made no attempt to decide how the National Government would be represented in the conference. I had no authority to make a decision on that subject, that is the prerogative of the National Government. It is altogether proper for me to express to you my candid opinion which is that the President and Generalissimo of the National Government of China, known internationally as the Republic of China, will be recognized as the representative of China at the conference and the President alone, in my opinion will select the staff which will accompany him. The conference at San Francisco is to be a conference of nations, not of political parties within nations. The Communist Party of China is not a nation and, as far as I know, no one has recognized it as a nation. It is one of the political parties of China. The only difference from the ordinary political party is that it is armed. I am further of the opinion that recognition by the conference of any armed political party in China other than the National Government would destroy the possibility of unification in China. I urge that Mao Tze-tung, your Chairman, and you, as Vice Chairman and my friends, consider only the methods by which you can unite with, be included in and cooperate under the National Government of China. On my return, I hope to be able to see Chairman Mao, you and General Chu and be in a position to discuss the situation fully with you.

49

Summary of Conversations Between Representatives of the National Government and of the Chinese Communist Party [2]

1. Basic policy on peaceful national reconstruction.—It was agreed that as China's war of resistance against Japanese aggression has been brought to a victorious conclusion, China is now on the threshold of a new era of peaceful national reconstruction, and that peace, democracy, solidarity and unity should form the basis of the nation's concerted efforts. It was likewise agreed that under the leadership of President Chiang, cooperation should be perpetuated and resolute measures taken to avert internal strife so that a new China, independent, free and prosperous, may be built and the Three People's Principles fully implemented. Both parties further agreed that political democratization, nationalization of troops and the recognition of the equal legal status of political parties, as advocated by President Chiang are absolutely essential to achieving peaceful national reconstruction.

---

[2] Issued by the Chinese Ministry of Information on October 11, 1945; *China Handbook, 1937–1945,* pp. 738–740.

2. On political democratization.—It was agreed that the period of political tutelage should be brought to an early conclusion, that constitutional government should be inaugurated and that necessary preliminary measures should be immediately adopted, such as the convocation of the National Assembly (People's Congress) and a Political Consultation Conference, to which all parties and nonpartisan leaders will be invited, to exchange views on national affairs and discuss questions relating to peaceful national reconstruction and the convocation of the National Assembly. Both parties are now conferring with various interested quarters on the membership, organization and function of the proposed council. It was agreed that, as soon as such consultations are completed, the proposed council shall be convened.

3. On the National Assembly.—Three proposals were advanced by the Chinese Communist Party, namely, reelection of all delegates to the National Assembly already held should be valid, but that the number of delegates may be reasonably increased and the increase should be legalized. As regards the May 5 Draft Constitution, the Government representatives reminded the Communists that the Draft Constitution had already been submitted to the public for study and suggestions for its revision were invited. No agreement was reached on those points. But the Communist representatives made it known that they do not wish to permit national unity to be ruptured by the differences. Both parties agreed that the points concerned shall be brought before the proposed Political Consultation Conference for settlement.

4. On the people's freedoms.—It was agreed that the Government should guarantee the freedoms of person, religion, speech, publication and assembly—the rights enjoyed by the people in all democratic nations in normal times. Existing laws and decrees should be either abolished or revised in accordance with this principle.

5. On the legality of political parties.—The Chinese Communists proposed that the Government should recognize the equality and the legal status of the Kuomintang and the Communist Party as well as that of all other parties. The Government stated that a common attribute of constitutional government is that all parties are equal before the law and that this fact will be given immediate recognition.

6. On the special service agencies.—Both parties agreed that the Government should strictly prohibit all offices other than law courts and police to make arrests, conduct trials and impose punishment.

7. On release of political prisoners.—The Chinese Communists proposed that all political prisoners with the exception of those guilty of treason should be released. The Government representatives stated that the Government is prepared to do this of its own accord and that the Chinese Communist Party may submit a list of people who they think should be released.

8. On local self-government.—Both sides agreed that local self-government should be vigorously promoted. General elections should be conducted from the lower level upward. However, the Government expressed the hope that this would not affect the convocation of the National Assembly.

9. On the nationalization of troops.—It was proposed by the Chinese Communists that the Government should effect an equitable and rational reorganization of the entire Chinese Army; decide on the program and different stages of recognition; redemarcate the military zones; and inaugurate a conscription and replenishment system with a view to unifying military command. Under this program, the Chinese Communists finally expressed their readiness to reduce the troops under their command to 24 divisions or to a minimum of 20 divisions.

The Chinese Communists further stated that they would take prompt action to demobilize their anti-Japanese troops now deployed in Kwangtung, Chekiang, southern Kiangsu, southern Anhwei, central Anhwei, Hunan, Hupeh and Honan (not including northern Honan), and that such troops as are to be reorganized will be gradually evacuated from the said areas, to be concentrated in the liberated areas north of the Lunghai Railway and in northern Kiangsu and northern Anhwei. The Government representatives stated that the national troops reorganization program is being carried out, and the Government is willing to reorganize the Communist-led anti-Japanese troops into 20 divisions, if the other issues coming up in the present talks could be satisfactorily settled. Regarding the garrison areas, the Chinese Communists may submit plans for discussion and decision.

The Chinese Communists proposed that the Communist military personnel should participate in the work of the National Military Council and the various departments under the Council, and that the Government should respect the personnel system of the army units and commission the original officers after their units have been reorganized. Discharged officers should be given training in different areas, and the Government should adopt a reasonable and satisfactory system of maintenance and political education.

The Government indicated that it was ready to consider the proposals and discuss details.

In reply to the Chinese Communists' proposal that all the militiamen in the liberated areas should be reorganized into local self-defense corps, the Government expressed the view that this matter will have to be determined in accordance with local conditions and needs. In order to formulate concrete plans in regard to all the questions mentioned in this section, it was agreed that a subcommittee of three, with one representative each from the Board of Military Operations of the National Military Council, the Ministry of War, and the Eighteenth Group Army, be formed.

10. On local governments in the liberated areas.—The Communist representatives proposed that the Government should recognize the popularly elected governments in the liberated areas. The Government representatives pointed out that after the unconditional surrender of Japan the term "liberated area" becomes obsolete and the integrity of the administrative authority of the country should be respected.

The initial formula advanced by the Communist representatives was to redemarcate the provincial and administrative areas according to the conditions that now obtain in the 18 liberated areas. And to preserve administrative integrity, the Communist Party would submit to the Government a list of officials of the popularly elected governments for reappointment.

The Government replied that the redemarcation of provincial boundaries would involve changes of unusual magnitude, and the question should be very carefully and thoroughly considered and could not be resolved in a short time. At the same time the Government representatives reiterated what President Chiang had stated to Mr. Mao Tse-tung, that after the unification of the military command and administrative authority, the National Government would take into consideration administrative personnel nominated by the Communist Party. The Government would consider retaining the services of those functionaries who have served in the recovered areas during the war on the basis of their ability and record without regard to party affiliations.

Upon this, a second formula was proposed by the Communist representatives, asking the National Government to appoint nominees of the Communist Party as chairman and members of the provincial governments of the Shensi-Kansu-Ningsia Border Region, Jehol, Chahar, Hopei, Shantung and Shansi. They further asked that Communist nominees be appointed deputy chairman and members of the provincial governments of Suiyuan, Honan, Kiangsu, Anhwei, Hupeh, and Kwangtung, and deputy mayors of the special municipalities of Peiping, Tientsin, Tsingtao and Shanghai. The Communist representatives also requested participation in the administration of the Northeastern Provinces.

After lengthy discussions on this topic, the Communist representatives modified their proposals by requesting the appointment of their nominees as chairman and members of the provincial governments of the Shensi-Kansu-Ningsia Border Region, Jehol, Chahar, Hopei and Shantung, as deputy chairman and members of the provincial governments of Shansi and Suiyuan, and as deputy mayors of the special municipalities of Peiping, Tientsin and Tsingtao.

The Government representatives replied that the Communist Party might nominate those members of the Communist Party, who possess administrative ability and have rendered commendable service during the war, to the Government for appointment. But if the Communist Party should insist upon nominating chairmen or deputy chairmen or members of the provincial government for specific provinces, this would not be sincerely endeavoring to achieve military and administrative integrity.

The Communist representatives then said they would withdraw their second suggestion and propose a third formula. They suggested that general elections be held in the liberated areas under the existing popularly elected government. Under the supervision of the Political Consultation Council the Communist Party would welcome members of all other political parties as well as members of various professions to return to their native places to participate in the elections. A popular election is to be held in any hsien in which the public officers of more than one-half of its chu or hsiang have been elected by popular vote. Likewise, a popular election is to be held in any province or administrative area in which public functionaries of more than one-half of its hsien have been elected by popular vote. In the interest of administrative integrity, the names of all the provincial, hsien or chu officials thus elected should be submitted to the National Government for appointment.

The Government representatives replied that this formula is not acceptable as such a process is not conducive to real administrative integrity. But the Government might consider the appointment of popularly elected hsien officials. Popular election of provincial government functionaries could only be held after the status of the province has been definitely defined following the promulgation of the constitution. For the time being, only those provincial government officials who have been appointed by the National Government should proceed to take up their posts, so that conditions in the recovered areas may be restored to normalcy at the earliest possible moment.

At this point, a fourth formula was proposed by the Communist representative: that all liberated areas temporarily retain their status quo until the constitutional provision for the popular election of provincial government officials has been adopted and put into effect. For the time being an interim arrangement is to be worked out in order to guarantee the restoration of peace and order.

Finally, the Communist representatives suggested that this particular problem be submitted to the Political Consultation Conference for discussion and settlement. The Government, desirous of the early establishment of administrative integrity so that peaceful reconstruction might not be delayed, hoped that an agreement could soon be worked out on this matter. The Communist representatives concurred. Discussions will continue.

11. On traitors and puppet troops.—The Communist representatives proposed that traitors be severely punished and puppet troops be disbanded. The Government representatives' reply was: in principle there is no question. But traitors should be dealt with according to due process of law and the disbandment of puppet troops should be carried out in such a manner that peace and order in the areas concerned would not be disturbed.

12. On accepting the surrender of Japanese army.—The Communist representatives asked that the Communist troops be allowed to participate in the task of accepting the surrender of Japanese troops and that the areas of surrender should be redefined. The Government representatives answered that the participation of the Communist Party in accepting the surrender of Japanese troops could be considered after the troops of the Communist Party accepted the orders of the National Government.

50

The Ambassador to China (Hurley) to President Truman [3]

[WASHINGTON,] *November 26, 1945*

MY DEAR MR. PRESIDENT: I hereby resign as Ambassador to China.

In tendering my resignation I wish you to know that I am in agreement with the foreign policy outlined by you in your recent Navy Day address.

I am grateful to both you and the Secretary of State for the support you have given me and for your kind offer in requesting me to return to China as Ambassador.

In one capacity or another I have been on the perimeter of America's influence since the beginning of the war. During the war I have served in Java, Australia, New Zealand, and generally in the southwest Pacific, in Egypt, Palestine, The Lebanon, Syria, Trans-Jordan, Iraq, Saudi Arabia, Iran, Russia, Afghanistan, India, Ceylon, Burma and China. Of all of the assignments China was the most intricate and the most difficult. It is a source of gratification to me that in all my missions I had the support of President Roosevelt, Secretary Hull, Secretary Stettinius, yourself, Mr. President, and Secretary Byrnes.

In the higher echelon of our policy-making officials American objectives were nearly always clearly defined. The astonishing feature of our foreign policy is the wide discrepancy between our announced policies and our conduct of international relations. For instance, we began the war with the principles of the Atlantic Charter and democracy as our goal. Our associates in the war at that time gave eloquent lip service to the principles of democracy. We finished the war in the Far East furnishing lend-lease supplies and using all our reputation to undermine democracy and bolster imperialism and Communism. Inasmuch as I am in agreement with you and the Secretary of State on our foreign policy I think I owe it to you as well as to the country to point out the reasons for the failure of the American foreign policy in reaching the objectives for which we said we were fighting the war. I will confine my remarks in this letter to Asia, although I wish to assure you that I will be at your service in discussing frankly other phases of our international relations.

---

[3] Transmitted through the Secretary of State.

I was assigned to China at a time when statesmen were openly predicting the collapse of the National Government of the Republic of China and the disintegration of the Chinese Army. I was directed by President Roosevelt to prevent the collapse of the Government and to keep the Chinese Army in the war. From both a strategical and diplomatic viewpoint the foregoing constituted our chief objective. The next in importance was the directive to harmonize the relations between the Chinese and American military establishments and between the American Embassy in Chungking and the Chinese Government. It will readily appear that the former objective could not be accomplished without the accomplishment of the secondary objective as a condition precedent. Both of these objectives were accomplished. While these objectives had the support of the President and the Secretary of State it is no secret that the American policy in China did not have the support of all the career men in the State Department. The professional foreign service man sided with the Chinese Communist armed party and the imperialist bloc of nations whose policy it was to keep China divided against herself. Our professional diplomats continuously advised the Communists that my efforts in preventing the collapse of the National Government did not represent the policy of the United States. These same professionals openly advised the Communist armed party to decline unification of the Chinese Communist Army with the National Army unless the Chinese Communists were given control.

Despite these handicaps we did make progress toward unification of the armed forces of China. We did prevent civil war between the rival factions, at least until after I had left China. We did bring the leaders of the rival parties together for peaceful discussions. Throughout this period the chief opposition to the accomplishment of our mission came from the American career diplomats in the Embassy at Chungking and in the Chinese and Far Eastern Divisions of the State Department.

I requested the relief of the career men who were opposing the American policy in the Chinese Theater of war. These professional diplomats were returned to Washington and placed in the Chinese and Far Eastern Divisions of the State Department as my supervisors. Some of these same career men whom I relieved have been assigned as advisors to the Supreme Commander in Asia. In such positions most of them have continued to side with the Communist armed party and at times with the imperialist bloc against American policy. This, Mr. President, is an outline of one of the reasons why American foreign policy announced by the highest authority is rendered ineffective by another section of diplomatic officials.

The weakness of American foreign policy has backed us into two world wars. We had no part in shaping the conditions that brought about these two wars. There is a third world war in the making. In diplomacy today we are permitting ourselves to be sucked into a power bloc on the side of colonial imperialism against Communist imperialism. I am opposed to both. I still favor democracy and free enterprise.

Our announced policy in the first world war was to make the world safe for democracy. That slogan was elaborated for the second world war by a definite statement of principles in the Atlantic Charter and the Iran Declaration. We won both wars but in both instances we failed to establish the principles for which we alleged we were fighting. America's foreign policy officials have always been divided against themselves. Consequently, we have always been a prey to the nations that give lip service to our ideals and principles in order to obtain our material support. The war that is now in the making is not even intended to defend or establish democratic ideals. Instead of putting our weight behind the Charter of the United Nations we have been definitely supporting the imperialistic bloc. At the same time a considerable section of our State Department is endeavoring to support Communism generally as well as specifically in China.

The Hydra-headed direction and confusion of our foreign policy in Washington during the late war is chargeable to the weakness of our Foreign Service. If our Foreign Service had been capable of understanding and sympathetic effectuation of our announced war aims it would not have failed so completely to couple our logistical strength with our foreign policy to obtain commitments to the principles for which we claimed to be fighting from the nations to which we gave the strength of our productivity and manpower.

I am purposely omitting from this short paper a discussion of my negotiations with Britain and Russia for the recognition of the territorial integrity and independent sovereignty of China and the procurement from both of these nations of an agreement to support the aspirations of the Chinese people to establish for themselves a free, united, democratic government. These negotiations as you know were successful and so far as Russia is concerned was solemnized in a treaty and exchange of letters.

A democracy must live on its intelligence and its integrity and its courage. The people of a democracy should be given all the facts to enable them to form correct opinions. The discrepancy between American foreign policy as announced in the Atlantic Charter and the Iran Declaration and in your recent Navy Day address and as carried into effect may be attributed in large measure to the secrecy which has shrouded the actions of the State Department. All too frequently information concerning the conduct of our foreign relations "leaks" out to the public in distorted, garbled, or partial form. The result is that the American people have too little basic information to judge the extent to which their State Department correctly interprets and administers the foreign policies of the nation.

During the war we had to maintain secrecy to prevent giving aid to the enemy. I grant that sometimes during the war we had to be expedient. Now we should endeavor to be right. I raise this issue because I am firmly convinced that at this particular juncture in our history an informed public opinion would do much to give intelligent direction and implementation to our international objectives.

With special reference to China and the other nations where I have served in the last four years, the blessings of factual publicity would be manifold. Now that the war is over I am willing that all my reports be made public, together with the reports made by those officials in the foreign service who have differed with the promulgated American policy.

Our true position in China is misunderstood abroad because of this confusion of policy within our own Government. This situation suggests the need for a complete reorganization of our policy-making machinery beginning at the lower official levels. No international policy can succeed without loyal and intelligent implementation. Because of the confusion in our own international policy, make no mistake, Mr. President, America has been excluded economically from every part of the world controlled by colonial imperialism and Communist imperialism. America's economic strength has been used all over the world to defeat American policies and interests. This is chargeable to weak American Foreign Service.

I wish to absolve from this general indictment some of our career men. Some of them are very admirable and well-equipped public servants who have fought in the State Department and in other countries against overwhelming odds to advance American ideals and interests.

America's economic and diplomatic policies should be coordinated. America's strength should not be allied with any predatory ideology.

America should support the amendment or revision of the San Francisco United Nations Charter to make it democratic. Our strength should be used to uphold the decisions of the United Nations rather than to support conflicting ideologies or war-making power blocs.

Respectfully,

PATRICK J. HURLEY

Annexes to Chapter IV: The Yalta Agreement and the Sino-Soviet Treaty of 1945

51

Treaty of Friendship and Alliance Between the Republic of China and the U.S.S.R., August 14, 1945 [1]

The President of the National Government of the Republic of China, and the Presidium of the Supreme Soviet of the U.S.S.R.,

Desirous of strengthening the friendly relations that have always existed between China and the U.S.S.R., through an alliance and good neighborly post-war collaboration,

Determined to assist each other in the struggle against aggression on the part of enemies of the United Nations in this world war, and to collaborate in the common war against Japan until her unconditional surrender,

Expressing their unswerving aspiration to cooperate in the cause of maintaining peace and security for the benefit of the peoples of both countries and of all the peace-loving nations,

Acting upon the principles enunciated in the joint declaration of the United Nations of January 1, 1942, in the four power Declaration signed in Moscow on October 30, 1943, and in the Charter of the International Organization of the United Nations.

Have decided to conclude the present Treaty to this effect and appointed as their plenipotentiaries:

The President of the National Government of the Republic of China ;

His Excellency Dr. Wang Shih-chieh, Minister for Foreign Affairs of the Republic of China,

The Presidium of the Supreme Soviet of the U.S.S.R. ;

His Excellency Mr. V. M. Molotov, the People's Commissar of Foreign Affairs of the U.S.S.R.,

Who, after exchanging their Full Powers, found in good and due form, have agreed as follows:

ARTICLE I

The High Contracting Parties undertake in association with the other United Nations to wage war against Japan until final victory is won. The High Contracting Parties undertake mutually to render to one another all necessary military and other assistance and support in this war.

ARTICLE II

The High Contracting Parties undertake not to enter into separate negotiations with Japan and not to conclude, without mutual consent, any armistice or peace

---

[1] *Department of State Bulletin,* Feb. 10, 1946, p. 201.

treaty either with the present Japanese Government or with any other government or authority set up in Japan which do not renounce all aggressive intentions.

ARTICLE III

The High Contracting Parties undertake after the termination of the war against Japan to take jointly all measures in their power to render impossible a repetition of aggression and violation of the peace by Japan.

In the event of one of the High Contracting Parties becoming involved in hostilities with Japan in consequence of an attack by the latter against the said Contracting Party, the other High Contracting Party shall at once give to the Contracting Party so involved in hostilities all the military and other support and assistance with the means in its power.

This article shall remain in force until such time as the organization "The United Nations" may on request of the two High Contracting Parties be charged with the responsibility for preventing further aggression by Japan.

ARTICLE IV

Each High Contracting Party undertakes not to conclude any alliance and not to take any part in any coalition directed against the other High Contracting Party.

ARTICLE V

The High Contracting Parties, having regard to the interests of the security and economic development of each of them, agree to work together in close and friendly collaboration after the coming of peace and to act according to the principles of mutual respect for their sovereignty and territorial integrity and of non-interference in the internal affairs of the other contracting party.

ARTICLE VI

The High Contracting Parties agree to render each other every possible economic assistance in the post-war period with a view to facilitating and accelerating reconstruction in both countries and to contributing to the cause of world prosperity.

ARTICLE VII

Nothing in this treaty shall be so construed as may affect the rights or obligations of the High Contracting Parties as members of the organization "The United Nations".

ARTICLE VIII

The present Treaty shall be ratified in the shortest possible time. The exchange of the instruments of ratification shall take place as soon as possible in Chungking.

The Treaty comes into force immediately upon its ratification and shall remain in force for a term of thirty years.

If neither of the High Contracting Parties has given notice, a year before the expiration of the term, of its desire to terminate the Treaty, it shall remain valid for an unlimited time, each of the High Contracting Parties being able to terminate its operation by giving notice to that effect one year in advance.

In faith whereof the Plenipotentiaries have signed the present Treaty and affixed their seals to it.

Done in Moscow, the Fourteenth August, 1945, corresponding to the Fourteenth day of the Eighth month of the Thirty-fourth year of the Chinese Republic, in two copies, each one in the Russian and Chinese languages, both texts being equally authoritative.

THE PLENIPOTENTIARY OF THE SUPREME SOVIET OF THE U.S.S.R.	THE PLENIPOTENTIARY OF THE PRESIDENT OF THE NATIONAL GOVERNMENT OF THE REPUBLIC OF CHINA.

52

Exchange of Notes Relating to the Treaty of Friendship and Alliance [2]

The People's Commissar for Foreign Affairs (Molotov) to the Chinese Minister for Foreign Affairs (Wang)

August 14, 1945

YOUR EXCELLENCY, With reference to the Treaty of Friendship and Alliance signed today between the Republic of China and the U.S.S.R., I have the honor to put on record the understanding between the High Contracting Parties as follows:

1. In accordance with the spirit of the aforementioned Treaty, and in order to put into effect its aims and purposes, the Government of the U. S. S. R. agrees to render to China moral support and aid in military supplies and other material resources, such support and aid to be entirely given to the National Government as the central government of China.

2. In the course of conversations regarding Dairen and Port Arthur and regarding the joint operation of the Chinese Changchun Railway, the Government of the U.S.S.R. regarded the Three Eastern Provinces as part of China and reaffirmed its respect for China's full sovereignty over the Three Eastern Provinces and recognize their territorial and administrative integrity.

3. As for the recent developments in Sinkiang the Soviet Government confirms that, as stated in Article V of the Treaty of Friendship and Alliance, it has no intention of interfering in the internal affairs of China.

If Your Excellency will be so good as to confirm that the understanding is correct as set forth in the preceding paragraphs, the present note and Your Excellency's reply thereto will constitute a part of the aforementioned Treaty of Friendship and Alliance.

I take [etc.]   V. M. MOLOTOV

The Chinese Minister for Foreign Affairs (Wang) to the People's Commissar for Foreign Affairs (Molotov)

August 14, 1945

YOUR EXCELLENCY: I have the honour to acknowledge receipt of Your Excellency's Note of today's date reading as follows:

"With reference to the Treaty of Friendship and Alliance signed today between the Republic of China and the U. S. S. R., I have the honour to put on record the understanding between the High Contracting Parties as follows:

---

[2] *Ibid.*, p. 204.

"1. In accordance with the spirit of the aforementioned Treaty, and in order to put into effect its aims and purposes, the Government of the U.S.S.R., agrees to render to China moral support and aid in military supplies and other material resources, such support and aid to be entirely given to the National Government as the central Government of China.

"2. In the course of·conversations regarding Dairen and Port Arthur and regarding the joint operation of the Chinese Changchun Railway, the Government of the U.S.S.R. regarded the Three Eastern Provinces as part of China and reaffirmed its respect for China's full sovereignty over the Three Eastern Provinces and recognize their territorial and administrative integrity.

"3. As for the recent developments in Sinkiang the Soviet Government confirms that, as stated in Article V of the Treaty of Friendship and Alliance, it has no intention of interfering in the internal affairs of China.

"If Your Excellency will be so good as to confirm that the understanding is correct as set forth in the preceding paragraphs, the present note and Your Excellency's reply thereto will constitute a part of the aforementioned Treaty of Friendship and Alliance."

I have the honour to confirm that the understanding is correct as set forth above.

I avail [etc.]   WANG SHIH-CHIEH

53

Exchange of Notes on Outer Mongolia[3]

The Chinese Minister for Foreign Affairs (Wang) to the People's Commissar for Foreign Affairs (Molotov)

August 14, 1945

YOUR EXCELLENCY: In view of the desire repeatedly expressed by the people of Outer Mongolia for their independence, the Chinese Government declares that after the defeat of Japan should a plebiscite of the Outer Mongolian people confirm this desire, the Chinese Government will recognize the independence of Outer Mongolia with the existing boundary as its boundary.

The above declaration will become binding upon the ratification of the Treaty of Friendship and Alliance between the Republic of China and the U.S.S.R. signed on August 14, 1945.

I avail [etc.]   WANG SHIH-CHIEH

The People's Commissar for Foreign Affairs (Molotov) to the Chinese Minister for Foreign Affairs (Wang)

August 14, 1945

YOUR EXCELLENCY: I have the honour to acknowledge receipt of Your Excellency's Note reading as follows:

"In view of the desire repeatedly expressed by the people of Outer Mongolia for their independence, the Chinese Government declares that after the defeat of Japan should a plebiscite of the Outer Mongolian people confirm this desire, the Chinese Government will recognize the independence of Outer Mongolia with the existing boundary as its boundary.

---

[3] *Ibid.*, p. 204.

"The above declaration will become binding upon the ratification of the Treaty of Friendship and Alliance between the Republic of China and the U.S.S.R. signed on August 14, 1945."

The Soviet Government has duly taken note of the above communication of the Government of the Chinese Republic and hereby expresses its satisfaction therewith, and it further states that the Soviet Government will respect the political independence and territorial integrity of the People's Republic of Mongolia (Outer Mongolia).

I avail [etc.]   V. M. MOLOTOV

54

Agreement Concerning Dairen [4]

In view of a Treaty of Friendship and Alliance having been concluded between the Republic of China and the U.S.S.R. and of the pledge by the latter that it will respect Chinese sovereignty in the control of all of Manchuria as an integral part of China; and with the object of ensuring that the U.S.S.R.'s interest in Dairen as a port of entry and exit for its goods shall be safeguarded, the Republic of China agrees:

1. To declare Dairen a free port open to the commerce and shipping of all nations.

2. The Chinese Government agrees to apportion in the mentioned port for lease to U. S. S. R. wharfs and warehouses on the basis of separate agreement.

3. The Administration in Dairen shall belong to China.

The harbor-master and deputy harbor-master will be appointed by the Chinese Eastern Railway and South Manchurian Railway in agreement with the Mayor. The harbor-master shall be a Russian national, and the deputy harbor-master shall be a Chinese national.

4. In peace time Dairen is not included in the sphere of efficacy of the naval base regulations, determined by the Agreement on Port Arthur of August 14, 1945, and shall be subject to the military supervision or control established in this zone only in case of war against Japan.

5. Goods entering the free port from abroad for through transit to Soviet territory on the Chinese Eastern and South Manchurian Railways and goods coming from Soviet territory on the said railways into the free port for export shall be free from customs duties. Such goods shall be transported in sealed cars.

Goods entering China from the free port shall pay the Chinese import duties, and goods going out of other parts of China into the free port shall pay the Chinese export duties as long as they continue to be collected.

6. The term of this Agreement shall be thirty years and this Agreement shall come into force upon its ratification.

55

Protocol to the Agreement on Dairen [5]

1. At the request of the U.S.S.R. the Chinese Government leases to the U.S.S.R. free of charge one half of all port installations and equipment. The term of

---

[4] *Ibid.*, p. 205.
[5] *Ibid.*, p. 205.

lease shall be thirty years. The remaining half of port installations and equipment shall be reserved for the use of China.

The expansion or re-equipment of the port shall be made by agreement between China and U.S.S.R.

2. It is agreed that the sections of the Chinese Changchun Railway running
from Dairen to Mukden that lie within the region of the Port Arthur naval base,
shall not be subject to any military supervision or control established in this
region.

56

Agreement on Port Arthur [6]

In conformity with and for the implementation of the Treaty of Friendship
and Alliance between the Republic of China and the U.S.S.R., the High Contracting Parties have agreed as follows:

ARTICLE I

With a view to strengthening the security of China and the U.S.S.R. against
further aggression by Japan, the Government of the Republic of China agrees to
the joint use by the two countries of Port Arthur as a naval base.

ARTICLE II

The precise boundary of the area provided in Article I is described in the Annex
and shown in the map (Annex 1). [7]

ARTICLE III

The High Contracting Parties agree that Port Arthur, as an exclusive naval
base, will be used only by Chinese and Soviet military and commercial vessels.

There shall be established a Sino-Soviet Military Commission to handle the
matters of joint use of the above-mentioned naval base. The Commission shall
consist of two Chinese and three Soviet representatives. The Chairman of the
Commission shall be appointed by the Soviet side and the Vice Chairman shall
be appointed by the Chinese side.

ARTICLE IV

The Chinese Government entrusts to the Soviet Government the defence of the
naval base. The Soviet Government may erect at its own expense such installations as are necessary for the defence of the naval base.

ARTICLE V

The Civil Administration of the whole area will be Chinese. The leading posts
of the Civil Administration will be appointed by the Chinese Government taking
into account Soviet interests in the area.

The leading posts of the civil administration in the city of Port Arthur are
appointed and dismissed by the Chinese Government in agreement with the Soviet
military command.

The proposals which the Soviet military commander in that area may address
to the Chinese civil administration in order to safeguard security and defence will
be fulfilled by the said administration. In cases of disagreement, such cases shall

---

[6] *Ibid.,* p. 205.
[7] Map not reproduced. See *ibid.,* pp. 202–203.

be submitted to the Sino-Soviet military commission for consideration and decision.

ARTICLE VI

The Government of U.S.S.R. have the right to maintain in region mentioned in Article II, their army, navy and air force and to determine their location.

ARTICLE VII

The Government of the U.S.S.R. also undertakes to establish and keep up lighthouses and other installations and signs necessary for the security of navigation of the area.

ARTICLE VIII

After the termination of this agreement all the installations and public property installed or constructed by the U.S.S.R. in the area shall revert without compensation to the Chinese Government.

ARTICLE IX

The present agreement is concluded for thirty years. It comes into force on the day of its ratification.

In faith whereof the plenipotentiaries of the High Contracting Parties have signed the present agreement and affixed thereto their seals. The present agreement is made in two copies, each in the Russian and Chinese language, both texts being authoritative.

Done in Moscow, August 14, 1945, corresponding to the 14th day of the 8th month of the 34th year of the Chinese Republic.

| THE PLENIPOTENTIARY OF THE PRESIDIUM OF THE SUPREME SOVIET OF THE U.S.S.R. | THE PLENIPOTENTIARY OF THE PRESIDENT OF THE NATIONAL GOVERNMENT OF THE REPUBLIC OF CHINA. |

57

Appendix to "Agreement on Port Arthur" Signed in Moscow on August 14, 1945 [8]

The territory of the area of the naval base provided for by paragraph II of the Agreement on Port Arthur is situated south of the line which begins on the west coast of Liaotung Peninsula—south of Housantaowan—and follows a general easterly direction across Shihe Station and the point of Tsoukiachutse to the east coast of the same peninsula, excluding the town of Dalny (Dairen).

All the islands situated in the waters adjoining the west side of the area on Liaotung Peninsula established by the Agreement, and south of the line passing through the points 39°00′ North latitude, 120°49′ East longitude; 39°20′ North latitude, 121°31′ East longitude, and beyond in a general northeasterly direction along the axis of the fairway leading to port Pulantien to the initial point on land, are included in the area of the naval base.

All the islands situated within the waters adjoining the eastern part of the area on Liaotung Peninsula and south of the line passing from the terminal point on land in an easterly direction towards the point 39°20′ North latitude, 123°08′ East longitude, and farther southeast through the point 39°00′ North

---

[8] *Ibid.*, p. 206.

latitude, 123°16′ East longitude, are included in the area. (See attached map, scale 1: 500,000.) [9]

The boundary line of the district will be demarcated on the spot by a mixed Soviet-Chinese Commission. The Commission shall establish the boundary posts and, when need arises, buoys on the water, compile a detailed description of this line, enter it on a topographical map drawn to the scale of 1: 25,000 and the water boundary on a naval map drawn to the scale of 1: 300,000.

The time when the Commission shall start its work is subject to special agreement between the parties.

Descriptions of the boundary line of the area and the maps of this line compiled by the above Commission are subject to approval by both Governments.

W. S.   V. M.

58

Agreement Regarding Relations between the Chinese Administration and the Commander-in-Chief of the Soviet Forces After the Entry of Soviet Troops Into the "Three Eastern Provinces" of China During the Present Joint Military Operations Against Japan [10]

The President of the National Government of China and the Presidium of the Supreme Council of the Union of Soviet Socialist Republics, desirous that relations between the Chinese Administration and the Commander-in-Chief of the Soviet forces after the entry of Soviet troops into the "Three Eastern Provinces" of China during the present joint military operations against Japan should be governed by the spirit of friendship and alliance existing between the two countries, have agreed on the following:

1. After the Soviet troops enter the "Three Eastern Provinces" of China as a result of military operations, the supreme authority and responsibility in all matters relating to the prosecution of the war will be vested, in the zone of operations for the time required for the operations, in the Commander-in-Chief of the Soviet forces.

2. A Chinese National Government representative and staff will be appointed for the recovered territory, whose duties will be:

(a) To establish and direct, in accordance with the laws of China, an administration for the territory cleared of the enemy.

(b) To establish the cooperation between the Chinese armed forces, both regular and irregular, and the Soviet forces in recovered territory.

(c) To ensure the active cooperation of the Chinese administration with the Commander-in-Chief of the Soviet forces and, specifically to give the local authorities directions to this effect, being guided by the requirements and wishes of the Commander-in-Chief of the Soviet forces.

3. To ensure contact between the Commander-in-Chief of the Soviet forces and the Chinese National Government representative a Chinese military mission will be appointed to the Commander-in-Chief of the Soviet forces.

4. In the zones under the supreme authority of the Commander-in-Chief of the Soviet forces, the Chinese National Government administration for the recovered

---

[9] Map not reproduced. See *ibid.*, pp. 202–203.
[10] *Ibid.*, p. 206.

territory will maintain contact with the Commander-in-Chief of the Soviet forces through the Chinese National Government representative.

5. As soon as any part of the liberated territory ceases to be a zone of immediate military operations, the Chinese National Government will assume full authority in the direction of public affairs and will render the Commander-in-Chief of the Soviet forces every assistance and support through its civil and military bodies.

6. All persons belonging to the Soviet forces on Chinese territory will be under the jurisdiction of the Commander-in-Chief of the Soviet forces. All Chinese, whether civilian or military, will be under Chinese jurisdiction. This jurisdiction will also extend to the civilian population on Chinese territory even in the case of offenses against the Soviet armed forces, with the exception of offenses committed in the zone of military operations under the jurisdiction of the Commander-in-Chief of the Soviet forces, such cases coming under the jurisdiction of the Commander-in-Chief of the Soviet forces. In disputable cases the question will be settled by mutual agreement between the Chinese National Government representative and the Commander-in-Chief of the Soviet forces.

7. With regard to currency matters after the entry of Soviet troops into the "Three Eastern Provinces" of China, a separate agreement shall be reached.

8. The present Agreement comes into force immediately upon the ratification of the Treaty of Friendship and Alliance between China and the U. S. S. R. signed this day. The Agreement has been done in two copies, each in the Chinese and Russian languages. Both texts are equally valid.

*Date*_____

ON THE AUTHORIZATION OF THE NATIONAL GOVERNMENT OF THE REPUBLIC OF CHINA.	ON THE AUTHORIZATION OF THE GOVERNMENT OF THE UNION OF SOVIET SOCIALIST REPUBLICS.

59

Agreement Between the Republic of China and the U.S.S.R. Concerning the Chinese Changchun Railway [11]

The President of the Republic of China and the Presidium of the Supreme Council of the U.S.S.R., desiring to strengthen the friendly relations and economic bonds between the two countries on the basis of the full observation of the rights and interests of each other, have agreed as follows:

ARTICLE I

After the Japanese armed forces are driven out of the Three Eastern Provinces of China the main trunk line of the Chinese Eastern Railway and the South Manchurian Railway from Manchuli to Suifenho and from Harbin to Dairen and Port Arthur united into one railway under the name "Chinese Changchun Railway" shall be in joint ownership of the U.S.S.R. and the Republic of China and shall be operated by them jointly.

There shall be joint ownership and operation only of those lands acquired and railway auxiliary lines built by the Chinese Eastern Railway during the time of Russian and joint Sino-Soviet administration and by the South Manchurian Railway during the time of Russian administration and which are designed for direct needs of these railways as well as the subsidiary enterprises built during

---

[11] *Ibid.,* p. 207.

the said periods and directly serving these railways. All the other railway branches, subsidiary enterprises and lands shall be in the complete ownership of the Chinese Government.

The joint operation of the aforementioned railway shall be undertaken by a single management under Chinese sovereignty and as a purely commercial transportation enterprise.

ARTICLE II

The High Contracting parties agree that their joint ownership of the railway shall be in equal shares and shall not be alienable in whole or in part.

ARTICLE III

The High Contracting parties agree that for the joint operation of the said railway the Sino-Soviet Company of the Chinese Changchun Railway shall be formed. The Company shall have a Board of Directors to be composed of ten members of whom five shall be appointed by the Chinese Government and five by the Soviet Government. The Board of Directors shall be in Changchun.

ARTICLE IV

The Chinese Government shall appoint one of the Chinese Directors as President of the Board of Directors and one as the Assistant President. The Soviet Government shall appoint one of the Soviet Directors as Vice-President of the Board of Directors, and one as the Assistant Vice-President. Seven persons shall constitute a quorum. When questions are decided by the Board, the vote of the President of the Board of Directors shall be counted as two votes.

Questions on which the Board of Directors cannot reach an agreement shall be submitted to the Governments of the Contracting Parties for consideration and settlement in an equitable and friendly spirit.

ARTICLE V

The Company shall establish a Board of Auditors which shall be composed of six members of whom three are appointed by the Chinese Government and three appointed by the Soviet Government. The Chairman of the Board of Auditors shall be elected from among the Soviet Auditors, and Vice-Chairman from among the Chinese auditors. When questions are decided by the Board the vote of the Chairman shall be counted as two votes. Five persons shall constitute a quorum.

ARTICLE VI

For the administration of current affairs the Board of Directors shall appoint a manager of the Chinese Changchun Railway from among Soviet citizens and one assistant manager from among Chinese citizens.

ARTICLE VII

The Board of Auditors shall appoint a General-Comptroller from among Chinese citizens, and an assistant General Comptroller from among Soviet citizens.

ARTICLE VIII

The Chiefs and Assistant Chiefs of the various departments, Chiefs of sections, station masters at important stations of the railway shall be appointed by the Board of Directors. The Manager of the Railway has right to recommend candidates for the above-mentioned posts. Individual members of the Board of Directors may also recommend such candidates in agreement with the Manager. If the Chief of a department is a national of China, the Assistant Chief shall be a national of the Soviet Union, and vice versa. The appointment of the Chiefs and assistant chiefs of departments and Chiefs of sections and station masters shall be made in accordance with the principle of equal representation between the nationals of China and nationals of the Soviet Union.

ARTICLE IX

The Chinese Government will bear the responsibility for the protection of the said Railway.

The Chinese Government will, also organize and supervise the railway guards who shall protect the railway buildings, installations and other properties and freight from destruction, loss and robbery, and shall maintain the normal order on the railway. As regards the duties of the police in execution of this Article, they will be determined by the Chinese Government in consultation with the Soviet Government.

ARTICLE X

Only during the time war against Japan the railway may be used for the transportation of Soviet troops. The Soviet Government has the right to transport by the above-mentioned railway for transit purpose military goods in sealed cars without customs inspection. The guarding of such military goods shall be undertaken by the railroad police and the Soviet Union shall not send any armed escort.

ARTICLE XI

Goods for through transit and transported by the Chinese Changchun Railway from Manchuli to Suifenho or vice versa and also from Soviet territory to the ports of Dairen and Port Arthur or vice versa shall be free from Chinese Customs duties or any other taxes and dues, but on entering Chinese territory such goods shall be subject to Chinese Customs inspection and verification.

ARTICLE XII

The Chinese Government shall ensure, on the basis of a separate agreement, that the supply of coal for the operation of the railway will be fully secured.

ARTICLE XIII

The railway shall pay taxes to the Government of the Republic of China the same as are paid by the Chinese state railways.

ARTICLE XIV

Both Contracting Parties agree to provide the Board of Directors of the Chinese Changchun Railway with working capital the amount of which will be determined by the Statute of the Railway.

Profits and losses and exploitation of the railway shall be equally divided between the Parties.

ARTICLE XV

For the working out in Chungking of the Statutes of joint operation of the railway the High Contracting Parties undertake within one month of the signing of the present Agreement, to appoint their representatives—three representatives from each Party. The Statute shall be worked out within two months and reported to the two Governments for their approval.

ARTICLE XVI

The determination, in accordance with the provisions in Article I, of the properties to be included in the joint ownership and operations of the railway by China and U.S.S.R. shall be made by a Commission to be composed of three representatives each of the two Governments. The Commission shall be constituted in Chungking within one month after the signing of the present Agreement and shall terminate its work within three months after the joint operation of the railway shall have begun.

The decision of the Commission shall be reported to the two Governments for their approval.

ARTICLE XVII

The term of this present Agreement shall be thirty years. After the expiration of the term of the present Agreement, the Chinese Changchun Railway with all its properties shall be transferred without compensation to the ownership of the Republic of China.

ARTICLE XVIII

The present Agreement shall come into force from the date of its ratification.

Done in Moscow, August 14, 1945, corresponding to the 14th day of the 8th month of the 34th year of the Chinese Republic, in two copies, each in the Russian and Chinese languages, both texts being equally authoritative.

THE PLENIPOTENTIARY OF THE PRESIDIUM OF THE SUPREME SOVIET OF THE U.S.S.R.

THE PLENIPOTENTIARY OF THE PRESIDENT OF THE NATIONAL GOVERNMENT OF THE REPUBLIC OF CHINA.

60[12]

Red Army "War Booty" Removals From Manchuria

60 (a)

State Department notes concerning Soviet removals

Secretary of State James F. Byrnes on February 9, 1946, instructed the American Embassies in Chungking and Moscow to present the following views to the Chinese Government and the Government of the U. S. S. R. respectively: [13]

"Current reports of discussions between officials of the Chinese Government and the Russian Government with regard to the disposition and control of industrial enterprises in Manchuria give concern to this Government.

"The Sino-Soviet Treaty and agreements signed August 14, 1945, provide for joint Sino-Soviet control over certain trunk railways in Manchuria, but these agreements exclude reference to any similar control over industrial enterprise in Manchuria. It is the understanding of the United States Government, which was kept informed of the course of negotiations which led up to the agreements, that exclusive Sino-Soviet governmental control over Manchurian enterprise would be limited to the railways dealt with in the aforesaid agreements. It is

---

[12] Parts A–C of this annex are extracts from a "Report On Japanese Assets in Manchuria to the President of the United States, July, 1946," by Edwin W. Pauley, Personal Representative of the President on Reparations.

[13] See also *Department of State Bulletin* of Mar. 17, 1946, p. 448.

therefore disturbing to this Government to receive reports that discussions are under way which might result in the establishment of exclusive Sino-Soviet control over industrial enterprises in Manchuria. Under present conditions, when free access to Manchuria is not open to nationals of other powers and equality of opporturnity in seeking participation in the economic development of Manchuria is denied Americans and other Allied nationals, it is felt that negotiation of agreements between the Chinese and Russian governments with regard to industries in Manchuria would be contrary to the principle of the Open Door, would constitute clear discrimination against Americans who might wish an opportunity to participate in the development of Manchurian industry and might place American commercial interests at a distinct disadvantage in establishing future trade relations with Manchuria.

"Directly related to this matter of the industries in Manchuria is the matter of reparations policy for Japan because the major portion of the industries of Manchuria were Japanese-owned prior to the defeat of Japan. This Government considers that the ultimate disposition of Japanese external assets, such as the industries in Manchuria, is a matter of common interest and concern to those Allies who bore the major burden in defeating Japan. This Government is now preparing a general policy outline for consideration by the concerned Governments with regard to Japanese reparations. It will be suggested that an inter-Allied Reparations Commission for Japan be established, and that one of the primary functions of this Commission will be the final allocation of Japanese external assets among the various claimant nations. It would seem, therefore, most inappropriate at this juncture for any final disposition to be made of Japanese external assets in Manchuria either by removal from Manchuria of such industrial assets as 'war booty' or by agreement between the Russian and Chinese Governments for the control of ownership of those assets.

"The Government of the United States desires to be cooperative with the Chinese and Soviet Governments in seeking a solution of the problems outlined above and it hopes that the other two Governments are animated by a similarly cooperative spirit. It would therefore appreciate being informed of any discussions which the two Governments may be having or may plan to have or any action they may have taken, in regard to the disposition or control of industrial enterprises in Manchuria and we would welcome full and frank discussion of the general problems."

The Secretary of State today [14] announced that he had received a reply from the Chinese Foreign Office, which reads in part:

"The Soviet Government declared in a memorandum addressed to Chinese Government on January 21, 1946 that all Japanese enterprises in the Chinese northeastern provinces which had rendered services to the Japanese Army were regarded by Soviet Union as war booty of Soviet forces. The Chinese Government considers this claim of Soviet Government as far exceeding the scope of war booty as generally recognized by international law and international usage and for this reason the two governments have not been able to reach a unanimity of views of fundamental principles involved.

"In another memorandum presented to officials of the Generalissimo's Headquarters in Changchun the Soviet Government declared that it proposed to hand over to China a part of the Japanese enterprises which Soviet Union regarded as war booty while remaining enterprises (including specified coal mines, power

[14] Mar. 5, 1946 ; see also *ibid.*

plants, iron and steel industries, chemical industries and cement industries) were to be jointly operated by China and Soviet Union. Chinese Government on its part has found it impossible to agree to this Soviet proposal because it goes beyond provisions of the Sino-Soviet agreements of August 14, 1945 and is contrary to the aforesaid stand of Chinese. Government regarding Japanese properties and enterprises in China."

60 (b)

The Personal Representative of the President on Reparations (Pauley) to President Truman

WASHINGTON, NOVEMBER *12, 1946*

DEAR MR. PRESIDENT: Under your instructions to me contained in your letter of April 27, 1945, and subsequent verbal orders you have issued to me, I present to you a report on Japanese assets in Manchuria.

This is a factual report based primarily on the first-hand observations and consultations with informed persons by myself and my Mission in Manchuria in June and July. In addition studies were made and appropriate personnel consulted in Washington and Tokyo prior to the arrival of our Mission in Manchuria.

It would not have been possible to carry through this assignment without the aid and assistance which was received from the Secretary of State and the Secretaries of the War and Navy Departments, and especially from General Douglas MacArthur and General George C. Marshall in the Orient. The Chinese National Government was most helpful in facilitating the activities of my Mission throughout areas under its control. In the Communist-held areas in North Manchuria, Chinese Communist and Soviet Railway officials were also of help.

Sincerely yours,

EDWIN W. PAULEY

60 (c)

General Summary of "Report on Japanese Assets in Manchuria"

A. SCOPE

The objectives of the 1946 Pauley Mission in Manchuria were: to survey Japanese assets subject to reparations; to ascertain the present productive capacity of industry; to estimate what immediate reparations removals from Japan could be utilized to improve or rehabilitate that industry; and to prove or disprove reports that crippling removals had been made from that area.

The Mission was organized in Washington in April 1946 pursuant to instructions from the President. It contained well-known American engineers specializing in various fields of industry. On May 4, 1946, the Mission departed from Washington for the Far East. After a short stay in Tokyo where the Mission was augmented by a number of industrial specialists from General MacArthur's headquarters, the group departed for Seoul for a survey of Korea. A base was established in Mukden, Manchuria, on May 27, 1946 and from there inspection trips were made to the various important industrial and mining centers. Among these were Mukden, Fushun, Liaoyang, Anshan, Penchihu, Kungyuan, Chinchow, Chinhsi, Peipiao, Fouhsin, Hulutao, Kaiyuan, Ssupingchieh, Hsian, Changchun, Kirin, Harbin and Mutanchiang. Dairen, the finest seaport in Manchuria, and an important industrial center, was not reached because authority for the visit could not be secured from the Soviet Government or local authorities. Antung, another important point was not visited because Chinese Communists refused permission. The work of the Mission was greatly facilitated by the whole-hearted cooperation of the Chinese National Government and of all United States Agencies in the Far East. Chinese Communists were of assistance in the visits in territory held by them in *Northern* Manchuria. The Mission left China on 15 July 1946 and returned to Washington on 21 July 1946.

The principal sources of data upon which this report is based are the following:

a. In Washington: Conferences with and studies made by appropriate Sections of the State, War, Navy and Commerce Departments, Office of Strategic Services, Foreign Economic Administration and other governmental agencies.

b. In Tokyo: Conferences with and studies made by agencies of Supreme Allied Commander. Interviews with Japanese responsible for the management of Manchurian industry and study of Japanese records.

c. In Manchuria: Inspection of industrial plants in the centers mentioned. On-the-spot interviews with persons who were present before, during and after the Soviet occupation were most fruitful. These included Chinese, Japanese, American and European Nationals. At the time of the survey many Japanese industrial executives had not yet been repatriated, so that many documents such as diaries and production records were available in Manchuria.

It is recognized that in the interviews with individuals, the Mission was dealing with hearsay evidence and that some of the information received was biased and exaggerated. Nevertheless, by comparing data from the different sources and balancing it against observed conditions, it is believed that an accurate picture was evolved and that this report is substantially accurate.

B. BACKGROUND

United States policy in the postwar Far East was predicated upon the establishment of China as a strong, stable, united nation, with a basic economic self-sufficiency, so that nation could take its proper part in the development of a peaceful Asiatic economy. During the years before and after Pearl Harbor the Japanese had created in Manchuria a tremendous industrial structure which was definitely tributary to the economy of Japan. Had this structure remained as intact as it was on the date of Soviet occupancy and had China remained peaceful, the Manchurian industrial complex could have readily been integrated with China's growing economy and so greatly accelerated the overall Chinese industrial development. The large capacities in basic industries in Manchuria would have made possible a rapid absorption by China of further processing equipment removed from Japan as reparations. At the same time this action would have lopped off from Japan one of the most important sources of strength in the Japanese war potential. It was presumed that China could fill at least partially, the economic vacuum resulting from the Japanese defeat and the consequent imposed reduction of Japan's productive capacity to a peacetime level. However, the damage which Manchurian industry has sustained since V–J Day has set back China's industrial progress for a generation and has thus materially delayed the implementation of announced U.S. policy.

Japan's interest in the Asiatic Mainland has been of long standing. The clash of Russian and Japanese interests there, resulted in the Russo-Japanese

War in 1904, and the acquisition by Japan of Russian concessions in South Manchuria. With the establishment of the South Manchurian Railway in 1906, Japan's exploitation of Manchuria took definite form. The railroad expanded into many industrial enterprises which furnished a wedge for further Japanese penetration on the continent. With the seizure of Manchuria from China by the Kwantung Army in 1931 and the creation of the Puppet State of Manchukuo, the exploitation was tremendously accelerated.

Impelling motives in Japan's development of Manchuria stemmed primarily from two sources. One, the ultra patriots including the military clique, the Black Dragon Society, and all dreamers of a Pan-Asiatic hegemony under Japanese domination, found in the conquest and exploitation of Manchuria an essential step in the march to empire. The Japanese Kwantung Army played no small part in advancing the aims of the military clique. The other source, the Zaibatsu (ruling commercial combines) saw in Manchuria an opportunity for an enormous source of profit. The Japanese Government and the puppet Manchukuo Government assisted the Zaibatsu in their exploitation with preferential treatment and subsidies. There was no altruism in these actions. Japan took care that management and technical skills remained in Japanese hands, using the local population primarily as a source of cheap labor.

Manchuria is a relatively rich country. It abounds in many natural resources which exist much more sparsely in the remainder of Asia. It is one of the few areas of great size which has consistently produced agricultural surpluses. Manchuria was fortunate in that the Japanese in their industrial development there provided a far greater capacity in finished products than in any other conquered country. It was Japan's apparent intention to make Manchuria industrially an integral part of the Japanese Empire and a source of economic strength for further military conquest. This is indicated by the fact that a great deal of construction and development of industrial and power facilities were still going on at the end of the war. From 1932 to 1944 coal production was more than doubled and the output of pig iron and iron ore was more than tripled.

The best estimate of the total of Japanese investments in Manchuria as of June 1945 is ¥11,000,000,000. In arriving at this estimate, figures cited by the Chinese Northeast Economic Commission, the British Ministry of Economic Warfare, the U.S. Foreign Economic Administration, and Japanese sources were also consulted.

The defeat of Japan caused the disruption of the production centers and trade channels built up by Japan in its empire-building and conquests, thus upsetting the entire economic structure of the Far East. U.S. policy is now directed toward the establishment of an economy that will promote a lasting peace in the Far East and to prevent the resurgence of Japanese economic domination.

U.S. policy has long held that all Japanese assets whether situated in Japan proper or in other areas were subject to claim as allied reparations. Japanese assets in conquered areas such as the Philippines, China, including Manchuria, and Korea, were to be taken from Japanese ownership and control and were to be operated for the benefit of the countries where the physical assets exist. Under what conditions full and complete title to these assets is to be vested in the local governments and under what conditions the ex-Japanese industrial plants are to be considered as part of the overall reparation allocation, is still under discussion and awaiting allied agreement. It was considered that this primary step was necessary in order to strengthen the economies of the countries which had been victims of Japanese aggression and further to keep the facilities operating in order to prevent loss of needed production and safeguard the livelihood of the local population.

The next step needed is the realignment of production areas and trade channels in the Far East so as to secure a properly balanced regional economy that can be both productive and profitable; an economy that does not have to rely upon subsidies, confiscation, and oppression to maintain itself. The United States reparations plan is aimed at achieving these two important steps: to turn over to local non-enemy governments control of the Japanese assets situated in those countries; and, to transfer surplus capacity from Japan to regions where it can best be used to process the natural resources so as to satisfy the needs of the Far East. In the steel industry, for example, where Japan has a much larger capacity than is needed for her normal peace requirements, the U.S. policy would remove this surplus capacity and place it near sources of iron ore and coking coal. Such areas can be found in Manchuria, China proper, and the Philippines.

C. FINDINGS

The difference in condition of the Manchurian industrial plant between Japanese surrender and the dates the Pauley Mission made its survey is appalling, as will be shown in the remainder of this report. How much of the wrecked condition is a direct result of Soviet removals, and how much may be ascribed to pillage, civil war, and other indirect consequences of the Soviet occupation cannot be accurately determined. In any case, the Soviet government must bear the major responsibility.

Soviet forces entered Manchuria on 9 August 1945. Japanese resistance was confined to Northern Manchuria and within a week this ended. Southern Manchuria, which contained over eighty percent of Manchurian industry, was taken practically unopposed and with little if any damage. There was ample opportunity for the orderly occupation of the entire area.

Japan was preparing to surrender prior to the Soviet entry into the Japanese war. The rolling up of the Southwest Pacific front, the rapid penetration of the Pacific defenses, and the powerful blows struck against the Japanese homeland forced Japan to seek means for halting the conflict. A partial chronology of important events from June 15, 1944, taken from General MacArthur's reports and other official sources shows the following:

Landings on Saipan . . . . June 15, 1944
Landings on Guam . . . . July 21
Landings on Leyte. . . . . October 20
First B-29 raids on Japan from Saipan . . . . November 24
Landings on Luzon . . . . January 9, 1945
U. S. Navy 3rd Fleet struck Tokyo and Nagoya-Kobe areas. . . . . February 16-17
Landings on Okinawa . . . . April 1
Abrogation by Soviets of Treaty of Neutrality with Japan . . . . April 5
Naval operations against Japanese homeland from North Hokkaido to Tokyo. . . . . . July 14-17
Potsdam Ultimatum issued to the Japanese Government. . . . . July 27
First atomic bomb dropped on Hiroshima . . . . August 6
Soviets declare war on Japan and invade Manchuria . . . . *August 9*
World receives news of Japan's acceptance of Potsdam Ultimatum . . . . *August 10*
General MacArthur acknowledges receipt of news of Japanese acceptance. . . . . *August 11*
Sino-Soviet Treaty signed at Moscow . . . . August 14
President Truman announces unconditional surrender of Japan. . . . . August 15
Japanese Commander in Manchuria appeals by radio to Soviets to cease attacks. . . . . . August 16
Unopposed Soviet air landing at Mukden . . . . August 18, 1945
Japanese delegation arrives in Manila to receive orders . . . . August 19
Unopposed Soviet air landings at Kirin and Changchun . . . . August 20
Eighth Army advance party landed at Atsugi Airdrome, Tokyo . . . . August 28
General MacArthur arrives at Atsugi . . . . August 30
Formal signing of surrender terms in Tokyo Bay . . . . September 2

Upon their arrival in the industrial areas of Manchuria, the Soviets began a systematic confiscation of food and other stockpiles and in early September started the selective removal of industrial machinery. It is apparent that they planned to complete these removals by 3 December 1945, the date originally set for the withdrawal of all Soviet military forces from Manchuria.

The term "stripping" as it has been used in the press in connection with removals from Manchuria may be confusing. The Soviets did not take everything. They concentrated on certain categories of supplies, machinery and equipment. In addition to taking stockpiles and certain complete industrial installations, the Soviets took by far the larger part of all functioning power generating and transforming equipment, electric motors, experimental plants, laboratories, and hospitals. In machine tools, they took only the newest and best, leaving antiquated tools behind. In the old Mukden Arsenal, for example, about one-third of the tools were taken, while in the new arsenal, virtually everything was taken or demolished.

Not only were buildings and structures damaged by the removal of the equipment, but the taking of some key equipment, such as generators and pumps from mines resulted in the loss of current production, and in irreparable damage to the mines by flooding. The removal of power facilities not only halted all current industrial production, but also made it impossible to maintain and protect the plants themselves. Water works and sewage facilities in the large cities were made inoperable because of lack of power.

After the removals, the Soviet forces permitted and even encouraged Chinese mobs to pillage, taking official movies of the process in some instances. Apparently the mobs were in search of objects of salable value and of wood for fuel to burn during the bitter Manchurian winter. The fuel problem was, of course, enormously intensified by the stoppage of a large part of coal production because of Soviet removals.

By far the greatest part of the damage to the Manchurian industrial complex occurred during the Soviet occupation and was primarily due to Soviet removals of equipment, and to Soviet failure to preserve order. After the Soviet withdrawal, Chinese Communist action resulted in further damage to some of the installations. It is a sad commentary that the small amount of benefit received by the Soviet Government in its removals from Manchuria could have been readily supplied by reparations removals from Japan proper at a much smaller cost to the world.

The Soviet forces also confiscated approximately three million U. S. dollars worth of gold bullion stocks and over a half billion Manchurian yuan from Manchukuo banks. They also circulated nearly ten billion yuan in occupational currency, almost doubling the total Manchurian note issue. In addition to the removals, mentioned above, occupational currency was used to purchase factories and properties and some privately-owned merchandise and materials.

It is difficult to ascertain in Manchuria the real reasons behind the Soviet actions there. The excuse that the articles removed were in the nature of "war booty" and were desperately needed to replace damage caused by the German invasion at home, does not fully cover the situation. As for reparations, the Soviet military effort in Manchuria which lasted only a few days is minute when compared with the long, tremendous and costly operations in the Pacific. Therefore, the Soviet Government would not be entitled to substantial reparations from Japanese-owned assets merely on the basis of their operations in this area. Obviously Japanese assets in Manchuria did not belong solely to the Soviet Government. Other nations too are logical claimants. In the allied reparations discussions at Moscow, Potsdam and Paris in 1945, the allies expressed as a principle that the greatest economic utility would result if the industrial equipment in Manchuria were left intact there, in the locations for which these items were specifically designed. Moving this equipment has destroyed a large part of its original value and the installations from which this equipment was removed have in many cases become total losses.

It can also be pointed out that there are now in the occupied zones of Germany (other than the Soviet occupied zone) reparations items which under the terms of the Potsdam Agreement were destined to be delivered to the Soviets. The nations occupying these zones are also entitled to Japanese reparations and so have a legitimate claim on the Japanese assets removed from Manchuria by the Soviet Government. Thus Soviet claims on German reparations in occupied zones could be counterbalanced by claims by other nations on the Manchurian removals. However this would require revision of the entire global reparations program.

Soviet actions in Manchuria are high-lighted by the entirely different policy followed in Korea where there were practically no capital removals or destruction of industry. In Manchuria the confiscation and removal of food stocks, the destruction attendant upon and following the removals of machinery, the almost complete halting of productive effort with no regard for the harmful effects upon the Chinese population, all indicate that there were long range strategic reasons behind the Soviet actions. The chaos caused by the Soviets has produced a condition of instability both politically and economically which will take a long time to correct. It left a populace hungry, cold, and full of unrest.

It is generally agreed that China's first economic need is communications, principally railways, transport, and domestic shipping. Less than 10,000 miles of railway is in existence in all of China exclusive of Manchuria and less than half of that is now operable. Manchuria with its abundant natural resources and industrial plant would have been the logical point to begin the rehabilitation of China's transport. If Manchurian industry had been left intact it could also have produced the steel, machinery and consumer goods so badly needed for restoration and for new construction in China.

China's continuing internal strife is a major factor in retarding her economic recovery. But even this cannot minimize the powerful set-back which the destruction of the Manchurian industrial plant has been to Manchuria, to China, and to the Far Eastern World.

D. Conclusions

The situation in Manchuria today is far from promising. The internal struggle continues intermittently. Dairen, by far the best port, has been practically sealed off by the Soviets for their own exclusive use, despite the fact that under the terms of the Sino-Soviet Treaty of August 14, 1945, Dairen is to be an open port and the Soviets are entitled to use only part of the port facilities. Railway communications to the few remaining secondary ports are under constant harassment by Chinese Communists. Thus, even if Manchurian industry were working full blast, it would be most difficult if not impossible to move any large quantity of finished products to China proper. It would be just as difficult to move into Manchuria the equipment necessary to rehabilitate industry.

Little can be done in the way of rehabilitation in China in the areas where fighting is going on or where the threat of armed action is present. This, however, should not delay the preparation of plans so that when peaceful conditions are resumed and communications restored, a rapid and orderly process of rehabilitation of the plants essential to primary needs of the inhabitants can begin. The natural resources are there. In restoring Manchuria's industrial complex, however, it must be remembered that Manchuria is practically surrounded by territory either wholly or partially under direct Soviet control. Manchuria will thus be vulnerable to further Soviet penetration.

In the meantime no effort should be spared in the industrial strengthening of the peaceful areas of other parts of China. China's urgent needs are manifold, but the prime need is for steel, for railroads, shipping, construction and consumer goods. One important steel producing area lies on the Yangtze River, near Hankow. There are others. These must be surveyed with a view to the immediate transfer to those areas as reparations from Japan, of such equipment as can be efficiently utilized. Similar recommendations have been made with respect to the Philippine Islands. The Chinese Government was urged to take action along these lines during Ambassador Pauley's conferences in Nanking on 25 May 1946. The necessity for immediate transfer of critically needed power equipment for the coal mining areas of Manchuria from Japan was also pointed out in a letter from Mr. Pauley to General MacArthur dated 20 June 1946. Training of additional Chinese personnel in engineering and management of the industrial equipment is also essential.

Manchuria's power installations are first priority in rehabilitation. This includes hydro-electric stations as well as thermal power plants at the coal mines. If sufficient power generating equipment can be quickly transferred from Japan, there is a good chance of salvaging one or two important coal mines that are now flooded or in grave danger of flooding.

Another possible and readily available but limited source of power is what remains of the hydro-electric development now in operation at Tafengmen near Kirin and which is furnishing power to Harbin and Changchun. Transmission lines to the South have been cut by Chinese Communists who will not permit repair. Until peace between the Communists and Chinese Nationalists is restored, this badly needed power is being wasted. Restoration of electric power in Manchuria will go far toward alleviating the immediate needs of the populace.

Given the best of conditions, China's rehabilitation is a matter of many years. In the meantime the stability of the entire Far East is in a large measure dependent upon satisfying the urgent needs of the populations of the various countries lying there. They all need materials and machines for reconstruction. Failure to supply these needs will result in continued unrest and instability.

Annexes to Chapter V: The Mission of General George C. Marshall, 1945–1947

61

President Truman to the Special Representative of the President to China (Marshall)

WASHINGTON, *December 15, 1945*

MY DEAR GENERAL MARSHALL: On the eve of your departure for China I want to repeat to you my appreciation of your willingness to undertake this difficult mission.

I have the utmost confidence in your ability to handle the task before you but, to guide you in so far as you may find it helpful, I will give you some of the thoughts, ideas, and objectives which Secretary Byrnes and I have in mind with regard to your mission.

I attach several documents which I desire should be considered as part of this letter. One is a statement of U. S. policy towards China [1] which was, I understand, prepared after consultation with you and with officials of the Department. The second is a memorandum from the Secretary of State to the War Department in regard to China. And the third is a copy of my press release on policy in China.[2] I understand that these documents have been shown to you and received your approval.

The fact that I have asked you to go to China is the clearest evidence of my very real concern with regard to the situation there. Secretary Byrnes and I are both anxious that the unification of China by peaceful, democratic methods be achieved as soon as possible. It is my desire that you, as my Special Representative, bring to bear in an appropriate and practicable manner the influence of the United States to this end.

Specifically, I desire that you endeavor to persuade the Chinese Government to call a national conference of representatives of the major political elements to bring about the unification of China and, concurrently, to effect a cessation of hostilities, particularly in north China.

It is my understanding that there is now in session in Chungking a Peoples' Consultative Council made up of representatives of the various political elements, including the Chinese Communists. The meeting of this Council should furnish you with a convenient opportunity for discussions with the various political leaders.

---

[1] Not printed; it did not differ substantially from the final text, for which see annex 62.
[2] See annex 62.

605

Upon the success of your efforts, as outlined above, will depend largely, of course, the success of our plans for evacuating Japanese troops from China, particularly north China, and for the subsequent withdrawal of our own armed forces from China. I am particularly desirous that both be accomplished as soon as possible.

In your conversations with Chiang Kai-shek and other Chinese leaders you are authorized to speak with the utmost frankness. Particularly, you may state, in connection with the Chinese desire for credits, technical assistance in the economic field, and military assistance (I have in mind the proposed U. S. military advisory group which I have approved in principle), that a China disunited and torn by civil strife could not be considered realistically as a proper place for American assistance along the lines enumerated.

I am anxious that you keep Secretary Byrnes and me currently informed of the progress of your negotiations and of obstacles you may encounter. You will have our full support and we shall endeavor at all times to be as helpful to you as possible.

Sincerely yours,

HARRY TRUMAN

[Enclosure]

MEMORANDUM BY SECRETARY BYRNES

[WASHINGTON,] *December 9, 1945*

For the War Department

The President and the Secretary of State are both anxious that the unification of China by peaceful democratic methods be achieved as soon as possible.

At a public hearing before the Foreign Relations Committee of the Senate on December 7, the Secretary of State said:

"During the war the immediate goal of the United States in China was to promote a military union of the several political factions in order to bring their combined power to bear upon our common enemy, Japan. Our longer-range goal, then as now, and a goal of at least equal importance, is the development of a strong, united, and democratic China.

"To achieve this longer-range goal, it is essential that the Central Government of China as well as the various dissident elements approach the settlement of their differences with a genuine willingness to compromise. We believe, as we have long believed and consistently demonstrated, that the government of Generalissimo Chiang Kai-shek affords the most satisfactory base for a developing democracy. But we also believe that it must be broadened to include the representatives of those large and well organized groups who are now without any voice in the government of China.

"This problem is not an easy one. It requires tact and discretion, patience and restraint. It will not be solved by the Chinese leaders themselves. To the extent that our influence is a factor, success will depend upon our capacity to exercise that influence in the light of shifting conditions in such a way as to encourage concessions by the Central Government, by the so-called Communists, and by the other factions."

The President has asked General Marshall to go to China as his Special Representative for the purpose of bringing to bear in an appropriate and practicable manner the influence of the United States for the achievement of the ends set forth above. Specifically, General Marshall will endeavor to influence the Chinese Government to call a national conference of representatives of the major political elements to bring about the unification of China and, concurrently, effect a cessation of hostilities, particularly in north China.

In response to General Wedemeyer's recent messages, the State Department requests the War Department to arrange for directions to him stipulating that:

(1) He may put into effect the arrangements to assist the Chinese National Government in transporting Chinese troops to Manchurian ports, including the logistical support of such troops;

(2) He may also proceed to put into effect the stepped-up arrangements for the evacuation of Japanese troops from the China theater;

(3) Pending the outcome of General Marshall's discussions with Chinese leaders in Chungking for the purpose of arranging a national conference of representatives of the major political elements and for a cessation of hostilities, further transportation of Chinese troops to north China, except as north China ports may be necessary for the movement of troops and supplies into Manchuria, will be held in abeyance;

(4) Arrangements for transportation of Chinese troops into north China may be immediately perfected, but not communicated to the Chinese Government. Such arrangements will be executed when General Marshall determines either (a) that the movement of Chinese troops to north China can be carried out consistently with his negotiations, or (b) that the negotiations between the Chinese groups have failed or show no prospect of success and that the circumstances are such as to make the movement necessary to effectuate the surrender terms and to secure the long-term interests of the United States in the maintenance of international peace.

62

Statement by President Truman on United States Policy Toward China, December 15, 1945 [3]

The Government of the United States holds that peace and prosperity of the world in this new and unexplored era ahead depend upon the ability of the sovereign nations to combine for collective security in the United Nations organization.

It is the firm belief of this Government that a strong, united and democratic China is of the utmost importance to the success of this United Nations organization and for world peace. A China disorganized and divided either by foreign aggression, such as that undertaken by the Japanese, or by violent internal strife, is an undermining influence to world stability and peace, now and in the future. The United States Government has long subscribed to the principle that the management of internal affairs is the responsibility of the peoples of the sovereign nations. Events of this century, however, would indicate that a breach of peace anywhere in the world threatens the peace of the entire world. It is thus in the most vital interest of the United States and all the United Nations that the people of China overlook no opportunity to adjust their internal differences promptly by means of peaceful negotiation.

The Government of the United States believes it essential:

(1) That a cessation of hostilities be arranged between the armies of the National Government and the Chinese Communists and other dissident Chinese

---

[3] *Department of State Bulletin*, Dec. 16, 1945, p. 945.

armed forces for the purpose of completing the return of all China to effective Chinese control, including the immediate evacuation of the Japanese forces.

(2) That a national conference of representatives of major political elements be arranged to develop an early solution to the present internal strife—a solution which will bring about the unification of China.

The United States and the other United Nations have recognized the present National Government of the Republic of China as the only legal government in China. It is the proper instrument to achieve the objective of a unified China.

The United States and the United Kingdom by the Cairo Declaration in 1943 and the Union of Soviet Socialist Republics by adhering to the Potsdam Declaration of last July and by the Sino-Soviet Treaty and Agreements of August 1945, are all committed to the liberation of China, including the return of Manchuria to Chinese control. These agreements were made with the National Government of the Republic of China.

In continuation of the constant and close collaboration with the National Government of the Republic of China in the prosecution of this war, in consonance with the Potsdam Declaration, and to remove possibility of Japanese influence remaining in China, the United States has assumed a definite obligation in the disarmament and evacuation of the Japanese troops. Accordingly the United States has been assisting and will continue to assist the National Government of the Republic of China in effecting the disarmament and evacuation of Japanese troops in the liberated areas. The United States Marines are in North China for that purpose.

The United States recognizes and will continue to recognize the National Government of China and cooperate with it in international affairs and specifically in eliminating Japanese influence from China. The United States is convinced that a prompt arrangement for a cessation of hostilities is essential to the effective achievement of this end. United States support will not extend to United States military intervention to influence the course of any Chinese internal strife.

The United States has already been compelled to pay a great price to restore the peace which was first broken by Japanese aggression in Manchuria. The maintenance of peace in the Pacific may be jeopardized, if not frustrated, unless Japanese influence in China is wholly removed and unless China takes her place as a unified, democratic and peaceful nation. This is the purpose of the maintenance for the time being of United States military and naval forces in China.

The United States is cognizant that the present National Government of China is a "one-party government" and believes that peace, unity and democratic reform in China will be furthered if the basis of this Government is broadened to include other political elements in the country. Hence, the United States strongly advocates that the national conference of representatives of major political elements in the country agree upon arrangements which would give those elements a fair and effective representation in the Chinese National Government. It is recognized that this would require modification of the one-party "political tutelage" established as an interim arrangement in the progress of the nation toward democracy by the father of the Chinese Republic, Doctor Sun Yat-sen.

The existence of autonomous armies such as that of the Communist army is inconsistent with, and actually makes impossible, political unity in China. With the institution of a broadly representative government, autonomous armies should be eliminated as such and all armed forces in China integrated effectively into the Chinese National Army.

In line with its often expressed views regarding self-determination, the United States Government considers that the detailed steps necessary to the achievement of political unity in China must be worked out by the Chinese themselves and that intervention by any foreign government in these matters would be inappropriate. The United States Government feels, however, that China has a clear responsibility to the other United Nations to eliminate armed conflict within its territory as constituting a threat to world stability and peace—a responsibility which is shared by the National Government and all Chinese political and military groups.

As China moves toward peace and unity along the lines described above, the United States would be prepared to assist the National Government in every reasonable way to rehabilitate the country, improve the agrarian and industrial economy, and establish a military organization capable of discharging China's national and international responsibilities for the maintenance of peace and order. In furtherance of such assistance, it would be prepared to give favorable consideration to Chinese requests for credits and loans under reasonable conditions for projects which would contribute toward the development of a healthy economy throughout China and healthy trade relations between China and the United States.

63

Press Release on Order for Cessation of Hostilities, January 10, 1946

We, General Chang Chun, Representative of the National Government, and General Chou En-lai, Representative of the Chinese Communist Party, have recommended to Generalissimo Chiang Kai-shek and Chairman Mao Tse-tung and have been authorized by them to announce that the following order has been issued to all units, regular, militia, irregular and guerrilla, of the National Armies of the Republic of China and of the Communist-led troops of the Republic of China:

"All units, regular, militia, irregular and guerrilla, of the National Armies of the Republic of China and of Communist-led troops of the Republic of China are ordered to carry out the following directive:

a. All hostilities will cease immediately.

b. Except in certain specific cases, all movements of forces in China will cease. There also may be the movements necessary for demobilization, redisposition, supply, administration and local security.

c. Destruction of and interference with all lines of communications will cease and you will clear at once obstructions placed against or interfering with such lines of communications.

d. An Executive Headquarters will be established immediately in Peiping for the purpose of carrying out the agreements for cessation of hostilities. This Headquarters will consist of three Commissioners; one representing the Chinese National Government, one representing the Chinese Communist Party, and one to represent the United States of America. The necessary instructions and orders unanimously agreed upon by the three Commissioners, will be issued in the name of the President of the Republic of China, through the Executive Headquarters."

As a matter of public interest we are further authorized to announce that the following stipulations regarding the above Cessation of Hostilities Order were agreed upon and made a matter of record in the minutes of the conferences.

1. Paragraph *b*, Cessation of Hostilities Order, does not prejudice military movements south of the Yangtze River for the continued execution of the plan of military reorganization of the National Government.

2. Paragraph *b*, Cessation of Hostilities Order, does not prejudice military movements of forces of the National Army into or within Manchuria which are for the purpose of restoring Chinese sovereignty.

3. Lines of communications, mentioned in paragraph *b*, Cessation of Hostilities Order, includes post communications.

4. It is further agreed that movements of the forces of the National Army under the foregoing stipulations shall be reported daily to the Executive Headquarters.

We are also authorized to announce that the agreements, recommendations, and directives of the Executive Headquarters will deal only with the immediate problems raised by the cessation of hostilities.

American participation within the Headquarters will be solely for the purpose of assisting the Chinese members in implementing the Cessation of Hostilities Order.

The Executive Headquarters will include an Operations Section, composed of the number of officers and men required to supervise adequately in the field of the various details.

It is agreed that separate and independent signal communications systems may be established for each Commissioner in order to insure rapid and unhampered communications.

The Headquarters will be located initially at Peiping.

CHANG CHUN
CHOU EN LAI

64

Resolution on Government Organization adopted by the Political Consultative Conference, January 1946 [4]

I. Concerning the State Council: Pending the convocation of the National Assembly, the Kuomintang, as a preliminary measure preparatory to the actual inauguration of constitutionalism, will revise the Organic Law of the National Government in order to expand the State Council. The following are the salient points of the revision under contemplation:

1. There will be forty (40) State Councillors, of whom the Presidents of the Executive, Legislative, Judicial, Examination, and Control Yuan will be ex-officio members.

2. The State Councillors will be chosen by the President of the National Government from among the Kuomintang members as well as non-members of the Kuomintang.

3. The State Council is the supreme organ of the Government in charge of national affairs.

4. The State Council will be competent to discuss and decide on:

A. Legislative principles.

B. Administrative policy.

C. Important military measures.

---

[4] Printed also in *China Handbook, 1937–1945*, pp. 744–745.

D. Financial schemes and the budget.

E. The appointment and dismissal of Ministers of State with or without port-folios, and the appointment of members of the Legislative and Control Yuan.

F. Matters submitted by the President of the National Government for consideration.

G. Proposals submitted by three or more State Councillors.

5. If the President of the National Government is of opinion that any decision of the State Council is difficult to be carried out, he may submit it for reconsid-eration. In case three-fifths of the State Councillors, upon reconsideration, up-hold the original decision, it shall be carried out accordingly.

6. General resolutions before the State Council are to be passed by a majority vote of the State Councillors present. If a resolution before the State Council should involve changes in administrative policy, it must be passed by a two-thirds vote of the State Councillors present. Whether a given resolution involves changes in administrative policy or not is to be decided by a majority vote of the State Councillors present.

7. The State Council meets every two weeks. The President of the National Government may call emergency meetings, if necessary.

II. Concerning the Executive Yuan.

1. All Ministers of the Executive Yuan are ipso facto Ministers of State. There may be three to five Ministers of State without portfolios.

2. Members of all political parties as well as individuals with no party affilia-tions may become Ministers of State with or without portfolios.

III. Concerning miscellaneous matters.

1. Whether the membership of the People's Political Council should be in-creased and its powers raised, pending the inauguration of the Constitution, will be left to the Government to decide in the light of the circumstances of the time.

2. All Government employees, whether of the Central Government or of the local Governments, should be selected on the basis of merit. No discriminations on account of party affiliations should be allowed.

NOTE: A. The appointment of State Councillors by the President of the National Government will be made on the nomination of the different parties concerned. In case he does not consent to the candidature of any given individual, the party concerned may nominate another one for the office.

B. When the President of the National Government nominates any individual with no party affiliations as State Councillor whose candidature is opposed by one-third of the other nominees, he must reconsider the matter and make a different nomination.

C. Half of the State Councillors will be Kuomintang members and the other half will be members of other political parties and prominent social leaders. The exact number of members of other political parties and prominent social leaders who are to serve as State Councillors will form the subject of separate discussions.

D. Of the existing Ministers under the Executive Yuan and the proposed Minis-ters of State without portfolios, seven or eight will be appointed from among non-Kuomintang members.

E. The number of Ministries to be assigned to non-Kuomintang members will form the subject of separate discussions after the PCC has closed.

65

Resolution on Program for Peaceful National Reconstruction Adopted by the Political Consultative Conference, January 1946 [5]

Now that the war of resistance against Japan has ended and peaceful reconstruction should begin, the National Government has invited representatives of the different political parties and prominent social leaders to the Political Consultative Conference to discuss national problems with the double objective of putting an end to the period of political tutelage and inaugurating constitutionalism at an early date. The present program is drawn up to serve as a guide for the Government, pending the actual inauguration of constitutionalism. Representatives of the different political parties and prominent social leaders will be invited to take part in the Government. It is to be hoped that one and all will give first consideration to the needs of the nation and the demands of the people, and that they will cooperate wholeheartedly and work for the realization of the program, whose main features are as follows:

I. GENERAL PRINCIPLES

1. The principles of the San Min Chu I will be regarded as the highest guiding principles for national reconstruction.

2. All forces of the nation will unite under the guidance of President Chiang Kai-shek in order to construct a new China, unified, free, and democratic.

3. It is recognized that the democratization of politics, the nationalization of troops, and the equality and legality of all political parties, as advocated by President Chiang, are necessary paths leading to peaceful national reconstruction.

4. Political disputes must be settled by political means in order to maintain peaceful national development.

II. THE RIGHTS OF THE PEOPLE

1. The freedoms of person, thought, religion, belief, speech, the press, assembly, association, residence, removal, and correspondence should be guaranteed to the people. Any existing laws that contravene these freedoms should be either revised or repealed.

2. Any organization or individual other than judicial organs and the police should be strictly forbidden to arrest, try, and punish the people. Anyone who violates this rule shall be punished. The Habeas Corpus Law which has already been promulgated by the Government should be put into practical operation by Government decree at an early date.

3. The political, social, educational, and economic equality of women should be guaranteed.

III. POLITICAL PROBLEMS

1. All national measures of the moment should take into consideration the proper interests of the people of all localities, classes, and professions, and allow for their equitable development.

2. In order to increase administrative efficiency, the different grades of administrative machinery should be revamped, their rights and duties should be unified and clearly delimited, all unnecessary Governmental agencies should be abolished, the administrative procedure should be simplified, and the principle

---

[5] Printed also in *China Handbook, 1937–1945*, p. 747.

of individual responsibility each for his own section of the work should be introduced.

3. A sound system of civil service should be established : competent individuals should be protected; Government employees should be appointed not on the basis of personal or party allegiance, but on that of ability and past experience; no one should be allowed to hold concurrent jobs or to be drawn into Government service through the exertion of purely personal influence.

4. The unity and independence of the judicial power should be guaranteed, precluding it from political interference. The personnel in the courts of law should be increased, their salaries and positions should be raised, the judicial procedure should be simplified, and prisons should be reformed.

5. The supervisory system should be strictly enforced; corruption should be severely punished; facilities should be given to the people to accuse corrupt officials.

6. Local self-government should be actively pushed forth, and popular elections beginning from the lower administrative units and gradually ascending to the highest unit should be carried out. Provincial, District, and Municipal Councils should be established throughout the country at an early date, and District Magistrates should be elected by the people.

In frontier provinces and districts where minority peoples live, the number of Provincial or District Councillors to be elected by these minority peoples should be fixed according to the proportion they occupy in their respective provinces or districts.

7. All national administrative matters which have to be carried out in the territory of a district which has attained complete self-government must be carried out under the supervision and control of the National Government.

8. The powers of the Central and local Governments should be regulated on the basis of the principle of "a fair distribution of powers". The local Governments may take such measures as are adapted to the special circumstances of the localities concerned, but the regulations issued by the Provincial and District Governments must not contravene the laws and decrees of the Central Government.

IV. MILITARY AFFAIRS

1. The army belongs to the State. It is the duty of the soldier to protect the country and love the people and to insure the unity both of military organization and of military command.

2. All military establishments should be adapted to the needs of national defense. The military system should be reformed in accordance with democratic institutions and the circumstances of the nation. The army and political parties should be separated from each other; military and civil authority should be vested in different hands; military education should be improved; equipment should be adequate; a sound personnel and finance system should be introduced. All these should be done in order to create a modernized national army.

3. The system of conscription should be improved and made to apply fairly and throughout the whole country. Some form of the volunteer system should be maintained and improved upon in order to meet the needs of a fully equipped army.

4. All troops of the country should be reorganized into a lesser number of units in accordance with the provisions of the "Military Reorganization Plan".

5. Preparations for the rehabilitation and employment of disbanded and retired officers and men should be made. The livelihood of disabled officers and men

should be guaranteed.   The families of fallen officers and men should be provided for.

6. A time limit should be set for the repatriation of the Japanese troops who have surrendered.   Adequate measures should be put into operation at an early date for the disbandment of puppet troops and the liquidation of roving armed bands.

V. FOREIGN RELATIONS

1. The Atlantic Charter, the Cairo Declaration, the Moscow Four-Power Declaration, and the United Nations Organization Charter should be observed.   China will take an active part in the UNO in order to preserve world peace.

2. All remnants of Japanese influence in China should be extirpated according to the provisions of the Potsdam Declaration.   The problem of Japan should be solved in cooperation with other Allied Nations in order to prevent the resurgence of Japanese Fascist-militarist forces and to guarantee the security of the Far East.

3. Friendly relations with the United States, the Soviet Union, the United Kingdom, France, and other democratic countries should be promoted; treaty obligations should be observed; and economic and cultural cooperation should be undertaken in order to work for the prosperity and progress of the world in conjunction with other countries.

4. Commercial treaties, based on the principles of equality and reciprocity, should be concluded at an early date with other nations when necessary, and the position of Chinese residents overseas should be ameliorated.

VI. ECONOMICS AND FINANCE

1. A plan of economic reconstruction should be formulated in accordance with the teachings of Dr. Sun Yat-sen's "Industrial Planning", and the cooperation of foreign capital and technique should be welcome.

2. Any enterprise which partakes of the nature of a monopoly or which cannot be undertaken by private initiative should be classified as a state enterprise; the people should be encouraged to undertake all other enterprises.   Such should be the principles for the first stage of economic reconstruction, which must be effectively carried out.   All existing measures should be examined and improved upon in the light of this principle.

3. In order to hasten the process of China's industrialization the Government should convene a National Economic Conference, to which will be invited social leaders interested in the problem of economic reconstruction.   In this way the Government will be able to sound out popular opinion and decide upon the measures to be taken.

4. The development of "official capitalism" should be forestalled.   Government officials should be strictly forbidden to take advantage of their official position to indulge in speculation and cornering, evade taxes, smuggle, embezzle public funds, and illegally make use of the means of transportation.

5. Active preparations must be made for the construction of additional railroads and highways, harbors and bays, irrigation and other projects.   Subsidies should be granted to those who construct houses, schools, hospitals, and other public buildings.

6. Farm rents and interest rates must be effectively reduced.   The rights of the lessee must be protected, and the payment of farm rents must be guaranteed.   More and larger loans to farmers must be made available, and usury should be strictly prohibited.   All these must be done in order to better the peasants' lot.

The land law must be put into operation so as to attain the objective of "He who tills the soil also owns it."

7. Active measures should be taken to help the people increase their productive power by afforestation and the growth of grass, the conservation of water and soil, the development of animal husbandry, the reorganization and further development of agricultural cooperation, the expansion of agricultural experimentation and research, and the utilization of modern equipment and methods to kill locusts and other insects.

8. Labor laws must be put into operation. The conditions of labor must be improved; the bonus system should be put on trial; unemployment and disablement insurances should be started; child and female labor should be given adequate protection; more workers' schools should be established in order to raise the cultural level of the working population.

9. Laws governing industrial association should be made at an early date, so that those engaged in industrial undertakings may form their own associations. Laws concerning factory management should be examined and revised on the assumption that there prevails a spirit of conciliation between capital and labor.

10. Financial accounts should be made public. The budget system and annual accounts system should be strictly adopted. Public expenditure should be curtailed, and revenues and expenditures should be balanced. Central Government finance and local finance should be sharply differentiated. The currency should be deflated and the monetary system should be stabilized. The raising of both domestic and foreign loans and the use to which they will be put should be made public and subject to popular supervision.

11. The system of taxation should be reformed. All illegal taxes and extortions should be completely abolished. The various offices for the collection of taxes should be amalgamated, and the procedure of collection should be simplified. Progressive taxes should be imposed on assets and incomes. National banks should be entrusted with special economic tasks in order to help develop industry and agriculture. Assets which have escaped to foreign countries or have been frozen should be commandeered to be used for the balancing of the budget.

VII. EDUCATION AND CULTURE

1. The freedom of learning should be guaranteed. Religious beliefs and political ideologies should not be allowed to interfere with school and college administration.

2. Scientific research and artistic creation should be encouraged in order to raise the national cultural level.

3. Compulsory education and social education should be made nation-wide; illiteracy should be actively wiped out. Professional education should be expanded in order to increase the professional ability of the people; normal education should be further developed in order to educate more qualified teachers for compulsory education. The contents of the teaching material in the various grades of schools should be revised in the light of the democratic and scientific spirit.

4. The proportion of the national budget to be devoted to education and cultural enterprises should be increased. The salaries and retirement annuities of teachers in the various grades of schools should be reasonably increased. Poor students should be subsidized, so that they can go to school and continue their studies. Endowments should be made for scientific research and creative literary and artistic work.

5. Privately endowed schools and cultural work among the people should be encouraged and subsidized.

6. In order to promote national health encouragement and assistance should be given to all forms of child welfare, public health installations should be made nation-wide, and physical exercise should be actively encouraged.

7. The wartime censorships of the press, motion pictures, the drama, letters, and telegrams should be abolished. Assistance should be given to the development of businesses in connection with publications, newspapers, news agencies, the drama, and motion pictures. All news agents and cultural enterprises operated by the Government should serve the interests of the entire nation.

VIII. REHABILITATION AND RELIEF

1. Social order in the liberated areas should be restored at an early date. The people must be relieved of all oppressions and sufferings which were heaped on them in the period of enemy occupation. The tendency for prices to rise in the liberated areas must be curbed. All corrupt practices of officials who were sent to the occupied territories to take over from the enemy should be severely punished.

2. Railroads and highways should be quickly repaired. Inland and coastal shipping should be quickly restored. Those people who have migrated to the interior in wartime must be helped by the government to return to their native districts. Homes and jobs should be found for them, if necessary.

3. Good use must be made of the UNRRA supplies in order to relieve the war refugees; medical supplies must be distributed to them in order to cure and prevent diseases; seeds and fertilizers must be given them in order to restore farming. The authorities in charge of this work will be assisted by popular agencies and organizations in the discharge of their duties.

4. Factories and mines in the liberated areas must be quickly made operative; the property rights of the original owners must be protected; work must be resumed at an early date, so that employment may be found for those without useful occupations. Enemy and puppet property should be properly disposed of in order to enable those factories and individuals who have made significant contributions to the war of resistance in the interior to take part in its exploitation.

5. The Yellow River must be quickly put under control. Other irrigation projects which have been damaged or allowed to lapse in the course of the war must be made good at an early date.

6. The Government's decrees to stop conscription and exempt the people from the payment of agricultural taxes for one year must be carried out to the letter by the different grades of Government. No conscription or agricultural taxes under a different guise should be allowed.

IX. CHINESE RESIDENTS OVERSEAS

1. Chinese residents overseas who have become destitute as a result of enemy oppression will be helped by the Government to reestablish their former business; those members of their families who may be living in China will receive proper relief.

2. Assistance will be given to Chinese residents overseas who have returned to China in the last few years in the course of the war, so that they may go back to their former place of residence. Facilities will be provided for them for the recovery of their property and the reestablishment of their business.

3. All educational and cultural enterprises of Chinese residents overseas will be restored and active assistance will be given them by the Government. Encouragement and assistance will be given to the children of Chinese residents overseas to come back to China for education.

ANNEX

1. In those recovered areas where the local government is under dispute the status quo shall be maintained until a settlement is made according to Articles 6, 7, and 8 of Chapter III on Political Problems in this program by the National Government after its reorganization.

2. A Committee for the Protection of the People's Liberties will be formed, composed of representatives of the local Council, the Lawyers' Association, and popular organizations. Financial assistance will be given to it by the Government.

3. Revisions will be made, in the light of the usual practices in democratic countries, in the Citizen's Oath-Taking and the examination of candidates for public offices.

4. Membership of the Supreme Economic Council of the Executive Yuan should be increased by the addition of economic experts representing the people at large and of experienced industrialists.

5. It is recommended that the Government put an end to the policy of control over nitrate and sulphur.

6. (a) Those workers originally employed in factories which have been removed to the interior in the course of the war, who now find themselves unemployed due to the closing up of the factories as a result of the war, should be granted a certain amount of financial.assistance by the Government.

(b) Those factories which have made significant contributions to the manufacture of military material in the course of the war should continue to receive Government patronage by the latter's purchase of their ready-made articles and as much of their material as possible.

7. The press law should be revised. The Regulations Governing the Registration and Control of Newspapers, Magazines, and News Services in Times of Emergency; Provisional Regulations Governing Newspapers, News Agencies, Magazines, Motion Pictures, and Broadcasts in Liberated Areas; Regulations Governing the Censorship of the Drama and Motion Pictures; Regulations Governing the Censorship of Letters and Telegrams, and other regulations of a similar nature should be repealed. Amusement taxes and stamp taxes on motion pictures, drama, and concert tickets should be lightened.

66

Resolution on Military Problems Adopted by the Political Consultative Conference, January 1946 [6]

I. Fundamental principles for the creation of a national army.

1. The army belongs to the State. It is the duty of the soldier to protect the country and love the people.

---

[6] Printed also in *China Handbook, 1937–1945*, p. 745.

2. The army shall be established in response to the necessities of national defense. Its quality and equipment shall be improved in the light of the progress made in general education, science, and industry.

3. The military system shall be reformed in the light of the democratic institutions and actual conditions prevailing at the time.

4. The system of conscription shall be reformed and applied fairly and universally. Some form of the volunteer system shall be preserved and reforms shall be introduced in order to meet the requirements of a fully equipped army.

5. Military education shall be conducted in the light of the foregoing principles, and shall forever be dissociated from party affiliations and personal allegiance.

II. Fundamental principles for the reorganization of the army.

1. Separation of army and party

A. All political parties shall be forbidden to carry on party activities, whether open or secret, in the army. So shall be all cliques based on personal relations or of a territorial nature.

B. All soldiers on active service who owe allegiance to any political party may not take part in the party activities of the district in which they are stationed, when they are on duty.

C. No party or individual may make use of the army as an instrument of political rivalry.

D. No illegal organizations and activities may be allowed in the army.

2. Separation of civil and military authorities.

A. No soldier on active service in the army may serve concurrently as civil officials.

B. The country shall be divided into military districts, which shall be made not to coincide with administrative districts as far as possible.

C. The army shall be strictly forbidden to interfere in political affairs.

III. Methods aiming at the civilian control of the army.

1. When the preliminary measures for the reorganization of the army have been completed, the National Military Council shall be reorganized into a Ministry of National Defense under the Executive Yuan.

2. The Minister of National Defense shall not necessarily be a soldier.

3. The number of troops and military expenditure shall be decided upon by the Executive Yuan and passed by the Legislative Yuan.

4. All troops shall be under the unified control of the Ministry of National Defense.

5. A Military Committee shall be established within the Ministry of National Defense to be charged with the double duty of drawing up schemes for the creation of a national army and of seeing to it that the schemes are faithfully carried out. Members of the Committee shall be drawn from various circles.

IV. Practical methods for the reorganization of the army.

1. The three-man military commission shall proceed according to schedule and agree upon practical methods for the reorganization of the Communist troops at an early date. The reorganization must be completed as soon as possible.

2. The Government troops should be reorganized, according to the plan laid down by the Ministry of War, into ninety (90) divisions. The reorganization should be completed within six (6) months.

3. When the reorganizations envisaged in paragraphs 1 and 2 have been completed, all troops of the country should be again reorganized into fifty (50) or sixty (60) divisions.

4. A commission for the supervision of the reorganization plan shall be established within the National Military Council. Members of the commission shall be drawn from various circles.

67

Agreement on the National Assembly by Sub-Committee of the Political Consultative Conference

Based on the resolution on this subject introduced by the Government representatives, the following agreement on the National Assembly was reached in the PCC Sub-Committee dealing with this problem by the various delegations:

1. That the National Assembly shall be convened on May 5, 1946.
2. That the power of the National Assembly is to adopt the Constitution.
3. That the Constitution shall be adopted by a vote of three-fourths of the delegates present.
4. That the 1,200 geographical and vocational delegates, who have been or are going to be elected according to the electoral law of the National Assembly, shall be retained.
5. That the geographical and vocational delegates for the Northeast provinces and Taiwan shall be increased by 150.
6. That 700 seats shall be added to the National Assembly and they shall be apportioned among the various parties and social leaders. The ratio of apportionment shall be decided later.
7. That the total number of delegates to the National Assembly shall be 2,050.
8. That the organ to enforce the Constitution shall be elected six months after the Constitution is adopted.

68

Resolution on the Draft Constitution Adopted by the Political Consultative Conference, January 1946 [7]

I. Establishment of a Reviewing Committee.

1. *Name:* Committee for the Reviewing of the Draft Constitution.
2. *Organization:* The Committee will have a total membership of twenty-five (25), of whom five (5) will represent each of the five groups composing the Political Consultation Conference. In addition, ten (10) technical experts outside of the PCC will be invited to take part in the work of the Committee. In selecting the technical experts reference should be made to the membership lists of the Association for the Promotion of Constitutionalism and the Association to Assist the Inauguration of Constitutionalism.
3. *Functions:* The PCC will establish the Committee for the Reviewing of the Draft Constitution, which will draw up a comprehensive scheme for the revision of the 1936 Draft Constitution on the basis of the principles recommended by the PCC and in the light of the recommendations made by the Association for the Promotion of Constitutionalism and the Association to Assist the Inauguration of Constitutionalism and opinions advanced by various other quarters. This

[7] Printed also in *China Handbook, 1937–1945*, pp. 746–747.

scheme will be submitted to the National Assembly for adoption. It may also be laid before the PCC for discussion, if necessary.

4. *Duration:* Two months.

II. Principles to be applied in the revision of the Draft Constitution.

1. Concerning the National Assembly.

A. The entire electorate, when they exercise the rights of election, initiative, referendum, and recall, are called the National Assembly.

B. Pending the election of the President by universal suffrage, he shall be elected by an electoral body composed of the District, Provincial, and National Representative Assemblies.

C. The recall of the President is to be effected by the same means as that employed in his election.

D. The exercise of the rights of initiative and referendum will be defined by appropriate laws.

NOTE: The convocation of the first National Assembly will form the subject of discussion by the PCC.

2. Concerning the Legislative Yuan: The Legislative Yuan will be the supreme law-making body of the State and will be elected by the electorate. This function corresponds to those of a Parliament in a democratic country.

3. Concerning the Control Yuan: The Control Yuan will be the supreme organ of control of the State and will be elected by the Provincial Assemblies and the Assemblies of the Self-Governing Areas of Minority Peoples. It will exercise the functions of consent, impeachment, and control.

4. Concerning the Judicial Yuan: The Judicial Yuan will be the Supreme Court of the State, and will not be responsible for judicial administration. It will be composed of a specified number of justices, who will be appointed on the nomination of the President of the National Government and with the consent of the Control Yuan. The different grades of judges shall all be without party affiliations.

5. Concerning the Examination Yuan: The Examination Yuan will be in the form of a committee, whose members will be appointed on the nomination of the President of the National Government and with the consent of the Control Yuan. Its functions will be mainly to examine candidates for civil service and technical experts. Members of the Examination Yuan shall be without party affiliations.

6. Concerning the Executive Yuan.

A. The Executive Yuan is the supreme executive organ of the State. The President of the Executive Yuan is to be appointed on the nomination of the President of the National Government and with the consent of the Legislative Yuan. The Executive Yuan is to be responsible to the Legislative Yuan.

B. If the Legislative Yuan has no confidence in the Executive Yuan as a whole, the latter may either resign or ask the President of the National Government to dissolve the former. But the same President of the Executive Yuan may not ask for the dissolution of the Legislative Yuan for a second time.

7. Concerning the Presidency of the National Government.

A. The President of the National Government may promulgate emergency decrees according to law when the Executive Yuan has so decided. But the action must be reported to the Legislative Yuan within one month.

B. The right of the President of the National Government to call the Presidents of the Executive, Legislative, Judicial, Examination, and Control Yuan into conference need not be written into the Constitution.

8. Concerning the system of local government.

A. The Province is to be regarded as the highest unit of local self-government.

B. The powers of the Province and the Central Government will be divided according to the principle of "a fair distribution of power."

C. The Provincial Governor is to be elected by the people.

D. The Province may have a Provincial Constitution, which, however, must not contravene the provisions of the National Constitution.

9. Concerning the rights and duties of the people.

A. All freedoms and rights which are generally enjoyed by the peoples of democratic countries should be protected by the Constitution and should not be illegally encroached upon.

B. If the freedom of the people is to be defined by law, it must be done for its protection and not with a view to restricting it.

C. Labor service should be provided for in the Law on Local Self-Government, and not written into the National Constitution.

D. The right of self-government must be guaranteed to minority peoples who live together in one particular locality.

10. A separate chapter on elections should be provided in the Constitution. Only those twenty-three years of age or over have the right to be elected.

11. Concerning fundamental national policies: A separate chapter in the Constitution should be devoted to fundamental national policies, including items on national defense, foreign relations, national economy, culture, and education.

A. The aim of national defense is to guarantee the safety of the Nation and preserve the peace of the world. All members of the Army, Navy, and Air Forces should be loyal to the State, love the people, and rise above all personal, territorial, and party affiliations.

B. Foreign relations should be carried on in a spirit of independence. Friendly relations with foreign countries should be promoted, treaty obligations carried out, the Charter of the United Nations Organization observed, international cooperation fostered, and world peace guaranteed.

C. Dr. Sun Yat-sen's principle of economic democracy (the Min Sheng Chu I) should serve as the basis of the national economy. The State must see to it that he who tills the soil also owns it; that workers have jobs; and that enterprisers have ample opportunities to carry on their business. These things must be done in order to attain the twin objective of fairness and sufficiency in the national economy and the people's livelihood.

D. It should be the aim of culture and education to foster the growth of the national spirit, the democratic attitude of mind, and scientific knowledge and technique. The general cultural level of the people should be universally raised; equality of educational opportunity should be made a reality; freedom of learning should be guaranteed; and scientific development should be pushed forth with vigor.

NOTE: The provisions in the Constitution relative to paragraphs (a), (b), (c), and (d) should not go too much into detail.

12. Concerning amendments to the Constitution: The right to amend the Constitution shall be vested in a joint conference of the Legislative and Control Yuan. The proposed amendments should be passed by that body in which is vested the right to elect the President of the National Government.

69

Press Release by Military Sub-Committee Concerning Agreement on Basis for Military Reorganization and Integration of Communist Forces into National Army, February 25, 1946 [8]

We, General Chang Chih Chung, representative of the Government and General Chou En-lai, representative of the Chinese Communist Party, constituting the Military Sub-Committee of which General Marshall is advisor have been authorized to announce that an agreement has been reached on the basis for military reorganization and for the integration of the Communist forces into the National Army.

The Military Sub-Committee is now preparing the detailed measures to carry the terms of the agreement into execution. The Executive Headquarters at Peiping will be charged with the responsibility of transmitting the necessary orders to the troops in the field and with supervision of their execution.

These measures will be carried out over a period of 18 months so as to insure a minimum of difficulty.

The object of the agreement is to facilitate the economic rehabilitation of China and at the same time to furnish a basis for the development of an effective military force capable of safeguarding the security of the nation, including provisions to safeguard the rights of the people from military interference.

The articles of agreement follow:

Basis for Military Reorganization and for the Integration of the Communist Forces Into the National Army

Article I—Command

Section 1. The President of the Republic of China being the Commander-in-Chief of the Armed Forces of the Republic of China exercises command through the Ministry of National Defense (or National Military Council). The commanders of the army groups and of the separate armies and the directors of the service areas herein provided for shall report to the Commander-in-Chief through the Ministry of National Defense (or National Military Council).

Section 2. The Commander-in-Chief shall have the power to appoint and relieve all subordinate officers provided, however, that in the event it becomes necessary during the process of the reorganization of the military forces to relieve the commander of any Communist-led unit or any Communist officer holding other position, the Commander-in-Chief shall appoint in the place of the officer relieved an officer nominated by the senior Communist member of the government.

Article II—Functions and Restrictions

Section 1. The primary function of the Army shall be to defend the Republic in time of war. In time of peace the principal function of the Army shall be training. It may be employed however, to quell domestic disorders, but only as provided in Section 2 of this article.

Section 2. When, in the event of domestic disorders, the governor of a province shall have certified to the Council of State that the local civil police, and the Peace Preservation Corps have been unable to cope with the situation, the Pres-

---

[8] Printed also in *China Handbook, 1937–1945*, pp. 755–758.

ident, in his capacity as commander-in-chief, shall, with the approval of the Council of State, employ the army to restore order.

ARTICLE III—ORGANIZATION

Section 1. The army shall consist of armies of three divisions each with supporting troops not to exceed 15% of their total strength. At the conclusion of 12 months the armies shall consist of 108 divisions of not to exceed 14,000 men each. Of these, 18 shall be formed from Communist Forces.

Section 2. China shall be divided into 8 service areas under directors responsible to the Minister of National Defense (or National Military Council) for the following functions within their respective areas:

The supply, quartering and pay of all military units located within the areas;

The storage, reconditioning and issue of the weapons and equipment collected from demobilized troops within the area;

The processing of demobilized officers and enlisted personnel within the area and the continued processing of demobilized officers and enlisted personnel passing through the area en route to their homes or other designated destinations;

The processing and elementary training of individual recruits received within the area as replacements for the armies;

The supply of military schools within the area;

The service area directors shall have no authority or control over the armies located within their areas and they are specifically prohibited from interfering with or influencing in any way whatsoever civil administration or affairs;

Each army commander within a particular service area shall maintain in the service area headquarters his own representative to insure that the needs of the forces under his command are fully and expeditiously met;

There shall be a meeting every second month within each service area and presided over by the service area director. These meetings shall be attended by the army and division commanders, or their duly appointed representatives, of each army located within that area. A representative of the Ministry of National Defense (or National Military Council) shall also be present. The instructions of the Ministry of National Defense (or National Military Council) shall be presented, and the state of supply and similar matters of the service area discussed.

ARTICLE IV—DEMOBILIZATION

Section 1. During the 12 months immediately following the promulgation of this agreement the Government shall demobilize all units in excess of 90 divisions and the Communist Party shall demobilize all units in excess of 18 divisions. The demobilization shall start immediately and shall proceed at the rate of approximately one twelfth of the total number to be demobilized during each month.

The Government shall prepare within three weeks of the promulgation of this agreement, a list of the 90 divisions to be retained and the order of demobilization of units during the first two months. The Communist Party shall prepare within three weeks of the promulgation of this agreement, a complete list of its military units stating character, strength, armament, names of brigades and higher commanders and location of units. This report shall include a list of the 18 divisions to be retained and the order of demobilization during the first two months. These lists shall be submitted to the Military Sub-Committee.

Six weeks after the promulgation of this agreement the Communist Party shall submit to the Military Sub-Committee a complete list of the army units to be demobilized and the Government shall submit a similar list.

On receipt of the foregoing lists and documents the Military Sub-Committee shall prepare a detailed plan for the execution of this agreement and submit it for the approval of both parties. After such approval the lists, documents and plan shall be transmitted to the Ministry of National Defense (or National Military Council).

Section 2. The arms and equipment of the army units demobilized may be utilized to complete the arms and equipment of the army units to be retained in service. A detailed statement of such transfers will be submitted to the Ministry of National Defense (or Nåtional Military Council) by the Executive Headquarters. The surplus material will be stored as directed by that Ministry (or Council).

Section 3. In order to prevent large scale hardship or lawlessness arising, as a result of the demobilization, the Government and the Communist Party shall initially provide for the supply movement and employment of their respective demobilized personnel. The Government shall take over unified control of these matters as soon as practicable.

Section 4. During the 6 months following the first 12 months the National divisions shall be further reduced to 50 and the Communist divisions shall be further reduced to 10 making a total of 60 divisions to be organized into 20 armies.

ARTICLE V—INTEGRATION AND DEPLOYMENT

Section 1. During the first 12 months after the promulgation of this agreement there shall be organized 4 army groups each consisting of 1 National and 1 Communist army. Each army shall consist of 3 divisions. The schedule for establishing these army groups shall be as follows: One army group shall be organized during the 7th month; another the 9th month; another the 10th month; and another the 11th month. The staffs of the army groups shall consist of approximately one half National and one half Communist staff officers.

Section 2. The deployment of the armies at the end of the first 12 months shall be as follows:

Northeast China—5 armies each consisting of 3 National divisions, each army with a National commander and 1 army consisting of 3 Communist divisions with a Communist commander—total 6 armies.

Northwest China—5 armies each consisting of 3 National divisions each with a National commander—total 5 armies.

North China—3 armies each consisting of 3 National divisions, each with a National commander; and 4 army groups each consisting of 1 National and 1 Communist army of 3 divisions. 2 army group commanders shall be National officers and 2 army group commanders shall be Communist officers—total 11 armies.

Central China—9 armies each consisting of 3 National divisions, each with a National commander; and 1 army consisting of 3 Communist divisions, with a Communist commander—total 10 armies.

South China (including Formosa)—4 armies each consisting of 3 National divisions, each with a National commander—total 4 armies.

Section 3. During the following 6 months the 4 army groups referred to in Section 2 above shall be reorganized, creating 4 separate armies each consisting of 1

National and 2 Communist divisions and 2 separate armies each consisting of 2 National and 1 Communist divisions. Thereafter, the organization of army groups shall be terminated.

Section 4. The deployment of the armies at the end of the second 6 months (i. e. at the end of a total of 18 months) shall be as follows:

Northeast China—1 army consisting of 2 National and 1 Communist Divisions with a National commander and 4 armies each consisting of 3 National divisions, each with a National commander—total 5 armies.

Northwest China—3 armies each consisting of 3 National Divisions each with a National commander—total 3 armies.

North China—3 armies each consisting of 1 National and 2 Communist divisions, each with a Communist commander; 1 army consisting of 2 National and 1 Communist divisions with a National commander; and 2 armies each consisting of 3 National divisions, each with a National commander—total 6 armies.

Central China—1 army consisting of 1 National and 2 Communist divisions with a Communist commander and 3 armies each consisting of 3 National divisions, each with a National commander—total 4 armies.

South China (including Formosa)—2 armies each consisting of 3 National divisions, each with a National commander—total 2 armies.

ARTICLE VI—PEACE PRESERVATION CORPS

Section 1. Each province shall be authorized to maintain a Peace Preservation Corps in proportion to the population of the province but the strength of the Corps for any one province shall not exceed 15,000 men. After it has become apparent that the civil police of any province have been unable to cope with the situation, the governor of that province is authorized to employ this Corps to quell civil disorders.

Section 2. The armament of the Peace Preservation Corps shall be restricted to the pistol, the rifle and the automatic rifle.

ARTICLE VII—SPECIAL PROVISIONS

Section 1. Executive Headquarters

The Executive Headquarters created in the agreement of the Committee of Three, signed 10 January 1946, shall be the agency through which this agreement shall be implemented.

Section 2. Common Uniform

A common distinctive uniform for the reorganized military forces of China shall be adopted for wear by all officers and enlisted men of the Army of the Republic of China.

Section 3. Personnel System

An adequate personnel system shall be established and the name, grade and assignment of each officer of the Army shall be carried on a single list without political prejudice.

Section 4. Special Armed Forces

Neither the Government nor any political party nor any group or association shall maintain, or in any way support, any secret or independent armed force, after the effective date of this agreement.

Section 5. Puppet and Irregular Troops

All troops which were maintained in China under the sponsorship, directly or indirectly, of Japan and all troops maintained by persons or factions other than the Government or Communist Party shall be disarmed and disbanded as soon as possible. The detailed plan (Article VIII, Section 1) shall provide for the execution of the provisions of this section in a definitely limited period of time.

ARTICLE VIII—GENERAL

Section 1. Upon approval of this agreement by Generalissimo Chiang Kai-shek and Chinese Communist Party Chairman Mao Tse-tung there shall be prepared and submitted to them for approval by the Military Sub-Committee a detailed plan of the schedules, regulations and specific measures to govern the execution of the provisions of this agreement.

Section 2. It is understood and agreed that the detailed plans above referred to shall provide that the demobilization shall start at the earliest practical date; that the organization of service areas shall be instituted gradually and that the detailed procedure of the integration of armies shall be carried out under the provisions of Article V.

It is further understood and agreed that during the initial period of transition, the Government and the Communist party shall be responsible for the good order, the supply of their respective troops and for their prompt and full compliance with the instructions issued to them by the Executive Headquarters.

General CHANG CHIH CHUNG
Representative of the Government
General CHOU EN-LAI
Representative of the Chinese Communist Party
General GEORGE C. MARSHALL
Advisor

CHUNGKING, CHINA
February 25, 1946

70

Memorandum by the Military Sub-Committee, March 16, 1946

1. The "BASIS FOR MILITARY REORGANIZATION AND FOR THE INTEGRATION OF THE COMMUNIST FORCES INTO THE NATIONAL ARMY," constitutes the general directive to Executive Headquarters covering demobilization, redeployment, and integration.

2. Executive Headquarters will be the medium for the execution of the Basic Plan. The Headquarters will form a Control Group for planning and for supervising the execution of the orders of the Executive Headquarters in these matters. This group will be composed of Government, Communist and U. S. military personnel. Executive Headquarters will utilize combined field teams to supervise on the ground for demobilization, redeployment and integration of the Government and Communist troops.

3. The reports required by the Basic Plan will form the basis for detailed plans and schedules prepared at Executive Headquarters.

4. The demobilization will require the gradual elimination of Military Commands on a higher level than Army headquarters.

5. Puppet units will be disbanded complete by D-Day plus 3 months. Military equipment and munitions in the hands of these units will be turned in to the local Service Area if established, or as directed by Executive Headquarters.

6. Executive Headquarters will direct each division designated to be retained by the Government or the Communist Party to assemble in its general area, and initiate a 12 week's basic training program pending receipt of more detailed instructions.

7. A school of elementary instruction for the 10 Communist Divisions designated for Army integration in the last six months, will be organized under the guidance of the Interim Military Advisory Group of the U. S. Army to conduct a series of basic courses of 3 months duration in organization, training procedure, and administration. Planning for the schools will be coordinated with Executive Headquarters.

8. Movements to effect the necessary redeployment and integration will be ordered by Executive Headquarters in accordance with the general directive of the Ministry of National Defense (or National Military Council). The logistic requirements for the demobilization, redeployment and integration will be coordinated with the Ministry of National Defense (or National Military Council). Executive Headquarters is authorized to deal direct with Directors of the Service Areas regarding logistic problems.

9. Executive Headquarters will prepare the detailed logistic and administrative plans for personnel to be demobilized.

> General CHANG CHIH CHUNG
> *Representative of the National Government*
> General CHOU EN-LAI
> *Representative of the Chinese Communist Party*
> General A. C. GILLEM, Jr.
> *Representing General G. C. Marshall*

CHUNGKING, CHINA
16 March 1946

71 (a)

Agreement on Establishment of the Executive Headquarters, Signed at Chungking, January 10, 1946

PREAMBLE

By joint agreement, we, General Chang Chun, authorized representative of the National Government, and General Chou En-lai, authorized representative of the Chinese Communist Party, do hereby establish, with the approval of the National Government of China, an Executive Headquarters empowered to implement the agreements for the cessation of hostilities.

FUNCTIONS

The Executive Headquarters will implement the agreed policies for the cessation of hostilities. The Headquarters will submit recommendations covering necessary additional subsidiary agreements to insure more effective implementation of the cessation of hostilities orders; such recommendations to include measures for the disarmament of the Japanese forces, restoration of lines of communication and coordination of the movement of Japanese soldiers to the coast for repatriation. The formal instructions unanimously agreed upon by the three Commissioners will be issued in the name of the President of the Republic of China.

ORGANIZATION

The Executive Headquarters will consist of three Commissioners with authority to vote, and to negotiate among themselves; one to represent the Chinese National Government; one to represent the Chinese Communist Party and one to represent the United States of America. The United States Commissioner will be invited to be the chairman.

The Headquarters will have within itself as its implementing agency a group to be called the Operations Section composed of the number of officers and men required to supervise in the field the various agreements, and to render the required reports. The National Government and the Chinese Communist Party will have an equal number of personnel in the Operations Section.

There will be included within the Executive Headquarters the necessary secretarial staff to support the Headquarters.

HOUSING AND SUPPLY

The National Government will furnish adequate living and office accommodations for the Executive Headquarters. The National Government will also furnish the subsistence for this Headquarters. Over all security will be furnished by the local authorities. Immediate security for offices, quarters, and installations will be provided by small units of each Army as required and agreed upon.

LOCATION

The Executive Headquarters will be located initially at Peiping.

PROCEDURE

The Executive Headquarters will operate as the executives of the National Government, the Chinese Communist Party, and the United States respectively.

The three commissioners shall each have one vote. All action must be by unanimous agreement.

The Executive Headquarters will issue the necessary formal orders, directives, and instructions in the name of the President of the Republic of China.

Daily reports will be prepared by the Operations Section to be rendered by the commissioners to their respective chiefs.

The Executive Headquarters will operate through its Operations Section.

The Operations Section will have a United States Army Officer as its director.

The Operations Section will supervise the publication and dissemination of all orders, directives, and instructions to all forces concerned.

The Operations Section may establish sub-stations and will dispatch supervisory and reporting teams as required to implement the policies and agreements.

The National Government, the Chinese Communist Party, and the United States may each maintain independent signal communications at the location of the Executive Headquarters.

DURATION OF AUTHORITY

The Executive Headquarters shall remain in existence and operate until this agreement is rescinded by the President of the Republic of China or the Chairman of the Central Committee of the Chinese Communist Party after due notification to the other party.

CHANG CHUN
CHOU EN-LAI

71 (b)

The Committee of Three to Generalissimo Chiang Kai-shek, Chungking, January 10, 1946

ORGANIZATION OF EXECUTIVE HEADQUARTERS

The approval by Your Excellency and Chairman Mao Tse-tung of the directive to cease hostilities makes it mandatory that the Executive Headquarters become operational at once. The Headquarters should be kept as small as possible for convenience and celerity of operation.

Mr. Walter S. Robertson, who has been nominated as the American Commissioner of the Executive Headquarters, will have initially a staff of not to exceed four persons; a political advisor, an aide, a stenographer, and a translator.

The Operations Section, under Colonel Henry A. Byroade, must contain the necessary personnel to operate various sub-headquarters in critical areas, maintain communications, furnish the required office and housekeeping overhead, etc. The American portion of this Section is initially planned to consist of approximately 26 American officers, 68 enlisted men, and 30 Chinese civilian employees.

Attached is the type of organization Colonel Byroade has planned for the American portion of the Operations Section. Request that you provide, as a matter of urgency, a similar group for the National Government's staff of the Operations Section.

Colonel Byroade will go to Peiping on 11 January 1946 to establish the Executive Headquarters and to assemble the American personnel.

Mr. Robertson will be ready to depart on 13 January 1946. It would be most advantageous if the Commissioner of the National Government, as well as the Communist Commissioner, could be prepared for departure together. General Marshall will provide his personal C–54 aircraft for this purpose.

The staffs for the Executive Headquarters and Operations Section should be organized immediately. The National Government and the Communist Party staffs should each, at least as a beginning, consist of not more than forty officers and ninety enlisted men.

It is very important that adequate facilities be available before arrival of this personnel. It is therefore recommended that the personnel to be assigned to the Operations Section be scheduled to start arrival in Peiping on 15 January. At least half of this personnel should have reported in Peiping by 19 January and the remainder not later than 26 January 1946.

A similar memorandum is being forwarded to Chairman Mao Tse-tung.[9]

CHANG CHUN
CHOU EN-LAI
G. C. MARSHALL

71 (c)

Memorandum on Operations of the Executive Headquarters

The Executive Headquarters was established at Peiping as the agency to implement the cessation of hostilities agreement signed at Chungking on January 10, 1946, and began its official functions on January 14. The functions of the Executive Headquarters were set forth in the document providing for its establishment as follows:

---

[9] Not printed.

"The Executive Headquarters will implement the agreed policies for the cessation of hostilities. The Headquarters will submit recommendations covering necessary additional subsidiary agreements to ensure more effective implementation of the cessation of hostilities orders; such recommendations to include measures for the disarmament of the Japanese forces, restoration of lines of communication and coordination of the movement of Japanese soldiers to the coast for repatriation. The formal instructions unanimously agreed upon by the three Commissioners will be issued in the name of the President of the Republic of China."

The Executive Headquarters was headed by three Commissioners: Lieutenant General Cheng Kai-min, representing the National Government, Lieutenant General Yeh Chien-ying, representing the Chinese Communist Party, and Mr. Walter S. Robertson, American Chargé d'Affaires, representing the United States and serving as Chairman. Decisions by the three Commissioners had to be unanimous, as stated in the agreement, and it was envisaged that matters on which they were unable to reach agreement would be referred to the Committee of Three for decision, a procedure which was ultimately followed. Immediately under the three Commissioners and directly responsible to them was a Director of Operations. In accordance with the agreement for the establishment of the Headquarters, a United States Army officer, Brigadier General Henry A. Byroade, was named as the Director of Operations. The Operations Division served as the implementing agency within the Headquarters for the execution of its decisions and directives. Various sections were established under the Operations Division: Plans and Operations Section, Logistics and Supply Section, Conflict Control Group, Communication Group, Army Reorganization Group and Public Relations Group. United States Army planes provided the transportation facilities for the movement of personnel and supplies between Peiping and the various points to which field teams were sent. In the absence of normal communications in China, the only possible means of transportation to the locations of practically all the field teams was by plane.

The key personnel in the functioning of the Executive Headquarters over widespread areas in China were the members of the field teams. They were composed of one representative of each of the three branches of the Headquarters and each branch included in its field team membership communications and interpreting personnel. These teams were sent to areas of conflict or threatened conflict to halt or prevent hostilities. Practical experience in the field revealed that the effectiveness of the field teams could be hampered and necessary investigations actually blocked in cases where one Chinese member of the team vetoed any proposal which might be disadvantageous to his side. When the United States branch of the Headquarters proposed, therefore, a revision of this requirement of unanimity in order to permit the United States team member as chairman to break a deadlock and direct the movement of the team for the purpose of investigating reported violations of the cessation of hostilities agreement—not including the results of the investigation or the action to be taken—the National Government branch approved this proposal but the Communist branch would not agree. At the beginning of May, as the Headquarters was being faced with increased instances of the blocking of team investigations by the refusal of the Communist team members to agree on the movement of the teams, the United States branch proposed that decision for investigation be reached by a majority vote. The National Government branch agreed to this proposal but the Communist branch again refused to assent on the basis that this was contrary to the principle of unanimity under which the Headquarters operated.

Each Chinese side, in approaching problems at issue, both in the Executive Headquarters and in the field, was too often intent upon protracted debate designed to wring the last possible advantage to its cause from the argument, rather than being interested in broad principles and compromise in order to create a spirit conducive to the settlement of differences between the two sides. One side or the other would be willing to block all investigation of reported violations of the cessation of hostilities order unless it received a *quid pro quo* from the rival party, even though there would be no relation between the incidents under discussion. Distrust between the two sides was further heightened by incidents involving field teams. The Communists complained that their team members were on several occasions arrested and beaten and that in some cases their representatives had been kidnapped and had not been heard of since their disappearance. In two cases Communist forces fired on and killed National Government team members and in another incident the United States member of a field team was wounded slightly by a Communist sniper's bullet. Each side apparently organized mass demonstrations in the areas under its control for the purpose of propagandizing the field teams. Such demonstrations sometimes grew out of hand and resulted in incidents leading to near attacks on members of the teams. While these incidents in themselves should not be magnified out of proportion, they were indicative of the bitterness between the two Chinese parties and show some of the difficulties under which the Executive Headquarters and its field teams functioned.

High praise can be given to the United States members of the field teams, who were often stationed in isolated places under primitive and difficult living conditions. The field teams were the key personnel in effecting the cessation of hostilities and it was they who supervised on the spot the carrying out of the directives issued by the Executive Headquarters. United States members of the teams were often under fire, travelled by jeep over near-impassable roads in the performance of their duties and in many ways accomplished miracles in their efforts to bring about cooperation between the two Chinese sides.

Every effort was made to ensure the impartiality of the United States members of the field teams, as their usefulness would have ended if they were felt to be biased. There was inevitably feeling, from time to time, that some United States team members had shown partiality, the majority of such accusations coming from the Communist side. It was believed, however, that this arose chiefly through Communist Party press and radio propaganda directed against United States aid to the Kuomintang, which, not always adhering too closely to the truth, naturally served to arouse bitter feeling among the lower echelons of the Communists forces. It was not believed that any United States member of a field team consciously or intentionally displayed partiality in dealing with problems handled by the teams, and that misunderstanding that arose was due chiefly to the above-described propaganda campaign and perhaps in some cases to honest and unintentional errors of judgment, which were inevitable under the circumstances and which may have been to the advantage of either side.

By September 1946 the total number of Executive Headquarters field teams was 36 and there had been established a wide network of communications facilities to link these outposts with the Executive Headquarters at Peiping. The chief task of the Executive Headquarters at the time of its establishment was that of effecting a cessation of hostilities. Other equally vital functions of the Headquarters, either envisaged in the original agreement for its establishment or in subsequent agreements reached by the Committee of Three (or the

Military Sub-Committee), were the restoration of communications, the repatriation of the Japanese military and civilian personnel and the demobilization and reorganization of the Chinese armies. It is an interesting commentary that the only one of the above-named functions that the Executive Headquarters was able to carry successfully to completion was that of repatriating the Japanese military and civilian personnel. The restoration of communications and the demobilization and reorganization of the Chinese armies were necessarily dependent upon the cessation of hostilities and neither of these two tasks could be carried to completion or even successfully begun so long as armed conflict continued and there was no solution of the political issues involved. The net result was that the Executive Headquarters functioned very successfully within the limits of its possibilities and that its success was governed largely by the over-all political situation. A deterioration in the relations between the National Government and the Chinese Communist Party was soon reflected in the increased difficulties experienced by the Executive Headquarters and among its field teams in effectively preventing violation of the cessation of hostilities order or in carrying out the directives and decisions already agreed upon.

In any event, the Executive Headquarters, as the agency for the implementation of the major non-political agreements reached between the two Chinese parties, played a necessary and vital part in the efforts to bring peace and unity to China and restore the economic life of the country. If its efforts were not completely successful, the responsibility can be charged not to the Executive Headquarters, but rather to those Chinese elements whose bitterness and distrust of each other defeated the peaceful purpose of the field teams.

71(d)

Memorandum Concerning Repatriation of Japanese

One of the objectives set forth in the President's statement of United States policy toward China on December 15, 1945 was that of effecting the repatriation of Japanese troops from China with a view to the elimination of Japanese influence in that country. In this statement it was pointed out that the United States had assumed a definite obligation in the disarmament and evacuation of Japanese troops from China and that the United States was assisting and would continue to assist the Chinese Government to that end.

Although this statement of policy indicated that the elimination of Japanese influence in China was to be achieved through the evacuation of Japanese troops, it was obvious that the elimination of Japanese influence in China also called for the repatriation of Japanese civilians, whose presence in China would permit continued Japanese influence and many of whom, if permitted to remain, would strive secretly for the resurgence of Japanese power and influence on the continent of Asia. It was recognized, however, that the Chinese authorities had expressed a need for the services of Japanese technicians and that the expulsion of all Japanese technicians from China, without an adequate number of trained Chinese to take their places in industry, communications, mining and other fields, would result in injury to the economic life of the country.

In a conference between Chinese Government and United States Armed Forces representatives in October 1945 agreement was reached that the Chinese Government would be responsible for the repatriation of Japanese disarmed military personnel and civilians from China and that, consonant with the terms of the Potsdam Declaration, the United States Government would assist in this repatriation program. The United States Seventh Fleet assumed responsibility for the water lift of Japanese.

The question of the repatriation of Japanese from China was closely related to the cessation of hostilities, as the continued presence of Japanese armed forces in North China represented a very definite threat to peace in that area. This was particularly true because of the continued use by the National Government of armed Japanese units in garrisoning certain points along railway lines in North China and the Communist Party's insistence on the right of its forces to accept the Japanese surrender. With these circumstances in mind, the subject of Japanese repatriation was taken up in the discussions of the Committee of Three regarding the cessation of hostilities and the establishment of the Executive Headquarters. In the agreement for the establishment of the Headquarters, provision was made for the submission by the Headquarters of recommendations for measures for the disarmament of Japanese forces and the coordination of the movement of those forces to the coast for repatriation. It was realized that the dearth of military equipment in China would prevent the carrying out of measures for the destruction of Japanese military equipment and in discussions of the Committee of Three it was agreed that this equipment would be used for units of the 60 divisions to be retained by the National Army.

The scheduled repatriation of all Japanese military and civilian personnel from South China was completed on April 25, from Formosa on April 23, from Central China on July 11 and from North China on August 11. Difficulties were encountered in planning for the repatriation of Japanese from Manchuria owing to the continued occupation of that area by Soviet troops, who did not withdraw from Manchuria until the end of April. A relatively small number of Japanese military personnel was represented in the final repatriation figures for Manchuria and it has been assumed that large numbers of these Japanese troops were removed from Manchuria into Siberia.

The total number of Japanese repatriated under this program at the completion of mass repatriation on December 31, 1946, was as follows: 1,233,244, military personnel; 1,750,306, civilian personnel; total repatriated 2,983,550. The major portion of the task of Japanese repatriation from Chinese territory had been accomplished by September 20, when a total of 2,711,951 Japanese had been evacuated to Japan.

This task was one of great magnitude, involving the movement of Japanese repatriates from various inland points via inadequate lines of communications to the ports of embarkation. It required careful and close coordination between the Executive Headquarters Communication Group (charged with carrying out Executive Headquarters' responsibilities in this program), the field teams, the United States Army repatriation teams at the ports of embarkation, the United States Navy authorities and the Supreme Commander for the Allied Powers, which controlled the bulk of the shipping used for repatriation purposes. It involved the timing and regulation of the flow of repatriates from the interior to the ports of embarkation in such a manner that there would be a minimum of delay in the departure of repatriation vessels without an overloading of the processing and billeting facilities available to the repatriation teams. It required the establishment of food dumps and billets at the necessary points en route. It is a tribute to the effectiveness of the planning and execution of the repatriation program that the evacuation from China of this tremendous number of Japanese was accomplished within a relatively brief period of time.

72

Ratification by Central Executive Committee of the Kuomintang of Resolutions Adopted by Political Consultative Conference, March 16, 1946 [10]

Chungking, March 16 . . .   The P. C. C. agreements were ratified unanimously by the C. E. C. at this morning's meeting, presided over by President Chiang Kai-shek, Tsungtsai. of the Kuomintang. Following the passage of the resolution, Dr. Sun Fo, President of the Legislative Yuan, announced that the Communist Party, the Democratic League and the Young China Party has agreed to certain revisions in the original P. C. C. agreement on the Draft Constitution.

The C. E. C. resolution pledged the Party's all-out observance and support of the P. C. C. agreements.

The resolution's accepting of the P. C. C. agreements expressed three "hopes". The three hopes were:

(1) After the reorganization of the Government, it is hoped that all parties will work sincerely for peace, unity and national reconstruction. It is especially hoped that the Communist Party in its own areas will practice democracy, allowing the freedom of thought, religious belief, expression, publication, assembly, and residence as well as the freedom of organization of other parties and so forth, and that the Communist Party will stop all atrocities against the people in the so-called "liberated areas".

(2) As the nationalization of armies is a prerequisite to national reconstruction, it is hoped the Communist Party will sincerely carry out the military subcommittee's basic agreement for the reorganization of the National Army and the integration of the Communist forces into the National Army and the cessation of hostilities and restoration of communications agreement and that the Communist Party will lift its blockade and siege of Government-held cities and cease drafting young men into its army, so that order will be fully restored in the interests of public welfare.

(3) As the Three People's Principles were accepted by the whole nation and also by the P. C. C. and because the five-power system is indispensable to the realization of the Three People's Principles, meaning that the two are indivisible, it is hoped that any amendments in the Draft Constitution which are contrary to the five-power system should be revised to accord with the plan for national reconstruction and the five-power system.

It is recalled that the P. C. C. agreements caused the longest and the hottest debate in the C. E. C. on March 7 and 8. The members' main objection was directed against the P. C. C. Draft Constitution agreement and they were suspicious of Communist sincerity in carrying out the P. C. C. agreements, especially the agreement on the nationalization of armies.

The chief points of conflict were over the principles of separation powers and the presidential system. The Kuomintang supported them while the other parties opposed them.

The Kuomintang insists that the National Army should be a real existing body, that the American presidential system and the principle of the separation powers be adopted and that federalism should be discarded, that is, provinces should not have their own constitutions.

---

[10] China News Service, Mar. 16, 1946.

The C. E. C. members regard the P. C. C. Draft Constitution agreement as diametrically opposite to Dr. Sun Yat-sen's plan for national reconstruction and the five-power system, which the other parties had agreed to observe.

The members' objection to the agreement was, however, considerably allayed when Dr. Sun Fo announced that at an interparty meeting yesterday the other parties had agreed to make three revisions in the agreement, namely, that the National Assembly should be made a real existing body, that the American presidential system be adopted and that provinces should not have their own constitutions and provincial governments should be provided for in organizational laws.

Dr. Sun said, however, that there are still many technical details to be thrashed out with the other parties.

On the motion of President Chiang Kai-shek, the C. E. C. resolved to give full powers to the C. E. C.'s Standing Committee to make decisions in regard to the Draft Constitution in the course of talks with the other parties.

MANIFESTO OF THE SECOND PLENARY SESSION OF 6TH KUOMINTANG CENTRAL EXECUTIVE COMMITTEE [11]

Following is a translation of the Manifesto issued by the Second Plenary Session of the Sixth Central Executive Committee of the Kuomintang on March 17, 1946:

Our war of resistance was won after the Fifth National Congress of the Kuomintang had met. That brought us into a new era of peaceful national reconstruction.

An opportunity to put Dr. Sun Yat-sen's "Plan for National Reconstruction" into operation presented itself after World War I, but it was lost in the hands of the lingering monarchists and the warlords. Now at the end of World War II we have secured, as a result of eight years of bitter fighting, another rare opportunity for rebuilding our nation. We must not let it pass by again. In order to preserve the fruits of our victory, we must take full advantage of this turning point in history.

To all of our Fellow Countrymen, we of this Plenary Session wish to point out the following:

First, we must achieve social stability, restore peace and order and complete the plan of national rehabilitation in order to inaugurate the task of peaceful national reconstruction. Peace is a requisite for national reconstruction; the two are absolutely indivisible. Confronted with the expensive damages of more than eight years of war, and having encountered numerous obstacles and difficulties in national rehabilitation during the last half year and witnessed the plight of our compatriots in various parts of the country; the suffering awaiting relief; the homeless, repatriation; the unemployed, re-employment; the oppressed, emancipation, we fully realize that no longer should there be turmoil and strife within the country. Nor should the phenomena of local disorder be permitted. We can validate the Party's struggle only by conforming our exertions with the needs of our country and our people. In the past six months the Government made great concessions in the interests of national rehabilitation. This Assembly regards such measures as correct. To bring about a favorable environment for peaceful national reconstruction we, in a spirit of tolerance, invited representatives of the other political parties and prominent social leaders to a Political Consultation Conference before the convocation of the National Assembly. We

---

[11] Special release by China News Service, Mar. 19, 1946.

admit that modifications in the procedure for national reconstruction, as laid down by our Party, might have been made, but our consistent Party spirit of placing the interests of the country and the people above everything else should be plain to all of our fellow countrymen. In conformity with this spirit we will stop at nothing to bring about the speedy completion of national rehabilitation.

Second, we must convene the National Assembly as scheduled to return the Government to the people in order to fulfill our long cherished wish of inaugurating constitutional government.

Our Party has all along advocated political democratization. It was openly declared by the Hsing Chung Hui (organized by Dr. Sun Yat-sen in 1892) as far back as fifty years ago. The revolutionary history of our Party is the history of democracy being fostered in China. Constitutional government would have been inaugurated according to our original program long ago had Japan not launched her campaign of aggression and had there been no military obstacles within the country. Our determination to inaugurate constitutional government at an early date has been made amply manifest by resolutions adopted by the Kuomintang on a number of occasions, as well as by the repeated statements of the Tsungtsai (Director General) of the Party. The Government has never slackened for comparing the way for constitutionalism, even in times of military crises. Our earnest desire has been to return the Government to the people, but we maintain that the convocation of the National Assembly is an essential step towards that end.

Third, we wish to affirm our sincere desire to implement fully the various agreements reached at the Political Consultation Conference and our determination to uphold the "Quintuple-Power Constitution." In view of the need of peace, stability and solidarity in the country and the urgent need of alleviating the people's sufferings, all of us should, after a careful study of the agreements reached at the Political Consultation Conference, very sincerely pledge to exert ourselves in concert with the other parties and prominent social leaders to carry out the agreements. But we maintain that the revision of the Draft Constitution must conform with Dr. Sun Yat-sen's teachings on the "Quintuple-Power Constitution."

The reason for our insistence on the "Quintuple-Power Constitution" is that the Three Principles of the People and the "Quintuple-Power Constitution" are inseparable. Minus the "Quintuple-Power Constitution," the Three Principles of the People cannot be fully carried out. This political system is Dr. Sun's great and profound discovery as a result of his study of the European and American constitutions, of their merits and demerits, as well as of the actual conditions in China, having as his object the laying of an enduring foundation for national peace and security.

A comprehensive and practicable constitution is necessary to insure a sound and firm political structure in our country. If the contents of the constitution should contravene the "Quintuple-Power Constitution", practical difficulties are certain to be encountered in its application, therefore placing the country at a disadvantage. The Kuomintang, therefore, will steadfastly uphold the "Quintuple-Power Constitution". This is indeed taking a long-range view of our national interests. We hope that the other parties and social leaders will appreciate our stand and understand our views.

Fourth, we must lay a foundation for peace and unity by thoroughly carrying out the nationalization of armed forces. The primary requisite of political democratization is the nationalization of armed forces. Only by nationalizing troops can administrative integrity and unity of military command be achieved. Democracy may be truly realized only when there is national unity in deed as well as in name. The existence of a state within a state and regional domination by armed forces are anti-democratic. Such phenomena could not be tolerated in any country. When administrative integrity and unity of military command are wanting and when local peace and order are constantly disturbed, there is no safeguard even for the people's basic need of being able to live and pursue their occupations in peace, let alone carrying out reconstruction measures.

There must be unqualified nationwide observance and thorough execution of the orders issued by the Government a month ago concerning the cessation of hostilities and the restoration of communications. The plans for military reorganization and the integration of the armed forces, recently arrived at at the three-man Military Subcommittee, should be similarly carried out. Only then can we say that the concessions we have made in the interests of national peace and solidarity have not been in vain and our long-harassed people will be given a chance to rest and recuperate. In examining the present situation, this Session feels compelled to demand that a halt be called immediately to the ceaseless military attacks and to acts impeding national unity, so that peaceful national reconstruction may proceed smoothly and the promotion of democracy may not result in empty talk.

Fifth, we must carry out the program bearing upon the people's livelihood as laid down by the Sixth National Congress of the Kuomintang. The fulfillment of the Principle of the People's Livelihood is the ultimate objective of the Three Principles of the People. In promoting the Principle of the People's Livelihood at this stage, efforts may be directed to treat both the symptoms and the causes.

Treatment of the symptoms should begin, first, with the enforcement of peace and order and the relief of the people's distress before embarking on large-scale economic reconstruction projects. Our foremost task now is to alleviate the sufferings of the starving or half-starving like the large farming and laboring classes, civil servants, school teachers, and officers and men who fought to defend the country. Ways and means must be devised to improve their living, and our own work must begin with stabilizing commodity prices and maintaining the value of the currency. The Government should spare no efforts to carry out the required measures.

We should furthermore restore production to increase supplies at home and purchase and transport foodstuffs to give necessary relief. A program of retrenchment should be adopted to curtail unnecessary expenditures. International economic cooperation should be established so that large supplies of goods, particularly production tools, may be imported.

The most urgent task of the moment is the restoration of communications. With communications disrupted at so many places, even the distribution of international relief supplies has not been possible. The destruction of communications, therefore, has not only been of great harm to the people; it is tantamount to condemning the people to death. This Session cannot refrain from frankly pointing this out in the hope that the Executive Headquarters will take effective measures to stop acts of obstructing road repairs and of violating communications administration.

Treatment of causes should stress the equalization of land ownership and regulation of private capital which are fundamental principles of this party which must be fulfilled. Similarly important are the relief of rural districts and the checking of the present trend of land annexation with a view to aiding farmers who till their own soil.

In carrying out our postwar five-year economic reconstruction programs, we have great need of international economic and technical assistance. The economic reconstruction programs adopted by the Fifth National Congress of the Kuomintang are most accurate. It is a matter for regret that they have not been extensively carried out in the past nine months on account of military clashes and rehabilitation work. Henceforth, we must urge the Government departments concerned to execute the measures alluded to so that the people may live and pursue their occupations in peace with eventual raising of the living standard.

Sixth, we must fully realize our primary aim in embarking on the war of resistance, namely, the preservation of our national sovereignty and the consolidation of world peace. Our fundamental foreign policy aims at safeguarding our territorial, sovereign and administrative integrity and at consolidating enduring world peace through faithful adherence to international treaties. This explains why we opposed Japanese coercion, designed to bring us into the anti-comintern pact, and resisted for more than eight years.

With the war of resistance at an end, we desire for our postwar reconstruction not only stability at home but peace all over the world. We do not wish conflicts and misunderstandings between nations which would revive the hope of the defeated aggressors for a resurgence. With utmost sincerity we have supported the United Nations Charter, while at the international conference tables our delegates have taken considerable pains to strengthen the cooperation of the major allies. This is a concrete demonstration of our policy.

In the interests of enduring peace in China and in the world as a whole, we must eliminate completely all chances of Japanese imperialism being revived. This calls for complete understanding and closest cooperation between our country and our allies, particularly the Soviet Union, with which we have the longest continuous border. It is our most sincere desire to further mutual confidence and friendship with the Soviet Union. We firmly believe that strict observance of the Sino-Soviet Treaty of Friendship and Alliance by both parties is the first and foremost prerequisite for the enhancement of mutual trust and friendship.

In the meantime, we welcome, for the completion of our economic reconstruction, financial or technical cooperation from any one of our allies as long as it does not violate Chinese law or contravene China's international commitments. Only when there is an independent, free, united and strong China can the resurgence of Japanese imperialism be effectively eliminated and a durable peace in the Pacific and in the whole world be maintained. We are convinced that with this recognition a reasonable and lawful solution can be found for the present Northeast problem. We will not allow a temporary phenomena to lessen our confidence or slacken our efforts.

At this time when the period of political tutelage is about to be concluded, and our revolutionary work is entering the new phase of national reconstruction, our fellow party members should be aware that, whereas in the past we led the revolution as the only revolutionary political party, we should henceforth work for national reconstruction as the largest political party. We will not evade our responsibility. Let us remember:

First, that the Republic of China was founded by Dr. Sun Yat-sen and the Kuomintang martyrs;

Second, that the task of weeding out the warlords and bringing about national unification was accomplished under the leadership of the Kuomintang;

Third, that the bondage of the century of unequal treaties was removed under the leadership of the Kuomintang; and

Fourth, that, again, it was under the leadership of the Kuomintang that the war of resistance was fought for more than eight years until a magnificent victory was won for the country and the nation.

Inasmuch as we have accomplished these four great missions in modern times, we are the more confident that our Party and our Tsungtsai will lead the entire nation to perform the still greater mission of peaceful national reconstruction.

In the departing period of political tutelage, there have been shortcomings in political and party affairs. We cannot escape responsibility although some mistakes were due to uncontrollable factors. The object of our revolution is precisely what Dr. Sun Yat-sen once said: "To rescue the people from suffering and hardship and lead them to peace and happiness." We are indeed aggrieved that immense difficulties still face the country and that the people are leading such a hard life. We revolutionary workers should bravely assume responsibility for effecting reforms. We should continuously and searchingly examine ourselves, to shoulder the great and difficult responsibility henceforwards, this plenary Session feels that we should consolidate our views, examine and strengthen ourselves, so as to renovate our Party activities; that we should endure hardships and exert our utmost to serve the people in pursuance of our revolutionary aims; and, above all, that we should, in a spirit of frankness and mutual trust, concert our efforts with the other parties and the entire people to insure the success of national reconstruction.

In the past, the Kuomintang, with the support of the entire nation, has accomplished one great mission after another. Now that victory is here, it is our duty to rebuild the Chinese Republic into a modern nation, prosperous, strong, healthy and happy. Let us raise the banner of the Three Principles of the People as we march on toward peaceful national reconstruction.

73

Memorandum by the Chairman of the Committee of Three (Marshall)

January 24, 1946

For General Chang Chun: [12]
  General Chou En-lai: [13]

While I do not find reference in the official documents concerning the truce agreements to the effect that the Executive Headquarters has no jurisdiction over hostilities in Manchuria, I am informed by Mr. Robertson, the U. S. Commissioner in Peking that the commissioners are of the opinion and have publicly announced that the Executive Headquarters has no jurisdiction in Manchuria.

In this connection, I have received reports of serious conflicts around Yingkow. I recommend that we here agree to direct Executive Headquarters to dispatch immediately a team to Yingkow.

I propose that further action in Manchuria under the terms of the "cease firing" order be directed by us from Chungking in each instance, but to be carried out by the Executive Headquarters.

If you indicate your agreement, I will dispatch the enclosed message to the Commissioners in Peking.

  Faithfully yours,

G. C. MARSHALL

---

[12] Representative of the Chinese National Government.
[13] Representative of the Chinese Communist Party.

74

The Committee of Three to the Executive Headquarters

CHUNGKING, *March 27, 1946*

We, General Chang Chih-chung, authorized representative of the National Government; General Chou En-lai, authorized representative of the Chinese Communist Party and General A. C. Gillem, Jr., acting for General G. C. Marshall; have agreed that Field Teams, with carefully selected personnel, will be sent into Manchuria immediately under the following instructions:

1. The mission of the teams will pertain solely to readjustment of military matters.

2. The teams should operate within the areas of the Government troops as well as the Communist troops, keeping clear of places still under Russian occupation.

3. Teams should proceed to points of conflict or close contact between the Government and Communist troops to bring about a cessation of fighting and to make the necessary and fair readjustments.

It is further agreed that included as a matter of record in the minutes of the Committee of Three conferences will be the following statement:

The Committee of Three will further discuss the military matters pertaining to Manchuria. As to political matters in Manchuria separate discussion will be held with a view to reaching an early settlement.

CHANG CHIH-CHUNG
Representative of the National
Government

CHOU EN-LAI
Representative of the Chinese
Communist Party

A. C. GILLEM, Jr.
Representing General G. C. Marshall

75

The Committee of Three to the Three Commissioners of Executive Headquarters

NANKING, *May 14, 1946*

This message from the Committee of Three is addressed to the three commissioners of Executive Headquarters. The following agreement has been reached by the Committee of Three and will be placed into effect without delay.

It is agreed that effective implementation of the cessation of hostilities agreements reached by this committee or by the commissioners of Executive Headquarters requires that field teams of Executive Headquarters be permitted to investigate without delay any violation of such agreements as may be reported to them.

To insure prompt investigation of such reported violations, it is agreed that:

1. The military and civil authorities of both the National Government and the Chinese Communist Party shall render all possible assistance to the activities of the field teams, without imposing any delay or restriction.

2. The military and civil authorities of both the National Government and the Chinese Communist Party shall assure the personal freedom and security of the field team members.

3. Equal opportunity for investigation shall be afforded to both the National Government and Communist Party within any team area, but this policy shall not be permitted to delay action or to interfere with the overriding principle that priority of investigation should be based upon the apparent seriousness and urgency of the violations reported to the team.

4. The procedure regarding priority of areas and matters for investigation shall be as worked out by the U. S. representative as the chairman of the team and unanimously agreed upon by the team members for implementation. In case of disagreement the American member will immediately report the disagreement to the commissioners, who will within twenty-four hours either render a unanimous decision or report their disagreement to the Committee of Three.

5. In the event it is established that a false report of violation has been submitted to a team for investigation, a report of the incident will be submitted by the commissioners to the Committee of Three for corrective action.

> Hsu Yung-chang
> *Representative of the National*
> *Government*
>
> Chou En-lai
> *Representative of the Chinese*
> *Communist Party*
>
> G. C. Marshall
> *United States Representative*

76 (a)

Statement by Generalissimo Chiang Kai-shek on Temporary Truce Period in Manchuria, June 6, 1946

I am issuing orders at noon today to my armies in Manchuria to halt all advances, attacks and pursuits for a period of 15 days commencing noon Friday, June 7th. I am doing this to give the Communist Party an opportunity to demonstrate in good faith their intention to carry out the agreements they had previously signed. In taking this action the Government in no way prejudices its right under the Sino-Soviet Treaty to take over the sovereignty of Manchuria.

The following matters must be satisfactorily settled within the 15 day period:

a. Detailed arrangements to govern a complete termination of hostilities in Manchuria.

b. Detailed arrangements, and time schedules, for the complete restoration of communications in China, and

c. A definite basis for carrying out without further delay the agreement of February 25, 1946, for the demobilization, reorganization and integration of the armed forces in China.

76 (b)

Statement by Vice Chairman of the Central Committee of the Chinese Communist Party (Chou) on Temporary Truce Period in Manchuria, June 6, 1946

The Chinese Communist Party is advocating all the time an unconditional and true termination of civil warfare, which applies to hostilities in China proper and in Manchuria as well. It is due to the persistence of the Chinese Communist Party, the aspiration of the Chinese people, and the efforts exerted by General Marshall, that the Generalissimo's issuance of orders to halt all advances, attacks and pursuits in Manchuria for a period of 15 days and negotiations in the following matters are secured:

a. Detailed arrangements to govern a complete termination of hostilities in Manchuria.

b. Detailed arrangements, and time schedules, for the complete restoration of communications in China, and

c. A definite basis for carrying out without further delay the agreement of February 25, 1946, for the demobilization, reorganization and integration of the armed forces in China.

Though we feel concerned over the shortness of the 15 day period, and that the inevitable involvement of political subjects pertaining to Manchuria, or even China as a whole, into the forthcoming negotiation would call for a longer period for discussion, we concur with the 15 day cease fire arrangement, having in mind that no opportunity for the realization of peace should be skipped over. In doing so, we will exert our best efforts toward bringing the negotiations to a success. We hope that the Kuomintang, in compliance with the desire of the Chinese people as well as nations abroad, would demonstrate in good faith their intention to carry out the agreements they had previously signed, and make the temporary armistice a lasting truce, with advances, attacks and pursuits stopped forever.

77

Directive by the Committee of Three for Reopening of Lines of Communication in North and Central China, June 1946

1. All lines of communications in North and Central China will be opened without delay for free and unrestricted interchange of goods, foodstuffs and ideas, and for free and unrestricted civilian travel.

2. Reconstruction of railways will proceed immediately and will progress as rapidly as is consistent with the time limitations necessarily imposed by labor and matériel requirements. Time estimate for construction of the railroad lines is covered in Appendix A.

3. All local commanders and all team members shall expedite construction by all means within their power. No commander nor team member will permit interference with the construction work or with the work of removal or destruction of fortifications for any reason whatsoever.

4. Construction will start before 30 June 1946 at each of the following points, under supervision of Communications teams and under control of the MOC:

Team No. 24 or 4—Lunghai RR from Hsuchow to Haichow.
Team No. 23—   "   "   "   "   Yucheng to Te Hsien.

Team No. 23 or 16—" " " "   Taian to Yenchow.
Team No. 24— " " " "   Hanchuan to Yenchow.
Team No. 21—Tsinan-Tsingtao RR from Kaomi to Fengtze.
Team No. 23 or 7—" " " "   Chengtien to Fengtze.
Team No. 24 or 4—Lunghai RR from Hsuchow to Haichow.

Construction on other railroad lines will be commenced at the earliest practicable date in conformance with the principles herein contained.

5. All mines, fortifications, blockades, blockhouses, and other military works lying within 1,000 meters on either side of the railroads listed above will be removed or destroyed simultaneously with construction, except those military works constructed for defense of, and lying within 1,000 meters of, vital railroad installations such as 1st or 2nd class railroad stations, tunnels, or bridges of total span of more than 5 meters, and within 200 meters of 3rd class stations. This work of removal or destruction will proceed in the direction of construction within each of the 7 construction areas above listed, at such rate that the removal or demolition will, at all times, be completed for a distance of not less than 1,000 meters in advance of completed construction of the railroad. At the same time, other military works along the operating portions of the above-mentioned lines will be removed or destroyed at a constant rate such that the removal or destruction will have been completed on or before the date of completion of the railroad within the area of control of each of the above 7 listed teams. When work of restoration of the other railroad lines in North and Central China is commenced, this same principle shall apply. However, the Lunghai railroad west of Cheng-hsien and the Peiping-Hankow railroad south of Cheng-hsien are specifically exempted from the program for removal or destruction of military works, and the destruction or removal of military works along the Lunghai railroad between Hsuchow and Cheng-hsien will be deferred until _____. No new fortifications will be erected except to meet attacks against the railroad itself and only after approval by a communications team.

6. Before through traffic is permitted over the reopened sectors of the railroads, qualified railroad personnel of the CCP may be taken into the employ of the MOC in accordance with a plan to be determined. The qualifications of such personnel will be determined by examinations conducted by communications teams or by the Communications Group of the Executive Headquarters.

7. Detailed plans for the restoration of all other lines of communications in accordance with General Directive 4 will be covered by later agreement. This directive shall not prejudice in any way General Directive 4.

Appendix A

Time Schedule

Tientsin Pukow RR from Tsang Hsien to Te-Hsien	75 days
Yucheng to Te-Hsien	60 days
Taian to Yenchow	60 days
Hanchuan to Yenchow	90 days
Tsinan Tsingtao RR	30 days
Lung-Hai RR, Hsuchow to Haichow	30 days
Peiping-Suiyuan RR, Hankow to Paotou	45 days
Peiping-Hankow RR, Yuanshih to Anyang	150 days
Tung-Po RR, Lingfen to Yunchang	50 days
Peiping-Ku Pei Kou RR	30 days
Tatung-Taiyuan RR	30 days

78

Agreement by the Committee of Three on Stipulations for the Resolution of Certain Disagreements Among Field and Communication Teams, and Executive Headquarters in Changchun and Peiping, June 24, 1946

I. FIELD AND COMMUNICATION TEAMS

a. In case of disagreement regarding matters of urgency, the American representative of the field or communication team may render his own report of the situation as he sees it direct to Executive Headquarters in Changchun or Peiping requesting instructions.

b. In case of disagreement, the American representative of the field team is authorized to make decision as to where and when the field team will move within his area to conduct investigations regarding military activities. Regarding the place of investigation, transportation difficulties should not be permitted to prejudice or delay the movement of the teams.

c. In case of disagreement regarding matters relating to cessation of hostilities and separation of forces the American representative of the field team is authorized to issue orders in the name of the Executive Headquarters to the field commanders on both sides to stop fighting at once and to effect the separation of the forces as prescribed in accordance with directives.

d. The area assigned to each field and communication team will be designated by Executive Headquarters.

II. EXECUTIVE HEADQUARTERS IN CHANGCHUN AND PEIPING

a. In case of disagreement the senior American official of Executive Headquarters in Peiping or Changchun may render his own report to Executive Headquarters in Peiping or the Committee of Three based on the situation as he sees it requesting instructions.

b. In case of disagreement regarding the implementation of orders or instructions from the higher level, the senior American official of the Executive Headquarters in Peiping or Changchun is authorized to direct the execution of that order or instruction unless amended or rescinded by the higher level itself.

79

The Committee of Three to the Three Commissioners of Executive Headquarters

[*June 26?*] *1946*

On the basis of the orders of June 6, 1946 halting all advances, attacks and pursuits for a period of 15 days commencing at noon of June 7th, which will be continued in effect, we, the Committee of Three, announce the following instructions to govern a complete termination of hostilities in Manchuria.

a. The terms of 10 January 1946 for the cessation of hostilities will govern except as hereinafter specifically modified, or later directed by the Committee of Three.

b. Commanders of forces in close contact or engaged in actual fighting will immediately direct their troops to cease fighting and will seek to secure a local truce by establishing liaison with the opposing commanders, pending the arrival of a field team. They should both immediately withdraw their respective troops from close contact.

c. The readjustment of troops found to be in close contact or actually engaged in fighting will be directed by the field team on the ground by requiring the withdrawal for specified distances, normally 20 li, of one or both forces according to the circumstances. The local situation believed to have existed at noon of June 7, 1946 will be the basis for determining the readjustment of the troops involved.

d. All movements of Government or Communist troops of a tactical nature will cease. Administrative and supply movements as authorized in the original cease fire order of January 10, 1946 may be carried out within the garrisoned areas if previously approved by a field team.

e. Within fifteen days after the issuance of this agreement, lists showing all units together with commanders of regiments and larger units, strength and locations in Manchuria will be submitted to the advance section of Executive Headquarters in Changchun.

f. The Government will move no additional combat units to Manchuria. However, individual replacements of the Government are authorized for the purpose of bringing up to approved strength those units authorized in the basic plan for the reorganization and integration dated February 25th, 1946, as hereafter amended.

g. Officers failing to carry out the terms of this agreement will be relieved and disciplined by their respective commanders.

80

Preliminary Agreement Proposed by the Chairman of the Committee of Three (Marshall), June 1946

The following conditions are agreed to by the Committee of Three and are to be included in the amendments to the document signed February 25, 1946, "Basis for Military Reorganization and for the Integration of the Communist Forces into the National Army". These conditions are established for the purpose of committing the Government and the Communist Party to certain understandings in order to facilitate the preparation and acceptance of the formal documents required and to permit the immediate issuance of instructions for the final termination of hostilities.

1. The specific disposition of troops in Manchuria and China proper must be finally agreed to at this time for both National and Communist troops. And it is understood that these assignments will refer to definite localities rather than to areas.

2. The ratio previously agreed to between the total strength of the Government and Communist forces will not be altered.

3. The periods previously established for the assignment of the troops into specified localities will be altered for the first phase (originally 12 months) to six months except where specifically stated to the contrary.

4. The Executive Headquarters will immediately determine the localities which have been occupied by the Government or Communist forces in China proper since January 13, 1946 and will require the troops involved to vacate those localities within 20 days after signing this agreement unless specifically directed otherwise.

5. The Executive Headquarters will immediately determine the localities occu-

pied by the Government or Communist forces in Manchuria afternoon of June 7, 1946 and will require the troops involved to vacate those localities within 10 days after the signing of this agreement unless specifically directed otherwise.

6. The Chinese Communist Party agrees to a Government garrison in Harbin of one regiment of not to exceed 5,000 men.

7. The Chinese Communist Party has agreed to concentrate its troops in specified localities, it being understood that the Government troops will not move into the areas thus vacated in China proper and that the present established civil governments and the Peace Preservation Corps for the maintenance of local security, will be continued. It is further agreed that in these areas no restrictions will be imposed on imports or exports, and free communication with adjacent regions will be assured.

8. It is understood and agreed that the formal amendment of the army reorganization plan of February 25, 1946 must be completed and signed within _____ days from the date of this document.

ANNEX PRELIMINARY AGREEMENT OF COMMITTEE OF THREE DATED JUNE 1946 TO GOVERN THE AMENDMENT AND EXECUTION OF THE ARMY REORGANIZATION PLAN OF FEBRUARY 25, 1946

In acordance with paragraph 7 of this agreement the Chinese Communist Party agrees that in implementing the Army Reorganization agreement of February 25, 1946 the following conditions will govern:

a. Communist troops will not be garrisoned or concentrated within any of the following areas:

Anwhei—All of the province after

Kiangsu—South of the latitude of Hwai-an exclusive, after   , and south of the Lunghai RR. after

Shantung—1. Tsaochuang area after

            2. Tsingtao-Tsinan R. R. after (including coal mines)

            3. Northeast Shantung after

            4. Te-Hsien after

Chahar—South of the latitude of Kalgan exclusive, within

Jehol—South of the latitude of Chengte exclusive, within   Chengte to be evacuated within

Hupeh-Honan Border Area—The Communist troops in that area will be moved to Hopei within

Shansi—Wen-hsi.

Manchuria—All provinces except Hei Lungchiang, Hsing-an, Central and Northern Nun-chiang and Eastern Kirin.

81

Manchuria Annex to Preliminary Agreement Proposed by Chairman of the Committee of Three (Marshall)[14]

The entire demobilization and integration program for Manchuria shall be completed before January 1, 1947. The ultimate strength of military forces in Manchuria shall comprise a total of 6 armies. There shall be 1 army composed of 1 National division and 2 Communist divisions with a Communist Commander, 1

_____

[14] Presented to the Representative of the Chinese Communist Party (Chou) on June 17, 1946.

army of 2 National divisions and 1 Communist division with a National Commander and 4 National Armies with National Commanders.

The necessary demobilization or increase in strength to realize the foregoing shall begin on June 22, 1946 and shall be completed before January 1, 1947. Redeployment of divisons to the localities designated hereinafter shall be completed before October 1, 1946. During the month of December 1946 integration of the two armies concerned shall be effected.

The location of armies shall be as follows:

1. One army composed of 1 National and 2 Communist divisions to be located within the three provinces of Hsin Hei Lung Kiang, Hsing-An, and Nun Kiang with one Communist division in Hsin Hei Lung Kiang and North and Central Nun Kiang, one Communist division in Hsung-An and North-Central Nun Kiang, and one National division in Southern Nun Kiang. The division headquarters of the above 3 divisions shall be located at Tsi-tsihar, Hailar and Paicheng respectively. The army headquarters shall be located at Tsitsihar.

2. One army composed of 2 National divisions and 1 Communist division to be located within the Provinces of Kirin and Sung Kiang with one National division in Central Kirin Province, one National division in Eastern Sung Kiang Province and one Communist division in Eastern Kirin Province. The division headquarters of the three divisions shall be located at the cities of Kirin, Mutankiang and Yenki, respectively. The army headquarters shall be located in the city of Kirin.

3. One national army shall be located within the provinces of Sung Kiang and Kirin with one division in Eastern and Central Sung Kiang and two divisions in Central and Eastern Kirin. The division headquarters of the above divisions shall be at Harbin and Changchun respectively. The army headquarters shall be located at Changchun.

4. One National army shall be located within Liao Peh and Liaoning Provinces with one division in Liao Peh Province and 2 divisions in Northern Liaoning Province. The division headquarters of the above divisions shall be located at Ssupingkai and Mukden respectively. The army headquarters shall be located at Mukden.

5. One National army shall be located within Liaoning and Antung Provinces with one division in Western Liaoning Province and two divisions in Antung Province. The division headquarters of the above divisions shall be at Penshi, Antung and Tunghuakai respectively. The army headquarters shall be located at Penshi.

6. One National army shall be located within Southern Liaoning Province. Two of the division headquarters shall be located at Chinchow and one at Yingkou. The army headquarters shall be located at Chinchow.

82

Radio Message by Generalissimo Chiang Kai-shek, July 1, 1946

Priority: Urgent
To: Directors, Generalissimo's Field Headquarters.
    Directors, President's Field Headquarters.
    Directors, Pacification Bureaus.
    Commanding Generals, War Areas.
    Commanding Generals, Pacification Areas.

Commanding Generals, Garrison Commands.

The Commanding General, Nanking Garrison Command.

Commanding Generals, Army Groups.

Commanding Generals, Armies (CG's, Reorganized divisions).

General Cheng Kai-ming, Commissioner, Executive Headquarters, Peiping.

Our Government has been extremely patient, disregarding the great injustice done to itself and conceded time and again, for the purpose of obtaining peace. But up to date, no successful solution is being reached on any problem. Now, for sake of urging the Communist Party to repent itself, so as to reach basis for reaching agreement and establishing peace and unity, the following stipulations are made: If Communist troops do not attack our forces, then our troops will not attack the Communist Forces. Should the Communist troops advance against our forces, then our troops, for sake of self defense, protecting lives and properties of the people, and to keep local law and order will concentrate their strength and counter attack them,—so as to do the duties of us Soldiers. This order is being distributed and strict compliance by all units is requested. Also date of receipt of this order will be reported.

Generalissimo CHIANG KAI-SHEK

83

Joint Statement by Mao Sse Tung[15] *and General Chu Teh,*[16] *July 1, 1946*

To: All Communist Field Commanders:

At any place, if the Nationalist troops do not attack our force, our army shall not take the initiative in attacking them. But in case of being attacked, our army shall resolutely take self-defensive measures in order to protect lives and properties of the people and to maintain law and order of the Democratic Governments.

MAO TSE TUNG
CHU TEH

84

Joint Statement by the Special Representative of the President (Marshall) and the Ambassador in China (Stuart), August 10, 1946[17]

General Marshall and Doctor Stuart have been exploring together every possibility for terminating the present growing conflict in China and for the initiation of the preliminary steps in the development of a truly democratic form of government. The desire for a peaceful solution to the political problems appears practically unanimous on the part of the people. The economic situation demands a prompt solution if a disastrous collapse is to be avoided. The fighting is daily growing more wide spread and threatens to engulf the country and pass beyond the control of those responsible. Both the Government and the Communist leaders are anxious to put an end to the fighting but there are certain issues concerned in the immediate settlements involved regarding which an agreement has not been found. It appears impossible for the two parties to reach a settlement of

---

[15] Chairman of the Central Committee of the Chinese Communist Party.

[16] Commander-in-Chief of the Chinese Communist Armies.

[17] *Department of State Bulletin,* Aug. 25, 1946, p. 384.

these issues which would permit a general order to be issued for the complete cessation of hostilities in all of China. Certain of the unsettled issues relate to the military redispositions of troops. However, these apparently present less difficulty of settlement than a more fundamental issue concerning the character of local or country governments to be maintained in the regions which will be evacuated as a result of the military redisposition pending a basic decision in such matters by the Constitutional Assembly.

85

Statement by President Chiang Kai-shek, August 13, 1946 [18]

My fellow countrymen:

Exactly one year ago today Japan surrendered unconditionally to the Allied Powers.

At the time when the war ended I realized that peace and unity in the country must be established before the people could live and produce, and before reconversion and reconstruction could progress. One year has passed but our national difficulties have not been lessened, nor have the people's sufferings been alleviated. In reviewing the past and looking toward the future, I feel the great responsibilities that fall upon me.

Our principal objective after victory was reconversion to peace. During the past year the government has moved from Chungking to Nanking. Wartime legislation restricting civil liberties has been removed or amended. The National army is being reorganized according to schedule; thousands of officers are being retired from active service. Universities in the interior are moving back to their original campuses. Ruined and broken cities and towns are being repaired, damaged dykes rebuilt.

In areas not occupied or affected by the Communists the main communications systems, such as the Canton-Hankow railway, have been restored. Relief is being given to the famine areas. Systems of election and assembly are being extended in the various provinces and districts. Bumper crops are reported throughout the country this year which give hope of alleviating the famine that followed the war. The taxation system has been improved. Since March the rate of banknote issues has decreased steadily and there was no new issue during July.

This much we have accomplished through hardship and industry during the past year.

However, we have much to regret in the slow progress of our reconversion. The most critical situation facing the country today is the stoppage of production, economic dislocation, the high cost of commodities and livelihood.

The prime reason for this situation is the disruption of communications. The number of vessels we possess is still inadequate. Our trunk railway lines— the Peiping-Hankow, Tientsin-Pukow, Kiaochow-Tsinan and Lunghai—have been repeatedly destroyed and disrupted. Because of this, our industrial centers lack raw materials, our agricultural and mineral products have no markets. While cargoes clog the commercial ports there is serious shortage of commodities and capital in the interior.

---

[18] English summary of statement on the first anniversary of the Japanese surrender as issued by the International Department of the Chinese Ministry of Information.

Furthermore, there are a number of places now occupied by the Communists who have established their own economic unit enforcing a blockade on food-stuffs, issuing and circulating their own currency, and living off the people in those areas. They have controlled the livelihood of the people in the adjacent areas. This situation has split the national economy and thus has hampered price control, currency stabilization, and reconversion as a whole.

The crux of the difficulties I have just enumerated is the continued disruption of peace and order, and our inability so far to reach a satisfactory settlement of political differences.

When the war ended, the government decided on a policy of "national unity" and "political democracy". It was hoped that through political measures party friction could be eliminated. We knew that the Communist Party was not an ordinary party with a democratic system. It is a party with an independent military force, an independent administrative system. It taxes the people within its areas and remains outside the realm of the National government.

However, the government exerted much effort hoping that the Communists would give up their military occupation of territory and change into a peaceful, law-abiding political party and follow the democratic road to reconstruction. We must not permit another state to exist within a state; nor permit a private army to operate independent of a national army. This is the main obstacle in the settlement of the present situation and is also the minimum demand the government has to put before the Communist party for the interest of the country and the people.

During the past year the government took the first step to open negotiations with the Communist representatives. Then, at the Political Consultative Conference in which all political elements were represented, five agreements were reached. Through the assistance of General Marshall an agreement was signed for ending all hostilities and for the restoration of communications. A plan for reorganization of the National army and integration of the Communist armies into the National army was also reached.

The future of the country and the prosperity of the people largely depended on the execution of these agreements and formulas.

Unfortunately, during the past seven months the Communists have taken advantage of the situation to expand their areas of occupation. They have increased their demands. They have refused to respect the decisions of the Executive Headquarters, in which the government, the Communists, and the Americans are represented and which was created to implement the agreements. They have continued to disrupt peace by their actions.

The people are forced to live in fear and it has increased the difficulties of the government.

Under the present domestic and international situation, China cannot permit another war to break out. However, no government in the world can shirk its responsibility to preserve order and protect the lives of the people.

The government will continue to favor a peaceful settlement of the present differences. Because of long years of war, hardships, sacrifices, and losses, the nation is like a person who has been seriously ill and needs gentle care during his period of recuperation.

The government will always abide by the agreements and formulas to which it is a party. A plan for reorganization of the National army is already being carried out by the government. Even when the Communists have violated the agreements and provoked clashes, the government has accepted the decisions of the Executive Headquarters. The record bears this out.

The government's policy will be:

1. To end the period of political tutelage and institute constitutional government without delay in spite of all obstacles. The National Assembly definitely will be held on schedule November 12.

2. To abide by the agreements reached by the Political Consultative Conference, and to execute them. Sound proposals on principles of constitutional law should be embodied in the draft constitution which will be presented to the National Assembly for adoption.

3. To enlarge the government's political basis by including members of all parties and non-partisans and to put into effect the Program of Peaceful Reconstruction as adopted by the Political Consultative Conference.

4. To abide by the January 10 truce agreement. Our only demand is that the Communists withdraw from areas where they threaten peace and obstruct communications.

5. To continue to use political means to settle political differences; but only if the Communists give assurance and evidence that they will carry out the truce agreement, restore communications, respect decisions of the Executive Headquarters, and integrate the Communist army into the National army, the government will be ready to negotiate all the pending problems.

6. To give protection and security to the people and their properties and to remove any threat to peace so as to enable the people to live in peace and carry on their daily livelihood.

My fellow countrymen:

In looking over the past year, if we had not suffered domestic strife, if a political party with armed forces had not insisted on expanding its territory, our country would be in a high and respected place, our people would have peace and prosperity.

If the Communists had carried out the three agreements reached since last January to cease hostilities, restore communications, and integrate their armies, and if they had, according to schedule, appointed representatives to participate in the National Government and attend the National Assembly, we could by now have instituted constitutional government. We could have completed our transition to political democracy and we would not be misunderstood and criticized by world opinion. The people of Northern Kiangsu, Hopei, and Shantung would not have had to go through again the sufferings of battle and floods.

I earnestly hope that the Communist party, reflecting on these facts, will come to this realization.

Today our one important demand is that the Communist party change its policy of seizing power by military force and transform into a peaceful party. We want them to help us win the peace in China.

We must have a deep understanding of the issues confronting our country and realize our responsibilities. We must put down rebellions, and make China a peaceful, democratic, unified, and strong country. But government officials, also, must review their own mistakes and shortcomings, and exert every effort to fulfill their duties to their country. Furthermore, the people must have faith, patience, and zeal. They must be able to differentiate between right and wrong, true and false, to speak up for justice; to complete the revolutionary work of the nation.

I dedicated myself to the cause of the revolution for the country and the people. I will not let the fruits of victory be lost in a day. I will not change my determination to establish a peaceful, unified, and democratic country. I will assume my responsibilities, and with the help of my fellow countrymen, follow the scheduled course to national reconstruction.

86

President Truman to President Chiang Kai-shek

WASHINGTON, *August 10, 1946*

I have followed closely the situation in China since I sent General Marshall to you as my Special Envoy. It is with profound regret that I am forced to the conclusion that his efforts have seemingly proved unavailing.

In his discussions with you, I am certain that General Marshall has reflected accurately the overall attitude and policy of the American Government and of informed American public opinion also.

The rapidly deteriorating political situation in China, during recent months, has been a cause of grave concern to the American people. While it is the continued hope of the United States that an influential and democratic China can still be achieved under your leadership, I would be less than honest if I did not point out that latest developments have forced me to the conclusion that the selfish interests of extremist elements, both in the Kuomintang and the Communist Party, are obstructing the aspirations of the people of China.

A far sighted step toward the achievement of national unity and democracy was acclaimed in the United States when the agreements were reached on January 31st by the Political Consultative Conference. Disappointment over failure to implement the agreements of the PCC by concrete measures is becoming an important factor in the American outlook with regard to China.

In the United States, there now exists an increasing school of thought which maintains that our whole policy toward China must be re-examined in the light of spreading strife, and notably by evidence of the increasing trend to suppress the expression of liberal views among intellectuals as well as freedom of the press. The assassinations of distinguished Chinese liberals at Kunming recently have not been ignored. Regardless of where responsibility may lie for these cruel murders, the result has been to cause American attention to focus on the China situation, and there is increasing belief that an attempt is being made to resort to force, military or secret police rather than democratic processes to settle major social issues.

American faith in the peaceful and democratic aspirations of the Chinese people has not been destroyed by recent events, but has been shaken. The firm desire of the people of the United States and of the American Government is still to help China achieve lasting peace and a stable economy under a truly democratic government. There is an increasing awareness, however, that the hopes of the people of China are being thwarted by militarists and a small group of political reactionaries who are obstructing the advancement of the general good of the nation by failing to understand the liberal trend of the times. The people of the United States view with violent repugnance this state of affairs.

It cannot be expected that American opinion will continue in its generous attitude towards your nation unless convincing proof is shortly forthcoming that genuine progress is being made toward a peaceful settlement of China's internal problems. Furthermore, it will be necessary for me to redefine and explain the position of the United States to the people of America.

I earnestly hope that in the near future I may receive some encouraging word from you which will facilitate the achievement of our mutually declared aims.

87

The Chinese Ambassador (Koo) to President Truman

WASHINGTON, *August 28, 1946*

MY DEAR MR. PRESIDENT: Referring to my acknowledgement of August 12 of your letter dated August 10 containing a message to President Chiang Kai-shek, I have the honor to transmit to your excellency, in accordance with instructions, the following reply:

"Referring to your message of August 10, I wish to thank you cordially for your expressions of genuine concern for the welfare of my country.

"General Marshall has labored most unsparingly to achieve our common objective; namely, peace and democracy in China, since his arrival. Despite all obstacles, I, too, have done my utmost to cooperate with him in the accomplishment of his task.

"The desire for peace has to be mutual, therefore, it means the Communists must give up their policy to seize political power through the use of armed force, to overthrow the government and to install a totalitarian regime such as those with which Eastern Europe is now being engulfed.

"The minimum requirement for the preservation of peace in our country is the abandonment of such a policy. The Communists attacked and captured Changchun in Manchuria and attacked and captured Tehchow in Shantung after the conclusion of the January agreement. In June, during the cease-fire period, they attacked Tatung and Taiyuan in Shansi and Hsuchow in northern Kiangsu. They have opened a wide offensive on the Lunghai railway in the last few days, with Hsuchow and Kaifeng as their objectives.

"Mistakes have also been made by some subordinates on the government side, of course, but compared to the flagrant violations on the part of the Communists, they are minor in scale. We deal sternly with the offender whenever any mistake occurs on our Government side.

"In my V-J Day message on August 14, I announced the firm policy of the government to broaden speedily the basis of the Government by the inclusion of all parties and non-partisans, amounting to the effectuation of the program of peaceful reconstruction adopted on January 13 by the political consultation conference. It is my sincere hope that our views will be accepted by the Chinese Communist party. On its part, the Government will do the utmost in the shortest possible time to make peace and democracy a reality in this country.

"I am cooperating with General Marshall with all my power in implementing that policy which has as its aim our mutually declared objective. Success must depend upon the sincerity of the Communists in response to our appeals. I am depending on your continued support in the realization of our goal. (Sgd.) Chiang Kai-shek."

I again offer my highest respects.

Yours most sincerely,

V. K. WELLINGTON KOO.

88

President Truman to President Chiang Kai-shek

WASHINGTON, *August 31, 1946*

DEAR PRESIDENT CHIANG: Your message was transmitted to me by letter on August 28 by the Chinese Ambassador Dr. Koo. I note with gratification your references to General Marshall. The strenuous efforts, indicated in the concluding paragraphs of your message, being made to effect the settlement of the internal problems now confronting you are greatly welcomed by me. It is earnestly hoped by me that a satisfactory political solution can soon be reached to bring about a cessation of hostilities, thereby making it possible for the great and urgent task of reconstruction to be continued by you and the Chinese people. With reference to the final paragraph of my policy statement of 15 December 1945, I hope it will be feasible for the United States to plan for assisting China in its industrial economy and the rehabilitation of its agrarian reforms. This can be rendered feasible, I believe, through the prompt removal of the threat of wide spread Civil War in China.

With my best wishes and highest regards.

Sincerely,

HARRY S. TRUMAN

89

The Head of the Chinese Communist Party Delegation (Chou) to the Special Representative of the President (Marshall)

MM 145 SHANGHAI, *September 15, 1946*

DEAR GENERAL MARSHALL: Since the fruitless June armistice, the Committee of Three has been in adjournment up to this moment. At the time when you declared the adjournment, it was presumed that some other means would be sought in order to break the deadlock and bring about the cessation of hostilities. Nevertheless, the Government, taking advantage of this opportunity, played a delaying tactic towards the negotiation and plunged itself headlong into a large-scale civil war. The meeting of the Committee of Five in early July, the entering of Dr. J. L. Stuart into mediation since mid July, the joint statements of yours and Dr. J. L. Stuart's as of 10 August, and Dr. Stuart's proposition advanced about a month ago for an Informal Group of Five, were all exploited by the Government authorities for dovetailing the talks into the fighting with a view to camouflaging the large-scale war which they had waged. Being solicitous for peace, the Chinese Communist Party did not hesitate to recede further ground, and eventually acceeded to the proposition of taking up the issue of government reorganization first in the hope of winning a guarantee for cease-firing. However, the Government authorities countered with dilatory tactics. Instead of giving an assurance for cease-firing, they went so far as to declare that the Chinese Communist Party must designate its representatives for the National Assembly before the promulgation of the order for the cessation of hostilities. At the same time, they intimated that the reorganization of the Executive Yuan would not be undertaken prior to the convening of the National Assembly, and that they had in mind continuing in governmental military occupation of the places recently occupied in Jehol, etc. As the matter now stands, the Kuomintang Government not only has no intention of cease-firing and is designing to realize its 5-point demand through continued military drive towards the areas covered by this demand, but also has thrown overboard one by one the procedures prescribed by the PCC resolutions. The foregoing moves best bear out that the Government authorities did violate the Cease Fire Agreement and overthrow the PCC resolutions, the most striking evidence being the grave fact that a nation-wide civil war is there and is still going on.

From 13 January when the Cease Fire Order came into effect till August, the Government forces in violation of that order have moved as many as 180 divisions (or reorganized brigades), threw 206 regular army divisions (or reorganized brigades) with a strength of 1,740,000 men, i.e. 85 percent of its total strength which is 256 divisions (or reorganized brigades) or about 2,060,000 men, into the offensive against the Communist Liberated Areas; they made 6,000-odd major and minor assaults, conducted over 300 bombing and strafing raids, and had seized and was continuing in occupation by 7 September of 76 cities thus seized. As a matter of fact, the Nationalist troops are everywhere on the offensive, no matter in Manchuria, North China, Central China or South China. Chengteh city has already fallen. Cities like Kalgan, Hwaiyin and Harbin are being made the immediate objectives of the Nationalist drive. Following the seizure of Chinchow-Chengteh Railroad, the fighting along the Chinese Changchun, Peiping-Kupeikow, Peiping-Suiyuan, Tungpu, Taiyuan-Shihchiachwang, Tsingtao-Tsinan, Lunghai, Tientsin-Pukow, and Peiping-Hankow Railroads also became intensified.

Notwithstanding the Kuomintang Government declares that its field forces have been reorganized, the strength of a present-day division in fact surpasses the actual strength of a former army. Now the Government is turning the demobilization back into a new mobilization. As a result of which, over 60 divisional districts originally established for conscription have been restored. This in fact is tantamount to an increase of more than 60 divisions. Furthermore, in order to meet the war requirement, the Government authorities incorporated large numbers of puppets and as in the case of Shantung and Shansi even Japanese war prisoners into the Nationalist army, the latter being recruited under false names.

Up to the present moment, not only the January Cease Fire Agreement has been thoroughly destroyed, but also the war situation has become graver than prior to the signing of that agreement, and from the viewpoint of its scale, it is unparalleled in the twenty years' history of the Chinese civil strife.

On the other hand, the vast assistance received by the Kuomintang Government from the United States for prosecuting the civil war is also unequalled in Chinese History. Since the V–J Day, the quantity of supplies which the Kuomintang Government has received under U. S. Lend-lease Bill, even according to official announcement of the U. S. Government, is equal to the amount delivered during wartime, both being over U. S. $600,000,000 worth. The actual amount presumably would be still more. Whereas during the anti-Japanese war, the American-equipped Chinese divisions had only been used in the India-Burma campaign and later on once in western Hunan; now nearly all of them are thrown into the offensive against the Communist Liberated Areas. Furthermore, the United States Forces also helped to move these troops by air and sea. As this was found still insufficient, the United States Forces further helped the Government by guarding the railroads, cities, towns as well as seaports and by joining its military operations. On the top of that, during the June armistice, the U. S. Government brought before the Congress a bill of 10-year extension of the lend-lease to China, which could serve no other purpose than to bolster up the war spirit of the Kuomintang Government. Later on, the U. S. Government turned over U. S. $825,000,000 worth of surplus properties including naval vessels and other equipment to the Kuomintang Government. It might well be questioned as to what an embarrassed position the large-scale assistance and armed intervention on part of the United States Government have placed you and Dr. J. L. Stuart as its envoys plenipotentiary and mediators into. You, in particular as the Chairman of the Committee of Three which is directing the Executive Headquarters, can well be imagined to be on the worst spot. Unless the U. S. Government has no intention to let its envoys plenipotentiary act as true mediators, and would rather leave them open to public criticism, it should weigh the necessity to change its erroneous policy of assisting the prosecution of the civil war by the Kuomintang, withdraw the American Forces in China, freeze the transfer of the surpluses and withhold all aids, so that you and Dr. J. L. Stuart will be in a position to exercise their fair and equitable mediation. Only under such conditions, peace in China will become highly hopeful, and the Sino-American cooperation will receive high benefit under its influence. It is my sincere hope that you would deeply think the matter over.

Since the June armistice, all intricate ways to solve the issue have proved futile and non-instrumental in breaking the deadlock. Instead they were merely exploited by the bellicose elements to gain time, to befog the public opinion, to enlarge the civil war, and to imperil the people. In view of this, I, as the official representative of the Chinese Communist Party with full authority, wish to advance to you, the Chairman of the Committee of Three, a straightforward proposition for the settlement of the issue, i. e., you would immediately convene a meeting of the Committee to discuss the question of cease-firing.

An immediate termination of the civil strife in China is the aspiration of the people throughout China as well as the call in the world. President Harry Truman's statement and the Moscow Communique of the three Foreign Ministers of last December all pointed towards this end. On this basis you were entrusted with the present mission. And on the invitation of both the Kuomintang and the Communist Parties you took up the role as mediator in the negotiation and became the Chairman of the Committee of Three. And it was on the basis of the Cease Fire Agreement between the two parties that the Peiping Executive Headquarters and the Changchun Advanced Section were established and field teams formed. Now that the situation has become so much worsened, the only hope lies in returning to this sole legal cease-fire agency for seeking a truce arrangement and a direct and simple solution. You as the Chairman of the Committee of Three are hereby requested to transmit our view to the Government and to arrange for the meeting of the Committee at the earliest possible moment in order to discuss the issue.

Your reply is eagerly awaited.

[Signed in Chinese]
CHOU EN-LAI

90

The Head of the Chinese Communist Party Delegation (Chou) to the Special Representative of the President (Marshall)

SM 827   [SHANGHAI,] *September 16, 1946*

MY DEAR GENERAL: Because of some business that requires my attendance, I am called upon to leave for Shanghai to-day. In case there is any matter that you want to communicate to me, please contact my associates Messrs. Liao Cheng-chih and Wang Ping-nan here.

As soon as you have decided to convene the Committee of Three, I will be back on your notice.

Faithfully yours,

[Signed in Chinese]
CHOU EN-LAI

91

The Special Representative of the President (Marshall) to the Head of the Chinese Communist Party Delegation (Chou)

OSE 446   NANKING, *September 19, 1946*

DEAR GENERAL CHOU: Dr. Stuart has informed me that he learns through Dr. Wang Ping Nan that you desire a formal written acknowledgement to your memorandum to me of September 15th in which you request me as Chairman of the Committee of Three to transmit to the National Government the view of the Communist Party of the situation as expressed in this memorandum, and to arrange for a meeting of the Committee of Three at the earliest possible moment.

I have transmitted to the National Government in Nanking a copy of your memorandum. Further when advised at Kuling by radio of your desire regarding Committee of Three meeting I took your proposal to the Generalissimo and was informed by him that he would not authorize the attendance of the Government member of the Committee of Three at such a meeting until there had been a meeting of the informal five man committee headed by Doctor Stuart, and some progress had been made towards an agreement for the organization of the State Council.

Doctor Stuart, I believe, had previously conveyed this information to Mister Wang Ping Nan.

Faithfully yours,

[GEORGE C. MARSHALL]

92

The Head of the Chinese Communist Party Delegation (Chou) to the Special Representative of the President (Marshall)

SHANGHAI, *September 21, 1946*

MY DEAR GENERAL MARSHALL: Your memo OSE 446 dated September 19 has been received.

The extremely serious situation at this moment, as I see, has gone far beyond the scope that it can be resolved by a discussion on government reorganization or any other similar procedure. Instead, the key to it rests with cease firing— a prompt and immediate cease firing. Inasmuch as the sole legal agency handling cease firing matters is the Committee of Three, you as its chairman are therefore called upon to hold joint discussion with the two Chinese parties on this paramount and most urgent problem, no matter what their respective views will be.

I wish to recall that it was largely due to your assuming the chairmanship of the Committee of Three in early January, that the cease fire agreement was concluded, and that the Executive Headquarters in Peiping and the various field teams became established, which in turn secured the implementation of that agreement, and ushered in the incipient rays of peace to China proper. It was due to the same event, that the prospect was opened for the fulfillment of the primary part of your mission in China. Again it was this course of events that entailed the successful conclusion of the PCC and the signing of the Army Reorganization Plan.

As the matter now stands, however, we find ourselves facing a state, which can only find a parallel in days prior to January 10, if not even worse. The only proper approach toward disentangling the many complexities lies therefore in effecting a prompt cessation of hostilities. The function as well as the past record of the Committee of Three further underscore your obligation to call its meeting at once. And the reasons are:

(1) The Committee of Three has been in adjournment for nearly three months, it thus not only bars the prospect for peace, but utterly deprives the Executive Headquarters and the field teams a guiding light amidst this turmoil.

(2) There is no precedent in the record of the Committee of Three that any Chinese party has ever rejected your invitation to its meeting. Nor is it conceivable that anybody would ever boycott such a meeting. In particular the Chinese Communist Party has never undertaken such a step.

I feel therefore all the more justified in requesting a prompt meeting of the Committee of Three at this moment.

As to the rejoinder that the Committee of Three should not be convened until there has been a meeting of the informal five man committee headed by Dr. Stuart, and some progress has been made towards an agreement for the organization of the State Council, it is but a too obvious unwarranted excuse, which I believe you are fully aware. For plainly the informal five man committee would not by itself bring forth a cessation of hostilities. At best, it would only open the way for a discussion on truce,—being still far off from our true objective of cessation of hostilities. Speaking about the reorganization of the State Council itself, it is not a complicated matter at all, unless the Kuomintang government would lavishly play an obstructionist policy. If the Kuomintang would agree to appropriate fourteen seats of the State Council to the Chinese Communist Party and the Democratic League, thus definitely ensuring a one-third vote to safeguard the PCC common program from being infringed upon, the whole issue of the State Council can be settled almost overnight. Would such a course be adopted, I am sure, that Dr. Stuart as the pre-assigned chairman of that committee can very well confer with both sides for a settlement. If a different course be chosen, then even the abandonment by the Kuomintang of its previous claim for a 8–4–4–4 ratio does not rule out the possibility that it may wreck the whole proceeding by substituting that claim with other terms. Facing such a situation, the debate would just go on endlessly without ever resolving the State Council issue, let alone the cessation of hostilities.

Time and again I have explained to Dr. Stuart, that the resolution of the State Council issue does not call for a formal meeting, as it can very well be achieved by informal talks with the two parties, thereby facilitating the discussion on the principal cease-firing issue. Any insistence on placing the informal five man committee before the Committee of Three is not only unwarranted, but merely a pretext for the purpose of obstruction.

In view of the foregoing I earnestly request that you would immediately call the Committee of Three together, and favour me with an early reply.

Should the Committee of Three nevertheless fail to meet, I can hardly convince myself that there is still a second way leading to cessation of hostilities. By reaching such a stage, I would feel myself forced to make public all the important documents since the armistice in June, in order to clarify the responsibility and appeal to the general public for judgement. I wish hereby to serve notice of my contemplated action.

Faithfully yours,

[CHOU EN-LAI]

93

The Special Representative of the President (Marshall) and the Ambassador in China (Stuart) to the Head of the Chinese Communist Party Delegation (Chou)

OSE 446   [NANKING] *September 26, 1946*

DEAR GENERAL CHOU: Since your departure for Shanghai we have been steadily hoping that you would return here and thus make possible a resumption of the efforts to end the spreading civil war. The disastrous consequences to the nation of a continuation of the present situation are apparent to all. We continue in our belief that both the Government and the Communist leaders sincerely desire peace and the establishment of a coalition government and the adoption of a democratic constitution, and that the difficulties are largely questions of procedure.

We desire to help in this to the utmost of our ability. We venture, therefore, on the basis of our past friendly relations and our personal esteem for you, to urge that you return to Nanking without further delay in order that we may together explore all conceivable ways and means for the objective we are seeking to achieve.

We have been informed that the Generalissimo returns to Nanking today or tomorrow, weather permitting.

G. C. MARSHALL
J. L. STUART

94

The Head of the Chinese Communist Party Delegation (Chou) to the Special Representative of the President (Marshall) and the Ambassador in China (Stuart)

NANKING, *September 27, 1946*

DEAR GENERAL MARSHALL AND AMBASSADOR STUART: Thank you for your letter dated 26 September, 1946.

The deterioration and seriousness of the present situation is apparent both to you and to all. I am not unwilling to return to Nanking for a discussion of the ways and means to stop the civil war. The government not only gives no signs for the cessation of hostilities but further is increasing its efforts by many folds in the active offensive upon Kalgan, Harbin, Antung, North Kiangsu, and other areas. A further adventure for negotiation will be nothing helpful to the real peace but a smokescreen for a free hand to make a full scale civil war on part of the government and for the deception of the people. This is why I would rather wait here in Shanghai for the convocation of the Committee of Three.

Your good friendship as expressed in your letter to urge me to return to Nanking is appreciated. However, inasmuch as the actual situation is still unknown, I am requesting Mr. Tung Pi-wu to approach you first on behalf of our side.

Should the government give factual evidence in reply to the demand for cease-fire and prove itself to have sincerity, I shall have no reason not to return to Nanking for a talk.

Sincerely yours,

CHOU EN-LAI

95

Draft of Statement for Generalissimo Chiang Kai-shek [19]

A continuation of the present political and military situation in China will be destructive of the interests of a long suffering people. It will render impossible the unification of our country and will threaten the peace of the world. Therefore, it is necessary that an early solution be found to the present conflict and that peace be restored to the land. But as the responsible head of the Government of China, I must see that the necessary measures are taken to safeguard the security of the nation, since we are dealing with a political party which maintains a large army to support or enforce its political policies.

In the past three months, I have stipulated certain conditions that must be met by the Communist Party before a peaceful accord could be achieved and to which they have thus far refused to agree. They now demand an immediate meeting of the Committee of Three of which General Marshall is the chairman. That committee reached an impasse in its negotiations the latter part of June and unless there are certain preliminary but vital agreements or understandings, a meeting of the committee would not only be ineffective but its future possible usefulness would be fatally impaired. I have insisted that the group of five men selected to reach an understanding between the Government and the Communist Party making possible the establishment of the coalition State Council should first meet under the chairmanship of the United States Ambassador, Doctor Stuart, to give evidence of the good intent of both the Kuomintang Party and the Communist Party towards the reorganization of the government in accordance with the resolutions of the Peoples Consultative Council. With this reassurance of good faith on both sides there would then be a new basis of trust for the termination of the hostilities now disrupting China. I have further stated that concurrent with the termination of hostilities the Communist Party should indicate its honest intention to cooperate in the reorganization of the government by announcing its delegates to the National Assembly to meet on November 12 to determine on a democratic constitution for the Government of China.

In view of the seriousness of the situation, the misunderstandings and public confusion, and the distrust and suspicions unfortunately prevalent, I now make the following public announcement of the conditions under which the Government is prepared to act to secure an immediate cessation of hostilities.

The Five Man Committee under the chairmanship of Doctor Stuart to meet immediately and at the same time the Committee of Three under the chairmanship of General Marshall with the following understandings:

(a) The opposing troops in close contact to be separated in accordance with the terms tentatively agreed to by the Committee of Three in June for the termination of hostilities in Manchuria.

---

[19] Prepared by the Special Representative of the President, (September) 1946.

(b) The restoration of communications to be immediately resumed in accordance with the agreement tentatively reached by the Committee of Three last June.

(c) The method for settling disagreements among the team members of Executive Headquarters and Commissioners at Executive Headquarters to be in accordance with the agreement tentatively reached by the Committee of Three last June.

(d) The implementation of the agreement for the reorganization and unification of the armies of China to be settled by the Committee of Three without delay.

(e) That whatever understanding is reached by the Five Man Committee headed by Doctor Stuart it is to be confirmed by the Steering Committee of the PCC without delay.

(f) All questions of local government to be settled by the newly organized State Council.

(g) Concurrent with the cessation of hostilities, the Communist Party to announce its intention of participating in the National Assembly by publishing its list of delegates to that Assembly.

96

The Head of the Chinese Communist Party Delegation (Chou) to the Special Representative of the President (Marshall)

SHANGHAI, *September 30, 1946*

DEAR GENERAL MARSHALL: Since the interruption of the talks during the June armistice, the Kuomintang Government thenceforth not only went further in ignoring all the previous commitments, but also tore the Cease Fire Agreement of January to pieces, and launched a large-scale drive in China proper. During the last three months they have occupied many cities, destroyed the popularly-elected local administrations of many a place, made ruthless air raids into Liberated Areas, killing and wounding countless civilians. They further advanced the insensible five-point demand setting forth the withdrawal of Communist troops and popularly-elected local administrations from a number of areas. When the Chinese Communists rightfully rejected their proposition on account of its incompatibility with the basic principles of the PCC Joint Platform, they threw their military drive into high gear, in order to achieve this demand by force, and aggrandize their occupation.

Thus, apart from taking away a series of places from the Communist led Liberated areas in Hupeh-Honan, north Anhwei, north Kiangsu, Shantung, Shansi, Hopei and Jehol, the Kuomintang authorities then used the Communist siege over Tatung as an excuse for making the announcement that they would launch ruthless drives for capturing Chengteh, Kalgan and Yenan. What then happened was that Chengteh was soon occupied by them, followed by such key cities like Tsining and Fengchen along the Peiping-Suiyuan rail line. Actually the Communist campaign around Tatung is merely calculated to divert the attacks launched by the Kuomintang troops in Shansi under Yen Hsi-shan and Hu Chung-nan, and as such it is of a besieging nature. Most recently the Communists even announced the formal lifting of the siege, thereby freeing Tatung from any kind of menace.

On the other hand, the Kuomintang troops are still up to the neck engaged in enlarging their occupation in Jehol and east Hopei. Most significantly, at this moment, a three-pronged attack is being formally launched against Kalgan. It thus became obvious that the Kuomintang Government shows even no hesitation to strike against one of the political and military centers of the Communist-led Liberated Areas—Kalgan—, in order to force the Kuomintang-Communist relation into the perilous state of an ultimate break.

Now I am duly instructed to serve the following notice, which I request you would kindly transmit to the Government: If the Kuomintang Government does not instantly cease its military operations against Kalgan and the vicinity areas, the Chinese Communist Party feels itself forced to presume that the Government is thereby giving public announcement of a total national split, and that it has ultimately abandoned its pronounced policy of peaceful settlement. When reaching such a stage, the responsibility of all the serious consequences should as a matter of course solely rest with the Government side.

[CHOU EN-LAI]

97

The Special Representative of the President (Marshall) to President Chiang Kai-shek

OSE 476   NANKING, *October 1, 1946*

YOUR EXCELLENCY: Since our conversation of Monday morning, September 30, and General Yu Ta Wei's call on me the same afternoon, I have carefully considered all the factors involved in the present status of negotiations and military operations. I have also taken into consideration the later developments;

(1) The Communist announcement of yesterday stating their refusal to nominate delegates to the National Assembly unless certain PCC conditions are met and the announcement of the governmental Central News Agency regarding the operations against Kalgan;

(2) The informal suggestions (Incl. 1)[20] of Doctor T. V. Soong for a series of actions as conditions precedent to a cessation of hostilities, which he mentioned to Doctor Stuart this morning, and

(3) The memorandum from General Chou En-lai to me (Incl. 2)[21] which was handed to me by Mr. Tung Pi Wu today.

I am not in agreement either with the present course of the Government in regard to this critical situation or with that of the Communist Party. I disagree with the evident Government policy of settling the fundamental differences involved by force, that is by utilizing a general offensive campaign to force compliance with the Government point of view or demands. I recognize the vital necessity of safeguarding the security of the Government, but I think the present procedure has past well beyond that point.

On the part of the Communist Party, I deplore actions and statements which provide a basis for the contention on the part of many in the Government that the Communist's proposals can not be accepted in good faith, that it is not the intention of that Party to cooperate in a genuine manner in a reorganization of the Government, but rather to disrupt the Government and seize power for their own purposes.

I will not refer to the circumstances connected with the ineffective negotiations since last March. I wish merely to state that unless a basis for agreement is

---

[20] Not printed.
[21] See annex 92.

found to terminate the fighting without further delays of proposals and counterproposals, I will recommend to the President that I be recalled and that the United States Government terminate its efforts of mediation.

[GEORGE C. MARSHALL]

AIDE MEMOIRE

Informal suggestion—without commitment

I. Five-men Committee to meet first to discuss Communist participation in State Council.

II. (a) Following this first meeting a 3-man Committee to meet and decide the areas to which Communist troops will be assigned.

(b) Dates will be set for the movement of Communist troops to designated areas.

(c) Truce teams will be sent to observe the movement of these troops.

(d) Upon the acceptance by the Communist delegates of the areas where Communist troops will be stationed and the dates set for their removal to those areas, cease-fire order will forthwith be given.

(e) When the Communist troops have reached the areas assigned to them, they will be incorporated into the National Army, and trained and equipped like other national divisions.

98

President Chiang Kai-shek to the Special Representative of the President (Marshall)

[Translation]

NANKING, *October 2, 1946*

Your Excellency's letter dated October 1, 1946, which was attached with a letter from General Chou En-lai under date of September 30, 1946 ·handed to you by Mr. Tung Pi-wu, has been received. The Government is more eager than any other party for an early cessation of hostilities, but past experience shows that the Chinese Communist Party has been in the habit of taking advantage of negotiations to obtain respite and regroup their troops in order to launch fresh attacks on Government troops who have been abiding by truce agreements (attached is a list of important evidences of Communist troops attacking Government troops during the truce periods), and that conflicts only ceased temporarily but flared up again after a short interval. Therefore effective means should be devised to assure that cease fire is permanent and not temporary. The Government, having the responsibility of restoring and maintaining order and security in the country, can not allow the chaotic situation to be prolonged indefinitely.

With a view to saving time and showing its utmost sincerity, the Government hereby, with all frankness, expresses its maximum concessions in regard to the solution of the present problem:

(1) The Chinese Communist Party has been incessantly urging the reorganization of the National Government. This hinges on the distribution of the membership of the State Council. The Government originally agreed that the Chinese Communist Party be allocated eight seats and the Democratic League, four, with a total of twelve. The Chinese Communist Party, on the other hand, requested

ten for themselves and four for the Democratic League with a total of fourteen. Now the Government makes a fresh concession by taking the mean and offering one seat for the independents to be recommended by the Chinese Communist Party and agreed upon by the Government, so that, added to the original twelve, it makes a total of thirteen seats.   But the Communist Party should without delay produce the list of their candidates for the State Council as well as the list of their delegates to the National Assembly.   This reassignment of seats should be decided by the proposed group of five to be confirmed by the Steering Committee of PCC.

(2) For immediate implementation of the program for reorganization of the army, the location of the eighteen Communist divisions should be immediately determined and the Communist troops should enter those assigned places according to agreed dates.   The above should be decided by the Committee of Three and carried out under the supervision of the Executive Headquarters.

If the Communist Party has the sincerity for achieving peace and co-operating with the Government, and is willing to solve immediately the above-mentioned two problems, a cease fire order should be issued by both sides, when agreement has been reached thereon.

Kindly forward the above to the Communist Party and let me know your esteemed opinion about it.

CHIANG KAI-SHEK.

99

The Special Representative of the President (Marshall) to the Ambassador in China (Stuart)

OSE 491   NANKING, *October 6, 1946*

DEAR DOCTOR STUART: I have outlined below my understanding of the arrangement agreed upon this morning between ourselves and the Generalissimo.

You are to notify Wang Ping Nan that we proposed to the Generalissimo a 10-day truce for the operations against Kalgan under the following conditions:

1) The purpose of the truce is to carry out the two proposals of the Generalissimo in his communication to me of October 2.   (copy attached)[22]

2) During the period of the truce, Executive Headquarters will check on its observance with teams at all critical points composed and directed as follows:

a. Teams within the Communist lines will not have a National Government member and teams within the Government lines will not have a Communist member.

b. The American member will have the authority to determine where and when the teams shall go and will himself report on any actions which in effect could be considered violations of the truce.

c. Between the two forces a team or teams may be located with both Government and Communist representatives.

3) The public announcement of the truce will be made by you and me, and the Government and the Communists are to refrain from any announcement.

---

[22] See annex 98.

100

Statement by the Chinese Communist Party

YENAN, *October 8, 1946*

1. The truce should be without a time limit because, based on previous experience, it would otherwise be unsatisfactory. The proposal would seem to be a strategy unless the Government troops were withdrawn to their original positions, thus demonstrating the sincerity of the Government.

2. The Communist Party wishes to have the Three- and Five-Man Committees to meet but the discussion should not be limited to the two paragraphs of the October 2nd communication of the Generalissimo. These topics dealt with under truce conditions may be regarded as under military coercion.

3. No reply has been sent to the communication of October 2nd because the Communist Party had been hoping to have some word from General Marshall and Dr. Stuart clarifying the situation for peace. The latest proposal implies that the situation has not changed much. General Chou is therefore preparing to send a formal written reply and sees no need for his returning to Nanking.

101

Joint Statement by the Special Representative of the President (Marshall) and the Ambassador in China (Stuart),[23] *Nanking, October 8, 1946*

On the morning of October 1st General Marshall received through the hands of Mr. Wang Ping-nan, the Communist representative, a memorandum dated September 30th from General Chou En-lai in Shanghai relating to the activities of the Kuomintang Party to which objection was taken and concluding with the following paragraph:

"Now I am duly instructed to serve the following notice, which I request you would kindly transmit to the Government: If the Kuomintang Government does not instantly cease its military operations against Kalgan and the vicinity areas, the Chinese Communist Party feels itself forced to presume that the Government is thereby giving public announcement of a total national split, and that it has ultimately abandoned its pronounced policy of peaceful settlement. When reaching such a stage, the responsibility of all the serious consequences should as a matter of course solely rest with the Government side."

In accordance with the request of General Chou the foregoing memorandum was transmitted to the Generalissimo, and on October 2nd he replied in a memorandum to General Marshall relating certain hostile acts of troops of the Communist Party. In this memorandum the Generalissimo proposed, with a view to saving time and as indicating the sincerity of the Government, the following as the maximum concessions the Government would make in the solution of the present problem:

"1) The Chinese Communist Party has been incessantly urging the reorganization of the National Government. This hinges on the distribution of the

---

[23] *Department of State Bulletin,* Oct. 20, 1946, pp. 723–724.

membership of the State Council. The Government originally agreed that the Chinese Communist Party be allocated eight seats and the Democratic League, four, with a total of twelve. The Chinese Communist Party, on the other hand, requested ten for themselves and four for the Democratic League with a total of fourteen. Now the Government makes a fresh concession by taking the mean and offering one seat for the independents to be recommended by the Chinese Communist Party and agreed upon by the Government, so that, added to the original twelve, it makes a total of thirteen seats. But the Communist Party should without delay produce the list of their candidates for the State Council as well as the list of their delegates to the National Assembly. This reassignment of seats should be decided by the proposed group of five to be confirmed by the Steering Committee of PCC.

"2) For immediate implementation of the program for reorganization of the army, the location of the eighteen Communist divisions should be immediately determined and the Communist troops should enter those assigned places according to agreed dates. The above should be decided by the Committee of Three and carried out under the supervision of the Executive Headquarters."

This communication was immediately transmitted to the Communist representatives and they, later on in the week, called on the American mediators with a request for information as to whether the memorandum of the Generalissimo of October 2nd was a reply to General Chou's memorandum of September 30th, as no mention of Kalgan was made.

There followed a series of discussions between the Generalissimo and General Marshall and Ambassador Stuart which finally resulted in the acquiescence of the Generalissimo that he halt the advance on Kalgan for a period of 10 days during which the Five Man Group and the Committee of Three would meet in order to consider the two proposals of the Generalissimo in his communication of October 2nd. The Generalissimo further agreed that during the period of this truce Executive Headquarters would check on its observance with teams at all critical points and that Government representatives would not accompany teams within the Communist lines while the Communist representatives would not accompany teams within the Government lines. Also that between the two forces, teams will be located with representatives from both sides. Further that the American member would have the authority to determine where and when the teams would go and would himself report on any actions which would, in effect, be considered violations of the truce.

The Generalissimo further agreed to the arrangement that the public announcement of the truce would be made by the American mediators and that the Government and the Communists were to refrain from any announcement.

This information was transmitted immediately at 1:30 on October 6th to the Communist representative, Mr. Wang Ping-nan for transmittal by him to General Chou En-lai in Shanghai.

Today, Tuesday October 8th, Mr. Wang Ping-nan delivered verbally the reply from Yenan through General Chou En-lai, the substance of which was as follows:

"1) The truce should be without a time limit because, based on previous experience, it would otherwise be unsatisfactory. The proposal would seem to be a strategy unless the Government troops were withdrawn to their original positions, thus demonstrating the sincerity of the Government.

"2) The Communist Party wishes to have the Three- and Five-Man Committees to meet, but the discussion should not be limited to the two paragraphs of the

October 2nd communication of the Generalissimo. These topics dealt with under truce conditions may be regarded as under military coercion.

"3) No reply had been sent to the communication of October 2nd because the Communist Party had been hoping to have some word from General Marshall and Dr. Stuart clarifying the situation for peace. The latest proposal implies that the situation has not changed much. General Chou is therefore preparing to send a formal written reply and sees no need for his returning to Nanking."

102

The Head of the Chinese Communist Party Delegation (Chou) to the Special Representative of the President (Marshall)

SHANGHAI, *October 9, 1946*

DEAR GENERAL MARSHALL: Your memo OSE 479 dated October 2, 1946, which you directed Colonel Caughey to send to me and which was attached with a memo from President Chiang under even date, has been duly received.

President Chiang's memo not only refused to reply to my demand expressed in my memo dated 30 September calling for an immediate termination of the military operations against Kalgan, but instead went so far as to raise two claims which directly run counter to the PCC resolutions and the Army Reorganization Plan. For this reason I refrained myself from making an immediate reply, but merely instructing Mr. Wang Ping-nan to deliver verbally my comment to Dr. Stuart, with a view to looking forward that you and Dr. Stuart would further exert fair and impartial efforts for the peace in China.

As was transmitted by Mr. Wang to Dr. Stuart, we could not accept President Chiang's terms for the following reasons:

1) According to the principles of the previous agreement, the Chinese Communist Party and the Democratic League must hold fourteen out of the forty seats in the state council, that is a little over one-third of the total vote, in order to ensure that the Peaceful Reconstruction Program would not be revised unilaterally. However, the Government proposal of thirteen seats could not provide such a safeguard. To regard one of the non-partisan members as belonging to the Chinese Communist Party or the Democratic League is also not in accord with the PCC resolution.

2) The list of National Assembly delegates can be produced only to the reorganized Government, and even so not until the draft constitution has been revised by the PCC, acknowledged as the only draft to be presented to the National Assembly, and the distribution of the membership of the National Assembly has been finally agreed upon. Whereas such is the procedure stipulated by the PCC resolutions, President Chiang demanded that the list of National Assembly delegates be produced to the one-party government, obviously in violation to those resolutions.

3) For an effective implementation of the Army Reorganization Plan, it is essential to determine as to where the troops of both parties will be located during the process of reorganization, and not to determine merely the location of the Communist army, while Government troops are being granted freedom to move around, to menace at any time and to attack at will the Communist troops and the populace in the Liberated Areas.

It was certainly not our expectation that that hope of ours was being mis-planted. On 7 October, I received your memorandum to Dr. Stuart under date of 6 October, thereby learning that President Chiang agreed merely under the con-dition that his two afore-mentioned demands would be carried out to postpone his military drive against Kalgan for ten days. This is obviously an ultimatum to force us to surrender. We feel therefore compelled to reject firmly that proposal.

Now, apart from instructing Messrs. Tung Pi-wu and Wang Ping-nan to trans-mit my views regarding this matter to you, I wish further to state the following, which I also request to be transmitted to President Chiang Kai-shek:

1. In my memo under date of 30 September, I have already made it clear that the military operations by the Government troops against Kalgan is a demonstra-tion of the Government determination not even to abstain from forcing a national split. At this hour, only an immediate calling-off once for all the drive against Kalgan coupled with a withdrawal of the attacking troops back to their original positions would bear ample evidence to the effect that the Government is willing to break the way for fresh negotiation and to avert a split. Failing which the responsibility for all serious consequences will automatically rest squarely with the Government.

2. With a view to showing its utmost sincerity and concessions, the Communist Party is willing, on Government immediate calling-off once for all its drive against Kalgan, to attend the Committee of Three and the informal five-man committee or the PCC steering committee, to join the simultaneous discussion on the two subjects: cessation of hostilities and implementation of the PCC resolutions. Regarding these the Chinese Communist Party has the following proposals to make:

A. Cessation of Hostilities (to be discussed by the Committee of Three):

a. Both armies shall restore their positions as of January 13 in China proper, and as of June 7 in Manchuria.

b. The location of both armies, instead of that of the Communist army alone, during the reorganization shall be determined.

c. The Government troops having been moved against previous agreements should be ordered to return to their original positions, so as to facilitate reorganization.

B. Implementation of PCC resolutions (to be discussed by the PCC Steering Committee or informal five-man committee):

a. The Chinese Communist Party and the Democratic League shall occupy fourteen seats in the state council, in order to ensure that the Peaceful Recon-struction Program would not be revised unilaterally. The distribution of these fourteen seats will be decided jointly by the Chinese Communist Party and the Democratic League.

b. The reorganization of the Executive Yuan will be taken up along with the reorganization of the state council.

c. The draft constitution, which is being revised by the PCC draft constitu-tion reviewing committee in accordance with the principles and the stipulated procedure of the PCC resolutions, will be presented to the National Assembly as the only basis for discussion. All parties and groups further pledge that they will ensure the adoption of that draft.

d. The final reconvening date of the National Assembly and the distribution of the additional National Assembly membership will be decided by the PCC steering committee.

e. After the government has been reorganized in accordance with paragraph B, items *a.* and *b.*, the various parties will produce to that government lists of their National Assembly membership following the arrangement of paragraph B, item *d.*

f. The local administrations will in accordance with the provisions of the Peaceful Reconstruction Program maintain a status quo, pending the introduction of local self-government after the reorganization of the Central government.

g. In order to ensure that the four promises regarding people's freedom and rights made by President Chiang at the PCC session on January 10 will be carried out first of all and without delay political prisoners should be released, the outrageous incidents occurred since last January should be thoroughly investigated, the culprits punished, the special service organizations should be abolished, and the newspapers, magazines, news agencies, bookstores and people's organizations banned since last January should be restored.

h. The PCC military resolution governing the divorce of military affairs from civil administrative affairs should be carried out, in order to effect demobilization.

All the afore-mentioned proposals in connection with the two big subjects, which originate from the Cease Fire Agreement, Army Reorganization Plan and the five resolutions of the PCC, are indeed the most infallible measures for solving the prevalent crisis. If the government authorities still has sincerity in implementing those agreements, there should be no reason why they do not accept them. If instead, they are but making idle talk about political settlement and implementation of the PCC resolutions, while actually they gear everything to military settlement and overthrow of the PCC resolutions, without even hesitating to force a national split by resorting to civil war and dictatorship, the Chinese Communist Party would feel itself forced to put up stubborn opposition till the very end.

With best regards   Faithfully yours,

CHOU EN-LAI

103

Address Delivered by President Chiang Kai-shek at Nanking, October 10, 1946

Fellow countrymen:

On this 35th anniversary of the birth of the Chinese Republic we commemorate the first October 10th since the return of the Government to Nanking.

To begin with, let us remember the difficulties that faced the Founder of our Republic, Dr. Sun Yat-sen, and of our Revolutionary predecessors in establishing the Republic. Let us review the fruits of sacrifices and struggles of our soldiers in resisting Japanese aggression.

Let us look ahead into the prospects for national unification and peaceful reconstruction in our country.

Let us appreciate fully the precarious nature of the position of our sovereignty and national freedom.

In view of all these we must without exception forge ahead conscientiously and with industry, to implement the teachings of Dr. Sun Yat-sen, to carry forward the task left unfinished by our Martyrs, and build a modern nation according to the Three People's Principles in order to bring about a rich, powerful and prosperous Chinese Republic.

Dr. Sun Yat-sen once said, "Like the building of a house, no rush job can be done of national reconstruction." It requires a spirit of utmost perseverance and a strength of utmost endurance.

Thirty-five years have passed since the Revolution of 1911. A comparison of our revolutionary work throughout this interval of 35 years will show that it has always been making headway. Its consummation, however, remains remote.

Our accumulated exertions from the establishment of the National Government in Nanking and the completion of the Northern Expedition, through the eight years of resistance, culminated in the defeat of Japan's aggressive might, thereby restoring to China the territory of Taiwan (Formosa) and the sovereignty of the Northeast. We have also won the abrogation of the unequal treaties and established the foundation of friendly cooperation with the rest of the world.

All these represent signal achievements of the National Revolution and should be a source of rejoicing to all, even the lost souls of the Revolution.

That our National Government was able to lead the entire nation and people with concentrated will and solidified strength to negotiate difficulty after difficulty, obstacle after obstacle, and to overcome every crisis, internal and external, until the winning of the final victory, is precisely because our program for revolution and national reconstruction corresponds with the wish and desire of the entire nation and people.

As we review our past achievements, we feel impelled to perpetuate and redouble our united efforts to safeguard our sovereignty and national freedom. Above all, we must carry out Dr. Sun Yat-sen's teachings of the Three People's Principles so that China may become unified and powerful enough to uphold peace in the Far East. On this commemorative occasion we must remember Dr. Sun Yat-sen's statement that the "objective in the founding of the Chinese Republic is peace".

A year ago today I pointed out that our future program was "national reconstruction first". Again on New Year's Day I emphasized the necessity of national unification and political democratization.

Unfortunately, as the last 10 months have gone by not one of our programs was implemented as scheduled. Even now disturbances continue unabated. It is painful indeed to see our fellow countrymen suffer directly or indirectly from national disunity, social disorder, and precarious living. I wish to take this occasion to outline for the information of my fellow countrymen just how our national foundation can be stabilized and how the abnormal state of affairs can be set straight.

The National Revolution has been aimed at the implementation of the Three People's Principles and the establishment of an equal, independent and free Chinese Republic. The basic conditions for national reconstruction are national unification and social stability. In the absence of the latter there could be no safeguard for the people's lives and property, still less for peaceful pursuit of happiness and vocations. Furthermore, increased agricultural and industrial production would be out of question and the general living standard could not be elevated.

Likewise, if national unification is not achieved, internal disturbance will multiply, democratic government will have no chance, national reconstruction will stand still, and the realization of the Three People's Principles will be impeded.

Safeguarding national unification, therefore, constitutes the first and foremost consideration of the Government in regard to the current situation in the country. It will seek unification through peaceful channels. We all know that the minimum requirements for national unification are the integration of military command and the unity of administrative decrees. To achieve integration of military command, we must carry out the nationalization of all the troops and thus establish a national army. To attain administrative unity, we must have decrees and regulations enforced throughout the country and eliminate regional domination. If and when in a nation there are two opposing armies and local governments assuming the proportions of regional domination, that nation no longer is a unified nation.

In order to win peace, therefore, we must consolidate our national unification. We may say that without national unification there can be no peace in China. National unification is the absolute condition for peace. Repudiation or violation of this condition would not only lengthen the ordeal of the people but also invite the ruin of the nation. This is a life and death issue for every citizen and also a bounded duty falling on the Government. Under no condition can the Government brook any attempt to prevent national unification or any rebellion aimed at national disintegration. Still less can the entire people and nation look on unconcernedly and allow the country and nation to be plunged headlong into an inextricable abyss. . . .

Today the peaceful avenue to national unification leads also to nationalization of all troops and political democratization. To attain political democratization, we must convoke the National Assembly and broaden the basis of the Government, thereby enabling the Government to return its rein to the people and the citizens to have actual exercise of their political power.

To attain nationalization of troops, we must follow the basis for army reorganization and integration of Communist troops into the National Army, decide where troops are to be located, decide upon the dates and set the time limit for carrying out the measures agreed upon so that no longer any party may fight for political power by force of arms. Only thus will China become a truly unified nation. . . .

Today the Government requests the various parties to participate in the National Government and to attend the National Assembly.

Today the Government asks the Chinese Communist Party to abandon its plot to achieve regional domination and disintegration of the country by military force and to participate along with all other parties in the National Government and National Assembly. Realization of this step will correspond with the agreement reached jointly by the various political parties and groups and the unanimous desire of the entire masses of the people.

It is also the hope of the Government that the various political parties and groups will bring forward according to schedule lists of their candidates to the State•Council of the National Government and their delegates to the National Assembly so that reorganization of the National Government may be carried out at an earlier date, and that the National Assembly may satisfactorily convene.

Another thing I wish especially to bring to the attention of my fellow countrymen today is the question of the cessation of armed conflicts. This has been the consistent wish of the Government. What the Government has been wishing for has been a total and permanent cessation of hostilities. The Military Committee of Three met in June this year primarily to seek agreement on restoration of communications and the determination of the location of the Communist troops thereby insuring the cease-fire order. The Committee was deadlocked on account of the obstinacy of the Communist Party.

Seeking permanent peace I, for one, during the last three months, have advanced certain proposals for consideration and acceptance by the Communists, but these were all rejected. The Communists subsequently demanded the immediate convocation of the Military Committee of Three under General George Marshall. . . .

Now the Chinese Communists have rejected the two proposals concerning the reorganization of the National Government and the implementation of the basis for army reorganization and the integration of the Communist troops into the National Army. They have also turned down the truce proposals from General Marshall and Ambassador Stuart, but the Government nevertheless is not going to abandon its policy of a peaceful settlement. It will continue to hope and seek for a settlement by mediation and consultation. The political and military conditions in the country as they are today must not be allowed to continue and thus intensify the ordeal of the people.

In view of the present tense situation and restlessness among some people due to their lack of understanding of the Government's policy, I may take this occasion to assert with all the force of emphasis that in order to break the deadlock in the current situation we must still resort to peaceful consultation in seeking the solution of some of the basic problems.

I wish to propose the convening of the twin committees at the same time. The Five-Man Group should meet to consider mutually acceptable measures for the reorganization of the National Government. The Committee of Three should meet to seek a solution of the problems bearing upon the implementation of the basis for army reorganization and integration of Communist troops into the National Army. As soon as an agreement is reached, the Government will immediately issue a "cease-fire" order provided that the Chinese Communists call a halt to their military operations and cease attacks on National troops.

The Government feels that if these suggestions materialize, the present difficulties will disappear. From the standpoint of the interests and future of the nation and people these are the only sure and passable avenues to peace.

In short, in dealing with the Chinese Communists the Government will under no circumstances whatsoever abandon its expectancy of frank and sincere negotiations if only the Chinese Communist Party will place national interest and the people's welfare above everything else, if only it will give up its prejudiced views, appreciate the Government's difficulties and carry out the aforementioned suggestions, then not merely cessation of hostilities will materialize as a natural consequence, but the mission of peaceful national reconstruction will also be accomplished smoothly.

Fellow countrymen, our undivided unity and hard struggle sustained us through eight years of resistance to foreign aggression and won for us the final victory. To pursue our heavy task of national reconstruction we must all follow with firm faith the prescribed course regardless of the difficulties. We must promote the enforcement of the Quintuple-Power Constitutional System and seek the full implementation of the Three People's Principles.

Above all, we must with concerted purpose and discerning mind consolidate national unification and stabilize social order so as to lay the framework of national reconstruction and accomplish the task of the National Revolution. Thus the nation will ever follow the road to democratic government and the nation will ever retain its glory of independence and freedom, and only thus can the unfinished work of the Founder of our Republic and our Revolutionary Predecessors be fully consummated.

104

Second Draft of Statement for Generalissimo Chiank Kai-shek [24]

A continuation of the present political and military situation in China will be destructive of the interest of a long suffering people. It will render impossible the unification of our country and will threaten the peace of the world. Therefore, it is necessary that an early solution be found to the present conflict and that peace be restored to the land. But as the responsible head of the Government of China, I must see that the necessary measures are taken to safeguard the security of the nation, since we are dealing with a political party which maintains a large army to support its political policies.

In the past three months, I have stipulated certain conditions that must be met by the Communist Party before a peaceful accord could be achieved and to which they have thus far refused to agree. They demanded an immediate meeting of the Committee of Three of which General Marshall is the chairman. That committee reached an impasse in its negotiations the latter part of June and unless there are certain preliminary but vital agreements or understandings, a meeting of the committee would not only be ineffective, but its future usefulness would be fatally impaired. I have insisted that the proposed group of five men under the chairmanship of the United States Ambassador, Dr. Stuart, selected to reach an understanding between the Government and the Communist Party for the establishment of the coalition State Council should first meet as an evidence of the good intent of both the Government and the Communist Party towards the reorganization of the government in accordance with the resolutions of the Peoples Consultative Council. With this reassurance of good faith on both sides, there would be a new basis of trust for the termination of the hostilities now disrupting China. I have further stated that concurrent with the termination of hostilities, the Communist Party should indicate its honest intention to cooperate in the reorganization of the government by announcing its delegates to the National Assembly to meet on November 12 to determine on a democratic constitution for the Government of China.

In view of the seriousness of the situation, the misunderstandings and public confusion, and the distrust and suspicions unfortunately prevalent, I now make the following public announcement of the conditions under which the government is prepared to act to secure an immediate cessation of hostilities.

The Five Man Committee under the chairmanship of Doctor Stuart to meet immediately and at the same time, the Committee of Three under the chairmanship of General Marshall, with the following understandings:

(a) The opposing troops in close contact to be separated in accordance with the procedures tentatively reached by the Committee of Three in June for Manchuria.

(b) The restoration of communications to be immediately resumed in accordance with the agreement tentatively reached by the Committee of Three last June.

(c) The method for settling disagreements among the team members of Executive Headquarters and Commissioners at Executive Headquarters to be in accordance with the agreement tentatively reached by the Committee of Three last June.

---

[24] Prepared by the Special Representative of the President (Marshall) and the Ambassador in China (Stuart), Oct. 14, 1946.

(d) The tentative agreement reached last June by the Committee of Three for the redisposition of troops in Manchuria to be confirmed.

(e) The government troops north of the Yangtze to continue in occupation of localities now under their control until the agreement by the Committee of Three is reached for the redistribution, reorganization and demobilization of troops, Government and Communist alike for the unification of the armed forces in China.

(f) Whatever understanding is reached by the Five Man Committee headed by Doctor Stuart, it is to be confirmed by the Steering Committee of the PCC without delay.

(g) Questions of local government to be settled by the newly organized State Council.

(h) The Constitutional Draft Committee to be convened immediately and the agreed draft to be submitted to the National Assembly as the basis for its action.

(i) Concurrent with the cessation of hostilities which is to be effected immediately following the agreement of the Communist Party to the foregoing procedure, that party is to announce its intention of participating in the National Assembly by publishing its lists of delegates thereto.

105

Statement by Generalissimo Chiang Kai-shek, October 16, 1946

In my October 10th broadcast to the nation, I stated that the Government has always adhered to the political solution of our domestic political problem and would not give up this policy of peaceful settlement under whatever circumstances. I further stated that the cessation of hostilities had also been the consistent policy of the Government.

The Chinese Communists rejected the recent proposal of October 2 by the Government and later also turned down the truce proposals from General Marshall and Ambassador Stuart. The Government, nevertheless, is not going to abandon its policy of "peaceful settlement" and will still seek for a settlement by mediation and consultation. The present political and military situation in the country must not be allowed to continue and thus intensify the suffering of the people. But as the responsible head of the Government of China, I must see that the necessary measures are taken to safeguard the peace and security of the nation, since we are dealing with a political party which maintains a large army to support its political policies.

In view of the new development of the situation, the earnest desire for peace by the whole nation and the hope for an early cessation of hostilities as expressed by the various parties and non-partisans in the last few days, I now reiterate the Government's sincerity in finding a peaceful solution and propose the following concrete and practical procedure, upon the Communist agreement of which, the Government is prepared to act and secure an immediate cessation of hostilities:

The Five Man Committee under the chairmanship of Doctor Stuart to meet immediately to discuss the reorganization of the National Government; and at the same time, the Committee of Three under the chairmanship of General Marshall, with the following understandings:

(1) The restoration of communications to be immediately resumed in accordance with the agreement tentatively reached by the Committee of Three last June.

(2) The method for settling disagreements among the team members of the

Executive Headquarters and commissioners at Executive Headquarters to be in accordance with the agreement tentatively reached by the Committee of Three last June.

(3) The tentative agreement reached last June by the Committee of Three for the redisposition of troops in Manchuria to be carried out according to a fixed schedule without delay.

(4) The Government troops and Communist troops in North China and Central China to continue in occupation of localities now under their control until the agreement by the Committee of Three is reached for the redistribution, reorganization and demobilization of troops, Government and Communist alike, for the unification of the armed forces in China.

(5) Whatever understanding is reached by the Five Man Committee headed by Doctor Stuart, it is to be confirmed by the Steering Committee of the PCC without delay.

(6) Questions of local government, excluding Manchuria, to be settled by the newly organized State Council.

(7) The Constitutional Draft Committee to be convened immediately and the agreed draft to be submitted to the National Assembly, through the National Government, as the basis for its action.

(8) Concurrent with the proclamation of the cessation of hostilities which is to be effected immediately following the agreement of the Communist Party to the foregoing procedure, that party is to announce its intention of participating in the National Assembly by publishing its lists of delegates thereto.

106

Proposals by the Third Party Group, October 1946

Peace is the consistent objective of the Central Government, and the cessation of hostilities has steadily been its hope. We are all moved by the sufferings of the people and realize that a speedy solution should be found. We have therefore proposed three points in the hope that both sides may reach an understanding and very promptly stop the fighting.

1. Both sides at once issue a cease firing order, the troops to remain in their present positions. The procedure for ceasing hostilities and restoring communications will be effected by the Three Man Committee through Executive Headquarters and its field teams. The troops of both sides are to be reorganized according to the previous agreements. Their allocation is to be dealt with by the Three Man Committee. (The location of Communist troops in Manchuria should be determined in advance in Tsitsihar, Peian, Chiang Mu-ssu.)

2. Local administration throughout the nation should be arranged by the reorganized State Council according to the PCC and Peaceful Reconstruction resolutions. Wherever there is dispute the military and civil issues should be separately dealt with without delay. But along the Changchun Railway, except for *hsien* already occupied by the Government, the Government should dispatch railway police to take over.

3. According to the resolutions of the PCC and the adopted procedure, the Steering Committee should be convened in order to plan the reorganization of the Government, in which case all parties will join the Government and discuss the question of calling the National Assembly, thus making it possible for all to

take part in its meetings. At the same time the Constitutional Draft Committee should be convened in order to complete its revision.

Mo Te-hui	Liang Shu-min
Carson Chang	Yu Chia-chu
Li Huang	Chang Po-chun
Huang Yen-pei	Chen Chi-t'ien
Miao Chia-ming	Lo Lung-chi
Tso Shun-sheng	Hsu Fu-liu

107

Initial Draft of Statement for Generalissimo Chiang Kai-shek [25]

On October 16th I made public a statement regarding the policy of the Government, with a series of proposals as a basis for the termination of hostilities. This was formally transmitted to the official representative of the Communist Party, but as yet no formal acknowledgement has been received. Today, on the eve of the meeting of the National Assembly, I wish to reassert the consistent policy of the Government to promote internal peace and national unity and to carry through to consummation the conclusion of the period of political tutelage and the inauguration of constitutional democracy. As a further evidence of the sincere desire of the Government to achieve a lasting peace and political stability for the country, orders have been issued for all Government troops to cease firing except as may be necessary to defend their present positions. Further, I wish to announce that the Government desires to reach an immediate agreement with the Communist Party for the unconditional termination of hostilities.

In accordance with the resolutions of the PCC, the National Assembly was to have been convened on May 5th, 1946. However, the Communist Party and the Democratic League declined to submit the list of their delegates. Later, on July 4th, an announcement was made by the Government to the effect that the National Assembly would be convened on November 12 thus leaving a period of four months for discussions and preparations by all parties concerned. There has been objection to this procedure made by minority parties on the grounds that certain steps in the reorganization of the Government under the PCC agreements had not yet been carried out. To these objections I would say that the general situation had greatly changed since the determination of the agreed procedure for the political development of the Government, serious fighting having developed in Manchuria and spread into North China. In this situation the normal procedure for reaching political agreements was rendered ineffective. However, any further postponement of the National Assembly would only serve to intensify the political and military instability as well as the sufferings of the people. Therefore, it is the decision of the Government that the Assembly be formally convened on November 12th.

The Government is prepared to agree to an immediate but temporary adjournment of the National Assembly after formal convocation until the following conditions shall have been fulfilled:

1. Sufficient time has been allowed to permit the selection and arrival of the delegates who have not yet been selected.

---

[25] Presented on Nov. 7, 1946, by the Special Representative of the President and the Ambassador in China.

2. Reorganization of the State Council has been agreed to by the PCC Steering Committee and the council established.

3. The Draft Constitution Committee shall have completed its work on a basis of the principles set forth in the PCC agreements.

When these conditions have been fulfilled, the National Assembly shall reconvene and proceed to the adoption of the Draft Constitution in the form presented.

As regards the reorganization of the Executive Yuan that, according to the PCC resolutions, is a function of the State Council. Furthermore, it involves a drastic change in the administration of the Government which must be approached with careful deliberation.

The next few weeks are of fateful importance to China. It is within our power to lay the foundations for a strong and prosperous democratic nation. We must overcome natural serious divergence of views as well as deep suspicion and bitterness. The time has come to rise above these difficulties and dedicate ourselves purely to the service of the people.

108

Statement by Generalissimo Chiang Kai-shek, November 8, 1946

On October 16th, I made public a statement regarding the policy of the Government, with a series of proposals as a basis for the termination of hostilities. I had hoped that this would evoke a response from the Communist Party leading to a final and complete cessation of war. Today, on the eve of the meeting of the National Assembly, I wish to reassert the consistent policy of the Government to promote internal peace and national unity and to carry through to consummation the conclusion of the period of political tutelage and the inauguration of constitutional democracy. As a further evidence of the sincere desire of the Government to achieve a lasting peace and political stability for the country, orders have been issued for all Government troops in China proper and the Northeast to cease firing except as may be necessary to defend their present positions.

In accordance with the resolutions of the PCC, the National Assembly was to have been convened on May 5th, 1946. However, the Communist Party and other parties declined to submit the list of their delegates. Later, on July 4th, an announcement was made by the Government to the effect that the National Assembly would be convened on November 12th, thus leaving a period of four months for discussions and preparations by all parties concerned. There has been objection to this procedure made by the minority parties, especially on the ground that certain steps in the reorganization of the Government under the PCC agreements had not been carried out. In this connection, I would say that the general situation changed greatly during the six months after the conclusion of the PCC conferences, serious fighting having developed in Manchuria and spread into the North China area, and the demobilization of Communist forces was not initiated as agreed upon and has not been started. Under these conditions the procedure for reaching political agreements was rendered ineffective. However, legally elected delegates to the National Assembly have already arrived in Nanking and any further postponement of the Assembly would serve not only to intensify political and military instability with the consequent sufferings of the people, but would deny the only legal step by which the Government can return political power to the people. Therefore, it is the decision of the Government that the Assembly be formally convened on November 12th as scheduled.

In my recent statement of October 16th, the Government showed a spirit of conciliation which it was hoped would be reciprocated by the Communists in order that a complete settlement could be reached on all pending problems. The Government stands ready to provide ample opportunity for the Communist Party and other parties to develop along truly democratic lines. Militarily, however, no political party should maintain a private army. All troops should be servants of the State.

In the meeting of the National Assembly, the Government will reserve quotas of the delegates for the Communists as well as for the other parties in the hope that they will participate in the making of the Constitution. The Government also hopes that the Communists will authorize their representatives to participate in meetings of the committees to discuss the immediate implementation of the measures for the cessation of hostilities, the disposition of troops, the restoration of communications and the reorganization and integration of armies as proposed in my statement of October 16.

It is hoped that an agreement for the reorganization of the State Council will be reached and the Council formally established. The reorganization of the Executive Yuan cannot be effected before the adjournment of the present National Assembly. As such reorganization involves a drastic change in the administration of the Government, it must be approached with careful deliberation.

As regards the draft of the Constitution, the Government will submit to the National Assembly the uncompleted draft of the Constitutional Drafting Committee. Within six months after the adjournment of the present National Assembly, a general election will take place according to the adopted Constitution. All parties and all citizens can then freely take part in this election, in order to bring into existence the next National Assembly which will exercise its functions as stipulated by the Constitution. Should any modification be found necessary in the next National Assembly, amendments still could be introduced by all parties.

The next few weeks are of fatal importance to China. It is within our power to lay the foundations for a strong and prosperous democratic nation. We must overcome the serious but natural divergencies of view as well as deep suspicions and much bitterness. The time has come to arise above these difficulties and dedicate ourselves purely to the interests of the people who so urgently need and desire peace and security. I appeal, therefore, to the members of my own and all other parties, to my colleagues in the Government and in the National Army, and to all others concerned to unite in a final effort to reach an agreement by peaceful means for achieving the "democratization of the Government" and "the nationalization of the armed forces".

109

The Head of the Chinese Communist Party Delegation (Chou) to the Special Representative of the President (Marshall)

NANKING, *November 8, 1946*

With reference to my memorandum under date of October 9th which I requested to be transmitted to the Generalissimo, I have not as yet received a reply.

As regards the Generalissimo's statement of October 16th, I have already on October 17th explained the Communist attitude and views to the Government representative, Wu Teh Chen, Shao Li Tze and Lei Cheng in Shanghai. I also explained the same to the Third Party Group on October 18th. On the same day, I received a copy of Generalissimo's memorandum to you under date of October 17th which was forwarded to me from your office. On return to Nanking I thereupon immediately explained our views to you and Dr. Stuart and I presume that you are familiar with those.

Since returning to Nanking all the negotiations were conducted through the Third Party. Through their good offices there is some possibility for the reconvening of the Committee of Three, the PCC Steering Committee and the Draft Reviewing Committee and we are still exerting efforts for this end.

CHOU EN-LAI

110

Address Delivered by President Chiang Kai-shek at Nanking, November 15, 1946 [26]

Fellow Delegates:

The National Assembly is being inaugurated today.

You, ladies and gentlemen, have come from all over China and from overseas to assemble here in the national capital with a vital assignment from the people, namely, to participate in the great task of adopting a Constitution for the Republic of China. The present occasion marks the beginning of China's evolution into the period of constitutional democracy. It is also the most august and grand convention throughout the history of the building of the Chinese Republic.

For this reason, I wish, on behalf of the National Government, to extend to you a warm welcome and to the Assembly sincere greetings.

We should all remember that the late Dr. Sun Yat-sen, in starting the National Revolution and engaging himself in a lifetime struggle, aimed to bring about the revival of China, the establishment of a republic and the implementation of the Three People's Principles, thereby converting China into a nation of, by and for the people, enjoying wealth, power and happiness. The Revolution of 1911 deposed the 4,000-year old monarchy and the Manchu despotism of more than two centuries. The significance of this incident is seen in the remark of Dr. Sun Yat-sen: "Through this revolution, democratic government became nationally acknowledged in China".

Following the founding of the Chinese Republic, however, while its foundation was yet to be strengthened and the Three People's Principles were yet to be implemented, ceaseless disturbances broke out among warlords seeking regional domination. The country was thrown into further chaos by incessant foreign inroads.

Dr. Sun Yat-sen, nevertheless, led and encouraged the revolutionary workers to carry on indomitably the struggle in spite of dangers and hardships. He explicitly made known to the entire nation his firm will and purpose when he said "China is susceptible to democracy" and "We do not concern ourselves with the mere name of republic but with actual sovereignty in the hands of the people".

The quintessence of Dr. Sun's Principle of Nationalism is "the depositing of power in the hands of the people". In other words, it is the form of government which enables the entire people to administer affairs of common concern.

---

[26] At the opening session of the National Assembly.

The formulation of the "Fundamentals of National Reconstruction" by our Republic Founder clearly charted the course of a revolutionary plan, namely, the transition from military and political tutelage to constitutional democracy. The object was to put popular government on a solid basis and to secure a strong safeguard for the republic.

The National Government, with a view to carrying forward the ideals of Dr. Sun, embarked arduously upon political tutelage as soon as it had successfully concluded the Northern Expedition in 1928. Its supreme aim was the inauguration of constitutional government and the consummation of national reconstruction.

I shall leave it to the various offices in charge to render detailed, comprehensive reports regarding preparations for the inauguration of constitutional government and the convocation of the National Assembly.

The election of delegates to the National Assembly took place throughout China shortly after the promulgation by the National Government of the Draft Constitution on May 5, 1936 and, later, of the organizational law and the electoral law of the National Assembly. Even before the war broke out in China, the Chinese Government had already decided to convene, on November 12, 1937, the National Assembly for the institution of a constitution. At that time, the election of delegates in the various localities was about to be completed.

When the war came on July 7, 1937, as a result of intensified Japanese aggression, the Government, however, could not help but pool the whole country's resources to fight for the sheer existence of the nation. The subsequent increased tempo of fighting naturally nullified democratic efforts in areas where the election of delegates was yet to be completed, and the convocation of the National Assembly ran into physical difficulties.

In spite of this, the Fifth Kuomintang Central Executive Committee at its Sixth Plenary Session in 1939 again decided to convene the National Assembly in November, 1940. Once more it was postponed, nevertheless, in view of the further spread of hostilities and the consensus of opinion of many members of the People's Political Council who urged the convocation be delayed.

At the Eleventh Plenary Session of the Kuomintang Central Executive Committee in 1943, it was decided it was necessary to definitely stipulate the date of convocation of the National Assembly. Hence, the resolution was adopted that "the National Assembly shall be convened within one year after the conclusion of the war."

I, for one, considered that the dual program of armed resistance and national reconstruction should be carried through to simultaneous consummation. The early convention of the National Assembly would bring about the early adoption of China's fundamental and vital charter and, in turn, the early realization of the long-cherished wish of the National Government to return political authority of the people. Acting upon this belief, I proposed at the plenary session of the Sixth Kuomintang National Congress in June 1945, that the National Assembly be convoked that year on November 12, the 80th birthday anniversary of Dr. Sun Yat-sen. This proposal was adopted and active preparations to that end began.

My idea at the time was that to inaugurate constitutional democracy was Dr. Sun's greatest wish, for which he had labored selflessly all his life. The temporary retirement of Dr. Sun from his success in the first year of the Republic and his consistent struggle in succeeding years were all in the interests of the welfare and freedom of the country and the people. With this in view, we and all the other people of China could not better remember Dr. Sun, our teacher of national revolution and national reconstruction, than by convening the National Assembly to adopt a constitution.

The National Assembly is meeting today already one year behind its original schedule. Fellow delegates, as we meet before the portrait of the great nation builder and recall the difficult struggle for democratic government, we must be filled with thoughts of reverence and admiration.

The foreign menace to the unification and democracy of our country was removed last year with the capitulation of Japan. But, nevertheless, ponderous difficulties beset the internal situation. The activities of an armed political party affect the nation's peace and stability while political dissensions also impair the nation's strength and power to rebuild after the war.

The National Government, on its part, is intensely aware that, following eight years of extraordinary ravages, the country must head immediately toward extraordinary reconstruction. Also, that the smooth progress of national reconstruction requires the entire nation's concerted efforts of sincerity and unity.

For this reason, the National Government, in January, this year, convoked a Political Consultation Conference wherein the representatives of the various parties and groups as well as social leaders met to discuss the vital problem of peaceful national reconstruction. Twenty days of conference yielded five agreements bearing on political and military matters. Those concerning the National Assembly included the proposal calling for the revision of the principles of the May 5th Draft Constitution, the increase of the number of delegates to the National Assembly, and the fixing of May 5, 1946 as the date of convocation of the Assembly.

As reflected in these agreements, the attitude of the National Government was consistently one of tolerance and conciliation. It approved the conclusion of every one of the agreements, inasmuch as it was guided unswervingly by a spirit to serve the interests of the country and the nation as well as by its consideration of the terrific post-war afflictions of the people and of the urgency of the national reconstruction program.

After the closing of the Political Consultation Conference, the National Government adhered faithfully to all its resolutions and carried them out one by one. The organizational law of the National Assembly was duly revised in accordance with the agreements.

In the meantime, however, numerous new difficulties cropped up and had to be surmounted. Consequently the National Assembly failed to convene on May 5 as scheduled. And until today we have been compelled to hold off the convocation of the long-expected National Assembly. All this I feel called upon to report to you, my fellow delegates, particularly those who have come long distances to the national capital and have been waiting here for so long.

The delegates to the Assembly today have come from various provinces, municipalities and localities. There are also in our midst those who have traveled from far beyond the seas to return to their fatherland for this occasion. Some of you, ladies and gentlemen, are regional delegates and some professional. Some have a vast experience in politics; others are socially preeminent.

However heterogeneous your background and representation, you must all be entertaining the unanimous, fervent hope and wish for the materialization of democracy, unity and progress in our country. Especially those delegates from the Northeast which has been under foreign rule for fourteen years and those from newly recovered Taiwan—their love and admiration for their fatherland, and their willingness and spirit to serve the country must be at an unusually high level.

I trust that you deeply appreciate the two famous sayings of Dr. Sun Yat-sen: "The foundation of a state lies in its people" and "Hundreds of millions of people are linked up to the nation." You will clearly see the relationship between the state and the people as well as the people's responsibility toward the state. You will, according to the law, discharge your respective duties bearing on the adoption of a constitution and thus introduce a good beginning for a constitutionalized China.

As we all know, the constitution of a nation is a fundamental and vital charter, in no way comparable by any ordinary law or regulation. It is an ordinance to be observed by the whole nation. On the one hand, a constitution must embody high and lofty ideals; on the other, the actual and realistic conditions in the country must be taken into consideration.

Our ideals are the Three People's Principles and the Quintuple-Power Constitutional System handed down by Dr. Sun Yat-sen: the reality of our country is that both our nation and society have, since the outbreak of the war of resistance, gone through a long period of evolution and progress. Only a constitution that embodies both ideals and reality will truly answer the needs of the country and be flawless and operative. It will insure for the nation an enduring peace and for the people a genuine well-being.

If we can dedicate ourselves to the institution of a flawless and operative constitution and thus lay down the framework of democracy and government by law, then the will of people in the various places, strata and vocations of the country, and the opinions of the various parties can all be expressed through legally charted channels. Hereafter all problems can be brought before public forums and decided thereby according to the law. Only thus will genuine independence, freedom, unification and democracy take root in our country. And only thus will our people be able to exercise true people's rights and fulfill their obligations as citizens, thereby furthering national prosperity and progress.

From the time I consecrated myself to national revolution under the leadership of Dr. Sun Yat-sen, it has always been my lifelong aim to build China into an independent, free, unified and democratic nation. Our chief war aim during the last eight years of resistance was to eliminate violence and aggression and thus to secure the independence and freedom of China. The victory finally was won through the efforts of all our people, civilian and military alike. Furthermore, along with the conclusion of new treaties with Great Britain, the United States and the Soviet Union during the war, Dr. Sun's wish to abolish all unequal treaties materialized.

Reviewing my life, however, I find my greatest regret in the fact that, from the Mukden Incident till the present moment, no constitution has yet been adopted and inaugurated. In the course of these thirty years, the wish has always been in my thoughts to conclude political tutelage and inaugurate constitutional government in order that the task of national reconstruction might be fully accomplished.

We have been carrying on the struggle of national revolution and reconstruction for the country and the people, for the realization of the Three People's Principles and democratic government based upon the Quintuple-Power Constitutional System. This is the ultimate objective in our revolution. As long as this ultimate objective remains unattained, unfulfilled remains the will of our republic founder. It will also mean that we are yet to fulfill our part towards the country, the people and the revolutionary predecessors of the last fifty years.

I wish especially to point out to you that the exercise of the political powers was delegated to the Chinese Kuomintang in 1931 by the People's Congress while the National Government was authorized to exercise the governing powers in accordance with the provisional constitution for the period of political tutelage.

Throughout these ten years and more, affairs of the state have been administered with utmost conscientiousness and feelings of responsibility.

By fighting the war to a victorious end, the National Government has barely been able to fulfill the trust of the nation. Its one and only wish now is to adopt a constitution and inaugurate constitutionalism at an early date, thus returning political power to all the people of the country and establishing a durable foundation for the Republic. And this sacred and solemn assignment to adopt a constitution is to fall squarely and equally on all of the delegates to the Assembly.

Ladies and gentlemen, after innumerable difficulties, hardships and nightmares, the present National Assembly has at long last become a reality.

In view of the difficulties Dr. Sun Yat-sen encountered in leading the revolution and of the ceaseless and bitter struggle of our revolutionary predecessors, we certainly must exert our utmost to make this Assembly worthy of Dr. Sun and the martyrs.

If only we turn our thoughts back to the Japanese aggression which impeded and delayed our program of national reconstruction, then all of us should, with might and main, accomplish this sacred mission in order that our soldiers and compatriots who gave their lives for the country during the war may not have died in vain.

Meanwhile, if we try to trace the cause for the political turmoil of the present day and also the sufferings of the people, we find that these are all due to the absence of the foundation of the state. And the present adoption of a constitution is a vital step towards stabilizing the foundation of the state and inaugurating constitutional democracy. Such is the solemn and important mission of all of the delegates.

It is indeed an unusual honor for me to attend this great convention. May I, with utmost sincerity, ask all of you to make your best efforts for the country and the success of the Assembly.

111

Statement by the Head of the Chinese Communist Party Delegation (Chou), [Nanking,] November 16, 1946

The National Assembly, a creation of the Kuomintang one-party rule Government, was convened yesterday. The convention, being called by the one-party Government alone, against the PCC decisions and the will of the people, is strongly and firmly opposed by the Communist Party. Not only the date for calling the meeting was not decided through agreement by political consultation, moreover, it is a nation-splitting National Assembly called by the Kuomintang alone, instead of a united one, joined by all political parties and groups.

According to the program and spirit of the PCC, the convention of the National Assembly is only possible, until all those PCC decisions are step by step carried out into working realities and Assembly itself directed by the reorganized Government. The PCC decisions is a temporary political charter agreed by all parties and groups. They are an integral whole which is not to be cut into disintegrating parts.

During the past ten months, all the decisions reached at the PCC have not been carried out to the least extent, furthermore, they have been totally ruined by the Kuomintang authorities. The cease fire agreement is one which has been approved by the PCC. But civil war, began from the Northeast, has extended to areas inside the Great Wall. The Government authorities have thoroughly destroyed the status quo as of Cease Fire Order of January. The four promises pledged by the responsible authority of the Government at the inaugural meeting of the PCC were utterly broken by the Kuomintang Gestapo rule from the time of the Chiaochangkou Incident in Chungking in February this year to the assassination of Li Kung-pu and Wen I-tou, leading members of the Democratic League. Up to the present, no final decision is agreed upon regarding the reorganization of the Government, thus, the peaceful national reconstruction program is also held back from its realization.

As to the local governments in the various Liberated Areas, the Kuomintang authorities in violation of the above-mentioned program, does not allow it to maintain a status quo. Furthermore, attempts have been made for the "taking over" of them. Not allowed, the Kuomintang took steps to capture the places by military occupation.

The underlying principle of the military agreements is the separation of military and civil administrations. Yet it is an obvious fact that at present almost all the provincial governors appointed by the Kuomintang Government are military men in active services.

Regarding the reviewing of the draft constitution, it is a work uncompleted in Chungking, which obliged the Communist Party to announce openly its reservation for its final approval. But this subject has been shelved up till this moment since the Government came back to Nanking.

The decision regarding the National Assembly is the last piece of compromise reached during the PCC sessions. The Kuomintang authorities at that time pledged not to call a National Assembly which is manipulated by one party alone, and which would entail a split. They also pledged to adopt the Constitution which the PCC will bring to completion, whereas all the other parties promised the acknowledgement of the delegates elected ten years ago under the Kuomintang sponsorship to be among the regional and professional delegates on the condition that delegates representing various political parties and the Liberated Areas be added. Moreover, only when the civil war is stopped, the PCC decisions are carried out, the people's freedoms are safeguarded and the reorganization of the Government is achieved, would they attend the convention, and regard the National Assembly as a united National Assembly participated in by all parties.

The National Assembly, being inaugurated now, is called in violation to the above-mentioned decisions and spirit. It is clear enough that even the date for its inauguration or postponement is decided by the one-party Government alone. According to PCC agreement, of the 2,050 delegates, there should be 410 delegates representing the various political parties and non-partisans and 200 representing the Liberated Areas. Yet the list of delegates promulgated by the Government on November 15 published names of 1,580 showing that the Government has illegally annexed 140 more seats. This exposes all the more profoundly that this National Assembly is ruled by one party and spells national split. The so-called reservation of seats for the Communists, itself a violation of the PCC agreement, is only a fraud to seduce all parties other than the Communists to join the meeting and to whitewash the Kuomintang autocracy.

In view of the painstaking efforts made by the third party group, the Chinese Communist Party has during the negotiations of the last month in Nanking made repeated representations to the effect that any form of parley will be agreeable, provided the decisions and program of the PCC are adhered to.

These, however, were again turned down by the Government authorities. And when the inauguration of the one-party National Assembly draws to a close, we firmly urged that this one-party National Assembly should be called off without delay, in order to afford an opportunity for the concurrent meeting of the military Committee of Three, the PCC Steering Committee and the Draft Constitution Reviewing Committee, which will straighten out the various current military and political problems on the basis of the Cease Fire Agreement, the Army Reorganization Agreement and the PCC decisions, and put them into effect. Amidst the peaceful atmosphere thus brought about, it would be feasible for a united National Assembly, participated in by all parties and groups, to take place. But the Government authorities, merely eager to whitewash their own dictatorship, would not pay the slightest thought to that.

The One-Party National Assembly, now being opened, denies the prospect of putting the advocacies of the Communist Party and the third party group put forward during the latest stage of negotiations into materialization. It thus destroyed once for all every resolution since the PCC, as well as the Cease Fire Agreement and the Army Reorganization Agreement, and wrecked the path of peaceful negotiations established since the PCC. At the same time, it unmasked also most drastically the fraudulent nature of the Government's "cease fire order" of November 8.

This unilateral National Assembly is now afoot to adopt a so-called "constitution", in order to "legalize" dictatorship, to "legalize" civil war, to "legalize" split, and to "legalize" the selling-out of the interests of the Nation and the people. Should that come to pass, the Chinese people shall fall headlong into the deep precipice of immense suffering. We, Chinese Communists, therefore adamantly refuse to recognize this National Assembly.

The door of negotiation has by now been slammed by the single hand of the Kuomintang authorities. All the shows that are going to be staged during the National Assembly, even the reorganization of the Government, are not worthy of our slightest attention. To attend such a National Assembly, to recognize all these shows, will constitute the throwing overboard of the PCC decisions, and the destruction of the track laid by PCC leading to peace, democracy, solidarity and unity. Regarding this issue there is no midway.

While the bloody war waged against the Liberated Areas is going on with full vigor, and the policy of the United States Government to assist Chiang in the civil war remains unchanged, a false peace, a false democracy cannot but fail to deceive the people. We, Chinese Communists, are ready to join hands with the Chinese people and all such parties which are truly working for democracy, to struggle for a genuine peace and genuine democracy to the very end.

112

The Representative of the Chinese Communist Party (Tung) to the Special Representative of the President (Marshall)

[NANKING,] December 4, 1946

MY DEAR GENERAL MARSHALL: General Chou En-lai requests the following message to be delivered to your hands :–

"With the inauguration of the one-party-manipulated National Assembly, the PCC agreements have been utterly destroyed by President Chiang Kai-shek, and there is short of a basis for the negotiation between the Kuomintang and the Chinese Communist Party. However, with a view to comply with the aspiration of the entire Chinese people for peace and democracy, our party takes the stand that if the Kuomintang would immediately dissolve the illegal National Assembly now in session, and restore the troop positions as of January 13 in accord with the Cease Fire Order, the negotiation between the two parties may still make a fresh start. Request the foregoing be transmitted to President Chiang."

Yours faithfully

(TUNG PI-WU)

113

Personal Statement by the Special Representative of the President (Marshall), January 7, 1947 [27]

The President has recently given a summary of the developments in China during the past year and the position of the American Government toward China. Circumstances now dictate that I should supplement this with impressions gained at first hand.

In this intricate and confused situation, I shall merely endeavor here to touch on some of the more important considerations—as they appeared to me—during my connection with the negotiations to bring about peace in China and a stable democratic form of government.

In the first place, the greatest obstacle to peace has been the complete, almost overwhelming suspicion with which the Chinese Communist Party and the Kuomintang regard each other.

On the one hand, the leaders of the Government are strongly opposed to a communistic form of government. On the other, the Communists frankly state that they are Marxists and intend to work toward establishing a communistic form of government in China, though first advancing through the medium of a democratic form of government of the American or British type.

The leaders of the Government are convinced in their minds that the Communist-expressed desire to participate in a government of the type endorsed by the Political Consultative Conference last January had for its purpose only a destructive intention. The Communists felt, I believe, that the government was insincere in its apparent acceptance of the PCC resolutions for the formation of the new government and intended by coercion of military force and the action of secret police to obliterate the Communist Party. Combined with this mutual deep distrust was the conspicuous error by both parties of ignoring the effect of the fears and suspicions of the other party in estimating the reason for proposals or opposition regarding the settlement of various matters under negotiation. They each sought only to take counsel of their own fears. They both, therefore, to that extent took a rather lopsided view of each situation and were susceptible to every evil suggestion or possibility. This complication was exaggerated to an explosive degree by the confused reports of fighting on the distant and tremendous fronts of hostile military contact. Patrol clashes were deliberately magnified into large offensive actions. The distortion of the facts was utilized by both sides to heap condemnation on the other. It was only through the reports of American officers in the field teams from Executive Headquarters that I could get even a partial idea of what was actually happening and the incidents were too

---

[27] *Department of State Bulletin*, Jan. 19, 1947, pp. 83–85.

numerous and the distances too great for the American personnel to cover all of the ground. I must comment here on the superb courage of the officers of our Army and Marines in struggling against almost insurmountable and maddening obstacles to bring some measure of peace to China.

I think the most important factors involved in the recent breakdown of negotiations are these: On the side of the National Government, which is in effect the Kuomintang, there is a dominant group of reactionaries who have been opposed, in my opinion, to almost every effort I have made to influence the formation of a genuine coalition government. This has usually been under the cover of political or party action, but since the Party was the Government, this action, though subtle or indirect, has been devastating in its effect. They were quite frank in publicly stating their belief that cooperation by the Chinese Communist Party in the government was inconceivable and that only a policy of force could definitely settle the issue. This group includes military as well as political leaders.

On the side of the Chinese Communist Party there are, I believe, liberals as well as radicals, though this view is vigorously opposed by many who believe that the Chinese Communist Party discipline is too rigidly enforced to admit of such differences of viewpoint. Nevertheless, it has appeared to me that there is a definite liberal group among the Communists, especially of young men who have turned to the Communists in disgust at the corruption evident in the local governments—men who would put the interest of the Chinese people above ruthless measures to establish a Communist ideology in the immediate future. The dyed-in-the-wool Communists do not hesitate at the most drastic measures to gain their end as, for instance, the destruction of communications in order to wreck the economy of China and produce a situation that would facilitate the overthrow or collapse of the Government, without any regard to the immediate suffering of the people involved. They completely distrust the leaders of the Kuomintang and appear convinced that every Government proposal is designed to crush the Chinese Communist Party. I must say that the quite evidently inspired mob actions of last February and March, some within a few blocks of where I was then engaged in completing negotiations, gave the Communists good excuse for such suspicions.

However, a very harmful and immensely provocative phase of the Chinese Communist Party procedure has been in the character of its propaganda. I wish to state to the American people that in the deliberate misrepresentation and abuse of the action, policies and purposes of our Government this propaganda has been without regard for the truth, without any regard whatsoever for the facts, and has given plain evidence of a determined purpose to mislead the Chinese people and the world and to arouse a bitter hatred of Americans. It has been difficult to remain silent in the midst of such public abuse and wholesale disregard of facts, but a denial would merely lead to the necessity of daily denials; an intolerable course of action for an American official. In the interest of fairness, I must state that the Nationalist Government publicity agency has made numerous misrepresentations, though not of the vicious nature of the Communist propaganda. Incidentally, the Communist statements regarding the Anping incident which resulted in the death of three Marines and the wounding of twelve others were almost pure fabrication, deliberately representing a carefully arranged ambuscade of a Marine convoy with supplies for the maintenance of Executive Headquarters and some UNRRA supplies, as a defence against a Marine assault. The investigation of this incident was a tortuous procedure of delays and maneuvers to disguise the true and privately admitted facts of the case.

Sincere efforts to achieve settlement have been frustrated time and again by extremist elements of both sides. The agreements reached by the Political Consultative Conference a year ago were a liberal and forward-looking charter which then offered China a basis for peace and reconstruction. However, irreconcilable groups within the Kuomintang, interested in the preservation of their own feudal control of China, evidently had no real intention of implementing them. Though I speak as a soldier, I must here also deplore the dominating influence of the military. Their dominance accentuates the weakness of civil government in China. At the same time, in pondering the situation in China, one must have clearly in mind not the workings of small Communist groups or committees to which we are accustomed in America, but rather of millions of people and an army of more than a million men.

I have never been in a position to be certain of the development of attitudes in the innermost Chinese Communist circles. Most certainly, the course which the Chinese Communist Party has pursued in recent months indicated an unwillingness to make a fair compromise. It has been impossible even to get them to sit down at a conference table with Government representatives to discuss given issues. Now the Communists have broken off negotiations by their last offer which demanded the dissolution of the National Assembly and a return to the military positions of January 13th which the Government could not be expected to accept.

Between this dominant reactionary group in the Government and the irreconcilable Communists who, I must state, did not so appear last February, lies the problem of how peace and well-being are to be brought to the long-suffering and presently inarticulate mass of the people of China. The reactionaries in the Government have evidently counted on substantial American support regardless of their actions. The Communists by their unwillingness to compromise in the national interest are evidently counting on an economic collapse to bring about the fall of the Government, accelerated by extensive guerrilla action against the long lines of rail communications—regardless of the cost in suffering to the Chinese people.

The salvation of the situation, as I see it, would be the assumption of leadership by the liberals in the Government and in the minority parties, a splendid group of men, but who as yet lack the political power to exercise a controlling influence. Successful action on their part under the leadership of Generalissimo Chiang Kai-shek would, I believe, lead to unity through good government.

In fact, the National Assembly has adopted a democratic constitution which in all major respects is in accordance with the principles laid down by the all-party Political Consultative Conference of last January. It is unfortunate that the Communists did not see fit to participate in the Assembly since the constitution that has been adopted seems to include every major point that they wanted.

Soon the Government in China will undergo major reorganization pending the coming into force of the constitution following elections to be completed before Christmas Day 1947. Now that the form for a democratic China has been laid down by the newly adopted constitution, practical measures will be the test. It remains to be seen to what extent the Government will give substance to the form by a genuine welcome of all groups actively to share in the responsibility of government.

The first step will be the reorganization of the State Council and the executive branch of Government to carry on administration pending the enforcement of the constitution. The manner in which this is done and the amount of representation accorded to liberals and to non-Kuomintang members will be significant.

It is also to be hoped that during this interim period the door will remain open for Communists or other groups to participate if they see fit to assume their share of responsibility for the future of China.

It has been stated officially and categorically that the period of political tutelage under the Kuomintang is at an end. If the termination of one-party rule is to be a reality, the Kuomintang should cease to receive financial support from the Government.

I have spoken very frankly because in no other way can I hope to bring the people of the United States to even a partial understanding of this complex problem. I have expressed all these views privately in the course of negotiations; they are well known, I think, to most of the individuals concerned. I express them now publicly, as it is my duty, to present my estimate of the situation and its possibilities to the American people who have a deep interest in the development of conditions in the Far East promising an enduring peace in the Pacific.

114

Statement by President Truman on United States Policy Toward China, December 18, 1946 [28]

Last December I made a statement of this Government's views regarding China. We believed then and do now that a united and democratic China is of the utmost importance to world peace, that a broadening of the base of the National Government to make it representative of the Chinese people will further China's progress toward this goal, and that China has a clear responsibility to the other United Nations to eliminate armed conflict within its territory as constituting a threat to world stability and peace. It was made clear at Moscow last year that these views are shared by our Allies, Great Britain and the Soviet Union. On December 27th, Mr. Byrnes, Mr. Molotov and Mr. Bevin issued a statement which said, in part:

"The three Foreign Secretaries exchanged views with regard to the situation in China. They were in agreement as to the need for a unified and democratic China under the National Government for broad participation by democratic elements in all branches of the National Government, and for a cessation of civil strife. They affirmed their adherence to the policy of non-interference in the internal affairs of China."

The policies of this Government were also made clear in my statement of last December. We recognized the National Government of the Republic of China as the legal government. We undertook to assist the Chinese Government in reoccupation of the liberated areas and in disarming and repatriating the Japanese invaders. And finally, as China moved toward peace and unity along the lines mentioned, we were prepared to assist the Chinese economically and in other ways.

I asked General Marshall to go to China as my representative. We had agreed upon my statement of the United States Government's views and policies regarding China as his directive. He knew full well in undertaking the mission that halting civil strife, broadening the base of the Chinese Government and bringing about a united, democratic China were tasks for the Chinese themselves. He

---

[28] *Department of State Bulletin,* Dec. 29, 1946, pp. 1179–1183.

went as a great American to make his outstanding abilities available to the Chinese.

During the war, the United States entered into an agréement with the Chinese Government regarding the training and equipment of a special force of 39 divisions. That training ended V–J Day and the transfer of the equipment had been largely completed when General Marshall arrived.

The .United States, the United Kingdom and the Union of Soviet Socialist Republics all committed themselves to the liberation of China, including the return of Manchuria to Chinese control. Our Government had agreed to assist the Chinese Government in the reoccupation of areas liberated from the Japanese, including Manchuria, because of China's lack of shipping and transport planes. Three armies were moved by air and eleven by sea, to central China, Formosa, north China and Manchuria. Most of these moves had been made or started when General Marshall arrived.

The disarming and evacuation of Japanese progressed slowly—too slowly. We regarded our commitment to assist the Chinese in this program as of overwhelming importance to the future peace of China and the whole Far East. Surrendered but undefeated Japanese armies and hordes of administrators, technicians, and Japanese merchants, totalling about 3,000,000 persons, had to be removed under the most difficult conditions. At the request of the Chinese Government we had retained a considerable number of American troops in China, and immediately after V–J Day we landed a corps of Marines in north China. The principal task of these forces was to assist in the evacuation of Japanese. Only some 200,000 had been returned to Japan by the time General Marshall arrived.

General Marshall also faced a most unpropitious internal situation on his arrival in China. Communications throughout the country were badly disrupted due to destruction during the war and the civil conflicts which had broken out since. This disruption was preventing the restoration of Chinese economy, the distribution of relief supplies, and was rendering the evacuation of Japanese a slow and difficult process. The wartime destruction of factories and plants, the war-induced inflation in China, the Japanese action in shutting down the economy of occupied China immediately after V–J Day, and finally the destruction of communications combined to paralyze the economic life of the country, spreading untold hardship to millions, robbing the victory over the Japanese of significance to most Chinese and seriously aggravating all the tensions and discontents that existed in China.

Progress toward solution of China's internal difficulties by the Chinese themselves was essential to the rapid and effective completion of most of the programs in which we had already pledged our assistance to the Chinese Government. General Marshall's experience and wisdom were available to the Chinese in their efforts to reach such solutions.

Events moved rapidly upon General Marshall's arrival. With all parties availing themselves of his impartial advice, agreement for a country-wide truce was reached and announced on January 10th. A feature of this agreement was the establishment of a unique organization, the Executive Headquarters in Peiping. It was realized that due to poor communications and the bitter feelings on local fronts, generalized orders to cease fire and withdraw might have little chance of being carried out unless some authoritative executive agency, trusted by both sides, could function in any local situation.

The Headquarters operated under the leaders of three commissioners—one American who served as chairman, one Chinese Government representative, and one representative of the Chinese Communist Party. Mr. Walter S. Robertson, Charge d'Affaires of the American Embassy in China, served as chairman until his return to this country in the fall. In order to carry out its function in the field, Executive Headquarters formed a large number of truce teams, each headed by one American officer, one Chinese Government officer, and one Chinese Communist officer. They proceeded to all danger spots where fighting was going on or seemed impending and saw to the implementation of the truce terms, often under conditions imposing exceptional hardships and requiring courageous action. The degree of cooperation attained between Government and Communist officers in the Headquarters and on the truce teams was a welcome proof that despite two decades of fighting, these two Chinese groups could work together.

Events moved forward with equal promise on the political front. On January 10th, the Political Consultative Conference began its sessions with representatives of the Kuomintang or Government Party, the Communist Party and several minor political parties participating. Within three weeks of direct discussion these groups had come to a series of statesmanlike agreements on outstanding political and military problems. The agreements provided for an interim government of a coalition type with representation of all parties, for revision of the Draft Constitution along democratic lines prior to its discussion and adoption by a National Assembly and for reduction of the Government and Communist armies and their eventual amalgamation into a small modernized truly national army responsible to a civilian government.

In March, General Marshall returned to this country. He reported on the important step the Chinese had made toward peace and unity in arriving at these agreements. He also pointed out that these agreements could not be satisfactorily implemented and given substance unless China's economic disintegration were checked and particularly unless the transportation system could be put in working order. Political unity could not be built on economic chaos. This Government had already authorized certain minor credits to the Chinese Government in an effort to meet emergency rehabilitation needs as it was doing for other war devastated countries throughout the world. A total of approximately $66,000,000 was involved in six specific projects, chiefly for the purchase of raw cotton, and for ships and railroad repair material. But these emergency measures were inadequate. Following the important forward step made by the Chinese in the agreements as reported by General Marshall, the Export-Import Bank earmarked a total of $500,000,000 for possible additional credits on a project by project basis to Chinese Government agencies and private enterprises. Agreement to extend actual credits for such projects would obviously have to be based upon this Government's policy as announced December 15, 1945. So far, this $500,000,000 remains earmarked, but unexpended.

While comprehensive large scale aid has been delayed, this Government has completed its wartime lend-lease commitments to China. Lend-lease assistance was extended to China to assist her in fighting the Japanese, and later to fulfill our promise to assist in re-occupying the country from the Japanese. Assistance took the form of goods and equipment and of services. Almost half the total made available to China consisted of services, such as those involved in air and water transportation of troops. According to the latest figures reported, lend-lease assistance to China up to V-J Day totalled approximately $870,000,000. From V-J Day to the end of February, shortly after General Marshall's arrival, the total was approximately $600,000,000—mostly in transportation costs.

Thereafter, the program was reduced to the fulfillment of outstanding commitments, much of which was later suspended.

A considerable quantity of civilian goods has also been made available by our agreement with China for the disposal of surplus property which enabled us to liquidate a sizable indebtedness and to dispose of large quantities of surplus material. During the war the Chinese Government furnished Chinese currency to the United States Army for use in building its installations, feeding the troops, and other expenses. By the end of the war this indebtedness amounted to something like 150,000,000,000 Chinese dollars. Progressive currency inflation in China rendered it impossible to determine the exact value of the sum in United States currency.

China agreed to buy all surplus property owned by the United States in China and on seventeen Pacific Islands and bases with certain exceptions. Six months of negotiations preceded the agreement finally signed in August. It was imperative that this matter be concluded in the Pacific as had already been done in Europe, especially in view of the rapid deterioration of the material in open storage under tropical conditions and the urgent need for the partial alleviation of the acute economic distress of the Chinese people which it was hoped this transaction would permit. Aircraft, all non-demilitarized combat material, and fixed installations outside of China were excluded. Thus, no weapons which could be used in fighting a civil war were made available through this agreement.

The Chinese Government cancelled all but 30,000,000 United States dollars of our indebtedness for the Chinese currency, and promised to make available the equivalent of 35,000,000 United States dollars for use in paying United States governmental expenses in China and acquiring and improving buildings and properties for our diplomatic and consular establishments. An additional sum of 20,000,000 United States dollars is also designated for the fulfillment of a cultural and educational program.

Before General Marshall arrived in China for the second time, in April, there was evidence that the truce agreement was being disregarded. The sincere and unflagging efforts of Executive Headquarters and its truce teams have succeeded in many instances in preventing or ending local engagements and thus saved thousands of lives. But fresh outbreaks of civil strife continued to occur, reaching a crisis of violence in Manchuria with the capture of Changchun by the Communists and where the presence of truce teams had not been fully agreed to by the National Government.

A change in the course of events in the political field was equally disappointing. Negotiations between the Government and the Communists have been resumed again and again, but they have as often broken down. Although hope for final success has never disappeared completely, the agreements made in January and February have not been implemented, and the various Chinese groups have not since that time been able to achieve the degree of agreement reached at the Political Consultative Conference.

There has been encouraging progress in other fields, particularly the elimination of Japanese from China. The Chinese Government was responsible under an Allied agreement for the disarmament of all Japanese military personnel and for the repatriation of all Japanese civilians and military personnel from China, Formosa and French Indo-China north of the sixteenth degree of latitude. Our Government agreed to assist the Chinese in this task. The scope of the job was tremendous. There were about 3,000,000 Japanese, nearly one-half of them

Army or Navy personnel to be evacuated. Water and rail transportation had been destroyed or was immobilized. Port facilities were badly damaged and overcrowded with relief and other supplies. The Japanese had to be disarmed, concentrated and then transported to the nearest available port. In some instances this involved long distances. At the ports they had to be individually searched and put through a health inspection. All had to be inoculated. Segregation camps had to be established at the ports to cope with the incidence of epidemic diseases such as Asiatic cholera. Finally, 3,000,000 persons had to be moved by ship to Japan.

American forces helped in the disarmament of Japanese units. Executive Headquarters and its truce teams were able to make the complicated arrangements necessary to transfer Japanese across lines and through areas involved in civil conflict on their way to ports of embarkation. American units also participated in the inspections at the port, while American medical units supervised all inoculation and other medical work. Finally, American and Japanese ships under the control of General MacArthur in Japan, and a number of United States Navy ships under the Seventh Fleet transported this enormous number of persons to reception ports in Japan.

At the end of last year, approximately 200,000 Japanese had been repatriated. They were leaving Chinese ports at a rate of about 2,500 a day. By March of this year, rapidly increased efforts on the part of the American forces and the Chinese authorities involved had increased this rate to more than 20,000 a day. By November, 2,986,438 Japanese had been evacuated and the program was considered completed. Except for indeterminate numbers in certain parts of Manchuria, only war criminals and technicians retained on an emergency basis by the Chinese Government remain. That this tremendous undertaking has been accomplished despite conflict, disrupted communications and other difficulties will remain an outstanding example of successful American-Chinese cooperation toward a common goal.

Much has been said of the presence of United States armed forces in China during the past year. Last fall these forces were relatively large. They had to be. No one could prophesy in advance how well the Japanese forces in China would observe the surrender terms. We had to provide forces adequate to assist the Chinese in the event of trouble. When it became obvious that the armed Japanese would not be a problem beyond the capabilities of the Chinese Armies to handle, redeployment was begun at once.

The chief responsibility of our forces was that of assisting in evacuation of Japanese. This task was prolonged by local circumstances. Provision of American personnel for the Executive Headquarters and its truce teams has required a fairly large number of men, particularly since the all important network of radio and other communications was provided entirely by the United States. The Executive Headquarters is located at Peiping, a hundred miles from the sea and in an area where there was the possibility of local fighting. Hence, another responsibility was to protect the line of supply to and from Headquarters. Another duty our forces undertook immediately upon the Japanese surrender was to provide the necessary protection so that coal from the great mines northeast of Tientsin could reach the sea for shipment to supply the cities and railroads of central China. This coal was essential to prevent the collapse of this industrial area. Our Marines were withdrawn from this duty last September. Other units of our forces were engaged in searching for the bodies or graves of American soldiers who had died fighting the Japanese in China. Still others were required to guard United States installations and stores of equipment, and to process these for return to this country or sale as surplus property.

At peak strength a year ago we had some 113,000 soldiers, sailors and marines in China. Today this number is being reduced to less than 12,000, including some 2,000 directly concerned with the operations of Executive Headquarters and will be further reduced to the number required to supply and secure the American personnel of Executive Headquarters and the air field and stores at Tsingtao.

Thus during the past year we have successfully assisted in the repatriation of the Japanese and have subsequently been able to bring most of our own troops home. We have afforded appropriate assistance in the reoccupation of the country from the Japanese. We have undertaken some emergency measures of economic assistance to prevent the collapse of China's economy and have liquidated our own wartime financial account with China.

It is a matter of deep regret that China has not yet been able to achieve unity by peaceful methods. Because he knows how serious the problem is, and how important it is to reach a solution, General Marshall has remained at his post even though active negotiations have been broken off by the Communist Party. We are ready to help China as she moves toward peace and genuine democratic government.

The views expressed a year ago by this Government are valid today. The plan for political unification agreed to last February is sound. The plan for military unification of last February has been made difficult of implementation by the progress of the fighting since last April, but the general principles involved are fundamentally sound.

China is a sovereign nation. We recognize that fact and we recognize the National Government of China. We continue to hope that the Government will find a peaceful solution. We are pledged not to interfere in the internal affairs of China. Our position is clear. While avoiding involvement in their civil strife, we will persevere with our policy of helping the Chinese people to bring about peace and economic recovery in their country.

As ways and means are presented for constructive aid to China, we will give them careful and sympathetic consideration. An example of such aid is the recent agricultural mission to China under Dean Hutchison of the University of California sent at the request of the Chinese Government. A joint Chinese-American Agricultural Collaboration Commission was formed which included the Hutchison mission. It spent over four months studying rural problems. Its recommendations are now available to the Chinese Government, and so also is any feasible aid we can give in implementing those recommendations. When conditions in China improve, we are prepared to consider aid in carrying out other projects, unrelated to civil strife, which would encourage economic reconstruction and reform in China and which, in so doing, would promote a general revival of commercial relations between American and Chinese businessmen.

We believe that our hopes for China are identical with what the Chinese people themselves most earnestly desire. We shall therefore continue our positive and realistic policy toward China which is based on full respect for her national sovereignty and on our traditional friendship for the Chinese people and is designed to promote international peace.

115

Press Release Issued by the Department of State, January 29, 1947

The United States Government has decided to terminate its connection with the Committee of Three which was established in Chungking for the purpose of terminating hostilities in China and of which General Marshall was Chairman. The United States Government also has decided to terminate its connection with Executive Headquarters which was established in Peiping by the Committee of Three for the purpose of supervising, in the field, the execution of the agreements for the cessation of hostilities and the demobilization and reorganization of the Armed Forces in China.

The American personnel involved in Executive Headquarters will be withdrawn as soon as possible.

Annexes to Chapter VI: The Ambassador-ship of John Leighton Stuart, 1947–1949

116(a)

Statement Issued January 20, 1947, by the Ministry of Information, Chinese National Government

893.00/1–2147

With a view to establishing constitutional rule and completing national reconstruction, the government has been consistently seeking for peace and unification. As far back as the beginning of the war of resistance, in order to pool together the nation's efforts, the government called the People's Political Council consisting of representatives of all political parties and independents.

From start to finish, the government has regarded the Communist problem as a political problem. The Kuomintang at its tenth CEC plenary session in 1942 and eleventh plenary session the following year persistently advocated an early solution through political means.

After May 1944 the government has been negotiating with the Communist Party without letup in the hope that a peaceful settlement could be reached.

When the Committee for Promotion of Constitutional Rule met on March 1, 1945, President Chiang Kai-shek, being convinced that the Communist problem, if left unsolved, would constitute a serious obstacle in the way of national unification and reconstruction, reiterated his determination of finding a peaceful solution without delay. He also proposed three steps leading toward constitutional government.

After victory, President Chiang Kai-shek invited Communist leader, Mr. Mao Tse Tung, to Chungking for discussions. These discussions resulted in the Double Tenth Agreement with the announcement that negotiations would be continued on the basis of mutual trust and concessions so that satisfactory results will be achieved.

Since the Political Consultative Conference last January, agreements have been reached between the Government and Communists on military and communications problems with the help of United States special envoy General George C. Marshall. These agreements raised hope throughout the world that the Communist problem in China would be solved through political means.

The Government and Kuomintang, especially in the resolution of the party's second plenary session, repeatedly pledged support to the PCC resolutions and expressed their willingness to implement them in cooperation with the other political parties and independents. The failure of realization of the PCC resolution is due to the following factors:

First, according to the Sino-Soviet treaty, the National Government should take over the administration in the nine northeast provinces. When the Soviet troops began withdrawing, Communist troops obstructed in various ways the takeover work of the national army. In the middle of March last year the Communists occupied various places already taken over by the government forces in Liaopei and attacked Ssupingchieh, Harbin and Tsitsihar. In order to fulfill its treaty obligations and assert its right to recover sovereingty over the northeast, the government on March 27 reached an agreement with the Communists for sending truce field teams to the northeast. Unfortunately nothing was achieved despite the efforts of the field teams under the Executive Headquarters, thus the northeast remains in chaotic conditions. The National Assembly scheduled by PCC to convene on May 5 had to be postponed.

Two. Since the Government returned to Nanking in May 1946, conflicts in the northeast were further intensified and communications in North China continued to be disrupted. The government jointly with the Communists issued a cease fire order for 15 days during which it hoped to put a full stop to the hostilities in the northeast, to restore communications lines throughout the country and to implement the army reorganization plan. On all these three points, the Government and the Communist Party had almost reached agreements. But though the deadline of the truce period was postponed three times, the Communists intensified their attacks during the interval, capturing Tehchow, Taian and attacking Tatung, Tsinan and the outer rim of Tsingtao. Again nothing was achieved.

Three. Before the National Assembly was convoked, in view of the confused domestic conditions and the countrywide demand for peace and especially the sincerity and earnest desire of the various political parties and independents for the early termination of hostilities, the government on October 16 proposed to the Communists an eight point peace program, in the hope that another cease fire order be issued and the National Assembly be called as scheduled to enact a constitution. But despite the strenuous mediatory efforts of the minority parties, and despite the government's intention to make concessions, the Communists stood adamant in its opposition to the compromise suggestion and demanded further postponement of the National Assembly. A deadlock was thus reached.

After the adjournment of the National Assembly, the government, with the date set for the enforcement of the constitution, made further efforts for the resumption of the peace talks. Through Doctor J. Leighton Stuart, United States Ambassador, the government informed the Communist Party of its willingness to send a representative to Yenan to resume the peace negotiations. But the Communists still insisted on the restoration of the troops dispositions extant on January 13 last year, and on the annulment of the constitution adopted by the National Assembly as the sine qua non conditions. But the fact is that great changes have occurred in the troops dispositions during the past year since January 13. It is practically impossible to revert to the original positions. Moreover withdrawal of government troops from recovered areas would surely endanger the peoples lives and property in those areas—a thing most incompatible with the government's obligation to restore order and protect the people and to prevent the recurrence of Communist terrorism.

If the Communists are really sincere to achieve peace, they should implement the army reorganization plan and other programs reached in the committee of three. If so, there should be no need for any dispute over the temporary dispositions of the troops.

As regards the annulment of the constitution, the National Assembly consisted of district, occupational and racial representatives and delegates from various political parties, in accordance with PCC resolution. The Assembly, therefore, was by no means a KMT-dominated Assembly. Moreover, the constitution adopted by the Assembly embodies the very principles laid down by the Communist Party and the other parties represented in the Political Consultative Conference, and in the draft constitution reviewing committee. Therefore, there should not be any reason for the Communists to object to the constitution.

The above stated fact clearly indicated that in order to achieve peace and unity, the government has made the greatest possible concessions to appeal to the reasonable consideration of the Communists. Since political democratization and nationalization of troops were common objectives of the PCC there seems to be no reason why the Communists should cling to their prejudices and suspicions.

Now the war has been over for more than a year, peace and unity must be achieved without delay. It is fervently hoped that the Communists will appreciate the government's earnest efforts to seek a political settlement and agree to resume negotiations. The government is still ready to meet the Communists with tolerance and sincerity.

The government thereby proposes the following four points for the resumption of the peace talks and government reorganization. The four points are:

1. The government is willing to send a representative to Yenan, or to invite Communist delegates to come to Nanking to resume the peace talks, or to call a round-table conference to be attended by representatives of the various parties and independents.

2. The government and the Communists will immediately order their troops to cease hostilities and remain at their present positions and negotiate effective measures to ensure cessation of hostilities.

3. The government is prepared to resume negotiations with the Communists for the enforcement of the army reorganization plan and then restoration of communication agreement in accordance with the principles laid down by the Committee of Three.

4. Before the full operation of the constitution, the government is willing to work out a just and equitable plan for solving the much controverted problem of regional administration.

116 (b)

Statement by Lu Ting-yi, Chief of the Department of Information, Central Committee, Chinese Communist Party

893.00/1-2947

[*January 29, 1947.*]

The entire content of the statement by the Kuomintang Ministry of Information is rejection of the two conditions raised by the Chinese Communist Party for restoring peace negotiations—it is rejection of nullification of Chiang Kai-shek's false Constitution and of restoration of military positions of January 13, 1946. Moreover, it raises four points of so-called peace proposal.

These four points have already been transmitted by Chiang Kai-shek to the Chinese Communist Party. It is clear that the so-called peace negotiations are complete fraud and the so-called four points are employed to reject prerequisites for real peace negotiations. Inasmuch as these prerequisites are rejected, what kind of sincerity or peace negotiations remain to be spoken of?

Nullifying Chiang Kai-shek's fake Constitution and restoring the military position of January 13 last year these objectives must and can be attained. If Chiang can utilize every means of fraud and force to transfer 90% of his military strength to attack liberated areas, why then cannot he transfer these armies back to the position of January 13 in pursuance of needs of peace? Already more than 300,000 war prisoners have been captured from Chiang's invading armies by people's liberation armies. From army and division commanders down to rank and file soldiers everyone expresses their unwillingness to fight civil war and everyone yearns to make peace and return to their original positions. Why then must Chiang Kai-shek plunge them into civil war to become cannon fodder? As for so-called "during past year changes in positions of both sides have been extremely great" and therefore restoration of military positions of January 13 last year is impracticable—is this not the clearest deception? Another reason for the statement of the Kuomintang Ministry of Information's rejecting restoration of military positions of January 13 last year is "as soon as the Government withdraws from territories already recovered, people in those areas would have nothing to rely on for their lives and properties" this is utter fabrication. Chiang Kai-shek's armies have occupied over 160 liberated area cities, 179,000 square kilometers of liberated area territory, where dwell over 20,000,000 people of liberated areas—equal to half the population of France. Before invasion and occupation [by] Chiang Kai-shek's troops peasants in these areas had already carried out "land to tillers", democratic governments had already been established, traitors, Japanese, collaborators had already been punished, people of all ranks and classes were living and working in peace and happiness. There were no scourges, no economic crises. After Chiang's troops invaded and occupied these places, the peasant's land was confiscated, Fascist secret police terrorized the populace, traitors, collaborators and local tyrants came back and were made officials by Chiang Kai-shek's Government. Chiang Kai-shek's officials and armies burned, murdered, raped, carried out exorbitant taxation, and conscription of soldiers and grain and corruption pervaded everywhere. Over 20,000,000 people again suffer from the boundless misery of Chiang Kai-shek's dictatorship.

Chiang Kai-shek in truth exhausts his energies in protecting traitors, secret police agents, evil gentry and corrupt officials. Where does he have even one minute in which to protect the lives and properties of people? Precisely for the sake of protecting the lives and properties of people, Chiang Kai-shek's armies should be withdrawn from all of the invaded and occupied territories.

As for the so-called truce at present positions Chiang Kai-shek's "peace proposal", everyone should remember that truce at present positions has taken place three times since the truce order of last January 13. The January truce order was the first time the March 27 cease fire order for Manchuria was the second time and the truce and peace negotiations of last January was the third time. In each case Chinese Communist Party made positive concessions, but the result of these concessions was that Chiang Kai-shek three times in succession broke the agreements. You don't mean to say that the Chinese people are all a bunch of block heads, and after all this must still give Chiang Kai-shek a fourth truce at present positions so that he can break it for the fourth time? So that he can entirely wipe out all liberated areas? Who can guarantee that he will not do this? The present so-called "truce at present positions" of the Kuomintang is truce at "present positions" after Chiang Kai-shek has completely torn up the truce order, PCC resolutions and launched unprecedented large-scale civil war.

This is in order to have the Chinese people recognize the results obtained by his use of military force in faithless betrayal of all agreements and trusts, and thus to encourage warlords to carry out the idle dream of unity through force, and to encourage the reactionaries recklessly to tear up all agreements and wage large-scale civil war. Chiang Kai-shek repeatedly says he believes in "political settlement" but his real activity is "military settlement". If the Chinese people were to agree to this, what hope for peace would there be? If the Chinese Communist Party were to agree to this, what could they say to the people? The Chinese Communist Party for the sake of the people's happiness absolutely cannot recognize the results achieved with military force thus in defiance of law. Therefore, the Chinese Communist Party absolutely cannot agree to so-called "truce in present positions". (which in reality is scheme to wipe *thirteenth* must be completely restored.) The 90% of Chiang Kai-shek's armies which have been illegally transferred must one and all return to their original positions. Otherwise there is absolutely no guarantee of peace.

With regard to the third and fourth points of Chiang Kai-shek's "peace formula"—reorganization of armies, restoration of communications, local governments, et cetera—they have been raised and talked over innumerable times in the past, but either no results were reached or if results were reached they were torn up by Chiang Kai-shek. Before Chiang Kai-shek nullifies the false Constitution and restores positions of January 13, these questions cannot be discussed at all. Hence the first point of Chiang Kai-shek's "peace formula" alleging that the "Government is willing to send a representative to Yenan for talks or even hold a round-table conference, et cetera" is not necessary before the two conditions of the Chinese Communist Party are carried out. Raising of such points by Chiang Kai-shek is but empty stalling to deceive people.

Chiang Kai-shek's fake Constitution must be nullified and can be nullified. This is the third fake Constitution since the country was called the Chinese Republic. Since the two fake Constitutions of Yuan Shih-kai and Tsao Kun were nullified why then cannot Chiang Kai-shek's fake Constitution be nullified since Chiang Kai-shek has treacherously betrayed and violated PCC decisions by unilaterally calling the "National Assembly" and passing the fake Constitution? The people have every reason to order him to nullify his fake Constitution.

The Kuomintang Ministry of Information states that the "Chinese Communist Party has no reason whatsoever to oppose" this Chiang Kai-shek fake Constitution. It can, however, be asked, what reason has Chiang Kai-shek for manufacturing such Constitutions? Did the Chinese people not have reason for nullifying the fake Constitutions of Yuan Shih-kai and Tsao Kun? Since Chiang Kai-shek has manufactured such a fake Constitution, not nullifying it would be tantamount to recognizing Fascist dictatorship, violating of laws and breaking of discipline by warlords; where then can there be talk of political democracy and nationalization of armies? Hence the fake Constitution must be nullified.

The overwhelming bulk of public opinion at home as well as abroad heaped imprecations in concert on the "National Assembly" called by Chiang Kai-shek. The Chinese Communist Party and democrats of all quarters long ago advised Chiang Kai-shek not to convene a one-party illegal National Assembly. But Chiang Kai-shek persisted in ignoring this. When Chiang Kai-shek's National Assembly opened we again advised him to dissolve it but he again refused to listen. Such unbridled lawlessness of Chiang Kai-shek will definitely not be permitted by the Chinese people. The Chinese people and real democrats will absolutely not recognize the validity of such an illegal National Assembly of division.

With regard to representatives of Chiang Kai-shek's "National Assembly" most of them were appointed handpicked and produced through bribed elections. Part of them were provisionally "supplemented" by Chiang Kai-shek and his cronies. Among them are traitors. This National Assembly is worse than the rump assembly of Tsao Kun. Where are the "representatives of all nationalities, all provinces and municipalities and all professions"? When was Chiang Kai-shek's fake Constitution ever finally examined by the Political Consultation Conference? Which of the main question of principles such as people's rights, autonomy of national minorities, relations between legislature and executive, distribution of powers between central and local governments in this fake Constitution accords with PCC principles? Refusal of Chiang Kai-shek to nullify the malodorous Fascist fake Constitution is really a "stubborn clinging to one's opinion," calamity to the entire country, betrayal of the people, betrayal of the nation and determination to be reactionary to the last!

Nullification of the false Constitution and restoration of the military positions of January 13 last year are minimum prerequisites for the restoration of peace negotiations. Reasons these are minimum prerequisites are: Chiang Kai-shek has already completely torn up his four promises, the truce order, the plan for reorganization of armies, the Manchurian cease fire agreement, and the PCC decisions. He has assassinated professors Li Kung-po, Wen I-to and other democratic figures. He has convoked an illegal "National Assembly," concluded the Sino-American commercial treaty of national betrayal, launched large-scale civil war throughout the country, invaded and occupied so much of the liberated areas. After perpetrating all these lawless deeds Chiang Kai-shek still wants to negotiate for peace—of course, this cannot be done without first carrying out a few prerequisites. Otherwise, who can believe he has even a shred of sincerity? If we speak according to law, all bellicose elements of the Kuomintang should be punished as war criminals, all Kuomintang reactionaries and secret police agents who broke PCC decisions should be punished as Fascists, the Kuomintang government officials who signed the Sino-American commercial treaty should be punished as traitors. Furthermore, they should have to compensate to people of liberated areas and of all China for colossal damages suffered from Chiang Kai-shek's launching of civil war. We have not raised all these just and equitable demands, however, but have only demanded nullification of the false Constitution and restoration of the military positions of January 13 last year. What is this if not the most extreme clemency toward Chiang Kai-shek?

To what degree of lawlessness has Chiang Kai-shek reached within the past year? If we do not ask him to carry out our two minimum points, if we "cease fire at present positions," forget all his past crimes and give him time to rest and regroup his troops, consolidate invaded areas, replenish his armies, "reorganize government" to get $500,000,000 or more loans and military aid from the United States Government, then when he has strength to launch a large-scale offensive again, Chiang Kai-shek will certainly be more lawless. What happened last year is a good example.

Therefore, if we still want independence, peace and democracy, we must ask Chiang Kai-shek to nullify his fake Constitution and restore positions of January 13 last year. We will never rest till this goal is attained. All deceptions will be in vain. Now that Chiang Kai-shek has rejected these two points and has brought forward his deceptive "peace proposals" in conflict he will have to bear responsibility for all consequences.

116 (c)

Statement Issued January 29, 1947, by the Ministry of Information, Chinese National Government

893.00/1–3047

It has been more than three months since the government issued a cease-fire order on November 8, 1946. The Communists did not comply with this order, but instead have taken advantage of the opportunity and launched a general offensive on all fronts from the northeast to the eastern section of the Lunghai railway. The Communist offensive has been further intensified recently. For the cause of peace and the interest of the country and the people, the government made one concession after another in the hope that a political solution could be found. It is indeed regrettable that the Communists refused both the government proposal of sending a representative to Yenan for the resumption of negotiations and the four point peace proposal of the government.

Following the adoption, in the National Assembly, of a democratic constitution embodying the principles agreed upon by all parties in the PCC of last January, and having started discussions and preparations for the governmental reorganization plan by inviting all parties and groups to take part in the State Council, the Legislative Yuan, the Executive Yuan and the Control Yuan with a view to broadening the basis of the government, the government on January 24 requested Dr. J. L. Stuart, United States Ambassador to convey to the Communists the following four points:

First, the government is willing to send a representative to Yenan or to invite Communist delegates to come to Nanking to resume the peace talks, or to call a round-table conference to be attended by representatives of the various parties and independents.

Secondly, the government and the Communists will immediately order their troops to cease hostilities and remain at their present positions and negotiate effective measures to insure cessation of hostilities.

Thirdly, the government is prepared to resume negotiations with the Communists for the enforcement of the army reorganization plan and the restoration of communications agreements in accordance with the principles laid down by the Committee of Three.

Fourthly, in the regions where hostilities are now taking place, the government is ready to negotiate with the Communists for a fair and reasonable solution.

Now, the Communists have formally refused all peace negotiations and insisted upon the government's acceptance of their dictates, namely the restoration of the military positions of January 13, 1946 and the abolition of the Constitution. This is equivalent to putting both the National Government and the National Assembly under the yoke of the Communist Party and subjecting them to the orders of the Communists. What would the Chinese Republic be like and what would be left of the rights of the people?

During the one-year period after the PCC and the Committee of Three, the government has spared no effort in inviting the Communist and the minority parties to join the government.

All such endeavors in achieving an understanding with the Communists have been in vain. Since the Communists have taken such an obdurate stand, the only course at present is for the government to carry out its fixed policy of "political democratization".

We hope that all party leaders as well as independents will participate in the government in accordance with their consistent patriotic attitude in order to expedite the preparations and scheduled realization of constitutional rule. We also hope that all parties will cooperate as one man in the gigantic task of national reconstruction, restoration of a balanced economy and improvement of the peoples livelihood.

116 (d)

Statement by Generalissimo Chiang Kai-shek, February 16, 1947

893.00/2–1647

When war ended, our long-tortured country desperately needed relief and rehabilitation, for which peace and unity are prime requisites. The first important postwar problem the Government undertook was to attempt a peaceful settlement with the Communists. With the disinterested mediation of the United States, negotiations were carried on for over a year, now and then glimmering with hopes of success.

However, when the Communists refused to join the National Assembly in November, negotiations came to an end. The people of this country will have decided by now upon whom to lay the blame, and we leave to them and to posterity to render a just verdict. On its part, the Government will confine its military efforts to the protection and restoration of communication systems so necessary for the economic life of the nation, and we shall spare no efforts to continue to seek for a political solution of the Communist problem.

Although settlement with the Communists has failed, at least temporarily, the Kuomintang will go ahead immediately on its historic mission of bringing democracy to the Chinese people. Within a few days we will organize a new State Council charged with the supreme policy making powers of government, and with the task of conducting an election to implement the new Constitution. Membership of the Council will be given to the best men the country could find irrespective of party affiliations. Non-partisans as well as members of all political parties will be given representation.

At the same time, the Executive Yuan and the other Yuans will be immediately reorganized in a similar way, to broaden the basis of government.

Today we are facing not a question of political parties, but the problem of the democratic development, and even the survival of the Chinese nation. I call on all patriots to join with me in working out the salvation of the country and to them I pledge my loyal cooperation.

China is today facing an acute economic crisis. Following the heels of Japanese devastation, internal strife has been raging with the Communist armies even during the period of negotiations. Communist armies have occupied large areas in North China and Manchuria, set up their own separatist Communist administrations, introduced their own currency, and set up economic blockades so that food and produce should not flow into Government-controlled areas. Railways were incessantly attacked and mines and industries were wantonly destroyed because the Communist armies could not hold them. The destructions and dislocation caused by the Communists during the last year exceeded in intensity a similar period of Japanese occupation.

I need only to give a few examples. China is rich in coal deposits and is normally a large exporter, but many of the coal mines and the communications leading to them were systematically destroyed by the Communists so that last year we were even obliged to import some coal from the United States for our industries. Before the war, China was selfsufficient in cotton and tobacco, but this year we have to import over 200 million dollars of foreign cotton and tobacco.

In a word, the economic crisis we are facing today is the cumulative effect of devastation and dislocation of eight years of war and one year of destructive peace.

Our Government last year pursued a liberal foreign exchange policy to enable the country to be supplied with the needs of foreign supplies denied during long years of blockade. However, with the economic situation aggravated by Communist destruction, we have to take new stock of our situation, and meet it realistically and steadfastly by the following emergency measures:

(1) Foreign exchange resources of the Government, including gold, will be conserved for raw material and machinery so that our communications and factories will be kept running, and the basic necessities of our people supplied. We need a new exchange rate bringing our domestic price level attuned to the foreign markets, and which will not be subject to constant fluctuations. After careful consideration, we are fixing the new exchange for both exports and imports at a flat rate of CNC (Chinese National Currency) 12,000 to one US dollar, commencing Monday, February 17. The new rate is much higher than the old rate, but even so it is no higher than the prevailing domestic price level.

(2) The purchase and sale of gold in the market, and circulation of and transaction in foreign currency are prohibited in order to stop speculation. At the same time, the Central Bank will provide sufficient foreign exchange for legitimate purchases.

(3) The Government will relieve the pressure of usurious interests on agricultural and industrial production through loans and other means.

(4) Government expense will be held to the absolute minimum, administration will be streamlined, and all new construction work will be postponed.

(5) The collection of revenues will be conducted with the utmost vigor. Since we have not yet developed a modern accounting system, the collection of income tax and other direct taxes have proved very ineffective. Rough and ready justice will now be applied, and if there are individual cases of suffering, it will have to be remembered by the propertied classes that this Government must be supported at all costs.

(6) In answer to general clamour public services have been kept much below cost, at a tremendous charge on the budget. The Government has decided on an all-out policy to bring about better equilibrium of the budget, and public services, such as the postal system, will have to pay their own way.

(7) During the National Government regime labor wages have been increased manifold, until today they are much higher than the corresponding pay of Government functionaries and the soldiers, and the Government is reserving its foreign exchange resources for the use of industries in which they are employed. We do not intend to take away the just dues of labor, but like all sections of the community, they should demonstrate their patriotic spirit, and there should be a ceiling to wage advances.

(8) All industries owned by the Government except those for national defense and public utilities should be speedily disposed of to private interests. The Government is not in business in competition to private interests.

(9) There will be instituted rigorous control of a few basic commodities such as rice, flour, cloth, food oil and fuel so that prices should not be allowed to run

away. Speculators, hoarders, and profiteers will be punished as severely as the crisis calls for.

(10) Some of the private banks mushroomed during the war have indulged in an orgy of speculation. The Ministry of Finance will inspect their accounts and mete out exemplary punishments.

In spite of the difficulties before us, we have made and are making economic progress. When the Government reoccupied Japanese-controlled areas, there were in running condition only 7,845 kilometers of railways, but today, in spite of Communist attacks, we are operating 11,887 kilometers of railways, an increase by 50 percent. At the end of the war we had only 314,835 tons of shipping, much of which had to be scrapped, today we have a tonnage of 692,071 tons. Last year we produced 960,000 bales of yarn, 8,000 tons of steel, 1,171,155 kilowatts of power, 300,000 tons of cement, and 13 million tons of coal. This year we will produce 2.379 million bales of yarn, 200,000 tons of steel, 1.638 million kilowatts of power, 900,000 tons of cement, and 23 million tons of coal. Compared to industrial nations, our production is still meagre, but it is heartening that we have made this advance during last year in spite of all obstacles.

In agriculture, while we have to import 75 percent of our needs in raw cotton and tobacco in 1947, after this year's crop we will be able to supply 75 percent of cotton and tobacco from our own production. With the 1948 crop we plan to be self-sufficient.

In exports we are rapidly organizing ourselves, and we will presently be able to sell to foreign markets much more yarn and cloth, soya beans, egg products, tea, minerals, essential oils and the varieties that make up Chinese exports. In the recovery of Taiwan with its rich resources of sugar, tea, camphor, and rice, and which in good years under Japanese occupation had a favorable annual balance of trade of over 250 million US dollars, the nation has recovered an asset of the first importance.

There is no reason for us to give way to panic. The basic factors of the agricultural and industrial situation are sound. If we only apply ourselves to our tasks with resolution and energy, we will overcome the immediate difficulties of the Japanese invasion. By so laboring, we are indeed on the way to exercise political freedom and recovery of the free economy that is the distinguishing characteristic of our people. I bespeak the sympathetic understanding of friendly nations as China labors to recover its economy, and equip itself for full participation in world trade and make its contribution to the cause of world peace.

117

Speech by Chou En-lai on January 10, 1947 [1]

893.00/1-1647

This day last year saw the signing of the cease-fire order, and the opening of the political consultative conference. Great were the changes in the situation, and rapid was the growth of the awakening of the people during the past year. Today a year ago, the people throughout the whole country were cheering for peace and cease-fire, but not before long, the nation was again plunged into the abyss of civil strife. All of us have realized that, unless the rule by militarists is put to an end, China can never have peace. The people of the whole nation were celebrating the success of the political consultative conference in January and Febru-

---

[1] Broadcast from Yenan on Jan. 14, 1947.

ary last year; but not before long, the PCC agreements were completely over-thrown by the reactionaries in the Kuomintang. All of us have realized that un-less the system of individual dictatorship is removed, the democratic PCC line can never be realized. The people of the whole nation were welcoming Presi-dent Truman's statement on China and General Marshall's mediation efforts in China a year ago, but not before long the true nature of the China policy of the American imperialists was exposed, and the high treason diplomacy of Chiahg Kai-shek's regime was also fully unmasked. Since then, from tens of thousands of students to the broad masses of residents in big cities all over China have been shouting these slogans: "US Army quit China," "oppose American interven-tion in China's internal affairs," "oppose Quisling style diplomacy," "oppose the Sino-American trade treaty," and the like.

In the changes during the past year, not only the KMT reactionaries have started anew the civil war and scrapped the PCC agreements, but also the Ameri-can witness who affixed his signature on the cease-fire agreement has never again mentioned the January cease-fire order. And the delegates of the Youth Party, the Social Democrats, and a great part of the so-called social leaders who took part in the PCC also participated in the illegal Kuomintang-controlled "National Assembly" which completely destroyed the PCC line, whereby they formulated a dictatorial constitution which runs diametrically counter to the PCC principles, thus deepening the split of the nation. Only the Chinese Communists, genuine democratic parties and groups, genuine civic leaders and the broad masses of the people have never in a moment ceased to uphold the January cease-fire agreement, to fight for the PCC line, and to fight for the realization of the demands that US troops withdraw from China, and the United States stop interfering with China's domestic politics. In looking back over the struggles during the past year, we can't help but think of the martyrs of the April 8 incident who clamored for a cessation of hostilities, and for the implementation of the PCC resolutions, and also of Messrs. Wen, Li and Tao. The spirit with which they fought bitterly against the reactionary bloc which had tried to destroy the cease-fire agreement, and the PCC resolutions has been a constant source of inspiration to us.

Exactly one year after, and on the eve of his departure from China, General Marshall issued a statement summarizing his mediation efforts during the past year. In the light of this statement of his, I will now briefly touch upon a few important points.

General Marshall admitted that there is a reactionary group in the Kuomintang which constitutes a dominant one in the Kuomintang government, and which includes military and political leaders. They oppose a coalition government, have no confidence in internal cooperation, but believe in the settlement of prob-lems by armed force. They have no sincerity in carrying out the PCC resolu-tions. All these remarks are true. But what is to be regretted is that he did not point out that Chiang Kai-shek is the highest leader of this reactionary group. Chiang Kai-shek said a coalition government is tantamount to overthrowing the government; inter-party conference is a spoils system conference. After the establishment of the executive headquarters in Peiping last year, Chiang Kai-shek and his group opposed the sending of field teams to Manchuria. After the sign-ing of the cease-fire agreement in Manchuria on March 27, Chiang Kai-shek ordered Tu Yu-Ming to launch a big offensive there. That the failure in the truce negotiations in June was caused by Chiang Kai-shek's insistence on the with-drawal of Communist troops from northern Kiangsu, Jehol and two other liberated areas—an act which is a breach of the PCC resolutions. Immediately after that, he conducted a large scale fighting in China proper, and up to now, he continues to act against the PCC agreements in massing 280 brigades (formerly divisions) 90 percent of his total military strength, to attack the communist-held liberated areas. Up to the end of last year, his armies invaded 174,000 square kilometers and took 165 cities in the liberated areas. What are they if these are not armed attacks?

The PCC resolutions were completely violated by members of the one party "National Assembly" and the decision of the constitution was made by Chiang Kai-shek. Therefore, the man who scrapped the cease-fire pact and the PCC resolutions was none other than Chiang Kai-shek himself.

Chiang Kai-shek's reactionary bloc wished by this means to maintain its feudal control. Even General Marshall admits that this further weakens Chiang's government. As to the disruption of economic and communication system, they are attributable to the civil war waged by Chiang Kai-shek. The yearly military expenses constitute 80 percent of the total state expenditures of Chiang's government. Added to these is the exploitation of the people by bureaucratic capital. How can economic ruin be averted?

General Marshall thinks that with the same bad government and still under the leadership of Chiang Kai-shek, but with the participation of a few Kuomintang liberals and minority parties such as the Social Democratic Party and the Youth Party, a good government can ultimately be formed. Will it not be too cheap? Without the participation of the Communists in a coalition government, the dictatorial system instituted by Chiang Kai-shek cannot be abolished, nor can a liberal government be formed.

General Marshall understands full well that the Chiang assembly convened last year is a violation of PCC resolutions and procedures, but he purposely says that the constitution passed by it is a democratic constitution and its main parts are in full agreement with the principles laid down by PCC. Even Communist demands are incorporated in it. This is a big bluff. The main parts of the constitution passed by Chiang's assembly are in direct contravention to the PCC principles. PCC favors the safeguarding the liberties of the people, but Chiang's constitution restricts them. PCC is in support of the granting of the right of self-government to racial minorities, but in Chiang's constitution, such a right is non-existent. PCC wants to make the province the highest unit for regional autonomy, and let it draft its own constitution so that there will be an equal division of power, but Chiang's constitution is pervaded with the idea of centralization of power and the stipulation about the drafting of the provincial constitution is cancelled. PCC desires the cabinet system to be instituted in the coalition government, but Chiang's constitution is all for the President system as contained in the May 5 draft constitution. General Marshall relies on the enforcement of Chiang's constitution and the reorganization of the government for prolonging Chiang's dictatorship, but in this he is mistaken. The consequences will be that Chiang's government will be further discredited and isolated and it will completely fail to gain the support of the people.

That being the case, will the Communists' opposition to Chiang's constitution and the participation in the government under the present circumstances and their demands of a return to the military positions of January 13, the abolition of Chiang's constitution and the convocation of an inter-party conference be considered as a sign of unwillingness to make a fair compromise as the Communists have been so accused by General Marshall? Quite the contrary. These are the most fair compromises and the lowest limit of the Communist demands for peace and democracy. Even General Marshall admitted that during last January and February the Communists were willing to reach a compromise. But, since last

February, the Kuomintang reactionary group has repeatedly violated the PCC resolution and the cease-fire pact. Up to now, the Communists have tried to reach a compromise on the basis of the cease-fire pact signed last January and thru the PCC line. These are really what General Marshall praised as a liberal and forward looking charter.

If we make a comparison, Chiang Kai-shek is violating the cease-fire pact and deviating from the PCC line, whereas the Communists are observing the cease-fire pact and following the PCC line. Is Chiang Kai-chek trying to annihilate the Communists in the liberated areas or are the Communists trying to overthrow the government? Is it fair if Chiang can refuse to accept the two Communist demands while the Communists must accept Chiang's constitution and the positions of the two troops not in accordance with the cease-fire pact?

No Chinese people will believe that the residents of the liberated areas are in the depth of their suffering. This is not an actual fact and is a blasphemy against the Communists. The Communists have worked for the welfare of the people for the last six years and have built up their reputation by their close attachment to the people. If the Communists agree to the occupation of the liberated areas by Chiang's troops and permit Chiang to force the residents to recognize the constitution and to acknowledge his dictatorship, it will be a complete disregard of people's suffering and the interest of the country. Besides, it will not lead to real peace.

There are many naive persons who are too eager to have peace and who are too easily deceived by the apparent peace .and do not want to struggle for the minimum safeguards for peace. Chiang Kai-shek has perceived their weaknesses. When it was advantageous for Chiang to launch an attack, he would not hesitate to attack. But when he was defeated and required time to regroup his troops, for instance (he was in such a pass last January and February), he would favor the halting of the war and conducted the so-called peace talks. Let me ask how a fair compromise could be reached. Never. A fair compromise must be built on a basis which is beneficial to the people. That basis is the cease-fire pact signed last January by General Marshall and Chang Chun, Chiang's representative, and the PCC resolutions passed by Chiang Kai-shek. In General Marshall's report, he mentioned the PCC resolutions, but not the cease-fire pact. That was not just a slip of his memory. It was his intention to absolve himself of the responsibility of appending his signature to a pact and try to find a way out for the three man military sub-committee and the Peiping executive headquarters. This further proves that the US Government has been helping Chiang to extend the civil war. It also explains why General Marshall hated very much the propaganda activities carried out by the Communists. Yes, the Communists had since last March repeatedly pointed out the error of the US policy in China, particularly the garrison of the United States forces in this country, their interference in the domestic affairs, and the invasion of the liberated areas. The Anping incident alluded to by General Marshall was one of the thirty-odd incidents.

The Chinese Communists have unremittedly exposed and lodged protests against American aid to Chiang Kai-shek's government troops in the form of transportation, lend-lease materials, surplus property, warships and airplanes, military advisors and technical training, and the colonial policy of the American imperialists (here broadcast was badly garbled). Instead, the Chinese Communists were blamed for their being unable to accept the American mediation, something we must repudiate. General Marshall thought that the above-mentioned kinds of propaganda tend to arouse a bitter, hatred of Americans, and are therefore of a vicious nature. The truth is that what aroused people is not abstract propaganda, but living facts. If facts such as those listed above continue to remain, then in the eyes of an independent and freedom loving people they are vicious.

General Marshall has now returned to the United States to take up the post of Secretary of 'State. I hope that he will, taking the stand of the late President Roosevelt's China policy and for the sake of the traditional friendship between and the interests of the two Chinese and American peoples review again the US China policy during the past year. I hope that the United States will not repeat the past mistakes but stop helping Chiang Kai-shek's government in waging the civil war, evacuate American troops from China, and not intervene again in China internal affairs, but readjust the relations between China and the United States. In so doing, it will be greatly helpful to the efforts of the Chinese people in their striving for peace, democracy, independence and freedom, and will also be beneficial to far faster pace and international cooperation.

We cannot forget this memorable day of the first anniversary of the issuance of the cease-fire order and the meeting of the PCC. We Chinese Communists pledge ourselves to continue to fight, and we believe that democratic people and our fellow countrymen throughout the country will fight for the complete realization of the PCC agreements and the PCC line. We will not cease our efforts until the aims are realized.

118

Memorandum Entitled "Explanation of Several Basic Questions Concerning the Postwar International Situation" by Lu Ting-yi, Chief of the Department of Information of the Chinese Communist Party [2]

893.00/6-2047

It is now the new year—1947. We wish to make an all-sided examination of the whole international situation in order to dispel certain misconceptions in this realm.

During the past year and more and right up to the present time, owing to the complicated changes in the situation and to demagogic propaganda intentionally spread about widely by the Chinese and foreign reactionaries, there are still some people in the camp of democracy in China whose understanding of several basic questions concerning the postwar political situation is not in accord, or not wholly in accord, with the real state of affairs. These people include some Communists, some left-wing critics, some middle of the road critics. The purpose of this article is to offer a general explanation of these several basic questions.

I. MAO TZE-TUNG'S PREDICTION

16 months have elapsed since the victory in the anti-Fascist war. These 16 months have been a period of extremely complicated changes in the international political situation. The course of changing affairs has taken many twists and turns—one sort of conditions prevailed at the London Foreign Ministers' Conference in September a year before last, there was a change at the time of the Moscow Foreign Ministers' conference in December of the same year, in February and March of last year another change took place, and from September of last year yet another change occurred. After the many changes of the past

---

[2] Printed in Yenan *Emancipation Daily*, Jan. 4 and 5, 1947.

16 months we have ample surety in saying: The development of the international situation is entirely in accord with the prediction of Comrade Mao Tze-tung.

In "On Coalition Government," a political report of Comrade Mao Tze-tung to the 7th National Convention of the Chinese Communist Party, in April, 1945, he made the following prediction of a new world situation following the World War II:

"This new situation differs greatly from that of the first world war and the so-called 'peaceful' period which followed. At that time there was not a Soviet Union like the present one, nor was there such a degree of consciousness as now expressed by the people of Great Britain, America, China, France, and other anti-Fascist Allies, and naturally there could not be such a present world unity headed by three great powers or five great powers. Now we are living in an entirely new situation. There now exist in the world peoples and their organized forces who have been awakened and united, and are in the course of becoming more so. This determines the objective to which the wheels of world history are moving, and the path which should be followed to attain it.

"The defeat of the Fascist aggressor countries and the emergence of a general peace situation do not mean that there will be no more struggle. The widely spread remnant forces of Fascism will certainly continue to make trouble. The anti-democratic forces remaining in the camp of the anti-Fascist war against aggression will continue to oppress the people. Therefore after the realization of international peace, the struggle between the anti-Fascist masses of the people and the remnant forces of the Fascists, and between democracy and anti-democracy will continue to occupy a major part of the world. A most widespread people's victory can only be the outcome of a long period of energetic forces to overcome the remnant Fascist forces and the anti-democratic forces. To attain this is certainly not very quick or very easy, but it will nevertheless certainly come. The victory of the anti-Fascist war—the just World War II— has opened the road to victory for the people's struggle in the post-war period, and it is only after such a victory that a stable and lasting peace can be guaranteed. This is the bright future lying before the people of the world."

I hope all readers will carefully read these words of Comrade Mao Tze-tung several times. This will be helpful to comprehension of basic questions concerning the present international situation.

II. Two Basic Points

These words of Comrade Mao Tze-tung bring out two basic points:

1. The victory in the anti-Fascist war has opened way to progress for democratic forces in all nations. The extent of progress of these democratic forces will be incomparably greater than after the first world war. The attack by the anti-democratic forces on peoples of all nations must of necessity come. But the democratic forces will in necessity of things be able to overcome the anti-democratic forces, secure their own victory and win a firm and lasting international peace. There are the two necessities here: (1) that the anti-democratic forces will of necessity attack and (2) that the democratic forces will of necessity be victorious.

Thus, all erroneous pessimistic contentions are swept clean away. These pessimistic contentions are: alleging that the extent of the progress of the democratic forces after World War II is smaller than that after World War I; allegations about "super colossal" reactionary strength of the American imperialism and Chiang Kai-shek and about how they will oppress the people of China and the whole world till they will be unable to draw a breath; alleging that the World War III is inevitable or will soon arrive; that a firm and lasting peace cannot be attained, etc. All these points of view are obviously erroneous. The reason for committing those errors have been misled by the temporary and outside appearance of might of international and internal reactionary forces or been blinded by reactionary propaganda thereby underestimating the strength of the people.

2. The struggle between the forces of democracy and anti-democracy will cover a greater part of the world. That is to say, in the world there is a socialist Soviet Union in which there has long been no anti-democratic forces and therefore there is no internal struggle between democracy and anti-democracy. Other places in the world besides the Soviet Union—that is the whole of the capitalist world—is filled with struggle between democracy and anti-democracy. Thus, following the World War II, the actual dominant political contradiction in the world between democratic and anti-democratic forces is within the capitalist world and not between the capitalist world and the Soviet Union and also not between the Soviet Union and the United States. Speaking more concretely, the present dominant contradictions in the world are contradictions between the American people and the American reactionaries, the Anglo-American contradictions and the Sino-American contradictions.

Thus, the propaganda of the reactionaries in China and abroad is thoroughly confuted so that all good hearted people will not be misled by such propaganda. Such demagogic propaganda is: that actual dominant political contradiction in the present world is between capitalist and socialist countries, that the Soviet-American contradictions are dominant and the Anglo-American and Sino-American contradictions are secondary; the socialist and capitalist countries cannot peacefully cooperate, the Soviet-American war is inevitable, etc.

We will elucidate below: 1. Who are anti-democratic forces? What is their present and will be their future? 2. Who are democratic forces? What is their present and will be their future?

III. WORLD REACTIONARIES, THEIR SMOKESCREEN AND THEIR REAL ACTIVITIES

After the World War II, the American imperialists took place of the Fascist Germany, Italy and Japan becoming a fortress of the world reactionary forces. So-called reactionary forces are precisely the American imperialists with addition of reactionaries in various countries (China's Chiang Kai-shek, Great Britain's Churchill, France's DeGaulle, etc.) and other Fascist remnants (Spain's Franco Government, Japan's Yoshida cabinet, Germany's von Papen and Schacht, etc.). The reactionaries of all countries and the Fascist remnants have now all become traitors directly or indirectly supported and protected by the American imperialists selling out the people of all countries.

The American wartime industrial production has more than doubled in comparison with prewar figures. During the war, American monopoly capital underwent tremendous development. At the same time, a batch of warlords arose in America. After the conclusion of the war, this batch of monopoly capitalists and militarists, this bloc of extremely small handful of fanatical aggressors, advocated a policy of imperialist aggression to expand markets, wrest away markets, colonies and semi-colonies of other capitalist countries, primarily oppressing the great colonial imperialist countries England and France and oppressing China while at the same time exercising a sole domination over Japan and Latin-America. The American imperialists are carrying out this aggression under slogans of "open door policy and equal opportunity" etc. to be in an overwhelming position to drive others away and monopolize the market. In addition to all this, the American imperialists are undertaking large-scale military preparations against all capitalist countries, colonies, and semi-colonial countries, under all sorts of pretext. Their military bases are spread over many countries, outside the Soviet Union. The American imperialists have through "peaceful" means occupied many "Pearl Harbors" in various countries, saying on the other hand that this is to "prevent another Pearl Harbor."

In February and March of 1946, the world reactionaries schemed to incite a war against the Soviet Union. This was characterized by the reactionary speech of Churchill. This speech has aroused a great vigilance of the people as it should. But Churchill's agitation has met with the opposition of the people of the whole world. The attempt of the reactionaries has suffered a bitter defeat.

The "anti-Soviet war" propaganda launched by Churchill was regarded as a treasure and inherited by the American imperialists. Why the American imperialists love this kind of propaganda? Their purpose is not to launch an anti-Soviet war at present, but to use it as a smokescreen in order to carry out their large-scale aggressive actions abroad and oppression of the American people at home.

What is the meaning of the "anti-Sovietism"? Hitler's "anti-Sovietism" meant enslaving of the German people and invading whole Europe. The Fascist Japan's "anti-Sovietism" meant oppressing the Japanese people and aggressing countries on both sides of the Pacific. The American reactionaries' "anti-Sovietism" at present only means enslaving the American people and world domination.

But the anti-Soviet slogan of the American reactionaries at present differs from that of the former Fascists Germany and Japan. Germany is close to Soviet Union. In addition to other conditions, Fascist Germany was able to attack the latter. Japan is also near the Soviet Union. Owing to the fact that its strength was weaker than Fascist Germany, Fascist Japan could only attack China and the Pacific and was defeated before it had time to invade the Soviet Union. The United States is far away from the Soviet Union with a large area lying between. In this neutral area, there are capitalist countries, colonial and semi-colonial countries of three continents, Europe, Asia, and Africa. In addition to other conditions, it is very difficult for the United States to attack the Soviet Union: therefore the actual meaning of the "anti-Soviet" slogan of America at the post-war period is only to oppress the American people and invade through "peaceful" means all countries besides the Soviet Union.

Certainly there is a contradiction between the American monopoly capital and warlords on the one side and the Socialist Soviet Union on the other. It is a contradiction between the new and old world, is one of the world basic contradictions. The social and political system of the Soviet Union is much stronger than the American capitalism. The Soviet Union is the defender of world peace. Ambition and graft of the American and world reactionaries are impossible to be realized as long as the Soviet Union exists, therefore the American and world reactionaries hate the Soviet Union, and they certainly will persist in an anti-Soviet struggle. But anti-Soviet propaganda is one thing and anti-Soviet war is another. We cannot say that the American imperialists do not want to attack the Soviet Union; but the American imperialists cannot attack the Soviet Union before they have succeeded in suppressing and putting under their control the American people and all capitalist, colonial and semi-colonial countries. To oppress and put under their control these countries is impossible. Therefore, the contradiction between the United States and Soviet Union, though it is one of the basic contradictions, is not an imminent one, not a dominant one in the present political situation. This has been proved by the development of events during the past 16 months. The actual policy of the American imperialists is to attack through "peaceful" means the American people and oppress all capitalist, colonial and semi-colonial countries. However, the American imperialists will keep under cover these activities that they are actually doing. The American imperialists have no way to attack the Soviet Union, yet they are talking loudly about the anti-Soviet war, obviously the slogan is only a smokescreen.

Why do the American imperialists use this smokescreen? Why should we expose this smokescreen? The purpose of the American imperialists in smokescreening is to divert the attention of the American people, the broad masses of all capitalist countries besides America and all colonial and semi-colonial countries so that they will be off guard against attacks of the American imperialists. With the unpreparedness of the American people and the other countries, the American imperialists can more easily fascistize their own country and turn other countries into American colonies and dependencies. If we fail to expose this smokescreen of the American imperialism or we fail to pay due attention to this important work, we will more or less be lured into the trap of the American imperialists or be a mouthpiece speaking for the American imperialists, the common enemy. Therefore, we should not be fooled by the smokescreen of the reactionaries and lose our own judgment, bewildered by such demagogic propaganda as: "The dominant contradiction in the present world is between capitalist and socialist countries", "the World War III is inevitable", etc. The only road to follow and the only duty for each and every one in the democratic camp to fulfill is to expose the reactionaries' smokescreen and to call the people in America, in all capitalist, colonial and semi-colonial countries to fight for their own existence and to resist the attacks and aggressions of the American imperialists, their real enemies.

IV. WORLD DEMOCRATIC STRENGTH

Standing against the world reactionaries—the imperialists of America and their running dogs in various countries—is the world democratic might.

Besides the Soviet Union, which is the main pillar, the world democratic forces are made up of three sections: the broad masses of the American people, the broad masses of the people of all capitalist countries besides America, and the broad masses of the people of all colonial and semi-colonial countries. In terms of class make-up, they include everyone from workers and farmers right up to patriotic elements and advocates of peace among the bourgeoisie.

The American people made heroic contributions during the anti-Fascist war. The object of their self-sacrificing struggle is the winning of world peace and democracy and happy life for themselves. After the conclusion of the war, however, the American people were faced with the following situation: After the defeat of foreign reactionaries loomed domestic reactionaries. They were precisely those monopoly capitalists who fattened on speculation and ill-gotten riches during the war. In the field of domestic policy this batch of monopoly capitalists and their reactionary spokesmen in the government raise prices of goods to press down living standards of the people, crack down on strikes in order to cancel people's liberties, encourage anti-Sovietism to divert attention of the American people so that they will be off guard against attacks of the monopoly capitalists. In the field of foreign policy, the American reactionaries do not call themselves "isolationists", but rather "internationalists". But these "internationalists", however, are international aggressionists and not democratic international cooperationists. These reactionary elements have their men in both American Democratic and Republican parties. The world aggression of these reactionaries has seriously spoiled the reputation of America, ruined the international friendship and is brewing a danger of war.

This is why the American people, including enlightened members of American bourgeoisie represented by Wallace, will certainly rise for a determined struggle with reactionaries.

Capitalist countries outside of America, principally England and France, suffered great wounds from war and compared to America they are second or third class countries. They are objects of the aggression by the American imperialism. The law of uneven development of capitalism forces them resolutely to resist the American oppression.

These capitalist countries are now struggling for economic recovery from wounds of war and are at the same time in the following situation: On the one hand is the democratic movement of the people of their own country, and the demand for independence and autonomy on the part of colonies and semi-colonial countries and on the other is a savage aggression of the American imperialism. The line being taken by the reactionaries like Churchill and de Gaulle within these countries is to rely on America to oppose the democratic movement of the people of their own country and the independence movement of the peoples of colonies and semi-colonies. The price paid for this reactionary line is that it inevitably leads these countries sinking to the position of American dependencies. The people in these capitalist countries have another line: winning the democratic and social reform for their own country and granting colonial and semi-colonial people's independence and autonomy and cooperation with the Soviet-Union, in order to resist the aggression of the American imperialism and maintain the national independence. Beyond all shadow of doubt, the people's line will be victorious. This line will obtain the endorsement of all classes of people including enlightened members of the bourgeoisie. On the other hand, the line of reactionaries must certainly fail, because it will meet with the opposition of the whole nation.

Take the most important among those capitalist countries—Great Britain for instance. In the post-war period, she is exerting her efforts to effect economic recovery. Her exports are gradually rising and this is something about which the American imperialist elements are not happy. The American imperialism schemes to break the sterling bloc by exploiting the need of England for loans and in the name of so-called "defense against Soviet Union's attacks" wants England to enter into a military alliance with her. These are all serious preparatory steps for swallowing up England. England's far-flung dependencies and colonies—Canada, South [Africa], Australia, Atlantic Islands, Middle-east, Palestine and Arabia, Egypt and Mediterranean and finally India, Burma and elsewhere—are all scenes of American imperialistic attacks on England under the American imperialist policy of the world domination. In certain places, these clashes have already become or are brewing up armed struggles. In the future, the possibility exists of America's inciting aggressive wars against other capitalist countries (first of all Great Britain).

The Attlee-Bevin Cabinet which continues the Conservative Party's foreign policy in Great Britain has done many evil deeds in concert with the American imperialism and on many questions has expressed a mutual sympathy and understanding or a common action with the American imperialism. The policy of American imperialism, however, cannot but force the English people gradually into consciousness. The gradual increase of votes in the British Lower House against Bevin's foreign policy is a proof of this. In circumstances of daily growing consciousness of the British people, it will be very difficult for Great Britain to continue her present foreign policy and the time for her to change her foreign policy is already not distant.

Thus it is with England and it will be even more so with France. In circumstances of daily growing consciousness of the French people, France certainly will not follow the road of American imperialists.

The American imperialistic policy of aggression on all capitalist countries must of necessity arouse the opposition of these countries. After the second World War, there are no grounds therefore for the so-called "capitalist encirclements of the Soviet Union". Just the contrary, because of the peaceful democratic international policies and policies of peaceful competition and the friendly commerce with all countries on the part of the Soviet Union and because England, France and other countries must resist the American aggression, escape blows of the economic crisis and furthermore restore their economies, these countries must cooperate and trade with the Soviet Union. So-called capitalist encirclement therefore does not exist.

The American policy with regard to all colonial and semi-colonial nations is to transform them into American colonies or dependencies. The American imperialistic policy towards China is a typical example. There is no difference in nature between the policy of American imperialism towards China and the policy of Japanese Fascists toward China, although there are differences in form. The venomous treachery of means employed by the American imperialism however surpasses that of the Japanese imperialism. After the defeat of the Japanese imperialism, America supports Chiang Kai-shek and other reactionaries in oppressing the Chinese people. In Japan, it supports Yoshida and other reactionaries in oppressing the Japanese people, and helps them to revive the policy of aggression towards China. At the present time the reactionaries of both China and Japan are occupying the same position as running dogs of America, and the peoples of both China and Japan are in the same position bearing oppression of the American imperialism. The self-defense war now being waged by the Chinese people against Chiang Kai-shek and the American imperialists is, in its nature, a war for the motherland. It is an all national war obtaining the full support of the entire nation. This kind of war for the motherland has been taking place in Indo-China, India, Iran, Greece etc. These wars are fought against the American imperialism and its running dogs in various countries. They are directly or indirectly against the American imperialism and for winning a world peace and democracy.

The contradiction between the American imperialism and the democratic forces in the capitalist world is not being slackened, but instead is growing and developing.

When the American economic crisis arrives, the American imperialists, because of this, tighten up their attacks, these contradictions will become sharp. Such a period is not far off because the American economic crisis will arrive this year or next.

V. UNITED FRONT ON WORLD SCALE

The world anti-democratic forces are the American imperialists and reactionaries in various countries. Since the world antidemocratic forces are in unison attacking the American people, the peoples of various capitalist countries, colonies and semi-colonial countries, the peoples of America, various capitalist countries, colonies and semi-colonial countries must also act in unison to form a world-wide united front against the American imperialism and reactionaries in all countries. This world-wide united front, this colossal army comprising well over one billion people is precisely the world democratic might.

This world-wide united front cannot possibly be of any other character than that of a united front hunting for world peace and democracy and independence of all nations against the American imperialism and its running dogs in various countries. This united front will undoubtedly have the sympathy and moral support of the socialist Soviet Union.

This united front on a world scale will characterize a new page in world history: that is the history of world from the end of second world war down to today when the stable and lasting peace of the world is ensured. The Chinese movement for independence, peace and democracy is an important part of this chapter of world history.

Within each capitalist country, colony and semi-colonial country, there will be an extremely broad united front as in China against the American imperialists and the reactionaries within each country.

The immediate cardinal task before the peoples and democratic forces of all countries is a struggle for the realization of this world-wide united front and an united front within each country.

VI. RELATIVE STRENGTH OF FORCES

Facts in more than one year following the victory in the anti-Fascist war prove that the rate of the world progress is very fast, and some events have developed faster than we had expected. The scope of development of democratic forces in all countries of the world is far greater than that after the world war one.

The progress of people in the capitalist world during the past year and more is manifested in: 1, firm establishment of new democratic regimes in various countries of the eastern and southern Europe; 2, progress by leaps and bounds of the peoples of England and France; 3, the flourishing development of the struggles of the peoples of colonies and semi-colonial countries with China at their head for independence and autonomy; 4, the rapid leftward trend of the peoples of Germany, Italy and Japan; 5, the high tide of American strike movement and the occurrence of Wallace incident (the Wallace incident expresses a split among the American bourgeoisie, just as the British Labour Party's opposition in England expressed a split among the British bourgeoisie); 6, a broad development of democratic forces in all countries of South America.

The scope and speed of the progress of people and the development of democratic forces in the capitalist world is really startling.

The international position of the most progressive country in the world—the socialist Soviet Union—has risen greatly. At present she is devoting all her strength to the peaceful constructive work of a new Five Year Plan. The completion of her first year's industrial production plan one month ahead of its schedule shows that it is entirely possible to complete and overfulfill this new plan for construction. Struggle of the Soviet Union in the realm of small nations achieved great victories in the recent foreign ministers conferences and the United Nations Assembly. A plot of American and British reactionaries to isolate the Soviet Union following Churchill's reactionary utterances of March last year has been smashed. Victories of the Soviet Union in economic construction and in foreign policy will greatly influence the history of world development, and will be beneficial to peoples of all countries.

The world reactionary forces are outwardly strong, but hollow inside. Moreover, they are becoming daily more isolated. The American imperialism reaches the highest peak of the capitalist development, but precisely because of this, it is weaker than the capitalism in any earlier period. The higher they climb, the harder they fall—the American economic crisis which will arrive this year or next cannot but be turbulent in its nature. The reactionary foreign and domestic policies of the American imperialists will necessarily lead, and have led, to the opposition of broadest masses of people both within and without the country. This will daily result in the masses turning against them and their allies deserting them. All running dogs of the American imperialists in various countries, as for example, China's Chiang Kai-shek, cannot but become traitors, and in their countries meet with the opposition of the entire nation. Therefore they cannot but rapidly isolate themselves, turned against by the masses and deserted by their allies. It is thus with China's Chiang Kai-shek and with reactionaries of all countries. The reactionary forces will collapse in the long run. They really appear very ferocious for a time, and can even frighten the feeble-minded people out of their will, so that they express pessimism and disappointment, lose their self-confidence, and even give in and surrender to reactionaries. But the broad masses of people and all men of strong will cannot be frightened away. The people in the course of their own practical experience will recognize not only the reactionary nature of the reactionaries, but also their feebleness. They will recognize that attacks of the reactionaries on the people can be smashed.

To sum up : the world progress, successes of the Soviet Union, and the American crisis are three factors of decisive significance in the history of future development of the world.

VII. Road to Victory

The present time is still a period when the world reaction can be cocky, baring its fangs and extending its talons. This is primarily because struggles of the peoples in the various countries have not entered a higher stage and at the same time this is also because the American economic crisis has not yet arrived. But even in this kind of period, the reactionary forces have already revealed that they are hollow within and outwardly strong. When struggles of the peoples of all countries reach a higher development and the American economic crisis has broken out, that will be the time when the grand arrogance of the reactionaries will collapse. This is already not far distant. Before the arrival of this time, the people of each country will meet with difficulties, and in individual countries and regions, may even meet with very serious difficulties. Difficulties of this kind, however, can and must be conquered. The present task is for every one to exert all efforts and to overcome these difficulties.

Following the development of three factors—world progress, Soviet successes and American crises—the democratic forces will become even stronger and the relative strength of the democratic and anti-democratic forces will become more beneficial to the people. But it is not to be imagined that the reactionary forces will voluntarily abdicate to the democratic forces. Therefore before we have attained what comrade Mao Tze-tung calls "broadest victory of the people" and the "ensurance of stable and enduring peace", there is still a long and tortuous struggle ahead. The Chinese Communists and the Chinese people will fear no difficulties. They will fight on till the complete victory of the democratic cause and winning of the peace and independence of their nation. We have the strongest confidence in this brilliant future, but the world bourgeoisie on the other hand have completely lost confidence in their future. The terrorism whipped up by the anti-democratic forces in various countries after the war against the forces of people, their terror at the strength of the Soviet Union, their fanatical oppression of the peoples, their horror of the truth, their complete reliance on lies for a living—these all are manifestations of their complete loss of confidence. It is certainly not accidental that all newspapers of the Chinese bourgeoisie express an unprecedental pessimism and disappointment with regard to their future.

In general, everything has changed after the second world war, and is still continuing to change. How strong the people have become—how conscious, how organized, determined, and full of confidence! How maniacally savage the reactionaries have become—outwardly strong yet inwardly feeble, turned against by masses and deserted by their allies, devoid of all confidence in their future! It may be forecast categorically that the face of China and the world will be vastly different after three to five more years. All comrades of our party and all people of China must resolutely fight for a new China and a new world.

119

Statement of the Central Committee of the Chinese Communist Party, February 1, 1947

893.00/2-747

The Political Consultative Conference, comprising all major political parties, groups and prominent social figures, convened on January 10, 1946 in accordance with stipulations of the summary of Kuomintang-Communist talks in Chungking on October 10, 1945, is universally recognized by the people of the entire country and world powers as the highest political body in China. Until China has a really democratic national parliament, all important internal and diplomatic affairs which would be passed by a parliament in democratic countries should pass through this Conference or obtain agreement of major political parties and groups before they can be regarded as effective.

Since January 10, 1946, however, Chinese Kuomintang government has not only enacted many arbitrary domestic measures but has also many times singly conducted diplomatic negotiations of a serious nature with certain foreign governments. In the course of understandings both oral and written, secret and open, without these agreements and understandings having been passed by the Political Consultative Conference or consulting opinion of this party and other parties and groups participating in Political Consultative Conference. These diplomatic negotiations include loans from foreign governments, continuation of Lend-Lease, buying and accepting of munitions and surplus war materials, forming of treaties regarding special rights in commerce, navigation, aviation and other economic and legal special rights.

These negotiations and agreements request or permit foreign land, sea and naval forces to be stationed in or operate on the seas, waterways, territories, and in the air of the country, and to enter or occupy and jointly construct or make use of military bases and points strategic to the national defense. They furthermore request or permit foreign military and other personnel to participate in organization, training, transportation and military operations of land, air and naval forces of the country, and to become conversant with military and other state secrets of the country. They also permit such serious matters as foreign intervention in internal affairs.

Those measures of the Chinese Kuomintang government are completely contrary to the will of the Chinese people and they have plunged and will continue to plunge China into civil war, reaction, national disgrace, loss of national rights, colonization and crises of chaos and collapse. In order to rescue the motherland from this calamity, to protect national rights and interests and the dignity of the Political Consultative Conference, the Chinese Communist Party solemnly states: This party will not either now nor in the future recognize any foreign loans, any treaties which disgrace the country and strip away its rights, and any of the above-mentioned agreements and understandings established by the Kuomintang government after January 10, 1946, nor will it recognize any future diplomatic negotiation of the same character which have not been passed by Political Consultative Conference or which have not obtained agreement of this party and other parties and groups participating in the Political Consultative Conference. This party furthermore will absolutely not bear any obligations for the above-mentioned.

120

Article by Mao Tse-tung, Chairman, Commemorating the 28th Anniversary of the Chinese Communist Party [3]

July 1, 1949, means that the Communist Party of China has passed through 28 years. Like a man, it has its childhood, youth, manhood, and old age. The Communist Party of China is no longer a child or a youth in its teens, but is an adult. When a man reaches old age, he dies. It is the same with the party. When classes are eliminated, all the instruments of class struggle, political parties, and the state apparatus, will, as a result, lose their functions, become unnecessary and gradually wither away, end their historical mission, and travel toward the higher plane of the society of mankind.

We are quite different from the political party of the bourgeoisie. They are afraid to talk of abolishing classes, state authority, and the party. But we, however, openly declare that we struggle hard precisely for the creation of conditions to accelerate the elimination of these things. The Communist Party and the state authority of the people's dictatorship constitute such conditions. Anyone who does not recognize this truth is no Communist.

Young comrades who have just joined the party and have not read Marxism-Leninism may not understand this truth. They must understand this truth before they can have a correct world outlook. They must understand that all mankind has to travel along the road of eliminating classes, state authority, and party. The question is only one of time and conditions.

PREPARATION FOR WORLD COMMUNISM

The Communists in the world are more intelligent than the bourgeoisie. They understand the law of the existence and development of things. They understand dialectics and see farther ahead. The bourgeoisie do not welcome this

---

[3] Broadcast by the New China News Agency on June 30, 1949: reprinted from Central Intelligence Agency, Foreign Broadcast Information Branch, *Daily Report of Foreign Radio Broadcasts,* Far East section, July 1, 5, 1949.

truth, because they do not want to be overthrown by the people. To be over-thrown—like the Kuomintang reactionaries being overthrown by us at present and like Japanese imperialism having been overthrown by us and peoples of various countries in the past—is painful and is inconceivable to the overthrown.

For the working class, laboring people, and Communists, the question is not one of being overthrown but of working hard and creating conditions for the natural elimination of classes, state authority and the political party, so that mankind will enter the realm of world Communism. We have here touched on the perspective of the progress of mankind to explain the following questions.

Our party has passed through 28 years. Everybody knows that they were passed not peacefully but under difficult surroundings. We had to fight against enemies within the country and abroad and within and outside the party. Thanks to Marx, Engels, Lenin, and Stalin who gave us weapons. These weapons are not machine guns but Marxism-Leninism.

Lenin in his book " 'Left-wing' Communism—An Infantile Disorder," written in 1920, described how the Russians sought for a revolutionary theory. After several decades of hardships and tribulations, they eventually discovered Marx-ism. Many things were the same or similar in China and Russian before the October revolution. The feudal oppression was the same. The economic and cultural backwardness was similar. Both countries were backward, and China is even more backward. Progressive people struggled hard to seek for revolu-tionary truth to bring about national recovery. This was the same.

WESTERN TEACHINGS SOUGHT

Since China lost the Opium War in 1840, the advanced Chinese underwent countless tribulations seeking for the truth from the Western countries. Hung Hsu-chuan, Kang Yu-wei, Yen Fu, and Sun Yat-sen represented this group of people who sought for truth from the West before the birth of the Communist Party of China.

At that time, the Chinese who sought for progress read all the books that contained new Western teachings. The students sent to Japan, England, Amer-ica, France, and Germany reached a surprising number. Efforts were made to learn from the West. The old examination system of officialdom was abolished and schools multiplied.

What I learned in my youth were also such things. They were the culture of Western bourgeois democracy, or the so-called new school of learning which included the sociological doctrines and natural sciences of that time and which were antagonistic to the culture of China's feudalism, or the so-called old school of learning. For quite a long time, people who learned the new knowledge were confident believing that it was sure to save China. Apart from people of the old school, very few of the new school expressed doubt. To save the country, the only way is to enforce reforms, and to enforce reforms, the only way is to learn from foreign countries. Of the foreign countries at that time, only the Western capitalist countries were progressive. They had successfully estab-lished the modern bourgeois state.

The Chinese also wanted to learn from the Japanese. To the Chinese of that time, Russia was backward and very few people wanted to learn from her. This was how the Chinese learned from foreign countries during the period from the 40's of the Nineteenth Century.

Imperialist aggression shattered the dream of the Chinese to learn from the West. Really strange, why do teachers always invade students? The Chinese learned much from the West, but what they learned could not be put into effect.

Their ideal could never be realized. The conditions of the country worsened day by day, the environment was such that the people could not live. Doubt sprang up, grew, and developed.

The First World War shook the whole world. The Russians carried out the October Revolution, creating the first socialist country in the world. Under the leadership of Lenin and Stalin, the revolutionary energy of the great Russian proletariat and laboring people, which had lain hidden and could not be seen by foreigners, suddenly erupted like a volcano. The Chinese and all mankind then looked differently at Russians. Then, and only then, the Chinese from the fields of ideology to life entered an entirely new era. The Chinese found the universal truth of Marxism-Leninism which holds good everywhere, and the face of China was changed.

POSSIBILITY FOR WORLD COMMUNISM CREATED

The patterns of the Western bourgeoisie, the bourgeois democracy, and the pattern of the bourgeois republic all went bankrupt in the minds of the Chinese people. The bourgeois democracy gave way to the people's democracy under the leadership of the proletariat, and the bourgeois republic gave way to the people's republic. A possibility has thus been created to reach socialism and Communism through the people's republic, and to attain the elimination of classes and attain world Communism.

Kang Yu-wei wrote a book about world Communism, but he did and could not find the road to it. The bourgeois republic existed in foreign countries but could not exist in China, because China is a country oppressed by imperialism. The only road to the elimination of classes and to world Communism is through the people's republic under the leadership of the working class.

All other things had been tried and had failed. Of those who yearned for something else, some had fallen, some had awakened to their mistake, and some are changing their minds. Events developed so swiftly that many people felt surprised and the need to learn anew. This state of mind of these people is understandable and we welcome such good intentions to learn anew.

The vanguards of the Chinese proletariat learned Marxism-Leninism after the October Revolution and established the Communist Party of China. Following this, it entered into political struggle and traveled a zigzag path for 28 years, before gaining a basic victory.

From the experiences of 28 years, just as from the "experiences of the 40 years" in the will of Sun Yat-sen, a common conclusion has been reached, namely: "The firm belief that to attain victory we must awaken the masses of the people and unite ourselves in a common struggle with those peoples of the world who treat us on the basis of equality."

Sun Yat-sen has a different world outlook from us, and started out from a different . . . standpoint to observe and deal with problems, but on the problem of how to struggle against imperialism in the 20's of the Twentieth Century, he arrived at a conclusion which was in basic agreement with ours.

"TRAVEL THE ROAD OF THE RUSSIANS"

The Chinese found Marxism through the introduction of the Russians. Before the October Revolution, the Chinese not only did not know Lenin and Stalin, but also did not know Marx and Engels. The gunfire of the October Revolution sent us Marxism-Leninism. The October Revolution helped the progressive elements of the world and China to use the world outlook of the proletariat as the instrument for observing the destiny of the country and reconsidering their own problems. Travel the road of the Russians—this was the conclusion.

In 1919 the "May 4" movement occurred in China, and the Communist Party of China was formed in 1921. During his period, Sun Yat-sen came across the October Revolution and the Communist Party of China. He welcomed the October Revolution, welcomed Russian help to Chinese, and welcomed the Communist Party of China to cooperate with him.

Sun Yat-sen died, and Chiang Kai-shek came into power. During the long period of 22 years, Chiang Kai-shek dragged China into hopeless straits. At this period, the antifascist Second World War, with the Soviet Union as its main force, defeated three big imperialist powers, weakened two other big imperialist powers, and only one imperialist country in the world, the United States of America, suffered no loss. However, the domestic crisis of America was very grave. She wanted to enslave the entire world, and she aided Chiang Kai-shek with arms to slaughter several millions of Chinese. Under the leadership of the Communist Party of China, the Chinese people, after having driven away Japanese imperialism, fought the people's war of liberation for 3 years and gained a basic victory.

Two Basic Experiences Gained

Twenty-four years have elapsed since Sun Yat-sen's death, and under the leadership of the Communist Party of China, Chinese revolutionary theory and practice have made big strides forward, fundamentally changing the features of China. Up to the present, the Chinese people have gained the following two basic experiences:

1. To awaken the masses in the country. This is to unite the working class, the peasant class, the petty bourgeoisie, and the national bourgeoisie into a united front under the leadership of the working class and develop into a state of the people's democratic dictatorship, led by the working class, with the alliance of workers and peasants as its basis.

2. To unite in a common struggle with those nations of the world who treat us on the basis of equality and the peoples of all countries. This is to ally with the Soviet Union, to ally with the new democratic countries of Europe, and to ally with the proletariat and masses of the people in other countries to form an international united front.

"You lean to one side." Precisely so. The 40 years' experience of Sun Yat-sen and the 28 years' experience of the Communist Party have made us firmly believe that in order to win victory and to consolidate victory, we must lean to one side. The experiences of 40 years and 28 years show that, without exception, the Chinese people either lean to the side of imperialism or to the side of socialism.

No Third Road Exists

To sit on the fence is impossible. A third road does not exist. We oppose the Chiang Kai-shek reactionary clique who lean to the side of imperialism. We also oppose the illusion of a third road. Not only in China but also in the world, without exception, one either leans to the side of imperialism or to the side of socialism. Neutrality is a camouflage, and a third road does not exist.

"You are too provoking." We are talking of how to deal with domestic and foreign reactionaries, that is, imperialists and their running dogs, and not of any other people.

With regard to foreign and democratic reactionaries, the question of provoking does not arise, for whether there is provoking or not does not make any difference as they are reactionaries.

Only by drawing a clear.line between reactionaries and revolutionaries, only by exposing the designs and plots of the reactionaries, arousing vigilance and attention within the revolutionary ranks, and only by raising our own morale and taking down the arrogance of the enemy can the reactionaries be isolated, conquered, or replaced.

In front of a wild beast you cannot show the slightest cowardice. We must learn from Wu Sung, (one of the 108 heroes in the famous historical novel, "All Men Are Brothers") who killed a tiger on the Chingyang Ridge. To Wu Sung, the tiger on the Chingyang Ridge will eat people all the same whether you provoke it or not. You have to choose between the alternatives of either killing the tiger or being eaten by it.

DIPLOMATIC RELATIONS BASED ON EQUALITY

"We want to do business." Entirely correct. Business has to be done. We only oppose domestic and foreign reactionaries who hamper us from doing business, and do not . . . people. It should be known that it is not any other than imperialists and their lackeys, the Chiang Kai-shek reactionary clique, who hamper us from doing business with foreign countries and even hamper us from establishing diplomatic relations with foreign countries.

Unite all forces at home and abroad to smash domestic and foreign reactionaries and there will be business, and the possibility of establishing diplomatic relations with all foreign countries on the basis of equality, mutual benefits, and mutual respect of territorial sovereignty.

"Victory is also possible without international aid." This is an erroneous thought. In the era when imperialism exists, it is impossible for the true people's revolution of any country to win its own victory without assistance in various forms from international revolutionary forces, and it is also impossible to consolidate the victory even when it is won. The great October Revolution was thus won and consolidated as Stalin had told us long ago. It was also in this way that the three imperialist countries were defeated and the . . . in East Europe liberated. This is and will be the case with the People's China at present and in the future.

Let us think it over. If the Soviet Union did not exist, if there were no victory of the antifascist Second World War, and especially, for us, no defeat of Japanese imperialism, if the various new democratic countries of Europe did not come into being, if there were no rising struggles of the oppressed nations in the east, if there were no struggles of the masses of peoples in the United States, Britain, France, Germany, Italy, Japan, and other capitalist countries against the reactionary clique ruling over them, and if there were no sum total of these things, then the international reactionary forces bearing down on us would surely be far greater than that at present.

Could we have won victory under such circumstances? Obviously not. It would also be impossible to consolidate the victory when it was won. The Chinese people have had much experience about this. The remark made by Sun Yat-sen before his death about joining hands with international revolutionary forces reflected this experience long ago.

NO NEED FOR U. S.-BRITISH AID

"We need the aid of the British and American Governments." This is also a childish thought at present. At the present time, rulers in Britain and the United

States are still imperialists. Will they extend their aid to a people's state? If we do business with these countries, or supposing that these countries are willing in the future to lend us money on the condition of mutual benefits, what is the reason for it? This is because the capitalists of these countries want to make money. The bankers want to gain interest in their own crises; there is no aid to the Chinese people.

The Communist parties and progressive parties and groups in these countries are now working to bring about business with us, and even to establish diplomatic relations with us. This is well meant, this is aid, and this cannot be spoken of in the same breath together with the acts of the bourgeoisie in these countries.

During his lifetime, Sun Yat-sen had many times appealed to the imperialist countries for aid. The outcome was futile and instead met with merciless attacks. In his lifetime, Sun Yat-sen received international aid only once and that was from the USSR. The reader can refer to the will of Dr. Sun, in which he did not ask the people to look for aid from imperialist countries, but earnestly bade them "to unite with those peoples of the world who treat us on the basis of equality." Dr. Sun had had the experience; he had been duped. We must remember his words and not be duped again.

Internationally, we belong to the antiimperialist front, headed by the USSR, and we can only look for genuine friendly aid from that front, and not from the imperialist front.

"You are dictatorial." Yes, dear gentlemen, you are right and we are really that way. . . . The experiences of several decades amassed by the Chinese people tell us to carry out the people's democratic dictatorship, that is, the right of reactionaries to voice their opinion must be deprived, and only the people are allowed to have the right of voicing their opinions.

Who are the "people" at the present stage in China? They are the working class, the peasants, the petty bourgeoisie, and the national bourgeoisie. Under the leadership of the working class and the Communist Party, these classes unite together to form their own state and elect their own government to enact dictatorships over the lackeys of imperialism—the landlords, the bureaucratic class, and the Kuomintang reactionaries and their henchmen, representing these classes to oppress them and only allow them to behave properly and not allow them to talk and act wildly. If they talk and act wildly they will be prohibited and punished immediately.

The democratic system is to be carried out within the ranks of the people, giving them freedom of speech, assembly, and association. The right to vote is given only to the people and not to the reactionaries. These two aspects, namely democracy among the people and dictatorships over the reactionaries, combine to form the people's dictatorship.

No Benevolence for Reactionaries

Why should it be done this way? It is very obvious that if this is not done, the revolution will fail, the people will meet with woe and the State will perish. "Do you not want to eliminate State authority?" Yes, but not at present. We cannot eliminate State authority now. Why? Because imperialism still exists, the domestic reactionaries still exist, and classes in the country still exist. Our present task is to strengthen the people's State apparatus, which refers mainly to the People's Army, People's Police, and People's Court, for national defense and protection of the people's interests, and with this as condition, to enable China to advance steadily, under the leadership of the working class and the Communist Party, from an agricultural to an industrial country, and from a new democratic to a socialist and Communist society, to eliminate classes and to realize world Communism. The Army, police and court of the State are instruments for classes to oppress classes. To the hostile classes, the State apparatus is the instrument of oppression. It is violent, and not "benevolent." "You are not benevolent." Just so. We decidedly do not adopt a benevolent rule toward the reactionary acts of the reactionaries and the reactionary classes.

We only adopt a benevolent administration among the people and not toward the reactionary acts of the reactionaries and reactionary classes outside the people.

The People's State protects the people. Only when there is the People's State is it possible for the people to use democratic methods on a Nation-wide and all-round scale to educate and reeducate themselves, to free themselves from the influence of reactionaries at home and abroad (this influence is at present still very great and will exist for a long time and cannot be eliminated quickly— NCNA) to unlearn the bad habits and thoughts acquired from the old society and not let themselves fall on the erroneous path pointed out by the reactionaries, but to continue to advance and develop toward a socialist and a Communist society.

The methods we use in this field are democratic, that is, methods of persuasion and not coercion. When people break the law, they will be punished, imprisoned, or even sentenced to death. But these are some individual cases and are different in principle from the dictatorship over the reactionary class as a class.

REEDUCATION WORK

After their political regime is overthrown, those of the reactionary classes and the reactionary clique will also be given land and work and a means of living to reeducate themselves anew through work, provided they do not rebel, disrupt, or sabotage. If they are unwilling to work, the People's State will compel them to work.

Furthermore, political work, propaganda, and educational work will be carried out among them, and moreover, carefully and adequately, as we did to capture officers. This can also be said to be benevolent administration, but this is what we enact through compulsion to those of a formerly hostile class, and it . . . be mentioned, beside concrete education work among revolutionary people.

Such reeducation of the reactionary classes can only be carried out in the State of the People's democratic dictatorship. If this work is well done, the main exploiting classes of China—the landlord and bureaucratic capitalist classes— will be finally eliminated.

As for the remaining exploiting class, the national bourgeoisie, much appropriate education work can be carried out among many of that class at the present stage. When socialism is realized, that is when the nationalization of private enterprises will be carried out, they can be further educated and reeducated. The people have in their hands a powerful State apparatus and are not afraid of the rebellion of the national bourgeois class.

The grave problem is that of educating peasants. The peasant economy is scattered. According to the experiences of the Soviet Union, it requires a very long time and careful work to attain the socialization of agriculture. Without the socialization of agriculture, there will be no complete and consolidated socialism.

BETRAYAL OF SUN YAT-SEN

And to carry out the socialization of agriculture, a powerful industry with State-owned enterprises as the main component must be developed. The State of the people's democratic dictatorship must step-by-step solve this problem of the industrialization of the country. This article will not go too much into the economic problem, which will not be dealt with here in detail.

In 1924 a well-known manifesto was passed by the Kuomintang First National Congress, which was directed personally by Sun Yat-sen and participated in by Communists. The manifesto stated: "The so-called democratic systems in countries of modern times are often monopolized by the bourgeois class and turned into an instrument for oppressing the common people. But the democracy of the Kuomintang is the common possession of the common people in general, and is not the private possession of a minority."

Except for the question of who is to lead and who is to be led, the democracy mentioned here, when viewed as a general political program, is consistent with the people's democracy or new democracy mentioned by us.

Chiang Kai-shek betrayed Sun Yat-sen and used the dictatorship of the bureaucratic capitalist class and the landlord class as an instrument for oppressing the common people of China. This counterrevolutionary dictatorship remained in force for twenty . . . years and was only overthrown by the Chinese common people under our leadership now.

The foreign reactionaries who vilify us for carrying out a "dictatorship" and "totalitarianism" are in fact the very people who are carrying out dictatorship and totalitarianism. They have been carrying out the dictatorship and totalitarianism of one class, the bourgeoisie, over the proletariat and other people. They are the very people referred to by Sun Yat-sen as the bourgeois class in countries of modern times who oppress the common people. Chiang Kai-shek's counterrevolutionary dictatorship was learned from these reactionary fellows.

Chu Hsi, a philosopher of the Sung Dynasty, wrote many books and made many speeches about which we have forgotten, but there is one sentence we have not forgotten, and this is: "Do to others what others do unto you." This is what we do. That is, do to imperialism and its lackeys, the Chiang Kai-shek reactionary clique, what they do to others. Simply this and nothing more.

IMPORTANCE OF WORKING CLASS

The revolutionary dictatorship and the counterrevolutionary dictatorship are opposite in nature. The former learned from the latter. This learning is very important, for if the revolutionary people did not learn the methods of ruling over counterrevolutionaries, they would not be able to maintain their regime, which would be overthrown by the reactionary cliques at home and abroad. The reactionary cliques at home and abroad would then restore their rule in China and bring woe to the revolutionary people.

The basis of the people's democratic dictatorship is the alliance of the working class, the peasant class, and the urban petty-bourgeois class, and is mainly the alliance of the working class and the peasant class because this class constitutes 80 to 90 percent of the Chinese population. It is mainly the strength of these two classes which overthrows imperialism and the Kuomintang reactionary clique. The passing from the new democracy to socialism mainly depends on the alliance of these two classes.

The people's democratic dictatorship needs the leadership of the working class, because only the working class is most far-sighted, just, unselfish, and richly endowed with revolutionary thoroughness. The history of the entire revolution proves that without the leadership of the working class, the revolution is bound to fail, and with the leadership of the working class, the revolution is victorious.

In the era of imperialism, no other class in any country can lead any genuine revolution to victory. This is clearly proved by the fact that the Chinese national bourgeois class led the revolution many times and failed.

The national bourgeois class is of great importance at the present stage. Imperialism is still standing near us, and this enemy is very fierce. A long time is required for China to realize true independence economically. Only when China's industries are developed, and China no longer depends on foreign countries economically, can there be real independence.

The proportion of China's modern industry in the entire national economy is still very small. There are still no reliable figures at present, but according to certain data, it is estimated that modern industry only occupies about 10 percent of the total production output in the national economy of the whole country.

To cope with imperialist oppression, and to raise the backward economic status one step higher, China must utilize all urban and rural capitalist factors which are beneficial and not detrimental to the national economy and the people's livelihood, and unite with the national bourgeoisie in the common struggle.

CAPITALISM WILL PLAY MINOR PART

Our present policy is to restrict capitalism and not to eliminate it. But the national bourgeois class cannot be the leader in the revolutionary united front, and also cannot occupy the main position in the state. The national bourgeoisie class cannot be the leader of the revolution and should not occupy the main position in the institutions of the state, because the social and economic status of the national bourgeois class has determined its feebleness, its lack of foresight, its lacking in boldness, and fear of the masses by many of them.

Sun Yat-sen advocated "awakening the masses" or "helping the peasants and workers." Who is going to awaken and help them? To Sun Yat-sen this meant the petty bourgeoisie and the national bourgeoisie. But this is in fact unfeasible. Sun Yat-sen's 40 years of revolutionary work was a failure. Why? Because in the era of imperialism it is impossible for the petty bourgeoisie and national bourgeoisie to lead any real revolution toward success.

Our 28 years were entirely different. We had plenty of invaluable experiences, and the following were our three main experiences: 1, A party with discipline, armed with the theories of Marx, Engels, Lenin, and Stalin, employing the methods of self-criticism, and linked up closely with the masses; 2, an army led by such a party; 3, a united front of various revolutionary strata and groups led by such a party.

These mark us off from our predecessors . . . on these three things we have won the basic victory. We have traversed tortuous paths and struggled against rightist and leftist and opportunistic tendencies within the party.

DIFFICULT ROAD AHEAD

Whenever serious mistakes were committed in these three things, the revolution suffered setbacks. The mistakes and setbacks taught us, making us wiser. Thus, we were able to do better work. Mistakes are unavoidable for any party or person, but we demand that less mistakes are committed. When a mistake is committed, correction must be made: The quicker and the more thoroughly the better.

Our experiences may be summarized and boiled down into the following single-point—the people's democratic dictatorship based on the workers' and peasants' alliance led by the working class (through the Communist Party—NCNA). This dictatorship must unite in concert with international revolutionary forces. This is our formula, our main experience, our main program.

In the 28 long years of the party we have only done one thing, and that is, we have won the basic victory. This is worth celebrating because it is the people's victory and a victory in a large country like China.

But there is plenty of work before us, and like walking, what has been done in the past is simply the first step in the 10,000-mile-long march. Remnants of the enemy have still to be wiped out, and the grave task of economic construction lies before us.

Some of the things with which we are familiar will soon be laid aside, and we are compelled to tackle things with which we are unfamiliar. This is difficult. The imperialists bank on the belief that we are unable to tackle our economic work. They look on and wait for our failure.

We must overcome difficulties, and master what we do not know. We must learn economic work from all who know the ropes (no matter who they are— NCNA). We must acknowledge them as our teachers, and learn from them respectfully and earnestly. We must not pretend that we know when we do not know. Do not put on bureaucratic airs. Stick to it, and eventually it will be mastered in a few months, one or two years, or three to five years.

At first, many of the Communists in the U.S.S.R. also did not know how to do economic work, and the imperialists also waited for their failure. But the Communist Party of the Soviet Union won. Under the leadership of Lenin and Stalin, they not only could do revolutionary but also reconstruction work. They have already built up a great and brilliant Socialist state.

The Communist Party of the U.S.S.R. is our best teacher, from whom we must learn. We can wholly rely on the weapon of the people's democratic dictatorship to unite all people throughout the country except the reactionaries, and advance steadily toward the goal.

121

The Ambassador in China (Stuart) to Secretary Marshall

893.00/5–2047

NANKING, *May 20, 1947.*

In a move to bring under some semblance of control the 2-weeks-old series of rice and student demonstrations and disorders. the Government on May 18 promulgated a series of decrees forbidding public mass demonstrations and setting up channels for the presentation of grievances. Coincidentally, the Generalissimo issued a statement calling for discipline and the application of the processes of law. The background and development of this mounting crisis appear to be as follows:

As already reported in previous despatches, the first outbreaks were looting of rice shops in areas as widespread as Shanghai and Chengtu, but predominantly in the lower Yangtze Valley. These outbreaks closely followed a spectacular increase in the price of rice, with the merchants refusing to sell accumulated stocks. In self-defense the rice dealers then began to organize themselves. Effective action by the police has reduced the number of rice riots and held them under control.

In the meantime, unrest in the University has increased to such a point that practically every academic center in the country is on strike. The demands in the original University demonstrations were somewhat fanciful in that they comprised such things as protesting the elimination of a course on navigation in the curriculum of the Hangchow Christian College, protests against examinations which are now scheduled, and demands for removal of certain colleges from one city to another. As the demonstrations spread, demands become more basic; now they are principally for an increase of Government subsidies to students and immediate termination of the civil war.

Giving added weight to the current seriousness of student demands is that the majority of sympathy among faculty members is with the students. The highlight in protests by professors came in the form of a manifesto issued by the faculty of the government's National Central University in Nanking which strongly condemns government neglect of education, small appropriations, and attempts to control academic freedom of thought. The manifesto demands higher pay for teachers, larger appropriations for education and purchase of books and scientific instruments. It further warns that unless there is a drastic revision of basic policy, placing education on a more important level, the educational system of China is rapidly heading for disaster.

Demonstrations are estimated at between 3 and 10 thousand students each.

Leadership and motivation of the demonstrations have shown definite signs of changing. Most competent observers believe the original impetus was given by the CC Clique which was desirous of inciting a series of disorders which would in time publicly discredit a political science group-dominated government by proving it incapable of maintaining order, and in the long run provide the justification for a strong-arm, right wing government coming into power either through a coup d'etat or through sweeping the elections to be held this fall. All this has coincided with growing public agitations for a new peace movement. Aside from repeated demands for peace in the liberal and independent press, two outstanding examples are the request by three members of the Peoples' Political Council that Communist representatives be invited to attend the session which convenes on May 20, and a petition signed by 13 members of the Legislative Yuan that the government forthwith offer new peace terms. With this kind of public backing it is now apparent that leadership in the disturbances organized by the CC Clique is passing into the hands of the Democratic League and the Communists. This development can hardly be displeasing to the CC Clique, which can now claim that lack of public order is attributable to their enemies. Just how much of the agitation is now under Communist leadership is debatable, but it must be assumed that the Communists are present and, if not already active, are prepared to exploit the situation should it become necessary or desirable.

Chang Chun's government is facing an important test. Having banned demonstrations on May 18, several thousand Shanghai students on May 19 proceeded to disregard the order and demonstrate for peace. No measures were taken against them. On May 20, students in Nanking organized a demonstration to demand peace at the opening session of the PPC. The government stationed troops around Nanking University to prevent movement in or out. Other university students, under the leadership of the National Central University, organized a movement to "liberate" their fellow students. They marched into the Nanking University, joined forces with students there and marched out. Again no action was taken by either police or soldiers beyond some blank rifle fire. As the students marched on the national assembly hall, where the PPC was meeting, they were confronted by barricades, fire hoses, and blackjacks which resulted in some disorder and a few injuries to students, as the PPC hastily adjourned for the morning.

Large bodies of students are still assembled in the vicinity of the national assembly hall confronting barricades manned by police and gendarmes. It remains to be seen what action the government will take in face of this public flouting of its authority, but it is apparent that there is in train a student movement of considerable proportions which if not halted soon will tend to expand and contribute to further deterioration of the already parlous politico-economic situation.

J. LEIGHTON STUART

122

The Ambassador in China (Stuart) to Secretary Marshall

893.00/6–447

NANKING, *June 4, 1947.*

Wide-spread and comprehensive action by the government was responsible in largely forestalling the projected development of the June 2 general student strike. This action took the form of numerous arrests, the imposition of martial law in many localities and concentration of force in areas where trouble was expected. Symptomatic of government intentions was a meeting between Generalissimo and academic members of the PPC, in which the latter stated that they were doing all they could do to prevent demonstrations but that if they did take place they begged the government to avoid use of violence. The Generalissimo replied that he had personally issued orders against demonstrations and that, therefore, there would be none, but that, if there were, any measures necessary would be taken to put them down. The Generalissimo further stated that the student movement was obviously Communist-led and inspired and, therefore, must be dealt with on those terms. The unfortunate coincident, from the student standpoint, that June second was date proclaimed last year by Communists as anti-civil war day was also responsible for causing many students to question advisability of carrying out their original plans on scheduled date. This argument was effectively used, particularly in Nanking, by faculty members in persuading students at least to delay.

Week-end action and developments were in brief as follows: In Shanghai martial law was imposed and student arrests reached the 200 mark. There was a rally on the campus of Chiaotung University but no violence. In Canton there was a fracas between students and unidentified elements resulting in several injuries. Nothing happened June 2. In Nanking there was a large and obvious increase of garrison strength, plans for June 2 were cancelled and *a peaceful rally* was held at the National Central University on June 3. At Hankow, on June 1, students clashed with the police, resulting in three deaths and many injuries among the students. Following this, Hankow faculties went on strike. In Chungking there were some 1,500 arrests, including approximately 20 reporters from independent papers. Tientsin was quiet. In Peiping communications were cut between the city and Yenching and Tsinghua universities. Barbed wire barricades were erected around universities within the city confining students to campuses and, as far as is known, one was killed and several were injured trying to break out.

These somewhat anti-climactic developments and superficial success of the government in preventing wide-spread disorders should not be taken as indicating that impetus of student discontent has been diffused or destroyed. Evidence indicates that, if anything, students are more determined than ever to make their views known and to ensure that their rights and security shall in the long run be secured. Educated opinion in Nanking is that the government will continue its repression, mostly through medium of arresting ringleaders, but that this in the end will prove ineffective because too many students are now aroused and in the face of repression are becoming increasingly cohesive in the drive for obtaining their objectives. This opinion believes that something has now been started which cannot be destroyed by force, especially as economic and military position of the government deteriorates during the summer months. There is also evidence that increasingly faculty members sympathize with student aims.

J. LEIGHTON STUART

123

The Ambassador in China (Stuart) to Secretary Marshall

893.00/5–3047

NANKING, *May 30, 1947.*

The Peoples Political Council on May 26 by a large majority passed a resolution inviting Chinese Communist representatives to come to Nanking for discussions on ways and means of bringing about the termination of civil war. The Resolution reads as follows:

"In view of the fact that peace is the unanimous desire of all the Chinese people, and of the delegates to the Peoples Political Council who have decided to do their utmost to solve the present national crisis.

We have therefore resolved to ask the delegates of the Chinese Communists to attend the PPC meeting to discuss national affairs."

It has been broadcast on all government radios.

This resolution points up one phase in the growing agitation, particularly among leftwing and intellectual circles, for a negotiated peace. The first aspect of this movement is that many, perhaps even most, of those involved in the agitation are sincere in their professed belief that the first essential step to the solution of any of China's multitudinous problems is peace. It is perhaps unfortunate that none of the groups or leaders involved have so far brought forth any constructive suggestions as to how this commendable objective is to be accomplished, nor has there been any suggestion that the Communists in their present and relatively favorable position may not be amenable to compromise.

The second aspect is that the government, since the agitation has arisen and presumably having a fairly realistic understanding of what the Communists could or could not be expected to do, may not be altogether displeased that the peace movement has developed as it has. If the words of prominent government spokesmen can be taken at their face value, they must believe that any overtures of peace negotiations would be either ignored or repulsed. Hence it is not unreasonable to assume the probability that the PPC resolution combined with similar agitation in the Legislative Yuan will in the predictable future be followed by a formal government offer to the Communists for negotiations.

J. LEIGHTON STUART

124

The Ambassador in China (Stuart) to Secretary Marshall

893.00/7–147

NANKING, *July 1, 1947.*

Communist military successes, the shrinkage of railway mileage in Nationalist hands, the depreciation and depletion of Nationalist equipment and supplies, the increasing friction between southern military forces and civil administrators on one hand and northern troops and the local civil population on the other, reports of a projected withdrawal of Nationalist forces to intramural China and the abandonment of Manchuria to the Communists, rumors of the early return of Marshal Chang Hsueh-liang to Manchuria, and the expanding economic stagnation suggest the following observations:

The recent Communist drive has met with little Nationalist resistance. Northeast Combat Command sources and military observers admit that many Nationalist withdrawals were premature and without military necessity. The words "strategic retreat" have lost all significance. As a result the Communists possess almost complete initiative and are able to maneuver practically at will. If Ssupingkai with its garrison of 17,000 falls, the Communists should be able to proceed successfully against bypassed Changchun and Kirin and thereupon gain unimpaired control over 90 percent of Manchuria. The fall of Yingkow would leave only ports on the west coast of the Liaotung Gulf in Nationalist hands. The only railway of any appreciable mileage in Nationalist hands is the Peiping-Liaotung main line. The Communist drive eastward through Jehol is threatening even these meager holdings and should this drive be successful and contact be established between these forces and those now in the vicinity of Yingkow, Manchuria will be effectively cut off from land and water communication with China, and Mukden itself will be virtually in a state of siege. Nationalist military intelligence has been outstandingly deficient. The Northeast Combat Command is seemingly in almost complete ignorance of Communist plans and is therefore being constantly outwitted. Northeast Combat Command headquarters officers admit they had no intelligence of the recent Communist drive on Changchun and then southwards, even though it is now known that such plans therefor had been formulated three months prior to the opening of the drive.

Rivalry (if not enmity) between General Hsiung Shih-hui, the Generalissimo's representative, and General Tu Li-ming, commanding the Northeast Combat Command, is openly discussed and the absence of closely integrated military and economic planning in Manchuria is attributed to it.

By holding the initiative, the Communists are able to keep the Nationalists scurrying over the countryside, thereby causing depreciation of Nationalist motorized mobile equipment and depletion of sorely needed supplies. Communist transport on the other hand consists almost wholly of draft animals. Persons in direct contact with the Nationalist troops in rural areas state there are insufficient small arms and ammunition to arm all combatant troops now in the field. These reports are so consistent, some, though not necessarily full, credence must be given them. The Communists also are underarmed, but by guerrilla tactics and surprise night attacks they are able to cause greater loss of weapons and expenditure of ammunition by the Nationalists than by themselves.

Nationalist southern military forces and civil administrators conduct themselves in Manchuria as conquerors, not as fellow countrymen, and have imposed a "carpet-bag" regime of unbridled exploitation upon areas under their control. If military and civil authorities of local origin were in control, they too would probably exploit the populace, but experience has shown that Chinese authorities of local origin, in general, never quite strangle a goose laying golden eggs, and furthermore, it is a human trait to be less resentful toward exploitation by one's own than toward that by outsiders. The result of this is that the countryside is so antagonistic toward outsiders as to affect the morale of non-Manchurian troops and at the same time arouse vindictiveness in southern military officers and civil administrators.

Nationalist withdrawals toward Mukden have progressively cut off Nationalist-held areas from the great food producing regions in Manchuria, thereby causing a potential Nationalist food shortage which was already apparent in extensive grain hoarding and speculation. Puerile efforts have been made toward price control and to combat hoarding, but in general, the results of these efforts have been largely to enforce the requisitioning of grain at bayonet point for controlled prices and to enable the resale of requisitioned grain at black market prices for the benefit of the pockets of rapacious military and civil officials. The common man is being crushed between the rising cost of living and the depreciating currency. (The cost of living index of May, 160 percent compared to 100 percent in April.) Local currency is pegged to Chinese National Currency and has not only fallen with CNC, but also because of the wholesale exodus of families of Nationalist officials and the resulting flight from local currency incidental to frenzied buying of CNC and gold bars. The black market value of the U. S. dollar at Mukden is now TP dollars 3,300 against TP dollars 1,000 March 1.

Little goods move between Mukden and its hinterland. Business is rapidly approaching a standstill, exports from Manchuria have practically disappeared and imports have reduced to a trickle of the normal. Almost all capital has been expended in long-range investment since the Nationalists took over Manchuria and no such capital, government or private, is being invested today. All commodity markets are purely speculative.

The evidence is growing daily that the people of Manchuria not only are prepared for but are keenly desirous of a change in the government. But what change? Most are undecided even though voluble in discontent of the present way of living and the trend of events. It is safe to state that the overwhelming majority in the nation are as dissatisfied with, dislike and would welcome freedom from the present Nationalist regime. A like majority fear and would therefore not welcome the Communist regime. Many talk "revolution" even aloud in public places, but few are able to define their conception of revolution other than as change from the present way of living and even fewer envisage revolution involving armed resistance. There seems no likelihood that an armed uprising would be more than abortive, at least until the national morale and military might has suffered devastating deterioration. One platform on which Manchus seem almost unanimous is "out with Heilien (outsider) Chinese and Manchuria for the Manchus." The return of Ma Chan-shan lent heart to those who look to restoration of Manchu rule under a "native son," but his relegation to figurehead status in a position of impotence has dampened their hopes. Eyes are today turned toward the possibility of the return of the young Marshal to power in Manchuria. His vices, weaknesses and "playboy" tendencies are known but he is nevertheless associated in the minds of the people with prosperity and progress which Manchuria enjoyed under Chang Tso-lin regime. He or some other pre-Manchu leader could serve as a central figure for rallying the Manchu people. Such a change would in all likelihood herald the return of warlordism to Manchuria, but even so Manchuria would remain Chinese with nominal allegiance at least to China and not a "Manchu peoples republic" as it may become if the Communists succeed in sweeping the Nationalists back into intramural China.

There is every reason to believe that punitive military action against the Communists, unless succeeded by overwhelming military occupation will not save Manchuria to China. It is high time for Nanking to be realistic and to replace its present impotent disliked regime in Manchuria with one which will be supported by the local population and would thereby serve to weaken the Communist movement. It may be, and some think that it is, too late to accomplish this purpose. Without some such effective measure there are many indications that it will be only a matter of some months, perhaps six to nine, before Manchuria will be lost.

125

The Ambassador in China (Stuart) to Secretary Marshall

893.00/4–547

NANKING, *April 5, 1947.*

Review of the labors and accomplishments of the Third Plenary Session of the Kuomintang Central Executive Committee reinforces the tentative conclusions which I suggested in my report of March 23. The two principal points of interest were: (1) the efforts of certain factions within the Kuomintang to obstruct reorganization of the government and (2) the struggle for power and position, mainly between the CC–Clique and the Political Science Group.

On the first point, the Generalissimo, supported by the Political Science Group and liberal elements, was successful in blocking the drive to stop reorganization.

In the struggle between factions, the Generalissimo emerged in a· stronger position than ever before and higher in the esteem of his party. At the same time the CC-Clique also seems to have emerged in a stronger position, to the detriment of other factions; but full confirmation must await the publication of personnel to the State Council and the Yuan. Evidence of his political astuteness, as well as the strength of his roots in the past, is found in his present trip to his home to sweep the tombs of his ancestors which he can combine with a brief period of "absent treatment" for the third parties. He stopped off for a few hours in Shanghai for business in connection with his position as President of the Executive Yuan.

The CC-Clique (the most fanatically anti-Communist group in China) is far and away the most disciplined Kuomintang faction, and because of its comprehensive organization, reaching into every *hsien* in the country, is able to fulfill the Generalissimo's needs in this phase of his struggle with the Communists.

The tragic paradox of his position, of which he may be unaware, is that he is being compelled by circumstances to utilize the qualifications which the CC-Clique can offer. At the same time this clique exploits its preferred position to render more firm its hold on the Party and the country; and with time the Generalissimo therefore may well become less and less able to dispense with them or to circumscribe their activities, which can only serve to aggravate those social conditions basically giving rise and strength to the Communist movement.

There are many evidences that the Chen brothers are now attempting to insert themselves into the economic field and that Chen Li-fu desires to become Vice-Chairman of the National Economic Council.

It is more difficult to estimate the position now of other groups, such as the Political Science Group, Sun Fo and other liberals. Certainly General Chen Cheng, and probably parts of the military cliques, went along with the CC-Clique and will continue to do so. The Political Science Group was instrumental in helping to unseat T. V. Soong, though in the process it failed in its objectives to consolidate its hold on financial affairs because the CC-Clique was successful in gaining headship of Central Trust. Though having failed to control the

Party, the Political Science Group did block CC attempts to nullify the process of reorganization. In this struggle it was supported by Sun Fo and his followers. The most serious Political Science Group concern now is economic. Wong Wen-hao has said that if Chen Li-fu did become Vice-Chairman of the National Economic Council, it would be impossible for him, and perhaps for others around him, to continue on the Council. Such an eventuality would be somewhat balanced by what now appears to be the certainty that Sun Fo would be Vice President of the reorganized State Council and General Chang Chun President of the Executive Yuan. These factors, of course, must remain to a certain extent speculative until appointments are actually announced since the Generalissimo gives his complete confidence to no one.

On balance, it would appear that the struggle will be continued between the liberals who will control most of the high government positions and have a major interest in the economic world and the CC-Clique largely controlling the Party organization and an influential section of the army, and attempting to inject itself into finance. During the Central Executive Committee the liberals showed their fundamental lack of cohesive organization and their unwillingness or inability to defend each other publicly against the unrelenting CC attack. How far this compromises their standing can only be demonstrated when reorganization has been accomplished.

Recently Chen Li-fu has shown some interest in plans for basic agrarian reform and restriction of corruption within the Party, which are, after all, the two measures which can offer a social as opposed to a military solution of the Communist question. Various liberal elements within the Party who accept the inevitability for the time being of CC-Clique influence are encouraging this interest on his part. It remains to be seen how successful they can be but account must be taken of his past record and the known narrowness of his economic and political views. Those who know him well are by no means sure that he really understands the urgency of the agrarian problem in China or the measures which could reform it.

The economic proposals which Chen Li-fu submitted and which were passed by the Central Executive Committee are being made subject of a dispatch.

The political resolutions are comprehensive, skillful and well designed to secure the avowed intention of tightening Party control and discipline in the face of pressures and disintegration arising from the civil war. It is reported that CC-Clique is putting its main effort in preparing for the elections which will precede implementation of the Constitution on December 25, 1947.

In accordance with the Central Executive Committee resolution, preparations proceed for termination of the period of political tutelage. The Executive Yuan has approved ten basic laws on organization and elections. Negotiations on reorganization are proceeding slowly. In the interim a game of political musical chairs being played by the third parties, the Social Democrats have finally agreed to enter the government, though Carson Chang himself will not; and it is now the turn of the Youth Party to be difficult and increase its demands. Based on the experience of the last few months, it is by no means impossible that the positions of these two minor parties will shortly be reversed. The Foreign Minister remarked the other day on the irony of a situation where the Generalissimo, having been made self-conscious about his ability to dictate political settlement and consequently reluctant to use bludgeoning tactics, finds himself in endless political dickering which only delays that reorganization which his liberal advisors have been urging on him.

126

Summary of the Manifesto Issued by the Kuomintang Central Executive Committee [4]

893.00/3–2547

The present plenary session of our party has taken place just a year after the conclusion of the second plenary session. During the year, the greatest accomplishment in China's political development was the convocation of the National Assembly and the promulgation of the Constitution of the Republic of China.

It is three months since the promulgation of the constitution. We rejoice that the date for the institution of constitutional government is drawing near and that our long-cherished desire of nation building is nearing realization. But as we survey the present situation in our country, we cannot help feeling deeply regretful that our nation is still beset with difficulties and we realize all the more keenly the weightiness of our responsibility for the national revolution.

Now, the plan for broadening the basis of the government is being carried out. Reorganization of the national government will end the political tutelage of the country under our party. Henceforth, the Government of China will no longer be the sole responsibility of one party. And the status of our party and its relations with the government will also differ from those in the past. But the sincere efforts of our party in promoting the welfare of our country and the people must be pushed vigorously forward.

In the light of the internal situation of our country, we wish to enumerate below five important tasks on which we should concentrate our efforts in the future:

1. Complete preparations for the institution of constitutional government and the drafting of a pattern for nation building.

The consistent objective in our party's struggle for the past 50 years has been the destruction of all obstacles standing in the way of democracy and the building of China based on Three People's Principles. After eight years of armed resistance Dr. Sun Yat Sen's Three People's Principles are now subscribed to by the entire nation. During the current interim period preceding constitutional government, the formulation of laws and regulations pertaining to the enforcement of the constitution, the guarantee of liberties and rights of the people, the revision of existing laws and regulations, the establishment of the systems of central and local governments and the holding of elections are all basic measures for laying a sound foundation for constitutional government. Our party should sincerely cooperate with other parties and they should help one another in advancing the welfare of the nation. Meantime, our members should go into and among the masses and help educate them in constitutional government.

2. Remove all obstacles to national unification and consolidate the foundation of the country.

During the past year, the national government issued cease fire orders three times and carried out continuous mediation and negotiations. But the Chinese Communists, pinning their implicit faith in armed force and acting in violation of good faith took advantage of the government's tolerance, and each time when the government made a concession, they carried out general mobilizations in their illegally occupied areas. Now they have launched an all-out offensive and wherever their military force reaches, the people are either displaced from their homes or are plundered and killed. As a consequence, unity of the country

---

[4] Released by the Central News Agency, Nanking, Mar. 24, 1947.

is undermined and economic reconstruction and rehabilitation are likewise hindered because of the Communists' wanton and systematic destruction of communications. For the sake of preserving the existence of the country and the nation, and for the sake of delivering the people from their present state of distress, this plenary session deems it imperative that the national government should take resolute and speedy measures to suppress the armed rebellion.

3. Carry out the principle of people's livelihood and stabilize national economy.

Another serious obstacle to the development of our nation is economic maladjustment. This plenary session considers that the only way to remedy this situation is to carry into effect the principle of people's livelihood by reforming our economic policies. Thus, all the economic policies of the government must be aimed at promoting the welfare of the masses, including the farmers. Economic rehabilitation and reconstruction must not be confined to large cities but extensively pushed to all rural areas. Further, there should be rational administration of finance, improvement of procedures for extending loans to productive enterprises and extensive establishment of cooperatives. At the same time, the nation as a whole should sincerely observe all the laws and ordinances pertaining to the enforcement of emergency economic measures.

4. Uphold international justice and strive for world peace.

The supreme objective of our foreign policy has always been the maintenance of national independence and equality and the promotion of international justice and peace. The stand we take in our relations with others conforms with our traditional spirit of "not to oppress the weak nor fear the strong."

Our country has never harbored any ambition of dominating the world. Nor will it permit itself to become a pawn in international relations. It is the firm belief of our party that an independent, free and strong China is the *sine qua non* to the maintenance of world peace. As long as world peace is not ensured, China will not be able to pursue her task of national reconstruction unhindered.

At present, the world situation is in a state of confusion and instability, but the wisdom gained by mankind through the tragic sacrifices made in the recent world war should be the main force for establishing world peace and security. We fervently hope that the United Nations Organization will grow quickly and become strong and that through it all international complications may find their satisfactory solution.

5. Vitalize the educational program so as to build up the potential strength for national reconstruction.

What is generally regarded as a matter of great regret in our work of national reconstruction is the inadequacy of our educational measures and the slackening of school discipline.

The youths of our country are dissipating their energy in empty and vague political activities. To build up the nation, it is necessary to have persons specialized in various kinds of technical professions. But many young men today cannot set their mind at peace to receive practical technical training. The government should henceforth lay greater emphasis on education.

Our party, having dedicated itself to the cause of national revolution, thinks only of duty and minds, not power. To whatever is of benefit to the country, we will address ourselves, even at the cost of our lives. It behooves our comrades to resolutely keep faith in their mission, sincerely do their duty, rectify their shortcomings, strive to improve themselves, serve the people and be loyal to the country. Thus, we may not fall short of the expectations of the founder of our Republic, the martyrs of the war of resistance and our distressed fellow countrymen in the postwar period.

127 (a)

Statement by President Chiang Kai-shek Announcing the Reorganization of the State Council [5]

893.00/4–2047

The reorganization of the State Council, which takes effect Monday is another step in the transition from Kuomintang tutelage to constitutional government in China. It gives representation on the nation's highest policy making body to minor parties and to independent.

The composition of the State Council under this reorganization is as follows:
The Presidents of the Executive Yuan (ex-officio)—five seats.
Kuomintang 12 seats; Democratic Socialist party—4 seats.
Young China Party—4 seats; independents—4 seats.

At present the Yuan Presidents are all Kuomintang members, so that the total Kuomintang seats number 17. But assumption of these posts by members of other parties or by independents automatically would reduce the Kuomintang representation.

It was originally planned that the membership of the State Council consist of 40, with the Kuomintang members numbering 20. At present 29 seats have been occupied. If the remaining 11 should be filled, the Kuomintang membership will be 17 out of 40, or less than half.

In the case of the Democratic Socialist and Young China Parties, the individuals were selected by the groups themselves. In the case of the independents, I made the selections after consultation with the individuals concerned.

The broadening of political representation on the State Council follows the election of minority party members to the Legislative and Control Yuan and the established multi-party government. The next step is the forthcoming reorganization of the Executive Yuan under the new Premier, with Cabinet ministries assigned to minority parties and independents as well as the Kuomintang.

The effect of the reorganization on the Chinese Government is as follows:
Control of the Government, hitherto exclusively under the Kuomintang, is broadened to control by the KMT, the Democratic Socialist Party, the Young China Party, and Independents. The State Council will direct China's affairs during the transitional period, carry out the mandates of the last National Assembly, and prepare for the inauguration of constitutional government on December 25, 1947.

China's postwar political history has been divided into two phases. First, came an attempt with American mediation to persuade the Communists to join the government and merge their army into the national army.

The second phase began with the National Assembly. The participation by the Democratic Socialists, the Young China Party, and Independents in that body and in the adoption of the constitution meant that they supported the government's effort to bring in the constitutional era.

The world is not static. China's need for peace and reconstruction becomes more urgent every day. China must push vigorously ahead to achieve unity by the quickest means possible. Progress toward democracy and constitutionalism cannot wait indefinitely for the Communists.

---

[5] Released by the Central News Agency, Nanking, Apr. 18, 1947.

If the Chinese Communist Party abandons its policy of seizing power by force and cooperates to achieve the unity of the nation, it still has the opportunity to join the government and participate in the work of national reconstruction. For the sake of China's suffering people, it is hoped that the Communists will change their present attitude of open rebellion.

127 (b)

Text of the Political Program of the National Government of China [6]

893.00/4–1847

The National Government of the Chinese Republic, with a view to establishing constitutional government and promoting democracy has since the political consultation conference (January 1946) decided to reorganize the government and to invite individuals from political parties and groups other than the Kuomintang, as well as independents, to participate. More than one year's persistent efforts have just resulted in a jointly formulated and agreed upon procedure for immediate completion of the government reorganization. Besides, a political program for the National Government after the reorganization, evolving from comprehensive and careful deliberations by all parties concerned, has just been approved, respectively, by the standing committees of the Young China Party, the Democratic Socialist Party and the Chinese Kuomintang; it has also been agreed upon by the Independents who took part in the discussions. The embodiments of the political program, which will be adhered to jointly by the reorganized National Government, are as follows:

One. The program of peaceful national reconstruction shall be the guiding principle of administration for the reorganized National Government, while all participating parties and independents shall be jointly responsible for completing the interim procedure for inauguration of constitutional government.

Two. Cooperation among the various parties and groups shall be based upon the principles of "political democratization" and "nationalization of armed forces" under this common principle, no efforts will be spared toward political progress and national stability.

Three. In order to promote world peace and uphold the United Nations charter, China should pursue a foreign policy of equality and good neighborliness, without discrimination, toward all friendly nations.

Four. Settlement by political means shall remain the basic principle for solution of the Chinese Communist problem. If only the Chinese Communists show willingness for peace and the railway system can be completely restored, the government will seek national peace and unity through political channels.

Five. The responsible Executive Yuan system shall be enforced as an experiment, in accordance with the spirit of the provisions of the constitution. The Executive Yuan should abide by any decisions of the State Council and assume full responsibility for their execution, thus conforming to the principle of "authority and responsibility". Equal respect should be accorded to the functions and powers of the Legislative Yuan. In presenting a bill to the Legislative Yuan, the Executive Yuan authorities shall be present to offer explanations, thereby insuring coordination between the executive and legislative authority.

Six. Pending the inauguration of constitutional government any nomination

---

[6] Published by the Government on Apr. 17, 1947.

to the presidency of the Executive Yuan shall be made by the President (of the Republic) with the previous concurrence of the various parties.

Seven. Provincial administrations shall be governed by principles making a clear distinction between the military and civil authorities and allowing expediencies as local conditions warrant. In matters of personnel, and legislation, a thoroughgoing checkup will be made and reform instituted in order to enable the provincial governments to attain the highest degree of efficiency possible.

Eight. All laws promulgated and all institutions established to meet the needs of political tutelage shall, after reorganization of the National Government, be rescinded and abolished.

Nine. Thorough adjustments shall be made in the tax system and financial setup, the procedure of levying taxes shall be simplified, and the categories of land tax and additional levies shall be reduced, in order to alleviate the burdens of the people.

Ten. Strict guarantee shall be accorded to the people's freedom of person, freedom of speech, freedom of publication and freedom of assembly. Any illegal arrest or interference shall be strictly forbidden. Where restrictions are deemed essential for the maintenance of social order or to avert a crisis, laws governing such restrictions shall be approved by the State Council.

Eleven. Foreign loans henceforth to be contracted shall all be earmarked for purposes of stabilizing and improving the people's livelihood and of production and reconstruction.

Twelve. As far as possible, there should be participation of political parties and independents in the political councils or provisional councils of the provinces, municipalities and hsiens. Local governments in the various provinces should also include representatives of various parties and independents, based on the principle of "selection of the able and efficient."

127 (c)

Statement on April 23, 1947, by the Chinese Minister of Information (Peng)

893.00/4–2347

I am happy to be able to announce that one-party rule in China has come to an end today. The Kuomintang has fulfilled its promise of handing over the political power to the people and carrying out its program for establishing constitutional government after the tutelage period. The formal completion of the process came with the inaugural meeting of the new multiparty State Council, at which the Executive Yuan was reorganized to include representatives of other parties and independents.

This action, following the election of members of different parties to the Legislative and Control Yuan, means that the multiparty transition government has now been fully set up and is ready to govern the country in the spirit of the constitution until the new government provided by that charter is elected.

The composition of the Executive Yuan is as follows: President, Chang Chun; Vice President, Wang Yung-wu; Minister of Interior, Chang Li-sheng; Minister of Foreign Affairs, Wang Shih-chieh; Minister of National Defense, Pai Ch'ung-hsi; Minister of Finance, O. K. Yui; Minister of Economic Affairs, Li Huang; Minister of Education, Chu Chia-hua; Minister of Communications, Yu Ta-wei; Minister of Agriculture and Forestry, Tso Shun-sheng; Minister of

Social Affairs, Ku Cheng-kang; Minister of Food, Ku Cheng lun; Minister of Water Conservancy, Hsueh Tu-pi; Minister of Justice, Hsieh Kuan-sheng; Minister of Land, Li Ching-chai; Minister of Public Health, Chow I-chun; Chairman of National Resources Commission, Wong Wen-hao; Chairman of Mongolian and Tibetan Affairs Commission, Hsu Shih-ying; Chairman of Overseas Chinese Affairs Commission, Liu Wei-chih; Ministers without Portfolio, Chang Nai-chih, Li Ta-ming, Chiang Yuen-tien, Miao Chia-min, Peng Hsueh-Pei, Lei Chen.

127 (d)

Inaugural Radio Speech by the President of the Executive Yuan (Chang)[7]

893.00/4–2347

My fellow countrymen, four months have passed since the promulgation of the Constitution of the Republic of China. The Kuomintang is now in the process of concluding its political tutelage. It has broadened the basis of the Government. Furthermore, in accordance with the spirit of the Constitution, it has advanced the practice of the responsible Executive Yuan system.

The next eight months will be a period of transition from political tutelage to constitutional democracy. The government must complete preparations for implementation of the Constitution. It must seek to restore national unity and stability. At the same time it must exert its utmost to resolve the serious financial and economic problems of the moment. These tasks are extremely difficult. On their accomplishment depends the fate of the country for generations to come.

It is with much apprehension, and awareness of my own limitations, that I am assuming the premiership at this hour. Fortunately, we have as our highest guiding principles the "fundamentals of nation reconstruction" which were laid down by Dr. Sun Yat-sen, father of the republic. For political and economic reforms during this period, we have also the sound resolutions adopted at the recent Third Plenary Session of the Kuomintang Central Executive Committee. As to the administrative policies to be followed after reorganization of the government there is an agreement reached among the different parties and nonpartisans. These will enable me, under the leadership of the President and in deference to public opinion, to attempt the execution of a difficult task.

We can well anticipate the possible difficulties and obstacles born of long years of war. However, I shall begrudge no effort or labor. Nor shall I be influenced by personal loss or gain. I will give what I have and what I am in the interest of national unity, democracy, peace and reconstruction. On my assumption of office today, I wish to outline a few of my administrative policies and appeal for the solidarity and cooperation of my countrymen.

The first and foremost need for China today is internal stability and unity. This is the prerequisite to national reconstruction. Ever since V–J Day, the Government has, with the greatest zeal and patience, been seeking a political solution of the Chinese Communist problem. During the past year, on instructions of the President, I have time and again participated in the negotiations for peaceful unification. Unfortunately, the situation has deteriorated so that today the Chinese Communists are in an all-out armed rebellion against the state, thus slamming the door for further negotiations and nullifying all past

---

[7] Released at Ministry of Information press conference, Apr. 23, 1947.

efforts toward peace. In order to restore social order and safeguard national unity the Government is constrained to take effective military measures to quell the rebellion. It is the challenge of the time. It is the demand of the people. It is, above all, the duty of any government. In discharging this grave responsibility, however, the Government has not failed to realize the serious consequences or the pains and sufferings necessarily involved. It is my fervent hope that such military measures will quickly bring about a fundamental solution, eventually by political means, of the internal strife and thus successfully restore national unity.

Eight long and difficult years of war have sapped China's economy, and have made life miserable for her people. Another year of internal disturbances has rendered the financial, social and economic crisis of the country more acute than ever before.

As a move to weather the present crisis, the Government has already promulgated a set of emergency economic measures. These will continue to be enforced. In removing the causes of the crisis, the Government will have to carry out step by step the economic program already formulated. In view of the general depression and suffering throughout the country, it is imperative that past mistakes should not be repeated. Special caution must be taken in policy making. Piecemeal action should be avoided, and emphasis must be placed on measures for a fundamental solution. Matters not immediately related to the balancing of the budget, the stabilization of currency, or the requirements of the people's livelihood are not to tax the attention of the Government. Progress should be sought through stability. Above all, no effort should be spared to encourage privately operated economic enterprises in order to divert idle capital to productive channels. And the basis for all progress and reform is the faith and confidence the Government is able to inspire.

As for political reform, the Government will take the responsibility to revitalize the administrative machine. It will uphold strict discipline, eradicate corruption, and break up bad habits of shoddiness and procrastination in order that administrative efficiency may be increased. I appeal to all responsible officials of all levels to carry out Government policies, and to set personal examples of self-discipline, selflessness and fairmindedness. In this way, the rule of law may be secured, and a wholesome political atmosphere created.

The guarantee of civil freedoms and rights is a most essential item in the preparation for constitutional government. The Government will, in accordance with the constitution and the new administrative policies, safeguard all civil freedoms and rights according to law. At the same time, it is my hope that all the people of the country will fully respect the divinity of the law, enhance their law abiding spirit, and realize their responsibility towards the state. In so doing, freedom and law will go hand in hand, thus ensuring the successful development of a constitutional democracy in China.

In the field of foreign relations, what China sincerely hopes to see is a peaceful, righteous, friendly and cooperative world. The Chinese Government therefore reaffirms its consistent stand to live at peace with all friendly nations of the world. Towards her wartime allies such as the United States, the Soviet Union, Great Britain and France, China will spare no effort to perpetuate the friendship and comradeship cemented through a common struggle for a common cause. In the case of any unsettled problem that may adversely affect friendly relations, she is willing and prepared to seeks a reasonable solution through customary diplomatic channels. In the interest of world peace she will also exert her utmost to increase mutual understanding and harmony among her allies.

For the settlement of the various pending postwar issues among nations and the establishment of the peace, order and cooperative relations of the world, China will not fail to contribute her share of the responsibility. Nor will she permit impairment of the standing she has secured in the family of nations. She will support the United Nations Charter, abide faithfully by treaty obligations, and respect the legitimate rights and interests of friendly states. She is equally determined to preserve her own sovereignty and independence as well as her own status among nations.

A most crucial moment has arrived in China's history. On her hands there are a host of practices, either to be initiated or to be reformed. However, China's potential is vast, and her entire populace is enthusiastic for an orderly government. While we should in no wise under-rate our present difficulties and obstacles, I see no ground for pessimism and skepticism about the prospect of China's renaissance if only we can marshal and organize the will and strength of the whole people for developing the potential of the country.

Out of the multifarious tasks pressing for attention and action, the Government will select the most essential ones and tackle them energetically and solidly. Each of us, individually, must shake off his inertia, faithfully observe the laws and regulations and take part in the recovery. Government can lead the way, but there must be patriotic and energetic cooperation by all the people to make leadership successful.

Should it so happen that the laws and decrees of the Government are not faithfully enforced, or should the sufferings or wishes of the people have escaped the attention of the Government, I hope that public opinion will prevail to help repair the shortcomings. The Government will welcome any constructive, helpful and concrete suggestions.

Although I shall make no claim of achievements throughout my thirty years of military and civil service, I find it gratifying that I have never permitted myself to overstep the confines of the law for personal reasons or expediency. Nor has personal gain or loss ever been in my consideration.

As I assume office today, at this time of national distress, I fully realize the grave responsibility on my shoulders. I shall do my duty to my country, faithfully and loyally. I shall try to repay the sympathy and fulfill the aspirations my fellow countrymen and party comrades have shown for me. Animated by a spirit of selflessness and confident of the people's cooperation, I hope this Government will successfully restore national unity, complete the preparations for constitutional government, surmount the economic crisis, and ameliorate the people's livelihood.

128

The Ambassador in China (Stuart) to Secretary Marshall

893.00/4–1947

NANKING, *April 19, 1947*

It is too early to assess with any accuracy the eventual effect of State Council reorganization announced April 17, and any such assessment must be approached with caution in the light of a series of past Chinese Government reorganizations which have been largely for external effect and have brought little effective change to the Chinese domestic scene.

The Embassy's initial impression, however, is that the caliber and standing of Kuomintang appointees indicates real effort to place in positions of power and responsibility the most capable and modern figures of the Party. It is indeed promising that in the case of Kuomintang appointees there is a notable exclusion of persons closely affiliated with the CC-Clique. A possible exception to this is the appointment of Wu Chung-hsin sometime governor of Sinkiang province.

It is also encouraging that the Political Science Group is well represented by its most prominent and ablest members including Chang Chun, Wong Wen-hao, Wang Chung-hui, and Wan Shih-chieh. Chen Pu-lei and Chiang Mon-lin, although not generally considered as members of the Political Science Group, may be expected to support Political Science Group policies.

The appointment of Sun Fo as Vice President of the National Government is no doubt intended to strengthen the progressive or liberal elements and to set the pattern to the Government. The inclusion of Shao Li-tze and T. V. Soong indicates at least a drift away from the traditional aspects of Chinese political conservatism.

Chu Chen, Yu Yu-jen, Tai Chi-tao, Chang Chi, and Chou Lu can be best classified as Party elders, faithful to the Generalissimo and essentially conservative in political outlook, but generally accepted as being in support of high standards of public morality.

A disappointing aspect of the announcement was the failure to change any of the Presidents of the Five Yuan, with the exception of Chang Chun, who replaces T. V. Soong as President of the Executive Yuan and relieves the Generalissimo of his temporary assumption of the office. It had been originally planned that Chang Chun-mai (Carson Chang), leader of the Social Democratic Party, would be appointed President of the Judicial Yuan and that Tseng Chi, leader of the Youth Party, would be given the presidency of one of the other four Yuan. The final refusal of Carson Chang to accept office in the Government, even though sanctioning the participation of his party made it impossible to carry out this plan and for the time being at least all Yuan Presidencies remain in Kuomintang control.

In the case of the Social Democratic Party, even in the final stages of reorganization of the State Council, there was continued reluctance on the part of members of the party to join the government and on the evening of April 17 it was only possible for the Social Democrats to name three members of their allotted four. It has been announced that they will appoint the fourth member as soon as possible.

Youth Party and Social Democratic Party appointees are largely unknown quantities. They represent in the case of the Youth Party a group of Szechuan scholar-landlords who have tended in the past to be affiliated with the right wing of the Kuomintang. The Social Democratic Party appointees are a group of elderly scholars without important political following in the country.

On the other hand, the independent appointees offer considerable promise, particularly in the case of Chen Kwan-pu (K. P. Chan), the most able private banker in China with a high reputation for his statesmanlike judgment and probity in New York and Washington as well as China. Wang Yun-wu, present Minister of Economic Affairs, seems also a satisfactory appointment as an independent. Both K. P. Chen and Wang Yun-wu are sympathetic to the Political Science Group and will tend to strengthen its position in the State Council. Mo Teh-hui has obviously been appointed because of his long affiliation with events in Manchuria. Pao Erh-han (Burkhan), a Turki and present Vice-Chairman of the Sinkiang Provincial Government is no doubt intended as a placatory gesture toward the minorities of the northwest. In this same general connection it will be noted that among the Kuomintang appointees there is included Chang Chia-hutuktu, a Tibetan.

In summary, the composition of the State Council is as regards the Kuomintang and independents as good as could be expected in the circumstances. Whether or not the State Council, which will constitute itself on April 23, if its members can reach Nanking by that date, will assert itself in such a manner as to bring about substantial social and economic reform in China remains, of course, a question depending upon many factors not the least one being the attitude of the Generalissimo toward it and his ability to control the Kuomintang as the still dominant political party in China.

It is interesting to note that at the same time as the appointment of Kuomintang State Councillors, a separate political committee of the Kuomintang was established. The Secretary General of this committee is Chen Li-fu and it is a safe assumption that this committee will have an important role in controlling the Kuomintang political machine and establishing party policies.

Eleven seats in the State Council have been left vacant for the Democratic League and the Communist Party in the event that they wish to join the interim government. On the night of April 17 Lo Lung-chi made known to the Embassy that Democratic League participation was at this time "impossible". Furthermore, it seems extremely unlikely that there will be any Communist participation in the government between now and the end of the year when the new constitution comes into force.

The reorganization of the Executive Yuan which will be carried out by the State Council will offer some indication of how assertive and energetic the Council will be and in what direction the government may be expected to move. Concessions to the CC-Clique, however, because of its control of Kuomintang machinery, may be expected to ensue in this reorganization.

In face of the magnitude of Chinese internal problems, aside from the existence of a state of civil war, to expect too rapid change would be unrealistic, but the calibre of Kuomintang and independent appointees to the State Council offer reasonable ground for hope that there will be an effort made to achieve healthy and substantial change. Such change will come slowly, however, and in the process it must be borne in mind that the CC-Clique, while at the moment not in the forefront, is still substantially in the control of the Kuomintang party machinery. The inclusion of non-Kuomintang groups at least offers promise for the stimulation of political activity and the development of non-Communist opposition, but in the final analysis the major imponderable is whether or not the Generalissimo will be capable of seeking and being guided by the advice of liberal-progressive public servants rather than acceding to the reactionary henchmen personally loyal to him.

STUART

129

The Ambassador in China (Stuart) to Secretary Marshall

893.00/7–547

NANKING, *July 5, 1947*

Following is the text of the resolution on general national mobilization passed by the State Council July 4:

With a view to delivering the people from Communist-held areas, safeguarding the existence of the nation, and consolidating national unity, it is herein proposed that a national general mobilization be enforced to quell the rebellion of the Chinese Communists and remove obstacles to democracy, thereby inaugurating constitutional government according to schedule and implementing thoroughly the program of peaceful national reconstruction:

Following the conclusion of the war, the government immediately embarked upon rehabilitation in order that reconstruction might be launched to resuscitate the people. Admittedly, not all of its administrative measures succeeded as expected.

With regard to the acts of the Chinese Communist Party in carrying out its regional domination through its own army, ravaging towns and cities, and staging armed rebellion against the state, the government consistently and steadfastly held to the policy of political settlement and, to seek its materialization, exercised utmost tolerance and made most liberal concessions.

Since October last year, however, the Chinese Communist Party have renounced the cease-fire orders issued by the Government, boycotted the National Assembly, and furthermore, rejected the Government proposal to send a representative to Yenan for peace negotiations. Lately, the Chinese Communists, through their propaganda organ, flatly turned down the peace proposal initiated by the People's Political Council.

While the Government is concentrating on the reorganization of the army the Chinese Communists are expanding their armed forces to coerce the people. While the Government is engaged in rehabilitation and reconstruction the Communist rebels are everywhere obstructing the work and destroying communications and industrial and mining enterprises. While the Government is devoting itself to the realization of democratic rule and the preparation for inauguration of constitutional government, the Communist rebels are advocating democracy and persecuting people at the same time.

In recent months, the Communist rebels launched large-scale offensives against National troops in North and Northeast China to prevent the Government from taking over national territory and sovereignty. Their intention of destroying the nation is evident and their rebellious actions of instigating riots to disturb social peace and order are obvious.

The Communist rebels, in openly starting their all-out armed rebellion, have practically ostracized themselves from the people of China. In fact, they have long considered themselves as an armed rebellious group rather than a political party. Apparently they are ready to go any length to antagonize the nation. They are so obdurate and incorrigible that the Government's policy to achieve peaceful national reconstruction can no longer be realized through political means.

The suffering of our compatriots in Communist-devastated North China and regions near Communist-held areas is daily aggravating. The Government should no longer fail to redeem its negligence and remain callous to the people's afflictions. The people of the nation, in order to live and work peacefully, must make every effort to remove this greatest obstacle to national reconstruction. Otherwise, they cannot safeguard the foundation of the nation and stabilize social order to ensure security for the country and the people.

It is the duty and responsibility of the Government to achieve unity in the nation and safeguard the survival of its people. If the Communist rebellion is not speedily suppressed, not only constitutional democracy cannot be realized, but unity and security of the nation will not be ensured. It is, therefore, with great reluctance that the Government has determined to quell the Communist rebellion. To remove the obstacles in the way of constitutional democracy, and to attain the final aim of national reconstruction, we must intensify our campaign against the Communists and, at the same time, redouble our efforts in reconstruction, which are to be achieved only through a singleness of purpose and marshalling of national resources.

With this purpose in view, it is proposed that the State Council order a national general mobilization and encourage the people to help in its execution. Plans concerning the acceleration of economic reconstruction, the reform of local governments, the mobilization of manpower and resources, the improvement of food and conscription administrations, the maintenance of social order, the mitigation of the people's sufferings, the protection of their basic rights, the practice of thrift, the increases of agricultural and industrial production, and the amelioration of the treatment of officers and men shall be carefully drafted by the competent authorities and enforced in accordance with law. The competent authorities shall also be instructed to guard against abuses in the execution of those plans.

STUART

130

Central News Agency Bulletin Dated July 5, 1947 [8]

893.00/7-847

General Chang Chun, President of the Executive Yuan, declared in an exclusive interview with Central News this evening that the government is determined to restore national unity through the suppression of the Communist rebellion and to accomplish national reconstruction and rejuvenation by hard self-exertion.

General Chang said that the Executive Yuan received instructions from the National Government yesterday to enforce national general mobilization, to remove obstacles to democracy and to carry out the peaceful reconstruction policy. This is an important step taken by the government for speeding up national reconstruction and it will be put into execution immediately, General Chang added.

Explaining the reason why the government should enforce a national general mobilization to quell the Communist rebellion, General Chang said that the government is deeply concerned over the sufferings of the people and is forced to take military action immediately to quell the Communist rebellion which, otherwise, would probably destroy the whole nation.

China had hoped to embark upon national reconstruction, to democratize her government and to industrialize her economy immediately after the Sino-Japanese war, General Chang recalled, but unfortunately, during the war the Communists took advantage of national grievance, expanded their armed forces which after the war have constituted a serious obstacle to the reconstruction of the country.

The protracted peace negotiations between the government and the Communists, the convocation of the Political Consultation Conference and the mediation of American friends have all failed to stop the Communists' sinister ambition to seize political power by military force, General Chang remarked. During the past two months, the Communists have further intensified their subversive activities, starting open armed rebellion, persecuting the people and destroying whatever construction work the government has done, he added.

The significance of the general mobilization is to rally the national will and strength to speed up political and economic reconstruction by removing all

[8] Transmitted by the Ambassador from Nanking, July 8, 1947.

obstacles, General Chang asserted. It is a struggle between the constructive force and destructive force as well as a struggle between the democratic force and the anti-democratic force. It is quite unexpected that China in the course of national reconstruction should have to pass through such a period. Now that it has been forced upon us, we must rally our national strength to overcome all difficulties. We are determined to restore national unity through the suppression of the Communist rebellion and to accomplish national reconstruction through hard self-exertion. The stronger is our will the shorter will be this difficult period, General Chang opined.

The national general mobilization is more positive for national reconstruction than for the suppression of the Communist rebellion, General Chang said. When the nation is striving for peace and unity, the Premier said, all the people should place the interests of the state above their own. The government should respect the rights and freedoms of the people and the people should also respect law and strengthen their sense of responsibility toward the state.

During the period of national general mobilization, the government will see that all orders are faithfully and promptly carried out he said. Government officials should win the confidence and cooperation of the people and coordination among various government departments should be further strengthened. Corruption and delinquency among government officials and armed forces should be wiped out, General Chang emphasized.

Reviewing the history of national revolution, General Chang expressed the belief that China's national reconstruction can never be obstructed by any reactionary force. Now that the government has determined to suppress the Communist rebellion and consolidate national unity, the people all over the country are expected to support the government's policy and contribute their share to bring the task to consummation, General Chang concluded.

131

Radio Broadcast on July 7, 1947, by President Chiang Kai-shek [8a]

893.00/7–1147

My Fellow-countrymen:

On this, the tenth anniversary of the Double Seventh, I feel called upon to earnestly inform you of the following major happenings since the conclusion of the war: the change of our national situation, the crisis confronting our nation as a whole, and the factors that will determine our destiny.

It was primarily to defend her domain, recover the Northeast and preserve her sovereign and territorial integrity that China fought the Japanese aggressor. She will never attain her war aim so long as her sovereignty and territorial administration in the Northeast remain unrestored, nor will the death of millions of Chinese soldiers and civilians be vindicated. The responsibility, therefore, falls equally on the shoulders of the survivors.

In the Northeast, as everybody knows, there were no Chinese Communist rebels prior to the Japanese capitulation. In the one and a half year, however, since National troops entered that part of the country to take over sovereignty there, Communist rebels at different times launched five offensives against Na-

---

[8a] Issued by the National Government Information Office, Nanking, July 7, 1947.

tional troops. They besieged and attacked areas already taken over by the Government, carved up the territory, and slaughtered the populace.

Lately, the Communists' reply to the peace proposal from the People's Political Council was first, a barrage of vituperatives through their propaganda machine, and then a series of fanatical thrusts outside of the Great Wall. The latest Communist offensive in the Northeastern provinces, because of its unprecedented magnitude, is especially significant. Since early May, the Communists, in powerful thrusts, have thrown more than 300,000 men against various strategic bases. Finally, they focussed their attacks on one single locality, Szepingkai, employing a force that outnumbered the defenders ten to one. The battle raged for 18 days and nights.

Thanks to the fighting stamina of our forces developed during the war against Japan, the invading Communists were given a decimating blow. Their plot to encircle Changchun and Kirin and seize Shenyang (Mukden) was crushed, and the tide of war turned in our favor.

Under no circumstances, however, will the Communist rebels abandon their consistent, insidious design of ruining their own fatherland. It cannot be conceded that the Ssupingchieh victory may have fundamentally removed the crisis facing the Northeast. Everyone knows well just how the Chinese Communist rebels entered the Northeast and how the various rebellious units there were organized.

The Chinese Communists patently are heir to imperialistic Japan and the "Manchoukuo" puppets, and they are now in the process of carrying out the pernicious plot to distintegrate China which was left unfinished by their Japanese predecessors. That plot would not permit restoration of Northeast sovereignty to the Chinese nation nor would it allow the Chinese nation to enjoy territorial and administrative integrity.

Worse still, the Chinese Communists have even made a cat's paw of remnant Japanese troops to ravage our territory and people at their command. In perversion, malignancy and treachery, the Chinese Communists indeed are worse than any bandit, traitor or puppet in Chinese history.

Fellow-countrymen, we must realize that, in thus engaging in armed rebellion, the Communists aim to disintegrate all of China and our whole nation. They seek total elimination of our national spirit and hereditary virtues, eternal enslavement of our race, and the complete deprivation of the basic human attributes of independence and freedom.

Should the Communists, indulging in such bestial acts of destroying human instincts and suppressing human ethical concepts, be allowed to continue to exist, the Chinese nation would in the near future suffer the disaster of national extinction with indiscriminate, wholesale massacre, collective banishment and eternal slavery for all the composite racial groups.

The aim of our National Revolution is to build a new, independent, free China—of the people governed for the people and by the people—on the basis of the Three People's Principles. To build such a nation requires, first of all, national unity and peace. Without national unity, however, there can be no national peace. Nor can there be democracy and liberty. National unity is all the more important for the people's welfare. Therefore, if national unity cannot be achieved, the ideal of national reconstruction will remain illusory and the Principles of Nationalism, Democracy and People's Livelihood can never be realized. The people naturally cannot enjoy normal life when their land is being devastated, their economy monopolized, their production destroyed and their communications disrupted by the Communists.

You may still remember my earnest appeal to the Communist Party after V-J Day: "With the devastating war barely ended, there should not be any civil strife." No responsible government or patriotic individual would let the country and the people fall into another war when they are still suffering from the ravages of a large-scale war.

We have never attempted to castigate communism as a theory or ideal. We continued to hope that the Communists might follow the course of democracy, as the Communists in Great Britain and the United States have done for so many years, by appealing to the electorate for support of their platform. We have been consistent for the past ten years, and even more so in the last year and a half, in our attitude toward the Communists. We have practised extreme tolerance and we have made substantial compromises and concessions, in the hope that the Communists would refrain from disrupting national unity, carrying on military regional domination, and undermining the foundation of the nation, and that they would contribute their share in national reconstruction. The Government was willing to give full consideration to their opinions. But no peace talk, no mediation, has succeeded in dissuading the Communists from staging a rebellion. We had no way of appealing to their conscience to give up their destructive policy in the interest of the nation and the people.

The activities of the Communist rebels in the past year or so were centered in the destruction of communication lines, industrial and mining plants and the already-depleted farms. Every attempt of the Government to appeal for peace and every issuance of a cease-fire order only brought further expansion and attacks of the Communist rebels, which added more difficulties to the National Armies and increased the sufferings and sacrifices of the people, thus creating unparalleled difficulties in our postwar social revival. Now, all fellow countrymen can rest assured that the Communists, whose rebellious character does not seem to change for the better, have no faith in repentance, and apparently are determined to rebel to the last. Their ambition and intrigues will not be halted until the country is ruined and the world as a whole menaced. If we do not discern the treacherous plots of the Communists, and if we are not determined to quell their rebellion, not only will the people's livelihood be impoverished, but the whole country will be disintegrated.

It was the pre-determined policy of the Chinese Communists to rebel against the Government after the conclusion of the war. After V-J Day, they openly launched the so-called "join-the-army movement," "social struggles," and "people's liquidation," in the rebel areas. They looted what food and clothing they could find in order to conserve their rebellious strength. Not even the old men and women or the children are spared from their terrorism and wantoness. Youngsters in rebel areas must either follow their dictates or perish, and burial alive or torture are meted out if the slightest opposition is shown. If a man escapes from rebel control, his whole family is executed. Thousands upon thousands of our compatriots in rebel areas have become sacrifices to the Communists, who have opposed the Government and menaced the people.

In provinces away from the front, especially in large cities of Central and South China, there are still many who do not realize the gravity of our national crisis and the vicious and sinister terrorism of the Communists. They are deluding themselves into false security. They must realize that if it had not been for the struggles of our soldiers to quell the Communist rebellion, they could not maintain their normal living and would be placed in the same tragic conditions as people in North and Northeastern China. Therefore, if we weaken the strength of the National Army, we will deprive the people of their right to exist. Because the people remote from the front are not aware of the realities of the situation, the Communists instigate their reactionary elements everywhere to disseminate anti-civil war and anti-conscription of food and soldiers slogans in an attempt to confuse right and wrong, drug people's minds, bewilder the masses and finally weaken the national foundation. This has been done to prevent us from mustering our man power and resources for suppressing the Communist rebellion and hastening reconstruction.

We can say that our people are being poisoned by Communist propaganda. It is evident that the Communists, in order to implement their plot to betray the country and the people, are trying to blindfold us and deaden our conscience. The aim of the Communists is to confuse the people so they will ignore their national consciousness and the disaster which confronts them and lose their faith in self-improvement and independence, thus falling spiritual captives to the Communists.

The existing confused situation is what the Communists hoped to create. An old saying goes: "A bird nesting on a falling bough is unaware of imminent disaster." As a matter of fact, if the nest eventually falls, none of the eggs will remain unbroken. Fellow-countrymen, procrastination now will bring death in the near future. It will be too late for regret if we fall into the same pit as our compatriots in the rebel areas. Our country and the destiny of all our people face such a serious crisis that I cannot delay calling upon you to be on the alert.

Fellow-countrymen, there are two ways before us and we must immediately choose between them. The first is to vacillate before the ravages and devastation of the Communists and our whole people will perish. The other is to face the facts realistically, put down the rebellious elements and salvage our nation as well as ourselves. Shall we choose to quell the Communist rebellion with concerted efforts, so as to protect our sovereignty, hasten national unity and attain the goal of freedom and democracy? Or, shall we procrastinate before Communist vandalism and see our villages pillaged, our kinsmen humiliated, our children compelled to become instruments of betrayal, and eventually our national life ruined? We must remember how our compatriots are passing their days in North and Northeastern China.

The people in the Northeast underwent more than a decade of Japanese subjugation and enslavement. But since the war ended, Communist terrorism, suppression, looting, and massacring have superseded imperial Japan's despotic rule. During the war, people of North China sustained the greatest losses and underwent the severest tribulations. After the war, instead of having a breathing spell, they were again overrun, this time by the Communists, and thrown into another dark abyss. In their recent offensives the Communists made the "peoples' militia" spearhead the attacks. Wherever the Communists hit, they looted and took prisoners, not sparing even dogs and poultry. Their wantonness surpassed even that of the Japanese. Whenever the Communists occupy a place, tens of thousands of the inhabitants at great risk move into the Government-controlled areas to find shelter, leaving their homes and property behind them. Their lamentations are the most tragic human utterances. How can those of us remote from the front who have the same ancestral origin, remain indifferent to their lot. The aim of the Communist rebels is to exterminate the country and enslave us all. We must suppress the Communist rebels, otherwise we shall undergo the same sufferings in the near future.

With our rehabilitation work yet to be completed, I am fully aware that our people in the recovered areas are leading a hard life. At any rate, they obviously are far better off than their brethren in rebel areas where personal freedom, physical or spiritual, is absolutely forbidden. No whisperings are allowed even between father and son, husband and wife.

Therefore, not only does our suppression of the Communist rebels help to save our compatriots in the rebel areas, but it also helps to save ourselves. If we let the Communist rebellion spread unchecked, we would be inviting ruin. The ambition of the Communists is obvious, and it is our responsibility to quell them.

We suffered cruelly and sacrificed the lives of millions of soldiers and civilians during our war against the Japanese invaders. If we let the Communist rebels attain their goal of destroying the Government and erasing the history of our war of resistance, thus completing the unfinished task of the Japanese to exterminate China, how can the losses we suffered during the war be redeemed?

Suppression of the Communist rebellion, therefore, is aimed at preserving the highest interests of the state and the basic rights of existence, democracy, and liberty of the people. Our struggle against the Communist rebels is as sacred as was our resistance against the Japanese aggressor.

The call to crush the Communist rebels is a continuation of the unfinished task of national reconstruction after our war against Japan. This is necessary, as I have told you, if we are to preserve the fruits of victory. Such a struggle is inevitable if we are to secure national independence and liberty. This being the case, the National troops who have fought and died for the cause should be respected by the people the same as those who fought and died in the Sino-Japanese war. Our 450,000,000 people must not shirk the responsibility of supplying sufficient food and munitions to the National troops at the front. In this task of saving the nation and protecting the people, all persons in areas at the front and in the rear should share their joys and sorrows and decide to live and die together.

Fellow-countrymen, the Communist rebels' ambition has been completely exposed in the recent battles in the Northeast. The national crisis has become more and more serious. Our people should not harbor the illusion that they may avoid participating in the struggle through some lucky occurrence or temporary peace. We must concentrate on our strength and redouble our efforts in suppressing the Communists and reconstructing the nation, so as to eliminate the seeds of misfortune for our future generations. We must achieve national general mobilization with the same spirit as we did during the war of resistance, and we must multiply our efforts in eliminating the deficiencies we had during the war of resistance. We must not hesitate to contribute all our manpower, material strength and lives, if necessary, to the war of suppressing the rebellion in a common effort to save our country and people. Only in this way can we preserve the fruits of our victory over Japan, achieve national independence and liberty and retain the hope of again securing social peace and order.

Fellow-countrymen, the National Government has issued an order for the enforcement of national general mobilization. The purpose of the order is to awaken the people of the whole country to unify their purpose and concentrate their efforts for the struggle. We must call on all patriotic Chinese to rise for the salvation of their country and themselves.

All the measures taken by the Government will be in accordance with law. The Government has implicit faith in the people's patriotic conscience and will let the people themselves serve the country spontaneously on the basis of the principle of nationalism. Every compatriot must love the country and the people, observe national laws and perform his duty. He must make every effort to contribute his part in the suppression of the Communist rebellion and the promotion of national reconstruction.

The nation's social leaders should guide the people in promoting the cause in every possible way. Our youths in particular, upon whom our national existence depends, must discern right from wrong and fair from foul and promote nationalism to safeguard national existence. Unless the youths of China are willing to be Communist instruments and are indifferent about national extinction, they must recognize that they are descendents of Huang Ti and nationals of the Republic of China. If they wish the nation to achieve independence and existence, so that they may have freedom of thought without oppression by the Communists, they must be determined to face the national crisis. Those who go to schools should devote themselves to study, and those who are engaged in agriculture, industry and business must devote themselves to production, so as to increase national strength. Everybody must play his part and do his duty in an effort to stabilize social peace and order in the rear.

Our people must know that the nation-wide Communist rebellion is coordinated and linked up with the Communists' well-planned destruction of social order. Ever since the beginning of our resistance against the Japanese, the Communist Party has consistently disparaged the war efforts of the Government with vituperative propaganda in an effort to undermine the Government. This was done to arouse discord between the Government and the people, weaken our strength in the war, relegate the international position of the nation, erase the history of our war of resistance, minimize the people's faith in winning the war and deaden the people's patriotism.

The Communists not only spread rumors and instigate riots in schools, among the people, in factories and in financial markets, but they also openly declare that such riotous and destructive actions are "the second front" as distinguished from "the first front," military operations. These two fronts are interdependent, so that military operations can disturb the community in the rear and riots in the rear can affect the troops at the front. This is malicious intrigue, and I must call it to your attention so that you may take timely precautions.

I can assure you that the Government's enforcement of national general mobilization will be in accordance with law. All military and administrative organs will respect the basic rights of the people. But anyone who disregards the national crisis and principle of nationalism, and who is willing to take part in the work of "the second front," disturbing social order and jeopardizing public safety under Communist direction, will be punished by the Government according to law, which is responsible for the maintenance of national existence and people's welfare.

At this time, when the war of suppression against the Communist rebels is developing and National troops are fighting at the front, all our patriotic countrymen must struggle with one object in view,—unified strength, definite aim and positive efforts,—so as to solidify our military strength and achieve early suppression of the rebellious forces.

The Government's policy regarding the present situation can be seen in the resolution of the State Council. The national general mobilization has been promulgated not only for the suppression of the Communist rebellion, but also for national reform and reconstruction. Therefore, I wish to point out the following two matters:

First, we must work for national reconstruction. To carry the reconstruction work to completion, we must concentrate today on the suppression of the Communist rebellion by marshalling our spiritual and physical strength, thereby realizing internal unity. We must at the same time intensify our efforts to increase agricultural and industrial production so as to frustrate the Communist intrigue to undermine the national economy by throwing obstacles in the way of reconstruction.

The progress made in the promotion of and the preparation for the inauguration of constitutional democracy will not be impeded by the suppression campaign. The Communists renounced constitutional democracy by boycotting the National Assembly and obstructing the progress of national reconstruction, although they have proclaimed that they are dedicated to democracy. From this, we can see that the Communists are fundamentally opposed to the enforcement of constitutionalism in China and to the accomplishment of national reconstruction. If the Constitution is enforced in China, the Communists will have to relinquish their military forces, and they will be deprived of their chief reliance, rebellion.

If China adopts political democracy, the people will become masters of their own destiny, and dictatorship of the proletarian, advocated by the Communists, can never be realized. Following the institution of constitutional democracy, the Government will embark on the necessary work of economic reconstruction, and the Communists will be unable to create social disturbances and capitalize on them to establish a Soviet regime.

It is on this basis that I want to emphasize to my fellow-countrymen, and especially to those who are actually striving for the realization of freedom in China and the democratization of our Government, that to attain constitutional democracy we must first eliminate the Communist rebels whose principles run counter to constitutional democracy and peaceful reconstruction. To save China from terror and chaos, we are duty bound to expedite the preparations for constitution enforcement, carry out completely the Principle of People's Livelihood and safeguard the people's basic rights. This being our consistent policy, we shall never slacken our efforts toward its realization.

Second, we must exert our utmost to effect administrative reforms. We have committed ourselves to a dual political program: to quell the Communist rebellion and introduce governmental reforms. Admittedly many defects exist in our administration. Weaknesses can also be found in our way of life. Immediately after the conclusion of the eight-year war, the Communist rebellion began, thus, we have been given no time to put our house in order. Our material resources, already drained by the war, are practically exhausted. The defects and weaknesses in the Government and in our way of life, which first made their appearance in the war, have now become more apparent. The sufferings of the people have immeasurably increased. Unless drastic reforms are introduced, China may not be able to exist in the family of nations. Therefore, political, educational, economic and social reforms, which should be made, shall not be delayed until the conclusion of the suppression campaign, but will be initiated right away.

We should seek to increase our national strength, mitigate the people's sufferings, and concentrate our will power to effect a thorough going reform so as to overcome all difficulties confronting us. Constructive criticisms and suggestions from the people on our political and economic policies and especially ways to alleviate the people's afflictions will be sincerely received by the Government, and measures for improvement will be instigated. It is also expected that people will report, with substantial evidence, mistakes made by governments of all levels, so that reforms may be made.

It was for the purpose of concentrating our efforts to effect an over-all reform and remove all obstacles in the way of national reconstruction that national general mobilization was ordered. It is therefore positive rather than negative in nature; it is nation-wide rather than local in scope. It is obligatory not only for the people, but for governments of all levels to seek improvement.

Dedicated to national revolution, I have struggled for the existence of the country and the people, the realization of the Three People's Principles, unity in the nation and the inauguration of constitutional democracy. I have never been mindful of personal gains or losses, glories or eclipses. All I can offer you is my sincerity to save the country and the people. I cannot betray our founding father and our martyrs. I cannot betray the cause of national revolution, for which I have fought so long. I cannot betray the soldiers and the civilians who died in the War of Resistance. I must preserve to the best of my ability the achievements of the eight-year war. I must lead the nation to crush the enemies who are obstructing the realization of our principles, destroying national unity and interfering with our efforts for peaceful reconstruction. I shall not waver till the final aim is achieved.

My fellow-countrymen! On this solemn occasion, I call for a rededication to the unfinished task of national reconstruction and a revival of the same spirit and energy manifested when we fought against the aggressors. At the conclusion of the war I said that the task of national reconstruction would be ten times more difficult than the military victory. In view of the accumulated effects of internal troubles and external aggressions over the last hundred years and the infirm basis on which this Republic was founded, we cannot make a new, indepedent, powerful and prosperous China in a day. But we can count on our long history, large population and the moral strength of our people. I am sure with these assets we shall be able to destroy the force that is hampering our reconstruction.

If only the entire population will rise up against the Communist rebels as they did against the Japanese, if only they will use the same determination and perseverance to deal with the Communist insurgents as they did in the War of Resistance, then the suppression of the Communist rebellion can be effected within a short period of time. Once this great difficulty is overcome, and the final obstacle removed, China will enter upon a glorious stage. We should not be distracted by Communist propaganda or dismayed by present difficulties, but should retain our self-confidence.

I hope we shall always remember our unflinching faith in ultimate victory during the War of Resistance and our strong determination to carry the work of national reconstruction to completion. By quelling the Communist rebellion and overcoming the last obstacle, we can expect to accomplish the important task of national reconstruction, and vindicate the sacrifice of soldiers and civilians who died in the War of Resistance and in the suppression campaign.

132

The Ambassador in China (Stuart) to Secretary Marshall

893.00/7–2147

NANKING, *July 21, 1947*

Following was published in Central News Agency English Service, dated July 19:

"Following is the text of 'The Outline for the Implementation of Mobilization to Suppress Rebellion and Complete Constitutional Government' which was adopted by the State Council today (July 18, 1947), to become effective immediately:

"Article 1. This outline has been formulated in accordance with the stipulations of the program for the enforcement of national general mobilization to suppress the Communist rebellion, remove obstacles to democracy and realize constitutional government as scheduled, which was adopted by the State Council, and the provisions of the National General Mobilization Act (promulgated by the National Government on March 29, 1942, and put into effect on May 5, 1942).

"Article 2. Enforcement of constitutional government and conducting of elections in connection therewith shall all be expedited as stipulated.

"Article 3. Manpower necessary for military, labor and other services required to suppress the rebellion shall be fully mobilized. Any action to evade or obstruct such services shall be punished in accordance with law.

"Article 4. All materials required to suppress the rebellion, including foodstuffs, clothing, medicine, oil, coal, iron and steel, transportation and communication equipment, and other supplies needed by the military, shall be immediately mobilized. Any action to evade or obstruct requisitioning of such supplies, hoard them or profiteer from them shall be punished in accordance with law.

"Article 5. Close cooperation shall be maintained between management and labor in all enterprises. All disputes shall be mediated or arbitrated in accordance with law. Sabotage, tne in-outs or any other actions hampering production or disturbing social order shall be punished in accordance with law.

"Article 6. In order to stabilize the people's livelihood, the government may institute restrictions or controls over market prices of .daily necessities, salaries and wages, the flow of materials, use of capital and other financial activities.

"Article 7. The Government shall, in accordance with law, take punitive measures against assemblies where speeches or other actions incite the people to rebellion.

"Article 8. In areas recovered from rebels, authorities concerned shall consolidate security measures and maintain social order. When necessary, loans may be extended, taxes in the areas suspended and social relief and medical aid carried out.

"Article 9. Refugees from rebel-held areas shall be given adequate relief, assistance and accommodation by authorities concerned.

"Article 10. Authorities concerned shall direct needs. In case of a shortage in capital, government banks may grant loans in order to increase supplies. If necessary, the Government may exercise control over finished products.

"Article 11. In areas free from the Communist rebels, local administration shall be revamped and social peace and order safeguarded. To improve the people's livelihood, priority shall be given to urgent projects of production, transportation, irrigation and water conservancy.

"Article 12. Equitable taxation shall be increased and unnecessary expenditure curtailed in order to finance the suppression of the rebellion.

"Article 13. Measures shall be formulated to enforce thrift and increase efficiency, for observance by both the Government and the people.

"Article 14. Basic rights of the people shall be fully respected and adequately safeguarded. Any impingement thereupon shall be strictly prohibited, unless necessitated by laws and decrees required for the implementation of mobilization and the suppression of the rebellion.

"Article 15. Where there is need for separate detailed measures for the implementation of the outline, such measures shall be drawn up by the Ministers and commissions of the Executive Yuan concerned, and, after their approval by the Yuan, promulgated by mandates for enforcement.

"Article 16. Violation of Articles 3 to 7 of the outline or any action that would be outlawed and restrained in accordance with the stipulations of these articles shall be punished in accordance with the provisional penal regulations for obstructors of National General Mobilization Act (promulgated by the National Government on June 29, 1942, and put into force on August 1, 1942).

"Public functionaries who, in the exercise of authority delegated to them under the outline, break the law or neglect their duties shall be punished in accordance with law.

"Article 17. In addition to the stipulations of the outline, the Executive Yuan may, in accordance with the provisions of the National General Mobilization Act, at any time issue mandates to expedite the suppression of the rebellion.

"Article 18. The outline shall be promulgated for enforcement after approval by the State Council."

133

Summary of Remarks Made by Lieutenant General Albert C. Wedemeyer Before Joint Meeting of State Council and All Ministers of the National Government August 22, 1947 [9]

121.893/8–2547   TAXATION:

Approximately 80 percent of the people of China are hard working peasants, their crops are visible and officials can easily appraise the amounts the peasants are able to give toward government. Corrupt officials in many instances take more than the peasants are able to give and this results finally in the peasants leaving the land and forming bandit groups.

In contrast to the taxation of peasants, Chinese businessmen and rich Chinese resort to devious and dishonest methods to avoid payment of proper taxes to their government. It is commonly known that Chinese business firms maintain two sets of books, one showing the true picture of business transactions and the other showing a distorted picture so that they do not pay as much tax as they should.

MILITARY:

For the first year after the war, in my opinion it was possible to stamp out or at least to minimize the effect of Chinese Communists. This capability was predicated upon the assumption that the Central Government disposed its military forces in such a manner as to insure control of all industrial areas, food producing areas, important cities and lines of communication. It was also assumed that the Central Government appointed highly efficient and scrupulously honest officials as provincial governors, district magistrates, mayors, and throughout the political and economic structure. If these assumptions had been accomplished, political and economic stability would have resulted, and the people would not have been receptive, in fact, would have strongly opposed the infiltration or penetration of communistic ideas. It would not have been possible for the Chinese Communists to expand so rapidly and acquire almost undisputed control of such vast areas. I believe that the Chinese Communist movement

---

[9] Transmitted by the Ambassador in China (Stuart) to Secretary Marshall, Nanking, Aug. 25, 1947.

cannot be defeated by the employment of force. Today China is being invaded by an idea instead of strong military forces from the outside. The only way in my opinion to combat this idea successfully is to do so with another idea that will have stronger appeal and win the support of the people. This means that politically and economically the Central Government will have to remove corruption and incompetence from its ranks in order to provide justice and equality and to protect the personal liberties of the Chinese people, particularly of the peasants. To recapitulate, the Central Government cannot defeat the Chinese Communists by the employment of force, but can only win the loyal, enthusiastic and realistic support of the masses of the people by improving the political and economic situation immediately. The effectiveness and timeliness of these improvements will determine in my opinion whether or not the Central Government will stand or fall before the Communist onslaught.

During the war while serving as the Generalissimo's Chief-of-Staff, I tried to impress upon all Chinese military officials the importance of re-establishing excellent relationships between officers and enlisted men. I explained that officers must show sincere interest in the welfare of their men both in times of war and in peace. Wounded must be evacuated from the battlefield and cared for in hospitals or aid stations. Officers should visit their men in the hospital and find out if they can visit them in any way. Officers should play games with their soldiers such as basketball and soccer. The junior officers should know all of their men in the unit by name. They should talk to them and encourage them to discuss their problems. Explain to them why they are fighting. Explain the objectives of their Government and encourage open discussions. This will create a feeling of mutual respect and genuine affection. Discipline acquired through fear is not as effective as discipline acquired through affection and mutual respect. It would be so easy for the Chinese officers to win the respect and admiration of their men who are simple, kindly and brave and who will gladly endure hardships and dangers if they are properly led and cared for.

CONSCRIPTION:

I have received many reports that the conscription of men for military service is not being carried out honestly or efficiently. Again, as in taxation peasants are expected to bear the brunt of conscription, although in the cities there are thousands and thousands of able-bodied men, who should be under the conscription laws eligible for military service. Rich men's sons by the payment of money avoid conscription and the sons of rich men are being sent to school abroad instead of remaining here to help their country in a time of great crisis.

RELATIONSHIP BETWEEN MILITARY AND CIVILIANS:

I cannot emphasize too strongly the importance of establishing and maintaining good relationship between military forces and the civilian population. Officers and men in the army and air corps should be very careful to be courteous, friendly, cooperative and honest in all of their contacts with civilians. In Manchuria, I was told by many sources that the Central Government armies were welcomed enthusiastically by the people as deliverers from Japanese oppression. Today, after several months of experience with these Central Government armies, the people experience a feeling of hatred and distrust because the officers and enlisted men were arrogant and rude. Also they stole and looted freely; their general attitude was that of conquerors instead of that of deliverers. In Formosa the reports are exactly the same, alienating the Formosans from the

Central Government. All of this is a matter of discipline. Of course if the officers themselves are dishonest or discourteous, one can hardly expect the enlisted men to be otherwise. Good relations between the military forces and the civilians are absolutely essential if the Central Government expects to bring about successful conclusion of operations against the Communists. At first the Communist armies were also crude and destructive and made the people hate even, but in the past few weeks, they have adopted an entirely new approach which requires their officers and men to be very careful in' all their relations with civilian communities. You can understand therefore how important it is that your own military forces adopt steps immediately to improve the conditions that I have mentioned.

Promotion in the military service should be by merit and merit alone. Older officers or incompetent ones should be retired and relieved. The retired officers should realize that they must make room for the younger ones and they must accept retirement patriotically and philosophically. There are entirely too many Generals in the Chinese Army. Most of them are not well-educated and are not well versed in modern combat. Generals should never be used in civilian posts of responsibility, for example, as governors, mayors and magistrates, except perhaps as Minister of Defense. Military men should not be permitted to belong to a particular political party. After the constitution goes into effect on December 25, they should be permitted to cast a vote, in other words, exercise the right of suffrage, but no military men should be permitted to hold government office or be active members of a political party.

GOVERNMENT ORGANIZATION :

I have carefully studied the existing organization of the government. In my opinion a definite clear-cut delineation of the authorities and functions of each major division of the government from the State Council on down to sub-divisions of the ministries, is urgently required. At present there is an over-lapping of responsibilities and authorities causing frictions and inefficiencies. Also a tremendous streamlining program is necessary within each government ministry or bureau. There are entirely too many employees, this would effect economy in manpower and in funds and I am sure would bring about efficiency. In studying your government organization, for example, I could not determine the exact authority and function of the National Assembly and Legislative Yuan with regard to the enactment of legislation. There must be a streamlined organization and clear cut enunciation in the duties of all of the ministries and bureaus of the government. In April a year ago I discovered that there were well over 60 sections in the National Military Council with duplicating functions and conflicting authorities. There was little coordination between the various groups or sections. Actually there were some groups within the National Military Council that were handling matters which had nothing whatsoever to do with national defense matters. Today in the Ministry of Defense we have grouped 60 sections under 6 general heads and reduced the personnel about 50 percent. Actually over 75,000 individuals were eliminated.

CORRUPTION :

One hears reports on all sides concerning corruption among government officials, high and low and also throughout the economic life of the country. With spiralling inflation, the pay of government officials both in civil service and in military service is wholly inadequate. I am sure that persons who are presently practicing dishonest methods would never consider doing so were it not for the fact that they receive insufficient remuneration to meet the bare necessities of life. Many of them are not trying to acquire vast fortunes, but are just trying to provide a standard of living commensurate with their position. On the other hand, certain rich families, some of whom have relatives in high positions of the government, have been greatly increasing their fortunes. Nepotism is rife and in my investigations I have found that sons, nephews and brothers of government officials have been put in positions within the government, sponsored firms, or in private firms to enable them to make huge profits at the expense of their government and their people. It would be interesting and revealing if you would conduct an investigation into various large banking organizations and other newly created business organizations, to ascertain how much money has been made by such organizations and to what individuals or groups of individuals the money has been paid. To reduce corruption, it will be necessary to establish an index of the standard of living and as the exchange rises the pay of civil service and military service must be increased accordingly. I should emphasize that I am sure many patriotic and selfless Chinese are eking out a bare existence under difficult conditions. They are a great credit to China. However, it must be very discouraging to them to realize that many who already had amassed great fortunes have taken advantage of the present unfortunate situation in China to increase their wealth.

NATIONAL ASSETS AND RESOURCES:

I have just completed an extensive tour in England and on Continental Europe. I made a survey of conditions in those areas such as I have just completed in China. The people in Europe are hungry. They have very limited fuel to keep them warm and to run the utilities such as electric power and to provide water. It is difficult for them to obtain as much as 1500 calories a day, which is barely enough to keep a healthy person moving about. Here in China there are untold resources, food, raw materials and manpower. It should be at once apparent that organization and honest, efficient administration will strongly contribute to alleviate your problems.

There are approximately ten million Chinese citizens living abroad. These Chinese in many instances are financially able to help their country in this time of dire necessity. Also there are many Chinese here in China who have vast sums of money invested abroad. They should be required to make a complete report on their holdings in securities and capital goods. It has been conservatively estimated in America that they could raise at least one billion United States dollars from these sources. China is far from bankrupt in a financial sense or with regard to material resources. China is practically bankrupt in spiritual resources. If the people of China really love their country and want it to emerge strong and united, they should be prepared to come forward and make any sacrifice, including their lives if necessary. Again I should like to emphasize that it is predominantly the poor people, the peasants, who are making great sacrifices and predominantly the rich class who are not coming forward to assist their country.

PUNISHMENT AND SECRET POLICE:

I have had reported to me many instances of misdirection and abuse in meting out punishments to offenders political or otherwise. In Formosa there are many so-called political offenders who are still in prison without any charges or sentences. Some have been released but only after paying large sums of money and being required to sign a statement to the effect that they were guilty of an offense against the government. Actually in their hearts and minds they did not feel that they were guilty of such offense. Secret police operate widely, very much as they do in Russia and as they did in Germany. People disappear. Students are thrown into jail. No trials and no sentences. Actions of this nature do not win support for the government. Quite the contrary. Everyone lives with a feeling of fear and loses confidence in the government.

RESTORATION AND REVITALIZING CHINESE ECONOMY

State ownership should be discouraged. Many Japanese Government and private Japanese properties in Formosa, Manchuria and other parts of China have been taken over by the Central Government. This was perfectly normal procedure, but the government should dispose of these properties as quickly as possible to private individuals or groups to encourage free enterprise. It should be a standing rule that persons in government service, civil or military, should not participate in speculative businesses, in banking and commercial enterprises.

FINAL REMARKS

The Government should not be worried about criticism. I think constructive criticism should be encouraged. It makes the people feel that they are participating in government; that they are members of the team. I have mentioned earlier the terrible economic conditions that exist in England. Criticism of the government is expressed freely in meetings on the streets, and in the press, and on the radio. This is in my opinion a healthy condition. The Government should point out that it is made up of human beings who are of course fallible and can make mistakes. The Government should emphasize, however, that once the mistakes are pointed out, effective steps will be taken to remedy them. The Government should publish information freely concerning expenditures, taxation. Let all the people know how much income tax each individual, particularly wealthy people and big business firms are paying. Announce publicly when any official or any individual has been guilty of some crime or offense and also indicate the punishment meted out. By the same token, announce publicly the accomplishment or good work of individual Government activities. All of these matters would contribute to confidence on the part of the people in the Government. They want to know what is going on and they have a right to know. Open and public official announcements on the part of the Government will also serve to stop malicious conjectures and adverse propaganda of opponents of the Government.

I realize that many of the ideas that I have expressed are quite contrary to Chinese tradition. However, I have carefully studied the philosophy of Confucius and I am sure that all of these ideas are in consonance with the fine principles of conduct that he prescribed. I have confidence in the good sound judgment and in the decency of the bulk of the Chinese peoples. I hope sincerely that you will accept my remarks in the same spirit in which they were given, namely, in the interest of China. Anything that I can do to help China become a strong, happy and prosperous nation, I would gladly do. Anything I could do to protect the sovereignty of China and to insure her a place of respect in the eyes of the world in the family of nations, I would gladly do.

ADDITIONAL POINTS:

1. A sign of general frustration on the part of Chinese officialdom.
2. Generalissimo's dabbling in all strata of government.
3. Weak Executive Yuan.
4. Urge closer relationship with the Generalissimo who should encourage criticism.

134

Statement of August 24, 1947, by Lieutenant General Albert C. Wedemeyer on the Conclusion of His Mission in China [10]

As promised in the initial press release, the inquiry into economic, political, military and social conditions has been undertaken without commitment or prejudgment.

All members of the mission have striven for objectivity and impartiality. To that end we have traveled widely to escape influences peculiar to any one area, visiting Mukden and Fusan, Manchuria; Peiping, Tientsin, Tsingtao and Tsinan in North China; Nanking, Shanghai and Hankow in Central China; Canton in South China, and also Taiwan (Formosa).

Successful efforts were made to reach all classes and categories of people as measured by economic position, intellectual attainment and divergent political viewpoints. Foreign business men and officials were interviewed. We have seen officials of national and local governments, members of various political organizations, many of whom were frankly critical of the government and some of whom were far Left in their views.

We have received approximately 2,000 letters, a small proportion of which were anonymous. These letters contained suggestions which we were able to follow up advantageously.

The last week of our stay in China was devoted chiefly to analyzing an enormous mass of data and in relating political, economic and other items together to reach sound judgments and conclusions.

Varied as were the views, there is one point on which all the hearts and minds of China unite: Throughout strife-torn China there is a passionate longing for peace, an early, lasting peace. I wish the means of attaining it were as easily discernible.

After V–J Day the Chinese people rightfully expected to enjoy the fruits of hard-earned victory. They endured hardships and dangers and suffered untold privations in their efforts to expel the ruthless invader.

In China today I find apathy and lethargy in many quarters. Instead of seeking solutions of problems presented, considerable time and effort are spent in blaming outside influences and seeking outside assistance.

It is discouraging to note the abject defeatism of many Chinese, who are normally competent and patriotic, and who instead should be full of hope and determination.

Weakened and disrupted by long years of war and revolution, China still possesses most of the physical resources needed for her own rehabilitation. Recovery awaits inspirational leadership and moral and spiritual resurgence which can only come from within China.

---

[10] Reprinted from the New York *Herald Tribune,* Aug. 25, 1947.

While I am fully aware of the interests and problems of particular individuals or groups within the country, I am profoundly concerned over the welfare of the Chinese people as a whole. It is my conviction that if the Chinese Communists are truly patriotic and interested primarily in the well-being of their country, they will halt the voluntary employment of force in efforts to impose ideologies. If they are sincere in a desire to help the Chinese people, they can better do so by peaceful means, in lieu of the violence and destruction which have marked these tragic months.

Equally important, the existing Central government can win and retain the undivided, enthusiastic support of the bulk of the Chinese people by removing incompetent and/or corrupt people who now occupy many positions of responsibility in the government, not only national but more so in provincial and municipal structures.

There are honorable officials who show high efficiency and devotion to duty, who strive to live within ridiculous salaries and such private means as they possess, just as there are conscientious businessmen who live up to a high code of commercial ethics. But no one will misunderstand my emphasis upon the large number whose conduct is notoriously marked by greed, incompetence or both.

To regain and maintain the confidence of the people, the Central government will have to effect immediately drastic, far-reaching political and economic reforms. Promises will no longer suffice. Performance is absolutely necessary. It should be accepted that military force in itself will not eliminate Communism.

On taking leave, all members of the mission join in expressing sincere gratitude for the assistance uniformly given by the Generalissimo and all patriotic Chinese with whom we had contact. All Americans hope and pray that China will achieve the unity, prosperity and happiness which her people so richly deserve and of which they have been unjustly deprived for so many years.

135

Report to President Truman by Lieutenant General Albert C. Wedemeyer, U. S. Army

19 September 1947.

MEMORANDUM FOR THE PRESIDENT [11]

MY DEAR MR. PRESIDENT: In compliance with your directive to me of 9 July 1947, the attached "Report on China-Korea" is respectfully submitted.

In consonance with your instructions, advisors from State, Treasury, War and Navy Departments accompanied me on a two months fact-finding mission in the Far East. The principal cities and some rural areas in China and Korea were visited. Successful efforts were made to reach all categories of people as measured by economic position, intellectual attainment and divergent political viewpoints. Conferences were held with public officials and with private citizens in all walks of life. Approximately 1,200 memoranda from individuals and groups were received and considered.

---

[11] All references to Korea have been deleted from General Wedemeyer's report itself as irrelevant to this paper.

The report includes pertinent data in appendices which may be of interest and assistance to appropriate government departments and agencies. The report presents against a global background my estimates of the situations, current and projected, in both China and Korea, and recommends what I deem to be sound courses of action for achievement of United States objectives in the Far East.

Respectfully yours,

A. C. WEDEMEYER,
Lieutenant General, U. S. Army.

MEMBERS OF MISSION

16 July-18 September 1947

Captain James J. Boyle	Aide-de-Camp—Secretary, War Department.
Captain Horace Eng	Aide-de-Camp—Interpreter, War Department.
Lt. Colonel Claire E. Hutchin, Jr	Military Advisor, War Department.
Mr. David R. Jenkins	Fiscal Advisor, Treasury Department.
Mr. Philip D. Sprouse	Political Advisor, State Department.
Rear Admiral Carl A. Trexel	Engineering Advisor, Navy Department.
Mr. Melville H. Walker	Economic Advisor, State Department.
Mr. Mark S. Watson	Press and Public Affairs Advisor, Baltimore Sun, Baltimore, Md.
Lt. General A. C. Wedemeyer	Special Representative of the President of the United States.

INDEX

REPORT TO THE PRESIDENT

CHINA

PART I—General Statement

China's history is replete with examples of encroachment, arbitrary action, special privilege, exploitation, and usurpation of territory on the part of foreign powers. Continued foreign infiltration, penetration or efforts to obtain spheres of influence in China, including Manchuria and Taiwan (Formosa), could be interpreted only as a direct infringement and violation of China's sovereignty and a contravention of the principles of the Charter of the United Nations. It is mandatory that the United States and those other nations subscribing to the principles of the Charter of the United Nations should combine their efforts to insure the unimpeded march of all peoples toward goals that recognize the dignity of man and his civil rights and, further, definitely provide the opportunity to express freely how and by whom they will be governed.

Those goals and the lofty aims of freedom-loving peoples are jeopardized today by forces as sinister as those that operated in Europe and Asia during the ten years leading to World War II. The pattern is familiar—employment of subversive agents; infiltration tactics; incitement of disorder and chaos to disrupt normal economy and thereby to undermine popular confidence in government and leaders; seizure of authority without reference to the will of the people—all the techniques skillfully designed and ruthlessly implemented in order to create favorable conditions for the imposition of totalitarian ideologies. This pattern is present in the Far East, particularly in the areas contiguous to Siberia.

If the United Nations is to have real effect in establishing economic stability and in maintaining world peace, these developments merit high priority on the United Nations' agenda for study and action. Events of the past two years demonstrate the futility of appeasement based on the hope that the strongly consolidated forces of the Soviet Union will adopt either a conciliatory or a cooperative attitude, except as tactical expedients. Soviet practice in the countries already occupied or dominated completes the mosaic of aggressive expansion through ruthless secret police methods and through an increasing political and economic enslavement of peoples. Soviet literature, confirmed repeatedly by Communist leaders, reveals a definite plan for expansion far exceeding that of Nazism in its ambitious scope and dangerous implications. Therefore in attempting a solution to the problem presented in the Far East, as well as in other troubled areas of the world, every possible opportunity must be used to seize the initiative in order to create and maintain bulwarks of freedom.

Notwithstanding all the corruption and incompetence that one notes in China, it is a certainty that the bulk of the people are not disposed to a Communist political and economic structure. Some have become affiliated with Communism in indignant protest against oppressive police measures, corrupt practices and mal-administration of National Government officials. Some have lost all hope for China under existing leadership and turn to the Communists in despair. Some accept a new leadership by mere inertia.

Indirectly, the United States facilitated the Soviet program in the Far East by agreeing at the Yalta Conference to Russian re-entry into Manchuria, and later by withholding aid from the National Government. There were justifiable reasons for these policies. In the one case we were concentrating maximum Allied strength against Japanese in order to accelerate crushing defeat and thus save Allied lives. In the other, we were withholding unqualified support from a government within which corruption and incompetence were so prevalent that it was losing the support of its own people. Further, the United States had not yet realized that the Soviet Union would fail to cooperate in the accomplishment of world-wide plans for post-war rehabilitation. Our own participation in those plans has already afforded assistance to other nations and peoples, friends and former foes alike, to a degree unparalleled in humanitarian history.

Gradually it has become apparent that the World War II objectives for which we and others made tremendous sacrifices are not being fully attained, and that there remains in the world a force presenting even greater dangers to world peace than did the Nazi militarists and the Japanese jingoists. Consequently the United States made the decision in the Spring of 1947 to assist Greece and Turkey with a view to protecting their sovereignties, which were threatened by the direct or inspired activities of the Soviet Union. Charges of unilateral action and circumvention of the United Nations were made by members of that organization. In the light of its purposes and principles such criticisms seemed plausible. The United States promptly declared its intention of referring the matter to the United Nations when that organization would be ready to assume responsibility.

It follows that the United Nations should be informed of contemplated action with regard to China. If the recommendations of this report are approved, the United States should suggest to China that she inform the United Nations officially of her request to the United States for material assistance and advisory aid in order to facilitate China's post-war rehabilitation and economic recovery. This will demonstrate that the United Nations is not being circumvented, and that the United States is not infringing upon China's sovereignty, but contrarywise is cooperating constructively in the interest of peace and stability in the Far East, concomitantly in the world.

The situation in Manchuria has deteriorated to such a degree that prompt action is necessary to prevent that area from becoming a Soviet satellite. The Chinese Communists may soon gain military control of Manchuria and announce the establishment of a government. Outer Mongolia, already a Soviet satellite, may then recognize Manchuria and conclude a "mutual support agreement" with a de facto Manchurian government of the Chinese Communists. In that event, the Soviet Union might accomplish a mutual support agreement with Communist-dominated Manchuria, because of her current similar agreement with Outer Mongolia. This would create a difficult situation for China, the United States and the United Nations. Ultimately it could lead to a Communist-dominated China.

The United Nations might take immediate action to bring about cessation of hostilities in Manchuria as a prelude to the establishment of a Guardianship or Trusteeship. The Guardianship might consist of China, Soviet Russia, the United States, Great Britain and France. This should be attempted promptly and could be initiated only by China. Should one of the nations refuse to participate in Manchurian Guardianship, China might then request the General Assembly of the United Nations to establish a Trusteeship, under the provisions of the Charter.

Initially China might interpret Guardianship or Trusteeship as an infringement upon her sovereignty. But the urgency of the matter should encourage a realistic view of the situation. If these steps are not taken by China, Manchuria may be drawn into the Soviet orbit, despite United States aid, and lost, perhaps permanently, to China.

The economic deterioration and the incompetence and corruption in the political and military organizations in China should be considered against an all-inclusive background lest there be disproportionate emphasis upon defects. Comity requires that cognizance be taken of the following:

Unlike other Powers since V–J Day, China has never been free to devote full attention to internal problems that were greatly confounded by eight years of war. The current civil war has imposed an overwhelming financial and economic burden at a time when resources and energies have been dissipated and when, in any event, they would have been strained to the utmost to meet the problems of recovery.

The National Government has consistently, since 1927, opposed Communism. Today the same political leader and same civil and military officials are determined to prevent their country from becoming a Communist-dominated State or Soviet satellite.

Although the Japanese offered increasingly favorable surrender terms during the course of the war, China elected to remain steadfast with her Allies. If China had accepted surrender terms, approximately a million Japanese would have been released for employment against American forces in the Pacific.

I was assured by the Generalissimo that China would support to the limit of her ability an American program for the stabilization of the Far East. He stated categorically that, regardless of moral encouragement or material aid received from the United States, he is determined to oppose Communism and to create a democratic form of government in consonance with Doctor Sun Yat-sen's principles. He stated further that he plans to make sweeping reforms in the government including the removal of incompetent and corrupt officials. He stated that some progress has been made along these lines but, with spiraling inflation, economic distress and civil war, it has been difficult to accomplish fully these objectives. He emphasized that, when the Communist problem is solved, he could drastically reduce the Army and concentrate upon political and economic reforms. I retain the conviction that the Generalissimo is sincere in his desire to attain these objectives. I am not certain that he has today sufficient determination to do so if this requires absolute overruling of the political and military cliques surrounding him. Yet, if realistic United States aid is to prove effective in stabilizing the situation in China and in coping with the dangerous expansion of Communism, that determination must be established.

Adoption by the United States of a policy motivated solely toward stopping the expansion of Communism without regard to the continued existence of an unpopular repressive government would render any aid ineffective. Further, United States prestige in the Far East would suffer heavily, and wavering elements might turn away from the existing government to Communism.

In China [and Korea], the political, economic and psychological problems are inextricably mingled. All of them are complex and are becoming increasingly difficult of solution. Each has been studied assiduously in compliance with your directive. Each will be discussed in the course of this report. However, it is recognized that a continued global appraisal is mandatory in order to preclude disproportionate or untimely assistance to any specific area.

The following three postulates of United States foreign policy are pertinent to indicate the background of my investigations, analyses and report:

The United States will continue support of the United Nations in the attainment of its lofty aims, accepting the possible development that the Soviet Union or other nations may not actively participate.

Moral support will be given to nations and peoples that have established political and economic structures compatible with our own, or that give convincing evidence of their desire to do so.

Material aid may be given to those same nations and peoples in order to accelerate post-war rehabilitation and to develop economic stability, provided:

That such aid shall be used for the purposes intended.

That there is continuing evidence that they are taking effective steps to help themselves, or are firmly committed to do so.

That such aid shall not jeopardize American economy and shall conform to an integrated program that involves other international commitments and contributes to the attainment of political, economic and psychological objectives of the United States.

Part II—China

Political

Although the Chinese people are unanimous in their desire for peace at almost any cost, there seems to be no possibility of its realization under existing circumstances. On one side is the Kuomintang, whose reactionary leadership, repression and corruption have caused a loss of popular faith in the Government. On the other side, bound ideologically to the Soviet Union, are the Chinese Communists, whose eventual aim is admittedly a Communist state in China. Some reports indicate that Communist measures of land reform have gained for them the support of the majority of peasants in areas under their control, while others indicate that their ruthless tactics of land distribution and terrorism have alienated the majority of such peasants. They have, however, successfully organized many rural areas against the National Government. Moderate groups are caught between Kuomintang misrule and repression and ruthless Communist totalitarianism. Minority parties lack dynamic leadership and sizable following. Neither the moderates, many of whom are in the Kuomintang, nor the minority parties are able to make their influence felt because of National Government repression. Existing provincial opposition leading to possible separatist movements would probably crystallize only if collapse of the Government were imminent.

Soviet actions, contrary to the letter and spirit of the Sino-Soviet Treaty of 1945 and its related documents, have strengthened the Chinese Communist position in Manchuria, with political, economic and military repercussions on the National Government's position both in Manchuria and in China proper, and have made more difficult peace and stability in China. The present trend points toward a gradual disintegration of the National Government's control, with the ultimate possibility of a Communist-dominated China.

Steps taken by the Chinese Government toward governmental reorganization in mid-April 1947 aroused hopes of improvement in the political situation. However, the reorganization resulted in little change. Reactionary influences continue to mold important policies even though the Generalissimo remains the principal determinative force in the government. Since the April reorganization, the most significant change has been the appointment of General Chen Cheng to head the civil and military administration in Manchuria. Projected steps include elections in the Fall for the formation of a constitutional government, but, under present conditions, they are not expected to result in a government more representative than the present regime.

Economic

Under the impact of civil strife and inflation, the Chinese economy is disintegrating. The most probable outcome of present trends would be, not sudden collapse, but a continued and creeping paralysis and consequent decline in the authority and power of the National Government. The past ten years of war have caused serious deterioration of transportation and communication facilities, mines, utilities and industries. Notwithstanding some commendable efforts and large amounts of economic aid, their overall capabilities are scarcely half those of the pre-war period. With disruption of transportation facilities and the loss of much of North China and Manchuria, important resources of those rich areas are no longer available for the rehabilitation and support of China's economy.

Inflation in China has been diffused slowly through an enormous population without causing the immediate dislocation which would have occurred in a highly industrialized economy. The rural people, 80 per cent of the total Chinese population of 450 million, barter food-stuffs for local handicraft products without suffering a drastic cut in living standards. Thus, local economies exist in many parts of China, largely insulated from the disruption of urban industry. Some local economies are under the control of Communists, and some are loosely under the control of provincial authorities.

The principal cause of the hyper-inflation is the long-continued deficit in the national budget. Present revenue collections, plus the profits of nationalized enterprises, cover only one-third of governmental expenditures, which are approximately 70 per cent military, and an increasing proportion of the budget is financed by the issuance of new currency. In the first six months of 1947 note-issue was tripled but rice prices increased seven-fold. Thus prices and governmental expenditures spiral upwards, with price increases occurring faster than new currency can be printed. With further price increases, budget revisions will undoubtedly be necessary. The most urgent economic need of Nationalist China is a reduction of the military budget.

China's external official assets amounted to $327 million (US) on July 30, 1947. Privately-held foreign exchange assets are at least $600 million and may total $1500 million, but no serious attempt has been made to mobilize these private resources for rehabilitation purposes. Private Chinese assets located in China include probably $200 million in gold, and about $75 million in US currency notes. Although China has not exhausted her foreign official assets, and probably will not do so at the present rates of imports and exports until early 1949, the continuing deficit in her external balance of payments is a serious problem.

Disparity between the prices of export goods in China and in world markets at unrealistic official exchange rates has greatly penalized exports, as have disproportionate increases in wages and other costs. Despite rigorous trade and exchange controls, imports have greatly exceeded exports, and there consistently has been a heavy adverse trade balance.

China's food harvests this year are expected to be significantly larger than last year's fairly good returns. This moderately encouraging situation with regard to crops is among the few favorable factors which can be found in China's current economic situation.

Under inflationary conditions, long-term investment is unattractive for both Chinese and foreign capital. Private Chinese funds tend to go into short-term advances, hoarding of commodities, and capital flight. The entire psychology is speculative and inflationary, preventing ordinary business planning and handicapping industrial recovery.

Foreign business enterprises in China are adversely affected by the inefficient and corrupt administration of exchange and import controls, discriminatory application of tax laws, the increasing role of government trading agencies and the trend towards state ownership of industries. The Chinese Government has taken some steps toward improvement but generally has been apathetic in its efforts. Between 1944 and 1947, the anti-inflationary measure on which the Chinese Government placed most reliance was the public sale of gold borrowed from the United States. The intention was to absorb paper currency, and thus reduce the effective demand for goods. Under the circumstance of continued large deficits, however, the only effect of the gold sales program was to retard slightly the price inflation and dissipate dollar assets.

A program to stabilize the economic situation was undertaken in February 1947. The measures included a wage freeze, a system of limited rationing to essential workers in a few cities, and the sale of government bonds. The effect of this program has been slight, and the wage freeze has been abandoned. In August 1947, the unrealistic official rate of exchange was replaced, for proceeds of exports and remittances, by a free market in foreign exchange. This step is expected to stimulate exports, but it is too early to determine whether it will be effective.

The issuance of a new silver currency has been proposed as a future measure to combat inflation. If the government continued to finance budgetary deficits by unbacked note issue, the silver would probably go into hoards and the price inflation would continue. The effect would be no more than that of the gold sales in 1944–1947, namely, a slight and temporary retardation of the inflationary spiral. The proposal could be carried out, moreover, only through a loan from the United States of at least $200 million in silver.

In the construction field, China has prepared expansive plans for reconstruction of communications, mines and industries. Some progress has been made in implementing them, notably in the partial rehabilitation of certain railroads and in the textile industry. Constructive results have been handicapped by a lack of funds, equipment and experienced management, supervisory and technical personnel.

On August 1, 1947, the State Council approved a "Plan for Economic Reform." This appears to be an omnibus of plans covering all phases of Chinese economic reconstruction but its effectiveness cannot yet be determined.

Social—Cultural

Public education has been one of the chief victims of war and social and economic disruption. Schoolhouses, textbooks and other equipment have been destroyed and the cost of replacing any considerable portion cannot now be met. Teachers, like other public servants, have seen the purchasing power of a month's salary shrink to the market value of a few days' rice ration. This applies to the entire educational system, from primary schools, which provide a medium to combat the nation's grievous illiteracy, to universities, from which must come the nation's professional men, technicians and administrators. The universities have suffered in an additional and no less serious respect—traditional academic freedom. Students participating in protest demonstrations have been severely and at times brutally punished by National Government agents without pretense of trial or public evidence of the sedition charged. Faculty members have often been dismissed or refused employment with no evidence of professional unfitness, patently because they were politically objectionable to government officials. Somewhat similarly, periodicals have been closed down "for reasons of military security" without stated charges, and permitted to reopen only after new managements have been imposed. Resumption of educational and other public welfare activities on anything like the desired scale can be accomplished only by restraint of officialdom's abuses, and when the nation's economy is stabilized sufficiently to defray the cost of such vital activities.

Military

The overall military position of the National Government has deteriorated in the past several months and the current military situation favors Communist forces. The Generalissimo has never wavered in his contention that he is fighting for national independence against forces of an armed rebellion nor has he been completely convinced that the Communist problem can be resolved except by force of arms. Although the Nationalist Army has a preponderance of force, the tactical initiative rests with the Communists. Their hit-and-run tactics, adapted to their mission of destruction at points or in areas of their own selection, give them a decided advantage over Nationalists, who must defend many critical areas including connecting lines of communication. Obviously large numbers of Nationalist troops involved in such defensive roles are immobilized whereas Communist tactics permit almost complete freedom of action. The Nationalists' position is precarious in Manchuria, where they occupy only a slender finger of territory. Their control is strongly disputed in Shantung and Hopei Provinces where the Communists make frequent dislocating attacks against isolated garrisons.

In order to improve materially the current military situation, the Nationalist forces must first stabilize the fronts and then regain the initiative. Further, since the Government is supporting the civil war with approximately seventy per cent of its national budget, it is evident that steps taken to alleviate the situation must point toward an improvement in the effectiveness of the armed forces with a concomitant program of social, political and economic reforms, including a decrease in the size of the military establishment. Whereas some rather ineffective steps have been taken to reorganize and revitalize the command structure, and more sweeping reforms are projected, the effectiveness of the Nationalist Army requires a sound program of equipment and improved logistical support. The present industrial potential of China is inadequate to support military forces effectively. Chinese forces under present conditions cannot cope successfully with internal strife or fulfill China's obligations as a member of the family of nations. Hence outside aid, in the form of munitions (most urgently ammunition) and technical assistance, is essential before any plan of operations can be undertaken with a reasonable prospect of success. Military advice is now available to the Nationalists on a General Staff level through American military advisory groups. The Generalissimo expressed to me repeatedly a strong desire to have this advice and supervision extended in scope to include field forces, training centers and particularly logistical agencies.

Extension of military aid by the United States to the National Government might possibly be followed by similar aid from the Soviet Union to the Chinese Communists, either openly or covertly—the latter course seems more likely. An arena of conflicting ideologies might be created as in 1935 in Spain. There is always the possibility that such developments in this area, as in Europe and in the Middle East, might precipitate a third world war.

PART IV—Conclusions

The peaceful aims of freedom-loving peoples in the world are jeopardized today by developments as portentous as those leading to World War II.

The Soviet Union and her satellites give no evidence of a conciliatory or cooperative attitude in these developments. The United States is compelled, therefore, to initiate realistic lines of action in order to create and maintain bulwarks of freedom, and to protect United States strategic interests.

The bulk of the Chinese are not disposed to Communism and they are not concerned with ideologies. They desire food, shelter and the opportunity to live in peace.

China

The spreading internecine struggle within China threatens world peace. Repeated American efforts to mediate have proved unavailing. It is apparent that positive steps are required to end hostilities immediately. The most logical approach to this very complex and ominous situation would be to refer the matter to the United Nations.

A China dominated by Chinese Communists would be inimical to the interests of the United States, in view of their openly expressed hostility and active opposition to those principles which the United States regards as vital to the peace of the world.

The Communists have the tactical initiative in the overall military situation. The Nationalist position in Manchuria is precarious, and in Shantung and Hopei Provinces strongly disputed. Continued deterioration of the situation may result in the early establishment of a Soviet satellite government in Manchuria and ultimately in the evolution of a Communist-dominated China.

China is suffering increasingly from disintegration. Her requirements for rehabilitation are large. Her most urgent needs include governmental reorganization and reforms, reduction of the military budget and external assistance.

A program of aid, if effectively employed, would bolster opposition to Communist expansion, and would contribute to gradual development of stability in China.

Due to excesses and oppressions by government police agencies basic freedoms of the people are being jeopardized. Maladministration and corruption cause a loss of confidence in the Government. Until drastic political and economic reforms are undertaken United States aid can not accomplish its purpose.

Even so, criticism of results achieved by the National Government in efforts for improvement should be tempered by a recognition of the handicaps imposed on China by eight years of war, the burden of her opposition to Communism, and her sacrifices for the Allied cause.

A United States program of assistance could best be implemented under the supervision of American advisors in specified economic and military fields. Such a program can be undertaken only if China requests advisory aid as well as material assistance.

PART V—Recommendations

It is recommended:

That the United States Government provide as early as practicable moral, advisory, and material support to China in order to contribute to the early establishment of peace in the world in consonance with the enunciated principles of the United Nations, and concomitantly to protect United States strategic interests against militant forces which now threaten them.

That United States policies and actions suggested in this report be thoroughly integrated by appropriate government agencies with other international commitments. It is recognized that any foreign assistance extended must avoid jeopardizing the American economy.

China

That China be advised that the United States is favorably disposed to continue aid designed to protect China's territorial integrity and to facilitate her recovery, under agreements to be negotiated by representatives of the two governments, with the following stipulations:

That China inform the United Nations promptly of her request to the United States for increased material and advisory assistance.

That China request the United Nations to take immediate action to bring about a cessation of hostilities in Manchuria and request that Manchuria be placed under a Five-Power Guardianship or, failing that, under a Trusteeship in accordance with the United Nations Charter.

That China make effective use of her own resources in a program for economic reconstruction and initiate sound fiscal policies leading to reduction of budgetary deficits.

That China give continuing evidence that the urgently required political and military reforms are being implemented.

That China accept American advisors as responsible representatives of the United States Government in specified military and economic fields to assist China in utilizing United States aid in the manner for which it is intended.

APPENDIX TO PART I—GENERAL STATEMENT

Directive to Lieutenant General Wedemeyer

You will proceed to China without delay for the purpose of making an appraisal of the political, economic, psychological and military situations—current and projected. In the course of your survey you will maintain liaison with American diplomatic and military officials in the area. In your discussions with Chinese officials and leaders in positions of responsibility you will make it clear that you are on a fact-finding mission and that the United States Government can consider assistance in a program of rehabilitation only if the Chinese Government presents satisfactory evidence of effective measures looking towards Chinese recovery and provided further that any aid which may be made available shall be subject to the supervision of representatives of the United States Government.

In making your appraisal it is desired that you proceed with detachment from any feeling of prior obligation to support or to further official Chinese programs which do not conform to sound American policy with regard to China. In presenting the findings of your mission you should endeavor to state as concisely as possible your estimate of the character, extent, and probable consequences of assistance which you may recommend, and the probable consequences in the event that assistance is not given.

When your mission in China is completed you will proceed on a brief trip to Korea to make an appraisal of the situation there with particular reference to an economic aid program in Korea and its relation to general political and economic conditions throughout the country. Before going to Korea you will communicate with General MacArthur to ascertain whether he desires you to proceed via Tokyo.

You will take with you such experts, advisers and assistants as you deem necessary to the effectiveness of your mission.

Approved
HARRY S. TRUMAN

July 9, 1947

APPENDIX "A" TO PART II—CHINA

POLITICAL

INDEX

Résumé of United States Policy Toward China

The fundamental bases of United States policy toward China have remained unchanged since the Open Door notes of Secretary of State John Hay in 1899 and his circular note to the Powers during the Boxer Rebellion: equality of trade and the preservation of China's territorial integrity. Russian and Japanese aggression in Manchuria in the early 1900's and Japanese demands to China during the first world war threatened these principles. During these years the United States protested, often futilely, foreign infringement of the Open Door Policy. In 1921–22 formal international agreement to these principles was expressed in the Nine-Power Treaty. While the United States adopted a non-recognition policy at the time of the Japanese Twenty-one Demands and reiterated this policy at the time of Japanese occupation of Manchuria, the United States was not prepared to take stronger steps to uphold Chinese sovereignty or American trade rights if they involved the risk of war. At the outbreak of Sino-Japanese hostilities in 1937, the United States restated her policy and offered her good offices for mediation, but a meeting of the signatories of the Nine-Power Treaty resulted in no concerted action against Japan. The American neutrality legislation was not invoked since it was felt that enforcement of its provisions would have hurt China more than Japan. Repeated American diplomatic protests proving useless, restrictions were gradually imposed on exports to Japan and material aid to China was progressively expanded. Confronted with the issue of American security in the face of Japanese domination of eastern Asia and possible Japanese and German domination of the world, the United States was for the first time prepared to run the risk of war in upholding her policy. The result was the Japanese attack on Pearl Harbor and United States entry into the world war. Strategic consideration caused concentration of Allied military strength in Europe initially, rather than in Asia, and China received relatively little material aid. This produced some Chinese resentment but the United States attempted to give China various forms of material and moral aid and endeavored to build up China's prestige as one of the major powers. The United States also stressed to China the importance of a strong unified nation and attempted to use influence to that end. Following the Japanese surrender, however, widespread civil war between the National Government and the Chinese Communists threatened. The position of the United States and the Soviet Union was of importance. As a result of the Yalta Agreement, to which the United States was a party, a Sino-Soviet Treaty was signed in August 1945, granting certain rights in Manchuria to the Soviet Union. Although both the United States and the Soviet Union were committed to the return of Chinese territory to Chinese Government control, the Soviet Union utilized its occupation of Manchuria to hamper the Chinese Government and to assist the Chinese Communists. The United States aided the Chinese Government by transporting its troops to former Japanese-occupied areas and thus found itself in the midst of an undeclared civil war. At this juncture President Truman sent General Marshall to China to mediate between the two factions and stated that the United States would be prepared to aid China as it moved toward peace and unity. The early agreement reached by the Chinese factions gradually broke down and civil war was renewed on an increasing scale. Since the end of the American mediation effort in January 1947, the United States has continued to withhold aid to China in the hope that an improvement in the Chinese internal situation would permit the extension of effective aid toward rehabilitation and development of economic stability.

The effect of American policy toward China from the time of the Hay Open Door notes until 1941 was not to preserve China's territorial integrity or provide equality of trade; mutual suspicion among the Powers probably was the only factor that saved China from dismemberment in the early 1900's. When Japanese aggression in 1937 threatened the territorial integrity of China and equality of trade, the United States, as in the past, found diplomatic protests unavailing. It was not until the United States felt her own security and interests seriously endangered that it was finally prepared to accept the risk of war to protect her security and interests. China was thus saved from Japanese domination and control. The American mediation effort, which for the time being stopped the civil war, was accompanied in its later stages by the spread of hostilities in first one and then in another area as the National Government occupied important Communist-held areas. In spite of increased Chinese Government efforts to destroy the Communist forces following the end of the American mediation effort, the civil war has brought no recent major successes to its arms except in Shantung Province. The Communists threaten to occupy all of Manchuria and their strength appears to be increasing in that area. In view of the continued economic deterioration in National Government areas, it may be said that the American mediation effort has been to the advantage of the Chinese Communists and conversely to the disadvantage of the National Government.

Current Political Situation

China is confronted with civil war, a deteriorating economic situation, social unrest and the psychological reactions inevitable under such conditions. Among the people themselves, there is a unanimous desire for peace at almost any cost. There seems, however, to be no possibility of any peaceful settlement in the foreseeable future between the National Government and the Chinese Communist Party, owing to recent Communist military successes in Manchuria, added to Communist awareness of the Government's increasing economic difficulties. The National Government has issued a General Mobilization Order with the object of establishing powers and creating forces in order to destroy the Chinese Communist forces; however, to the detriment of the government it is also being used to suppress opposition which is not Communist at all.

The Chinese Government is headed by Generalissimo Chiang Kai-shek and dominated by the Kuomintang under his leadership. The reactionary character of Kuomintang leadership, the repressive nature of its rule and the widespread corruption among Government officials and military officers have cost the Government heavily in terms of the confidence and support of the people. There is a widespread belief that under present conditions, unless the National Government takes drastic measures of reform, it will, through a slow and gradual process, disintegrate.

The Chinese Communists are self-professed Communists bound ideologically to the Soviet Union. They proclaim as their eventual aim the establishment of a communist state in China. The Chinese Communists constantly foster anti-American feeling in areas under their control, picturing the United States as an imperialistic power which has as its objective the enslavement of the world. Their ruthless tactics of land distribution and oppression of the Christian missionary movement have made for them bitter enemies among many Chinese in the rural areas. Some sources say that Communist land reforms have benefitted the poor peasants who comprise the majority of the rural population and who, therefore, support the Communists, while other sources say that Communist terroristic tactics have alienated the vast majority of peasants. Where local government, regardless of ideology, is competent, honest and humane, there is no local revolt. Whether by suasion or by intimidation, the Communists have in many areas been successful in organizing the countryside against the National Government.

Middle of the road groups in China, desirous of the essentials of democratic government, are caught between the misrule and repression of the Kuomintang and the totalitarian ruthlessness of the Chinese Communists. Yet in the moderate and constructive views of these Chinese, many of them in the Kuomintang, lies one of the greatest possibilities for a governmental program which would be acceptable to the mass of Chinese. The trouble is that these views are not boldly and confidently asserted and cannot be against the present uncompromising power of the extremists. The minority parties, with present leadership and following insufficient to defy intimidation and to assert a vigorous policy, offer little hope in the situation. Existing provincial opposition to the National Government is not yet an important factor, but separatist movements would probably occur in the event of an imminent collapse of the National Government.

The Chinese Government's position in Manchuria has been seriously weakened by Soviet actions. In spite of the Sino-Soviet Treaty of 1945 and its related documents, the Soviet Union has hindered the efforts of the Chinese Government to restore its control over Manchuria, has not given the "moral support and aid in military supplies and other material resources" provided for in these documents and has not permitted the Chinese Government freely to take over the civil administration of Dairen and the Port Arthur area. Rather, the Soviet Union has assisted the Chinese Communists in Manchuria by the timing of the withdrawal of Soviet troops and by making available, either directly or indirectly, large quantities of surrendered Japanese military equipment. Soviet machinations in western Sinkiang and among the Mongols have further embarrassed the Chinese Government. In brief, the Soviet Union has given no indication of any effort to assist the Chinese Government and has, instead, taken action which has aided the Chinese Communists in Manchuria. The result has been to strengthen the Chinese Communist position in Manchuria, with political, economic and military repercussions on the National Government's position both in Manchuria and China proper, and to make more difficult the attainment of peace and stability in China.

Steps Taken and Projected to Improve Internal Political Situation

At the time of General Marshall's departure from China, he stated that while the form for a democratic China had been set forth in the new constitution, practical measures would be the test to see to what extent the Chinese Government would give substance to the form.   In mid-April the Chinese Government announced the reorganization of the State Council and shortly thereafter the reorganization of the Executive Yuan.   The caliber of the appointees to the State Council indicated that an effort had been made to name some of the most capable, moderate and progressive members of the Kuomintang, qualities which also characterized the non-party appointees to the Council.   The only other parties to join the Government were the Youth Party and the Socialist Democratic Party, but their appointees were without particular significance.   Seats were also left vacant on the Council for the Communist Party and the Democratic League in the event they wished to participate in the Council at a later date, but this was viewed chiefly as a political gesture.   However, the possible effectiveness of the Council was largely nullified by the simultaneous creation of a new Kuomintang Political Committee, the chief figure in which was Chen Li-fu. The important role played by this Committee in controlling the Kuomintang and its policies was seen in the subsequent consolidation of the position and strength of the CC Clique (dominant right wing of the Kuomintang led by Chen Li-fu and Kuo-fu).   The reorganized Executive Yuan under General Chang Chun gave similar promise but the political maneuvers of the CC Clique, which was strongly opposed to General Chang and his political colleagues, the pace of military and economic developments, and domination by the Generalissimo tied its hands and neutralized its efforts to take effective action to meet pressing problems.   In effect, therefore, there was a limited reorganization of the Government but it was one which failed to bring about any significant changes.   Control of the Government and its policies remained, in general, in the same few hands and within this framework the Generalissimo has continued to be the main determinative force in Chinese Government policy.

Since the time of the above-described reorganization, few changes in the Government have occurred.   Perhaps the most significant has been the appointment of General Chen Cheng, Chief of Staff, as Director of the President's Office at Mukden to succeed General Hsiung Shih-hui and the consolidation of civil and military administration in Manchuria under his control.   This change represents an effort to correct the weaknesses of the National Government position in Manchuria, but it may have come too late and may not be sufficiently far reaching to achieve the desired effect.

Projected steps include elections in areas under National Government control within the next few months in accordance with the new constitution as a prelude to the formation of a constitutional government.   However, under conditions of civil war, Kuomintang refusal to permit the minority parties to organize and campaign freely for the elections and control by the Kuomintang CC Clique throughout National Government territory, there is no likelihood that the elections will result in the immediate creation of a government representative of the people's will or the formation of a government any more democratic than the present regime. Even so, the elections should serve as a step forward along the road to representative government.

Implications of "No Assistance" to China or Continuation of "Wait and See" Policy

To advise at this time a policy of "no assistance" to China would suggest the withdrawal of the United States Military and Naval Advisory Groups from China and it would be equivalent to cutting the ground from under the feet of the Chinese Government. Removal of American assistance, without removal of Soviet assistance, would certainly lay the country open to eventual Communist domination. It would have repercussions in other parts of Asia, would lower American prestige in the Far East and would make easier the spread of Soviet influence and Soviet political expansion not only in Asia but in other areas of the world.

It is possible that the adoption of a "wait and see" policy would lead to the Generalissimo's finally carrying out genuine reforms which in turn would enable the United States to extend effective aid and which themselves would furnish the best answer to the challenge of communism. Because of an inevitable time lag in its results, however, such a policy would permit for an appreciable time the continuation of the process of National Government disintegration. At some stage of the disintegration the authority and control of the National Government might become so weak and restricted that separatist movements would occur in various areas now under Government control. At this point, conceivably there might emerge a middle group which would be able to establish a modicum of stability in the areas under its control. It would then be possible for the United States to extend support, both moral and material, to any such group or combination of groups which gave indication of ability to consolidate control over sizable portions of the country and whose policies would be compatible with our own. This, however, represents conjecture regarding a possible future course of events in China. There is the further possibility that such a policy would result at some point in the Generalissimo's seeking a compromise with the Chinese Communists, although it is likely that he would not do so until his position became so weak that the Communists would accept a settlement only on terms assuring them a dominant position in the government. At worst, under a process of continued National Government disintegration, it may be expected that there would be a long period of disturbance verging on chaos, at the end of which the Chinese Communists would emerge as the dominant group oriented toward the Soviet Union.

Reforms Needed to Improve the Internal Political Situation

Reforms to improve the internal political situation should, in general, include measures which would (a) make for efficient government, (b) protect the basic freedoms of the people from arbitrary acts of repression, (c) remove civil administration from military control, and (d) contribute to the welfare of the people. These measures might include, *inter alia*, reforms such as the following: Complete separation of the Kuomintang from the Government and the emergence of the Generalissimo as the leader of the nation rather than of the party; reorganization of the National Government, including both the Executive Yuan and the State Council, to ensure participation by responsible Chinese without regard to party affiliations; a clear-cut delegation of responsibility in the Government to increase efficiency, foster initiative, prevent the domination of governmental affairs and policies by one person and encourage entry into Government service of capable and progressive Chinese now unwilling to serve in the Government; the strengthening of the Control Yuan to ensure the removal and punishment of corrupt officials; the abolition of the existing secret police system; the cessation of arrests of civilians by military organs; the prompt and public trial of persons arrested and the full exercise of the right of *habeas corpus;* the cessation of the use of force and intimidation against teachers and students and the reinstatement of university professors and students dismissed solely for their political views; the carrying out of a land reform program which would lighten the burdens of usury and taxation on the peasant as well as provide him land; decentralization of governmental power to permit more local autonomy and local participation in administration; removal of military officers from posts in civil government while on active status; and publication of complete information regarding fiscal policies and their implementation and of detailed data covering government revenues and expenditures, including National, Provincial and Municipal budgets.

APPENDIX "B" TO PART II—CHINA

ECONOMIC

INDEX

Financial

China has reached a condition of hyper-inflation, and it is difficult to estimate how long the deterioration can continue before the present monetary system ceases to function. During the past six months, two serious upsurges in prices have occurred, each followed by a few weeks of temporary stability and readjustment. The recent history of Chinese inflation, as indicated by the price of rice and by the black market price for U. S. dollars (the two best general indicators of the overall financial situation) has been one of increasingly violent convulsions separated by short intervals of relative stability.

China's hyper-inflation is a classical currency inflation, occurring in a predominantly agrarian country. It requires a longer time to run its course than a comparable inflation would in an urban industrial society. The recurrent price upsurges occur first in the large cities, are diffused gradually through the smaller cities, and finally permeate the countryside. There is some credit inflation through loans by the Government banks for purposes approved by the Government, but this credit inflation is a secondary cause, not to be compared in magnitude or impact with the swelling flood of notes.

A tendency towards panic on the part of the Government officials in the Ministry of Finance and Central Bank very easily develops, since personal responsibility for each crisis is difficult to avoid. It is difficult to explain to the Generalissimo and to such bodies as the People's Political Council and the Legislative Yuan that hyper-inflation results from years of unbalanced budgets and a debilitated economy, and that sudden upsurges in prices are to be expected in a hyper-inflation. Since personal responsibility is frequently assigned and scapegoats found, partly for political reasons, no individual wishes to take remedial action which might result in a price upsurge. Such administrative inertia aggravates the situation, and makes practical measures to forestall or smooth out the fluctuation doubly difficult. Thus, the official rate of CN$12,000 to one U. S. dollar remained in effect from February 11, 1947, until the middle of August, although the black market rate had proceeded by erratic leaps to 40,000. On a number of occasions between February and August it should have been easier than in August to effect a change or abandon the official rate. The weight of administrative inertia, however, was too great. Now that the change has been made, the accumulated maladjustments, the opportunities for market manipulation by exchange speculators who are among the keenest in the world, and the failure to prepare an administrative machine for Central Bank support of the market, will eventually combine to aggravate the crisis, and sooner or later produce another price convulsion which may be more violent than it need have been had the readjustment been made earlier.

Disinvestment—The disorganization in Chinese economy, caused by civil war and hyper-inflation, has resulted in massive disinvestment. This disinvestment has taken principally the forms of living off capital, and capital flight to the United States, Hong Kong, Europe and South America. Disinvestment is also occurring through the deterioration of physical assets, abuse of capital equipment, neglect of maintenance, and overloading of power facilities. In a very real sense, the economy functioned, and is continuing to function, by consuming reserves accumulated by the Japanese, materials purchased with dollars provided by the United States during the war years, and UNRRA and surplus property supplies. The hyper-inflation and the uncertainties of the civil war have further strengthened a traditional Chinese tendency towards the quick exploitation of capital assets, without provision for their maintenance or replacement.

The long-term consequences of disinvestment are very serious for the Chinese economy. The magnitude of this factor is difficult to estimate, because statistics of production and depreciation are not available, but it must be taken into account in any long-term estimate of China's reconstruction needs. Long continuance of the civil war will result in a degree of disinvestment which will make recuperation painfully slow and difficult. The result, a weak and dependent China, promising poor returns on investments for a long period, should be taken into account in planning for the distribution in Asia of United States resources.

Fiscal and Monetary Situation—The expenditures in the budget for the year 1947 were originally estimated at CN$9.4 trillion, against estimated revenues of CN$7.4 trillion. On May 7, a new budget of CN$18 trillion for 1947 was approved. With further increases in prices, new budget revisions will undoubtedly be made to provide for increased governmental expenditures. Receipts from taxes and government-operated enterprises cover approximately one-third of expenditures. The emission of new currency is therefore the principal means of financing the national budget. Increases in the note issue, with static or declining production, bid up prices and in turn require larger government expenditures. This spiralling effect has been evident in China for several years. During the past 18 months it has reached the stage of a hyper-inflation, in which the price increase is proceeding faster than the increase in note issuance. In the first six months of 1947 the note issue increased three times, but cost of living increased fivefold, and rice prices increased seven-fold. Experience in other countries suggests that there is a limit to the process of inflation. In China this limit is more elastic than elsewhere, due to the fact that about 80 per cent of the population live in relatively self-contained village economies. It is obviously unwise to attempt specific or precise predictions of how long the trend of the last six months can continue before there is a disintegration of the authority of the National Government with a possible reversion to regionalism accompanied by a collapse of the urban economies. China might then enter a period of chaos from which it might take as long as a generation to emerge. While the existence of a strong Communist movement makes the recrudescence of a simple pattern of warlordism of the period 1911–27 unlikely, it is doubtful whether the Communists would have the power or the technical skills to unify the country and rapidly bring it under control.

REVENUE OF THE CHINESE GOVERNMENT

Total revenue and expenditures, with percentage breakdown by sources of revenue based on monthly receipts of the Chinese National Treasury.

Month	Receipts and Expenditures (CN Trillions)	Revenue From Taxation (Percent)	Receipts From Public Borrowing (Percent)	Bank Advances (Currency Issuance) (Percent)	Other Receipts (Percent)
1947					
January	1.2	17.9	2.9	70.9	8.3
February	1.0	22.1	7.4	66.2	4.3
March	1.5	19.5	0.6	73.7	6.2
April	2.0	19.9	0.1	53.4	26.6
May	1.9	22.3	4.4	49.8	23.5
June	3.1	18.2	9.5	62.8	9.5

Source: Minister of Finance, O. K. Yui.

CURRENCY NOTES OUTSTANDING IN MANCHURIA, TAIWAN AND SINKIANG

(Billions)

Month	Northeastern Currency Notes (CBC issue for Manchuria)	Taiwan Currency Notes (Bank of Taiwan)	Sinkiang Provincial Bank Notes
1946			
June	4.5	3.7	6.2
July	6.0	4.0	6.6
August	10.1	4.2	7.1
September	15.0	1.2	8.5
October	18.8	2.8	10.0
November	22.9	4.0	11.4
December	27.5	5.0	13.0
1947			
January	36.2	5.7	14.8
February	40.2	6.4	16.6
March	47.5	7.0	18.0
April	55.9	7.5	----
May	64.4	8.9	----
June	74.6	---	----

Source: Minister of Finance, O. K. Yui.

CURRENCY ISSUANCE AND PRICES IN CHINA

Month	Notes Outstanding (Trillions)	Percentage Increase Over Previous Month	Whole Price Index (Shanghai)	Percentage Increase Over Previous Month
1946				
January	1.15	11	92	4
February	1.26	9	175	89
March	1.35	6	255	45
April	1.53	13	258	0
May	1.80	17	380	47
June	2.11	17	372	97
July	2.16	2	407	9
August	2.38	10	428	5
September	2.70	13	509	18
October	2.98	10	536	5
November	3.30	10	531	99
December	3.73	13	571	7
1947				
January	4.51	21	686	20
February	4.84	7	1066	55
March	5.74	18	1120	5
April	6.90	20	1847	64
May	8.38	21	2845	53
June	9.94	16	2993	17
July	11.46	15	3116	5

Source: Minister of Finance, O. K. Yui, "Financial Statistics for Wedemeyer's Mission" August, 1947

Balance of Payments Situation—Official foreign exchange assets of the Chinese Government reached their peak about V–J Day and have since declined. Total gold and short-term dollar assets of the Chinese Government and Chinese nationals were estimated at U. S. $949 million on December 30, 1945, the official portion being $835 million; in addition there were private Chinese long-term assets in the United States amounting to at least $220 million. The official assets held by the Central Bank of China had declined to $327 million on June 30, 1947, and an additional amount of over $123 million was held in other government banks. Private gold and short-term assets have almost certainly increased very substantially from the estimated figure $114 million at the end of 1945. While some private accounts have been drawn down to finance imports, amounts which more than compensate for this decrease have been added through private accumulation of gold and U. S. currency in China, and through flight of capital via Hong Kong, and through other means. Gold sales to the Chinese public out of the 1942 Congressional loan amounted to $150 million, most of which is still in Chinese private hands. There are an estimated $50–75 millions of U. S. currency in private hands in China, a substantial part of which is held by Chinese Nationals; and the flight of capital via underestimation of the value of exports, overestimation of the value of imports, diversion of remittances, etc., has undoubtedly been heavy. A plausible estimate of private Chinese holdings of gold and hard foreign exchange at home and abroad, recently made by the U. S. Treasury Attaché in Nanking, was approximately U.S. $500 million. Estimate of private Chinese foreign exchange assets have gone as high as several billion, but the private assets in the United States which could be identified as Chinese are probably nearer the U.S. $500 million figure.

Chinese Government estimates of the dollar deficit in the international balance of payments for the second half of 1947 are between $106 and $120 million. At the higher rate of usage, the official assets in the Central Bank would be drawn down to $206 million by the end of 1947, and would be exhausted by the end of 1948 or early in 1949. The dollar assets in other government banks would, of course, be intact.

TABLE A

Official Foreign Exchange Assets of China, July 1, 1947, in Deposits, Cash and Investments, Net of Forward Contracts and Margin Deposits

	Millions
U.S. dollars	U.S. $177.3
Pounds sterling	21.9
Hong Kong dollars	12.0
Rupees	0.4
Gold	85.7
Silver	29.4
Total	U.S. $326.6 millions

(Items rounded to nearest U.S. $100,000, therefore slight discrepancy in total.)

TABLE B

U. S. Dollar Holdings of Government Banks, July 1, 1947

	Millions
Bank of China	U.S. $94.8
Bank of Communications	16.6
Farmers Bank of China	2.4
Central Trust of China	4.6
Postal RSB	4.2
Total	U.S. $122.6 millions

Source: Minister of Finance, O. K. Yui.

INTERNATIONAL BALANCE OF PAYMENTS POSITION OF CHINA

(September 1947 to September 1948)

(Official Tentative Estimate by Ministry of Finance in Millions of U.S. Dollars)

EXPENDITURES

	Millions
Imports:	
Raw cotton.	U.S. $100
Rice, wheat and flour.	40
Coal and Coke.	2
Schedule I imports.	24
Schedule II and extra quota.	215
Schedule III (a).	30
Financed by private exchange holdings.	100
Total.	511
Approved Financial Services:.	55
Government Expenditures:	
Gasoline for military.	31
Munitions.	10
Debt Services.	35
Industrial Supplies, etc.	20
Foreign Services, etc.	25
Total.	687

RECEIPTS

Exports.	200
Remittances.	100
Foreign Expenditures in China.	25
Charities, etc.	14
Repatriation of Capital.	100
Total.	439
Deficit.	248

Source: The Minister of Finance, O. K. Yui.

There are several considerations which suggest that China's dollar resources will last at least a year and may last longer than 18 months. The most recent Central Bank estimate of China's balance of payments in the next 12 months anticipate in addition to the loss of $120 million of foreign exchange for Government imports and expenditures abroad, a deficit on current account of about the same amount. This estimate is based on fairly realistic assumptions concerning the extent of increase in exports and receipts from overseas remittances as a result of the new foreign exchange policy. Part of this deficit will be met by $30 million from post-UNRRA relief. Therefore, the Central Bank's total net loss of official foreign exchange assets in the next 12 months will be $210 million, leaving $117 million of official foreign exchange assets. This is, of course, a dangerously low figure. Nevertheless, it indicates that China has not yet reached the bottom of her official till, and has not yet tapped the substantial foreign hoards of Chinese nationals.

A complete picture of the balance of payments must also allow for smuggling and flight of capital. If the new regulations, and the recent agreement with Hong Kong, have more than a temporary effect, then smuggling of imports and flight of capital may not amount to more than $110 million, which should be compensated by smuggled exports and diversions of overseas remittances, plus depletion of Chinese private assets.

Private external assets, as indicated above, probably approximate $500 million. The National Government has never made a serious attempt to mobilize these assets for imports, and with a continued deterioration in the financial and economic situation its ability to do so would decrease rather than increase. Any substantial improvement in the general economic situation would undoubtedly begin a reflow of these assets to China and their gradual release for current use. A striking example of the Chinese private holder's unwillingness to invest foreign exchange in the development of China's industry is provided by the Hwainan Coal Mine. This mine is the best mine in Central China in actual operation and thus occupies a crucial position in the event of military failures in or the cutting of communications with the North China coal mining areas. The Hwainan Coal Mine is about 200 miles north of Nanking on a spur of the Tientsin-Pukow railroad, and its production of 90,000 tons a month could be substantially increased with further capital investment. The mine is 80 per cent owned by the China Finance Development Corporation, a Soong-Kung corporation with wide interests and extensive foreign exchange assets. After V-J Day the rehabilitation of the mine was financed by a CN dollar loan from the government and the advance of over U.S. $1 million by the N.R.C. for the purchase of essential transportation equipment. The China Finance Development Corporation did not put up any foreign exchange for this rehabilitation, and will not invest any foreign exchange for its further development. China Finance Development Corporation's attitude can be explained only in terms of short-sighted selfishness and lack of faith in the future of Kuomintang China.

The above calculations indicate that the Chinese Government has sufficient dollars in its official account to maintain the import program for at least one year, more probably for 18 months. The conclusion is that a shortage of official foreign exchange holdings for financing essential imports is not an immediate problem, but it may become acute if there is continued deterioration in China's capacity to produce and export commodities and her ability to prevent excessive diversion of overseas remittances. The essential problem is not one of advancing the foreign exchange required to make up the deficit in China's international balance of payments, as this would be a process which would have to be repeated indefinitely until forces are set in motion to rectify the deficit situation. Rather it is a problem of establishing the conditions which will eliminate the deficit, and of securing the capital for reconstruction and development from Chinese as well as foreign sources.

Currency Stabilization—Since 1942 the Chinese Government has sought to secure financial assistance from the United States for the purpose of stabilizing the Chinese national currency. In 1945 China raised the possibility of a loan of $500 million to be used as a currency reserve fund. This proposal was rejected by the United States on the grounds that China's foreign exchange assets, including the remainder of the 1942 loan, were sufficient to provide a reserve, and that any effort at stabilization would be futile unless the fiscal policy of the Government was changed. Between 1942 and 1946, $400 million was used by the Chinese Government for "economic stabilization purposes." U. S. dollar denominated savings certificates of up to 3-year maturity and bonds redeemable within 10 years were sold for CN currency at the rate of CN $20 to U.S. $1, and $150 million worth of gold was sold to the public by the Central Bank to stabilize prices. The history of these stabilization measures was one of criticism from the United States Government that valuable foreign exchange resources were being dissipated to no avail, and repeated unsubstantiated claims from the Chinese that the anti-inflationary measures would be effective. There were several scandals in connection with the sale of dollar certificates and bonds and gold to insiders and officials on a preferential basis. Notable examples were the gold scandals of March, 1945, in Chungking and February, 1947, in Shanghai.

Since V–J Day there has been continuous discussion of the issuance of a new currency. Recently the principal proposal has been the issuance of a metallic silver currency as an intermediate step in stabilization. The present fiscal situation is inopportune for the introduction of a new currency or the adoption of even an intermediate step towards stabilization. Experience in other countries indicates that after hyper-inflation has reached a certain stage it must run its course before the currency system can be effectively reorganized and stabilized. Mistakes in timing are apt to prove costly and actually serve to delay stabilization.

Proposed Silver Loan—During the past three months proposals have been advanced by the Chinese Government for a silver loan from the United States. It has been proposed to borrow between $200 and $250 million worth of silver from the United States to mint silver coins for circulation in China. Under the proposal it has been suggested that coins would be issued at a fixed rate with CN notes, and would eventually replace the paper currency.

The principal weakness of this proposal is that the Government would presumably continue to finance its budget by the issuance of paper currency. Unless the Government decided to withdraw paper currency from circulation entirely, replace it by silver and thereafter issue no more paper currency, the silver would go into hoards and hyper-inflation would continue. No attempt has been made by the American or Chinese proponents of the silver currency scheme to avoid this dilemma. Their case has been mainly based on four considerations:

(1) China had a relatively stable silver currency in the past, and great psychological importance has been attached to this fact;

(2) The world price of silver has declined from 90¢ to 64¢ during the past year and silver producers in the United States would welcome loans of silver to foreign countries;

(3) The war-time history of the silver lend-lease operations with India set a precedent for lending silver out of U. S. reserves;

(4) U. S. silver stocks are in any case of little use to the United States.

The proposed silver loan for currency stabilization cannot be seriously considered until a real start has been made to solve the Chinese budgetary problem. The issuance of silver coins as a subordinate currency alongside paper currency would have no more effect on the Chinese price level than would the sale to the public of an equivalent amount of metal in silver or gold bars. As the devaluation of the paper currency continued, silver coins would be hoarded for their metal content. On the other hand, if the paper currency were totally withdrawn and permanently replaced by the silver dollars, the Government would have to finance its national budget entirely out of taxation and public borrowing.

A silver loan to China would have many of the features of a budgetary loan. The silver coins would be sold to the public for paper currency and thereafter would be lost to the Government, in the same sense that the gold from the 1942 Congressional loan which was sold to the public in 1945–46, has not been mobilized as a foreign exchange asset for Government use. Therefore, the prospects of repayment would be very slight, and any proposed silver "loan," secured by no physical assets as collateral, might, more properly, be considered as a proposed gift of dollars. The Congress is the only body which can decide to make such a gift. It is suggested that other forms of aid should be considered as having a higher priority, since under existing conditions a gift of silver would have a minimal likelihood of benefit to China, and would carry with it the maximum risk of misuse.

Financial Advisors—The National Government has employed foreign financial advisors for many years, as part of its general policy of using foreign technicians. Most financial advisors have been employed on a personal contract basis. Useful work has been done by American advisors in planning and supervising foreign exchange operations of the Central Bank, but with one or two outstanding exceptions such advisors have usually not had any substantial effect on monetary or fiscal policies. Numerous problems have arisen in private employment of financial technicians, mainly over the difficulties of avoiding involvement in Chinese politics, or avoiding being called upon to exert pressures and exploit their contacts in Washington for specific projects. There have been notable examples of advisors such as Dr. Arthur Young avoiding both these difficulties and performing loyal and useful service to the National Government. The deepening of China's economic crisis, however, and the intensification of the need for foreign financial aid, may make those two difficulties increasingly acute.

One of the major difficulties confronting official American representatives, assigned as advisors to China, would be the increasingly nationalistic trend which is evident in the Chinese Government. Opposition to any policy recommendations from the United States might be based on objection to infringement on Chinese sovereignty. Unless the policy responsibilities of the official advisor were clearly defined by clear-cut agreement between the two governments, it is possible that American financial advisors would be absorbed into the Chinese system and faced with the two problems, indicated above, which have always confronted private American advisors employed by the Chinese Government.

Industry

Chinese vital transportation and communications facilities, mines, utilities and industries have been seriously damaged during 10 years of war. In Manchuria there was considerable stripping of Japanese-developed industrial and power generating equipment by the Russians. Reliable statistics are not available in all cases, but the report of the Working Group on Reconstruction of Devastated Areas for Asia and the Far East, of the United Nations, estimated that 58 per cent of the productive capacity of the cotton textile industry, 90 per cent of the machine and light metal industries, and 70 per cent of the coal, electric power, and iron and steel industry were lost. Chinese Government data indicate that the textile industry has been able to restore 50 per cent of its pre-war capacity, and the machine and light metal industries 25 per cent. The coal industry is up to 53 per cent but is handicapped by loss of mines damaged or held by Communists and by lack of transport. Electric power capacity is 60 per cent restored—in Shanghai nearly 100 per cent—but is in a rundown precarious condition. Since V–J Day, 3,816 km of railways have been restored, using materials and equipment furnished by UNRRA and cannibalized from branch lines and sidings, but on an emergency basis with temporary timber bridges and other substandard materials. Deficiencies in transport are a major obstacle to economic recovery, but until the political situation in North China and Manchuria is resolved, only the lines in Central and South China are available for permanent rehabilitation. Since V–J Day 20,000 km of additional highways have been restored in some measure and added to the 50,000 km regarded in operable condition. Some 20,000 trucks and 60,000 metric tons of highway equipment have been received from UNRRA and the United States.

Ten per cent of the main telecommunication lines have been restored. Some 800,000 tons of shipping have been obtained by the Chinese as compared with a pre-war total of 1,300,000 tons. There is reported an acute shortage on the Yangtze of passenger vessels and cargo vessels with passenger accommodations. Port facilities have deteriorated seriously through the war years and require extensive repairs, but little if any expansion under present conditions. Cement production, an essential element in reconstruction plans is currently 30 per cent of pre-war production. Less than 50,000 tons of steel were produced in pre-war years, though large amounts of ore were mined and shipped to Japan. Accurate figures are not available but iron and steel production appears to be running at less than the pre-war.

It will be noted that, notwithstanding UNRRA and United States assistance, efforts to revive China's communications and industries have not been entirely effective. High labor and raw material costs, shortage of power and fuel, delays in deliveries of vital repair parts from abroad and the critical shortage of qualified supervisors who have the practical "know how," have been deterrents but the major obstacles to recovery are inflation and the lack of capital. A serious threat to China's industrial future and material welfare is imposed at present by the denial to the nation of most North China and Manchurian resources. If this condition were to become complete and final, it would constitute nothing short of a calamity to Chinese prospects for industrialization.

Coal—China's most important natural resource is coal, ranking among the major reserves of the world. The reserves according to National Government data are approximately as follows:

	Million Metric Tons
Coking	2,728
Anthracite	46,001
Bituminous	188,167
Total	236,896

plus 4,738 million metric tons of lignite. The reserves are located mostly in North China, particularly in Shansi Province, and also in Manchuria and Southwestern China.

According to Chinese reports, coal production in 1937 totalled 32 million tons, 12 from Manchuria, 11 from the Northern Provinces and 9 from the remainder of China. During the war, production for all of China reached approximately 72 million tons. Due primarily to disruption of mines and transport by the Communists, production during 1946 was only 15,000,000 tons, and for the first six months of 1947 was 8,577,000 tons.

Since coal is practically the sole source of power except in Manchuria and Taiwan, and of fuel for water transportation, industrial processes, maintenance of essential community services and domestic heating and cooking, this deficit has not only retarded economic recovery but has contributed to discomfort, sickness and unrest among the people. It has also prevented export of coal which would be important to China's exchange position, and to the economic recovery of Japan and other Far Eastern countries.

The complete loss of Manchuria's coal to China would be a crippling blow, and the additional loss of North China sources would be even more serious, for without at least those from the Northern Provinces, China cannot' hope to achieve any substantial industrialization, the only hope for a balanced economy and a strong free China.

Lack of transport has played a part in the present coal shortage. At the Kailan Mines in North China, by far the largest remaining producing mine in

China, 500,000 tons of coal have accumulated and been stock-piled for lack of adequate rolling stock to remove all of the daily production for shipment to Chinhuangtao (and Shanghai) and Tientsin. This mine which is currently producing 15,000 tons per day, is frequently in jeopardy from Communist operations. Its loss under present conditions would be disastrous.

Most of the coal mines in China are operated by the National Resources Commission which has had a survey made by foreign consultants and prepared a program of rehabilitation. A loan of $1,500,000, U. S. has been obtained and also considerable quantities of equipment and materials through UNRRA, not much of it yet installed. The mines which are receiving first attention are Yilo near Loyang and Chungfu in Honan Province, Hwantung mines in Kiangsu, Hsiangtan mines in Hunan, Pinghsiang mines in Kiangsi, and those in northern Taiwan, but rehabilitation is going slowly and will require some time to complete. The privately owned Hwainan mines in Anhwei are reported to have uncovered additional deposits and to have plans for expansion as previously mentioned. Other mines proposed for rehabilitation and development are in the politically unsettled North and not available for rehabilitation. The importance under the circumstances of protecting and holding the Kailan Mines is indicated.

Electric Power—There are some 1,350,000 kilowatts of electric power installed in China, with about 900,000 kilowatts actually available, much of it was damaged and deteriorated or obsolete. Since the war, a considerable number of packaged power units, 2,000 kilowatts and smaller, have been obtained through UNRRA, primarily with a view to revival of industry. The principal plants or systems are located in Shanghai, Tientsin-Peiping area, Tsingtao, Canton, Nanking, Hankow, Taiwan, and Manchuria, though the last have largely become unavailable by reason of Communist operations. With the exception of the Shanghai Power Company, Hankow Water Works and Electric Power Company, Nanking Electric Company, and two plants in Tientsin, they are all public owned, and operated by the National Resources Commission, which has prepared a program of rehabilitation and expansion of the North Hopei, Tsingtao, Shanghai, Canton and Taiwan systems. While rehabilitation of plants is undoubtedly needed, any expansion proposed should be carefully coordinated with anticipated industrial expansion and additional power requirements. In Shanghai there is a serious power shortage, and an existing connected load of some 60,000 kilowatts, not in operation and awaiting only the availability of additional power, and this deficit will grow to 100,000 kilowatts or more in the four years required to install additional capacity. A project has been prepared by the Shanghai Power Company to construct a new efficient base load plant to serve, on a wholesale basis, all the power companies in the adjacent area. From an investment standpoint, domestic or foreign, this is a needed and worthy project, provided a franchise be granted and suitable assurances given with respect to servicing and amortization of loans. Taiwan offers many advantages to industrial expansion, a strategic shipping location, appreciable natural resources, adequate transportation, a literate and industrious population and low cost hydro-electric power, and some expansion of power facilities may be indicated, particularly if the fertilizer and other industries are greatly expanded. There is, however, a considerable installed capacity not now available because of damaged transmission lines and sub-stations. In North China, political difficulties will need to be resolved before any permanent improvement or expansion of power systems would be justified.

Railways—The railways of China, operated by the Ministry of Communications as a government monopoly, may be grouped as follows:

	Total	—Kilometers— Operable (by Natl Govt)
Manchuria	11336	1647
North China	5749	2362
South and Central China including Lunghai Railroad	8837	6199
Taiwan (Formosa)	3925	3925
Hainan Island	289	. . . .
Totals	30136	4133

From July 1937, when Japan initiated war against China, to October 1938, China lost virtually all railway lines to the enemy or through her own scorched earth policy. On V–J Day 8772 km were in operation in China proper and approximately 11000 km in Manchuria, but since then 3649 km in China proper and 9353 km in Manchuria have been captured or destroyed by the Communists.

With railroad materials and rolling stock furnished by UNRRA, and cannibalized from branch lines and sidings, since V–J Day, 3816 km of railways have been restored in China proper, but largely on an emergency basis with temporary timber bridges and other sub-standard materials.

Deficiencies in transport are a major obstacle to economic recovery but until the political situation is resolved in Manchuria and North China, no rehabilitation of railways in those areas, except on an emergency basis, is feasible. This includes the Lunghai Line which, since the change in course of the Yellow River to the old bed, is now considered in Central rather than North China. Proposed railway rehabilitation programs have therefore been confined to lines south of the Yangtze River, the important North and South artery between Canton (Kowloon) and Hankow, (1242 km main, 106 km branch) and nearly complete rebuilding of the diagonal Chekiang-Kiangsi Railway, from Hangchow to Chuchow (1076 km main, 68 km branch) where it connects with the Canton-Hankow Railway; and the Hunan-Kwangsi-Kweichow line which runs from Hengyang to Kweilin and Tuyun. The latter line could probably be rebuilt at least in part with materials salvaged in rebuilding the other two lines.

Estimates run high, up to $100,000,000 and more, for this program and include such maintenance of way material, rolling stock and railway shop equipment which must be imported. A major obstacle to additional investment in these lines on a loan basis is the heavy and involved capital structure, which is completely out of line with the present deteriorated plant value. Financial reorganization is indicated, with assumption by the National Government of war damage.

Shipping—Inadequacy of coastal and river shipping is a contributing factor to the existing breakdown in trade within China, as well as foreign commerce, upon which national unity and prosperity depend. In this case, however, the situation could be improved, despite the civil war, were it not for the spirit of nationalism and monopoly which characterizes the Chinese government's policy. Foreign flag vessels are no longer allowed to engage in Chinese coastal trade as before the war, and important former ports, such as Hankow, are not open to foreign ships.

In July 1937 when Japan launched an intensified campaign against China, there were 4008 ships of all categories with a gross tonnage of 1,286,000 tons engaged in China's trade. Of these 3457 with a gross tonnage of 576,000 tons were under Chinese registry. As a result of the blockade and seizure of the China Coast and harbor areas by Japanese armed forces, all the sea-going vessels and some of the river steamers together with 7450 junks and 30,000 fishing boats were lost. All ship yards and repair facilities were also lost.

After the war, 60,000 tons of British shipping were leased and numbers of ships obtained, nearly all from the United States. Ships purchased by the National Government and operated by China Merchants total 137 of a gross tonnage of 283,800 tons and those by private (Chinese) firms total 114 of a gross tonnage of 253,400 tons. There is a total, government and private, of 1017 sea going ships of 628,900 gross tons and 1501 river and small craft of 179,893 tons or a total gross tonnage of 808,815. Many of these ships are, however, old and costly to maintain and operate, so that the total falls short of actual needs. There is a reported shortage on the Yangtze of passenger vessels and cargo vessels with passenger accommodations. There is also a serious shortage of ship repair and docking facilities. Rehabilitation of docking and repair facilities at Keelung (Taiwan) will meet a part of this requirement. One major deterrent to resumption of normal shipping traffic is its relatively high cost, due principally to the increased cost of coal and high cost and inefficiency of maritime and cargo-handling labor.

Harbors—All Chinese harbors were occupied by the Japanese after July 1937, and except in North China and Manchuria very little was done to improve or even to maintain them adequately. As a result, at the end of the war, waterfront structures and godowns were in a deteriorated and in some cases damaged condition, and harbors and channels were in some instances, notably in Taiwan, blocked by sunken vessels.

In the early part of 1946, a survey was made by Chinese and American engineers and plans made to rehabilitate and improve a number of the harbors. Some of these plans would appear to be unrealistic and inadvisable, specifically the Whangpoa project at Canton and the Tangku Harbor project in North China. The less ambitious but more realistic Inner Canton Harbor project, and the improvement of the channel and entrance of the Hai Ho River, sponsored by the Hai Ho Conservancy Commission, would seem to be more in consonance with reasonable requirements and funds which can probably be made available. All harbor projects need to be carefully reviewed for economic justification and conformance to the general economic rehabilitation program for China.

Tangku Harbor Project—For more than 40 years, shipping to Tientsin, the commercial and communication center of North China, has been carried on in two types of ships, the majority in small coastwise steamers which crossed the Taku bar at high water, and contingent upon draft proceeded either to Tangku or Taku, or on up the Hai Ho River to Tientsin the remainder in deeper draft ships which anchored outside the bar and were discharged or loaded by special sea-going lighters. Although little cargo was ever lost, there were some delays due to weather, and there was agitation for a deep water port. The Gulf of Chihli contains no natural deep draft harbors nor does it lend itself to their economic construction south of Chinhuangtao because of the shallow water along the coast and the heavy silt content of rivers which discharge into it.

The Japanese undertook the construction of a harbor on the North side of the mouth of the Hai Ho River with a lock connection into the river with a view to shipping coal and salt to Japan. The Tangku Harbor Administration created under the Ministry of Communications has expanded this original Japanese project into a full fledged deep draft harbor. As originally conceived it consisted of a protected dredged harbor with a lock connection into the Hai Ho River and stone jetties extending 16,800 metres (10 miles) over the mud flats to deep water. The approximate estimate at that time was U. S. $30 million. It has already been determined that much more than the originally estimated quantity of stone would be required for the jetties, due to the soft silt bottom, and that even the original quantity of stone was beyond the capacity of the railroad to carry. The Tangku Harbor Commission therefore proposed to substitute cellular construction of steel sheet piling. In view of the soft bottom conditions it is open to question whether this alternative will be satisfactory. The difficulties and high cost of construction under such conditions are well known. In any case, the 80,000 tons of steel required will appreciably increase the cost and the foreign exchange requirements. It is probable that the total cost of the project will exceed U. S. $50 million. Operating difficulties and costs are also likely to be heavy. The mud banks along the harbor and channel will slough indefinitely and require continuous maintenance dredging, and ice conditions inside the harbor and channel, located between the outlets of two fresh water rivers, are likely to be severe, with no appreciable current to facilitate clearance. Difficulties from silting and ice are likely to be encountered in operation of the lock. Since it would be costly and imprudent, if not fatal, to rely solely upon the lock to pass shipping to Taku and Tientsin, it will be necessary to keep open the Hai Ho entrance channel, and since this channel will normally service the bulk of the traffic at nominal cost, the heavy operating and capital costs of the Tangku Harbor project would have to be borne by the deep draft ships. For a fraction of the Harbor cost, worthwhile channel (Koku and Nan Kai cuttings) and entrance (jetty) improvements could be made to the Hai Ho River which would benefit the majority of the vessels normally serving Tangku, Taku and Tientsin. In this connection it is interesting to note as evidence of the need for a coordinating agency, that there are two Government agencies, one under the Ministry of Communications and the other under the Ministry of Water Conservancy, competing, working at cross purposes and devoting their attention and efforts to the same basic problem, namely providing adequate harbor facilities for the Tientsin-Peking area.

Textiles—The textile industry, next to food, is China's largest consumer goods industry and by the same token, the most important toward reviving her economy and meeting her vital clothing need. It was in textiles that China first embarked on her modern industrial development. Before the war there were in China, including Manchuria, 6 million machine spindles and over 50,000 power looms, of which 2.1 million were lost and 1.6 million damaged but susceptible of repair. It is estimated that approximately 3 million spindles are now in operation, and that 4 million may be in operation in another year. These capacities will only partially meet requirements. Cotton production is also below the pre-war, largely because of the disturbed political situation in the North. The cotton summary and outlook for the 1946–1947 and 1947–1948 seasons are shown on the following page. Substantial assistance has been extended to China, largely through UNRRA in the form of clothing, cotton textiles and raw cotton totalling $115 million U. S., and through an Eximbank loan for the purchase of cotton. The former Japanese enterprises which comprised a large part of the pre-war industry have been taken over by a government corporation, the China Textile Industries, Inc., and the earnings of this corporation since V–J Day have provided the government with substantial revenues. It is the intention of the Chinese Government, under the corporation's charter, to sell the mills which it now operates to private enterprise, and appraisals of their worth are currently being made with this object in view. Some inquiries are being made concerning the prospects for investment in these mills by United States textile interests. In view of unsettled political and financial conditions, the latter undoubtedly would require assurances regarding financial control of any enterprise jointly established with Chinese interests, as well as provisions for remission of profits and debt service, fair assessment of taxes, and guarantees of maintaining operations at capacity.

TENTATIVE ESTIMATE CHINA COTTON SUMMARY AND OUTLOOK FOR THE 1946-47 AND 1947-48 SEASONS

	500 lb. Bales, in Thousands
August 1, 1946–July 31, 1947	
Estimated carryover of cotton in warehouses and mills on August 1, 1946	750
Arrivals of UNRRA cotton from August 1, 1946 up to July 31, 1947	258
Arrivals of foreign commercial cotton from August 1, 1946 up to July 31, 1947	568
Total domestic cotton estimated to be available for mills during period ending September 30, 1947, mostly arriving before July 31	800
	2,376
Calculated mill consumption, August 1, 1946–July 31, 1947	1,500
Mill and undistributed stocks	876

TENTATIVE ROUGH FORECAST FOR AUGUST 1, 1947–JULY 31, 1948

Estimated amounts available to mills from domestic crop to September 30, 1948, mostly arriving before July 31	1,100
Total available supply at manufacturing centers or in the country	1,976
Requirements	
Estimated mill consumption, August 1, 1947–July 31, 1948	1,750
Mill and other visible stocks needed for safe carryover	600
	2,350
Imports needed to July 31, 1948	347
UNRRA cotton to arrive	124
Commercial or other imports scheduled to arrive	150
Further imports needed	100
Third quarter allocation	97

Fertilizer—One of the outstanding needs in China is chemical fertilizer. China is predominantly an agricultural country. More than 80 per cent of her population are farmers, most of them barely able to eke out an existence, with practically no purchasing power or ability to improve their miserable lot. If there is ever to be any real improvement in Chinese economy and standards of living, it must come in large part from increased agricultural production. There is no more effective means of increasing the productivity of land and farmers than by the use of fertilizers. Natural fertilizers traditionally used are inadequate to restore the fertility of the soil, and oil cake wastefully used as fertilizer could more profitably be fed to animals whose by-products—milk, eggs and meat—would greatly improve the diet and health of the people. A good theoretical case can be made for the use of chemical fertilizer, because even at the very high prices to the Chinese farmers, it can produce three to four times its value in crops. A practical problem remains of satisfactory financing arrangements.

In Taiwan 300,000 tons of commercial fertilizer were used annually before the war. In South China about half that amount was used profitably for rice and sugar on the depleted triple-cropped soils of that area, but the bulk of Chinese farmers have no knowledge of its advantages. Merely as a measure of possible requirements, if the same amount were applied as in Japan, Chinese requirements would total 11,000,000 tons annually. Probably only a fraction of that amount will ever be used, primarily because of the prohibitive cost to the farmers, due to the primitive means of transport in the interior of China, and the difficulties of providing any such quantities. It is not feasible for China to import the fertilizers she needs, because of short world supply, and exchange requirements.

The Yungli Chemical Company, privately owned, has a plant near Nanking with a capacity of 30,000 tons per year, of ammonium sulphate, which it is expanding to capacity of 60,000 tons; and has also obtained an Eximbank loan in the sum of $16,000,000 toward the construction of a new plant at Hsiangtan in Hunan Province of a capacity of 90,000 tons of ammonium sulphate per year.

The National Resources Commission has made a survey with the aid of American consultants, and has made plans to develop a production of 705,000 tons of chemical fertilizers annually—481,000 tons of ammonium sulphate and nitrate, 12,000 tons of calcium cyanamid, and 212,000 tons of super-phosphate, and has requested an Eximbank loan in the sum of $50,000,000 to implement them. The projects consist of the rehabilitation and expansion of five existing plants in Taiwan to increase the pre-war capacity of 34,000 tons of both phosphatic and nitrogenous fertilizers to a production of 75,000 tons by 1949; also the construction of two new plants in Taiwan, one an ammonium sulphate plant with a capacity of 181,900 tons annually and the other a super-phosphate plant with a capacity of 170,000 tons annually. The construction of an ammonium sulphate plant at Canton with a capacity of 278,800 tons annually is also proposed. Taiwan is a more favorable location because of the availability of low cost electric power. The proposed construction of the super-phosphate plant may require further consideration because of the present lack of satisfactory phosphate rock. The rock from Haichow is inferior, and the proposal to import from Indo-China and Christmas Island cannot be regarded as a satisfactory solution for a costly permanent installation of this kind. The Japanese are thought to have discovered a large deposit in China, but it has not yet been found. The need to pursue prospecting diligently is evident.

Iron and Steel—The mining and tempering of iron has been practiced in China for several thousand years, but the lack of technical skill has kept the industry at a low level of development. There are few available data on the Chinese pre-war iron industry. There was a rather considerable production of iron ore— perhaps 2 million metric tons annually, largely from the Lungyen Mine in the Liaoning District and the Tayeh Mine in the Yangtze Valley, but most of it went to the Japanese steel industry. Pig iron production in China proper in 1936 was about 155,000 tons, largely from native furnaces, and in Manchuria about 475,000 tons. Less than 50,000 tons of steel were produced. During the war in Free China, iron and steel making facilities were small, primitive and unproductive. In 1944 only 44,000 tons of iron and 13,000 tons of steel were produced. In 1945 steel production was down to 8,000 tons but there has been some revival and the Chinese Government hopes, optimistically, to produce 200,000 tons in 1947.

The National Resources Commission has had a survey made by American consultants, of the iron and steel potential of China. While known iron ore deposits of China are substantial—if all recovered they would produce 300,000,000 tons of steel—they are not impressive for a country as large and populous as China, and in the United States they would suffice for less than six years. The importance of continuing the search for additional high grade deposits, persistently and continuously, is indicated, as well as making a more careful survey and appraisal of the low grade deposits. The latter appear to be considerable and add appreciably to the possibility of creating an iron and steel industry of considerable magnitude in China.

As a result of the survey, the National Resources Commission is proceeding with plans for the construction of a steel plant in the Yangtze Valley, at Tayeh, on the south branch of the Yangtze River about 135 kilometers east of and downstream from Hankow, and is soliciting U. S. funds in the sum of $35,000,000 to undertake this project. The proposed initial capacity of this first plant is 375,000 metric tons per year, of rails, fittings, plates, blooms, billets, structurals, merchant bars, sheets and tin plate. Additional plants are proposed later at Peiping with a capacity of 300,000 tons, at Chungking of 80,000 tons, and at Canton of perhaps 250,000 tons. Neither Manchuria nor Taiwan was considered in this survey. Before final decision is made on the Tayeh site, a further study should be made, and consideration given to a location on Taiwan, inasmuch as the design of the proposed Tayeh plant was predicated on imports of iron ore from Hainan, to the South.

Cement—The development of the cement industry in China has taken place in comparatively recent years. In China proper the production in 1937 was 1,000,000 tons. In 1946, the output was only 300,000 tons and 600,000 tons were imported. Cement is an important element in the reconstruction of industries, harbors, railways, roads and buildings, and plans have been made for the expansion of the industry. Fortunately China has abundant raw material resources. Plans have been made by the National Resources Commission for the rehabilitation and expansion of three plants in Taiwan, at Kao-hsiung, Tsu-Tung and Suao (the latter is poorly located and was badly damaged by bombing) ; by the Kwa Hsin Cement Company for the development of a new plant at Tayeh, for the rehabilitation and expansion from 200 to 500 tons per day of the North China Cement Company, and the development of the Hunan Cement Company with a capacity of 500 tons per day. The last two projects, both sponsored by the National Resources Commission, should have further study. Funds in the sum of $2,700,000 US have already been obtained for the Taiwan plants, $1,600,000 from UNRRA, $500,000 Eximbank, $260,000 Canadian and $340,000 National Resources Commission, and orders in approximately this amount have been placed for overseas materials and equipment. The present cement output of 150,000 tons per year in Taiwan is adequate for present local requirements. By June 1948, with the increased capacity, it is hoped to produce 600,000 tons per year, 300,000 for local requirements including hydro-electric expansion, and 300,000 tons for export.

The Hwa Hsin Cement Company has undertaken the construction of a modern 1,000 tons per day plant at Tayeh on the site of a pre-war plant of one-fifth that capacity, which was moved to Chengchi in Free China on the approach of the Japanese. The major part of the required machinery has already been ordered from Allis-Chalmers and other U. S. manufacturers and they have received aid from UNRRA in the form of cement mixers, structural steel, earth-moving equipment and miscellaneous items, but they are now seeking a $2,000,000 Eximbank loan to cover the U. S. cost of a 3½ kilometer aerial tramway, conveyors, quarrying equipment, etc., required to complete the project.

Crop Conditions

China's winter and summer food harvests this year, assuming no changes in present summer crop conditions, are expected by the American Agricultural Attaché to be significantly larger than last year's fairly good returns. Poor distribution, however, will result in a serious lack of food in at least five large areas in China which are possible famine districts. It must be emphasized that

China's food stocks since the war have been much lower than normal. Therefore a potentially dangerous situation will continue to exist until food stocks have been built up.

The most important food shortage areas, approximately in order of their importance are:

1) The coastal strip in Kwangtung from Swatow south to the Canton delta country. This area, a large food deficit area in normal times, suffered from the early June floods which occurred in the East, West and North River valleys. The Pearl River estuary and delta and the Han River area around Swatow are expected to be the centers of the shortage. Early reports indicate a good start for the second rice crop.

2) South Hunan in the hsiens around Hengyang. The rest of Hunan expects a good rice crop, but this area, which suffered starvation last year, was damaged again by a flood in the middle of June. It is not clear how badly the June floods damaged south Hunan. Damage may have been overestimated, in which case supplies from within the province will be more than sufficient if properly distributed. However, proper distribution within Hunan is questionable when other areas offer better prices.

3) Northern Kwangsi areas which are part of the extension of the south Hunan shortage area. UNRRA reports state that starvation in this area is partly due to heavy exports of rice to large coastal cities where higher prices for rice are offered.

In early June 100,000 acres of farm land were flooded in Kwangsi along the West River from Nanning to Wuchow. The first rice crop in this area was reported destroyed, but in the rest of Kwangsi crop conditions were reported good.

4) Two areas in Honan, one in the north near the Hopei border, and one in the southeastern reclaimed Yellow River areas. The shortage area in the north, which includes Linhsien, Tangying and Linchang, is apparently suffering from the winter wheat drought as well as fighting. The information on this area is based on reports that have yet to be confirmed.

The southeastern area lacks food since this was in the Yellow River flood area in recent years. In many parts no crops have been harvested since the river was diverted across Shantung. This area also includes parts of the Yellow River flooded areas in North Anhwei.

5) Food shortages are reported by UNRRA in western and northern Shantung, especially in the areas adjacent to the Yellow River. Food is particularly short in the Tehsien area on the Hopei border. There is a definite need for food for the migrants leaving the lowlands and bed of the Yellow River which has been diverted back into northwest Shantung.

6) Recent press reports indicate floods in north Kiangsu both north and south of Hsuchow, with the Peihsien and Suchien areas claimed completely inundated. This area, as well as local areas in southwest Shantung, were the scene of civil war fighting last summer and fall and will undoubtedly require assistance. Actual flood damage to crops in north Kiangsu is still being assessed so that reliable estimates of relief needs are not yet available.

Local areas which are suffering or anticipating food shortages include:

1) the south Jehol mountainous area,

2) some hsiens on the Liaotung Peninsula north of Dairen in Manchuria,

3) scattered areas in Shansi, including the Tatung locality,

4) the Hoo Li area in Chahar will be short until harvest this fall,

5) scattered hsiens in Hopei. Hsiens mentioned by UNRRA as short of food are Mancheng, Tingshing, Jungcheng, Chingyuen and Mingho.

6) Famine conditions are expected in Ningteh hsien in north central Fukien. Some of the Fukien coastal hsiens are short of food.

7) UNRRA anticipates famine conditions in the Pescadores Islands.

8) Local flooded areas in south Kweichow, south Kiangsi, southwest Kwangsi and along the rivers in the Chengtu basin in Szechwan.

Shortages may generally develop in north China if summer crops are poor, especially in Shansi, Hopei and Shantung. Crop conditions in north China so far, however, have been reported at least average, except for the flooded areas mentioned above.

During late July and early August an estimated 12 million shih mow (2 million acres) were flooded in the lower Liao River valley south of Mukden. Early reports tentatively indicate that more than a million people in this area were affected by the unusually heavy seasonal flood. Suffering and food shortages in this area are expected as a result of the flood and poor distribution from other parts of Manchuria. However, a surplus production of food is definitely expected for the whole of Manchuria. Nationalist-occupied Manchuria is expected to have a food surplus for the year also, although much smaller than that of the Communist areas.

Taiwan's rice acreage and production appear to have returned to pre-war figures, aided by the use of some land in the southern part of the island that was formerly used for sugar-cane production. As UNRRA Agricultural Rehabilitation men point out, this is significant since this is the first large rice-producing or exporting area in the Far East which apparently has returned to pre-war averages and production.

Problems Confronting American Business in China

In each of the localities visited conferences were held with American businessmen. Much valuable information concerning the situation in China was gained from these sources and from memoranda prepared by the American Chambers of Commerce in Shanghai and Tientsin. American business representatives strongly expressed the view that it would be undesirable for the United States to extend further financial assistance to China, in the present situation, unless strict conditions were attached to assure effective use of the proceeds of any loan for purposes consistent with United States policies. As stated in a Joint Memorandum of the Far East-American Council of Commerce and Industry, Inc., and the National Foreign Trade Council, Inc., submitted to the Department of State June 17, 1947, these two councils are strongly on record in support of a procedure under which, from now on, any public funds which the United States Government may provide or make available to the Government of China, either for relief or general reconstruction purposes, should be only on the basis of strictest control as to handling, end-use, and disposition.

American businessmen stated that the present Chinese Government has been apathetic in its efforts at economic improvement, and has taken refuge in the thought of foreign assistance for solution for China's problems. The American businessmen felt that it would prejudice achievement of necessary reforms in China, if financial assistance were to be provided in any large amount with control of its use to be left in Chinese hands. They regarded this, for example, as a basic defect in the $500 million loan of 1942.

The following are the principal problems which American business is facing in China at the present time. Complaints include the administration of import and exchange controls, particular stress being placed upon the methods used in allocation of import quotas, delays and inefficiency in obtaining import licenses, and the practice on the part of the import licensing board of discriminating against foreign concerns to favor newly established Chinese companies, including those organized by "favored families." It was universally acknowledged that conditions of corruption among lower officials in the import control and customs services were widespread. Legitimate enterprise is restricted under the regulations, but goods which are on the list of prohibited imports can move and do move into China by bribery. Smuggling via Hong Kong is widespread with established fees and procedures.

From the standpoint of China's commercial relations with the rest of the world, as well as of maintaining what historically has been one of the most important sources of revenue to the Chinese Government, great importance attaches to the maintenance of an efficient and honest Chinese Maritime Customs Service. In pre-war years, the reputation of the Chinese Maritime Customs for efficiency and honesty of administration was unexcelled throughout the world. At the present time, in contrast, corruption among the lower officials is widespread, more so it was learned than at any time in the last 94 years. For analogy, comparison would have to be made with the period between 1842 and 1853 when conditions of bribery and corruption were so rampant as to lead to the establishment of the Inspectorate General of Customs. The basic cause for the situation which exists is to be found in the completely inadequate level of wages for customs employees. They are paid a starting wage of around CN $1,500,000 per month and employees who have been employed for six years, now earn around $2 million CN per month (equivalent to U. S. $50.00 at present market rate). These sums are completely inadequate to cover the essentials of life for any man with a family. With opportunity for bribery frequently present, almost the inevitable result is widespread corruption. A similar or worse situation exists in other Chinese tax bureaus. A rise in the wages paid to customs officials would not only do more than any other single factor to restore the integrity of the Maritime Customs but undoubtedly would repay the National Government many fold in terms of receipts acquired.

The most common form of corruption in the customs is understood to be the payment of what is called "convenience money," i. e., a payment made by an importer to expedite action on his case and movement of goods through customs. Much less frequent is an alteration in the amount of custom payment or the sum which goes to the National treasury. In this respect, the record of the Maritime Customs is relatively good. Administrative costs of collecting duties run 9–11 percent. In the Direct Tax Bureau of the Ministry of Finance, it is reported, the "administrative" expense of tax collection runs as high as 60 per cent.

Scarcely any reforms which could be instituted would be more important for China's commercial relations than the taking of measures to restore the efficiency and integrity of its Maritime Customs service.

American business is also concerned with the fact that profits from trade in China cannot be remitted to the States through regular exchange channels. They stress that if China desires the assistance of foreign capital in development of its commerce and industries, provision must be made to permit remission of legitimate profits to the States by American investors. The National Government has recently recognized this fact in principle but stresses the emergency character of the present situation and China's inability with its present small exchange holdings to permit such remission of profit.

Another principal complaint of American business relates to discrimination in the enforcement of various Chinese taxes, particularly the business tax and the income tax. There exists a technical provision in the existing income tax law, and its enforcement regulations, under which many American corporations are required to pay greater income taxes than those paid by Chinese groups ; and also for some American corporations to pay an excess profits tax as well, which they would not have had to pay if they had been incorporated under Chinese instead of American law. The principal complaint of American business, however, is that the income tax is collected in practice from only a small proportion of Chinese companies, and, if collected, the sum is a matter of arrangement by payment of a bribe to the local tax official. American companies, on the other hand, are required to pay taxes to the full letter of the law.

American business firms operating in Shanghai are particularly concerned at the operations of the buying and selling agencies of the National Government, and particularly of the developing channel by which China's principal exports, such as bristles and tung oil, have been exported through the Central Trust, a subsidiary of the Central Bank of China, and the Universal Trading Corporation, organized under the State of New York. The Universal Trading Corporation also functions as a purchasing agent on both governmental and private account and forwards its products to China for sale through the Central Trust. During the first six months of 1947, 33 per cent of the exports from Shanghai to the United States were consigned to the Universal Trading Corporation. Development of this channel serves to undermine the position of established American trading firms and agency representatives in China. The recent decision of the Chinese Government to terminate the Chinese Supply Commission in Washington as of 1 August would be welcome were it not for the fact that the Supply Commission functions were announced as being transferred to the Universal Trading Corporation. Recognizing the concern with which American business and government officials may be expected to regard this transfer, it is possible that the National Government will modify the intended functions of the Universal Trading Corporation, as well as of the Central Trust.

Immediate Steps to Strengthen the Economy

The handling of foreign trade through normal private channels with rigorous nondiscriminatory enforcement of import controls is urgently needed. The Central Trust should be taken out of foreign trade and its functions restricted. A free market in foreign exchange, within a system of import controls, and managed by the Central Bank with full cooperation of the Appointed Banks, should provide incentives for private exporters. All ports, including Hankow, should be open to foreign vessels, at least temporarily. A rigid control of smuggling would also be a major step towards the restoration of foreign trade.

China should move towards stabilizing the currency by first attempting to restore a balance between Government receipts and expenditures. Any attempt at currency stabilization through the issuance of a new currency, either paper or silver, will be premature, unless the Government has already taken steps to live within its income. The ultimate objective should be a limit or ceiling on the currency circulation and on borrowing from the Central Bank. Full publicity should be given to the activities of the Central Bank in controlling the issuance of the Chinese National Currency. These measures might help to slow down the rate of price increases, protect the position of the CN dollar as a national currency, and forestall any attempts by provincial authorities to issue separate local currencies.

The economy would be strengthened by disposing of Government-owned industrial concerns and monopolies to private Chinese enterprise, both on the mainland and in Taiwan, through open and honest sales—preferably for foreign exchange or gold—to the highest bidder. This step would increase production by giving an incentive which is at present lacking. The disposal of industrial plants would eliminate expenditures from the national budget to finance Government enterprise, reduce the number of functionaries who are in a position to make private profit at the public expense, bring in large amounts of revenue for the national budget, and assist in retarding the rise in prices. A prohibition against public officials as directors in private corporations would also strengthen the morale of the Government service.

Progress towards a balanced budget should become possible through the foregoing measures, and through increased revenue from taxation and public borrowing. Even under the present tax laws, revenue could probably be increased by strict and punctual enforcement. A tax on profits secured from speculation in commodities would be a useful addition. If there is any prospect of success in stabilizing prices and limiting currency issuance, the public would be encouraged to buy Government bonds and repatriate funds which have been sent abroad, thus materially helping the Government to balance the budget. Improved efficiency in the collection of the land tax in kind would increase the yield and reduce the burden of its incidence. Stability of the Government in the countryside could be rapidly undermined if the incidence of conscription and the land tax in kind becomes too severe. The recrudescence of *likin*—local transit taxes—and military requisitioning at nominal prices should be severely discouraged.

The administrative inefficiency and corruption, which are paralyzing the economy and crippling China as a military power, should be eliminated as rapidly as possible, and the administrative inertia overcome by a delegation of executive power and authority.

Considerations on United States Economic Assistance

Budgetary Deficits—Inflation is China's central economic problem, and the most urgently required assistance is that which can first check the depreciation of the Chinese currency and later permit of its stabilization. The main inflationary pressure comes from budgetary deficits, financed by issuance of paper currency, to cover the increasing burden of military expenditures. Reduction of such deficits requires drastic action by the Chinese government in two principal ways, (1) in reducing military expenditures by setting China's military objectives within the capacities of its economy (with such assistance as the United States can appropriately give), as well as by reforms aimed at eliminating inefficiency and corruption from the Chinese army itself; and (2) by increasing Chinese government revenues, possibly by levying new taxes, but initially by increased efficiency in the collection of existing taxes.

The above reforms are not easy; they call for measures which would alienate many local Army leaders, and require ruthless weeding out of corrupt tax officials and payment of a living wage to tax collection employees. They cannot be accomplished quickly. But unless effective efforts are made in this direction no attack on China's economic problems can hope to succeed.

United States assistance in meeting these problems could best be rendered by making available the services of experienced advisors in the budgetary and taxation fields, and by providing military advisory personnel to assist in developing and supervising an efficient military service of supply. The United States government, in our view, should not extend financial assistance with a view to covering China's budgetary deficit. Nor should financial assistance be extended on any substantial scale for reconstruction projects or to relieve pressure on China's balance of payments unless these basic steps are first taken.

Economic Reconstruction Projects—The Mission has not endeavored to prepare a plan for China's economic reconstruction. It is, however, greatly impressed with the need of a realistic formulation by the National Government of a practical program for economic reconstruction. Most necessary is a greater coordination of effort by military and economic agencies of the National Government, as well as between the National and Provincial governments and private enterprise, both in the formulation and in the implementing of reconstruction projects. China's own resources should be marshalled for solution of her economic problems before there can be assurance that requests for foreign assistance are soundly conceived and can be carried out effectively.

In connection with the Marshall Plan, European nations have been called upon for their plans for economic reconstruction. If the same principle were to apply in the Far East, difficulties would be encountered, because of China's lack of a coordinated program of economic reconstruction and of the personnel and centralized responsibilities for developing one.

The Mission accordingly would recommend, as a prerequisite to United States financial assistance, the establishment by the National Government of a high-level planning and screening agency to review carefully and impartially the projects and programs submitted by various sponsor-Ministries, Commissions, Administrations, provincial, local authorities and by private enterprise, with a view of establishment of an overall priority list of projects on the basis of which China's available resources can be directed towards China's most vital programs and projects. Such a screening and planning agency should assess the economic justification and self-liquidating potentialities of any project submitted; review the technical feasibility and estimated costs; coordinate such project with essential corollary projects of other Ministries, such as power and transportation projects which need to be accomplished prior to or concurrently with a given project; determine the manner of financing and indicate data or revision required to qualify for financing; and finally assign a position on the overall priority list.

Some such agency and procedure are considered essential to a coordinated and effective economic rehabilitation program. Such an agency would be the third place (Ministry of Finance and Ministry of War being the first two) where the services of United States economic advisors could be most effectively employed. They should be assisted also by a staff of qualified technical personnel. Such advisors would not have authority to extend financial assistance. Their job would be to assist in developing a program capable of realistic implementation; to assure that so far as possible China's resources were directed toward most pressing economic reconstruction projects, and to assure, in those cases in which United States financial assistance was required, that the projects were soundly conceived and presented for United States consideration.

Investment of Private Chinese Funds—Under conditions of inflation and financial insecurity Chinese investors are not disposed to place their capital in long term productive enterprises. Short term advances under inflation conditions command interest rates of from 15% to 30% per month. Private capital goes also into hoarding of commodities as a hedge against inflation, and for speculative purposes. The current psychology is entirely an inflationary one, and is not conducive to efforts at longer run economic reconstruction. This is a further compelling reason why the Chinese government must take definite steps toward fiscal reform and a stabilized currency, as a pre-requisite to economic reconstruction, which in large measure requires the investment of private Chinese and foreign capital.

Export-Import Bank—Under date of June 27, 1947, the National Government applied to the Export-Import Bank for loans aggregating almost $270 million to cover the dollar costs of a number of reconstruction projects, and subsequently a $200 million credit for raw cotton. Conclusions with respect to the situation in China as it affects generally the matter of loans from the Export-Import Bank follow:

In framing requests for Export-Import Bank credits the Chinese authorities appear not to have been sufficiently concerned with the requirement of economic and technical justification for individual projects to be considered. They have decided apparently upon a lump sum total of a credit to be requested, and assigned amounts for individual projects to approximate in the aggregate the desired total. Although the National Government has employed the services of a number of outstanding American engineering consultant firms to survey its needs in such fields as transportation, mining, electric power and harbor development, the studies made by these firms—submitted by the Chinese in justification for the projects requested of Export-Import Bank—appear to suffer from a basic defect. Under instruction from the National Government they are drawn up to provide China facilities which are comparable to the best in use in the United States, strictly from the engineering standpoint, and are not realistically drawn up in terms of local needs, capacity for repayment of investment, and of utilizing local resources. A case in point is the Canton-Hankow Railroad for which the Chinese made a credit application originally of $42,654,000, subsequently reduced to $37,500,000. The original construction cost of this line was equal approximately only to $20,000,000. The instructions under which the Morrison Knudsen Company undertook this survey reflect an apparent desire on the part of the Chinese Government planners for the best in modern transportation and industrial equipment. Their survey, however, is not an adequate basis for consideration of a loan request. A loan application should provide a realistic appraisal of the traffic potentialities of the road, its contribution to trade and production in the area, how the National Government proposes to meet the local currency costs of its development, the extent to which the necessary development has been met by the bridge materials, track, ties, locomotives, and rolling stock which have been provided by UNRRA, the financial plan according to which the National Government proposes to meet its earlier outstanding indebtedness on the line, the status of its agreement with the Boxer Indemnity Commission under which the British Government financed the construction of the central section of the line and in accordance with which it was agreed that all materials for this section should be purchased in the United Kingdom, etc., etc. None of this data, to our knowledge, has been provided by the Chinese Government in support of any loan application for the Canton-Hankow Railroad.

The mission was impressed with the extent to which Chinese Government requests for Export-Import Bank assistance are being made on behalf of state-owned and operated enterprises. This was particularly apparent in Formosa where the National Resources Commission owns and operates, either itself or in conjunction with the provincial Government, all principal industries on the island except coal, tea and pineapple. The Commission owns and operates, and in most instances has sought Export-Import Bank loans, for such widely diversified industries as electric power, petroleum refining, sugar refining (the Commission owns 250,000 acres of land under sugar cane), cement manufacturing, shipbuilding, machine shops, artificial fertilizer, and paper manufacture. The pattern of development which the National Resources Commission desires is evident. They wish United States financial assistance, but not United States management or control, to provide necessary foreign exchange for materials and equipment to be acquired in the United States, and to hire foreign technicians when necessary to assist in bringing into operation the facilities acquired. In the case of the Takao Refinery now operated by the Chinese Petroleum Corporation, an NRC subsidiary, the National Government refused American oil companies an opportunity to participate in the ownership and operation of the plant, but requested an Export-Import Bank loan to provide foreign exchange financing, and hired foreign technicians to assist in running the plant. On failing to obtain an Export-Import Bank credit the National Government apparently did not find difficulty in providing itself the foreign exchange required to place this refinery in operation. Whatever the statements made by the National Government regarding the extent to which foreign investments in China are to be welcome, the fact remains that at present there exists in China a strong tendency towards state ownership and operation over wide fields of industry. This raises a problem of policy from the standpoint of United States financial assistance, particularly Export-Import Bank financing, since credits from this institution are intended wherever possible to give support to private enterprise. Obviously it would be undesirable from the standpoint of United States policy to be doctrinaire or completely inflexible in granting loans to Government-owned or operated enterprises. A railroad credit, for example, in China would seem a desirable loan to a Government body and there could be other similar examples. In the present situation, however, in which the National Resources Commission is operating in every major field of industry in China except textiles—in which the bulk of Chinese productions by another Government Corporation, the China Textile Industry, Inc.—there is reason to consider carefully every project in its impact on private enterprise, Chinese as well as American.

The fact that individual credit applications for Export-Import Bank funds must be guaranteed by the Central Bank of China places difficulties in the way of giving consideration to what might be worthwhile small projects proposed either by provincial authorities or by private enterprise. In the more effective coordination of reconstruction projects in China, some method must be found to open the way to financing of locally sponsored projects, both provincial, municipal, and private.

As long as present conditions of civil war and inflation continue, and lack of confidence in the situation in China by Chinese investors themselves exists, there is a general difficulty with respect to the possibility for external financing on banking terms. Among the statutory requirements to Export-Import Bank loans is the proviso that there must exist a reasonable assurance of repayment of any loan made. Even though an individual project may be meritorious from the standpoint of meeting China's basic needs, assurances of repayment cannot exist when the value of the Chinese yuan and the general credit or exchange position of the National Government is deteriorating. Until some effective steps are taken towards greater stability in China's public finances and currency, it is difficult to see how ordinary banking loans can be made with adequate assurances for repayment. The Chinese place emphasis upon the desirability of proceeding now with individual projects in areas which are sheltered from the civil war and hence from attacks or destruction by the Communists. There is, however, in China no industrial area which now is sheltered from the effects of currency inflation and depreciation of the National currency.

The credits which China needs for reconstruction projects for the most part will be long term credits for example from 15–20 years. It is doubtful whether the Export-Import Bank desires to undertake such financing over a period that long. Its policies are understood to aim more at shorter term credits, and largely of the exporter-credit type on particular sales of American manufactured materials or equipment. In any event, it is clear that Export-Import Bank loans could not be used to finance local currency expenditures in China for materials and labor required to be purchased there in connection with any project.

Therefore, there are in China now very few projects which can qualify for Export-Import Bank financing. As the situation is improved, particularly in terms of steps towards fiscal and currency stabilization and towards more realistic formulation of economic reconstruction projects, it is possible that increased opportunities will exist for Export-Import Bank financing, particularly of projects sponsored by American and Chinese private enterprises.

Balance of Payments Assistance.—Another necessary approach to the problem of economic stability in China must relate to the exchange value of the Chinese currency, to checking its depreciation and establishment of conditions under which the foreign exchange value of the yuan eventually may be stabilized. Such stabilization may require United States assistance, but in our view is not a practical possibility until definite steps are taken towards fiscal reform and restoring confidence of the Chinese people, and until production in China increases to permit expansion in exports more nearly (with remittances from overseas Chinese) to pay for imports. Again there is need to emphasize the interdependence of China's economic, political, and military problems, and the sequence envisaged for budgetary, reconstruction, and currency stabilization measures of assistance.

Immediately China has the problem of financing its imports, which even on a restricted basis and not counting UNRRA imports, are running at a level several times its exports plus remittances of overseas Chinese, and drawing down external official exchange holdings at the rate of around $200 million per year. It is anticipated that such official assets at the present rate of usage will be drawn down to around $220 million by the end of 1947 and would be exhausted by the end of 1948 or early in 1949. It is hoped that the recently introduced system of partial linking of exports and imports and other measures will result in expansion of exports and improvement of China's foreign exchange position. At best, however, there will be a period of months in which the drain on China's external official holdings of exchange will continue. It may be desirable, therefore, as an interim measure prior to any currency stabilization loan, to give some assistance towards financing a part of China's principal industrial imports, e. g., raw cotton, to prevent too great an impairment of China's official exchange holdings.

Congressional Aid—United States objectives and interests require that positive and constructive aid be rendered to China to arrest the deterioration of economic conditions, and thus to help to develop and maintain a government whose philosophy and aims are compatible with our own. This recommendation is consonant, not only with the present world situation, but with the historical ties—between the United States and China. For reasons stated above, it is not believed feasible that necessary financial assistance can be provided China from the Export-Import Bank. The need in any event is for an integrated program of assistance which would require clarification and authorization by Congress of its intended military, economic and political phases.

Certain major prerequisites to assure effective utilization of any aid extended have been indicated. With concrete evidences of performance in these respects, and with firm commitments for continued progress, it is recommended that the United States government, under Congressional authorization, provide financial assistance to China to assure an early undertaking of projects essential for that country's economic reconstruction, and eventually for stabilization of its currency system. The amount of such aid and specific means of its implementation would be subject to determination by Congress acting upon the recommendations of appropriate agencies of the United States government. However, it would be desirable to inaugurate before July 1, 1948 key reconstruction projects relating to transportation, electric power, coal, and artificial fertilizer, even though more substantial assistance for currency stabilization were to be made available at a later date. This emphasizes that a lump-sum financial grant to be handed over to China is not considered justifiable. It indicates the need for Congressional support for a program of assistance over a period of at least five years in which aid can be made available when, as, and if it can be effectively utilized for the purposes intended.

The priority list for reconstruction projects submitted by the National Government should be prepared by a screening and planning agency in the government assisted by American economic and engineering advisors. In connection with any individual projects so presented, and approved, it is contemplated that suitable provision will be made for financial and technical supervision by United States personnel to assure effective utilization of the aid extended.

APPENDIX "C" TO PART II—CHINA

SOCIAL AND CULTURAL

The unending war has inevitably paralyzed China's ambitious pre-war plans for social and cultural advancement. It has been impossible even to hold such slender gains as were made in the few years between internal revolution and Japanese invasion. The primary schools and the adult education enterprises which in those years had barely started their attack upon the nation's mass illiteracy have lost buildings and textbooks and teachers and even contact with pupils. Today, with depreciated money they are unable to replace their buildings and equipment or to encourage their teachers with adequate pay. The middle schools are no better off. The universities limp along under burdens which almost cause despair even in a nation in which scholarship continues to command universal respect to a degree unknown in the Occident. Most of the universities, being seated in eastern China, were driven out by invasion, thus losing buildings and books and equipment. During the war they kept alive by pooling their scant resources in common properties in interior cities. After the war they rushed back home only to find libraries and laboratories gone and often buildings as well. Endowment and other funds had become so small and so unproductive that teachers' salaries and students' scholarships had vanished: what once would have supported a student for one year now might buy him one notebook. In this situation numerous universities have again pooled their poor resources in an effort to carry on, but with feeble success. That the teaching institution still exists to a respectable degree must be attributed largely to the devotion of the teaching profession whose members, receiving hopelessly insufficient salaries, survive only by selling their possessions item by item or by finding odd jobs to do in spare time. There are fewer nobler examples of patriotism.

Beyond the troubles listed, the universities have lately suffered in another respect. Strong political demonstrations among the students have been sharply punished, in defiance of the students' traditional freedom of expression and, still more seriously, in defiance of the libertarian principle of open trial. Faculty members have been replaced because of their political views. In these cases the National Government defends its suppressive arrests by declaration that the prisoners' actual offense has been sedition rather than merely opposition-thinking, but the fact remains that this sort of suppression does not exist in free lands, and the actual disappearance of victims, untried by any known law process, is itself intolerable. That the universities should be forced to live under this sort of shadow is one of the chief tragedies in China's higher education today.

The professions and technological groups mark time. Not only are individual incomes reduced by inflation, but access to professional magazines and reports, by which under normal conditions proficiency is maintained and increased, remains most difficult (the United States Information Service libraries do what they can toward meeting this acute lack). Newspapers have for the most part become party organs, with a few honorable exceptions. Free expression risks closing down of the newspaper by government order "for reasons of military security" with reorganization under altered direction a requisite to renewed operation. University presses have ceased to operate. Cultural assemblies of every sort, save for political purposes and these thoroughly shepherded, are rare and spasmodic, offering in this field no such continuity of public information as in normal times.

The effects of prolonged social disorder are bad in any land, but a nation which is highly literate can live for a time on the cultural resources of its individuals. In a nation where there already is so wide a gap between a small but select intelligentsia and a mass of mankind largely illiterate, a new blockade in education is far more serious. Public literacy is essential to public readiness for effective self-government.

The steps to revive education which have been taken already are largely local and hence variable. The national program is in existence, but translating it from paper to performance requires, first of all, far more money than China has available for education. In a land at war most revenues are consumed in the insatiable maw of the military, and such funds as do come to civilian departments' hands are likeliest to be diverted to food and other unquestionably urgent necessities, rather than to education. Hence, National Government plans for reopening schools and buying books and desks and granting a somewhat better wage to teachers are not supported by funds. Much the same thing is true of those universities and middle schools which once were generously supported by foreign churches, now grown uncertain about the institutions' future.

There are other uncertainties in education. The very principles of former years are being re-examined—whether to continue sending Chinese students to America (save for training as teachers, committed to prompt return to China's schools) or rather to prevail on Americans who once taught in China to return quickly to China to resume instruction work there. There is a growing feeling that at this stage the cost of sending students to America would more profitably be expended in bringing teachers to China. Not the least consideration for several years to come is the desirability of toning Chinese students to the environment in which they expect to work as adults, rather than to that of the United States.

China's national mechanism for educational direction and supervision has suffered as much as the schools themselves. It will revive best by being put to work, but that, like the restoration of individual schools, must await the provision of funds.

APPENDIX "D" TO PART II—CHINA

THE MILITARY SITUATION IN CHINA AND PROPOSED MILITARY AID

INDEX

Military Situation

Since General Marshall's departure from China, the overall military situation of the Chinese National Government has deteriorated. In March 1947, following the Nationalist capture of Yenan and at the beginning of an all-out Government effort against Communists, the Nationalist Chief of Staff announced that the main Communist armies would be crushed within three months. Like previous predictions of this nature, his statement never came true and fighting between Nationalists and Communists continues, principally in Manchuria, Hopei, and Shantung.

Communist operations in Manchuria have practically rendered Nationalist forces in that area militarily impotent and prompt action is necessary to prevent Manchuria from becoming a Soviet satellite. Continued successful Communist operations could make untenable the entire Nationalist position in Manchuria where they control only a slender finger of territory. Now, with the cessation of rains, it appears that the Chinese Communists will launch an offensive against both flanks of this narrow Nationalist salient. Simultaneously, Communist guerrilla activities and raids in other provinces, such as Hopei, Shantung, and Jehol, will be intensified so as to pin down other Nationalist forces, prevent guerrilla activities and raids in other provinces, such as Hopei, Shantung, reinforcement and interrupt important Nationalist lines of communication. Meanwhile the National Government has done very little to improve its position in the light of these developments. The Generalissimo has designated General Chen Cheng, a capable commander, as the overall commander of Manchurian forces, but it is doubtful that he can weld a strong unified force in view of the continued serious shortages of both supplies and capable subordinates.

Total Nationalist forces of about a million and a half combat troops plus another million service troops are opposing less than a million Communist combat troops and militia supported by an unknown number of service troops. Unfortunately, less is known about Communist forces than ever before, for at the present time there are no competent foreign observers with them. Chinese information on Communist supply, equipment, casualties, and manpower is completely unreliable and inaccurate.

The underlying military reason for Communist success is that they retain the initiative, striking at places of their own selection with local superiority of forces and with a mission of destruction. Nationalist forces, on the other hand, with a mission of protection, are forced to what amounts to a perimeter defense of scattered areas and of long connecting lines of communication. Such widespread defense offers little chance of lateral coordination and mutual support, thus immobilizing forces that would otherwise be available for offensive action. Communist drives appear to meet with little substantial resistance, while Nationalist withdrawals are generally premature and the words "strategic retreat" have lost all significance.

The Generalissimo has never waivered in his contention that he is fighting for national independence against forces of an armed rebellion nor has he been completely convinced that the Communist problem in China can be resolved except by force of arms in spite of the fact that his efforts to suppress Communists by military force alone have failed. The present course, unfortunately, functions as a stimulus to the progressive expansion of Communism.

It is essential that the Generalissimo revise his present course, since, particularly in view of the vast areas involved, it is impossible to conceive of complete suppression of Communists by the sole use of any military force which the National Government could foreseeably field and support, even with external aid, in the future. Hand in hand with action to improve the current military situation, social, political and economic reforms must be instituted in order to maintain a happy and satisfied, and therefore loyal, population in Nationalist areas.

All in all, the military situation in China appears to be governed predominantly by Communists enjoying substantial military successes in Manchuria, in Shantung and in Hopei. These successes can be attributed mainly to the lightness and efficacy of their hit-and-run guerrilla type forces, to their mission of destruction as opposed to the Nationalist mission of protection, to the ineptitude and incompetence of Nationalist high command, to the shrinkage of Nationalist communications, to the general depreciation and depletion of Nationalist equipment and supplies, both ground and air, to increased friction between military forces from the south and civil administration in the areas under attack, and to the stigma attached to troops which so often live off the local civil population.

Strategic Importance

Any further spread of Soviet influence and power would be inimical to United States strategic interests. In time of war the existence of an unfriendly China would result in denying us important air bases for use as staging areas for bombing attacks as well as important naval bases along the Asiatic coast. Its control by the Soviet Union or a regime friendly to the Soviet Union would make available for hostile use a number of warm water ports and air bases. Our own air and naval bases in Japan, Ryukyus and the Philippines would be subject to relatively short range neutralizing air attacks. Furthermore, industrial and military development of Siberia east of Lake Baikal would probably make the Manchurian area more or less self-sufficient.

On the other hand, a unified China friendly or allied to the United States would not only provide important air and naval bases, but also from the standpoint of its size and manpower, be an important ally to the United States even though her poor communications and lack of modern industrial development would make her contribution less effective than would otherwise be the case.

An important factor in analyzing the strategic importance of Manchuria and North China is the role of these two areas in the formation of an industrial crescent capable of complementing the economy of either Siberia or China in which the potentiality of these areas for the manufacture of arms and ammunition, for the development of coal and iron resources, and for the operation of arsenals and machine tooling facilities would be possible. This is important in a positive sense in that China requires these areas to complete her economy and it is important in a negative sense in that both these areas must be denied to the Soviet Union.

While Communist success in China would serve Soviet interests through expansion of control of a regime oriented to and sympathetic with the Soviet Union, a continuation of political and economic chaos accentuated by protracted civil war would also produce the same general result. This appears to fit into a pattern of progressively staged Soviet expansion at the expense of China, a pattern which has already resulted in Soviet absorption of Tannu Tuva and Outer Mongolia.

The military problem in China is inextricably involved in psychological, moral, political and economic factors. Moral support of the National Government by the United States will, in bringing about *military* success for the National Government, be of importance in proportion to the degree of actual material assistance, provided there are concurrent drastic political and economic reforms. United States support of a Chinese request to the United Nations for immediate action to bring about a cessation of hostilities would serve as a prelude to further steps which could be taken to prevent the establishment of a Communist Government in Manchuria.

Military Aid and Assistance

In order to improve the current serious military situation, Nationalist forces must first stabilize the fronts and then regain the initiative. Further, since the Government is supporting civil war with approximately seventy percent of its national budget, steps must be taken to decrease the size of the military establishment while increasing its effectiveness and efficiency.

Whereas some rather ineffective steps have been taken to revitalize the command structure, and other more sweeping reforms are projected for the future, the effectiveness of the armed forces requires a sound program of equipment and improved logistical support. The present industrial potential of China is inadequate to support military forces effectively. Hence outside aid in the form of munitions (most urgently ammunition) and technical assistance are essential before any plans of operations can be undertaken with reasonable prospect of success.

The purpose of conditional American military aid to China should be to facilitate reorganization of her armed forces; to regain public confidence in the armed forces; to insure successful resistance of further Communist advances into Nationalist China; to aid in establishing stability. Such aid could be conditioned to foster the emergence of a regime which would develop along lines satisfactory to the United States, at the same time engaging in a holding operation against the progressive spread of militaristic Communism. A program for such military aid to China would necessarily have to be an integrated element of our worldwide policy of military assistance to specified nations.

Extension of military aid by the United States to the National Government might possibly be followed by similar aid from the Soviet Union to the Chinese Communists, either openly or covertly—the latter course seems more likely. Tension between the United States and the Soviet Union might therefore increase, even as it is now in European and Middle East areas.

Military aid and assistance to China could take essentially three forms or a combination thereof: Material, advisory, or active participation in operations by American personnel. This last form is rejected as contrary to current American policy. In all cases, China should take the initial step of requesting United States aid and should inform the United Nations of steps taken.

Consideration has been given to what the Chinese can do themselves to improve their situation as regards military matériel. It is believed that they can do little to help themselves because of their basic deficiency in industrial capacity. However, they can help themselves by implementation of a carefully prepared logistical plan based upon supervised material aid. They can further help themselves by demonstrating a real willingness to achieve stabilization of military fronts, by improving command, by regrouping forces, by reducing the total military force to one which can be supported by the Government with such outside aid as may be furnished, and by implementing necessary social, political and economic reforms.

Material aid programs visualized include:

Completion of the General Pai Motor Vehicle Parts Project
Purchase of additional military equipment
Ammunition Supply
Completion of the 8⅓ Group Program plus augmentation in military air transport
China Mapping Program
Transfer of Ships

Motor Vehicle Parts Project. Sixteen-thousand motor vehicles, chiefly trucks, are inoperative because of lack of parts. It would materially benefit China's military forces and her transportation system to have this program completed by arrangements which would enable the Chinese to purchase these parts on as favorable a basis as possible. The United States is morally obligated to complete this program by virtue of a contract between the National Government and the Foreign Liquidation Commission, which would have made available the required parts from surplus stocks. The United States has unilaterally voided this contract as the required surplus stocks are not available and no legal way for furnishing them exists.

Purchase of Additional Military Equipment. Since completion of the 39 division program nearly two years ago, very little has been supplied. Thus, there are many shortages in military equipment which react to the disadvantage of Nationalist military efforts. Credits should be established for China to purchase the necessary military equipment needed to effect a supervised revitalization of her ground and air forces. Without such aid, American equipment purchased during and subsequent to the war is, or soon will be, valueless since maintenance parts will not be available to continue the equipment in use.

In many cases, reliance upon artillery has been a handicap. Artillery is often a logistic drain, limiting mobility in a fluid situation, and causing the Nationalists to be overly cautious for fear of having it captured; it has, however, been useful in the few instances when Communists have made determined large-scale assaults against Nationalist positions or when they have attempted to hold positions against Nationalist attack. Mortars, automatic weapons and rifles have been the most valuable weapons to either side in the current mobile warfare.

Ammunition Supply. In July, the Navy abandoned 335 tons of ammunition in Tsingtao which was recovered by Nationalists. However, Nationalist armies continue to complain of shortages in ammunition of all types and calibers. There will be severe shortages in the near future unless replenishment from foreign source is accomplished. There is an implied moral obligation to assist the Chinese Government to obtain ammunition.

Completion of the 8⅓ Group Program and Possible Augmentation in Military Air Transport. Major deficiencies which exist in the Chinese Air Force include the lack of an adequate system of logistical support, of a proper maintenance or supply system, of a reclamation system, and of supply and maintenance facilities. All these deficiencies are due to the critical condition of the Chinese economy plus the fact that the 8⅓ group program has not yet been completed. To remedy these deficiencies, the Chinese Air Force would require supplies for first and second echelon maintenance for all types of aircraft, complete fulfillment of the 8⅓ group program which includes equipment for supporting service units; equipment for a complete training program including aircraft spare parts and training aids; and initial TE equipment for two additional air transport groups (C–46). A realistic National Government effort to resolve major logistical problems of its armed forces will necessarily demand the fullest utilization of air transport since in many areas, it is the only remaining means of communication.

China Mapping Program. Because of lack of available United States resources in China, this program, undertaken by special agreement, has been reduced in scale to the mapping of Taiwan only. Such a program is of strategic value to the United States in furnishing up-to-date post-hostilities maps of areas already or potentially involved in conflict. It would also provide China with up-to-date maps of her own territory and thus be of military aid to her. The present program should be expanded to include other areas of vital strategic importance.

Transfer of Ships. Navy Department plants to furnish to China by transfer without compensation, some 137 vessels, craft, and floating dry docks; along with such plans, blueprints, documents, and other information in connection with these vessels and other technical information as is necessary in connection with organization and maintenance of a naval establishment. Cost of repairs, outfit and equipment to these vessels and the transfer of any material will be on the basis of a cash reimbursement by Republic of China. Ninety-three of these vessels are now under lend-lease to the Chinese Government and will be recaptured under terms of the Naval Lease Agreement Charter and retransferred under Public Law Number 512 which authorizes a maximum transfer of 97 similar type vessels through Oflc for use by Chinese Maritime Customs. However, there are still several vessels in the Maritime Customs Program yet to be delivered. As part of a program for aid to China, delivery of vessels under Public Law 512 could be completed.

Occupation of Japan. There is an agreement between United States and China which specifically charges China with logistical support of Chinese Occupation Forces but recognizes that some additional support will be required from the United States. To date, China has taken no action under this agreement and appears to have no inclination to take action in the future. This agreement expires 30 June 1949.

Military Advice to Chinese Armed Forces

Military advice is now available to Nationalist ground, sea and air forces on a General Staff level through American Military and Naval Advisory Groups. The Generalissimo repeatedly expressed to the Head of this Mission a strong desire to have advice and supervision extended in scope to include field forces, training centers and particularly logistical agencies.

Under present instructions, the Advisory Groups have confined their activities to the highest echelons of the Chinese Armed Forces except for assisting in operating schools and for limited technical advice in handling ships and airplanes. They are not allowed to assist directly in actual training of troops which take part in civil war.

Under the basic assumption that the United States "Hands Off" policy is relegated to the past, there remain only two alternatives or lines of action with respect to our present military advisory role: To continue the present scale of advice on a ministry and general staff level or to increase the scope of this advice. Should the latter alternative be adopted, there are several courses of action which could be followed.

A considerable number of forces engaged in combat have lost their effectiveness due to losses in personnel and equipment and in lowered morale. There are now a number of divisions which need to be withdrawn, reorganized and retrained. The scope of the Advisory role could be extended so as to provide assistance in this training.

The United States would be subject to serious charges if it were to become involved in any way in actual combat against Chinese Communists. Although advice indicated above does provide advice *indirectly* to tactical forces, it should be carried on outside operational areas to prevent the criticism that American personnel are actively engaged in fratricidal warfare.

Advice in connection with training technical specialists in the United States and in China should be continued. In addition consideration must be given, not only by the Advisory Groups but also by Chinese industrialists, to preservation of the nuclei of specialists already trained and schooled.

There are two points which should be given consideration by American advisors. First, conscription should be conducted on an equitable basis, to include sons of rich or influential families as well as of the poor. Such is not now the case. Secondly, better relationships and foundations for respect and comradeship between officers and enlisted men should be evolved.

Conclusions

The military situation in China is grave. Communists have the tactical initiative in Manchuria and in North China.

The Nationalist position in Manchuria is precarious, and in Shantung and Hopei provinces strongly disputed. Continued deterioration of the situation may result in establishment of a Soviet satellite government in Manchuria and ultimately in a Communist-dominated China which would be inimical to United States interests.

This spreading internecine struggle within China threatens world peace. Positive steps should be taken to end hostilities immediately.

Soviet aims in the Far East are diametrically opposed to and jeopardize United States interests in China in that their aims envisage progressive expansion of Soviet control and dominant influence. Realization of their aims in China would threaten

United States strategic security. Time works to advantage of the Soviet Union.

The Soviet Union, in achieving her aims, is being actively assisted by the Chinese Communist Party, which by its actions and propaganda is proven to be a tool of Soviet foreign policy.

The only working basis on which national Chinese resistance to Soviet aims can be revitalized is through the presently corrupt, reactionary and inefficient Chinese National Government.

The National Government is incapable of supporting an army of the size it now has in the field.

In order to preclude defeat by Communist forces, it is necessary to give the National Government sufficient and prompt military assistance under the supervision of American advisors in specified military fields.

American military aid to China should be moral, material and advisory. It should be an integrated element of our worldwide policy of military assistance to certain nations. China should take the initial step of inviting the United States to provide such aid.

American military aid to China, ground, sea and air, would if appropriately supervised, contribute to gradual development of stability in the Far East and lessen the possibility of a Communist-dominated China.

Recommendations

It is recommended:

That the United States provide as early as practicable moral, advisory and material support to China in order to prevent Manchuria from becoming a Soviet satellite, to bolster opposition to Communist expansion and to contribute to the gradual development of stability in China.

That China be advised to request the United Nations to take immediate steps to bring about a cessation of hostilities in Manchuria and request that Manchuria be placed under a Five-Power Guardianship or, failing that, under a Trusteeship in accordance with the United Nations Charter.

That China be advised to take steps to reduce its military expenditures in the national budget and at the same time increase the effectiveness and efficiency of the military establishment.

That China give continuing evidence that urgently required military reforms are being implemented.

That China, with the advice and support of the United States, develop and implement a sound program of equipment and improved logistical support.

That arrangements be made whereby China can purchase military equipment and supplies, (particularly motor maintenance parts), from the United States.

That China be assisted in her efforts to obtain ammunition immediately.

That the 8⅓ Air Group Program be completed promptly and that consideration be given to expansion of its air transport.

That the China Mapping Program be extended in scope where practicable.

That the program for transfer of ships to China be completed as rapidly as China is able to utilize them effectively.

That the occupation of Japan program be dropped, but only with the concurrence of the National Government of China.

The military advice and supervision be extended in scope to include field forces, training centers and particularly logistical agencies.

136

The Consul General at Shanghai (Davis) to Secretary Marshall

121.893/9–247

SHANGHAI, *September 2, 1947.*

Premier Chang Chun in an exclusive interview with the United Press today declared there will be no change in either the domestic or foreign policy of the Chinese Government as a result of the Wedemeyer Mission and said "There were many things which Wedemeyer did not know".

The Premier said while he met Lieutenant General Albert C. Wedemeyer several times during the American envoy's visit to China, Wedemeyer did not hold any "serious" discussions with him. "General Wedemeyer paid more attention to people outside the government than in it", Chang said.

The Prime Minister said that many of the reforms suggested in the Wedemeyer farewell statement "were already being carried out before the General visited China. Perhaps General Wedemeyer thought he was not away from China for a long time and still knows China well" Chang said.

"There were many people who wanted to see Wedemeyer and could not. And there were many things not known to the General." Chang said Wedemeyer got lots of help from his advisers "and the General perhaps thought these materials were quite enough."

CRITICIZED BY PEOPLE

The Premier said that he personally was good friends with Wedemeyer and recognized the good intentions of the General "but as a representative of the President of the United States Wedemeyer's statement caused a lot of criticism among the Chinese people."

The Prime Minister said he hopes that in time the critics will understand Wedemeyer's good intention "and Wedemeyer will understand the persons who criticized his statement".

Asked whether his assertion that there would be no change in Chinese domestic policy as the result of the Wedemeyer statement means that he did not agree with Wedemeyer's contention that "drastic and far reaching political and economic reforms" were necessary, Chang replied that such changes were already provided for in the form of the new constitution and forthcoming national election.

QUESTION OF METHOD

Chang said that such changes however must be made "step by step" according to a schedule already decided upon by the Chinese Government. "We are improving", the Premier said. "Minor affairs should not be mixed up with matters of policy. It is a question of method. Chinese policy is fixed and will not change either domestically or foreign.

"Our American friends say the Chinese Government is not efficient. We are studying ways and means and we know we have a lot to learn from the United States and western countries. But changes in China involve many things— old customs, system and procedures. This does not mean we are not trying to improve our present administration and there are many things we can do now. But many must wait.

"We know, for example, that the period of political tutelage is not good and we are trying to conclude it as soon as possible. But it is not feasible to end the tutelage period until the constitution is put into operation. Many similar changes can only be done after the constitution is operative."

The Premier said that even since the government reorganization the national government has heavier responsibility and much more work but nevertheless it is bending all effort to usher in the constitutional period.

GOVERNMENT DETERMINED

"In spite of all obstacles, the government is determined to finish this work this year," Chang asserted.

He said a lot of people had expressed doubts about whether the government really intended to hold the national elections this fall and has suggested that they might be postponed because of the civil war. "The policy is to hold the elections," Chang declared. "And the government is not going to change that policy in spite of obstacles."

The Premier touched on other matters which had been the subject of criticism from "American friends" such as export and import regulations about which business men felt keenly and he said the government was effecting improvements but foreign critics should not expect a change over night.

Chang said the specific reactions of the Chinese Government to the Wedemeyer Mission were contained in a note handed to Wedemeyer a few days prior to the General's departure which he said represented both his views and the views of the Chinese Government.

Chang received me in his spacious office at the Executive Yuan late in the afternoon. He was dressed in a gray civilian suit and spoke Chinese during the formal part of the interview and English during the informal chat. The interview lasted 45 minutes. Samson Shen of the Chinese Information Office acted as the interpreter.

137

The Ambassador in China (Stuart) to Secretary Marshall

121.893/8–3047

NANKING, *August 30, 1947.*

Following is substance of Communist radio comment following departure of Wedemeyer mission.

"North Shensi, August 28th: People here all laugh at Wedemeyer's August 24th departing statement. They say that he is playing another deceptive trick to cover up his imperialistic activities in China by 'criticizing' Chiang's Government, talking of 'peace'.

"However, from Wedemeyer's statement one can clearly see these three points: 1. There is no way to cover up corruption of Chiang Kai-shek's dictatorial rule. 2. There is no way to deny the demand of the Chinese people for ending Chiang's dictatorial rule and U.S. aggression. 3. Even the imperialist Wedemeyer cannot distort the fact that the might of the people of liberated areas, especially that of the people's liberation army, is invincible. The statement shows that even a blood-thirsty butcher like Wedemeyer now sees that to support this evil government of Chiang is difficult under the present circumstances when the peoples of the world including the U.S. are so bitter against Fascists like Chiang. Although Wedemeyer has quit China and has unhappily accepted that 'military force in itself will not eliminate Communism', yet his promise to equip

Chiang's troops and other plots are being put into practice. It is very possible that he will urge Washington for further aid to Chiang to prop up the Kuomintang government from imminent collapse. Chiang Kai-shek will also exert all his effort for a final struggle and American imperialists will rush aid to Chiang.

"People of the liberated areas have known these things too well and they will never be cheated by 'peace' uttered by a hypocrite like Wedemeyer. Real peace can only be attained when Chiang's corrupt rule is thoroughly smashed and American imperialistic force completely driven out of China."

Stuart

138

Memorandum from the Chinese Government to Lieutenant General Albert C. Wedemeyer [12]

121.893/9–647

On V–J Day the Chinese Government found itself confronted with the following problems:

1. The question of the Chinese Communists who were maintaining a regular armed force of 310,000 men in addition to a larger number of their so-called "militia". The presence of a large number of yet unsurrendered and undisarmed Japanese and puppet government troops in Manchuria was offering opportunities to the Chinese Communists to acquire more and better equipment.

2. An inflation, which had developed during the long years of war and was threatening the economic life of the nation.

3. The complete standstill of over 90% of China's railways and the acute shortage of inland shipping which made the work of repatriation and of restoring order in areas formerly held by the Japanese or puppet forces extremely difficult and rendered it impossible for many pre-war industries to revive even though the plants were partially recovered.

4. The need for the rehabilitation of rural economy after eight years of neglect and destruction during enemy occupation resulting in widespread shortage of farm labor, livestock and fertilizers and in consequent critical reduction of agricultural production. The total annual production of cotton, for example, was reduced to about 5,320,000 piculs or shih tan, $\frac{1}{3}$ of the 1937 level, which was 16,180,000 piculs or shih tan.

5. There were in China proper more than one million Japanese soldiers and approximately an equal number in Manchuria; 600,000 puppet government troops scattered in various parts of China proper and another 330,000 of them in Manchuria; and as a result of Soviet participation in the Far Eastern war, a large Soviet force estimated at 600,000 to 700,000 men deployed in different parts of Manchuria.

6. And at last, but by no means the least, the question of the fulfillment of commitments made by the Government, before and during the war, of the convocation of the National Assembly, the drafting and adoption of a national constitution, the return by the Kuomintang of the responsibility of government to the people, the termination of one-party rule, and the lifting of censorship. These were the most difficult problems that the Government had to deal with all at once on V–J Day. The weight of responsibility that so suddenly fell on the

---

[12] The memorandum handed to Lt. Gen. Albert C. Wedemeyer before his departure and transmitted to Secretary Marshall by Ambassador Stuart Sept. 6, 1947.

Government was far greater than the Government machine then existing could adequately cope with.   Not only were the tasks themselves heavy and complicated but they were also in many cases new to the experience of the Government.

In the repatriation of Japanese soldiers and civilians and in the timely dispatch of Chinese troops by air and by sea to many areas to take over from the enemy, the Chinese Government was substantially aided by the United States forces in China.   Credit must also be given to UNRRA and CNRRA for their contribution toward the solution of many problems in connection with the repatriation of displaced persons and such relief and rehabilitation work as could be undertaken immediately.   Meanwhile, the Government itself was tackling all the problems it could in the circumstances.   (1) It set about reorganizing the army and reducing the national budget.   (2) An immediate attempt was made following V–J Day to restore communications systems, such as railways, highways, waterways, public utility services and conservancy works.   (3) Mines and iron works (including a number of those the equipment of which had been largely removed by the Soviet Army from Manchuria or destroyed by the Communists) were reopened and textile and other precarious industries were salvaged.   (4) Efforts were made afresh to lay down the foundations for local self-government, such as the reorganizing and re-staffing of municipal and hsien offices, the organization of Pao-Chia system in villages and towns, and the rehabilitation of schools of various grades.   (5) Wherever practicable, measures were also taken to revitalize rural economy.   In the case of cotton, the extension work carried out by the Government in the past one and one-half years is now expected to result in a production of eleven million piculs or shih tan this year, a 100% increase over the production for the year of the V–J Day.   Each of these jobs involved considerable administration, funds and personnel.

When one assesses the work of the Government in this period one should bear in mind the fact that social institutions in China were not yet fully adapted to modern conditions, that a large portion of her territory was under enemy occupation for many years, and that the new economic foundations that had been prepared since 1927 were impaired by the enemy.   The immensity and complexity of the task of recovery that followed in the wake of victory must be taken into account.

There can be no doubt that the Government would have achieved greater results and China's politico-economic position would be brighter if the greater part of the Government's constructive effort had not been thwarted at each turn by the non-settlement of the Communist issue and the continuance of the war-time legacy—inflation.

The infiltration of the Chinese Communists into Manchuria during and following the Soviet occupation constituted a new factor in the Communist impasse after V–J Day.   The armed opposition of the Communists was the greatest single destructive force against all the effort of the Government in carrying out rehabilitation and in restoring law and order, particularly in areas formerly held by the Japanese.   When every possible effort was being made, for instance, to restore the main communication lines, mobile Communist squads were actively engaged in demolition work disrupting newly repaired railways, cutting telegraph and telephone lines, and causing havoc in the countryside.

As a result of the inability on the part of the Chinese Government to disarm and accept surrender from the large number of Japanese and puppet government troops in Manchuria, the attitude of the Communists towards the Government became increasingly challenging and uncompromising.   After the meeting of the National Assembly last November and December, the Communists openly denounced the adopted constitution. It was then clear that all hopes of a political settlement had gone. For, by that time the Communists had decided on the immediate launching of a large-scale military offensive. No one could feel more profoundly disappointed than the Government itself at such a turn of events, at a time when so much reconstruction work called for its undivided attention and immediate action.

While the Communist issue remained unsettled, the plan for army reorganization could not materialize owing to Communist obstruction thus hampering the reduction of the armed forces. As a result, a policy of retrenchment in national budget could not be put into effect, and inflation developed to such an extent as to threaten every fabric of our political and economic life. It led to the lowering of the efficiency of the Government administration and the undermining of the morale of the army. The bulk of the civil servants were not paid enough to meet anew the requirements of a bare subsistence. As a result, many Government employees were forced to seek concurrent work in order to maintain their living, while others turned to more lucrative jobs.

To this day there has been no substantial improvement in the treatment of these long-suffering civil servants. However, considering the straitened circumstances of the civil servants in general, it is astonishing to find that the great bulk of them are carrying on without failing in their duties. The loyalty of these people recalls to mind the stolid endurance of the Chinese masses who bore the brunt of the long war against Japanese aggression.

Whatever one may say of the national Government in China, one cannot possibly accuse it of not having steadily pursued the preparatory work for a democratic government as laid down by their leader Dr. Sun Yat-sen. It has always been the unanimous opinion of the leaders of the Kuomintang that unless it could lead the nation into a multi-party and representative government, it could not be said to be in any way carrying out the principles on which the party was founded. No one of any importance in the party has ever questioned the need to terminate the so-called "period of political tutelage" as soon as the basic conditions stated by Dr. Sun have been fulfilled. In this respect, the party as a whole, never once swerved from its aim.

When Sino-Japanese hostilities broke out in 1937, the momentous decision to resist the enemy was accompanied by a nation-wide effort to preserve, as, far as possible, the political and economic foundation that had been laid since 1927. Above all, the general opinion of the party was such that the interlude of war should not nullify the preparatory work for representative government that had already been undertaken.

In 1938, the People's Political Council was founded to provide a broader basis of representative opinion for the guidance of government policy. Except for matters of military strategy and security, the Council served as a war-time organ of public opinion. Here, in the midst of a life-and-death struggle, the national Government decided to invite and accept open questions and criticism and thus to promote representative government. This invaluable tradition has happily continued to this day. Although the 200 members of the first People's Political Council were all elected by the Government from different professions and on the basis of geographical distribution, it was widely acknowledged to be a fairly representative body of the politically conscious sections of the country. Early in 1940, the second People's Political Council met with 240 members, of which 90 were for the first time elected by the various provisional provincial and municipal councils, both on a regional and a professional basis. When the third People's Political Council met in 1942, 164 out of the total 240 members were elected by the provincial and municipal councils. Today, the People's Political Council, in the last phase of its existence, has 362 members, of which 227 were reelected by provincial and municipal councils.

In September, 1938, two months after the first People's Political Council held its inaugural meeting, the national Government promulgated the regulations of the provisional provincial council. Today, such councils have been organized in nearly all the provinces. Here again, the percentage of elected councillors was increased after each meeting, so that in many provinces the members of such councils are now entirely elected representatives. The municipal and hsien councils have also been conducted along the same lines. Thus, while the war was being fought and its priority acknowledged, no effort was spared in preserving the continuity of the effort towards the building up of basic democratic institutions and practices.

Shortly after V–J Day, press censorship was lifted in spite of the existence of a number of factors which might still have argued for its continuance. The National Assembly was convened and the draft constitution adopted in November 1946. The one-party rule had come to an end, although the Kuomintang was still by far the majority party in the Government. The Youth Party and the Demo-Socialist Party are now also represented in the Government.

No observer who is acquainted with Chinese events in the past can possibly fail to notice the existence today of a far greater body of public opinion than had ever existed before. This has come about since V–J Day as a result of the lifting of censorship, the convocation of the National Assembly, the presence of other parties in the Government, the emergence of a responsible Cabinet in the new Executive Yuan and above all, the effect of the periodic open discussions at the People's Political Council. The defense by the Government of its own policy and administration has in turn a stimulating effect on the growth of public opinion. It brings the Government closer to the people.

Since the Kuomintang gained power it may have committed errors in regard to methods for the attainment of its political goal, but never has it for any period deviated from its general political direction. Exigencies of circumstances may at times have retarded the progress of its work, but in the 20-odd years of its government, it has never been known to recede from a step once it has been taken.

China's critics are prone to lose sight of the vastness of the country, the weaknesses of its traditional political, economic and social structures, and the complexity of the problems with which she is confronted. Their views and judgment are apt to be based too much on the situation of a given moment without due regard to the background.

It may be well for us to review briefly the period between 1927 and 1937, a period in which the strength of the Kuomintang was put for the first time to a real test, and in which the Government never had a continued peace for more than a few months. In 1926, when the Government was still in Canton, it launched upon a punitive expedition against the war lords. In 1927, when the national Government was established in Nanking there were still war lords to reckon with; there was internal political opposition to overcome from the Communists as well as remnants of the old regime who were ever ready to lend a hand in any port against the Government; there was no street in Chungking where one could not find public opium dens and such conditions prevailed in many other cities; extraterritorial rights continued and the attitude of the major powers, not excluding the United States, towards the new Government was one of critical skepticism. Since September 18, 1931, when the Japanese started her open aggression, the Government had to resist the enemy on the one hand and on the other to suppress the armed rebellion of the Communists in the south.

But in spite of all this, the Government during this hard-pressed period of ten years was able to launch upon a national constructive program.

In 1937, it had completed almost 5,000 kilometers of railways, 100,000 kilometers of highways; had built schools, parks, hospitals and civic centers in many cities, trebled the number of middle schools and doubled that of universities and colleges. The number of middle school and vocational school students totalled nearly 600,000 in 1936. It was estimated that illiteracy decreased by almost 20% in those ten years. Modern ordnance works began in 1926 and at the time of the Lukouchiao incident, China was already able to supply, from her own arsenals, practically all her infantry divisions with rifles, hand grenades, machine guns, trench mortars and various accessories. A national anti-narcotic movement was launched during this period. The number of drug addicts rapidly decreased and by the end of 1938 no public opium den was to be found in areas under the control of the national Government.

When the full-fledged war broke out in 1937, Japanese financial experts predicted that China's finances would collapse within a few months of the war. During the eight years of war China faced financial problems as enormous as they were complicated but as a result of certain vigorous measures taken before the war, such as the adoption of a managed currency, concentration of gold and silver reserves, the reform of the taxation and banking systems, the Chinese Government was able to pass through the early—in fact the most critical—part of the war without any serious financial crisis.

In short, the period between the establishment of the national Government in Nanking in 1927 and the beginning of the war with Japan in 1937 was one of severe trial for the Kuomintang. However, the Government concentrated its effort on the two-fold task of suppressing Communist rebellion and resisting the Japanese aggression and this gigantic undertaking received the singleminded support of the entire populace. Moreover, the relations between China and her neighbors were at that time not so complicated as they are. The Government was therefore able to turn this difficult decade into a constructive period. Commerce and industries developed while the people both in rural districts and cities were able to plan and look ahead. Industrial production reached in 1936 a level higher than in any previous year. A general feeling of prosperity and growth prevailed.

The complexity of the problems of today may be greater than those of the pre-war years, but the dangers and difficulties which beset the present Government are reminiscent of those that confronted the nation during the early years of war (1937–1942), when China was forced to fight Japan singlehanded. Whether the present Government, for which the Kuomintang is practically still responsible, will be able to overcome these fresh dangers and difficulties as it did in the war and pre-war periods remains to be seen.

It is, however, clear that there is no weakening of determination on the part of the present Government and the Kuomintang to face the new challenge. As to the lines of policy with which the Government will meet the challenge, several things are uppermost in the minds of its leaders. First, the Communists as an armed political party must be suppressed. No half measures should be considered. The Government fully realizes that the success or failure of this fight against the Communist peril will not only decide its own fate but also the life or death of China as a sovereign power. In fact, the outcome of the struggle is bound up with the peace and security of the whole of the Far East. Second, the inflation menace must be brought under control; there should be no further delay in initiating some effective program in this regard because this is the very root of many political, economic and social ills.   Third, in the provinces which are free from Communist menace, economic rehabilitation work must be intensified as far as Government resources permit. This must be accompanied by necessary political reform in the local government. Last the Government must pursue its political goal, the building up of a democratic constitutional government, without fear or hesitation. Whatever difficulties the present Communist rebellion and other political factors may cause to the accomplishment of this task, the Government must proceed to give effect to the constitution adopted at the end of last year. No real form of democracy is built in a day and it is the consensus of opinion of the Government that the best way to achieve it is to start it as soon as you can.

139

The Ambassador in China (Stuart) to Secretary Marshall

893.00/8–1147

NANKING, *August 11, 1947*

I have the honor to report a visit with President Chiang last evening.[13] This followed upon the most recent interview General Cheng Kai-min had with him. General Cheng and I have of late been frequently in consultation in our efforts to persuade President Chiang to commit himself wholeheartedly and without further delay to the democratic way. General Cheng had recently submitted to him a memorandum with various concrete suggestions of this nature (a translation of which has been given to General Wedemeyer).

After discussing a brief trip to Tsinan from which I had just returned, he opened the way for me to say what I had in mind. My comments could be summarized as follows:

(1) China should join the democratic group of nations in opposition to aggressive Communism.

(2) The United States has been consistently ready to aid China by such means as are proper and possible, provided only that the present government can give convincing evidence of reforms in this direction and in doing so recover the support of its non-Communist people.

(3) The procedure might well include such measures as these:

(a) The *Kuomintang* should be completely dissociated from the Government and given the status of any other party in a democracy. (President Chiang had already asked General Cheng to secure an outline of the organization of the two principal American parties for him to study.)

(b) *Military Affairs.* The reorganization of the army along the lines of the P. C. C. proposals and with the help of the American Army Advisory Group might be begun on a basis that had due regard for the realities of the civil war. A small army, well-trained and equipped, with adequate physical treatment and a new morale, would be far more effective and less costly than the present one. The problem of deactivating the surplus officers and men could not be neglected.

(c) *Administration.* The rampant venality and similar evils among civil officials could be improved at the outset by enlarging the powers of the Control Yuan and holding it accountable. The civil rights provided for in the Constitution might be declared as taking effect now, in advance of the date set for its

---

[13] Aug. 6, 1947.

enforcement (December 25). But what was more essential than any of these measures was a new revolutionary spirit, with fresh enthusiasm and a dynamic conviction as to the real meaning and value of democracy. This should be incarnated in him. He was too much the head of a Party when he should be the leader of the whole Nation.

There was little new, of course, in any of this, even in previous conversations of mine with him. He made occasional comments as I went along and when I had finished said that he had come to essentially these conclusions.

He said that he had determined to increase the pay alike of civil and military employees of the Government and that this would bring a measure of relief.

As to the military reorganization, he reminded me of his request to you in my presence that you become Supreme Advisor with all the authority that he himself possessed. He said that he was ready to make the same offer to General Wedemeyer and earnestly hoped that this might be accepted.

He claimed that freedom of the press, for instance, was already in existence and cited the unrestrained publicity allowed in discussing the affairs of the two big companies in which members of the Soong and Kung families were involved. I replied that the newspaper editors were by no means aware that such freedom could be relied upon and that it would be in order to issue an unequivocable proclamation supported by a description of means for redress or protection.

He said in conclusion that he was giving this whole subject very careful thought—as is undoubtedly the case—and I remarked that when he was ready to make the rather radical changes involved it might be desirable to issue a very clear announcement.

He left this morning for Kuling where he plans to spend several days alone in order to think over the momentous decisions he must soon be making and some of the detailed issues involved.

140

The Ambassador in China (Stuart) to Secretary Marshall

[Extract]

893.00/8–1947

NANKING, *August 19, 1947.*

The activities of the Wedemeyer Mission have of course aroused a great deal of Chinese comment ranging from vituperative Communist denunciation and the serious misgivings of the liberals who fear that it will play into the hands of reactionaries to the overconfident hopes of many in the Government. The reliance of these latter upon our country to solve their problems for them irritates or angers or at times is merely amusing. But there is a growing number both within the Government and outside of it with whose opinions I must confess to a large measure of sympathy. They admit the logic of all that we argue about what Chinese should do to help themselves, get their own house in order first, etc., but feel utterly impotent in view of the conservatism, feudalistic ideas, selfishness, narrow prejudices and similar limitations prevalent among those who have the power to effect reforms, while the Communists are rapidly making gains. The best among these would not have chosen such a course nor do they intend to stand idly by while we attempt to do it all, but things being as they are in this country, they simply do not see any other way out. Nor do I. Where I perhaps differ from many of them is in being somewhat more hopeful of the moral and psychological influence upon the responsible leaders and the public generally once they all begin to see some hope ahead.

The signs of willingness and ability to institute progressive reforms are still sadly lacking but there are some. President Chiang recently summoned the Provincial Governors for a conference and along with some vehement criticism and pertinent instruction promised certain benefits. From now on provincial revenues should be principally used for provincial needs. Officials from Central Government Ministries and other agencies should be under the provincial authority. He has since then argued with me that, while in theory these governors should be civilians, yet until the Constitution is actually in force and the army reorganized, it would be very difficult for any civilian to hold out against military domination. He added that under existing conditions the best men could not be induced to accept such posts as he had learned from several such efforts. He is making definite plans to dissociate the Kuomintang from the Government at the coming meeting, September 9th, and compel it to accept a status somewhat analogous to our political parties. He has been studying memoranda on this subject. He is also working on the scheme for enlarging the powers of the local police and having them deal with such matters as civil liberties, rather than the military police (practically accountable to him alone), the secret service men, etc. I pointed out that when he is fully prepared to effect this change there should be civilian trials, prompt and public, and authoritative statements explaining the new policy and procedure. The reduplication in Central and local bureaus, in the ordinary officials and those representing him, in unnecessary employees, should be corrected both to reduce expenditure and for greater efficiency. Slight beginnings are being made. Much of this is due to the age-long suspicions by the Central Authority of those away from the Capital and the system of protective devices employed. President Chiang has practiced to the full this method of personalized control. In his case it is acutely aggravated by his fear of ubiquitous Communism which largely explains, if it does not excuse, the terroristic measures against the student strikes last May and similar repressive violations of civilian rights.

141

The Ambassador in China (Stuart) to Secretary Marshall

121.893/8–2647

NANKING, *August 26, 1947*

The Wedemeyer Mission departed August 24 after a busy month at Nanking, Shanghai, Peiping, Tientsin, Mukden, Canton and Hangkow where members of the Mission interviewed Chinese and foreigners and received written communications representing widely differing viewpoints.

The Mission met a few individuals who admitted they were Communists but alleged no direct contact with the Party. In any event these limited contacts had no effect upon Communist Party propaganda which remained vituperative of the Mission throughout its stay, particularly of General Wedemeyer personally, and generally suspicious and critical of the objectives of the Mission. The resumption of Kuomintang-Communist peace talks through American initiative was urged by few individuals, but it was clear that prevailing sentiment was to the effect that such a move was impracticable.

On August 22, General Wedemeyer spoke to the members of the State Council, Cabinet Ministers, and about forty other prominent Chinese including the

President and Madame Chiang. This specific act of General Wedemeyer will continue to have important repercussions as the tenor of his remarks becomes more widely known in Chinese circles (as will certainly result). As the Department is aware, General Wedemeyer made exceedingly frank statements with regard to Government shortcomings, but prefacing and concluding his comments with obviously sincere declarations of his friendship for China and his desire to be helpful. Those present at the gathering were predominately of the old scholar class to whom blunt public statements for a foreign visitor seemed offensive. It has been reported reliably that the president of the Examination Yuan, Tai Chi-tao, actually wept after the meeting adjourned. It was proposed by the State Council that none of the members go to the airfield to bid General Wedemeyer farewell, but President Chiang over-ruled this proposal. The reactions of those present at the meeting resulted partly from regard for "face" but included also the fear that such language from a Presidential envoy might encourage the Communists and arouse more opposition to the Government among non-partisans. There was also the consideration of disturbances in the money market resulting therefrom.

It is interesting to note that prior to General Wedemeyer's talk before the State Council the Generalissimo telephoned the Ambassador and suggested that he might caution General Wedemeyer against being too critical of the Government inasmuch as the State Council and others present represented a very heterogeneous group. The Ambassador informed the Generalissimo that he did not feel in a position to attempt to influence the scope of General Wedemeyer's remarks inasmuch as they were being made at the suggestion of the Generalissimo.

En route to the airfield General Wedemeyer called on President Chiang for an official farewell. The President remonstrated with him over his reported refusal to receive groups of substantial persons in the cities he had visited, such as representatives of Chambers of Commerce and the People's Political Council. General Wedemeyer protested that he had been ready to receive as many of all types as time permitted and that the schedule in each city had been arranged by the local American consuls who were well acquainted with local dignitaries and other persons. General Wedemeyer also stated that some persons who had asked to see him later withdrew their requests without apparent reason and the presumption of intimidation was therefore raised. President Chiang insisted that his orders had been that the Mission should be free to see whomever they wished.' He evidently felt that the groups he had mentioned would have been less critical of the Government than some of the groups with whom the Mission talked.

The Generalissimo also renewed a previous attempt to induce General Wedemeyer to give him a list of names in the General's possession of those Chinese with large financial holdings abroad. The Generalissimo used rather strong language stating that since he wished to force these Chinese to contribute to the national need and General Wedemeyer had advised this course, his unwillingness to facilitate in this respect was an unfriendly act. General Wedemeyer held to his position that since these names had been given him in the strictest confidence he could not do otherwise than refuse. General Wedemeyer parted with the Generalissimo in a friendly if not cordial atmosphere. The leading officials of the Government were at the airfield to wish General Wedemeyer farewell and Wu Ting-chang was present representing the Generalissimo. On the evening of August 25 the Generalissimo called Phillip Fugh, the Ambassador's personal secretary, to his residence and quizzed him at some length with regard to the background of the Wedemeyer Mission. He wished to know whether the Ambassador had had any part in its organization or dispatch, and why it was necessary to send such a mission to China uninvited as long as the Ambassador and his staff were reporting on matters Chinese.

More interesting however, in this unusual procedure was the Generalissimo's apparent preoccupation with whether or not the United States had the intention of forcing his retirement or by any other means wished his removal. The Embassy is not aware in detail of how Fugh handled this conversation except that he has informed the Ambassador that he was "careful" and "non-committal".

The Generalissimo's preoccupation with the possibility that the United States may desire his withdrawal from the scene probably arises from the use of the phrase "inspirational leadership" used by General Wedemeyer as a need in China, and the possibility that Americans felt that he was no longer capable of such leadership. The Ambassador has been informed by sources in which he has confidence that the Generalissimo has personally directed that critical comment of General Wedemeyer's final press release be restricted and that there has also been issued a down-hold order on press speculation with regard to the General's State Council address inasmuch as otherwise comment might be far too critical and vehement against the United States.

Press comment on the Mission in general will be the subject of separate messages.

There can be little question but that General Wedemeyer's talk before the State Council and his final press release have been a rude shock to the Chinese Government, although in the course of the Mission's stay it seemed to have become apparent to many prominent Chinese that they could expect little encouragement from the Mission's visit in the way of unencumbered material aid either economic or military.

The Ambassador has taken occasion to point out to the Generalissimo and to Chang Chun and other prominent Chinese that the State Council speech and all else that has been said by General Wedemeyer on this trip has been with the utmost sincerity and kindest intentions toward China. This as well as facts which brought about such seemingly harsh words, all of these individuals admit, and most politically conscious non-partisan and liberal Chinese undoubtedly largely endorse all that the Mission has said.

142

The Ambassador in China (Stuart) to Secretary Marshall

893.00/9–1747

NANKING, *September 17, 1947.*

The following manifesto was issued by the Fourth Plenary Session of the Sixth Kuomintang Central Executive Committee and published in the Central News Bulletin datelined September 13, 1947:

"Ever since Dr. Sun Yat-Sen led us in our national revolution, our party has undertaken one historical mission after another for the nation. At every such juncture, our party, after reexamining the past, came forth with a new front of solidarity to carry its mission to a successful conclusion.

"Toward the end of the Manchu dynasty, under the leadership of Dr. Sun, the Hsin Chung Hui (China Regeneration Society was reorganized into the Tung Men Hui (Revolutionary League). This subsequently led to the birth of the Republic of China. Then in the third year of the Chinese Republic (1914), the

Kuomintang became the Chung Hua Ke Ming Tang (the Chinese Revolutionary Party). This brought about the downfall of the Yuan Shih-kai monarchy and the reestablishment of the Chinese Republic. In the thirteenth year of the Chinese Republic, the Chung Kuo Kuomintang (Chinese Nationalist Party) came into being as the result of another reorganization. This was soon followed by the Northern Expedition which ended with the elimination of the warlords and the unification of the country. In the twenty-seventh year of the Chinese Republic (1938), important resolutions reached at the extraordinary party congress and the formation of the San Min Chu I Youth Corps, laid the foundation for victory after eight long years of war against Japanese aggression. Now in this post-World War II period, history is again calling upon our party to take up the responsibility of quelling a domestic revolt and carrying on war-delayed reconstruction. Whereupon, our party has reached the momentous decision of combining the party and the San Min Chu I Youth Corps.

"This step is taken, in the light of Dr. Sun's own experience in party reorganization, to rally all party members, and unify our system of command, both for the sake of greater strength. In this way we shall be consolidating the foundation for our revolution, reinforcing our party's leadership in ideology, and enhancing the party's revolutionary spirit. With our forces thus marshalled, we can proceed to tackle the important and difficult tasks at hand, until we attain success in the second phase of our revolution.

"The overthrow of the Manchu dynasty, the founding of the Chinese Republic, the eradication of the warlords, the abolition of unequal treaties, the victorious conclusion of the war of resistance, all these epochal events of the past fifty years have borne witness to our party's important achievements in the cause of the principle of nationalism and that of people's rights. The establishment of representative assemblies at various levels in recent years, the promulgation of a constitution last December, and the forthcoming termination of the period of political tutelage, have given further evidence of our party's determination to persist in its efforts for the realization of democracy. The present military campaign to suppress the Communist rebellion and the general mobilization are for the purpose of unifying China and preserving her sovereignty and territorial integrity. On their outcome will depend China's chance of continued existence as an independent nation and the world's chance of a lasting peace.

"As to the consummation of the principle of people's livelihood, it has been a principal aim of our party all these years. The pressing need of the moment is to relieve the people of their sufferings. In pre-war years, our accomplishments in reconstruction projects with a direct bearing on the people's livelihood were meager, but even this little has been destroyed as a result of the war and postwar spoliation by the Communist rebels. Therefore, no more time must be lost in beginning anew those economic reconstruction projects as directly concern the people's livelihood. In this, as in other types of reconstruction, we should first exert our own utmost. Our party wishes to set this as a goal in our present endeavors.

"We are aware of the difficulties now besetting our efforts, but at the same time we should be equally aware of the fact that our revolutionary strength is really greater than it has been during any previous period in our struggle. Previously with comparatively weak revolutionary strength at our disposal, we managed to overcome such difficulties as arose in various stages of our endeavors. Henceforth, so long as we respect ourselves but not to the extent of egoism, look within ourselves without becoming discouraged, and have confidence in ourselves without feeling self-satisfied, as before, we shall be able to attain our goals.

"We must realize that unless we can continue to gather strength, ours cannot be called a revolutionary party. Those of us who cannot endure injustices and slights, and those who cannot stand trials and tribulations, are not qualified as members of a revolutionary party.

"Our wish is that through unity and struggle, we can create a new life for the party, which will in turn generate a new revolutionary force to effect comprehensive political and economic reforms.

"Bearing in mind the 2,000-year-old Chinese proverb, 'One handling public affairs need not say too much but should try his best under the circumstances,' we' are henceforth willing to let deeds speak for themselves and actions bear witness to our determination.

"We must not hesitate to make sacrifices if this is necessary to safeguard our national existence, nor should we hesitate to struggle for the realization of constitutional democracy; nor should we fear to exert our efforts to improve the people's living conditions.

"Our nation is now entering a period of constitutional government. To protect the Chinese Republic and safeguard our nation is a sacred duty, which neither our party as a whole, nor individual party members, can justifiably shirk. We wish to offer this as a common creed of guidance. We are particularly desirous that all our fellow-countrymen, out of our common conceptions of a nation-state, and national consciousness, will, as one man, unite to work for the creation of a new China dedicated to the fulfillment of the Three People's Principles."

STUART

143

The Ambassador in China (Stuart) to Secretary Marshall

893.00/9–2047

NANKING, September 20, 1947

There was considerable surprise several weeks ago when the Kuomintang announced that the Fourth Plenary Session of the Central Executive Committee would be held on September 9, since the Third Plenary Session had been held only last spring. The announced purpose of the meeting was to consolidate the San Min Chu I Youth Corps with the Kuomintang. Until ten days prior to the meeting there was little speculation about it but when comment did appear, it was generally assumed there was a more important reason and rumors developed accordingly, mostly along the lines of a drastic reform in the Government and a comprehensive purging of so-called undesirable elements. Despite official denial most sources generally considered the rumors of reform as an aftermath of the Wedemeyer Mission and as a desire to impress the United States with the ability and intention of the Chinese Government to comply with American requirements for substantial assistance. The rumors failed to reveal any particularly clear outlines which this reform might follow.

As for the consolidation of the Youth Corps with the Party, it was apparent there were two main reasons for this step. The first one was the desire to draw into the Party the younger elements in the country and to make use of their youth, energies and ideas. The second one was a desire to eliminate the growing friction between the Kuomintang, now largely dominated by the CC-Clique on a local and organizational basis though with a primarily Political Science Group national administration, and the Youth Corps, largely dominated by the CC-Clique but also resisting that influence through army inspiration. The Youth

Corps had become increasingly noisy in its demands for larger participation in Party affairs but had been resisted in its ambitions by the Party which looked with disfavor on the autonomous features of Corps activities. The CC-Clique favored the consolidation in the hope of continuing its hold, and the Generalissimo hoped to eliminate dissension. Though formally accomplished, the consolidation is reported as so far not having been very successful. As far as can be ascertained, the Central Executive Committee otherwise actually accomplished very little and such political manipulation as did take place was well-concealed from the public view. The first few meetings were devoted to hearing reports from ranking officials in the Government. These were largely routine and devoid of any particular interest except for speeches by the Generalissimo and the Prime Minister.

The main interest in what the Generalissimo had to say was his scathing condemnation of the Party for failure to solve China's problems, his absolution of himself from all responsibility, and his announcement that henceforth China would never again be dependent upon the United States for assistance. The balance of his remarks were devoted to the usual clichés on the extermination of the Communists and the need for rejuvenation in the Party. It should be noted parenthetically that what the Generalissimo said was largely a repeat of a speech he had given to the Standing Committee of the Central Executive Committee last spring.

The main interest in what the Prime Minister said touched on foreign affairs: (1) China was considering the despatch of warships to Indonesia for the protection of Chinese interests; and (2) Chinese policy on Japan generally coincided with that of the Soviet Union and was opposed to American policy and that therefore China would be obliged to strengthen its relations with Russia while at the same time preserving its traditional tie of friendship with the United States.

Another salient point of the meeting was the attempt at reform within the Party and the purging of "undesirable" elements. To this end an elaborate if general program of reform was proposed and all indications were it would be adopted. At one of the final sessions the Generalissimo put in a strong demand that the reform program be dropped and that in lieu thereof the Party proceed to carry out unfulfilled promises made during the last two years. As a result of this demand, the final manifesto of the session was couched in most general terms and said nothing that has not already been said innumerable times.

The specific accomplishments of the session, therefore, appear to have been negligible—a preliminary sparring for position prior to the Standing Committee meeting and any reshuffling of the Government would have to come from that present meeting. There may indeed be reform and purge of a kind since the program for consolidation of the Youth Corps provides for a reenlistment of all Party members. It is difficult at this stage to predict what form it will take or what its nature will be, though it can be assumed that it will conform to the desires and ambitions of the dominant clique. In this connection it should be noted that indications are the CC-Clique has emerged in a stronger position than previously because it controls the Youth Corps and because it has been able to exploit current internal and international conditions.

The uncertainties in the Chinese mind concerning the outcome of the Wedemeyer Mission unquestionably played an important role. The Government had assumed—and so advertised it—that the Wedemeyer Mission would bring with it substantial aid or at least specific promises thereof. This would, of course, have greatly strengthened the Political Science Group government which could

take credit for the acomplishment. As these hopes have so far failed to materialize, the CC-Clique has been in a position to point an accusing finger thereby weakening the administration in power. This is not to say of course that the CC-Clique
basically liked the Wedemeyer statement any more than did the administration,
but it was and is able to make political capital of it. That the CC-Clique did not
go farther than it did is partly attributable to the continuing uncertainty as to
the forthcoming aid and partly to what must be the reluctance of the Generalissimo
to take any unduly strong position during the period of uncertainty. His own
words were the strongest used by a prominent figure and must have been compounded of anger, disappointment and political maneuvering.

144

The Ambassador in China (Stuart) to Secretary Marshall

893.00/9–2047

NANKING, September 20, 1947.

Political, military and economic position of Central Government has continued
to deteriorate within recent months in accordance with previous expectations.
Currently, the cumulative effect of the absence of substantial, financial and
military assistance expected from the Wedemeyer Mission and renewed Communist military activity are intensifying the Chinese tendency to panic in times
of crisis.

Department will have noted renewal of Chinese efforts to obtain favorable
action on ammunition supplies and despite Embassy's statements that ammunition question is one for decision in Washington, constant inquiries are received
with regard to action taken. More recently there has emanated a series of
thinly-veiled suggestions from senior officials of the Government obviously intended to convince the Embassy that if aid is not soon forthcoming from the
United States, it may become necessary for China to seek assistance from the
Soviet Union. It has even been suggested to the Ambassador that the Soviet
Ambassador to China, whose return is expected shortly, might be asked to mediate
in the civil war and that he would be glad to accept.

Although the Embassy does not overlook the remote possibility of a Sino-
Soviet rapprochement and is following the situation closely, it considers that
such talk is primarily for effect on the United States and secondarily reflects a
feeling of desperation among Chinese leaders. The Department will realize that
under present circumstances, and prior to any action as a result of General
Wedemeyer's report and recommendation, a Chinese paper flirtation with the
Soviet Union by the Vice-President and President of the Executive Yuan is a
maneuver reminiscent of similar Chinese tactics in the past, of Dr. Sun Fo's letter
to <i>New York Times</i> in January 1942. An added element in the over-all situation,
of course, is the increasing Chinese fear that the United States is tending more
and more to shift the center of gravity of its Far Eastern policy from China to
Japan.

At the moment the most serious concern of the Government is the sweeping
large-scale raid of Liu Po-cheng into Anhwei and southern Honan which commenced about August 12 and has been increasing in momentum since that time.
There is much speculation with regard to Liu's ultimate objective which is variously interpreted to be the crossing of the Yangtze River at some point between
Wuhu and Hankow and advancing southward to establish Communist bases in
Fukien or Kwangtung or even to make connection with the Communist-led forces
of Ho Chi-minh in Indo-China. It is more likely that Liu has no more concrete

objective in view than to harass a wide area, further embarrass the Government and cause it to withdraw troops from critical areas in pursuit.

Three divisions have already been withdrawn from southwestern Shantung and despatched in pursuit of Liu. Concurrently Yeh Chien-ying, alleged by the Government to have been contained in Shantung in the Yellow River delta area, has moved his troops southwestward and crossed the Yellow River in the vicinity of Tungo, with a force of approximately 40,000 men. The possibility suggested in my report of August 28 appears now to have become fact and recent Government optimism with regard to Shantung has been proven largely unwarranted.

In Manchuria the military situation remains quiescent. The arrival of Ch'en Ch'eng and the military reforms inaugurated by him have had an excellent effect upon over-all military and civil morale. However, the sixth Communist offensive in Manchuria is imminent and seems to be waiting only upon further drying of the roads which has been delayed this season by unusually heavy rains. It is doubtful that changes made by Ch'en Ch'eng will be in sufficient time to counteract serious decay which set in under Hsiung Shih-hui and Tu Li-ming regime. Furthermore, it is likely that the on-coming Communist offensive will be coordinated with Communist military activity in North China to preclude the despatch of adequate replacements or reinforcements outside the wall. Current activities of Liu Po-cheng in Central China and Yeh Chien-ying in Shantung now tend to confirm this belief. Communist radio broadcasts state that the offensive to "liberate" China north of the Yangtze has been launched, but it is unlikely that the Communists will be successful in attaining this objective within the foreseeable future. Their maneuvers, however, will undoubtedly further shake the economic and political structure of the Central Government throughout China but critically so in the north.

Most disheartening features of present Chinese situation in economic as in other spheres are overt reliance on *deus ex machina* of American aid to extricate China from its pressing problems and corresponding lack of self-reliance and self-help in tackling them. While introduction of the "official" open market rate of exchange on August 17 marked a welcome departure in this respect, toying with a premature and ill-considered project for the introduction of silver coinage, expectation that China's balance of payments deficit will be partly covered in some form or other by the United States, and continued passivity in the face of mounting hyperinflation clearly reflect a dominant trend of dependence on outside assistance. While there is a *prima facie* case for foreign aid, for instance, to cover part of the balance of payments deficit, it would be immeasurably strengthened if there were signs of a concerned and aggressive policy on the part of the Government.

Too early to judge what impact of establishment of "official" open market rate of exchange on China's balance of payments will be, as much depends on whether political pressures will counteract the influence of foreign advisers who rightly wish to hug the black market rate for United States currency. Nevertheless, its establishment is a healthy if belated step in the right direction. The Central Bank had been losing foreign exchange at the rate of $30,000,000 a month, $20,000,000 for financing the gap between commercial imports and receipts from exports, et cetera, and $10,000,000 for Government imports and expenditures abroad. In its first month of operations the Exchange Equalization Committee's receipts have slightly more than covered outgo on commercial imports, but unless this trend can be maintained, China's existing foreign exchange assets of $260,000,000, including 45,000,000 ounces of silver, is barely sufficient to last another nine months.

145

The Ambassador in China (Stuart) to Secretary Marshall

893.00/10–2947

NANKING, *October 29, 1947*

SIR: I have the honor to comment on political trends in China perhaps more as a record of my present impressions than because of any substantial objective changes. Most of this may therefore be mere repetition of what is already familiar.

COMMUNIST PARTY

There is no evidence of any weakening either in fighting power or in morale. Rather the opposite. They seem to be relatively well supplied with ammunition, money and other material necessities, and to be confident of their ability to carry on for the two or three years which they estimate as the time required to get control of the territory north of the Yangtse River. They are steadily improving their organization and discipline. Officers and men share the same hardships and have the enthusiasm of those who are devotedly fighting for a cause which transcends all thought of selfish ambition or enjoyment. There is little if any evidence of material assistance from Moscow but there is undoubtedly very close and conscious affinity in aims, methods and objectives. This will probably become more apparent as the rift widens between the United States and the Soviet Union. The hatred against America is said to be more vocal now than even against Chiang Kai-shek. Reports indicate that the younger student type is more unreservedly pro-Russian or international in its sympathies than the older leaders with whom the nationalistic loyalties aroused by foreign aggression still linger. The younger people argue that if America can help the Kuomintang why should not Russia be allowed to help them. On the other hand the official pronouncements have always been at pains to disavow any such aid or connection realizing the unfavorable effects of this upon the general public. There are numerous and well-authenticated reports of the merciless cruelty of the Communists, especially in newly occupied areas, and of the terrorism this inspires. There is no slightest question but that they intend to carry on their destructive tactics until the present government succumbs. They will then agree to any temporary compromise or coalition that will enable them to extend their control until they achieve their goal of a thoroughly communized China. Nor is there any doubt in my mind but that their control will follow the invariable Communist pattern of a police-state, with no freedom of thought or action and with brutal slaughter or expropriation of all who seem to be in their way.

KUOMINTANG

The corruption and the reactionary forces pervading the Kuomintang are too familiar to call for further emphasis. It should be kept in mind, however, that single-party control always tends to be corrupt, that the period during which this party has been in power has been one of incessant conflict, that the mounting costs of living have greatly aggravated an age-long tradition in China, and that the mood of defeatism in an increasingly hopeless outlook has caused a creeping paralysis upon all creative effort. Even so the men at the very top are of high integrity and continue to struggle bravely against terrific difficulties. There are many more like them within and outside of the Government.

OTHER PARTIES

The minority parties are rather disappointing. Those now absorbed into the Government are contributing but little and are busily seeking office for their members. The Democratic League continues to arouse suspicion of its communistic proclivities and offers little prospect of serving as a nucleus for liberal action. My chief concern at present is that the Government through ill-advised persecution will discredit itself further for high-handed oppression thus winning sympathy for the League from those who stand for enlightened constitutional procedure, while the League members will be driven further leftist and to underground activities.

Another factor which is becoming more apparent is the infiltration of Communists not only into bodies like the League but also into the Government itself. The seizures in Peiping following the discovery of a Communist headquarters are grim evidence of this. But of the arrests in other cities because of documents found there all but two have been Government employees. With a revitalized program, supported alike by their colleagues and the public, such men could be largely immunized. Otherwise their members and their sinister influence will tend to increase.

The best hope of the country seems to be in her educated youth. This group should be broadened so as to include those who once were ardently patriotic students, have become more or less cynical or discouraged in their depressing environment, but might be expected under better conditions to recover much of their lost enthusiasm. Assuming American aid of the nature which has in general been under consideration, these young people could be enlisted as "shock troops". If we can manage to sublimate our military and monetary aid into a movement to bring peace, freedom from oppression and economic recovery under democratic principles, including the responsibility of the people to take part in reforming their government, this can win the allegiance of youth and neutralize their suspicions of American imperialism, reliance on force, strengthening an effete regime as an anti-Soviet policy, et cetera. The student class is intensely nationalistic and now thoroughly alarmed. The genius of the Chinese people is naturally democratic rather than communistic. By making our objectives transparently clear we can help toward a resurgent moral awakening aiming at government reform and a better livelihood for all, with students past and present as the animating heart of it. This is what actually happened in the Revolution of 1911 and in the anti-Japanese resistance. It can come again. The convictions of democratic youth will thus match those of communist youth and which of those of the present generation wins will largely determine the destiny of China. Nor need we fear this if we really believe in the democratic way of life and in its ability to win over its greatest rival in our time when the contest is out in the open as this would be. If this process cannot conquer Communist ideology and machinations nothing else will. But a challenge on this high plane ought to have far-reaching consequences in other parts of Asia.

When I stopped off in Nanking in May of last year to pay my respects to the Generalissimo on my return from the United States, he asked me what I thought of the situation. I replied that it was worse than I had reason to expect from press reports in America but that I believed it could be changed if he would lead wholeheartedly in a new revolutionary movement with the adventurous and unselfish zeal of the Kuomintang when he first joined it, rallying present-day youth as it had done when he was one of them. The rallying cry might well be that of patriotic loyalty expressed now in reforming, unifying and constructive effort, and of treason as consisting in all that hinders these. It would be less easy for him now but with our help I still think of this somewhat visionary solution as in the end the most practical one.

Respectfully yours,

J. LEIGHTON STUART

146

Article Published in Central News Agency Bulletin, October 28, 1947 [14]

893.00/11-347

On the charge of complicity with the Chinese Communists in their armed rebellion against the state, the Democratic League has been outlawed, declared a spokesman of the Ministry of Interior, in a statement issued yesterday.

The spokesman said that henceforth all government offices responsible for peace and order will prosecute the activities of the Democratic League and its sympathizers in accordance with the temporary regulations for punishment of saboteurs of the national general mobilization and the regulations for dealing with the Communists in our rear. This puts the Leaguers in the same category as the Communists. The statement asserted that the Ministry was impelled to take this action to stop the activities of the Democratic League which has been playing the part of accomplice to the Communists' boom in the front and the rear against the security of the state. The spokesman cited concrete examples of his charges of the Democratic League's conspiracy with the Communists to overthrow the Central Government. According to the spokesman the League had dispatched Li Ping-chen to take charge of armed activities against the government in the northeast, and Kung Chung-chow, League leader in north eastern China had attempted a revolt in Sian. The League also instigated the student disturbances in May and the recent labor trouble in Shanghai. The statement charged that Li Ying-feng, influential member of the League, has been enlisting brigands for an uprising in Szechuan. Other charges against the League included the open denunciation of the government's general mobilization order by the League's Hong Kong and Singapore branches.

STUART

147

Announcement by the China Democratic League, November 6, 1947 [15]

[Translation]

893.00/11-1347

The China Democratic League has consistently maintained its firm stand for democracy, peace and unity. Unfortunately, the war has become more and more intensified. In the face of this calamity, we, the Leaguers, could only grieve being unable to do anything effective to serve the country. Recently, the Government ordered the outlawing of the League, prohibiting it from engaging in any activities. We, the Leaguers, could no longer be active. So we unanimously elected Huang Yen-Pei, member of the Standing Committee, as our representative, and dispatched him to the Capital from Shanghai to ne-

---

[14] Transmitted to Secretary Marshall by Ambassador Stuart Nov. 3, 1947.
[15] Transmitted by the American Consul General at Shanghai (Davis), Nov. 13, 1947.

gotiate with the Government concerning the problems relating to the dissolution of the League. Following are the measures proposed by the Government:

"(1) The Government has already outlawed the League and hopes that the League will dissolve itself voluntarily, so that the responsible officials of the League can be relieved of their responsibilities.

"(2) Concerning houses and other properties: (a) The properties belonging to the Communist Party, now in the League's custody, should be turned over to the Government; (b) the houses belonging to the League can be retained for the time being; (c) the houses appropriated by the Government for use of the League should be returned to the Government, and if they cannot be vacated immediately, they can be used temporarily; (d) the private residences of League members will not be disturbed and (e) the houses located at Rue Chu Pao San, originally rented by the Communist Party, now in the League's custody, should likewise be handed over to the Government. If the houses are now used for school purposes and can not be vacated, arrangements for the use of the houses by the school should be worked out."

Mr. Huang Yen-Pei gave the following answers to the above proposals:

"(1) Since the League has been outlawed by the Government, its only course it to notify all the Leaguers to cease all party activities, and, following the issue of the notification, the Leaguers themselves will be held personally responsible for their own activities and utterances.

"(2) The various points with respect to houses will be duly observed. However, one further point needs clarification, namely: While it is not known that the League originally had properties of its own, if there should prove to be any such properties, they should be disposed of by the League itself. Furthermore, the League submits the following two requests:

"(3) That the League members in various places be exempted from registering with the Government and enjoy all civil liberties to which they are legally entitled.

"(4) That League members in various places who are considered by the Government as having violated the law, and those who are already under arrest, should be treated by the Government in accordance with the law, and that the Measures for Dealing with the Communists in the Rear should not be applied to League members arrested under alleged but unproven Communist affiliations.

"As to whether or not points (2), (3) and (4) can be carried out, we now await your reply. As for the various documents published in the press critical of the League, they are quite contrary to facts. However, we do not intend to argue or offer refutations now."

Following is the reply made by the Government:

"(1) If the League would obey the order announced by the spokesman of the Ministry of the Interior and formally declare its voluntary dissolution as well as cessation of all activities, then all League members everywhere could be exempted from registering with the Government and would be assured freedom within the law. However, if hereafter some still engage in illegal activities under false pretexts, they will be prosecuted by the security agencies in various places according to law.

"(2) If, after proper investigations by the judicial authorities, League members under arrest for alleged offenses, are found not to be Communist nor working for Communists, then the Measures for Dealing with the Communists in the Rear will not be applied to them.

"Furthermore, all the points relating to houses and other properties will be carried out."

While publishing the foregoing record of the negotiations, we at the same time hereby notify all League members to stop all political activities as from this date. All personnel of the League's General Headquarters will resign en bloc as from this date and the General Headquarters will also dissolve as from this date.

CHANG LAN, *Chairman of the China Democratic League*

148

The Ambassador in China (Stuart) to Secretary Marshall

893.00/11–547

NANKING, *November 5, 1947.*

SIR: I have the honor to refer to the Embassy's messages concerning the Central Government's declaration outlawing the Democratic League and to set forth in more detail the events immediately prior and subsequent to the Government's action.

Commencing on October 21, 1947 there was published prominently on the front page of the *Chung Yang Jih Pao*, an official Government organ, a public announcement issued jointly by the Nanking Garrison Commander and the Mayor of Nanking that all Communist agents and persons connected with them should register their secession from the Chinese Communist Party prior to October 31, 1947. The announcement stated that those failing to register within the prescribed period would be liable to arrest and punishment according to law. There is enclosed for the information of the Department a copy in translation of the announcement.

The Department will recall that as early as October 14 Democratic League leaders expressed their concern to the Ambassador with regard to the probable outlawing of the League by the Government. It will also be recalled that on October 15, the Ambassador took the occasion of a visit to the Prime Minister to raise the question of repressive measures against the Democratic League, and to suggest that the League request for a conference between Government-appointed representatives and representatives of the League be favorably considered primarily for the sake of the Government itself.

On the morning of October 24 Dr. Lo Lung-chi, a Democratic League leader, called upon an officer of the Embassy to say that commencing on the night of October 23 the Democratic League headquarters had been surrounded by approximately twenty persons. Dr. Lo assumed that these individuals were secret police operatives. He said that residents of the League headquarters had not been molested in any way but that he was being constantly followed by persons in plain-clothes riding in an unmarked jeep. Dr. Lo was in a state of great perturbation and referred to the public announcement by the Nanking Garrison Commander and the Mayor of Nanking which he interpreted as being directed primarily at the League in as much as it was unlikely that there were any actual Communists in Nanking who would appear at the Nanking Garrison Headquarters for registration. Dr. Lo alleged that there was in existence a list containing approximately 600 names who would be arrested following the expiration date for registration mentioned in the Garrison Commander's announcement. On the same morning Dr. Lo also called on the Ambassador to express his growing concern with regard to the Government's attitude.

Dr. Lo's greatest concern stemmed from his conviction that the persons surrounding the League headquarters were members of the military secret police, and that in the event of arrest he anticipated secret action by military tribunals which in many past cases had resulted in the permanent disappearance of persons so arrested.

In passing it is interesting to note that Dr. Lo's fears in this connection are borne out to some extent by checking the registration number of the jeep which followed Dr. Lo to the Ambassador's residence and to the Chancery on October 23 and succeeding days. With the assistance of the Provost Marshal of the Army Advisory Group, the Embassy ascertained that the jeep which followed Dr. Lo was registered with the Secret Affairs Bureau of the Ministry of National Defense and the registration record of the vehicle showed that it had been formerly registered with the office of General Tai Li.

In the early morning of October 28 a spokesman of the Ministry of Interior announced that the Government could no longer tolerate an organization which opposed the national constitution and aimed at the overthrow of the Government and that the Democratic League was therefore pronounced an illegal organization. This announcement was published in the vernacular press on the morning of October 28 and a copy of the announcement in translation is enclosed. At approximately 10:00 a. m. on the morning of October 28 Dr. Lo Lung-chi called an officer of the Embassy by telephone to seek an appointment which was granted. Shortly thereafter Dr. Lo called again to say that he had been refused permission to leave the Democratic League headquarters. Approximately one hour later, however, Dr. Lo was granted permission to leave his place of residence after he expressed to his guards a desire to call upon the American Ambassador and accepted the condition that his car would drive slowly in order that a police vehicle could follow it. Dr. Lo proceeded to the Ambassador's residence and spoke briefly with the Ambassador. It was necessary, however, for the Ambassador to leave to keep an appointment with the Foreign Minister and the Ambassador directed an officer of the Embassy to come to his residence to talk with Dr. Lo. An Embassy officer proceeded to the Ambassador's residence and accompanied Dr. Lo in Dr. Lo's car to the Chancery where Dr. Lo again expressed at considerable length his grave concern at the trend of events. Dr. Lo appeared convinced that the announcement by the Ministry of Interior could not have been made without its having been authorized by the highest authority. Dr. Lo believed that instructions had been issued by the Generalissimo, otherwise the Ministry of Interior would not have dared to take responsibility for such action. In this same general connection, an Assistant Naval Attache, while calling on the Municipal Police headquarters with regard to an unrelated matter, was informed by a responsible municipal police official that orders outlawing the Democratic League had been issued personally by the Generalissimo. There is also enclosed a memorandum of conversation between an officer of the Embassy and an American employee of the Government Information Office which also bears on this point.

In the course of conversation with Dr. Lo at the Chancery on October 28, an officer of the Embassy informed Dr. Lo that following the conversation of the League leaders with the Ambassador on October 14 the Ambassador had taken occasion to point out to the Prime Minister, the Ministry of the Interior, and to the Generalissimo's personal secretary the possible adverse effect both abroad and internally of the course of action to which the Government seemed committed. It was also mentioned to Dr. Lo that the Ambassador had in mind mentioning this matter to the Foreign Minister in the course of his conversation on the morning of October 28. It was pointed out to Dr. Lo, however, that the League could not expect the Embassy or the United States Government actively to intervene on its behalf, although he was informed that the Embassy was naturally interested in developments and would appreciate his keeping the Chancery informed.

On October 28 Dr. Lo had lunch with an officer of the Embassy whose residence is in the Chancery compound and while waiting to keep this engagement Dr. Lo had opportunity to speak to a number of foreign correspondents who called at the Chancery during this period and who had previously been refused admission to the League headquarters. Following his luncheon engagement, Dr. Lo proceeded to the Ambassador's residence where he met Hwang Yen-p'ei, another leader of the League, who, in the meantime, had arrived from Shanghai. On October 28, therefore, Dr. Lo was on Embassy property for approximately five hours and this apparently gave rise to the allegation in the headlines of certain minor Shanghai vernacular papers that Dr. Lo was in hiding at the American Embassy. The text of the stories, however, did not bear out the headlines and therefore the Embassy issued no formal denial although the Department was informed that these reports had no foundation in fact.

Since October 28 there has developed a considerable amount of confusion with regard to the current status of the Democratic League. As far as the Embassy can ascertain the action taken by the Ministry of Interior has not been approved by the Executive Yuan, and although the Government continues to regard the League as an illegal organization it has not taken steps to order its dissolution and in fact appears very reluctant to take such action. There have been no important changes in the situation since the Embassy's report of October 31, 1947. There would appear to be little question, however, but that extreme rightist elements in the Government continue convinced of the necessity for complete suppression of the Democratic League. For the time being the indirect action taken by the Embassy and the obvious interest expressed by the foreign correspondents in the Government's move against the League has forestalled a wide scale "witch hunt" and has probably impressed upon the more enlightened elements of the Government the growing need for control of their extremist colleagues. The ability of the former to control the latter, however, is dubious.

The Embassy was gratified to learn from the Department that its action in connection with the Government's move against the League had the full approval of the Department.

For the Ambassador
WILLIAM T. TURNER
First Secretary of Embassy

[Enclosure 1—Translation]

Official Announcement by the Nanking Garrison Headquarters and Nanking Municipal Government

No. 2110   *October 21, 1947*

The resolution concerning the plan for dealing with the Communists in the rear, passed by the 19th Meeting of the Executive Yuan, has been published. Those Communists hiding in Nanking municipality should apply for registration. The measures for the application for registration of secession from the Communist Party drafted in accordance with Article 6 of the plan passed by the Executive Yuan are hereby published. The period from the publication of the measures to October 31 is set for the application for registration and those who fail to register within this period will be liable to arrest, and to be punished according to law. The measures for the application for registration of secession from the Communist Party are hereby publicly announced and it is hoped that registration will be completed within the period established.

MEASURES FOR THE APPLICATION FOR REGISTRATION OF SECESSION FROM THE COMMU- NIST PARTY IN NANKING MUNICIPALITY ARE AS FOLLOWS:

(1) These measures are based on Article 6 of the plan for dealing with the Communist rear areas published by the Executive Yuan.

(2) These measures apply to Nanking and its environs.

(3) All Communist agents and persons connected with them, no matter whether they worked for the Communist Party in the past or are working for it at present, should register.

(4) Application for registration should be filed within the period from October 21 to October 31. Those who fail to register within this period will be liable to arrest.

(5) Applications for registration should be filed with the Garrison Command.

(6) Applications for registration should be filed with the Garrison Command during its office hours within the period established.

(7) Application forms may be obtained at the Garrison Command and should be completed there.

(8) These measures will go into effect as of today.

Garrison Commander CHANG CHEN
Mayor SHEN YI

[Enclosure 2—Translation]

Announcement by the Chinese Government Declaring the Democratic League Illegal

October 28, 1947

The Chinese people have known for a long time that the Democratic League has linked with the Communists and joined the rebellion. According to reports made by various local authorities who are responsible for the preservation of peace and order the following examples are outstanding: Lo Ping-chi, a League member has instigated mutiny among the troops in Manchuria; the responsible League member for the Northwest was responsible for the rebellion of Kung Chung-chou; the student strikes in May and the recent labor strikes in Shanghai were incited by the League. Since the promulgation of the General Mobilization Order by the Government for the suppression of the Communist rebellion the Hongkong and Malaya branches of the League have publicly opposed the Order and indicated clearly that the League action and the action of the Communists are one and the same. Recently, Li Ying-fen, an important League member mustered bandits in Szechuan in order to rise in rebellion and to cooperate with the Communist bandits of Li Hsien-nien. Other plots and underground work carried on by the League of which we have concrete proof are too numerous to mention. In view of the seriousness of the Communist rebellion and the rampant activities carried on by the League, the Government can no longer tolerate an organization which opposes the National Constitution and aims at the overthrow of the Government. For the preservation of peace and order in the rear this Ministry has to take adequate steps to check the activities of the League. The Democratic League is hereby pronounced illegal and local authorities responsible for the preservation of peace and order shall halt the illegal activities of the League and effect punishment according to the measures for the treatment of Communists stated in the General Mobilization Order.

[Enclosure 3]

Memorandum of Conversation [16]

Mr. Votaw, American Adviser, Chinese Government Information Office, in discussing the Government order declaring the Democratic League an illegal organization said that a special committee of the Executive Yuan considered the question on October 27 and that Dr. Hollington Tong, Director of the Chinese Government Information Office, was present at the meeting. Dr. Tong vehemently opposed the suppression of the League as an organization and as a result of his recommendation, and that of other members of the Yuan, it was decided to disapprove such action. Although the suppression order was issued by the Minister of Interior at 2:30 AM, October 28, the Ministry steadfastly, until noon of that same day, denied to the CGIO that such action had been taken or was even contemplated. Mr. Votaw maintains that Dr. Tong, up to the present moment, has still been unable to get in touch with the Minister of Interior to ascertain why and how the order was promulgated. Mr. Votaw adds, however, that one of the leading figures in the case was Tao Shih-shen, Vice-Minister of Information of the Kuomintang and a strong supporter of Chen Li-fu. He also adds that Li Wei-kwo, Minister of Information of the Kuomintang, was not privy to the developments.

Mr. Votaw said that the more enlightened elements in Government and party are seriously disturbed at the action against the League; that the action represents another step of the CC Clique in its drive toward the elimination of all opposition and for its own complete and final control of the Kuomintang. He does not believe there is much that moderate elements in the party can do to save the situation unless the Generalissimo himself actively intervenes in favor of the League.

149

The Ambassador in China (Stuart) to Secretary Marshall

[Extract]

893.00/1–948

NANKING, *January 9, 1948*

Full text December 25 statement by Mao Tse-Tung has already been sent airmail to Department. . . . The Embassy gains two dominant impressions: (1) the note of triumphant conviction that the essentials of the Communist struggle for victory in China have been achieved, though Mao is careful to point out that additional great sacrifices will be required, and (2) the continuous and vitriolic attacks on the United States as the great enemy of the world and the agent responsible for the continuing civil war in China. Endlessly Mao reiterates the point that reactionary American imperialism is a major enemy of the people of China. Even though the recent months have witnessed heightening attacks on the United States, this is the first time that one of the top leaders of the party has publicly joined the hue and cry.

[16] Conversation between Maurice Votaw, American Adviser in the Chinese Government Information Office, and John F. Melby, Second Secretary of Embassy at Nanking.

Mao's elaboration of Communist military tactics and strategy is a remarkably candid explanation of how precisely Communist armies operate as far as the Embassy has been able to determine. It is perhaps a mark of Communist contempt for Nationalist military thinking and intelligence that the Communists have so little hesitation in explaining their strategy, which, it must be admitted, has to date not been without success.

Considerable attention in the manifesto is given to explaining the need for relentless pursuit of the land reform program in order to satisfy the aspirations of peasant groups regardless of cost to those who now hold the land. This is in accordance with other scattered and fragmentary reports received by the Embassy in recent months about the stepping up of the land program.

It is interesting to note the appeal for support from the middle group of peasants whom Mao says he believes will be willing to make certain personal sacrifices for the common weal. The threat that any opposition can expect no mercy rather suggests, however, that the Communists are not yet prepared to rely solely upon goodness of heart in securing cooperation. Nor should the gesture of conciliation to the middle groups yet be considered as anything more than a propaganda device which can be reversed at will.

It is significant that this statement moves even farther away than the New Year's message of Lu Ting-I of a year ago, from the lip service to conciliation and moderation which characterized Mao's report to the 7th National Congress of the Chinese Communist Party in April, 1945. It seems to the Embassy there is a striking similarity between the argument and invective advanced by Mao and that of other Communist leaders throughout the world. It also seems to the Embassy that more than at any other time in the past Chinese Communist thinking, with some exceptions made necessary by contemporary conditions, is following the line of reasoning advanced by Lenin in his April theses. All current evidence indicates Communist willingness and intention to adopt and exploit any means possible or necessary to securing the ultimate objective, namely, full power. Not even the obscure vocabulary can obscure the fact that this is precisely what Mao is saying or becloud his conviction that it will work.

150 (a)

The Ambassador in China (Stuart) to Secretary Marshall

893.00/2–548

NANKING, *February 5, 1948.*

Symptomatic, we believe, of the increasing unrest and of disillusionment with the present Chinese Government were the recent disturbances in Shanghai. More than other races, the Chinese are inclined to look for a scape-goat when things go wrong and in this case we have noticed an increasing tendency to blame the Generalissimo and to seek for an alternative to his regime.

Within a five day period, January 29 to February 2, there were three major civil disturbances in Shanghai culminating in outbreaks or mob violence with destruction to property and loss of life and injury to both police and members of the mob. The government's explanation of these events was given in press conference of Shanghai mayor on February 3 in which he stated that disturbances were "Communist stage-managed" and that "Shanghai is main objective of organized red mass uprising headquarters for the Yangtze valley area".

We feel that question of Communist participation in these civil disorders is in large degree academic. While Communists undoubtedly eager exploit events to own ends, these situations are intrinsically manifestations of government's alienation of popular support through administrative ineptitude which has now progressed to a degree endangering government's stability. In each instance of civil unrest, an organized group appeared convinced that government had acted unreasonably and arbitrarily against group's economic or political interests. Government made no adequate arrangements for orderly settlement of points at issue, leaving group no alternatives except to abandon demands or present them through mass action. Government policing of individual situations was inept and exacerbated mass feeling to point where group became mob bent on violent retaliation for real or fancied wrongs. Police unable, or possibly unwilling, to restrain mob until after acts of violence had been committed.

These specific, local situations faithfully mirror government's predicament on national level, which is also largely of government's own making and for which government's sovereign remedy has so far also been force ineptly applied. In most of China north of Yangtze, principal elements opposing government are Communist organized. In remainder of the country still under its control, government's futile attempts to eliminate all opposition and compel support and its failure to devise and implement adequate constructive policies for improvement in its position is rapidly bringing it to the verge of severe crisis which it can hardly hope to survive. Increased urban civil unrest on a large scale may well be the factor precipitating crisis, which the Communists obviously are prepared to exploit.

Growing pessimism and despondency of high Chinese civil and military officials with regard to economic, political and military deterioration has long been apparent. Recently there seems to have developed a sharper awareness of the fact that the government may soon lack the minimum of popular support necessary for its survival. This trend approaches conviction on the part of most that the government lacks capacity to extricate itself from the plight without foreign assistance and fear on the part of many that the government's position is hopeless even though foreign aid is forthcoming.

In this situation several types of response are taking shape. The Generalissimo and those most loyal to him favor strategy of continued resistance to the Communists and repression of other dissident or potentially dissident elements, while effecting such minimum reforms as are possible without antagonizing the most reactionary groups. This group hopes to sustain itself with whatever aid it can get, believing that in the final analysis it will be saved by a Soviet-American war.

Another indefinite grouping responds to the situation with the idea of seeking a negotiated peace with the Communists through the mediation of the Soviet Union, hoping to retain dominant influence and authority in a coalition government which would result from this mediation. Recent reports, unconfirmed but from credible sources, indicate that this group is gaining many adherents among the military and is already exploring means to contact the Soviets to negotiate mediation. While this group may not have yet achieved status of an anti-government movement, probably because of lack of firm leadership, many factors strongly favor such development. Since the military elements in the group are preponderant, the possibility of defection among the armed forces cannot be overlooked.

The situation is very definitely one to cause pessimism. If American aid should materialize in adequate measure and palatable form, the tide may turn quickly in our favor. On the other hand, when details of American aid are announced, they will be weighed carefully by all factions and if our plans are deemed to be insufficient or unpalatable, or unlikely to be effective, it is more than likely that disaffection of some elements now in the government may ensue. Such disaffection may well result in the replacement of present dominant elements with the group desirous of effecting union with the Communists through the good offices of the Soviet Union. As we have previously reported, the Generalissimo is unalterably opposed to such a move and if those favoring an arrangement with the Communists came into the ascendancy, his retirement from the scene would be inevitable.

STUART.

150 (b)

The Ambassador in China (Stuart) to Secretary Marshall

893.00/2–648

NANKING, *February 6, 1948.*

We are by no means convinced that the general breakdown of law and order in Shanghai is imminent, although we believe further sporadic civil disturbances probable. There is as yet no indication that the Communists are so organized as to be capable of creating and controlling a state of chaos at Shanghai. As we have already reported on February 5, we continue to believe that basic causes of civil disturbances at Shanghai are economic rather than political and must be dealt with by economic measures in conjunction with determined police control. It seems to us that the government is well aware of the need to maintain itself at all costs in the lower Yangtze valley, and at this time we can see no serious threat to its position in this area. However, the fact remains that government control of Shanghai is likely to be endangered by policy of extremist elements in the government in using party secret police to suppress even legitimate dissatisfaction caused by maladministration and thus solidify discontented elements into organized opposition. In such a situation the advantage is thrown to the Communists. Moderate elements who would prefer to deal with the situation by firm but rational methods are handicapped by lack of unified administrative control. For example, the Mayor of Shanghai has no authority over garrison command or over party secret police. Mayor Wu has requested such authority and we are very informally supporting his request with the Generalissimo, pointing out that the deterioration in the Shanghai situation seems to call for firm measures and centralized authority. We consider this feasible because of competence of the Mayor, his loyalty to the Generalissimo and the high regard in which the latter holds him.

In the situation prevailing at Shanghai there is reason for concern but no immediate cause for alarm. In fact, manhandling of Mayor Wu and the apprehension of some leaders may have sobering effect. Shanghai foreign community has long tended to panic over relatively insignificant political developments. This tendency is infectious and inevitably contributes to general unrest and feeling of insecurity.

We do not wish to minimize potentialities of situation at Shanghai but for time being we feel Chinese Government can retain control over situation. Furthermore, there are factors in situation, such as pending American aid, which will undoubtedly have substantial effect on public morale thus tending to stabilize at least temporarily.

151 (a)

The Ambassador in China (Stuart) to Secretary Marshall

893.00/3–1748

NANKING, *March 17, 1948.*

Political and military disintegration is now rapidly approaching the long expected climax. The most spectacular evidence of this is the breakdown of military morale seen not only in lethargy and passive unconcern, but also in refusal to obey orders or even to act in defiance of orders given. Chinese describe this latter phenomenon as deliberately suicidal in terms of national interest. Civil and military officials, both high and low, are grafting or are planning their escape. In the highest circles, Generalissimo listens only to such civilians as Tai Chi-tao, the Chen brothers, and T. V. Soong, but Chen Kuo-fu is now in disfavor and his brother is less in favor than hitherto. Relations between the Generalissimo and Tai are not cordial, and T. V. Soong is concentrating on his job in south China. Among many of those hitherto most loyal to the Generalissimo, there are definite signs of discontent with his policy. Nor are there any indications of any intention on his part to make the requisite radical changes. In their despair, all groups blame America for urging structural changes, many of which they claim have been undertaken, or reforms which they feel they themselves would carry out if their immediate internal problems were not so acute, while America still delays the long promised aid upon which the survival of democratic institutions depends. At the same time they are proposing that someone be sent to Washington to plead for immediate and adequate assistance. Such names as those of T. V. Soong and Yu Tai-Wei have been mentioned to me of late for this purpose.

There is a growing tendency to postpone the National Assembly due to convene March 29. Tai Chi-tao supports postponement on the ground that in their efforts to settle controversies over the election of delegates they are using authoritarian methods not unlike the Communists whom they are fighting. Others support postponement on the ground of present inexpediency, or because a suitable name for Vice President has not emerged. Vice President candidates being discussed are Yu Yu-jen, Sun Fo, Ho Ying-chin, Cheng Chien, Fu Tso-yi, and Li Tsung-jen. Li is opposed by the inner circles around the Generalissimo because of factional bickering and as being too strong a personality to be willing to leave the Generalissimo in complete power. Some urge that the Vice President should be a civilian. Present indications are that Generalissimo will support Yu Yu-jen with all that implies.

Various rather inconsequential attempts are being made among liberals to organize or to issue appeals, but the controlled press and fear of high-handed repression tend to nullify their efforts. There is, however, a nucleus within the party leadership which is planning something of the sort with some hope of results. I have been asked to advocate their cause with the Generalissimo, but have replied that I have repeatedly suggested to the Generalissimo without success, that he himself lead such a movement, and that while I still think his endorsement is not entirely impossible, I could perhaps be of more influence in supporting the general idea after their movement had attained substantial proportions. I have added that it seemed to me to be of primary importance that the liberals ensure freedom of publication in party papers for their proposed manifesto.

The long expected climax is rapidly approaching, and although we cannot see the Generalissimo voluntarily relinquishing his power almost anything can happen. There is most definitely accelerated demoralization, dismay and frantic search to save something from the wreckage, coupled with a psychopathic inability to do anything.

STUART

151 (b)

The Ambassador in China (Stuart) to Secretary Marshall

893.00/3–3148

NANKING, *March 31, 1948*

Demoralization and deterioration of situation portrayed in our report of March 8, have continued at an accelerated pace. There is an increased feeling of helplessness in government circles as elsewhere and a fervent searching for some means of bringing a stop to civil war and economic and political uncertainties resulting from it. There is an increasing realization, shared even by the Generalissimo, that military victory over Communists is impossible and that some other solution must be reached if Communist-domination of all China is to be avoided. There is a realization that old methods are inadequate and that a new approach is needed. There is, we believe, a sincere search for an effective new approach yet no one has found the formula. No one seems capable of taking positive action towards peace. Each one looks to another for initiative. Those in position to influence the Generalissimo to take positive effective measures fear his anger and are reluctant to put forward their ideas of reform. He has need of more courageous advisers around him and perhaps his reorganized government will supply this need. As straws in the wind and as possible portent of future trends are recent proclamations by intellectual groups advocating reforms. What they are afraid to do individually, they are beginning to do collectively.

The Chinese people do not want to become Communists yet they see the tide of Communism running irresistibly onward. In midst of this chaos and inaction the Generalissimo stands out as the only moral force capable of action. We know that he plans to reorganize his Government yet we question a mere shifting of portfolios can result in effective action. Little, if any, new blood seems available. What is needed is inspired leadership, of which so far the Generalissimo seems incapable. Possibly, however, the desperateness of his situation will serve to stimulate him as in the past to leadership required.

In any event, there is ever so slight an indication that the Generalissimo may at last deem the situation so acute that he is prepared to accept and follow sound advice. He is taking measures to improve military situation in Mukden and if he can save Mukden, and it begins to look as though he may do so; if he can bring himself to begin institution of political and economic reforms needed to make his government more acceptable to the people, and there are signs here also that he may have reached that stage; and if we can continue and, if possible, expand our present support, as now seems likely from the Congressional consideration of Aid to China Bill; then the situation may not be entirely beyond redemption.

It is nevertheless desperate and if the Generalissimo does not act and act promptly, there are increasing indications that growing opposition to him within the party may find leadership, possibly under the Political Science Group, and will remove him from the scene, accepting the best possible accommodation with the Communists. Should this stage be reached, we could expect Soviet Ambassador designate, Roschin, to assume his duties at Nanking and could look for acceptance of Soviet offer of mediation. Contrary, however, to belief expressed in our report of March 8 we now incline to the opinion that Soviet mediation would result in a coalition government rather than in territorial arrangement. That road to power is better known to Communists and would, we believe, be more acceptable to dissident elements in government. Under a territorial arrangement the present disposition of Communist forces would likely involve giving them jurisdiction over everything north of Yangtze and east of Sian— a division of territory unlikely of acceptance even by dissident elements of government. On the other hand, we hear expressed on many sides belief that under coalition government fundamental characteristic of Chinese would assure that pattern of Czechoslovakia could be resisted and that democratic government in some form would eventually succeed.

Developments in the National Assembly now in session should throw light on the future. Choice of a vice president will give an indication. China is once more at crossroads. The Generalissimo sees structure he labored so long and so hard to create collapsing about him and he may be expected to fight with his usual courage and ability. Either those of weak heart will prevail and we will find ourselves with a Soviet-sponsored coalition government, or those of stout heart will rally round a Generalissimo in some way reinspired to restore benevolence to his despotism sufficient to attract once more a public following necessary to overcome Communist threat. We hope for the latter but we fear the former.

152 (a)

The Ambassador in China (Stuart) to Secretary Marshall

893.00/4–248

NANKING, *April 2, 1948*

We are informed that the Generalissimo has definitely given consideration to the possibility of accepting the Presidency of Executive Yuan reported on March 18. Dr. Hu Shih, who has been very active in organizing the National Assembly, informs us that this subject is being widely discussed and may have merits. He points out that the office of President, under the Constitution, may become, as in France, largely ceremonial while the President of Executive Yuan will exercise great authority. Also once appointed, the President of Executive Yuan should be secure in office as two-thirds vote of the Legislature Yuan is required to unseat him. Hu Shih also mentioned the fact that the Generalissimo had not announced his candidacy for President. In this connection, Chu Cheng, incumbent President Judicial Yuan and qualified for ceremonial office, has announced his availability for election as President.

Sun Fo is actively campaigning for election as Vice President and as President of the Legislative Yuan as well, maintaining that constitutional prohibition against holding other government office when elected President of Legislative Yuan does not apply to elective offices such as those of President or Vice President of the Republic.

The Vice Presidential campaign has now narrowed to Sun Fo and Li Tsung-jen, but should the Generalissimo decide to seek Executive Yuan Presidency, some arrangement is entirely possible whereby Sun Fo would be elected President of the Republic and would appoint the Generalissimo to the Presidency of Executive Yuan leaving the Vice Presidency free for Li Tsung-jen.

STUART

152 (b)

Speech by Generalissimo Chiang Kai-shek Before the Central Executive Committee of the Kuomintang on April 4, 1948 [17]

893.00/4–948

The convocation of the National Asssembly is a great event in the history of China. On the current situation as well as on the course of political development in decades to come it is bound to exercise a most profound and decisive influence. Problems confronting the National Assembly are many. In tackling any one of them, especially that of the presidency and vice-presidency, we must have all the seriousness of mind and a sense of grave responsibility to the nation and posterity. We must carefully study our revolutionary history, analyze the prevailing circumstances, understand the people's psychology and visualize the future of the country. Above all, we must uphold our late leader Dr. Sun's lofty ideal "everything for the people", and make our choice with far sight and circumspection. I, therefore, propose to explain to you with all sincerity the conclusions I have drawn on these questions after careful deliberation.

Before I present to you my views on the question of the presidency and vice-presidency, I wish to make clear three points: First, the ultimate aim of our Party is to save and reconstruct the country. Aside from the paramount interest of the State, the Party has no interest of its own. We have no partisan or personal considerations. Secondly, the only ambition our comrades should have is how to serve the country and the people. We can best render our service only when we perform our duty wholeheartedly, each in his respective post. Thirdly, our late leader Dr. Sun, when leading the revolutionary movement, always took cognizance of the past and gave practical and realistic consideration to existing circumstances. The above three points are what we have to bear in mind when we take decisions on momentous issues. Hence I wish to remind you of a bitter lesson of history and draw a parallel between it and the present situation.

At the beginning of the Republic Dr. Sun Yat-sen was the president of the Provisional Government. Hardly had three months elapsed when the majority of party comrades advocated Dr. Sun's withdrawal from the government in order to make the peace negotiations between the North and South a speedy success. They were mistaken in regarding the provisional constitution, the parliament and the cabinet as constitutional democracy itself. They did not realize that Peiping still was the citadel of reactionary influence with the northern warlords actually in control of everything. In other words, the foundation of the Republic was extremely feeble. At that juncture, our Party, in order to safeguard this foundation, should not have relinquished the presidency. But to Dr. Sun's pleadings our comrades turned a deaf ear. So he failed. And his failure was also that of the Revolution of 1911. The result was the tragic history of the last thirty-odd years and the enormous sufferings of the people. The situation today is, however, fundamentally different from that of 1911. On account of the contributions we made during the Northern Expedition and the War of Resistance the foundation of the Republic has been greatly strengthened. The idea of democracy has become a popular sentiment. In these circumstances, our Party does not need to keep the post and honor of the presidency. On

---

[17] Transmitted by Ambassador Stuart from Nanking, Apr. 9, 1948.

the contrary, we should develop Dr. Sun's ideal "everything for the people" to the fullest extent. In other words, we can entrust to persons outside the Party the grave responsibility of making the Constitution a living thing. Only in this manner, I believe, shall we rally the support of the people in our common and gigantic task of rebellion, suppression and national reconstruction.

After careful deliberation I consider that the qualifications for the first president should be as follows: First of all, he must be a person who comprehends the essentials of the Constitution. He must have the ability and will to uphold the Constitution, observe it and carry it into practice. To choose the man capable of obeying and enforcing the law is the surest guarantee of the success of constitutional democracy. In the second place, he must be a person inspired by the ideals of democracy and imbued with a democratic spirit. I believe that a true democrat is always a true patriot. I believe that he will, in accordance with the Constitution, carry out the Three People's Principles and build up China as a country by the people, of the people, and for the people. In the third place he must be a person loyal to the basic policy of rebellion, suppression, and national reconstruction. It takes a true democrat to fully comprehend the incompatability between a dictatorship and a constitutional government. In the fourth place, he must be one who has a profound understanding of our history, culture and national traditions. It is evident that the Communists are determined to undermine the very existence of our country. They are equally determined to destroy our history, culture and national traditions. Finally, he must be one who follows world trends and has a rich knowledge of contemporary civilization. He will lead China towards the ideal of universal brotherhood, make China an independent and self-respecting country and guide her to take her rightful place in the family of nations. I sincerely hope that my views will be shared by all of you, especially those who are holding responsible positions. Let a person outside of our Party with such qualifications be nominated as candidate to the presidency. Let all of us support him and help him to be elected. As for myself, being the leader of the Party, I may be the logical candidate for nomination by the Party to the presidency. I believe, however, that since you have been with me for so many years, you must understand that I do not care for high honor and important post. My only concern has always been how to give my best to serve my people. I am ever ready to assist the president in carrying out the democratic principles embodied in the Constitution. I shall contribute what I have and what I am as a soldier to defend the country.

As long as the nation remains disunited, I am determined not to run for the presidency.

This does not mean that I shall shirk the responsibility towards our revolutionary cause and our beloved country. Aside from the presidency and vice-presidency, I shall not fail to answer the call of the new Government. I have been with my people and army throughout these twenty years of great trials and tribulation. Patriotic soldiers and citizens have supported me in uniting and defending the country. They have given their very best. They have sustained great sacrifices. I have the moral obligation to do my utmost so as not to disappoint them and to forfeit the confidence they have placed in me. I shall contribute whatever I can to cooperate with the people, the army and my party comrades towards our common goal. For the good of the country and the good of the people, I am convinced that I should not run for the presidency. This is not mere modesty. It is my sincere conviction. The only hope I cherish is: how to lay a sound and solid foundation for China's constitutional government.

In a word, I propose that our Party will nominate an outstanding non-partisan to be candidate to the presidency.

Comrades : I hope you will appreciate my sincerity, trust my judgment, endorse my opinion and make a decision !

152 (c)

The Ambassador in China (Stuart) to Secretary Marshall

893.00/4–548

NANKING, *April 5, 1948*

During a tense all-day meeting of the Kuomintang's Central Executive Committee on April 4, the Generalissimo affirmed his unwillingness to be a candidate for the presidency and advised both Cheng Chien and Li Tsung-jen not to run for vice president, but to leave both offices open to civilians. Cheng Chien agreed immediately, but Li is reported to have become very angry and to have said it was too late for him to withdraw. After an all night meeting with his associates he has decided to run independently of the Kuomintang, and if he is defeated there may be trouble.

Strong opposition to the Chen brothers is manifest among delegates, and any motion suspected of being sponsored by them is denounced. Also, revolt against party domination is read into the applause which follows reference to such domination.

The Generalissimo today openly advised party members to vote for Hu Shih and Sun Fo for president and vice president respectively, maintaining both are civilians.

STUART

152 (d)

The Ambassador in China (Stuart) to Secretary Marshall

893.00/4–648

NANKING, *April 6, 1948*

The consequence of the Generalissimo's announcement of a desire to withdraw from the presidential race and serve the country in another capacity and his advice to the Kuomintang to select non-party man as its presidential candidate has been to confirm him in a presidential position, rally full support of the party to his leadership and enhance his authority.

Whether wholly calculated or not, the Generalissimo's action was a masterful political maneuver. Original motivation for action was doubtless need more cohesion within the party weakened by factionalism and by mounting discontent with the quality of his leadership. Apprehensive lest the National Assembly serve as a source from which elements within the party could attack his policy and so bring about party split, the Generalissimo apparently decided to risk assuming minor role in new government through quitting presidential race and recommending non-party candidate for party support. Initial reaction of the party to proposal was feeling of vast dismay. Although under the new constitution presidential powers are greatly reduced, the bulk of Kuomintang has long been accustomed to equating party leadership with the presidency and the presidency with control of the government. Thus, the Generalissimo's move encountered violent opposition on the basis that party's control of the government would be weakened and on the basis that the present crisis demands a strong hand at the helm of the ship of state. Following a series of party meetings, CC Clique refused to cooperate with any government not headed by the Generalissimo as president and Whampou group threatened to go over to the Communists rather than serve under any president other than Chiang. The party leaders joined in the refrain that the Generalissimo is indispensable man in presidential role. Thus, bowing to the party mandate the Generalissimo today consented to enter presidential race.

As suggested above this maneuver greatly strengthens Generalissimo's position. He has answered Communist criticism of "personal rule" by attempting to seek less significant position in new government. Thus Communists are now forced to attack "KMT Government" instead of "Chiang Government." Also he has answered other critics at home and abroad by his public advocacy of broadening base of new government by the inclusion of non-party elements in insignficant posts and by his demands that such posts be filled by persons with civil rather than military backgrounds. By facing his critics within the party with unpalatable possibility of their being forced to attempt to dominate the government without him in key position, he has secured from them clear and firm mandate to continue his rule and probable uncritical acceptance of his policies in future. Finally, since under new constitution the president is Commander-in-Chief of the armed forces, he will be able to maintain control over the army.

In the course of discussions the Generalissimo insisted that vice-presidential elections be held on free and competitive basis with party having no candidate of its own. He declined to give personal backing to any candidate. These circumstances will probably improve chances of Li Tsung-jen winning vice-presidential election especially since Sun Fo, having encountered intense opposition to his desire to hold both vice presidency and head Legislative Yuan, now inclines to be content with the latter office only.

STUART

152 (e)

The Ambassador in China (Stuart) to Secretary Marshall

893.00/4–1948

NANKING, April 19, 1948

The National Assembly today elected the Generalissimo first constitutional President of China by a vote of 2,430 to 269. The Assembly yesterday passed temporary rebellion suppression authorizing the President to take emergency measures free of restrictions imposed by Articles 39 and 43 of the Constitution but subject to veto of Legislative Yuan under the procedure prescribed in Article 57, Section 2. If the end of the rebellion suppression period is not proclaimed prior to December 25, 1950, a special meeting of the Assembly is to be called to consider extension of the act.

The effect of the act is to permit the President, in conjunction with Executive Yuan, to issue emergency decrees at any time without prior concurrence of legislative Yuan, but subject to revision or revocation by a two-thirds majority vote in Legislative Yuan. From what is known of the composition of the newly-elected Legislative Yuan, it appears very unlikely that a two-thirds majority could ever be mustered against a decree of the executive, so that act, in effect, gives the President practically unlimited power.

STUART

152 (f)

The Ambassador in China (Stuart) to Secretary Marshall

893.00/4–2348

NANKING, *April 23, 1948.*

Someone who has just seen the Generalissimo reports he is still wavering on acceptance of the presidency though it may be assumed he will accept. He had had three long conferences with Hu Shih trying still unsuccessfully to persuade him to be a candidate as he felt the President should be some internationally known figure. He opposed Chu Cheng for this reason, and Chang Po-ling was rejected as too old. He is said to have had more than one stormy argument with his party and with the military over his refusal to run, they insisting that if he would not become President, the elections must be postponed. Finally he had agreed to run as being the only one able and willing to face the responsibility. The Generalissimo is opposed to Li Tsung-jen as Vice President which lessens Li's chances and increases the possibility that Li may make trouble if defeated. The Generalissimo is urging Chang Chun to continue as Premier and intends to have the Executive Yuan function in a more constitutional manner.

It was reported that when the Generalissimo was reminded that he ought to give more authority to others in the Central Government and in the provinces and that under his concept of centralized administration, things had been getting steadily worse, the Generalissimo had replied that others refused to take sufficient responsibility or were unsatisfactory so that he was compelled to act as he did.

Here we have the picture of a strong, resourceful man unquestionably sincere and courageous, yet persisting in a policy which is frustrating his own aims. I am convinced that he does not seek for dictatorial prerogatives from selfish motives, but insists on exercising these to his own detriment and that of the nation. The worse things become under his leadership, the more does he feel impelled to carry the whole burden.

I do not believe he is conceited or intoxicated with power in the usual sense, yet he is dangerously self-opinionated and confident that he understands the situation better and has more experience than anyone else. This is all the more tragic because he is so largely right in these assumptions, and because there really seems to be no one else who could take his place. Yet the election has eliminated Li Tsung-jen in particular and produced in general an unfavorable reaction in China and probably abroad. If the Generalissimo had the vision to take the occasion of becoming President under the constitution to alter radically his procedure, these unfortunate tendencies might be neutralized, but the probabilities, as I see them, are against this.

STUART.

152 (g)

The Ambassador in China (Stuart) to Secretary Marshall

893.00/4–2348

NANKING, *April 23, 1948*

Persistent reports from informed sources close to Li Tsung-jen state he has made a complete break with the Generalissimo and in event of defeat in vice presidential race plans to take some "action" the type of which is unspecified.

Other less qualified sources feel this may take the form of local military revolt. The bulk of troops in the vicinity of Nanking are Kwangsi and Kwangtung units whose loyalty, whether to Li or to the Generalissimo, is unknown to us. On the basis of present information, we consider armed coup only a remote possibility, though conceivable. Li may act in the heat of anger at what he considers his ill treatment at the hands of the Generalissimo and because of a feeling of frustration over the Kuomintang party machine's rejection of his services to the nation in its present crisis. We believe "action," if any, will take place later; probably in conjunction with Hong Kong and south China dissidents with whom evidence suggests Li is in close contact. Vice Presidential election will probably not be concluded until June 24 or 25.

STUART

152 (h)

The Ambassador in China (Stuart) to Secretary Marshall

893.00/4–2548

NANKING, *April 25, 1948*

In the early morning hours of April 25 Cheng Chien and later Li Tsung-jen announced retirement from the vice presidential race, leaving Sun Fo as the sole remaining candidate. At the Assembly meeting this morning, amidst considerable disorder on the part of delegates, the meeting was adjourned without any action being taken. This morning local vernacular press carried stories of the retirement of both candidates, and Li's supporters issued statement in the form of an advertisement that his withdrawal is in the interest of securing national harmony and to secure vindication from scurrilous rumors being circulated to the effect that he intends to force the Generalissimo to leave the country. At the morning Assembly meeting with Yu Yu-jen acting as chairman, delegates stated that Li's retirement from the race could only be effected with the concurrence of his supporters, and appealed to the chairman for agreement. Yu Yu-jen, weeping copiously, stated that the whole affair was regrettable and that a new set of elections should be held.

As we have previously reported, Li has been under heavy pressure from the Generalissimo to withdraw candidacy and Li has consistently refused. Li's associates say that Li is interested in the vice-presidency as a platform for criticizing shortcomings of the government and suggesting remedial measures, and that he will retire from the army and do so as a private citizen if his campaign fails. Li's supporter, Governor Li Pin-Hsien of Anhwei, has been the target of organized student demonstration and local vernacular paper supporting Li and critical of Sun Fo has been wrecked by a mob, reportedly led by delegates supporting Sun Fo, without interference from the police. Presumably reliable source informs us that the Generalissimo has summoned Pai Chung-hsi and directed him on pain of secret court martial to switch support from Li to Sun Fo.

Our initial reaction to these developments is that Li has been subjected to extremely heavy pressure from party machine and Whampoa army clique. He defies this pressure by resignation of candidacy, thus putting himself in the position of being sought by the office rather than seeking office, in compliance of traditional Chinese practice, and so focusing attention of the general public and all interested parties on opponents' maneuvers to prevent his position. In a free and uninfluenced election Li would almost certainly have majority vote. The bulk of delegates, desirous of effecting efficient government and frustrated by machine control Assembly equate Li's election with satisfaction of their aims. The effect of the latest developments on temper of the delegates may be judged by the remark of one, "this is worse than Tsao Kun's election, at least he paid for his."

We repeat, at this stage tempers on both sides are running high, and eventual course of action adopted by either is unpredictable. However, there is no doubt but what the Kuomintang is severely split over matters of principle, in distinction to ordinary party cleavage on matters of self-interest. The principle at stake is efficacy of present leadership and its policies. It is not difficult to conceive of a situation where attempts would be made to reject this leadership, or where leadership, including the Generalissimo and his closest supporters, would prefer to retire in response to popular demand, since the Generalissimo has not formally accepted the presidency and is understood not yet to have made up his mind to accept.

In the present circumstances the ultimate consequences are difficult to foretell. Reliable sources state resolution of the situation will be forthcoming within the next 24 hours. We will continue to report significant occurrences.

STUART

152 (i)

The Ambassador in China (Stuart) to Secretary Marshall

893.00/4–2648

NANKING, *April 26, 1948*

On the afternoon of April 25 Sun Fo announced his withdrawal from the vice-presidential race, stating that he felt it would be undemocratic to run without opposition. His withdrawal was made at the Generalissimo's direction. In the afternoon the Central Executive Committee of the Kuomintang met and passed a resolution stating candidates withdrawals all invalid. The Assembly did not convene today. Li Tsung-jen's associates state that his withdrawal was a political maneuver designed to focus attention on threats and intimidation directed against his supporters by the Generalissimo, Kuomintang bosses and Whampoa clique. He made the decision when the Generalissimo ordered Pai Chung-hsi to withdraw his support of Li under threat of punitive action and to coordinate his move with Cheng Chien. Pai yesterday issued a statement that Li withdrew because his supporters were continually subjected to intimidation and under those conditions free election was impossible. Cheng's cooperation with Li seems to have begun when the Generalissimo summoned him, asked him to withdraw and throw vote to Sun Fo, and offered to reimburse him for the entire costs of his campaign, which proposition Cheng refused.

Intense political maneuvering by all factions continues today, and even best informed circles are bewildered and uncertain as to outcome. However, it is abundantly clear that recent developments have seriously split the Kuomintang. Rank and file of party and independents, including probably majority of civil servants and army officers, have come to believe that country can survive present crisis only through more liberal effective vigorous leadership than has been evident in past. This group hoped that such leadership might be forthcoming in an orderly manner through implementation of the new constitution. Interference of Generalissimo and party machine with elections to Assembly and the new Yuan, with deliberations of Assembly on constitutional amendment question and flagrant intervention in vice presidential election has thoroughly convinced those desiring effective constitutional government that Generalissimo intends to use new constitution as vehicle for continuation of his personal rule in same close cooperation with CC Clique dominated party machine and Whampoa clique dominated High Military Command as has obtained in past.

There seems little doubt but what vast majority of politically articulate Chinese who are not intimately associated with KMT party machine are aroused over present situation and place blame on Generalissimo. In early stages of vice presidential contest Generalissimo left Sun Fo campaign in hands of Chen Li-fu but intervened personally to influence outcome, despite his pledge of free election, when Sun's defeat appeared likely. The character of Generalissimo's intervention has definitely outraged many of his supporters. Hitherto, respect for Generalissimo's service to nation, tendency to regard him as indispensable man and fear of retaliation have combined to prevent non-Communist elements in Nationalist China from acting or speaking covertly against him. However, action of Cheng and Li and statement of Pai on reasons for Li's withdrawal forces development of political alignments over issue of democratic constitutional government versus personal autocratic rule through entrenched reactionary cliques. Notwithstanding native Chinese genius on techniques of political compromise, the fact that the present issue is clear-cut and open and involves popularly supported challenge to vested authority by groups convinced that continuation of that authority in power must inevitably by reason of its autocratic character and long record of failure and incompetence, involve country in ruin, mitigates strongly against lasting compromise.

The assembly is now slated to reconvene the morning of the 27th with delegates voting on acceptance of the withdrawal of each candidate in turn. Li's managers now claim 1800 votes. The bulk of the Kuomintang is now out of control by party leaders. The Youth party is insisting on free elections and Carson Chang's Democratic Socialists are cautious and irresolute. In this situation it appears entirely possible that democratic, constitutional and anti-Generalissimo propensities of the delegates may result in Li's election. How the Generalissimo would accommodate himself to such defeat involving rejection of his leadership is impossible to foretell. One of the many possibilities is refusal to accept the presidency. Despite the many disturbing features in this situation, we are encouraged by the undeniable fact that democratic forces are now appearing and making themselves felt in protest against autocracy and reaction.

Following the conference, all three contenders have just announced their intention to re-enter race.

152 (j)

The Ambassador in China (Stuart) to Secretary Marshall

893.00/4–2748

NANKING, *April 27, 1948*

The confusion which has characterized political maneuvering in the vice presidential race continued through most of yesterday, but some clarification is apparent this morning. On the morning of the 26th Hu Shih, speaking on behalf of the special committee appointed by the Central Executive Committee of the Kuomintang to deal with impasse in vice presidential elections, stated that all candidates had agreed to reenter race. Shortly thereafter Li's followers began passing out word that Li would not run and was planning to return to Peiping. At this juncture the Generalissimo informed Hu Shih committee of his pleasure at the decision of all the candidates to remain in the race, exhorted the party to act in accordance with his earlier expressed wishes that delegates have freedom of choice in voting, and stated that candidates should not spread slanderous rumors against one another. Adding to the confusion, Li himself then told correspondents of his intention to abandon the race and fly to Peiping today. This statement was immediately denied by Hu Shih. The Generalissimo summoned Li for conference last night and after an hour's discussion persuaded Li to reenter contest. The Assembly will meet tomorrow to proceed with elections.

Li's stand has strengthened his position and gained the sympathy of the delegates who continue to blame the Generalissimo and the party machine for the undemocratic interference in the election procedure. The Youth Party and Democratic Socialists have issued statements calling on the Kuomintang to be "more democratic". On the basis of present information it appears that liberal and independent elements have successfully challenged control of the CC Clique dominated party machine and the election of Li seems likely.

STUART

152 (k)

The Consul General at Shanghai (Cabot) to Secretary Marshall

893.00/4–2748

SHANGHAI, *April 27, 1948*

Reference statement in previous message to effect that, since the Communist supporters believe present regime confirmed and continued in power by recent American aid, more violent anti-American propaganda campaign by the Communists can be anticipated.

Of the politically alert population of nationalist China, there is a very large proportion which is fundamentally anti-Communist and anti-revolutionary; which considers however that Nanking regime as presently constituted must inevitably collapse through incompetence, corruption, and lack of popular support against the Communists; which feels that drastic purge and reform of that regime offers only hope of salvation; and which views American aid prior to revitalization of government with open hostility or grave misgivings as merely serving to confirm rotten regime on its path to disaster. Hopes of these people, who include students, intellectuals, businessmen and many others, have to a significant extent been pinned on National Assembly and especially on Li Tsung-jen's candidacy which, rightly or wrongly, many identify with reform and progress.

If proceedings of National Assembly result in Li's election or other developments involving real change in complexion of government and introduction of new vigorous elements which offer some promise of effecting drastic reform, there is good reason to hope that this important segment of articulate Chinese public will largely swing over to support of liberal forces in government and of American aid.

If, on the contrary, results of the National Assembly are the rejection of Li and other popularly regarded "liberal" forces and the confirmation of stand pàt Kuomintang politicians in their domination of government and influence over the Generalissimo, consequent wave of disappointment and revulsion against government, whether or not productive of immediate violence, is bound to be serious. Many of those who have been wavering with respect to support of the government will turn toward Communists and revolution as only alternative.

Their opposition to American aid would be revived and the coincidence of the aid's timing with the National Assembly's confirmation of rightist control of the government would invite a new wave of anti-American feeling.

Despite American aid, or really because of it, if it does in fact assist continuance of CC control, large masses of people will follow exiled liberal leaders in supporting Communist Civil War or at best apathetically regarding Nanking efforts. Either will result in an inevitable extension of Civil War with further destruction and chaos in larger and larger areas where Chinese Communism of a more and more Soviet nature can take root and thrive.

That Communists are preparing to exploit such contingencies would seem to be indicated by report that Chou En-lai is advocating more emphasis on wooing of liberals and by article by Communist "theoretician" Jen Pi-shih published in the April issue of Hong King Communist publication MASSES. While we have not seen this article, we have learned from two good sources that it has caused excitement in local intellectual and liberal circles; and that its main thesis is an admission that Communists have been too severe toward landowners (small, middle and large), industrialists and intellectuals, and will have to treat them more considerately. With respect to intellectuals, the article is said to be aimed directly at those who have lost faith in the government but have hitherto feared persecution by the Communists and to play skillfully on theme of "futility of supporting rotten regime" when good existence under Communists is guaranteed.

In summary, results of unclarified United States aid to China program will be: (1) strengthening of far left groups; (2) indefinite continuation and extension of Civil War; and (3) fostering of anti-Americanism in liberal groups through latter's claim of non-support and in reactionary groups by their claim of inadequate support.

It would seem to us that, while situation now evolving at Nanking thus holds serious potentialities from American standpoint, something can be done toward softening anti-American outburst which may eventuate.

The question has been asked locally why a United States official statement to the press has not been made clarifying our position as one of giving aid to the Chinese people regardless of their government, provided the government is not Communist dominated. and that the United States Government is therefore completely disinterested in the outcome of Nanking political maneuvering. The opportune time for such a statement would be on release of terms of letter of intent. If properly worded, such statement would serve to correct popular misunderstanding that American support of the Generalissimo means underwriting his reactionary coterie, to counteract much Chinese Communist propaganda, and to enhance or help salvage (depending on the National Assembly outcome) American prestige among Chinese liberals.

CABOT

152 (I)

The Ambassador in China (Stuart) to Secretary Marshall

893.00/4–2948

NANKING, *April 29, 1948*

Following the agreement of the three leading contenders to withdraw their withdrawals from the vice presidential race, and vote of the Presidium of the National Assembly to continue with the election, a third ballot was held on April 28 and resulted in 1156 votes for Li Tsung-jen; 1040 for Sun Fo; and 515 for Cheng Chien. The decrease in Li Tsung-jen's support and the general attitude and apathy apparent during the third ballot, led many observers to surmise that possibly sufficient pressure and coercion had been brought to bear to insure that on the fourth and final vote Sun Fo would emerge victorious.

Fourth ballot held on April 29 and resulted in 1438 votes for Li Tsung-jen and 1295 for Sun Fo. The Presidium immediately thereupon proclaimed Li as Vice President. The voting was quiet and orderly until near the end of the counting when it became apparent that Li would win and his supporters became increasingly noisy in expressing their approval of the vote and centered their demonstrations around Madame Li, who was present on the floor of the Assembly.

Public interest in Nanking during fourth ballot was apparent. The proceedings of the Assembly were broadcast and it seemed as though every radio in Nanking was tuned in on it with crowds of people gathered in streets wherever a radio could be heard.

The Embassy will subsequently elaborate its estimate of what this development means. The preliminary appraisal is that it represents a smashing defeat for the CC Clique, a serious setback for the Generalissimo whose determined support of Sun Fo was no secret, and a successful challenge by opposition elements of the party to dictation by party machine centering around CC Clique and Whampoa clique. It remains to be seen how the Generalissimo will accommodate himself to these developments and whether opposition elements can organize effectively to implement a reform program which Li professes. Li appears to have been rallying point for all discontented and opposition elements in Assembly. Question now is whether he can provide effective leadership which can and will coalesce this feeling into an effective and progressive opposition.

STUART

152 (m)

The Ambassador in China (Stuart) to Secretary Marshall

893.00/5–348

NANKING, *May 3, 1948.*

The National Assembly which was convoked solely to elect the president and vice president developed quickly into something far more basic. Success of the Generalissimo's 1948 version of the retreat to Fenghua confirmed him in power personally, but struggle over the vice presidency ended in rejection of his policies. Unquestionably the vice presidential race was the most significant development in the Assembly. There can be no question but the balloting was above the slightest suspicion of fraud. Sun represented the dead reactionary aim of the party machine and his election would have meant the unchallenged continuation of the old political policies, preservation of vested interests, and the elimination of any prospect of that revitalization of the party and government which was necessary to give hope of ultimate success in the face of a dynamic Communist movement. Whatever he may turn out to be in practice, Li Tsung-jen during the campaign became the symbol and the rallying point of discontented and progressive elements who had lost faith in those controlling the government and who demanded new faces and new and more effective policies. Li represented a demand for effective government in contrast to the lack of achievement of the discredited group in power. Lacking experience or organization, his supporters challenged the party machine and won. It now remains to be seen whether Li can provide that kind of dynamic leadership which will coalesce these elements into effective opposition and give substance to the program on which Li based his candidacy. Li's victory was a disastrous blow to the CC clique which not only failed to deliver in one of the most important jobs ever assigned to it but also seriously undermined the position of the Generalissimo himself by misinforming him on what he could expect. Most of the opposition criticism was directed at the person of the Generalissimo for attempting to nullify democratic procedures. Much of the criticism directed at him should more properly have been turned on the CC clique but the adverse effect on his prestige exists nonetheless. The Generalissimo's position is made doubly difficult by the fact that he openly and bitterly opposed the man with whom he must now work. It remains to be seen how he will accommodate himself to this situation. In this sense he continues to be as in the past—the key man. If he attempts to oppose Li and to box him in, he will drive Li to increasingly desperate moves since Li gives all indications of intending to be active in the national life. The Generalissimo on the other hand is a practical man and a politician. If he concludes that Li represents the dominant force in nationalist China and decides that he cannot destroy him, he may well decide to join him, at the same time discarding his previous sources of power. He is reported to have been exceedingly angry over the election of Li. He may indeed now be too old and has been in undisputed power too long to adjust himself, or he may again demonstrate that he is still the master politician in China. The decision is his.

The Kuomintang was originally a revolutionary party and the revolutionary tradition remains strong within it. The party is still committed to the activation of the principles of Sun Yat-sen. Kuomintang dissident groups in Hong Kong and abroad have adopted reform slogans and policies, and in recent months even more conservative groups within the party have been talking in similar terms. The source of this interest in change is the pressure of the success of the Communist revolution. The action of the Assembly confirmed the Generalissimo in power but rejected his anti-reform policies. In his present constitution position he can either accept and implement, or deny the popular demand for change.

However, Li's election also gave this demand a constitutional and legal status, and it may be this circumstance which will constrain the Generalissimo to include new talent in his government and adopt the policies which will represent an attempt to combat revolution by social change. Further proof this is realized is that the two principal defeated candidates, Sun and Cheng Chien, have already started to organize what they call reform groups.

There has yet been no reaction from the Communists. Unless, as is rumored, they have substantial reason to believe that Li is prepared to compromise with them and to take them into a coalition government more or less on their own terms, they must be disappointed, realizing that the election of Sun would have favored continuous growth of a situation calculated to foster Communist causes.

The other group to be considered is the Kuomintang Revolutionary Committee in Hong Kong. This committee claims to have a definite time schedule now for the removal of the Generalissimo. It is known that the committee and T. V. Soong have been making the coyest kind of eyes at each other from afar, just in case such a misalliance might prove convenient. The committee claims that it has maintained closest contact with Li Tsung-jen during recent months. If these allegations are correct, then it may well be that the claimed time-table has foundation and that the struggle in the Assembly was but the first round in a life and death struggle between the Generalissimo, the CC clique and the Whampoa clique on the one hand, and Li and his associates on the other.

If the civil war and economic deterioration continue on their present disastrous course Li and his associates seem assured of eventual success, with increasing probabilities that Li from choice or necessity will be driven into an understanding with the Communists. We shall have to watch developments with extreme care, yet our efforts should, we believe, be directed toward influencing the Generalissimo to accept the situation and support more liberal policies.

STUART

152(n)

Editorial from the New China News Agency Entitled: An Old China is Dying, a New China is Marching Ahead

893.00/5-2748

[PART 1] [18]

The final play which Chiang Kai-shek wanted to enact in his 21 years' rule over China has been performed. From March 29th to May 1st, he convened a gang of henchmen and puppets in Nanking to inaugurate a so-called "National Assembly" which has "elected" him "president". But they have enacted this play so malodorously that people do not know whether they are enacting a jubilant event or a funeral.

All Chinese and foreign papers, periodicals and news agencies in Chiang Kai-shek controlled areas, including those of the various KMT cliques, without exception daily publicised and ridiculed unceasingly all sorts of odious news about the "National Assembly". The "National Assembly" was filled with rifts and divisions, with confusion and despair. Even Chiang Kai-shek blamed his "National Assembly Delegates" as not fit to be "Constitutional Models" while "National Assembly Delegates" counter-blamed Chiang Kai-shek for concealing the real state of the war in his report. They cursed and beat each other, and at the same time opposed the people in concert and made this and that resolution against the people. But as a foreign correspondent puts it, the delegates spoke words of bravado like the frightened child who whistles as he passes a graveyard.

In face of the people's democratic revolutionary upsurge, it is in such panic and despair that they have Chiang Kai-shek make up and appear on the stage. Is it not true that even his masters, the American imperialists, contemplate Chiang Kai-shek's abdication to go abroad at a certain moment after his election as president?

The people of the whole country do not pay the least attention to Chiang Kai-shek's calling of the so-called "National Assembly" and becoming the so-called "president". What the people pay attention to is only how to strike down Chiang Kai-shek swiftly· The people of liberated areas are actively unfolding a victorious people's liberation war. Within the period of the "National Assembly" alone, more than 50 cities and towns including Yenan, Loyang and Weihsien have been liberated. The people in Chiang Kai-shek controlled areas are continuing their movement against hunger and oppression. Since inauguration of the "National Assembly" the student movement has, in particular, begun

---

[18] Broadcast by the North Shensi Radio on May 24, 1948, and transmitted by Ambassador Stuart from Nanking, May 27, 1948, with the following comment: "This editorial presents a fascinating, if completely inaccurate, picture of what took place at the National Assembly, together with a somewhat less fascinating but equally inaccurate picture of what would take place if the Communists were in power."

a new high with Peiping as a starting point, and on May 4th, after Chiang Kai-shek was "elected president", students in Shanghai publicly burned effigies of American aggressors and the dictator of China in "celebration". It can be definitely said that the Chinese people will, in the not distant future, send this "government for implementing the constitution" and its makers into their self-dug graves.

Why does Chiang Kai-shek meet with such a fate? This is because he is the representative of the most corrupt and most reactionary feudal compradore bloc in China. This bloc resolutely carries out an anti-popular policy of national betrayal, civil war and dictatorship and a policy of opposing the vanguard of the people—the Communist Party.

As far back as three years ago, in April 1945, comrade Mao Tze-tung in his book "On Coalition Government" raised the warning: "any government that excludes the Communist Party outside its doors will not be able to achieve any worthy thing. This is the basic characteristic of China in the historical stage of new democracy. In the past eight years of the anti-Japanese war, although the KMT Government has up till now not openly declared general war against the Communist Party because there is a Japanese invader facing them, but is employing measures of localized war, suppression by the secret police, blockades, insults, preparation for civil war and opposition to the organization of a Coalition Government to exclude the Communist Party, it has created for itself such a situation that the more it excludes the Communist Party, the more down slope it goes. If in the future it continues to do this then it is preparing to go downslope to the bottom".

In January 1946, because of the urging of the people and the Communist Party, the Chiang Kai-shek block convened and participated in the Political Consultation Conference and expressed willingness to cooperate with the Communist Party and other democratic parties and groups. And because of this, they, in a certain sense and to a certain extent, evoked the hope of the Chinese people towards them for the last time. But after facts, democracy was only a piece of deception. Treacherous Chiang Kai-shek tore up the Truce Agreement, and started an all out civil war, tore up the PCC resolutions and convened the fake "National Assembly" of cleavage and dictatorship. Chiang Kai-shek and his backer, American imperialism, entertained the delusion that American aid would enable Chiang Kai-shek to do as he liked, but no quantity of American dollars, airplanes and guns could ultimately change comrade Mao Tze-tung's scientific prediction—the more they exclude the Communist Party, the more downslope they go.

When Chiang Kai-shek excluded the Communist Party in October 1946 and unilaterally issued the order to convene the "National Assembly" he had deceived the people and started on the downslope. But he was then enthralled by his momentary military progress; he still entertained illusions about the rosy prospects before him. But only after a month when he was calling his so-called "National Assembly for framing the constitution", his good but short dream was completely shattered. Up to the present opening of the "National Assembly for implementing the constitution" when the so-called "president" proclaimed the China under his rule a "constitutional", his rule is a symbol of all the confusion and despair of the present odious plan in Nanking, advantageous for the reactionary ruling class.

The new trick that the reactionary clique can now put out is only to use the so-called "anti-Chang" Li Tsung-jen as the "vice president". It is said that the Chinese and American reactionary cliques are preparing to replace Chiang Kai-shek with Li Tsung-jen. The record of his rule over the people and in the eyes of the people is that Li Tsung-jen is not only as counter-revolutionary as Chiang Kai-shek but a partisan in Chiang Kai-shek's long term counter-revolutionary collaboration. Li Tsung-jen's so-called "anti-Chiang" term has nothing in common with the people's anti-Chiang. The people entertain no illusion whatsoever about him. Therefore, even if the Chinese and American reactionary cliques actually use Li Tsung-jen to replace Chiang Kai-shek, it will also be utterly impossible to because of the Chinese people.

Of course, the plot of the Chinese and American reactionary cliques will not succeed at this. When Li Tsung-jen proves incapable of maintaining their support they will also pick out Hu Shih and other figures. Under such circumstances, the sign "liberalism" recently put up by the political science clique paper "Ta Kung Pao", and the Social Economic Research Association organized under the slogan of the "Third Road" by T. V. Soong's subordinates, Chien Chang-chao and company, and other activities of the same kind will still parade about and mislead the masses, adopting new poises to preserve the essence of the reactionary cliques' rule. Especially when Chiang Kai-shek has collapsed and the main forces of his army have exterminated or routed. The reactionary clique will further adopt a certain policy of concealment and will even find certain unsteady figures from among the present anti-Chiang peoples as their protective charm to conceal and rally their force for what they regard as the proper opportunity for the comeback of reactionary forces. Because at that time, Chiang Kai-shek, who is bitterly hated by all, will have fallen from power while the reactionary clique will also adopt a policy of concealment, and it is possible that a part of the people will relay their vigilance. Therefore, today we should tell the people all this beforehand and ceaselessly expose the various plots of the reactionary clique so as to carry out China's new democratic revolution to the very end.

The new democratic revolution is not only to overthrow thoroughly Chiang Kai-shek's personal rule, but also the foundation of Chiang Kai-shek's rule, that is, thoroughly eliminate the imperialism and the system of China's feudalism and bureaucratic capitalism so that any rule of Chiang Kai-shek's pattern will permanently not revive and not reincarnate.

To point out the correct policy of struggle for people throughout the country, the Central Committee of the Chinese Communist Party issued slogans for the current situation on May 1st, the very day the bogus "National Assembly" came to a close. These slogans called for broadening of the united front against imperialism, feudalism and bureaucratic capitalism; swift convening of a new political consultation conference by all liberals, democrats and independent groups and organizations and all social luminaries to discuss and approve the calling of a People's Congress to establish a Democratic Coalition Government. Timed with the advance of the people's war of liberation and the people's democratic movement, these slogans very clearly map out the path for the Chinese people. Without doubt, the Chinese people must resolutely carry the revolutionary war to the end, for the enemy who unleashed the war has not yet been disarmed. Without doubt, the Chinese people must thoroughly eliminate the rule of imperialism, feudalism and bureaucratic capitalism because this is the prerequisite of an era of freedom and peace for the people. Also without doubt, there can be no "third road" in the death struggle between the Chinese people and their enemy. The only path that exists before China today is to continue to preserve the armed forces and prerogatives of the people's enemy. This is the line of semi-feudalism, and semi-colonialism, national betrayal, civil war and dictatorship led by the big landlord bourgeoise class· This is the people's democratic line of the workers, peasants, independent labour, and no matter from what corner they come or what banner they fly, all movements, which in essence preserve the armed forces prerogatives of the people's enemy, show there is no "third road", but only another guise of the counter-revolution army line. This is the path of new democracy; this is the path of the united struggle against imperialism, feudalism, and bureaucratic capitalism; this is the path of the political consultation conference which the present stage of Chinese history determines that China's big landlord, big bourgeoise class cannot join China's democratic ranks and that these ranks can only be led by the working class and its political representative, the Chinese Communist Party. The two years of history since the failure of the political Consultation Conference in 1946, though only a history of two short years, have demonstrated this truth so vividly and fully! Today the people of China, have, through suffering, universally come to know this truth. This insures that the old China of the reactionary clique cannot but wait its doom and the new China of the people cannot but win out.

[PART 2] [19]

When their rule meets with the opposition of the people and there is a crisis, the reactionary ruling class frequently recall and change their representative political figures who have lost prestige and replace them with representative figures whose reactionary face has not yet been completely exposed or with regard to whom the people still entertain illusions, in order to . . . people's opposition, dull the people's vigilance and continue to maintain their rule. The ruling class represented by Chiang Kai-shek today see their rule heading towards doom. They also badly want to do the following: attempt to find a "suitable" figure to replace Chiang Kai-shek who is bitterly hated by all, to carry on their rule. This is why Hu Shih was suggested as a possible "presidential" candidate and Li Tsung-jen has been elected "vice president". This is also why American imperialism and certain reactionary newspapers in the country do their utmost to boost Hu Shih and Li Tsung-jen. It would actually have been a craftier and more advantageous . . . for the reactionary ruling class if they could today find a figure whose reactionary face has not yet been completely unveiled or about whom the people still entertain certain illusions, and who could take the place of Chiang Kai-shek in carrying on their rule. But the Chinese reactionary ruling class is so corrupt and desperate that it is absolutely impossible for them to find out a comparatively "suitable" figure to replace Chiang Kai-shek, and consequently they cannot but put up this Chiang Kai-shek hated by all, to be the "president" and rely on him to maintain their tottering rule.

The new trick that the reactionary clique can now put out is only to use the so-called "anti-Chiang" Li Tsung-jen as the "vice-president". It is said that the Chinese and American reactionary cliques are preparing to replace Chiang Kai-shek with Li Tsung-jen at the proper moment. But of what use is this? In the record of his rule over the people and in the eyes of the people, Li Tsung-jen is not only as counter-revolutionary as Chiang Kai-shek but is also Chiang Kai-shek's long-term counter-revolutionary collaborator. The people entertain

---

[19] Broadcast by the North Shensi Radio on May 30, 1948, and transmitted by the Ambassador from Nanking, June 7, 1948.

no illusion whatsoever about him. Therefore, even if the Chinese and American reactionary cliques actually use Li Tsung-jen to replace Chiang Kai-shek, it will also be utterly impossible to deceive the Chinese people.

Of course, the plot of the Chinese and American reactionary cliques will not stop at this. When Li is also incapable of maintaining their rule, they will also feel out Hu Shih or other figures. Under such circumstances, the signboard of "liberalism" recently put up by the Political Science clique's paper "Ta Kung Pao", and the Social Economic Research Association organized under the slogan of the "third road" by T. V. Soong, Chien Chang-chao and Company, and other activities of the same kind, will still parade about and mislead the masses, adopting new poises to preserve the essence of the reactionary cliques rule. Especially when Chiang Kai-shek has collapsed and the main forces of his army have been exterminated or routed, the reactionary clique will further adopt a certain policy of concealment and will even find certain unsteady figures from among the present Anti-Chiang . . . as their protective charm to conceal and rally their forces to wait for what they regard as the proper opportunity for the comeback of reactionary forces. At that time, Chiang Kai-shek, bitterly hated by all, will have fallen from power and the reactionary clique will also adopt a policy of concealment, and it is possible that a part of the people will relax their vigilance. Therefore, today we should tell the people all this beforehand and ceaselessly expose the various plots of the reactionary cliques so as to carry out China's new democratic revolution to the very end.

The new democratic revolution is not only to overthrow thoroughly Chiang Kai-shek's personal rule, but also to overthrow thoroughly the foundation of Chiang Kai-shek's rule, that is: thoroughly eliminate the prerogatives of imperialism in China and the system of China's feudalism and bureaucratic capitalism so that any rule of Chiang Kai-shek's pattern will not permanently revive nor reincarnate.

To point out the correct policy of struggle for the people throughout the country, the Central Committee of the Chinese Communist Party issued slogans for the current situation on May 1st, the very day the bogus "National Assembly" came to a close. These slogans called for a march on Nanking to take alive the bogus president Chiang Kai-shek; consolidation and broadening of the united front against imperialism, feudalism, and bureaucratic capitalism; swift convening of a New Political Consultation Conference by all democratic parties and groups of all people's organizations and all social luminaries to discuss and realize the calling of a People's Congress to establish a Democratic Coalition Government. Timed with the advance of the people's war of liberation and the people's democratic movement, these slogans very clearly map out the path for the Chinese people. Without doubt, the Chinese people must resolutely carry the revolutionary war to the end, for the enemy who unleashed the war has not yet been disarmed. Without doubt, the Chinese people must thoroughly eliminate the rule of imperialism, feudalism, and bureaucratic capitalism because this is the prerequisite of a life of freedom and peace for the people. Also without doubt there can be no "third road" in the life and death struggle between the Chinese people and their enemy. Only two paths exist before China today: either continue to reserve the armed forces and the prerogatives of the people's enemy—this is the line of semi-feudalism, national betrayal, civl war and dictatorship led by the big landlord, big bourgeoise class—or liquidate the armed forces and prerogatives of the people's enemy—this is the people's democratic line of the workers, peasants, independent labourers, intelligentsia, liberal bourgeoise and other patriots against imperialism, feudalism, and bureaucratic capitalism. No matter from what corner they come or what banner they fly, all movements, which in essence preserve the armed forces and prerogatives of the people's enemy, constitute no "third road" but is only another guise of the counter-revolutionary line at the end of its. . . . All persons advocating the liquidation of the armed forces and prerogatives of the people's enemy have only one . . . differing from the counter-revolutionary one. This is the path of new democracy; this is the path of the united front against imperialism, feudalism, and bureaucratic capitalism; this is the path of the new political consultation conference.

The basic characteristics of the present stage of Chinese history determine that China's big landlord, big bourgeoise class, cannot join China's democratic ranks, and that these ranks can only be led by the working class and its political representative, the Chinese Communist Party. The two years of history since the failure of the Political Consultation Conference in 1946, though only a history of two short years, have demonstrated this truth so vividly and fully! Today the Chinese people have, through their own experience, universally come to know this truth. This insures that the old China of the reactionary clique cannot but meet its doom, and the new China of the people cannot but be victorious.

153 (a)

The Ambassador in China (Stuart) to Secretary Marshall

[*May ?*] *1948*

Our best information at the moment is that the Generalissimo has refused to agree to reforms demanded by Ho Ying-chin and has commanded Chang Chun to remain as Premier and form a new Cabinet.

Nevertheless, when I called on the Generalissimo on May 6 he indicated agreement with various points I felt it desirable to raise with him. In the first place, he promised support for Jimmy Yen's reconstruction plan and agreed with me when I enlarged upon the fact that the Communist issue could not be settled merely by military means; that unless there were drastic reforms in government policy convincing the people that their lot was better than it would be under Communist control, no amount of military effort or American aid could be successful. He continued to agree when I expressed my belief in the extreme gravity of the outlook in the military, financial and economic fields, and particularly in respect of morale among the people as well as with the government. The only hope, it seemed to me, lay in radical reform that would convince the people that the government had stopped merely speaking and intended to act. Now that he had been elected President, I said, the constitution was coming into effect, American aid was beginning to arrive, and he had a superlative opportunity to take the requisite leadership and that if he didn't do so now, it might soon be too late for him to play any part in the steps which must inevitably take place. His expression indicated that he understood I had the revolt surrounding Li Tsung-jen in mind. I went on, with the Generalissimo agreeing, that in my opinion the great majority of Chinese, even the more radical student element, did not want China to be communized, but that they were dissatisfied with the present government. It became, therefore, a question of winning this large majority by demonstrating that the government was more modern, up to date, democratic and liberal than the Communists who, I stressed, represented the last vestige of out-moded, totalitarian and dictatorial political organization. As I saw it, and he seemed to agree, the problem was primarily spiritual rather than military or material and that somehow the spirit of the populace and of the troops would have to be aroused or all his plans and all the American assistance would be useless. Mme. Chiang, who was present, agreed most emphatically with this and I believe will exert her influence toward improving the situation.

In response to his request for specific suggestions, I remarked that the Premier's ten-point program seemed to offer a framework for action and that now was the time to give proof that these points were not just a literary essay, but represented an intention of the government which would be implemented without further delay.

The above doesn't sound too hopeful, yet we are afraid it represents the present attitude of the Generalissimo. He will assent, as he did, but we find it difficult to believe that he is any longer capable of the leadership necessary to instill new spirit into the people or that he has any intention of really instituting necessary reforms.

153 (b)

The Ambassador in China (Stuart) to Secretary Marshall

893.00/5–1948

NANKING, *May 19, 1948.*

The Generalissimo is meeting this afternoon with his top advisers in an attempt to find a workable solution to the present Executive Yuan impasse. Among his most active advisers is Chen Li-fu who, since his election as Vice President of the Executive Yuan, has been extremely vocal in expressing his conviction that the primary need is party unity and that thereafter the government can proceed on questions of reform. Chen's views seem to reinforce the growing conviction of the Generalissimo that Chang Chun is not the man to head the new Cabinet because of his inability to provide forceful leadership. The CC-Clique is urging the Generalissimo to name T. V. Soong as president of the Executive Yuan and the Generalissimo appears inclined to go along with this suggestion. Soong has arrived in Nanking for consultations on this question and will probably accept it if the offer is definitely made. Chen is further urging that Ho Ying-chin be made Vice-Premier and that Pai Chung-hsi be retained as Minister of National Defense in order to heal the rift between the Generalissimo and Li, and to draw the latter into active partnership with government. It is impossible to forecast how this manipulation will turn out. Given past performance, the possibility must not be overlooked that this is another skillful manipulation on the part of the CC-Clique to regain its waning hold on government. On the other hand, the possibility must also be kept in mind that Soong, who has been flirting with the CC-Clique ever since his retirement from the premiership, might be able to provide sufficiently strong leadership to keep CC-Clique activities within bounds. The CC-Clique for some months has been attempting vocally to assume leadership of the reform movement. Only a practical test could determine whether this is merely lip service or honest conviction. Furthermore, there is no indication as to whether Li Tsung-jen would accept the line offered him or would remain wary.

In general the situation remains fluid.

STUART

153 (c)

The Ambassador in China (Stuart) to Secretary Marshall

893.00/5–2248

NANKING, *May 22, 1948.*

The inauguration of the new President was held on the morning of May 20 at a simple but impressive ceremony. The Generalissimo delivered a brief inaugural address in which he said nothing to which anyone could take exception and whose content, if carried out, would go a long way toward solving the internal problems of China. The only flaw in the ceremony was that Li Tsung-jen was largely ignored and was kept in the background at the presentation of the Diplomatic Corps.

Meanwhile, the impasse over the Legislative Yuan is entering a new and more serious phase. Chang Chun abandoned all pretense to the office by departing for Chungking May 21. Chen Li-fu had previously informed the Generalissimo that Chang Chun could have no expectation of securing a vote of confidence in the Legislative Yuan. Two leading contenders now are T. V. Soong and Ho Ying-chin, both of whom are uncertain they can command sufficient majority in the Legislative Yuan to persuade them yet to accept office even though Soong is the CC-Clique candidate.

The struggle now seems to have passed beyond the stage of personalities and into the realm of a major rebellion within interior party circles to the leadership of the Generalissimo. The failure of Soong as the CC-Clique candidate to obtain assurances of a large majority is one indication thereof. Another indication is that on May 20, the Generalissimo ordered a certain motion passed by the Central Executive Committee and lost it. He blames Chen Li-fu for this failure and has ordered him to resign from the Central Executive Committee. The Embassy will attempt to ascertain the nature of the motion. The evening of May 20 the Generalissimo entertained the Central Executive Committee at a tea party. Less than two-thirds of the members showed up. Disobedience of such a request, which normally would have been considered as a royal command, combined with the inability to form a Cabinet, is reported to have the Generalissimo in a highly nervous and irresolute state of mind.

The present course of action devised by the CC-Clique has the Generalissimo's approval:

(1) Ho Ying-chin is to be given a final offer of the Premiership and made to make his position very clear. The greatest possible pressure will be used on Ho.

(2) If Ho refuses it will be offered to Soong. He will accept if he feels he can command sufficient majority of the Legislative Yuan.

(3) If Soong refuses, Ho will be ordered to assume it and take his chances with the legislature, thus attempting to force Central Executive Committee opposition to the Generalissimo into the open. Soong might well then be put in charge of administering the American aid program. In the light of developments during the past week, prognostication of future developments is, of course, open to revision without notice.

This intra-party rebellion is doubtless more serious than that which the Generalissimo faced in the election of Li Tsung-jen because it is a rebellion in the inner circle on which the Generalissimo has for years based his strength. If he fails at this juncture it will be difficult for him to re-establish his control. It must also be admitted that Chen Li-fu has given a good account of himself in the face of enormous odds. Confronted with a major revolt throughout the entire length and breath of the party he still holds a major hand and he plays it well. Unlike many other party leaders he is demonstrating ability to play politics in the open as well as behind the scenes.

The activities of Li Tsung-jen during this period are still obscure. As far as can be ascertained at the moment, he seems to be largely passive. This may be partially due to a nervous let-down after a strenuous campaign. It may be also partially due to a weakness of leadership. He has stated privately that he does not know what to do now because the Generalissimo controls the Army, the government finances and the party machine. For a brief period he even appeared to have given some consideration to going to the United States on the grounds that he could accomplish more there than here.

Another development of some importance is the report, apparently true, that General Wang Yao-wu is being relieved of his military command and his governorship of Shantung. He would be a serious loss to the National Government because he is one of the ablest military commanders in China and has had a highly successful and distinguished record as Governor of Shantung, which is his native province. There is one factor against him. It must be known by the Central Government by this time that Wang, for almost a year now, either directly or through trusted lieutenants, has been considering the establishment of an autonomous regime in Shantung under his own leadership; that he has discussed this question with various Americans, and that in recent months he has approached American officials on the possibility of obtaining American financial and military support for his regime should he feel developments in Nanking warrant such action on his part. The situation in Shantung is hardly improved by the possibility that Wang would be succeeded by General Teng Wen-yi who has never commanded troops and has been a conspicuous failure as military spokesman in Nanking, but is a Whampoa man and completely loyal personally to the Generalissimo. Telegram has just been received from the Shantung Provincial Assembly requesting financial and military aid for Shantung apart from that for the National Government.

STUART

153 (d)

The Ambassador in China (Stuart) to Secretary Marshall

893.00/5-2448

NANKING, *May 24, 1948.*

Prior to my departure for a brief visit to Taiwan, the Generalissimo asked me to call on him. I found him in a calmer frame of mind than he had been reported to be on previous days. Madam Chiang was not present, possibly because of the delicacy of her position in view of the possibility that her brother might be named Premier.

I took advantage of the occasion to express a few of my opinions on the current situation in China and what I believed the general course of action should be. I told the Generalissimo that the American people were gravely disturbed over the friction which had arisen in the Nationalist Assembly and which was now becoming increasingly apparent in the Legislative Yuan. I said that now is the time for strong and decisive action and that someone should be appointed as Premier who could undertake such action. The Generalissimo interposed at this moment that he agreed completely and that he had honestly hoped himself to assume the position of Premier and deeply regretted his plans had gone astray.

I then went on to point out that the reform movement which Li Tsung-jen symbolizes represents a new force in China which cannot be quenched; that now is the time for reforms; and that unless the Generalissimo gives it, some one else will. I suggested that the first step should be the dissolution of the CC-Clique. The Generalissimo expressed his general agreement and said he hoped I would feel free at any time to express to him anything I might have on my mind. He said he realized the criticalness of the present position and that much of the future will depend on what happens now. He then went on to say that Chang Chun is out of the question as Premier because he lacks forcefulness. In answer to my query, he ruled out T. V. Soong on grounds he could not receive a majority in the Legislative Yuan and is so desperately needed in Kwangtung. The Generalissimo said he had every expectation that Ho Ying-chin would accept the position.

I asked the Generalissimo if he had any objections to my trip to Taiwan. He replied at once that he did not; if he needed me, he would ask me to return.

Subsequent to this interview, Philip Fugh called on Ho Ying-chin who expressed great surprise at the Generalissimo's confidence that he would accept the post as Premier. Ho said that whereas he was still considering the matter, the question depended in large measure on who would be Minister of Finance. He did not indicate whom he would like to see as Finance Minister though I do know he would not accept Chang Kia-ngau who at present appears to be a strong possibility since he has resigned as Governor of the Central Bank and has been replaced by O. K. Yui.

With the elimination of Chang Chun and T. V. Soong, both of whom have already left Nanking; and in the event that Ho finally refuses, I would venture to suggest the possibility that the position might be offered to Wang Shih-Chieh who commands general respect for his intelligence, integrity and honesty but who would hardly provide strong leadership and has no substantial following in the party.

STUART

153 (e)

The Ambassador in China (Stuart) to Secretary Marshall

893.00/6–2348

NANKING, *June 23, 1948*

The initial reception of Prime Minister Wong Wen-hao and his Cabinet by the Legislative Yuan and the press is highly critical. Wong's administrative report to the Legislative Yuan on June 12 was vague and full of generalities, as were reports of his Ministerial colleagues. No new policies nor specific panaceas for improvement were offered. Comments of legislators on the Yuan floor were violently critical and caustic. Though the ministers were not personally attacked and though the legislators put forward no specific program of their own, their lack of confidence in the Cabinet was apparent. The vernacular press controlled by the CC-Clique also was censorious, and almost no papers offer the Cabinet any support. This position is a faithful reflection of the general public sentiment of disgust with a government which does not govern.

The Premier and the Cabinet are generally regarded as personal retainers of the Generalissimo and attacks on them are viewed as attacks on the President himself. Up to the present the Generalissimo has failed to defend the Cabinet and apparently is willing to let them receive the blame for the continuing deterioration of the government position. The government's inability to control food prices, which has led to rice riots in Chungking, Ningpo and the Yangtze delta towns, is greatly increasing popular discontent and provides critics with additional ammunition which they use unsparingly.

The present Cabinet was a deliberate creation of the Generalissimo who wanted a compliant group through which he could continue to exercise his personal authority over all aspects of government. Under these conditions we do not expect the Cabinet to come forth with any concrete and specific program of its own, nor do we expect the Premier to provide any dynamic or constructive leadership.

Since the Generalissimo refuses to delegate authority, since he still fails to exercise in any positive or constructive way the authority he has concentrated in his own hands and since the Cabinet is so completely subservient to him, we see few, if any, reasons to believe that more efficient and effective government can be anticipated in the near future. And since the Cabinet is so generally regarded as the Generalissimo's personal machine, criticism of its inevitable shortcomings will be visited equally on the Generalissimo, to the further detriment of his personal prestige.

STUART

154

The Ambassador in China (Stuart) to Secretary Marshall [20]

893.00/6–548

NANKING, *June 5, 1948.*

It is with real regret that I find myself compelled to take cognizance publicly of a growingly dangerous situation which affects not only the interests of the United States, but, I am firmly convinced the vital interests of China as well. I am, of course, referring to the campaign against American policy in Japan. I know you will understand that my sorrow at having to do this is all the greater because most of my life has been spent in Chinese academic circles and because the primary object of my life work has been to assist them in some small measure in increasing the welfare and the mature responsibility of Chinese students to themselves and their country.

It is therefore difficult for me to have to admit that the core of anti-American agitation on the question of Japan is coming from the Chinese student groups. I do not pretend to know who initiated this agitation or for what purpose. I have received varying reports as to its origin and intent. Perhaps all reports are partially valid. What I do know is that it is seriously damaging the traditional cordiality between the United States and China and that if it continues it can have most unfortunate results. It is all the more regrettable that this movement should start at a time when the United States is embarking upon a large-scale and serious program to assist China in its present tragic plight. At a time when the American people are being called upon to assist in the rehabilitation of war-torn areas throughout the world and, I should add, are only too glad to do so, they may well wonder when these efforts are greeted by unreasonable and irresponsible attacks on American policy.

I would be most reluctant to believe that university circles which initiate or follow the anti-American agitation really believe the arguments which they use

---

[20] Transmitting the Ambassador's statement of June 4, 1948, concerning anti-American student agitation.

against my country. We are charged with fostering the restoration of Japanese military and economic imperialism. These charges are demonstrably false. Immediately after the victorious conclusion of our war against Japan, the United States on behalf of the Allied Powers who destroyed Japanese power, proceeded to disband the Japanese Army, Navy, Air Force and General Staff. I defy anyone to produce a single shred of evidence that any part of Japanese military power is being restored or that there is any intention on the part of the United States other than to assure that it will never rise again. The basis of Japanese aggression was its overseas empire. It has now lost that empire and cannot regain it without military power. You may rest assured the American people and government will make sure it does not do so.

As for Japanese economic and industrial power, the United States again on behalf of the Allied Powers, proceeded to destroy or dismantle all Japanese war industries. We are now faced with a situation where we must restore enough of Japanese economic life to enable the Japanese people to become self-supporting. No one can expect the American taxpayer to continue indefinitely paying the Japanese bills. Japan must be allowed a chance for self-support or it will be a continuing liability not only to the United States but also to China. An indigent country can never become a peace-loving and democratically-minded people. If it be argued that industry can be converted to war-time purposes, I admit the truth of the allegation. In modern warfare, any production is susceptible of war uses. Food is a war product. Textiles are a war product. Any of the articles of consumption are necessary in modern warfare. It will be our responsibility to insure that these products are used for peaceful purposes. This task will be made immeasurably easier if we cooperate thereon. It will be immeasurably more difficult if we squabble among ourselves.

If it be charged that the revival of Japanese economy will be a threat to Chinese economy, then I deny it. Certainly the demands of the peoples of the world for goods and services are far greater than anything all the countries in the world in the predictable future can hope to satisfy. On the contrary, the indefinite continuation of an indigent Japan will continue to lower the standards of living of the world. The world will be deprived of what Japan can produce. It will continue to be a drain on our already depleted resources. As a hungry and restless people, it will continue to be a threat to peace. Such a situation is made to order for Communism. If we are sincere in our profession, that Communism, in the general interest, must be stopped, then we must remove the causes which encourage Communism.

If those of you who agitate or who participate in the agitation against the United States on the question of Japan disagree with what I have said, then you must be prepared to face the consequences of your actions. If in your hearts you know that I am right, and still continue your agitation for other and secret purposes, then I say to you that it is time you examined your consciences. If by dishonest means you are attempting to accomplish some clandestine purpose, you are not only damaging the United States, you are also damaging your own country. You are also damaging your own standing and reputation as students and intellectuals of China whose best and most honest efforts are so desperately needed today by your country. You are the ones who are in the best position in China to know the truth. If you betray it you also betray yourselves. If you are not true to yourselves then most assuredly you cannot be true to any one or any thing else.

I hardly need protest my affection for Chinese student groups. If my life has not proven that, then it has been a total failure. I trust then that you will take the harsh words I have felt compelled to speak in the spirit in which they are intended. My greatest wish is the peace and welfare of all peoples of the world. Unless China and the United States can approach each other with mutual trust and confidence, that peace and welfare are endangered. I have confidence that the students of China will not knowingly lend themselves to evil purposes or betray the trust which has been placed in them by their country.

At the same time I want to assure you that I am fully aware of how much the Chinese people suffered at the hands of the Japanese and how heroically China resisted aggression. I was a prisoner of the Japanese myself and I know what it meant. I also know that the American people are aware of the tremendous Chinese sacrifices and are deeply grateful for that selfless contribution to the defeat of our common enemy. But I would also say that despite the understandable bitterness of China toward Japan, the best guarantee against a recurrence of the tragedy is wisdom, calmness and unity of purpose. In the present distraught situation of the world, misunderstanding among ourselves is the luxury we can least afford.

Your interests in Japan and those of my country are identical. We do not want a Communist Japan, and our surest method of preventing such a calamity is to enable the Japanese people to earn their own living.

155

The Ambassador in China (Stuart) to Secretary Marshall

893.00/8–2048

NANKING, *August 20, 1948*

Local vernacular press carries following text of order issued August 17 by Executive Yuan:

In rebelling against the nation, the Communist bandits are not only engaged in manslaughter, arson, and pillage by force of arms, but also have set spies, circulated rumors and instigated workers' and students' strikes in the rear. The responsible authorities may not have taken strict precautions or handled the situation in earnest. During the bandit suppression period, preservation of social order and elimination of bandit spies are essential to ensuring the safety of the people and guarding the foundation of the state. Attention is hereby called to the following four points:

(1) In accordance with Article 3 of the Prosecution Law of the Criminal Code, in making arrests according to law judicial and police agencies may search residences and other places without a warrant if there is sufficient evidence for establishing the crime of the accused and if the situation is urgent. But places of military secrecy may not be searched without the permisison of the officer-in-charge.

(2) Liaison will be established with responsible administrative agencies in banning bandit-inspired strikes or other activities interfering with production. Those who disobey the ban will be turned over to the special criminal court for punishment according to law.

(3) Student bodies which interfere with the bandit suppression campaign by calling strikes, staging demonstrations, presenting petitions, and making oral or written propaganda on behalf of the bandits are to be dissolved or prohibited from doing so. Chief offenders will be turned over to the special criminal court for treatment according to law.

(4) Those in charge of government agencies, civic bodies, and schools are responsible for ensuring order within their organizations. When they find their fellow members instigating the activities set forth in (2) and (3), they are to report to the local peace preservation agencies and, insofar as possible, help collect evidence. Those who fail to do so will be punished.

STUART

156 (a)

The Consul at Shanghai (Pilcher) to Secretary Marshall

893.00/6–2448

SHANGHAI, June 24, 1948

According to the press, the City Councilor's meeting for the Sixth Plenary Session was explosively attacking the Central Government, particularly its economic policies. The tone of the first three meetings of the Session was unprecedentedly critical ·of ¡both the Central and local government. Chairman Pan Kung-chan, at the opening meeting on the 21st, is reported to have severely criticized Nanking officials for "blunders, incompetency and apathy" and said they should be held responsible for the economic crises. He is said to have suggested that the Central Government officials refrain from talking before finishing their plans, as senseless talk was causing the recent price upheaval. Pan is also reported to have compared conditions in Shanghai settlement days when residents had more legal protection and self-governing power. Mayor Wu following Pan said he "agreed in principle" with Pan and "agreed 100 percent" with his remarks on economic conditions.

The third day of the meeting of the Council was highlighted with a proposal made by two councillors and supported by one hundred others that application to the Central Government be made to dismiss Finance Minister Wang Yun-wu on the ground of incompetence, as he had made no move to check the steadily deteriorating economic situation. The City police was also under attack for incompetence and corruption. One proposal asked for disbanding of the economic police because it had accomplished nothing towards stabilization of commodity prices and had unjustly harassed the people.

156 (b)

The Ambassador in China (Stuart) to Secretary Marshall

893.00/7–648

NANKING, July 6, 1948.

Within the past month the prestige and authority of the Central Government has sunk to an all time low, emphasized by a military debacle on the Kaifeng front and the collapse of the Chinese dollar on the commodity and foreign exchange markets. From information available to us, it appears that, with the exception of Fu Tso-Yi, Nationalist commanders are avoiding combat and are abandoning their positions when combat threatens. The Chinese Supreme Headquarters in Nanking admits that Kaifeng was taken by Communists without resistance from the defending garrison and that the attacking force was even joined by certain Nationalist units. Similar conditions appear to characterize recent military activities in southern Shantung and we are forced to the conclusion that, except in isolated instances, Government armies can no longer be counted on to fight.

Deterioration in the economic sphere is also noteworthy. The new cost of living index, issued just after depreciation in the value of the dollar, is arousing protests of wage earners and salaried groups who argue correctly that their incomes, as based on this index, will be insufficient to permit them to purchase the necessities of life. While their argument is valid, an increase in the index to a point where their basic needs would be satisfied would bankrupt both Government and private enterprise. Commodity prices are stable at the moment but there is little or nothing to prevent other spectacular jumps, with the consequent increase in discontentment and civil unrest.

In this situation, and as has been the case previously, the Government appears to have no remedies. The Military appears unable to stabilize any of the fighting fronts or restore the situation there to the Government's advantage. Civil officials admit frankly that they do not know what to do to curb the present violent inflation.

As we have reported, the Generalissimo is generally and directly blamed for this state of affairs and is criticized for his inability to take any effective action to cope with the situation. He is doubtlessly aware of this criticism and of its implication. He responds to it only by trying to safeguard his own position through placing individuals on whose loyalty he can personally count, in positions of trust, regardless of the fact that these individuals have long records of incompetence or corruption or both.

It is this failure of the Generalissimo to use his authority for the improvement of conditions, that forces provincial military and civil leaders to consider adoption of regional understandings and formation of regional political associations against the day when the government in Nanking either falls or loses the last vestiges of its authority. We have received reports from two independent sources that the purpose of General Li Tsung-jen's present visit to north China is to consult with Fu Tso-yi, Wei Li-haung, Wang Yao-wu, and certain other northern leaders, on the formation of a third government which would control northern China. It has been reported that this government will be independent of both Nationalist and Communist control, that it will reach some sort of an agreement with the Communists and that if necessary, it will include "some Communists." We have reported in the statement of T. V. Soong that he is adopting military measures for the protection of the south and his determination to defend that area should disaster overtake the Generalissimo. Also, there are indications that a provisional government which Marshal Li Chi-sen states he intends forming in the near future, may be essentially regional in character, comprising several provinces in the southwest.

As we noted above, regionalism and particularism is the natural response of those who would preserve, or make a new place for themselves, as the authority and power of the present Government inevitably declines. It is impossible to say what event would precipitate a break between the Generalissimo and any potential regional leader. This could result from an overt move by the Kuomintang Revolutionary Committee or from any comparable occurrence detrimental to the Generalissimo's prestige. In any event, our role in this situation is not a happy one. In the popular mind, we are associated with the Government and are regarded as the principal means by which it keeps itself in power. We are asked with increasing frequency why we adopt the policy of perpetuating in the power a government seemingly bent on its own destruction and facile only in paving the way for the spread of Communism. While we answer such queries by referring to the Generalissimo's adamant stand against Communists, we are forced to admit that it is a stand in name only. A continuation of his regime will almost certainly either plunge the entire country into profound chaos whereupon the Communists will seize power, or result in the seizure of power by local leaders anxious to safeguard themselves.

156 (c)

The Consul General at Tientsin (Smyth) to Secretary Marshall

893.00/7–1448

TIENTSIN, *July 14, 1948*

On my recent return to Tientsin after five months' absence, I found the local Chinese military, civil leaders, press, and many civilians increasingly bitter over the National Government's policy of favoring the south against the north. They consider that North China has been deserted by the National Government, and feel that this area has been discriminated against as regards to relief supplies, military supplies, allotment of foreign exchange, and other ways.

Present opinion among the Chinese here is that the National Government is making a deliberate effort to create the impression with American authorities that North China is lost and should not be considered in any American aid plans. The Chinese here do not concur in this defeatist theory. They consider the military situation of North China much better than Honan, Shantung, Hupeh, et cetera. Particularly since the Fu Tso-yi assumption of control six months ago, military operations against the Communists have been conducted with more ability and success than in other areas. They state that competent military leaders in North China have been unable to conduct full effort against the Communists, due to lack of cooperation, funds, and military supplies from the Central Government.

Chinese officials here assert that North China can be held against the Communists if given a fair proportion of American economic and military aid before it is too late. They point out that military aid should accompany economic aid to the Kailan mines and it would be more secure if the mines and railways have more adequate military protection. According to these Chinese, Fu Tso-yi has raised and partially trained 100,000 local militia in North China, but they have no arms; they say if arms for this number can be supplied, North China can be held against Communists.

Chinese here mentioned reported plans to use American aid to develop and improve mines, railways in South China, harbors, docks, Canton and Shanghai power plants, water works, industries in South China, and comment on apparent aid to North China not be neglected and be given a fair share. The recent visit of the Stillman group to Tientsin has given some encouragement, but the Chinese here feel that the National Government will block aid to North China unless American pressure is applied. Chinese here consider that if North China is lost, the rest of China will follow sooner or later, also, if North China is lost, due to deliberate refusal, the National Government would meet a bitter resistance in a future effort to recapture that area.

North China people in general, do not want Communism and would prefer to continue allegiance to the National Government if this Government would assist North China and effect some reforms. The Chinese here feel that if the National Government continues to refuse help, North China will have to decide on the future policy, whether to continue to resist or endeavor to make other arrangements. Mere government promises to help will be futile, only concrete action in the form of aid visibly arriving in North China will be effective.

During Stillman's trip to Tientsin, July 7 to 9, he visited the Kailan mines and had discussions with the Mayor of Tientsin and representatives of North China railways, power and other utilities, and Tangku new harbor, also Chinese and American businessmen. His visit and proposed visit of Mr. Lapham, have created a good impression and raised the hopes of North China.

The Tientsin American Chamber of Commerce is sending a memorandum to Lapham, urging strongly aid for North China. Copies are being forwarded to the Department, Embassy, Shanghai, and Peiping.

156(d)

The Ambassador in China (Stuart) to Secretary Marshall

893.00/7–1748

NANKING, *July 17, 1948*

I have the honor to report that on the morning of July 16 I called on President Chiang Kai-shek with the intention of giving him the only advice that seemed to me to have any promise in the present extremely critical situation. He asked me if I had any news and I replied that the news which seemed to me most important was the Communist general meeting to be held next month with the idea of a coalition government on the program, and the news reaching the Embassy from Hong Kong that Li Chi-shen was planning to start his Southwestern Provincial Government in the quite near future with the intention of proposing a coalition with the Communists. These developments taken in connection with the Chinese Communist broadcasts denouncing Tito and others openly committing themselves to world communism under the dictatorship of the Kremlin all supplied the background for the suggestion I had come to make. This was that he summon a small group of leaders who were generally respected and urge them to sink all personal and political differences in view of the real danger China was now facing, which was the loss of her national independence after the Communists triumphed. It had ceased to be merely an issue of Kuomintang factional politics as against Chinese Communists but was also part of a struggle between the fundamental principles of democracy and freedom on the one side and the domination of a minority controlled from Moscow on the other. The revolution and the war against Japan had been fought to win national independence which was now again jeopardized. In such a crisis he and all others ought to put the nation above all minor issues. I mentioned by name Fu Tso-yi, Li Tsung-jen, Pai Chung-hsi, and Li Chi-shen. As to this last, he should be given the opportunity and if he failed to comply on such a basis he should be denounced as preferring Russian communism to national independence. I hoped that this would result in a joint declaration appealing to all who wanted a free nation to face the realities and support the cause. The financial crisis and the economic hardships were very real, but even these were less important than the basic issue. It should be thought of primarily as a war of ideas and he ought to beat the others to it with skillfully prepared publicity. He said that he agreed in principle and would think it over very carefully, and added that he had been planning for a conference to reorganize the Kuomintang. I said that I was quite familiar with this but that my concern was more in personal relationships among the outstanding leaders and that this ought to be as dramatic as possible in order to convince the public.

He then asked about American opinion and I told him that Governor Dewey's announcement about increased aid to China had produced quite a bit of unfavorable editorial and other comment. I had with me the latest USIS bulletin on this subject, which I gave his secretary for reference.[21] I added, however, that if there should be a movement of the kind I was advocating which showed vitality, it would help to neutralize the feeling in the United States that this Government had been too weakened to make any assistance to it of much use. I told him that after all the greatest help that America could give was not money nor military advice but the dynamic force of our ideals which were shared by a great many Chinese but were being misrepresented and replaced by those of the Soviet Union.

He said that Americans tended to overrate the importance of Li Chi-shen, to which I replied that the man himself and his immediate followers need not be taken too seriously but that the whole nation was desperately anxious for peace and that with this popular mood any movement that held out the hope of peace through an understanding with the Communists might find more hearty support than he expected. It seemed to me, therefore, that whatever he did ought to be done with as little delay as possible. He said again that he would think the matter over carefully.

In attempting to draw conclusions from this interview the dominant impression is one of futility. I seriously question whether President Chiang has that quality of greatness which would enable him to assemble those leaders not already completely subservient to him and so to treat them as comrades as to draw out their own ideas in reaching a consensus of opinion and a group decision. The habits of twenty years, reinforced by Chinese traditional concepts, would be hard to alter. If he makes the attempt to cooperate with such a body he probably could not bring himself to do so graciously and with the unreserved sharing of minds which alone would win their confidence and impress the public. Any jointly issued statement would reflect these limitations and be unconvincing. He would also tend to draw in those upon whom he can depend which would further vitiate the effect. But nothing less than such a unified appeal, dramatic in its note of sincerity and urgency, would startle the now apathetic or disillusioned people of the country into realizing that something new and inspiring was actually happening on the highest level of their Government. Any effort to urge him further than I have done would either have to imply much more American aid than is possible or would over-persuade him to relinquish his own judgment. In either case he would cease to be true to himself and the results would almost certainly be unfortunate. It would seem, therefore,

---

[21] The following is the excerpt from the USIS Bulletin of July 17 (Foreign Service Digest—"Not for Publication") referred to by Ambassador Stuart in his conversation with the Generalissimo :

"CHINA : Gov. Dewey's recent criticism of the Truman Administration for its alleged 'Niggardly' aid to China and his assertion that the U. S. should provide 'far greater assistance' to preserve free China against the Communists has been echoed by a number of commentators. Disturbed by reports of increasing Communist activity throughout Southeast Asia, these observers contend China is 'bulwark of stability in the Far East and the only safeguard possible against Soviet expansion' (Manchester, N. H., Union). Criticism of U. S. policy also comes from Far Eastern expert Owen Lattimore and Henry Wallace.

"On other hand, some despair of pouring more American dollars and arms into China, arguing that its economy is 'floundering' and its leaders 'corrupt'. 'The rat hole in Asia is even more capacious than that in Europe', said the Chicago Tribune. 'Mr. Dewey had better indulge in a little reflection before he starts stuffing dollars into both ends of the hole'. And the Christian Century speculated that while the Republicans 'will undoubtedly have widespread backing in calling for more aid to China, unless their proposals for extending such aid are clearly outlined, they may do harm rather than good'."

that he must be allowed to go his own way, modified to be sure to some extent by suggestions from others, or that sooner or later there will be a movement which will force him out of his present ascendancy. He seems unable to think of Communism as an extreme form of social unrest which cannot be extirpated by the combination of military force and gracious compassion which he thinks to be the method taught by Chinese history. It is tragic that the very qualities of grimly inflexible determination and enduring courage which fitted him preeminently for incarnating the popular will to resist Japan are now in some real sense a hindrance to him in problems calling for very different mental processes.

157 (a)

The Ambassador in China (Stuart) to Secretary Marshall

893.515/8–2348

NANKING, *August 23, 1948*

In summary, we can find no basis for optimism regarding the Gold Yuan's future.

The Cabinet is staking its life on the success of its currency and economic measures. If we assume vigorous, ruthless and effective Government action against hoarders, black marketeers and cheaters (in whose hands control of the wealth of the country largely lies), it would still seem that the most this program can accomplish is three or four month's surcease from the upward flight of prices. In fact, there is surprisingly frank admission in official circles that the Government's eyes are glued to a sympathetic Republican Congress in January and that this program is a plank thrown across the intervening chasm.

The only important, concrete and immediate effect of the currency reform is the invigorating effect on exports which legalizing the black market rate should produce. It is also true that the physical inconvenience of lugging around bales of paper money is removed. Otherwise, the basic factors seem to us to be unchanged. The assets which are announced as backing the present currency are the same assets which, in theory at least, underlay the Chinese National Currency. The Government's budgetary deficit, which is what keeps the printing presses rolling out paper, remains with us, and even given maximum economy where economy is possible, the deficit will of necessity remain unmanageable as long as war goes on.

The measures appear calculated to take advantage of the dramatic effect on the Chinese public of the physically new currency notes. It is probable that this is sufficient temporarily to reduce the velocity in circulation calculated by the Central Bank for early August at a rate approximating 17 times per month. Simultaneously, the Central Bank and Central Trust are reported to be releasing stocks of commodities in Shanghai and Canton, particularly cotton yarn, and restricting bank credit. The combined effect of these measures should at least temporarily stabilize prices and thereby reduce the demand for dollars.

The remainder of the program as it is now constituted consists largely of declarations against: (1) increase in prices of goods and services over the August 19 levels; (2) hoarding of commodities; (3) publication of black market prices of gold and silver foreign exchange or of "daily necessities"; (4) payment of wages and salaries on a cost-of-living index basis; (5) lock-outs of strikes.

Declarations were also made requiring of all natural and juristic persons: (1) surrender of gold, silver and foreign currency held in China to the Central Bank for Gold Yuan notes of, at option of holder, for purchase of Chinese Government

United States dollar gold bonds of 1947, or for dollar deposit with the Central Bank to be drawn for payment of licensed imports, etc.; (2) sale of all gold produced in China to the Central Bank; (3) registration of foreign exchange assets held abroad by Chinese nationals including current and fixed deposits, currencies, gold, stocks, bonds, debentures, land titles, insurance policies, etc.; (4) upon registration of the foregoing, transfer of such assets to the Central Bank. The enforcement of item four aided by the provision of payment of 40 percent in the former's fee.

The announced reserve behind the currency of $200 million is gold, silver and foreign currency does not in fact exist in that amount. Already there is evidence of public skepticism of this part of the program.

As previously reported, the regulation limits the total gold yuan issue to two billion, equivalent approximately to ten times the present note issue. The difference between the amount needed to replace outstanding CNC and NEC will be used by the Central Bank to meet the continuing budget deficit, which there will be, even in the promised increase in tax collections and other revenue, and a reduction of expenditures, are forthcoming. Unless an extremely drastic decrease in the velocity of circulation occurs, there is no possibility apparent that the Chinese economy can absorb such an increase within the next few months without accelerating the inflation. Out payments of additional gold yuan will be largely through wage and salary payments. No significant increase in production is anticipated and imports are to be cut a minimum of 25 percent.

The black market, particularly for gold bars and dollars cannot be eliminated by fiat. Assuming the regulations achieve price stability and a reduction in the demand for dollars for the maintenance of value and liquidity of wealth, there can be only slight weakening of the demand for dollars arising from the flight of capital from areas of military and political insecurity, and for payment of unlicensed imports. This demand alone is sufficient to create black markets for dollars which must be at a premium over official rates and which inevitably will pull prices upward as well.

Against possible deflationary influences arising from the contraction of the money supply and the reduction in velocity, off-setting inflationary factors are reduction of imports, undervaluation of the Gold Yuan in terms of the dollar by 10 to 20 percent, inertia of previously rising prices, reluctance of small entrepreneurs and farmers to accept the psychological effect of the prices of their goods and services amounting to a few Gold Yuan cents when they were previously expressed in millions, and finally, the difficulties of enforcement. A real danger exists that these inflationary forces may go out of control at which time all confidence in the currency would be lost, since the Chinese Government has promised so much in attendant publicity.

157 (b)

Secretary Marshall to the Chinese Minister for Foreign Affairs (Wang)[22]

893.50 Recovery/8–2548

Thank you for your message[23] forwarded to me by Ambassador Stuart. I have just received information regarding the emergency financial and economic measures proclaimed by President Chiang and am now having a careful study

---

[22] Transmitted to Ambassador Stuart on Aug. 28, 1948.
[23] Message of Aug. 25, 1948 ; not printed.

made of them. I am gratified at your determination, as well as that of your colleagues, to enforce measures designed to help meet China's serious economic problems and view sympathetically the measures of self-help taken by the Chinese Government.

I look forward to seeing you at the United Nations Assembly in Paris and to having the opportunity of discussions on these and several others matters. My warm regards to you.

157 (c)

The Ambassador in China (Stuart) to Secretary Marshall

893.50/10–1548

NANKING, *October 15, 1948*

The China August 19 economic reform appears now to be hastening to its denouement. Efforts and gestures of the last two months may well soon be forgotten and will be back on the basis of the open printing press and all but the open hedging and the speculation in foreign exchanges and commodities. (The black-market trading is now out of hand.) With few exceptions, as public utilities are fixed, the prices are fictions. In Shanghai, where enforcement started off spectacularly and where control has been most stringent, there is now a noticeable lack of zeal and decreasing effectiveness on the part of the police. The several really big names who were early arrested are still in confinement but their trials are dragging on through protracted adjournments and appeals. Chiang Ching-kuo's heralded plans for an industrial resurgence, the "second phase" of the August 19 program, have just been announced; they are uninspiring and follow the same old pattern of "conservation of foreign exchange" and the concentration of authority in the central trust and the trade guilds. The accompanying registration of industrial commodities and the inspection of warehouses are tapering off with no apparent results.

The China note issue is now probably in the neighborhood of Gold Yuan 1.25 billion which represents a quantity of money say five times as great as that in circulation on August 19. This money is not going back to the government in taxes nor into the production enterprise but rather is accumulating and idle in the cities building up the inflationary pressure which has recently been evidenced by:

1. Shanghai's last week retail buying spree which has now spread to other cities stripping shops of their exposed goods;

2. Increasing unavailability in all cities of daily necessities except under the counter and at prices far above the fixed levels;

3. Short-term interest rates are so low as to be practically negligible by Chinese standards (i. e. 4 percent per month);

4. Reestablishment of "organized" black markets in gold bullion and United States currency.

In Peiping and Tientsin where police surveillance has been only nominal, gold is selling for Gold Yuan 1,000 per ounce and United States dollars at Gold Yuan 16 compared to the respective official quotations of Gold Yuan 200 and Gold Yuan 4. In Canton the Hong Kong dollar is up in the past week to Gold Yuan 1.25 as compared to the official .75. In Shanghai where to date the operators have been most circumspect, there is now a good volume of business in currency at Gold Yuan 6 to 7 with TTs bringing about 20 percent premium; the shopkeepers are beginning to again quote and surreptitiously to accept United States dollars; the volume of telephone calls is this week picking up showing the resumption of black-market transactions as pretty much on a "normal" basis.

With the concurrent discouraging military developments, it seems to us impossible that the government much longer can continue to imitate Canute before the economic tide. It appears equally unlikely that it can publicly abandon the program on which so much was staked. What is more likely is that we are seeing the slackening of the pretence of enforcement and a yielding full rein to economic forces which at the moment are so precariously held in check.

158

The Consul General at Shanghai (Cabot) to Secretary Marshall

893.00/11–248

SHANGHAI, *November 2, 1948*

STATEMENT BY CHIANG CHING-KUO NOVEMBER 1, 1948

After past seventy days of my work I feel that I have failed to accomplish the duties which I should have accomplished. Not only did I not consummate my plan and mission but in certain respects I have rather deepened the sufferings of the people which they experienced in course of execution of my task.

I will never shift to others any responsibility which should be borne by me. I will never give up my political platform just because of setbacks I have sustained. I firmly believe that direction I have pointed out as regards "whither Shanghai" is absolutely correct.

Today aside from petitioning to government for punishment so as to clarify my responsibility I wish to take this opportunity of offering my deepest apology to citizens of Shanghai. But in so doing I do not want to be accorded an understanding by them. I only mean to point out to the people here the responsibility which I should bear. I sincerely wish the citizens of Shanghai to use their own strength to prevent unscrupulous merchants, bureaucrats, politicians and racketeers from controlling Shanghai. I firmly believe that a bright future lies ahead for Shanghai.

159

Editorial from the "Chung Yang Jih Pao," November 4, 1948 [24]

893.00/11–548

"LOSE NO TIME IN WINNING THE PEOPLE'S CONFIDENCE"

Recent military reverses in the Northeast are facts which the Government no longer tries to hide and everybody is suffering terribly from the new high prices. The masses of people live under a feeling of fear and are pursued relentlessly by difficult living conditions. Such facts are so undeniably true that they can no longer be ignored just because some people find them unpleasant to the ear, nor can they be white-washed by beautiful words.

At this moment when the nation's fate is flickering, and when the people are suffering terribly, what comfort and hope is there for them? The special privileged classes still enjoy their privileges, and the people can do nothing to them. Those plutocrats who have made their money because of personal or political relations, are either having a nice time abroad, or keeping right on with their

---

[24] Transmitted by Ambassador Stuart from Nanking, Nov. 5, 1948.

activities in fleecing the people. Even now nothing can be done to these public enemies of the people who are able accomplices of the Communists. No one has applied political pressure on them to make them disgorge their money to finance bandit suppression and to relieve the people. Nobody even dares to touch them ever so slightly. Nepotism rides on just as it has always done and the masses of people have no right to say anything. What are we going to do with national affairs like that, with each lao pa hsin with a bellyful of resentment? If nothing is done to release a fraction of that resentment in the bosoms of the 400 million people who are the masters of the country, how can we face the soul of our National Father who devoted his entire life to helping the nation and helping the people? How can we face the souls of our brave warriors who died for the revolution? And how can we face the suffering people who are our brethren?

In the process of bandit suppression, most people pay attention only to equipment and to the methods of combating Communists—in short, to tangible factors only. No emphasis is given to the spiritual factor, particularly political reform. We should all know that "military affairs are only an elongation of political affairs." How can we have satisfactory military conditions if our political affairs are not healthy to begin with? If our politics are not solid and bubbling with life, how can our military affairs be satisfactory? The present state of affairs should be sufficient to make us thoroughly realize that if we want to eradicate the Communists and retrieve the present unfavorable military conditions we should, while it is important to strengthen the tangible equipment of our army, tackle political reform which will give strength to our army. What does this mean exactly?

In the second half of the 19th Century, the Communists enjoyed considerable power in Germany. What did Germany do to cope with the situation? Dr. Sun Yat-sen told us that Bismarck boldly decided to adopt national socialism, and took over from the hands of the Communists their most tantalizing issues. As a result, the Communists could do nothing in Germany. This proves that Bismarck was an able statesman. China today is experiencing troubles unprecedented in seriousness since the Tai Ping Rebellion. Of course our present troubles are enhanced by international intrigue, but we must admit that fundamentally it is because of the many defects that exist in our social system. While the essential purpose of the Communists is to grasp political power, on the surface they capitalize on these social defects in order to attract the people to their banner. This explains why Communist eradication has been such a difficult task. If we want to eliminate the Red menace, we must do what Bismarck did in coping with the German Communists; take over from the hands of the Communists all those tantalizing issues. At present, a handful of people are enjoying all the privileges. They live snobbishly and luxuriously. They do not have to part with one farthing. They will not yield one single man to serve in the army. The entire burden of military service and contribution of food falls on the shoulders of the poverty-stricken masses. How can one feel that it is just? How can we prevent our opposers from using this as an excellent pretext?

With our national affairs as they are at the present, it is imperative that we sacrifice the handful of people to help the masses. Only by doing so can we retrieve the situation. The final test as to whether we are revolutionary or anti-revolutionary lies in our choice of ways: whether we will go along with the masses, or with the handful of people. If we choose to walk with the small minority, then no matter how loudly we shout our revolutionary slogans we are *de facto*, anti-revolutionary. If we choose to walk with the masses, even if we do not speak of being revolutionary the lao pa hsing will know that we are revolutionary. If we can truly rule the country with a heart absolutely free from selfishness, employ officials because of their merits, keep the villains out of our way, remove all officials who do harm to the people, severely punish those who fleece the people by virtue of their power, and transfer the burden now resting on the masses to the shoulders of the plutocrats, we are sure that the people will feel that a new era has indeed dawned—the morale of the troops will bolster like magic. What is this small task of eradicating the Communist bandits?

Giving full allowance for the worst, the area that lies south of the Yangtze River is big enough to contain more than ten European nations and has a population of more than 200 million. There is easy access to the sea, there is an abundance of all kinds of products and adequate transportation facilities. Compared to the time of the Northern Expedition, conditions today are far more favorable. Why then should there be pessimism? This is because something is fundamentally wrong with ourselves. If we can gain full control and make full use of the manpower and material resources within this large tract of land, we have more than the strength we need in eliminating the Communists. However, the key to the full mobilization of this manpower and material resources lies in our winning of the people's confidence and we must realize that the people's confidence cannot be won by the mere issuance of an official order on a sheet of paper. It can only be revived by having the responsible parties of the Government do several things which will remove the feeling of resentment. Facts must be used to prove absence of selfishness and that bandit suppression is not for the purpose of protecting the interests of the privileged classes but for the protection of territorial integrity, freedom and democracy for the people, and our history and culture. If we can accomplish this we are sure to expect a sudden change in the situation.

Waste no time in winning the people's confidence. This is our last chance.

160

The Ambassador in China (Stuart) to Secretary Marshall

893.00/11–148

NANKING, *November 1, 1948*

The following is the full text of two articles twice broadcast by the North Shensi Chinese Communist radio on October 30 and 31:

The American State Department and American espionage organization are jointly undertaking a big plot to destroy national liberation movements of China and various countries of Asia, according to reliable reports obtained by well-informed quarters in Shanghai.

To explain the necessity for this plan, its framers emphasize in their report to Truman the "menace" to America of peoples liberation movements in Asia, especially China. The report holds that "Chinese Communist-controlled areas" are deciding the fate of Communism in Asia. Describing Chinese liberated areas, the report says that for the first time in the history of China, the Chinese people now have a really clean and honest government. Agrarian reform there has not only satisfied the demands of peasants, but has also solved many hitherto unsolved economic problems in "Communist-controlled areas". As a result, the political system there has become a highly effective organization, the report says.

The report admits the complete failure of American economic and military aid to Chinese reactionaries. Economic and military aid to China cannot transform soldiers unwilling to fight into troops with combat power, the report says. In its conclusion the report holds that after the end of World War II, the situation in Asia has become a "powerful and deadly menace" to Western Colonial Powers, first of all to American positions, at a time when America's need for Asia has become more pressing than at any period in the past. The report says that loss of position in Asia will bring with it irreparable and crushing blows to America. It points out that Asia's social life has entered an era of great events and only a carefully thought out plan of action can counteract it.

The report proposes a plan for the setting up of a joint political organization in Washington, especially devoted to opposing the so-called Communistic activities in Asia. The organization is to include departments for work in various parties and groups and trade unions, military work, work among students and women, and espionage and intelligence activities.

The tasks of this joint political organization are stipulated as follows: (1) use all possible means to support "legal government" in various countries; (2) organize and give financial backing to "center parties and groups" to split and destroy national movements; (3) strive to reach understanding with elements with Leftist leanings in Socialist parties; (4) develop anti-Communist activities in trade unions and peasant organizations; (5) stir up discord between Leftist leaders and destroy their prestige; (6) stir up and utilize friction between national groups especially in India, Amman, Burma and Malaya; (7) actively absorb renegades from peoples movements in various countries to do work; (8) gather and study intelligence of peoples government movements.

It is stipulated that the above work is to be under the unified leadership of United States Ambassadors in various countries. The Shanghai report states that this American plot will be linked up with recent American measures in China and Japan. A central espionage organization participated in by American and Japanese spies has recently been set up in MacArthur's staff headquarters in Japan. This organization specifically undertakes disruption of Japan's democratic organizations and opposition to leaders of democratic movement. Many Japanese secret police agents participate in this organization. Among them is the notorious General Arisue. On American instructions, a society of retired Japanese servicemen is still carrying on secret activities, and has established an organization for the specific purpose of disrupting democratic movements.

A China office of U. S. Strategic Services has been set up in Shanghai to collaborate with Kuomintang secret police organizations to destroy any democratic movement in China. This office of U. S. Strategic Services has recently shipped large quantities of radio sets, radio location detectors, and cameras to China to be used for espionage work. American espionage organizations have worked out a specific plan to destroy democratic movements in China. This plan has been approved by Leighton Stuart and Chiang Kai-shek. The organization to execute this plan has decided to set up its headquarters in Nanking, and its local organizations in Manchuria, North China, Central China and Southeast China.

The second article begins: The following is the full text of an important New China News Agency editorial entitled "China and Asia Friends of American People, Bitter Enemies of American Reactionaries."

Today we published a report from Shanghai on the fact that American reactionaries are actively employing every conspiratorial means of disrupting national democratic movements of China and Asia. We have frequently reported facts on oppression, aggression, and armed intervention of American imperialism against peoples of China and Asia.

What is new about this report is:

(1) American reactionaries admit that peoples revolutionary movements of China and Asia have obtained support of broad masses of people. They admit that government, born of the peoples revolution, is truly loyal to the people and very effective.

(2) American reactionaries regard obtaining of due and sacred rights by peoples of China and Asia a "powerful and deadly menace," thus proving how thoroughly the American Government has scrapped its promise of "respecting the right of all peoples to choose their form of government" in Atlantic Charter of August 1941, and also thus proving that American reactionaries are mortal enemies of the people of China and Asia.

(3) American reactionaries admit that the reactionary governments of China and Asia are rotten to the core, so that even such enormous military and economic aid as given by the United States to the Kuomintang Government in China cannot block the victorious development of peoples revolutionary movements.

(4) Under the above conditions, American reactionaries consider that they can now no longer rely on open "legal" methods to save reactionary rule and colonial systems in China and Asia from extinction, but must rely on illegal methods which cannot meet the public eye—methods of secret police organizations. As prescription for prolonging the life of imperialism, American reactionaries have decided to rely on the Gestapo methods of Hitler and Himmler, and to cooperate with the darkest forces of China, Japan and various countries of Asia.

The stupidity of the American Government's reactionary plan is obvious. Himmler could not prolong Hitler's rule. Secret police aid decidedly cannot solve problems that no military or economic aid can solve. Strengthening the activities of American secret police organizations in China and various countries of Asia can only accelerate the fall of ruling blocs in these countries into abysses of isolation and disintegration. However, the peoples of China and Asia should draw important lessons from the vicious schemes of the American Government.

Since the American secret police scheme stresses provocations within the camp of the Left, it behooves the camp of the Left to answer with further consolidation of its own unity.

Since the American secret police scheme stresses buying up "political parties of the center," and developing the "anti-Communist" movement, it behooves those who have illusions about the middle road to abandon their illusions, reject all "anti-Communist" inducements, and to be on guard against the danger of playing into the hands of imperialist conspirators in an off-guard moment. At a time when Chiang Kai-shek, America's number one running dog in China, is bankrupt and useless and it is decided to replace him with the number two running dog, Li Tsung-jen, people self-styled "in the center" should examine their conduct carefully to avoid falling into the trap of American imperialism. This moment is probably very near at hand. Since the American secret police plan stresses utilization of discord among various nationalities, it behooves all oppressed nationalities, and especially various nationalities of multi-national countries, firmly to abandon all kinds of mistaken narrow nationalist thinking for the sake of the common struggle against imperialism. Since the American secret police plan stresses utilization of renegades and spies, of espionage, it behooves all revolutionary organizations to redouble their vigilance and to strengthen the fight against spies, so that all these skulking forces are brought out into the light of day, where they are powerless to realize their schemes.

There will still be difficulties in the way of liberation movements of the peoples of China and Asia. Courage which blasts path through thorny difficulties, and the caution of these who walk on the brink of perilous chasms, are needed to attain our objective; but if only we can act in this manner, we will certainly be able to attain our objective.

American reactionaries in their scheme regard the peoples of China and Asia as their bitter enemies and regard liberation of peoples of China and Asia as a "powerful and deadly menace" to them. This is because American reactionaries wildly think of making the peoples of China and Asia their permanent colonial slaves. But the peoples of China and Asia will never be enemies of American peoples. American reactionaries, Truman, Dewey and their ilk, have received and will continue to receive "irreparable and crushing blows" from the peoples of China and Asia. The America of the people, however, the America of Wallace and the Progressive Party, and the America of laborers and the Communist Party of the United States of America has obtained, and will continue to obtain, the friendship of the peoples of China and Asia. No matter whether American reactionaries like it or not, the peoples of China and Asia will ultimately achieve liberation, while those of American reactionaries in various countries and American reactionaries themselves, will eventually meet their doom. All schemes and conspiracies of American imperialism will, of necessity, crumble to pieces, whereas the friendship of the peoples of China and Asia and America will live forever.

STUART

161

The Ambassador in China (Stuart) to Secretary Marshall

893.00/8–1048

NANKING, August 10, 1948

1. Military: The Communists continue to win the civil war. They have retained the initiative with all the advantage given by the offensive and government troops just do not seem to have the will or the ability to fight. There are many reports of defections to the Communists but none from Communist ranks. Occupying as they do most of north China east of Sian and north of the Yangtze River except for a few scattered urban centers such as Peiping and Tientsin and certain lines of communication the Communists now appear intent on removing the last vestiges of government strength from Shantung Province, a prelude possibly to full-scale attack south to Nanking or possibly to an all-out attack on Peiping-Tientsin area. In Central China south of the Yangtze scattered Communist bands operate throughout the countryside creating confusion and disorder with the obvious intent of further weakening the government and preparing the way for some future large-scale operation. In South China though less active Communist guerrilla units operate more or less at will and the government has no forces to employ against them.

It is a gloomy picture and one would expect the government to clutch at any means of improving the situation. Nevertheless it ignores competent military advice and fails to take advantage of military opportunities offered. This is due in large part to the fact that government and military leadership continue to deteriorate as the Generalissimo selects men on the basis of personal reliability rather than military competence. In the distribution of desperately needed military supplies men of proven military competence such as Fu Tso-yi are given low priority and are almost left to fend for themselves. Long contemplated plans for training new armies and replacements are not being implemented or are moving too slowly materially to affect the situation in the coming desperate months.

There is an awareness of the desperateness of the military situation yet no evidence of a will or capability to cope with it.

2. Economic: The inflationary spiral continues at an accelerated pace. Prices have become astronomical and their rise so rapid that the government has been unable to print sufficient money to meet day-by-day needs with the result that barter is becoming more and more the rule. Prices increasingly are quoted either in US dollars, silver or gold. In the interior silver dollars are coming back to use. Thus government has introduced measures to control inflation but the effects have been only temporary and palliative. The fact is that the government in the absence of assured continuing and massive loans from the United States cannot hope to find an answer as long as circumstances require the maintenance of the present military establishment. A renewed and concerted attack on the periphery of the central problem now impends but at best it can only provide a breathing spell.

3. Psychological: After years of war and destruction the all-consuming urge of the people today, and this includes both low and high ranking members of the government and Communist areas as well, is for peace. This urge becomes all the more insistent as most people can see no ray of hope under present conditions. A spirit of defeatism is prevalent throughout the country reaching even men of cabinet rank. Almost without exception there is no longer faith that the present government can bring a return to even a bearable standard of living without some radical reorganization. With this frame of mind a cessation of hostilities is desired at almost any price. There is an overwhelming desire for peace yet the Generalissimo wants only military victory over the Communists and no one has yet found a way to surmount the Generalissimo's objections and win out to peace.

4. The Generalissimo himself: Universally the Generalissimo is criticized for his ineffective leadership and universally no one can suggest any one to take his place. He is the one who holds this vast country together. Without him disintegration seems inevitable yet long experience with him suggests that he is no longer capable of changing and reforming or of discarding inefficient associates in favor of competent ones and unless he can summon the resources to reverse the present trend he will inevitably and in time be discarded. Nevertheless the Generalissimo is a resourceful man and there are signs that he is trying to find a way to continue the fight against the Communists and at the same time prevent a return of the country to regionalism. He has sent former Prime Minister Chang Chun to the north and to the southwest offering regional autonomy in return for continued allegiance to Nanking and there is reason to believe Chang Chun's trip has not been entirely unproductive of results. There is active and violent agitation for reorganization of the Kuomintang which will permit liberal voices greater weight in government circles and there is evidence that under Wong Wen-hao the government is making a valiant effort toward economic and financial reform which may be announced shortly. Unless, however, these drastic measures which are contemplated produce a miracle and result in the retention of the Generalissimo and the Kuomintang in control we may expect to see some kind of an accommodation with the Communists or a regional breakup or a combination of the two. The third possibility seems the most likely.

Even though at present some form of coalition seems most likely we believe that from the standpoint of the United States it would be most undesirable. We say this because the history of coalitions including Communists demonstrates all too clearly Communist ability by political means to take over complete control of the government and in the process to acquire some kind of international recognition. We question whether a Communist government can in the foreseeable future come to full power in all China by means other than coalition. We would recommend therefore that American efforts be designed to prevent the formation of a coalition government and our best means to that end is continued and, if possible, increased support to the present government. Nevertheless deterioration has already progressed to the verge of collapse and it may already be too late for our support to change the course of events. To assure success we should likely have to involve ourselves in great responsibilities, military, economic, political for we should have to undertake the direction of Chinese affairs on a large scale and a scale in fact that would likely involve responsibilities beyond our resources.

162(a)

Secretary Marshall, temporarily in Paris, to Under Secretary Lovett

893.00/11–648

PARIS, *November 6, 1948*

Dr. T. S. Tsiang, Chinese delegate to the United Nations, called on me this morning with a message from Foreign Minister Dr. Wang.

(1) Would the United States agree to the appointment of United States officers in actual command of the Chinese army units under the pretense of acting as advisers?

(2) Would the United States appoint an officer of high rank to head the special mission, primarily for advice and planning on an emergency situation?

(3) Will the United States expedite the supply of munitions?

(4) What was the thought as to the advisability of Chinese appeal to the United Nations because of Soviet training and equipping of Japanese military and also the Koreans?

I explained the efforts regarding the supply of munitions and stated I would request you to press for urgent action. I did not offer encouragement beyond present efforts.

I said I would refer the requests under (2) and (3) to Washington without making any comment to reference (1).

I remarked regarding (2) that the proposition inherently involved great difficulties if favorably considered; that if the individual did not know China it would require months for him to grasp understanding of the possibilities of the situation, and it would therefore be a very serious matter for the United States to send an officer to almost certain failure.

Regarding (4) I said I would have to consult my colleagues of the United States delegation to develop various possibilities; that offhand I thought it an inadvisable procedure and discussed possible Soviet moves to take advantage rather than to counter such a move. Dr. Tsiang told me the proposition had been put to him three times and each time he had recommended against such action.

MARSHALL

162(b)

Secretary Marshall, temporarily in Paris, to Under Secretary Lovett

893.00/11–848

PARIS, *November 8, 1948.*

Your report of November 6 shows why the visit of a high-ranking United States officer to China would be undesirable and unproductive. Even if the record of the repeated failure of the Chinese Government in the past to accept U. S. advice did not exist, it would be foolhardy for the United States, at this stage of disintegration of the Chinese Government authority in civil as well as the military sphere, to embark upon such a quixotic venture. We are doing everything possible to expedite the shipment of military matériel under the $125 million grants. The pattern of defections and other accompaniments of the fall of Tsinan, Chinchow and the Manchurian debacle, although Chinese Government troops had adequate arms, indicate the will to fight is lacking. With respect to the Chinese Government appeal to the United Nations regarding Soviet treaty violations, this is a matter for Chinese decision, but could not be expected to change the internal situation in China.

You are authorized to inform the Foreign Minister that the National Military Establishment is making every effort to expedite the shipments of military matériel under the $125 million grants. You should point out to him the inherent difficulties involved in an attempt on the part of a foreign official to advise the Chinese Government regarding its courses of action even in the unlikely event such official could be completely conversant with all the complexities of the situation, and the even greater difficulties for a foreign official not familiar with China. You should state that it is not believed that the inspection visit of a high-ranking U. S. officer would or could offer the solution to China's problems. With respect to the Chinese Government appeal to the United Nations, you should reply in the sense of the final sentence of the preceding paragraph.

163

President Chiang Kai-shek to President Truman [25]

893.50 Recovery/10–1648

I have the honor to acknowledge receipt of Your Excellency's reply dated October 16, 1948, for which I am deeply grateful.

The Communist forces in Central China are now within striking distance of Shanghai and Nanking. If we fail to stem the tide, China may be lost to the cause of democracy. I am therefore compelled to send to Your Excellency again a direct and urgent appeal.

The general deterioration of the military situation in China may be attributed to a number of factors. But the most fundamental is the non-observance by the Soviet Government of the Sino-Soviet Treaty of Friendship and Alliance, which, as Your Excellency will doubtless recall, the Chinese Government signed as a result of the well-intentioned advice from the United States Government. I need hardly point out that, but for persistent Soviet aid, the Chinese Communists would not have been able to occupy Manchuria and develop into such a menace.

As a co-defender of democracy against the onrush and infiltration of Communism throughout the world, I appeal to you for speedy and increased military assistance and for a firm statement of American policy in support of the cause for which my Government is fighting. Such a statement would serve to bolster up the morale of the armed forces and the civilian population and would strengthen the Government's position in the momentous battle now unfolding in North and Central China.

My Government would be most happy to receive from you as soon as possible a high-ranking military officer who will work out in consultation with my Govern-

[25] Delivered to the White House on Nov. 9, 1948, by the Chinese Ambassador. Text as transmitted by the Department to the Embassy in Paris, Nov. 12, 1948.

ment a concrete scheme of military assistance, including the participation of American military advisers in the direction of operations.

As the situation demands your Excellency's full sympathy and quick decision, I shall appreciate an early reply.

CHIANG KAI-SHEK

164

President Truman to President Chiang Kai-shek [26]

893.50 Recovery/11–1248

MY DEAR PRESIDENT CHIANG: This is in acknowledgment of your letter delivered to the White House on November 9 through the good offices of your Ambassador, Dr. V. K. Wellington Koo.

As I stated in my letter of October 16, 1948, everything possible is being done to expedite the procurement and shipment to China of the weapons and ammunition being obtained in this country under the China Aid Program. I am again emphasizing to the appropriate officials the urgency of your needs and the necessity of prompt action. In this connection, I have just been informed that one shipment of arms and ammunition sailed from Guam on November 4 and another from Japan on November 7 en route to China. I have also been informed that a further shipment of ammunition sailed from the West Coast of the United States on November 9 and is scheduled to reach China about November 24.

A message of November 9 from the Secretary of State to Ambassador Stuart, containing Secretary Marshall's reply to a request from the Chinese Foreign Minister for military aid and the visit of a high-ranking United States officer to China, apparently crossed Your Excellency's message in transmission. The Secretary authorized Ambassador Stuart to inform the Foreign Minister that the United States National Military Establishment was making every effort to expedite shipments of military matériel purchased in this country under the China Aid Act. He also authorized Ambassador Stuart to point out the inherent difficulties involved in an attempt on the part of a newly appointed foreign official to advise the Chinese Government regarding its courses of action in the present dilemma, even if such an official would be completely conversant with all the numerous complexities of the situation, and to point out the even greater difficulties for a foreign official not familiar with China.

However, Major General Barr, Director of the Joint United States Military Advisory Group in China, is conversant with the current situation and his advice has always been available to you.

Your attention may have been called to my public statement on March 11, 1948, in which I stated that the United States maintained friendly relations with the Chinese Government and was trying to assist the recognized Government of China maintain peace. I also stated that I did not desire Communists in the Chinese Government. Secretary Marshall stated publicly on March 10, 1948, that the Communists were now in open rebellion against the Chinese Government and that the inclusion of the Communists in the Government was a matter for the Chinese Government to decide, not for the United States Government to dictate. I believe that these statements and the action of my Government in extending assistance to the Chinese Government under the China Aid Act of 1948 have made the position of the United States Government clear.

You will understand the desire of the United States Government to support the cause of peace and democracy throughout the world. It is this desire that has

---

[26] Text as transmitted by the Department to the Embassy in Nanking, Nov. 12, 1948.

led this Government to extend assistance to many countries in their efforts to promote sound economies and stable conditions without which the peoples of the world cannot expect to have peace and the principles of democracy cannot grow. It was with that hope that the United States Government has extended assistance in various forms to the Chinese Government. I am most sympathetic with the difficulties confronting the Chinese Government and people at this time and wish to assure Your Excellency that my Government will continue to exert every effort to expedite the implementation of the program of aid for China which has been authorized by the Congress with my approval.

Very sincerely yours,

HARRY S. TRUMAN

165(a)

The Ambassador in China (Stuart) to Secretary Marshall

893.00/11–548

NANKING, *November 5, 1948*

I have the honor to enclose for the information of the Department the text as released by the Central News Agency in Peiping on October 31, 1948 of a statement made by President Chiang Kai-shek to Mr. Arthur T. Steele of the New York Herald Tribune in reply to a series of ten questions.

The major portion of the President's statement consists of the usual redundancies concerning China's contributions to peace and civilization, a tirade against Communists and the customary assurances that conditions in China are really not as bad as many people think. Some passages are, however, of more than passing interest.

After stating that the Chinese Communists have not the slightest concern for the welfare of the people, the President gives his explanation for the recent Manchurian debacle. It is difficult to deduce from his statement just what he has in mind, but it is apparent that he ignores the real reasons for the defeat and prefers to consider the capture of Mukden by the Communists as being of little significance. He denies any pessimism on his part and states that if the Government should receive moral and financial help from friendly nations the situation could be speedily reversed.

Perhaps the most telling comment he makes, certainly from the standpoint of world opinion, is the parallel he draws between contemporary events in Manchuria and those of 1931. The President says that when Japan invaded Manchuria he pointed out to the world that the Second World War had thereby begun. He says he wishes now to warn that Chinese Communist conquests of the Northeast must be considered the starting point of the Third World War if the Communists are permitted to secure control of the rest of China. He reaches this conclusion because the Soviets' desire to control all Asia and China is the decisive pivot of the area.

The President then makes the interesting statement that the ruthlessness and treachery of Chinese Communists cannot be compared with that of Communists elsewhere. In conclusion he says, "The center of endeavor in Asia must be China. This is the great task unprecedented in human history. I hope that the American people and their statesmen will dedicate their lives to this task."

Shortly thereafter several prominent newspapers echoed the President's sentiments editorially. Typical were the comments of KMT Chung Yang Jih Pao and the Army Ho Ping Jih Pao which pointed out that the problem of China is the problem of the world and that if the United States wishes to avoid a Third World War it had better do something about China soon.

The contents of this statement suggest that it was designed in the main to influence American opinion, particularly because of the emphasis placed on the Japanese invasion of Manchuria and prospects that the Chinese Communists' seizure of the area portends a Third World War. It must be admitted that the President has made an effective point.

For the Ambassador
LEWIS CLARK
Minister-Counselor

[Enclosure]

Statement by President Chiang Kai-shek to Mr. Arch T. Steele of the New York Herald Tribune

Mr. A. T. Steele, New York Herald Tribune China correspondent, submitted to President Chiang Kai-shek ten questions of which the President made the following observations:

In answer to the question what is the basic reason for the temporary setbacks of Government troops at the present moment, the President said the sole aim of the Government military policy adopted in the war of resistance and in the bandit suppression campaign has always been to preserve China's territorial integrity and sovereignty and also to protect the people's lives and property. This accounts for the fact that no city or place has ever been given up lightly.

The original purpose of fighting the eight long years war of resistance was to recover the Northeast. With the conclusion of the war Government troops took over at great risk important Northeastern regions and consequently could not lightly resort to withdrawal. The traditional ideal and conception of duty of the Chinese soldier decree is that it is imperative for him to die if the city falls or to live if he can hold it and that it is a disgrace for him to withdraw from or give up a city for this reason.

During the past three years, with defense posts scattered all over the areas under Red menace Government forces are availing themselves of this weakness. Communist bandits have employed the tactics of breaking individual posts in isolated areas.

As the Government belongs to the people, the enlistment of men into the army service and the collection of military foodstocks should be done without overburdening the people or violating the law and rulings of the nation. The Communists, however, have not the slightest concern for the people. They issue in different regions, bogus currency notes as they like. They confiscate at any time the people's property, enforce arbitrary conscription and ferret out all foodstuffs they can lay their hands on. Their ways and means cannot be more cruel and inhuman. During the past year, under the pretext of land reform they have resorted to draining the pond in the hope of netting a final catch of the fish. With what they have thus squeezed from the people, they are able to expand their armed forces on a large scale. The scorched earth policy taken on their withdrawals and the human sea tactics in their offensives are certainly not what Government troops should like to follow.

Consequently, while Government troops can surely score victory when they concentrate their forces and engage the main enemy forces in fighting, they would now and then be put into such a position that with troops inferior in number and isolated from main forces they had to suffer setbacks. All this is the fundamental reason for which Government troops for the moment undergo losses. At present, therefore, the Government cannot but subject the strategy and tactics of its Communist suppression campaign to some change. Besides, its military education should undergo thorough reform. The necessity to take the whole situation into consideration so as to ensure ultimate success relieves the Government of contending with feelings of the gain or loss of a city for a moment in isolated areas.

Moreover, I should like to point out that the Communist bandits with whom the Government is engaged in fighting is linked up with Japanese and Korean Communists who in turn receive support of the Communist International.

To the serious nature of this fact, we should be fully awake. A people with long cumulative weakness, we have never been afraid of aggression and violence. We engaged ourselves in eight years of war in resistance against Japanese militarists and we have been fighting for 25 years the Communist bandits fully equipped with arms and brutality from 1924 to 1945.

During the Northern Expedition the Communist bandit suppression campaign and the war of resistance against Japanese aggression, the national revolutionary army in each of the long periods of fighting underwent many setbacks and experienced heavy losses, but eventually in all cases won glorious victories.

Within the two score and five years the Government had more than once encountered situations far more critical than what it is facing at present. But again without any exception it has overcome all the difficulties and the eventual victories were invariably followed immediately after the heaviest losses.

Through our bitter experiences we build up our firm faith with persevering courage. We shall put up a relentless and unflinching struggle. We have a deep faith in the fact that the bandit suppression campaign and national reconstruction will this time also reach the final success.

After this failure, I am not at all pessimistic. Now, instead, I feel confident China expects that its people and soldiers become thoroughly awake to the national crisis and rise to a man for the national salvation.

What we have relied on was the spirit of nationalism and the Three People's Principle and these cannot be destroyed by whatever intrigues and outrages. We do not think lightly of the gravity of the Communist menace, but we are sure the torturous and dastardly extortion the Communists imposed upon the people so that they have been able to launch offensives one after another, will spell their own doom as they are heading for the old rut they had traversed during the period of 1935 and 1936 when they suffered a total defeat in Kiangsi.

Should the Government be able to receive moral as well as material help from the friendly nations and the support of international righteousness ultimate success, it is sure, could be speedily scored.

The President's answer to the question whether or not the Government will hold Mukden with its full strength is as follows:

It has been the invariable decision of the Government to maintain the territory of and sovereignty over the Northeast since September 1931. In view of the fall of Chinchow and Changchun, the situation in the Northeast as a whole has reached an unfavorable stage. Consequently, Mukden as a city in the Northeastern deadlock, is not as vital as it used to be.

The present situation in Mukden is indeed critical. Government troops, however, are still exerting their last strength to fight against the bandits there at any cost. This is being done to discharge their heaviest duty towards both their people and the world. Of the most important international problems, the Northeast is one. It has significant bearings on the world situation particularly on those nations maintaining close relations with the Pacific throughout the past three years.

Such a heavy and hard task has been shouldered by China only. We, being unable to fulfill our part feel quite regretful. Seventeen years ago with the outbreak of the September 18 incident, I signalled to Democratic nations and the League of Nations a warning confirming that the disaster of a world war had since then begun. Although this warning was not considered important by the various countries, history eventually evidenced the truth that the Northeast question was the prelude to World War II.

History is now repeating itself. If international right cannot prevail and extend its influence and if democracies maintain the same stand by watching the fire ablaze across the river, the world is bound to tread the former path of disaster. Should, unfortunately, Communist bandits control China, another world war would surely descend upon this globe. And should the Communists rule over the nine Northeastern provinces, it would mean the virtual beginning of another world catastrophe. What is more obvious, is that without an integral Northeast, there will be no independent Korea, nor will there be a peaceful East Asia. This much I can firmly say the ominous and treacherous clouds will gather with the trouble in the Northeast as their starting point.

The question as to the serious nature of China's role in the world anti-communist struggle, her position in another world war and if the worst should come to the worst, the effect of the Communist control over her on the world situation, the President answered as follows:

China is endeavoring to exterminate the powerful factor threatening the world peace in order to prevent the outbreak of the third world war, consequently I am not inclined to express my views on that position China should hold. In the world war to come of the 2,100,000,000 population, the Asiatics number over 50 percent and of the 1,100,000,000 population of Asia, the Chinese claim one-third.

The importance of Asia's position in the world and of China's in Asia is too obvious to need superfluous remarks. What I should like to point out is (1) In political organization, economic life, social foundation or cultural standard, Asiatic races lag behind the Europeans. In the West, in the prevailing times of poverty and starvation, it is easier for Communist propaganda and organization to achieve effect, (2) The traditional policy of the Communist Internationale in enforcing its world revolution and the present direction of its expansion center upon Asia. And since the future of Asia revolves around China as its decisive pivot, it is the Communist principle that in order to control the world, it is essential to control Asia and in order to control Asia it is essential to control China. I can decidedly affirm that in case China should be subjugated by the Communists, the third world war would surely follow and mankind would once again be precipitated into a tragic disaster.

If the Chinese Government is able to extirpate the Communist today, the factor lurking in Asia and conducive to the next world war will on this account be eliminated. The Chinese Communists hold armed forces, and the ruthlessness and treachery of the Chinese Communists cannot be compared with those of the believers in communism in any other democratic countries. In spite of the difficult circumstances, the Chinese Government has never given up its responsibility towards the nation and the time adhered to international pledges and sense of duty and in addition endeavors to fulfill moral obligations in the past war against aggression. Now it does the same. I deeply believe, that in the anti-communist struggle, the world should present one whole front. There should have been no difference between West Europe and East Asia in signifi‌cance. However, in West Europe, nations are advanced in industries and enjoy a higher standard of civilization, nationalism and democracy.

Since a history of over one and a half centuries are deeply rooted in the life and thoughts of the people, it is far less urgent for them to rely on the material and moral aid from the United States in their resistance against communism than for Asiatic races. If the American people and their statesmen are sincere in their work for the welfare of mankind they should start to work in the most vast and the most populous area whose people suffer most in their livelihood. There, the former should lift the living as well as cultural standards of the latter and help them to secure their freedom and independence in order to spare mankind the catastrophe of the third world war. It is particularly necessary to come to Asia's rescue. The center of endeavor in the salvation of Asia must be China. This is the great task unprecedented in human history. I hope that the American people and their statesmen will dedicate their lives to this task..

165 (b)

The Ambassador in China (Stuart) to Secretary Marshall

893.00/11–648

NANKING, *November 6, 1948*

We gathered together senior military personnel JUSMAG and Service Attachés, who, after discussing military situation, were unanimous that short of actual employment of U.S. troops no amount of military assistance could save present situation in view of its advanced stage of deterioration. Agreeing that employ‌ment U.S. troops impossible, it was conclusion of group that there was no military step China or U.S. could take in sufficient time to retrieve the military situation. It was agreed that Fu Tso-Yi could not resist attack by forces which Com‌munists can mass against him in North China, and that against Nationalist forces known to be of inferior caliber in Hsuchow area, Chen Yi could reach Yangtze River in vicinity Nanking in two weeks.

We reluctantly reach conclusion, therefore, that early fall present Nationalist Government is inevitable. It is too early to say with certainty whether that Government will be replaced by a Communist Government or by a Communist-dominated coalition. In either event, we shall have to make the best of a bad situation and save what we can from the wreckage.

Embassy will remain Nanking unless developments indicate contrary course desirable, in which case Department's instructions will be requested.

STUART

165(c)

The Consul General at Shanghai (Cabot) to Secretary Marshall

893.00/11–2948

SHANGHAI, *November 29, 1948.*

After discussion regarding possibility transfer of power in Shanghai [a high-ranking Chinese Government official] commented extensively on our China policy. He said he felt it was vital to our national security to keep the "flame of democ‌racy" alive in China. When I pointed out many people doubted that present Government could win against Communists regardless of amount of aid we furnished, he said he fully agreed and added that Government was now detested by great majority of people. He said we could be greatly mistaken, however, if we thought we could do business with Communists and mentioned Chinese knew that liquidation had already started in Tsinan. He then suggested 4-point plan and said that in view gravity of situation U.S. should demand its fulfillment threatening aid otherwise. I pointed out gravity of interference in Chinese internal affairs. Program follows:

(1). Generalissimo should remain head of Government but surrender all real power.

(2). Responsible cabinet should be formed representing all non-Communist elements in China and should assume responsibility for war against Communists.

(3). U.S. supreme military adviser should be appointed in effect to run Chinese armies and should be furnished with massive shipment of arms and munitions.

(4). Primarily to stiffen soldiers morale U.S. should lend 250 million ounces of silver to China to pay soldiers.

The official pointed out that such a cabinet could make clear to Chinese people that this was a war against foreign imperialism. I said that deeply moved as I was by plight of China I could only report what he had said to Washington.

CABOT

165(d)

The Ambassador in China (Stuart) to Secretary Marshall

893.00/12–1648

NANKING, *December 16, 1948.*

Chang Chun, acting as Generalissimo's emissary, sent for me morning December 13. He said that Generalissimo was hearing on all sides that he should withdraw from active control of Government and that this view was shared by Americans; that Generalissimo would like my opinion and advice on such step. We talked about two hours and in true Chinese fashion he did not come to point until near end, but that was burden of his mission. He emphasized report that it was Americans who felt Generalissimo should withdraw. I finally replied that it was certainly impression of most of Americans that I had talked to that great mass of Chinese people felt that Generalissimo, as principal obstacle to termination of hostilities, should step down from his position of authority; that what people of China thought and wanted was dominant factor in our policy formation. Chang Chun continued that according to Generalissimo's reports Americans did not believe there was any close connection between Chinese Communists and U.S.S.R., nor that U.S.S.R. was backing CCP. I replied that in my experience Americans were sure there was close connection between aims and methods of CCP and U.S.S.R., and that former represented faithfully policy of U.S.S.R. in China. This did not mean, I added, that in American opinion Soviet soldiers and technicians were actually participating in civil war on Communist side. I continued that what American Government and people wanted were establishment and general application of human liberties and preservation of independence of China. I said that the present Government should make these objectives theirs and should make them known to people of China as its program; that the Kuomintang should stand on these declared principles in any negotiations with other side, and if it were able to inspire people of China with significance of these principles and reenlist their support in sacrifice and suffering and exile against the threat of totalitarian dominion, the National Government could be sure of active sympathy and support of Government of U.S. wherever in free China it might have to move to continue fight. I said that if peace in China could be achieved on basis of human liberties and national independence, well and good, but that there should be no compromise with principles and that if they required continued resistance the Nationalists would have the support and sympathy of entire non-Communist world.

In response to suggestions for outside help on mediation in present stage, I emphasized over and over that present decisions must come from Chinese, that it must be Chinese initiative which either makes peace on honorable terms or inspires people of China to further resistance of totalitarian aggression. I said that we were interested in what Chinese people wanted and were willing to support; that issues must be clarified and confidence of people secured by Chinese leaders themselves and their policies. I continued that these policies should no longer be on a partisan basis of for or against Chiang Kai-shek or his party or his Government, but that they should be lifted to higher non-partisan plane of individual human rights and national independence.

Chang Chun said he thought he understood and would think very seriously about what I had said. I said that he would have to do more than think about it; that he and other Chinese leaders in and out of Government would have to do something constructive and do it fast.

STUART

165 (e)

The Ambassador in China (Stuart) to Secretary Marshall

893.00/12–1948

NANKING, *December 19, 1948*

On morning December 17 I visited Sun Fo at his request. He was extremely harassed. He at once said he wanted my advice as an old friend of China, should they go on with war or sue for peace. I explained that I could not give such advice without implicitly representing my country and that my instructions on the matter were explicit. He then asked me to help him on personal grounds as far as I felt would be permissible. I described the American dilemma: We are opposed to spread of communism all over world and anxious to assist in preventing this in China, but on other hand, we cannot do this through a Government that has lost the support of its own peoples; to do so would be contrary to those democratic principles, the violation of which is a principal reason for our objection to communism. In reply to further questions or comments, all of which revealed his genuine perplexity, I pointed out that the all but universal desire of the people was for peace, and that, although this could not be registered by any constitutional process, yet it was as evident to everyone as had been the popular will to resist and the consequent support of the Government during the Japanese wars; that President Chiang's determination to resist to the end, then as now, was magnificent in its personal courage and patriotic purpose, but that his own problem as Premier would seem to lie in whether to support the President, in the face of contrary public opinion and the unfavorable military and fiscal trends, or to have the Cabinet discuss and decide the issue for presentation to the President; that, in other words, it might be helpful to the President if he were advised to relinquish his emergency powers and delegate more authority to the Executive Yuan, or if this were too cumbersome, to a small group who had his confidence and could in some real sense represent or at least interpret the people's will; that this did not necessarily involve the President's resignation, but it ought to mean that the delegation of authority was complete and real.

Dr. Sun asked if I had any special information as to results of Madame Chiang's mission and present attitude of General Marshall. I replied that I knew of no changes in American policy resulting from her visit to Washington; that the Secretary of State was still deeply solicitous over Chinese affairs but that he was probably very much perplexed as to what America could do to help; that nothing more was possible until after Congress had assembled; and that I questioned wisdom of Chinese authorities allowing their decisions to be influenced by any expectation of American military aid under existing conditions.

He then put series of questions as to whether Communists wanted peace, or would abide by their promises, or would not continue to use their armies to overrun China since they had the power, et cetera. I replied that these were all pertinent, but that I had no answers that were more than guesses. He asked if I had any direct contact with the CP leaders and when I replied in the negative he remarked that part of the problem was how to reach them and ascertain their views. He wondered if they were in touch with Soviet Embassy and whether he might not undertake to mediate. When I rather discouraged this approach he expressed hope that U. S. and U. S. S. R. might jointly undertake this, to which I replied that such proposal would have to come from the two Chinese parties before it could even be considered seriously, but that I personally inclined to opinion that Chinese had better try to find their own solution despite all the quite obvious difficulties. He remarked that any decision for peace or war by Executive Yuan would be subject to review by Legislative Yuan which, while in a sense representative of people, had about one-third its membership under CC Clique control, and that it would also involve much argument and publicity.

I then tried to sum up my advice to effect that he and his colleagues would have to debate whether in view of all factors they could from now on fight communism more effectively by military or political methods, and that no outside elements could or should decide this for them nor influence their choice; that I was confident that a very large element of the politically conscious people of country were strongly against communism and its ruthless totalitarism policy; that they should think in terms of preserving individual liberties and national sovereignty as the fundamental issues rather than of the retention of the KMT and its present leadership as against some other procedure; that I could assure them of continuing American sympathy and readiness to help in whatever ways seemed to be beneficial to the Chinese people and their national independence; and I was personally much more sympathetic than my replies to his questions might seem to indicate.

STUART

165 (f)

The Ambassador in China (Stuart) to Secretary Marshall

893.00/12–2148

NANKING, *December 21, 1948*

May I outline below my personal views re political outlook in China and bearing of this on American policy. This is partly for record but chiefly in order to have full benefit of your instructions.

As you are well aware my original hope had been that by military aid to Chiang Government especially in form of advice upon which all else would be conditioned, it might have been possible to keep area south of Yangtse intact and clear coastal region from Nanking northward of militant Communism. It

would have been expected that again with American technical advisers and
economic aid there would be improvements in local Government and in people's
livelihood which would compare favorably with conditions in Communist territory. National Government would guard its frontier but carry on no aggressive
warfare against Communists. This would allow public opinion to take form
in both sections and be basis for some sort of negotiated settlement. Whether
this would have proven practicable and results have justified our efforts now is
immaterial.

Dealing with present realities one must begin as always with President
Chiang. It is distressing to observe how completely he has lost public confidence
in recent months and how widespread is desire he retire. This sentiment is
shared by most officials of all ranks in Government and is almost universal
among politically conscious citizens. Opposition to him is primarily because of
conviction that war as he has been conducting it is hopeless and is bringing upon
people almost unendurable economic and other distress. View is not infrequently
expressed that he is best asset Communists have. It is ironical therefore that he
refuses to turn over active direction of affairs as he has been repeatedly advised
to do because this would be in his opinion tantamount to allowing Communists
overrun country. Issue is thus confused in his mind as apparently in case of
many in U. S. as though American military aid to him were only alternative to
complete Communist domination of China. But it would be in violation of basic
principle of democracy to maintain in power man who has lost support of his
own people. It would arouse greater sympathy for Communist cause and violent
anti-American feeling.

In any case our military men all seem to be agreed that such aid would be too
late, even under new leadership. It is probable that resistance groups will carry
on for some time in south and west and may form a loose federation. But our
military aid to these would at this state be in my opinion very unwise and would
certainly complicate matters in coastal provinces and central area.

Government leaders are all constantly asking what American policy is going to
be or what our advice to them would be or, more insistently whether it would not
be in order for us to advise President to retire or go abroad for trip or in some
way eliminate himself from absolute control of affairs. He meanwhile is coercing
Sun Fo to form new Cabinet without delay but new Premier in addition to having
undergone rather painful operation and being met by refusals as he invites one or
another of inner circle of party members, is being thwarted by President's interference as he attempts to make up his list. Dr. Sun is therefore in mood of frustration and Government lacks even semblance of functioning Cabinet. President
has been advised by various people to organize small emergency group in Cabinet
to which he could delegate full administrative authority while he exerted only his
constitutional prerogatives. It is generally recognized that this would only be
possible if he withdrew to Kuling or elsewhere under some pretext which at present he has no serious thought of doing. However after having repeatedly tried
without success to persuade Hu Shih to become Premier he has induced him to
come to Nanking for consultation. He is proposing that Hu form a sort of advisory group as "braintrust" but as Hu points out this would be in effect paper-
cabinet and would have no more real power than one it would supersede.

On December 17 I had long talks in each case at their request, with Sun Fo
and Hu Shih, and these only served to accentuate quandary that Government
is in. The conversation with Hu was especially saddening because he represents
finest type of patriotic idealism in his attempt to be loyal to Chiang Government.
Hu's argument is that Communism is so implacable and intolerant, so diaboli-

cally thorough in its indoctrination and so ruthless in enforcing its totalitarian control even in China that Chiang Kai-shek should be supported despite his shortcomings because he alone sees this and has been uncompromising in resisting it, also because he almost alone among KMT leaders has been free from taint of avarice or other typical vices of Chinese officialdom. He believes that if Chiang were forced to retire Central Government would disintegrate and Communists take over virtually on their own terms. He wonders therefore if America could even now be persuaded to recall JUSMAG and assist Chiang in carrying on war rather than allow Communists dominate country and mold it to their own ends. Tears came to his eyes when he asked me, on basis of our long friendship, to tell him what he should say to President Chiang and what else he could do now that he had determined to give up academic career for service to nation. I told him that primary weakness of Chiang Government was moral rather than military, in sense that troops had lost fighting spirit and people had lost confidence in Government's ability to provide for them as well as in cause for which they were being asked to suffer. America was powerless under these conditions. I had repeatedly urged upon President Chiang supreme importance of rallying public opinion behind him but had failed. I wondered if Hu could lead in another "new thought movement" or "literary revolution" on issues of freedom and democracy as he had done with brilliant success thirty odd years ago. He said he bitterly regretted not having used talents in this field since V-J Day rather than selfishly returning, as he had, to more congenial academic activities. This lengthy comment is to prepare way for discussion of our policy if coalition Government will in course of time be formed. Presumably CP will dominate at outset. But whether they continue to do so or will allow their original [position?] to be diluted or modified will depend on number of factors. One of these is extent to which non-Communist elements will participate and exert liberalizing influence. Another is necessity for CP to adopt tolerant course at beginning because of their own limitations. This would doubtless be nothing more than temporary tactics but in that period inter-action between their own ideology and more liberal ideas might have permanent effects.　　　　　　　　　STUART

165 (g)

The Ambassador in China (Stuart) to Secretary Marshall

893.00/12–2948

NANKING, *December 29, 1948*

I called on General Wu Te-chen, new Vice Premier and Acting Foreign Minister yesterday morning. His concern briefly summed up is that Government has failed in its military action against Communists; that for first time new (#') that in announcement of readiness to consider "an honorable peace" there has been no response from Communists. He is, therefore, greatly puzzled as to what Communists want, and what American advice is.

I explained on this last that American hostility to Communism and interest in welfare of China and her people were both unchanged but that it was inherently impossible for U. S. to make any suggestions or promises that might influence solution of their present problems by Chinese themselves. I added that I had greatest admiration for resolute will-power of Generalissimo in fighting Communism by military means, and that, whatever decision responsible leaders should make as to present crisis, I hoped they would all show that same resolute will in resisting the evils of Communism by every available means. They ought not to think of situation as hopeless and irretrievable. They would probably have some very distasteful and even bitter experiences and outlook might seem very depressing, but more thorough cooperation among themselves and grim determination were called for. They should also win support of people in whatever course of action they undertook. I reminded him in leaving that the U. S. was watching with keenly solicitous interest and readiness to help in whatever ways might seem justifiable and effective when time came.

In course of conversation he raised question of the four other members of "Big Five" undertaking to mediate, and I explained difficulties. His mood is one of being quite aware of desperate military failure and on bafflement over unresponsive attitude of Communists.

He apparently is unaware of negotiations in which Vice President has been involved or at least made no reference to them.

STUART

165 (h)

The Ambassador in China (Stuart) to Secretary Marshall

893.00/12–3048

NANKING, *December 30, 1948*

A successful formation of the Sun Fo Cabinet does not promise to alter prevailing political trends. Agitation for peace both within and without the government is reaching a crescendo, yet nothing can be done without the assent of the Generalissimo. By virtue of action by the National Assembly, the Generalissimo holds emergency powers allowing him to make virtually all policy decisions. The Cabinet can only advise and assist in implementing the Generalissimo's will. Thus as long as the Generalissimo can exercise command over Nanking garrison and police, he has both de facto and de jure authority to continue the war or adopt a peace policy.

Various reports of the impending retirement of the Generalissimo should not be taken as positive indication of the Generalissimo's intentions in spite of the fact that he summarily removed Wu Ting-chang, his faithful Secretary General and replaced him with Wu Chung-hsin solely because of the latter's known ability as a negotiator and for the avowed purpose of arranging the retirement of the Generalissimo. In the present deteriorating military situation it may be assumed that the Generalissimo has given thought to peace as an alternative to continued hostilities. He is under strong pressure to retire and it is conceivable that he may be persuaded to step aside or that Pai Chung-hsi whose troops now garrison Nanking may force his hand by coup d'etat assisted by Chang Chun, Chang Chih-chung and those others demanding peace. His retirement from the scene is prerequisite for any negotiations with the Communists.

The principal motivation of governmental peace advocates appears that if the Generalissimo retires, the government can negotiate with the Communists and a considerable segment of the present Kuomintang can be preserved as a bloc in the coalition government. This view was strengthened by Li Chi-shen on December 20 in the Hong Kong press announcement which indicated that the present government, less the Generalissimo, would be recognized by the Communists as having legal status as a temporary government for the purposes of negotiation. However, in the December 22 Reuter-AP Hong Kong story, "spokesman for one of major groups of 10 anti-Chiang parties exiled Hong Kong" states

Communists not prepared to enter the coalition government which would have representation from the present Nanking regime. We reported December 16 that Li Tsung-jen has a man in Hong Kong negotiating this point and it is possible that Li Chi-shen's statement is a result of these negotiations.

However, that may be, we consider it unlikely that the Communists will permit the Kuomintang to enter the coalition government as a bloc, but will rather permit participation by individual Kuomintang members selected with care. As we see it, should Generalissimo be persuaded to retire or be forced out, Li Tsung-jen as leader of the government would seek through his proclamation to open negotiations with the Communists. He has little with which to bargain, however, and we think it unlikely that the Communists will be willing to treat with him except in terms amounting to unconditional surrender. Their military forces gathered north of Nanking and already moving to encircle the city are overwhelming. Proclamations promising safety and good treatment to technicians both within and without the government and the precedent set in Tsinan and Mukden make it highly likely that sufficient government and public utility officials would remain in their jobs to ease the problem of running the government which will confront the Communists. Even the Kuomintang leadership is offered the opportunity of getting off the blacklist of war criminals or at least being permitted to survive, by proof of acceptable service to the Communist victory.

Therefore, with anticipated refusal of the Communists to negotiate, with the loss of the Generalissimo's leadership should he have retired command, with the deathblow to what remains of military morale in government forces which would result from publicized effort to negotiate, we believe there is little likelihood that the government can continue to rally sufficient support to maintain resistance as a unit. It would be more likely to disintegrate, leaving the autonomous areas in the west and southwest to make their own accommodations with the Communists.

The central point in the present situation remains, however, the fact that the Generalissimo has not yet taken the final step to relinquish his control and that until he has done so, his opposition to Communism will continue as heretofore. He has said that he would remove to Nanchang, then Canton, and Taiwan if necessary and that he would resort to guerrilla tactics if forced into it, but that he would fight the Communists unto death. Those insisting on peace may succeed in persuading him that he is harming the Chinese people by continued resistance, yet his deep conviction in the inhumanity of Communism with the resulting oppression of the Chinese people may lead him to carry out his threat. It would certainly be a more glorious end and more in the traditional pattern than if he were meekly to step aside to spend his dying days in exile.

STUART

166

A Series of Chronicle Summaries by the American Embassy in Nanking to the Department of State during 1948 on the General Situation

NANKING, *February 17, 1948.*

The Chinese lunar New Year celebrations have just come to an end, and we shall take that as a pretext for sending you this second round-up of our thinking on the China scene. As the Chinese arrange matters, or rather try to arrange matters, everyone embarks on the New Year with a clean slate—a new suit of clothes, a full stomach, all debts paid and past sins forgiven. While this may be true for the individual citizen, it is certainly not so for the body politic. Indeed, with the coming of the New Year, we see no reason to believe that it promises anything better for the people of China than the year of the Pig, which has just passed.

Perhaps the most spectacular occurrences in China during the past month were the riots in Canton and Shanghai. The Canton affair, to judge from the way in which the matter was handled by the Government-controlled press, had its beginnings in a calculated attempt by certain elements in Kwangtung to distract public attention from the domestic crisis by an appeal to the xenophobia generally latent in the Chinese intelligentsia and student groups. The appeal was successful, and there is much to suggest that those who roused the feeling of the mob, went on to lead it to acts of vandalism. That the whole affair was a source of considerable embarrassment to Dr. T. V. Soong, could not but be gratifying to its instigators. The Shanghai disorders, except for the demonstration against the British Consulate General, had a totally different character. Here the students of Tungchi University, the taxi dancers and cabaret employees and the cotton mill workers had long standing grievances over what they felt to be the failure of the Government to meet their political and economic requirements. There was, and is, widespread unhappiness with the economic and political outlook, which is so deepseated as to spring into unrest at the slightest provocation. Disgruntled at their lack of success in negotiating their differences with Government representatives, they turned to force, and, in the end, could only be restrained by force. We may expect more of this unless conditions improve sufficiently to inspire hope of a better day.

In recent weeks, besides the disturbances in Shanghai and Canton, we have had reports of unrest in predominantly rural areas of Southern and Southeastern China. The perennial banditry seems to be on the increase and is occasioned we believe by an increasing feeling on the part of the common people that the Government is unwilling or unable to improve conditions. In spite of the increasing tendency on the part of the Government to cry "Communist" at every disturbance, in none of the civil disturbances of which we have heard do we have any credible information that they were instigated by Communist agitation, or that in their totality they form a pattern of Communist subversive activity. This is not to say, of course, that the Communists will refrain from exploiting to the utmost this tendency on the part of the people to solve their economic and political problems by force. In addition, as civil unrest continues, we may expect that the Communists will try to organize and direct it to their own ends. However, for the time being, it appears that the Government police and military can meet force with force, and keep the situation under control.

The lack of confidence in the Government which is becoming general among the common people, and which has occasionally resulted in open opposition, has a parallel development among certain military and civil officials. Here the discontent is founded on the Government's failure in the purely military phases of the civil war, and its general lack of success in dealing with the problems arising therefrom. We have, for some time, been reporting that a deeply pessimistic and defeatist psychology is growing in Government circles, and we have noticed through the past months as the situation has continued to deteriorate, that this feeling is becoming more widespread and more profound. It is easy to understand how officials underpaid as they are and suffering all the ills of inflation (the Vice Minister for Foreign Affairs gets the equivalent of US$35.00 per month) are becoming more and more convinced that the differences between the Government and the Communists cannot be settled by purely military means, or at least cannot be settled in a way that would leave the authority of the Government preponderant and unchallenged. Basically the Chinese are opportunistic, and an increasing number has its finger in the air to make sure which way the wind is blowing.

There are good grounds for pessimism over the Government's ability to force a favorable military decision. In Manchuria, Government armies remain under siege in a few of the principal cities, and a large, well equipped relieving force from Shantung, which was transported by sea to Hulutao, has not been able to open land communications between that port and the Mukden area. Depending entirely on air transport for supply and reenforcement, and with troops and matériel being depleted in defensive engagements, the position of the Government's Manchurian armies is serious, if not critical. As this is being written, we learn of an extraordinary conference of native Manchurian political and military leaders which is to be convened shortly in the capital; extraordinary in the sense that the Government has not, in the past, shown any disposition to forget past differences and consult with Manchurians on Manchurian problems. Despite the Government's announced determination to hold Manchuria at all costs, we feel that even in its highest echelons the Government is coming to regard its Manchurian venture as a very forlorn hope. Thus, if the conference appraises the Manchurian problem realistically, it can hardly do other than recommend the rescue of Government forces now committed there by withdrawal. If this is attempted we are not altogether convinced that the operation would be tactically feasible.

Elsewhere, in China proper, the Government's military position is no brighter. In Hopei, Gen. Fu Tso-yi's forces are mainly engaged in constructing fortified positions in Jehol, roughly parallel to the Great Wall. This is evidently in anticipation of a Government military collapse in Manchuria, which would release Communist armies there for an offensive in China proper. General Fu can scarcely hope to defend this position in strength, and, at the same time, cope with the Communist armies in southern and central Hopei, should they coordinate an offensive with a drive to the south by the Manchurian Communists. The recent reappearance of regular Communist forces in northern Kiangsu has forced the Government to concern itself with the defenses of the northern approaches to Shanghai and of the capital itself. To the west of Hankow, the Communists even have a foothold on or near the north bank of the Yangtze, and will, in all likelihood, soon be able to interdict river shipping unprotected by naval convoy between Szechuan and middle and lower Yangtze ports.

In the sphere of economics, the Government has apparently done better than in its military operations. Vigorous policing of the black market in foreign currency, better smuggling control and a more restricted allotment of foreign exchange for imports has stemmed the advance of the Chinese dollar in terms of foreign currencies. However, this has operated in restraint of export trade and a consequent gain of foreign exchange, since prices of native commodities continue to spiral upwards. Also, recent measures for the centralization of financial controls in the Bank of China, which thereby becomes a national bank in effect, if not in form, provides a more rational banking structure for the country, and brings it under the direction of more responsible political elements than has hitherto been the case. However, the one fact in the economic situation which impresses most Chinese is the upspring in commodity prices unaccompanied by comparable increases in wages and salaries. It is this fact, as much as any other, that is responsible for the growing opposition of the people to their government.

The flow of American relief supplies to China, which is now under way, and the prospect of further aid in the near future has met with a mixed reception. The higher officials of the Government, while expressing suitable gratification, openly say that this aid will be of value only in so far as it may be the forerunner of greater things to come. At least one of the Government's foreign economic advisors has stated that aid as now contemplated will not ameliorate the Government's economic plight to any appreciable degree. Liberal intellectual and even business circles oppose aid on the ground that the Government is certain to misuse it, and that at best it will serve as only a temporary prop for the groups in power and so prolong a civil war which the Government will lose in any event.

Given the conditions we have described above, there is nothing surprising in the fact that many Chinese, both civil and military officials, as well as groups outside the Government, are actively seeking a means to end the civil war. They are aware that this can come only through a negotiated settlement with the Communists, but we doubt that there is any realization that such a settlement would in all likelihood result in either a coalition government in which the Communists would play the dominant role, or in a territorial arrangement which would give the Communists time to consolidate their gains and reform their forces for the next offensive stake. That such an accommodation is likely, is denied by many high government officials, particularly those closest to the Generalissimo. However, we have much information to the effect that even in the Army there is strong sentiment for a negotiated peace.

As we have stated before, the main barrier to a negotiated settlement is the intransigence of the Generalissimo and his closest supporters on one hand, and the Communists on the other. As yet there appears to be no effective, organized opposition to the Generalissimo, yet such opposition seems to be forming. The recently announced candidacy of Gen. Li Tsung-jen for the Vice Presidency may well provide leadership for opposition to the Generalissimo on this matter, and, if General Li should be elected, he would have means for making this opposition effective.

There seems to be some evidence that the Communists would, at this time, view with favor a chance for a negotiated settlement. They are now in a position militarily and politically to demand as much or more than in 1945–1946, and the Government—less the Gimo—might be willing to accede to these demands. Also, the Communists may feel a compulsion to consolidate their political control over the areas they now occupy, or would receive from a negotiated settlement, to train administrative personnel for the government of these areas and to make the necessary preparations for the political penetration of the rest of the country. . . .

Thus, the New Year which confronts the Chinese people presents a picture of little hope, much travail, and small prospect of a solution of their problems. We have noted a tendency to hold everything until the extent and the character of the Aid-to-China program is known. We have endeavored to counteract this tendency by pointing out to all who would listen that the major effort must come from the Chinese themselves and that the best way to insure American aid would be for the Chinese to initiate definite measures for their own economic betterment, but we have encountered expressions of intentions to do just that which were tinged with insincerity.

NANKING, *March 18, 1948.*

At the time our last letter was written, the Generalissimo had secluded himself at Kuling for a winter vacation. His absence from the helm of the ship of state lasted more than three weeks, and through this period he saw no one of consequence in his government. As may be imagined, this excursion in ergophobia gave rise to the wildest rumors, not the least sensational of which was that he had become convinced of his incompetency in governing, and so was selecting his successor. However, better informed and more knowledgeable persons agreed that he had retired to consult with himself as to what measures might be effective in the present exigency, and that on his return to the capital he either would or would not promulgate radical changes in policy. If the latter were true, it was held this could be taken as an indication that the Generalissimo is satisfied that his present policies are adequate to the task at hand.

Over two weeks have elapsed since the Generalissimo's return. In this period he has made no notable policy statements, nor have we any indication that any are contemplated. He has exhorted his officials to improve and purify their administration of public affairs, and he has informed the nation of the government's intention to defend Manchuria come what may, but he has in no wise indicated that he has any new solution for the tasks confronting him. If this be so, and we are of the belief that it is so, we take it as an indication that the Government has no new solution, and so we can see no reason to hope for a halt in the processes of decay and disintegration which have characterized the China scene these past several years.

We have not noted, since our last letter, any particularly spectacular examples of further disintegration in the Government's over-all position. However, the decline continues, and there is little doubt but what the Government will soon be faced with new crises. What is, perhaps, the salient characteristic of the Government's present situation is the fact while certain of its leaders have excellent and feasible plans for solving certain specific problems, there does not exist in the Government a complete and dynamic leadership to integrate such plans, implement them and carry them out. For example, Gen. Wei Li-huang, the Government commander in Manchuria, has an adequate plan for the continued defense of the Mukden area, yet the Government shows no signs of meeting Wei's fairly modest requirements. At the same time, Manchurian leaders have advised the Government that much support could be won from the Communists in the Northeast if the people of Manchuria were given more responsibility and authority in the management of their own affairs, under their own leaders. By way of reply, the Government offered honorary titles to the Manchurian leaders, announced its intention to hold Manchuria at all costs, and seemingly paid no heed to this advice. Similar examples of the attitude of the Government to the problems of China proper could be cited at great length, an attitude expressed in a policy of passive resignation to the many vicissitudes confronting it.

As we have reported before, the people of China, both officials and ordinary citizens regard with increasing disfavor this government which does not govern, or at most governs through inertia. Bitter criticism of its leadership is commonly expressed. The Generalissimo, once regarded as the unfortunate victim of incompetent advisors, is now viewed as personally responsible for his country's ills and feeling runs strong that any great prolongation of his leadership must certainly involve the entire country in ruin. In this situation many officials, particularly those outside the capital, believe that the time has come when they must look to their own interests as a matter of self preservation, and are so proceeding to develop a direct and personal control in the regions where they are assigned. We have been informed that Dr. T. V. Soong now seeks to increase his military resources in Kwangtung, and to integrate Hunan, Kwangsi, Kiangsi and Fukien into his province. In Hopei and Chahar there is some evidence to suggest that Gen. Fu Tso-yi may already have attained some degree of independence from Nanking control in the military sphere. Likewise, the Muhammadan leaders in Ninghsia show signs of questioning the authority of the Central Government, and in Shantung the provincial governor, Gen. Wang Yao-wu, has been openly critical of Government policies and has evinced a desire to seek American aid on a semi-independent basis. From these and similar indications, we conclude that local leaders in several parts of the country are, from lack of faith in the Central Government to continue to perform its functions, beginning to exhibit particularistic tendencies.

Besides this new growth of regionalism, we note, as we have reported, that the Government's ineptitude, particularly as regards the prosecution of the civil war, has brought some officials to consider the advisability of a mediated settlement with the Communists. Despite official Government denials, through its recent military attaché, Gen. Roschin, the Soviet Government informally suggested to certain Government leaders that the good offices of the Soviet Union could be obtained to arrange a mediated end to the present civil strife. The fact that, subsequent to his having made this suggestion, the Government, aware that he had done so, accepted General Roschin as the new Soviet Ambassador to China, leads us to believe that accommodation with the Communists must be favored by many influential persons within the government as preferable to a continuation of the status quo. The Chinese with whom we talk are of the opinion that accommodation means coalition government, and that through participating in a coalition government the Communists might come to control all of China by political means. Yet, faced as they are with mounting defeats in the civil war, and with the most colossal chaos in the administration of the nation's affairs, they cling to a forlorn hope that more can be salvaged from a mediated peace than would be saved if the entire country were to fall into Communist hands as the political disintegration develops.

The fact that at least some members of the Government look with favor on a Soviet offer to mediate an end to the civil war does not, in our opinion, necessarily indicate a firm trend for the Government to orient itself toward the Soviet Union, rather than the United States. Soviet mediation would, we feel, be accepted by non-Communist Chinese only with great reluctance, and only if it were clear that the negotiations with the Communists could come no other way. Except in very limited circles, the U.S.S.R. has no following in non-Communist China, and it is almost universally feared, disliked and mistrusted there. However, the possibility remains that the Soviets may succeed, perhaps through the insistence of their Chinese party, in forcing the Government to accept them as mediators.

In this situation, the slow increase of anti-American sentiment in the country is noteworthy. The origins of this sentiment are complex. In its most vocal expression, as it occurs in the statements of such public personages as Dr. Sun Fo, it is but little more than irresponsible and malicious talk. In other instances it is probably the result, direct or indirect, of Communist propaganda which reiterates the simple, but effective, theme of the Alliance between American imperialism and the rapacious and corrupt reactionary, Chiang Kai-shek. Effective as the Communist propaganda is, it largely serves to reinforce a common conviction, which we have referred to elsewhere, that the Generalissimo is, in fact, leading the country to ruin and chaos, and that he could not do so if it were not for the support which the American government has given him. Regardless of the validity of this idea, it is, as we say, commonly held. Although it is not, of course, found in the Government controlled press, this opinion is held by the intellectuals who staff the press, and so causes them to attack us and our policies for other matters, not directly pertinent to this issue.

As we have suggested above, the main political issue before most non-Communist Chinese today is how a settlement with the Communists can be reached which will leave a maximum of political control with non-Communist elements. It seems clear now that even those Chinese who are most strongly anti-Communist feel that this must be achieved by political means since it cannot be done by military methods. At the moment, the principal barrier to a political settlement is the Generalissimo and some of his closest followers, for, even though they might be inclined to accept such measures, there is no likelihood that the Communists would negotiate with any government led by the Generalissimo and participated in by some of his associates. In these circumstances, the question arises as to whether the Generalissimo would retire so as to make such negotiations possible. We feel sure that he will not do so as long as he has any hope that our military assistance to him will be of a scale and scope sufficient to allow him to gain a military decision or to prolong the civil war until such time as other events may force us to intervene decisively in his favor.

However, regardless of the fact that the Generalissimo may himself decide to depend on a military decision for a settlement of the civil war, there are some strong indications, as we have suggested, that he may not be allowed to do so, for opposition to this course of action continues to mount, and is becoming concrete and organized. It is in this connection that the vice-presidential candidacy of Gen. Li Tsung-jen is significant. General Li's candidacy was announced without reference to the Generalissimo. He has attracted support from Dr. Hu Shih, from other academicians and intellectuals, and, we believe, from many political personages of importance. There is some evidence to suggest that he will have a large amount of support from army circles, and possibly from Marshal Li Chi-shen and his followers. General Li's principal opposition lies in the C. C. Clique, which will support Yu Yu-jen. It is likely that Yu will have the Generalissimo's backing as well. Since the election will be held in the Legislative Yuan, which is almost entirely packed by the C. C. Clique, it is likely that Yu will be elected. However, this cannot be taken as a certainty, for provincial leaders will exercise much influence over provincial delegations, and a real contest may develop. In any event, dissatisfaction with the activities of the Government's leadership will be freely expressed.

As will be noted from the foregoing, we are now entering an era of political change in China. Not all of the forces which make for this change are immediately clear. Though some of the larger outlines are beginning to emerge, any comments as to how current trends will work out must be highly speculative. However, we are on relatively sure ground when we point out, as we have above, that present Government leadership is in the process of being repudiated by those who have formerly supported it; that opposition to this leadership is becoming concrete and organized, and is primarily based on opposition to the Government's policy of settling the Communist question by military means; that the present leadership must almost certainly go unless actively sustained in power by us; and, that if there is a change in leadership, the new leaders will reach a political settlement with the Communists which may very likely result in some form of coalition.

NANKING, *May 1, 1948*

Whatever the ultimate result of the recent session of the National Assembly and the elections of the first President and Vice President under the Constitution, it seems to me that two phenomena were made clear: Firstly, the Gimo, by masterful political strategy, coupled, I believe, with at least a certain amount of sincerity, refused to be a candidate for the Presidency, with the result that he finds himself elected to that office with confirmed authority, albeit somewhat battered by the fray. He succeeded in establishing his indispensability at. this stage, even though his policies have been repudiated, and in demonstrating that he, and he alone, can hold together the present governmental structure based, as it is, on the support of more or less independent Generals, with their more or less personal armies, who are restrained from declaring their complete regional autonomy by self-interest, of course, but also largely by their loyalty to the Generalissimo. Should he disappear from the scene at this time, they would inevitably revert, I believe, to the regionalism that existed prior to the march north of the Kuominchun and we would see an era of *sauve qui peut.*

Secondly, the liberals, or the reformers, or whatever you wish to call them— those who were rapidly becoming desperate in their desire to bring new life into a government that was slowly, but surely, committing suicide—were able to demonstrate and make effective their strength by rallying behind Li Tsung-jen, who has emerged, whether he is qualified or not, as the great reformer, and elected him Vice President despite the most violent efforts of an efficient CC Clique machine, supported by an irate, but arrogant and not too adept Generalissimo. The reactionary, who agreed to a secret ballot in that election, will now rue the day he did so. I am told that when Li Tsung-jen's strength became evident, the Generalissimo called Chen Li-fu on the mat and there were heated words as to why Chen had not been able to control the vote as he had promised. Maybe now Chen will once more, as he has in the past, express a desire to visit the U.S. to study "democratic institutions" !

Our interest during the past few weeks, has, of course, been largely centered on these meetings of the National Assembly. Its activities have had pride of place in the press and have formed the topic of conversation everywhere. Even the shopkeeper, avid for his gain, kept one ear on the radio, while the other was listening to his customer. Also, wherever there was a loud-speaker on the streets of Nanking, crowds could be found listening to the results.

Going back a little bit, our information indicates that in the elections to the National Assembly and to the new Legislative Yuan, as well as during the first meetings of the Assembly, it was evident that the party bosses of the KMT regarded the establishment of constitutional government as an exercise in machine politics. It was obviously their intention to use the party machine and the prestige of the Generalissimo to control the new Government as they had the old, and they were prepared to use whatever means were necessary to accomplish this end. They were aghast, therefore, when the Generalissimo, without, I believe, real prior consultation with his supporters, announced his intention not to stand for President. It was the decision he had made in Kuling over the Chinese New Year and which had been long and expectedly awaited although no one, I believe, had previous knowledge of the nature of the decision he had made. To the party machine, the Generalissimo was an indispensable man. He had helped create and had protected the machine and since he ruled through it, it was indispensable to him as well. The Whampoa Generals, the Paoting Generals, and the Generals of no Clique whatsoever, including the Mo-hammedan Generals of the West, all of whom care little for the Nationalist Government, insisted that if he left the Ship of State, so would they. This situation cannot have been unknown to the Generalissimo, and it is for this reason, even though we do not question his sincerity, that we credit him with a masterful political tactic when he refused to stand for President. Having let himself be persuaded, which, if our assumption is correct, was not a difficult task, that he was indispensable to the country, the circumstances of his past forced him once again to strive to bring the party machine with him in full power into the new Government, to exclude its opponents, and to amend the Constitution so as to make the new Government susceptible to his personal control as had been that Government which was passing. Through an amendment to the Constitution, he obtained the full powers necessary to maintain his personal control and he sought continued power for the party machine through his support of Sun Fo for the Vice Presidency, with every indication that the party machine would find some way to see that Sun Fo remained also as the elected President of the Legislative Yuan.

The machine had rigged the elections to the National Assembly and had thus retained an almost solid bloc of delegates which could be strictly controlled, and which included politically experienced individuals well able to stir the Assembly and to control its deliberations. Also, it had at its disposal a disciplined corps of political workers skilled in such minor political arts as bribery and intimidation. It had a controlled press, which could be counted on not to expose its more flagrant violations of the amenities of democratic procedure and it had at its service, at least so most delegates thought, the secret police. Finally, through its affiliation with the Whampoa Generals, an affiliation so close as to make them, to all intents and purposes, a part of the machine, it had with it the bulk of the Army High Command.

Thus, the party machine was an organized political force of no little magnitude. Yet it was committed in support of reactionary principles, which had been implicitly, if not openly and explicitly, rejected by the rank and file of the KMT, and by independent individuals and groups within Nationalist China. These principles involved essentially the perpetuation of the personal autocratic rule of the Generalissimo and his closest followers.

The opponents in the KMT of this reactionary leadership had, and still have, no cohesive organization. Such union as is found among them is based on their common dissatisfaction with the Government's lack of concrete achievement, on their well-grounded fear that the Government, as at present constituted, cannot prevent the further spread of Communism, and on their belief in democracy and in constitutional government. A benevolent despotism had remained despotic while ceasing to be benevolent. The community of interest and views among opponents of the party machine would not, in the ordinary course of events, suffice to move them to united action, yet the flagrant intervention of the machine in the elections and the all too obvious intervention of the machine and of the Generalissimo in the deliberations of the Assembly and in the Assembly's Vice Presidential elections, moved most delegates to consider ways and means of protecting their interest and of representing their constituents.

As a result, revolt against party solidarity developed. The clash came to a head in the Vice Presidential elections. Independent delegates had shown disgruntlement when the party machine, during the meetings of the Assembly, had successfully prevented free debate of the shortcomings of the Government, and they felt further frustration when the Generalissimo and the party machine intervened, all too openly, to prevent the election of Li Tsung-jen. (We are told on good authority that the Generalissimo called in Li Tsung-jen and demanded his withdrawal and that at one stage he offered Ch'eng Ch'ien, who was running third, complete reimbursement for all his campaign expenses if he would withdraw in favor of Sun Fo.) The frustration of these independent delegates and of the disgruntled members of the KMT coalesced in support of Li Tsung-jen as the one who had campaigned for reform.

Aroused by this evidence of mounting dissatisfaction and organized opposition, the KMT machine threw all its resources into the battle, vilifying Li and intimidating his supporters. These tactics aroused violent resentment and Li, in a masterful manoeuvre, announced his withdrawal from the race in order to demonstrate clearly the nature and source of the attacks to which he and his supporters were being subjected. There is evidence that his withdrawal was concerted with that of Ch'eng Ch'ien. As was anticipated, Li's move, supported by that of Ch'eng Ch'ien, gained the sympathy of the general public and of those delegates to the National Assembly not under strict machine control. Blame for the situation was increasingly placed on the Generalissimo, and since Ch'eng Ch'ien, the only other nonmachine candidate remaining in the race, had withdrawn in sympathy with Li, the Generalissimo was forced to direct Sun Fo to withdraw his candidacy as well. Also, in order to persuade Li and Ch'eng to re-enter the race, the Gimo was compelled to give absolute assurances, both private as well as public, that the Vice Presidential race would henceforth be free and without party duress, each member of the National Assembly being allowed to vote as his conscience dictated. Incidentally, to make sure the Generalissimo didn't go back on his promises, the Assembly delegates took elaborate precautions to see that the vote was not only secret, but that the ballots were also accurately counted. The result of all this, as is known to you, was the election of Li Tsung-jen as Vice President by 143 votes (1,438 to 1,295), or, in other words, a photo finish.

It remains to be seen whether the emergence of Li Tsung-jen, as what might be called leader of a reform group, can be confirmed. Those who supported him are of divergent views, and of his qualities as a political leader, we know little, though he shows promise. We can only hope that these stirrings of democracy which were so evident in the Vice Presidential election may grow into legitimate and effective opposition to the reactionary elements in the Government. What existed as opposition to the Generalissimo and to the KMT party machine was, in essence, we believe, a demand for change and reform which had not yet become an organized political force. Having shown sufficient strength to elect Li Tsung-jen as Vice President in spite of the strenuous efforts of the CC Clique, backed by the Generalissimo, the reformers now have a spokesman, and their chosen leader can speak with authority if he plays his cards well. Nevertheless, the Generalissimo and the machine control the key posts in the Government, and how they will accommodate themselves to the pressure for change remains to be seen. We can only hope that the liberal elements which have thus expressed themselves will be able to assert strength toward reform within the Government and within the country sufficient to give some hope that the present onsweep of Communist expansion may be checked and some day reversed.

In the meantime the lull in military activities does not warrant, we believe, any confidence in the ability of the Government at the moment to checkmate any Communist move which Communist strategy may dictate. The Generalissimo announced on New Year's that the Communists would be of no military importance between the Yellow and Yangtze Rivers in six months. Yet months have gone by and we see little sign of action toward accomplishing that end. Weihsien in Shantung, the first walled city to go by frontal attack supported by heavy artillery, is only one more example of the incapability of the National Leadership to direct an offensive. Here, as elsewhere, the Nationalist troops encamp behind walls and wait for the Communists to come pick them off. Present indications are that the Communists may by-pass Mukden, and strike toward Chinhuangtao.

Yet we see no real activity to counter this move. Fu Tso-yi in Peiping, as has Wang Yao-wu in Shantung, is showing increasing tendencies toward independence, and we find it difficult to believe that he will remain in that area under serious Communist threat. We are watching the situation closely in hope that we can give Americans in that area sufficient advance warning should we become convinced that Fu Tso-yi will not fight, but will withdraw toward Chahar and Suiyuan. Wang Yao-wu has already warned Americans in Shantung to seek places of safety, and the situation in Central China looks none too good. There are already creditable rumors that the Communists have penetrated south of the Yangtze and that we will be hearing in due course from new concentrations. Unless some means can be found to revive the spirit of the Nationalist troops and possibly, just barely possibly, Li Tsung-jen and his backers may be able to accomplish this, there seems little hope of effective resistance to continued expansion of the Communists where and when they will.

We have been interested in the failure of Roschin, the former Soviet Military Attaché in Nanking, who has been Soviet Ambassador Designate here, to return to Nanking. We were told the other day that he has asked for a visa and is expected here early in May. We feel that the timing of his arrival has some meaning, but as yet we have no good guess.

One element in the Li Tsung-jen candidacy which has worried us, has been the possibility that he might seek an accommodation with the Communists, and there is recent evidence that he may have had, and may maintain, contact with the KMT Revolutionary Committee in Hong Kong. It is not entirely beyond the realm of possibility, therefore, that Roschin's return to Nanking at this time may in some way be connected with developments in the National Assembly.

NANKING, *June 12, 1948*

Although the military situation has been deteriorating at an alarming rate during the past month, the attention of Government leaders has been directed almost entirely to political maneuvering and the election of a new Government.

With the selection of the Premier and the Cabinet, Government under the new Constitution has finally come into being. The personnel of the new Government is largely recruited from the old, and the new elements present are so dominated by the groups which held power before that no far-reaching changes in policy are likely.

In general, the reaction of the country to the new Government is most unfavorable. We have heard few expressions of faith that it is competent to improve the situation, and there is much talk that it will soon be replaced. When the National Assembly met, it was hoped by many that somehow, through its deliberations, a political renaissance would be effected, which would culminate in the creation of a strong Government capable of halting the spread of Communism. The Generalissimo was given extraordinary powers to achieve this end, and his critics offered their advice and their services to assist him. What was wanted of the Generalissimo was dynamic, effective leadership. The Generalissimo, however, has failed to respond to this demand. While he has retained his almost unlimited authority, he has come forward with no new program. His rejection of the services of Li Tsung-jen as an advisor, and his continued reliance on incompetent men to head the new Ministries combine to convince most people that his leadership will continue to be uninspired and essentially disruptive. Since it has become apparent that he intends to continue his personal rule, and has no intention of responding to the popular demand for change, widespread dissatisfaction develops, and the Generalissimo has become more unpopular than at any time in his career.

In view of this increasing dissatisfaction with the Generalissimo and his Government, it is surprising that there is no apparent popular demand for his removal from office. The opposition elements within the Government talk mainly in terms of supplanting the C. C. Clique and of offering the Generalissimo better and more disinterested advice. If there were open agitation for the Generalissimo's removal, rather than covert dissatisfaction with his rule, Li Tsung-jen and certain groups in the Government would probably respond to it. But there is no popular, open movement in this direction, although the Generalissimo loses in prestige each day he fails to provide that leadership necessary to rally the people in defense against Communism. The prevailing mood is one of despair and resignation to what is regarded as the inevitable victory of Communism. Furthermore, there is a growing belief that Communism would be a not unattractive alternative to the present ineffective regime, particularly since such a change would bring with it an end to civil war.

As an accommodation with the Communists might be expected to include the removal from the scene of the Generalissimo with whom the Communists may be expected to refuse to deal, the question of his successor immediately arises and there is no obvious person available. The Generalissimo has dominated the scene for so long, no one stands out as capable of replacing him. Li Chi-shen of the Kuomintang Revolutionary Committee is, of course, "available" yet we have no way of gauging the strength of his support. It might easily be someone within the Kuomintang itself. Nevertheless, we find it difficult to believe that the Generalissimo can be removed from the scene except at the expense of national unity. It was demonstrated most clearly in the Presidential election that it is the Generalissimo that holds this vast country together and that without him it would likely fall apart. Should he leave the scene and should regionalism result, the Communist task would be made much more easy.

In the military field, it is obvious that the Communists continue to gain and the Government appears incapable of saving that part of China not yet in Communist hands. The military position of the Government is deteriorating rapidly and has become critical in several areas. The Government armies in Manchuria are virtually isolated, must inevitably be contained in their present positions by siege and cannot influence the military decision in China proper, even though their capitulation should be long postponed. The Communist offensive in Jehol is succeeding in reducing the local Nationalist garrisons, and Fu Tso-yi finds himself under heavy attack along the Jehol border. While General Fu should be able to stop the initial assault against his northern defenses, the fact that he has large Communist armies on his flanks and his rear makes his situation dangerous. It is probable that, as the campaign progresses, the Manchurian Communists will be able to secure a foothold on the North China Plain.

Except for a minor Nationalist victory in Northern Kiangsu, there have been no Nationalist successes through the past month. A large Communist concentration has crossed the Yellow River without opposition northwest of the junction of the Lunghai and Tsinpu railroads. The Tsinpu has been cut near Taian, isolating Tsinan. Lin-yi, the last Government garrison in Southern Shantung, is now under attack, and is not expected to offer prolonged resistance. The Communists are in sufficient force just north of the Lunghai to besiege Hsuchou, or to by-pass that point and drive toward the north bank of the Yangtze, near Nanking. While their intentions are not yet clear, the latter move remains a strong possibility.

Observers report no improvement in the morale of the Nationalist forces, now at a dangerously low ebb. Field Commanders and troops are unwilling to fight, except as a last resort, and large-scale defection of combat elements confronted with battle can be expected to continue. While the Government's military situation has probably not yet become critical in the sense that a general military collapse is imminent, only inspired and dynamic military leadership can long postpone, let alone avert, that eventuality, and there are no officers having such qualities in positions of authority.

The general public is well aware of the continuing deterioration in the political, military and economic spheres and is disillusioned and despairing of improvement. In this situation, the notion that stability can come only through the cessation of the civil war has become an *idee fixe*, the currency of which spreads rapidly. Thus, the people of Nationalist China become less and less inclined actively to resist Communism. In this state of mind, our China Aid Program is condemned, even by its direct beneficiaries, as a factor prolonging the civil war. Since the Government prohibits anti-civil war propaganda, this condemnation of our aid is sublimated and transferred into an attack on our policies in Japan by student groups and other elements of the population. This nascent anti-American feeling is, of course, exploited and fanned by Communist propaganda organs, and is further fostered by some elements of the Government-controlled press, which uses this means to distract attention from the Government's own shortcomings. There is inherent in this situation a very grave danger to the American position in China. We still have in this country a large backlog of good-will, particularly among the educated classes. However, in their present suffering the people of China do not discriminate between friend and enemy. Nor do they clearly perceive where their interests lie. In the eyes of many Chinese, we bear the onus for supporting and keeping in power an unpopular regime which does not have the interests of the country at heart. We are blamed for preventing its replacement by a government which promises, as they see it, to be an improvement. And we are further condemned because the regime we support patently fails to meet the minimum requirements that any people asks of those who rule it. This state of mind, we believe, is playing no small part in the present student anti-American campaign.

On the other hand, recent reports from Communist territory indicate that the Communists have difficulties of their own. The principal of these is a shortage of qualified administrative personnel for political posts, and a lack of personnel with the more advanced economic skills. Their revolutionary program and propaganda are now designed to secure the support of potential administrators, but the violence and brutality which has characterized their political activity continue to alienate many. However, in appealing to administrators and to persons possessing knowledge of advanced agricultural, industrial and commercial techniques, the Communist leaders have had to jettison their practice of economic egalitarianism. This costs them at least some of the support of the agrarian and industrial proletariat which forms the mass basis for their revolution. Although the Communists have been spectacularly successful in the military sphere, their victories have been over a most incompetent opponent. Should the efficiency of the Government armies be restored, even to its war-time level, the Communists could no longer hope for cheap victories. Indeed, as the military situation now stands, the Communists may be forced to undertake campaigns involving formal, positional warfare. The Communists have yet to win a battle under such conditions, and should the Government armies dictate the conditions of battle, as they are capable of doing, some large Communist defeats can be anticipated.

It is a black picture, yet in the final analysis, we incline to the belief that the situation of the Government, critical though it is, is not entirely beyond repair. The adoption of only a few positive policies would improve its position immensely. What the Government now suffers from as much as anything is that its own personnel and its own supporters have no confidence in it. To cite a single instance, a high ranking Chinese Government Army officer has told one of the staff officers of AAG that the Executive Yuan is refusing to provide funds for certain military expenditures on grounds that the civil war is already lost.

We are doing what we can to bolster morale in Government circles and we are leaving no stones unturned in our efforts to assure that advantage will be taken of the respite afforded by the Aid to China Program to institute the reforms and find the leadership necessary to rally the people and encourage them to resist Communist expansion. If those vast numbers who do not want to be Communists can be given even one ray of hope it may yet be possible to turn the tide though time is rapidly running out.

NANKING, *August 24, 1948*

In recent weeks the Chinese political scene has been characterized by obscurity. Trends and developments which had been clear and traceable became less evident, and the various definite patterns of political activity which we had been watching became ill-defined and indistinct. It became evident, however, that certain stabilizing factors are beginning to retard the recent rapid decline in the Government's position. We do not feel that these factors will be permanently effective in the sense that they will halt once and for all the general deterioration pervading Nationalist China. Disintegrating forces are still dominant. However, we feel that the Government is in somewhat less danger of collapse than was the case a month or six weeks ago. In fact, the Gimo and his new Cabinet under Wong Wen-hao are showing signs of determination to survive.

The principal dangers to the Government continue to be the progressive deterioration of the military situation, the prospect of a breach in Nationalist ranks through the formation of regional political associations, the crisis in the national economy and the inability of the Government to exercise effective political controls in many spheres of public and private activity. The Government is well aware of the gravity of this situation, and, in its own way, is developing means for meeting it.

The most important recent event, of course, is the series of financial and economic measures promulgated by the Executive Yuan on August 20. A new currency called the Gold Yuan is established, the bank notes themselves being the so-called Sun currency which was actually printed about three years ago. CNC is to be converted to the Gold Yuan at the rate of three million to one, and the Gold Yuan itself has a gold content valuation which works out at four to one U.S. dollar. The Government announced that this currency will be backed by holdings of bullion, specie and foreign exchange amounting to U.S. $200,000,000 and the pledge of securities in Government-owned enterprise, on which latter a valuation of U.S. $300,000,000 has been placed. There is a provision that the Gold Yuan cannot be issued in an amount exceeding the value of this backing. At the moment this is academic since it is calculated that the U. S. dollar value of total CNC and NEC outstanding is only in the neighborhood of U.S. $70,000,000. The difference between that sum and the total "backing" is the .authority to the printing presses to meet the deficit in the coming months. So much for the highlights of the currency measures.

The currency reform was accompanied by a series of measures designed to accomplish the near-balancing of the Government's budget, and the reduction of the export-import deficit. Many of these measures involve future executory acts, clarifying regulations, and the establishment of enforcement machinery. Exports are to be stimulated, imports cut, wages and prices frozen as of the August 19 levels, strikes banned, and holdings of gold, silver, and foreign currency, at home and abroad, are to be nationalized. In connection with the latter, there is a whale of an informer's fee; to wit, 40% of the Government's recovery in any individual case.

All of this represents Wong Wen-hao's supreme effort. It has been received so far with complete skepticism by sophisticates and some genuine expressions of hope and relief by rick-shaw boys. Real effort is being made to appeal to the patriotism of all the Chinese people and the Gimo has thrown his full influence behind it. It might work, but if it does it will only be because the Government executes the program with ruthlessness, courage and effectiveness.

So far as the future of the Gold Yuan is concerned, it seems to us the only real change is, first, the acceptance and legalization of the black market rate as the new official exchange rate. If internal prices can be, in fact, frozen as is the intention, this should have a highly beneficial effect on exports. The second accomplishment is nominal. It is the removal of the daily inconvenience which has been entailed in handling bales of CNC for even minor transactions. Otherwise, the basic factors remain just what they were before the measures were promulgated; there is no more backing to the new currency than existed for the old, and the budget of the Government is just as hopelessly out of balance today as it was last week. We don't want to appear unduly pessimistic, but our guess is that we will have a very few weeks of relative stability in prices and then the new Gold Yuan will start sliding in terms of the U.S. gold dollar, picking up where the late, unlamented CNC left off.

In the military field the Government's efforts continue ineffectual. The bulk of its field commanders have proven themselves incompetent in battle, and ignorant or neglectful of the primary objective of military operations—the destruction of the enemy. The Government can still compel and entice its armies to continue resistance, but it does not appear able to mobilize its military and other resources and use them in the offensive effort necessary to restore the military situation to its own advantage. A case in point is now shaping up in the Hsuchow area. The Governor has been anticipating strong Communist attack on Hsuchow and has been concentrating troops in that area. As matters now stand, General Chen-yi, with his strong Communist columns, is maneuvering in the area around Yingchow in Northwest Anhwei. He has gotten himself into such a position that it would be a not too difficult task for the Government troops to encirclé him and annihilate his forces. This they plan to do, yet our experience cautions us to anticipate that inability of the Government to compel obedience to its commands, lack of uniform command in the theater, unwillingness of one Government General to cooperate with another or come to the aid of another, and the traditional Chinese inclination to leave an avenue of escape open so as to avoid real battle if possible, will all result in much maneuvering, little actual fighting, and the retirement North of Chen Yi's forces practically intact.

If the Government troops should surprise us and actually encircle and annihilate Chen Yi, which we are informed by competent authority is within their capability, such an action should change the course of military events for some time and might serve as the inspiration needed to spur others on to victory.

Until we are convinced, however, that Government troops are capable of taking strong offensive action, we feel that were it not for the fact that the Communist armies themselves have difficulties, a general military collapse on the part of Government forces would likely occur. It does not appear at the moment, however, that the logistic services of the Communists are such that they can support a massive, protracted assault of sufficient weight and duration to reduce and take any of the more strongly garrisoned Nationalist centers. Under these conditions, the Communists must perforce keep to their strategy of containment, attrition, and limited attack. Changchun is now starving and will fall of its own weight one of these days. This strategy will bring them no quick victory unless there should intervene political and economic factors which contribute to break the will of the Nationalists to continue their resistance; but, as the battle now goes, their victory will be delayed beyond what might have been expected several months ago.

The steps which the Government can take to improve the military picture continue limited. The sheer inertia of a war-weary populace, plus the fact that the Government cannot control many of its own members who place self-interest above the welfare of the nation, militate against the development of an all-out war effort. Given the complex personal and political relationships of the Officer Corps, it is all but impossible to remove incompetent Officers of high rank, or to reward the few men of merit with suitable promotions and authority.

The threat of the formation of independent regional governments appears less imminent than was the case of a month ago, when well-founded reports indicated that the forces of disintegration were actively at work. While there is little doubt that regional leaders, and such dissident organizations as the KMTRC, are still thinking in terms of separatism and still planning to that end, it looks very much as though they have come to think that an overt break with Nanking is not feasible at the present time. This is not to say that the dissidents and potential dissidents have effected any sort of a reconciliation with Nanking, or that they have abandoned the thought that they must prepare to set up their own regime or regimes against the day when the present government disappears. Their liking for the Gimo has not increased, nor has their confidence in his leadership. However, it seems at the moment that they do not intend to influence the course of events by an overt move which would help unseat the Gimo. Rather, it appears that they intend to wait for what they regard as the inevitable collapse of the Nanking Government before venturing on the establishment of their own independent political associations.

If this appraisal is correct, we believe that the reluctance of the dissidents to make an open break very likely stems from a new realization that the present Government still performs for them certain indispensable functions. Principal among these at the moment is Nanking's role in channeling American aid to the Provinces. We have made it abundantly clear that we support the Nanking Government. We have also made it plain that we intend to consult the Nanking Government on the allocation of our economic aid, and it is a well-known fact that the disposition of military aid is Nanking's responsibility. In this situation, the potential dissident, who cannot dispense with American aid, is bound to Nanking by very strong ties. Also, Nanking continues to supply such vital necessities as air and sea transportation, money and civil governmental organization. . . .

Manchurian regionalism also appears quiescent. The Northeastern politicos cannot move without the concurrence of Wei Li-huang, and Wei cannot dispense with the supplies and air transport that he receives from Nanking via Chinchow. Thus, he is even less likely to favor a break with the Gimo than Fu Tso-yi. In this connection, for the past several days the vernacular press has been quoting unidentified "informed sources in Government circles" to the effect that the Young Marshal is soon to be released. Government spokesmen, including Hollington Tong, make no comment on the report. This story appears at irregular intervals, generally when the Northeastern leaders become restive, and is doubtlessly designed to quiet them. We have no reason to believe, however, that the Gimo has changed his hitherto adamant refusal to release the Young Marshal under any circumstances.

The picture remains still black. Yet it is not as black as it has been and there is some evidence that the Government has obtained a new lease on life. If the economic measures can afford the breathing spell required and if the Government succeeds in taking even a part of the drastic action planned for reform, and if, by some miracle, it can bring a real victory in the military field, collapse of the Government may be postponed indefinitely. As we have said so often in the past, the bulk of the Chinese people does not want to be Communist and would cooperate heartily with any regime which gives promise of an efficient alternative. On the other hand, as one Chinese intellectual remarked to us recently: "You can't deny the lessons of history, and history will show that in China, periods of chaos are inevitably followed by periods of tyranny." We are certainly experiencing a period of chaos.

NANKING, *November 8, 1948*

Within the past few weeks, the Government's military power and economic position have so deteriorated that we seriously question its ability to survive for long. There is just no will to fight in Nationalist Government armies and in high official circles there is only befuddlement. We have reported on the various crises that the Government has had to face, and for that matter still faces, and there is no need to recount them here. It will suffice to say that at no time has the Government been able to devise measures adequate and suitable to the tasks confronting it, and that most of the measures adopted have actually operated to the Government's detriment. There is little or no confidence in official Chinese circles that the Gimo has mustered, or can muster, the resources needed to rescue his regime. While there are some in the Government who say that increased American assistance can still save the day, we are inclined to believe that most of those who take this line are not, in fact, convinced that any practicable amount of aid can save them. The departure of the Gimo has been mooted in the Legislative Yuan, and peace has been advocated editorially in the Tientsin vernacular press. These sentiments are widely, if not generally, held, and it cannot be long before further military and economic debacles and their translation into effective political action.

Precisely when and exactly how the present Government will go is impossible to foretell. There are so many imponderables involved that no firm prediction can be made. However, when it goes there must be sooner or later a new government for China, and this must be either wholly Communist in character, or one in which the Communists play a leading role. There will very likely be certain sections of the country that will hold aloof for the time being to see how the wind blows. Nevertheless, it appears at the moment that the new "Central" Government will result from an association of the Communists with the minority parties and a segment of the KMT. In this case the degree of control which the Communists exercise will always be enough to insure that their opponents cannot combine to eliminate them by force. Actually, the extent of this control is virtually at their pleasure, for they can very likely maintain the preponderance of military power which they now hold and so enforce their will against their opponents. Thus, insofar as the opposition cannot, through the foreseeable future, develop the military potential needed for a counter revolution, the new government must be very much what the Communists choose to make it.

If there is one thing certain in this situation, it is that the problems facing the new government will be of an almost indescribable magnitude. The native agrarian economy is in grave crisis, and that segment of the national economy organized along Western lines is in an equally serious plight. At almost all levels political institutions no longer function as they were intended to, so that a state of loosely controlled anarchy obtains. Only a part of the general chaos is directly attributable to the civil war; many of the crises stem from the deeper contradictions of Chinese society. We can assume that the new government will soon succeed in ending civil strife, though conflict may continue briefly in peripheral areas and may flare up anew from time to time. We can also assume that the new government will display more administrative ability and that it will, at least in initial stages, have a higher degree of probity than the present regime. From these assumptions we may expect it to make some substantial progress in solving those problems which are the products of civil war and bad government, and so contribute to its own stability.

We have often pointed out just how the present Government has been wont to do those things it ought not to do, and to leave undone those things it ought to do, and how, in so doing and not doing, it was bringing on its own downfall. The main problem facing the new government is to do those things it ought to do in meeting the minimum requirements any government must provide for those it rules. Here we may fairly question whether the new government has this capacity, and from all indications it would appear that the answer is in the negative. Briefly, the basic problem of the new government will be the ordering of the national economy so as to insure a livelihood to all, and at the same time acquire from the nation's production a surplus for its own support. This involves the rehabilitation of the national economy—not only in terms of repair and replacement to physical plant—but also reconstruction of economic institutions, and it involves the reorganization of the economy in terms of a new economic and social philosophy which is altogether an import and has no real roots in the country. To do these things, the new government will need a feasible program, good administrative personnel, and it will need, above all, matériel. Whether its program is feasible remains to be seen. It is certainly true that it has not worked too well in the agrarian areas which the Communists have held. It may work on a national scale if sufficiently amended, but deep and vital changes will be difficult without doing violence to the Communists' basic, underlying dogma. Good administrative personnel they lack, as do the Nationalists. Indeed, effective, trained administrators are in short supply throughout China. The material most needed are capital goods which cannot be produced within the country and must be imported. There is little prospect in the foreseeable future that, however and by whomever managed, the national economy can produce a surplus, over and above the requirements of the State for its own maintenance, to pay for the imports needed.

The difficulties we mention, while basic, are only a few of the many that will arise. However, on a short term basis the prospects are that a new government will achieve some success, and will gain a considerable measure of popular support. For one thing, it will have brought about an end to the civil war, the consummation devoutly to be wished as far as most Chinese are concerned, regardless of the manner of its coming. Also, it will at the outset likely be able to do certain things of benefit to the masses, which any "good" government could do. Indeed, it may well, over a considerable period of time, be regarded by the body politic as a vast change for the better. But as it must come to grips with its fundamental problems, its chances of giving a satisfactory performance diminish. . . .

Our foregoing comments concern the longer view, rather than the immediate future. As we say, what will come in the next several months, or even weeks, is almost impossible to predict. The fall of Mukden, which occurs as this is written, is likely the beginning of the final series of military debacles for Nationalist arms. At the moment it appears that the isolation of Hsuchou has begun. In this situation, of all the Government there are few, if any, save the Gimo who even profess confidence that the tide may yet be turned. Only a few days before Mukden fell, the Government had five well equipped, supplied and trained armies in the Manchurian field, the most formidable striking force at its command, and within few days these armies were lost. They were lost not from battle casualties, but from defection, although among their commanders were numbered officers long associated with the Gimo, and in whose loyalty he trusted implicitly. The troops at Hsuchou are far inferior to the former Mukden garrison, and their commanders are already resigned to defeat. There is no reason to believe in their will or ability to resist an offensive. And when they are gone, Nanking has no defenses worthy of the name.

It is not difficult to see why the Gimo retains some confidence in his star. His beginnings were modest, and from them, against great odds, he led a revolution and was the principal architect of a new state. For a time his government was successful. More than that he was able to maintain it through the eight years of his war with Japan and in the end to regain the territories that he had lost. His achievements are by no means inconsiderable, and they testify to his qualities. There is a tendency on our part to forget that Chiang succeeded as a revolutionary, and that he still regards his party as a revolutionary party. It was his fate that there should develop in China another revolution in competition with his own, and that, in the broader view, the KMT has become to the Communist revolution what the old, war-lord regimes were to Chiang as he rose to power. The Gimo does not understand this, and so, to some extent, he regards himself as the protagonist of a revolution which must in the end succeed because all men must recognize that it is essentially right. To that extent he must regard his triumph was inevitable and his reverses as but setbacks incidental to the temporary perversion of natural order. These are, in general, the reasons which constrain him to continue the struggle when it has become apparent that it is a lost cause.

There appears no reason to believe that the Gimo has, or will consider, a negotiated peace with the Communists, even should they agree to deal with him. This intransigence will prolong the conflict as long as there are any who will stand by him. It remains to be seen how many of his followers will remain when the news of Mukden becomes generally known. Their members will be appreciably less when the assault on Hsuchou begins. Whether he will have enough of a following to attempt a defense of Nanking is problematical, even doubtful, but it seems clear that once he has left Nanking in flight, he will never again be really effective political force in this country.

167

New Year Message, 1949, of President Chiang Kai-shek [27]

My Fellow Countrymen:

On this thirty-eighth anniversary of the founding of the Republic of China and the first anniversary after the introduction of constitutional Government, I observe with great regret that our national reconstruction efforts have come to a state of suspension and the Three People's Principles still remain to be achieved.

Since the end of the war against Japan, the main object of the Government has been to lay down a firm foundation for peace and reconstruction so as to alleviate the sufferings of the people. The task which the Government considered as of great importance was to recover the Northeast, thereby preserving China's national sovereignty and territorial integrity. But, unfortunately, we have not been able to do this.

On the other hand, Tsinan was lost to the Communists and Chinchow, Changchun, and Mukden fell into their hands in succession. The Mukden tragedy of 1931 has repeated itself. Commercial and industrial cities as well as cultural centers in North and East China are now being menaced by the Communists.

During this national crisis I cannot but blame myself for my inadequate leadership. I am sorry that I have not lived up to the high expectation of the people.

WILL NOT ABANDON LIBERTY

The military situation has entered upon an exceedingly perilous stage. The fate of the nation and the historical and cultural continuity of our people will soon be decided. The issue of this struggle will determine whether the Chinese people will continue to live as free men and women or as slaves, and whether they will live at all or perish.

Everyone is concerned over the policy which the Government has pursued in dealing with the situation. We are convinced that all patriotic citizens will not tolerate the Communist method of "liquidation" and "struggle" and that they are not willing to abandon their liberty and to remain inactive at this critical moment.

But we are also fully aware that military operations have increased the people's burden and that they hope for an early conclusion of the war. Shouldering the responsibility of the conduct of national affairs, I have carefully studied the situation and considered the wishes of the people.

The Father of our Republic once said: "The aim of national reconstruction of the Republic of China is peace." Being a strong believer in the Three People's Principles and abiding by Dr. Sun Yat-sen's bequeathed teachings, I did not have any intention to fight the Communists at the end of the war.

Immediately after V-J Day, the Government declared its principles for peace and reconstruction. Later it went one step further by seeking to solve the Communist question by means of political consultation.

In the subsequent one and a half years, the Communists disregarded every agreement and obstructed every peace effort that was made. As a result, these agreements and the programs which were agreed upon were not implemented.

In the end, the Communists started an all-out rebellion, thereby endangering the very existence of the nation. Unwillingly, the Government was forced to order a general mobilization and to proceed with the anti-Communist campaign. I am sure that these historical facts are still vivid in your minds.

---

[27] Reprinted from *China Information Bulletin* (New York), vol. II, Jan. 7, 1949.

Communism has already had a history of twenty-five years in China. In this period I have never for a moment given up the hope that the Communists would place the national interests above that of their own, would follow the regular courses as befitting a political party, and would join hands with the Government in finding ways to work for peace and national existence.

CHALLENGES REDS' SINCERITY

Such was the purpose of the political consultation which took place shortly after the war, and such remains the objective of the Communist-Suppression Campaign. The key to the problem of peace or war and to the happiness or suffering of the people is not in the hands of the Government, nor can the problem be solved by popular appeal for peace to the Government alone. The problem can be decided only by the Communists. So the sincerity of the Communists for peace must be ascertained before the problem can be solved.

If the Communists are sincerely desirous of peace, and clearly give such indication, the Government will be only too glad to discuss with them the means to end the war.

If a negotiated peace is not detrimental to the national independence and sovereignty, but will contribute to the welfare of the people; if the Constitution is not violated and constitutionalism preserved, the democratic form of government maintained, the entity of the armed forces safeguarded; and if the people's free mode of living and their minimum living standard are protected, then I shall be satisfied.

In my devotion to the cause of the National Revolution, I have known nothing except loyalty to the nation, service to the people and the realization of the Three People's Principles, thereby fulfilling my sacred duties as a Revolutionist. If peace can be secured, I am not at all concerned about my own position. In this I will follow only the consensus of the people.

If, on the other hand, the Communists are not sincerely desirous of peace and will insist on continuing their armed rebellion, the Government, with no other alternative, will fight them to the finish. As the political nerve center of the country, the Nanking-Shanghai area will be held at all costs, and the Government is determined to throw in all available forces for a decisive victory. I firmly believe that the Government will win out in the end, and it also will mark the turning point of the war.

The people of the nation should realize that only by carrying on this war of self-defense can a real peace be secured; and only by making sacrifices can a glorious victory be won. It has been almost forty years since I joined the National Revolution. In every major and prolonged battle, I have suffered many setbacks and have been subjected to vicious propaganda. No matter how serious was the reverse, I never lost confidence in the final victory. And as a rule, victory was obtained in the end.

National spirit, justice, and righteousness, such as they are generally recognized, must constitute our mainstay in this fight. The brutal force of the Communists can wrest from us the Northeast, but it can never subdue our national spirit.

The Communists can penetrate into our heartland, but they can never soil our national character. Righteousness is the strength for victory, and right will always triumph over might. We of this generation have seen the greatest cataclysm in our history; we have on our shoulders an unprecedented mission.

We can, we must, endure temporary afflictions and sacrifices and struggle for the existence of the nation, the continuity of our history and culture, our free way of living, and the prosperity of our offspring.

My countrymen, at this time of national crisis, I feel all the more keenly the weightiness of my responsibilities and the difficulties in fulfilling my mission. It is my hope that all patriotic countrymen will advise me and join hands in the fight for the sanctity of the Constitution, the maintenance of China's territorial and sovereign integrity, the freedoms of the people, and the continuance of our culture.

Dr. Sun said: "Final victory belongs to the one who struggles until victory." I hope that all of us will bear this motto in mind.

168

The Chinese Foreign Minister (Wu) to the Ambassador in China (Stuart)

893.00/1-849

AIDE-MÉMOIRE

NANKING, *January 8, 1949*

The Chinese people, true to their peaceful traditions, have always devoted themselves to the pursuit of international as well as domestic peace. In their long history, it was only when they were in the face of the danger of aggression that they took up arms in self defense. For this reason, the people rose to resist the Japanese invaders, and later, through their close cooperation with their allies, World War II was carried to a successful conclusion. On the eve of victory, China took an active part in organizing and founding the United Nations in the hope that a foundation for world peace might thus be laid and international disputes settled by pacific means. For, it has long been through the maintenance of peace that the continuity and development of human civilization can be ensured.

Following the surrender of Japan, the National Government immediately took steps to initiate and carry on peace negotiations with the Chinese Communist Party. Through the good offices personally offered by General Marshall the Political Consultative Council was set up and a number of meetings took place. Unfortunately, the failure to reach a mutually satisfactory settlement led to a renewal of hostilities. Although these efforts proved abortive at the time, the government and the people have never since abandoned the hope that hostilities may still be brought to an end.

However, in the wake of the long, gruelling struggle against Japan, this renewed conflict has inflicted untold suffering upon the masses and prevented the government from carrying out the plans of reconstruction which it had prepared during the war with Japan. The ravages of war followed by rapid deterioration of the economic life of the nation make it imperative that peace be restored as soon as possible.

As nations today are unavoidably interdependent and international peace and stability depends largely upon degree to which international cooperation can be achieved, it would be difficult for any nation to confine the effect of its own unsettled conditions to itself. The Chinese Government is, therefore, most anxious that her internal situation would not in any way become an impediment to the progress of world peace.

In consideration of the above facts, the President of the Republic of China, in his New Year message on January first, announced without hesitation his determination for the restoration of peace in the country. The decision thus proclaimed by the President has since received the general support of the people, who have through numerous messages and public statements echoed their prompt support for a peaceful settlement of the questions at issue between the government and the Communists.

The United States Government has on many occasions in the past demonstrated its friendly concern over the state of affairs in China and has cooperated with the Chinese Government for the promotion of international peace. The Chinese Government wishes hereby to assure the United States Government of its sincere desire for a peaceful settlement with the Chinese Communist Party and particularly avail itself of this opportunity to ascertain in the views of the United States Government on this subject. The Chinese Government will welcome any suggestion by the United States Government which may lead to an early restoration of peace in China. The Chinese Government further signifies its readiness, through the possible intermediary of the United States Government, to initiate negotiations with the Chinese Communist Party with a view to attaining the end stated above.

Similar notes are being communicated to the French, the Soviet and the British Governments. An early reply from the United States Government will be greatly appreciated.

169

Memorandum on the Situation in Taiwan [28]

Background

The Formosan Chinese greeted the surrender of Japanese authority to the Chinese with immense enthusiasm on October 25, 1945. After fifty years under Japanese control and intensive economic development they welcomed a return to China, which they had idealized as the "Mother Country". The richness of the island and the relatively light population pressure had made rapid economic and social developments possible. Agriculture, food processing and light industry in the best years produced an overseas trade valued at U.S. $225,000,000. To improve Taiwan's economic value the Japanese had raised the general standard of living. Public health standards were high and literacy widely spread among the masses. Formosans had come to place a high value on orderly procedures in the courts and on the orderly enforcement and observance of government regulations, for they found order both profitable and necessary in a complex and semi-industrialized economy.

With the removal of the Japanese the Formosans looked forward to a return to profitable trade and an expansion of their already established industries, with the markets of China ready to receive all that they could produce. The surpluses which had always gone to Japan would now, they thought, go to China. They expected to return to control of the properties taken from them by the Japanese through fifty years and expected a larger share in the management of their own enterprises. Under pressure of the Japanese overlords who were alien to Taiwan, they had developed an island-wide sense of social solidarity. They were free of all internal political strife. The Japanese had rigorously excluded all Communist influence and activity, and had indeed filled the people with fear, dislike and distrust of Communist doctrines. They revered the Generalissimo,

[28] Submitted by Ambassador Stuart to President Chiang Kai-shek on Apr. 18, 1947.

believed the Three People's Principles meant new opportunities, and looked forward expectantly to participation in the Central Government. The year 1946 was one of increasing disappointment. Though the majority of petty officials, clerks and office boys of the new Administration were Formosans, they were virtually excluded from all important government offices and from important administrative posts. The legal necessity to place all confiscated Japanese properties and enterprises under Government control led to the creation of syndicates and combines in every field in which the Japanese had had an interest. Though the Government owns (and must heavily subsidize) these companies, the salaried and priviledged administrators are in a position to squeeze freely. It is alleged that raw and finished materials and agricultural products find their way into the hands of unscrupulous officials for their use in private trading and smuggling. Judging from Taiwan's former capacity to produce and the fact that its enterprises continue, qualified Formosans estimate that published records show only one-tenth of actual receipts. As an example, it is alleged by persons formerly connected with the Department of Agriculture and Forestry that fishing boats were withdrawn from their normal bases in 1946 and were used for smuggling in the interests of the authorities concerned.

Formosans have been virtually excluded from the higher levels of economic administration. These persistent allegations of corruption lead them to place responsibility on members of the Government who appear and reappear in lucrative posts as Commissioners, members of Committees, and Directors in a manner which concentrates full control of the total economy in the hands of a clique close to the Governor.

There was a progressive decline in Formosan economic enterprise, especially where there was competition with ex-Japanese interests. Unemployment among Formosans has progressively increased, either through direct discharge (frequently to make room for unqualified newcomers) or by the suspension or abolition of various established enterprises which failed to be profitable under the new management. Whereas about 50,000 Formosans had been employed normally in industrial work, by January 1947 UNRRA officials estimated that less than 5,000 were so employed. Whereas the top government officials created a Taiwan Industrial and Mining Enterprises Syndicate with a capital of two billion Taiwan yen, in which the Commissioners and their associates play leading roles, the Department of Mining and Industry announced an appropriation of only eight million Taiwan yen for loans in aid of private (i. e. Formosan) industrial enterprises after June 1946.

The Quarantine Service broke down and the Public Health Service was badly shattered. Cholera epidemics occurred for the first time in about 30 years; bubonic plague appeared after an even longer absence. Educational standards in the schools were markedly lowered. Friction spread through the schools between Formosans and mainland students and teachers. Trouble between mainland police and local petty officials increased. The press was filled with public charges and counter-charges of corruption and lawless acts among government officers. Formosans claimed that corruption and nepotism among mainland officials increased rather than abated during the year. The cost of living soared. Bank of Taiwan wholesale commodity price indices show advance as follows from November 1945 to January 1947: foodstuffs 3,323 to 21,058; clothing 5,741 to 24,483; fuel 963 to 14,091; fertilizers 139 to 37,559; building materials 949 to 13,612. (Pre-war June 1937 is used as a basis.) Prices shot up most rapidly during February 1947. These figures on the whole reflect the drain of Taiwan wealth from the island, with little or no return to it.

Although the two rice harvests of 1946 were good, a rice shortage grew acute in December 1946 and January 1947. The Government instituted a tax in kind for rice lands, ostensibly to secure an equal distribution, and repeatedly threatened to use military force to punish private hoarders which it blamed for the shortages. In fact there is substantial evidence to support the Formosans in their charges that large quantities of grain were smuggled out or went into private control of officials. It is popularly believed that the army is shipping unpublicised quantities to the northern front on the mainland.

Three governmental acts

Against this background of increasing economic and social dislocation three governmental acts in January and February appear to have crystallized Formosan resentment toward economic policies and toward individuals in the Government.

(1) Throughout 1946 Formosans sought permission to elect city mayors and *hsien* magistrates, in order to ensure themselves of some direct control over local police and over economic functions and public services. The announcement of China's new Constitution was greeted with relief. Prominent Formosan leaders counseled that demands for local elections could wait until the Constitution would become effective at the end of 1947. In early January, however, the Governor General announced that although the Constitution would be effective on the mainland on December 25, 1947, it would be impossible for the Government to allow local elections of mayors and magistrates in Formosa until December 1949. This had an effect which stirred political discussion to a new pitch. Formosans state that until they can elect their own representatives at all levels of local government they will have no security of person ; they cannot control the local police, ensure the enforcement of law nor enjoy security of property.

(2) On February 1 the Government announced a new policy for the disposal at auction of certain large categories of Japanese property—principally real estate abandoned by the Japanese and now occupied by Formosans on a low rental basis. The announced procedures were such that it was widely believed that Formosans without great wealth and its influence would be unable to buy real estate which they had believed would be available, especially in view of the fact that it had been taken from them more or less forcefully by the Japanese over the course of fifty years.

This announced procedure was interpreted as a threat to the security of low-income level Formosans who, having lost their former homes during the war, are not anxious to face eviction from houses now occupied if, as they anticipate, new mainland landlords should suddenly greatly increase rentals. (Rental is the one item in living costs which has not risen excessively since 1945, due to the removal of several hundred thousand Japanese.)

(3) The third governmental act was a February 14 announcement of a series of complex financial and trading regulations which Formosans believed effectually concentrated monopoly control in the hands of a small group of officials. It is believed by some observers that these were announced precipitously and rashly in the belief that the crisis in Shanghai was about to provide an opportunity long awaited to establish a semi-autonomous economy for Taiwan, giving into the hands of a few mainland people an absolute control of all external trade and a general control of internal production and business as well.

As an island people, Formosans have been sensitive to overseas trade, and after the Japanese surrender they anticipated the reestablishment and expansion of seaborne commerce. They had proposed to organize their capital for production and individual business, out of which they had expected to be taxed in support of the Central Government and of the local island administration. These new measures seemed to the Formosans not only a threat to return them to the subservient position they had suffered under the Japanese, but to threaten to destroy the very means to create wealth within the island.

THE FEBRUARY INCIDENT

Spontaneous protest and unorganized riots

On the evening of February 27 certain armed Monopoly Bureau agents and special police agents set upon and beat a female cigarette vendor, who with her two small children, had protested the seizure of her small cash as well as her allegedly untaxed cigarettes. She is reported to have died soon after as a result of the beating at police hands. An angered crowd set after the agents, who shot at random, killing one person before they escaped into a civil police station. Their Monopoly Bureau truck and its contents were burned in the street, although the agents were allowed to be taken away, on foot and unmolested, from the police station by military police called for that purpose.

On the morning of February 28 a crowd estimated at about 2,000 marched in orderly fashion from the area in which the incident had occurred, past the American Consulate and toward the Monopoly Bureau Headquarters. Placards and banners announced that they intended to protest the action of special armed agents, to demand a death sentence for the responsible man, and to demand the resignation of the Monopoly Bureau Director.

Unfortunately, as they made their way across the city, two Monopoly agents were discovered in a side street molesting a vendor. They were beaten to death by an angry crowd which was not taking part in the initial demonstration. This happened near the Taipei Branch Monopoly Bureau Office buildings which the crowd began to sack. Its contents were burned in the streets. Mainland employees were driven out and if caught were beaten mercilessly. The crowd's anger enlarged to include employees and property of the Trading Bureau, another monopolistic organization greatly disliked. The Consul and the Vice Consul observed the orderly gathering before the Monopoly Bureau Headquarters, where no Monopoly Bureau official would receive the petition which had been brought about noon. Monopoly Bureau police and a few military police were guarding the entrances.

Meanwhile at about one o'clock someone announced to the radio audience that demands were being made on the Government to put an end to its monopolies. All Formosans were urged to support the movement.

The parade, meanwhile, left the Monopoly Bureau for the Governor's office where it was intended to present the petition for reform. At about two o'clock it reached a wide intersection adjacent to the government grounds. Without warning a machine gun mounted somewhere on the government building opened fire, swept and dispersed the crowd and killed at least four. Two consular officers drove through the square immediately after the shots were fired. Two of the dead were picked up a few minutes later by an UNRRA officer.

This shooting was the signal for a citywide outburst of anger against all mainland Chinese, regardless of rank or occupation. Many were beaten, cars were burned and in some few cases offices and houses of minor officials were sacked and the contents burned in the streets. It was observed that the Formosans refrained from looting. One Formosan was found attempting to take cigarettes from a burning heap; he was forced to kneel and beg forgiveness from the crowd and was then driven away. Another was severely beaten. Tires and other equipment were observed to have been left untouched on overturned cars, and remained in evidence until the Formosans lost control of the city March 9. Martial law was invoked in the late afternoon February 28. Armed military patrols began to appear in the city, firing at random wherever they went.

At 10 o'clock a. m., March 1, the Chairman of the Taipei Municipal People's Political Council invited the Council, representatives of the National and Provincial P.P.C. Councils and the Taiwan representatives to the National Assembly, to form a committee for settling the so-called Monopoly Bureau incident. It was decided to send a delegation to call on the Governor General, requesting, among other things, that a committee be formed to settle the problems jointly by the people and the Government. These men recognized that with the firing on the crowd at the government building, the issues had become much greater than mere punishment of Monopoly Bureau agents and a financial settlement for the injured and dead. They urged the Governor to lift martial law so that the dangers of a clash between the unarmed civil population and the military would be averted. This the Governor agreed to do at midnight, March 1, meanwhile forbidding meetings and parades.

On that day busses and trucks, filled with squads of government troops armed with machine guns and rifles, began to sweep through the streets, firing indiscriminately. Machine guns were set up at important intersections. Shooting grew in volume during the afternoon. At no time were Formosans observed to have arms and no instances of Formosan use of arms were reported in Taipei. Nevertheless, the military were evidently allowed free use in what appeared to be an attempt to frighten the people into obedience.

At approximately 5 o'clock, the Governor General broadcast a message which appears to have increased the anger of the people. He stated that the Monopoly Bureau incident had been settled by a generous payment of money. Without referring to the machine gun fire from his own office he accused the Formosans of increased rioting, but generously promised to lift martial law at midnight.

"There is one more point," the Governor broadcast. "The P.P.C. members wished to send representatives to form a committee jointly with the Government to settle this riot. This I have also granted. If you have any opinion, you can tell me through this Committee." (*Hsin Sheng Pao*, March 2, 1947.)

While he was broadcasting, members of the American Consulate staff witnessed a severe clash between armed government forces and unarmed crowds. Mounted troops had killed two pedestrians near the compound. A crowd gathered. A few hundred yards away Railway Administration special armed police suddenly opened fire from within the Administration building and killed two more pedestrians. The crowd turned on any mainland Railway Bureau employee found nearby. Two more pedestrians who looked like coolies were shot about 300 feet from the Consulate gates. Then as the bodies were carried off the crowd was observed to assemble again some distance from a mounted patrol near an intersection. Suddenly, with no warning, a long burst of machine gun fire swept the area. Some of the wounded and dead were carried past the Consulate gates; it is stated reliably that at least 123 were felled by this burst and that 25 died. How many of the injured walked away is not known.

On this afternoon 25 mainland officials from the neighboring Railway Administration compound took refuge in the Consulate. Although the crowd observed them enter, no attempt was made to pursue them. They were removed eight hours later under police guard.

Organization for settlement recognized by General Chen

The temper of the populace was uncertain. Inflammatory handbills and posters began to appear in increasing numbers. There was a general demand that the Government of Taiwan must be thoroughly reformed.

At 12 noon March 2 the "Untaxed Cigarette Incident Investigation Committee of the Taipei Municipal P.P.C." called on the Governor General, and with this began the attempt to meet and clarify the fundamental political and economic problems which lay back of the uprisings. The Governor had with him the Secretary-General, the Commissioners for Civil Affairs, Communications, and Industry and Mining.

The Governor appears to have been told by the Committee that there could be no peace as long as roving armed patrols were permitted to sweep the streets with gunfire and so paralyze all normal activity.

It is believed that if fully determined the people could have overpowered and ended the patrols which were moving only in the central part of the city.

The Governor therefore agreed to several "temporary demands", i.e., stipulations of conditions to be maintained while the people organized their fundamental demands for reform in government. These included (1) an agreement that a schedule of fundamental reforms should be prepared for discussion by March 10, after representatives of the people throughout the island could be consulted; (2) a promise that the Government would not bring additional troops into the city while these consultations were in progress; (3) a volunteer youth organization under the supervision of the Mayor and the municipal Chief of Police (a mainlander) would maintain law and order temporarily; (4) communications would be restored at once in order to avoid a food shortage.

The Governor agreed to broadcast at 3 o'clock p. m. and agreed to reduce the armed patrols gradually, meanwhile ordering them to patrol with rifles and other arms down on the floor of the trucks and busses, for use only if crowds were found disturbing the peace.

At 2 : 30 o'clock the first general meeting of the Governor's representatives (the Commissioners of Civil Affairs, Police, and Communications, and the Taipei Mayor) and the Settlement Committee met in the Public Hall, with a capacity audience of spectators. It was announced that as a result of the morning conference the Governor had decided to readjust the Committee to bring into it representatives of the Chamber of Commerce, the Labor Union, student organizations, popular organizations, and the important Taiwan Political Reconstruction Association which has been for many months the most outspoken and emphatically nationalist group urging reform in General Chen's government.

The following temporary demands were formulated:

1. All people arrested in connection with the riots will be released;
2. The Government will pay death gratuities and compensations to the wounded;
3. The Government will not prosecute persons involved;
4. Armed police patrols will be stopped immediately;
5. Communications will be restored immediately.

While in session the meeting was disturbed by volleys of shots outside. When the Governor's promised 3 o'clock broadcast was postponed for almost two hours, it began to be rumored that he was delaying in hope that troops would reach the city from the south and he would not be forced to make public acceptance of the demands.

At approximately 5 o'clock, March 2, the Governor again broadcast, concluding his speech with the statement:

"A committee will be organized to settle the incident. Besides Government officials and members of the P.P.C., representatives from the people of all walks of life will be invited to joint the committee so that it may represent opinions of the majority of the people." (*Hsin Sheng Pao*, March 3, 1947)

On the night of March 2, word reached Taipei that the Governor actually had attempted to get troops to the city. Citizens near Hsinchu city, however, were reported to have halted the troop carriers by removing rails from the main line.

From this time (March 3) the confidence of the people appears to have been undermined. The moderate and conservative element represented by the Committee members were willing to trust the Government's word and to proceed with negotiations. The more skeptical elements agreed to support the Committee in its efforts but at the same time determined to prepare resistance to any military action which might be set against them.

This delegation, received by five Government Commissioners and Chief of Staff Ko, urged that the patrols be withdrawn, for they were still firing wildly in the streets despite the Governor's promises. After long discussion the Government representatives agreed:

1. All troops to be withdrawn by 6 p. m., March 3;

2. Public order to be maintained by a temporary Public Security Service Corps including gendarmes, police, and youths;

3. Communications to be restored at 6 p. m.;

4. Military rice stores to be released to avert crisis;

5. Any military personnel making a disturbance to be sent to General Ko for punishment;

6. Any civilians disturbing the peace to be punished according to law, on the guarantee of the Committee;

7. Troops absolutely would not come from the south to the north. (General Ko is reported to have promised "to commit suicide" if his personal guarantee were broken.)

Meanwhile, a Taipei City Provisional Public Safety Committee was organized by the Settlement Committee. Its members were recommended by the Committee and were to constitute a "Loyal Service Corps." Its effective period was to end on the day normal conditions were restored in Taipei. Meanwhile, events at Taipei were known throughout Taiwan. It appears that Formosans became deeply alarmed at persistent rumors that troops were coming from the mainland, and began to arm themselves to resist a military occupation, insisting, however, that they wanted reform, not civil war. Formosans began to take over local administrative posts everywhere held by mainland Chinese. Government troops offered some resistance but it appears that in many places mainlanders agreed to relinquish their posts peacefully, as at Hualienkang (Karenko). The aborigines are reported to be cooperating fully with the Formosan Chinese. Without prearrangement or preparation, by March 5, Formosan-Chinese were in the ascendency or in control throughout the island.

This called for larger organization in order to prevent ruffians under guise of "local patriotism" from taking advantage of confusion. On March 4, the Settlement Committee enlarged its representative character by creating 17 sub-divisions or local Settlement Committees throughout the island. Circumstances beyond control forced the Committee to so enlarge its duties, and in doing so it announced:

"We should acknowledge the aim of this action, that there is no other desire except to demand a reformation of Government." (*Hsin Sheng Pao*, March 5, 1947)

This was without doubt necessary, for the absence of mainland office-holders from their duties threatened to paralyze the administration.

The Governor and his Commissioners received the Committee's representatives at 3:30 p. m., March 4, and the Governor took occasion to remind them that his duties were related to both national administration and local government and expressed his hope that the people would come forth with more proposals for local administration. He stated that he had ordered the police and gendarmes not to carry weapons.

March 5 was quiet at Taipei. Shops were open and primary schools resumed classwork. The city appeared to be returning to normal while the Settlement Committee worked toward a reform program which would remove the sources of conflict between administration and people.

There was intense popular anxiety, however, for rumors of impending troop movements grew stronger. It was said that the March 10 date set for presentation of the reform proposals would be too late. Each rumor strengthened the arguments of the men who desired to organize resistance and made the task of the officially recognized Settlement Committee more difficult. In an attempt to clarify its own position and to strengthen its influence over dissident elements the Settlement Committee published basic Articles of Organization clearly defining its temporary character.

A Youth League of considerable potential significance came into being, stressing as basic principles a desire to make Taiwan a model province of China and to hasten Dr. Sun Yat-sen's program of National Reconstruction. The founder, former president of the Chamber of Commerce, Chiang Wei-chuan, said:

"We absolutely support the Central Government but will eradicate all corrupt officials in this province. This is our aim which I hope every one of you fully grasp." (*Chung Wei Jih Pao*, March 6, 1947)

Spurred by fears of a military invasion, on March 6 the Settlement Committee completed its draft of items of reform which the Governor had agreed to discuss and to refer to the Central Government wherever necessary. The Committee's executive group acted as sponsors and included four members of the National P.P.C., six members of the Taiwan Provincial P.P.C., five members of the Taipei Municipal P.P.C. and two "reserve members". Everyone of these men had received the approval of the Government as P.P.C. members and represent in fact the most conservative elements in Taiwan. One is a former Consul General at San Francisco, and ex-Mayor of Taipei. The reform proposals, made possible March 7, are set forth on pages 15–18 of this despatch.

The Army's explicit promise that the Central Government would not send troops

On March 8 Major-General Chang Wu-tao, Commander of the Fourth Gendarme Regiment, at 12:00 noon called on the Settlement Committee at its headquarters. According to the press and to witnesses he made the following categorical statement:

"I can guarantee that there will be no social disturbances if the people do not try to disarm the soldiers. I want especially to report to you that the demands for political reforms in this province are very proper. The Central Government will not dispatch troops to Taiwan. I earnestly entreat the people of Taiwan not to irritate the Central Government, but to cooperate to maintain order. I can risk my life to guarantee that the Central Government will not take any military actions against Taiwan. I speak these words out of my sincere attachment to this province and to the nation. I hope Taiwan will become a model province after these political reforms." (*Hsin Sheng Pao*, March 9, 1947.)

The landing of Government troops and subsequent terrorism

Foreign observers who were at Keelung March 8 state that in mid-afternoon the streets of the city were cleared suddenly by machine gun fire directed at no particular objects or persons. After dark ships docked and discharged the troops for which the Governor apparently had been waiting. Fairly reliable sources estimate that about 2,000 police were landed, followed by about 8,000 troops with light equipment including U. S. Army jeeps. Men and equipment were rushed to Taipei. It is reported that about 3,000 men were landed at Takao simultaneously. Troops were reportedly continuing to arrive on March 17.

Beginning March 9, there was widespread and indiscriminate killing. Soldiers were seen bayonetting coolies without apparent provocation in front of a Consulate staff residence. Soldiers were seen to rob passersby. An old man protesting the removal of a woman from his house was seen cut down by two soldiers. The Canadian nurse in charge of an adjacent Mission Hospital was observed bravely to make seven trips under fire into the crowded area across the avenue to treat persons shot down or bayonetted, and once as she supervised the movement of a wounded man into the hospital the bearers with her were fired upon. Some of the patients brought in had been shot and hacked to pieces. Young Formosan men were observed tied together, being prodded at bayonet point toward the city limits. A Formosan woman primary school teacher attempting to reach her home was shot in the back and robbed near the Mission compound. A British business man attempting to rescue an American woman whose house was being riddled with machine gun fire from a nearby emplacement was fired upon and narrowly escaped, one bullet cutting through his clothing and another being deflected from the steering gear of his jeep. Another foreigner saw a youth forced to dismount from his cycle before a military policeman, who thereupon lacerated the man's hands so badly with his bayonet that the man could not pick up his machine.

Anyone thought to be trying to hide or run was shot down. Looting began wherever the soldiers saw something desirable. In the Manka area, near the Consulate, a general sacking by soldiers took place on March 10; many shopkeepers are believed to have been shot.

On March 11 it was reported that a systematic search for middle school students had begun during the night. School enrollment lists were used. A broadcast earlier had ordered all youths who had been members of the Security Patrol or the Youth League to turn in their weapons. Concurrently, all middle school students were ordered to remain at home. If a student was caught on the street while trying to obey the first order he was killed; if the searchers found a weapon in his house, he met a like fate. If a student was not at home his brother or his father was seized as hostage. A reliable estimate was made that about 700 students had been seized in Taipei by March 13. Two hundred are said to have been seized in Keelung. Fifty are reported to have been killed at Matsuyama and thirty at Kokuto (suburbs of Taipei) on the night of March 9.

From March 8 the Government instituted searches for all members of the Settlement Committee and for all editors, lawyers and many prominent businessmen who had in any way been identified with the activities of the Committee between March 1 and 8. Wang Tien-teng, Chairman of the Settlement Committee, was seized and is alleged to have been executed about March 13. Tan Gim, a leading banker, was taken from his sick bed; Lim Mo-sei, editor of the *Min Pao*, was seized in the night and taken without clothing. Gan Kin-en, head of a large private mining interest, was arrested.

Middle school and normal school teachers began to be seized or to disappear March 14. One teacher who had been deprived of his license as a public prosecutor after exposing a case of police corruption in early 1946, was taken on March 15. Another public prosecutor involved in the arrest and punishment of mainland police officers convicted in court of killing an official of the Taichung Court, is said to have been literally dragged out of the Taipei Higher Court by the convicted man who had apparently won release after March 8. A minor accountant in the Taiwan Navigation Company at Keelung was called out and shot, with the explanation that the Manager did not think well of him.

On March 13 a tense crowd was observed near the homes of the Vice Consul and the U.S.I.S. Director; wailing women who came away incoherently said that two students had just been beheaded. UNRRA personnel observed bodies lying along the road between their hostel and the city office. Unclaimed bodies were reliably reported to be lying in the ditches and along an embankment within 2,000 feet of the foreign mission compound. A foreigner reported that on March 10 while at the Army Garrison Headquarters he observed some 15 well-dressed Formosan-Chinese bound and kneeling, with necks bared, apparently awaiting execution. On March 14 and 15 many bodies began to float into the inner harbor at Keelung. Foreigners saw sampans tow them in for possible identification by anxiously waiting people. It is estimated by a reliable Keelung observer that some 300 people had been seized and killed there.

After three days in Taipei streets, government forces began to push out into suburban and rural areas. Mounted machine gun patrols were observed along the highroads 15 to 20 miles from Taipei shooting at random in village streets in what appeared to be an effort to break any spirit of resistance. Manhunts were observed being conducted through the hills near the UNRRA hostel. Foreigners saw bodies in the streets of Tamsui.

By March 17 the order of seizure or execution seemed to have become, successively, all established critics of the government, Settlement Committee members and their aides, men who had taken part in the interim policing of Taipei, middle school students and teachers, lawyers, economic leaders and members of influencial families, and finally, persons who in the past had caused members of the Government or their appointees serious loss of face. On March 16 it was rumored that anyone who spoke English well, or who had close foreign connections was being seized "for examination", and that many Japanese technicians in the employ of the Government were being taken.

On March 9, the Committee began to publish retractions, modifications and denials of acts and proposals made during the preceding ten days. Only the Government's paper, the *Hsin Sheng Pao*, appeared March 9. On that date the Taiwan Garrison Headquarters issued the ambiguous statement that "all illegal organizations must be abolished before March 10 and meeting and parades are prohibited . . ." (Communiqué no. 131, March 9, 1947).

On March 10, General Chen issued the following statement:

"On the afternoon of March 2, I broadcast that members of the national, provincial and municipal P.P.C.s, Taiwan representatives to the National Assembly and representatives from the people may jointly form a committee to receive the people's opinion concerning relief work for the February 28 incident.

"Unexpectedly, since its formation, the committee has given no thought to relief work such as medical care for the wounded and compensation to the killed and so forth. On the contrary, it acted beyond its province and on March 7 went so far as to announce a settlement outline containing rebellious elements. Therefore, this committee (including *hsien* and municipal branch committees) should be abolished. Hereafter, opinions on political reforms concerning the province may be brought up by the Provincial P.P.C., and those concerning the *hsien* and municipalities by their respective *hsien* on municipal P.P.C.s. People who have opinions may bring them up to the P.P.C. or to the Government-General direct by writing." (*Hsin Sheng Pao*, March 11, 1947)

On March 13, it was announced that all but three government-sponsored papers were banned or suspended for having published accounts of the uprising and activities of the Committee. The *Min Pao* press was destroyed effectively on March 10.

By March 17, the Government forces were pushing down the main railway lines toward the center of the island. Martial law was rigorously enforced from 8 o'clock p. m. until 6 :30 o'clock a. m.

THE DRAFT REFORM PROGRAM

Hereafter, events in Formosa and the development of Chinese administration there may be better understood in the light of the draft reform program—the so-called 32 Demands—which are here set forth. Though the rioting after February 27 was spontaneous and the creation of the Settlement Committee an unplanned event, these requests for specific reforms in local government are rooted in fundamental economic and administrative problems which must some day be solved.

It must be pointed out that the Settlement Committee, aware of its responsible official character, was greatly hampered and embarrassed by many impossible demands made on it by individuals and groups who were not authorized to develop a reform program for the Governor's consideration. For example, there were published demands that only Formosans be allowed to hold arms on Taiwan and that all Central Government troops be withdrawn. Some extreme threats to individuals in the Government appeared in handbill and poster form.

Here the Committee's proposals are regrouped as they appear designed to achieve (1) equality in government; (2) security of person and (3) security of means of livelihood. Certain of the measures were clearly open to compromise and negotiation.

Reforms to ensure equality for Formosans in local government

1. A provincial autonomy law shall be enacted and shall become the supreme norm for political affairs in this province so that the ideal of National Reconstruction of Dr. Sun Yat-sen may be here materialized.

2. The appointment of commissioners shall have the approval of the People's Political Council (after new elections have been held.) The People's Political Council shall be newly elected before June 1947. In the meantime such appointments shall be submitted by the Governor General to the Committee for Settling the February Incident for discussion and approval or rejection.

3. More than two-thirds of the Commissioners shall be appointed from those who have lived in this Province for more than ten years. (It is most desirable that such persons only shall be appointed to the Secretariat and to be Commissioners of the Department of Civil Affairs, Finance, Industry and Mining, Agriculture and Forestry, Education, and Police.)

4. Unarmed gatherings and organizations shall enjoy absolute freedom.

5. Complete freedom of speech, of the press and of the right to strike shall be realized. The system requiring registration of newspapers to be published shall be abolished.

6. The Regulations in force covering the formation of popular organizations shall be abolished.

7. The Regulations governing the scrutiny of the capacity of candidates for membership in representative organs of public opinion shall be abolished.

8. Regulations governing the election of members of various grades in representative organs of public opinion shall be revised.

9. A Political Affairs Bureau of the Settlement Committee must be established by March 15. Measures for its organization will be that a candidate be elected by representatives of each village, town and district, and then newly elected by the prefectural or city People's Political Council. The numbers of candidates to be elected in each city or prefecture are as follows:

[Total 30—figures and allocations here omitted]

10. The Office of the Governor General shall be converted into a Provincial Government. Before this reform is approved by the Central Government, the Office of the Governor General shall be reorganized by the Settlement Committee through popular elections so that righteous and able officers can be appointed.

(NOTE: It has been indicated by a Formosan lawyer that the thought behind this was to provide for the interim period leading to the peace treaties and the legal return of sovereignty to China, until which time, it is widely held, a legal Provincial Government cannot be established.)

Reforms to ensure security of person and property

1. Popular election of prefectural magistrates and city mayors shall be held before June of this year and at the same time there shall be new elections of members to all prefectural and municipal political councils.

(NOTE: The reason given for this is the establishment of control over the police systems and to ensure the supremacy of, and respect for the courts.)

2. The posts of the Commissioner of the Department of Police, and of the directors of all prefectural or municipal Police Bureaus ought to be filled by Formosans. The armed Special Police Contingents and the armed police maintained by the Railway Department and the Department of Industry and Mining shall be abolished immediately.

3. No government organs other than the civil police can arrest criminals.

4. Arrest or confinement of a political nature shall be prohibited.

5. All chiefs of local courts of justice and all chief prosecutors in all local courts of justice shall be Formosans.

6. The majority of judges, prosecutors and other court staff membership shall be Formosans.

7. More than half the Committee of Legal Affairs shall be occupied by Formosans and the Chairman of the Committee shall be mutually elected from among its members.

Measures to ensure a revision and liberalization of economic policy and a reform of economic administration

1. A unified Progressive Income Tax shall be levied. No other sundry taxes shall be levied except the Luxury Tax and the Inheritance Tax.

2. Managers in charge of all public enterprises shall be Formosans.

3. A Committee for Inspecting Public Enterprises, elected by the people, shall be established. The disposal of Japanese properties shall be entirely entrusted to the Provincial Government. A Committee for management of industries taken over from the Japanese shall be established. Formosans shall be appointed to more than half the Committee posts.

4. The Monopoly Bureau shall be abolished. A system for rationing daily necessities shall be instituted.

5. The Trading Bureau shall be abolished.

6. The Central Government must be asked to authorize the Provincial Government to dispose of Japanese properties.

Reforms affecting military administration on Formosa

1. The military police shall arrest no one other than military personnel.

2. As many Formosans as possible shall be appointed to Army, Navy and Air Force posts on Taiwan.

3. The Garrison Headquarters must be abolished to avoid the misuse of military privilege.

Reforms affecting social welfare problems

1. The political and economic rights and social position of the aborigines must be guaranteed.

2. Workmen's protection measures must be put into effect from June 1, 1947.

3. Detained war criminals and those suspected of treason must be released unconditionally.

(NOTE: This is stated as designed to secure the release of a number of wealthy and prominent Formosans who have been held for more than a year on general charges of "treason" and "war crimes", who are alleged to be paying continual ransom to ensure the lives of those detained and to ensure the security of their extensive holdings.)

Demands which are subordinate measures or subject to compromise

1. The abolition or unification of the Vocational Guidance Camp and other unnecessary institutions must be determined by the Political Affairs Bureau of the Settlement Committee, after discussion.

(NOTE: An internment camp for persons the Government decides to make into "useful citizens".)

2. The Central Government must be asked to return funds for the sugar exported to the mainland by the Central Government.

3. The Central Government must be asked to pay for 150,000 tons of food exported to the mainland, after estimating the price in accordance with the quotation at the time of export.

In preparing these proposals for reform the Settlement Committee believed that it was preparing a basis for discussion with the Governor and through him with the Central Government. For an examination of public statements by the Governor and his representatives and from the direct testimony of Committee members, it is believed that the Committee was justified in considering itself empowered officially to propose such reforms in administration. These were not put forth as minimum or unalterable demands; they were clearly understood to be intended as a means for reflecting popular opinion. March 10 was mutually agreed upon as a date for presentation in order that people throughout Taiwan could contribute their ideas to the Committee.

AFTERMATH AND SETTLEMENT

Public opinion, Nationalism and Communism

However bitter their criticism of local administrative policy before these uprisings, there can be no question that the Formosan-Chinese have felt loyalty to the Central Government and toward the Generalissimo. Fifty years under Japanese rule had sharpened their sense of Chinese nationality and race and in doing so developed a strong sense of island-wide social unity. Formosans have been ambitious to see Taiwan become a model province of China. From February 28 until March 9, while Formosans were in effective control of the island, the leaders in the Settlement Committee, leaders of the Youth Groups and editors of newspapers which have been most critical of the local government all took great pains to emphasize their fundamental desire to become a model province in China, proud of their race and nationality and proud to be taking part in the National Reconstruction.

(For specific reference, see editorials and speeches quoted in the *Chung Wai Jih Pao*, March 6; *Min Pao*, March 6; *Hsin Sheng Pao*, March 5; and other journals of that week.)

Reference has been made earlier to the intense distrust and fear of communism which was fostered intensively by the Japanese. There are a few Formosans who have been suspected of interest in overseas communism but they have always been counted of little importance. Of direct external influence a few communist pamphlets of mainland origin were found in the autumn of 1946 but they were not especially designed for Taiwan. So long as the living standard remained at a relatively high level there was little danger of communist doctrine finding a reception on Formosa. A large number of Formosans who had been conscripted into Japanese army labor battalions were repatriated from Hainan Island in conditions of extreme poverty in 1946. They had not been treated as "liberated Chinese" but as defeated enemies after the surrender. Failure to find employment on Formosa in the months since has undoubtedly increased their discontent and made them susceptible to the arguments of any confirmed communists who may have come back with them.

It may be therefore said with a high degree of assurance that as of March 1, 1947, communism in any form was of most negligible importance on Taiwan.

However, a local form of communism is not only possible but is believed to be a highly probable development if economic organization collapses under the pressure of continued military occupation.

The military commitment and possible economic consequences

If the Central Government chooses to support a policy of suppression of all criticism of the government and to confirm the authority of present officials by establishment of military garrisons throughout the island, the cost will be very high and will not diminish. Firm control will necessitate the maintenance of troops at all large cities, at all important rail and highway junctions and in the vicinity of the power plants upon which the normal economy depends. The ports and harbors must be garrisoned. Almost 14,000 square miles will have to be policed by military force.

It is not possible before March 17 to assess the truth of some Formosan claims that large supplies of arms had been seized in the central part of the island and transported into hiding. The opportunity presented itself and was probably taken.

It is presumed that the Formosans, if oppression continues, will not attempt a resistance from fixed positions, but will continue to harry Government troops, creating a continuous drain upon men and supplies, and will use the mountainous hinterlands as cover. Perhaps no single province in China involved so little military expenditure as that needed for Formosa before March 1, 1947. It may now well become one of the most costly, if the economic losses in production and hampered transportation are added to outright military costs.

It is significant that throughout the trouble the local government has emphasized the fact that the Army represents the Central Government most directly. Thus, when it began to be clear that the word given by the highest ranking military officers was to be broken, Formosans began to lose faith in the Central Government as well.

With industry in such a precarious condition in February 1947, it must be presumed that the dislocations attendant upon the present trouble and a military occupation will hasten the disintegration of the industrial structure of Taiwan. China loses thereby an asset of immeasurable value. This established industrial structure (including the food processing units which make agriculture so profitable) has a substructure of semi-skilled local labor. UNRRA investigations have shown that young Formosans are no longer able to go into industrial schools or apprenticeships as in the past, but enter the common labor market as they see industry after industry shrivel up as capital investments dwindle and small industries close. Unemployment will increase with acceleration of this trend.

The rice crisis in January indicated that in present circumstances Formosa may have no immediate food surpluses upon which to draw. The addition of large numbers of troops, feeding on the countryside, will further diminish available supplies. Rice and other foods will go into hiding. Sabotage and slow-down tactics may be anticipated.

The total losses of a military occupation are incalculable. Prominent Formosan-Chinese—conservative, liberal and extremists—and many young men have been killed or seized or are driven into hiding. The educational development of the island, especially in the technical schools of middle grade, will be greatly retarded at a time when China needs every trained man. Highly qualified mainland doctors and foreign medical personnel predict that the public health system may break down badly within the year, bringing on a larger scale the cholera epidemics which appeared in 1946.

A state of near anarchy is a distinct possibility for Formosa by the end of 1947 if drastic efforts to revise policy and effect governmental reforms (free of military pressure) are not undertaken speedily. Having known a relatively high standard of living under the Japanese regime, the Formosans are not going to lose what they have without a struggle directed against the forces which they hold responsible. If the Central Government meets increasing difficulties compounded of economics and military struggles of the mainland, the Formosans will be tempted to increase their resistance in proportion.

For eighteen months Formosan-Chinese blamed the provincial administration and at the same time assured themselves that if the Generalissimo were made fully aware of conditons he would reform the system in effect on Taiwan. Later it was assumed that the application of the new Constitution would bring to Taiwan the measure of self-government needed to restore the total economy to its former high level of production, to the permanent benefit of China.

There may be a sullen peace achieved by military action, but it cannot be enforced. Further uprisings of far more serious proportions than these recent spontaneous outbursts may occur at a time when the over-all peace settlement in the Far East is underway, and problems are being reviewed for inclusion or exclusion in the conference agenda. Anyone who wishes to embarrass China will find good material in a revolutionary situation on Taiwan.

Formosa should be put to work earning foreign credit for China. Its peculiar character as an industrialized and technically developed province should be sheltered from the greater economic difficulties found on the mainland. Taiwan was returned to China as an outstanding economic asset, and example of the advanced technological economy toward which all other provinces of China are striving. Two years of concentrated rehabilitation effort in Formosa hereafter will produce permanent assets of two kinds. Raw materials and products such as fertilizers, cement, foodstuffs and industrial chemicals will become permanently available to China in increasing amounts. Others such as tea, camphor, sugar, industrial salt, pineapples and light manufactures can be directed to overseas markets. A moderate share of the foreign credit so created must be returned to Formosa for rehabilitation and expansion of state-owned industries and the expansion of private enterprise. Formosan-Chinese must be admitted to greater participation in all aspects of economic administration and reasonable profit if the island is to prosper and to return to the high and constant level of production achieved in former years. Economic stability and expansion must be founded on a sound political and social administration. Now is the time to act. To encourage and ensure wholehearted effort the Formosan-Chinese must be allowed to take a larger part in government at all levels. Changes in personnel as well as in the structure of the administration must be thoroughgoing; it is felt that half-way measures and palliatives now will only postpone a larger repetition of the current protests against corruption, maladministration and autocracy in the provincial government. Formosa can be restored to its former high level of political allegiance and of economic production by prompt and fundamental reform.

The following developments have been reported as occurring during the end of March and the first part of April:

The continuing presence of fresh bodies in Keelung Harbor and other evidence indicate that the elimination of the informed opposition is continuing. The bodies of at least two men known to neutral sources as having taken no part in any activities during the recent incidents have been identified. It is reported at Taipei that although shots and screams in the night have become less frequent, they continue, and that there is no palpable difference in the tense atmosphere of the city. Mainlanders generally are reported to be apprehensive of further trouble, and many of them are said to feel that Formosan cooperation under present circumstances will be difficult for an indefinite time in the future. Of serious import is the reported continued undermining of Taiwan's advanced economic structure.

Annexes to Chapter VII: The Military Picture, 1945–1949

170

Oral Statement by President Truman to Dr. T. V. Soong Concerning Assistance to China, September 14, 1945

The United States is prepared to assist China in the development of armed forces of moderate size for the maintenance of internal peace and security and the assumption of adequate control over the liberated areas of China, including Manchuria and Formosa. The arrangements for the provision of such assistance should include the method of discharge by the Chinese Government of the financial obligations incurred in connection with the supplies furnished and services rendered by the United States.

Having in mind statements by the Generalissimo that China's internal political difficulties will be settled by political methods, it should be clearly understood that military assistance furnished by the United States would not be diverted for use in fractricidal warfare or to support undemocratic administration.

The exact amount of assistance which can be provided by the United States will need to be agreed between the U.S. and Chinese Governments and will depend on a detailed study by the Chinese and U.S. military authorities. It appears practicable at this time, subject to suitable mutual arrangements concerned with the provision of equipment and supplies to complete the 39-division program, to furnish certain naval craft, particularly those suitable for coastal and river operations, and to equip an air force of commensurate size. After consulting General Wedemeyer further and when the problem has been considered by the Joint Chiefs of Staff and other U.S. agencies concerned and we have completed our determination of availability of equipment, we will be in a position to determine what assistance, if any, beyond the 39-division program will be feasible.

The exact size, composition and functions of an advisory mission will be dependent upon the status and character of the mission and on the size and composition of the Chinese armed forces which may be agreed between the U.S. and Chinese Governments. As to the status and character of the mission, it might be more desirable to relieve officers from active duty for appointment by the Chinese Government than for this Government to organize and appoint such a group.

A U.S. advisory mission composed of officers on active duty can only be established under the emergency powers of the President. Consequently legislation would be required to continue the mission after the expiration of these powers.

It is suggested that Generalissimo Chiang Kai-shek immediately formulate a plan, in collaboration with General Wedemeyer, for the post-war Chinese armed forces and an estimate of U.S. assistance desired and indicate to this Government his views as to the financial and other governmental arrangements which must be made.

171

Study of American Military Matériel and Services Provided to the Chinese Government since V–J Day

I

SINO-AMERICAN COOPERATIVE ORGANIZATION AGREEMENT (SACO)

Item	Amount
Payment of lump sum of expenses of training 40 Chinese students as obligated by article 17, SACO agreement	$200,000.00
Equipage, shore bases	585,045.18
Public-works construction and maintenance	79,304.37
Ordnance supplies and equipment	14,284,067.80
Communications	14,746.58
Clothing	2,309.60
Radio equipment and supplies	1,320,664.26
Fiscal codes, aerology	957,782.27
Medical equipment	159,493.57
Aviation supplies and materials	67.25
Furniture and fixtures	63,448.82

Total estimated value of issues, V–J Day to March 2, 1946 . . . . $17,666,929.70

AMMUNITION DUMPED AND TRANSFERRED BY THE U. S. MARINES IN NORTH CHINA, APRIL–SEPTEMBER 1947

A) The following ammunition was abandoned by the First Marine Division during the months of April–May 1947, in the Peiping-Tientsin Area:

Type	Units
Rockets, HE, AT 2.36 in	3,646
Rockets, HE, AT 4.50 in	300
20 MM	9,493
37 MM	4,993
60 MM Mortar	47,678
80 MM Mortar	20,916
75 MM Gun	5,577
105 MM How	64,538
155 MM How	18,726
155 MM Prop. charge	10,725
Grenades, hand	55,529
Grenades, rifle	23,038
Demolition blocks	47,438
TNT, lbs	29,787
Charges, M–12, prop	2,420
Bangalore torpedoes	3,020
Mines, anti-personnel	1,014
Mines, anti-tank	2,636
Small arms, .30 cal	2,195,370
.45 cal	94,100
.50 cal	225,515
Grenade adapters	8,592
Flame throwers, portable	35
Flame thrower cylinders	302
Bombs, 500 lbs. GP	62
Demolition charges	3,248
Artillery fuses	16,975
Pyrotechnics	13,174
Blasting caps	32,913

Type	Units
Blasting, fuse, feet	100, 500
Firing Device	2, 575
Detonators	460
Shaped charges	288
Detonating cord, feet	366, 200
Firecrackers, M–11	1, 200
Ignition cylinder, M–1	3, 000
Napalm, gals.	12, 751
Bomb fuses, AN, M–230	48
Shells, shotgun, 12GA	9, 000
Lighter fuse	72, 581

B) The following ammunition was transferred to the Chinese Navy:

(1) Ammunition charged to Lend Lease Account, transferred from storage at Tsingtao airfield (previously removed from magazines of vessels transferred):

Type	Units
3″/50	1, 246
40 MM	6, 592
20 MM	169, 560
50 cal.	38, 150
45 cal.	250
30 cal.	99, 000

(2) Ammunition charged to Lend Lease Account transferred in ships' magazines:

Type	Units
3″/50	1, 781
40 MM	37, 767
20 MM	208, 835
50 cal.	80, 255
45 cal.	29, 520
30 cal.	157, 414
22 cal.	55, 560

(3) Ammunition charged to Lend Lease Account, transferred at Shanghai after special shipment from U. S. as training allowance:

Type	Units
3″/50	250
40 MM	100, 000
20 MM	150, 000
30 cal.	20, 000

C) Unserviceable ammunition in the hands of the Fleet Marine Force, Western Pacific, was abandoned by dumping small quantities at a time in revetments near Tsangkou Airfield, Tsingtao. The Chinese National Army Garrison Commander, was informed of the intention to abandon this ammunition. Dumping operations began on 19 May 1947, and were completed on 13 September 1947. During this period, the following ammunition was dumped:

Type	Units
105 MM Howitzer	24, 665
81 MM Mortar	30, 903
60 MM Mortar	28, 042
75 MM Howitzer	9, 337
155 MM Prop charge	6, 485
155 MM Prop charge	929
Grenade, hand, fragmentation	27, 575
Grenade, hand, all others	13, 640
Grenades, rifle, all types	9, 650
Bangalore torpedoes	1, 810
Small arms, cal. .30, carbine & rifle	1, 488, 490
Mines, anti-tank	372
Mines, anti-personnel	686

Type	Units
Shaped charges 40#	634
Shaped charges 10#	200
Grenade adapters, all types	4,272
Shell, 37 MM, all types & shot	1,035
Rocket, HE, AT	321
Flares, trip, all types	911
Device, firing, pressure type	980
Device, firing, pull type	1,410
Device, firing, push type	340
Device, firing, release type	1,040
Lighter, fuse, waterproof	102,000
Lighter, fuse, friction type	55,000
Pyrotechnic signals, ground	1,010
Fuse, igniting, hand grenade	7,725
Shells, shotgun # OOB	720
Cord, detonating, (Prima) 500 ft. Spools	280

TRANSFER OF U. S. NAVAL VESSELS UNDER PUBLIC LAW 512 (GRANT)

PR 4
DE 6
DE 47
PCE 867
PCE 869
AM 257
AM 258
AM 259
LST 537
LSM 155
LSM 157
LSM 285
LSM 457
LSM 431
AM 260
AM 266
AM 273
AM 276
AM 246
AM 274
AM 286
PC 1247
PC 1549
PGM 20
PGM 26
PGM 12
PGM 13
PGM 14
PGM 15
SC 648
SC 698
LSM 433
LSM 442
LSM 456
LCI (L) 233
LCI (L) 631
LCI (L) 417
LCI (L) 418
LCI (L) 630
LCI (L) 632
LST 557

LST 755
LST 1030
LST 993
LST 716
LST 717
LST 1017
LST 1050
LST 1075
LCI (L) 514
LCI (L) 517
AG 124
LCT 512
LCT 515
LCT 849
LCT 892
LCT 1143
LCT 1145
LCT 1171
LCT 1213
AOG 42
AFDL 34
25 LCM
25 LCVP
AM 287
AM 216
YMS 339
PC 490
PC 492
PC 593
PC 595
SC 704
SC 708
SC 722
SC 723
SC 735
AOG 22
AFDL (c) 36
ARL 41
DE 102
DE 103
DE 104
DE 112

Total procurement cost of above 131 vessels : $141,315,000.

II

PUBLIC LAW 512—79TH CONGRESS
CHAPTER 580—2D SESSION
H. R. 5356

AN ACT

To provide assistance to the Republic of China in augmenting and maintaining A Naval Establishment, and for other purposes.

Be it enacted by the Senate and House of Representatives of the United States of America in Congress assembled, That notwithstanding the provisions of any other law, the President is authorized, whenever in his discretion the public interests render such a course advisable, or will assist in relieving United State forces of duty in China or putting the Government of the Republic of China in a better position to protect or improve the safety of navigation in its waters, to provide to the Republic of China such naval services, training, plans, and technical advice as he may deem proper; and to dispose of naval vessels and craft, not to exceed two hundred and seventy-one vessels and craft under authority of this Act, which are in excess of the naval needs of the United States, floating drydocks of capacity sufficient to accommodate any vessel or craft disposed of under authority of this Act, and material necessary for the operation and maintenance of the vessels and craft disposed of under authority of this Act and for the training of the crews of such vessels and craft, to the Republic of China by sale, exchange, lease, gift, or transfer for cash, credit, or other property, with or without warranty, or upon such other terms and conditions as he may deem proper : *Provided*, That prior to the disposition under the authority of this Act of any battleship, aircraft carrier of any type, cruiser, destroyer (but not destroyer escort), or submarine the President shall first obtain the authority of Congress in each instance : *Provided further*, That no information, plans, advice, material, documents, blueprints, or other papers, bearing a secret or top-secret classification shall be disposed of or transferred under authority of this Act.

Sec. 2. The President is authorized, upon application from the Republic of China, and whenever in his discretion the public interests render such a course advisable, to detail not to exceed one hundred officers and two hundred enlisted men of the United States Navy and Marine Corps to assist the Republic of China in naval matters : *Provided*, That United States naval or Marine Corps personnel shall not accompany Chinese troops, aircraft, or ships on other than training maneuvers or cruises : *Provided further*, That the Secretary of the Navy is authorized to pay to such persons such additional compensation as may be necessary to make appropriate adjustment for increased cost of living occassioned by reason of detail to such duty : *And provided further*, That while so detailed such officers and enlisted men shall receive the pay and allowances thereunto entitled in the United States Navy or Marine Corps and shall be allowed the same credit for longevity, retirement, and for all other purposes that they would receive if they were serving with the forces of the United States.

Sec. 3. The provisions of this Act shall terminate five years after the date of its enactment.

Approved July 16, 1948.

III

EXECUTIVE ORDER

AUTHORIZING THE SECRETARY OF THE NAVY TO TRANSFER CERTAIN VESSELS AND MATERIAL AND TO FURNISH CERTAIN ASSISTANCE TO THE REPUBLIC OF CHINA

WHEREAS the act of July 16, 1946, Public Law 512, Seventy-ninth Congress, provides, in part:

"That notwithstanding the provisions of any other law, the President is authorized, whenever in his discretion the public interests render such a course advisable, or will assist in relieving United States forces of duty in China or putting the Government of the Republic of China in better position to protect or improve the safety of navigation in its waters, to provide to the Republic of China such naval services, training, plans, and technical advice as he may deem proper; and to dispose of naval vessels and craft, not to exceed two hundred and seventy-one vessels and craft under authority of this Act, which are in excess of the naval needs of the United States, floating drydocks of capacity sufficient to accommodate any vessel or craft disposed of under authority of this Act, and material necessary for the operation and maintenance of the vessels and craft disposed of under authority of this Act and for the training of the crews of such vessels and craft, to the Republic of China by sale, exchange, lease, gift, or transfer for cash, credit, or other property, with or without warranty, or upon such other terms and conditions as he may deem proper: *Provided,* That prior to the disposition under the authority of this Act of any battleship, aircraft carrier of any type, cruiser, destroyer (but not destroyer escort), or submarine the President shall first obtain the authority of the Congress in each instance: *Provided further,* That no information, plans, advice, material, documents, blueprints, or other papers, bearing a secret or top-secret classification shall be disposed of or transferred under authority of this Act.

"Sec. 2. The President is authorized, upon application from the Republic of China, and whenever in his discretion the public interests render such a course advisable, to detail not to exceed one hundred officers and two hundred enlisted men of the United States Navy and Marine Corps to assist the Republic of China in naval matters: *Provided,* That United States naval or Marine Corps personnel shall not accompany Chinese troops, aircraft, or ships on other than training maneuvers or cruises. . . ."

WHEREAS the Republic of China has requested the United States to transfer to it certain specified naval vessels, craft, and floating drydocks, and to furnish it certain technical advice and assistance in connection with the organization and maintenance by it of a naval establishment; and

WHEREAS such vessels and craft are in excess of the naval needs of the United States; and

WHEREAS it appears that the transfer of such vessels, craft, and floating drydocks, and the furnishing of such advice and assistance to the Republic of China would be in accordance with the conditions and limitations of the said act of July 16, 1946, and would be in the public interest:

Now, THEREFORE, by virtue of the authority vested in me by the said act of July 16, 1946, and as President of the United States and as Commander-in-Chief of the Army and Navy of the United States, it is hereby ordered as follows:

Section 1. Subject to the conditions and limitations contained in the said act of July 16, 1946, the Secretary of the Navy is authorized:

(a) To transfer to the Republic of China without compensation the said vessels, craft, and floating drydocks.

(b) To repair, outfit, and equip the vessels, craft, and floating drydocks which are to be transferred under paragraph (a) of this section, and to transfer material deemed by the Secretary of the Navy to be necessary for the operation and maintenance of the vessels and craft so transferred, all on the basis of cash reimbursement of the cost thereof by the Republic of China.

(c) To furnish to the Republic of China such plans, blueprints, documents, and other information in connection with such vessels, craft, and floating drydocks, and such technical information and advice in connection with the organization and maintenance of a naval establishment by the Republic of China which has not been classified as secret or top-secret as the Secretary of the Navy may deem proper.

(d) To train personnel for the operation of such vessels, craft, and floating drydocks, and for such other naval purposes as the Secretary of the Navy may deem proper.

(e) To detail not more than one hundred officers and two hundred enlisted men of the United States Navy or Marine Corps to assist the Republic of China in naval matters under such conditions and subject to such rules and regulations as the Secretary of the Navy may prescribe.

Section 2. The authority hereby granted shall be exercised by the Secretary of the Navy subject to concurrence by the Secretary of State; and if at any time the Secretary of State shall determine that the transfer of further vessels and craft or material would not be in the public interest, such transfers shall be discontinued.

HARRY S. TRUMAN.

THE WHITE HOUSE,
April 25, 1947.

IV

OFLC SHIPMENTS OF ARMS AND AMMUNITION TO CHINA

ACCUMULATED FIGURES—JANUARY 1, 1948 TO MARCH 31, 1949

Item	Quantity shipped	Procurement cost	Sales price
Air Force			
Aircraft P47-D	42	$3,999,534.00	$147,000.00
Aircraft P47-N	70 [1]	5,771,220.00	350,000.00
Aircraft C46-F	13 [2]	3,292,991.00	292,500.00
Aircraft P51-D	53	2,781,917.00	397,500.00
Aircraft Engines	683	8,729,563.50	1,210,077.00
Aircraft Spares	Mixed-bulk		
Parts and Tools	Shipments	11,729,011.45	2,023,745.32
20mm Guns	200	332,827.36	33,282.74
TOTALS		36,637,064.31	4,454,105.06
Other equipment			
Chemical	M/T 273.92	29,992.28	3,749.04
Engineer	M/T 439.91	77,037.09	9,629.64
Medical	M/T 77.05	42,500.28	5,312.54
Ordnance	" 7,072.63	1,590,699.39	198,837.43
Quartermaster	" 1,011.14	309,224.55	38,653.07
Signal	M/T 182.42	214,443.58	26,805.45
TOTALS	M/T 9,057.07	2,263,897.17	282,987.17

Accumulated Figures—January 1, 1948 to March 31, 1949—Continued

Item	Quantity shipped	Procurement cost	Sales price
Ammunition			
Cal. 30	37,972,793 rnds	$1, 865, 421. 86	$24, 621. 46
Cal. 50	18,571,550 rnds	2, 540, 350. 79	41, 913. 07
Cal. 45	1,836,600 rnds	71, 878. 38	4, 259. 50
20mm	138,696 rnds	42, 977. 50	4, 708. 26
37mm	346,874 rnds	848, 689. 56	42, 989. 04
60mm	152,411 rnds	452, 660. 67	4, 526. 62
81mm	83,475 rnds	432, 546. 24	4, 325. 44
4.2 m	36,918 rnds	415, 327. 50	41, 717. 34
75mm	151,933 rnds	1, 499, 335. 68	61, 070. 58
105mm	354,780 rnds	5, 484, 691. 89	155, 800. 95
155mm	287,732 rnds	1, 293, 128. 48	64, 805. 22
155mm (propelling charge)	8,889 rnds	63, 310. 65	3, 150. 69
Grenades	216,668	317, 665. 76	32, 062. 24
Mines	52,133	208, 532. 00	20, 853. 20
Bombs, grenades and mines (mixed) . .	L/T 5,666	2, 691, 336. 23	26, 913. 36
Bombs (photoflash)	200	6, 200. 00	620. 00
Ammunition—(mixed, bulk)	L/T 4,125	2, 989, 866. 52	29, 898. 67
Metallic Links	Mixed-Bulk	15, 169. 01	620. 00
Boosters, Flares, Fuses, etc.	L/T 696	330, 495. 03	3, 304. 95
Clusters.	M/T 506	137, 952. 35	1, 379. 52
TOTALS.	. . . .	21, 707, 536. 10	569, 071. 80
GRAND TOTALS	. . . .	60, 608, 497. 58	5, 306, 164. 03

[1] Delivered to Taiwan in September and December of 1948 in combat operational condition.
[2] Delivered to airfields in China in mid-1948 in operational condition.

V

PUBLIC LAW 472—80TH CONGRESS

"CHINA AID ACT" [Excerpt]

Sec. 404. (a) In order to carry out the purposes of this title, there is hereby authorized to be appropriated to the President for aid to China a sum not to exceed $338,000,000 to remain available for obligation for the period of one year following the date of enactment of this Act.

(b) There is also hereby authorized to be appropriated to the President a sum not to exceed $125,000,000 for additional aid to China through grants, on such terms as the President may determine and without regard to the provisions of the Economic Cooperation Act of 1948, to remain available for obligation for the period of one year following the date of enactment of this Act.

VI

THE PRESIDENT'S LETTER TO THE SECRETARY OF STATE, JUNE 2, 1948

THE WHITE HOUSE
WASHINGTON

June 2, 1948

MY DEAR MR. SECRETARY: I am in general in accord with the position expressed in your memorandum to me of May 14, 1948, regarding the provision of additional aid to China as authorized by Section 404 (b) of the China Aid Act of 1948. It is my desire that the grants to China under this section of the Act be made under the following procedures:

1. The Chinese Government will, from time to time, submit to the Department of State requests for payment with respect to commodities or services procured by it, supported by invoices or other appropriate documentation evidencing the transactions.

2. The Department of State will examine the documentation submitted by the Chinese Government to determine that the request is not in excess of the total represented by the invoices or other supporting data, and will authorize the Treasury to make the appropriate payments to the Chinese Government.

3. The Secretary of State will request from the Chinese Government monthly reports showing in as much detail as possible the purposes for which expenditures have been made out of the funds provided to it under the authority of Section 404 (b) of the Act.

Attached is a copy of my letter to the Secretary of the Treasury informing him of this procedure and making an allocation of $13,500,000 to carry out the provisions of Section 404 (b) of the China Aid Act of 1948.

Sincerely yours,

HARRY S. TRUMAN.

Attachment.

VII

THE PRESIDENT'S LETTER TO THE SECRETARY OF THE TREASURY, TYPED JUNE 2, 1948

THE WHITE HOUSE
WASHINGTON

June 2, 1948

MY DEAR MR. SECRETARY: Pursuant to the authority of Section 404 (b) and Section 406 of the China Aid Act of 1948 (Title IV, Public Law 472, 80th Congress), I hereby allocate to you the sum of $13,500,000 out of the funds advanced by the Reconstruction Finance Corporation to carry out the provisions of the said China Aid Act of 1948. Please take the necessary steps to effect this allocation.

Out of the funds allocated hereunder disbursements are to be made by you to the Chinese Government upon certification by the Department of State that the amounts requested are supported by invoices submitted by the Chinese Government, which the Department has examined to determine that the request is not in excess of the total represented by these invoices. A record of these disbursements should be forwarded monthly to the Department of State.

The Secretary of State will further advise the Chinese Government to furnish him monthly reports showing in as much detail as practicable the purposes for which expenditures have been made out of the funds made available under the authority of Section 404 (b) of the China Aid Act of 1948.

At such time as appropriations may become available for the purpose of carrying out Section 404 (b) of the China Aid Act of 1948, further allocations will be made out of such appropriations, to be disbursed in accordance with the terms of this letter.

Sincerely yours,

HARRY S. TRUMAN

VIII

NOTE FROM THE UNDER SECRETARY OF STATE TO THE CHINESE AMBASSADOR, JUNE 28, 1948

June 28, 1948

EXCELLENCY: I have the honor to inform you that, in accordance with the authorization contained in Section 404 (b) of the China Aid Act of 1948 (Title IV of the Foreign Assistance Act of 1948) and subject to the provisions of the Act appropriating funds thereunder, the Government of the United States is prepared, for the period of one year following the date of the enactment of the Act, to extend to the Government of the Republic of China additional aid through grants in the amount of $125,000,000 which have been appropriated for this purpose by the Congress in the Foreign Aid Appropriation Act of 1949. As stated in Section 404 (b) of the China Aid Act of 1948, this aid is to be extended on such terms as the President of the United States may determine and without regard to the provisions of the Economic Cooperation Act of 1948.

Pursuant to the authorization under the Act, the President of the United States has determined that the extension of additional aid under these grants shall be governed by the following terms:

1. The Government of the Republic of China shall, through its authorized representatives in Washington, present from time to time to the Secretary of State formal written requests for payment with respect to commodities or services procured or to be procured by it, supported by invoices, contracts or other appropriate documentation evidencing the transactions.

2. The Secretary of State shall upon the receipt of such requests, supported by invoices, contracts or other appropriate documentation evidencing the transactions, authorize the Secretary of the Treasury to make the appropriate payments to the Government of the Republic of China.

3. The Government of the Republic of China shall furnish the Secretary of State monthly reports showing in as much detail as practicable the purposes for which expenditures have been made out of funds provided to it under the authority of Section 404 (b) of the China Aid Act of 1948.

I should appreciate receiving notification of your Government's agreement to the terms set forth above for the extension of this additional aid under Section 404 (b) of the China Aid Act of 1948. Upon the receipt of a note indicating your Government's acceptance of these terms, the implementation of this Section of the Act may be promptly undertaken.

Accept [etc.]

For the Secretary of State:
ROBERT A. LOVETT
Under Secretary

IX

NOTE FROM THE CHINESE AMBASSADOR TO THE SECRETARY OF STATE, JULY 1, 1948

July 1, 1948

SIR: I have the honor to acknowledge the receipt of your note dated June 28, 1948, stating that, in accordance with the authorization contained in Section 404 (b) of the China Aid Act of 1948 (Title IV of the Foreign Assistance Act of 1948) and subject to the provisions of the Act appropriating funds thereunder, the Government of the United States is prepared, for the period of one year following the date of enactment of the China Aid Act of 1948, to extend to the Government of the Republic of China additional aid through grants in the amount of $125,000,000 which have been appropriated for this purpose by the Congress in the Foreign Aid Appropriation Act of 1949. It is understood that this aid is to be extended on such terms as the President of the United States may determine and without regard to the provisions of the Economic Cooperation Act of 1948.

My Government has authorized me to inform you of its agreement to the terms determined by the President of the United States to govern the extension of additional aid under these grants as set forth in your note under acknowledgement.

It is understood that the Government of the Republic of China shall, through its authorized representative in Washington, present from time to time to the Secretary of State formal written requests for payment with respect to commodities or services procured or to be procured by it, supported by invoices, contracts or other appropriate documentation evidencing the transactions. It is understood that the Secretary of State shall upon the receipt of such requests, supported by invoices, contracts or other appropriate documentation evidencing the transactions, authorize the Secretary of the Treasury to make appropriate payments to the Government of the Republic of China. It is also understood that the Government of the Republic of China shall furnish the Secretary of State monthly reports showing in as much detail as practicable the purposes for which expenditures have been made out of funds provided to it under the authority of Section 404 (b) of the China Aid Act of 1948.

My Government concurs in the understanding expressed above.

Accept [etc.]   V. K. WELLINGTON KOO

X

THE PRESIDENT'S LETTER TO THE SECRETARY OF STATE JULY 28, 1948

THE WHITE HOUSE
WASHINGTON

July 28, 1948

MY DEAR MR. SECRETARY : My letter of June 2, 1948, addressed to you concerning the provision of additional aid to China as authorized by Section 404 (b) of the China Aid Act of 1948 is amended to read in pertinent part as follows :

"It is my desire that the grants to China under this Section of the Act, which grants are hereby made, shall be paid under the following procedures :

1. The Chinese Government will from time to time submit to the Department of State requests for payment with respect to commodities or services procured or ordered by it, supported by purchase orders, contracts, invoices, or other appropriate documentation evidencing the transactions.

2. The Department of State will examine the documentation submitted by the Chinese Government to determine that the request is not in excess of the total represented by the supporting data and will authorize the Treasury to make the appropriate payments to the Chinese Government. The Treasury Department shall make the payments in accordance with such authorization.

3. In those cases in which the Chinese Government wishes to arrange for the procurement or furnishing of supplies or services by any department, agency, or establishment of the United States Government, subject to the approval

of the Secretary of State as to the availability of funds prior to the procurement or furnishing of such supplies or services and pursuant to Sections 403 and 113 (a) of the Foreign Assistance Act of 1948, such department, agency, or establishment is authorized to submit to the Department of State requests for reimbursement of appropriations or for advance payments. On the basis of such requests, the Department of State will authorize the Treasury Department to make reimbursements or advance payments to such department, agency, or establishment.

4. The Secretary of State will request from the Chinese Government monthly reports showing in as much detail as possible the purposes for which expenditures have been made out of the funds provided to it under the authority of Section 404 (b) of the Act."

Attached is a copy of my letter to the Secretary of the Treasury advising him of this decision.

Sincerely yours,

HARRY S. TRUMAN

Attachment.

XI

THE PRESIDENT'S LETTER TO THE SECRETARY OF DEFENSE JULY 28, 1948

THE WHITE HOUSE
WASHINGTON

July 28, 1948

MY DEAR MR. SECRETARY: I enclose copies of letters addressed by me to the Secretary of State and to the Secretary of the Treasury setting forth the procedures to be applied to the additional aid to China authorized by Section 404 (b) of the China Aid Act of 1948. I also enclose a copy of a memorandum addressed to me by the Secretary of State with reference to facilitating the procurement of military supplies by the Chinese Government. There are further enclosed copies of an exchange of letters on the same subject with Chairmen Bridges and Taber of the Senate and House Appropriations Committees.

Will you please take such action as may be appropriate in the circumstances to facilitate the acquisition by the Chinese Government of such military supplies as the Chinese Government may request, either by making available existing stocks of the National Defense Establishment or by arranging for the procurement of such supplies on behalf of that Government.

Sincerely yours,

HARRY S. TRUMAN

Enclosures

XII

THE PRESIDENT'S LETTER TO THE SECRETARY OF THE TREASURY JULY 28, 1948

THE WHITE HOUSE
WASHINGTON

July 28, 1948

MY DEAR MR. SECRETARY: My letters of allocation under Section 404 (b) of the China Aid Act of 1948 (Title IV, Public Law 472, 80th Congress), dated June 2 and July 16, 1948 are hereby amended in pertinent part to conform with the attached letter addressed to the Secretary of State establishing procedures under which payments under that Act shall be made.

Sincerely yours,

HARRY S. TRUMAN

Attachment.

XIII

DEPARTMENT OF STATE, WASHINGTON
July 30, 1948.

EXCELLENCY: I have the honor to refer to my note of June 28, 1948 in which were set forth the terms decided upon by the President of the United States to govern the extension of additional aid to the Government of the Republic of China through grants authorized under Section 404 (b) of the China Aid Act of 1948 and to your note of July 1, 1948 indicating your Government's acceptance of those terms.

I am now authorized to inform you of the following procedure established by the President by which United States Government departments, agencies or establishments may assist the Chinese Government in arranging for the procurement or furnishing of supplies or services under Section 404 (b) of the China Aid Act of 1948:

In those cases in which the Chinese Government wishes to arrange for the procurement or furnishing of supplies or services by any department, agency or establishment of the United States Government, subject to the approval of the Secretary of State as to the availability of funds prior to the procurement or furnishing of such supplies or services and pursuant to Sections 403 and 113 (a) of the Foreign Assistance Act of 1948, such department, agency or establishment is authorized to submit to the Department of State requests for reimbursement of appropriations or for advance payments. On the basis of such requests, the Department of State will authorize the Treasury Department to make reimbursements or advance payments to such department, agency or establishment.

Accept [etc.]

For the Secretary of State:
ROBERT A. LOVETT
Under Secretary

XIV

CHINESE EMBASSY, WASHINGTON
August 6, 1948

SIR: I have the honor to refer to your note of July 30th, 1948, stating that, pursuant to the following procedure established by the President, departments, agencies or establishments of the United States Government may assist my Government in arranging for the procurement or furnishing of supplies or services under Section 404 (b) of the China Aid Act of 1948:

"In those cases in which the Chinese Government wishes to arrange for the procurement or furnishing of supplies or services by any department, agency or establishment of the United States Government, subject to the approval of the Secretary of State as to the availability of funds prior to the procurement or furnishing of such supplies or services and pursuant to Sections 403 and 113 (a) of the Foreign Assistance Act of 1948, such department, agency or establishment is authorized to submit to the Department of State requests for reimbursement of appropriations or for advance payments. On the basis of such requests, the

Department of State will authorize the Treasury Department to make reimbursements or advance payments to such department, agency or establishment."

I am authorized to inform you in reply that my Government accepts the procedure set forth above, which, together with the terms communicated to me by your note of June 28th, 1948, and accepted by my Government in my note to you of July 1st, 1948, no doubt will greatly facilitate the procurement programs of my Government.

Accepted [etc.]

V. K. WELLINGTON KOO

XV

REPORT RECEIVED FROM THE CHINESE EMBASSY ON THE USE OF FUNDS OBTAINED UNDER THE $125 MILLION GRANTS

Summary of the Use of Funds Received—Total Accumulative

Category	Amounts ($)
(a) Chinese Air Force	
1. Aircraft	$2,867,700.00
2. Aircraft Parts	8,088,203.38
3. Aircraft Engines	2,690,895.78
4. Aircraft Accessories & Parts	520,796.71
5. Casing, Tube, Rubber Materials	310,267.87
6. Fuel & Lubricant	7,528,903.83
7. Electrical Supplies & Accessories	8,247.16
8. Gunnery Equipment	21,947.50
9. Flying Shoes	112,500.00
10. Radio Equipment	28,901.00
11. Tools & Equipment	223,882.72
12. Field & Hangar Equipment	459,473.64
13. Armament & Ammunition	90,282.25
14. Raw Materials & Hardware	4,034.60
15. Photographic Supplies	6,831.28
16. Chemicals, Gas & Oil	4,604.38
17. Rubber & Hose	273,570.24
18. Medicine	42,566.96
19. Critical Items	129,868.08
20. Shipping Charges	534,253.07
21. Insurance & Handling	58,986.50
22. Services	3,984.283.05
SUBTOTAL	28,000,000.00
(b) Chinese Army	
1. Ordnance, Weapons & Ammunition	42,604,465.47
2. Ordnance, Materials for Arsenals	12,512,779.61
3. Transportation, Trucks	359,987.64
4. Transportation, Vehicle Spare Parts	9,706,094.39
5. Transportation, Tools & Equipment	375,646.33
6. Transportation, Materials	124,020.57
7. Signal, Field Communication Equipment	4,133,465.87
8. Signal, Equipment & Supplies	332,763.76
9. Signal, Miscellaneous	1,038.00
10. Engineer, Supplies & Equipment	397,114.51
11. Armored Force, Equipment & Supplies	1,000,033.43
12. Intelligence, Equipment	90,000.00
13. Intelligence, Miscellaneous	702.09
14. Medical Supplies	7,000,000.00
15. Petroleum Products	8,375,000.00
16. Shipping Charges	483,274.85
17. Insurance Premiums	3,373.88
18. Miscellaneous Charges	239.60
SUBTOTAL	87,500,000.00

Category	(c) Chinese Navy	Amounts ($)
1. Vessels, Guns & Ammunition, Equipment & Supplies		$6, 557, 020. 00
2. Petroleum Products		2, 942, 980. 00
SUBTOTAL		9, 500, 000. 00
TOTAL		125, 000, 000. 00

XVI

Monthly Shipments Under China Aid Program, Authorized by Sec. 404 (b), China Aid Act of 1948, June Through December 1948

June—Miscellaneous aircraft spare parts purchased from private companies in the U. S. . 19, 197. 74

July—Approximately 10,000 tons of small arms and artillery ammunition (procurement cost $8 million) and miscellaneous aircraft spare parts 344, 869. 09

August—Aviation gasoline, aircraft spare parts, and communications equipment 1, 043, 026. 74

September—P–47 fighter aircraft (procurement cost $4 million) Aviation gasoline and other petroleum products, aircraft spare parts, communications equipment, reconditioning naval vessels 1, 913, 942. 17

October—Ammunition, aircraft spare parts, ordnance supplies, naval supplies and services, aviation gasoline and other petroleum products. 7, 006, 893. 91

November—Small arms and ammunition, naval supplies and services, aircraft parts, aviation gasoline and other petroleum products 20, 644, 970. 71

December—Small arms and ammunition, fighter aircraft, tanks, medical supplies, naval supplies and services, aviation gasoline and other petroleum products 28, 219, 461. 65

Undistributed [1]. 1, 766, 429. 37

TOTAL AS OF DECEMBER 31, 1948 .... 60, 958, 791. 38

[1] Records not yet available showing exact month in which shipment was made. This figure reflects miscellaneous shipments of aviation supplies known to have been made on a countinuing basis beginning in August 1948 and deliveries of petroleum products transferred primarily from bonded stocks in China which were available to the Chinese Government in August 1948.

XVII

Shipments Under China Aid Program by Agencies of U. S. Government and by Chinese Agencies, Authorized by Sec. 404 (b), China Aid Act of 1948, as of December 31, 1948

A. *Items Procured through U. S. Government Agencies*

(1) **Department of the Army**

    a) U. S. S. *Algol*—Sailed from the U. S. Nov. 9; arrived Shanghai Nov. 29, 1948.

        Small arms and ammunition **$16, 127, 081. 91**

    b) U. S. S. *Washburn*—Sailed from the U. S. Dec. 1; arrived Taiwan Jan. 4, 1949.

Rifles .30 cal.	$4, 491, 621. 00
Auto. rifles and sub-MGs	360, 970. 00
Johnson rifles and Johnson MGs	315, 151. 06
Bayonets	423, 034. 80
Grenades and rockets	408, 471. 50
Small arms ammunition	5, 457, 394. 83
	11, 456, 643. 19

    c) U. S. S. *Yancey*—Sailed from the U. S. Dec. 16; arrived Taiwan, Jan 4, 1949.

Rifles .30 cal.	1, 632, 000. 00
Auto. rifles and sub-MGs	657, 806. 00
4.2″ Chemical mortars	199, 500. 00
75 mm. Pack howitzers w/fire control equip	1, 400, 416. 00
Powder and propellants	558, 816. 25
.30 cal. ammunition	388, 552. 50
Quonset huts	48, 420. 00

(1) Department of the Army—Continued
   c) U. S. S. *Yancey*—Continued

Blankets.	$31,726.12
Dry cell batteries	22,206.29
Medical supplies.	2,353,727.19
Miscellaneous ordnance material.	456,913.82
Spare parts for weapons and vehicles.	1,250,000.00
Transportation, packing and handling of above-listed supplies	918,541.12
	$9,918,625.29

   d) Arms and ammunition from Far East Command—shipments completed, 16 November 1948 .... 2,225,102.62

   e) Explosives and demolition equipment from Hawaii—arrived Shanghai, 3 December 1948 .... 218,382.75

   f) Surplus ordnance material from Shanghai. 72,364.33

         TOTAL, DEPARTMENT OF THE ARMY 40,018,200.09

(2) Department of the Navy

a) Fuel, lubricants and petroleum products	19,000.00
b) Military vessels and watercraft	746,000.00
c) Technical navy equipment	315,000.00
d) Ordnance and ordnance stores	2,768,000.00

         TOTAL, DEPARTMENT OF THE NAVY 3,848,000.00

(3) Department of the Air Force

a) Ammunition and armaments		73,676.00
b) Aviation fuel and lubricants—shipped in October 1948		1,387,781.14
c) Miscellaneous supplies and equipment		160.50
d) Miscellaneous administrative expenses, applicable to above.	$41,633.43	
e) Ocean transportation	232,388.49	

         TOTAL, DEPARTMENT OF THE AIR FORCE. 1,735,639.56

(4) Bureau of Federal Supply, Treasury Department

a) Motor gasoline, from off-shore sources.	526,785.00
b) Kerosene, from off-shore sources.	5,150.26
c) Diesel oil, from off-shore sources.	115,136.00
d) Fuel oil, from off-shore sources	134,145.71

         TOTAL, BUREAU OF FEDERAL SUPPLY 781,216.97

(5) Office of the Foreign Liquidation Commissioner

   a) Ammunition (10,000 tons), the bulk of which was shipped on July 3 and 16, 1948 .... 336,916.05

   b) Aircraft—delivered in September and December 1948 .... 582,250.00

   c) Aircraft spare parts and armament parts 296,568.60

       TOTAL, OFFICE OF THE FOREIGN LIQUIDATION COMMISSIONER 1,215,734.65

       TOTAL U. S. GOVERNMENT AGENCIES $47,598,791.27

B. *Items Procured Directly by Chinese Government*

(1) Chinese Air Force

a) Aircraft.	$260,000.00
b) Aircraft engines.	205,780.00
c) Aviation gasoline and motor oil	4,701,626.31
d) Tires and tubes	126,008.52
e) Flying boats	110,880.00
f) Snow plows and trucks	112,466.70
g) Portable heaters	110,776.26
h) Aircraft parts and miscellaneous air force equipment	1,511,179.55
i) Shipping charges, including insurance	361,852.62
j) Miscellaneous services rendered	25,062.78

         TOTAL, CHINESE AIR FORCE 7,525,632.74

B. *Items Procured Directly by Chinese Government*—Continued

(2) Chinese Military Procurement Technical Group
    a) Signal equipment and supplies $671,027.50
    b) Ordnance material 590,702.09
    c) Transportation equipment 148,000.00
    d) Armored Force equipment 285,531.17
    e) Gasoline, fuel oil and other petroleum products 3,652,457.88
    f) Shipping charges 486,648.73

        TOTAL, CHINESE MILITARY PROCUREMENT TECHNICAL GROUP   5,834,367.37
        TOTAL, ITEMS PROCURED DIRECTLY BY CHINESE GOVERNMENT $13,360,000.11
        GRAND TOTAL 60,958,791.3

XVIII

REPORT RECEIVED FROM THE CHINESE EMBASSY ON SHIPMENTS UNDER THE $125 MILLION GRANTS

Period of Report: January 1–January 31, 1949

Part I—Chinese Air Force

Description	Value ($)	Weight	Name of vessel	Date of sailing	Port of embarkation
(1) ITEMS PROCURED BY CHINESE AIR FORCE					
Aircraft Engines	$132,500.00	82,500 lbs	Belleville	Dec. 19, 1948	Miami.
Mechanics Tools	149.44	38¼ lbs	Manderville . .	. . do	New York.
Flying Boots	1,620.00	766 lbs	Pioneer Cove . .	Dec. 29, 1948	Do.
Portable Ground Heaters.	191.42	385 lbs	. . do	. . do	Do.
Fuses for Aircraft	111.86	60 lbs.	Mount Davis .	Dec. 31, 1948	Do.
Jeep Replacement Parts .	4,765.00	3,509 lbs.	. . do	. . do	Do.
Regulators	2,324.92	809 lbs	. . do	. . do	Do.
Radio Compass	4,037.60	5,739 lbs	. . do	. . do	Do.
Power Unit Canopy Actuator.	2,575.59	96 lbs	. . do	. . do	Do.
Valve-Oil dil.	3,202.70	1,230 lbs	. . do	. . do	Do.
Diaphragm . . . . . , .	446.26	183 lbs	. . do	. . do	Do.
Airplane Parts	726.85	187 lbs	. . do	. . do	Do.
Generator	330.75	150 lbs	. . do	. . do	Do.
Accumulator	2,307.64	311 lbs	. . do	. . do	Do.
Airplane Part	19,417.24	4,192 lbs	. . do	. . do	Do.
Aircraft (P-51) (Machine Guns) (20).	260,000.00	320,700 lbs . . .	Colorado	. . do	Houston.
Merlin Aircraft Engines.	73,280.00	169,700 lbs . . .	. . do	. . do	Do.
Brake Assemblies . . .	5,715.00	1,978 lbs	. . do	. . do	Do.
Strut Assemblies	420.00	100 lbs	. . do	. . do	Do.
Aircraft Parts & Bomb Sight and Isopropanol.	896,767.35	150,834 lbs . . .	. . do	. . do	Do.
Pump and Refueling Unit Ass'y.	17,170.00	16,600 lbs	Transocean A. L.	Jan. 7, 1949	Oakland.
16 P-51 D Airplane . . .	208,000.00	251,600 lbs . . .	Ferndale	Jan. 15, 1949	Houston.
Total	1,636,059.62	1,011,667¼ lbs.			

Part II—Chinese Army and Navy

Description	Value ($)	Weight	Name of vessel	Date of sailing	Port of embarkation
(1) ITEMS PROCURED BY CHINESE MILITARY PROCUREMENT TECHNICAL GROUP					
Armored Force					
Periscopes, Head Assemblies & Tank Tracks 469 Cs.	$18,843.17	73,301 lbs	S. S. Courser . .	Dec. 1, 1948	Honolulu.
Ordnance					
Calculating Machine, 1 Pc.	702.09	94 lbs	C. N. A. C. . . .	Dec. 16, 1948	San Francisco.
Telescopes 350 Pcs. . . .	3,535.34	814 lbs.	Mt. Mansfield .	Jan. 22, 1949	New York.
Signal					
Calculating Machine, 1 Pc.	702.09	94 lbs.	C. N. A. C. . . .	Dec. 16, 1948	San Francisco.
Typewriters, 2 Pcs. . . .	335.91	252 lbs.	Philippine Bear.	Jan. 18, 1949	Do.
Paraffin Wax 98 Cs. . . .	2,184.16	20,249 lbs.	Philippine Transport.	Dec. 28, 1948	Do.
Zinc Chloride, 82 Dms. .	6,515.84	52,172 lbs. . . .	Grete Maersk. .	Jan. 18, 1949	New York.
Graphite Powder 66,000 .	4,290.00	67,652 lbs.	Mt. Davis . . .	Dec. 31, 1948	Do.
Switchboard BD–72 620 Pcs.	7,440.00	87,200 lbs.	. . do.	Dec. 31, 1948	Do.
Field Telephone EE8 4000 Pcs.	30,004.92	54,910 lbs.	. . do.	Dec. 31, 1948	Do.
Field Tel. EE8, 1530 Pcs.	13,064.90	21,349 lbs.	President Fillmore.	Jan. 7, 1949	Do.
Field Telephone EE8 900 Pcs.	8,569.92	12,412 lbs.	Mt. Mansfield .	Jan. 22, 1949	Do.
Switchboard BD–72, 180 Pcs.	3,083.92	20,250 lbs.	. . do.	. . do. . . .	Do.
Switchboard BD–71 250 Pcs.	4,060.31	27,982 lbs.	. . do.	. . do. . . .	Do.
Radio Tubes 20 Cs. . . .	20,179.82	6,681 lbs.	. . do.	. . do. . . .	Do.
Zinc Sheet 100 Cs. . . .	15,015.21	61,605 lbs.	. . do.	. . do. . . .	Do.
Ammonium Chloride 582 bbls.	12,819.26	174,600 lbs.	. . do.	. . do. . . .	Do.
Transportation					
Retreading & Recapping Stock, T2.	38,253.06	167,610 lbs. . . .	Philippine Bear.	Jan. 18, 1949	San Francisco.
Retreading & Recapping Stock, T2.	38,938.55	166,352 lbs. . . .	Lakeland Victory.	Jan. 29, 1949	Los Angeles.
Spare Parts for Motor Vehicles T3.	531,964.81	631,026 lbs. . . .	Philippine Bear.	Jan. 18, 1949	San Francisco.
Do.	16,314.86	7,496 lbs.	Lakeland Victory.	Jan. 29, 1949	Los Angeles.
GMC 2.5T 6x6 Army Truck 38 Cs.	134,099.06	394,900 lbs. . . .	Philippine Bear.	Jan. 18, 1949	San Francisco.
Auto Spark-Plugs 46 Cs.	22,562.78	12,532 lbs	Mt. Mansfield .	Jan. 22, 1949	New York.
Rubber Compd. & Tire Patches 56 Cs.	25,650.63	27,526 lbs	. . do	Feb. 5, 1949	Los Angeles.
Testing Apparatus Electric 46 Cs.	46,018.32	15,565 lbs	. . do	Feb. 10, 1949	San Francisco.
SUBTOTAL (items on 1)	1,005,148.93	2,104,624 lbs. . .	. . . .	. . . .	

Part II—Chinese Army and Navy—Continued

Description	Value ($)	Weight	Name of vessel	Date of sailing	Port of embarkation
(2) ITEMS SUPPLIED BY U. S. ARMY AND NAVY					
SCR 522 Radio Sets 150 Pcs.	43,534.16	150,867 lbs . . .	U. S. S. Washburn.	Dec. 16, 1948	Bangor.
Signal Equipment Parts 246 Bxs.	78,285.20	42,000 lbs	Philippine Transport.	Dec. 28, 1948	San Francisco.
Navy Jackets & Coats 1,500 Pcs.	18,250.00	8,800 lbs.	R. C. S. Tai-Ho.	Jan. 11, 1949	Norfolk.
SUBTOTAL (items on 2)	$140,069.36	201,667 lbs . . .	. . . .	. . . .	
(3) ITEMS SUPPLIED BY U. S. BUREAU OF FEDERAL SUPPLY					
Navy Lubricating Oil 587 x 55 Gals.	16,759.59	257,400 lbs. . . .	M. S. Belleville.	Jan. 12, 1949	New Orleans.
Navy Lubricating Oil 3857 x 54 Gals.	61,959.59	1,697,520 lbs. . .	S. S. City of Alabama.	Jan. 25, 1949	Do.
Auto-Gasoline 10,000 x 53 Gals.	217,300.00	3,800,000 lbs. . .	Philippine Bear	Jan. 18, 1949	San Francisco.
Auto-Gasoline 9,943 x 53 Gals.	216,061.39	3,778,340 lbs. . .	Lakeland Victory.	Jan. 29, 1949	Los Angeles.
SUBTOTAL	$512,080.57	9,533,260 lbs. . .	. . . .	. . . .	
TOTAL (Army and Navy)	1,657,298.86	11,839,551 lbs. . . (5,381.6 long tons)	. . . .	. . . .	

Part III—Summary

	Approximate total value ($)	Approximate total weight (long tons)
Chinese Air Force.	1,636,059.62	459.9
Chinese Army and Navy	1,657,298.86	5,381.6
GRAND TOTAL	3,293,358.48	5,841.5

XIX

REPORT RECEIVED FROM THE CHINESE EMBASSY ON SHIPMENTS UNDER THE
$125 MILLION GRANTS

Period of Report: February 1–February 28, 1949

Part I—Chinese Air Force

Description	Values ($)	Weight	Name of vessel	Date of sailing	Port of embarkation
(1) ITEMS PROCURED BY CHINESE AIR FORCE					
Aircraft Parts.	7,542.18	5,860 lbs.	Luxembourg V..	Jan. 19, 1949	Los Angeles.
Static Dischargers. . . .	414.00	50 lbs.	.. do.	.. do.. . . .	Do.
Aircraft Parts.	1,935.00	426 lbs.	.. do.	.. do.. . .	Do.
Do.	5,546.85	2,578 lbs.	.. do.	.. do.. . .	Do.
Do.	1,513.75	508 lbs.	.. do.	.. do.. . .	Do.
Do.	8,950.00	4,600 lbs.	.. do.	.. do.. . .	Do.
Transport Tires & Tubes.	79,204.10	159,057 lbs. . . .	.. do.	.. do.. . .	Do.
AT–6 Aircraft.	330,000.00	179,520 lbs. . . .	.. do.	.. do.. . .	Do.
Truck Tires & Tubes.. .	34,408.29	62,598 lbs..	.. do.	.. do.. . .	Do.
Attachment Screw. . . .	154.00	54 lbs.	.. do.	.. do.. . .	Do.
R–100—Hose.	806.74	869 lbs.	.. do.	.. do.. . .	Do.
Expander Tubes. . . .	2,278.19	744 lbs.	.. do.	.. do.. . .	Do.
Airplane Tires.	1,527.90	972 lbs.	.. do.	.. do.. . .	Do.
Hose.	1,214.51	1,195 lbs.	.. do.	.. do.. . .	Do.
Airplane Tubes.. . . .	750.00	1,802 lbs.	.. do.	.. do.. . .	Do.
Airplane Engines.. . . .	64,000.00	103,800 lbs. . . .	Fernfield..	.. do.. . . .	New York.
Do.	78,200.00	47,650 lbs..	.. do.	.. do.. . .	Do.
Generators.	1,560.00	340 lbs.	.. do.	.. do.. . .	Do.
Airplane Parts.	6,103.65	395 lbs..	.. do.	.. do.. . .	Do.
Radio Tubes.	1,236.00	636 lbs.	.. do.	.. do.. . .	Do.
Disc. Etc..	1,825.40	113 lbs.	.. do.	.. do.. . .	Do.
P–47 Tires & Tubes. . .	11,168.88	6,899 lbs.	.. do.	.. do.. . .	Do.
Radio Compasses.. . . .	4,851.00	2,233 lbs.	.. do.	.. do.. . .	Do.
Coil Assembly.	2,544.00	154 lbs.	.. do.	.. do.. . .	Do.
Protectors.	31.75	7 lbs.	.. do.	.. do.. . .	Do.
Relays, Reg.	1,295.94	761 lbs.	.. do.	.. do.. . .	Do.
Airplane Parts.	68,531.00	59,634 lbs.. . . .	. do.	.. do.. . .	Do.
Aircraft Parts.	349.35	140 lbs.	Lakeland, Vic. .	Jan. 29, 1949	Long Beach.
AT–6 Aircraft.	20,185.00	89,760 lbs.. . . .	.. do.	.. do.. . .	Do.
Propeller Ass'y for C–46.	5,445.00	12,100 lbs.. . . .	.. do.	.. do.. . .	Do.
Do.	1,485.00	3,300 lbs.	.. do.	.. do.. . .	Do.
AT–6 Aircraft.	20,185.00	89,760 lbs.. . . .	Mt. Mansfield..	Feb. 6, 1949	Los Angeles.
Aircraft Parts.	1,500.00	230 lbs.	.. do.	.. do.. . .	Do.
Do.	4,025.00	6,752 lbs.	.. do.	.. do.. . .	Do.
Truck Tires & Tubes.. .	11,528.72	24,952 lbs.. . . .	.. do.	.. do.. . .	Do.
P–47 Tires & Tubes. . .	692.12	631 lbs.	.. do.	.. do.. . .	Do.
P–47 Airplanes K/D with Machine Guns.	35,000.00	118,525 lbs.	.. do.	Feb. 14, 1949	Houston.
Merlin, V–1650–7 New Engines, Aircraft.	18,320.00	41,600 lbs.. . . .	.. do.	.. do.. . .	Do.
Internal Combustion Eng.	31,900.00	85,550 lbs.. . . .	.. do.	.. do. . . .	Do.
P–51 Airplanes K/D with Machine Guns.	127,500.00	268,744 lbs. . . .	.. do.	.. do.. . .	Do.
Aircraft Engines (Pratt & Whitney).	212,000.00	13,200 lbs	.. do.	.. do. . . .	Do.
24 cc Pertussis Endotoxid Vaccine.	13,527.00	1,475 lbs.	Airlines	Feb. 16, 1949	Washington, DC.

Part I—Chinese Air Force—Continued

Description	Value ($)	Weight	Name of vessel	Date of sailing	Port of embarkation
(1) ITEMS PROCURED BY CHINESE AIR FORCE—Continued					
100's Penioral Tablets, Buffered Penicillin.	$9,020.00	466 lbs	Airlines	Feb. 16, 1949	Washington, D.C.
Aircraft Clock A-11. . .	195.00	20 lbs.	Titania.	Feb. 18, 1949	New York.
Airplane Engine Parts. .	125.50	56 lbs.	. . do.	. . do.	Do.
Airplane Engines .•. . .	115,920.00	140,700 lbs	. . do.	. . do. . . .	Do.
Snow Plow Parts Auto .	17,039.52	11,690 lbs	. . do.	. . do. . . .	Do.
Aircraft Engine Parts. .	1,676.40	405 lbs	. . do.	. . do	Do.
Pumps & Refueling Unit	1,875.00	1,900 lbs. . . .	. . do.	. . do	Do.
Aircraft Engine Electric Relay Assembly.	4,721.76	1,983 lbs	. . do.	. . do	Do.
R37S-1 Spark Plugs. . .	67,103.02	66 lbs.	. . do.	. . do. . . .	Do.
Lead Assemblies	4,832.40	486 lbs	. . do.	. . do. . . .	Do.
Bolts	97.85	225 lbs	. . do.	. . do. . . .	Do.
Aircraft Magneto	437.75	35 lbs.	. . do.	. . do. . . .	Do.
Leather Packing	1,566.72	69 lbs.	. . do.	. . do. . . .	Do.
Contact Springs and Lead Assembly.	5,207.26	563 lbs	. . do.	. . do. . . .	Do.
Aircraft Material	1,125.60	348 lbs	. . do.	. . do. . . .	Do.
Carburetor Air Filters. .	8,401.00	4,733 lbs.	. . do.	. . do. . . .	Do.
Gun, Automatic 20mm M2 & parts.	33,134.00	48,664 lbs	. . do.	. . do. . . .	Do.
Aluminum Sheets. . . .	1,498.00	3,373 lbs.	. . do.	. . do. . . .	Do.
Aircraft Batteries	1,473.00	1,432 lbs.	Axel Salen . . .	. . do. . . .	Do.
Spark Plugs.	1,152.00	282 lbs	. . do.	. . do. . . .	Do.
Engine Rad.	9,970.64	3,708 lbs.	. . do.	. . do. . . .	Do.
Motor Assembly	370.80	128 lbs	. . do.	. . do. . . .	Do.
Aircraft Parts	2,278.85	770 lbs	. . do.	. . do. . . .	Do.
Dic. Ass'y Snubbing Super-Vision.	582.12	1,280 lbs	. . do.	. . do. . . .	Do.
Engine Parts Misc. . . .	8,116.63	2,326 lbs	. . do.	. . do. . . .	Do.
100/130 Octane Aviation Gas.	970,127.54	15,819,174 lbs . .	General Guisan .	Feb. 19, 1949	St. Rose, La.
AT-6 Airplanes	20,185.00	89,760 lbs	Chas. E. Dant .	Feb. 21, 1949	Long Beach.
Carburetors	2,700.00	1,245 lbs	Tantara	. . do. . . .	Los Angeles.
Aircraft Parts	7,977.60	1,625 lbs	. . do.	. . do. . . .	Do.
Do.	2,150.00	1,140 lbs	. . do.	. . do. . . .	Do.
Auto Tires with Tubes Ins.	51,586.40	101,672 lbs	. . do.	. . do. . . .	Do.
Aircraft Parts	84.00	38 lbs	. . do.	. . do. . . .	Do.
Do.	980.70	917 lbs	. . do.	. . do. . . .	Do.
Propeller Assembly . . .	12,720.00	16,080 lbs	. . do.	. . do. . . .	Do.
Aircraft Parts	3,031.00	897 lbs	. . do.	. . do. . . .	Do.
Auto Cleaning Equip. and Supplies.	18,259.30	12,810 lbs	. . do.	. . do. . . .	Do.
Airplanes	20,185.00	89,760 lbs	. . do.	. . do. . . .	Do.
Propeller Assemblies . .	2,176.02	3,025 lbs	Jesse Lykes . .	Feb. 23, 1949	Houston.
R-2600-29 Wright Engines.	46,440.00	53,100 lbs	. . do.	. . do. . . .	Do.
(9) R-2600-29 Wright Engines.	17,550.00	26,550 lbs	. . do.	. . do. . . .	Do.
(13) Airplanes P-47 K/D	136,500.00	308,165 lbs . . .	. . do.	. . do. . . .	Do.
Links	19,644.11	76,300 lbs	Chas. E. Dant .	Feb. 27, 1949	San Francisco.
TOTAL	2,851,452.89	18,228,140 lbs . .	. . . .	. . . .	. . . .

Part II—Chinese Army and Navy

Description	Value ($)	Weight	Name of vessel	Date of sailing	Port of embarkation
(1) ITEMS PROCURED BY CHINESE MILITARY PROCUREMENT TECHNICAL GROUP					
Armored Force					
Spare Parts for Truck, GMC 176 Items.	217,701.68	84,915 lbs. . . .	Mt. Mansfield .	Feb. 11, 1949	San Francisco.
Engines & Spare Parts for Tank 876 cs.	170,184.18	405,718 lbs. . . .	. . do.	Feb. 18, 1949	Honolulu.
Tank Tracks 589 Pks . .	9,358.84	562,500 lbs. . . .	President Buchanan.	Feb. 19, 1949	New York.
Auto Mechanics Tool Set 100 Cs.	29,087.20	25,142 lbs. . . .	. . do.	. . do. . . .	Do.
LVT Gun Shields etc. 400 Pcs.	26,475.07	155,930 lbs. . . .	Gen. Meigs . . .	Feb. 2, 1949	Honolulu.
Ordnance					
Cartridges Balls 2800 Cs ORD-6.	262,005.65	177,200 lbs. . . .	President Buchanan.	Feb. 19, 1949	New York.
Signal					
Field Telephones EE-8 1,550 Pcs.	14,015.15	21,037 lbs. . . .	. . do.	. . do. . . .	Do.
Transportation					
GMC 2.5T Army Truck 22Cs TRANS-1.	77,628.49	250,800 lbs. . . .	China Victory .	Feb. 18, 1949	Los Angeles.
Dry Storage Batteries 185 Cs T-10.	9,845.83	36,515 lbs. . . .	. . do.	. . do. . . .	San Francisco.
Machinery & Parts 3 Plants T-4.	82,131.03	130,164 lbs. . . .	President Buchanan.	Feb. 19, 1949	New York.
Tire Repair Equipment 45 Cs T-5.	11,692.53	15,060 lbs. . . .	. . do.	. . do. . . .	Do.
Auto Carburetors & Parts 23 Cs T-8.	24,965.77	11,926 lbs. . . .	. . do.	. . do. . . .	Do.
Auto Storage Batteries 821 Cs T-9.	36,953.21	93,378 lbs. . . .	. . do.	. . do. . . .	Do.
SUBTOTAL (items on 1).	972,044.63	1,960,285 lbs. . .	. . . .	. . . .	.
(2) ITEMS SUPPLIED BY U. S. ARMY AND NAVY					
Navy Ships Spare Parts & Communication Equipment.	607,000.00	330,000 lbs. . . .	U.S.S. Warrick .	Feb. 2, 1949	San Francisco.
Army Tubes & Tires & Medicals.	. . . . . .	725,139 lbs. . . .	Mt. Mansfield .	Jan. 23, 1949	New Jersey.
Items for Ord, Trans, Med, Sig.	. . . . . .	5,594,398 lbs. . .	Seminole	Feb. 19, 1949	Bangor.
Items for Trans, Sig, Ord, 661MT.	. . . . . .	336,600 lbs. . . .	President Buchanan.	. . do. . . .	New York.
Items for Trans etc. 655 T.	. . . . . .	552,200 lbs. . . .	Pacific Transport	Feb. 24, 1949	San Francisco.
SUBTOTAL: (items on 2 Navy).	607,000.00	7,538,337 lbs. . .			
(items on 2 Army).	3,000,000.00	. . . .			
	3,607,000.00	. . . .	. . . .	. . . .	.

Part II—Chinese Army and Navy—Continued

Description	Value ($)	Weight	Name of vessel	Date of sailing	Port of embarkation
(3) ITEMS CONTRACTED BY U. S. BUREAU OF FEDERAL SUPPLY					
Chinese Army					
Hydraulic Brake Fluid 105 x 54 gals	15,309.00	52,290 lbs	China Victory .	Feb. 11,1949	Los Angeles.
Motor Gasoline 4,636,000 AG	1,344,400.00	12,980 tons . . .	Ex-ware-Shanghai by Texas Co.	. . . .	
Fuel Oil A-3	435,150.00	15,000 tons . . .	. . do	. . . .	
Lubricating Oil 59,000 AG	22,597.00	195 tons.	. . do	. . . .	
Greece [Grease]	4,719.00	33,000 lbs	. do	. . . .	
Motor Gasoline 2,452,500 AG	846,855.00	6,867 tons	Ex-ware-Canton by Texas Co.	. . . .	
Chinese Navy					
Hydraulic Brake Fluid 43 x 54 gals	6,153.30	18,700 lbs	China Victory .	Feb. 11,1949	Los Angeles.
Hydraulic Brake Fluid 45 x 54 gals	5,346.00	19,800 lbs	. . do	Feb. 4,1949	New York.
Motor Gasoline 527,900 AG	160,490.00	1,478 tons. . . .	Ex-ware-Shanghai by Texas Co.	. . . .	
Kerosene 26,593 AG . . .	7,646.26	80 tons	. . do	. . . .	
Diesel Oil.	705,856.00	15,470 tons . . .	. . do	. . . .	
Fuel Oil	560,190.00	19,000 tons . . .	. . do	. . . .	
Lubricating Oil 177,882 AG	71,466.79	586 tons.	. . do	. . . .	
Motor Gasoline 66,000 AG	20,460.00	185 tons.	Ex-ware-Canton by Texas Co.	. . . .	
Kerosene 5,000 AG . . .	1,635.00	15 tons	. . do	. . . .	
Diesel Oil	140,400.00	3,000 tons	. . do	. . . .	
SUBTOTAL: (items on 3 Army)	2,669,030.00	85,290 lbs & 35,042 long tons	. . . . . .	. . . . . .	
(items on 3 Navy)	1,679,643.35	38,500 lbs & 39,814 long tons	. . . . . .	. . . . . .	
	4,348,673.35	123,790 lbs & 74,856 long tons	. . . .	. . . . . .	
TOTAL (Army and Navy)	8,927,717.98	79,230 long tons on wt. basis as last month.	. . . .	. . . . . .	

Part III—Summary

	Approximate total value ($)	Approximate total weight (long tons)
Chinese Air Force	2,851,452.89	8,285.5
Chinese Army and Navy	8,927,717.98	79,230.0
GRAND TOTAL	11,779,170.87	87,515.5

XX

REPORT RECEIVED FROM THE CHINESE EMBASSY ON SHIPMENTS UNDER THE
$125 MILLION GRANTS

Period of Report: March 1–March 31, 1949

Part I—Chinese Air Force

Description	Values ($)	Weight	Name of vessel	Date of sailing	Port of embarkation
(1) ITEMS PROCURED BY CHINESE AIR FORCE					
C-46 Tires	4,750.75	5,980 lbs.	Chas. E. Dant .	Feb. 26, 1949	San Francisco.
Truck Tires and Tubes .	14,349.55	28,391 lbs..	. . do.	. . do.. . . .	Do.
Truck Tires.	12,986.96	23,986 lbs..	. . do.	. . do.. . . .	Do.
AT-11 Tires and Tubes .	485.75	323 lbs.	. . do.	. . do.. . . .	Do.
Fuel Hose.	3,358.09	3,588 lbs.	. . do.	. . do.. . . .	Do.
Discs and Gaskets. . . .	408.23	150 lbs.	. . do.	. . do.. . . .	Do.
11 AT-6 Airplanes. . . .	165,000.00	89,760 lbs.	Phil. Transport .	Feb. 25, 1949	Los Angeles.
Truck Tires and Tubes .	19,317.50	36,928 lbs..	. . do.	Feb. 28, 1949	San Francisco.
C-6 Tools and Spare Parts.	6,783.77	1,611 lbs.	Axel Salen . . .	Mar. 2, 1949	Los Angeles.
Airplanes P-47 K/D (3) .	27,000.00	72,000 lbs.. . . .	Almeria Lykes . .	. . do.. . . .	Houston.
Internal Combustion Engines.	21,000.00	15,600 lbs..	. . do.	. . do.. . . .	Do.
Aircraft Parts.	670.00	989 lbs.	Mongabarra . .	Mar. 10, 1949	Los Angeles.
Do..	152.00	105 lbs.	. . do.	. . do.. . . .	Do.
Do..	900.00	172 lbs.	. . do.	. . do.. . . .	Do.
Do..	2,079.00	164 lbs.	. . do.	. . do.. . . .	Do.
Do..	4,210.60	1,211 lbs.	. . do.	. . do.. . . .	Do.
Do..	391.50	114 lbs.	. . do.	. . do.. . . .	Do.
Aircraft Equipment. . .	6,463.19	500 lbs.	. . do.	. . do.. . . .	Do.
C-46 Aircraft Parts . . .	25,681.80	16,532 lbs..	. . do.	. . do.. . . .	Do.
Aircraft Parts	4,422.00	4,604 lbs.	. . do.	. . do.. . . .	Do.
13 AT-6 Aircraft.	195,000.00	106,080 lbs.	. . do.	. . do.. . . .	Do.
Aircraft Parts	3,632.90	708 lbs.	. . do.	. . do.. . . .	Do.
Paint Thinner	1.00	38 lbs.	. . do.	. . do.. . . .	Do.
35 R-1340 Aircraft Engines.	80,500.00	57,950 lbs..	. . do.	. . do.. . . .	Do.
17 R-2800-75 Converted to R-2800-59 Airc. Engines.	21,436.01	55,250 lbs..	. . do.	. . do.. . . .	Do.
1 Pratt & Whitney Engine.	1,000.00	3,100 lbs.	. . do.	. . do.. . . .	Do.
T11BK Ctg. .50 Cal. M2.	3,805.53	8,176 lbs.	. . do.	Mar. 13, 1949	San Francisco.
T11CN Ctg. Cal. .50 Belted.	716.89	1,638 lbs.	. . do.	. . do.. . . .	Do.
Aircraft Parts	502.50	252 lbs.	. . do.	. . do.. . . .	Do.
AT-6 Aircraft (11). . . .	165,000.00	89,760 lbs.	Indian Bear. . . .	. . do.. . . .	Long Beach.
Air Brake Assembly. . .	3,750.00	1,390 lbs.	. . do.	. . do.. . . .	Do.
Truck Tires and Tubes .	29,980.50	61,782 lbs..	. . do.	Mar. 18, 1949	San Francisco.
C-46 Tires and Tubes . .	15,048.90	17,314 lbs..	. . do.	. . do.. . . .	Do.
C-46 De-Icer Parts . . .	295.96	14 lbs.	. . do.	. . do.. . . .	Do.
Aluminum Rivnuts. . .	17.70	11 lbs.	. . do.	. . do.. . . .	Do.
Aircraft Repl. Parts. . .	20,961.31	21,250 lbs..	Howell Lykes. .	Mar. 15, 1949	Houston.

Part I—*Chinese Air Force*—Continued

Description	Values ($)	Weight	Name of vessel	Date of sailing	Port of embarkation
(1) ITEMS PROCURED BY CHINESE AIR FORCE—Con.					
P-51 Airplane Parts. . .	3,118.20	2,367 lbs.	Howell Lykes. .	Mar. 15, 1949	Houston.
Do.	4,367.80				
Do.	318.97				
Gauge Fuel Level. . . .	112.50	65 lbs.	. . do.	. . do. . . .	Do.
P-47 Airplanes with Machine Guns.	180,000.00	480,000 lbs. . . .	. . do.	. . do. . . .	Do.
Glass Assy for P-51, incl. Canopy.	1,754.53	8,111 lbs.	. . do.	. . do. . . .	Do.
B-24 Spare Parts					
Aircraft Parts	2,152.50	898 lbs	Ivarah	Mar. 18, 1949	New York
Aluminum Sheets. . . .	1,619.50	5,740 lbs	. . do.	. . do. . . .	Do.
Do.	654.25	1,629 lbs	. . do.	. . do. . . .	Do.
Airplane Prop. Assembly.	8,095.80	10,275 lbs	. . do.	. . do. . . .	Do.
Aircraft Material	1,152.27	675 lbs	. . do.	. . do. . . .	Do.
Vix Syn-Packing	618.62	45 lbs	. . do.	. . do. . . .	Do.
Carburetors and Parts. .	1,786.50	869 lbs	. . do.	. . do. . . .	Do.
Aircraft Accessories . . .	853.98	260 lbs	. . do.	. . do. . . .	Do.
Emulsion Spray Outfit .	872.50	1,688 lbs	. . do.	. . do. . . .	Do.
Oil Pressure Gages . . .	290.00	85 lbs	. . do.	. . do. . . .	Do.
Harness Assy—Ignition Comp.	1,200.00	2,215 lbs	. . do.	. . do. . . .	Do.
Military Windlasses. . .	867.00	1,167 lbs	. . do.	. . do. . . .	Do.
LE45 Spark Plugs. . . .	11,256.00	2,061 lbs	. . do.	. . do. . . .	Do.
Internal Comb. Engines.	6,250.00	7,000 lbs	. . do.	. . do. . . .	Do.
Spare Parts	4,809.26	214 lbs	. . do.	. . do. . . .	Do.
Chamois Leather	690.00	108 lbs	. . do.	. . do. . . .	Do.
Cylinder and Valve Assy.	2,292.87	1,168 lbs	. . do.	. . do. . . .	Do.
P-47N Repl. Parts. . . .	11,496.32	8,335 lbs	. . do.	. . do. . . .	Do.
Airplane Parts	1,230.00	325 lbs	. . do.	. . do. . . .	Do.
Aircraft Repl. Parts . . .	842.44	831 lbs	. . do.	. . do. . . .	Do.
W-670-24 Aircraft Engines.	53,900.00	39,600 lbs	. . do.	. . do. . . .	Do.
Aircraft Engines	21,887.37	140,700 lbs . . .	. . do.	. . do. . . .	Do.
0-435-11 Aircraft Engines.	60,000.00	27,400 lbs	. . do.	. . do. . . .	Do.
Tank Units; Electric Fuel.	1,329.50	188 lbs	. . do.	. . do. . . .	Do.
Plug Valves.	280.28	14 lbs	. . do.	. . do. . . .	Do.
Aircraft Tools	11,001.64	1,890 lbs	. . do.	. . do. . . .	Do.
11 AT-6 Aircraft.	165,000.00	89,760 lbs	Lakeland Victory.	Mar. 26, 1949	Long Beach.
T11 BK Ctg. Armor Piercing Cal. .50 M2 Grade MG.	4,724.95	100,000 lbs . . .	Arizona.	Mar. 27, 1949	San Francisco.
Do.	4,174.57	88,440 lbs	. . do.	. . do. . . .	Do.
Do.	4,049.96	85,890 lbs	. . do.	. . do. . . .	Do.
Do.	2,513.05	53,240 lbs	. . do.	. . do. . . .	Do.
TOTAL	1,438,623.02	1,890,674 lbs. . .	. . . .	. . . .	

Part II—Chinese Army and Navy

Description	Values ($)	Weight	Name of vessel	Date of sailing	Port of embarkation
(1) ITEMS PROCURED BY CHINESE MILITARY PROCUREMENT TECHNICAL GROUP					
Armored Force					
Spare Parts for Truck 2½ T 150 cs A-3.	$1,355.86	88,530 lbs	President Buchanan.	Mar. 8, 1949	San Francisco.
Spare Parts for Tank 1,363 cs A-5.	4,000.00	315,728 lbs . . .	Pioneer Mail . .	Mar. 21, 1949	Honolulu.
Army Engineer					
Barbed Wire Machine 4 pcs E-11.	16,798.66	23,680 lbs	President Van Buren.	Mar. 19, 1949	New York.
Testing Apparatus & Magnetos 5 cs E-5, 14.	1,580.33	546 lbs	. . do	. . do	Do.
Road Grader Parts etc. E-9.	4,844.73	10,756 lbs	. . do	. . do	Do.
Crates Pneumatic Chain Saw 5 cs E-21.	3,000.34	825 lbs	. . do	. . do	Do.
Boring Bars & Parts 10 cs E-15.	4,692.00	2,050 lbs	. . do	. . do	Do.
Ordnance					
Brass Plate 652 Cs 0-9, 10.	81,474.28	285,665 lbs	. . do	. . do	Do.
Cartridges Balls 3750 Cs O-6.	357,722.72	239,250 lbs . . .	. . do	. . do	Do.
Transportation					
Machinery & Parts 2 plants T-4.	54,754.02	86,776 lbs	. . do	. . do	Do.
Auto Accessories 59 Cs T11.	8,931.71	15,403 lbs	. . do	. . do	Do.
Machinery & Parts 4 Sets T13.	33,409.20	48,992 lbs	. . do	. . do	Do.
SUBTOTAL (items on 1).	$572,563.85	1,118,201 lbs or 500.00 long tons.	. . . .	. . . .	
(2) ITEMS SUPPLIED BY U. S. ARMY					
Army Tubes and Tires .	60,000.00	96,687 lbs	Pioneer Mail . .	Mar. 4, 1949	Do.
Items for Ordnance . . .	10,000.00	285,409 lbs . . .	. . do	. . do	Do.
SUBTOTAL (items on 2)	70,000.00	382,096 lbs or 170.50 long tons.	. . . .	. . . .	

Part II—*Chinese Army and Navy*—Continued

Description	Values ($)	Weight	Name of vessel	Date of sailing	Port of embarkation
(3) ITEMS CONTRACTED BY U. S. BUREAU OF FEDERAL SUPPLY					
Chinese Army					
Motor Gasoline 70 Octane 899,993 A G.	332,997.41	2,520.00	Ex-ware-China by Standard Oil Co.	. . . .	
Commercial St. Fuel Oil A-3.	184,453.12	5,902.50	. . do	. . . .	
Industrial St. Diesel Oil A-4.	69,012.50	1,290.00	. . do	. . . .	
Motor Oil SAE 30 & 40 174,996 A G.	72,338.40	532.00	. . do	. . . .	
Chinese Navy					
Lubricating Oil N-8, 9, 10, 89,557 A G.	37,412.29	271.00	. . do	. . . .	
Red Engine N-16 17,606 A G.	6,778.31	53.50	. . do	. . . .	
SUBTOTAL					
(items on 3 Army).	658,801.43	10,244.50 long tons.	. . . .	. . . .	
(items on 3 Navy).	44,190.60	324 50 long tons	. . . .	. . . .	
	702,992.03	10,569.00 long tons.			
TOTAL (Army and Navy).	1,345,555.88	11,239.50 long tons on wt. basis as last month.			

Part III—*Summary*

	Approximate total value ($)	Approximate total weight (long tons)
Chinese Air Force	1,438,623.02	859.4
Chinese Army and Navy	1,345,555.88	11,239.5
TOTAL	2,784,178.90	12,098.9

XXI

REPORT RECEIVED FROM THE CHINESE EMBASSY ON SHIPMENTS UNDER THE
$125 MILLION GRANTS

Period of Report: April 1–April 30, 1949

Part I—Chinese Air Force

Description	Values ($)	Weight	Name of vessel	Date of sailing	Port of embarkation
(1) ITEMS PROCURED BY CHINESE AIR FORCE					
Aircraft Engine Parts . .	27,596.88	8,670 lbs.	Tarifa	Mar. 31, 1949	New York.
Clocks	97.50	9 lbs.	. . do.	. . do. . . .	Do.
Seal Disc Assy	670.65	16 lbs.	. . do.	. . do. . . .	Do.
Aircraft Repl. Parts . . .	457.69	95 lbs.	. . do.	. . do. . . .	Do.
Magneto Repair Parts .	873.00	70 lbs.	. . do.	. . do. . . .	Do.
Shaft and Casings . . .	326.16	63 lbs.	. . do.	. . do. . . .	Do.
Stromberg Carburetor Tools.	11,473.82	2,660 lbs.	. . do.	. . do. . . .	Do.
Aircraft Engines	29,900.00	20,500 lbs. . .	. . do.	. . do. . . .	Do.
Breaker, Slip Ring . . .	1,083.00	94 lbs.	. . do.	. . do. . . .	Do.
Airplane Parts	657.11	193 lbs.	. . do.	. . do. . . .	Do.
Aircraft Engines	18,023.10	117,250 lbs. . . .	. . do.	. . do. . . .	Do.
Airplane Parts	2,284.00	271 lbs.	. . do.	. . do. . . .	Do.
Aircraft Engine Parts . .	53,900.00	39,600 lbs. . . .	. . do.	. . do. . . .	Do.
Aircraft Engines	16,616.77	46,800 lbs. . . .	. . do.	. . do. . . .	Do.
Propeller Assy	3,000.00	5,400 lbs.	President McKinley.	Apr. 4, 1949	Los Angeles.
11 AT–6 Aircraft	165,000.00	89,760 lbs. . . .	. . do.	. . do. . . .	Do.
Do	165,000.00	89,760 lbs. . . .	Philippine Bear .	Apr. 8, 1949	Long Beach.
AT–6 Tools and Spare Parts.	174.30	85 lbs.	. . do.	. . do. . . .	Do.
AT–11 Aircraft (5) . . .	437,500.00	90,400 lbs. . . .	China Victory .	Apr. 22, 1949	Do.
C–46 Tires and Tubes . .	5,199.73	7,020 lbs.	Philippine Bear .	Apr. 27, 1949	San Francisco.
Aircraft Hose	321.18	316 lbs.	. . do.	. . do. . . .	Do.
De-Icer Parts	1,057.50	340 lbs.	. . do.	. . do. . . .	Do.
Aircraft Parts	31.50	12 lbs.	Vingnes.	Apr. 21, 1949	Los Angeles.
Do.	6,598.00	1,757 lbs.	. . do	. . do. . . .	Do.
11 AT–6'Aircraft	165,000.00	89,760 lbs. . . .	. . do.	. . do. . . .	Do.
Aircraft Parts	11,202.67	18,643 lbs. . . .	. . do.	. . do. . . .	Do.
Do.	1,168.02	1,893 lbs.	. . do.	. . do. . . .	Do.
Do.	2,303.50	2,504 lbs.	. . do.	. . do. . . .	Do.
Do.	13,182.30	10,424 lbs. . . .	. . do.	Apr. 25, 1949	San Francisco.
5 AT–11 Aircraft	437,500.00	90,400 lbs. . . .	Pacific Trans. .	Apr. 27, 1949	Los Angeles.
Aircraft Parts	537.60	35 lbs.	. . do.	. . do. . . .	Do.
Do.	4,391.70	1,408 lbs.	. . do.	. . do. . . .	Do.
Do.	23,376.00	3,008 lbs.	Lisholt	Apr. 25, 1949	New York.
Ring Leather Packing . .	1,684.23	67 lbs.	. . do.	. . do. . . .	Do.
Aircraft Engines	22,050.00	16,200 lbs. . . .	. . do.	. . do. . . .	Do.
Brush Assy Slip Ring . .	3,900.00	50 lbs.	. . do.	. . do. . . .	Do.
Disc. Assy for Fuel Seles.	43.35	6 lbs.	. . do.	. . do. . . .	Do.
Automotive Carb. & Parts.	1,080.00	658 lbs.	. . do.	. . do. . . .	Do.
58289 Diaphragm	248.75	90 lbs.	Pan American A. L.	Apr. 27, 1949	San Francisco.
Oxygen Regulators . . .	550.00	1,122 lbs.	S. S. Fernbay . .	Apr. 16, 1949	New York.
Airplane Spare Parts . .	222.20	68 lbs	. . do	Apr. 16, 1949	Do.
Do	1,236.75	17 lbs	. . do	Apr. 16, 1949	Do.
Carburetor Tools	3,853.05	304 lbs	. . do	Apr. 16, 1949	Do.

Part I—*Chinese Air Force*—Continued

Description	Values ($)	Weight	Name of vessel	Date of sailing	Port of embarkation
(1) ITEMS PROCURED BY CHINESE AIR FORCE—Continued					
Airplane Spare Parts . .	$298.60	25 lbs	S. S. Fernbay. .	Apr. 16, 1949	New York.
Do	218.85	34 lbs	. . do	Apr. 16, 1949	Do.
Do	8,856.00	754 lbs	. . do	Apr. 16, 1949	Do.
Do	336.00	86 lbs	. . do	Apr. 16, 1949	Do.
Leather "V"	372.06	22 lbs	. . do	Apr. 16, 1949	Do.
Carburetor Overhaul Tools.	1,376.67	263 lbs	. . do	Apr. 16, 1949	Do.
Aircraft Engines	53,900.00	39,600 lbs	. . do	Apr. 16, 1949	Do.
Replacement Parts . . .	11,292.01	7,837 lbs	. . do	Apr. 16, 1949	Do.
Auto Parts	74,004.27	137,493 lbs	. . do	Apr. 16, 1949	Do.
R-2800 Aircraft Engines .	15,750.00	20,100 lbs	. . do	Apr. 16, 1949	Do.
Mobile Grease Aero . . .	2,482.88	10,440 lbs	. . do	Apr. 16, 1949	Do.
TOTAL	1,810,159.35	964,452 lbs . . . (438.4 long tons) .	. . . .	. . . .	

Part II—*Chinese Army and Navy*

Description	Values ($)	Weight	Name of vessel	Date of sailing	Port of embarkation
(1) ITEMS PROCURED BY CHINESE MILITARY PROCUREMENT TECHNICAL GROUP					
Army Engineer					
Parts for H. Machine & Tools E13, E27.	$16,935.00	6,982 pounds. . . .	President Jefferson.	Apr. 2, 1949	New York.
Parts for H. Machine E-2, E-10.	6,260.00	2,727 pounds . . .	Marine Snapper.	Apr. 13, 1949	Do.
Misc. Tools E-22, E-26, E-28.	8,295.00	3,853 pounds . .	. . do.	. . do. . . .	Do.
Blasting Machine, Galvanometers E12.	10,282.00	1,804 pounds . .	China Victory .	Apr. 29, 1949	San Francisco.
Cylinder Reconditioning Outfit E17.	1,956.50	1,153 pounds . .	. . do.	. . do. . . .	Do.
Ordnance					
Cartridges Ball 1,750 Cs .	156,596.69	109,250 pounds .	President Jefferson.	Apr. 2, 1949	New York.
Cartridges Balls 2,000 Cs.	173,946.66	124,000 pounds .	Marine Snapper.	Apr. 13, 1949	Do.
Brass Plates 68 Cs Ord-10.	8,171.35	27,242 pounds . .	. . do.	. . do. . . .	Do.
Signal					
Radio Tubes for 2nd Div. 7,820 Pcs.	4,445.70	723 pounds . . .	. . do.	. . do. . . .	Do.
Transportation					
Dry Storage Batteries T10 412 Cs.	21,546.80	79,298 pounds . .	President Van Buren.	Apr. 7, 1949	San Francisco.
Auto Accessories T11 8 Cs.	714.98	1,040 pounds . .	President Jefferson.	Apr. 2, 1949	New York.
Auto Accessories T11 85 Cs.	20,694.56	19,223 pounds . .	Marine Snapper.	Apr. 13, 1949	Do.
Lubrication Equipments T7 307 Cs.	56,618.86	99,539 pounds . .	. . do.	. . do. . . .	Do.
Spare Parts for Trucks T3 196 Cs.	85,699.90	82,100 pounds . .	China Victory .	Apr. 29, 1949	San Francisco.
SUB-TOTAL (items on 1).	572,164.00	558,934 pounds or 250 long tons.	. . . .	. . . .	

Part II—Chinese Army and Navy—Continued

Description	Values ($)	Weight*	Name of vessel	Date of sailing	Port of embarkation
(2) ITEMS SUPPLIED BY U. S. ARMY					
Ord. Misc. Surplus Items.	$122,039	526 long tons . .	LST No. 799 . .	Apr. 4, 1949	Manila.
Med. Misc. Tools & Parts.	10,000	4 metric tons . .	President Jefferson.	Apr. 2, 1949	New York.
Ord. Maintenance Materials.	10,000	83 metric tons . . .	. . do.	. . do. . . .	Do.
Sig. Radio Sets	230,000	112 metric tons .	. . do.	. . do. . . .	Do.
Sig. Intelligence	. . . . . .	0.2 pound . . .	. . do.	. . do. . . .	Do.
Trans. Tires & Parts . .	869,097	4,160 metric tons.	. . do.	. . do. . . .	Do.
SUB-TOTAL (Jefferson).	$1,119,097	4,359.2 metric tons or 1,000 long tons approx.	. . . .	. . . .	
AFC Guns	1,540	8 metric tons . .	John Towle . .	Apr. 24, 1949	San Francisco.
Med. Medicines & Misc.	300,000	108 metric tons .	. . do.	. . do. . . .	Do.
Ord. Maintenance Materials.	30,000	471 metric tons .	. . do.	. . do. . . .	Do.
Sig. Batteries	48,000	67 metric tons .	. . do.	. . do. . . .	Do.
Trans. Tires & Parts . .	354,325	1,396 metric tons	. . do.	. . do. . . .	Do.
SUB-TOTAL (John Towle).	733,865	2,050 metric tons or 800 long tons approx.	. . . .	. . . .	
Med. Instruments & Drugs.	$30,000	31 metric tons .	China Victory .	Apr. 29, 1949	San Francisco.
Ord. Maintenance Materials.	2,000	5 metric tons . .	. . do	. . do	do.
Trans. Tire & Tubes . .	136,400	551 metric tons .	. . do	. . do	do.
SUB-TOTAL (China Victory).	$168,400	587 metric tons or 160 L/T approx.	. . . .	. . . .	
Med. Drugs & Misc . .	$500,000	295 metric tons .	Explorer	. . do	New York.
Ord. Maintenance Materials.	200,000	203 metric tons .	. . do	. . do	do.
Sig. Radio Sets	380,000	180 metric tons .	. . do	. . do	do.
Sig. Intelligence	. . . . . .	0.4 metric ton .	. . do	. . do	do.
Trans. Tires & Parts. . .	604,261	2,640 metric tons	. . do	. . do	do.
SUB-TOTAL (Explorer).	$1,684,261	3,318.4 metric tons or 1000 L/T approx.	. . . .	. . . .	
Ord. Pig Lead	$1,343,865	2,525 long tons .	Cotton State . .	Apr. 30, 1949	Tampico, Mexico.
SUB-TOTAL (Items on 2).	5,171,527	6,011 long tons .	. . . .	. . . .	
TOTAL (Items 1 and 2).	$5,743,691	6,261 long tons on wt. basis as last month.	. . . .	. . . .	

* "Metric tons" in this column should read "measured tons."

Part III—Summary

	Approximate total value ($)	Approximate total weight (long tons)
Chinese Air Force	1,810,159.35	438.4
Chinese Army and Navy	5,743,691.00	6,261.0
GRAND TOTAL	7,553,850.35	6,699.4

172

Categories of American Military Aid Extended to China Since V–J Day

The following table outlines briefly the categories and totals of military aid extended since V–J Day, figures being in millions of United States dollars:

Military Aid	Sales of U. S. Government Excess and Surplus Property				
	Grants	Credits	Procurement Value	Realization by U. S.	
				Init.	Ult.
1. Lend-Lease ($694.7 million)	$513.7	$181.0			
2. Military Aid Under SACO	17.7				
3. Sale of excess stocks of U. S. Army in West China		20	(^{1})	(^{2})	^{2} $20
4. Ammunition Abandoned and transferred by U. S. Marines in North China (over 6500 tons)	(^{3})				
5. Transfer of U. S. Navy Vessels (PL 512) .	141.3	(^{4})			
6. Sales of surplus Military equipment (total shipped)			102.0	6.7	6.7
7. $125 Million Grant Under China Aid Act of 1948	125				
TOTAL MILITARY AID	$797.7	$201.0	$102.0	$6.7	$26.7

[1] No information regarding procurement value available.

[2] Down payment covered under Bulk Sale Agreement of August 30, 1946.

[3] No estimate of total value available.

[4] Vessels valued at procurement cost.

LEND-LEASE

Though lend-lease terminated for most countries on June 30, 1946, in order to continue assistance to the National Government lend-lease to China was extended on a reimbursable basis under terms of a military aid agreement of June 28, 1946.

As of June 30, 1948, a grand total of $781.0 million in post V–J Day lend-lease transfers had been reported to the Treasury Department by United States Government agencies. Of this amount, $50.3 million represented deliveries on 3(c) credit terms under the lend-lease "pipeline" agreement, and $36 million covered United States Navy vessels originally lend-leased to China but subsequently transferred under the terms of PL 512 to which consideration is given later in this paper.

Of the balance of $694.7 million, $181.0 million is considered subject to payment. Settlement of this amount is now under negotiation.

Listed below are the major categories of Post V–J Day lend-lease supplies:

Ordnance and Ordnance Stores	$117, 869, 076. 94
Aircraft and Aeronautical Material	43, 683, 604. 63
Tanks and other Vehicles	96, 009, 610. 08
Vessels and other Watercraft	49, 940, 642. 57
Miscellaneous Military Equipment	99, 762, 611. 71
Facilities and Equipment	36, 198. 74
Agricultural, Industrial and other Commodities	37, 918, 928. 21
Testing and Reconditioning of Defense Articles	2, 338. 88
Services and Expenses	335, 817, 910. 56
Total	$781, 040, 922. 32

These transfers included by tonnage equipment sufficient to complete the war-time program to equip 39 Chinese divisions which as of V–J Day was approximately 50 per cent complete. The transfer also included the bulk of the 936 planes and other equipment provided under lend-lease for the 8⅓ group program for the Chinese Air Force.

Also included in the lend-lease transfers were many thousands of military vehicles, of great importance in giving the Government's forces mobility. As of V–J Day the Government had an overwhelming superiority over the Communists in combat equipped troops conservatively estimated at 5–1 and a virtual monopoly of all heavy equipment. This already existing superiority in men and arms reveals the significance of American aid in transporting Government troops to north China and in furnishing transport equipment, which properly employed would have enabled the Government to bring to bear its superior forces.

SINO-AMERICAN COOPERATIVE ORGANIZATION AGREEMENT

The military transfers under the Sino-American Cooperative Organization Agreement (SACO) consisted primarily of ordnance supplies furnished the Chinese between September 2, 1945 and March 2, 1946 by the United States Navy. These transfers were accomplished in fulfillment of a wartime agreement calling for the furnishing of equipment in exchange for certain services provided by the Chinese Government. A detailed breakdown of the figures is provided in Annex I, part 1.[5]

WEST CHINA SALE

The sale of a broad assortment of military supplies in west China was made on the departure of United States forces from that area. This property was transferred for a sales price of $25 million (U. S.) plus $5.16 billion (Chinese). Down payments of $5.16 billion (Chinese) and $5 million (U. S.) were made in the form of offsets against the United States indebtedness to China. (The $5 million (U. S.) down payment was incorporated in the realized return to the United States under the surplus property sales agreement of August 30, 1946). It was agreed that $20 million (U. S.) would be paid over a period of time by China. The terms of repayment are subject to negotiation.

AMMUNITION ABANDONED BY UNITED STATES MARINES

Between April and September 1947 the United States Marines abandoned or transferred to the Chinese Government approximately 6,500 tons of ammunition in connection with their withdrawal from north China. Included was a wide variety of small arms and artillery ammunition, grenades, mines, bombs, and

---
[5] See annex 171, section I.

miscellaneous explosives. No estimate of the total value of this material transferred is provided in Annex I, Part 2,[6] which includes figures on certain naval ammunition transferred in the same operation but charged against lend-lease.

TRANSFER OF UNITED STATES NAVY VESSELS

Public Law 512 of the 79th Congress authorized the President to transfer 271 naval vessels to the Chinese Government on such terms as he might prescribe. On December 8, 1947 an agreement was signed between the United States Government and the Republic of China relative to the implementation of this act. The text of this agreement was published by the Department of State in the Treaties and Other International Acts Series 1691. A total of 131 vessels with a procurement cost of $141.3 million had been transferred to the Chinese Navy under PL 512 as of December 31, 1948 on a grant basis. This figure includes approximately $36 million representing vessels originally lend-leased to China but subsequently transferred under PL 512.

The naval vessels transferred included destroyer escorts, patrol ships, landing craft and many other types of vessels, which, after conferences between appropriate American and Chinese naval Personnel, were selected for their suitability in meeting Chinese naval requirements. Of the 131 vessels transferred under PL 512, the 96 which had originally been lend-leased had all their combat equipment. Of the remainder some were still combat equipped. Ammunition for these was made available during the summer of 1947 when the 6,500 tons of ammunition were transferred in north China, and in the fall of 1948 under the $125 million grants. A list of the vessels transferred is attached as Annex I, Part 3,[7] together with copies of Public Law 512 and as Executive Order authorizing its implementation.

SALE OF SURPLUS MILITARY EQUIPMENT

The United States continues to make military equipment available to the Chinese Government following the termination of lend-lease, through the transfer of surplus United States equipment at a small fraction of its original procurement cost. The following is a listing, in summary form, of military surplus shipments:

Commodity and Source	Procurement Cost	Sales Price
1) 130 million rounds of 7.92 ammunition (sold by Office of the Foreign Liquidation Commission under contract dated June 25, 1947).	$6,564,992.58	$656,499.27
2) 150 C–46 airplanes (sold by War Assets Administration under contract dated December 22, 1947).	34,800,000.00	750,000.00
3) Additional Office of the Foreign Liquidation Commission transfers:		
Ammunition, Cal. 30 to 155 Howitzer	21,707,536.10	569,071.80
Air Force material and equipment, including 178 aircraft and 683 engines	36,637,064.31	4,454,105.06
Ordnance, Signal, and other military equipment (over 9,000 tons)	2,263,897.17	282,987.17
TOTAL	$101,973,490.16	$6,712,663.30

[6] See annex 171, section I (B).
[7] See annex 171.

A portion of the total military surplus shipments was financed by the Chinese Government from the $125 million grants authorized under the China Aid Act of 1948. A detailed breakdown of Office of the Foreign Liquidation Commission transfers from January 1, 1948 to March 31, 1949 is included in Annex I, part 4.[8]

$125 MILLION GRANTS

Section 404 (b) of the China Aid Act of 1948 (Title IV of Foreign Assistance Act of 1948) authorized to be appropriated to the President a sum not to exceed $125,000,000 for additional aid to China through grants on such terms as the President might determine.

It was evident from Congressional debate on Section 404 (b) of the China Aid Act of 1948 that the grants were to be expended by the Chinese Government for whatever purpose it desired, though it was expected that the funds would be used for the purchase of military equipment. It was likewise evident that the funds were to be expended by the Chinese Government on its own option and responsibility. Under terms decided upon by the President the Chinese Government was required to submit to the Department of State requests for payment with regard to goods or services procured, with supporting documentation evidencing the transaction. The terms also stated: "The Department of State will examine the documentation submitted by the Chinese Government to determine that the request is not in excess of the total represented by the invoices or other supporting data, and will authorize the Treasury to make the appropriate payments to the Chinese Government." The initiative in the expenditure of the funds lay wholly with the Chinese Government and no payments were made unless that Government submitted a request for disbursement.

The Chinese Government did not submit its first request for withdrawals from the funds until July 23, 1948 although the Department had transmitted the President's terms to the Chinese Ambassador on June 29, 1948, in a note dated June 28, and the Chinese had accepted the terms in a note dated July 1, 1948. The Chinese Government however utilized approximately $10 million from the grants to pay for military material purchased under contracts made during the late spring and early summer of 1948 prior to the submission of the first request on July 23.

As a means of assisting the Chinese Government in purchasing desired material the Department took the initiative in arranging a procedure whereby American Government departments, establishments, and agencies were authorized to transfer equipment from their own stocks or to procure for the Chinese material to be paid for from the grants. Such a procedure had not been specifically provided for in the legislation on the grants. The President's directive authorizing such action was issued on July 28, 1948.[9]

The grants have been used by the Chinese for the most part to purchase items of a military nature. As of April 1, 1949 the Department of Treasury had disbursed the total $125 million appropriated. Disbursements were made to the Chinese Government direct or to American Government agencies requested by the Chinese Government to engage in procurement activities as follows:

---

[8] See annex 171, section IV.

[9] The text of Section 404 (b) of the China Aid Act of 1948, copies of directives from the President, to various agencies of the Government, appropriate communications among agencies of the Government, and communications between the Department of State and the Chinese Embassy with respect to the grants are attached as annex 171, section V.

Agent	Item	Disbursement
Department of the Army . . .	Arms, ammunition, medical supplies, motor vehicles, spare parts, etc.	$64, 595, 178. 25
Department of the Navy . . .	Naval vessels, reconditioning of naval vessels, ammunition	6, 892, 020. 00
Department of the Air Force .	Miscellaneous air force equipment and aviation gasoline	7, 750, 000. 00
Bureau of Federal Supply . .	Petroleum products, ordnance raw materials	13, 765, 522. 12
Office of Foreign Liquidation Commissioner	Surplus aircraft, aircraft spares, ammunition, etc.	[10] 2, 690, 910. 88
Republic of China	Miscellaneous supplies and equipment, from commercial sources	29, 306, 368. 75
TOTAL	. . . .	$125, 000, 000. 00

[10] In addition, OFLC has received by direct payment from the Chinese Government $1,045,693.80 of the $29,306,368.75 paid to the Chinese Government by the Treasury Department.

The first significant shipments of military material paid for out of the $125 million grants consisted of approximately 10,000 tons of small arms and artillery ammunition purchased by the Chinese Government from the Office of the Foreign Liquidation Commissioner at a fraction of the procurement cost and shipped to China in two ships which left Hawaii on July 3 and July 16, 1948. Fifty-one fighter aircraft purchased from the same agency with funds from the grants were delivered to China in September, 1948 in combat operational condition, and aviation gasoline, aircraft spare parts, and communications equipment were shipped to China during the above period.

The most significant Chinese purchases under the grants were made through the Department of the Army and covered equipment for 7 Armies and 3 Divisions. The Chinese request for disbursement of funds to cover this purchase was received in the Department of State on September 27, 1948 and payment by the Treasury was authorized on October 1, 1948. The requests at the program for small arms and small-arms ammunition were placed ahead of those for the United States Army. The first shipment of military materiel purchased under this requisition arrived in China on November 11, 1948 and subsequent major shipments reached Chinese ports on November 29, 1948 and January 4, 1949 (two shipments on this date). An additional shipment of Army-supplied cargo procured under the above and allied purchases reached China and in mid-March, four full cargoes being shipped without charge to the Chinese in United States Navy owned vessels. Following are figures showing certain Chinese requests under this program and the amount of material delivered according to the latest figures available:

Item	Number Requested	Number Delivered
U. S. Rifles, Cal. 30	124, 383	132, 851
Browning Automatic Rifles, Cal. 30	8, 104	8, 793
Heavy Machine Guns, Cal. 30	1, 566	1,707
Sub. Machine Guns, Cal. 45	8, 920	12, 975
Rocket Launcher	1, 134	1, 196
Grenade Launcher	5, 592	5, 758
30 Cal. Ammunition	291, 104, 500	231, 221, 082
45 Cal. Ammunition	26, 760, 000	26, 577, 498
Rocket Ammunition	90, 720	66, 380
Grenades	559, 200	280, 560

In certain categories as revealed above, more than the originally specified amount of equipment was provided, following discussions between American and Chinese military officers in which the desire of the Chinese representatives to obtain the additional amount of equipment was expressed. Chinese requests for mortars and mortar and artillery ammunition were for the most part unfulfilled since funds transferred to the Department of the Army were inadequate to pay for these. Decision concerning use of the grants rested solely with the Chinese Government and if that Government had desired, funds used for purchasing other items of less immediate military value, such as raw materials for arsenals, could have been made available to the Department of the Army for further purchases under the 7 Army, 3 Division program. It should be noted, however, that shipments of surplus ammunition from the Pacific during 1948 contained large quantities of mortar and artillery ammunition.

The pricing formula adapted in mid-1947 during implementation of the aid programs for Greece and Turkey was applied to Chinese requests under the $125 million grants. Since most of the items desired were not surplus but had to be replaced in Army stocks, the Chinese were charged replacement costs.

At the time the first of the above shipments of arms was arriving in China, United States Army forces in Shanghai transferred (abandoned) without cost to the Chinese approximately $500,000 worth of small arms and ammunition.

There are attached in annex 171, section XV, tables showing:

a) Summary of the use of funds received—a report submitted to the Department by the Chinese Embassy;
b) Reports on monthly shipments to China of goods purchased under the grants (the reports covering 1949 were prepared by the Chinese Embassy);
c) Report on major shipments of material by agencies of this Government, and by Chinese procurement agencies.
d) Department of the Army report on the China Aid Program.

Following the rapid deterioration of the military situation in north and central China and in view of the danger that stocks delivered to China proper might eventually fall into the hands of the Communists, the Chinese Government late in December 1948 requested that shipments of material purchased under the grants be delivered to Taiwan. Pursuant to this request, subsequent shipments have been made to Taiwan. At the end of February 1949 the Acting President requested that shipments of munitions be stopped pending reorganization of the Executive Yuan. In accordance with a later request from him they were again renewed during the latter half of March.

173

Transfer and Sale of Ammunition and Matériel to the Chinese Government during 1947 and 1948

On the same date (May 26, 1947) the Chinese were informed that the Department would approve the sale to China of 130 million rounds of surplus 7.92 rifle ammunition, and would approve applications for export licenses for transport planes and for spare parts for all equipment, including combat items previously transferred under the 8⅓ Group Program.

Subsequent to this date the Chinese on June 25, 1947 purchased the 130 million rounds of 7.92 rifle ammunition for $656,499.27 or 10 per cent of procurement cost.

Shipment of this ammunition was made from Seattle on July 14 and August 11, 1947.

In July 1947, the Chinese expressed a desire to purchase 43 C–47 aircraft but wanted these considered part of the 8⅓ Group Program. Since the quota of C–47's under the Program had been fulfilled, the Chinese were informed that transport planes would be made available through normal surplus channels. The Chinese signed a contract with the War Assets Administration for the purchase of 150 C–46's on December 22, 1947, purchasing for $5,000 each planes which had a procurement cost of $232,000 each.

The contract covering civilian end-use items in the Pacific for the 8⅓ Group Program was concluded on November 6, 1947 at 12½ cents on the dollar.

On December 9, 1947, the Chinese Government signed a commercial contract for 6,500,000 rounds of .50 caliber ammunition.

On December 16, 1947, the Chinese were informed of the availability of surplus ammunition and explosives and combat matériel including combat planes for the 8⅓ Group Program. In March and April of 1948 the Department of the Army provided the Department of State for transmission to the Chinese certain information on the quantity and type of surplus ammunition available in Hawaii and the Pacific. Prior to this, however, the Chinese, following negotiations with the OFLC, concluded on January 7, 1948, an open-end contract for the purchase of all surplus ammunition in the Marianas at the nominal cost of one cent on the dollar. As the result of further negotiations, a contract was signed on January 30, 1948, for the purchase at 17½ cents on the dollar of all surplus stocks in the United States, including Hawaii, available for the 8⅓ Group Program, except combat aircraft, which were available and were separately negotiated. (This contract was revised on March 16, 1948.)

On January 31, 1948, a contract supplementing that of November 6, 1947, was signed covering the sale of surplus combat equipment in the Pacific applicable to the 8⅓ Group Program, the ammunition component being sold at the nominal cost of one cent on the dollar.

On April 29 and June 11, 1948, contracts were signed covering the sale of surplus ammunition located on Hawaii.

On May 22, 1948, a contract was concluded for the sale of the surplus ammunition remaining in the Pacific and not included in previous contracts. The bulk of the ammunition covered by this contract was located at Okinawa.

174

Statement Submitted by Brigadier General T. S. Timberman to the Committee on Foreign Affairs of the House of Representatives, June 21, 1949

History of the China Aid Program

Public Law 472, 3 April 1948, and Public Law 793, 28 June 1948, authorized an Aid Program to China involving a grant of $125,000,000.

The terms of Public Laws 472 and 793 did not provide specifically for participation of the U.S. military establishment in the program, nor for the transfer of funds to its Departments to permit the necessary replacement of those items withdrawn from military stocks to meet the requirements of the Chinese military program.

On the 28th of July 1948 Presidential letters to the Secretaries of State, of Defense, and of the Treasury authorized not only assistance to the Chinese Government by the National Military Establishment, but also the transfer of funds allocated to the China Aid Program to United States governmental agencies participating in the supply program. The Secretary of Defense, by memorandum to the three Service Secretaries dated 29 July 1948 forwarded copies of the Presidential letters of 28 July 1948 and requested the implementation of the China Aid Program by the Army, Navy and Air Force.

On 2 August 1948 the Department of the Army established a procedure for fulfilling the Army requirements of the Chinese Government.

By August 1948 the Department of the Army had disposed, in the main of all surplus supplies of World War II procurement, and particularly of those items which the Chinese listed as their priority requirements.

Nevertheless, availability studies based upon Chinese requirements were initiated by the Department of the Army on 3 August 1948. Paralleling the availability studies was the computation of the prices which the Department of the Army would have to charge in order that those supplies issued directly from stock could be replaced.

The Chinese representatives in Washington, in the hope of obtaining supplies at the lowest possible price, canvassed a number of possible commercial sources. The Chinese representatives were reluctant to place orders with the Department of the Army until they had completed the canvassing of all possible commercial sources and the Department of the Army had completed computation of prices. The Chinese wanted to compare prices before making a definite commitment for purchases.

The Department of the Army gave highest priority to the study of availability and computation of prices of caliber .30 rifles and ammunition. On 19 August the Chinese representatives were informed that the Department of the Army could supply, if the Chinese so desired, caliber .30 rifles and ammunition in sufficient quantities to meet the total requirements. On 31 August the Chinese were further informed that the Department of the Army could supply caliber .30 carbines and caliber .45 ammunition. They delayed placing their order for small arms and accessories for about a month.

The Department of the Army completed and delivered to the Chinese representatives data as to availability and pricing for Signal, Quartermaster, and Medical supplies in the period 7–9 September and that for Engineer supplies and the remaining Ordnance supplies on 19 September.

On 10 September the Department of the Treasury transferred to the Department of the Army as the result of a Chinese request, the sum of $25,130,431.55 for payment in connection with firm requests which the Chinese were concurrently preparing. The items requested by the Chinese for purchase with this sum were raw materials, such as metals and powder base for the Chinese arsenal program; radios for Chinese signal communications; tires and tubes; spare parts for motor transportation and demolition supplies. Demolition materials were immediately available from surplus stocks still existing in Hawaii. They were ordered shipped without delay; transportation was arranged and, approximately 1,000,000 pounds of TNT, sold at surplus prices were moved in November via commercial shipping from Hawaii. The Department of the Army had available from stock approximately 65% of the motor vehicle spare parts requested. These supplies were likewise moved immediately to a port for shipment. The remaining items, however, of the specific types required by the Chinese in this request, are not carried in stock by the Department of the Army and consequently must be manufactured expressly to fill the Chinese requirements. Contracts were negotiated in accordance with statutory requirements. Delivery of some of these types of items will not be completed (as the Chinese were fully aware when their request was submitted) until the Fall of 1949.

The Chinese Ambassador, Dr. Koo, delivered to the Secretary of Defense on 20 September 1948, a revised list of requirements for the Military Aid Program. This list included primarily weapons and ammunition. It voided all previous Chinese requests and action by the Department of the Army with respect to these particular items. The Department of the Army on 21 September initiated new availability studies and computation of prices, considering them in the light of possible free transportation and 1945 list prices. It was immediately apparent that this revised list of requirements for weapons and ammunition, at the lowest possible price which the Department of the Army could arrange, would amount to more than $50,000,000. In a meeting with the Chinese representatives it was learned that approximately $40,000,000 remained available in the China Aid Fund with which to purchase the supplies of this new list. The Chinese were thereupon advised to show the requirements in the order of the most urgent priority. The priorities were submitted to the Department of the Army on 24 September and on 4 October the Chinese specified destinations in China for shipment of these supplies. These destinations and the approximate percentages of the supplies to be delivered thereto follows:

Shanghai	60%
Tsingtao	10%
Tientsin via Tsingtao	30%

Also on 4 October 1948 the Department of the Army received from the Treasury Department $37,783,386.68, transferred from the China Aid Fund at the request of the Chinese representatives in Washington in payment for the arms and ammunition of the revised list. Upon receipt of these funds, and without awaiting the completion of the availability study or the computation of prices, the Department of the Army ordered the preparation for shipment of weapons and ammunition in fulfillment of the requirements contained in Priority I of the revised program. Based upon informal information received from the Navy Department on 9 October and later confirmed in a letter from the Secretary of the Navy to the Secretary of the Army, ports were selected for handling and loading these supplies, utilizing U.S. Navy vessels for transportation free of charge to the Chinese. In an effort to transport the maximum quantity of urgently needed supplies in the shortest possible time, the Department of the Army ordered the shipment, in first priority, of ammunition from depots throughout the U. S. to the selected port on the West Coast. Following inspection, preparation of packages and marking with shipping instructions, the actual movement of this ammunition to port commenced early in the week of 25 October. The first Navy vessel, of 5,000 ton capacity, reached the port on 1 November and commenced loading immediately. This vessel departed 9 November for the port of Shanghai. Approximately 2500 tons of ammunition remaining at the port following departure of the first vessel, together with such weapons as had arrived at the port by that time, were loaded on a second naval vessel of 5000 tons capacity which reached the port about 21 November. This second vessel completed its loading and departed for the same destination on 1 December. A third shipment, comprised of the remaining weapons, and miscellaneous supplies departed from the port on 16 December. It should be noted that in order to meet this schedule it was necessary to place the inspection, necessary repair and preparation for shipment of the rifles of this program ahead of a similar program in connection with the expansion of our own armed forces.

In a further effort to ship weapons and ammunition to China in the shortest possible time, the Department of the Army on 5 October transmitted the entire list of Chinese requirements to General MacArthur and requested that he make a survey of his entire Command and report those items which he could supply immediately. The Department of the Army in making this request offered to replace in his stocks any supplies which he could make available for the Chinese. Subsequently it was determined that the Commander of the Naval Forces Western Pacific could provide transportation for shipment of these supplies free of charge. After coordinating his report with the action underway in the U.S., General MacArthur was ordered on 27 October to prepare and deliver to the port of Yokohama those supplies which he had reported available. These supplies, amounting to approximately 1200 tons of small arms and ammunition, actually reached China by mid-November.

The first vessel with Army supplied cargo which departed from a U.S. West Coast port on 9 November, reached Shanghai on 29 November, discharged 60% of its cargo for Shanghai, an additional 30% for onward shipment to Tientsin because of better facilities available in Shanghai for transferring the cargo to smaller vessels, and then proceeded to Tsingtao where discharge of the remaining 10% was completed on 7 December. Meanwhile on 6 December 1948 the Department of the Army was notified that the Chinese Government desired all future shipments of the Aid Cargo then en route and to be shipped to Shanghai be diverted to Keelung, Taiwan (Formosa). The subsequent shipments via U.S. Navy vessels and commercial vessels alike have been routed to Taiwan in accordance with this request. In all, four full shiploads of Army supplied cargo were transported to Chinese ports free of charge in U.S. Navy owned vessels. The last of these departed from the West Coast of the U.S. on 19 February.

Although some supplies which were procured from commercial concerns expressly for the China Aid Program were shipped free of charge on board the four U.S. Navy vessels, these vessels carried mainly the items which were immediately available from Army stocks. Since the readily available items were thereby virtually exhausted, shipments thereafter depended upon the rate of completion of manufacture by the commercial sources from which the supplies were being procured. In addition there were small amounts of supplies being requested by the Chinese for purchase with the residue of funds remaining after computation of the cost of the large purchases made earlier. Nevertheless, supplies becoming available would arrive at the port in less than shipload lots. To permit accumulation would have delayed the program. It was decided thereupon to contract with commercial shippers to move the cargo as it reached the ports. This procedure will be followed until completion of the program which it is estimated will continue with small shipments until the Fall of 1949.

Sale of Military Supplies by the Department of Army in Accordance With China Aid Act of 1948

In accordance with the China Aid Act of April 3, 1948, and the July 28, 1948, implementing directives of the President, the Department of the Army has furnished and is continuing to furnish military supplies as they are requested by the Chinese Government. These supplies, when available, are furnished direct from existing stocks or, if unavailable in stock, are procured from commercial sources normally used by the Department of the Army.

The prices charged by the Department of the Army for supplies furnished the Chinese Government are in accord with pricing formula adopted in mid-1947 during the implementation of the aid program for Greece and Turkey as authorized by Public Law 75, Eightieth Congress. Briefly stated, the pricing formula is as follows:

(a) Items entirely surplus to the needs of the United States armed forces are sold at surplus prices, averaging 10 percent of 1945 procurement cost price.

(b) Items stored as war reserve, i. e., needed to equip units in event of a mobilization, are sold at 1945 procurement cost price.

(c) Items needed for current use of the United States armed forces and which if disposed of must be replaced immediately are sold at current replacement costs.

Of course, items which are not available in stock must be procured and are charged to the foreign government at the exact price charged by the manufacturer, plus any costs involved for handling and shipping.

All appreciable quantities of surplus items had been disposed of prior to the implementation of the China Aid Act. They had been previously applied to the foreign military assistance programs, including Greece and Turkey, and in addition virtually all surplus items in the Pacific and Far East areas, except in the Philippines, had been sold to China as surplus under the Soong-McCabe agreement (bulk sales). Moreover, aside from the exhaustion of stocks of surplus supplies, the Surplus Property Act after June 30, 1948, could no longer be used for disposition of surplus supplies in the continental United States, and, therefore, was no longer a valid instrument for possible implementation of the China Aid Act had there in fact been a surplus. Overseas, surplus supplies that did exist were already committed, much of them to China in bulk sales arrangements.

The Military Establishment was first authorized to furnish supplies and service to the Chinese Government in connection with the China Aid Act of 1948, as a result of a Presidential directive of July 28, 1948. Implementation of a definite program commenced on August 3, 1948. As stated above virtually no surplus stocks remained at this time, consequently, relatively few items requested by the Chinese Government could be made available at the surplus prices. Regardless of the priority given the China aid program we proceeded to its immediate implementation. In fact for delivery of some items, notably small arms and small arms ammunition, the China aid program was placed ahead of the supply of the United States Army. It was by such a priority that the first shipload of United States Army procured supplies for China departed from the west coast on November 9 or little more than a month after the Chinese had placed a firm request for their needs on the Department of the Army.

It should be noted that of the $125,000,000 appropriated, the Chinese Government has placed orders with the Department of the Army for an amount approximately only $64,500,000. The remainder of the funds have been allotted for purchases from the United States Air Force, United States Navy, and purchases by the Chinese themselves direct from commercial sources. The Department of the Army has furnished supplies to the Chinese in all categories of prices—a small quantity at surplus prices, considerably more at 1945 procurement cost prices, but the majority at either replacement cost prices or at the price actually charged by the majority at either replacement cost prices or at the price actually charged by the manufacturer, where the supplies were procured expressly for the Chinese. Through the use of Army channels for procurement, the Chinese Government has been given the advantage of any special considerations provided by commercial enterprises to the United States Government.

Of the $64,500,000 authorized for purchases from or through the United States Army, supplies valued at $47,081,500 have been shipped from the west coast to date. Delivery of supplies available direct from Army stocks has been completed except for new requisitions recently received from Chinese. However, shipments are continuing at a normal rate paced by the rate of deliveries from the commercial sources of procured supplies that were not available in Army stocks. One exception is a small quantity of ammunition in Hawaii which has been blocked from shipment by the longshoremen's strike. The Department of the Army has attempted to offset this delay by making available additional ammunition of the same type for immediate shipment from the west coast of the United States. Two new requisitions were received from the Chinese during the past week. One for tool sets for fifth echelon repair of tanks, the other for 37 twin Diesel engines for M–5 tanks. Incidentally, the latter item will be furnished at the surplus price as were the tanks for which they are intended.

To relate the China aid program to the aid programs for Greece and Turkey, it must be recalled that the latter were initiated by Public Law 75 passed May 22, 1947. Hence supplies were furnished to Greece a full year before the implementation of the China aid program. In the main, the requirements for Greece and Turkey were fulfilled from military surplus stocks. All surplus items were sold at surplus prices. During the same period surplus supplies also were sold to other foreign governments, notably to China. The items sold to China likewise were sold at surplus prices. As a result of all these sales the surplus stocks of the Army were largely depleted when the China aid program was initiated. It might be noted that the aid programs for Greece and Turkey were continued by Public Law 472, the same law which initiated the China aid program. The provisions of law for continuation of the programs for Greece and Turkey, unlike the China aid program, were such as to permit continued implementation by the National Military Establishment. Hence it was possible to supply to Greece and Turkey such surplus items as existed so long as those items lasted. Because of these factors, including the previous sale of surplus supplies to the Chinese at surplus prices as well as to Greece and Turkey, there simply was little available when the China aid program commenced. The pricing formula has been applied alike in the furnishing of supplies in the fulfillment of all programs. When surplus stocks became exhausted subsequent sales to Greece and Turkey were at the higher prices depending upon the category of the item in accordance with the formula.

In the handling within the Department of the Army of requests from the Chinese Government in comparison with the handling of those from Greece and Turkey, there has been no difference except that at the outset of the China aid program the programs for Greece and Turkey were already operating smoothly as the result of a year's experience. All of this experience which was applicable was adapted immediately to the program for China and served to reduce considerably the time that normally would have elapsed in the solving of new problems.

Annexes to Chapter VIII: The Program of American Economic Aid, 1947-1949

175 (a)

Message From President Truman Transmitting Recommendation That the Congress Authorize a Program for Aid to China in the Amount of $570,000,000 to Provide Assistance Until June 30, 1949

To the Congress of the United States:

On several occasions I have stated that a primary objective of the United States is to bring about, throughout the world, the conditions of a just and lasting peace. This is a cause to which the American people are deeply devoted.

Since V–J Day we have expended great effort and large sums of money on the relief and rehabilitation of war-torn countries to aid in restoring workable economic systems which are essential to the maintenance of peace. A principle which has guided our efforts to assist these war-torn countries has been that of helping their peoples to help themselves. The Congress is now giving careful consideration to a most vital and far-reaching proposal to further this purpose—the program for aid to European recovery.

I now request the Congress to consider the type of further assistance which this country should provide to China.

A genuine friendship has existed between the American people and the people of China over many years. This friendship has been accompanied by a long record of commercial and cultural association and close cooperation between our two countries. Americans have developed a deep respect for the Chinese people and sympathy for the many trials and difficulties which they have endured.

The United States has long recognized the importance of a stable Chinese nation to lasting peace in the Pacific and the entire world. The vast size and population of China make her an important factor in world affairs. China is a land which has a rich tradition and culture and a large and energetic population. It has always been our desire to see a strong, progressive China making a full contribution to the strength of the family of nations.

With this end in view, we have supported the National Government of China since it first came to power 20 years ago. China and the United States were allies in the war against Japan, and as an ally we supported China's valiant war efforts against the Japanese. Since the Japanese surrender we have provided a great deal of additional assistance. Military aid was given the Chinese Government, not only to help defeat the Japanese invaders but also to assist in reoccupying Japanese-held areas. The United States contributed the major share of the extensive aid received by China under the program of the United Nations Relief and Rehabilitation Administration. We made available to the Chinese Government at minimum cost large quantities of surplus goods and equipment of value to China's economy. We are currently extending further aid to China under our foreign-relief program.

Nevertheless, the Chinese Government and people are still laboring under the double and interrelated burden of civil war and a rapidly deteriorating economy. The strains placed upon the country by 8 years of war and the Japanese occupation and blockade have been increased by internal strife at the very time that reconstruction efforts should be under way. The wartime damage to transport and productive facilities has been greatly accentuated by the continued obstruction and destruction of vital communications by the Communist forces.

The civil warfare has further impeded recovery by forcing upon the Government heavy expenditures which greatly exceed revenues. Continual issuances of currency to meet these expenditures have produced drastic inflation, with its attendant disruption of normal commercial operations. Under these circumstances, China's foreign-exchange holdings have been so reduced that it will soon be impossible for China to meet the cost of essential imports. Without such imports, industrial activity would diminish and the rate of economic deterioration would be sharply increased.

The continued deterioration of the Chinese economy is a source of deep concern to the United States. Ever since the return of General Marshall from China, the problem of assistance to the Chinese has been under continuous study. We have hoped for conditions in China that would make possible the effective and constructive use of American assistance in reconstruction and rehabilitation. Conditions have not developed as we had hoped, and we can only do what is feasible under circumstances as they exist.

We can assist in retarding the current economic deterioration and thus give the Chinese Government a further opportunity to initiate the measures necessary to the establishment of more stable economic conditions. But it is, and has been, clear that only the Chinese Government itself can undertake the vital measures necessary to provide the framework within which efforts toward peace and true economic recovery may be effective.

In determining the character and dimensions of the program which might be suited to this purpose, we have had to take into account a number of diverse and conflicting factors, including the other demands on our national resources at this time, the availability of specific commodities, the dimensions and complexities of the problems facing the Chinese Government, and the extent to which these problems could be promptly and effectively alleviated by foreign aid. United States assistance to China, like that provided to any other nation, must be adapted to its particular requirements and capacities.

In the light of these factors, I recommend that the Congress authorize a program for aid to China in the amount of $570,000,000 to provide assistance until June 30, 1949.

The program should make provision for the financing, through loans or grants, of essential imports into China in the amount of $510,000,000. This estimate is based upon prices as of January 1, 1948, since it is impossible at present to predict what effect current price changes may have on the program. Revised dollar estimates can be presented in connection with the request for appropriations if necessary. The essential imports include cereals, cotton, petroleum, fertilizer, tobacco, pharmaceuticals, coal, and repair parts for existing capital equipment. The quantities provided for under this program are within the limits of available supplies. The financing of these essential commodity imports by the United States would permit the Chinese Government to devote its limited dollar resources to the most urgent of its other needs.

The program should also provide $60,000,000 for a few selected reconstruction projects to be initiated prior to June 30, 1949. There is an urgent need for the restoration of essential transportation facilities, fuel and power operations, and export industries. This work could be undertaken in areas sheltered from military operations and could help in improving the supply and distribution of essential commodities.

As in the case of aid to European recovery, the conduct of this program of aid should be made subject to an agreement between China and the United States setting forth the conditions and procedures for administering the aid. The agreement should include assurances that the Chinese Government will take such economic, financial, and other measures as are practicable, looking toward the ultimate goal of economic stability and recovery. The United States would, of course, reserve the right to terminate aid if it is determined that the assistance provided is not being handled in accordance with the agreement or that the policies of the Chinese Government are inconsistent with the objective of using the aid to help achieve a self-supporting economy.

Pending establishment of the agency which is to be set up for the administration of the European recovery program, the assistance to China should be carried forward under the existing machinery now administering the foreign-relief programs. Legislation authorizing the Chinese program should make possible transfer of the administration of the Chinese program to the agency administering our aid to European recovery. The need for authority in the administering agency to make adjustments in the program from time to time will be as great here as in the European recovery program.

The proposed program of aid to China represents what I believe to be the best course this Government can follow, in the light of all the circumstances. Nothing which this country provides by way of assistance can, even in a small measure, be a substitute for the necessary action that can be taken only by the Chinese Government. Yet this program can accomplish the important purpose of giving the Chinese Government a respite from rapid economic deterioration, during which it can move to establish more stable economic conditions. Without this respite the ability of the Chinese Government to establish such conditions at all, would be doubtful. The achievement of even this limited objective is of such importance as to justify the proposed program of aid.

I recommend, therefore, that this program be given prompt and favorable consideration by the Congress.

HARRY S. TRUMAN.

THE WHITE HOUSE, *February 18, 1948.*

175 (b)

Statement by Secretary of State Marshall regarding the China Aid Program, February 20, 1948

In consideration of a program of assistance to China, it should be recognized that for the main part the solution of China's problems is largely one for the Chinese themselves. The great difficulty in determining a basis and procedure to justify a program of assistance lies in the conditions which exist in China, military as well as economic.

Thus far, the principal deterrent to the solution of Chinese economic problems is the civil war which has drained the Chinese Government's internal and foreign-exchange resources, continued the destruction of property and the constant disruption of economic life, and has prevented recovery. The Communist forces have brought about the terrible destruction to wreck the economy of China. This is their announced purpose—to force an economic collapse.

The Chinese Government is in dire need of assistance in its present serious economic difficulties. However, the political, economic, and financial conditions in China are so unstable and so uncertain that it is impossible to develop a practical, effective, long-term over-all program for economic recovery. Nevertheless, it is desirable that the United States Government render assistance to China in her present critical situation in order to help retard the present rapid rate of economic deterioration and thus provide a breathing space in which the Chinese Government could initiate important steps toward more stable economic conditions.

While there are a multitude of factors in China that are involved in the consideration of such a program, the following appear of first importance:

China is a country of vast area and population. Through communications north of the Yangtze River are almost nonexistent except by coastal shipping. Local governments are often so corrupt that they are undependable for assistance in the administration of relief measures. The political control by long-entrenched groups is a great difficulty to be overcome in the restoration of China to economic stability. The conduct by the Government of the civil war now in progress, particularly in view of the geographic disadvantages—exposed and lengthy communications, and the inherent difficulties in dealing with guerrilla warfare—demands a high order of aggressive leadership in all major echelons of command, which is lacking. The civil war imposes a burden on the national budget of 70 percent or more and the financing is now carried on by means of issuance of paper money. Industrial production is low and transportation facilities are poor, the lack of adequate transportation affecting particularly the movement of foodstuffs. The results are an extreme, really a fantastic, inflation of currency, and the inevitable speculation in commodities as well as hoarding.

In considering the measures to be taken by the United States to assist China, it is very necessary, I think, to have in mind that a proposal at the present time cannot be predicated upon a definite termination for the necessity of such assistance as in the case of the European-recovery program. Provision of a currency stabilization fund would, in the opinion of our monetary experts, require large sums which would be largely dissipated under the present conditions of war financing and civil disruption. In view of this situation, the program should not involve the virtual underwriting of the future of the Chinese economy. The United States should not by its actions be put in the position of being charged with a direct responsibility for the conduct of the Chinese Government and its political, economic, and military affairs.

The proposed program of aid for China would provide economic assistance in the amount of $570,000,000 for the period ending June 30, 1949. Of this amount, $510,000,000 would cover minimum imports of essential civilian type of commodities, chiefly foodstuffs and raw materials, and $60,000,000 would be for key reconstruction projects. The program concentrates on those commodities believed to be of maximum aid to Chinese civilian economy and those which will insure the greatest aid per dollar spent.

While the total import needs of China cannot be accurately estimated, in view of the generally disturbed and, in certain regions, chaotic conditions of production and trade, the need for the commodities listed can be demonstrated, we feel, with reasonable assurance. The program will therefore meet the most essential commodity requirements. China will need other imports, of course, including civilian-type commodities not included in the program, and military supplies. In addition, China has certain international financial obligations.

To meet these additional needs for foreign exchange, China will have available certain financial resources of her own. These include proceeds from exports, miscellaneous receipts from such sources as overseas remittances, the sale of surplus property, and foreign government and philanthropic expenditures in China; and finally, to be called upon if necessary China's reserves of gold and foreign exchange which were estimated as totaling the equivalent of $274,000,000 as of January 1, 1948. This amount would be increased to the extent the Chinese are able to bring about an improvement in their net foreign exchange receipts. On the other hand, the amount will be reduced to the extent that reserves must be used, for lack of other available funds, to make necessary payments after January 1, 1948.

It is proposed, in the program submitted, that it would be administered by the agency or establishment of the Government created by law for the purpose of administering programs of assistance to foreign countries or, pending the establishment of such agency, temporarily by the Department of State in cooperation with the other agencies of the Government directly concerned. The conditions under which assistance is to be extended should be spelled out in an agreement with the Chinese Government, which would be based on the same considerations underlying the conditions for assistance to European countries but of necessity adjusted to the different conditions in China.

176

Statement Issued by the Ambassador in China (Stuart) upon the Presentation to Congress of the China Aid Bill [1]

893.00/12–2247

A personal message to the people of China.

From President Truman's statement to Congress you know something of the proposed efforts of the United States to assist the people of China. May I, therefore, take this opportunity to attempt to interpret to you the purposes controlling American policy toward China, and the problems involved. I do this from the standpoint of one who was born and has spent most of his life in your country and who is as deeply concerned over its welfare as any of you.

Fortunately the government and the people of the United States desire for China precisely what all truly patriotic Chinese themselves are struggling to achieve; its freedom and independence, internal peace and prosperity, the establishment of a genuinely modernized and democratic government. We Americans earnestly desire all of this but nothing more.

Our problem has been how to help the common people who have been the chief sufferers from the devastating internal conflict which has continued since V–J Day. What the common people need is peace and productive activity under a government that cares for their welfare.

More specifically the problem is how to benefit the common people and to protect them alike from the extreme reactionary or selfish elements and from the extreme radicals with their brutally destructive revolutionary tactics. Both of

---

[1] Issued on Feb. 20, 1948.

these groups are highly organized. Both place their partisan or their individual interests far above those of the suffering people.

We Americans believe thoroughly in democracy and we are convinced it will work in China if given a fair chance and sufficient time. Negatively, a democratic government guarantees freedom from forcible interference in the daily pursuits of the people and freedom from fear. Positively, it fosters conditions under which the more intelligent and progressive leaders can educate and in other ways assist the ordinary people to appreciate the duties and the rights of citizens in the democratic way of life and to apply constitutional procedures in exercising these under rule of law rather than under caprice of individuals.

As has always been true in Chinese history, the masses will follow educated leaders in whose moral character they have confidence. By adapting this ancient democratic Chinese process to modern constitutional procedures, the corrupt or incompetent elements in the present regional, provincial and local governments can be gradually eliminated and replaced by those whom the people freely choose to administer public affairs for the public good.

Personally from my long association with Chinese students I have confidence in their patriotic idealism. They, whether having already graduated and occupying responsible positions in government, in education, in business, or any other walks of life, or whether still in school, should be the ones to lead in this latest form of patriotic, public-spirited effort. By their public-spirited and unselfish example, they should be able to surmount those at the other extreme who are so fanatically devoted to their party, so intolerant of all other political faiths, so utterly ruthless in the methods they employ, that they are willing to destroy public and private property and inflict upon the helpless people all the horrors of rapine and war in the attainment of their own arbitrary objectives.

We Americans, under the leadership of Mr. Marshall, did our utmost to prevent the development of the situation which now exists and all the suffering it entails for the Chinese people. Nevertheless, with the traditional friendship between the American and Chinese peoples, and given our belief that the economic well-being of the Chinese people will redound to the benefit of the world, we are proposing, through a program of economic assistance to China, to provide a further opportunity to the Chinese Government and people to take the initial steps toward laying a solid foundation for economic recovery and stability in China.

The real task, the responsibility, however, rests with the Chinese people themselves. No amount of American material assistance nor any number of skilled American technical advisers can accomplish what is required to bring political stability and economic recovery to China. The major effort must be Chinese and there must be a sincere and deep-seated determination to put selfishness aside and strive unceasingly for the common good.

The meanings of freedom and democracy have been confused by the wholly different interpretations being put upon these terms today. There should be no misunderstanding of these issues. Under a totalitarian system there can be no intellectual freedom—those who attempt to think for themselves either succumb to regimentation or are promptly liquidated. Democracy is government not only for the people, but also by the people. In this truly democratic sense the people must, however, continuously bring the weight of enlightened public opinion to bear upon the conduct of government to prevent misuse of power by those in office. This requires, therefore, freedom of debate and publication and free access to news objectively reported. In a totalitarian system these freedoms cannot exist. Instead, news becomes propaganda scientifically developed. It depends for its effects upon unrestrained vituperation and incessant repetition without regard for the truth.

China today is faced with insidious dangers which will require the united effort of all public spirited citizens to overcome. This calls for clear-sighted vision, a high degree of courage and grim determination. It is hoped that the freedom-loving patriots of China, together with all elements of the population, will join in a constructive evolutionary process that will bring unity and peaceful progress to the entire nation.

177

Statement by the Department of State, the Department of the Treasury, and the Federal Reserve Board on Possible Use of Silver for Monetary Stabilization in China in Connection With China Aid Program

[February 1948]

The China Aid Program does not provide for the use of silver to bring about monetary stability in China. It does not do so for three main reasons: *one*, because conditions in China do not now furnish a basis for any lasting currency stabilization; *two*, because even if basic conditions now favored stabilization of the currency and price level it would not be practical to restore the silver standard in China; and *three*, because the introduction of silver as an emergency measure at this time would involve such technical difficulties as to make it a costly and uncertain venture.

I

No provision was made for a fund for currency stabilization because under present conditions of civil war and economic disruption, such provision would result in the inevitable dissipation of large sums of money.

The basic cause of inflation in China is the massive budgetary deficit of the Chinese Government. This deficit is, of course, immediately occasioned by military expenditures and therefore depends on the exigencies of civil war. Overall military expenditures are estimated to have accounted for not less than 65 to 70 percent of total government expenditures in 1947. Instead of being financed by taxes and loans these expenditures are financed by expanding the note issue. As long as the expenditures of the Chinese Government continue vastly to exceed its revenues, and as long as the deficit continues to be financed by increasing the money supply, inflation will persist in China. When the total amount of spending is, by reason of this deficit, greatly in excess of the available supply of goods at any given price level, prices will continue to rise regardless of the kind or kinds of monetary units employed. It is therefore not feasible to contribute effectively to monetary stabilization in China until this deficit is reduced to manageable dimensions.

Since inflation in China is essentially an internal problem, the basis for a permanent solution will ultimately have to be provided primarily by the Chinese themselves. Funds are, therefore, not provided for currency stabilization in the proposed China Aid program. The program does, however, assure a continued supply from abroad of commodities and raw materials essential to the prevention of starvation and the maintenance of industrial output, and in this sense is anti-inflationary.

II

Even if basic conditions in China favored measures to restore monetary stability, there would be serious disadvantages in any attempt to restore the silver standard in China.[2] While the eventual reform of the currency in China might provide for the use of subsidiary metallic coins, including silver coin in reasonable amounts, silver is too bulky for efficient handling and shipment of large sums of money, especially in a country like China where transportation is so costly. Moreover, the progressive demonetization of silver throughout the world has brought about very unstable prices and market conditions for silver. The result is that the external value (foreign exchange rate) of a Chinese currency based on silver would be exposed to the risks of radical fluctuations in the price of silver unrelated to economic conditions in China. These fluctuations would in turn have disturbing repercussions on the Chinese economy and would inhibit the freedom of the Chinese authorities in pursuing desirable fiscal and monetary policies at home.

Finally, it must be pointed out that China, a member of the International Monetary Fund, has committed herself in principle to stability of exchange rates in terms of gold. When conditions permit, it is presumed that China will take steps to establish a stable monetary system and a stable exchange value for the Chinese currency in terms of gold. To assist China to establish a silver standard currency would appear to be inconsistent with the principles of the Fund Agreement, and consequently with established United States international financial and monetary policy.

III

To try to mitigate monetary instability in China now by injecting silver into her currency system would be a hazardous as well as a costly undertaking.

The mechanics of putting silver into circulation in China would be highly complex and technical even if the operation were handled most efficiently and without abuses. The Chinese Government would probably use silver coins for its expenditures and make a standing offer to redeem paper currency with silver coins. Overnight conversion would be impossible in China and a short-period redemption offer would amount to a repudiation of a large part of the currency. On the other hand, to make expenditures in silver without standing ready to redeem outstanding notes would accelerate the flight from the paper currency. While acceptance of notes in payment of taxes might tend to retard their depreciation,

---

[2] It has been suggested that China successfully employed a silver monetary system for hundreds of years, that China would still be on the silver standard if the United States' silver purchase policy in 1934 and 1935 had not forced its abandonment, and that the historical silver base should be re-established. Actually China has only had a modern national monetary system since 1933 when the old silver *tael* (not a coin but a unit of weight in silver) and various circulating silver coins were abandoned as legal tender, and the Sun Yat Sen dollar was first minted by the new National Mint in Shanghai. From 1933 until November 1935 China was on a unified silver standard system. On November 4, 1935 this system was abandoned as a result of high and unstable silver prices. A managed paper currency system backed by adequate gold and dollar reserves was substituted. The Government undertook to maintain the stability of the yuan by buying and selling foreign exchange at fixed rates in unlimited quantities. These reforms of 1935 were successfully carried through, and China enjoyed markedly stable prices and exchange rates for at least two years until after the outbreak of hostilities with Japan in 1937.

While fluctuating silver prices precipitated the abandonment of the silver standard in China, the announced tendency of Chinese monetary policy was already in the direction of a monetary system based on reserves of gold and foreign exchange, and the Chinese people quickly and easily adapted themselves to the use of paper currency. Without such a system China would have found it impossible to finance the war against Japan.

the Government, in the absence of unlimited convertibility of paper currency into silver, would probably recognize this depreciation by continually altering its official "conversion" rate between silver and paper; such action would itself tend to accelerate the depreciation.

Since the Government could not afford to have the existing currency collapse, for reasons of prestige and because it would wish to make some expenditures in paper currency (at times and places that silver was not on hand), both spending in silver and redemption of paper on demand would be necessary. The Government would therefore require to have on hand very large physical stocks of silver in order to maintain unlimited convertibility. Estimates of the amount of silver that would be required for such an operation range from 500 million to over one billion ounces.

If China is not able concomitantly to take the measures required to reestablish fiscal equilibrium, further large amounts of silver would be required to meet the continuing budgetary deficits. As pointed out above, as long as deficit spending continues on a large scale and the deficit is financed by increasing the money supply, inflation will continue regardless of the kind of monetary units employed. Even if silver coins are introduced and used in considerable quantities, the continuing increase in their supply will result both in increased prices of commodities in terms of silver and in a continued drain of silver into hoards or into black market channels for export. The leakage of silver into foreign markets through such channels would provide a means for financing unauthorized and luxury imports and further flight of capital abroad and thus would not reduce the deficit in the balance of payments which must be met out of official foreign exchange holdings and foreign aid. Moreover, it would disrupt the New York silver market unless the United States Treasury spent large sums in order to support this market. Such an operation would not give China a permanently stable monetary system, and would be a purely palliative measure.

Thus the use of silver as a temporary monetary expedient would be an extremely expensive as well as hazardous means for the possible attainment of a limited objective.

Any silver provided for Chinese domestic monetary purposes would thus have to be *in addition* to the aid already proposed, for it would not obviate or lessen the necessity for providing assistance in the form of supplies of badly needed imports as is proposed in the recommendations now before Congress.

178(a)

Secretary Marshall to the Ambassador in China (Stuart)

893.00/1–1248

WASHINGTON, *January 12, 1948.*

For your confidential information the final decisions regarding the China aid program have not yet been made by the Secretary, and thereafter proposed legislation will have to be reviewed by the National Advisory Council and submitted to the Bureau of the Budget before it is presented to Congress. Accordingly it is not possible to send authoritative information to the Embassy at this stage. It is suggested that pressure on the part of the Chinese for details of the program can be met by indicating Congress' prior rights in receiving such a message from the President. A report containing sufficient data will of course be sent you for communication personally to the Generalissimo and the Foreign Minister a day or so before public presentation.

The question of the appointment of technicians in connection with implementing the aid program will form part of the proposed legislation and no definitive action can be taken until at least the attitude of Congress manifests itself. Incidentally it is not clear how the Generalissimo's request for a "supreme economic adviser" and his suggestion of Blandford for that position jibes with his memorandum in which it is stated that the Chinese Government wishes to employ its own American or foreign technicians. No doubt the United States will have to send to China additional personnel to act in a supervisory and advisory capacity in connection with the aid program, but these may well be very limited in number due to the unavailability of experienced personnel. There are, however, two obvious and serious disadvantages to appointment of a "supreme economic adviser": First, there is the basic question of how effective under present circumstances in China he can be and secondly, and more important, the strong implication that his presence would carry of continuing United States responsibility for economic, financial and governmental situation in China, a responsibility which the United States cannot assume and which China and other countries must not be misled to believe has been or is going to be assumed.

This is no less applicable to the civil war. Consequently, the activities of the Military Advisory Group must be carefully delimited and they are not regarded as constituting an integral part of the aid program, which is essentially economic in character. It is expected that decisions regarding certain changes in the Military Advisory Group's directives and what additional military training center can be appropriately authorized will be made before General Barr's departure.

The importance of the considerations set forth above is reinforced by certain current indications that elements in the Chinese Government are looking more to external assistance than to their own exertions in meeting China's problems and seem to be directing their efforts towards shifting to the United States the responsibility for the conduct and the course of the civil war, the welfare of the Chinese people and the efficacy of the regime.

178(b)

Secretary Marshall to the Ambassador in China (Stuart)

893.50 Recovery/4–1448   WASHINGTON, *May 7, 1948*

The Department is studying United States policy aspects of the problem of furnishing qualified advisers to the Chinese Government and agrees that some advisory assistance is necessary in connection with the aid program. With regard to top level advisers for functions involving policy, the Department is of the opinion that if provided by the United States, they should be limited to a small number for highly select fields. Account must be taken not only of the limited number of competent advisers available, but also of the significance of their proposed fields of action from the standpoint of the objectives of the aid program and the extent to which reasonable prospects exist for implementation of recommendations made. The fields of advice and the relationship of the advisers to the Chinese Government and the aid Mission should minimize the possibility for undesirable involvement of the United States Government in the course of developments in China and its implied responsibility therefor. This is particularly true for certain aspects of fiscal policy and operations where the fundamental solution cannot be reached under present civil war conditions and where the United States effort to exert pressure, control, and the reduction of military expenditures might imply United States responsibility for the Chinese Government military effort and be exploited to obtain commitment in that regard. This would be contrary to the intent of Congress as described earlier.

The Department believes certain basic fiscal and other policy problems, such as those above, cannot be solved through technical advice, but that continuous effort can and should be made in the direction of improvements by well-timed informal pressure at top levels, e. g., by the Chief of the ECA Mission and top Embassy officials.

The assignment of United States technical personnel as advisers at the operational level should also be highly selective and primarily for functions directly related to implementation of the aid program, such as reconstruction projects financed by United States appropriation and/or the Chinese currency account. In exceptional cases, technical personnel might be assigned to advise operations indirectly related to the aid program which involve a minimum of policy issues, such as certain aspects of the foreign exchange operations of the Central Bank. The largest number of technical personnel in an advisory capacity probably should be provided for reconstruction. United States technical assistance to Chinese Government agencies responsible for control or operations of the distribution of expendable U. S. aid commodities should be rendered by members of the aid Mission in the course of the performance of the normal functions of observation and reporting, and not by United States personnel in the capacity of advisers assigned to the Chinese Government agencies concerned.

Departmental thinking now is that specific recommendations on types of advisers should be deferred until the Chief of the ECA China Mission has had opportunity to study the question in China and is able to determine the exact needs of the Chinese Government and their abilities to use advisers in terms of the China Aid Program. In the meantime the Department is studying the best methods to correlate the provision of technical assistance under the Smith-Mundt Act with the China Aid Program.

179

China Aid Act of 1948

(TITLE IV OF PUBLIC LAW 472)

Sec. 401. This title may be cited as the "China Aid Act of 1948".

Sec. 402. Recognizing the intimate economic and other relationships between the United States and China, and recognizing that disruption following in the wake of war is not contained by national frontiers, the Congress finds that the existing situation in China endangers the establishment of a lasting peace, the general welfare and national interest of the United States, and the attainment of the objectives of the United Nations. It is the sense of the Congress that the further evolution in China of Principles of individual liberty, free institutions, and genuine independence rests largely upon the continuing development of a strong and democratic national government as the basis for the establishment of sound economic conditions and for stable international economic relationships. Mindful of the advantages which the United States has enjoyed through the existence of a large domestic market with no internal trade barriers, and believing that similar advantages can accrue to China, it is declared to be the policy of the people of the United States to encourage the Republic of China and its people to exert sustained common efforts which will speedily achieve the internal peace and economic stability in China which are essential for lasting peace and prosperity in the world. It is further declared to be the policy of the people of the United States to encourage the Republic of China in its efforts to maintain the genuine independence and the administrative integrity of China, and to sustain and strengthen principles of individual liberty and free institutions in China through a program of assistance based on self-help and cooperation: *Provided*, That no assistance to China herein contemplated shall seriously impair the economic stability of the United States. It is further declared to be the policy of the United States that assistance provided by the United States under this title should at all times be dependent upon cooperation by the Republic of China and its people in furthering the program: *Provided further*, That assistance furnished under this title shall not be construed as an express or implied assumption by the United States of any responsibility for policies, acts, or undertakings of the Republic of China or for conditions which may prevail in China at any time.

SEC. 403. Aid provided under this title shall be provided under the applicacable provisions of the Economic Cooperation Act of 1948 which are consistent with the purposes of this title. It is not the purpose of this title that China, in order to receive aid hereunder, shall adhere to a joint program for European recovery.

SEC. 404. (a) In order to carry out the purposes of this title, there is hereby authorized to be appropriated to the President for aid to China a sum not to exceed $338,000,000 to remain available for obligation for the period of one year following the date of enactment of this Act.

(b) There is also hereby authorized to be appropriated to the President a sum not to exceed $125,000,000 for additional aid to China through grants, on such terms as the President may determine and without regard to the provisions of the Economic Cooperation Act of 1948, to remain available for obligation for the period of one year following the date of enactment of this Act.

SEC. 405. An agreement shall be entered into between China and the United States containing those undertakings by China which the Secretary of State, after consultation with the Administrator for Economic Cooperation, may deem necessary to carry out the purposes of this title and to improve commercial relations with China.

SEC. 406. Notwithstanding the provisions of any other law, the Reconstruction Finance Corporation is authorized and directed, until such time as an appropriation is made pursuant to section 404, to make advances, not to exceed in the aggregate $50,000,000, to carry out the provisions of this title in such manner and in such amounts as the President shall determine. From appropriations authorized under section 404, there shall be repaid without interest to the Reconstruction Finance Corporation the advances made by it under the authority contained herein. No interest shall be charged on advances made by the Treasury to the Reconstruction Finance Corporation in implementation of this section.

SEC. 407. (a) The Secretary of State, after consultation with the Administrator, is hereby authorized to conclude an agreement with China establishing a Joint Commission on Rural Reconstruction in China, to be composed of two citizens of the United States appointed by the President of the United States and three citizens of China appointed by the President of China. Such Commission shall, subject to the direction and control of the Administrator, formulate and carry out a program for reconstruction in rural areas of China, which shall include such research and training activities as may be necessary or appropriate for such reconstruction : *Provided*, That assistance furnished under this section shall not be construed as an express or implied assumption by the United States of any responsibility for making any further contributions to carry out the purposes of this section.

(b) Insofar as practicable, an amount equal to not more than 10 per centum of the funds made available under subsection (a) of section 404 shall be used to carry out the purposes of subsection (a) of this section. Such amount may be in United States dollars, proceeds in Chinese currency from the sale of commodities made available to China with funds authorized under subsection (a) of section 404, or both.

Approved April 3, 1948.

180

The Ambassador in China (Stuart) to Secretary Marshall

893.50 Recovery/5–1048

NANKING, *May 10, 1948*

The Embassy agrees that a bilateral aid agreement should be negotiated in Nanking and that the period of its negotiations presents time and opportunity to continue to press the Chinese Government for undertakings regarding self-help and tangible acts in the execution of the Premier's January 28 statement. Pressures in these directions have been applied by the Embassy whenever and wherever the occasion was offered. The Embassy agrees that they should be intensified now and during the period of bilateral negotiation with implicit but not an explicit link.

Two important factors, however, must be borne in mind in any advance estimate of progress which may be made with the Chinese Government. In the first place, any broad or powerful bargaining position vis-a-vis the Chinese Government disappeared on the date Congress passed the China Aid Act of 1948. Our position rests basically now on the more tenuous ground of Chinese hopes for the continuation and expansion of aid beyond the time period covered by the present Act. It is true, however, that we retain and should make full use of our bargaining position in the bilateral negotiations with respect to (1) methods of procurement for aid commodities, (2) methods of distribution of aid commodities in China and (3) utilization of Chinese National Currency proceeds from the sale of aid commodities provided under the grant. On the broad front of governmental reform and positive, self-generated fiscal and economic action, we rely for all practical purposes today, in the Embassy's opinion, on the effectiveness of moral pressure and not on a trading position.

The second element to be considered is the limitation on the Chinese Government's ability as opposed to its willingness to take bold constructive and effective action. The economic and financial status is deteriorating with increased momentum, as witnessed by the doubling within the past week of the black market CNC rate for the United States dollar. The military situation shows no improvement nor signs of any in prospect. Politically, there is a paralysis of leadership at the top which has permitted, for example, the tangle over the membership of the Legislative Yuan to make it impossible, until a settlement has been reached, for the Generalissimo to appoint his new Cabinet.

Under these circumstances, the Embassy strongly recommends that we display no haste in the negotiation or conclusion of the bilateral agreement. The exchange of interim letters provides an entirely satisfactory basis on which to operate in the coming weeks. Moreover, working out in practical terms with the Chinese officials the procedures and operational methods under which the new aid program is to be handled will make more meaningful the language finally agreed upon and imbedded in the bilateral agreement. Delay will give time, presumably, to learn at least what individuals will head the Ministries directly concerned. Finally, it will extend the period in which our pressures can be applied.

In the Embassy's opinion, the Generalissimo, under the emergency powers granted him by the National Assembly, can sign a bilateral agreement without the necessity of ratification by the Legislative Yuan. We believe it safe to proceed on this assumption, though wê are checking in various governmental quarters, recognizing, however, that no one is in a position to give an authoritative answer in advance of an announcement of the Cabinet and the membership of the Judicial Yuan. The Embassy, accordingly, recommends that the opening of negotiations be deferred until June 1. Meanwhile, pressure for reform will be continued and discussions with the Chinese operating officials of procedures, drawing on experience, should be pushed.

With respect to topics to be covered in corollary discussions, the Embassy believes the Premier's Ten Points of January 28 provide comprehensive agenda with desirable emphasis to be placed on implementation of land reform, on extension of rationing and on fiscal and economic measures to maximize exports. It is presumed that protection of private trade channels can be achieved in the course of specific bilateral negotiations on methods of procurement and distribution of aid commodities.

181

Economic Aid Agreement between the United States of America and the Republic of China, July 3, 1948 [3]

PREAMBLE.

The Government of the United States of America and the Government of the Republic of China:

Considering that it is the policy of the Government of the United States of America to extend economic assistance to the people and the Government of China in accordance with the provisions of the China Aid Act of 1948; and

Considering that it is the policy of the Government of China to undertake a vigorous program of self help in order to create more stable economic conditions in China, and to improve commercial relations with other countries;

Have agreed as follows:

ARTICLE I.

The Government of the United States of America undertakes to assist China, by making available to the Government of China or to any person, agency or

---

[3] Treaties and Other International Acts Series 1837. Printed also in Economic Cooperation Administration, *Economic Aid to China under the China Aid Aut of 1948* (Washington, Feb. 1949), pp. 113–122.

organization designated by the latter Government such assistance as may be requested by it and approved by the Government of the United States of America. The Government of the United States of America will furnish this assistance under the provisions, and subject to all of the terms, limitations and conditions, of the China Aid Act of 1948 (other than Section 404 (b) thereof), acts amendatory and supplementary thereto and appropriation acts thereunder, and will make available to the Government of China only such commodities, services and other assistance as are authorized to be made available by such acts. The Government of the United States of America may suspend or terminate at any time the assistance under this Article.

ARTICLE II.

1. In order to achieve the maximum improvement of economic conditions through the employment of assistance received from the Government of the United States of America, the Government of China undertakes

(a) to adopt or maintain the measures necessary to ensure efficient and practical use of economic resources available to it, including

(1) such measures as may be necessary to ensure that the commodities and services obtained with assistance furnished under this Agreement are used for purposes consistent with this Agreement;

(2) to the extent practicable, measures to locate, identify and put into appropriate use in furtherance of its efforts to improve economic conditions, in China, assets, and earnings therefrom which belong to nationals of China and which are situated within the United States of America, its territories or possessions. Nothing in this clause imposes any obligation on the Government of the United States of America to assist in carrying out such measures or on the Government of China to dispose of such assets;

(b) to promote the development of industrial and agricultural production on a sound economic basis;

(c) to initiate and maintain financial, monetary, budgetary and administrative measures necessary for the creation of more stable currency conditions and for the promotion of production and marketing of goods for domestic consumption and export; and

(d) to cooperate with other countries in facilitating and stimulating an increasing interchange of goods and services with other countries and in reducing public and private barriers to trade with other countries.

2. The Government of China will take the measures which it deems appropriate to prevent, on the part of private or public commercial enterprises, business practices or business arrangements affecting international trade which have the effect of interfering with the purposes and policies of this Agreement.

ARTICLE III.

1. The Government of China undertakes to make all practicable efforts to improve commercial relations with other countries, including measures to improve the conditions affecting the carrying on of foreign trade by private enterprises in China.

2. The Government of China, in carrying out the provisions of paragraph 1 of this Article, will, among other measures, administer such import and exchange controls as are, or may be, made necessary by the exigencies of China's international balance of payments and the foreign exchange resources available to the Government of China, in a uniform, fair and equitable manner.

3. The Government of the United States of America and the Government of China will consult, upon the request of either, regarding any matter relating to the application of the provisions of this Article.

ARTICLE IV.

1. All commodities provided by the Government of the United States of America pursuant to this Agreement shall be processed and distributed by commercial enterprises or by private or Chinese Government agencies, and in accordance with terms and conditions, agreed upon from time to time between the Government of the United States of America and the Government of China.

2. The Government of China, in consultation with representatives of the United States of America, will take all appropriate steps designed to achieve fair and equitable distribution within the areas under its control of commodities provided by the Government of the United States of America pursuant to this Agreement and of similar commodities imported into China with other funds or produced locally. To the extent that circumstances and supply availabilities permit, a distribution and price control system shall be inaugurated or maintained in urban centers of China with the intent of insuring that all classes of the population shall receive a fair share of imported or indigenously produced essential civilian supplies. In permitting expendable commodities made available under this Agreement to be utilized in support of the Chinese efforts to improve consumption and price controls, it is understood that the Government of the United States of America takes no responsibility for the success of these urban programs.

3. The prices at which supplies furnished by the United States of America pursuant to this Agreement will be sold in China shall be agreed upon between the Government of the United States of America and the Government of China.

ARTICLE V.

1. The provisions of this Article shall apply only with respect to assistance which may be furnished by the Government of the United States of America on a grant basis pursuant to this Agreement.

2. The Government of China agrees to establish a special account in the Central Bank of China in the name of the Government of China (hereinafter called the special account) and to make deposits in Chinese currency to this account as follows:

(a) The unencumbered balance at the close of business on the day of the signature of this Agreement in that special account in the Central Bank of China in the name of the Government of China established pursuant to the Agreement between the Government of the United States of America and the Government of China made on October 27, 1947, and any further sums which may from time to time be required by such Agreement to be deposited in that special account. It is understood that subsection (E) of Section 114 of the Foreign Assistance Act of 1948 constitutes the approval and determination of the Government of the United States of America with respect to the disposition of such balance referred to in that Agreement, and

(b) The unencumbered balances of the deposits made by the Government of China pursuant to the exchange of notes between the two Governments dated April 30, 1948.

(c) Amounts commensurate with the indicated dollar cost to the Government of the United States of America of commodities, services and technical information (including any costs of processing, storing, transporting, repairing or other services incident thereto) made available to China on a grant basis pursuant to this Agreement less, however, the amount of deposits made pursuant to the exchange of notes referred to in sub-paragraph (b). The Government of the United States of America shall from time to time notify the Government of China of the indicated dollar cost of any such commodities, services and technical information and the Government of China will deposit in the special account at such times as may be specified by the Government of the United States of America a commensurate amount of Chinese currency computed at a rate of exchange to be agreed upon between the Government of the United States of America and the Government of China. The Government of China will upon the request of the Government of the United States of America make advance deposits in the special account which shall be credited against subsequent notifications pursuant to this paragraph.

3. The Government of the United States of America will from time to time notify the Government of China of its requirements for administrative expenditures in Chinese currency within China incident to operations under the China Aid Act of 1948 and the Government of China will thereupon make such sums available out of any balances in the special account in the manner requested by the Government of the United States of America in the notification.

4. The Government of China will further make such sums of Chinese currency available out of any balances in the special account as may be required to cover : A. Expenditures required to carry out the purposes of the Joint Commission on Rural Reconstruction in China as provided for by Section 407 of the China Aid Act of 1948 ; and B. Costs (including port, storage, handling and similar charges) of transportation from any point of entry in China to the consignee's designated point of delivery in China of such relief supplies and packages as are referred to in Article VII.

5. The Government of China shall dispose of any remaining balance in the special account only for such purposes as may be agreed from time to time with the Government of the United States of America including in particular : A. Sterilization as a measure of monetary and financial stabilization ; B. Expenditures incident to the stimulation of productive activity and the development of new sources of wealth including materials which may be required in the United States of America because of deficiencies or potential deficiencies in the resources of the United States of America ; C. Expenditures upon projects or programs the external costs of which are being covered in whole or in part by assistance rendered by the Government of the United States of America or by loans from the International Bank for Reconstruction and Development; or D. Expenditures upon uncompleted relief or work relief projects undertaken pursuant to the Agreement between the Governments of the United States of America and of China of October 27, 1947.

6. The Government of China will maintain the value in terms of United States dollar equivalent of such amount of the special account as is: A. Indicated by the Government of the United States of America as necessary for administrative expenditures referred to in paragraph 3 of this Article ; B. Required for the purposes of paragraph 4 of this Article ; and C. Agreed between the two Governments to be necessary to defray the expenses in Chinese currency associated with reconstruction projects or programs the external costs of which are met in whole or in part by assistance rendered by the Government of the United States of America pursuant to the Agreement. The Government

of China will carry out this provision by depositing such additional amounts of Chinese currency as the Government of the United States of America may from time to time determine after consultation with the Government of China.

7. Any unencumbered balance remaining in the special account on April 3, 1949, shall be disposed of within China for such purposes as may hereafter be agreed between the Governments of the United States of America and of China, it being understood that the agreement of the United States of America shall be subject to approval by act or joint resolution of the Congress of the United States of America.

ARTICLE VI.

1. The Government of China will facilitate the transfer to the United States of America for stockpiling or other purposes of materials originating in China which are required by the United States of America as a result of deficiencies or potential deficiencies in its own resources upon such reasonable terms of sale, exchange, barter or otherwise and in such quantities and for such period of time as may be agreed to between the Governments of the United States of America and of China after due regard for the reasonable requirements of China for domestic use and commercial export of such materials. The Government of China will take such specific measures as may be necessary to carry out the provisions of this paragraph. The Government of China will, when so requested by the Government of the United States of America, enter into negotiations for detailed arrangements necessary to carry out the provisions of this paragraph.

2. The Government of China will, when so requested by the Government of the United States of America, negotiate such arrangements as are appropriate to carry out the provisions of paragraph (9) of subsection 115 (b) of the Foreign Assistance Act of 1948 which relates to the development and transfer of materials required by the United States of America.

3. The Government of China, when so requested by the Government of the United States of America, will cooperate, wherever appropriate, to further the objectives of paragraphs 1 and 2 of this Article in respect of materials originating outside of China.

ARTICLE VII.

The Government of China will, when so requested by the Government of the United States of America, enter into negotiations for agreements (including the provisions of duty free treatment under appropriate safeguards) to facilitate the entry into China of supplies of relief goods donated to or purchased by United States voluntary non-profit relief agencies and of relief packages originating in the United States of America and consigned to individuals residing in China.

ARTICLE VIII.

1. The two Governments will, upon the request of either of them, consult regarding any matter relating to the application of this Agreement or to operations or arrangements carried out pursuant to this Agreement.

2. The Government of China will communicate to the Government of the United States of America in a form and at intervals to be indicated by the latter after consultation with the Government of China:

(a) detailed information regarding projects, programs and measures proposed or adopted by the Government of China to carry out the provisions of this Agreement;

(b) full statements of operations under this Agreement, including a statement of the use of funds, commodities and services received thereunder, such statements to be made in each calendar quarter;

(c) information regarding its economy and any other relevant information which the Government of the United States of America may need to determine the nature and scope of operations, and to evaluate the effectiveness of assistance furnished or contemplated under this Agreement.

3. The Government of China will assist the Government of the United States of America to obtain information relating to the materials originating in China referred to in Article VI which is necessary to the formulation and execution of the arrangements provided for in that Article.

ARTICLE IX.

1. The Government of China will keep the people of China fully informed of the progress achieved by the Government of China in implementing the undertakings contained in this Agreement designed to achieve more stable economic conditions in China, and it will provide continuously information to the people of China regarding the nature and extent of assistance furnished pursuant to this Agreement. It will make such information available to the media of public information and will take practicable steps to ensure that appropriate facilities are provided for the dissemination of such information.

2. The Government of the United States of America will encourage the dissemination of such information and will make it available to the media of public information.

3. The Government of China will make public in China in each calendar quarter full statements of operations under this Agreement, including information as to the uses of funds, commodities and services received.

ARTICLE X.

1. The Government of China agrees to receive a Special Mission for Economic Cooperation which will discharge the responsibilities of the Government of the United States of America in China under this Agreement.

2. The Government of China will, upon appropriate notification from the Ambassador of the United States of America in China, consider the Special Mission and its personnel as part of the Embassy of the United States of America in China for the purposes of enjoying the privileges and immunities accorded to that Embassy and its personnel of comparable rank. The Government of China will further accord appropriate courtesies to the members and staff of the Joint Committee on Foreign Economic Cooperation of the Congress of the United States of America and will grant them the facilities and assistance necessary to the effective performance of their responsibilities.

3. The Government of China will extend full cooperation to the Special Mission and to the members and staff of the Joint Committee. Such cooperation shall include the provision of all information and facilities necessary to the observation and review of the carrying out of this Agreement, including the use of assistance furnished under it.

ARTICLE XI.

1. The Governments of the United States of America and of China agree to submit to the decision of the International Court of Justice any claim espoused by either Government on behalf of one of its nationals against the other Govern-

ment for compensation for damage arising as a consequence of governmental measures (other than measures concerning enemy property or interests) taken after April 3, 1948 by the other Government and affecting property or interests of such national including contracts with or concessions granted by duly authorized authorities of such other Government. It is understood that the undertaking of each Government in respect of claims espoused by the other Government pursuant to this paragraph is made in the case of each Government under the authority of and is limited by the terms and conditions of such effective recognition as it has heretofore given to the compulsory jurisdiction of the International Court of Justice under Article 36 of the Statute of the Court. The provisions of this paragraph shall be in all respects without prejudice to other rights of access, if any, of either Government to the International Court of Justice or to the espousal and presentation of claims based upon alleged violations by either Government of rights and duties arising under treaties, agreements or principles of international law.

2. The Governments of the United States of America and of China further agree that such claims may be referred in lieu of the Court to any arbitral tribunal mutually agreed upon.

3. It is further understood that neither Government will espouse a claim pursuant to this Article unless the national concerned has exhausted the remedies available to him in the administrative and judicial tribunals of the country in which the claim exists.

ARTICLE XII.

1. This Agreement shall become effective on this day's date. It shall remain in force until June 30, 1950, and, unless at least six months before June 30, 1950, either Government shall have given the other notice in writing of intention to terminate the Agreement on that date, it shall remain in force thereafter until the expiration of six months from the date on which such notice shall have been given. Article V shall remain in effect until all the sums in the currency of China required to be disposed of in accordance with its own terms have been disposed of as provided in such Article.

2. This Agreement may be amended at any time by agreement between the two Governments.

3. The Annex to this Agreement forms an integral part thereof.

4. This Agreement shall be registered with the Secretary-General of the United Nations.

In witness whereof the respective representatives duly authorized for the purpose have signed the present Agreement.

Done at Nanking in duplicate in the English and Chinese languages, both texts authentic, this third day of July 1948, corresponding to the third day of the seventh month of the thirty-seventh year of the Republic of China.

J. LEIGHTON STUART,
For the Government of the
United States of America.

WANG SHIH-CHIEH,
For the Government of
The Republic of China.

ANNEX.

1. It is understood that the requirements of paragraph 1 (a) of Article II, relating to the adoption of measures for the efficient use of resources would

include, with respect to commodities furnished under the Agreement, effective measures for safeguarding such commodities and for preventing their diversion to illegal or irregular markets or channels of trade.

2. It is understood that the Government of China will not be requested, under paragraph 2 (a) of Article VIII to furnish detailed information about minor projects or confidential commercial or technical information the disclosure of which would injure legitimate commercial interests.

3. It is understood that the Government of the United States of America in making the notifications referred to in paragraph 2 of Article X would bear in mind the desirability of restricting, so far as practicable, the number of officials for whom full diplomatic privileges would be requested. It is also understood that the detailed application of Article X would, when necessary, be the subject of intergovernmental discussion.

NANKING, *July 3, 1948*

J. LEIGHTON STUART
WANG SHIH-CHIEH

182

Informal Memorandum Regarding Basic Reforms, Handed by Ambassador Stuart to President Chiang Kai-shek on May 22, 1948

The American people noted with deep interest the statement issued on January 28, 1948, by the President of the Executive Yuan which comprised ten financial and economic reform measures which the Chinese Government intended to undertake. The United States Government, including the Congress during its debate of the Aid to China Act, accepted this statement as a program which the Chinese Government would vigorously pursue in order to insure by its own actions that financial assistance from the United States Government would provide the maximum results for the Chinese people.

The Premier's statement represented a coherent and promising framework for individual measures and actions of the Chinese Government. A number of measures in execution of this program have been taken with respect to these objectives but they have often appeared as isolated acts, unnoted and even unrelated to the program as a whole. And in some important areas it has seemed that no appreciable progress can be measured in the past four months. Some of these areas, apparently vacant insofar as effective action and visible results are concerned, are noted below. The numbering of the paragraphs below follows the numbering of the Premier's ten points.

1. On control of Government expenditures, even granting all the difficulties, little seems to have been accomplished. The first steps would appear to be to establish standardized accounting with firm budgetary controls in the hands of a central fiscal authority possessing the power to determine allocations for all expenditures whether military or civil. Needless to say, this authority would require the unremitting personal support of the President. Another step would be the ruthless elimination of all non-productive expenditures. In both the civilian and military establishments there would appear to be room for the removal of duplicatory or unnecessary services and individuals.

2. With respect to securing an increase in tax yields and distributing the tax burden more equitably, it is recognized that the severity of the inflation of the

currency accentuates the Government's difficulties. It is a truism, however, that public confidence in the currency can only be recaptured if a drastic reduction in curtailable expenses is accompanied by a massive increase in tax collections. Even to the casual observer the administration of existing tax collection measures can be greatly improved. It is my impression, for instance, that urban real estate taxes are low compared to tax rates in the country districts. Increased reliance on ad valorem taxes and taxes collected at the source should help to compensate for loss of real revenues due to currency depreciation. The projected sale of certain Government assets is surely another step in the right direction which could be effectively followed by further acts of the same sort.

3. Although superficially increases in wages of civil servants and soldiers will add to the budgetary difficulty, it would seem essential that equitable adjustments must be made if loyalty and efficiency are to be retained. The weeding out of unnecessary personnel should be tied directly to the program of upward salary adjustments.

4. The rice and flour rationing program seems by general agreement to have been a substantial success, particularly in Shanghai, Canton, Peiping and Tientsin, and to lesser degree in Nanking. It would seem that this experience urgently justifies increasing the number of urban centers in which a rationing system is installed and, equally important, increasing the number of commodities covered. I have particularly in mind the addition of edible oils, cotton cloth, kerosene and automotive gasoline. Accompanying this would be the institution of practical measures to get commodities such as kerosene and cotton yarn flowing into the agricultural areas to provide the incentive for increased production and collection of foodstuffs.

5. It would appear that the fifth objective of the Prime Minister can only approach achievement if reduction of expenditures and increase in tax collections are vigorously and successfully pursued as a first step.

6. It would seem that the Central Bank has made some progress in its efforts to check speculation and pursue a deflationary credit policy. Loopholes, however, obviously continue to exist through which capital finds refuge in foreign currency and transfers abroad. The loss, both of Government customs revenues and foreign exchange, appears to be substantial in the two-way smuggling operations which by common report are widespread. The intensification of the present campaign against smuggling would yield returns to the Government on both scores. The Maritime Customs will need support and re-equipping to play their part.

7. Internal measures can reduce Chinese dependence upon the large imports now needed but only if such measures are accompanied by successful efforts to increase exports from China can the foreign exchange crisis be surmounted. There are many measures which the business community has repeatedly pointed out would contribute to an increase in exports. One such measure would be the directing of incentive goods referred to above into the interior areas of production. Another would be the establishment of realistic exchange rates for foreign currencies. Another would be the reduction in red tape now involved in arranging exports. Finally, the Government could do much by concentrating its encouragments on exporting industries which could increase their exportable surplus if for example, they were given priorities for securing spare parts and raw materials which must be imported.

8. On import controls, a clear policy of encouraging private enterprise by simplification of procedures would seem to promise the best results. Such acts

as the recent issuance of regulation No. 131 by the Central Bank should be considered in these terms in advance of promulgation. The result of this particular regulation has been to bring the import trade to a complete standstill and to deepen the already deep discouragement.

9. The recommendations of the joint Sino-American Agricultural Mission, many of which have been only partially acted upon, seem to provide a comprehensive framework for action in this important field. If there is any single area where reform in deeds and not words is most necessary and most sought by the people, it is land reform. The Land Law of April 29, 1946 contains a carefully considered program regarding limitations on land ownership, land redistribution, and of utmost importance, control and reduction of rents and taxes. Subsequent regulations dealing with particular aspects of land reform have been contained in such measures as the Principles Governing the Administration of Areas Aimed at Achieving Social Stability and Relieving the People, passed by the Supreme National Defense Council on October 23, 1946 and the "Measures for Disposition of Land Ownership in Pacification Areas," promulgated by the Executive Yuan on October 26, 1946. One hears on all sides that reforms have not yet been carried out, and the special investigators of the Executive Yuan have reported on various occasions regarding the non-implementation of these measures. Carefully prepared measures extending land reform to wider areas were strongly recommended by the Ministry of Land Administration to the Conference of Pacification Areas Commanders held in Nanking in March 1948. Successful policies which have related land and agrarian reform to the problem of defense seem to have been applied in the 10th Adminstrative Area of Hopei Province, which might merit extension to other areas.

10. Under the difficulties imposed by internal strife and shortage of materials, the restoration of the Chinese railroads has been inspiring. In the broad field of communications and reconstruction of industry important steps have been achieved. There are some related areas where it would seem China's self-interest would dictate action. For example, the closure of the River ports to foreign flag ocean shipping is contrary to the policy of great nations. This situation damages China's own interests in that transportation costs are heavily increased on American Aid oil shipments to Hankow, to take one case. The delay in reaching agreement in the long drawn out negotiations on the restoration of pre-war cable facilities is another case in point. Meanwhile certain difficulties which have arisen in connection with the Sino-U. S. Bilateral Air Transport Agreement remain unresolved.

In conclusion, the Premier's statement seems as cogent and comprehensive today as on the date when it was issued. There would seem to be nothing to add to this statement of objectives but there would seem much still to be done in attaining them. China does not seek a subsidy but it has looked to the United States for help in this difficult period in order that it might the better help itself. It was in this spirit that the United States Government has responded and it is in these terms that the American people and the American Congress in the coming months will follow with acute interest the progress that the Chinese Government makes in solving the broad and pressing problems of economic and financial reform.

183

Exchange of Notes between the United States Government and the Republic of China, Signed in Nanking on August 5, 1948, Providing for the Establishment of a Sino-American Joint Commission on Rural Reconstruction [4]

The Ambassador in China (Stuart) to the Chinese Minister for Foreign Affairs (Wang)

EXCELLENCY: I have the honor to refer to Section 407 of the China Aid Act of 1948 enacted by the Government of the United States of America (hereinafter referred to as the Act), which provides, among other things, for the conclusion of an agreement between China and the United States of America establishing a Joint Commission on Rural Reconstruction in China. In pursuance of the general principles laid down in the Act, and in particular section 407 thereof, I have the honor to bring forward the following proposals regarding the organization of the Joint Commission and related matters:

1. There shall be established a Joint Commission on Rural Reconstruction in China (hereinafter referred to as the Commission) to be composed of two citizens of the United States of America appointed by the President of the United States of America and three citizens of the Republic of China to be appointed by the President of China. The Commission shall elect one of the Chinese members as chairman.

2. The functions and authority of the Commission shall, subject to the provisions of the above-mentioned section of the Act, be as follows: (a) to formulate and carry out through appropriate Chinese Government agencies and international or private agencies in China a coordinated program for reconstruction in rural areas of China (hereinafter referred to as the program); (b) to conclude arrangements with the agencies referred to in the preceding paragraph establishing a basis for their cooperation; (c) to recommend to the Governments of the United States of America and of China within the limits prescribed by the Act the allocation of funds and other assistance to the program, and to recommend to the Government of China the allocation of such other funds and assistance as are deemed essential to the success of the program; (d) to establish standards of performance for implementation of the program, including the qualifications, type and number of personnel to be used by cooperating agencies in the program, and to maintain a constant supervision of all phases of the program with authority to recommend changes in or stoppage of any phase of the program; (e) to appoint such executive officers and administrative staff as the Commission deems necessary to carry out the program, it being understood that the chief executive officer shall be a citizen of China. Salaries, expenses of travel, and other expenses incident to the administrative functions of the Commission itself shall be paid from funds made available under Section 407 (B) of the Act.

3. In its program the Commission may include the following types of activity to be carried out in agreement with the agencies referred to in paragraph 2 (a): (a) A coordinated extension-type program in agriculture, home demonstration, health and education for initiation in a selected group of Hsien in several

---

[4] Printed in Economic Cooperation Administration, *Economic Aid to China under the China Aid Act of 1948* (Washington, Feb. 1949), pp. 126–129.

provinces to include a limited number of subsidiary projects suited to conditions in the areas where the program is developed, in such fields as agricultural production, marketing, credit, irrigation, home and community industries, nutrition, sanitation, and education of a nature which will facilitate the promotion of all projects being undertaken; (b) Consultation with the Chinese Government concerning ways and means of progressively carrying out land reform measures; (c) Subsidiary projects in research training and manufacturing to be carried out in suitable locations to provide information, personnel and materials required by the program; (d) Projects to put into effect over a wider area than provided for in the coordinated extension-type program specified in (a) any of the above lines of activity which can be developed soundly on a larger scale, of which examples might be the multiplication and distribution of improved seeds, the control of rinderpest of cattle, the construction of irrigation and drainage facilities and the introduction of health and sanitation measures; (e) Related measures in line with the general objectives of this program; (f) The distribution of the assistance in this program on the principle of giving due attention to strengthening rural improvement in areas where selected projects can be progressively developed and where their development will contribute most effectively to the achievement of purposes for which this program is undertaken but that the principle of distributing aid will not be controlled by proportionate or geographical consideration *per se.*

4. In respect of any decision of the Commission, the approval of the Government of China shall be obtained prior to its execution if the Commission or its chairman, with the concurrence of the Chinese members, deems it necessary.

5. The Commission shall publish in China and transmit to the Government of the United States of America and the Government of China, in such form and at such times as may be requested by either of the two governments, full statements of operations, including a statement on the use of funds, supplies and services received, and will transmit to the two governments any other matter pertinent to operations as requested by either of the two governments. The Government of China will keep the people of China fully informed of the intended purpose and scope of the program and of the progress achieved by the Commission in implementing the program, including the nature and extent of the assistance furnished by the Government of the United States of America.

6. The Government of China will, upon appropriate notification of the Ambassador of the United States of America in China, consider the United States members and personnel of the Commission as part of the Embassy of the United States of America in China for the purpose of enjoying the privileges and immunities accorded to that Embassy and its personnel of comparable rank. It is understood that the Ambassador of the United States of America in China in making the notification will bear in mind the desirability of restricting so far as practicable the number of officials for whom full diplomatic privileges and immunities would be requested. It is also understood that the detailed application of this paragraph would, when necessary, be a subject of inter-governmental discussion.

7. All supplies imported into China for use in the program shall be free of customs duties, conservancy dues, and other charges imposed by the Government of China on similar supplies which are imported through regular commercial channels.

8. The Government of the United States of America and the Government of China will consult with respect to problems incident to the interpretation, implementation and possible amendment of the terms of the agreement embodied in

this exchange of notes whenever either of the two governments considers such action appropriate.

9. The Government of the United States of America reserves the right at any time to terminate or suspend its assistance or any part thereof provided under this exchange of notes. Assistance furnished by the Government of the United States of America under Section 407 of the Act and pursuant to this exchange of notes shall not be construed as an express or implied assumption by the Government of the United States of America of any responsibility for making any further contributions to carry out the purpose of Section 407 of the Act or of this exchange of notes.

10. This note and Your Excellency's reply accepting the above proposals on behalf of the Government of China will constitute an agreement between the two governments in the sense of Section 407 of the Act. Subject to the provisions of paragraphs 8 and 9, this exchange of notes will remain in force until June 30, 1949, or, upon the request of either government transmitted to the other government at least two months before June 30, 1949, until the date of termination of the Economic Aid Agreement between the two governments concluded on July 3, 1948.

I avail myself [etc.]

J. LEIGHTON STUART

The Chinese Minister for Foreign Affairs (Wang) to the Ambassador in China (Stuart)

EXCELLENCY: I have the honor to acknowledge receipt of your note of today's date which reads as follows:

[Here follows text of preceding note.]

On behalf of the Government of China I have the honor to accept the proposals contained in the note quoted above.

In recognition of the importance of the program as one of the essential means of achieving the objectives in which the Governments of China and of the United States of America unite in seeking under the Economic Aid Agreement between the two governments concluded on July 3, 1948 the Government of China undertakes to afford to the execution of the program the full weight of its support and to direct cooperating agencies of the Government of China including the local officials concerned to give such assistance and facilities as are essential to the success of their undertakings under the program.

I avail myself of this opportunity to renew to your Excellency the assurances of my highest consideration.

WANG SHIH-CHIEH

184

Economic Aid to China under the China Aid Act of 1948 [5]

PART I—INTRODUCTION

At the time the China Aid Act was passed, China was in the grip of the longest sustained inflation in modern history. Her external resources had dwindled from approximately a billion dollars on V–J Day to less than one-quarter of that

[5] Excerpts from document published by the Economic Cooperation Administration Washington, February 1949.

sum at the beginning of 1948. Foreign trade was at a low ebb. Continuation of deficit financing to support the civil war against the Communists kept the fires of inflation burning; the currency inflation in turn caused production and other constructive business activity to stagnate and contributed greatly to a popular loss of confidence in the National Government. While the military strength of the Communists was increasing, Nationalist strength was being sapped by military defeats, sinking morale among the troops, and a crumbling economic front in the rear of the Government's armies.

Character of the 1948 Economic Aid Program for China

The China Aid Program was not originally conceived as something that could by itself turn back or even arrest these trends. It was described as an effort to "assist in retarding the current economic deterioration and thus give the Chinese Government further opportunity to initiate the measures necessary to the establishment of more stable economic conditions."

The program of economic aid was organized and carried on against a background of continuing civil war and progressive contraction of the area and resources under the control of the National Government. It has been directed toward bringing economic assistance as directly as possible to areas and people who have needed the type of assistance which could be supplied by the use of U.S. dollars.

Food has been provided through a controlled ration system to nearly 13,000,000 inhabitants of seven major Chinese cities. Cotton financed under the program has kept the mills operating in China's largest industry, providing cloth for direct consumption, for barter to encourage the bringing of indigenous food into the cities, and for export to earn foreign exchange that can be used to pay for more imports. Petroleum has kept in operation basic utilities, transport facilities and industries, and also provided goods for which the farmers in the countryside are prepared to exchange their produce. Fertilizer imports have been planned for use in the production of spring crops in 1949. A Joint Commission on Rural Reconstruction has been established, and has formulated principles and a program for attacking some of the root causes of poverty and unrest among China's vast rural population. An industrial program of replacement machinery and reconstruction projects has been initiated with the participation of private American engineering firms; although actual procurement and construction had to be suspended for the most part due to uncertainties connected with the civil war, much useful engineering survey work has been done. A "counterpart" fund in local currency, established by agreement with the Chinese Government and managed jointly by Chinese and Americans, has been used to maintain many hospitals, welfare programs, and dike-building projects.

In spite of the growing chaos around them, these activities, by and large, have been managed with care and have been carried out successfully within their own limited terms of reference. In the case of the commodity program particularly, the supplies provided have been an important and at times crucial factor in keeping unrest to a minimum in the main cities of the coastal areas controlled by the Nationalist Government. In this narrow but significant sense, therefore, the efforts of EcA in China have been constructive and useful. Supplies financed by the U.S. have been and are being effectively distributed to the people intended to receive them.

Economic Aid in a Setting of General Deterioration

But the atmosphere surrounding these efforts has been one of continuing discouragement and defeat for those who had hoped the Chinese National Government, after a decade of upheaval and in face of all difficulties, could and would do the things that needed to be done if it were to provide an adequate counter-force to the Communists in China. The incapacity of the Government to put into effect the reforms which it had in January announced its intention of initiating; the inability of the Nationalist commanders to lead and inspire an effective military effort against the growing Communist threat; a series of ill-conceived economic and financial measures which made the situation behind the lines even worse than it needed to be; the widening breach between the people and their Government—all these were factors so demoralizing in their effect that it became only a matter of time until the Government would reach the brink of disaster.

Chinese economic problems cannot be separated from problems which are ordinarily termed political and military. The inflation itself, dramatic as it has been, is only a symptom of broader and deeper problems. The prodigious increase in the issue of currency has been a devastating economic fact, but the reason for it is to be sought in the military fact that more than two-thirds of all currency issued has been used directly to support the Government's military efforts. Sudden increases in the velocity of circulation can be related directly to sudden drops in public confidence due to military defeats.

On August 19, 1948, the Chinese Government published a series of apparently sweeping financial reforms, in an attempt to arrest the runaway inflation of the Chinese National Currency (CN), and draw in for public use the large private holdings of foreign exchange. The drastic and dramatic reforms, including the introduction of a new Gold Yuan (GY) currency, seemed to hold the inflation in suspense for more than a month. But they did nothing to increase revenues or to reduce expenditures; thus they failed to attack the basic cause of the inflation, which is the gross imbalance of the Government's budget. Internal contradictions in the new regulations soon appeared. A new commodity tax was not put into effect because it would have meant breaking the price ceilings set forth in the same regulations. Although the Government reported collection of more than US$150 million worth of foreign exchange, it had to pay out in return so large an amount of the new Gold Yuan currency, without any compensating increase in supplies or production, that the new currency rapidly depreciated further both in real value and in the esteem of the Chinese people.

With these economic influences at work, the resumption of the inflationary spiral and a breakdown of the attempt to maintain August 19 ceiling prices was inevitable. Attempts to enforce arbitrary price ceilings in Shanghai, and to a less extent in other cities, brought about an almost complete stagnation of economic activity. The more strictly the regulations were enforced, the less food came into the cities, and the worse the situation became. Finally, in November, the regulations became so ineffective and disruptive of economic activity that they were officially revoked in the face of a downward slide of the Gold Yuan which has continued thereafter.

Internal financial deterioration and the maintenance of artificial exchange rates have held down official receipts by the Chinese Government from exports and inward remittances. Although China has had to draw down also some $100 million from her contracted dollar assets, official holdings of foreign exchange may have exceeded slightly, at the end of 1948, the balance existing when the China Aid Act was passed. This has been due in part to the existence of the China Aid Program itself, which has paid for most of China's basic commodity imports since June 1948. But it has been due also to two factors unfavorable to China: first, the fact that imports outside the ECA program were held to a level so low as to impair seriously production and trade; and second, the fact that private exchange holdings were called in under the August 19 regulations in such a way as to heighten the inflation and at the same time to wipe out extensively, middle class savings. Thus the balancing for a time of China's official international payments accounts was achieved at a prohibitive internal cost.

China's drawings upon restricted foreign exchange resources were largely for current requirements, not for importations of capital equipment. The Government even sold valuable productive properties in order to meet current outlays.

A further debilitating effect of the civil war was to be found in the phenomenon of "disinvestment" within China, which contrasted with the process of expanding investment in the ECA-aided countries of Europe. In a setting of spiralling inflation and universal uncertainty as to the future, private capital was almost wholly directed into non-productive channels of financial speculation and hoarding of goods for sale at higher prices; banks demonstrated an increasing reluctance to extend long-term credit for industrial investment. As a result, not only did China's productive plant fail to expand, but existing productive facilities deterioriated. The lack of repairs and rehabilitation of productive capacity has lowered output.

These facts, taken together, point to a steady decline in the overall productive capacity of the Chinese economy during 1948.

The relationship between military defeat and economic deterioration has been further demonstrated in the case of coal and food supplies.

Coal production in China during 1948 was at about the same level as 1947. Supplies reaching consuming areas, however, were sharply reduced, particularly during the latter half of the year, as mining centers were cut off or fell into Communist hands. An especially serious loss, toward the end of the year was that of the output from the Kailan Mines north of Tientsin, which were supplying more than half of the coal produced in the whole of Nationalist China.

The output of foodstuffs in 1948 reached a postwar peak at a level roughly equal to that of prewar years. In spite of this recovery in the agricultural regions, China's urban centers were able to meet their food requirements only with the continuing assistance afforded by substantial shipments from abroad. Factors contributing to this situation were Communist occupations of producing areas in Manchuria and much of north China and the consequent disruption of distribution patterns; and, in accessible areas—particularly, during the autumn months—an increasing unwillingness on the part of farmers to market their crops in view of rigid price controls and continuing currency depreciation.

Similar trends could be noted in every other sector of the economy. Mill output of cotton textiles held up during the first half of the year at 1947 levels and then began to drop sharply. Operable rail mileage in Nationalist hands was reduced by 2,500 kilometers despite the rehabilitation of lines in the south. Shipping capacity was maintained but the pressure of military needs reduced the amount available for commercial requirements. Costly air traffic increased under the necessity of supplying cities besieged by Communist armies. During the last few months of the year, important cities in north and central China were virtually cut off from major supply sources and economic activity became thoroughly demoralized. ECA imports, in the latter part of the year, played an increasingly large role in supplying urban areas with essential food and raw materials.

Preliminary Review of the ECA China Aid Program

Within a few weeks after the Economic Cooperation Administration came into being, economic aid to China was an operating reality. Initial funds from the

Reconstruction Finance Corporation were advanced to ECA, a "Program No. 1" for using these funds was approved by the Administrator, and the first procurement authorization was issued. An exchange of notes between the Secretary of State and the Chinese Ambassador in Washington set up interim arrangements for providing assistance pending conclusion of a formal bilateral agreement. Mr. Roger D. Lapham was appointed Chief of the ECA Mission to China, arriving at his post in Shanghai the first week of June. The Chinese Government created a Council for U.S. Aid, a cabinet level committee to deal with the ECA Program. To "backstop" the Mission, a China Program Division was created in the ECA Headquarters office. And on July 3, three months after the Foreign Assistance Act was approved, the formal Economic Aid Agreement between China and the United States was signed by the Chinese Foreign Minister and the U.S. Ambassador to China.

The ECA Mission to China was faced with the problem of getting itself organized quickly for the job ahead. To speed up the process, it took over and adapted to the new purpose the China Relief Mission which had been responsible in China for the U.S. Foreign Relief Program under Public Law 84 (Eightieth Congress). ECA also inherited some continuing functions of a relief character, including the distribution of P. L. 84 supplies which had not reached end-users by the time that law expired, on June 30, 1948. ECA likewise continued support to a number of special projects started by the China Relief Mission and financed from a local currency "Special Account."

Operating under a strict limitation on dollar administrative expenses, the Mission has made a maximum use of alien staff, paid in local currency. ECA has arranged for a part of the work of supervising and controlling portions of the program to be done by private firms and voluntary relief agencies.

The program itself has consisted of three parts: the provision of a limited number of basic commodities (food, fuel, cotton, fertilizer and coal); the initiation of an industrial replacement and reconstruction program; the formation and support of a Joint Commission on Rural Reconstruction in China. In addition, ECA has participated in the management and use of a Special Account, or "counterpart" fund, in Chinese currency provided by the Chinese Government. Of the total $275 million appropriation for the ECA China Program, $203.8 million was earmarked for commodities, $67.5 million for the industrial program, $2.5 million for dollar expenditures on the rural reconstruction program, and $1.2 million for administration.

The commodity program called for average ECA imports into China of supplies costing roughly $20 million a month. As of December 31, $194 million of the commodity funds had been authorized for procurement, and about $112 million worth of these supplies had arrived in China. The commodity program was, therefore, well up to schedule. But obligations against the industrial program had been limited to allotments of money for "preproject" engineering survey work. Toward the end of the year, some of the projects were about ready to start actual procurement and construction work; but in December, it was necessary to suspend allocations for such work pending clarification of the political and military situation in China. Similarly, the Rural Reconstruction Commission was only emerging from the planning stage at the end of 1948, and had tapped only a small part of the $2.5 million set aside for its U.S. dollar expenses.

In all phases of the program, as much emphasis as practicable has been placed on the use of commercial channels of supply and distribution. The food program is the sole exception as regards supply; rice from southeast Asia and wheat and flour from the U.S. have been bought and shipped by the Commodity Credit Corporation, an agency of the U.S. Department of Agriculture. The major portion of the petroleum products, most of which originate in the Persian Gulf, have been procured and shipped by private oil companies. American cotton has been shipped by American firms and received in China by American cotton importers. Fertilizer, coming from a variety of sources under allocations by the International Emergency Food Committee, has likewise been supplied through private commercial channels.

After each commodity shipment arrives in China, the ECA Mission keeps track of its receipt, processing, distribution, and end use. Food is distributed through the first general civilian rationing system ever developed in China's urban areas, with the Chinese Government and ECA each providing a part of the total ration requirements. Cotton becomes yarn, yarn becomes cloth, and the end-products are used for export, for barter and for domestic sale—all under the watchful observation of a Joint Management Board in which ECA participates. Petroleum products are distributed by the importing companies, who themselves assist in end-use control and reporting, and provide detailed sales records for each product to the ECA Mission. As of December 31, 1948, fertilizer had not been distributed since it was for use in 1949 spring production; a part, it was planned, would be handled in direct exchange with farmers for rice, a part sold through commercial channels and a part used by the Rural Reconstruction Commission. The small amount of coal imported before the end of the year went directly to utilities and other users under the supervision of the ECA China Mission. Medical supplies imported by ECA's predecessor in China, the U.S. China Relief Mission, are distributed by a special group set up by agreement between the Ministry of Health and voluntary agencies. Pesticides, also inherited from the China Relief Mission, have been distributed largely through commercial channels, the remainder being earmarked for agricultural demonstration purposes.

The industrial program started with an intensive investigation of proposed replacement and reconstruction projects conducted by a special Reconstruction Survey Group. This group faced a double problem—an extensive need for replacement and reconstruction equipment, and a serious lack of the engineering and management skills needed in China to make certain that such equipment would be effectively absorbed into the economy. The group prepared tentative recommendations for allocation among approved projects from the $67.5 million set aside for this purpose. The projects thus recommended were largely limited to the field of basic industry and transportation—the largest provisional allotments proposed being for power plants, coal mines, the rehabilitation of railroads, and the manufacture of fertilizer. The Survey Group also developed procedures for making maximum use of private American engineering firms as "project engineers" to help individual projects in drawing up plans, procuring the right equipment, and making sure that equipment is correctly installed and effectively operated. To manage the whole scheme, ECA and the Chinese Government agreed to retain a high-grade American firm of management engineers.

The uncertainties in the China situation had in December caused the suspension of all but survey work under this program, leaving open the possibility of selected projects being carried forward as circumstances permit. The technique adopted for administering this program may prove to be of significance in relation to future programs involving industrial projects in underdeveloped countries.

The Joint Commission on Rural Reconstruction in China was established in accordance with Section 407 of the China Aid Act to "formulate and carry out a program for reconstruction in rural areas of China." Initiated on August 5 by an exchange of notes between the Chinese and U.S. Governments, the Joint

Commission consisted of three Chinese and two American members, appointed in September by the Presidents of China and of the United States.

Intensive planning and survey work were undertaken by the Commission after the members had agreed on the general statement of objectives and principles. In general, the Commission has been moving in the direction of: assisting people in rural areas to improve their living conditions, increase food production, and develop local self-government; strengthening and improving the operations of government agencies concerned with rural problems; stimulating local movements and private agencies in efforts on behalf of the rural people; and affording to progressive elements in the population real opportunities to participate in the program. The Joint Commission operates under the supervision of the Administrator, who has delegated his authority in this field to the Chief of the ECA Mission to China. The American members and staff of the Commission are ECA staff members engaged in full-time work with the Commission.

A special concern of the ECA in connection with the China Program has been the development of sources of strategic materials required by the U.S. Although China is a major producer of three such materials—tin, tungsten, and antimony—the limitations upon funds for stockpiling purposes have made it impracticable to pick up antimony and tungsten which are available for purchase in China. Extensive investigations on the development and supply of tin concentrates and tin metal, however, had resulted before the end of December 1948, in a tentative arrangement for tin purchasing as part of a general scheme for rationalizing the supply of metal and the development of processing facilities in Yunnan Province.

The special local currency account, or counterpart fund, provided for in the Economic Aid Agreement with China, differed from corresponding accounts in Europe, two of its features being unique. The first is an arrangement for deposits of local currency, which leaves the timing of deposits in the discretion of the U.S. Government; this discretion is used to relate deposits to actual needs for the local currency, without large surpluses which would rapidly shrink in value. The second unique feature is a "maintenance of value" clause which provides that for certain important uses the Chinese Government would protect appropriations made from the special account against currency depreciation, by expressing the appropriation in terms of some more stable unit, such as U.S. dollars or a basic commodity like rice or cotton yarn.

Since it was clear from the outset that the sterilization of the entire special account would not by itself be an important influence toward control of the inflation, the Chinese Government and the ECA, after consultation with the National Advisory Council in Washingon, followed a policy of making expenditures from the account for important public purposes which might not otherwise be provided for, if such expenditures were of demonstrated urgency. The main categories of expenditures have been for administrative costs, the expenses of delivering relief packages and supplies in China, local currency costs of projects sponsored by the Joint Commission on Rural Reconstruction, expenditures on special projects in the field of water conservancy, health and welfare, and the internal costs to date of the replacement and reconstruction program, in cases where money could not be raised from other sources. It was estimated, according to the plans envisaged during 1948, that the total of these expenditures would amount to less than half of the total potential account.

By the end of December 1948, notifications of U.S. grant aid had been given to the Chinese Government to the amount of $94,470,926. According to preliminary and tentative estimates, pending final determination upon a formula for computing exchange rates, Gold Yuan equivalent to approximately $9,543,000 had been requested for deposits, and the equivalent of approximately $5,839,000 had been spent.

PART II—ECONOMIC AID PROGRAM FOR CHINA TO DECEMBER 31, 1948

Scope and Rationale

The President, in his message of February 18, 1948, to Congress on aid to China recommended authorization of an economic aid program in the amount of $570 million, to provide assistance over a fifteen-month period extending to June 30, 1949. Of this amount, $510 million was estimated as required for financing essential commodity imports into China, "which would permit the Chinese Government to devote its limited dollar resources to the most urgent of its other needs," and $60 million was recommended for "a few selected reconstruction projects to be initiated prior to June 30, 1949." "Essential imports" cited included cereals, cotton, petroleum, fertilizer, tobacco, pharmaceuticals, coal and repair parts for existing capital equipment. Reduced to a twelve-month basis, the program of economic assistance proposed by the President would have called for approximately $403 million for commodity shipments to China and an additional $60 million for aid to selected reconstruction projects.

The China Aid Act of 1948 authorized for expenditure during the ensuing twelve-month period (April 3, 1948, to April 2, 1949) $338 million for economic assistance to China, of which $275 million has been appropriated, and an additional $125 million for aid to China through grants "on such terms as the President may determine and without regard to the provisions of the Economic Cooperation Act of 1948."

The program of economic aid to China administered by the ECA during 1948 has been limited to expenditures within the $275 million appropriated by the Congress.

In Section 407 of the China Aid Act of 1948 (Public Law 472, Title IV), the Congress authorized for "a program for reconstruction in rural areas in China," an amount "equal to not more than 10 per centum" of the funds made available for economic assistance under the Act, which amount could be "in United States dollars, proceeds in Chinese currency from the sale of commodities made available . . . or both." Thus a third category of assistance was specified. The China Aid Act did not further stipulate the relative magnitude of expenditures to be incurred in behalf of the three general types of limited assistance contemplated, namely: a commodities program, an industrial reconstruction program, and a rural reconstruction program.

Related to these three types of aid within China and available for helping to carry them out was a special local currency or "counterpart" fund, established by the Chinese Government pursuant to the terms of an "Economic Cooperation Agreement between the United States of America and the Republic of China." (The text of this bilateral Agreement is quoted below, under the heading, "Documents.")

In administering economic aid to China, as approved by Congress, the ECA has faced the obligation to ensure as efficient use as possible, under prevailing conditions, of the $275 million appropriation provided by Congress, recognizing that the assistance thus furnished would, to be fully effective, have to be supplementary to, and not a substitute for, vigorous efforts on the part of the Chinese Government and people.

With limited resources and under prevailing conditions in China, it has not been possible for the ECA to undertake a comprehensive approach to China's broad problems of budgetary and financial stabilization and economic recovery. It has been necessary, instead, to concentrate upon a few restricted activities designed to furnish some assistance at critical points in the Chinese economy; to maximize in the aid program, where possible, the use of private trade channels as one means of sustaining a degree of normal economic activity; and to devise effective end-use controls designed to ensure efficient utilization of all the economic aid provided.

Initiation of the Program

On April 30, 1948, notes were exchanged between the Secretary of State and the Chinese Ambassador in Washington, setting up interim arrangements for the initiation of the China Aid Program, pending the negotiation of a bilateral economic aid agreement. These notes (a) confirmed the Chinese Government's adherence to the purposes and policies set forth in Section 2 of the China Aid Act of 1948; (b) specified that prior to the conclusion of an agreement under Section 405 of the China Aid Act and until July 3, 1948, the extension of aid to China as authorized by Section 404 (a) of the Act, would be provisionally governed, subject to agreed modifications, by the Agreement negotiated in connection with the United States Foreign Relief Program, dated October 27, 1947; and (c) recorded an understanding relating to the establishment of special mission for economic cooperation to China, together with an assurance that the Chinese Government would extend the fullest cooperation to representatives of the United States Government concerned with operations in implementation of the China Aid Act.

Bilateral Agreement

Section 405 of the China Aid Act provided that an agreement should be "entered into between China and the United States containing these undertakings by China which the Secretary of State, after consultation with the Administrator for Economic Cooperation, may deem necessary to carry out the purposes of this title and to improve commercial relations with China." Consequently, negotiations were begun in early June between the United States Embassy in Nanking and the Chinese Ministry of Foreign Affairs regarding the terms of a bilateral economic cooperation agreement between the two countries. These negotiations were concluded satisfactorily and the Agreement was signed on July 3, 1948 by Ambassador J. Leighton Stuart and the Chinese Minister of Foreign Affairs, Wang Shih-chieh. (The full text of the Agreement is quoted below in the section entitled "Documents.")[6]

In general, the Agreement with China followed the pattern of the bilateral agreements being negotiated simultaneously between the United States and those European countries which participated in the Organization for European Economic Cooperation. The language of certain articles was made almost identical for those undertakings specified by Title I of the Foreign Assistance Act which applied in principle to the Chinese as well as to the European situation. Because of certain basically different aspects of the Chinese situation, however, some standard articles were modified considerably in the China Agreement, or unique provisions were added. In view of conditions prevailing in China, the scope of joint control, particularly with respect to prices and allocations, was broader under the terms of the China Agreement than under the European bilateral agree-

---

[6] See annex 181.

ments. One unique article in the China Agreement, that calling for improvement of commercial relations, was required specifically by Section 405 of the China Aid Act.

The Agreement with China set forth a number of undertakings by the Chinese and/or the U. S. Government relating to the following:

provision of aid to the Chinese Government in accordance with the terms of the China Aid Act of 1948 (other than Section 404 (b) thereof) ; measures for improvement of general economic conditions including effective use of aid goods, appropriate use of private Chinese assets in the U. S., development of industrial and agricultural production, creation of more stable currency conditions, cooperation with other countries to increase international trade, and prevention of commercial arrangements which interfere with the purposes of the Agreement;

improvement of commercial relations with other countries, with particular reference to the conditions affecting foreign trade by private enterprises in China;

fair and equitable distribution of aid goods, and of similar goods produced locally or imported with other funds, and the method of determining terms, conditions and prices for distribution of aid goods;

deposits of Chinese currency in value commensurate with the value of U. S. aid provided on a grant basis, and the principles governing disposal of such deposits;

facilitating the acquisition by the U. S. from China of materials in short supply in the U. S.;

negotiation of duty-free treatment for imports into China of relief goods by private agencies or individuals;

joint consultation, and provision of information by the Chinese Government, regarding matters relevant to the Agreement;

publicity within China regarding provision of aid under the Agreement;

establishment in China of, and treatment to be accorded to, a U. S. Special Mission for Economic Cooperation;

settlement, by reference to an agreed upon international tribunal, of claims espoused by either government on behalf of its nationals against the other government for compensation for damage arising as a consequence of governmental measures taken after April 3, 1948;

entry into force, amendment and duration of the Agreement.

Advisory Bodies

Two advisory bodies have on request furnished helpful counsel and guidance on broad questions relating to the planning and conduct of the ECA China Aid Program: The National Advisory Council on International Monetary and Financial Problems, established by Congress, and the Public Advisory Committee for the China Program, appointed by the Administrator under authority granted in Public Law 472, Section 107 (b).

Members of the National Advisory Committee for the China Program have been: Isaiah Bowman, president-emeritus of Johns Hopkins University and a member since 1940 of the Permanent International Commission for China and the United States; Arthur B. Foye, senior partner of the international public accountant firm of Haskins and Sells and, since 1945, president of the Far East-America Council of Commerce and Industry; Paul V. McNutt, former ambassador and United States high commissioner to the Philippines, and president and chairman of the Board of United Service to China ; Elizabeth Luce Moore, former chairman of the USO Council, one of the founders in 1940 of United China Relief, and a trustee of Wellesley College, of the China Institute in America, and of the United Board for Christian Colleges in China; and Walter S. Robertson, former minister-counselor for economic affairs at the United States Embassy in Chungking, and a principal assistant to General George C. Marshall during his special mission to China in 1945–1946.

ECA Mission to China

Authority for the establishment of a special ECA Mission to China is contained in Public Law 472, Sections 109 and 403.

The organization of the China Mission began with the appointment of Roger D. Lapham, former mayor of San Francisco, as Chief of the Mission. The appointment was made on May 5, 1948, and Mr. Lapham arrived in China on June 7, accompanied by initial members of a Reconstruction Survey Group. Staffing of the Mission has been kept at a minimum consistent with the efficient performance of ECA economic aid functions in China. As of December 31, 1948, 89 Americans and 355 non-Americans were on duty with the Mission.

Clearances between ECA Headquarters and the China Mission are conducted through a China Program Division in Washington. This is a staff office of 20 persons which facilitates the integration, without needless duplication, of China operations within the general framework of ECA financing and supply operations.

RELATIONS WITH THE CHINESE GOVERNMENT

To provide for an orderly conduct of relations between the Chinese Government and the ECA China Mission, the Government appointed a Council for United States Aid (CUSA), with the Prime Minister as Chairman, which includes in its membership the Ministers of Foreign Affairs, Finance, and Communications, the Governor of the Central Bank, the Chairman of the National Resources Commission, the Mayor of Shanghai and the Chairman of the Chinese Technical Mission to the United States.

The Economic Cooperation Agreement between the United States and the Chinese Governments, signed at Nanking on July 3, 1948, by the United States Ambassador and the Chinese Minister for Foreign Affairs, provided the framework of understanding and agreements on the basis of which ECA operations in China have been conducted. The text of the Agreement appears in the final section of this paper.

TAKEOVER FROM U. S. CHINA RELIEF MISSION

The first organizational problem faced by the Chief of the ECA Mission to China was the need to make provision for the orderly transition from the work of the U. S. China Relief Mission, which had been responsible for the $45,000,000 interim relief program in China, previously provided under Public Law 84, to the new program under ECA direction. Arrangements were made for the temporary transfer of considerable numbers of the personnel in the China Relief Mission, in order to ensure the orderly liquidation of that Mission's ressponsibilities under the supervision of ECA, and at the same time to utilize, for the benefit of the ECA program, the experience of personnel already available in China, who had been working with a program similar in certain respects to the China Aid Program.

Takeover responsibilities included principally the receipt and distribution of residual China Relief Mission supplies, responsibility for residual proceeds from the sale of such supplies, and the carrying on or liquidation of various local currency projects agreed to by the China Relief Mission.

Approximately 25,000 tons of CRM rice and flour valued at about $3.8 million were on hand on June 30, 1948, which were taken over and distributed under the supervision of the ECA Mission through the rationing system. Approximately $5.2 million worth of medical supplies and $670,000 worth of pesticides were on order in the United States, to be delivered during the early months of the ECA program. The general policy governing distribution of medical supplies has been to distribute them for the greater part free of charge and in large part in outlying areas where it has not been feasible to ship ECA bulk supplies. About a third of the pesticides has been reserved for the use of the Rural Reconstruction Commission, the remainder being sold through normal commercial channels or distributed free by the Ministry of Agriculture through agricultural demonstration centers.

There was virtually no cash balance in the CRM local currency account at the time of the ECA takeover. However, commitments had been entered into for over 260 projects predicated on anticipated proceeds from the sale of undistributed rice and flour. The ECA, accordingly, assumed responsibility for the orderly completion or liquidation of these projects. In July and August, the equivalent of US $197,600 was disbursed from the local currency Special Account for these purposes, about 55 percent for public works, 43 percent for medical purposes, and 2 percent for miscellaneous projects. After August, considerable weeding out was done in order to reduce the number of projects to a number which would permit adequate supervision and these have been included in the overall ECA-CUSA program for the Special Account.

ORGANIZATION

Headquarters of the ECA Mission to China were established in Shanghai, and regional offices in Nanking, Peiping, Tientsin, Tsingtao, Canton and Taipeh (on Taiwan or Formosa).

The approved pattern of the Mission as of December 31, 1948, is reflected in the accompanying organizational chart. The principal functions of each organizational unit within the Mission are set forth in the Appendix.

Assistance has been given to the Mission by ECA Headquarters in the recruitment of American personnel and the coordination of personnel procedures, fiscal activities, and administrative management in accordance with Headquarters procedures and in compliance with foreign service requirements of the State Department.

ADMINISTRATIVE EXPENSES

The ECA China Program has operated under a limitation, for administrative expenses incurred in U. S. dollars, of $1.2 million—less than one-half of one percent of the amount appropriated for the current China program. This necessitated rigid economies in the planning of staff requirements, and a maximum use of other agencies and means in order to develop an effective field organization. The $1.2 million ceiling did not apply to administrative costs provided from counterpart local currency funds in China, from which source approximately three-fifths of the administrative costs of the Mission are being met.

Administrative expenses, with the benefit of special arrangements referred to below, were held, up to the end of December 1948, within an amount provisionally estimated at approximately $560,000. However, a large percentage of these expenses were incurred during the last quarter of the calendar year 1948. This was attributable chiefly to two factors: (a) the fact that the ECA China Mission was not fully staffed, and operations in China were not in full swing, until the October–December quarter; and (b) the necessity of incurring increased expenses (nottably for extensive transfers of supplies and personnel, including the removal of some dependents) as a result of unsettled and uncertain conditions in north and central China. A third factor contributing to higher costs was beginning to appear at the end of the year, namely, the necessity, with the excessive rate of depreciation of Chinese currency, of meeting certain administrative expenses out of U.S. dollars instead of local currency.

Payment for expenses incurred on behalf of American members of the Mission, including travel for members and dependents, is governed by U. S. Foreign Service regulations which are mandatory with respect to ECA employees.

Military developments in China have made necessary budgetary provisions for the voluntary removal of certain dependents and household effects from threatened areas. As of December 31, 1948, some dependents and women employees with children were being evacuated, and some members of the Mission had been reassigned in accordance with changing program plans.

The use of consulting engineers or engineering firms on a contract basis, in connection with the development of surveys and plans for reconstruction projects in the industrial field, has made it possible to have competent engineering surveys and to prepare for supervising this part of the program without incurring direct administrative expenditures in excess of the ceiling on administrative costs.

A similar saving has been effected in the case of the rural reconstruction program. As indicated above, the Congressional appropriation for this program, to be supervised by a Joint Commission on Rural Reconstruction, was "an amount equal to not more than 10 per centum" of the appropriation for economic aid to China, which amount could be in U.S. dollars, proceeds in Chinese currency from the sale of commodities made available to China, or both. From the ceiling of $27.5 million thus established for the rural reconstruction program, $2.5 million was tentatively earmarked for availability in U.S. dollars, to be used principally for salaries, dollar administrative requirements and essential procurement of agricultural supplies and educational media. The Joint Commission's allotments for both program and administration represent a program cost and are thus not chargeable to the limitation on administrative funds for the China Mission.

To avoid needless administrative duplication and expense, administrative arrangements were entered into between the State Department and the China Program of ECA, in which the State Department agreed to provide communication facilities and to assume disbursing functions with respect to U.S. dollars and to perform such minor services, in return for which ECA would reimburse the State Department, either through direct payment or through the provision of agreed services as needed by American or alien personnel.

Economies in time and space facilities were effected by the takeover of office and warehouse space and equipment previously utilized by the China Relief Mission operating under P.L. 84. Effective coordination with the Chinese Government Council for U.S. Aid (CUSA) was facilitated by a provision for CUSA offices in the same location as those of the ECA China Mission.

The civil war, with its attendant disruption of rail services, has made necessary an almost exclusive use of air travel on the part of the members of the

Mission in China, including chartered flights when necessary. Telegraph workloads in excess of available capacities through diplomatic or military channels have necessitated a considerable use of commercial telegraph facilities for unclassified operational messages.

Through the economies and special arrangements outlined above, direct administrative expenses charged against the ECA program in China were, as of December 31, 1948, within an administrative budget based upon the $1.2 million limitation for the one-year period of the authorizing legislation. And it was expected that administrative expenses incurred in the course of operations through April 2, 1949, would, despite the rising costs referred to above, be kept within this limitation.

COMMODITIES PROGRAM

The commodities program has had as its aim the provision of a continued flow to China of certain key commodities essential to the maintenance of minimum economic activity and subsistence in the urban centers of China. As indicated above, resources available for ECA commodity imports into China were not of a sufficient order of magnitude to reduce substantially the great imbalance in the Chinese national budget or to solve the nation's balance of payments problem by providing all essential imports which could not be financed by the Chinese themselves. It was essential, therefore, to concentrate upon the commodities which were of most strategic importance in helping to bolster China's internal economy. Commodities procured under the ECA program have included food, cotton, petroleum, fertilizer, and coal. In addition, as mentioned above, some residual medical supplies and pesticides were taken over by the ECA, from the earlier U.S. Foreign Relief Program, for distribution. The scope and character of each of these commodity programs are discussed below.

Procurement and Shipment

Following consultation with the National Advisory Council, ECA decided to finance commodities for China entirely on a basis of grants, not loans. The reason for this action lay in the state of the Chinese Government's external finances, as described in an earlier section of this paper.

Commodity procurement has been conducted by two methods—through private trade channels for cotton, fertilizer, petroleum and coal, and through the U.S. Department of Agriculture for rice, wheat and flour.

Cotton has been purchased through ECA financing by the Chinese Textile Industries, Inc., a quasi-government corporation, from U.S. cotton brokers submitting bids through agents in Shanghai. Fertilizer has been purchased by the Central Trust of China from suppliers presenting bids, over-all quantities purchased being governed by the size of International Emergency Food Committee allocations to China. Petroleum products have been purchased from suppliers on the basis of recommendations submitted by a joint Chinese-American subcommittee of CUSA, these recommendations being based on the prewar supply pattern; although this method of selecting suppliers has to some extent reduced the scope of price competition, prices paid for petroleum have been carefully scrutinized in the light of Section 202 of Public Law 793.

Procurement of wheat and flour has been from United States surpluses, purchases being made by the Commodity Credit Corporation of the U.S. Department of Agriculture from private suppliers on the basis of competitive bidding. These purchases have been against U.S. Department of Commerce allocations, determining the total quantity of U.S. wheat exportable to China. Rice has also been procured by the Commodity Credit Corporation, pursuant to Section 121, Public Law 472, chiefly in Siam and Burma, purchases being made against IEFC allocations.

Up to December 31, 1948, more than 99 percent of the ECA-financed cargo tonnage originating in the United States and delivered to China had been shipped in U.S.-flag vessels; this was far in excess of the over-all requirement for ECA (in section 111 (a) (2) of Public Law 472) "that at least 50 per centum of the gross tonnage of commodities, procured within the United States out of funds made available under this title and transported abroad on ocean vessels, is so transported on United States-flag vessels to the extent such vessels are available at market rates."

Procurement and Pricing of Commodities in China

Aid in providing essential commodities has been regarded by the ECA as a supplement to, and not a substitute for, production and supply efforts by the Chinese Government. This has been especially true with regard to the food program, in connection with which the ECA China Mission has undertaken to secure as effective performance as possible by the Government in providing from indigenous sources a substantial share of the food supplies required for the cities receiving ECA food shipments. In order to minimize the degree of subsidy to private consumers at the expense of government income, the China Mission has undertaken, with varying results, to exert its influence in favor of the selling of rationed food at, or near to, actual market prices; the same is true with respect to cotton goods and petroleum products. Similar influence has been exerted, as far as practicable, with regard to prices for coal, rates for electric power, or levels at which any enterprise, directly or indirectly assisted by ECA, sells its products.

End-Use Control

Measures essential to effective end-use control have been carefully developed for each of the commodity programs, in order to assure that supplies provided through ECA would go to the recipients for which they were intended, to furnish maximum assistance to people and institutions within China, to support efforts of the Government to increase production and stabilize economic conditions, and generally to secure the best results attainable through the expenditure of ECA dollars.

Food has been distributed through controlled rationing systems in major cities of China, and a detailed record has been kept of individual recipients of this aid; ECA representatives attend as observers the meetings of City Food Committees, and ECA investigators inspect and report on all phases of operations under the rationing program. The cotton aid program is directed in China by a Joint Management Board whose decisions require CUSA and ECA concurrence; a system has been established for following cotton through conversion into yarn, the conversion of yarn into cloth, and the subsequent domestic use or export of the resulting textiles. Petroleum has been distributed primarily by major oil companies which themselves help to make sure that ECA-financed oil goes only to the uses for which it is allocated; a joint CUSA-ECA Petroleum Committee estimates requirements and supervises distribution. Control arrangements are being developed to insure that fertilizer will be distributed in a way that will achieve maximum effect in increasing food production.

Further details with respect to end-use controls are contained in the description below of the several commodity programs, and in the Appendix.

Food

The interior of China—including countryside, towns and cities—has normally been relatively self-sufficient in foodstuffs, but the larger coastal cities have in recent decades become increasingly dependent, for part of their food supply, on imports from abroad. As previously indicated, the problem of food supplies for these cities became acute in the spring of 1948 due to the disruption of communications and trade by the civil war, spiralling inflation, and increasing strains upon the Government's foreign exchange resources.

INCEPTION OF FOOD RATIONING IN POSTWAR CHINA

Food rationing in postwar China was first developed in the program of the United States China Relief Mission. Under this program the U. S. Government provided—for the five major coastal cities of Shanghai, Nanking, Canton, Peiping and Tientsin—approximately 200,000 tons of rice, wheat and flour, of which more than 150,000 tons was distributed before the end of June 1948. Contributions from the Chinese Government approximately matched this tonnage, with the result that between March and the close of June about 300,000 tons of food was sold at prices considerably lower than those prevailing on the open market to between 11 and 12 million inhabitants of these cities.

Each individual, under the rationing program, was limited to a monthly purchase of 16.5 pounds of rice or flour, although no one was limited in the amount that might, if available, be purchased at inflated prices on the open market.

This program was an innovation in China. Food rationing on a major scale had not previously been practiced there as it has in most other countries of the world where shortages posed a problem of equitable distribution of available supply. Chinese officials considered the matter long and carefully before undertaking the responsibility for a program which depended for its success upon the development and maintenance of relatively complicated administrative machinery. However, once started, the administration of the program was carried out with a record of competence, precision and honesty that became a source of gratification to all parties concerned, including the Chinese officials responsible for the operation.

SEVEN-CITY RATIONING PROGRAM

Following the first arrival of ECA food supplies in China, it was decided that the rationing program should be continued as the best means of applying U.S. aid in an equitable manner, of retarding somewhat the rapid rate of price increase, and of providing an added source of revenue to the Government. Under the ECA program, the number of cities participating in rationing was extended to include Swatow and Tsingtao. In the latter city, the U. S. Navy maintained a base in an area which was surrounded by Communists and cut off from local sources of food supply.

The somewhat fluctuating population of the seven cities participating in the rationing program ranged, in total, between 12.7 and 13 million during 1948.

Under arrangements agreed upon between the ECA China Mission and the Chinese Government Council for U. S. Aid (CUSA), agreement was reached on the setting up, within the Chinese Government's Ministry of Food, of an Office of Emergency Food Procurement (OEFP), which was to handle indigenous purchasing for the rationing program. The OEFP undertook initially to procure from indigenous sources approximately 60 percent of the total food required for the operation of the rationing system, and ECA approximately 40 percent.

EMERGENCY FEEDING PROGRAMS

In addition to this rationing program for seven cities, a limited emergency feeding program for Mukden was developed while that city remained in Nationalist hands. Nearly one thousand tons of flour delivered under this emergency program were cooked and fed directly to key groups of workers with appropriate publicity. The resultant increase in morale was notable until, with the Communist assault on Mukden, the program had to be suspended. Some 400 tons of ECA flour in Chinchow awaiting airlift to Mukden were captured by the Communists during their rapid advance in that sector.

In order to cope with the heavy influx of refugees into Tsingtao from the war zones and to compensate for the reduced supplies of indigenous food coming into the city because of communist occupation of surrounding territory, the ECA China Mission has also provided, in that city, continuing support for a special Refugee Feeding Project originally instituted under the CRM program. This project, conducted outside the rationing program in cooperation with municipal authorities, consists of open-air kitchens which prepare and serve daily portions of rice congee to an estimated 100,000 refugees. Damaged rice, sweepings and poorer grades of rice unsuitable for rationing, which are received in ECA shipments from southeast Asia, are set aside for this project in Shanghai, for transshipment to Tsingtao. The bulk of shipments have been made via vessels of the U.S. Navy, which considers the project a necessary emergency measure effective in the maintenance of orderly conditions in Tsingtao. Requirements for the project are 1,300 tons per month.

AUGUST 19 REGULATIONS AND INDIGENOUS PROCUREMENT

An element of subsidy was inherent in the seven-city rationing plan. But it was never intended that the prices of rationed cereals would be allowed to fall far below open market prices. At first, prices for rationed foods were adjusted monthly to a level approximately 5 percent below prevailing open-market rates and held there throughout the ensuing month, regardless of price rises in the open market. Thus the Government was in a position to obtain much needed revenue from sales of rationed rice and flour, even though some slight subsidy accrued to the people, for the U.S. supplies thus sold cost the Government nothing and all local currency returns from this sale constituted a net gain.

Under the Government's August 19 reform measures, however, ration prices, particularly in the central and north China cities, were set well below market prices, with the result that the dependence of the program on governmental subsidies became heavy during the period until November when these measures were drastically revised. As the military, political and economic situation deteriorated, the Government deemed it expedient to use the rationing programs to provide an outright subsidy to all the people in the urban coastal cities in an effort to mitigate public discontent. At this time, wages were lagging so far behind essential commodity prices that the city populations began to be unable to purchase minimum requirements of daily necessities. ECA officials reluctantly acquiesced in the selling of U.S.-contributed food supplies along with indigenous supplies, at what to the Government were ruinously subsidized prices, but warned that the policy would prove exceedingly costly.

Since ECA funds for food procurement were limited, it appeared advisable at the outset to conserve them in large part to provide foodstuffs for the 1948–49 winter and spring months and thus assure rationing supplies at the time of the year when food is normally less plentiful. The Chinese Government agreed to find and deliver the foodstuffs needed for rationing during the last quarter of

1948, with the understanding that the Eca would undertake to supply a major portion of the ration during the first quarter of 1949 and to deliver additional food thereafter to the extent of availability of funds from the 1948 appropriation.

Difficulties developed in the implementation of this plan. The obtaining of indigenous supplies by the Chinese OEFP was slow and erratic; its attempts to purchase domestic food supplies were inspired by lack of sufficient appropriations and by the disparity between official and black-market prices. There was a failure to act quickly to procure domestic supplies in quantity when the harvests were in. Anticipated purchases of rice in Burma did not materialize. Some flour was collected at Shanghai for the ration in the cities of north China, but commandeering by the military of the ships selected for the transport of these supplies caused considerable delay in their movement. As indicated above, the unsuccessful economic regulations promulgated by the Government on August 19, 1948, resulted in the exclusion from China's major cities of normal free-market supplies of indigenous foods. The acute shortages, dramatized by all-night queues in front of food shops, were intensified by a partial breakdown of the rationing system during October. At the middle of October none of the cities except Canton and Tsingtao had even been able to start the October ration, and one city was still trying to fulfill the September ration commitment.

Throughout this period, the Eca China Mission pressed for the lifting of arbitrary food price ceilings in the cities, for a realistic pricing of rationed foods, and for more vigorous efforts by the OEFP to procure indigenous supplies.

SPEED-UP OF ECA DELIVERIES

Steps were also taken to speed up Eca deliveries of wheat, previously scheduled for the first quarter of 1949, in order to move up to November and December the resumption of Eca's contribution to the ration system. Some success was achieved in the acceleration of Eca shipments to China—which proved to be of crucial importance in allaying unrest in major cities—and in the development of more realistic pricing for rationed food, but indigenous procurement efforts by the Chinese Government continued to lag.

Reported shipments as of December 31, 1948, under procurement programs 1, 2 and 3 (for the second, third and fourth quarters of 1943, were valued at approximately $37,000,000 for the purchase of 129,000 tons of rice and 107,000 tons of wheat and flour. In addition, about 25,000 tons of rice and flour had been received as residue from the China Relief Mission and 9,000 tons of rice had been borrowed from Hongkong to relieve a threatened November food shortage in Shanghai. Of these amounts, approximately 120,000 tons of rice and 30,000 tons of wheat and flour had before the end of December been released for the rationing programs. Additional Program 3 stocks either en route, loading or waiting for shipment, at the end of 1948, totaled 27,000 ton of rice from Siam and Burma and 56,000 tons of wheat and flour from the United States.

SUPERVISION OF RATIONING PROGRAM

Although administered by Chinese Government officials, the Eca food program in China has been carefully supervised by Eca representatives who have insisted upon the maintenance of high standards of performance and honesty. Mindful of the considerable pilfering and misuse of food supplies previously delivered under the UNRRA program, Eca has paid utmost attention to the problem of end-use control. Strict supervision and careful checking have been applied to every phase of distribution in order to assure that all Eca-financed food supplies allocated to the rationing program actually reach the end recipient. A detailed description of rationing and end-use control under the ECA food program is contained in the Appendix.

The United States has delivered its contributions to the rationing programs regularly and on time. ECA officials in China have manifested constant concern that the rationing program should be conducted for the benefit of the people as a whole. These facts are well known to the millions of persons affected, and has done much to sustain their faith in the friendship of the American people.

Cotton

The first step in the cotton program involved an easing of pressure upon China's strained foreign exchange resources by ECA financing of existing consignment contracts with early delivery dates; these contracts were between the China Textile Industries, Inc., and the agents in Shanghai of American cotton shippers. All of the cotton involved was programmed for supply from the United States. In the course of authorizing procurement of this cotton, provision was made for joint supervision, by the Government and the ECA China Mission, of processing and distribution of raw cotton after arrival in China.

The total cotton program developed under the current China Aid Program involved an expenditure of nearly $70 million. During October 1948, the first of this cotton reached the mills and the system of control and reporting of end use was perfected. As of December 31, cotton in the amount of 299,038 bales, costing approximately $52.7 million, had arrived in China and was being allocated and distributed to the mills; 51,000 bales of yarn and 557,000 bolts of cloth (40 yards each) had been received back from the mills.

Under the ECA China aid program, all cotton is procured through private trade channels. Cotton shipments to China are continuing under schedules designed to maintain production and employment while avoiding any undue advance stockpiling.

The Chinese textile industry with about 3,900,000 operable spindles is China's largest manufacturing industry and raw cotton is one of China's vital imports. Not only are the cloth and yarn produced of great significance to the Chinese economy, but a high level of employment among the textile workers is important to the maintenance of relative stability in industrial centers, particularly in Shanghai.

RAW COTTON SUPPLY PROBLEM

Before the war, cotton grown in China supplied the bulk of the fibre required to keep the textile mills in operation. Due to some reduction in cotton acreage and, more important, to the extensive disruption of internal transportation trade caused by the civil war (see accompanying map), indigenous cotton has gone largely into household use and China has had to depend on imports for more than a third of the cotton used in her mills. In the year 1947–1948, mill consumption was about 1,950,000 bales; imports of cotton were about 700,000 bales (as compared with a prewar level of imports of 340,000 bales). Procurement was in considerable part from India, and limited quantities were purchased also from British East Africa, Burma and Egypt.

Provision of the necessary foreign exchange for cotton importation has been for China a problem of increasing proportions. The ECA program, which financed 300,000 bales in 1948 and in January of 1949 was in process of financing an additional 100,000 bales, has been a major factor in the sustaining of production and employment in China's textile industry during the latter part of 1948.

USE AND CONTROL OF ECA COTTON IMPORTS

The plan developed for the use of ECA cotton imports called for the conversion of the cotton into yarn under arrangements involving processing or trading at a fixed ratio under which raw cotton is paid for by the processing and in most cases by conversion of the resulting yarn into cotton cloth. The Council for United States Aid (CUSA) and the ECA Mission to China agreed upon a division of the yarn and cloth produced from ECA cotton, with 50 percent to be used for domestic consumption and the rest to be exported—the proceeds to be used for purchase of additional raw cotton. Exports under this program had up to December 31, 1948, earned an equivalent of more than $4.5 million in foreign exchange, all sales being to countries of southeast Asia. Domestic distribution is largely by direct sale through commercial channels; some of the textiles, however, have been used in barter schemes, as described below, designed to bring more food into the cities. More than 2,000 bales of yarn and cloth made from ECA cotton were bartered in Nanking, Shanghai and Nanchang for 33,000 piculs of rice at a time when no other grain was moving into these cities from producing areas.

The arrangements adopted followed careful planning and careful negotiation by the Mission with the Chinese Government. The conversion, storage and disposition of ECA-financed cotton shipments to China are under the control of a Joint Management Board, and full records of each stage of the process are kept for end-use control purposes. Details of the end-use control mechanism developed are presented in the Appendix.

Petroleum

Since production of crude oil in China is negligible, the country is almost wholly dependent upon imports of petroleum products required in the operation of utilities, transport facilities, and manufacture and for household use. The cutting off of coal from north China, as a result of the civil war, increased greatly during the year the relative importance of petroleum products for power and industrial units in which they could be substituted for coal.

Taken as a whole, petroleum imports were vital to the operation of China's limited transport facilities and industrial plant. Diesel and fuel oil were essential to the operation of power plants and other utilities. These types, as well as motor and aviation gasoline and lubricants, were essential to the operation of water, rail and air transport. The use of kerosene, normally in wide demand for household lighting and fuel in rural districts and towns lacking electric power, has been restricted by disruptions in transport, but there has been continuing demand in the more accessible areas.

USE OF NORMAL TRADE CHANNELS

The petroleum program involved, at first, negotiations on the part which each of the petroleum distributing concerns and the large end users in China would play in the importation and distribution of the products. The problems involved were largely settled about the middle of 1948, and firm authorizations were thereupon prepared for issuance.

As a result, the importation and distribution of petroleum products under the ECA China Aid Program have been entirely through normal trade channels and the bulk of the business is handled by the Standard Vacuum Oil Co., the Shell Company of China, Ltd., the California Texas Oil Co., and the Chinese Petroleum

Corporation (an agency of the Chinese Government). A number of small importers and distributers have also participated in the program. The oil companies at first charged somewhat higher prices for petroleum products to China than to other destinations in order to recover thereby the foreign exchange component of internal distribution costs. Such price differentials were not satisfactory either to the Chinese Government or ECA: consequently ECA has indicated its willingness to finance only such petroleum shipments as are priced on a cost-and-freight basis and are within the U.S. market price as provided in Section 202 of the appropriation act (Public Law 793).

As of December 31, 1948, the Central Bank of China had financed petroleum brought into China under the ECA China Aid Program to a value of about $28 million, for which amount the Central Bank of China was to be reimbursed by ECA as rapidly as the requisite documentation is furnished ECA by the Central Bank of China.

In view of the Central Bank's straitened foreign exchange position, ECA Headquarters on November 26, 1948 authorized an advance of $15 million to the Central Bank to enable it, pending reimbursement by ECA, to continue financing the release and distribution of petroleum products in China. Shortly before the end of the year, the reimbursement procedure was abandoned, and arrangements were made to finance all future petroleum shipments (and releases from bonded tanks of products already in China) by letter of commitment to U.S. banks. In connection with the new procedure, the ECA Mission to China was given the responsibility of approving each shipment or release in advance, in order to avoid undue stockpiling of petroleum products in Chinese ports.

ADMINISTRATION OF PETROLEUM PROGRAM

Requirements programs have been prepared on a quarterly basis by the CUSA-ECA Petroleum Committee, which includes both active members and observers from CUSA and ECA. Up to the end of 1948, prices within China were determined by the Oil Allocation Committee, with approval of the Executive Yuan; the CUSA-ECA Petroleum Committee has sought Executive Yuan approval of a plan to authorize a CUSA-ECA-EIB (Export-Import Board) Price Adjustment Committee in Shanghai to make periodic reviews and price adjustments on its own initiative, in order to keep prices on a realistic basis and prevent the oil companies from sustaining losses because of currency fluctuations.

With ECA assistance, production has been continued at the Kao-hsiang refinery in Taiwan to which, at the end of 1948, 225,000 barrels of crude oil were being provided monthly, for conversion into motor gasoline, diesel and fuel oil and kerosene. The plan under which this assistance has been given was developed on the basis of recommendations by an independent firm of engineers engaged for the purpose by the Chinese Government upon the suggestion of ECA.

End-use control of the petroleum products imported into China has presented fewer administrative problems for the ECA than end-use control of other commodities. Distribution of ECA-financed petroleum products in China is generally of two types: distribution to large users (for example, fuel oil for the Shanghai Power Company) and distribution by individual companies to end users (for example, retail distribution of gasoline through filling stations to car owners). Since the companies are the distribution agents, and the major distributors are two American companies and one British company, these firms themselves provide a considerable measure of end-use control and are able to do most of the end-use reporting required, subject to necessary spot-checking by the ECA Mission.

Fertilizer

Procurement of fertilizer has proceeded within the limitation of availabilities for China from existing world supplies, as reflected in allocations by the International Emergency Food Council. Although increased use of fertilizers offers promise of substantial increases in indigenous food production, its widespread application during the postwar period has been impeded by a lack of extensive previous experience in the use of chemical fertilizers in China, except in Formosa; by a shortage of extension personnel and organization to train Chinese farmers in the effective application of modern fertilizers; and by the difficulty of devising effective distribution and end-use control systems within China. Under plans being perfected at the end of 1948, it was expected that substantial distribution to end users, particularly in Formosa and south China, would occur during the first quarter of 1949, and that a reasonable minimum of fertilizer could be made available in China for the spring planting.

ECA PROCUREMENT OF FERTILIZERS

Under the current China Program, ECA is financing the procurement of approximately 75,000 metric tons of chemical fertilizers, at a cost of approximately US$8.9 million; this should be of material benefit in increasing rice production in some districts, particularly in sections of Formosa and south China. It was at first planned to spend U.S. $13.8 million on fertilizers. Subsequently, arrangements were made whereby the Bank of China, the Central Bank and the Taiwan Provincial Government undertook to finance from their own resources the procurement of a portion of the nitrogenous fertilizers allocated to China by the International Emergency Food Committee; ECA thereupon reduced its fertilizer commitment by 4.9 million dollars. Under these arrangements China is in a position to acquire during 1948–49, through ECA and Government procurement, 116,000 metric tons of ammonium sulphate and ammonium phosphate. Having been used by Chinese farmers who have previously employed chemical fertilizers, these types are considered the most practical under prevailing agricultural practice.

AID TO FOOD PRODUCTION IN CHINA

Fertilizers provided by ECA are primarily for use in increasing yields of lowland rice, which should mean a corresponding decrease in dependence upon importations of rice from abroad.

It has been found, through scientific experimentation and practice, that one unit of nitrogenous fertilizer can produce an average increase in yield of at least 2 units of clean rice or about 3 units of paddy rice, all by weight. Theoretically, therefore, one dollar's worth of fertilizer should produce three dollars worth of grain (in terms of each equivalent to the import cost of an equal amount of food). However, owing to high transportation and internal handling costs and low price of rice at producing centers in China, a somewhat smaller gain is realized. Nevertheless, the use of chemical fertilizer is the most effective means known to augment food production in China.

The total annual domestic production of chemical fertilizers in China, at the 1948 rate, was only about 81,000 metric tons (36,000 ammonium sulphate, 35,000 superphosphate and 10,000 calcium cyanamide). A provisional allotment from ECA of $5.5 million to China's domestic fertilizer industry, aimed to increase substantially production capacity, had to be suspended at least temporarily, toward the end of the year, due to disturbed civil war conditions.

At the end of 1948, the first 10,000 tons of Eca fertilizer was scheduled to reach Shanghai in January 1949. This installment, on the basis of an agreement with the Farmer's Bank, was to be distributed to farmers who, during November and December, had advanced rice for the food rationing program. Plans were developed for the distribution, through commercial channels in south China and Taiwan and through the Joint Rural Reconstruction Commission, of additional shipments totalling about 61,000 tons.

Coal

China's principal coal-producing centers have been in north China and Manchuria. As indicated on the accompanying map, military developments together with the cutting of vital transportation routes during 1948 interrupted the flow of coal from north China producing areas to consuming areas in central China.

Arrangements were made, therefore, for Eca procurement on an emergency basis of limited stocks from Japan through the Supreme Command, Allied Powers, Pacific (Scap) organization. Before the end of 1948, coal in the amount of 15,000 tons had been obtained from Japan at a cost of about $280,000, and there was a prospect that further emergency procurement would be required.

Medical Supplies

About $5 million worth of medical supplies were procured for China under Public Law 84, the U. S. Foreign Relief Program. Most of these supplies arrived in China after the expiration of the China Relief Mission on June 30, 1948; they became, therefore, an Eca responsibility. As of December, nearly 90 percent of the supplies programmed by the China Relief Mission had arrived in China.

The reception, storage and transportation phases of the medical supply program have worked smoothly and losses from pilferage and improper handling have been negligible. Special medical warehousing units established have operated with a high degree of efficiency. On the basis of careful allocation and distribution planning by the Council for U. S. Aid, the Eca Mission to China, the Ministry of Health and the International Relief Committee, the distribution of these supplies was proceeding regularly at the end of 1948.

Distribution from Shanghai was being accelerated in view of the rapidly changing political and military situations; additional warehouses were being stocked in Canton and Taipeh (on the island of Taiwan), leaving in Shanghai only supplies required in that area. It was expected that final distribution of medical supplies to end users would be completed by May 31, 1949.

Pesticides

Eca also took over from the China Relief Mission responsibility for $537,000 worth of pesticides which reached China during 1948; most of these supplies arrived too late for distribution during the lifetime of the China Relief Mission.

Plans were developed and agreed upon between Eca and the Chinese Government in September, for allocations of 35 percent of these pesticides to the Joint Rural Reconstruction Commission, 15 percent to the Ministry of Agriculture and Forestry for free distribution at agricultural demonstration centers, and the remaining 50 percent for sale through commercial channels. Sales during October and November were principally in south Kiangsu and north Chekian areas bordering the Shanghai district and were concluded in time to give needed protection to crops. When seasonal demand from farmers in these districts ceased, sales efforts were directed to south China where, with a long growing season, the need for insecticides continued during ensuing months. In Taiwan, where the use of agricultural insecticides is best known, the only channels through which farmers had been accustomed to obtain their supplies in the past had not, at the end of the year, been utilized in accordance with original plans due to lack of requisite cooperation in making supplies quickly available to consumers.

Special Barter Arrangements

A barter program, of an emergency nature, was developed initially on a small scale. Difficulties experienced by the Chinese in obtaining their quota of domestic food supplies for the rationing program were such that CUSA and ECA undertook to exchange limited quantities of cloth and yarn (maunfactured from aid cotton) for rice and other indigenous food grains.

About two hundred tons of cloth were sent to Nanking, for example, to be used in exchange for rice, about 150 pounds of rice being obtained for each piece of grey cloth 40 yards long.

In villages near Shanghai a similar type of exchange was developed, and in Changsha, commercial center of a large rice-producing area in northern Hunan, a beginning was made. Such exchanges up to the end of 1948, were experimental in character. The results attained indicated that considerable quantities of rice could be obtained in this manner, and it was planned that regular supplies of yarn and cloth to be used for this purpose would shortly be advanced to Office of Emergency Food Procurement, with ECA observing OEFP operations and ensuring strict end-use accounting.

In North China ECA representatives were, at the end of November, negotiating with representatives from General Fu Tso-yi's headquarters and local grain dealers. A contract was under consideration calling for 120,000 pieces of cloth to be used in exchange for domestic wheat, flour, and coarse grains, the foodstuffs to be used in a selective rationing plan for workers in essential services. This plan was disrupted by military developments in the Peiping-Tientsin area.

Two principal purposes were served by such barters of cloth and yarn for food: (a) the obtaining of additional supplies of food for use in the rationing programs and (2) the distribution of yarn and cloth in interior areas, in many cases direct to the farmers without passing through middlemen, thus reducing opportunities for cloth and yarn to fall into the hands of speculators.

Shipping

Mention has been made of the fact that more than 99 percent of ECA-financed commodities shipped from the United States to China during 1948 were carried in U.S. vessels.

Internal administrative rulings defining what types of transportation expenditures are eligible for reimbursing from ECA funds, written principally for application to Europe, are generally applied to China. However, due to emergency conditions in China the Administration has seen fit to depart from its general rules on special occasions. These departures involve the payment of partial freight in dollars to certain Chinese ships chartered to move rice from Siam and Burma. The rice, procured by U.S. representatives using ECA funds, has been moved to China on an exacting schedule to meet ECA's feeding program in principal Chinese cities. About $727,000 for freight thus provided before the end of December 1948 made possible the movement of 39 Chinese ships carrying about 155,000 metric tons of rice.

These movements of rice from southeast Asia to China have not taken place exclusively in Chinese ships; funds are made available to U.S. representatives to enable them to use American ships interested in the traffic. However, only one American ship was used for this purpose in 1948; the cost via this vessel was $7.50 per ton as compared with the current Chinese rate of $2.00 per ton from Siam. The Chinese rate toward the end of 1948 was $3.50 per ton from Burma as compared with an estimated $10.00 per ton in American vessels. It is considered doubtful whether the dollars provided the Chinese cover the out-of-pocket expenses of the ships involved, which do receive some additional compensation in Chinese currency from counterpart funds.

The reason for close scheduling of shipping carrying food into China has been to import sufficient amounts to prevent starvation and riots, at the same time avoiding stockpiling of quantities that might be lost as a result of the war. In addition to scheduling rice shipments, considerable authority was delegated to the ECA Mission in China to divert U.S. wheat and flour shipments, as well as shipments of other commodities, to meet changing situations. When the military situation in the vicinity of Tientsin deteriorated, several American ships about to discharge in ports serving that area were diverted to Tsingtao.

INDUSTRIAL RECONSTRUCTION AND REPLACEMENT PROGRAM

A total of $70 million was originally programmed for industrial reconstruction and replacement projects in China. The legislative history of the China Aid Act indicated considerable Congressional interest in this significant aspect of proposed assistance to China. Extensive, painstaking preparations were made, including the sending to China of a special Reconstruction Survey Group, in order to ensure the most productive use of the funds made available for industrial reconstruction and replacement purposes.

Necessity for Suspension

However, due to developments in the civil war situation in China, it became necessary for the Administrator, on December 21, 1948, to announce that work on the reconstruction and replacement program was, to a large extent, being suspended—exceptions being made in connection with the completion of certain pre-project engineering studies which had already reached an advanced stage of development. Preparatory work on some of the projects, located in areas of Manchuria or north China involved in or threatened by military developments, had already in fact been suspended. The series of defeats sustained by the Nationalist forces in the fall and early winter of 1948, jeopardizing the Government's position not only at its remaining bases in north China but also in the Yangtze Valley, had resulted in chaotic conditions and major uncertainties throughout many of the regions in which reconstruction and replacement projects had been planned.

The suspension did not eliminate the possibility of renewed activity on selected projects in areas remaining accessible, in the event that such a partial resumption of the reconstruction and replacement program should at any future time be deemed feasible and expedient. At the time of suspension, all of the projects were still in the pre-project engineering stage, no funds having as yet been actually committed for procurement.

The following paragraphs present a brief summary of the problems encountered in the field of industrial replacement and reconstruction, the planning and preparatory work undertaken, and the practical arrangements developed for the initiation and execution of replacement and reconstruction projects in China. A listing, with brief descriptions, of the projects for which "provisional allotments" were made prior to the suspension of this part of the program, appears in the Appendix.

Planning and Preparatory Work

Initial planning had called for an expenditure of $60 million for reconstruction and $10 million for replacement work; as a result of the work of the Reconstruction Survey Group, however, much greater proportionate emphasis was placed upon replacements needed to increase the productivity of existing enterprises.

Initial members of the Survey Group reached China on June 7, 1948. The Group, consisting of 4 engineers, 2 economists, a lawyer and a businessman (Charles L. Stillman) who served as its head, operated as a part of the ECA Mission to China. After several months' reviews of conditions in China by the members of this Group, the ECA Mission developed, in agreement with the Chinese Government, a tentative program designed to make a significant start toward the reconstruction or rehabilitation of certain railroads, electric power plants, fertilizer manufacturing units, and coal, tin and antimony mines—all in non-Communist China.

The program finally recommended by the Survey Group and tentatively approved by the Administrator prior to the enforced suspension of this aspect of ECA assistance to China, called for approximately $25 million worth of new reconstruction or development, $35 million to be spent for replacement assistance, and $7.5 million for engineering services and reserves, making a total of $67.5 million; the remaining $2.5 million was earmarked for foreign exchange expenditures required in connection with the rural reconstruction program. Most of the projects planned were in the fields of basic industry and transportation—approximately $13.5 million being provisionally allotted for railway rehabilitation, $17.25 million for power plants, $11 million for coal mines and $5.5 million for fertilizer manufacture.

Following extensive consideration within ECA of the possibility of extending assistance to certain types of replacement and reconstruction projects on a loan basis, and after subsequent consultation with the National Advisory Council, it was tentatively determined that projects currently under consideration would be provided on an outright grant basis, leaving open the possibility of future reconsideration of loan proposals.

Problems of Industrial Reconstruction in China

The Chinese, in taking back control of their country after eight long years faced many problems. The areas reoccupied had been swept over by Japanese armies, by Chinese armies, and by Chinese and American airforces. Communist raids and damage by armies of both sides in the civil war had continued in many regions. Nearly all existing industrial facilities were in deplorable condition due to a variety of causes dating back to the opening of the Sino-Japanese War in 1937. Railroads, partially restored during the UNRRA period, needed further assistance. Further problems were presented for foreign exchange shortages, internal economic and financial difficulties evidenced in extreme inflation, seriously inadequate transportation and a general disruption of Government and of industrial management, both public and private.

Elimination of much foreign participation in Chinese affairs, as a result of the war and the ending of extraterritoriality, inevitably left a gap in the nation's economic and industrial life. Particularly in the industrial areas, foreign participation in management and control of properties had been of significance in their development and effective operation. Following the war, foreign-flag shipping was excluded from Chinese river and coastal waters, resulting in higher transportation costs and less adequate services. The Chinese were unable to develop comparable services in a short time.

When Taiwan (the island of Formosa) was returned to *de facto* Chinese control after fifty years of Japanese occupation, U.S. military forces removed nearly all Japanese from the island. The removal of those who had exercised management control and possessed requisite technical knowledge meant that this relatively highly developed island had to be staffed at management and technical levels with Chinese personnel who lacked previous knowledge of the properties involved and who faced, in addition to normal maintenance problems, a large replacement problem resulting from bombing damage inflicted during the war by U.S. airforces.

Considerable quantities of industrial materials and equipment had been made available to China through previous aid programs, notably the UNRRA program, and through Chinese Government procurement from the Pacific islands of United States surplus supplies after the war. China had not been able to absorb all of these supplies during the first three post-war years. The ECA faced, therefore, the problem not only of making sure that equipment under the ECA China aid program was put to effective use, but of helping also to get into operation residual stockpiles of equipment already in China.

Most of China's industrial plant had been badly undermaintained throughout the long war years, and requisite training of personnel had been largely discontinued. Although China's industrial development was still in its early stages, the effective functioning of the nation's limited industrial plant was regarded as vital for the production of goods essential to the reducing of China's dependence upon external aid, and for an effective approach to the problem of inflation.

The essence of the problem facing ECA, then, was an extensive need for replacement and reconstruction equipment and a lack of the foreign assistance in engineering and management requisite to the effective absorption of such equipment into the Chinese economy. A solution to this problem required a unique approach. Engineering and management assistance would have to be furnished along with the equipment. The ECA, in approaching this problem, needed also to bear in mind objectives implicit in the legislative history of the ECA: to maximize the use of private trade channels, to encourage both internal production and international trade and to avoid impairment of the U.S. economy.

Insufficiency of technical knowledge and experience in management had been a recurrent problem encountered in efforts to help Chinese industry. This made necessary a provision of technical and managerial help along with material assistance. The Survey Group developed a unique plan of action for the meeting of this need. It recommended that each industrial project applying for, and receiving a tentative allotment for, ECA assistance be required to engage the services of a private engineering firm to help in surveying and planning the work needing to be done and in the procurement and installation of requisite equipment. The Survey Group further recommended that the Chinese Government and ECA jointly engage a high-grade American engineering management firm to assist in supervising the entire scheme, in order to ensure that this part of the China Aid Program would, as a whole, be conducted with the benefit of outstanding engineering talent and experience. These recommendations contemplated ECA payment for such engineering services under the "technical assistance" provision in Section 111 (a) (3) of the Foreign Assistance Act of 1948. These recommendations, in which the Chinese Government concurred, were approved by the Administrator as a tentative basis on which further development of the program might proceed.

In anticipating the types of firms best equipped to undertake, on behalf of provisionally approved projects, the requisite work of pre-project engineering analysis and subsequent assistance in procurement and installation, consideration was given both to engineering firms without previous experience in China and to concerns which had been active in developing production and trade in China. Some of the latter, with worldwide connections, extensive local experience and competent resident managers and staffs of engineers, both Chinese and foreign, could, it was believed, make valuable contributions, under appropriate safeguards, to the success of the program.

Practical Arrangements Developed

After consideration of all aspects of this complicated program, the Chinese Government and the ECA Mission to China agreed to form a non-voting consultative Joint Committee composed of three representatives of the Chinese Government and two representatives of the ECA Mission to supervise the carrying out of the replacement and reconstruction projects. This arrangement was in accord with the principles of the Economic Aid Agreement between China and the United States which specifies that programs are to be carried out by mutual agreement.

It was decided to engage the services of an outstanding American management engineering firm to assist the Joint Committee. This was a distinct change from methods hitherto employed for previous aid programs by either government or by the United Nations for the UNRRA program. Previous practice had involved efforts to coordinate the work of Chinese and non-Chinese staffs, without use in most cases of special engineering consultants or of normal business and trade channels for functions which might be performed efficiently and economically by private enterprise. The Joint Committee, representing both governments, decided to retain in a technical capacity the J. G. White Engineering Corporation of New York City. The principal function of this corporation, it was agreed, would be to furnish technical supervision, with a group of from six to ten U. S. engineers, of the projects approved under the tentatively authorized $70 million ECA replacement and reconstruction program in China. The staff was not itself to undertake any "projects", but to assist the Joint Committee in selecting, recommending for approval, and supervising a wide range of industrial projects.

The procedure adopted may be outlined briefly as follows:

Private or public enterprises desiring assistance under the program would present initial applications to the Joint Committee which would refer them to the J. G. White Corporation for analysis and recommendation; projects provisionally approved by the Joint Committee were to be given "provisional allotments".

As soon as a "provisional allotment" was made, the successful applicant was to select an engineering firm as its "project engineer", this selection requiring ratification by the Joint Committee set up by the Chinese Government and the ECA China Mission.

The project engineer would draw up a bill of materials with detailed specifications, search world markets for necessary equipment and supplies which could be procured on the most expeditious and economical terms, and present a fully justified "project" to the Joint Committee.

Upon approval of the project by the Joint Committee, the project engineer would arrange for the procurement and delivery of approved equipment and material, and assist the applicant in achieving prompt installation and use.

Financing was to be done by ECA by a letter of commitment to a U. S. bank, in effect guaranteeing letters of credit (a) to suppliers of equipment or materials under approved projects, and (b) to the project engineer for his approved fee.

At each stage of this procedure, the J. G. White Engineering Corporation was to act as technical staff to the Joint Committee, the Committee taking action only after receiving the recommendations of its technical staff on such matters as: approval of the selection of project engineering firms, approval of fees and charges by these firms, approval of the detailed specifications and sources of procurement of equipment for the projects, and approval of prices of materials to be procured. Before any program was approved, the applicant and the project engineer would be required to submit to the Joint Committee a sworn affidavit containing information with respect to their profit margins and their methods of seeking materials, including competitive bidding. Arrangements could be made for the technical staff of the Joint Committee to accept sealed bids on items where relationships between the project engineer and the supplier indicated that such protection would be desirable.

These procedures taken together represented a new pattern for publicly financed industrial projects in underdeveloped areas. As such, they provided a unique approach toward the solution of a large continuing problem, that of grafting branches of modern technology onto the great trunks of agrarian economy in Asia and other underdeveloped parts of the world. An uninterrupted testing of this approach was unfortunately precluded by events in China.

RURAL RECONSTRUCTION PROGRAM

During the deliberations of the House Foreign Affairs Committee in February and March of 1948 on prospective aid to China, consideration was given to the fundamental and extensive needs of the Chinese economy in the field of rural reconstruction. Some new light had been thrown on this problem by a special agricultural mission sent to China by the President in 1946. Valuable experience in dealing with certain aspects of the problem had been gained through the Chinese Mass Education Movement headed by Dr. James Y. C. Yen. Information from these and other sources was weighed by the Committee with the result that rural reconstruction was included in subsequent China aid legislation as a specific field in which program funds might be spent.

Section 407 of the China Aid Act

Authorization for inclusion of a special rural reconstruction program was provided in Section 407 of the China Aid Act of 1948—the full text of which appears in the Appendix. This Section authorized the Secretary of State, after consultation with the Administrator, "to conclude an agreement with China establishing a Joint Commission on Rural Reconstruction in China, to be composed of two citizens of the United States appointed by the President of the United States and three citizens of China appointed by the President of China." Such Commission, it was provided, subject to the direction and control of the Administrator, was to formulate and carry out a program for reconstruction in rural areas of China, including such research and training activities as might be necessary or appropriate for such reconstruction.

The Act authorized an expenditure, for this rural reconstruction program, of an amount equal to not more than 10 percent of the funds made available for economic aid to China under the China Aid Act. This placed an upper limit of $27.5 million upon the funds which could be used for the rural reconstruction program. It was stipulated that the amount could be made available in U.S. dollars, proceeds in Chinese currency from the sale of ECA commodities, or both.

Establishment of Rural Reconstruction Commission

Following a period of negotiation, notes were exchanged on August 5, 1948, between the United States Ambassador to China and the Chinese Government Ministry of Foreign Affairs, providing an agreement for the establishment of a Rural Reconstruction Commission in accordance with the terms of the China Aid Act of 1948. The texts of these notes are quoted in the section on Documents, below.

Following the conclusion of this agreement, appointments were made by the Chinese and the United States Governments to the Rural Reconstruction Commission, the Chinese members being Dr. Chiang Monlin (former President of the Peking National University, former Minister of Education, and recently Executive Secretary of the Chinese Government Executive Yuan), Chairman; Dr. James Y. C. Yen (for 25 years the leader of China's internationally known Mass Education Movement) ; and Dr. T. H. Shen (outstanding Chinese agriculturist). The United States members appointed by the President on September 19, 1948, were Dr. John Earl Baker (former Director of the China International Famine Relief Commission and former adviser to the Chinese Government), and Dr. Raymond T. Moyer (U.S. Department of Agriculture authority on Chinese agriculture). On October 1, the Commission held its first meeting.

Objectives and Principles

The problem of rural reconstruction in China is one of enormous magnitude and complexity. Intensive and lengthy discussion was required to reach general agreement among members of the Commission with respect to questions of aim, emphasis, organization and methods of work. On October 18, 1948, agreement was reached on a general statement of the objectives and principles of the Joint Commission on Rural Reconstruction. The text of this statement follows:

"I. *Objectives*
A. To improve the living conditions of the rural people.
B. To increase the production of food and other important crops.
C. To develop the potential power of the people to reconstruct their own communities and the nation, thus to lay the foundation of a strong and democratic China.
D. To help build up and strengthen appropriate services of government agencies—national, provincial and *hsien*—that are established to carry out measures pertaining to rural reconstruction.
E. To help stimulate and revitalize enterprises of the Rural Reconstruction Movement and other private agencies doing rural reconstruction work.
F. To offer liberals, educated youths and other constructive elements, opportunities to participate in a program of service.

"II. *Principles*
1. Relating to Program
A. The emergency nature of the present situation shall be given paramount consideration in deciding on the nature and location of program and projects.
B. First consideration shall be given to projects which will contribute most directly and immediately to the welfare of the rural people, with special emphasis to be given to the improvement of their economic conditions.
C. A literacy program, supplemented by audiovisual aids, shall be an essential

part of this program, as a means of furthering education, organizing the people, and developing and selecting rural leadership.

D. New projects in rural reconstruction deserve encouragement, but unless they can show evidence of self-help and self-support for a reasonable length of time, financial aid shall not be considered.

E. Projects which already have been proved successful, under rural conditions, and which are reasonably simple and inexpensive, shall be broadcast on a large scale.

F. In general, preference shall be given to those agencies engaged in rural reconstruction having a sound foundation and experienced staff and organization.

2. Relating to Procedure

A. The program formulated by the Commission shall be carried out in cooperation with existing agencies.

B. A correlated approach shall be adopted wherever possible, since the various aspects of rural reconstruction are interrelated, the success of one depending on the success of the other.

C. A direct extension-type of adult education shall be emphasized as the most effective and quickest means of promoting the understanding, acceptance and correct use of recommended practices.

D. Local initiative shall be fostered and local resources, both human and material, shall be mobilized for the purposes of the program.

E. Assistance to a project in any province shall be contingent upon the willingness of the provincial and local officials concerned to cooperate fully in efforts to carry it out, and to take other steps, themselves, that are essential to the attainment of results expected of the project."

On October 26, 1948, "A Memorandum of Understanding Between the Economic Cooperation Administration and the Joint Commission on Rural Reconstruction in China, Defining Their Respective Spheres of Administrative Responsibility" was signed by the Chairman of the Joint Rural Reconstruction Commission and the Acting Chief of the ECA Mission to China. This agreement established procedures for the presentation of budget estimates by the Joint Commission and the allocation of U. S. dollar funds for material and technical assistance and of local currency from the counterpart funds for expenses incurred within China. And arrangements were agreed upon for the recruitment, administrative supervision and direction of Commission personnel.

Based on the objectives and principles quoted above, the Commission worked out the main outlines of a program, which was divided into four parts with the following aims:

To increase in supplying areas the domestic production of agricultural commodities currently in serious short supply in China and supplied in part by the United States ECA program, particularly foodstuffs;

To establish centers in which a broad integrated program would be started under appropriate agencies of the Government, through projects related to local government administration, land reform, agriculture, rural public health and rural social education;

To carry out a large-scale effort in adult education as a means of developing the potential power of the people and raising their level of understanding, thus enabling them to participate more intelligently in solving their present problems; and,

To assist significant projects in rural reconstruction established in numerous centers through local initiative and resources.

When Nanking became threatened by military action, it was decided to move the Commission's operational headquarters to Canton. At the same time, a decision was made to focus major attention first on the development of a program in provinces south of the Yangtze River, and to concentrate upon projects susceptible of prompt development and usefulness, in such fields as irrigation, dyke repair, public health, and the control of serious animal diseases.

Surveys and Organization

To put this initial program promptly into effect a trip was taken by members of the Commission to Szechwan and Hunan provinces to inspect existing efforts on behalf of the rural population and to consult with responsible persons concerning projects for which assistance had been requested. Steps also were taken to set up regional officers in Chungking (Szechwan), Changsha (Hunan), and Kweilin (Kwangsi), and a central office in Canton (Kwangtung), while retaining a regional office in Nanking. Tentative plans to carry out some phases of a rural program from two offices in north China had to be suspended on account of troubled civil war conditions there. Headquarters of the Commission were moved to Canton on December 5, 1948.

To assist the Commission in carrying out its plans, competent persons were selected as heads for three of the four divisions of work, and, at the end of the year, able appointees were under consideration for the fourth division and to represent the Commission in three of the most important regional offices. A staff of Chinese and American specialists was being assembled to advise the Commission and help carry out its program, although uncertainties in the general situation caused the Commission to proceed gradually in building up such a staff.

The impression gained by the Commission in visits to provinces in west and south China was that these provinces were at the time relatively free from the acute tension then felt in the lower Yangtze area, and that local officials and private agencies were anxious to proceed with rural reconstruction measures along the general lines formulated by the Joint Commission. Steps were taken, therefore, to get into operation, in an initial program, specific projects to which the Commission was prepared to allocate assistance.

Initial Projects

Projects for which detailed plans were being developed included the following:

A broad integrated program in rural reconstruction in the third prefecture of Szechwan province, initiated by the Mass Education Movement and local leaders, assistance to include grants for the development of educational, agricultural and farm organization projects, and loans for irrigation and weaving projects.

The completion of 11 irrigation projects already underway in Szechwan province, which would provide for the irrigation of 191,000 mow (about 30,000 acres) of land by the end of April 1949.

The establishment of a system to multiply and distribute improved rice, corn and cotton varieties in Szechwan province.

The repair of dykes in the Tung T'ing Lake area of Hunan province, which would restore to production and protect from flooding land normally producing around two-thirds of the amount of rice annually imported into China before the war, to be completed by the end of April 1949.

An integrated program of rural reconstruction in Hunan, for which definite plans were yet to be received and agreed upon.

The establishment in Hunan province, the "rice bowl" of central China, of the beginnings of an improved system of rice production and marketing, including the multiplication and distribution of improved seed varieties and the establishment of more modern milling and warehousing centers.

Projects involving cooperation with various Ministries of the National Government were being considered in consultation with these Ministries after specific project plans were reasonably well developed. Steps were being taken to set up appropriate committees of specialists to advise the Commission and to assist in carrying out phases of the rural reconstruction program; the first committee established was for work in the field of public health in rural areas, with a former Minister of Health as Chairman. In accordance with a request of the Rural Reconstruction Commission, a private public relations firm completed in November a special study of the facilities available for a widespread educational effort under the Commission's sponsorship.

Detailed plans for the irrigation projects in Szechwan, for the dyke repair project in Hunan, for certain parts of the program sponsored by the Mass Education Movement in Szechwan, and for several other projects were being reviewed in December with a view to early allocations of funds. The Commission also expected to make early announcement of projects to which it would initially allocate assistance in Kwangtung province, and trips were planned to Kwangsi, Fukien and Taiwan to study projects for which aid had been requested.

Specific plans for broader programs with a major emphasis on education, it was anticipated, might not be completed before the end of February 1949. Tentative planning, conditional upon developments, called for an extension of some assistance to such integrated programs during the spring of 1949. It was expected, however, under prevailing conditions, that available funds under the current program would necessarily be allocated principally to projects of a short-range nature, emphasizing increases in agricultural production and improvements in rural health conditions.

STRATEGIC MATERIALS

Article VI, paragraph 1, of the Economic Cooperation Agreement between the United States and the Republic of China (the full text of which is quoted in the section on Documents, below) provided that the Chinese Government would facilitate the transfer to the United States, for stockpiling or other purposes, "materials originating in China which are required by the United States of America as a result of deficiencies or potential deficiencies in its own resources upon such reasonable terms of sale, exchange, barter or otherwise and in such quantities and for such period of time as may be agreed to between the Government of the United States of America and of China for domestic use and commercial export of such materials." The Government of China agreed to undertake "such specific measures as may be necessary to carry out the provisions of this paragraph" and "when so requested by the Government of the United States of America, to enter into negotiations for detailed arrangements necessary to carry out the provisions of this paragraph."

Article V, paragraph 4, of the same agreement, provided that expenditures in Chinese currency from the Special Account (described below) would be "only for such purposes as may be agreed from time to time with the United States of America, including expenditures incident to the stimulation of production activity and the development of new sources of wealth including materials which may be required in the United States of America because of deficiencies or potential deficiencies in the resources of the United States of America."

A preliminary investigation was conducted by members of the Reconstruction Survey Group, with a view to promoting increased production and export to the United States of strategic materials available in China and required by the United States, particular attention being given to tin, antimony and tungsten in south and southwest China. Such procurement, it was felt—to the extent that it could be developed—would, in addition to increasing the supplies of minerals needed by the United States, serve the double purpose in China of increasing local employment and augmenting the country's slender foreign exchange resources.

Production and Procurement Problems

It was found that foreign exchange policies and controls connected therewith since V–J Day, related to the Government's attempts to deal with the inflation, had exerted a depressing influence upon the production and export of these minerals, making it impossible for exporters, by and large, to obtain by negotiations through official channels fair and realistic prices for their goods. Only on rare occasions, when official exchange rates were for short periods realistic, were such exporters able to secure reasonable returns upon their produce. Initial negotiations looking toward the acquisition of these materials were aimed in part at securing the agreement of the Chinese Government to changes of policy designed to remove some of the obstacles to the flow of materials through legitimate channels of trade to the U.S., at prices fair to the producers.

Additional difficulties in procurement and export of such materials to the United States were attributable to shortage of productive equipment in China and to lack of transportation facilities from relatively inaccessible parts of China where such materials existed. Efforts toward helping to meet both these needs were clearly needed if production and procurement were to be developed on any appreciable scale.

Initial Arrangements

Following the aforementioned survey, the ECA China Mission before the end of 1948 began to work out arrangements with Chinese tin interests to make their product available for export to the United States. After receipt of pertinent information from ECA, the Reconstruction Finance Corporation in Washington offered to purchase from China considerable quantities of tin concentrates, to be refined in the U.S. where efficient smelter operation could extract a maximum percentage of high-grade tin; and to buy some tin metal in China for stockpile purposes. Preliminary negotiations were in progress at the end of the year to effect procurement arrangements, which were complicated by the necessity of effecting purchases through barter by the use of commodities or silver, instead of depreciated local currency.

SPECIAL LOCAL CURRENCY ACCOUNT

Provision for the establishment of a special local currency account, or counterpart fund, was contained in Article V of the Economic Cooperation Agreement between the Governments of China and the United States; the full text of this Agreement appears in the section on Documents, below.[7]

---

[7] See annex 181.

Unique Provisions in the Bilateral Agreement

The article referred to provided for two unique features in connection with the special local currency account, or counterpart fund, in China. The first was a provision that deposits would be made in the account only when requested by the United States; thus deposits could be requested at a rate sufficient to cover actual expenses that had to be met currently, without the accumulation of large balances which would rapidly depreciate in value as a result of the inflation. The second was a provision that the Chinese Government would "maintain the value" of allotments made from the Special Account—for such important purposes as administrative costs, rural reconstruction and the internal expenses of industrial projects—by "depositing such additional amounts of currency as the Government of the United States of America may from time to time determine after consultation with the Government of China." The value of allotments, to be thus maintained, could be recorded in terms of such standard and relatively stable measures of value as quantities of cotton yarn, rice or American dollars.

Support for China Relief Mission Projects

Shortly after the establishment of the ECA Mission in China, discussions were initiated with the Chinese Government pertaining to the setting up and operation of the special local currency account. While these discussions were in progress, provisional arrangements were made for the use of counterpart funds made available by the Chinese Government in support of existing projects in the fields of medical services, relief and welfare, conservancy work, and agricultural improvement which had been previously supported from a local currency account created in connection with the operation of the U.S. China Relief Mission. These projects which had theretofore been regarded as ending on June 30, 1948, were in some cases selected by action of the Chinese Government in consultation with the ECA for continuation after that date.

Preliminary Studies and Proposals

After careful study of special questions involved in setting up the special local currency account in China, and in light of discussions with the Government, the ECA China Mission prepared in September 1948 a tentative proposed program of local currency utilization which outlined in some detail projected uses for the counterpart funds in the fields of conservancy, public works, agriculture, medical and health activities and welfare.

Concurrently, analysis was undertaken of the financial and economic problems in China which needed to be considered in determining the manner in which the counterpart funds would be utilized. These problems included: the extensive deficit spending of the Government, concomitant with the continued prosecution of the civil war; the inflationary effect of the enforcement of the Government's short-lived August 19 economic regulations; the continuation of certain inflationary practices of the Government; the progressive deterioration in economic production; the disruption of transportation in disturbed areas; and the loss of public confidence in the currency resulting in widespread hoarding of supplies and excessively rapid turnover of the currency.

Technical problems requiring study included determination of the exchange rates governing payments of local currency counterpart funds into the Special Account; the timing of deposits; and policies to be followed with regard to the disposition of Special Account funds.

Studies and proposals received from the Mission, in relation to these problems, were further analyzed in Washington prior to consultations with the National Advisory Council.

Establishment of the Special Account

Following these consultations, authorization was given to the ECA China Mission to negotiate with the Chinese Government on questions relating to the establishment of the Special Account, deposits into such account, and purposes for which funds from the account might be utilized.

The Special Account was established in the Central Bank of China. It was agreed that, in order to avoid depreciation of cash balances in the account as a result of the inflation, deposits would be made only as called for by the ECA China Mission, in most cases a short time before withdrawal and expenditure.

Utilization of Counterpart Funds

It was further agreed that withdrawals would be made to cover all mandatory expenditures from the account, as called for in the Bilateral Agreement, including the Chinese currency portion of the following expenses: administrative costs of the ECA China Mission; costs of delivering private relief gift packages in China; and costs of the Joint Commission on Rural Reconstruction. It was estimated that expenditures of these types would amount to roughly 12 percent of the total account.

From the outset, it was clear that "sterilization" of local currency Special Account funds could not of itself be the key to controlling the Chinese inflation. The basic cause of the inflation was the magnitude of the Government's deficit financing, which in turn was due to the exigencies of the civil war and shaken public confidence in the currency which led to excessively rapid rates of circulation of the note issue.

On the other hand, it was apparent that an easy money policy in the use of the Special Account would be inflationary, the effect of such a policy being similar to that of greatly increasing the Government's monthly budget deficit through excessive note issue.

The ECA China Mission, in the light of discussions of this problem with the National Advisory Council in Washington followed, therefore, a policy of agreeing only to expenditures from the account which could be regarded as of demonstrated urgency and which in many cases would have offsetting deflationary benefits. Broad categories of non-mandatory expenditures on which the ECA China Mission could agree with the Chinese Government as being appropriate uses for the Special Account included: emergency expenditures which, at the discretion of the Chief of the ECA China Mission, could be considered as consistent with the objectives of the China Aid Act—expenditures envisaged in this category being for such purposes as emergency procurement of indigenous food for the rationing programs; expenditures on certain carefully screened projects, chiefly in the fields of conservancy, health and welfare; and expenditures, when necessary, to insure prompt installation and proper utilization of capital equipment under the replacement and reconstruction program. The total of these expenditures, it was expected, should amount to less than half of the potential local currency account.

Exchange Rates

A persistent problem with respect to the Special Account has been that of agreeing with the Chinese Government upon appropriate rates at which deposits would be made in terms of U.S. currency—that is, rates reflecting commensurate value in Chinese currency, at given times, for U.S. dollar aid provided. A rapid decline in the value of the new gold yuan and reluctance of the Chinese Government to negotiate formally on a basis other than official exchange rates led, pending a settlement of this question, to deposits being made as advances, without final agreement before the end of 1948 on commensurate value in terms of U.S. dollars.

Deposits and Withdrawals

As of December 31, 1948, deposits into the Special Account totalled, in round numbers, 157,289,000 gold yuan, equivalent (on the basis of rough tentative estimates prior to agreement on applicable exchange rates) to US$9,543,000. Withdrawals on the same date totalled, in round numbers, 150,333,000 gold yuan, equivalent, according to similarly tentative estimates, to US$5,839,000—the equivalent of approximately $1,342,000 being for Eca administrative expenses in China, $2,498,000 for administrative expenses of the Chinese Council for United States Aid, $1,803,000 for special projects, $53,000 for engineering services, and $143,000 for expenses incurred by the Joint Commission on Rural Reconstruction.

Before the end of 1948, the local counterpart funds thus jointly managed by Eca and the Chinese Government had enabled many worthy institutions and projects to continue operations in spite of inflation and civil war.

185

Summary of United States Government Economic, Financial, and Military Aid Authorized for China Since 1937

[Washington,] *March 21, 1949*

Since the commencement of hostilities between China and Japan in 1937 the United States Government has authorized aid to China in the form of grants and credits totalling approximately $3,523 million, of which $2,422 million has been in the form of grants and $1,101 million as credits. About 40 percent of the total, or $1515.7 million, was authorized prior to V–J Day to contribute toward the stabilization of China's wartime economy and to enable the Chinese Government to obtain military, agricultural and industrial goods essential to the conduct of the war with Japan.

United States Government grants and credits to China authorized since V–J Day have amounted to approximately $2,007.7 million, representing sixty percent of the total, of which $1,596.7 million has been as grants and $411 million on credit terms. This aid was designed to assist the Chinese Government in the reoccupation of liberated areas and the repatriation of Japanese, to meet some of China's urgent relief and rehabilitation needs, and, in the case of the present Eca program, to help retard the rate of economic deterioration in China and to encourage the adoption of effective self-help measures on the part of the Chinese Government. The Chinese Government has elected to use $125 million authorized by the China Aid Act of 1948 (included in the total of grants above) to purchase items of a military nature.

The totals of United States aid given above do not include sales to the Chinese Government of United States Government military and civilian-type surplus property which have been made since V–J Day, except where these sales were made on credit terms. In such cases, the amount of the credit involved has been included in the total of United States credits authorized. Surplus property with a total estimated procurement cost of over $1,078.1 million has been sold China for an agreed realization to the United States of $232 million, of which $95.5 million is to be repaid on credit terms. There are no available estimates of the fair value of this surplus property at the time of its sale. Neither do the aid totals include certain ammunition transferred by the United States Marines in connection with their withdrawal from north China.

United States aid to China reviewed herein does not reflect assistance through provision of advisory personnel in cultural, economic and military fields; nor does it include United States contributions through certain United Nations' programs in China—the International Children's Emergency Fund, the International Refugee Organization, the World Health Organization, and advisory social welfare services.

The various measures of United States Government aid authorized for China since 1937, together with the miscellaneous sales to China of United States Government surplus property, are summarized in the table below and described briefly in the text that follows.

United States Government economic, financial and military aid to China since 1937

[In millions of U. S. dollars]

	Grants	Credits	Sales of U. S. Government Excess and Surplus Property		
			Procurement value	Realization by U. S.	
				Initial	Ultimate
	(1)	(2)	(3)	(4)	(5)
					(Sum of Columns 2 & 4)
Pre-V–J Day:					
ECONOMIC					
1. Export-Import Bank Credits Authorized	. . . .	$120	. . . . .	. . . . .	. . . . .
2. Stabilization fund agreement, 1941	. . . .	50	. . . . .	. . . . .	. . . . .
3. 1942 Treasury Credit (PL 442)	. . . .	500	. . . . .	. . . . .	. . . . .
TOTAL ECONOMIC AID	. . . .	$670	. . . . .	. . . . .	. . . . .
MILITARY					
4. Lend-lease ($845.7 million)	$825.7	20	. . . . .	. . . . .	. . . . .
TOTAL MILITARY AID	$825.7	20	. . . . .	. . . . .	. . . . .
TOTAL PRE-V–J DAY AID	$825.7	$690	. . . . .	. . . . .	. . . . .
Post-V–J Day:					
ECONOMIC					
5. Lend-lease "pipeline" credit	. . . .	51.7	. . . . .	. . . . .	. . . . .
6. UNRRA—US Contribution	474.0	. . . . .	. . . . .	. . . . .	. . . . .
7. BOTRA—US Contribution	3.6	. . . . .	. . . . .	. . . . .	. . . . .
8. Export-Import Bank Credits Authorized	. . .	82.8	. . . . .	. . . . .	. . . . .
9. Civilian Surplus Property Transfers (Under August 30, 1946, bulk sale agreement)	. . . .	55	$900	$120	$175
10. OFLC dockyard facilities sales	. . . .	4.1	n. a.	. . . . .	4.1
11. Maritime Commission ship sales	. . . .	$16.4	$77.3	$9.8	$26.2
12. U. S. Foreign Relief Program	$46.4	. . . . .	. . . . .	. . . . .	. . . . .
13. ECA Program	275	. . . . .	. . . . .	. . . . .	. . . . .
TOTAL ECONOMIC AID	$799.0	$210.0	$977.3	$129.8	$205.3

United States Government economic, financial and military aid to China since 1937—Continued

[In millions of U. S. dollars]

	Grants	Credits	Sales of U. S. Government Excess and Surplus Property		
			Procurement value	Realization by U. S.	
				Initial	Ultimate
	(1)	(2)	(3)	(4)	(5)
Post V–J Day—Continued					
MILITARY					
14. Lend-lease ($694.7 million)	513. 7	181. 0	. . . . .	. . . . .	. . . . .
15. Military Aid Under SACO	17. 7	. . . . .	. . . . .	. . . . .	. . . . .
16. Sale of excess stocks of U. S. Army in West China.	. . . . .	20	n. a.	(ᵃ)	(ᵃ)20. 0
17. Ammunition Abandoned and Transferred by U. S. Marines in North China (over 6,500 tons) .	(ᵇ)	. . . . .	. . . . .	. . . . .	. . . . .
18. Transfer of U. S. Navy Vessels (PL 512)	ᶜ 141. 3	. . . . .	. . . . .	. . . . .	. . . . .
19. Sales of surplus military equipment (total accepted by Chinese Govt.)	. . . . .	. . . . .	100. 8	6. 7	6. 7
20. $125 Million Grant Under China Aid Act of 1948 .	125	. . . . .	. . . . .	. . . . .	. . . . .
TOTAL MILITARY AID	$797. 7	$201. 0	$100. 8	$6. 7	$26. 7
TOTAL POST-V-J DAY AID	1, 596. 7	411. 0	1, 078. 1	136. 5	232. 0
GRAND TOTAL	$2, 422. 4	$1, 101. 0	$1, 078. 1	$136. 5	$232. 0

ᵃ Down payment covered under Item 9. See textual explanation.

ᵇ No estimate of total value available.

ᶜ Vessels valued at procurement cost.

DESCRIPTION OF INDIVIDUAL CATEGORIES OF U.S. AID

(Paragraph numbers correspond with numbers of items listed in table above)

1. *Pre-V–J Day Export-Import Bank Credits:* Export-Import Bank credits extended prior to V–J Day were general commodity credits, used to purchase a considerable variety of American industrial and agricultural products and services. Repayment was arranged by contracts between United States and Chinese Government agencies for the sale of strategic minerals or wood oil. Of the $120 million total authorized, $117 million was disbursed and the balance, approximately $3 million, expired. Of the amount disbursed, $112.8 million had been repaid as of December 31, 1948. Credit authorizations were as follows:

		Million
Universal Trading Corporation	12/13/38	$25. 0
Universal Trading Corporation	3/7/40	20. 0
Central Bank of China	10/17/40	25 .0
Central Bank of China	11/30/40	50. 0
Total		$120. 0

2. On April 1, 1941, the Secretary of the Treasury entered into an agreement with the Government of China and the Central Bank of China to purchase Chinese Yuan up to an amount equivalent to U. S. $50 million to further the monetary and financial cooperation of the two governments and the stabilization of the United States dollar–Chinese Yuan rate of exchange. This agreement did not provide for collateralization of such purchases, as did a previous stabili-

zation agreement of 1937 which therefore cannot be considered as representing aid to the Chinese Government in the strict sense of the term. It was further agreed in connection with the 1941 agreement that a Stabilization Board be established, to which the Chinese Government banks were to contribute $20 million. Purchases of Chinese Yuan under this agreement amounted to U. S. $10 million and were repaid in April 1943.

3. *1942 Treasury Credit (PL 442)*: On February 7, 1942, Congress passed Public Law 442, authorizing the Secretary of the Treasury, with the approval of the President, to make available to China funds not to exceed $500 million and promptly made appropriations for this purpose. An agreement of March 21, 1942, between the United States and China established this amount as a credit in the name of the Chinese Government. Between the date of the agreement and V–J Day, the Chinese Government drew on this credit to the extent of $485 million, the balance having been drawn since V–J Day.

At the time of this congressional action, strategic bases of the United Nations were being lost to the Japanese offensive in the Pacific and southeast Asia, and effective land lines of communication with China were being severed. It was of vital importance to the United States Government that China, which had resisted Japanese aggression for 5 years, should be strengthened and encouraged to continue the war against Japan. Since opportunities for giving effective material aid to China, such as was being rendered to allies in more accessible areas through lend-lease, were not great, the $500 million credit was characterized by the Secretary of the Treasury and in House Report No. 1739 as "the financial counterpart of lend-leasing war materials."

Funds provided under the agreement of March 21, 1942, were used mainly by the Chinese Government to purchase gold for sale in China as an anti-inflationary measure and to provide reserves for the redemption of Chinese Government savings and victory bonds denominated in United States dollars. A total of $220 millions was withdrawn in gold, much of which was shipped to China, largely during 1945, to be sold internally in an effort to control inflation by reducing currency in circulation and keeping down the price of gold.

A total of $200 million was reserved out of the 1942 credit for the redemption of Chinese Government United States dollar security issues. A reserve of $100 million was established for payment of Chinese United States dollar savings certificates, and another $100 million was earmarked for the payment of Chinese United States dollar victory bonds. In 1946, this earmarking was abandoned, and the funds became available for imports and other foreign payments as measures were promulgated governing payment of foreign currency bonds held in China which provided that such bonds would be redeemed in Chinese currency. It was also provided, however, that registered bondholders outside China would be paid in foreign currency.

Of the balance of $80 millions of the credit, $55 million was spent for purchase of bank notes in the United States, and $25 million was used to import textiles into China.

Final settlement of the terms of this credit has not yet been negotiated.

4. *Pre-V–J Day Lend-Lease:* China was declared eligible for lend-lease aid on May 6, 1941. During that first year until the blocking of the Burma Road in April 1942, lend-lease aid was aimed especially at improving transport over the Burma Road, which, due to the Japanese blockade, was the only land route into China. Although amounts carried by this route were greatly increased, they were still small. Delivery by air cargo plane from Assam in India over the 18,000-foot hump of the Himalayas, begun in April 1942, was the only means of lend-lease

supply until the completion in January 1945 of the Ledo Road from India across Burma. Lend-lease materials supplied prior to V–J Day were primarily military in character, but included considerable quantities of industrial and transportation equipment essential to the Chinese war effort. All but approximately $20 million of the $845.7 million in lend-lease aid extended prior to V–J Day is considered to have been on a grant basis. Terms of settlement of the $20 million balance are subject to negotiation.

The following table presents a break-down by major categories of Pre-V-J Day lend-lease aid:

Ordnance and Ordnance Stores	$153, 333, 189. 94
Aircraft and Aeronautical Material	187, 339, 849. 94
Tanks and Other Vehicles	94, 177, 927. 72
Vessels and Other Watercraft	35, 561, 264. 12
Miscellaneous Military Equipment	47, 085, 115. 94
Facilities and Equipment	9, 928, 803. 33
Agricultural, Industrial and Other Commodities	46, 505, 983. 26
Testing and Reconditioning of Defense Articles	204, 393. 63
Services and Expenses	271, 611, 693. 00
Total	$845, 748, 220. 88

These figures are compiled from reports received by the Treasury Department from United States Government agencies as of June 30, 1948.

5. *Lend-Lease "Pipeline" Credit:* An agreement between the United States and China dated June 14, 1946 authorized the delivery on 3 (c) credit terms of civilian-type equipment and supplies contracted for but undelivered on V–J Day under the wartime lend-lease program. It was subsequently determined that a total of $51.7 million in equipment and supplies could be furnished under contracts covered by this agreement. The Chinese Government had been billed for "pipeline" shipments totalling $50.3 million in value as of November 30, 1948.

6. *UNRRA:* The UNRRA program for China was estimated on December 31, 1947 to involve the procurement of goods valued at approximately $517.5 million, allocated as follows:

	(Millions)
Food	133. 2
Clothing	113. 4
Medical Supplies	31. 7
Agricultural Rehabilitation	72. 5
Industrial Rehabilitation	166. 7
Total	517. 5

The estimate of the total value of the goods procured under the UNRRA program has since been revised upward to $526.8 million. This figure does not include shipping and insurance costs, which, in the case of China, are roughly estimated to have added an average of about 25 percent. This brings the total estimated cost of the UNRRA China program to $658.4 million. Since the United States contribution to all UNRRA funds was approximately 72 percent, it may be said that the United States contribution to the China program amounted to 72 percent of $658.4 million, or $474.0 million.

7. *BOTRA:* $5 million of UNRRA funds were allocated to the Board of Trustees for Rehabilitation Affairs (BOTRA), an international body established by the Chinese Government to control the use of UNRRA supplies and funds remaining after the conclusion of its China program. Since the United States contribution to the entire UNRRA program was approximately 72 percent, it may be esti-

mated that the United States contribution to the Botra fund was $3.6 million.

8. *Post-V–J Day Export-Import Bank Credits:*

(a) *Credits Authorized for China:* Export-Import Bank credits have been authorized for China since V–J Day for specific rehabilitation purposes. Individual credits are as follows:

Borrower	To Finance	Date	Amount (Millions)
Yungli Chemical Industry . . .	Machinery, equipment and services [1] .	3/21/45	$16. 0
Central Bank of China	Cotton	1/3/46	33. 0
Republic of China	Cargo Vessels	2/20/46	4. 2
Republic of China	" "		
Republic of China	Equipment, materials and engineering services	2/20/46 2/20/46	2. 6 8. 8
Republic of China	Railway Repair Materials	2/20/46	16. 7
Republic of China	Coal mining equipment, materials and supplies	3/13/46	1. 5
Total	. . . .	. . . . .	$82. 8

[1] Legal documents of guaranty not available until 1947.

Of the $82.8 million credit authorized since V–J Day, $65.4 million had been disbursed as of December 31, 1948. Thus a balance of $17.4 million remains undisbursed, including the $16 million credit to Yungli Chemical Industries, Ltd. Owing to the delay in concluding the detailed arrangements for disbursing the Yungli credit it was necessary for the Export-Import Bank to postpone the expiry date until December 31, 1950.

Of the total amount disbursed since V–J Day, 12.2 million had been repaid as of December 31, 1948, leaving 53.2 million outstanding.

(b) *The $500 Million Earmark for China:* In recognition of the magnitude of China's requirements for reconstruction and the possibilities for economic development under orderly conditions, the United States Government gave consideration after V–J Day to making available substantial funds for this purpose. In April 1946, following the recommendation of General Marshall and approval by the National Advisory Council, the Export-Import Bank authorized the earmarking until June 30, 1947 of $500 million of the Bank's funds for the possible extension of individual credits to the Chinese Government and private Chinese interests. It was contemplated that such credits would be confined to particular projects and would be subject to the usual criteria governing the Bank's lending operations. No implementing agreements were consummated between the Bank and the representatives of the Chinese Government.

During 1946 and the first half of 1947, the Chinese Government discussed numerous proposals for credits with the Export-Import Bank, for some of which General Marshall and the Department of State recommended favorable consideration. Most of the proposals were not adequately supported by economic and financial data and analysis, and many of them were overlapping and without any indication of priority. The principal reason, however, for the Bank's refusal to take favorable action on Chinese credit proposals was its inability to find reasonable assurances of repayment.

In accordance with the terms of its authorization, the earmarking of $500 million for China lapsed on June 30, 1947. However, on June 27, 1947, the Export-Import Bank announced that, the expiration of the earmarked funds notwithstanding, it was prepared to consider Chinese credit applications in accordance with its general policies. While the Chinese Government has subsequently applied for substantial credits, none have been extended by the Bank, primarily, again, because of inability to find reasonable assurances of repayment.

9. *Civilian-type Surplus Property Sales (Under August 30, 1946 Bulk Sale Agreement)*: The sale to China of United States surplus fixed installations and movable property located in India and China and on seventeen Pacific islands was authorized or recognized under an agreement between the two governments dated August 30, 1946. The property sold under this agreement included every type of supply used by an expeditionary force except combat matériel, vessels, and aircraft, all of which were specifically excluded from the contract. The total procurement cost of the property involved, initially computed at approximately $824 million, is now estimated at $900 million. Vehicles of all types account for about one-third of the total, construction equipment about one-sixth, and air force supplies and equipment about one-eighth. The remainder was composed principally of communication equipment, tools, shop equipment, industrial machinery, electrical equipment, medical equipment, and chemicals. Approximately $873.4 million at procurement cost had been declared surplus under this agreement as of September 30, 1948.

Property originally valued at $240 million, included in the above total, had been sold under a number of miscellaneous sales contracts prior to the conclusion of the agreement but incorporated in whole or in part in the consideration set forth in the agreement. This property consisted chiefly of fixed installations and stocks of equipment in China and India and small ships from the Pacific area. The sales value of this property was agreed in the contract as $74 million. It had been turned over, for the most part, to the Chinese Government prior to August 31, 1946, and consisted of the following individual transactions:

(a) The Calcutta stock pile, having a sales price of approximately $25,000,000. This group of property, which had been sold to China under an earlier agreement, was composed largely of trucks and spare parts together with other supplies related to the repair and maintenance of motor vehicles.

(b) The small-ship program, with the sales price of approximately $28,000,000. Ships included in this program cover all varieties of small noncombat types.

(c) Materials and supplies required for the support of air forces with a sales value of approximately $6,000,000. This package of equipment, originated as a part of the lend-lease program, had already been assembled for subsequent delivery to the Chinese when hostilities terminated.

(d) The Army's sale of property in west China, having a basic sales price of $25,000,000 (U.S.) plus $5,160,000,000 (Chinese) of which the $5,000,000 down payment is incorporated in the consideration covering the bulk sale. This sale was occasioned by the withdrawal of the Army from west China in 1945, and included a broad assortment of expeditionary supplies.

(e) Miscellaneous small sales with a sales value of approximately $10,000,000. These cover all types of property which had been purchased by the Chinese Government prior to the date of the bulk sale. Two major categories, which combined represent almost one-half the total, are railroad equipment purchased in France and an assortment of quartermaster supplies composed largely of mosquito bars, blankets, and bath towels.

The agreement of August 30, 1946 provided for a total realization by the United States of $175 million, as follows: 1) $150 million offset against the United States' wartime indebtedness to China, 2) the equivalent in Chinese currency of U.S. $20 million to be available over 20 years to the United States for research cultural, and educational activities in China, and 3) the equivalent in Chinese currency of U.S. $35 million to be available over 20 years for acquisition by the United States of property in China and for current governmental expenses. While these considerations total $205 million, the United States at the same time agreed to establish a $30 million fund to be used by China to cover the cost of shipping and technical services arising out of the property transfer. Thus the United States' net realization under the agreement was $175 million.

10. *OFLC Dockyard Facilities Sales:* On May 15, 1946 OFLC agreed to furnish the Chinese Government surplus supplies and equipment for dockyards at Shanghai and Tsingtao, with repayment to be mâde in thirty annual installments. However the agreement provided that the United States might, at its option, request of China certain goods and services for United States Navy and other Government-owned vessels, with the cost of such goods and services considered as part of China's annual payments of interest and principal. Transfers of United States surplus under this agreement have now been completed. As of October 31, 1948, OFLC sales totalled $4.1 million at fair value.

11. *Maritime Commission Ship Sales:* Since V–J Day the Maritime Commission has sold the Chinese Government 43 vessels with a total sales price of $26.2 million under the Merchant Ship Sales Act of 1946. Of this amount, $16.4 million was on Maritime Commission credit terms. The balance was paid in cash, obtained in part through an Export-Import Bank credit. (See item 8 above.) The total wartime procurement cost of the 43 vessels was $77.3 million.

The following sales are included in the total:

No.	*Type*	*Sales Price*
10	N–3	$4, 300, 000
10	Liberty and	
8	N–3	9, 300, 000
8	C1–M–VI and	
4	C1–S–AY1	10, 000, 000
3	VC2–A–P2	2, 600, 000
TOTAL	. . . .	$26,200,000

12. *U. S. Foreign Relief Program:* Public Law 84, approved May 31, 1947, authorized the initial appropriations for the United States Foreign Relief Program. China's allocation out of these appropriations amounted to approximately $28.4 million. A supplementary appropriation of $18 million for the China program was authorized under Public Law 393, approved December 23, 1947. Deliveries to China under the United States Foreign Relief Program were made during the first half of 1948, as follows:

Cereals	$35, 412, 900
Seeds	88, 400
Pesticides	609, 900
Medical Supplies	5, 185, 300
Estimated shipping costs	5, 084, 500
TOTAL	$46, 381, 000

13. *ECA Program:* The current program of economic aid for China was authorized on April 3, 1948, in the China Aid Act of 1948 (Title IV of the Foreign Assistance Act of 1948). This Act authorized to be appropriated $338,000,000 for economic assistance to China, to be available for obligation for a period of one year from the date of enactment. The Act further provided for creation

of a Joint Commission on Rural Reconstruction in China. It was specified that insofar as practicable a maximum of ten percent of the funds made available for economic assistance should be allotted to the Rural Reconstruction Program, in the form of United States dollars, proceeds in Chinese currency from the sale of Eca commodities, or both.

The appropriation act passed on June 28 (PL 793) appropriated $275,000,000 for economic aid to China of which not more than $1,200,000 was to be obligated for administrative expenses.

The original Eca Program for China consisted of the following four major categories of expenditures:

a) A commodity program, through which Eca finances the importation of food, petroleum, cotton, fertilizer, and coal into China, and supervises the use within China of these commodities $203, 800, 000
b) Participation with the Chinese Government in a Joint Commission on Rural Reconstruction 2, 500, 000
c) A program of industrial replacement and reconstruction, together with related engineering services 67, 500, 000
d) Administration in Washington, D. C. and China 1, 200, 000

TOTAL $275, 000, 000

The following amounts had been authorized for procurement under the Eca commodity program by March 11, 1949:

Rice $44, 580, 000
Wheat/Flour 20, 617, 000
Petroleum. 46, 000, 000
Cotton. 69, 790, 000
Fertilizer 9, 202, 000
Coal 286, 000

TOTAL $190, 475, 000

Dollar expenditures for the rural reconstruction program to date have amounted to less than $50,000. The Commission's expenses have been met largely through withdrawals of Chinese currency from the "counterpart fund" provided by the Chinese Government.

Procurement authorizations under the industrial reconstruction and replacement program have been suspended due to the military situation in China, but pre-project engineering is continuing on a number of projects. A total of $1,550,500 had been authorized for expenditure as of March 11, 1949, mainly for engineering surveys.

14. *Post V-J Day Lend-Lease:* Lend-Lease aid was furnished China after V-J Day to assist the Chinese Government in the reoccupation of liberated areas and in the disarmament and evacuation of Japanese troops. Under the direction of General Wedemeyer, Chinese armies were moved by air to their new reoccupation assignments at a cost of approximately $300 million. Though the "thirty-nine division" program ceased as of V-J Day, transfers of army ground material and equipment were continued. Lend-lease transfers of aircraft and air equipment after V-J Day were effected in order to assist the Chinese in the creation of a modern air force. A military-aid agreemnt of June 28, 1946, provided for the continuation of military lend-lease on a reimbursable basis. This agreement authorized expenditures up to $25 million for the reoccupation of China between June 30 and October 31, 1946, and up to $15 million for training Chinese military, air force, and naval personnel between June 30, 1946, and December 31, 1947. Expenditures under these programs are included in the total figure of lend-lease aid.

As of June 30, 1948 a grand total of $781.0 million in post-V-J Day lend-lease transfers had been reported to the Treasury Department by United States Government agencies. Of this amount, $50.3 million represented deliveries on 3 (c) credit terms under the leand-lease "pipeline" agreement (see item 5 above), and $36 million covered United States Navy vessels originally lend-leased to China but subsequently transferred under the terms of PL 512 (see item 18 below). Of the balance of $694.7 million, $181.0 million is considered subject to payment. Settlement of this amount is now under negotiation.

Listed below are the major categories of Post-V–J Day Lend-Lease supplies:

Ordnance and Ordnance Stores	$117, 869, 076. 94
Aircraft and Aeronautical Material	43, 683, 604. 63
Tanks and Other Vehicles	96, 009, 610. 08
Vessels and Other Watercraft	49, 940, 642. 57
Miscellaneous Military Equipment	99, 762, 611. 71
Facilities and Equipment	36, 198. 74
Agricultural, Industrial and Other Commodities	37, 918, 928. 21
Testing and Reconditioning of Defense Articles	2, 338. 88
Services and Expenses.	335, 817, 910. 56
TOTAL	$781, 040, 922. 32

15. *Military Aid Under SACO:* Supplies valued at $17,666,929.70, consisting primarily of ordnance, were furnished China between September 2, 1945 and March 2, 1946 by the United States Navy under the Sino-American Cooperative Organization agreement. The supplies were made available in exchange for certain services provided by the Chinese Government.

16. *Sale of Excess Stocks of United States Army in West China:* The sale of a broad assortment of military supplies in west China was made on the departure of United States forces from that area. This property was transferred for a sales price of $25 million (U. S.) plus $5.16 billion (Chinese). Down payments of $5.16 billion (Chinese) and $5 million (U. S.) were made in the form of offsets against the United States indebtedness to China. (The $5 million (U. S.) down payment was incorporated in the realized return to the United States under the surplus property sales agreement of August 30, 1946—see item 9 above.) It was agreed that $20 million (U. S.) would be paid over a period of time by China. The terms of repayment are subject to negotiation.

17. *Ammunition Abandoned and Transferred by U. S. Marines in North China:* Between April and September 1947 the United States Marines abandoned or transferred at no cost to the Chinese Government over 6,500 tons of ammunition in connection with their withdrawal from North China. Included was a wide variety of small arms and artillery ammunition, grenades, mines, bombs, and miscellaneous explosives. No estimate of the total value of this material is available.

18. *Transfer of United States Navy Vessels Under P. L. 512:* PL 512 authorized the President to transfer 271 naval vessels to the Chinese Government on such terms as he might prescribe. On December 8, 1947, an agreement was signed between the United States Government and the Republic of China relative to the implementation of this act. A total of 131 vessels with a procurement cost of $141.3 million had been transferred to the Chinese Navy under PL 512 as of December 31, 1948 on a grant basis. This figure includes approximately $36 million representing vessels originally lend-leased to China but subsequently transferred under P. L. 512.

19. *Sales of Surplus Military Equipment:* The United States continued to make military equipment available to the Chinese Government following the termination of lend-lease through the transfer of surplus U. S. equipment at a small fraction of its original procurement cost. As of November 30th, 1948, China had accepted declared military surplus totalling $100.8 million in value at procurement cost,

or \$6.7 million at sales price. Of the total accepted, \$99.8 million (procurement cost) had been shipped. The following is a listing, in summary form, of military surplus shipments:

	Procurement Cost	Sales Price
1) 130 million rounds of 7.92 ammunition (sold by OFLC under contract dated June 25, 1947) . . .	\$6, 564, 992. 58	\$656, 499. 27
2) 150 C–46 airplanes (sold by War Assets Administration under contract dated Dec. 22, 1947)	34, 800, 000. 00	750, 000. 00
3) OFLC transfers, Jan. 1, 1948–Nov. 30, 1948 :		
Ammunition, Cal. .30 to 155 Howitzer	21, 419, 116. 91	554, 534. 33
Air Force matériel and equipment, including 159 aircraft and 683 engines	34, 895, 332. 52	4, 365, 929. 29
Ordnance, signal, and other military equipment (10,304 tons)	2, 158, 938. 17	269, 867. 29
TOTAL	\$99, 838, 380. 18	[1] \$6, 596, 830. 18

[1] A portion of the total military surplus shipments was financed by the Chinese Government from the \$125 million grants authorized under the China Aid Act of 1948 (see item 20 below).

20. *\$125 Million Grant Under the China Aid Act of 1948:* Section 404 (b) of the China Aid Act of 1948 (Title IV of the Foreign Assistance Act of 1948) authorized to be appropriated to the President a sum not to exceed \$125,000,000 for additional aid to China through grants, on such terms as the President might determine. The legislative history of the Act made it clear that the Congress intended that these funds should be made available to the Chinese Government for such purposes as it might specify. The grants have been used by China to purchase items of a military nature. As of March 11, 1949 the Department of the Treasury had paid a total of \$124,148,891.99 of the \$125 million appropriated. Disbursements were made to the Chinese Government direct or to United States Government agencies requested by the Chinese Government to engage in procurement activities, as follows:

Recipient	Materials Procured	Amount
U. S. Government Agencies:		
Department of the Army	Arms, ammunition, medical · supplies, motor vehicles, spare parts, etc.	\$64, 437, 061. 68
Department of the Navy	Naval vessels, reconditioning of naval vessels, ammunition	6, 892, 020. 00
Dept. of the Air Force	Miscellaneous air force equipment and aviation gasoline	7, 750, 000. 00
Bureau of Federal Supply . . .	Petroleum products, ordnance raw materials	13, 765, 522. 12
Office of Foreign Liquidation Commissioner.	Surplus aircraft, aircraft spares, ammunition, etc.	[1] 2, 690, 910. 88
Republic of China	Miscellaneous supplies and equipment, from commercial sources.	28, 613, 377. 31
		\$124, 148, 891. 99

[1] In addition, OFLC has received by direct payment from the Chinese Government \$1,045,693.80 of the \$28,613,377.31 paid to the Chinese Government by the Treasury Department.

As of December 31, 1948, materials purchased for $60,958,791.38 under the $125 million grants had been shipped to China.

In accordance with the President's Directive of June 2, 1948, the Department of State examines the documentation submitted by the Chinese Government to determine that the request is not in excess of the total represented by the invoices or other supporting data, and authorizes the Treasury to make the appropriate payments to the Chinese Government. Under the President's Directive of July 28, 1948, the Chinese Government may arrange for the procurement or furnishing of supplies or services by any agency of the United States Government, subject to the approval of the Secretary of State as to the availability of funds. In such instances, the agency concerned is authorized to submit to the Department of State requests for reimbursement of appropriations or for advance payments. The Department has been able to certify fully documented requests for payment by the Treasury Department within a few days after receipt.

186

Secretary Acheson to Senator Tom Connally, Chairman of the Senate Committee on Foreign Relations

March 15, 1949.

The following comments on S. 1063 are offered in response to your request as conveyed by Mr. O'Day, Clerk of the Committee on Foreign Relations, in his letter of February 28, 1949. It is the Department's view that the Bill proposes aid of a magnitude and character unwarranted by present circumstances in China.

Despite the present aid program authorized by the last Congress, together with the very substantial other aid extended by the United States to China since V–J Day, aggregating over $2 billion, the economic and military position of the Chinese Government has deteriorated to the point where the Chinese Communists hold almost all important areas of China from Manchuria to the Yangtze River and have the military capability of expanding their control to the populous areas of the Yangtze Valley and of eventually dominating south China. The National Government does not have the military capability of maintaining a foothold in south China against a determined Communist advance. The Chinese Government forces have lost no battles during the past year because of lack of ammunition and equipment, while the Chinese Communists have captured the major portion of military supplies, exclusive of ammunition, furnished the Chinese Government by the United States since V–J Day. There is no evidence that the furnishing of additional military material would alter the pattern of current developments in China. There is, however, ample evidence that the Chinese people are weary of hostilities and that there is an overwhelming desire for peace at any price. To furnish solely military material and advice would only prolong hostilities and the suffering of the Chinese people and would arouse in them deep resentment against the United States. Yet, to furnish the military means for bringing about a reversal of the present deterioration and for providing some prospect of successful military resistance would require the use of an unpredictably large American armed force in actual combat, a course of action which would represent direct United States involvement in China's fratricidal warfare and would be contrary to our traditional policy toward China and the interests of this country.

In these circumstances, the extension of as much as $1.5 billion of credits to the Chinese Government, as proposed by the Bill, would embark this Government on an undertaking the eventual cost of which would be unpredictable but of great magnitude, and the outcome of which would almost surely be catastrophic. The field supervision of United States military aid, the pledging of revenue of major Chinese ports in payment of United States aid, United States administration and collection of Chinese customs in such ports, and United States participation in Chinese tax administration, all of which are called for by the Bill, would without question be deeply resented by the Chinese people as an extreme infringement of China's sovereignty and would arouse distrust in the minds of the Chinese people with respect to the motives of the United States in extending aid. While the use of up to $500 million in support of the Chinese currency, as proposed in the Bill, would undoubtedly ease temporarily the fiscal problem of the Chinese Government, stabilization of the Chinese currency cannot be considered feasible so long as the Government's monetary outlays exceed its income by a large margin. After the first $500 million had been expended, the United States would find it necessary to continue provision of funds to cover the Chinese Government's budgetary deficit if the inflationary spiral were not to be resumed. That China could be expected to repay United States financial, economic and military aid of the magnitude proposed, which the Bill indicates should all be on a credit basis, cannot be supported by realistic estimates of China's future ability to service foreign debts even under conditions of peace and economic stability.

The United States has in the past sought to encourage the Chinese Government to initiate those vital measures necessary to provide a basis for economic improvement and political stability. It has recognized that, in the absence of a Chinese Government capable of initiating such measures and winning popular support, United States aid of great magnitude would be dissipated and United States attempts to guide the operations of the Chinese Government would be ineffective and probably lead to direct involvement in China's fratricidal warfare. General Marshall reflected these considerations when he stated in February 1948 that an attempt to underwrite the Chinese economy and the Chinese Government's military effort represented a burden on the United States economy and a military responsibility which he could not recommend as a course of action for this Government.

Despite the above observations, it would be undesirable for the United States precipitously to cease aid to areas under the control of the Chinese Government which it continues to recognize. Future developments in China, including the outcome of political negotiations now being undertaken, are uncertain. Consideration is being given, therefore, to a request for Congressional action to extend the authority of the China Aid Act of 1948 to permit commitment of unobligated appropriations for a limited period beyond April 2, 1949, the present expiration date of the Act. If during such a period, the situation in China clarifies itself sufficiently, further recommendations might be made.

Index

Index